Western Liberalism

A History in Documents from Locke to Croce

Edited by E. K. Bramsted and K. J. Melhuish

Longman
London and New York

Longman Group Limited London

Associated companies, branches and representatives throughout the world

Published in the United States of America by Longman Inc., New York

© Longman Group Limited 1978

First published 1978

ISBN 0 582 48830 3 cased
ISBN 0 582 48831 paper

Library of Congress Cataloging in Publication Data

Main entry under title:
Western Liberalism.
  Bibliography: p.
  Includes index.
  CONTENTS: General introduction. The roots of liberalism: the eighteenth century. Classical liberalism. Major aspects of continental liberalism in the nineteenth century. Liberty and democracy. Epilogue: Liberalism challenged, revised, maintained, 1900-1950.
  1. Liberalism – History – Sources. I. Bramsted, Ernest Kohn. II. Melhuish, K. J.
JC571.W39   1978   320.5'1'08   77–5713

ISBN 0–582–48830–3

Printed in Great Britain by
Richard Clay (The Chaucer Press) Ltd,
Bungay, Suffolk

Dr Trevor Reese
In Memoriam

Acknowledgements

We are grateful to the following for permission to reprint copyright material:

George Allen & Unwin (Publishers) Ltd for extract from *History as the Story of Liberty* by Benedetto Croce, trans, by Sylvia Sprigge, 1941, and extract from *History of Europe in the Nineteenth Century* by Benedetto Croce, trans. by Henry Furst, 1934; Barrie & Jenkins for extract from *Why I Am A Liberal* by Sir William Beveridge, published by Herbert Jenkins 1945; S. Fischer Verlag for extract from 'Das Problem der Freheit' from *Reden Und Aufsätze* Band II by Thomas Mann. © Katja Mann, 1965, Reprinted by permission. Translated by E. K. Bramsted & K. J. Melhuish; Keynes Trust for extract from *The End of Laissez-Faire* by John Maynard Keynes, 1927; Macmillan Administration (Basingstoke) Ltd., for extract from Vol. IX *Essays in Persuasion* of the Collected Writings of John Maynard Keynes. Reprinted by permission of the publishers; Thomas Nelson & Sons Limited for extract from Book iv 'The Social Contract' from *Rousseau's Political Writings*, trans. and edited by F. M. Watkins; Oxford University Press for extracts from *Liberalism* by L. T. Hobhouse, 1911 and *Democracy in America* by Alexis de Tocqueville, trans. by Henry Reeve, abridged and edited by H. S. Commager (World's Classics editions 1946); Phaidon Press Limited for extract from *The Meaning of Freedom* by Gilbert Murray, Forword by Lord Samuel, London 1957; Routledge & Kegan Paul Limited and The University of Chicago Press for extract from *The Road to Serfdom* by F. A. Hayek (1944); Routledge & Kegan Paul Limited and Oxford University Press for extract from 'The Discipline of Freedom' by Karl Mannheim from *Freedom, Power and Democratic Planning*, Eds. H. Gerth & E. K. Bramsted, copyright 1950 and renewed 1977 by Oxford University Press, Inc. Reprinted by permission; Martin Secker & Warburg Limited and Random House Inc., for extracts from 'The Coming Victory of Democracy' from *Order Of The Day*: Political Essays and Speeches of Two Decades by Thomas Mann, trans. by Agnes Meyer, Copyright 1942 and renewed 1970 by Alfred A. Knopf, Inc; Weidenfeld & Nicolson Limited for extracts from *Sketch for a Historical Picture of the Progress of the Human Mind* by The Marquis de Condorcet, trans. by June Barraclough, London 1955;

We regret we have been unable to trace the copyright owners of the following– extracts from *Manual of Spanish Constitutions 1808–1931* by Arnold R. Verduin; and extract from document by Salvador de Madariaga 'Rettet die Freiheit. Ausgewählte Aufsätze in der Neue Zürcher Zeitung 1948–1957' article 'Europa und die liberalen Grundsätze' Berne 1958 – and any information which would enable us to do so would be appreciated.

Contents

Foreword   xvii

**General introduction
Major strands of liberalism**   1

Introductory   3

1. The doctrine of human rights   5

2. The classical economists and the utilitarians   12
   by Dr John R. Dinwiddy

3. Aesthetic individualism   25

4. The desire for constitutional government   29

5. From 'classic' to 'hyphenated' liberalism   35

6. Radicalism as an aspect of English liberalism   42

7. Aspects of liberalism and radicalism in France   52

8. Liberals and radicals in Germany – some aspects   80

Notes and References   91

**A. Roots of liberalism
   – the eighteenth century**   103

1. The civil State – representative government: introduction   105

Document 1.   JOHN LOCKE:
   (a) From the Natural State to the Civil State   173
   (b) Of the Ends of Political Society and Government   175
   (c) Of the Extent of the Legislative Power   177
   (From: 'The Second Treatise of Government', 1690)

2. Religious toleration: introduction   110

Document 2.   JOHN LOCKE: 'A Letter Concerning Toleration'
   (1689)   182
Document 3.   VOLTAIRE:
   (a) Whether Intolerance is Consistent with Natural
   Law;   184
   (b) An Account of a Controversial Dispute in China;   185
   (c) A Prayer to God   186
   (From: *A Treatise on Toleration*, 1764)
Document 4.   TURGOT: Memorial to the King 'On Toleration' (June
   1775)   187

3. 'The Spirit of the Laws': introduction   117

Document 5.   MONTESQUIEU:
   (a) Political Liberty with regard to the Constitution
   and the Separation of Powers   190
   (b) Political Liberty in Relation to the Subject   193
   (c) Of Laws in Relation to the order of things which
   they determine   193
   (From: *The Spirit of the Laws*, 1748)

4. 'Government is a Necessary Evil': introduction   122

Document 6.   THOMAS PAINE: The Origin and Design of
   Government   195
   (From: *Common Sense*, February 1776)
Document 7.   THOMAS PAINE: The First Principles of
   Government   197
   (From: *Dissertation on First Principles of Government*,
   1795)

5. Freedom through the general will: introduction   126

Document 8.   JEAN-JACQUES ROUSSEAU:
   (a) The Social Contract   200
   (b) Sovereignty is Inalienable   201
   (c) Sovereignty is Indivisible   202
   (d) Whether the General Will is Subject to Error   202
   (e) The General Will is Indestructible   203
   (From: *The Social Contract*, 1762)

6. Natural law and the economy –
the doctrine of *laissez faire*: introduction   135

(i) TURGOT: The harmony between the economic interests of the individual and those of society   135

Document 9.   TURGOT: 'Eloge de Gournay' (1759)   205
Document 10.   TURGOT: Letter to the Abbé Terray 'Sur la Marque des Fers', (24 Dec. 1773)   210

(ii) ADAM SMITH: 'The Wealth of Nations'   140

Document 11.   ADAM SMITH:
(a) Of the Natural and Market Price of Commodities   213
(b) Of the Rent of Land   217
(c) Of Restraints upon Importation from Foreign Countries   220
(d) The System of Natural Liberty   223
(From: *The Wealth of Nations*, 1776)

7. The doctrine of the rights of man: introduction   146

Document 12.   The Declaration of Independence, 4 July 1776   224
Document 13.   Declaration of the Rights of Man and Citizen, 27 Aug. 1789   227
Document 14.   THOMAS PAINE: The Voice of an English Supporter   229
(From: *The Rights of Man*, 1791)
Document 15.   JEREMY BENTHAM: The Voice of an English Critic   231
(From: *Anarchical Fallacies*, 1824)

8. The belief in progress: introduction   162

Document 16.   THE MARQUIS DE CONDORCET: *The Future Progress of the Human Mind* (1795)   236

Notes and References   165

B. Classical liberalism   241

1. The utilitarian approach to government: introduction   243

Document 17.   JEREMY BENTHAM: The End of Legislation – the Greatest Happiness to the Greatest Number   294
(From: *An Introductory View of the Rationale of Evidence*)
Document 18.   The Principle of Utility   294
(From: *An Introduction to the Principles of Morals and Legislation*, 1789)
Document 19.   The Duties of a Citizen – to Obey and Censure   296
(From: *A Fragment on Government or a Comment on the Commentaries*, 1776)
Document 20.   The Leading Principles of a Constitutional Code   298
(From: *Leading Principles of a Constitutional Code for Any State*, 1823)

Document 21. JAMES MILL: Good Government 301
              (From: *Essay on Government*, 1820)
Document 22. JOHN STUART MILL: The Ideally Best Form of
              Government is Representative Government 303
              (From: *Considerations on Representative Government*)

2. Economic liberalism: introduction   250

              (i) Free trade and *laissez faire* in Britain   250

Document 23. DAVID RICARDO: On Foreign Trade and the Benefits to
              be Derived from Free Trade 310
              (From: *On the Principles of Political Economy and Taxation*)
Document 24. RICHARD COBDEN: Free Trade and the Argument
              against the Corn Laws (Speech, 8 Feb. 1844) 315
Document 25. JOHN STUART MILL: The Grounds and Limits of the
              Laisser-Faire or Non-Interference Principle 317
              (From: *Principles of Political Economy*, 1848)

              (ii) Some trends on the Continent   259

              France: 259
Document 26. W. E. GLADSTONE: On Economical Government 321
              (From: *The Financial Statements of 1853, 1860–63*)
Document 27. JEAN BAPTISTE SAY: On the Limits of Government
              Interference 326
              (From: *A Treatise on Political Economy*, 1803)
Document 28. FREDERIC BASTIAT: Free Trade and Competition 328
              (From: *Harmonies of Political Economy*, 1850)
              Germany: 264
Document 29. FRIEDRICH LIST: Petition on behalf of the *Handelsverein*
              to the Federal Assembly, April 1819 330
Document 30. JOHN PRINCE SMITH: On Freedom of Trade in Relation to
              Political Freedom 332
              (From: *Uber Handelsfeindseligkeit*)

3. The superiority of the middle classes: introduction   268

Document 31. JAMES MILL: On the Superior Wisdom and Virtue of the
              Middle Classes 334
              (From: *Essay on Government*, 1820)
Document 32. FRANÇOIS GUIZOT: On the Middle Classes as the Basis
              of the New Society 335
              (From: *Mémoires pour servir a l'histoire de mon temps*)
Document 33. DAVID HANSEMANN: The Middle Class in Prussia 337
              (From: 'Memorandum on Prussia's Position and Politics,
              August–September, 1840')

4. Aesthetic individualism – '*The object of all mankind should be
individuality*': introduction   271

Document 34. WILHELM VON HUMBOLDT:

(a) 'The Purpose of Man'   340
(b) 'The Purpose of the State'   341
(From: *The Sphere and Duties of Government (Ideen zu einem Versuch)*

Document 35.   JOHN STUART MILL: Of Individuality, as One of the Elements of Well-Being   346
(From: *On Liberty*, 1859)

5. The belief in international harmony: introduction   278

(i)   Through free trade and non-intervention   278
(ii) Non-intervention and the image of the British abroad   284

Document 36.   JEREMY BENTHAM: In International Dealings, Justice and Beneficence   352
(From: *The Constitutional Code*)

Document 37.   RICHARD COBDEN: 'Commerce is the Grand Panacea'   354
(From: *England, Ireland and America*, 1835)

Document 38.   JOHN PRINCE SMITH: On the Significance of Freedom of Trade in World Politics   357
(From: *Uber die weltpolitische Bedeutung der Handelsfreiheit*)

Document 39.   JOHN BRIGHT: On Non-Intervention as a Principle of Foreign Policy (Speech, 13 Oct. 1853)   359

Document 40.   Emile de Girardin: On the Principle of Non-Intervention (Speech, 24 Aug. 1850)   361

Document 41.   JOHN STUART MILL: Non-Intervention is a Legitimate Principle of Morality   363
(From: 'A Few Words on Non-Intervention', 1859)

Document 42.   FRANCISQUE BOUVET: International Arbitration and Universal Peace (Speech, 28 Nov. 1848)   370

Document 43.   RICHARD COBDEN: International Arbitration (Speech, 12 June 1849)   374

Document 44.   EMILE DE LAVELEYE: On the Causes of War, and the Means of Reducing their Number   379
(From: Cobden Club Essays)

Notes and References   288

C. Major aspects of continental liberalism in the nineteenth century: Attitudes and ideas in France, Germany, Italy and Spain (1815–1881)   385

Introductory   387

1. The constitutional State: introduction   388

(i) Limitation of Power – the role of the Monarch 388

France: 431

Document 45. DESTUTT DE TRACY: A Commentary on
Montesquieu's 'Spirit of the Laws' 431 ·
(From: *Commentaire sur l'esprit des Lois*, 1814)

Document 46. BENJAMIN CONSTANT: On Constitutional Powers
and Political rights 434
(From: *Course de politique constitutionelle*, 1818–20)

Spain: 438

Document 47. Political Constitution of the Spanish Nation (1812) 438
(From: *Manual of Spanish Constitutions 1808–1931*)

Germany: 443

Document 48. KARL VON ROTTECK: Extract from 'Konstitution' in
the *Staatslexikon* 443

Document 49. K. T. WELCKER: The Responsibility of Princes and
the Ministers of State 446
(From: *Staatslexikon*)

Document 50. DAVID HANSEMANN: The Formation of the
Constitution in Prussia 447
(From: 'Memorandum on Prussia's Position and Politics,
August–September 1840')

Document 51. HEINRICH VON TREITSCHKE: Political Freedom
and its Limitations 449
(From: *Die Freiheit*, 1861)

(ii) The English model 391

France: 455

Document 52. MME DE STAEL: On Liberty and Public Spirit among
the English 455
(From: *Considérations sur les principaux événements
de la Révolution française*, 1818)

Document 53. MME DE STAEL: Can a limited Monarchy have other
Foundations than those of the English Constitution?
(op. cit.) 458

Germany: 461

Document 54. FRIEDRICH CHRISTOPH DAHLMANN: 'On
Constitution' (1815) 461
(From: *Kleine Schriften und Reden*)

Document 55. FRIEDRICH CHRISTOPH DAHLMANN: 'On
Discussions in Parliament' 465
(From: *Die Politik auf den Grund und das Maass der
gegebenen Zustaende zurueckgefuehrt*)

Document 56. DAVID HANSEMANN: England as a Model for the
Formation of a Constitution 466

Italy: 467

Document 57.   CAMILLO DI CAVOUR: 'The Chartist Revolution and the
              British Government' (1848)   467
              (From: *Scritti Politici*)

2. Freedom and the individual: introduction   394

   (i) The rights of the individual   394

Document 58.   MME DE STAEL: On the Love of Freedom   469
              (From: *Considérations sur les principaux événements
              de la Révolution française*, 1818)
Document 59.   F. de LAMENNAIS: The Conditions of Liberty   472
              (From: *Paroles d'un Croyant*)
Document 60.   The Fundamental Rights of the German People
              (Section VI of the Constitution for the German
              Empire, 1849)   477
Document 61.   GIUSEPPE MAZZINI: Liberty   479
              (From: 'On the Duties of Man')
Document 62.   EDOUARD LABOULAYE: Freedom, Ancient
              and Modern (1863)   484
              (From: *L'Etat et ses limites*)
Document 63.   ADOLPHE THIERS: On the Principles of 1789
              (Speech, 26 Feb. 1866)   487

   (ii) Freedom of speech, of the press, and
   of association   397

Document 64.   JOSEPH GORRES: Freedom of Speech   492
              (From: *Rheinischer Merkur* No. 50, 1 May 1814)
Document 65.   FRANCOIS GUIZOT: Thoughts upon the Liberty of the
              Press (1815)   493
              (From: *Memoirs to Illustrate the History of my Times*)
Document 66.   PIERRE PAUL ROYER-COLLARD: On Freedom of
              Speech and Publication (Speech, 1819)   496
Document 67.   F. de LAMENNAIS: The Doctrines of *L'Avenir*
              (7 Dec. 1830)   498
              (From: *Oeuvres complètes*)
Document 68.   K. T. WELCKER: On the Political Salutariness and the
              Danger of Free Associations   502
              (From: *Staatslexicon*)
Document 69.   GIUSEPPE MAZZINI: Association – Progress   505
              (From: 'On the Duties of Man', 1858)
Document 70.   ADOLPHE THIERS: The 'Indispensable Liberties'
              (Speech, 11 Jan. 1864)   507
Document 71.   LEON GAMBETTA: The Belleville Manifesto
              (1869)   509
              (From: *L'Avenir National*, 15 May 1869)

3. Freedom from the Church and freedom for the Church:
introduction   407

France: 408

Document 72.   COUNT DE MONTLOSIER: Concerning a Religious and Political System tending to overthrow Religion, Society and the Throne   512
(From: *Mémoire à consulter sur un système religieux et politique tendant à renverser la religion, la société et le trône*)

Document 73.   F. DE LAMENNAIS: Freedom for the Church (Letter, 5 Sept. 1830)   514

Document 74.   F. DE LAMENNAIS: On the Separation of Church and State   515
(From: *L'Avenir*, 18 Oct. 1830)

Document 75.   COUNT CHARLES MONTALEMBERT: An Explanatory Note on the Formula 'A Free Church in a Free State' (1863)   521
(From: *L'Eglise libre dans l'Etat libre*)

Italy: 410

Document 76.   CAMILLO DI CAVOUR: 'For Liberty of Conscience and of Worship (1848)   524
(From: *Scritti Politici*)

Document 77.   GIUSEPPE MAZZINI: Humanity and the Papacy (1849)   525
(From: 'Rome and the French Government')

Document 78.   The *Syllabus Errorum* of Pope Pius IX, 8 Dec. 1864   527

Germany: 413

Document 79.   SYLVESTER JORDAN: On the Freedom of Faith and the Separation of Church and State (Speech, 21 Aug. 1848)   530

Document 80.   IGNATZ DOLLINGER: On the Freedom of Belief and the Separation of Church and State (Speech, 22 Aug. 1848)   532

Spain: 415

Document 80a.   Articles on Religion and Religious Cults in the Constitutions of Spain 1837–1931   533
(From: *Manual of Spanish Constitutions 1808–1931*)

4. Freedom, power and the nation-state: Germany 1814–1881: introduction   418

Document 81.   ERNST MORITZ ARNDT: On Freedom and Fatherland   535
(From: 'Katchismus für den deutschen Kriegs und Wehrmann', 1814)

Document 82.   ERNST MORITZ ARNDT: The Constitution and the Peasants   536
(From: *Der Wächter*, 1815)

Document 83.   FRIEDRICH CHRISTOPH DAHLMANN: On the Right of Resistance (1835)   538

(From: *Die Politik auf den Grund und das Maass der gegebenen Zustaende zurueckgefuehrt*)

Document 84. DAVID HANSEMANN: Freedom and Patriotism. The Necessity of Freedom 539
(From: 'Memorandum on Prussia's Position and Politics, August–September 1840')

Document 85. THE OFFENBURG PROGRAMME of the South West German Democrats, 10 September 1847 541

Document 86. THE HEPPENHEIM PROGRAMME of the South West German Liberals, 10 October 1847 542

Document 87. German Liberals at the Crossroads – For or Against Bismarck 1863–66 543
(a) Hermann Baumgarten to Heinrich von Sybel, 22 May 1863; 543
(b) H. von Sybel to H. Baumgarten, 26 May 1863; 544
(c) H. Baumgarten to H. von Sybel, 11 May 1866; 545
(d) *do.* 23 June 1866 546

Document 88. HERMANN BAUMGARTEN: German Liberalism: A Self-Criticism (1866) 547
(From: *Der deutsche Liberalismus: Eine Selbstkritik*, 1866)

Document 89. Programme of the Progressive Party in Prussia, 6 June 1861 550
(From: *Die deutsche Parteiprogramme*)

Document 90. Programme of the National Liberal Party, 12 June 1867 552
(From: *Die politischen Parteien in Deutschland*, vol. II)

Document 91. KARL TWESTEN: Draft of the foundation programme of the National Liberal Party (1867) 554
(From: *Deutscher Liberalismus im Zeitalter Bismarcks. Eine politische Briefsammlung*, vol. I)

Document 92. G. G. GERVINUS: A Warning Voice in Time of National Victory. Memorandum for the Peace: To the Royal House of Prussia (1870) 557
(From: 'Denkschrift zum Frieden. An das Preussische Königshaus')

Document 93. The Liberals and the New Empire 1871–1881 558
(a) Hermann Baumgarten to Max Weber, 30 May 1878; 558
(b) H. Baumgarten to Heinrich von Sybel, 27 Dec. 1879; 559
(c) H. Baumgarten to H. von Sybel, 21 July 1880; 559
(d) H. Baumgarten to H. von Sybel, 1 Jan. 1881; 560
(e) H. von Sybel to H. Baumgarten, 8 Jan. 1881; 560
(f) H. Baumgarten to H. von Sybel, 29 Mar. 1881. 561

Document 94. EUGEN RICHTER: Liberalism and National Unity. The Split within the Liberal Camp (1874) 563
(From: *Die deutsche Fortschrittspartei und die nationalliberale Partei*)

Document 95. The Anti-clerical Reaction of the German Liberals. The

Slogan of the 'Kulturkampf' against the Catholic
Church   564
(From: The programme of the Progressive Party, 1875)

Notes and References   427

D. Liberty and democracy   567

Introductory   569

1. Are liberty and democracy compatible?: introduction   569

Document 96.   ALEXIS DE TOCQUEVILLE: The influence of
               Democratic Opinions and Sentiments on Political
               Society   605
               (From: *Democracy in America*)
Document 97.   FRANÇOIS GUIZOT: On the Government of the Majority
               and the True Doctrine of Representation   609
               (From: *History of the Origin of Representative Government
               in Europe*)
Document 98.   MICHEL CHEVALIER: Association as a Danger to
               Liberty   612
               (From: *The History of Political Economy Taught by the
               History of Freedom of Labour*)
Document 99.   LEON GAMBETTA: Speech at Grenoble, 26 Sept.
               1872   615
Document 100. W. E. H. LECKY: Democracy does not Harmonise well
               with Liberty   617
               (From: *Democracy and Liberty*, 1896)
Document 101. FRIEDRICH NAUMANN: Democracy and
               Monarchy   620
               (From: *Demokratie und Monarchie*, 1912)

2. The tyranny of majority and the right to non-conformity:
introduction   577

Document 102. ALEXIS DE TOCQUEVILLE: The Unlimited Power of the
               Majority in the United States and its Consequence   624
               (From: *Democracy in America*)
Document 103. JOHN STUART MILL: On the Dangers Arising from
               the Rule of the Numerical Majority   628
               (From: *Considerations on Representative Government*)
Document 104. LORD ACTON: On the Will of the Majority   632
               (From: 'Sir Erskine May's *Democracy in Europe*')

3. The limitations and the scope of the State:
introduction   583
               (i) Anti-etatism intensified   583

Document 105. HERBERT SPENCER: Over-legislation (1859) 634
    (From: *Essays, Scientific, Political, Speculative*)
Document 106. EMILE FAGUET: The Rights of the State 638
    (From: *Le Liberalisme*)
Document 107. PAUL LEROY-BEAULIEU: The Functions and
    Limitations of the State 643
    (From: *The Modern State in Relation to Society and the
    Individual*)

    (ii) The case for moderate State intervention   589

Document 108. T. H. GREEN: 'Liberal Legislation and Freedom of
    Contract' 1881 652
Document 109. JOSEPH CHAMBERLAIN: The Main Lines of Liberal
    Progress 657
    (Speech at Hull, 5 Aug. 1885)
Document 110. LEONARD T. HOBHOUSE:
    (a) The State and the Individual 662
    (b) Social Service and Reward 667
    (From: *Liberalism*, 1911)

4. Freedom and power: introduction   598

Document 111. LORD ACTON: 'The History of Freedom in
    Antiquity' (Address, 26 Feb. 1877) 669
Document 112. ALAIN (Emile August Chartier):
    (a) Traps for a Minister (1911) 672
    (b) Politics of the Citizen (1923) 672
    (From: *Eléments d'une doctrine radicale*)

Notes and References   602

E. Epilogue: Liberalism challenged, revised, maintained 1900–1950   675

Introductory   677

Document 113. BENEDETTO CROCE: History as the Story of Liberty
    (1941) 700
Document 114. BENEDETTO CROCE: Towards a Liberalised
    Europe 703
    (From: *The History of Europe in the Nineteenth Century*)
Document 115. JOHN MAYNARD KEYNES: The Liberal Position
    Re-defined (1926) 705
    (From: *The End of Laissez faire*)
Document 116. JOHN MAYNARD KEYNES: 'Liberalism and Labour' 709
    (From: *Essays in Persuasion*)
Document 117. WILLIAM BEVERIDGE: Liberal Radicalism and
    Liberty (1945) 712

(From: *Why I am a Liberal*)

Document 118. THOMAS MANN: The Problem of Freedom (Address, Sept. 1939)   717

Document 119. THOMAS MANN: The Social Renewal of Democracy   719
(From: *The Coming Victory of Democracy*)

Document 120. KARL MANNHEIM: The Discipline of Freedom   721
(From: *Freedom, Power and Democratic Planning*)

Document 121. F. A. HAYEK: The Great Utopia   728
(From: *The Road to Serfdom*)

Document 122. GILBERT MURRAY: The Meaning of Freedom (1949)   735

Document 123. SALVADOR DE MADARIAGA: Europe and the Liberal Principles (23 May 1948)   744

Notes and References   697

Biographical List   749

Index   791

Foreword

This collection of documents from the history of liberalism mainly in Western Europe including Britain, is intended to throw light on both the basic tenets and the variety of liberal thought and ideology. There can be little doubt that liberalism was a major doctrine, in substance if not always in name, from the seventeenth to the nineteenth centuries and that it has had significant, if diminishing, repercussions in our own century. Seen in historical perspective, liberalism grew into a complex web, although it was not conceived as such. Deeply influenced by the Enlightenment, by the revolutionary events in the USA in 1776 and in France in 1789, it was closely allied with the rise and later with the defence of the middle classes, in a period of growing industrialisation.

By and large liberalism, an approach in existence well before the term was coined early in the nineteenth century in Spain, emphasized reason instead of tradition, contract rather than status, the present and the future instead of the past, the value and rights of the individual instead of that of existing power-holders, whose claims based on the superiority of cast or creed it challenged. Basically liberalism has been an attitude in defence of the individual man and citizen in defiance of the arbitrary acts of government. It has been anti-authoritarian in its desire to challenge and limit the strength and scope of the powers that be.

Reflecting the self-assertion of the middle classes, particularly of its upper strata, liberalism favoured institutions safeguarding the role of the law and the right of the citizen to private property. No less significant was its insistence on constitutional government with a division of powers and clearly defined tasks for the legislature, the executive and the judiciary. Although there were great discrepancies in the attitudes of the basic liberal schools, the 'Rights of Man' school and the school of utilitarianism, they both initially favoured a *laissez faire* approach to the economy. Since Adam Smith the classical economists have had an unrivalled influence on the liberal outlook, which only began to recede towards the end of the nineteenth century.

Liberalism, it has been said, is both 'a habit of mind and an ideology'.[1]* One of the reasons for this is its ever-expanding concern for the individual which gradually went far beyond the early emphasis on mere freedom from the intervention of the state in commerce and industry. The respect for the individual citizen meant civil equality of all before the law. It also indicated his right to express opinions and to associate for lawful purposes with others. It did not mean equality of property or of opportunity. Whereas classic liberalism undertook to protect the individual from arbitrary actions of the government and its agencies, later liberalism developed a broader concept of the individual. In line with a trend of thought going back to the days of the Renaissance it viewed the individual as potentially unique and spontaneous. The individual had to be rescued not only from the arbitrariness of power-holders but also from the tyranny of the majority, which in the modern democracy claimed increasingly that its standards and *mores* were binding for everyone. Individualism as a 'habit of mind', as the right of the individual to follow his own preferences and tastes within the limits imposed by the law instead of having them dictated by the conventions of society, became an additional strand in the liberal attitude. Gradually the rights of minorities as well as the rights of the majority formed part of the platform.

Early liberalism shared with anarchism a dislike and distrust of government and of the existing powers. However, while anarchism in the last instance wanted to do away with government altogether, liberalism only desired to limit its powers and to put it on a rational, controllable basis. The ineradicable optimism, so characteristic of much liberal thought, tended to the belief that governments can be controlled by the citizens and that abuses of their power can be prevented. Such optimism wore thin towards the end of the nineteenth century when a liberal of the integrity and astuteness of Lord Acton insisted that 'all power tends to corrupt and absolute power corrupts absolutely'.

The student of history has to deal with both liberalism and liberalisms. He must not overlook the manifold specific features of the liberal approach, its variety in different periods and countries. One of the major distinct traits of Continental liberalism when compared with the British type was its anti-clericalism which differed widely from non-conformity in Britain. Anti-clericalism has been strong in countries in which the Roman Catholic Church was powerful and had been part of the power-groupings of the *ancien régime*. While a good deal of scepticism and the demand for toleration are characteristic of the majority of

*Superior numerals apply to the Notes and References at the end of this Foreword.

liberals, anti-clericalism was a specific attitude of belligerency which frequently equalled the intolerance of its opponent. In any case, the struggle for freedom from the Church, later accompanied by one for freedom for the Church, is characteristic of much nineteenth-century liberalism in Western and Southern Europe.

Political and economic ideas in the neatness and aloofness of a theoretical system are one thing, but are another as an instrument, a weapon in the political arena, in the competitive struggle for change or preservation of the existing social and political order. A political theory is not identical with a political programme, but it can be adapted or transformed for this purpose. Theories, it has been aptly said by a student of Bentham, 'relate in different ways to their settings; and such aspects include not simply some general social background or historical period, but complex social traditions that are often in conflict, theories and explanations that are most certainly in conflict, and a writer's more immediate and personal circumstances – his temperament, education, moral outlook and tastes . . .' [2]

These factors have to be considered when one is faced with the varied and often contradictory thoughts and statements of philosophers, economists and reformers who put forward what they regard as liberal ideas and points of view. Of them, as of the makers of rival political creeds, it can be argued that 'some apply in their political thinking general techniques that they have previously developed in considering the problem of knowledge or of moral obligation; other men start in the political field and look elsewhere for convenient or plausible techniques to take over. Most men mix such methods and add a quota of current dogma or prejudice'. [3]

Like other doctrines in modern history liberalism was spread through a multiplicity of channels. The theorist, be he philosopher or economist, the journalist and pamphleteer, the orator and organizer, the deputy and the statesman all undertook to formulate, to develop or simply to spread the liberal message. Some theorists like David Ricardo and J. B. Say were primarily interested in developing a coherent and convincing doctrine of *laissez faire*, others like Frédéric Bastiat, in France, or John Prince Smith, in Germany, wanted to persuade the public or the governments and convert them to the message of free trade. Publicists such as Joseph Goerres or Lamennais agitated through their journals trusting to the power of the printed word whereas a radical leader like Léon Gambetta preferred to rely more on the power of his oratory. Some liberal academics decided to enter the political arena. Guizot and Thiers in France, Professors Rotteck, Welcker and Treitschke in Germany, belong to this group though the reputation of Rotteck and Welcker as champions of constitutionalism originated as much from their political encyclopaedia, the *Staatslexikon* as from their addresses in the Baden Diet. Turgot and Hansemann tried to promote their ideas of reform by way of memoranda to their monarch, while the utilitarian philosophers addressed themselves in the first instance to the educated layers of the middle classes. Writers of great repute like Voltaire in the eighteenth century or Thomas Mann in the twentieth protested against intolerance and suppression. Historians used their interpretation of history, from Condorcet to Croce and from Guizot and Thiers to the liberal 'political historians' in Germany, in the service of liberal ideas and pleas.

Many later adherents of 'liberalism' were influenced by the liberal tradition in their own country or by model liberal patterns and regimes they discovered abroad. From the days of Montesquieu to those of Madame de Staël and Guizot the constitutional monarchy in Britain fulfilled the function of a model in the eyes of many Continental liberals. With de Tocqueville the democracy in the United States became a model if not in all respects then at least in some.

There were other traditions which could be appealed to by liberals and radicals. The memories of 1789 were again and again invoked in France from Madame de Staël and Constant to Thiers and Gambetta although their interpretations differed greatly. Perhaps in some ways the continuous flashback to the earlier traditions and slogans of the French revolution and the constant need felt for gaining prestige by referring to this wider ideological umbrella contributed to weaken the role of liberalism as such in nineteenth-century France. In Germany on the other hand no revolutionary traditions could be appealed to by liberals and radicals. The dilemma of German liberals in the same century was different. Their position became complicated − by the simultaneous desire for a constitutional *Rechtsstaat* and for the overall integration of a nation-state, a new Empire. This was one of the reasons why German liberals on the whole were less anti-*étatist* than liberals in other countries. The pressing problems of national unification also affected, though to a lesser extent, Italian liberals and intensified the dividing line separating them from a radical such as Mazzini. In the Habsburg Empire the tensions between a multitude of nationalities accentuated the differences between German, Hungarian, Czech and Polish liberals. In addition the fact that liberalism in Central Europe had often a romantic tinge explains perhaps why the 'unromantic' utilitarian approach to liberalism made little progress with the liberals in that region. 'National-liberalism', like 'social-liberalism' is thus of considerable significance for an understanding of the complexity of the liberal phenomenon.[4]

Liberalism has to be seen both in its national variety and in its universal aspects. The model function of the British constitutional system for Continental liberals has been mentioned. Later the belief in free trade as a means of bringing the nations together, as an instrument for advancing international cooperation and peace instead of the divisiveness of national power-politics leading to war, became an international platform. In the middle of the nineteenth century Richard Cobden was a revered figure for liberals in Western Europe. They shared his belief that free trade would lead to peaceful association of the peoples in contrast to the Machiavellian power-politics of the old 'conservative' regimes, controlled by the aristocracy and implemented by military and bureaucratic forces.

While it is hoped that the 'anti-positions' of the liberal ideology and of liberal parties become evident from the documents, for reasons of economy it has not been possible to include reactions to the liberal doctrines from the conservative Right or from the socialist Left. There is one exception, the *Syllabus Errorum* of Pope Pius IX (1864), for without it the *Kulturkampf* later waged by the German Liberals (and by Bismarck) against the Roman Catholic Church would not be understandable. The editors have been sparing with extracts from party programmes, especially in the case of English liberalism, as these are available in a number of specialized books. For the twentieth century in particular economic considerations have obliged them to concentrate on liberal thought and ideology to the exclusion of party programmes and manifestos. In general a good deal of material on European liberalism not easily obtainable in English has been included.

It is a truism to state that liberalism as an organized political force has declined since the First World War. Yet much of the liberal legacy, of the hard core of the liberal approach in many countries has been absorbed by both the moderate Right and the moderate Left, by 'liberal' Conservatives as well as by 'liberal' Social Democrats. While the orthodox *laissez faire* attitude in economics and politics is now largely a matter of the past, the idea of human rights as well as the emphasis on the value of the individual in the spheres of living and of cultural production remain relevant, so long as men do not wish to exist on the level of robots.

In conclusion, this book will have fulfilled its role if it helps the reader to ask searching questions on the nature, the evolution and the variety of liberal thought and ideology, on its relationship with the self-assertion and the self-defence of the middle classes, on the strength and weakness of a doctrine which over a span of two and a half centuries connects the days of John Locke with those of Benedetto Croce.

The documents were selected and edited jointly by E. K. Bramsted and K. J. Melhuish.

The General Introduction was written by E.K.B. with the exception of the section on 'Classical economists and utilitarians' (pp. 12–25) contributed by Dr John R. Dinwiddy. K.J.M. wrote the Introduction to Section A and parts of the Introductions to Sections B and D. (B: 'Economic Liberalism: Free trade and *laissez faire* in Britain'; D: 'Moderate State Intervention'). Otherwise the responsibility for the sectional introductions

B to D lies with E.K.B. The Biographical List was compiled by K.J.M.

The Editors wish to express their appreciation to Dr Dinwiddy for his contribution and for his comments on some of the sectional introductions. They also have pleasure in thanking Professor Alan Shaw and Dr Ian Nish, who read parts of the introductions, for their valuable advice and criticism.

Dr Melhuish wishes to acknowledge the assistance she has received from a Macquarie University (Sydney) Research Grant towards expenses for research and typing of the manuscript.

June 1977

E.K.B.
K.J.M.

Notes

1. Harold J. Laski, *The Rise of European Liberalism,* London, 1936, p. 15.
2. Wilfred Harrison in his introduction to Jeremy Bentham, *A Fragment on Government* and *An Introduction to the Principles of Morale and Legislation,* Oxford 1948, p. xvii.
3. Ibid.
4. These forms of 'hyphenated liberalism' are discussed in the 'General Introduction', pp. 35–42.

General Introduction

Major strands of liberalism

Introductory

In the history of Western Europe liberalism existed as an attitude of mind long before Liberalism arrived as a political label. The use of the latter dates back only to the beginning of the nineteenth century when in the Spanish Cortes of 1820 the *Liberales* representing the bourgeoisie successfully confronted the *Serviles*, the deputies of the Estates, the nobles and the clergy who traditionally supported the absolute monarchy. The *Liberales* had in 1812 succeeded in the acceptance of a Constitution giving the Spanish nation the right to determine its fundamental laws. Yet two years later Absolutism returned in the person of King Ferdinand VII. But the term 'liberals' caught on in other countries of the West. In England it was first a term of xenophobic abuse bestowed on the more progressive Whigs by their Tory opponents. However in due course the word was to become respectable and the name of a major party.

As a political movement everywhere liberalism emphasized the rights and the potential of the individual facing the forces of tradition and of the old Establishment. There was a major emphasis on a division of powers and on the role of Parliament as an unfettered forum of the nation. The individual and his property were regarded as sacrosanct so long as they did not conflict with existing laws. Liberalism (with a capital L) usually indicates 'whatever the Liberal Party stands for'. It is 'not so old as liberalism' (with a small l) which, especially in England, often does not go 'beyond the simple demand for the minimal state'.[1]* Long before Liberals opposed Conservatives or Clericals, philosophers had laid the basis of a liberal ideology, by putting a high premium on individual liberty. It served as a weapon in the rise of the middle classes, of its struggle over the claims of the feudal aristocracy and of absolutism. While the insistence on economic freedom bursting the fetters of Mercantilism proved an important aspect of the liberal outlook, it was preceded in time by the demand for freedom of conscience and of thought. John Locke's classic insistence at the end of the seventeenth century on the rights of the individual to 'life, liberty and property' is unthinkable without the earlier plea for freedom of conscience which had slowly and painfully emerged from the struggles of the Reformation and its aftermath.[2] The fact that after the Reformation there existed three competitive Christian creeds on the Continent instead of one, led at the end of the devastating Thirty Years' War to a compromise. While the sovereign ruler of a territory determined its religion, members of religious minorities were at least entitled to emigrate with their possessions. A rough coexistence of the officially recognized creeds, the Catholic, Lutheran and Calvinist

---

* Superior numerals apply to Notes and References listed on p. 91.

churches, made for a minimum amount of tolerance, however grudgingly conceded. Five years before it was written into the Peace of Westphalia (1648) John Milton, the poet and seer, in his *Areopagitica* (1643) made an eloquent plea to Parliament in England for freedom of thought by insisting on 'Unlicenced Printing'. Though he admitted it was a concern of Church and Commonwealth to keep a watchful eye on publications that might infect the nation with dangerous mischief, he felt it was a still greater danger to fetter the expression of opinion. 'We should be wary', Milton wrote, 'what persecution we raise against the living labours of living men, how we spill that seasoned life of man, preserved in books.' 'Truth can never be achieved without freedom to persue it'. . . . [3] Therefore Milton's plea: 'Give me the liberty to know, to utter, and to argue freely according to conscience, above all liberties.' [4]

Milton demanded both freedom of religion and freedom of thought. The problem of freedom of the conscience flared up in England after the Restoration of the Monarchy. In 1662 2,000 ministers of the Church of England defied *The Act of Uniformity* which insisted on strict conformity of all ministers with the doctrines of the Common Prayer Book. The dissenting ministers who refused to sign a declaration of 'unfeigned assent and consent to all and everything contained and prescribed' in that Book were driven out and deprived of their ecclesiastical livelihood. These ministers, their elders and the supporting families were hard pressed but could not be silenced. 'Nonconformity positively flourished and grew in stature during the trial.' [5]

A change came with the Act of Toleration, passed in Parliament in 1689, after the 'Glorious Revolution'. The persecution of the Dissenters ceased, but the political and social disabilities imposed on them under Lord Clarendon and by the Test Act of 1673 still continued. The members of the non-conformist churches ranging from Baptists to Quakers, from emotional Methodists to the rationalist Unitarians, remained a despised minority. In spite of considerable differences between the non-conformist sects, they all agreed on one point, 'the rights of conscience against all human authority'. They gradually established the freedom of conscience as 'a natural and inalienable right'. Their joint body, the Board of Dissenting Deputies during the next 200 years managed to remove one disability after another with the result that in the end 'religion was a no-man's land where the state must not intrude to help or hinder'. [6] It soon became clear that a plea for religious liberty was closely interrelated with one for civil liberty. By the end of the eighteenth century leading Dissenters like Joseph Priestley, Robert Hall and Richard Price stressed the duty of Dissenters to support and promote civil liberty in general. [7] The considerable share of the nonconformist conscience in the shaping of the Liberal movement in Britain up to 1914 has no counterpart on the European Continent. That conscience 'opposed the pretentiousness of Establishment and favoured the minimal state'. [8]

In the long run the Protestant insistence on an independent examination proved a first step in the direction of modern rationalism. Another was the development of philosophy and science in the seventeenth century. In some minds Newton's law of gravity began to take the place of God. In Catholic France Cartesianism, as Professor Ruggiero has observed:

'achieved truth and certitude by the very same process by which the religious consciousness attained its God. ... It was a kind of lay Methodism far more radical in its application than religious Methodism, because it never stopped short of any dogma or at any rate it postulated an unlimited possibility of progress along the road of criticism'. [9]

There developed a case of *La Raison* among the more educated people in France. The upper bourgeoisie prospering in manufacture could be called 'in a popular sense of the word Carthesian, in its cult of common sense, which is nothing but *la raison* in small change'. [10]

---

1. The doctrine of human rights

The close alliance between the liberal ideology and modern rationalism becomes evident when one considers the evolution of the movement emphasizing the significance of human rights for every person. The insistence on rational thought and on acknowledgement of human rights have moved forward together in modern society. Not that the rationalism of the Human Rights School is of recent origin; on the contrary it has a long tradition. Through the theory of natural law the doctrine of human rights is rooted in antiquity. To the Stoics nature meant the true realm of reason permeating the cosmos and shaping its inner structure. The law of nature was reasonable and valid for all nations. Natural law was no invention of man, but was created by divine reason itself. The Stoics believed in the original equality of people through their reasonable nature. Although the mediaeval Christian doctrine did not share the optimism of the Stoics, and their belief in man, which according to Christianity had been corrupted by man's fall, nevertheless in the elaborate theology of a Thomas of Aquinas the natural law of the Stoics had its place. Of divine origin, natural law pointed to everything constructive in life and, as with

5

the Stoics, Thomas regarded it as valid for all peoples and ages. Natural law laid down that agreements and treaties, once concluded between men, must be kept. It was seen as permanently valid in contrast to the changing positive laws, required by man's imperfection and fickleness. But these positive laws should model themselves on the pattern of Natural Law.

The modern theory of natural law, as it developed in the seventeenth and eighteenth centuries,[1] gradually freed itself from the theological background. The modern efforts were partly founded on the premise '. . . that the moral principles have a greater evidence than these teachings even of natural theology and, therefore, that natural law or natural rights should be kept independent of theology and its controversies'.[2] Like the Stoics, modern theorists believed in the reasonable character of nature. But with the progress of science they became convinced that nature too could be investigated and even measured. There remained the discrepancy between natural law and positive law as one between ideal and reality, between norm and fact. This discrepancy had been visualized in biblical terms in Milton's *Paradise Lost*: Man's fall, through the sinful enjoyment of the forbidden fruit, destroyed the original state of harmony and unity, created egoism, distrust, antagonism and desire for power. The murder of Abel by his brother Cain inaugurated the evil of violence and made organized State power inevitable.

A hundred years later J. J. Rousseau took up the same theme in a different form. He saw the state of innocence and complete harmony personified by the primitive people, recently discovered in the islands of the South Pacific. The fall, which had ended this happy state of things elsewhere, came about not through erotic desire, as the Bible suggested, but through the rise of private property. With its introduction 'the natural state of things was replaced by the law, right by violence'.[3] Yet men found a way out from this dilemma by concluding the social contract. They could not return to the state of nature which in the long run was a state of anarchy; what they required was security. To obtain it men agreed for themselves and for their families to conclude a social contract with each other. Each gave up part of his natural rights but gained security of the remainder within a new social order.

The construction of the social contract had been interpreted in various ways by the champions of Natural Law. One Group of thinkers, men like Grotius, Pufendorf and Thomas Hobbes, used the construction to justify the existing social order of the absolutist states. This school argued that the people after accepting the social contract with each other had concluded a second contract with a ruler, voluntarily agreeing to submit themselves to him, to transfer their rights to him and to put themselves under his protection. Once the contract had come into operation, it was binding and the people were not entitled to dissolve it and to depose the ruler. In the case of Hobbes the result was Leviathan, the omnipotent

6

State which did not depend on or acknowledge any valid higher norm.

However, a second school rejected the idea of a second contract. In their opinion the original social contract pointed to a limitation of government thus making absolutism in any shape impossible. To this school belonged Althusius, Milton and John Locke in the seventeenth century, Rousseau, Christian Wolff and Thomas Paine in the eighteenth century. In spite of variations in their thought, they 'continuously developed that system of inborn, inalienable human rights which in the end appeared as the proper core of the entire theory of natural law'.[4]

They were all anti-étatist in the sense that to them the state was not an abstract entity of unlimited powers. They viewed the state in fact as nothing but the association of the people. In the last instance only the sovereign people could issue laws and suspend them. Governments should only have limited power, as any government was commissioned by the sovereign people and had its mandate from them. This mandate could be revoked by them at any time and the government was accountable to the people for its actions and measures.[5]

The social contract, as understood by the second school, was the instrument by which to protect the inborn rights of the individual. It was above all John Locke who in his fundamental *Two Treatises on Government* (1689) emphasized both the innate rights of the individual and the necessity of limiting the powers of the government (see Section A, pp. 105–10). In fact the protection of the rights of the individuals, entitled to their 'Lives, Liberties and Estates', was seen by Locke as the main function of the government. 'The State has power only for the protection of natural law. Its province ends when it passes beyond those boundaries.'[6] As Locke expressed it with remarkable lucidity: 'A Government is not free to do as it pleases ... the law of nature stands as an eternal rule to all men, legislators as well as others.' Locke maintained that 'wherever "the people" or "the community", i.e. the majority, have placed the supreme power, they still retain "a supreme", power to remonstrate or alter the established government, i.e., they still retain a right of revolution.'[7]

At the same time a decisive aspect in Locke's thought – and even more so in the history of liberalism – is his doctrine of property: for to him the end of civil society is 'the preservation of property'. The chief reason why men unite themselves in a community and put themselves under government is 'the preservation of their property'. The individual has 'still in himself the great foundation of property ... Civil society merely creates the conditions under which the individuals can pursue their productive-acquisitive activity without obstruction.'[8]

The ideas of human rights and of the social contract did not remain confined to the academic ivory tower. They left their traces in two revolutionary manifestos issued on either side of the Atlantic during the last quarter of the eighteenth century. Both the Declaration of

Independence of 4 July 1776 (doc. 12), put forward by the thirteen independent states of America and the Declaration of the Rights of Man and Citizen, proclaimed by the French National Assembly on 27 August 1789 (doc. 13), were solemn protests against the wrongs of a rejected political and social order. While these manifestos were the products of specific and different circumstances, they claimed nevertheless a supranational and universal validity. Both took the rights of man for granted, although they defined them in different terms.[9] The American Declaration proclaimed 'life, liberty and the pursuit of happiness', the French Declaration 'liberty, property, security and resistance to oppression' as 'inalienable rights'. In the French case only the rights are described as 'natural and sacred', while in the American Declaration under the influence of Locke's thought the state guarantees the rights of the individual. No such guarantee is to be found in the French Declaration. Its article 3 'The source of all sovereignty resides essentially in the nation', can even be interpreted in a collectivist sense which puts the nation and its survival before the freedom and independence of the individual. But such contradiction between the rights of the individual and those of the nation which strikes the reader today did not concern contemporaries. They saw the French Declaration mostly as a radical challenge to the obsolete *ancien régime* and often as a great step forward on the road to the liberation of the individual and the nation.

In spite of differences in tenor and emphasis between them the Declarations share some major assumptions which were to leave their mark on the further development of liberal thought. In the American document the most pregnant aspects were two: firstly the insistence that all men are equally endowed with certain inalienable rights by their Creator; secondly that governments, far from taking their origin from divine grace, derive their powers from the consent of the governed. If a government fails to perform its duties, the people are entitled to alter or to abolish it. The United States had seceded from Britain because the King of Britain had as his first object 'the establishment of an absolute tyranny over these States'.

In the French Declaration a similar rebellious attitude towards the antiquated claims of the powers-that-be is evident. What was required by the Third Estate, the *spiritus rector* of the Revolution, was equality of all citizens before the law, the opening of positions and careers to all who possessed the necessary qualifications, and equality of the three Estates or Orders in the field of taxation. The sovereignty of the monarch was replaced by that of the nation and the fact that the natural rights of man include 'the resistance to oppression' clearly reflected the anti-absolutist tenor of the National Assembly.

Undoubtedly the French Declaration of 1789, which expressed the ideals of the rising French bourgeoisie, profited from the American example. But while the influence of America is beyond question, 'this is not to say that without America the French Declaration would not have seen the light. The whole philosophic movement in France in the eighteenth century pointed to such an act; Montesquieu, Voltaire and Rousseau had collaborated in its making. In reality, America and France, like England before them were alike tributaries to a great stream of ideas which, while expressing the ascendancy of the bourgeoisie, constituted a common ideal that summarized the evolution of western civilization'.[10]

The French Declaration is not free of some glaring metaphysical assumptions and contradictions.[11] Yet the two declarations created a pattern of insistence on the self-evidence of human rights, a pattern both repeated and modified later.

None of the manifestos of human rights issued in the nineteenth century proved of the same significance as did those of 1776 and 1789, but at least they indicate the further evolution of the idea. A year after the formation of Belgium as an independent state in 1830 a Constitution was drafted which included a list of rights of all Belgians. Among them the rights of property, of personal freedom, of freedom of opinion and of the press, the protection of the individual from arbitrary interference by others, including the organs of the Government, deserve to be mentioned. More elaborate, and perhaps cumbersome, was the 'Declaration of the Fundamental Rights' of the German National Assembly in Frankfurt passed after lengthy deliberations towards the end of 1848. It presented 'the accumulated fruits of political liberalism of the previous half century'.[12] Again freedom of the person, of speech, of assembly, of the press and of expression featured largely. The customary emphasis on liberty of religion and of conscience was accompanied by insistence on freedom of science and of university teaching. There were other new freedoms which resulted from specific needs of the situation in Germany. The vision of a united German Empire led to the emphasis on the right of freedom of movement for everyone within its boundaries, thus ending the restrictions on it long imposed by some of the German states. This insistence on the right of free movement was dictated by German patriotism as well as by the practical need for greater economic and social mobility at a time of growing industrialisation. While equality of all citizens before the law was reiterated, the draftsmen of the Frankfurt Assembly took a further step towards it by declaring the independence of the judiciary a condition of the freedom and welfare of the citizen.[13]

Seventy years later, after the immense upheaval of the First World War and the unexpected revolution of November 1918, the Constitution of Weimar once more hoisted the flag of human rights. It contained a special section devoted to the 'Fundamental Rights and the Fundamental Duties of the Germans'. These have to be seen against the political background of the new Republic, which was based on a coalition government of the moderate Social Democrats with two middle-class parties, the Catholic Centre and the German Democratic Party. Professor Hugo Preuss, a legal expert and the chief draftsman of the Weimar Constitution, wanted to confine the section on Rights and Duties to a few essentials, reiterating the principles of freedom of the nineteenth century. However the influential coalition parties and pressure groups managed to mould the text of that section on lines favourable to their specific interests. The outcome was a mixture, 'neither uniform nor clear'.[14] While the classic basic rights of the citizen were largely maintained, additional articles corresponded to a changed social and cultural situation. The protection of the family, the status of religious denominations, the position of workers and white-collar employees reflected new and often differing group interests in a pluralistic society.[15]

Property was 'guaranteed by the Constitution', though with the somewhat cryptic proviso that 'its content and limitations follow from the law' (art. 153). Other modern features were 'the right to work', first voiced in the French Revolution of 1848, and the idea of unemployment benefits. Every German was 'to be given his chance of earning his livelihood through work in the national economy'. If an adequate possibility of work was not forthcoming 'his necessary subsistence' would 'be provided for' (art. 163). The economic freedom of the individual was no longer viewed as unlimited. A balance had to be struck between it and the need for a dignified life for every citizen.[16]

The stipulation that there was to be no State Church (art. 137) was bound to satisfy the freethinkers as well as the Roman Catholics who in the Second Empire had resented the close ties between the Protestant State Church and the Hohenzollerns. Now all the churches were to enjoy an independence from the state unknown before. At the same time the rights of the adherents of non-Christian religions and of non-believers were acknowledged by the provision in the same article that 'religious denominations are regarded as equal with the associations which set themselves the task of jointly cultivating a philosophy (*Weltanschauung*)'. In this manner freedom was assured to a wide spectrum of religious as well as non-religious views ranging from Christian believers to atheists. The mixture of traditional and progressive liberal aspects in this complex catalogue of human rights is also discernible in the article on marriage (art. 119).[17]

Although the provisions on human rights in the Weimar Constitution thus reflect some new trends in contemporary society, they were still devised, like their forerunners, within the socio-political framework of one nation. By contrast the 'Universal Declaration of Human Rights' issued by the United Nations in Paris in December 1948 was the expression of a post-war global situation, an attempt to formulate a world-wide system of human rights. It was designed to apply not only to Frenchmen, Germans or Americans, but to every human being, irrespective of his or her nation, religion or social group. None of the previous statements of human rights had reached the universality of approach of the UNO Declaration directed to all mankind. The Preamble to its

International Covenant on Economic, Social and Cultural Rights (1966) speaks of 'recognition of the inherent dignity and of the equal and inalienable rights of all human members of the human family' as 'the foundation of freedom, justice and peace in the world'. It optimistically asserts that 'Member States have pledged themselves to achieve, in cooperation with the United Nations, the promotion of universal respect for and observance of human rights and fundamental freedoms.'

The thirty articles of the Universal Declaration reveal the vast extension of the range of human rights, political and social, demanded by major movements in the present century. Some of them, like the right to work, had been anticipated 100 years earlier by Louis Blanc and the Paris workers of 1848. But whereas freedom to work is, as we have seen, a traditional liberal demand, the *right to work*, to free choice of employment, to just and favourable conditions of work and to protection against unemployment' (art. 23 (1)) was the outcome of the pressure of the labour movement during the previous eighty years. The same is true of the provision that 'everyone has the right to form and to join trade unions for the protection of his interests' (art. 23 (4)). The stipulation too, that 'Men and women of full age, without any limitation due to race, nationality or religion have the right to marry and to found a family', and 'are entitled to equal rights as to marriage, during marriage and at its dissolution' (art. 16). would have been unthinkable without the movement for the emancipation of women which already 100 years earlier had found an articulate champion in the great liberal J. S. Mill.

A similar extension and refinement of other points in previous Declarations is also noticeable. Under the auspices of UNO the principle of security of the individual from arbitrary action by power-holders, from unlawful interference by the State has been amplified by the formula: 'No-one shall be subjected to arbitrary arrest, detention or exile' (art. 9). Again whereas the right to freedom of movement and of residence within the borders of each state was customary, new was the addition that 'Everyone has the right to leave any country, including his own and to return to his country' (art. 13 (2)). Although earlier Declarations had delineated the respective rights of the state and the churches, it was only now that 'everyone's right to education' was expressly acknowledged. [18]

As pointed out, in 1789 the citizens of France had been solemnly assured that 'the principle of all sovereignty rests essentially in the nation'. By contrast the Universal Declaration viewed the problem of the nation much more from the standpoint of the individual and of his or her rights by proclaiming that 'everyone has the right to a nationality' and 'No-one shall be arbitrarily deprived of his nationality nor denied the right to change his nationality' (art. 15).

The traditional liberal insistence on freedom of thought and religion, too, was amplified and re-defined at the forum of the United Nations. It now expressly included the individual's 'freedom to change his religion or belief, and freedom either alone or in community with others and in public or private, to manifest his religion or belief in teaching, practice, worship and observance' (art. 18). Correspondingly 'the right to freedom of opinion and expression', valid for everyone, was made more articulate and international by the addition that it included 'freedom to hold opinions without interference and to seek, receive, impart information and ideas through any media and regardless of frontiers' (art. 19).

Altogether, the Universal Declaration of Human Rights is not only much more complex and elaborate than any of its predecessors, it also has integrated elements from outside the liberal tradition, such as impulses from the struggle of the labour movement and the socialist camp. It further reflects the fight of national groups for their own identity, as well as the attitude of colonial nations in their insistence on independence from their former masters.

An entire spectrum of new ideas and attitudes had contributed to its making. Nevertheless the UNO Declaration basically stands in the tradition of the movement for human rights and thus remains in the wake of a major strand of international Liberalism.

2. The classical economists and the utilitarians

It is necessary to offer some definition of the two schools as interpreted for the purposes of this section. The term 'classical economists' will be interpreted in a broad sense to cover the writers who belonged to the mainstream of English (or rather Anglo-Scottish) economic thought between the 1770s and the mid-nineteenth century: Adam Smith, T. R. Malthus, Jeremy Bentham, David Ricardo, James Mill, Robert Torrens, J. R. McCulloch, Nassau Senior, John Stuart Mill. They cannot be regarded as a homogeneous school, and a few of them – Malthus and Bentham, for example – diverged sufficiently from some of its central doctrines to make their inclusion controversial. But it will be assumed here that there are sufficient links between those in the list to justify their being grouped together generically. One may also include along with them David Hume, whose essays on economic subjects anticipated some of the main elements in Smith's economic thought, and the Frenchman J. B. Say, who was the main interpreter on the Continent of Smithian economics and was himself a significant contributor to classical doctrine.

The term 'utilitarian' will be interpreted in a narrower sense. It *can* be used rather loosely, to describe those in the history of ethics who have regarded the maximization of happiness as the basic criterion of moral judgement. In this sense the utilitarian tradition can be traced back at least into the seventeenth century, and one can include within it on the one hand conservative thinkers such as Hume and William Paley and on the other hand a virtual anarchist such as William Godwin. But the word 'Utilitarian' was originally coined to describe the school of thought formed by Jeremy Bentham, and it is in this sense, as more or less interchangeable with 'Benthamite', that the term will be used in this introduction. From the point of view of moral and political thought the most important members of the school, apart from its founder, were James Mill and John Stuart Mill, though the latter moved away from strict utilitarianism in some important respects. Also connected with the school were Ricardo, the social reformer Edwin Chadwick, the Westminster radical Francis Place, and the loose group of politicians and journalists who came to be known as the Philosophic Radicals.

Between classical economics and utilitarianism there was a substantial, though not complete, overlap. The utilitarians (though Bentham and J. S. Mill were both in some ways unorthodox) did generally subscribe to the main body of classical economic doctrine, and indeed some of its most zealous propagators were Benthamites. But the question of how many of the classical economists accepted utilitarianism is more complex. Adam Smith, himself a moral philosopher of importance, explicitly maintained that sympathy rather than utility was the basis of moral judgement. Malthus did adhere to a principle of utility, but probably derived it from Paley rather than Bentham. Ricardo came under Benthamite influence with regard to politics and could describe himself in 1821 as 'a disciple of the Bentham and Mill school',[1] though he does not seem to have developed much interest in utilitarian ethics. J. B. Say was an admirer and correspondent of Bentham, but Torrens, McCulloch and Senior, though in frequent contact with the Benthamite circle, would not have regarded themselves as Benthamites. It has been pointed out by one scholar that the classical economists did all subscribe to 'the principle that the test of policy is to be its effect on human happiness'; but another scholar has argued that to classify them all on these grounds as 'utilitarians' would be to give the term an unusefully wide meaning.[2]

In looking first at the classical economists we shall not attempt any general description or assessment of their place in the history of economic thought. We shall concentrate on two questions: in what senses classical economics can be described as a doctrine of economic liberalism; and how far it implied or carried with it a liberal outlook in politics. In considering the first question one should recall that classical economics was originally developed in reaction against the mercantilism of the early modern period. It is true that the two schools were not wholly antithetical and that many of the key concepts of classical theory can be found in mercantilist writings, but the fact remains that the general tendency of these writings was not in favour of economic freedom. The mercantilists were concerned with securing a favourable balance of trade, which they regarded as both a source and a symptom of national economic strength; and they believed that in fostering native commerce and industry in competition with those of other countries, and in directing private effort into the channels most conducive to the public advantage, the state had an important role to play. In England the State did rely to a considerable extent, in the seventeenth and eighteenth centuries, on regulations of the kind which the mercantilist writers advocated — tariffs, prohibitions, bounties, monopolies. But government control over the economy was not so comprehensive and rigid as the economic authoritarianism which prevailed in France, and the first concerted plea for a more *laissez faire* approach to economic policy came not from the English classical economists but from the Physiocrats, a school of French economists whose main works appeared in the third quarter of the eighteenth century. Their distinctive belief that only the agricultural sector could produce net additions to wealth made them particularly critical of Colbertist policies for the direct stimulation of commerce and industry, and they believed that the main requirement for increased agricultural prosperity was greater freedom of trade in grain — both freedom of domestic trade and freedom of exportation. Their arguments against excessive regulation involved some notable analytic insights into the benefits derivable from competition and free enterprise. But they resorted at times to a rather metaphysical belief in the existence of natural laws which, if allowed to operate with the minimum of interference, would bring about a providential harmony in the economic order.

There are traces of natural law thinking and terminology in the writings of the classical economists; but their case for economic freedom had a more complete rationale than that developed by their predecessors, and did not need to be helped out by assertions about the providential beneficence of natural laws. While the notion of a 'natural harmony' resulting from spontaneous economic forces did play an important part in their system, they believed that the mechanisms which produced such harmony could be empirically explained.[3]

Given certain conditions (of which more will be said later), they maintained that economic freedom would maximize wealth — basically through giving the greatest possible scope to what Malthus called 'that animated activity in bettering our own condition which ... forms the masterspring of public prosperity'.[4] The argument was set out in its simplest form by Bentham. The wealth of a community consists of the wealth of the individuals who compose it; 'each individual bestowing more time and attention upon the means of preserving and increasing his portion of wealth than is or can be bestowed by government, is likely to take a more effectual course than what in his instance and on his behalf would be taken by government'; hence both individual and collective wealth can be most effectively increased by leaving each person free to pursue his own interests.[5] It was further shown that the desire of each individual to make the most remunerative use of his own share of the factors of production could be relied upon to secure an efficient allocation of resources. Smith, in particular, showed how 'the private interests and passions of men naturally lead them to divide and distribute the stock of every society among all the different employments carried on in it as nearly as possible in the proportion which is most agreeable to the interest of the whole society'.[6] He argued that any attempt to direct the 'industry of private people' into the most advantageous channels would be quite superfluous, and, because it would require a degree of wisdom and knowledge which no government could possess, would in practice be damaging to national wealth.[7] It was generally agreed by the classical economists that (at least in relatively advanced countries) governments should not attempt to produce economic growth directly. Instead, they should concentrate on enlarging the area of free trade and competition and on removing obstacles and disincentives to private enterprise and frugality. It was argued that the wider the effective trading area, the more opportunity there would be for each country to specialize in the types of production for which it was best suited, and the more opportunity there would be within each country for the division of labour. The division of labour was regarded as a crucial source of increases in productivity. Competition operated in the same direction: the less protection and privilege there were in an economy, the more scope there would be for competition to enforce efficiency and stimulate improvement. But perhaps the factor which was most heavily emphasized in the classical theory of growth was the accumulation of capital. This was the *sine qua non* for increasing the quantity as well as the efficiency of productive activity; and it depended on private saving, especially (it was thought) on that arising from the drive of the capitalist classes to build up their fortunes and businesses. It was chiefly as a hindrance to this process of accumulation that Ricardo attacked the Corn Laws: he argued that agricultural protection had the effect of pushing up food prices and wages and reducing the general level of profits, thereby checking the accumulation of capital or actually causing it to seek more profitable outlets abroad. In general, for the sake of a high rate of accumulation it was considered important that the rewards of enterprise and 'abstinence' should be subject to as little encroachment and insecurity as possible.

With all this emphasis on incentives for the entrepreneur and the capitalist, what incentives were envisaged for the working man? The market economy did offer, for some, the opportunity of raising themselves into the property-owning class. But the basic incentive it provided for the worker was the need to maintain himself and his family through his own exertions and prudence. It was because of its supposed tendency to undermine this incentive that the classical economists showed so much hostility to the Old Poor Law. Outdoor-relief, supplementation of wages and family allowances were thought to encourage idleness, improvidence and a rate of population growth which tended to outstrip its means of support; and the New Poor Law of 1834, for which Senior and Chadwick were mainly responsible, was a stern measure designed to restore working-class self-reliance. The classical economists were by no means indifferent to the welfare of the working class; but they were convinced that its best chance of ameliorating its condition lay in limiting the increase of its own numbers, and in cooperating with the capitalists to ensure a 'progressive' economy and thus a high demand for labour. They generally took the view that the interests of capital and labour were closely identified, and that the latter could not hope, except in the very short term, to improve its position at the expense of the former. Successful attempts by labour to raise wage-levels at the expense of profits would be likely to rebound on employment by checking the accumulation of the funds from which labour was paid. Thus economic liberalism could not offer the working classes any easy or rapid means of raising their standard of life. It did offer them certain kinds of freedom; but those it offered – freedom of choice as consumers, freedom to dispose of their own labour as they wished – were often in practice extremely limited.[8]

A question that remains to be considered is how far, in the opinion of the classical economists, the forces of free enterprise did need to be controlled or supplemented by the state.[9] Although the main burden of their message to their contemporaries was in favour of liberalization, it would be misleading to describe them without qualification as advocates of *laissez faire*. They would all have accepted, for a start, Smith's basic list of the responsibilities of the State: first, defence; secondly, justice, or 'the duty of protecting, as far as possible, every member of the society from the injustice or oppression of every other member of it'; and thirdly the erection and maintenance of public works and institutions the provision of which could not be left to private initiative.[10] This list could be interpreted as justifying a considerable range of governmental functions; and some of Smith's successors would have wished to extend it. The most dogmatic advocates of *laissez faire* and free trade were not the classical economists but the publicists, politicians and businessmen – Harriet Martineau, James Wilson of *The Economist*, Richard Cobden and the 'Manchester School' – who used their ideas in a simplified and one-sided form. The economists themselves looked at problems of state intervention in a pragmatic rather than a doctrinaire fashion, as is clear from the variety of economic and social measures which one can find recommended in their writings. These included, to give some notable examples, nationalization of the note-issue, government responsibility for public health and education, State-assisted emigration and colonization, regulation of the working hours of children, and the granting of compensation or special assistance to workers displaced by machinery. It is worth adding, however, that systematic analysis of the scope and theory of economic policy is rare in classical writings, and for such treatment one needs to look particularly to the Benthamite members of the school. Between the Benthamites and the other members there was no general disagreement over the criteria of policy, but there was some difference of emphasis and approach – as might be expected from the fact that the Benthamites (excluding Ricardo) were not primarily economists. They viewed economics as merely one of the areas which had to be mastered by anyone concerned with the general field of politics and legislation; and the principles on which their approach to legislation was based – their utilitarian concern with *net* effects on happiness – gave them a special awareness of the need not only to maximize growth but also to minimize its costs. In Bentham's *Constitutional Code,* written in the 1820s, there is an unprecedentedly detailed exposition of the legislative and administrative methods which an ideal polity might use for, *inter alia*, the elimination or prevention of various social evils, the spread of education and useful knowledge, and the regulation (though not the 'factitious encouragement') of economic activity. Two decades later, John Stuart Mill provided in his *Principles of Political Economy* the first general attempt to examine the defects of the market and to define the proper limits to the principle of *laissez faire.*

The final problem to be discussed with regard to the classical economists is the relationship between their economic and their political views.[11] J. B. Say said in the introduction to his *Traité d'économie politique* that the new science of political economy should be regarded as distinct from that of politics:[12] Wealth is essentially independent of political organization. Under any form of government, a state can prosper if it is well administered. Nations have been known to enrich themselves under absolute monarchs ... If political liberty is more favourable to the development of wealth, it is indirectly so.' That there was no necessary connection between economic liberalism and political liberalism is shown by the fact that the Physiocrats were believers in absolute monarchy; and among the classical economists in England there was a considerable variety of political attitudes. Still, there were certain respects in which adherence to classical economic doctrines might be expected to carry with it – and in England usually did – a liberal outlook in politics. It was natural that men who were opposed to an excess of government interference in the economy should have favoured a political system which imposed general limitations on the exercise of power. Malthus, the most conservative member of the classical school, was sufficiently whiggish to write in the *Edinburgh Review* that 'the great advantage of a free country' lay in its being 'fenced against the folly or wickedness of a sovereign'[13] and McCulloch considered it likely 'that the right of property will be more respected, that the exercise of industry will be less fettered, and that the public income will be more judiciously levied and expended' under a free government than under an autocratic one. [14]

As this last quotation indicates, one of the reasons for the classical economists' distrust of arbitrary government was their concern for the security of property: the more absolute were the sovereign's powers, the more danger there would be of his violating the property of his subjects. The same argument could be used, as James Mill pointed out in his *Essay on Government*, against placing effective power in the hands of an aristocracy;[15] but in fact some of the classical economists were willing to defend a predominantly aristocratic government, regarding it as more likely to safeguard liberty and property than to endanger them. Malthus, for example, believed like Burke that an aristocracy was of crucial importance for 'the protection of a people equally from the tyranny of despotic rulers, and the fury of a despotic mob'.[16] Ricardo and James Mill, however, developed anti-aristocratic views, which accorded with their particular version of political economy. Whereas Smith and Malthus thought that the economic interests of landowners were generally in tune with those of the rest of the community, Ricardo and Mill maintained that there was a conflict between the interests of landowners and those of other classes. Mill seems to have been the first to draw political conclusions from this conflict.[17] When he wrote his first economic pamphlet in 1804, he thought that if the landowners could be persuaded that a measure such as the bounty on the exportation of corn was against the long-term interests of the nation, they would be sufficiently public spirited to relinquish it; but by 1807 he had come to feel that the landed interest was bent on exploiting its dominant position in the legislature, and the Corn Law of 1815 seemed to provide decisive confirmation for this belief. He concluded that political reform was necessary if the full benefits of economic freedom were to be secured, and he helped to bring Ricardo round to the same point of view. In 1820 Ricardo was writing that only after a reform of parliament would any ministry be likely to succeed in 'sweeping away many of our commercial restrictions, particularly the greatest, the restraints on the importation of corn'. [18]

It was not surprising that men who believed in economic liberalization and growth should have favoured a moderate reform which increased the political influence of the middle classes; and most of the classical economists did give their support to the Reform Bill of 1832 (even Malthus accepting it retrospectively). It was also to be expected that – at least in the circumstances of the late eighteenth and early nineteenth centuries – they should have been unfriendly towards a more democratic brand of reform. Hume's basic argument in favour of entrusting political power to the propertied classes had been that they alone could be relied upon to respect and uphold the laws and conventions (especially those relating to property) on which the stability and prosperity of society depended. This opinion, reinforced by the French Revolution, remained

The classical economists and the utilitarians

very widespread among the upper and middle classes in England far into the nineteenth century, and it was shared by many of the classical economists. McCulloch and Senior both expressed themselves in strong terms against universal suffrage.[19] Ricardo was more radical than they were, but he recognized the seriousness of the objection that democracy would lead to economic levelling: that although it would not in reality be in the interests of the poorer classes to invade the property of the rich, it was hardly likely that they would be sufficiently well-informed and far-sighted to recognize this and to refrain from using political power for redistributive purposes. He conceded therefore that if it could be plausibly maintained that there were strata of society in which 'a sacred regard to the rights of property' was currently lacking, those strata should be excluded from the franchise until they were properly enlightened.[20] Bentham and James Mill did commit themselves to universal suffrage, at least in principle. They were confident that the mass of the people *could* be persuaded to respect property; but critics of utilitarian political thought, such as Macaulay, found this an unconvincing assumption,[21] and in the face of the new socialist doctrines which were beginning to circulate in the 1820s and 1830s there were doubts on this question even in Benthamite circles.

In their hostility to socialism Bentham and James Mill were at one with the other classical economists.[22] Mill went so far as to say that if socialist ideas were to spread the result would be 'the subversion of civilized society; worse than the overwhelming deluge of Huns and Tartars'.[23] After what has been said above, the economic reasons for such hostility need only be briefly sketched. It was argued that the abolition of private property would remove the motives to individual prudence and 'moral restraint', and would thus produce a rate of population growth which would soon outrun subsistence. Also, it was thought that socialism would be fatal to 'abstinence': it would destroy the current mode of capital accumulation, and the classical economists could not envisage any workable alternative. All incentives, they believed, would be weakened or removed, and coercion would become necessary to maintain production: Bentham warned that 'the gentle motive of reward' would have to be replaced by 'the doleful motive of punishment'.[24] In general, with regard both to individual freedom of choice and to allocative efficiency, many of the arguments used in championing the market economy against mercantilism could be brought to bear against a socialist system. The one major figure in the classical tradition who showed a more sympathetic, if somewhat ambivalent, attitude towards socialism was John Stuart Mill.[25] But the kind of socialism that attracted him, largely on ethical grounds, was that of Owen and Fourier – a decentralized socialism based on cooperative associations, rather than a collectivist regime. He never considered that the organization of a national economy from the centre was feasible, and indeed he always had doubts

19

about the practical operation of socialism at any level. By the end of his life he had definitely concluded that in the 'imperfect degree of moral cultivation' which men had so far reached there was no general substitute for self-interest as an incentive, and that the economic benefits derived from competition considerably outweighed its ill-effects; while on the political and social side he was afraid that under socialism individual freedom and self-development would be seriously curtailed.

In surveying the views of the classical economists it has been necessary to say something about the ideas of the leading utilitarians on politics and legislation, in so far as those ideas seemed relevant to their standpoint on political economy. But the time has now come to concentrate more directly on the utilitarians and their relationship to the liberal tradition. Much turns on how far the ideas of Bentham himself can be regarded as liberal, and to suggest some answer to that question one needs to sketch the outlines of his philosophy.

His basic psychological assumption was that what men actually seek in life is pleasure or happiness; and his basic value-judgement was that pleasure is the only thing which can be regarded as good in itself. He considered that each man was the best judge of what would give him pleasure, and that in the sphere of 'private ethics' it was right that men should pursue their own happiness. In the public sphere, he considered that the only end which could be reasonably and acceptably postulated for a society at large was the maximization of aggregate happiness, the greatest happiness of the greatest number; and the principle of utility laid down that actions and institutions were to be judged by how far they were conducive to this end. Bentham did not believe that in a properly ordered society the real long-term interests and happiness of individuals would conflict with the happiness of others or of the society in general. The task of the utilitarian legislator was to realize the potential harmony between private and communal interests. This was to be done partly by the creation of laws and other sanctions which would penalize and discourage anti-social behaviour; and partly by so moulding men's desires that they would seek their own pleasure in ways which were either innocuous or actually conducive to the general happiness.

There were obvious liberal implications in the assumption that each man was generally the best judge of his own happiness, and Bentham definitely stated that 'the care of providing for his enjoyments, ought to be left almost entirely to each individual'.[26] His works show a genuine tolerance of the variety of human tastes, and an awareness of the dangers of one man's presuming to decide what is good for another. Yet it appears that his tolerance applied essentially to men's private as distinct from their social activities. With regard to those aspects of life which came within the purview of the legislator Bentham was prepared, in the interests of the greatest happiness of the greatest number, to countenance a large degree of control and manipulation. He thought for example that a government inspired by utilitarian principles might influence, even 'dictate', the judgements of public opinion by issuing political and moral codes; and it could hope by these and other means to strengthen the 'moral sanction', the pressure exerted by public opinion in favour of behaviour which conformed to the requisite norms.[27] People whose conduct was noxious or disreputable or who became a charge on the community were − under Bentham's schemes for the management of criminals and paupers − to be subjected to a thoroughly coercive regime, primarily for the good of the community and indirectly for their own benefit.[28] But it was above all through the education of the young − the 'art of education' being defined as a branch of the art of government − that the legislator could adjust people's inclinations and behaviour to the requirements of the greatest happiness. By means of education they could be helped to derive pleasure from benevolence, and they could be diverted from inclinations which would be damaging to the happiness of others and of themselves. While it could be argued that there was nothing illiberal in such aims, the same could hardly be said of the methods recommended for implementing them. The conditioning process Bentham envisaged for the young was to involve relentless supervision and discipline. He anticipated objections to his scheme on the grounds that it suppressed the 'liberal spirit and energy of a free citizen' and constructed 'a set of *machines* under the similitude of *men*'. But he could see no force in any such objection. 'Call them machines', he said: 'so they were but happy ones, I should not care.'[29]

Bentham made it clear that he did not value liberty for its own sake. He equated pure liberty with absence of government and law, and what many people thought of as liberty he preferred to treat as security: personal security against injury at the hands of others, political security against maltreatment by those in authority. To him liberty was an emotive term, the use of which in politics distracted attention from the fact that it was essentially by restrictions on freedom that happiness was made possible. In an early manuscript he compared the use of the word with the use of brandy in one's diet: 'both cloud the understanding and inflame the passions'.[30] And he wrote[31] towards the end of his life:

'There are few words which, with its derivations [liberal, liberalism], have been more mischievous than this word liberty. When it means anything beyond mere caprice and dogmatism, it means good government; and if good government had had the good fortune to occupy the same place in the public mind which has been occupied by the vague entity called liberty, the crimes and follies which have disgraced and retarded the progress of political improvement would hardly have been committed.'

This passage shows that Bentham's approach to the concept of liberty was not altered by his conversion to democracy. Having in the earlier part of his life shown little disposition to criticize the structure of existing governments, he became in his sixties – in the years after 1809 – a thorough-going radical. A commitment to democracy did in fact seem to be a logical outcome of his thought, especially once the 'self-preference principle' (which was not clearly formulated in his early writings) had hardened into a basic tenet. It followed from this principle that the actual end of any government would be the happiness of the governors; the principle of utility laid down that the greatest happiness of the greatest number should be the end pursued; and it followed from the two principles together that the means of securing good government was a contrived 'junction of interests' which would bring 'the particular interest of rulers into accordance with the universal interest'.[32]

A distinguished scholar has said that Bentham was never a liberal but passed directly from monarchical authoritarianism to democratic authoritarianism.[33] It is certainly true that, having once decided that the will of a majority of the people was the only admissible guide to the maximization of their happiness, he treated any check to popular sovereignty as unjustified. In the *Constitutional Code*, which he composed in the last years of his life, he advocated republican and unicameral government, universal suffrage, and an elaborate set of measures designed to ensure that the people's agents were given as little opportunity as possible to diverge from the people's will. Moreover, in his *Deonotology* (a work on ethics which he was also writing in his last years) he envisaged a growing reliance on public opinion as a means of influencing social behaviour. He maintained that as enlightenment spread, the popular judgement of right and wrong would grow increasingly reliable, and with each person becoming more and more dependent upon the good opinion of others the 'moral or popular sanction' would steadily strengthen its hold over people's conduct. Eventually, he wrote, 'A whole kingdom, the great globe itself, will become a gymnasium, in which every man exercises himself before the eyes of every other man. Every gesture, every turn of limb or feature, in those whose motions have a visible influence on the general happiness, will be noticed and marked down'.[34] The concept seems uncomfortably close to the 'absolute dependence of each on all, the surveillance of each by all', which J. S. Mill was to regard as an intolerable feature of communism.[35]

It needs to be asked whether in the thought of Bentham's followers liberty occupied a more elevated place than it did in his own philosophy. Much the most important propagator of his ideas was James Mill. By the time Mill first met Bentham in 1808 he himself was already moving – for reasons which have been indicated above – towards a belief in parliamentary reform, and his influence may have helped to precipitate Bentham's conversion to political radicalism. But in the years that followed it would appear to have been Bentham rather than Mill who led the way in pursuing the utilitarian argument for democracy to its logical conclusion. Bentham said of Mill that his radical beliefs derived 'less from love for the many, than from hatred of the few'.[36] While strongly anti-aristocratic, Mill did explicitly put his faith in the middle classes rather than in the mass of the people. He was prepared to follow the logic of Benthamism to the extent of committing himself in principle to universal male suffrage. But unlike Bentham he was willing to take the view that certain exclusions from the franchise (not only the exclusion of women but also that of the lowest strata of society) *might* be made without damage to good government; and one feels that the only thing which made it possible for him to countenance a wide popular franchise was his declared belief that the opinions and votes of the bulk of the electors would be guided by the educated middle classes. He assigned to this section of the community a paternalistic responsibility for influencing and 'directing' the minds of the people which he denied to the old ruling class.[37] What in his view made such a role legitimate for the middle classes was the fact that it would depend not on pressure but on persuasion. He was confident that the truths established by the moral and social sciences could be passed on by the educated in a simple and cogent form which would command the assent of the people at large.

If Bentham was (or became in his last years) a democratic authoritarian, James Mill's acceptance of democracy was combined rather uneasily with authoritarian tendencies of a different, more élitist, kind. He himself had been trained in his early days to be a preacher in the Scottish Presbyterian Church and had earned his living as a tutor; and although he subsequently lost his religious faith he always retained a strongly moralistic and didactic outlook. One may illustrate this from an article of his called 'The Church and its Reform', published near the end of his life in 1835. He proposed that, instead of supporting an established church whose ministers performed religious ceremonies, the State should employ a largely secularized 'clergy' whose duties would be those of moral and civil instruction. 'We think it of great importance', wrote Mill, 'that all the families of a parish should be got to assemble on the Sunday – clean, and so dressed as to make a favourable appearance in the eyes of one another. That alone is ameliorating.' Instead of a church service, the occasion would be used for moral discourses (designed 'to make, as deeply as possible, all the impressions which lead to good conduct') or for lectures on subjects of public importance: 'there is no branch of political knowledge which ought not to be carefully taught to the people in their parochial assemblies on the day of rest'.[38] One would hesitate before applying the term 'liberal' to a reformism which could embrace this kind of indoctrination. It is true that in earlier works Mill had advocated freedom of the press,[39] believing that in conditions of free competition the right ideas were bound to prevail. But his vigorous certitude could hardly be combined with a genuinely tolerant and open-minded attitude to other values and modes of thought.

J. S. Mill, while less convinced of the exclusive truth of utilitarian doctrine, resembled his father in the importance he sometimes attached to the 'authority' of the educated.[40] But he did not share his father's confidence that in a democratic system the working classes would follow the lead of the middle classes, and he was pessimistic about the implications of what Bentham had called 'the omnipotence of the many'.[41] He wrote in 1838 that universal suffrage would mean giving power to 'unskilled manual labourers', and that the effect would be 'to make one narrow mean type of human nature universal and perpetual, and to crush every influence which tends to the further improvement of man's intellectual and moral nature'.[42] He probably had Bentham in mind when he wrote in his essay *On Liberty* that some reformers of the generation previous to his own had replaced the traditional liberal aim of limiting the power of rulers with the newer aim of identifying the rulers with the people. In their view, he said, 'The nation did not need to be protected against its own will. There was no fear of its tyrannizing over itself.' [43] But it was just this danger that J. S. Mill set out to combat, both in his arguments for the political representation of minorities and in his case for limiting the social pressures of 'collective opinion'. One should not exaggerate the differences between Bentham's ideas and those of the younger Mill. The latter continued to regard himself as fundamentally a utilitarian; and there was a close similarity between Bentham's insistence that each man should be allowed to pursue his own private happiness in his own way and Mill's arguments for complete freedom in 'purely personal conduct'. But there were elements in Mill's thought – his hatred of conformity and mediocrity, his belief in 'the Greek ideal of self-development', his conviction that progress depended on the initiatives of exceptional men – which gave it a different emphasis and some quite different values from those reflected in Bentham's work.

In spite of Bentham's democratic views, the influence of Benthamism in nineteenth-century England seems to have been largely confined to the intelligentsia. The cerebral and at times dogmatic approach of the Philosophic Radicals, together with their commitment to orthodox political economy, tended to distance them from the masses: Bagehot said baldly that 'the people did not like them or their ideas'.[44] At the same time, their ideas had little appeal for conventionally-minded members of the propertied classes. The parliamentary reform movement was influenced far more at the popular level by natural rights doctrines (which Bentham regarded as intellectually worthless), and at a higher social level by the Whig theory of the representation of interests, than it was by utilitarian arguments. It was in the fields of social and legal reform that a more significant impact could be claimed for Benthamism – an impact made through individual members of the Benthamite circle who helped to expose various problems and abuses and to devise systematic regulations and administrative machinery for coping with them.[45] It was once believed that the influence of Benthamism had been in the direction of *laissez faire*, but this view is now largely discredited. In fact the Benthamites tended to think that existing governments were *too* inclined towards a *laissez faire* attitude. Chadwick, writing in 1828 in the Benthamite *Westminster Review*, protested that the object of most of the country's rulers was apparently

'not to commit themselves, *i.e.* to do nothing or to evade difficulties neatly and speciously, and cover with pomp or a blind routine the *dolce far niente* of office, averting their heads from calamities so long as they are unnoticed, and letting evil principles work themselves out on the community, unless they are forced into notice by clamour.' [46]

Thomas Paine had written in his *Rights of Man*: 'The more perfect civilization is, the less occasion has it for government, because the more it does regulate its own affairs, and govern itself'.[47] The Benthamites mark the transition to a different view. In 1862 J. S. Mill explicitly recognized that the tendency was for the functions of the State to widen as civilization advanced.[48] It is true that, in spite of what James Mill called their 'passion for the improvement of the condition of mankind',[49] the utilitarians' economic views made them very cautious about attempts to improve the lot of the lower classes through any actual redistribution of wealth or income: although Bentham did recognize the principle of the diminishing marginal utility of money and its egalitarian implications, he was not willing to approve any measures for the equalization of wealth if they threatened to undermine the incentives on which production depended.[50] None the less, the Benthamite brand of reformism – as applied in fields such as education, public health and factory legislation – was more positive than that of most contemporary liberals. To describe it as liberal one needs to use the term not in its classical nineteenth-century sense, but with some of the connotations it has acquired in the twentieth century.[51] Indeed in some respects (as several scholars have suggested) the approach which Benthamism most accurately foreshadowed was the social engineering of the Fabians.[52]

3. Aesthetic individualism

In their specific ways both the Human Rights School and the utilitarians emphasized the need for liberating man from traditional fetters, from the excesses of the established monarchical and aristocratic forces. Bentham and James Mill regarded men as basically motivated by self-interest, seeking to secure a maximum of pleasure and to avoid a maximum of pain. Though these thinkers concentrated on freeing the individual from the shackles of an arbitrary and obsolete political and legal order, by a rational method, they were not interested in raising the potential of the individual. Man should be free to follow his own bent, but to improve and develop his talents and aptitudes was no more than a sideline in their reflections. It was no concern of the elder utilitarians whether people preferred poetry to gin, or paintings to beer. They wanted people to obtain a maximum of happiness but they did not inquire into the nature or degrees of this happiness. They neither wished to develop personality and character, nor did they deplore an imitative behaviour. They were concerned with the desirability, but not with the quality of happiness.

However a third strand in the complex texture of liberal thought pointed in a different direction. If it also claimed freedom of the individual *from* the tutelage of the State and from the pressure of public opinion, it wanted to make use of this freedom *for* advancing towards an ideal, for a norm of individualism. Though it is true, the cult of the many-sided personality, of the appreciation of the individuality as a work of art did not begin with Wilhelm von Humboldt and the younger Mill, only they gave it that modern note and consideration which one can describe as 'qualitative liberalism' or aesthetic individualism. It was the young Wilhelm von Humboldt who paved the way for the self-improvement of the individual, for its formation under the classical idea of *Bildung* with his essay on the 'Limits of State Action', written in 1792–93 but only published, in 1851, many years after the author's death.[2] An English edition which appeared in 1854 seems to have impressed John Stuart Mill while he composed his outstanding essay *On Liberty*. When Humboldt gave his reasons for confining the activities of the State to a mininum, he was under the spell of the idea of *Bildung*, of the perfectibility of man. It was an image of man far removed from that of Bentham's felicific calculus. 'The end of Man', Humboldt wrote in a notable passage of his essay quoted with approval by J. S. Mill, 'that which is prescribed by the eternal or immutable dictates of reason, and not suggested by vague and transient desires, is the highest and most harmonious development of his powers to a complete and consistent whole.'[3] The great object of human endeavour was 'the individuality of power and development' which could only be achieved with the help of two prerequisites, 'freedom and variety of situation'. Together they can bring about 'individual vigour and manifold diversity', in other words 'originality'. In the perspective of this civilized individualism making for harmony and a sense of proportion the danger signals were one-sidedness, disproportion, unthinking conformity and lack of originality. What mattered was self-realization. This kind of liberalism was not functional but normative. If Humboldt had a social concept it was that of an ensemble of highly individualistic beings, each of them eager to develop his potential to a maximum degree. Indeed, for Humboldt, 'harmony', one can feel reasonably sure, was a matter of the aesthetics of personality, perceived by taste or feeling, as one perceived beauty, not by a crypto-Benthamite calculation of the odds. It might coincide with the greatest quantitative realization of potentialities, but it was not logically equivalent to it. 'No utilitarian, but Shaftesbury, was surely the ancestor of this conception of Humboldt'.[4]

Though J. S. Mill probably did not realize it, by accepting Humboldt's idea of individuality and of *Bildung* – this concept of individual wholes, constantly changing but following an inner norm – Mill acknowledged a scale of values quite different from that of Bentham and James Mill. They would never have approved of his view on human nature which he conceived 'not as a machine to be built after a model and set to do exactly the work prescribed for it, but a tree which requires to grow and develop itself on all sides, according to the tendency of the inward forces which make it a living thing.' [5]

This 'organic view of man' was hardly compatible with utilitarian ethics, which, in J. S. Mill's own words,[6] simply describes 'the multiplication of happiness' as 'the object of virtue', [7] but says nothing about the quality of happiness. Mill was unable to solve the problem by conceding that 'some *kinds* of pleasure are more desirable and more valuable than others'.[7] On the other hand, while accepting Humboldt's norm of self-realization, Mill did not indicate its relationship to happiness, though he conceded to call it 'indisputable that the being whose capacities of enjoyment are low, has the greatest chance of having them fully satisfied; and a highly endowed being will always feel that any happiness which he can look for, as the world is constituted, is imperfect.'[8]

J. S. Mill's scale of values is clearly indicated by his asking: 'What more or better can be said of any condition of human affairs than that it brings human beings themselves closer to the best thing they can be?' It has been rightly said, that 'nothing in the estimation of pleasure could be less utilitarian than the spirit of this question. It did not much matter to Bentham and James Mill what men are like, whether they are highly developed individuals or ape-like imitators', 'provided only that they are happy, that they have as much pleasure as possible and as little pain.' [9]

By his unequivocal assertion that 'it really is of importance not only what men do, but also what manner of man they are who do it', [10] J. S. Mill opened the way to an evaluation of types of men unknown to his utilitarian predecessors. The younger Mill expressly approved of people endowed with energy and character. Conversely he depreciated the kind of man 'whose desires and impulses are not his own, (who) has no character, no more than a steam-engine has character',[11] a characteristic comparison in the early days of technology. He discovered that then the forces making for spontaneity and individuality were at a discount and that consequently many English people cared less for freedom than they thought they did. What mattered in the modern town was conformity. 'From the highest to the lowest classes' everyone lived 'under the eyes of a hostile and dreaded censorship' with the result that such cultural egalitarianism abhorred 'peculiarity of taste and eccentricity of conduct'.[12]

The emphasis on spontaneity, character, originality in human beings led J. S. Mill to a cultural élitism. Taking it for granted that 'originality is a valuable element in human affairs', his élite consists of the rather few persons who dare to experiment. Their experiments, if adopted by others, would be likely to lead to an improvement on established practice. These genuine few improvers 'are the salt of the earth, without them, human life would become a stagnant pool'.[13] Seventy years later a severe critic of liberalism, Vilfredo Pareto, viewed the social process as an incessant circulation of political élites. Being one of the motivating forces of history, he argued, these élites 'rise up from the lower strata of society, mount up to the higher strata, flourish there, and then fall into decadence, are annihilated or disappear'.[14]

J. S. Mill was far removed from such a socio-political view. He regarded élitism not as a political but as a cultural phenomenon of high significance. Dreading the growing danger of conformity of tastes and attitudes which seriously threatened the display and scope of individuality, he felt that if the claims of the latter were ever to be asserted, the time was now to prevent a deadly conformity. No one before him, not even the much more self-assured aristocrat Humboldt, had argued so forcefully for the need for a plurality of attitudes and tastes, for the right of the individual to his own cultivation, in short for a qualitative liberalism, superior to the mere conventions and calculating practices of *laissez faire*.

The cult of the personality perhaps took deeper root on the Continent than in England. At every possible occasion the educated German bourgeoisie liked to quote Goethe's maxim that the 'highest happiness of the children of this earth is yet personality'.

In the 1850s G. G. Gervinus, one of the few independent German liberals, saw individualism as a major force, but at the same time as part of a new democratic age, which stressed the individuality of the many rather than the cult of the few. 'The feeling of individuality and personal importance', he wrote, 'has become too strong in mankind not to loosen their respect for political institutions, not to dissolve closed corporations, the states within the state, not to equalize all differences of caste and class.' For Gervinus individualism and the stride towards equal rights for all were interconnected. As he put it, 'The struggle for equality in all the relations of life, for the liberty of man towards man, is necessarily founded on the importance of the individual.'[15]

The trend in the present age, he observed, was favourable to the individualities of the many but not to the great individuals of the past, to its princes, statesmen, warriors and authors. 'The attraction of the history of former days' had been 'purchased at the disheartening price of inaction among the people, to whom they only furnished the material which the leading men of the age used for their purposes.' The greatness of the present age lay in the fact that though 'the pre-eminence of highly gifted minds' had decreased 'the number of gifted minds of a secondary capacity' was increasing. The reputation of the present century did 'not depend as much on the quality and high cultivation of the individual as on the quantity, the extent, the spread of cultivation among the many'.[16] It was this different emphasis which separated that stubborn liberal democrat from the refined élitism of Humboldt and J. S. Mill.

4. The desire for constitutional government

The urge for constitutional government in Western Europe goes back to the seventeenth and eighteenth centuries. It was strongly reinforced through Montesquieu's insistence on the need for a separation of powers as he saw it ideally implemented in the British political system (doc. 5a). To liberals on the European continent early in the nineteenth century constitutional government often seemed the panacea to cure all political ills. Already some of the moderate reformers in the 1780s before the French Revolution had pleaded for a constitution which should clearly define the rights and limitations of the royal prerogative, break the impact of the hereditary aristocracy and make government accountable to representatives of the people who were to be chosen by a fixed electoral procedure.

French reformers in particular had witnessed from afar the novel spectacle of people across the Atlantic creating a new type of constitutional government. They had learned of the constitutional conventions through which the citizens in North America had set up machinery for devising constitutions first for individual states and then in 1787 in Philadelphia for creating the Constitution of the Federal Government of the United States. In all these cases 'the convention, acting as the sovereign people, proceeded to draft a constitution and a declaration of rights. . . . It was the Constitution that created the powers of government, defined their scope, gave them legality, and balanced them one against another. The Constitution was written and comprised in a single document.'[1]

With the creating of a Constitution the constituent power had finished its work:

'The constituent power went into abeyance, leaving the work of government to the authorities now constituted. The people, having exercised sovereignty, now came under government. Having made law, they came under law. They put themselves voluntarily under restraint. At the same time, they put restraint upon government. All government was limited government; all public authority must keep within the bounds of the Constitution and of the declared rights.'[2]

After the breakdown of Jacobin rule and the Napoleonic dictatorship, it seemed to many European, and particularly to French liberals that the Constitution they thought necessary had to some extent to be patterned on the (still monarchical) French Constitution of 1791. Before this all powers to make law, to enforce it and to interpret it in France had originated from the absolute ruler. Also the hereditary aristocracy had enjoyed great privileges. Both the absolute power of the monarch and aristocratic privilege had been eliminated by the Constitution of 1791. Its Preamble clearly stated that 'no privilege or exception to the common law for all Frenchmen any longer exists for any part of the nation or for any individual'.[3] The Constitution also guaranteed a long list of natural and civil rights, including liberty of movement, speech, publication, religion, assembly, petition, property, relief of the poor, work for the unemployed and observation of patriotic holidays. The fact that the Constitution of 1791 had been subsequently abandoned by the Jacobin rulers gave it a certain halo in the eyes of the liberals of 1814. Their leader Guizot, it has been aptly said, might well have been one of the advisers of Louis XVI and one of the framers of the Constitution of 1791.[4]

The first post-revolutionary liberal constitution on the continent, proclaimed by the Spanish Cortes in Cadiz in March 1812, had many features in common with the French Constitution of 1791. Although it soon proved premature and remained in operation for a few years only, it was at the time hailed by other continental liberals as a shining beacon light (doc. 47).[5] It proclaimed that the Spanish nation was 'free and independent' and not 'the patrimony of any family or person'. Sovereignty was, with the nation, 'obliged to preserve by just and wise laws the civil liberty, the property and the other legitimate rights of all individuals belonging to it'. A clear demarcation line was drawn between the person of the king and the extent of his power. The person of the king was declared 'sacred and inviolable and not subject to responsibility'. On the other hand ministers were responsible to the Cortes for any orders they authorized contrary to the Constitution and the law, and the excuse that they had been ordered to do so by the king was declared unacceptable.

Most French liberals shared the admiration for the British Constitution and constitutional monarchy which to some extent went back to Montesquieu's classic *L'esprit des Lois* (1748). Montesquieu favoured a separation of powers and saw the model for it in the British Constitution. Though this view did not fully correspond to the political reality of Britain, it was continually accepted by many French and other continental liberals after 1814. Guizot and some of his contemporaries were impressed by the parallels they found between Britain in 1660 and France in 1815 and later between England in 1688 and France in 1830. They concerned themselves more with the British than with the North American model which, however, through Alexis de Tocqueville's great work *Democracy in America (La Démocratie en Amérique*, 1835) was to receive a fresh and up-to-date interpretation.

The French liberals were understandably critical of the *Charte Constitutionelle* of 1814 for it was presented as a voluntary concession, a gift from the Bourbon king which could be withdrawn at any time. The intention of the Charter was by no means liberal or democratic. It served not liberal but legitimist purposes. If its authors paid only lip-service to the idea of a constitution, its very existence showed that the desire for a social order in which the rights and limitations of the political factors were to some extent laid down could not be ignored by the returning Bourbons. At least the Charter declared that the king was to rule through his ministers, though these were only responsible to him and not to the two chambers.[6] The idea of representation of the king's subjects was acknowledged by the provision of two chambers, a house of peers nominated by the monarch and an elected assembly chosen on a property basis. This 'legitimist' Charter was soon imitated by some South German states, where its validity survived considerably longer than in France herself.

Liberal constitutionalism made some advances through the revised French Charter of 1830 and the new Constitution of Belgium of 1831. The French Charter took sovereignty away from the king without unambiguously transferring it to the people. Laws could now be initiated by the chambers as well as by the king. But King Louis Philippe was reluctant to acknowledge the validity of the maxim of the revised Charter as expressed by Thiers, then leader of the Opposition, 'The King reigns but he does not govern.' On the other hand, the maxim certainly applied to the more precise Belgian Constitution. While Louis Philippe, now described as 'King of the French' and no longer as 'King of France', still tried to extend his power surreptitiously, in Belgium the sagacious Leopold I fully accepted the limited power of the monarchy. He took an oath to honour the Constitution. It provided for two houses of parliament, the members of which were elected by the people on a property basis, and for an independent judiciary. It also contained a modernized declaration of the Rights of Man and Citizen which had special articles including both freedom to worship and freedom *not* to worship.

During the first half of the nineteenth century liberals in Western and Central Europe took little exception to the property basis on which the right to vote and to represent the voters were based. They favoured equality of all citizens before the law but by no means equality of voting rights. In England there existed considerable property qualification for the vote both in the counties and in the boroughs. A member of the House of Commons in the counties had to own a landed estate of £600 a year and a member from the boroughs one of £200 a year. These qualifications, which reflected a bias towards landed and agricultural interests, were removed in Scotland in 1832 but in the rest of the United Kingdom only in 1858. According to the French Charter of 1814 electors had to pay 300 francs in direct tax and candidates for election as deputies 1,000 francs.[7] Further, voters had to be at least 30 years old and prospective deputies at least 40. After the revolution of 1830 the tax-qualification for voters was lowered to 200 francs and for prospective deputies to 500 francs. The age-limit, too, was reduced to 25 years for voters and 30 years for deputies.

Constitutionalism also meant to most continental liberals the assurance of a clear demarcation line between Church and State. In the tradition of Voltaire many liberals (and radicals) distrusted clerical influence intensely and particularly so in the case of Roman Catholicism. It is true the attitudes of continental liberals to the Catholic church varied a good deal, from Lamennais' attempt to liberalize the Church and Cavour's expedient formula 'A free Church in a free State' to Gambetta's later battle-cry 'Clericalism — there is the enemy'. In Belgium Catholics and Liberals co-operated to produce the Constitution of 1831 acceptable to both. In Spain the Constitution of the Cortes of 1812 (doc. 47), patterned to some extent on the French Constitution of 1791, and hailed by liberals elsewhere as a beacon of progress, took a critical attitude towards the all-powerful Church. The conflict between the Church and the liberal forces had both economic and ideological roots. Traditional and liberal Spain clashed over the maintenance of the Inquisition which was abolished by the Constitution of 1812 (see Section C, pp. 415–6). Clerical jurisdiction was also ended, but the suppression of the monasteries provoked the regular orders into a bitter counter-crusade. Throughout the century the position of the Church remained a controversial issue between traditional and liberal-radical forces in Spain.

In the 1840s in Switzerland the conflict between Catholic and Protestant cantons, between clericals and liberals over issues of education and of the religious orders even threatened the very existence of the Confederation. The dissolution of monasteries in the Canton of Aargau was followed by the Great Council of Lucerne inviting the Jesuits to undertake theological preaching within its confines. This in its turn led to a fierce anti-Jesuit campaign in other parts of the country. Armed clashes occurred and the turmoil caused six predominantly Catholic Cantons to form a defensive alliance, the *Sonderbund*. The majority formed by the other cantons remaining in the Swiss Diet declared the *Sonderbund* dissolved, expelled the Jesuits from the country and demanded a reform of the Constitution. In a brief civil war the forces of the *Sonderbund* were quickly beaten. Under the new Constitution of September 1848 Switzerland became for the first time a nation-state on a federal basis with a bicameral legislature and a fairly efficient central executive. While the *Ständerat* was composed of the representatives of the cantons, two in each case, the members of the *Nationalrat* were elected by the entire adult male population. At the same time the separate constitutions of the cantons and the rights and liberties of their citizens were expressly recognised.[8] The reforms were carried out in a spirit of moderation and with the resolve that the common ties of confederation should not be obliterated by cantonal and confessional differences. Through its wise liberality the new Swiss Constitution was as successful in tackling the relation between Church and State as earlier had been the Belgian Constitution of 1831. In both cases Church and State were clearly separated. In Belgium the clergy of all denominations was paid out of State funds, though it remained independent from the State.

The evolution of liberalism in Germany suffered from the multiplicity of her states. Some of the southern states had been granted constitutions, however restricted, by their princes soon after 1815, while Prussia remained without a national constitution and parliament until the revolution of 1848. Just as the earlier constitutions in Germany had followed the pattern of the French legitimist example of 1814, the revolution of 1830 in Paris forced the rulers of Saxe, Kurhesse and Hanover to grant constitutions to their citizens soon afterwards. When in 1837 the new ruler of Hanover, Ernest Augustus, revoked the Constitution, granted by his predecessor in 1834, some liberal professors at the University of Göttingen protested against this autocratic step. They were summarily dismissed only to be hailed as martyrs of constitutionalism by fellow-liberals in the more advanced South German states.

The special difficulty for liberals both in Italy and Germany lay in the fact that they were concerned with two different but, in their eyes, closely intertwined major issues against a background of growing industrialization. The desire for a constitution and for constitutional government with a clearly marked separation of powers was one difficulty, the urge to achieve national unity and sovereignty the other. In both Italy and Germany 1848 saw the muddled efforts of liberals to achieve both goals simultaneously.

Here we are only concerned with the constitutional aspect. In Italy the *Statuto* of 1848 was granted by Charles Albert, King of Piedmont-Sardinia, without consulting any elected assembly beforehand. Half legitimist, half liberal, it stated that the king received his office 'by the grace of God and the will of the nation'. As in the French Constitutions of 1814 and 1830 the vote was made dependent on taxation, confining the total voters in the state of Piedmont-Sardinia to a mere $2\frac{1}{2}$ per cent of the population. Yet the *Statuto* at least provided a two-chamber system and contained considerable concessions to the freedom of the press. With all its restrictions it became the constitutional loadstar for liberals all over Italy and after 1859 the basis, with some modifications, for the Constitution of United Italy.

In Germany the National Assembly at Frankfurt in 1848–49 drafted a much more elaborate and comprehensive constitution for the entire German people. The system of basic rights was to be valid in the envisaged *Reich*. There was to be equality of all citizens before the law. The aim was a parliamentary monarchy, a *Rechtsstaat* patterned to some extent on the constitution of the United States of 1787 and to a lesser extent on that of France in 1791. There were checks and balances for the government. The constitutional hereditary Emperor and his government would have to face a bi-cameral system, consisting of a People's Chamber to which ministers would be responsible, and which was based on universal manhood suffrage without property qualifications. Members of the Upper House, on the other hand, were to be appointed by the individual State governments and diets.

Although the events of 1849 illustrated the futility of the constitution-makers of Frankfurt, the idea of constitutionalism could not be suppressed. There is much truth in the observation by Professor C. J. Friedrich that 'even such "Macchiavellians" as Bismarck and Cavour could unify their countries only through the adoption of a constitution' [9]; yet an astute left-wing liberal, the renowned historian Theodor Mommsen, had good reasons for accusing Bismarck's Constitution of the Second Empire that it provided only the appearance, but not the essence of constitutionalism. To him it was a product of *Scheinkonstitutionalismus*. There were certainly no references to individual rights and guarantees in the Constitution of 1871. Yet Bismarck felt obliged to make some concessions to the liberal demand for representation of the people. He even conceded universal manhood suffrage for all citizens over 25. It was a sop to the National Liberals who had sided with the Chancellor after 1866, a compromise on a federal basis between some liberal principles and much authoritarian power, between the postulates of a *Rechtsstaat* and the autocracy of the old ruling class in Prussia. It was significant that there existed no Reich Cabinet but only a Reich Chancellor responsible to the Emperor and signing all laws jointly with him. The Chancellor appointed the heads of departments of the Empire, who were nothing but his assistants. At the same time he was Premier Minister of Prussia, just as the Kaiser was simultaneously King of Prussia. The fact that most liberals (though not all) shared Chancellor Bismarck's fear of political catholicism, as well as of international socialism, was an additional handicap to furthering the idea of parliamentary constitutionalism. What emerged was in the end a mixture of

Rechtsstaat and *Obrigkeitsstaat,* of an authoritarian regime based on a semi-liberal constitution.

'For more than fifty years Germany, under the leadership of Prussia, held out against parliamentary government under a constitution which separated the powers as much as they had been separated under the *Charte Constitutionelle* and other monarchical constitutions. During this period the same drift toward parliamentary supremacy which had transformed the English and the French constitutions manifested itself in Germany, but before it could culminate, the First World War broke out, Germany was defeated, and her constitutional evolution was revolutionized after 1918' [10]

Compared with the semi-constitutionalism of the highly industrialized German Empire, Tsarist Russia through most of the nineteenth century remained undeveloped both as regards industrialization and constitutional government. Only after the revolution of 1905 was the Tsar obliged to grant a parliament, a Duma, just as half a century earlier his relative King Frederick William IV had to consent to an elected National Assembly in Prussia under the impact of the Berlin revolution of 1848. Even after 1905 Russian liberalism never took real roots. The four Dumas before 1914 wielded little power. The *juste milieu* Kadets – orientated as they were on the model of Western liberalism – experienced this inadequacy as much as the Zemstvo gentry had done before them. Both these carriers of liberal reform, Zemstvo gentry and Kadet intelligentsia, in the words of a recent American analyst, 'confronted the same central liberal dilemma, the dilemma of attaining complex specifically-Western objectives in an illiberal, underdeveloped society'. [11]

Seen in historical perspective, the liberal plea for constitutionalism, which originated in the Anglo-Saxon world and in France, spread widely, but it met with varied responses in different countries at different times. [12] Its intensity depended on the strength of anti-authoritarian and parliamentary traditions and on a balancing of social and political forces. While often restricted and even paralysed by illiberal and totalitarian forces, it gradually spread over the globe. Today it is in the Third World under the changed conditions of recent industrialization and worldwide technology that the fight for and against liberal constitutionalism takes place.

---

5. From 'classic' to 'hyphenated' liberalism

In spite of the variations in the three main strands of liberalism, the features which classic liberals from Locke to John Stuart Mill had in common should not be overlooked. Rooted largely in the outlook of

Enlightenment there was a constant emphasis on man's fundamental rationality and reasonableness. Privileges of the ruling strata based on mere tradition and custom were questioned and often rejected. Everywhere we encounter a strong urge to expand the rights of the individual and to reduce the powers of the State and of the government. However widely their arguments differed, liberal thinkers of the period 1690–1850 argued mainly in favour of the rights and the social usefulness of the individual citizen and stressed the need for parliamentary control of the powers of the government and of the accountability of its civil servants. Throughout, liberalism presumed a pluralism of existing political and religious opinions; everywhere it tended to make a plea for the rights of minorities, rights which should be protected. Civil disabilities on account of religious or political dissent were to be abolished, provided the dissenters kept their activities within the rule of the law. The right to own property and the obligation of the government to safeguard it were essential features of the liberal ideology. It was not accidental that most liberals insisted on property qualifications to be attached to the right to vote. Between 1814 and 1848 French liberals were adamant on this point, whereas in England in the 1850s John Stuart Mill visualized a practically universal manhood suffrage. However, considerable differences between moderate and radical liberals can be noted in Britain as well as in the countries of Western Europe. While by no means all liberals shared Guizot's famous slogan *'Enrichissez vous!'*, people without property were not much respected by most of them, but were regarded as the concern of charity, if not of socialists and anarchists. Instead liberals busied themselves with the belief in a rational political order, based on a constitution and promoted by a government with limited powers. Ministers were to be responsible to Parliament.

The belief in progress, in an advancing civilization, was another characteristic of most liberal thought. From Turgot and Condorcet to Guizot and the German professors Rotteck and Welcker, a strong faith prevailed in the progress of civilization despite errors and setbacks. The continuous improvement of mankind, helped by the advance of science and the new self-confidence of the diligent middle classes, was never seriously doubted. However, such great post-classic liberals as Alexis de Tocqueville and Acton refused to take for granted this belief in the continuous progress of mankind (J. S. Mill was a borderline case). Their insight into the contradictions between liberty and equality, into the sinister aspects of the thirst for power under any political regime, into the tyranny of the majority in democracies, its threat to originality and individuality, the pressures towards conformity in the industrial age were phenomena unknown to the basically harmonious concept of man and society held by earlier liberals. De Tocqueville, Acton and later Benedetto Croce still maintained the ardent belief in freedom, but they did not share the classic faith in the basic harmony between the interest of the individual and that of society or at least of its major sections. They were convinced that conflict and disharmony played a permanent and much bigger role in human life than had been realized earlier.

Owing to the growing complexity of life in industrialized society the older classic liberalism was more and more replaced by what might be called 'hyphenated liberalism'. Its two main forms, 'National-Liberalism' and 'Social-Liberalism' will now be briefly discussed.

National-Liberalism

After 1815 the different political and social conditions in European countries outside the Anglo-American orbit made a re-interpretation of liberalism imperative. These countries were either not yet united by nationhood or were under stress by the tensions between competing nationalities and races in a multi-national structure. In the multiple States of Germany and Italy – some of them large and ambitious, others small and backward – national unity was by the middle of the century still a day-dream. The desire for more freedom meant both freedom for the individual and for the nation. In a multi-national Empire like the Habsburg monarchy, national minorities became conscious of their identity and worked openly or secretly for liberation from the yoke of the ruling German master or later from that of the 'master races'. In these circumstances liberty and liberalism obtained a different connotation as they were applied to both individual and collective freedom. Liberalism aimed at a constitutional framework in which not only the rights of the individual but also those of the nation or of national groups had to be safeguarded.

Against such a background, very different from that of England or France, national-liberalism developed its own problems and perils. After 1830 in most Continental countries liberals stressed the need for national identification, for a national State rooted in the rule of law. In it the educated and propertied classes would participate in the running of the country. At the same time the traditional freedoms of classic liberalism were to be maintained. There arose sometimes a problem of priorities. Some German liberals before 1848 argued that to achieve individual and constitutional freedom in the individual State was more important than to obtain freedom and unity in a larger German nation. As a south German, P. A. Pfizer, put it in 1832:

'Freedom in our internal life and independence from the foreign world or personal liberty and nationality are the two poles towards which the entire life of the century is orientated. The French nation has become the first in the world because it has absorbed these two basic trends of the present age most purely and has demonstrated their inseparableness most forcefully and decisively.'[1]

Many German and Italian liberals argued that true individual freedom

General Introduction

was only possible in a national State, based on a constitution with a Parliament, a true *Rechtsstaat*, a State under the ruie of law.

Yet if a choice had to be faced between individual freedom or national unity, other liberals expressed a preference for the first alternative. Karl von Rotteck preferred the constitutional State of Baden to a united but reactionary Germany. As he said in 1832: 'I do not desire national unity in any other way than with freedom and I prefer freedom without unity to unity without freedom.' A group of radicals in Baden who, fifteen years later in September 1847, gathered in Offenburg declared in their manifesto (doc. 85) that: 'Justice and Freedom in our internal life, a firm position in facing foreign countries were due to them as a nation.' They saw individual freedom and national power as complementary, not as contradictions. While German unity was the ultimate aim it had to be visualized in terms of the rights of free citizens. An assembly of more moderate men meeting soon afterwards in Heppenheim, another town in Baden, emphasized too that German unity could not be obtained by the rule of force, but only 'through and together with freedom' (doc. 86).

As the nineteenth century advanced, more and more German liberals came to desire a State which was based both on law (*Rechtsstaat*) and a new Empire (*Nationalstaat*). In 1848 the National Assembly at Frankfurt spent many hours on drafting a long list of individual freedoms including the freedom of the press, the right to free assembly, freedom of teaching and of conscience, freedoms largely derived from the English and French models. Twenty years later not a few liberals in Prussia, impressed by Bismarck's success in strengthening the power of that country, left the old Progressive People's Party – with its strong diehard liberalism, opposed to Bismarck's Macchiavellian tactics – and made their peace with the man they had fought so passionately. These members of the new 'National-Liberal Party' aimed at the unity of Germany, 'a unity tending towards Power and Freedom'. The new satellites of Bismarckism took the line that 'the German state and German freedom must be achieved simultaneously by the same means' (doc. 90).

It was a position far removed from the anti-étatism of classic Anglo-Saxon liberalism. Not that the National-Liberals did not care for freedom; they gave it a different meaning. While insisting on freedom *from* the fetters of aristocratic and semi-absolutist rule, they equally put emphasis on freedom *for* the unfettered economic activities of the citizens in a united nation enjoying a secure existence under a Constitution and the rule of law.

In the end the German National-Liberals acquiesced in compromise with Bismarck's Macchiavellian power politics, in a mixture of the *Rechtsstaat* with semi-authoritarian institutions. In Italy on the other hand the man who united the country was a 'National-Liberal' *sui generis* himself. Camillo de Cavour, the architect of modern Italy, in a unique way combined 'theoretical liberalism with practical

38

Macchiavellism'. [2] Deeply influenced by utilitarianism and French constitutionalism he saw constitutional monarchy as 'the only type of government which can reconcile liberty with order'. In Cavour's youth Bentham had been his favourite philosopher and it is characteristic that Cavour once defined 'Christianity as orthodox utilitarianism'. His scientific education certainly came from the school of Manchester Liberalism. This man of action from the Piedmontese landed nobility attained 'a wholly modern conception of the economic function of Society'. To English radical liberals from Bentham to James Mill 'Cavour owed not only a general view of the laws governing exchange, but also something deeper and more intimate, not to be expressed in abstract scientific terms: a consciousness of the expansive power of modern industrial society, and a confidence in individual initiative and enterprise. [3] By modernizing the economy in Piedmont, he aimed at setting up a model for the whole of Italy. Not without a touch of cynicism, in the difficult circumstances of Italy his 'National-Liberalism' had to be flexible and opportunistic in contrast to the doctrinaire attitude of an idealistic democrat and visionary such as Mazzini.

Internal reforms towards an industrialized society were required to make the building of a nation worthwhile. As with the National-Liberals in Germany only reforms within a constitutional framework and economic progress could make the citizens willing to fight for king and country. In 1846 Giacomo Durando, a contemporary of Cavour, expressed this aspect of the inter-relationship between internal feedom and national defence with remarkable clarity:

'If a civil people at the first beginning of its political regeneration, is surprised and threatened by an external or internal enemy, it will not undertake the defence of the State with the necessary resolution, unless it is fully assured that the new order of things will be safeguarded in exchange for its sacrifices. It will not hasten to the frontiers, or it will do so only with reluctance, if it leaves behind it silenced speakers and a silent press, the sure mark of tyranny renewed or imminent.' [4]

Social-Liberalism

If the Continental desire for nationhood and the birthpangs suffered on its achievement created one type of 'hyphenated' liberalism, a more universal phenomenon – the rapid pace of industrialization, the excesses of practically unlimited *laissez faire,* the plight of the masses in the slums of Manchester, London, Paris, Marseilles and the Ruhr – produced another. The era of intensified industrialization and urbanization favoured the growth of what may be called in retrospect 'Social-Liberalism'. Discarding the earlier liberal emphasis on the minimal State and on the severe limitation of its functions this school argued that the

State should and could assist in freeing the underprivileged. It should help in achieving a higher standard of their health, of the education of their children, and general welfare. Averse to the more drastic remedies for the existing social evils, proclaimed by Marxists and other pioneers of socialism, social-liberalism realized that in a changed socio-economic situation a mere reiteration of the formulae of classic liberalism would be inadequate.

As early as the 1840s some far-sighted Rhenish industrialists with a sense of responsibility felt the need for a modification of the liberal message. These entrepreneurs, successful as well as public-spirited, saw the necessity for putting some restrictions on free enterprise in the interest of social welfare. While pressing for constitutional reform in Prussia they realized that social reform was also desirable. They were critical of the ruthlessness of some of their fellow-industrialists whose sharp practices could, in their view, only be compared with those of the *condottieri* of renaissance Italy. As Friedrich Harkort saw it, their power depended on the hired mercenaries whom they used mercilessly in a life and death struggle with their competitors. They had an utter contempt for human rights. 'Although I personally am one of the leaders of industry', Harkort wrote in 1844, 'from the bottom of my heart I despise that creation of value and wealth which is based on the sacrifice of human dignity and the degradation of the working class. The purpose of the machine is to free man from animal servitude, not to fashion a more terrible bondage.' [5]

Opposed to the extremes of the old individualistic liberalism on the one hand and of the new socialist collectivism on the other, the champions of social-liberalism in the Rhineland 'first had to make their case restricting free enterprise in the interests of social welfare and second had to show why a total surrender to collectivism was unnecessary or undesirable'. [6]

Though Harkort was not an étatist, he would not accept the old liberal doctrine of the minimal state. On the contrary he advocated government action on several levels to improve the position of the working classes. This meant State intervention to guarantee a livelihood to the workers in the 1840s and facilities for their better education. Yet men like Harkort, Gustav Mevissen and Karl Biedermann, who thus moved away from the old doctrinaire liberalism trying to readjust it to a new position remained isolated forerunners in their country, to be followed only in the 1880s by the men of the 'Verein für Sozialpolitik' who equally realized the need for pursuing a more constructive social policy. While in Germany 'social-liberalism' was a concern of men of action or of economists, [7] in England it occupied the attention of such major thinkers as T. H. Green and later L. T. Hobhouse. Earlier the utilitarians had mainly 'looked at politics from the point of view of the legislator and were largely concerned with saying what the state ought not to do'. [8] It was their conviction that individuals left to themselves worked in complete harmony. Each individual aiming unhindered at his own happiness, would produce the happiness of all.

The idealistic philosophy of T. H. Green and the sociological realism of L. T. Hobhouse did not presume such a natural harmony.[9] The utilitarians had viewed the masses 'from the calm height of the scientific legislator, like Bentham, or of the civil servant of India House, like James Mill'. On the other hand T. H. Green looked at them from the standpoint of the ordinary citizen. Green argued that the good life was the end of all social activity. 'It cannot exist without freedom. The State can only further it indirectly, and may, by mistaking its sphere and capacities, do harm. But the State compulsions are not the only hindrance to Liberty.' There were others perhaps equally or even more damaging to an implementation of freedom. The good citizen will consider the economic and social hindrances which prevent the living of the good life. He will 'ask whether the State's compulsion may not be so used in the removal of these harmful conditions so as to produce an addition of real liberty'.[10]

While the plea for the right of the individual to adhere to his own religious and political ideas was never sacrificed by the later liberals, their attitude to the scope of the State, to the responsibility of society for the fate of the individual differed greatly from that of earlier liberals. It is true that the old anti-étatism of the classical school found a new champion in the writings of the rigorous individualist Herbert Spencer, who continued to demand freedom of the individual from the State, but T. H. Green and after him L. T. Hobhouse emphasized the chances for achieving greater freedom and security of the individual with the help of the State. These champions of social-liberalism saw the dignity of the individual becoming debased in conditions of poverty, bad housing and little chance of social mobility. Towards the end of the century many younger liberals felt that Gladstone's political formula of 'peace, retrenchment and reform' was inadequate. Freedom of contract, that basic tenet of classic economic liberalism, 'freedom in all the forms of doing what one will with one's own' was declared by T. H. Green in a lecture in 1881 as 'valuable only as a means to an end'. That end he described as 'freedom in the positive sense ... the liberation of the powers of all men equally for contributions to a common good'. 'No one', he argued, had 'a right to do what he will with his own in such a way as to contravene this end.' It was 'only through the guarantee which society gives him that he has property at all or, strictly speaking, any right to his possessions. This guarantee is founded on a sense of common interest'.[11] Green clearly realized the hopeless position of the dispossessed multitude. In his view a man who possesses nothing but his powers of labour and who has to sell these to a capitalist for a bare daily maintenance, might as well, in respect of the ethical purpose which the possession of property should serve, be denied rights of property altogether.

Some twenty-five years later L. T. Hobhouse declared that 'the restraint of one man in one respect is the condition of the freedom of other men in that respect'. Hobhouse drew a definite important distinction between 'social freedom' and 'unsocial freedom'; unsocial freedom 'was the right of a man to use his power without regard to the wishes or interests of anyone but himself'. 'Social freedom', on the other hand, 'rests on restraint. It is a freedom that can be enjoyed by all the members of a community, and it is the freedom to choose those lines of activity which do not involve injury to others.' [12] In the vision of social-liberalism liberty thus became 'not so much a right of the individual as a necessity of society'. It rested 'not on the claim of A to be let alone by B, but on the duty of B to treat A as a rational being'. [13]

In the 1880s Anthony Trollope, a shrewd commentator on the British political scene, could observe of the conscientious English liberal: 'what is really in his mind is – I will not say equality, for the word is offensive and presents to the imagination of man ideas of communism, of ruin, and insane democracy – but a tendency towards equality.' [14] With the extension of the suffrage in Britain through second and third Reform Bills, with the introduction of universal manhood suffrage in Germany and France after 1870 at least equality of the right to vote was accepted by liberals everywhere. Even liberals who did not care much for social-liberalism had to concede it. At the end of the century a middle-of-the-road English liberal and later Prime Minister, asked once more the basic question 'What do we mean by Liberalism of which we talk?' and gave the answer:

'I should say it means the acknowledgment in practical life of the truth that men are best governed by men who govern themselves; that the general sense of mankind, if left alone, will make for righteousness; that artificial privileges and restraints upon freedom, so far as they are not required in the interests of the community are hurtful; and that the laws, while of course, they cannot equalize conditions, can at least avoid aggravating inequalities, and ought to have for their object the securing to every man the best chance he can have of a good and useful life.' [15]

It was a formula very much in accord with the message of 'Social-Liberalism'.

---

6. Radicalism as an aspect of English liberalism

Radicalism played a greater role in England and was more relevant to her politics between 1780 and 1914 than in other European countries. Radicalism was dissent, dissent from those in authority. It felt superior to and challenged the Establishment.

Radicalism as an aspect of English liberalism

The terms 'Radical' and 'Radicalism' proved somewhat ambivalent. During the years between 1760 and 1914 they meant different things to different groups of people. Radicalism as an attitude highly critical of the existing political order demanded a change, but the content of its blueprint varied according to changing circumstances. While in politics 'radical' forms a contrast term to 'moderate', what is considered 'radical' in one age may be looked upon as 'moderate' in the next. Although English radicals were at all times ardent reformers, they were basically non-revolutionary, desiring to change the existing political and in some cases the social order through persuasion and mass appeal but on the whole not through violence.

Compared with the position on the Continent English radicalism had some distinct features.[1] It was largely an urban affair, with its impetus strong in provincial towns which had been greatly reshaped through the impact of the industrial revolution. 'It represented the industrial interest, the town-dwellers against the landlord and the country man.' It was the voice of rising middle-class entrepreneurs, often non-conformists, who fought the supremacy of the landed gentry and of its ally, the Church of England. Later it also expressed the protest of men of the under-privileged lower classes who wanted a better education for their children. Radicals were orientated towards the future and to an improvement of society.

They distrusted the expansionist policies of the ruling classes which, as the Radicals saw them, tended to involve the masses in costly and destructive wars. Radicals liked to believe in a conspiracy of governments against the people. Radicalism was often pugnacious and recognized the need for agitation. While some of its roots lay in the tradition of the Enlightenment, others were determined by Protestant non-conformity, going back to the seventeenth century – an ideological and social phenomenon which has no equivalent on the Continent.

The use of the term 'radical' is first to be found in English politics during the last quarter of the eighteenth century. As one of the earliest and most tenacious fighters against the privileges of the landed aristocracy and its control of the House of Commons, Major John Cartwright, declared in 1777:

'We must go to the bottom of the stinking sore and cleanse it thoroughly: we must once more infuse into the constitution the vivyfying spirit of liberty and expel the very last dregs of this poison. Annual Parliaments with an equal representation of the commons are the only specific in this case; and they would effect *a radical cure*. That a house of commons, formed as ours is, should maintain septennial elections, and laugh at every other idea is no wonder. The wonder is, that the British nation, which but the other day, was the greatest nation on earth, should be so easily laughed out of its liberties.'[2]

This 'radical cure' meant largely a restoration of the political liberties of Englishmen then declared to be lost. Cartwright also talked of

General Introduction

'reformation', favouring an attempt 'to bring about a thorough and compleat reformation'. The Radicals, as men desiring a reform of the parliamentary system they viewed as corrupt, wanted to go back to the 'roots', to the 'original fountain of power'. This can be clearly seen from a major speech by John Wilkes on parliamentary reform in the House of Commons on March 21 1776, in which he pleaded for a more democratic suffrage. 'We ought always to remember this important truth, acknowledged by every free State, that all government is instituted for the good of the mass of the people to be governed; that they are the original fountain of power, *and even of revenue,* and in all events the last resource....'³

By and large Radicals in England stood for 'renovation' rather than 'innovation' (to use a phrase of Bentham) and frequently stressed the need for pursuing their aim of parliamentary reform within the Law. Characteristic in this context are perhaps the following words in 'A Second Address from the Committee of Association of the County of York to the Electors' (1781): 'Far, therefore from wishing to promote confusion, or to prompt their fellow-citizens to deeds of violence and desperation; they exhort them with conscientious sincerity to confine their efforts within the bounds of legality.' ⁴ But whereas the members of this Committee of Association pleaded for 'the more moderate plan for the Reformation of Parliament', the idea of a 'radical reform' did not disappear.

About 1797 Charles James Fox and Horne Tooke had come to an agreement to demand 'a radical reform'. In 1811 Cartwright returned to this term, contrasting '*the radical reformer* who offers the nation the constitution itself' in all its simplicity of excellence with '*the moderate reformer* who offers something of his own fabrication which (as he himself admits) is complex and very imperfect'.⁵ It was from then onward that the adjective *radical* and the substantive *reformer* were used with growing frequency. But only since 1819 was the adjective radical turned into a substantive.⁶ In the same year Jeremy Bentham published his *Plan of Parliamentary Reform, in the Form of a Catechism* with an 'Introduction showing the necessity for Radical Reform and the insufficiency of Moderate Reform'. Bentham distinguished between three political groups: the Tories who were opposed to all of the various forms of reform; the Whigs who advocated or supported moderate reform; and finally those who backed 'the universal interest – the interest of the whole people' whom Bentham called 'People's Men'.⁷ His main confrontation was between 'the uncorrupted portion of the people' on the one hand and the Tories and the Whigs, on the other. The latter, he argued, were both representing 'the same seductive and corruptive interest' which was definitely 'opposite to that of the whole uncorrupt portion of the people'.⁸ The difference between Tories and Whigs, Bentham added sarcastically, was not fundamental. 'It was simply that what the Tories have in posses-

44

sion ... the Whigs have before them in prospect and expectancy.' [9]
According to this stern critic the greater proportion of the Tories were indebted for their seats in Parliament 'partly to proprietorship, partly to
terrorism (not to speak of bribery) '. The Whigs in their turn were indebted 'to the same instrument of subjection, to the same extinguisher of
freedom'. Bentham maintained that without any deliberate need of concert 'a sort of tacit cooperation' has been kept up 'between the two con-
tending parties: an alliance in form only defensive', but 'in effect too
offensive, against the people and their interest'. [10] Bentham maintained
in another publication a few years later that the confrontation between
the parties was merely a game.

Bentham's radicalism became more intense as the years passed by. In
1790 he had asked for moderate parliamentary reform, but when later he
wrote his Introduction to the *Plan of Parliamentary Reform* he displayed
an acute sense of fury. 'What once had been merely an intransigent
sinecure-ridden oligarchy has turned for him into a terrifying, sickeningly
corrupt military despotism.' He indulged in medical metaphors: 'The
country was poisoned to the depths; only the most recent radical surgery
could now save it; and that knife-thrust was radical parliamentary
reform, that is, virtually universal suffrage.' [11]

In fact the *Plan of Parliamentary Reform* itself, written in 1809, is a
much milder prescription than the Introduction added some years
afterwards. It had taken Bentham, says a recent biographer, 'several
years of post-war hunger, unemployment, riots and massacre to make
him a complete radical. But he was at no time a revolutionary; at no time
did he preach republicanism for England' [12] – though he admired the
republican United States. [13] Even in his introduction to the *Plan of
Parliamentary Reform* he denied that he desired the extinction of the
monarchy or the suppression of the peerage. As regards their property,
he declared, 'leaving with all my heart the full benefit of it to monarchy
and aristocracy, to the *ruling few*; my aim and wishes confine themselves
to securing, if it be possible a participation in that same benefit to
democracy, to the *subject many,* to the poor suffering and starving
people. [14] In fact 'radical reform' meant to Bentham popular suffrage,
voting by ballot, administrative centralization and the supremacy of the
reformed Commons over the Lords.

In 1818 a resolution on those lines, favoured by Bentham's forthright
and tireless pupil James Mill, was introduced in the House of Commons
by Sir Francis Burdett. It attacked the existing parliamentary system
as a citadel of aristocratic power. The 'Philosophical Radicals' around
Bentham and Mill were 'distinctly not a third party, but definitely a
political group' (J. S. Schapiro). While in theory they favoured at least
universal suffrage not excluding women, in practice they accepted a
qualified suffrage which meant a lowered property qualification for
voters.

General Introduction

A distinction between 'Liberals' and 'Radicals' was gradually made after 1830 when the term 'Liberal' began to replace the older term of 'Whig'. Liberals and Radicals were both opposed to the preponderance of the landed gentry and to its control of parliament by way of the 'rotten boroughs'. Both wanted to take government out of the hands of 'the special interests' and make it responsible to the multitude. But it was the early radical Bentham who systematically denounced these 'sinister interests' and indefatigably campaigned for ousting them. Both liberals and radicals emphasized the freedom of the individual, the need for loosening his ties with the established stratified society and for strengthening his chance to enter upon new associations pursuing new demands. For liberals in politics, as well as in economics, 'the source of action was (or ought to be) the rational, independent individual'. [15] But whereas the Liberals shared with the traditional Whigs the belief in parliament, the later Radicals wanted parliamentary government subject to democratic control. 'The majority should rule not because it is arbitrarily sovereign, but because it, and it alone can be trusted to speak with the voice of the whole people.' [16] Towards the end of the century, after the passing of the Third Reform Act in 1884 Joseph Chamberlain claimed 'At last we have a Government of the people by the people.'

Things had been very different sixty years earlier before the First Reform Bill had found a majority in the House of Commons. In a cogent analysis of the British constitutional system in his *Essay on Government* (1820) James Mill had exposed the control of political life by the landed aristocracy which was determined to maintain its interests against those of the people. Philosophical Radicals like James Mill realized that Bentham's earlier picture of the reactionary Whigs was too simple. They welcomed it when a 'left wing' of the Whigs developed, which favoured plans for moderate radical reforms. As landlords who had additional interests in the city these 'enlightened' Whigs conceded that some reform was inevitable in order to avoid a working-class uprising. As Macaulay pointed out in the Commons on 2 March 1831 it was also vital 'to admit the middle class to a large and direct share in the representation' to secure middle-class support and to ensure that it did not ally with 'the great body of the labouring classes' against the governing class. [17]

The 'liberal' Whigs accepted the claims of the Philosophical Radicals that their aims were not subversive. In 1820 Bentham published a pamphlet *Radicalism not dangerous* in which he insisted 'that radical reform, if carried into effect, would not be productive of any preponderant evil, but on the contrary of preponderant good'. In particular, the 'subversion of the rights of property would not be among the effects of it'. [18]

At this time large sections of the middle classes approved of radicalism, but disliked and perhaps feared what has been described as 'ultra-radicalism'. 'Antagonized as they might be by Pension List, rotten boroughs and State Church abuses ultra radical insurrectionism and ultra-radical journalism (Cobbett's *Political Register*) made them uneasy.'[19] Perhaps the demarcation line between 'radicalism' and 'ultra-radicalism' of the kind of the men of Peterloo, of the section of the Chartists around O'Connor and their pamphlets, is indicated by the fact that the Radicals, as we saw, eschewed violence and also had no affinity with revolutionary movements on the Continent. The Chartists, on the other hand, 'veered between schemes for working-class education and dreams of physical force. They favoured both cooperation and revolution.'[20] They 'were out of step with the progress of the age towards industrialism and the thrusting businessmen and utilitarians who made up the Radical party in Parliament.'[21]

In 1832 John Stuart Mill could claim 'that there was nothing definite and determinate in politics except radicalism'. Radicalism, i.e. 'liberalism of the Benthamite type', had indeed become the political faith of the time. Its triumph was signalized by the Reform Act.

This statement needs some modification. The Philosophical Radicals held the centre position in the Reform Movement which led to the passing of the Reform Bill. To their immediate right were the more advanced Whigs, led by Durham and Brougham, willing to give up the rotten boroughs and favouring a new electoral system based on the middle class. Further to the right we find, in this order, men like Lord John Russell and Earl Grey, who, while prepared to acquiesce in these changes, were in their hearts rather conservative, certainly more so than Durham and Brougham. Russell declared himself out of sympathy with 'the two hostile parties' of diehards and Radicals, 'neither agreeing with the bigotry of those who would reject all Reform, nor with the fanaticism of those who contend that only one plan of Reform would be wholesome or satisfactory'.[22] On the left, prepared to extend the vote on a property basis, were spokesmen of the working classes like Francis Place and his Westminster Radicals. However, they did not agree with an extreme demand for universal suffrage and annual parliaments. On the political scene 'Place and his friends were to (Joseph) Hume and the Parliamentary Radicals what Hume was to Brougham, and Brougham in his turn to Lord Grey and Lord John Russell.'[23]

There existed remarkable differences between the popular Radicals and the more moderate reformers. The latter represented powerful urban mercantile and manufacturing groups who reluctantly realized that they needed direct representation in Parliament to look after their interests. Among the Radicals various political unions sprang up. In London one was founded by Francis Place in 1831 while in Birmingham Thomas Attwood engineered the 'Political Union of the Lower and Middle Classes' (1829). They were supported in varying degrees by such different men as Burdett and Cobbett, Joseph Parkes, a utilitarian, and followers of Robert Owen. The existence of the political unions and of the frequently radical forces behind them proved an important factor in pushing the reluctant Whigs towards the Reform Bill of 1832. In the early decades of the nineteenth century Radicals were often regarded as the lunatic fringe of the Whigs and later of the Liberals. But by the middle of the century successful leaders with character and propaganda appeal like Richard Cobden and John Bright helped to change the image of radicalism. Oddly enough it was Palmerston who gave greater respectability to Radicals by opening the way for some of them, including Bright and Harcourt, to the Front Bench. [24] Through the successful campaign of the Anti-Corn Law League and later through anti-war propaganda during the days of the Crimean War, the radicalism of men like Cobden and Bright with their belief in the international solidarity of the peoples who should join to forestall the war-mongering tendencies of their governments, provided radicalism with a pacifist edge. 'Peace, retrenchment and reform' became the liberal slogan during the second half of the nineteenth century. When in the 1860s radicalism led to promotion and office, 'the personal quality of the Radicals changed rapidly from lunatic fringe to a cluster of brilliance'. [25]

Who were the Radicals who had then managed to enter Parliament? They had advanced in the service of two different causes. The secular Radicals 'were individuals, in a small minority in all classes, who became Radicals through their identification with some Radical tenet'. On the other hand there were 'the great Radicals, predominantly dissenting, who represented the social challenge of an order collectively Radical and economically and politically powerful'.[26] Their nonconformity was stern and uncompromising and provided them with a compass in political as well as in business affairs. Samuel Morley is characteristic of this type of successful man of action who endeavoured to set an example in the family and the chapel as well as in his business transactions and parliamentary activities. [27]

In the 1860s three generations were clearly distinguishable among the secular Radicals: 'the survivors of the 1830s, the [anti-Corn Law] League and aldermanic Radicals of the 1840s and 1850s and the cocksure intellectuals of the 1860s'.[28]

'The Radicals from the 1830s, "aristocratic, Byronic, almost adventurers', were merely relics of the past; to the second group belonged prominent politicians of the Manchester School, the pioneers of Free Trade as a panacea for all ills, including Cobden and Bright. By the 1860s J. S. Mill had become the lodestar of a much more refined radicalism, which attracted academically-trained writers and politicians like Dilke, Trevelyan, Fawcett and John Morley, men able to bridge "the gap between popular Radicalism and the educated public".' [29]

As the nineteenth century advanced public opinion in a variety of shades played an increasing role. It expressed itself through extra-parliamentary political associations and pressure groups in which

Radicals often took the lead. They had begun in the eighteenth century with John Wilkes's 'Society for Supporting the Bill of Rights' (1769) and the 'London Corresponding Society' (1792) which emphasized the incompatibility of aristocracy and democracy and the solidarity of English reformers with the French Revolution. Thirty years later Daniel O'Connell's Catholic Association of Ireland (1823) and the Chartist groups were significant and noisy extra-parliamentary groupings. Particularly important among the single issue associations was the Anti-Corn Law League (1839), the structure of which set a pattern for later associations with a specific purpose such as the National Reform Union, the National Reform League and the National Education League of the 1860s. Most of these political associations were only concerned with one single, if major, piece of legislation and were normally dissolved after its aim had been achieved. It is worthwhile noticing that from William Wilberforce's 'Anti-Slavery Society' (1823) to Joseph Chamberlain's National Education League 'the line of development in form and organization and in tactics is from Liberal to Radical models – away from Parliamentarism and towards direct democracy'.[30]

By 1885 the publication of *The Radical Programme*[31] reflected both a different position of a radical left-wing among the Liberals and a shift in the general attitude of the people who called themselves 'Radicals'. After the passing of the Third Reform Bill, Joseph Chamberlain could assert in his Preface to the *Programme* that the gap between the parliamentary parties and the mass of the people had lessened. At last 'the majority of the nation' would be 'represented by a majority of the House of Commons' and 'ideas and wants and claims' which had 'hitherto been ignored in legislation' would 'find a voice in Parliament' and would 'compel the attention of the statesmen'. The National Liberal Federation, formed in 1877 and much approved by Chamberlain, would enable 'the people to take part in framing the Party Programme and would see to it that candidates for Parliament were selected by associations in the constituencies'. Chamberlain claimed triumphantly that 'radicalism which had been the creed of the most numerous sections of the Liberal Party outside the House of Commons', would 'henceforth be a powerful factor inside the walls of the popular Chamber'.

The image of radicalism was indeed changing. Chamberlain denied that the objectives of 'advanced liberalism' were 'simply destructive' and argued that 'although the ground has to be cleared in many places, the new necessities of the time can only be fully met by constructive legislation'. Radicalism was now far removed from emphasis on *laissez faire* individualism and a fundamental suspicion of the activities of the State. 'New concepts of public duty, new development, new estimates of the national obligation of the members of the community to one another' had 'come to the fore', and in Chamberlain's view deserved consideration.

The Radical Programme of 1885 went far beyond the earlier specific or single cause type of radicalism. In 1877 Chamberlain had dissolved his single-cause association, the National Education League, which had served the idea of free education. The formation of the Liberal Federation on the other hand 'would avoid the waste of a plurality of separate reformist organizations such as the Education League, a Reform Union or a Liberation Society by providing one body that could speak on any question that might arise with all the authority of the voice of the nation'. [32]

In *The Radical Programme* one can detect a striking absence of most of the sectional reform causes and 'fads' which had been characteristic of radicalism in England for several decades and of the pluralism which was to disturb the Liberal Party even in the 1890s. There was no reference to the repeal of the Contagious Diseases Act and temperance was hardly discussed. As an article in the radical *Fortnightly Review* of July 1883 emphasized, it was now the purpose of the Radicals 'to get away from the "Radicalism of the crotchet-mongers"' and to replace it by a radicalism that represented 'the *general* opinion of the most advanced section'. [33] Therefore, the manifesto insisted, 'the mere circumstance that a man holds extreme views on some single subject or group of subjects gives him no claim to be considered a radical'. A wide gulf was said to exist between 'the constructive Radical and the irresponsible crotcheteer'. The constructive Radical 'may be in favour of the repeal of the Vaccination Act or of the Contagious Diseases Acts; he may be prepared to put down vivisection . . ., but as a question of practical politics he regards all these matters as details, subordinating them to the broader topics on which the entire party is agreed.' [34]

Radicals were reminded that the power of the State need not be that of a leviathan. In the right hands it can work for the benefit of the whole people for now 'every citizen is a partner of the State'. [35] Though this moralizing claim may seem far-fetched, even a recent critical analyst of the formative years of the British Liberal Party admits that it had some justification in the shifts of the social scene. Over whole areas, it was certainly true of the bulk of the Radical Liberals that

'to vote Liberal was closely tied to the growing ability of whole new classes to stand on their own feet and to live independent lives. The great moral ideal of liberalism was manliness, the rejection of the various forms of patronage from soup and blankets upwards, which had hitherto been the normal part of the greatest number. . . Thus *being* a Liberal . . . was something that could not come about without great changes in the circumstances and horizons hitherto outside the political nation'. [36]

By the 1880s this progress was well advanced and it was widely realized that the State need not necessarily be a machine, an instrument hostile to the masses but that they could play a part in determining its actions. As Joseph Chamberlain suggested in 1885 Radical reform therefore should take an overall view and improve society by 'constructive legislation'. [37] He did not deny that he had no time for *laissez faire*, that the State should move towards intervention 'on behalf of the weak against the strong, in the interests of the masses against the privileged, and in order to eliminate want and suffering by attacking luxury and ease. Again and again he re-iterated his belief in the necessity of free education, graduated taxation, and a reform of land law.' [38]

Chamberlain reformulated the radical tradition in an up-to-date manner (and in a way which would not have displeased Bentham) when he sternly pronounced in a speech at Birmingham in January 1885 that 'how to promote the greater happiness of the masses of the people, how to increase their enjoyment of life, that is the problem of the future'. He was certainly then in line with the modified form of 'social-liberalism' stretching from T. H. Green to Hobhouse and C. P. Scott which has already been discussed. Without the longevity of Gladstone and Chamberlain's breach with the Grand Old Man over his obsession with Home Rule, Joseph Chamberlain might well have become the leader of a Radical Liberal Party. After his turning away from the Radical movement for reasons partly rooted in his personality, that movement once more degenerated into a cluster of 'crotchety fads in the 1890s, as revealed by the Newcastle Programme and the dissension within the Liberal camp up to 1905.' [39] Joseph Chamberlain's policies reflected a situation in which the problem of individualism and collectivism required a fresh approach. If radicalism decreased and was divided after Chamberlain's departure from the Liberal Party, at least it obtained support from the growing Trade Union Congress. In the 1880s and 1890s its members served as an auxiliary of the radical wing of the Liberal Party. The few elected Labour members in the House of Commons before 1905 were 'generally regarded as belonging to the loose radical group of the Liberals in the Commons'. [40] Its secretary Sir Charles Dilke had close contacts with the trade union leaders.

Such contacts were an indication that the dividing line between progressive liberalism and socialism remained quite fluid, certainly much more so than on the Continent. At the beginning of the twentieth century the 'progressive movement' in Britain attempted to build a bridge between the 'apparently competing claims of collectivism and individualism, democracy and knowledge, social force and rational progress'. [41] Socialism was not anathema, but its nature was debatable. The new liberalism of Hobhouse, Hobson and Graham Wallas, which did not favour Marxism, has been described as 'an attempt to define true socialism as a special case of Liberalism'. [42] These men, like Ramsay MacDonald of the Labour Representation Committee, argued that 'the political democracy which Liberalism had won must now be translated into a social democracy'. [43] Hobhouse found it even permissible to speak of a 'liberal-socialism' without any intention of sacrificing any major liberal tenets. [44] Before 1914 there was 'nothing in the socialism of Tawney or MacDonald which made a gulf between their political philosophy and the liberalism of Hobhouse or Hobson or Wallas'.[45] For some years even the formation of a single Progressive Party composed of former Liberals and Labourites was 'a distinct possibility'.[46]

Whether from a practical point of view it was wise for the progressive Liberals to nurse political Labour as their infant is another question. The fact remains that the New Liberals, who included C. P. Scott, the tenacious editor of the *Manchester Guardian*, welcomed Labour in Parliament. Massingham's *Nation*, which viewed the Liberals as 'the practical progressive party' in England, interpreted socialism as 'partly a competitive and partly a cooperative idea'.[47] It also looked at the Independent Labour Party 'with a gentle sense of irony as occupying about the same relation to Liberal Politics as the Salvation Army to the regular Churches'.[48]

It was the First World War which dissolved the Progressive Alliance. There were growing dissensions within the Liberal camp and Lloyd George's hardly concealed affinity to the Conservatives did not endear him to Labour. Although progressive ideas continued to play their role in both parties, 'the political alliances between them had inevitably broken down and the power of Labour was increasing commensurately with the Liberal decline'.[49] Radicalism in the nineteenth century sense was no longer an issue.

---

7. Aspects of liberalism and radicalism in France

(a) Liberalism 1814–48

French political thinking in the early nineteenth century took up a position half-way between the metaphysical abstractions of the German idealistic school and English pragmatic utilitarianism. Influenced to some extent by both, French liberal thought was much more moulded by the lessons learnt from the traumatic convulsions of French society in the previous twenty-five years. The ideology of the early years of the French Revolution with its framework of a constitutional monarchy encouraged the post-1814 liberals, while the often sinister memories of Jacobin terror and lawlessness coloured their thought and created a barrier against Utopian promises. Whereas France had gone astray after 1791, suffering from the excesses of Jacobinism and dictatorial autocracy, the English constitutional monarchy had weathered the storm. To most French moderates England became therefore a panacea for all political ills. England was seen as offering the right combination of freedom and order, a model for the Charters of 1814 and 1830. French liberals were equally averse to the return of the *ancien régime* of which some of the returned emigrés and 'Ultras' dreamed, and to 'democratic' Jacobinism, the intellectual father of which in their eyes was Rousseau. There were, however, considerable differences within the liberal camp. Though all 'liberals' desired a limited monarchy, the constitutional liberals still believed in the preponderance of the monarchy while the parliamentary liberals favoured the right of the Chamber to select ministers who had its confidence.

There was no liberal party before 1848, only a variety of liberal attitudes. On the Right we find a liberal aristocrat with strong Catholic leanings like René Chateaubriand. He differed greatly from the cosmopolitan anglophiles Madame de Staël and Benjamin Constant. There were the liberals of the Centre, the doctrinaires Guizot and Royer-Collard and finally the liberals of the Left, men like La Fayette, Destutt de Tracy, Manuel, who played a role towards the end of the Restoration period.

In retrospect, Madame de Staël, the brilliant daughter of Necker and determined opponent of Napoleon, regarded the French Revolution as having been inevitable. Its ferocity was in her eyes a reaction to the vices of the *ancien régime*. Before 1789 she pointed out, France had been governed only by customs and the whims of kings and courtiers, but not by laws. The early years of the Revolution had been promising, when France seemed to be on the road to a limited constitutional monarchy. In her opinion the Charter of 1814 moved into the same direction; 'whilst guaranteeing the good principles of the Revolution it was the safeguard of the throne and of the country'.

For Madame de Staël the model of a constitutional monarchy was England (as it was for the more pedestrian Guizot). She believed that England's prosperity was closely connected with the role of liberty. It seemed to her 'that thinking men have not even yet discovered principles of monarchical and constitutional liberty other than those which are admitted in England'. [1] Madame de Staël was an élitist, both patriotic and internationally minded. While she loved her country, having travelled widely she looked beyond its frontiers. There existed, she argued, an international of friends of liberty. It was

'remarkable that at a certain level of depth among all people, there does not exist one enemy of liberty from one end of the world to the other, the friends of liberty communicate with each other through reason just as religious people do through their emotions, or to express it better, reason and emotions are reunited in love of liberty just as they are in that of the Supreme Being. When it is a question of the abolition of slavery, of the treatment of negroes, of freedom of the press, or of religious tolerance, Jefferson thinks like La Fayette and La Fayette like Wilberforce, and those who are no longer alive count for two in the holy pact. Is it then from the calculation of interest, is it from bad motives that men, so superior, in such different positions and countries, should be in so much harmony in their political opinions?' [2]

General Introduction

Benjamin Constant

Benjamin Constant, friend and lover of Madame de Staël, was versatile, excelling in politics as well as being a prominent journalist and novelist. He acquired a reputation as a political theorist and from 1818 until his death in 1830 was a Deputy in the French Chamber. In his youth in sympathy with the Gironde and the First Republic, he later assisted Napoleon during the Hundred Days of his return with the drawing up of the *Acte Constitutionnelle*. Afterwards he became a supporter of the constitutional monarchy, though without great enthusiasm. His education outside France, in Switzerland, Germany and Scotland gave him a wider experience than had some other liberals. Constant was instinctively opposed to any arbitrary action and violence. Shortly before his death (1830) he claimed that he had 'defended the same principle for 40 years: liberty in everything, in religion, philosophy, literature, industry, politics; and under liberty I understand the triumph of individuality – as much over the authority which would govern through despotism as over the masses who claim the right to enslave the minority under the majority. Despotism has no right.' [3]

In another context Constant described liberty succinctly as

'the right of each person to seek his opinion, to choose his own opinion and to follow it, to dispose of his property, even to misuse it, to come and go without obtaining permission and without rendering an account of his motives or movements. It is the right of each person to associate with other individuals, either to discuss their interests or to practice the form of worship they prefer; or simply to fill the days and hours in a way which best suits their inclinations and fancies.' [4]

The post-1814 liberals were more concerned with freedom of the individual than with justice for the many; they were liberals but not democrats. They resented the cult of the people popular with the Jacobins. [5] To maintain and rescue 'the indispensable liberties' was their main concern which incidentally made them blind to the requirements arising from a changing social structure during the early days of industrialization. Constant was a middle-of-the-road theorist on his own terms; although fickle in many ways, after 1815 his principles remained fairly stable. They were elucidated in the distinction Constant drew in 1819 between the ancient and the modern concepts of liberty. The ancient Greeks had enjoyed a collective liberty. They discoursed in public on the issues of war and peace, on the conclusion of alliances, they voted on laws, they examined the deeds and the management of the magistrates. Yet at the same time the individual was completely subordinated to the authority of the collective. There was no margin left for his independence, no matter whether his opinions, his approach to business or his religious attitudes were concerned. In condemning the liberty of the

54

ancient world Constant clearly had the Jacobins in mind.[6]

The modern concept of individual liberty as developed in the West, particularly in England, France and the United States was different. It implied the right of everybody to be subject to the law only; it meant freedom from arbitrary arrest, or detention or maltreatment by the arbitrary power of one or several persons. Everyone was entitled to express his own opinion, to choose and exercise his occupation, to dispose of his property, even to misuse it, to move about without needing a permit from the authorities and without accounting for his motives or for his actions. [7]

If freedom meant to the ancients the sharing of social power between all the citizens of the country, to the moderns it means the security of the individual as regards his private possessions and the guarantees accorded by the institutions to these possessions.[8] Constant drew a clear distinction between individual rights and political rights and regarded the latter as the guarantee of the former (doc. 46). To him the rights of the individual person comprised personal liberty, trial by jury, religious freedom, occupational freedom, inviolability of property and last but not least, freedom of thought.[9]

A Protestant himself, Constant favoured full religious freedom; neither deism nor even atheism should be proscribed. Different from Guizot and Royer-Collard he was an ardent champion of the freedom of the press. It was to him the touch-stone of freedom of opinion. Only if a full range of different opinions could be voiced was it possible to remedy the vices of all existing regimes. In order to protect the individual against arbitrary acts by the holders of power, Constant regarded the system of juries as indispensable as the need for making judges irremovable. The Deputy Constant stood up for people whom he thought threatened or who had suffered by arbitrary acts of the executive. His liberalism was not, as Emile Faguet later alleged, cold and dry. His belief in the freedom of the individual and the need to protect it was genuine. He 'had nothing of the sceptic attached only to his own tranquillity'. [10]

In common with Guizot and Royer-Collard, Constant rejected the unlimited sovereignty of any power. No power on earth was unlimited: not the power of kings, of representatives of the people, not even that of the laws which in the last resort express the will of a ruler or of the people. These limits were set by justice and by the right of the individuals who remain the ultimate source of justification for everything. Like Locke, he insisted that the power of society vis à vis the individual must be confined to a minimum. The realm of authority was largely negative. It should only prevent individuals from doing harm to each other. Government was in Constant's eyes a necessary evil. [11]

To Constant the best reinsurance against arbitrary and unfair acts of the power-holders was an independent judiciary. For it alone was able to protect the citizens from molestations by those in power. While the immovability of the judges remained a precondition for their independence, equally important was the responsibility of the executive.

Perhaps the fact that Benjamin Constant came out in favour of the constitutional Monarchy only in 1814 (even then he preferred a troublesome republic to an absolute monarchy), was the reason why he constructed a constitutional system of five powers. He felt the need for safeguards against absolutism and revolution through a balanced system of powers in which the Royal Power (*Pouvoir neutre*) was only one of five. It impressed him that within the framework of the English Constitution the Royal Power prevented any dangerous in-fighting between the other powers and maintained harmony between them. [12]

Article 13 of the Charter of 1814 declared that 'the person of the King is inviolable and sacred, his ministers are responsible. To the King alone belongs the executive power'. This formula only partly coincided with Constant's concept of a limited monarchy. In fact the practice in France soon went further than the Charter as it became a custom for the ministers to counter-sign the royal edicts. However, the principle of the non-responsibility of the Head of the State and of the responsibility of the Executive was only fully implemented in the Third Republic. In article 14 the Charter provided for the right of the king to issue by-laws and ordinances required for the execution of the laws and the security of the State, a formula which Constant viewed with suspicion and alarm. What mattered to him was the significance of the responsibility of the ministers and the need for penalties in case ministers neglected or failed in their responsibility.

Like Madame de Staël, Constant desired an upper Chamber. He regarded a House of Peers as indispensable; on the one hand it would be a safeguard for the monarchy, on the other as guarantee against despotism. To him an hereditary monarchy could not function properly without an hereditary class. However by 1818 Constant had his doubts about the wisdom of creating a new aristocracy after the failure of the old. His was less a preference for the aristocracy than one for the well-to-do.

Living one century and a half later it is perhaps difficult for us to understand how Constant could regard people as being prejudiced in their political activities by poverty and ignorance, but not by wealth and property. He thought it desirable that in general representative functions should be reserved to 'men, if not belonging to the opulent class, at least to that of the well-to-do'.[13]

Only a certain degree of economic independence, the possession of property which involves regular tax-payments or a long-term lease of land should entitle a man to the vote. To be dependent on others by way of a salary ruled him out. While Constant in his *Principes de Politique* (1815) regarded only the owning of landed property as a sufficient qualification for the vote, in the second edition of his *Réflections sur les*

Constitutions he extended it to industrial property as well. [14] By then he seem to have realized its growing importance in a still largely agricultural society. To him the patriotism of the lower classes, of the agricultural and industrial workers was undoubtable. But while it showed itself in their courage to die for their country, a different form of patriotism expressed itself in the ability to understand properly what was in the interest of France. Birth and nationality alone were not enough for a man to be given the vote. He must have the necessary leisure to gain insight and to arrive at proper judgements. Only property enables such leisure; and thus 'makes men capable to exercise political rights'.

In the end Constant came to the same conclusion as the more pragmatic Guizot. 'The necessary aim of the propertyless', he argued, 'is to arrive at securing property. They should reach it through labour.' [15] In an article, written in 1818, Constant described 'the great benefit from the Revolution (of 1789)' as 'the introduction of the middle classes to the affairs of the State'. He argued that the only aristocracy possible in France was one born from the nature of things; this means a kind of mobile aristocracy, founded on property, but circulating with it and following it in the different hands through which it passes. The soil has ceased to be the true, or even the main wealth and the aristocracy should therefore always seek its base in what constitutes the most real and the most powerful wealth; in our present state this is industry and it is therefore on industry that the still admissible aristocracy should repose.' [16] While Constant does not seem to have had an urge to keep the propertyless down, he did not bother to show them ways and means of how 'to arrive'.

It is strange that this celebrated novelist and writer did not favour 'la propriété intellectuelle', the intellectuals or liberal professions. He wanted to see them excluded from the vote as they were working 'far from the practical sphere'. Constant seems to have been filled with a fear of 'idéologues', of the literati, mathematicians and scientists who came out with extreme or odd opinions, which only proved that their work had little to do with social and political reality.

The industrious middle class stimulated Constant to an extraordinary lyricism:

'In the industrial class', he insisted, 'resides independence, because everyone is in need of it and it is in need of no one. In that class resides the spirit of equality because it is too large in order to gain prerogatives necessarily confined to a small number as in the case of the big proprietors. In that class resides patriotism, because its interests cannot isolate themselves, like those of pure capitalists, from the national interests'. [17]

Perhaps only Constant's fear of arbitrary action, his trauma of chaos and revolution, shared by many others of his generation, can explain this eulogy of a very restricted vote. It is true during the 1820s Constant wanted to lower the taxation limit of 300 francs for the right to vote but otherwise he strongly upheld *le vote censitaire,* the severely restricted franchise. There was no question for him as for other French liberals of conceding universal suffrage, although of all the prominent liberals only Guizot had the hardiness to prophesy in 1847: 'The day of the universal suffrage will never come.'

François Guizot

Guizot had three careers: as a civil servant, as an historian and professor at the Sorbonne whose books on French and English history as well on the wider compass of the history of European civilization were widely read, and as politician cum statesman. Elected a member of the Chamber of Deputies in 1830, Guizot played a major role in many of the cabinets of Louis Philippe whom he served as Prime Minister from 1840 to the end of the regime in 1848.

An adroit parliamentarian, Guizot has frequently been accused of opportunism, but recent research has stressed the constancy of his doctrines.[18] What were its fundamentals? Although a Calvinistic Protestant inclined to pessimism, Guizot believed in the rule of reason. Though, like every other power the human intellect was not free from 'a natural vice, a principle of feebleness and abuse', reason mattered. Guizot's concept of reason was neither Kantian nor utilitarian; it meant 'a principle of reasonableness and not of rationalism'.[19] It was eminently reasonable in politics to avoid extremes, to aim at the 'juste milieu' between reaction and anarchism. To Guizot and his fellow 'doctrinaire' Royer-Collard prudence was identical with shunning excess, with avoiding a return of the arrogant claims of the first two Estates under the *ancien régime* as well as the mob rule of the ignorant masses. Different from Bentham, Guizot did not reject the idea of human rights altogether, but drew a clear distinction between civil and moral rights, which had universal validity, and political rights, to be confined to men of property and education, to the *beati possidentes* who alone had the prerequisites for exercising political judgement. This was the ideological justification for the *pays légal,* the limited number of men who while paying 300 francs or more in annual taxes were entitled to vote.[20]

It was one of the lessons of 1789 for French liberals of Guizot's kind that a stable government had to be based on support from the property owners. From Barnave to Madame de Staël the rule of the propertyless had been regarded as the rule of crime. In reverse Guizot and his friends saw reliance on the middle classes as the only safe plank for a sound government.[21]

Oddly enough, this determined champion of the middle classes and of their virtues did not believe in the existence of class distinctions. He agreed that under the *ancien régime* society had been sharply divided;

Aspects of liberalism and radicalism in France

nobility and bourgeoisie, urban and rural populations, landowners and manufacturers had all been antagonistic to each other. But such divisions belonged to the past. As Guizot saw it, after 1814 there existed no more social antagonism. With an astonishing simplicity he told the Chamber of Deputies in February 1842: 'All classes, all social forces amalgamate, combine and live in peace within the great moral unity of French society'.[22] He was convinced that people who had the vote could and would represent those who had not. Guizot thought little of the political judgement of the fickle and ignorant masses. Although the multitude desired guarantees for security and freedom for their possessions, it did not seek power or wish to take part in government. On the whole the masses were concerned only with their private affairs.

Of course Guizot never regarded the middle classes as a tight caste. For him they were open to all. By their own endeavours people could acquire property and then qualify for the right to vote. In 1789 the Third Estate had done away with a false system of privileges, now its successor, the middle classes, would protect society from future revolutionary upheavals. In old age Guizot asked in an article published in 1865 'Who can say where the middle classes begin and where they leave off?' [23] Thirty years earlier he had assured the Chamber of Deputies: 'The movement of ascension is nowhere stopped. With work, good sense, good conduct one can rise as high as it is possible to rise in the social hierarchy'.[24] To him as to many contemporary French and English liberals poverty and economic failure were essentially the fault of the individual and not of society.

In one important respect, Guizot, so adroit in managing political power, differed from fellow liberals like Benjamin Constant and Royer-Collard. He did not share their distrust of any government as such. A sound regime would avoid excesses, steering a constructive middle course. Men of property and education were likely to find this course. In any case effective government should be in the hands of those most capable of discerning justice.

Guizot was not in favour of majority rule. Different from liberals of the left, like Lafitte or Destutt de Tracy, he defended the complete freedom of the king to choose his ministers, although under Louis Philippe they were in fact chosen from the ranks of the Deputies. While after 1848 Guizot was one of the first to realize the importance of a system of political parties, he never allowed any party in opposition the same right as the party behind the government. Much as he admired the English parliamentary system, he was not prepared to allow the opposition a constitutional role.

At a time when industrialization spread in France and her commerce expanded, the cult of the middle classes which Guizot and his friend Royer-Collard shared with Constant was perhaps not surprising. It was a comfortable belief for those who held it. If the French radicals

General Introduction

began to question it in the 1840s, the brutal events in Paris in June 1848 destroyed this myth and it became much more difficult to assert it during the second half of the century.

On the left of the Doctrinaires

To the left of the 'doctrinaires', Guizot and Royer-Collard, were the so-called Independents or Liberals of the Left. A mixed crowd, they included a big landowner like Voyer d'Argenson, leading bankers such as Lafitte and Casimir Périer, and the aged General Lafayette, elected Deputy in 1818. Lafayette, who in his youth had fought in the American War of Independence by then was 'a bit the grandfather of liberal and radical Europe' (Girard).[25]

The Independents were sharply critical of the clerical regime of King Charles X and his ministers. Among their followers were business people, shop-owners, commercial travellers etc., who met in masonic lodges and reading rooms. Apart from General Lafayette they did not favour a Republic but supported the July Revolution. The determined young journalist Adolphe Thiers and Armand Carrel, his fellow editor of the newspaper *le National*, even became revolutionaries in order to maintain liberalism. These two men were 'the most extreme liberals but they were not democrats, for they did not accept the doctrine of the sovereignty of the people'.[26] However, if there were differences among the liberals in the political field, there existed none in the economic sphere. Neither theorists nor politicians questioned the fundamentals of the standard view on a liberal economy. For Destutt de Tracy the legitimacy of property was based on nature. People are all property-owners! Men own their land, large or small, and everyone at least possesses his person. Nature is the basis of the existing inequality. Jean Baptiste Say, an ardent follower of Adam Smith, who believed in eternal and inevitable economic laws, set the tone (doc. 27). The economy must be free. Everyone had the right to produce, to exchange, to buy and sell a product and human labour was only a product like others. The individual, motivated by his personal interest, should be the sole agent in the economic sphere. The State on the other hand had no right to intervene though a certain amount of protectionism to safeguard the national economy against foreign dumping might sometimes be necessary.[27] The 'economic laws' valid for all ages and countries, did not allow for any State intervention in favour of the lower classes. Should and could the State do something to improve the position of the lower classes? Nothing or very little, answered Jean Baptiste Say and the other Liberals concurred. J. B. Say rejected the idea of public assistance, just as anything like the English Poor Laws was unacceptable to Guizot. On the other hand Duchatel, the economist of the left-liberal *Globe* and a pupil of Malthus, recommended to the lower classes: 'Work, economy, prudence in marriage' whilst Destutt de Tracy

60

declared it 'in the interest of human beings in every respect, to diminish the effects of their fertility'.[28]

Alexis de Tocqueville

Among the French liberals of his time Tocqueville holds a unique position through his penetrating sociological approach and historical perspectives. He saw French politics in terms of a historical process and at the same time he gained fresh insight by contrasting France with a different type of society, that of the United States.

Tocqueville never gave a clear-cut definition of liberty but his belief in it sometimes had religious undertones. The claims of liberty were to him fundamental. 'I regard, as I have always done, liberty as the greatest of all goods', he declared; it was 'in truth a sacred thing'. While he would not have disagreed with Constant's definition of freedom, to him it did not cover all its aspects. Tocqueville saw liberty threatened in a society on the road to an egalitarian democracy. The period of the *ancien régime* with its three Estates was over; that of democracy, was about to come. He regarded 'the gradual development of equality of conditions as a providential fact'. The trend in history during the last 700 years had worked towards that equality. 'The noble has gone down on the social ladder and the *roturier* has gone up', he wrote in 1835; 'the one descends as the other rises. Every half-century brings them nearer to each other, and they will very shortly meet.' [29]

As he saw it, society was in a state of flux, of transition which had its specific dangers. While the majority of the citizens were going to enjoy a greater degree of prosperity, a dangerous impasse had been reached: 'The spell of royalty is broken, but it has not been succeeded by the majesty of the laws; the people has learned to despise all authority, but fear now extorts a larger tribute of obedience than that which was formerly paid by reverence and by love.' [30]

The advantages of the old state of affairs had gone. The old aristocracy had lost its spell and was *passé*, while nothing really had taken its place. In America already 'an almost complete equality of conditions' prevailed while Europe was on the way to it. Therefore Tocqueville studied American society as a mirror of the society Europe had to expect. In America he saw 'more than America', he 'sought the image of democracy itself, with its inclinations, its character, its prejudices, and its passions, in order to learn what we have to fear or to hope from its progress'. [31]

Although Tocqueville never quoted Constant, there is no reason to believe that he was in disagreement with Constant's definition of liberty. Like Constant and other liberals he wished to see the sovereignty of the State or of the monarch severely curtailed. Realizing that the former privileges of the aristocracy had ceased, he did not share the arrogant wish-dreams of the ultras who wanted to turn the wheel of history back nor did he favour the *régime censitaire,* confining the vote to a small stratum of tax-payers. The citizen, Tocqueville argued, should not simply have his freedom guaranteed, but he should also participate in public affairs and play a part, as far as possible, in decision-making. Tocqueville was filled with the sense of responsibility of the aristocrat for the common weal. He acknowledged the right of the individual not to be badgered by the power of the State or by the social pressures of the tyrannical majority. The individual should be entitled to 'an area of activity free from the intrusion of others whether these others are private individuals or public authorities, an area in which the individual can make decisions, follow wishes, exercise choices without being impeded by any alien will. This he believed was necessary both as a recognition and an assertion of the individual's status as a moral being.' [32] Yet at the same time Tocqueville rejected what he called 'individualism', the attitude of the individual in democratic countries to withdraw from public affairs into a private circle of friends and acquaintances. He did not deny that democratic communities had 'a natural taste for freedom', but their passion for equality was more intense and ardent: 'They call for equality in freedom;' but 'if they cannot obtain it they will call for equality in slavery'. But when equality prevails, the individual reacts by withdrawing in himself. He indulges in 'individualism', which is in a democratic society what 'egotism' was under the previous social system. The fact that Tocqueville devoted an entire chapter to that theme in his *Democracy in America* is significant. He described individualism as 'a mature and calm feeling, which disposes each member of the community to sever himself from the mass of his fellow-creatures; and to draw apart with his family and his friends; so that, after he has thus formed a little circle of his own, he willingly leaves society at large to itself'. Individualism was to him a specific disease of a democratic society which threatened 'to spread in the same ratio as the equality of conditions'. [33]

With the close ties between men through guilds, church membership, and other social agencies which existed under the *ancien régime* having been eroded, there developed an attitude, which was the negative side of *laissez faire,* as we would perhaps call it today. People 'owe nothing to any man; they expect nothing from any man; they acquire the habit of always considering themselves as standing alone, and they are apt to imagine that their whole destiny is in their own hands'.[34] That negative concept of individualism – unknown at the time in England or Germany – was then more widespread in France than Tocqueville seems to have realized. For after the Revolution of 1830 other prominent French authors like Balzac, Sainte-Beuve, Lamartine, Lamennais, expressed an anxiety about what they called 'the odious individualism'. [35] Radical writers blamed the French Revolution for the attitude, said to be widespread, of everyone for himself only, 'resulting in a cut-throat competition and a struggle of all against all'. Whereas socialists like Louis Blanc saw the most deplorable manifestation of modern individualism not in the French Revolution but in the ruthless exploitation of man by man in history, Tocqueville deplored individualism as an attitude of the individual's will to isolation, as a kind of self-chosen social isolation, an unfortunate by-product of the new democratic society.

As a thinker, an historian and a political scientist Tocqueville had an intuitive eye for essentials but as a practising politician, a member of the French Chamber between 1839 and 1848 and for a short time a Foreign Minister of France in 1849, his grip was less steady and forceful. He was unable to identity himself with any of the political groupings at a time when political parties in the modern sense did not yet exist. While never doubting Guizot's sincerity Tocqueville was repelled by his lack of mobility, his intransigence in the question of enlarging the realm of Frenchmen entitled to vote, and perhaps also by his eclecticism. On the other hand the historian Guizot had made an impact on the young Tocqueville when he attended his lectures on 'The History of Civilization in France'. The wider perspective indicating a chain of events, the belief that inexorable laws control the process of history, even the tendency to a growing equalization between nobles and commoners, these ideas, so significant in *Democracy in America* have their roots in Guizot's lectures.[36] Although de Tocqueville shared Guizot's concern for a constitutional monarchy, he detested his pact with the propertied bourgeoisie and his encouragement of the propertied middle class under Louis Phillipe was denounced in Tocqueville's *Mémoires* in the sharpest terms. Guizot's advice to the lower classes to enrich themselves and thus work their way to obtaining the vote was to de Tocqueville only an encouragement of the odious individualism he so much disliked.

From more left-wing liberals in the Chamber before 1830, like Constant, Manuel, and Laffitte, Tocqueville was separated by their positive insistence on the revolutionary tradition, but even more so on account of their Voltairian attitude of indifference or hostility to religion. Tocqueville surprised many of his friends and relatives by taking the oath to the Orleans Monarchy which he was to denounce so bitterly twenty years later. On the other hand he then looked back with nostalgia to the '*grand parti liberal*, to which I had the glory of belonging'. [37]

Basically Tocqueville was a moralist. He denounced the rule of the French middle classes during the July monarchy when

'all political power, every franchise, every prerogative, and the whole government was confined and, as it were, heaped up within the narrow limits of this one class, to the statutory exclusion of all beneath and the actual exclusion of all above. Not only did it thus rule society, but it may be said to have formed it. . . . Master of everything in a manner that no aristocracy has ever been or may ever hope to be, the middle class, when called upon to assume the government, took it up as an industrial enterprise; it entrenched itself behind its power, and before long, in their egoism, each of its members thought much more of his private business than of public affairs; of his personal enjoyment than of the greatness of the nation.' [38]

In fact, in the eyes of Tocqueville the middle-class rulers were not only mediocre, they also lacked a true sense of liberty. For as he put it in '*The Ancien Régime and the Revolution*', with reference to the people under the despotism of the eighteenth century, only liberty was 'able to wrest them from the cult of money and from the petty daily worries of their individual affairs in order to make them realize and feel at every moment the fatherland (*la patrie*) above them and beside them; only it replaces the love of comfort from time to time by more powerful and higher passions.'[39]

It was not wise to close one's eyes to the advancing democratization of society. The Americans had had the great advantage over the French people that they had arrived 'at a state of democracy without having to endure a democratic revolution. And that they are born equal, instead of becoming so'. [40]But they had also been wise to combat the tendency of equality to keep men asunder by establishing free institutions and so they managed to subdue it. [41]Participation of many men in local government, so different from the centralism and the powerful bureaucracy in France, had contributed to it.

In France many people regarded 'equality of conditions as one evil, and political freedom as a second. When they are obliged to yield to the former, they strive at least to escape from the latter'. But de Tocqueville regarded this as erroneous. For those who wanted to fight the evils which equality might produce there was 'only one effectual remedy – namely political freedom'.[42]

(b) Liberalism during the second half of the nineteenth century

Adolphe Thiers

Different from England and Germany no liberal party made its bow in France. This does not mean that the liberal tradition did not operate or that liberal ideas played no role. Liberal ideas were part of the baggage of Radicalism which will be discussed separately (see pp. 70–9). Before and after 1870 radical Republicanism carried major elements of liberalism. During the last years of his rule even Napoleon III favoured a 'liberal empire', while theorists like Laboulaye and Vacherot developed an elaborate system of liberal politics. The liberals were then a sector of an unofficial opposition which ranged from a 'moderate' liberal like Thiers to a 'radical' like Jules Simon, not to mention his younger rival Léon Gambetta. What liberals of all shades in the Second Empire had in common was the demand for a constitutional government in which the security of the individual would be safe and public opinion could express itself through the press and through elections to an unfettered parliament.

It is debatable whether Adolphe Thiers, that complex, astute and protean figure, who, with intervals played a major role in French politics from 1830 to 1873, should be called a liberal. Yet during the Second Empire he came out constantly in favour of safeguards for the freedom of the individual and for a constitutional monarchy. In a way he remained faithful to the precise formula he had coined under Louis Philippe, 'The King rules but he does not govern.' A Deputy in the French Chamber from 1863 onward his speeches reflected the desire of industrial and business circles for both 'order' and 'liberty'. To Thiers they were the social principles on which modern society was based. Again and again they had been seriously threatened in Thiers' lifetime; it was therefore essential to him that they should now be firmly ensconced. The main task was to 're-establish the constitutional regime step by step'.[1] In his addresses before the Corps Législatif between 1863 and 1870 he constantly reiterated the 'indispensable liberties': security of the citizen from individual violence and arbitrary use of State power, freedom but not impunity of the press, freedom of elections, freedom of the citizens to elect their representatives and freedom for the majority in parliament to determine the course and the actions of the government.[2]

It is significant how Thiers interpreted the traditions of 1789 which were still sacrosanct to many Frenchmen. In a speech before the Legislative Body in February 1866 (doc. 63) Thiers' stance was that of an anti-revolutionary liberal. His aim was the restoration of liberty in the Second Empire without revolution, for, as he put it, 'every new revolution would be a postponement of liberty'. What made life so difficult in France were the numerous revolutions they had passed through. In the eyes of Thiers the French Revolution had had a social as well as a political aim. The social aim was 'the sacred equality which is called equality before the law', but *not*, as he emphatically stated, 'the chimerical equality of socialism'. The political aim was a constitutional monarchy, a system, under which 'the king not only listened to the advice of the country, but was also obliged to follow it'. The goal Thiers maintained through all the changes and vicissitudes of his long career was parliamentary government. 'Coupled with free elections and personal security for its citizens, it provided all that the country needed.'[3]

Thiers had confided to Nassau William Senior in 1852 that by birth he belonged to the people, by education he was a Bonapartist, by taste an aristocrat; he had also assured him that 'he had no sympathy with the bourgeoisie or with any system under which they were to rule'.[4] After 'he had made a fortune and entered the coveted circles of the haute bourgeoisie' Thiers became conservative in the defence of their interests. Yet at the same time he remained in the wake of the ideas of 1789.[5] As a liberal he stuck to its 'immortal principles' which continued for him 'to take the place of religion'. That irreverent selfmade realist was both '*a man of movement*' who did not value tradition for its own sake and saw in the monarchy of every shade a thing of the past, never to return, and '*a man of resistance*' who closed his eyes to the advance of the new social strata for whom Léon Gambetta became the eloquent spokesman.[6]

Thiers' moderate liberalism was that of a shrewd practitioner, of a manipulator of politics, little inclined to indulge in ideology or political thought. In the end his attitude was traditional, semi-conservative and therefore rather negative. The emphasis was more on 'freedom from' than on 'freedom for', with one exception, freedom for unfettered economic activity. He appreciated it as the president of a very successful mining firm, the Anzine Mine Company. Yet even this unlimited economic freedom was not absolute, for Thiers favoured 'prudent protection from foreign competition'.[7]

Two Liberals in the Third Republic: Emile Faguet and Paul Leroy-Beaulieu

Although no liberal party existed in France under the Third Republic, there were liberals of some sort in most of the non-socialist and non-clerical parties. During the first thirty years of the Republic, middle-class liberals 'had really very little to complain from the Government and the majority of the cabinets in office during those years were, under various labels, composed of representatives of the Liberal tradition.'[8] Emile Faguet (1847–1916), Professor of French literature at the University of Paris and a fertile writer on politics, was critical and stimulating, but also playful and indulging in *bon mots* for their own sake. He frequently argued as an anti-etatist although at other times he admitted that the position of the poor, public health and conditions of labour were matters for the State within clearly defined limits. Faguet feared the rising tide of collectivism and was opposed to socialism. He also emphasized the inadequacies of the parliamentary system and the follies of an inefficient bureaucracy.

The men of 1789, he felt, should have chosen between the liberalism of Montesquieu and the democratic collectivism of Rousseau. Not averse to the idea of human rights, Faguet nevertheless argued that they were not a prior construction or a divine gift like Moses' Ten Commandments but the outcome of the development of society and social process. He was also critical of the rights added in 1848, the right to work and the right to charity, and firmly denied that these should be a concern of the State.

Faguet drew a characteristic distinction between the small State and the big State (doc. 106). The small State is not menaced by external enemies whereas the big State is threatened by them. It is only in the big State that an army is required in addition to a system of justice and a police force. While in a small-scale State the government may have other objectives such as patronage of the arts, education, even a paternal supervision over the moral health of the family, the large-scale State should confine its activities to a budget, a police force and an army. Like Herbert Spencer, Faguet saw in the State a necessary evil, but also a remedy, 'i.e. a small evil that one invents in order to get rid of a big one'.

Faguet saw both the need for State power and for limiting it. In fact he went beyond Benjamin Constant when he desired 'a government to be very strong in its legitimate sphere and helpless outside it – that is, asking from citizens what it needs to defend the country, govern it and administer justice', yet 'without any interference in religion, in private consciences, in teaching in the discussion of ideas, or in propaganda'.[9] He was severely critical of the cumbersome and inefficient government machinery. Parliamentarians shirked their responsibilities and Cabinet Ministers were often appointed without any adequate qualification for their job. Private enterprise and professional efficiency outside the State operated much better. There was a 'cult of incompetence' in the State bureaucracy. 'Generally the Minister of Education is a lawyer; the Minister of Commerce an author; the War Minister a doctor; the Minister for the Navy a journalist.'[10]

Stimulating as Faguet's critique could be, it was often not more than a *jeu d'esprit*: for instance, when he alleged that France was one of the least free countries and one of the least liberal[11] and that he had never met a Frenchman who was truly liberal. All Frenchmen, he alleged, were passionately favouring their party ties. Even a patriotic Frenchman was only able to conceive the progress of France in terms of the triumph of his party. Faguet was worried by reflecting that full liberty would give an undue advantage to rival parties.

With all his anguish over the excesses and follies of the State, Faguet's patriotism kept his anti-étatism within limits. Whereas he would not recommend the cult of the ego to individuals, he insisted that 'to a country the cult of itself must be presented as a duty'. In retrospect it becomes clear that the contemporary struggle between the Big Powers on the Continent cast its shadow over this brand of liberal philosophy. For that reason Faguet found it necessary 'to praise and exalt patriotism as the first among duties and the most essential among virtues without which all others would be useless'.[12]

Emile Faguet's liberalism was more anti-egalitarian than anti-étatist. He realized the difficulties of reconciling liberty with equality, an equality which would lead to despotism. There was something unreal in his attempt to revive the traditions of 1789 by regarding 'fraternity' as the factor which could overcome the antinomies between liberty and equality.

Paul Leroy-Beaulieu (1843–1916) shared with Faguet the attitude of a marked though not unqualified anti-étatism. Both denounced many aspects of the Third Republic and yet admitted that the State, however defective, was indispensable. As professor at the Collège de France and editor of *L'Economiste Français,* Leroy-Beaulieu had the edge over Faguet because his insight into the economic and political trends of the Third Republic[13] was more astute and professional than the polished armchair reflections of Faguet.

A strong supporter of *laissez faire* Leroy-Beaulieu admired Herbert Spencer's acid criticism of State interference and incompetence but thought his method too deductive, too much argued 'from above'.

The instability of parliamentary majorities, the financial crises and scandals of the 1880s are reflected in many of Leroy-Beaulieu's arguments. Highly critical of the idolatry of the State which he detected in some contemporary German economists, he regarded the State as a *parvenu*, as superficial, unstable, 'precarious, vague, always changing, eternally provisional', dating in its present form back only a century instead of twenty centuries. The State was seen as a necessary evil, necessary because its two major legitimate functions, security and justice, cannot be provided by individuals. The State was based on a division of labour which enables the individual to devote more time to his private pursuits.

The main point in his criticism of the State was its complete lack of inventive ability. The State was not a creative, but a critical organ, vulgar and imitative. If John Stuart Mill saw in the few original though eccentric minds the salt of the earth, Leroy-Beaulieu regarded the 'individuals without a mandate', 'the prophets and inspired teachers' as 'the fermentation of the human mass which is naturally inert'.[14]

This anti-etatist and pro-capitalist bias is strikingly revealed when he compares the structure and the activities of the State with those of joint stock companies. [15] The members of the latter are affluent, sound and imbued with 'all those habits of patience and orderliness which competency generally confers'. The shareholders are free from the influence of passion which during political elections upsets the life of the State. The joint stock companies are by their very nature protected from sudden changes. They preserve a respect for tradition, for established rules, for continuity of action which stands in striking contrast to the tendencies prevailing in the modern State.

If incapable managers and administrators in joint stock companies do not answer energetically to the stimulus of competition, their enterprises are eventually eliminated. On the other hand an extravagant scheme of public works, contrary to all good sense, might still be approved of by a majority in parliament. Regrettably the State has no competitors, it is 'a personality without rival'. During the 1880s the point was highlighted by a chain of unfortunate interventions by the French State in the field of public transport and by the vested interests guiding many Deputies in conjunction with it. The frequent purchase of privately-owned railway companies by the State was a thorn in the flesh of both Faguet and Leroy-Beaulieu. Faguet saw in it 'in the first place, a means of exploiting the company'.[16] The disastrous outcome of the so-called 'Freycinet Plan' was to him only one major example of 'the disorderly outbreak of public works, ill-considered, badly directed, badly utilized which has run riot everywhere during the last 15 years'.[17]

Leroy-Beaulieu felt the danger lay in State intervention and not in the greed of unscrupulous entrepreneurs and Deputies.[18] Yet he admitted that the State had to provide for the 'common wants' of the nation, which the individuals cannot adequately secure by themselves. To maintain a system of justice and of national security was beyond the reach of mere individuals or even groups; to determine judicial rights and responsibilities was beyond their competency. While not denying the State's obligation towards the weak, Leroy-Beaulieu maintained that modern society rather tended to exaggerate its extent. The State was not bound 'to bring about universal happiness'. To lose sight of the 'very nature of things' which meant 'that each person is responsible for his own weaknesses and must suffer for them' was equivalent to running a serious risk of ennervating society and rendering it less capable of progress.

It reflected the feeling of insecurity on the Continent when both Leroy-Beaulieu and Faguet emphasized the need for a guarantee of the collective security of the nation and for the personal security of the individual and his rights more strongly than did contemporary English thinkers. The fear of Bismarckian power-politics, the French panic in the war crises of 1875 and 1887, contributed to Leroy-Beaulieu's insistence that it was most essential for the nation to 'keep its life, preserve its frontiers, be subject to no oppression and no tribute from abroad'. It 'should have sufficient confidence in the organization of its (military and diplomatic) forces not to be distracted from its daily task by panic'.[19] When does an anti-etatist turn etatist and patriot? Answer: when the *raison d'état* forces him to do so. 'Anything in the constitution of a State', Leroy-Beaulieu declared categorically, 'which endangers the cohesion of the national forces, their preparedness in times of peace, their continuity of practice with respect to armaments and the direction of foreign policy, must be considered as contrary to the very idea of State and a source of peril to the nation.'[20] He put this point more strongly than Faguet did, but he would have undoubtedly approved of the latter's insistence on the need for patriotism. 'When patriotism is no longer a virtue', Faguet wrote, 'it will be a necessity as long as there are other races among whom it is still fashionable.'[21]

At that time the German National-Liberals reasoned on similar lines. Liberalism on the Continent then was inclined to fade away when the fatherland was in danger or, more often, was simply declared to be so. This was perhaps one of the reasons why during the first thirty years of

General Introduction

the Third Republic, middle-class liberals 'had really very little to complain of from the Government. . . . and the majority of the cabinets in office during those years were, under various labels, composed of representatives of the Liberal tradition.'[22]

(c) Radicalism

1820–1870
The loose dividing line between liberals and radicals in France is often difficult to discern. Although in the 1820s the term 'radical' was borrowed from England, it developed a different meaning in France under the impact of the traditions of the French Revolution. It soon acquired a Republican emphasis alien to the English model. Although in the course of the nineteenth century French radicals were sometimes little more than liberals in stern and provocative disguise, 'radical' gradually became a less equivocal label than 'liberal'. On the whole French radicals were distrustful of the Establishment, and of State power. Most, though not all of them, would grant only a necessary minimum to the State. In this the influence of Bentham on the sporadic first radicals in France after 1820 was significant. Different from the liberals they were dissatisfied with the narrow limits of the electorate both before and after 1830 and strongly pressed for universal manhood suffrage, possibly in the frame of a Republic. When after an attempt on the life of King Louis Philippe in 1834 the usage of the term 'republican' was officially banned, the word 'radical' was often substituted by the Left for it.[1] While radicals wanted to improve the lot of the masses and to secure 'the greatest happiness of the greatest number', they still thought more in moral than social terms.

In 1835 Alexis de Tocqueville compared the French radicals unfavourably with their English counterpart. While admitting that there existed 'basic analogies' between them, he regarded the differences as more striking. In England the radicals were strictly law-abiding and applied only legal means to win a majority, whereas 'the most characteristic trait of the French radical' was 'a wish to use the power of some to secure the happiness of the greatest number'. 'His most important means of government' was 'material force and a contempt for law'. He had 'the greatest mistrust of property; and ready to violate it in practice he attacks it in theory'. Equally characteristic was his 'flaunting not only of anti-Christian opinions, but also of the anti-social ideas'. The English radicals Tocqueville had met were recognized as 'gentlemen' and 'almost all of them had a careful education. They were men who argued their opinions and liked discussion'. By contrast the French radical was 'almost always very poor, often boorish still more often presumptuous, and profoundly ignorant of political science'.[2] He understood only the use of force and dealt 'in empty words and superficial generalization'.

70

Perhaps Tocqueville's most devastating comment was the remark that 'an enlightened man of good sense and good will would be a radical in England' whereas he had 'never met those three qualities together in a French Radical'.[3] This was hardly a fair description, as Tocqueville seems to have included Utopian socialists among the radicals. He was much impressed by the free and orderly political discussion in a society which lacked strong revolutionary traditions and had recently passed the political compromise of the Reform Bill. Although in their speeches and publications French radicals emphasized the traditional ideals of 'liberty, equality and fraternity', they were on the whole more concerned with liberty and solidarity than with equality. It is true that Louis Blanc, a radical, later called himself a socialist, but Ledru-Rollin, the leader of the radicals in the 1840s, was more a populist than a socialist. Son of a physician and a brilliant law student he represented the level of culture which Tocqueville had found missing in French radicals. In 1834 Ledru-Rollin submitted a memorandum to the French Chamber denouncing the atrocities committed by soldiers against people of the lower classes in Paris. His radical faith was based on feeling as well as on reason and a romantic touch permeated his addresses.[4]

On the eve of the February Revolution of 1848 Ledru-Rollin announced sternly: 'We are ultra-radicals, if you understand this word as meaning the party which wants to bring to the reality of life the great symbol of liberty, equality and fraternity, yes, all of us who are here, are ultra-radicals. The word frightens only children.'[5] Whereas another radical, Hippolyte Carnot, still maintained in 1847 that 'the efforts of the radicals should concentrate on the one goal of achieving universal suffrage', Ledru-Rollin, stirring up public opinion by the new propaganda device of public banquets held first in Paris and later in various provincial centres, demanded a Republican State. Yet even then the radical emphasis was still more on political than on social issues; on closer contacts between electors and deputies. The political rights of the workers mattered still more than their social plight and depressed status.

The February Revolution of 1848 carried radicals and other republicans to power. Ledru-Rollin became Minister of the Interior and Louis Blanc, who presided over the 'Commission of Government for the Workers', proclaimed the right to work and a ten-hour day. Ledru-Rollin, too, approved of the organization of labour and demanded a moderate intervention of the State in economic affairs. But the tide soon turned against radicals and social democrats alike. In the Constituent Assembly, out of 900 Deputies there were fewer than 100 radicals and socialists and only 50 could be described as radicals.

In the elections to the Legislative Assembly of 1849 radicals and socialists combined in the 'Comité democratique socialist' (commonly called 'Comite montagnard'). In fact more radical than socialist, the programme of this organization combined the traditional formula of 'liberty, equality, fraternity' with the less exalted notions of 'order, unity and progress'.[6]

The arrival of Louis Bonaparte and his coup d'état of 2 December 1852 put an end to the political activities of the Left. Ledru-Rollin and Louis Blanc went into exile and in the 1850s neither the liberals nor the radicals counted. By the early 1860s a new generation of radicals appeared who discarded the earlier populist romanticism, replacing it by a positivistic faith in science and rational enquiry. Auguste Comte was a strong influence on the new generation of prominent liberals and radicals. Gambetta, Allain-Targé, Pelletan, Clemenceau received their education at the universities under the Second Empire and came under the influence of the new cult of science by the efforts of men like Charles Renouvier to establish a science of the moral order ('*Science de la morale*'). The belief in science as a factor of beneficial progress, widespread among students and scholars, contradicted the claims of the Catholic Church and pleaded for an education free from its allegedly pernicious influence. Future Republican leaders, such as Gambetta and Ferry, looked at the Free-masons as an enlightened counter-force to the Church which seemed more intolerant than ever since Pius IX issued the *Syllabus Errorum* in 1864.

From the point of view of the Right the terms 'liberal' and 'radical' seemed interchangeable. When Edouard Laboulaye in 1864 published his work *The Liberal Party, its programme and its future*,[7] he was accused of being 'radical'. The author replied that the name did not frighten him and he accepted it as praise. 'If it means to demand a free government in a free society', he declared, 'then I am a radical to the last degree.'[8] What he offered in fact in this work as in others was a clear and 'useful, if unexciting statement of what may be called the orthodox liberal programme of the 'sixties'.[9] He reiterated the old liberal demands of freedom of teaching and of association and added to them freedom of worship and the need for separation of State and Church. Laboulaye was afraid of the ceaseless appetite of the government to take over everything and he deplored the fact that some classical liberals in France approved of this. While emphatic on the separation of Church and State, he deplored it if some were afraid of Christianity and others of liberty; both had the same origin. 'If the individual today has a right to be sovereign', he argued, 'it is because Christ has freed our spirit and forever broken the despotism of the State.'[10]

A sharper language was used in Jules Simon's work *La Politique Radicale* (1868) published at a time when Napoleon III was obliged to make more and more concessions to the liberal *Zeitgeist*. Jules Simon was then one of the few oppositional Deputies in the Chamber and the acknowledged leader of the radicals. Only the radicals, he argued in his Preface, could have a programme. They differed from the middle-of-the-road liberals who, he said 'are liberal, but limit their liberalism to the degree required by the situation. One can strictly risk advancing a bit further on the day after a victory.' [11]

Simon proclaimed, 'the system of total liberty'. What did it mean? 'In the case of science, of theory, total freedom without restriction and reserve; in the case of the practice of politics, as basis of the national sovereignty; as measure of the least action; as guarantee for publicity and responsibility at all stages.'[12]

Like Laboulaye and other liberals, Jules Simon was anxious to avoid the two extremes of despotism or unlimited authority and of anarchy or uncontrolled liberty. He was highly critical of the State and of power altogether. His formula regarding State power was not 'no action' but 'the least action'. In his eyes the progress of liberty was identical with the gradual elimination of power. In 1868 Jules Simon, who later in the Third Republic became the first convinced Republican to be Prime Minister, attempted the squaring of the circle. In *La Politique Radicale* he opted for 'a power strong, but restricted, strong because it was restricted'. He even argued optimistically that 'power, if it is faithful to its mission must work with persevering energy towards its own elimination'.[13] 'Total liberty' should extend to the press, to education, to freedom of conscience which meant no stipends from the State for the clergy, no alliance with Rome, no Concordat. While reiterating the traditional liberal demands such as universal suffrage, uniformity of taxation, responsibility of ministers, he emphasized the need for the responsibility of administrative officials on all levels and more freedom for local communities, townships and parishes in the running of their affairs. Though Simon regarded himself as a radical, his radicalism did not extend to the social question. To him the fixing of working hours or wages meant to deprive manufacturers of their freedom. The social demands of socialists and communists, he argued, added the evil of hatred to that of poverty, while with 'competition, the evils it produced' were 'temporary evils that must neither be denied nor exaggerated'.[15]

The radical platform of Léon Gambetta's celebrated 'Manifesto of Belleville' (1869) (doc. 71) did not differ greatly from the theses in Simon's work. Yet the well-phrased, if somewhat academic, approach of a political doctrinaire like Simon became in the hands of the agile orator and lawyer Gambetta a political gospel.[16] It secured his victory over the rival candidate, Hippolyte Carnot, also a radical, in the most turbulent and radical constituency in Paris. The message of this Manifesto by and large remained valid for radicalism until 1905 when a main point in it, the separation of Church and State, was finally carried through. It was Gambetta's political style, his 'know how', his close contact with his electors, which make this Manifesto an important landmark. Therefore the Belleville Manifesto commences with a 'Memorandum from my Electors' (doc. 71). 'In the name of universal suffrage, the basis of all political and social organisation' it asked the citizens 'to give a mandate to our deputy to reaffirm the principle of radical democracy'. The electors were emphatic on 'freedom of meetings without impediments and traps, with the right to discuss all religious, philosophical, political and social questions'. They solemnly demanded 'the abolition of standing armies, the cause of the ruin of the finances and the business of the nation, the source of hatred between the peoples and of distrust at home'. Other points were somewhat vague, but expressed a similar moral indignation, for instance the demand of 'the abolition of privileges and monopolies which we define by the words: *"a bonus for idleness".*' In his lively reply Gambetta assured his electors that universal suffrage was to him the key to carrying out the demands made by the electors. [17]

Although directed to the electors in a constituency in which the lower classes, the petit bourgeoisie and the workers, prevailed, the political issues in the Manifesto had clearly pride of place before the social issues. It is true the electors recommended that the evolution of the social problem, 'although subordinated to political change, should be constantly studied and investigated in the name of the principle of justice and social equality', for only that principle, 'generalized and applied' could 'bring about the disappearance of the social antagonism'. But at its best this was a Populist approach; at its worst, an ostrich-like attitude towards the now important social question.

During the Third Republic

After the unexpected fall of the Second Empire in 1870 the survival of the Republic born out of national collapse and defeat was by no means certain. Not only was the new State threatened by the two rival Monarchist factions, the Bourbonites and the Orleanists, but also a large portion of the upper and middle sections of the bourgeoisie was hostile or lukewarm to it and at most the formula of President Adolphe Thiers appealed to them: that 'the Republic will be conservative or it will not be'. Gambetta astutely recognized that in order both to strengthen the Republic and advance his own career he had to appeal to social forces outside the old Establishment. In fact a gradual change of élites was taking place. The old élite of nobles, generals and the old bourgeoisie were now faced by aspiring new strata of citizens who had 'arrived', of solicitors, doctors, successful businessmen who welcomed the new State. Gambetta, artist and realist, had them in mind when in his speech at Grenoble in September 1872 he talked of the 'new social layers' which had entered political life. There was a new chance for shopowners as well as for small farmers who had only now become politically vocal. [18] Republicanism had a stronghold in the Freemasonic Lodges and it was perhaps symbolic that in a dramatic election in Paris in April 1873, fought between Thiers's man, the conservative candidate Charles Remusat, and the radical Desiré Barodet, supported by Gambetta, the latter, a leading freemason from Lyons, won.

Gambetta not only founded a radical newspaper *La République Française,* which first appeared in October 1871, he also encouraged the appearance of other papers with a similar orientation in the provinces. These newspapers were 'at the same time a means of expression and an instrument of association'; it was 'around a local organ that the militant supporters and even the sympathizers of radicalism regroup themselves; in the country the doctor, the teacher, the notary are the men of science facing the men of religious belief'.[19] They played the role of activists believing in evolution and progress in contrast to the backward men of order.

As Gambetta put it in an election address in October 1871: 'The people, of the lower bourgeoisie, the workers and the peasants realize from day to day more clearly the close connections between politics and their affairs and want to be represented by themselves. This is a revolution.'[20] By 1872 radicalism had become more complex and had to some extent changed its meaning. For Gambetta it meant struggle and opposition but also a trust in evolution, in an orderly development of things, 'radicalism of progress and radicalism of order, radicalism of refusal, but also radicalism of consent'.[21] Yet he declared that now the 'Republican party' was largely identical with the 'radical party' and that the latter no longer had any individuality. 'If one calls us Jacobins and Radicals, these are only words which each at its time have signified political necessities. But we are beings of our own hour and time and we belong to the Republican democracy of 1872.'[22] He found the label 'radical' no longer helpful.

In his Grenoble speech of September 1872 (doc. 99) Gambetta denounced 'political fear' as the chronic disease of France. As fear had become 'the expedient, the resource of their enemies,' it was the task of the Republican party, of the radical party, to cure France of this malady. 'And the remedy, the cure for this was prudence' (*la sagesse*).

By 1876 Gambetta's prudence was regarded by many radicals as a mere instrument of opportunism and as weakness. A split developed within the radical camp. It seemed to many that the supple Gambetta himself had become 'a conservative Republican'. It was not Gambetta but Clemenceau who in 1876 declared that the Belleville Programme was still valid: 'The conservative Republicans demand the minimum in the Republic, we the maximum.' 'We radical Republicans, we want the Republic for its natural consequences for the great and profound social reforms which it entails. The aim which we have set ourselves is the realization of the great renovation of 1789, inaugurated by the French bourgeoisie and abandoned by it before it was achieved.'[23]

Intransigent radicals like Clemenceau refused to close their eyes to the social questions which were taboo with large sections of the bourgeoisie still troubled by the memories of the Paris Commune of 1871. In the same election campaign Louis Blanc demanded that 'they should protect, instead of impeding every effort, either individual or collective, which aims at the gradual disappearance of the proletariat, the raising of the worker from the status of a wage-earner to that of a partner and to make more and more accessible to labour the enjoyment of the right of property, a fundamental right, inherent in human nature'. 'The regime of privileges', which added conventional inequalities to natural inequalities, should gradually make way for a regime that would assure the equal development of their unequal abilities to all'. [24]

It was this position which the intransigent radicals defended against the Republican 'opportunists' on the one side and against the slowly growing collectivistic socialists on the other. The 'opportunists' for their part restricted themselves to favouring a cautious development towards democracy, wanting to 'reassure the interests and win over the minds'. During the election campaign of 1881 Gambetta insisted that the country's problems had to be solved piecemeal and he warned of embracing too much. [25] On the other hand the radicals around Clemenceau accepted a measure of State intervention in the economy, a reason for labelling themselves 'radical socialists'; but they were opposed equally to doctrinaire egalitarianism and to the old fashioned liberal *laissez faire*.[26]

In their 'memorandum of the electors', the organizers of the 'radical socialist' committee which in 1881 offered Clemenceau the candidature as a Deputy in a Paris constituency included a number of social measures as targets. They were: reduction in law of the duration of working hours, foundation of superannuation funds and recognition of the civil status of trade unions. Clemenceau accepted these reforms which would help to 'prepare the great transformation which will be the completion of the French Revolution'. On the other hand, he rejected the dogma of the class struggle. It showed, he argued, a misconception of the nature of democratic politics. 'One has above all to guard one-self against letting the people believe that liberation could come to them suddenly from above, owing to a magic formula, outside the individual effort'. [27] In 1884 Clemenceau declared it necessary 'to make it clear to the disinherited of every kind that there exists no true emancipation for them outside the one which will come from their own efforts, in a milieu that the work of the politicians will make more and more favourable for them'. [28]

By 1881 when the Republic was definitely established and the Republicans in the Chamber outnumbered their opponents by nearly five to one, Gambetta had dropped the word 'radical' from the label of his *Union républicaine* which had over 200 deputies in the Chamber. On its left were two groups still proud to include the word 'radical' in their designation, *La Gauche radicale*, still prepared to cooperate with the *Union républicaine*, and *L'extrême Gauche radicale socialiste*, with Clemenceau, Louis Blanc and Pelletan, which drew a sharp dividing line between itself and the 'opportunists', led by Gambetta and Ferry. Only twenty years later the various groups of the Left outside the ranks of the strict socialists combined to form an organized Party which used the term 'radical'. In July 1901 the overall 'Republican Radical and Radical-Socialist Party' held its initial congress in Paris. It was the first organized major party in France under the Third Republic in the politics of which the power of the individual Deputy, not restrained by party discipline, had become a characteristic feature. [29] In any case it was a considerable achievement to combine the various groups calling themselves 'radical' or 'radical socialist' under one permanent roof. Its platform was wide. The congress, declared a circular distributed on the opening day: 'will not know enemies on the Left: it will not be called upon to establish a new programme', it will urge the country towards 'secular action against clericalism, democratic action against dictatorship and social action against misery' – a formula equally acceptable to the more moderate and the more 'advanced' elements. Considering the strong individualist element within the radical ranks, it was a major step towards integration. [30]

Here a word should be added about the left-wing radicals who during the first thirty years of the Third Republic endeavoured 'to lead France into the direction of a Welfare State'. [31] Favouring both political democracy, making for freedom, and industrial democracy which stressed equality, they were social-minded individualists who tried to combine their belief in the merits of personal initiative with an awareness of man's close contacts with society. In the 1880s and 1890s they desired State intervention in favour of industrial workers. Henry Maret, editor of *Le Radical*, argued against *laissez faire* liberals that the State 'intervened at all times only in favour of capital'. 'There should be not only laws for the protection of property but also laws protective of labour.' [32]

These left-wing radicals understood under 'socialism' – then still a term of many meanings – what was in fact social reform within the framework of small-scale private enterprise. They agreed with the socialists that the State should allow laws in favour of trade unions, grant workers the right to strike, prevent child labour, regulate the hours of workers and provide social security. But they did not favour extensive control and ownership of property by the State or nationalization of the means of production.

Towards the end of the nineteenth century, 'the radical's image of the workers' changed from 'that of a stalwart fighter for democracy into that of a restless insatiable troublemaker.' [33] The urban workers who, particularly in Paris, for a long time had supported the left-wing radicals, now turned towards more definitely socialist factions. Radicalism, once an urban phenomenon, now found its support in rural areas and in small towns. Although there were still friendly relations between radicals and socialists (until 1905 they combined in *Le Bloc*) within the new *Parti Republicain Radical et Radical-Socialiste* the left-wing members 'who generally called themselves radical-socialists, lost much of their former leadership of the (overall) left and a certain amount of their initiative in the social reform movement'.[34] On the whole the Radical Party moved much more to the Centre in the years before 1914. 'Since Clemenceau's Cabinet of 1906, its politicians became more cautious, won ministerial office, and gave scant attention to the ideals formulated by their predecessors during their days in the wilderness'.[35]

The parliamentary practice of the Third Republic with its many loose groupings, its lack of party cohesion, the emphasis of many Deputies on self-advancement while paying lip service to the glorious traditions of the Republic, not to mention political and financial scandals disillusioned millions of Frenchmen. It is in this context that the lonely voice of the radical critic and essayist Alain is significant.[36] His essays combined a deep distrust of all power with a spirited radical individualism.

Deeply steeped in the humanities and classic traditions, Alain unsensationally but adroitly exposed the abuse of power by those involved in the power game. He profoundly distrusted the Establishment in all its guises. Taking an active interest in adult education Alain sought friendship with his listeners in turning them 'against the Castles, the Academies and the Important Persons I don't love'.[37] 'The dream of the Important Person', he wrote in 1923 (doc. 112b), 'is to serve in order to command. And I understand that the only real politics, the politics of resistance and criticism, does not make sense and is without interest for them.' What Alain understood under 'real politics' was 'a continuous effort against the military and political despotism which are one'. All power, he maintained, 'should be reduced to civil power, which makes a minister simply a high-grade employee similar to the coach driver or the postman. Such power does not upset anyone. But the Importance, if one allows it to operate, upsets everybody. We have experienced it' (doc. 112b).

Alain resented being called 'the last radical', the representative of a dying species. On the contrary, he insisted in 1924, that radicalism was not old, it was 'still a child, in fact, the only new topic in politics, in which everything has already been said'.[38] In spite of all misgivings, he proclaimed that 'radicalism exists as a political doctrine, it has as a principle the government of the people by the people, as real and direct as possible'. Alain made a strong plea for direct democracy. It meant not only 'to maintain the universal suffrage loyally, assure the secrecy of the vote' – an old radical demand – but also

'to break the tyrannies which employ corruption or intimidation, assure the control of the Chambers, support the ministers against all around them who try to make them believe that they are the true masters and make them forget that they are the servants of the people, to crush the bureaucrats, the intriguers, the merchants of favours, the merchants of votes. Not to have any other law than that which conforms with the opinion of the largest number.'

That seemed to him a 'fine programme'.[39] Alain regarded it as 'impossible that the powerful, have not a passion for exercising power'. 'Every diplomat loves his schemes; every police commissioner loves order; every senior clerk works towards the extension of his right of control and of his prerogatives ... Altogether the abuse of power is a natural fruit of power; from it it follows that all people who fall asleep in liberty will wake up in servitude.'[40] While the army extends and establishes itself by its very nature, all the power-holders including the police, the judges and the industrialists, imitate it, with the President demanding new powers. Unfortunately people who call themselves democrats are naive enough not to see through this power-game. Hoodwinked, it suffices to them that 'the people are consulted from time to time, in such a way that they could choose other masters or confirm the present ones.'[41]

Alain proposed a different concept of leadership. The people should not elect chiefs, but *controllers*. The Head of State should not be seen 'as the head of all the State offices but as the delegate of the people, the model citizen who has the task to discover all abuses of power, and to put an end to them', a gigantic Ombudsman, as we would say fifty years after Alain.[42]

Alain was not an anarchist but an individualist averse to élites. He did not suggest that the citizen should reject all power. Some power was necessary in society, but the citizen must beware of blind obedience, of complacency in mere subordination. The true citizen should learn at the same time 'to obey and to resist. By obedience he assures the maintenance of order, by resistance he assures freedom.' Alain visualized a change of controlling power and to him radicalism meant 'the permanent control of the elected by the elector, of the minister by the elected deputy and finally of the administration by the minister himself'.[43]

In a way Alain reflected a widespread dissatisfaction with the power-game of the Third Republic. Although more symptomatic than effective his sophisticated radicalism was a far cry from the mere faith in the universal suffrage of Ledru-Rollin and the adroit stratagems of Gambetta and Clemenceau. To Alain the price of freedom was the radical vigilance of every citizen not only over his political enemies but equally over his political friends, in short over anyone exercising power (see section D, pp. 600–1).

8. Liberals and radicals in Germany – some aspects

There are a number of reasons why liberalism and radicalism in Germany in the nineteenth century were seldom unambiguous and definite concepts, as they were in England. Nor was the antinomy between 'liberal' and 'democratic' before 1847 as clearly marked in Germany as it was in France. Afterwards the terms 'radical' and 'radicalism' were used, but radicalism as a basic attitude was seldom conspicuous and relatively little in demand.

By and large the German political situation, differing from that in Western Europe, was conditioned by the fact that the 'liberal' movement after 1815 had not only to face the demand for individual freedom and human rights, but also recognize that individual freedom and constitutional guarantees could only be permanently safeguarded in an integrated nation.

During the years of *Vormärz*, the period between 1815 and the March revolutions of 1848, the organized sector of the liberal movement in Germany centred on seven very varying groupings. . . :

'A South German constitutional group which looked particularly to Rotteck and Welcker of the Baden Diet; a north-west 'classical' liberalism crystallized first around the diets of Hesse-Kassel and Hanover and then on the theory of Göttingen's Friedrich Dahlmann;[1] a Rhenish and an East Prussian movement within the state of Prussia, each using its provincial estates as its point of focus but drawing its real force from the industrial and commercial capitalism characteristic of these regions; church organisations which swung their masses behind the liberal political requirements of their clerical position – orthodox Catholicism in the Rhineland, the dissident 'German Catholics' and Protestant Illuminati movements in central Germany; these were the chief liberal groups connected with considerable interests or numbers in German society.'[2]

In those days officials, teachers and other *Gebildete* (educated people) formed a high percentage of the liberals.[3] Before 1848 these groups had few competitors as spokesmen for a progressive readjustment of public life. 'In a society without parties or pressure groups, without an extensive system of communications, and without a well-developed national market, university education, professional relationships, and above all the nexus of the State's bureaucratic institutions then were of unparalleled significance for the development of supralocal personal and political ties.'[4]

The multiplicity of many petty states, the lack of an Empire before 1871 together with the slow industrialization of the country before the 1850s provided a background less favourable to radical pressure on the evolution of German liberalism compared with the position in England. Different from England and France, the aristocracy in Germany maintained its political and social hegemony well into the middle of the century and even afterwards retained much of it. The fact that after 1815 the German nobility managed to keep its privileges for a considerable time, as well as the heavy and often woolly emphasis on speculative thought, a by-product of the impact of German idealism, contributed much to the political impotence of the middle classes.

The lack of any national representation in Prussia before the eve of the Revolution of 1848 was not favourable to a sharp line between 'moderate' and 'radical' thought among the opponents of the government. The same was to a more limited extent true also of the position in the South German states, where constitutions and with them some form of parliament had been granted soon after the Congress of Vienna. In the Chambers of Baden and Wuerttemberg representatives of the prosperous and educated middle class often argued that progress was only with them and not with the government. Its supporters were attacked as the 'Party of Reaction' or as 'Absolutist Party' in contrast to the liberals, the self-styled 'friends of the fatherland'. As one of their speakers maintained euphorically in the lower Chamber of Baden in 1840, the liberals 'favour Light and the rule of Law and certain guaranteed freedoms, they want constitutions which must be genuine (represent truth) and they demand freedom of the press'. On the other hand their opponents, the reactionaries, he alleged, 'demand darkness, tameness, a sense of servitude, the attitude of the Chinese, and they desire control of the press'.[5] In the Second Chamber the Freiburg professors Rotteck and Welcker proclaimed the idea of a constitutional monarchy which meant a belief 'in the eternal harmony of the true rights and interests of the throne, with those of the people'.[6]

By then a more radical movement had, however, developed in south-west Germany with rather vague idealistic conceptions of the sovereignty of the people and a democratic united Fatherland. This non-parliamentary opposition was considerably influenced by ideas from nearby France. The approach of the men behind the Festival at Hambach in the Palatinate in 1832 was radical in a rather vague and imprecise way. The protest against the tyranny of the ruling class, composed of officers and officials, was more drastically expressed there than in the less heated atmosphere of the Diets. At Hambach both nationalist and internationalist notes were struck. In his speech the radical leader P. J. Siebenpfeiffer visualized the day 'when a common German fatherland will arise which will welcome all sons as citizens and comprise all the citizens with equal love and equal protection'.[7] Siebenpfeiffer, a Republican, had also bold plans for a German Reform Association which aimed at fundamental changes of the socio-political structure by lawful means (*auf gesetzlichem Wege*).[8]

Concepts of 'radicalism' varied a good deal. A report on the Hambach Festival by the alarmed Prussian envoy in Baden to King Frederick William III noted as a 'highly important result' the distinction between the 'ultra radicals' and 'the less violent moderates'. At Hambach it had been loudly voiced 'how in spite of the narrow ties between all revolutionaries in Europe, who have their centre in Paris, the ultra-radicals in Germany certainly have a different relationship with them than is the case with the less violent men whom I call Doctrinaires who, however, also want to bring about a revolution'. In his report the same envoy calls 'Rotteck one of the greatest doctrinaires with a very revolutionary tendency'.[9] Yet Professor Karl von Rotteck was not at all pleased with the platform and propaganda of these 'ultra-radicals'. To him they were as obnoxious as the champions of the old order. 'Everywhere we see two opposed parties', he wrote in 1838, 'the favoured oligarchy and the plebeians and the big masses of the third estate who feel handicapped.' The existence of this antagonism seemed to him detrimental to the nation, partly because of the positions the opponents held in society and partly because their differing party ties transcended the frontiers of State and nation. He argued that in Germany a member of the oligarchy had closer ties with French and Spanish patricians than with his plebeian fellow-countryman. Similarly the German plebeian rejoiced with all his heart over the victory of the Greek liberation movement and of the anti-absolutist Spaniards, although he knew that both were a target of hatred to his ultra-aristocratic fellow-countrymen. According to Rotteck the only remedy against both these extremes was 'the spirit of the constitutional monarchy'. 'Only it gives the State authority such strength that it permeates all sectors of public life and makes impossible the resistance of any party, because it integrates all of them on a lawful (legal) basis and is not used for any of them but only for the general welfare of all classes in the nation.' [10]The State, as Rotteck understood it, had to care not for the exclusive welfare of patricians or plebeians, but for the good of all classes. [11]

The liberal 'doctrinaires' in Baden before 1848 interpreted the Constitution in a rather negative way. They denounced the government and its supporters as the reactionary '*Stillstandspartei*', the party of standing still, while the liberals regarded themselves as the 'anti-governmental' party, confining themselves to a mere conditional and therefore in the long run unproductive attitude. There was to be no cooperation between the government and a parliamentary majority. For a long time these liberals 'failed to form a clear concept of constitutional law as the French liberals had done before 1830'. In south Germany they suffered from the fact that 'on top of the bureaucratic, centralized State a constitution after the West European model had been grafted quite unorganically without any corresponding reforms in the structure of the State and without any preparations'.[12]

The Constitution of Baden of 1819 favoured the bourgeoisie and the towns as seats of the artisans and merchants and the candidates for parliament were largely selected by the local worthies – the

'*Honorationen*'. Under the parochial leadership of Professor Rotteck 'a friend-foe ideology' developed which insisted on the permanent dualism of the forces involved.[13] To Rotteck 'no cooperation between governmental and anti-governmental forces was permissible'. His insistence on displaying 'a manly pride in front of princely thrones' proved sterile.

Towards the end of the 1830s a split occurred in the Liberal camp, between a moderate wing ready to cooperate with the government and a 'radical' group led first by Itzstein and Rotteck and later by the more left-wing champions Struve and Hecker, who saw themselves as representative of the lower strata in society. There was little love lost between the 'moderate' and the 'radical' liberals. The radicals who claimed to be a 'People's Party' decried the moderates as servile and as 'enemies of the people' while the moderates, when later joining the government, denounced the 'Radicals' as 'enemies of the State'. [14]

On the eve of the Revolution of 1848 the dividing line between the 'moderates' and the 'radicals' in south-west Germany was clearly reflected in two political manifestos, issued in September and October 1847 (docs 85 and 86). The Offenburg meeting, with Hecker and Gustav von Struve as leaders, struck a more democratic note compared with the less drastic constitutionalism of the men who gathered a month later at Heppenheim. Both groups, the 'Half Ones' and the 'Total Ones', desired a united Germany with constitutional rights of the citizens, but they differed in the emphasis and the extent of their demands. The moderate Heppenheimers stressed 'the aim of uniting Germany through a German policy and a joint direction of national interest'. They wanted a considerable reform of the judiciary system, restrictions on police power, reform of the taxation system etc. The men of Offenburg, on the other hand, influenced as they were by radicals in nearby France and Switzerland, based their demands on the human rights ideology, emphasizing particularly freedom of conscience, and of teaching, and freedom of the press; also emphasized was the right of association and of freedom of movement within the overall German fatherland. There was sharp criticism of the police, which 'should cease to tutor and to torment the citizen'. Though at Heppenheim the introduction of a people's militia was considered, the Offenburg radicals were more definite in their demand for it. They argued that 'the citizen trained in the handling of arms and armed alone can protect the State'. At both meetings the need for taxation reform was pressed, the moderates demanding 'a just distribution of the public taxes for the alleviation of the lower middle classes and of the workers', while the radicals asked for 'just taxation' with everybody contributing 'to meet the charges of the State according to his ability'. The latter also stressed the need for the running of public affairs by the people. 'The citizen should be judged by his fellow-citizen and the system of justice should be a matter for the people.' There was sharp criticism of the State bureaucracy and it was urged that 'the place of the multiple regime of the officials should be taken by the self-government of the people'. But the most unorthodox point in the Offenburg programme was the stress on the position of labour. A 'readjustment in the disparity between labour and capital' was demanded. Society had 'the obligation to raise and protect labour'. The revolutionary élan in the programme of Offenburg reached its climax in its last article which insisted on 'the abolition of all privileges'.

When, in the wake of the February Revolution in Paris, the masses in Vienna, Berlin and South Germany began to move, the progressive intellectuals of all shades felt the moment had arrived to translate their programmes into reality. Earlier the United Provincial Diet of 1847 in Prussia had mapped out the road to a constitutional system, as the moderate liberals saw it, with a legitimate share of the liberals in the government but a refusal of direct mass action. The main point in the rather confused March revolution was the demand for constitutional reform of the German Confederation and in the German states. There was to be a breakthrough towards the legal rights of the individual to be underpinned by constitutional guarantees. The situation differed in the various states. 'In certain areas like the Rhineland and Berlin where the March risings took on proletarian socialist tendencies, the liberal opposition to them took on the appearance of a class struggle. In other sections like Baden, it took on the aspect of a political defence of constitutionalism against republican democracy.'[15] Already at the Pre-Parliament at Frankfurt in May 1848 the alternative arose between orderly reform through a national assembly, modifying but not radically removing the old authorities, and a far more drastic change through revolutionary committee and direct action. The will of the overwhelming majority of liberals and democrats prevailed, against a small group of radicals represented by Hecker and Struve, and decided in favour of a national assembly.

During the first months of the Frankfurt Assembly the loose groupings of the progressive deputies concentrated on the common demand for a Constitution limiting the absolutist rule, for clearly-defined rights of the individual and for a share of the population in administering the State. The Constitution makers of Frankfurt were convinced that they had devised a middle-of-the-road system in which both 'the princes' and 'the people' would have their proper place. Yet the events between the autumn of 1848 and the spring of 1849 showed that this assumption was doubtful. Whereas the moderates set store by a carefully phrased legal system of the rights of the individual and by a balanced constitution, the more radical group visualized a political democracy and felt concern about the plight of the lower classes. The finally accepted 'Fundamental Rights of the German People' were the outcome of accommodation between moderate and radical proposals, and the same was true of the entire German Constitution of 1849. While the moderates had gained their demand for the King of Prussia as hereditary Emperor, the radicals had secured democratic manhood suffrage and the supremacy of Parliament with a two-chamber system.

The autumn riots in Frankfurt and Baden, a second revolt in Vienna and the radical counter-parliament in Berlin made the frightened members of the propertied middle classes feel uneasy and more inclined to come to terms with the old powers. In the following year the refusal of King Frederick William IV to accept the Imperial Crown, followed by the dissolution of the frustrated National Assembly, led to serious riots in Saxony, in the Ruhr and above all in the Palatinate and Baden. In May a provisional democratic government was set up at Karlsruhe. People's associations sprang up everywhere in Baden with burgomasters, innkeepers, peasants and wine growers in their ranks. Even soldiers sympathized with the radical movement in Baden in which some Swiss, Poles and Frenchmen also participated. The Grand-Duke, who had fled to Frankfurt, obtained support from the big powers and soon two Prussian army corps made their appearance in his country as well as in the Palatinate. The revolt was quickly put down; only the rebels in the fortress of Rastatt held out for a fortnight. Afterwards twenty-seven revolutionaries, mostly soldiers, were put before a Prussian military court, sentenced to death and shot. In our context it is important to note that the Baden radicals had social as well as political aims. Their slogan 'Freedom, Prosperity and Education for All',[16] revealed a broad trend of egalitarianism, and social democracy. A small group of radical intellectuals, men like Gustav von Struve, Karl Schurz, Gottfried Kinkel and Ludwig Bamberger (later to be a prominent left-wing National Liberal in the Second Empire) fought and suffered with the insurgents, while the great bulk of the liberals accommodated themselves to the changed situation.

However in the 1850s some radical democrats like G. G. Gervinus 'criticized both the liberals' willingness to compromise with the established political powers and their eagerness to restrict the political influence wielded by the common man'.[17] Yet Gervinus who now favoured a Republic was to remain a lonely voice in the wilderness.[18] After 1849 hard facts and scientific data were more in demand in politics than the earlier idealistic phrases and philosophical speculation. The reactionary trend in Prussia became only too evident in the change from the Prussian Constitution of December 1848, based on the liberal model of the Belgian Charter conceding a declaration of rights, a constitutional army, a legislative chamber, and universal, if indirect manhood suffrage, to the Constitution of January 1850 with its restrictive three-tier voting system practically depriving the workers of the vote, with an army outside the constitution and a reduction of the taxation powers of the Diet.

The great majority of the liberal deputies at Frankfurt withdrew obediently from the Assembly on the order of their governments. When soon afterwards King Frederick William IV made a half-hearted attempt to secure the leadership in Germany for Prussia on his own terms, many moderate or constitutionalist liberals accepted this scheme of the 'Prussian Union' and some of the prominent men at Frankfurt participated in the 'Reichstag' in Erfurt in March 1850, convoked by Prussia for its promotion. Yet in the end nothing came of it as both Austria and Russia were sharply opposed to the self-aggrandisement of Prussia. But the willingness of most liberals to accommodate themselves to the changed circumstances, hoping for a compromise with the powers-that-be continued, an attitude equally reflected in the policy of the National Union (*Nationalverein*) founded in 1859 and in that of the National Liberal Party which sided with Bismarck after 1866. [19]

These liberals were indeed 'the party of the propertied and educated bourgeoisie, confident of its growing strength and although somewhat ineffectively critical of the reactionary aristocratic powers, determined not to be flooded by the gradually swelling proletariat'. [20]

After the collapse of 1849 the radical movement lost its momentum and organizational basis. The powerless protesters were forced into silence, but to some extent they also silenced themselves. Appalled by the highly unfair three-class electoral system in Prussia the radicals refused to vote in elections, thus depriving themselves of even a minimum of political influence. Nevertheless, a decade later they gathered new hope and a chance of representation with the formation of the German Progressive Party at Koenigsberg in 1861. In its programme it pursued the idea of German unification with a strong central power in the hands of Prussia and with manhood suffrage for all German citizens (doc. 89). At the same time it pressed for 'the firm and consequential realization of the *Rechtsstaat*', the constitutional State based on law. It also demanded 'a firm liberal government, which sees its strength in respecting the constitutional rights of the citizens and which knows how unrelentingly to impress its principles on all the strata of the bureaucracy thus creating respect for Prussia in the eyes of the other German tribes'. The programme of the new party obtained significance during the subsequent conflict between the liberal majority in the Prussian Diet and the new intransigent Prime Minister, Otto von Bismarck, in the early 1860s.

It is one of the distinguishing features of the political situation in nineteenth-century Germany, compared with that in England, that German radicals and socialists became separated at an early date. At first the dividing line was somewhat blurred. Such leading figures in the socialist camp as Ferdinand Lassalle, Wilhelm Liebknecht and August Bebel all began in the ranks of the radical wing of the liberal movement. Lassalle was a member of the German Progressive Party for a short time after its foundation. He worked in it 'for a democratic and national revolution on the unitary basis of an expanded Prussia'. Though a socialist, he then 'looked to liberalism for both the practical means and for reinforcing the ideal of present socialist endeavour'.[21] But by 1862 Lassalle's position had substantially changed. He attacked the liberal concept of the *Rechtsstaat* and in a speech in Berlin before listeners whom he addressed as 'Petty Bourgeois and Workers' he based his brand of political radicalism on the facts of political life which indicated a constant struggle for power. Soon afterwards at another meeting before workers he proclaimed that 'power always precedes right (*Recht*) ... until right gathers a sufficient force behind it to smash the power of wrong (*Unrecht*)'. 'The working man's idea of the State', his conception of the object of the State were, he insisted 'just as different from those of the bourgeois' as 'the principle of the working class, the claim of *all* to direct the will of the State, or universal suffrage' were 'different from the principle held by the Bourgeoisie, the census'.[22] A few months later in March 1863 Lassalle broke openly with the Progressive Party. In a manifesto he made an ardent plea for an independent working-class movement in Germany and thus threw down the gauntlet to the Progressives whom he accused of having not only failed 'to bring about the smallest real development of the interests of freedom' but also of being only concerned with 'the maintenance of the privileged position of the bourgeoisie'.[23] By then Lassalle identified himself completely with the interests of the Fourth Estate. Whilst insisting that 'the worker can expect the fulfilment of his legitimate interests from political freedom', he added that this 'political freedom meant to him only the use of universal suffrage as an instrument to conquer the State for the working class'. The representation of the working class in the legitimate bodies of Germany alone could 'satisfy its legitimate interests in politics'.[24]

In a savage critique Lassalle attacked a liberal radical whose economic ideas favoured *laissez faire* and State capitalism. Hermann Schulze-Delitzsch (1808–83) had been influenced by the writings of the French economist Frédéric Bastiat.[25] Steeped in Hegelian philosophy and Marxist economics Lassalle had little difficulty in pulling to pieces the dilettantic views of his opponent on capital and capitalism in a biting pamphlet.[26] However inadequate and superficial Schulze-Delitzsch's theoretical equipment was, Lassalle was anything but fair in lampooning him as a champion of the quasi-religious dogma of the profits of the speculative entrepreneur. In fact he hit 'the wrong target',[27] for Schulze-Delitzsch, pragmatic middle-class radical, was sincere in his tireless efforts to make the little men, and those without capital, economically viable through collective self-help. As a practical man he wanted to prevent their falling under the wheels of rapidly advancing industrialization. As early as the 1840s educational organizations which expressed Schulze-Delitzsch's ideas of self help had been formed with an aim of increasing the ranks of the self-employed. As the programme of one of the organizations in Hamburg put it fervently: 'Unite you German workers, apprentices, helpers or whatever you call yourselves, throw your lot in together in order to facilitate your education and training and thereby. . . . become a golden *Mittelstand* and begin a golden new age.' [28]

Different from his brilliant but erratic opponent Schultze-Delitzsch was a vigorous plodder who incessantly plugged the idea of workers' associations. Whereas Lassalle desired State help for his planned 'Production Associations' Schulze-Delitzsch favoured collective self-help. He shared the view of a fellow radical, Gustav von Struve, who rejected any State help for the working class, as it 'must always be accompanied by State tutelage'. [29]

A lawyer by training, Schulze-Delitzsch was for some years a judge in the Prussian State service. He was elected to the Prussian National Assembly in 1849 as a left-wing liberal. When he suggested there that citizens should refuse to pay taxes to the reactionary government he faced a trial for 'Insurrection'. Although acquitted, he was obliged to leave the State service. He then became the self-appointed 'advocate of the poor'. Whereas during the 1850s political associations of workers, such as the *Arbeiterverbrüderung* (Workers' Fraternal) of 1848, were no longer tolerated by the governments, the authorities did not object to workers' associations confined to improving the economic position of their members. Schulze-Delitzsch was thus able to organize artisans and workers into a variety of unions, all designed on the basis of collective self-help. Some served the purpose of savings or of investment, some offered assistance in the case of illness or death. Others provided loans for members or purchased raw materials on their behalf. These associations (*Genossenschaften*), which later were extended to *Konsumvereine* (cooperative associations for consumer goods), fulfilled a distinct need and gradually became part of the German socio-economic scene.

In 1858 Schulze-Delitzsch described this type of organized self-help as 'an association of the classes with little income, mainly performing manual work. Its aim was to enable individual forces, small and negligible in the exchange, through their combination to have at their disposal the advantage of a big force.' [30] Twenty years later he expressed the same ideas in a Reichstag election speech as a candidate for the Progressive Party in Wiesbaden. The aim of the German cooperative system was that 'unlike the socialists' it did 'not wish to be helped by the State', but it desired 'the education of the working population to their becoming efficient in every way'. It aimed 'at their moral improvement (*Sittliche Hebung*)' . . . 'Renouncing smaller enjoyments the working people shall create capital for themselves, not merely financial capital but also moral and expertise capital of skill.' For all this was necessary if one wanted to achieve property. He appealed to the socialists to join their ranks. There they would learn self-help. 'For your unreasonable demand for State-help does not mean anything but the exploitation of the proper-tied classes. ...' [31]

There was an odd discrepancy between theory and practice in the case of Schulze-Delitzsch. Theoretically he continued to cling to the Manchester doctrine, viewing the national economy in terms of rational self-interest and preaching the slogan: 'Nothing gratis, no service without payment.' [32] However, in practice he was by no means a harsh Benthamite, but proved helpful to thousands of people, mainly artisans and small-scale entrepreneurs. During the period from 1864 to 1874 the number of his *Genossenschaften* nearly doubled, whilst their membership nearly tripled and their capital increased by 800 per cent.

Rejecting the doctrine of the class struggle Schulze-Delitzsch hoped to break the monopoly of the big entrepreneur, to eliminate poverty among the workers, and to achieve a general level of prosperity. Such a belief appears rather Utopian in retrospect. His hopes to win over more and more workers to his ideals of social harmony were frustrated through the growing strength of the Social Democratic Party formed at Eisenach in 1869. In fact Schulze-Delitzsch was not so much concerned with the workers but with the small artisans whom he eulogized in the address of 1878 as 'the true nucleus of our bourgeoisie (*Bürgertum*). They must not break with big industry but must endeavour to put the means of big industry into their service on a modest scale.' The greater credit, the greater amount of capital, the possibility of purchasing in bulk were advantages of big industry and for this reason they should support it 'in order to make its great advantages available to the artisans too'. [33]

Schulze-Delitzsch's appeals succeeded with the small shop-keepers and artisans, but they never reached the property-less factory workers. In 1866 his credit unions, which mainly provided loans to small-scale manufacturers and merchants, had a membership of close to 200,000 whilst 'societies which were supposed to assist primarily the labouring masses lagged far behind'. [34] Yet during the years when Schulze-Delitzsch played a prominent part at the annual conferences of the German workers' associations, the delegates insisted on the right of the employees to combine and if necessary to strike. They also tackled problems of housing and of consumers' interests. By and large Schulze-Delitzsch's efforts proved economically successful but politically a failure. His concern for the working population was genuine, yet it found little echo even in his own Progressive Party.

On the other hand a small independent group of left-wing progressivists outside Prussia showed a better understanding of the plight of the lower classes. The German People's Party which had its focal point in South Germany, did not favour the idea of unlimited free trade, but upheld a measure of State intervention in economic affairs. Founded in 1865 it aimed at a federation of German states with the people participating in running its affairs. Neither Prussia nor Austria should rule the future German *Reich*. With their outlook, both radical and particularist, these men saw their model in a federal republic like nearby Switzerland and were 'opposed to autocracy, clericalism, jingoism, centralizing bureaucracy and restrictive regulations'. [35] An influential protagonist of the German People's Party and of its brand of social liberalism was Leopold Sonnemann (1831–1909), the son of a Jewish weaver, who rose to eminence as a banker and as founder of the progressivist quality newspaper *Frankfurter Zeitung*. A pioneer in the efforts for workers' education Sonnemann cooperated for some years with Bebel and Wilhelm Liebknecht as well as with Schulze-Delitzsch in the work of the organized German workers' associations. But he left them when they fell under the spell of international socialism and veered towards the new Social Democratic Party. It was characteristic of Sonnemann's line that in 1866 his *Frankfurter Zeitung* demanded that 'no dictatorship shall come over Germany neither that of Bismarck nor that of Marx'. [36]

As a democrat and a member of the Reichstag in the Second Empire from 1871–76 and again from 1878–84 Sonnemann had more influence than the numerical strength of his party warranted. (During his time in the Reichstag it never exceeded the figure of eight deputies.) To Sonnemann democratic radicalism was no empty phrase. He refused to accept Bismarck's suppressive measures against both the Catholic Church and the Socialists. Bismarck so much disliked Sonnemann's fearless criticism that before the Reichstag election of 1884 he gave instructions to the Conservatives and National Liberals in Frankfurt to vote for Sonnemann's Socialist rival candidate. [37] The plot succeeded and Sonnemann was beaten by the odd alliance of the supporters of two groups bitterly opposed to each other. But through his *Frankfurter Zeitung*, which was not uncritical of perverse acts of the Establishment and had some sympathy with the German Labour Movement, he proved that social liberalism existed in Germany, even if by and large the dividing line between it and socialism remained much more marked and less flexible than in England.

This was particularly true of the liberal representatives in the expanding big cities after 1890. The liberal *Honorationen* lost much of their prestige. They were no match for the new advancing mass movements. In the city councils there was on the whole little cooperation between the liberals and the social democrats or, in Catholic areas, with the men of the Centre Party. 'Once a beach-head for the liberal conquest of German politics, by 1914 the city had become a fortress in which liberals thought to defend their privileges and their cherished procedures against an increasingly hostile world'. [38]

Notes and References

Introductory

1. Maurice Cranston, *Freedom. A new Analysis.* (3rd edn) London 1967, p. 51.
2. It would, of course, be absurd to overlook the fact that a desire for political liberty is to be found in the Middle Ages. There was, however, much more emphasis in medieval thought on the community than on the individual and the principles of Political Liberty developed 'under the terms of the supremacy of law, not as something imposed on the community from outside, but as representing first the character and habit of the life of the community, and then the deliberate will of the community'. In the fifteenth century, Nicolas of Cusa had argued that 'Governments can only arise from the free consent of the subjects, just as laws can only be made by their consent.' A. J. Carlyle, *Political Liberty*, London 1963, p. 21.
3. J. Milton, *Areopagitica*, Bk. ii, p. 55, quoted in F. E. Hutchinson, *Milton and the English Mind*, London, 1949, p. 61.
4. Ibid., Book II, p. 95; Hutchinson, op. cit., p. 65.
5. Eric Routley, *English Religious Dissent*, Cambridge 1960, p. 117.
6. Raymond G. Cowherd, *The Politics of English Dissent*, London 1959, pp. 23–4.
7. Priestley's *Address to Protestant Dissenters*, Hall's *Apology for the Freedom of the Press* and Price's *Observations on the Nature of Civil Liberty*, all published before 1800, laid the foundations for the prominent part which Dissenters took in the agitation leading to the Reform Bill of 1832. Eric Routley, op. cit., p. 165.
8. Maurice Cranston, *Freedom. A new Analysis*, London, 1954, p. 80.
9. G. de Ruggiero, *The History of European Liberalism*, London, 1927, p. 21.
10. G. de Ruggiero, op. cit.

1. The doctrine of human rights

1. Willy Strzelewicz, *Der Kampf um die Menschenrechte*, Frankfurt a.M. 1968, p. 64.
2. Leo Strauss, *Natural Right and History*, Chicago 1953, p. 164.
3. W. Strzelewicz, op. cit., p. 73.
4. Otto Gierke, *Althusius und die Entwicklung der naturrechtlichen Staatstheorien*, Breslau 1902, pp. 113, 163.
5. W. Strzelewicz, op. cit. pp. 78–9.
6. H. J. Laski, *Political Thought in England from Locke to Bentham*, London 1930, p. 36.
7. Leo Strauss, *Natural Right and History*, p. 248.
8. Ibid., p. 245.
9. See Section A, pp. 146–56. It is interesting that only the French manifesto of 1793, inspired by Robespierre, was a *Declaration of the Rights and Duties of Man and Citizen*. But only the Declaration of 1789 became historically relevant.
10. Guido de Ruggiero, *The History of European Liberalism*, London, 1927, p. 69.
11. Georges Lefebvre, *The Coming of the French Revolution* (trans R. R. Palmer), Princeton 1947, pp. 214–15.
12. Koppel S. Pinson, *Modern Germany. Its History and Civilisation*, New York 1954, p. 102.
13. For extracts from the Frankfurt Declaration of Fundamental Rights see Doc. 60.
14. Erich Eyck, *Geschichte der Weimarer Republik*, I, p. 106.

15. Karl Dietrich Erdmann in *Bruno Gebhardt* (ed.) *Handbuch der Deutschen Geschichte* (8th edn), 1959, Bd. 3, p. 113.
16. 'The order of economic life has to correspond to the principles of justice with the aim of guaranteeing a dignified existence for all. Within these limits the economic freedom of the individual must be assured'. (Art. 151).
17. On the one hand marriage was described as 'the fundament of family life and of the preservation and augmentation of the nation', and therefore 'under the special protection of the Constitution'. On the other hand, it was 'based on equal rights of the two sexes' – a deliberate reference to the growing desire for recognition of the German women, who just had been given the vote for the first time. (Art. 119)
18. Education was to be free at least in the elementary and fundamental stages, whereas technical and higher education was to 'be equally accessible to all on the basis of merit' (art. 26 (1)).

2. The classical economists and the utilitarians

1. Piero Sraffa (ed.) *Works and Correspondence of David Ricardo* (10 vols) Cambridge 1951–5, IX, p. 52.
2. Lionel Robbins, *The Theory of Economic Policy in English Classical Political Economy*, London 1952, p. 177. A. L. Macfie, *The Individual in Society: Papers on Adam Smith*, London 1967, p. 155.
3. A recent and very useful survey is D. P. O'Brien, *The Classical Economists*, Oxford, 1975. See also Samuel Hollander, *The Economics of Adam Smith*, London, 1973.
4. T. R. Malthus, *Essay on Population* (Everyman edn, 2 vols), London 1914, II, p. 254.
5. Werner Stark (ed.) *Jeremy Bentham's Economic Writings* (3 vols), London 1952–4, III, pp. 333–4.
6. Adam Smith, *The Wealth of Nations* (Everyman edn, 2 vols), London 1910, II, p. 126.
7. Ibid., I, pp. 400–1; II, p. 180.
8. One should add, however, that McCulloch helped to secure the repeal of the Combination Laws (which had prohibited trade unions): see Graham Wallas, *The Life of Francis Place* (4th edn), London 1925, pp. 207–8.
9. For a collection of essays on this subject, with a bibliography, see A. W. Coats (ed.) *The Classical Economists and Economic Policy*, London, 1971.
10. Adam Smith, op. cit., II, pp. 180–1.
11. For an interpretation of the political ideas of the classical economists, see W. D. Grampp, *Economic Liberalism* (2 vols), New York 1965, II, Ch. 2.
12. J. B. Say, *Traité d'économie politique* (2nd edn, 2 vols.), Paris 1814, I, p. xiii.
13. *Edinburgh Review*, xiv (1809), 152; cited in Edward R. Kittrell, ' "Laissez faire" in English classical economics', *Journal of the History of Ideas*, xxvii (1966), 614n.
14. J. R. McMulloch, *Principles of Political Economy* (3rd edn), Edinburgh 1843, p. 57.
15. James Mill, *An Essay on Government,* ed. C. V. Shields, Indianapolis, 1955, pp. 53–4
16. T. R. Malthus, *Principles of Political Economy* (2nd edn), London 1836, pp. 381–2.
17. See James Mill, *Selected Economic Writings,* ed. Donald Winch, Edinburgh 1966, pp. 9–10.
18. *Works – Ricardo*, VIII, p. 304.
19. D. P. O'Brien, *J. R. McCulloch*, London 1970, p. 102; *Edinburgh Review*, lxxxi (1845), 29.
20. *Works – Ricardo*, V, pp. 500–2.
21. *Edinburgh Review*, xlix (1829), 180–3.
22. See L. Robbins, op. cit., Ch. 4.
23. Alexander Bain, *James Mill: A Biography*, London 1882, p. 364.

Notes and references

24. *The Works of Jeremy Bentham*, ed. John Bowring (11 vols), Edinburgh 1843, I, p. 312.
25. L. Robbins, op. cit., Ch. 5; Pedro Schwartz, *The New Political Economy of J. S. Mill*, London 1968, Ch. 7.
26. *Works – Bentham*, I, p. 301. Cf. Shirley R. Letwin, *The Pursuit of Certainty*, Cambridge 1965, ch. 12.
27. *Works – Bentham*, I, p. 568; II, p. 424.
28. See Gertrude Himmelfarb, *Victorian Minds*, London 1968, Ch. 2; 'Bentham's Utopia: the National Charity Company', *Journal of British Studies*, x (1970), 80–125.
29. *Works – Bentham*, IV, p. 64.
30. University College, London, Bentham MSS, box 100, fo. 170; cited in D. G. Long, 'The nature and development of the idea of liberty in the writings of Jeremy Bentham', Ph.D. thesis, University of London (1973), p. 288.
31. Bentham, *Deontology; or The Science of Morality*, ed. J. Bowring (2 vols), London 1834, II, p. 59.
32. *Works – Bentham*, IX, pp. 5–6.
33. Elie Halévy, *The Growth of Philosophic Radicalism*, trans. Mary Morris (2nd edn), London 1934, p. 375.
34. Bentham, *Deontology*, I, pp. 90–1, 100–1. Cf. S. S. Wolin, *Politics and Vision*, London, 1961, p. 348.
35. J. S. Mill, *Principles of Political Economy* (3rd edn, 2 ols), London 1852, I, pp. 195–6.
36. *Works – Bentham*, X, p. 450.
37. James Mill, *Essay on Government*, p. 90.
38. *London Review*, I (1835), 257–95.
39. See particularly his *Encyclopaedia Britannica* article on 'Liberty of the Press', reprinted in *Essays on Government, Jurisprudence, Liberty of the Press, and Law of Nations*, London n.d. [1828].
40. Cf. G. Himmelfarb, *On Liberty and Liberalism: The Case of John Stuart Mill*, New York, 1974, pp. 42, 54–5.
41. *Works – Bentham*, IX, p. 63.
42. J. S. Mill, *Dissertations and Discussions* (2 vols), London 1859, I, pp. 379–80.
43. J. S. Mill, *Utilitarianism, Liberty, Representative Government* (Everyman edn), London 1910, p. 67.
44. Walter Bagehot, *The Literary Essays*, ed. N. St. John-Stevas (2 vols), London 1965, II, p. 371.
45. For a recent guide to the controversy over the influence of Benthamism on nineteenth-century legislation, see A. J. Taylor, *Laissez-faire and State Intervention in Nineteenth-century Britain*, London 1972, pp. 32–8, 71–7.
46. S. E. Finer, *The Life and Times of Sir Edwin Chadwick*, London 1952, p. 14.
47. Thomas Paine, *The Rights of Man* (Everyman edn), London 1915, p. 159.
48. *Edinburgh Review*, cxv (1862), 347.
49. G. Wallas, *The Life of Francis Place* (4th edn), London 1925, p. 72. Cf. *Works – Bentham* X, p. 79.
50. Cf. C. B. Macpherson, *Democratic Theory*, Oxford 1973, pp. 7–8, 26.
51. Cf. W. D. Grampp, *The Classical Liberalism, Marxism, and the Twentieth Century*, Cambridge, Mass. 1960, p. 6.
52. See for example Mary P. Mack, 'The Fabians and Utilitarianism', *Journal of the History of Ideas*, xvi (1955), 76–88.

3. Aesthetic individualism

1. It had forerunners in the 'Uomo Universale' of the Italian Renaissance and in the theory of harmony of the development of the natural talents in man by the 3rd Earl of Shaftesbury (1671–1713), a pupil of Locke.
2. The German title is *Ideen zu einem Versuch, die Grenzen der Wirksamkeit des Staates zu bestimmen*. A recent English translation has been edited and introduced by J. W. Burrow under the title of *The Limits of State Action*, Cambridge 1969. See also pp. 271.
3. J. S. Mill, *On Liberty*, 1859, Ch. 3, p. 115. Humboldt's text, as rendered in the translation by Burrow, begins slightly differently: 'The true end of Man. . . .'
4. J. W. Burrow, in his introduction to *The Limits of State Action*, p. xxxii.
5. *On Liberty*, p. 117.
6. J. S. Mill, *Utilitarianism* (Everyman edn), Ch. 2, p. 7.
7. Ibid, p. 17.
8. Ibid. p. 9.
9. John Plamenatz, *The English Utilitarians* (2nd edn), Oxford 1958, p. 129.
10. J. S. Mill, *On Liberty*, p. 117
11. Ibid., p. 118.
12. Ibid., p. 119.
13. Ibid., p. 122.
14. Vilfredo Pareto, *Sociological Writings,* ed, S. E. Finer, London 1966, p. 134.
15. G. G. Gervinus, *Introduction to the History of the Nineteenth Century* London 1853, (Rev. translation), p. 126.
16. Ibid., p. 124.

4. The desire for constitutional government

1. R. R. Palmer, *The Age of Democratic Revolution*, Princeton 1959, I, pp. 214–15.
2. Ibid., p. 215.
3. Ibid., p. 517.
4. R. H. Soltau, *French Political Thought in the Nineteenth Century,* London 1931, p. 35.
5. This Constitution was the 'sacred codex' 'which defined Spanish liberalism as a political creed. This "codex" was to become the classical liberal constitution of latin Europe in the early nineteenth century'. R. Carr, *Spain, 1808–1939*, Oxford 1966, p. 94. Among the influences on it was the work of Bentham.
6. According to Article 13 of the Charter, 'The King is inviolable and sacred ... Executive power belongs only to the King.'
7. It is worth noticing that at that time more than half of the French nation were illiterate.
8. J. A. Hawgood, *Modern Constitutions since 1787*, London 1939, pp. 183–5.
9. C. J. Friedrich, *Constitutional Government and Democracy. Theory and Practice in Europe and America* (7th edn), Waltham, Mass. 1968, p. 29.
10. Ibid., p. 182.
11. George Fischer, *Russian Liberalism. From Gentry to Intelligentsia*, Cambridge, Mass. 1958, p. 203.
12. In Austria-Hungary for instance both parts of the Empire were granted constitutions after the *Ausgleich* of 1867. But universal manhood suffrage was conceded in Austria only in 1907, whilst in Hungary it never materialized during the lifetime of the monarchy.

Notes and references

5. From 'classic' to 'hyphenated' liberalism

1. A. P. Pfizer, 'Gedanken über das Ziel und die Aufgaben des deutschen Liberalismus' (1832), quoted in F. Federici, *Der deutsche Liberalismus*, Zürich 1946, p. 152.
2. D. Mack Smith, *Italy. A Modern History*, Michigan 1959, p. 22.
3. G. de Ruggiero, *History of European Liberalism*, London 1927, p. 310.
4. Giacomo Durando, *Della Nazionale italiana, saggio politico-militaire*, Paris 1846, quoted in G. Ruggiero, op. cit., p. 309.
5. Donald G. Rohr, *The Origins of Social Liberalism in Germany*, Chicago 1963, p. 136.
6. Ibid, p. 131.
7. See the study of the economist Lujo Brentano by James S. Sheehan, *The Career of Lujo Brentano*, Chicago 1966, Ch. 4.
8. Lord Lindsay in his Introduction to the *Lectures on the Principles of Political Obligation* by T. H. Green, London 1948, p. x.
9. On T. H. Green and L. T. Hobhouse, see documents 108 and 110.
10. Lord Lindsay, op. cit., p. xviii.
11. T. H. Green, *Liberal Legislation and Freedom of Contract* (1881), in R. L. Nettleship, (ed.) *Works of T. H. Green*, London 1888, III, pp. 370, 376.
12. L. T. Hobhouse, *Liberalism*. Introduction by A. P. Grimes, London 1971, p. 50.
13. Ibid, p. 66.
14. Anthony Trollope, *Autobiography* (1883), quoted in John Wilson, *C. B.: Life of Sir Henry Campbell-Bannerman*, London 1973, p. 232.
15. *The Liberal Magazine*, 1 January 1898, John Wilson, op. cit., p. 232.

6. Radicalism as an aspect of English liberalism

1. See J. W. Derry in the Introduction to *The Radical Tradition: Tom Paine to David Lloyd George*, London 1967, in which some of the features have been ably considered.
2. John Cartwright, *Legislative Rights of the Commonalty Vindicated*, (1777). Extract in S. Maccoby, *The English Radical Tradition, 1763–1914*, London 1952, p. 32.
3. Wilkes, S. *Speeches in Parliament*, 1777, I, p. 85 sqq. Quoted in S. Maccoby, op. cit., p. 32.
4. S. Maccoby, op. cit., p. 41.
5. Quoted in E. Halévy, *The Growth of Philosophic Radicalism*, p. 261.
6. Ibid.
7. J. Bentham, *Plan of Parliamentary Reform, in the Form of a Catechism*, London 1820, p. cccvi.
8. Ibid., p. cccvii.
9. Ibid.
10. Ibid., pp. cccix-x; see also J. Bentham, *The Book of Fallacies* (1824), p. 257 quoted in J. S. Schapiro, *Liberalism and the Challenge of Fascism*, New York 1949, p. 120.
11. Mary Peter Mack, *A Bentham Reader*, New York 1969, p. 307.
12. Ibid.
13. See J. K. Dinwiddy, 'Bentham's Transition to Political Radicalism, 1809–10', *Journal of the History of Ideas*, xxxv (1975) p. 693.
14. Mary Peter Mack, op. cit., pp. 316–17.
15. Samuel H. Beer, *Modern British Politics*, London 1965, p. 32.
16. Ibid., p. 41.
17. See G. M. Young (ed.) *Speeches by Lord Macaulay*, (World Classics), Oxford 1935, pp. 1–19.

General Introduction

18. 'Radicalism not dangerous', *The Works of Jeremy Bentham*, ed. John Bowring (11 vols), Edinburgh 1845, III, p. 604.
19. S. Maccoby, introduction to *English Radicalism 1832–1852*, London 1935, pp. 20–1.
20. J. W. Derry, op. cit. p. 156.
21. Ibid., p. 177.
22. Quoted in Asa Briggs, *The Age of Improvement*, London 1959, p. 240.
23. G. D. H. Cole and Raymond Postgate, *The British Common People 1746–1940*, London 1961, pp. 246–55.
24. John Vincent, *The Formation of the British Liberal Party 1857–1868*, London 1966, p. 55.
25. Ibid.
26. Ibid, p. 65.
27. See the *Life of Samuel Morley* by Edwin Holder (5th edn), London 1889, published shortly after his death. It is a hagiography rather than a critical biography.
28. Vincent, op. cit., p. 66.
29. Ibid., p. 67.
30. S. H. Beer, op. cit., p. 48.
31. Joseph Chamberlain, et. al., *The Radical Programme (1885)*, edited and with an introduction by D. A. Hamer, Brighton 1971, Preface. See also doc. 109.
32. S. H. Beer, op. cit., p. 53.
33. *The Radical Programme*, Introduction, p. xxxii.
34. Ibid.
35. Ibid., p. 222.
36. J. Vincent, op. cit., p. 14.
37. *The Radical Programme*, Preface
38. J. W. Derry, op. cit., p. 325.
39. D. A. Hamer, *Liberal Politics in the Age of Gladstone and Rosebery* Oxford 1972, pp. 235–6.
40. Philip P. Poirier, *The Advent of the Labour Party*, London 1958, pp. 11–12.
41. P. F. Clarke, 'The Progressive Movement in England,' *Transactions of the Royal Historical Society*. (Fifth Series), London 1974, p. 170. vol. 24.
42. P. P. Poirier, op. cit., p. 179.
43. Ibid.
44. On Hobhouse see Section D, pp. 596–8.
45. P. F. Clarke, op. cit., p. 171.
46. P. P. Poirier, op. cit., p. 71.
47. *The Nation*, 3 August 1907, p. 820.
48. Ibid.
49. P. F. Clarke, op. cit., p. 177.

7. Aspects of Liberalism and Radicalism in France

(a) Liberalism 1814–48

1. de Staël, *Considerations on the Principal Events of the French Revolution* (trans., 3 vols), London 1818, vol. III, Pt. VI, Ch. 9, p. 343.
2. Ibid, vol. III, pt. VI, Ch. 12, pp. 402–3.
3. B. Constant, *Mélanges de Littérature et de Politique*, Paris 1829, p. vi.
4. Quoted in Jack Lively, *The Social and Political Thought of A. de Tocqueville*, Oxford 1962, p. 11.
5. The cult of the people was soon to be proclaimed anew in the writings of Jules Michelet.

6. Constant's 'elaborate argument on this occasion was really in the same category as the impassioned claim which he made to the French voters in the next election: We do not want any revolution!' Irene Collins, *Liberalism in the Nineteenth Century*, London 1957, p. 7.
7. At the same time everyone was entitled to associate with others either for religious purposes or in order to influence the administration of the government by nominating all or some public servants, by making representations, by petitions or demands which the authorities are more or less obliged to consider.
8. These are listed in his book *Réflexions sur les Constitutions, la distribution des pouvoirs et les guaranties dans une monarchie constitutionnelle*, Paris 1814, Ch. 8; see Paul Bastid, *Benjamin Constant et sa Doctrine*, Paris 1966, II, p. 734.
9. Bastid, op. cit., II, p. 743.
10. Ibid., II, p. 848.
11. Providing a long list of the abuses of executive power, Constant noted three main categories: waste and embezzlement of public funds, unnecessary wars and last but not least attacks on the freedom of individuals.
12. P. Bastid, op. cit., II, p. 919.
13. Ibid., II, p. 971.
14. Ibid., II, p. 988.
15. Ibid., II, p. 989.
16. M. Girard, *Le Libéralisme en France de 1814 à 1848: Doctrine et Mouvement*. Premier partie, 'Le cours de Sorbonne', Paris, Centre de Documentation Universitaire n.d., p. 158.
17. P. Bastid, op. cit., II, p. 991.
18. D. Johnson, *Guizot. Aspects of French History 1787–1874*, London 1963, pp. 51–2, 60–1. Compare this view with that of R. H. Soltau, *French Political Thought in the Nineteenth Century*, New York 1959, pp. 56–9.
19. H. Pouthas, *Guizot pendant la Restoration*, Paris 1923, p. 318; and Vincent Starzinger, *Middlingness. Juste milieu political theory in France and England, 1815–1848*. Charlottesville 1965, p. 25.
20. Candidates for election to the Chamber had to pay 1,000 francs in taxes. While under the Bourbons 90,000 tax-payers were enfranchised, their number rose after the February Revolution of 1830 to 170,000. In 1847 it reached about 250,000.
21. Guizot to Reeve, November 4 1858, quoted in Johnson, op. cit., p. 75. As Guizot then put it in retrospect: 'They had to contend with both, the friends of the Bourbons (the legitimist party which would not accept the July monarchy) and the masses of the people of both towns and country, who neither cared nor understood anything about the constitutional system. . . . We had no support but the middle classes.'
22. D. Johnson, op. cit., p. 74.
23. Ibid., p. 76.
24. F. Guizot, *Memoirs*, VI, pp. 348–9.
25. Girard, op. cit., p. 152. Rejecting the Bourbons he favoured a Republic. In 1830 he was, however, prepared to accept a liberal monarchy under the Tricolor.
26. Girard, op cit., p. 273. On the other hand a democratic group which had been formed in 1827, and including La Fayette and the philosopher and economist Destutt de Tracy, had favoured it.
27. E. Labrousse, *Le Mouvement Ouvrier et les Idées Sociales en France de 1815 à la fin du XIX siecle*, Paris 1949, pp. 60–1.
28. Ibid., pp. 64–5.
29. Henry Reeve (trans.) *Democracy in America* (World Classics), Oxford 1947, Preface, p. 5.).
30. Ibid., Preface, p. 11.
31. Ibid., Preface, p. 16.
32. Jack Lively, op. cit., p. 221.
33. H. Reeve, op. cit., Ch. 24, p. 367.

General Introduction

34. Ibid., p. 368.
35. See the article by Koenraad W. Smart, ' "Individualism" in the Mid-Nineteenth Century (1826–1860)', *Journal of the History of Ideas*, vol. 23, 1962, p. 79.
36. Luis Diez Del Corral, 'Tocqueville et la Pensée Politique des Doctrinaires' in *Alexis de Tocqueville. Livre du Centenaire 1859–1959*, Paris 1960, p. 59.
37. Seymour Drescher, *Tocqueville in England*, Cambridge, Mass. 1964, p. 11.
38. Alexander Teixeira de Mattos (trans.), *The Recollections of Alexis de Tocqueville*, London 1949, pp. 2–3.
39. A. de Tocqueville, *L'Ancien Régime et la Révolution*, preface.
40. H. Reeve, op. cit., p. 370.
41. Ibid., p. 372.
42. Ibid., p. 375.

(b) Liberalism during the second half of the nineteenth century

1. See Henri Malo, *Thiers 1797–1873*, Paris 1932, p. 446.
2. See particularly his address on the five 'Indispensable Liberties' to the Corps Législatif, 11 January 1864 (doc. 70).
3. Theodore Zeldin, *France 1848–1945*, Oxford 1973, p. 608.
4. Nassau William Senior, *Conversations with M. Thiers, M. Guizot etc.*, London 1878, p. 39.
5. See his characteristic speech in 1866 'On the Principles of 1789' (doc. 63).
6. Jacques Chastenet, *Histoire de la Troisième République*, I, Paris 1952, p. 148.
7. T. Zeldin, op. cit., p. 608.
8. R. H. Soltau, *French Political Thought in the Nineteenth Century*, London 1931, p. 295.
9. Preface to Riou, *Aux Ecoutes de la France qui vient*, p. 33 quoted in Soltau, op. cit., p. 303.
10. Emile Faguet, *The Cult of Incompetence* (trans. Beatrice Barstow), London 1911, p. 92. Faguet even claimed that the well-known epigram by Beaumarchais 'The post required a mathematician – it was given to a dancing master' applied much more to a democracy than to an absolute monarchy.
11. E. Faguet, *Le Libéralisme*, Paris 1903, p. 307.
12. Ibid.
13. P. Leroy-Beaulieu, *L'Etat Moderne et ses Fonctions*, Paris 1890 (transn. *The Modern State*, London 1890). This, the author's major opus, became a bestseller and was translated into a number of languages.
14. Ibid., p. 88.
15. Ibid. Bk I, Ch. 3 pp. 128–54.
16. E. Faguet, op. cit., pp. 60–1.
17. P. Leroy-Beaulieu, op. cit., p. 37. For the 'Freycinet Plan' see Guy Chapman, *A History of the Third Republic of France*, I, London 1962, pp. 220–7.
18. P. Leroy-Beaulieu, op. cit., p. 162.
19. Ibid., p. 164.
20. Ibid., p. 165.
21. E. Faguet, *Politicians and Moralists of the 19th Century*, London 1928, p. 13.
22. R. H. Soltau, op. cit., p. 295.

(c) Radicalism 1820–1870

1. Jean-Thomas Nordmann, *Histoire des Radicaux 1820–1973*, Paris 1974, p. 31.
2. Alexis de Tocqueville, *Journeys to England and Ireland* ed. J. P. Mayer, London 1958, pp. 86–7.

98

Notes and references

3. Ibid.
4. 'His heart', he wrote, 'told him that at the sight of so much misery besetting the poorer classes God could not have wanted to expose them to eternal grief, to an endless helotry', while his reason 'loathed the idea that a society could impose obligations and duties on the citizen without bestowing on him in return some part of its sovereignty'. J.-T. Nordmann, op. cit., p. 35.
5. Ibid., p. 39.
6. In his *The 18th Brumaire of Louis-Napoleon Bonaparte* Karl Marx criticized this programme as 'petit bourgeois and social democratic'. See the English translation by Eden and Cedar Paul, London 1926, pp. 57–8.
7. E. Laboulaye, *Le Parti Libéral, sa programme et son avenir*, Paris 1864.
8. J.-T. Nordmann, op. cit., p. 54.
9. R. H. Soltau, *French Political Thought in the Nineteenth century*, New York 1959, p. 258.
10. See the extracts from Laboulaye's work *L'Etat et ses Limites*, (doc. 62).
11. Simon, *La Politique Radicale*, Paris 1868, p. 33. For Thiers' approach see his speech on the 'Indispensable Liberties' (doc. 70).
12. Ibid., p. 33–4.
13. J. Simon, *La Politique Radicale*, pp. 36–7.
14. As to foreign policy the echo of Cobden's voice can be detected in Jules Simon's plea: no secrets in foreign affairs, no wars of conquest, no standing army, only 'natural alliances which means alliances with liberal peoples'. *La Politique Radicale*, p. 35.
15. J. Simon, *La Liberté de Conscience*, Paris 1857, p. 295 and p. 300.
16. See also J. P. T. Bury, *Gambetta and the National Defence of France*, London 1936, p. 16.
17. At the same time he recalled the heritage of 1789, affirming 'that France, the home of an indestructable democracy, will encounter liberty, peace, order, justice, material prosperity and moral grandeur only through the triumph of the principles of the French Revolution.'
18. See Daniel Halévy, *La fin des notables*, Paris 1930, p. 111.
19. J.-T. Nordmann, op. cit., p. 67.
20. D. Halévy, op. cit., p. 124.
21. J.-T. Nordmann, op. cit., p. 66.
22. J. Kayser, *Les grandes batailles du radicalisme des origines aux porte du pouvoir 1820–1901*, Paris 1962, pp. 59–60.
23. J.-T. Nordmann, op. cit., p. 73.
24. Ibid., pp. 73–4.
25. As he said in a speech at Le Neubourg, 'Believe indeed that it would mean great danger to move too far ahead of (public) opinion.... Prudence consists of doing something every day but above all to abstain from wanting to do everything at the same time.' J. Reinach (ed.), *Discours et plaidoyers politiques de M. Gambetta*, Paris 1884, IX, pp. 456–66.
26. Sponsoring a new Paris daily *La Justice* in January 1880 in competition with *L'Egalité* the paper of the socialist Jules Guesde, Clemenceau argued that justice was 'in fact the essence, the joint expression of the traditional formula of ' "liberty, fraternity and equality".'
27. J.-T. Nordmann, op. cit. pp. 92–3.
28. Ibid.
29. Clemenceau's peculiar position as Senator from 1902 to 1905 is revealing in this respect. 'In a sense the original and most authentic Radical, Clemenceau was then supported by the Radical Group in Parliament, but did not take part in the Radical Congresses, nor did he belong to the executive committee of the party.' He 'was never more than a free-lance supporter' of the Radical Government under Combes. D. R. Watson, *Clemenceau. A Political Biography*, London 1974, p. 156.

General Introduction

30. The new organization was supported by 78 Senators, 201 Deputies, 476 committees, 155 freemason lodges, 849 conseilleurs generaux d'arrondissement, mayors and delegates of municipalities, lodges and associations and 215 republican, radical and radical socialist journals. J. Kayser, op. cit., p. 310.
31. See Leo A. Loubere. 'The Left-wing Radicals. Their Economic and Social Program since 1870', *American Journal of Economics and Sociology*, vol. 26 (1967) p. 189.
32. Ibid., p. 191.
33. Ibid., p. 201.
34. Ibid., p. 199.
35. Ibid., p. 203.
36. Alain was the pen-name of the Lycée professor Emile A. Chartier (1868–1951) who contributed many articles to respectable provincial newspapers like the *Depeche de Toulouse*. Later collected in books, many of them reached a wider public.
37. Alain on 'The Politics of the Citizen', *Elements d'une doctrine radicale*, Paris 1925, pp. 17–18.
38. Ibid., p. 13.
39. Alain, essay 'Radicalism exists', op. cit., pp. 17–18.
40. Alain, *Politiques*, Paris 1952, pp. 7–8.
41. Alain, essay 'Le Tribun', *Elements d'une doctrine radicale*, p. 14.
42. Ibid. This essay appeared on 15 May 1924.
43. C. Nicolet, *Le radicalisme*, Paris 1957, p. 39.

8. Liberals and radicals in Germany – some aspects

1. For Friedrich Dahlmann see docs 54, 55 and 83.
2. Leonard Krieger, *The German Idea of Freedom. History of a Political Tradition*, Boston 1957, p. 279.
3. In the National Parliament of 1848 at Frankfurt 80 per cent of the delegates had a university education, while less than 20 per cent of the delegates earned a living in some form of business or in agriculture. T. Hamerow, 'The elections to the Frankfurt Parliament', *Journal of Modern History*, vol. 33, (1961), pp. 15–32.
4. James J. Sheehan, 'Liberals and Society in Germany 1815–48', *Journal of Modern History*, vol. 45 (1973), p. 587.'
5. Werner Conze (ed.), *Staat und Gesellschaft im deutschen Vormärz 1815–1848*, Stuttgart 1962, p. 230.
6. L. Krieger, op. cit., p. 316.
7. For the test of the speech see Karl Obermann, *Einheit und Freiheit,* Berlin 1950, p. 119.
8. In a memorandum, copies of which were found by the police in his house in August 1832, Siebenpfeiffer listed the immediate aims as follows:
   1. Enlightenment and moral uplifting of all the national classes.
   2. Formation of patriotic associations of men and youths, of married and unmarried women in all the provinces and important cities of Germany.
   3. Efforts towards providing all German citizens with arms, not only the aristocratic privileged section, but all the citizens.
   4. A fraternal understanding with all other nations involved in the fight for freedom or about to begin such a fight.
   5. Spreading the view that partial concessions by the governments, granted against their will, are not a lasting and effective help, but only helpful is a fundamental reform based on the sovereignty of the people.
   6. Altogether the fate of a single German *Land* (State) means nothing as long as they had not a collective (national) union.

100

Notes and references

7. An account of the advantages of a truly democratic constitution of the State, of the communities and of the church, altogether documented from facts from North America.

8. Regarding the state administration, individual princes would not be mentioned either in praise or in criticism, but also the constitutional lie by that the ministers were the cause of all evil was to be abandoned. The description 'The Government' might suit best (for this purpose). K. Obermann, op. cit., pp. 123–4.

9. Veit Valentin, *Das Hambacher Nationalfest*, Berlin 1932, p. 125. Freiherr von Otterstedt the Prussian envoy in Karlsruhe to King Frederick William III on 7 June 1832.

10. W. Conze (ed), op. cit., p. 231.

11. Ibid.

12. Lothar Gall, *Der Liberalismus als Regierungspartei. Das Grossherzogtum Baden zwischen Restauration und Reichsgründung*, Wiesbaden 1969, p. 29.

13. Ibid., p. 36.

14. Ibid., p. 46.

15. L. Krieger, op. cit., p. 331.

16. See R. Stadelmann, *Soziale und Politische Geschichte der Revolution von 1848*, München 1948, p. 18.

17. Andrew Lees, *Revolution and Reflection. Intellectual Change in Germany during the 1850s*, The Hague 1974, p. 115.

18. Shortly before his death in 1871 he would bitterly deplore the annexationism of Bismarck in North Germany. See doc. 92.

19. The fact that Bismarck frustrated the Liberals with his Macchiavellian tactics 'did not prevent him from applying the economic legal and ideological programme of the liberal bourgeoisie in so far as it could be combined with the predominance of the landed aristocracy in a Protestant Prussian monarchy'. E. J. Hobsbawm, *The Age of Capital 1848–1875*, London 1975, p. 107.

20. Theodor Schieder, in Gebhardt's *Handbuch der Deutschen Geschichte* (8th edn), edited by H. Grundmann, 1959, Band 3, p. 156.

21. L. Krieger, op. cit., p. 375–6.

22. See Ferdinand Lassalle, Arbeiterprogramm (The Working Men's Programme) trans. Edward Peter, London 1884, 56.

23. L. Krieger, op. cit., p. 381.

24. F. Lassalle, *Gesamtwerke*, ed. Erich Bolum, Leipzig 1901, I, pp. 1–7.

25. For Bastiat see doc. 28.

26. F. Lassalle, *Herr Bastiat – Schulz von Delitzsch, der oekonomische Julian oder Kapital und Arbeit*, Leipzig 1863.

27. Hermann Oncken, *Lassalle. Eine politische Biographie* (4th edn), Stuttgart 1923, p. 422.

28. See James J. Sheehan's article 'Liberals and Society in Germany 1815–48', op. cit., pp. 597–8.

29. Theodore S. Hamerow, *The Social Foundations of German Unification. Ideas and Institutions*, Princeton 1969, p. 172.

30. Quoted in Werner Conze, *Möglichkeiten und Grenzen der liberalen Arbeiterbewegung in Deutschland*, Heidelberg 1965, p. 14.

31. *Hermann Schulze-Delitzsch's Schriften und Reden*, edited by F. Thorwart, Berlin 1909–13, p. 795.

32. W. Conze, op. cit., p. 16.

33. *Hermann Schulze-Delitzsch's Schriften und Reden*, p. 807.

34. T. S. Hamerow, op. cit., pp. 178–9.

35. T. S. Hamerow, op. cit., p. 150.

36. Dolf Sternberger, 'Leopold Sonnemann, Bürger and Gründer', *Frankfurter Allgemeine Zeitung*, 13 July 1974.

37. See the Introduction to *Zwölf Jahre im Reichstage. Reichstagsreden von Leopold*

Sonnemann 1871–1874 and 1878–1884. A tribute on the occasion of his seventieth birthday. Text by Alexander Giesen for a committee of the German People's Party, Frankfurt, 1901.,

38. James J. Sheehan, 'Liberalism and the City in Nineteenth Century Germany', *Past and Present,* No. 51, 1971, p. 137.

Section A

Roots of Liberalism
The Eighteenth Century

1. The civil State – representative government: introduction

(Documents 1a–c; pp. 173–81)

For the greater part of the eighteenth century the government of England, as established after the Revolution of 1688, was regarded by most Englishmen and also by educated people in Europe as a model of a civil state enjoying representative institutions. Among the writers who contributed to a greater or lesser extent to English political theory in the seventeenth century John Locke came to hold pride of place. His pre-eminent position was not due to the originality of his thought. It was due rather to the close relationship between his political thought and the political and social ideas of those who stood to gain most from the English form of representative government. As W. J. Gough has commented:

'The importance of his [Locke's] contribution to political thought lay not in its novelty but in its timelessness and its mode of expression. He summed up, and published in an easy, readable style, the accepted commonplaces of the political thought of his generation, at a moment when the successful accomplishment of the Revolution of 1688 made the government of England seem a model to be envied.' [1]

Contrary to what was once believed, Locke's *Two Treatises of Government* was not written to justify the Revolution of 1688. Although there is still some dispute among scholars, it is now generally held that the greater part of the *Two Treatises* was written between 1681 and 1683 at the latest, with the Second Treatise, *An Essay Concerning the True Original, Extent, and End of Civil Government,* being revised and some new paragraphs added prior to its publication in October, 1689.[2] A common factor in both periods of composition was the need to offer a refutation of absolute monarchy. Beyond that, Locke's book was unique. 'It was at once a response to a particular political situation and a statement of universal principle, made as such and still read as such.' [3]

Locke's concept of civil society was derived from two traditional and closely connected ideas: the social contract and natural law. It was argued that the social contract originated in a decision of will and was not imposed by force; and if men recognized the existence of natural law, then they must also recognize the existence of natural rights. Mediaeval thinkers and some of the seventeenth century apologists of royal absolutism had interpreted the social contract as being between the ruler and his subjects. During the seventeenth century it became more common to see that the social contract had a double aspect whereby a contract of society, which created a community, was a prior condition for the contract of government. When in the seventeenth and eighteenth centuries some political thinkers laid emphasis exclusively on the contract of society, the conclusions they drew varied greatly. Hobbes, for example, in *Leviathan,* contended that once the social contract came into existence, men handed over all their rights and powers to the sovereign; whereas Locke, and subsequently Rousseau, contended that the contract (or compact, as Locke preferred to call it) was exclusively between individuals when they agreed of their own free will to leave a state of nature and enter a civil or political society for the better securing of their rights.

The state of nature, as defined by Locke, is both a state of perfect freedom and a state of equality. In that state, every man has 'an uncontrollable Liberty, to dispose of his Person or Possessions'. It is governed by the law of nature; 'And Reason, which is that Law, teaches all Mankind, who will but consult it, that being all equal and independent, no one ought to harm another in his Life, Health, Liberty, or Possessions.' [4] The law of nature is also God's command; and so moral law is thus in accord with both reason and the will of God. [5]

Although men in a state of nature are naturally good, they are not perfect. Therefore, in order to secure the peace and preservation of mankind, every man holds the power to punish those who transgress the law of nature; for he who transgresses that law thereby shows that he lives 'by another Rule, than that of *reason* and common Equity' – reason being 'the common Rule and Measure, God hath given to Mankind'.[6] Why, then, do men need to leave the state of nature? They do so because of the need for collective power to punish offenders against the law of nature. By exercising the power of punishment collectively the rights of all can be better secured.

According to Locke's argument, men remain in a state of nature until, 'by their own consent', they agree to become members of a political society. This is the only social compact that Locke recognizes as forming a political society. From then onwards: 'Those who are united into one Body, and have a common establish'd Law and Judicature to appeal to, with Authority to decide Controversies between them, and punish Offenders, *are in Civil Society* with one another ...' [7]

Once men have formed a political society, and consented to be placed under its government, a majority can act for the whole (doc. 1*a*). The acceptance of majority rule is in the interests not only of freedom under the law, but also of stability and the preservation of property; for, as Locke contends, if a majority cannot act for the whole and command its obedience, government, and indeed the political society itself, will be dissolved.

Political power, according to Locke's initial definition, is 'a Right of making laws with Penalties of Death, and consequently all less Penalties, for the Regulating and Preserving of Property, and of employing the force of the Community, in the Execution of such Laws, and in the defence of the Common-wealth from Foreign Injury, and all this only for the Publick Good'.[8] Such a statement could be used, and was used during the eighteenth century, to justify the exercise of political power by a property-owning class; this meant that the many in England, who were propertyless, could only be represented indirectly in the governing majority.

Now, although the preservation of property was one of the reasons for men's entering into a political society, Locke's concept of property is only in part the generally accepted view of property as the private accumulation of wealth in land, money or other goods. According to Locke's broader definition of property: 'every Man has a *Property* in his own *Person*. This no Body has any Right to but himself. The *Labour* of his Body, and the *Work* of his Hands, we may say, are properly his'.[9] Hence the origin of property is to be found in God having given the world to men in common, and having given each man reason to make use of what nature offers to all: 'Whatsoever then he removes out of the State that nature hath provided, and left it in, he hath mixed his *Labour* with, and joyned to it something that is his own, and thereby makes it his Property'.[10] In this broad sense of the word, property is used by Locke to cover men's need to preserve their 'Lives, Liberties and Estates' from the insecurity of being invaded by others, including the imposition of arbitrary taxation; but on other occasions in the *Second Treatise,* he appears to be using the term in its more usual and limited sense.[11]

In order to preserve their 'Lives, Liberties and Estates' men need 'an *establish'd*, settled, known Law'. They also need '*a known and indifferent* [i.e. impartial] *Judge*, with Authority to determine all differences according to the established Law'; and finally there needs to be power to execute that law[12] (doc. 1*b*). Here is to be found the origin of the legislative and executive power, as well as the origin of government itself. Starting from this premise, Locke contends that the legislature must govern by 'establish'd *standing Laws*, promulgated and known to the People, and not by Extemporary Decrees'; that is, it must govern for the public good of society.

Although Locke states unequivocally that supreme power lies in the legislature, he does not use the term sovereignty for that supreme power (doc. 1*c*). Indeed, it is possible to contend that Locke is implying that although legal sovereignty lies in the legislature, political sovereignty remains in the community itself. Further, Locke does not expressly state that the supreme legislative power must necessarily be in the hands of a representative body, though this may be assumed from his remarks that the rule of the majority should be accepted, that the members of an assembly should not have interests different from those of the rest of the community, and that the consent of the majority, individually or through its representatives, must be given to taxation.[13] The criterion, irrespective of whether the supreme legislative power is in the hands of a representative body, either oligarchic or democratic, or in the hands of one individual, either hereditary or elective, is that the body or individual is exercising the common power of the political society; for the supreme legislative power is not and cannot be arbitrary power. [14]

In his statements on the origin and supremacy of legislative power, Locke is not free from ambiguity concerning consent and obedience. He can be interpreted as saying that each individual's consent is given directly to the establishment of a political society and therefore to its exercise of legislative power; but in succeeding generations it is then the duty of each member of society to obey, provided the laws ensure freedom, stability and the security of property. Those who exercise legislative and executive power are therefore in a position of trust, for they are entrusted with governing on behalf of the community. Political power is thus a fiduciary, or trustee, power. [15] If their exercise of political power fails to secure freedom and stability, and the safety of property, the community can withdraw the consent it once gave, and place its trust elsewhere. In that case, the community would be exercising its right of 'appeal to heaven', that is, exercising the right of resistance, for illegitimate or arbitrary power is an abuse of trust. [16] Here again, there are difficulties in interpreting Locke's thought. [17] The withdrawal of trust from those who exercise legislative and executive power is a recognition that the government is guilty of a breach of that trust; but this does not mean that the political society itself is dissolved, for the placing of trust in the government is something quite distinct from the original social compact. [18] However, it does mean that political power reverts to the community which can then decide to place its trust elsewhere. In other words, political sovereignty always remains with the community. [19]

Such arguments could undoubtedly be used to justify the events of November 1688, as they could equally well have served the political situation at the time of the Exclusion Bills in 1679–80 when Locke began to put together his thoughts on government. In viewing the task which lay before the Convention Parliament of 1689, Locke commented: 'the settlement of the nation on the sure grounds of peace and security is put into their hands, which can no way so well be done as by restoring our ancient government – the best possible that ever was, if taken and put together all of a piece in its original constitution . . .' [20]

Locke's understanding of the 'original constitution' and the 'ancient government' of England can be deduced from the text of his *Two Treatises of Government*. England was a 'mixed monarchy' in which power was shared by the monarch, the aristocracy and the commons; but the supremacy of Parliament had been recognized in the revolutionary settlement of 1688–89. [21] Locke pointed out the need for separating the legislative or law-making power from the executive power which administered that law. [22] However, in view of the English constitutional practice by which the king summons and prorogues Parliament, the head of the executive, that is, the king, could also be part of the

The civil State – representative government: introduction

legislature.[23] Locke saw Parliament as having only a limited life and not being continuously in session; and those entrusted with exercising legislative power should have the power of law making only for a time. In contrast to the legislature, the executive needed always to be in existence.[24] Locke did not stipulate that the judicial power was separate from the executive; but in the event, the political settlement of 1688–89 brought a long struggle to an end by establishing the independence of the judiciary. The other distinct power Locke recognized was a 'federative' power, that is, the conduct of relations with other political communities in peace or war; but in practice this power would be in the same hands as the executive power.[25]

Locke's emphasis on the aim of political society being the preservation of property, equally with life and liberty, was in keeping with his own acceptance of the social structure of seventeenth-century England and his personal position as a landed gentleman in addition to his being an academic. Further, Locke's family background associated him with industry and also with the Puritan tradition during the Civil War and the Protectorate. An emphasis on natural law, individual rights and the limitation of absolute power was part of that tradition; but Locke, like many Englishmen in the immediate years after the Restoration of Charles II in 1660 and again after the Revolution of 1688, also emphasized the need for order and stability. Owing to Locke's own background, and the circles with which he associated in the 1670s and 1680s, he could expect a sympathetic reading public for his *Two Treatises of Government* to consist of 'the English gentleman, the Member of Parliament, the administrator and politician, at home and overseas, but above all the landowner, the local notable'.[26] Among such people there would be little clash of interests between the government and the governed in the 1688–89 settlement. As property owners, they alone would fully be members of the political society.

In that Locke's arguments in the *Two Treatises of Government* are couched in general and universal terms, they are open to interpretations other than that of the eighteenth-century English constitution which developed from the 1689 revolutionary settlement. That settlement was based on the premise, not derived from Locke, that the contract between king and people had been broken by James II; but in the eighteenth-century the Lockean idea was widely accepted that Parliament held political power in trust. During the eighteenth century also, the general and universal nature of Locke's concepts provided Thomas Paine with arguments in favour of majority rule which would be truly democratic. Further, the American colonists in their political battles with George III's government in the 1760s, looked to Locke as an authority in support of their contention that the taxation levied on them by the British Parliament infringed their natural and constitutional rights.

According to the traditional view of the influence of Locke's political theories in the eighteenth century: 'Locke's general political doctrines continued to hold the field ... For all its imperfections, Locke's doctrine remained the basis of English constitutional government ... Nowhere was Locke's influence greater than across the Atlantic ...' [27]

This view can be challenged by distinguishing more carefully between political ideas and political practice in the eighteenth century. It is then found that to those who referred to Locke as an authority: 'The use of his name was more a feature of their effective life than a guarantee of any energetic conceptual exploration. It belonged to the rhetoric not to the analysis of politics ...' [28]

---

2. Religious toleration: introduction
(Documents 2–4, pp. 182–90)

If the end of political society and government is the preservation of men's 'Lives, Liberties and Estates', then freedom of religious belief is one of the chief of those liberties. When John Locke formulated his concept of civil society, religious toleration was rare in Europe; but the case for freedom of worship and of religious belief was stated clearly by Locke and others before the end of the seventeenth century in England and on the Continent.

Uniformity of religious belief in Western Christendom had been shattered by the Reformation; and from then onwards true faith was no longer associated only with the Catholic Church under the spiritual authority of the Pope. Other churches, including the Church of England and the various Lutheran and Calvinist churches, also claimed to hold and practise the true faith; and, like the Catholic Church, each of these churches was intolerant towards other churches and sects. Similarly, the secular princes and rulers, each claiming to uphold the true faith, denied religious freedom to their subjects. Churches and secular rulers alike believed that men must be forced to accept whichever religious beliefs each church or ruler regarded as the true faith. Uniformity of faith and worship would then be established and maintained by compulsion in each State or principality, even if not in Europe as a whole.

The most extreme manifestation of religious intolerance was the massacre of French Protestants on St Bartholomew's Day in 1572; and the memory of that massacre remained very much alive in France and elsewhere throughout the seventeenth century. During that century religious issues were important in the Thirty Years' War on the Continent and in the English Civil War. Religious attitudes current in England during the Civil War and Protectorate showed too that intolerance was likely to be just as strong among minority religious groups, such as the Puritans and Presbyterians, as in the established Church of England. When Locke began to formulate his concept of civil society, religious intolerance in England had been given legal form in the Clarendon Code of the 1660s and the Test Act of 1673. By these Acts, the rights of public worship and the holding of public office were denied to all, Catholics and Nonconformists alike, who did not accept the beliefs and practices of the Church of England. In France, persecution or limited toleration depended on the policy or the whim of the monarch; and in October 1685, with Louis XIV's Revocation of the Edict of Nantes, a new period of intolerance and persecution began for the Huguenots. Holland, by contrast, had an enviable reputation for tolerance and freedom, and so offered a refuge for Huguenots and others who were forced to leave their own countries.

The seventeenth century, unlike the eighteenth century with its rationalism and scepticism, was still an age of faith. To believe in and to practise the true faith was regarded as essential, not only for man's well-being on earth but also for his eternal salvation. Many sincerely religious men therefore believed that it was their duty to use either persuasion or force to bring those who had not the true faith to admit their error. A minority, recognizing the difficulties of reuniting Christians holding such widely differing views of what was the true faith, came to believe that agreement could be reached on a minimum of essential and common beliefs within a 'comprehensive' church; and, beyond that, differences in non-essential beliefs and in the forms of worship could remain. Other men, who rejected 'comprehension', put forward an important argument in favour of tolerating all the Christian faiths. This argument grew in strength in the latter decades of the seventeenth century. It came from sincerely religious men as well as from others who were more sceptical. Although their reasons were different, such men contended that true faith could not be forced on anyone. Each man must be personally convinced of the truth of his faith; and it was known only to God whether that man's faith was the true faith or not. As religious belief was essentially an individual and private matter, it followed that persuasion alone should be used to try to convince a man of his error. Further, in the matter of religious faith, the king or ruler had no special power of determining which was the true faith. Therefore it could not be the function of the ruler to force a man to accept a particular form of religious belief and practice against his own convictions, because such a belief would have no value in the sight of God.

These lines of thought on comprehension and toleration form the intellectual background to John Locke's arguments in favour of religious toleration; they are closely related to his concept of political society. If

111

the end of government is the preservation of men's 'Lives, Liberties and Estates', then the purposes for which the civil magistrate, that is, the government, may use force are not only clearly laid down, they are also clearly limited; and to enforce a particular set of religious beliefs and practices is outside the powers entrusted to government.

Locke's *Letter on Toleration* (doc. 2) was written in 1685 while he was in exile in Holland; but it was not published until 1689.[29] Since the 1660s Locke's attitude towards toleration had gradually become more liberal in the application of his principles, because he came to see that the Protestant dissenting sects, unlike the Roman Catholics, were not a danger to the peace of society or to the safety of the State. He also believed that the absence of toleration in England was causing an economic loss through the emigration of dissenters, whereas he saw in Holland a successful example of the combination of toleration and a prosperous economy based on trade.

Locke's argument in his *Letter on Toleration* is based on the premise that Church and State are separate because the functions of the State are quite different from those of the Church:

'The commonwealth seems to me to be a society of men constituted only for preserving and advancing their civil goods.

What I call civil goods are life, liberty, bodily health and freedom from pain, and the possession of outward things, such as lands, money, furniture, and the like ...

A church seems to me to be a free society of men, joining together of their own accord for the public worship of God in such manner as they believe will be acceptable to the Deity for the salvation of their souls.' [30]

Locke's advocacy of the separation of Church and State had no connection with anti-clericalism. He was personally convinced of the need for a sincere faith, though his own religious beliefs were nearer to unitarianism than to the orthodox teachings of the Church of England. As the passage quoted above indicates, Locke regard a church as 'a free and voluntary society' in which those men who have chosen to join that church will worship God in ways which they think will be pleasing to Him. Although he believed that true religion was necessary for man's salvation, Locke also admitted that no man can *know* whether his own religion is true or not: he can only practise it through faith and reason. [31]

Taken by themselves these arguments could suggest that Locke was advocating complete religious liberty. [32] In the conditions of the late seventeenth century Locke's advocacy of religious liberty was less sweeping and complete. He believed that religion was a man's private concern as long as the practice of any religion did not injure the rights of other men or affect the security of the State. For example, the State could interfere if a church introduced doctrines which would be immoral and lead to the destruction of civil society.[33] Nor could toleration be granted to a church which claimed authority over those who did not belong to that church, or refused to tolerate dissenters from its own faith. Although Locke does not say so directly, he is clearly implying in this and in other important exceptions that toleration could not be granted to the Catholic Church because of its own intolerance and its allegiance and duty to a foreign prince.[34] In the case of atheists, Locke is quite specific. They should be excluded from toleration because their ultimate aim is to destroy all religion; and civic and other oaths could not be binding on them when they had no belief in God.[35] Otherwise, mutual toleration among Christians was 'the chief distinguishing mark of a true church,' and it was in accord both with the teachings of the gospel and with reason.[36]

In his *Letter on Toleration*, as in his *Two Treatises of Government*, the arguments Locke put forward were of universal application; and, as far as England was concerned, they were broadly acceptable, for the most part, to many Englishmen in the late 1680s. However, the Act of Toleration, passed by the Convention Parliament in 1689 following the Glorious Revolution, was not as far-reaching as Locke would have wished. Whereas the Act allowed Non-conformists to worship publicly, but gave them no political or civic rights, Roman Catholics, Unitarians, atheists and Jews were still excluded. Even so, persecution of those who were excluded from the benefits of the Toleration Act, and the enforcement of the Corporation and Test Acts against Nonconformists, became a thing of the past. Once religious liberty had to some extent been granted in England by the Act of Toleration, freedom of thought on other matters came to be accepted generally in practice if not in law. Indeed, Locke had argued more for liberty of conscience, despite his qualifications, than for the toleration of religions other than the established or dominant one.

On the Continent French thinkers were given an immediate incentive to present the case for toleration by Louis XIV's Revocation of the Edict of Nantes in October 1685. Of these, the most outspoken in his advocacy of religious freedom was Pierre Bayle, then in exile in Holland. Bayle probably retained a personal belief in God despite his anti-clericalism; but, in contrast to Locke, he did not believe that there was a true religion or that certain beliefs were necessary for salvation. He saw no need for the organized religion of the churches; and, since he believed that morality could equally as well have a natural as a religious basis, it was freedom of conscience, rather than religious toleration, that Bayle advocated in his *Philosophical Commentary*.[37] There was, however, one important exception. On account of Louis XIV's Revocation of the Edict of Nantes, as well as the past history of intolerance in the Roman Catholic Church, Bayle excluded Catholics from toleration. Even more strongly than Locke had done, Bayle emphasized the contrast between the teachings of Christianity and the age-old practice of compelling men to accept certain doctrines. '*To compel them to come in*,' he said, 'means to ravage, hang, kill, devastate until the individual dare not refuse to join so kindly and true a religion.' [38]

French thinkers who were not in exile had perforce to use more indirect means of asserting the principle of religious toleration. Through the device of the *Persian Letters* Montesquieu put forward an argument that had already been heard in England in the seventeenth century: that a country suffered great loss when, as a result of religious persecution, an industrious and enterprising people [i.e. the Huguenots] left the country and took their talents elsewhere. [39] In the *Persian Letters* too, and later in *The Spirit of the Laws*, Montesquieu drew attention to two other arguments in the case against religious intolerance. First, that as all religious sects 'enjoin obedience' and 'preach submission', the toleration of several religions in a State would not affect its safety. [40] Secondly, the cause of intolerance was to be found in the 'spirit of proselytism', in the 'spirit of enthusiasm, the progress of which can only be regarded as a total eclipse of human reason.' [41]

As Montesquieu regarded toleration as a political principle he was not concerned with the truth or falsity of religion. His own personal belief in God was that of a deist, rather than a Christian; and because he believed in the principles of natural religion, he emphasized that reason and morality led to toleration. Conversely, intolerance and persecution, both being the outcome of enthusiasm, were unreasonable. An indictment of enthusiasm, that is, of fanaticism, and the unreasonableness of intolerance was also one of the most important elements in Voltaire's vigorous and sustained attack on *l'infâme*, which has variously been understood as being either clericalism, and particularly 'clerical superstition' in all forms, or the Catholic Church or even Christianity itself [42] (doc. 3*a*). As Bayle had done earlier, Voltaire contended that Christianity was no longer like Christ: for, says Voltaire, 'If you would resemble Jesus Christ, you must be martyrs, and not executioners.' [43] Voltaire also shared the anti-clericalism of the French *philosophes* in no small measure, although in his case it shaded into anti-Christianity on account of the superstition and fanaticism that he saw in Christianity (doc. 3*b*).

Certain events brought about by fanaticism provided Voltaire with the necessary opportunities in the 1760s for mounting his attack on *l'infâme*. Although active persecution of the Huguenots in France had become spasmodic and unpredictable rather than systematic by the middle of the eighteenth century, outbursts of persecution could still occur when economic distress, social unrest, and defeat in war encouraged renewed fanaticism among both Catholics and Protestants. In the Toulouse district in the south of France a few isolated but extreme cases of fanaticism and persecution occurred in 1761–62. The trial and execution of the Huguenot Jean Calas for the supposed murder of his son, who was thought to be a convert to Catholicism, and the condemnation of the Sirven family for the death of Elisabeth Sirven, who had been forcibly taught the Catholic faith, provided Voltaire with a weight of evidence for an attack on intolerance and fanaticism combined with cruelty and injustice.

Although Voltaire was at the most a deist who believed in a vague 'supreme being' (doc. 3c), but was more probably a sceptic or even an atheist,[44] he saw the necessity of some form of popular deistic religion which would act as a 'social cement' for the great unthinking majority, and so provide for social morality.[45] In the early 1750s, following the disastrous earthquake at Lisbon, Voltaire came to question the foundations and the validity of the eighteenth-century belief in optimism, that all was for the best in the best of possible worlds.[46] Out of Voltaire's pessimism about 'the best of possible worlds' came his conclusion in *Candide*, 'We must cultivate our garden.'[47]

To Voltaire, *l'infâme*, whatever its precise meaning, was the main hindrance to man's progress towards reasonableness (docs 3a, 3b); for toleration and justice were both ordered by nature, whereas fanaticism, the root cause of intolerance, was a disease created by superstition.[48] The harshness of the French legal code in the eighteenth century and the punishments imposed by law, including torture, were also irrational. The end of intolerance, cruelty and injustice was therefore closely connected with making the clergy subject to the State, instead of the Church continuing its long established practice of using the State as an agent for its own intolerance and inhumanity. In a reform of the legal code, State and civil interests must be separated from the interests of the Church. Then, once the guidance of reason and the rule of law was accepted by the State, freedom of thought could be allowed provided the civil peace was in no way disturbed.[49] So, freedom of thought and the removal of useless and irrational harshness from the legal code, as well as eliminating injustice from the operation of the law, were the ultimate ends Voltaire had in mind when he took up Jean Calas's defence in his *Treatise on Toleration*, and also while he compiled many of the articles for his *Philosophical Dictionary*, both of which were published in 1764.[50]

In the immediate circumstances of 1762, Voltaire's objective was to bring about a reversal of the unjust and inhuman sentence passed on Jean Calas. To do this, he set out to create an informed public opinion against intolerance and fanaticism, legal injustice and cruelty. The tone of the *Treatise on Toleration* is often polemical and Voltaire can be charged with exaggeration and even unfairness. Yet, because he was putting the case for tolerance and justice before a Catholic audience, the anti-clerical tone of the *Treatise* is noticeably softened in comparison

A. Roots of liberalism: the eighteenth century

with various articles in the *Philosophical Dictionary*. [51] The practical result of Voltaire's crusade against intolerance and injustice was the rehabilitation of Jean Calas in 1765 and the Sirven family in 1771. As for the broader issues in Voltaire's campaign, Theodore Besterman claims that Voltaire 'had shown, by evoking a vast response throughout the civilised world, that there was such a thing as public opinion, and that this opinion could be formed and harnessed'. [52] Further, as a result of Voltaire's defence of Jean Calas, 'Mankind suddenly became aware of the fact that not even the most crushing power can resist indignation provoked by injustice.' [53]

The reversals of acts of injustice in the Calas and Sirven cases certainly marked the changing and more humane climate of opinion which was developing in France with regard to religious toleration, at least as far as civic rights were concerned, and the uselessness of torture; and the attitudes of those members of the *parlements*, who came closest into contact with the emphasis placed on reason in the writings of the *philosophes*, were the most noticeably affected. [54] At the same time, during a period of peace lasting from 1763 to 1778, when France became involved in the American War of Independence against Great Britain, the economic and social strains which had in the past given rise to outbursts of fanaticism and intolerance were greatly lessened.

An illustration of the effects of reason and the Enlightenment on the thought and policy of an administrator is to be found in Turgot's advocacy of religious toleration. Unlike Voltaire, Turgot was not an anti-clerical. He retained his Catholic faith, although he gave up the prospect of a career in the Church for one in the royal administration. He accepted that 'on the belief and practice of a true or a false religion depends for man an eternity of happiness or of misery;' but his definition of religion was based on natural law as well as on divine law. [55]

Turgot's belief in religious toleration remained firm throughout his career in the royal administration. By the time he was appointed Controller-General by the new king, Louis XVI, in 1774, he had built up a reputation for himself as an enlightened administrator and economist. He regarded religious toleration as a political question; but he also saw that there were economic and social grounds for granting toleration to the Huguenots. The professions, including that of the law, would then be open to them; and with the granting of toleration, even if only by the restoration of the Edict of Nantes, many of the Huguenot emigrés, whose departure had been an economic loss to France, would return. [56] In line with the emphasis placed by the *philosophes* on the pursuit of happiness, Turgot had pointed out to Louis that the coronation oath should no longer include a promise to extirpate heresy but should emphasize instead the king's intention of maintaining the rights of his subjects and securing their happiness. Having failed in his object of persuading Louis to agree to an alteration in the wording of the coronation oath, Turgot put forward in his *Memorial* a reasoned argument in favour of full liberty of conscience in religious matters (doc. 4). During the course of Turgot's years as Controller-General from 1774 to 1776, Louis, like the higher clergy, wanted to stamp out the spirit of irreligion that was thought to be growing in France; and so Turgot's advocacy of a policy of ameliorating the harsh treatment suffered by Protestants met with strong resistance, in the same way as his enlightened economic and financial proposals stirred up a varied and powerful opposition before his fall in 1776.

In practice, systematic or even active persecution was becoming a thing of the past in France by the 1770s, although the disabilities against Protestants remained. Side by side with the changing climate of opinion towards persecution on religious grounds, the edicts of 1780 and 1788 abolishing the use of torture showed that public feeling was becoming more humane. In 1787, Loménie de Brienne, Archbishop of Toulouse, who had helped the spread of tolerance in his own archbishopric, marked the formal end of religious persecution under the French monarchy by persuading the king to issue an Edict of Toleration which gave the Huguenots legal recognition of civil rights. Two years later, freedom of religion and freedom of opinion were to become part of the argument surrounding the Declaration of the Rights of Man (doc. 13).

3. 'The spirit of the laws': introduction
(Documents 5a–c, pp. 190–5)

After John Locke the second major contribution to the development of liberal political ideas in the eighteenth century came from Charles-Louis de Secondat, Baron de Montesquieu. His family background and a short period in office in the important *parlement* of Bordeaux helped to shape both his view of society and his political outlook with its emphasis on law in relation to society. Even more importantly, the personal observations he made during extensive travels in Europe and England between 1728 and 1731 and wide reading in classical and modern thought, in the history of the ancient republics of Greece and Rome, in eighteenth century accounts of eastern despotisms as well as an acquaintance with natural science, were all reflected in Montesquieu's study of the structure of different societies and the relationship between customs, laws and institutions.

117

A. Roots of liberalism: the eighteenth century

Montesquieu sought to identify the spirit behind the formulation of law; and this purpose shows clearly in the title of his major work, *The Spirit of the Laws*, in which he defined laws as 'the necessary relations arising from the nature of things ... laws are the relations subsisting between [prime reason] and different beings, and the relations of these to one another'.[57] As man has need of law on religious, moral and political/civil grounds, there are natural or divine laws and positive man-made laws; and, of the latter, the political and civil laws of each country will be related to a number of factors, such as climate, geography, the occupations of the people, religion, wealth, manners and customs, and the degree of liberty in the constitution. [58] Montesquieu explained the design of his work in these words:

'I have first of all considered mankind, and the result of my thoughts has been, that amidst such an infinite diversity of laws and manners, they were not solely conducted by the caprice of fancy.
I have laid down the first principles, and have found that the particular cases follow naturally from them; that the histories of all nations are only consequences of them; and that every particular law is connected with another law, or depends on some other of a more general extent.' [59]

Montesquieu classified governments as republics (aristocratic or democratic), monarchies and despotisms.[60] Certainly the first two can still be distinguished from each other on the traditional ground of power being exercised by one person or by part or the whole of the people; but the distinction Montesquieu makes between monarchies and ancient and modern despotisms, such as Persia, China, Turkey and Russia, takes him on to new and different ground. For whereas republics and monarchies are both founded on the rule of law, no matter whether power is exercised by one or by many, despotisms are ruled arbitrarily so that religion and custom are the only restraints on the will of the ruler. [61] In his opinion, the republican form of government was suited only to small states. [62] Montesquieu therefore concluded that the monarchical form of government was the most suited to eighteenth-century Europe. Of the existing monarchies it was France, and not England, which came closest to his definition. This was because England, by the eighteenth century, exhibited some of the characteristics associated with both the aristocratic and democratic forms of a republic.

This distinction between England and France was highlighted when Montesquieu came to define what he regarded as the guiding principle which motivated political action in each of the three types of government. In a democratic republic this principle was political virtue, whereas in an aristocratic one it was 'moderation founded on virtue'; in a monarchy it was honour, but in a despotism it was fear.[63] In each type of government the execution of the laws should be in accordance with the guiding principle. Thus a democratic republic would be governed by its people out of

118

love of the republic and for the public good, and also in accordance with a love of equality and frugality.[64] In an aristocratic republic, a ruling aristocracy guided by moderation would ensure the public welfare and not seek excessive power and wealth for itself.[65] In a monarchy, guided by the principle of honour, the monarch in seeking his own and his kingdom's glory would respect both the fundamental laws which limited his power and the laws which he and his advisers promulgated; and in his administration of the law, the monarch would work through the traditional intermediary powers, the nobility, the Church and the *parlements*, so that those who served the monarch would serve him well in order to advance their own rank and privileges in a hierarchical society.[66]

Viewing France as the example *par excellence* of monarchy, according to his own definition of that form of government, Montesquieu showed that at heart and in mind he remained a noble of the robe and a supporter of the *parlements* as constitutional or intermediary bodies which would guard against royal despotism. Hence his famous aphorism: 'no monarch, no nobility; no nobility, no monarch.' [67]

Despite Montesquieu's predilections for the French type of monarchy, his observations of the English political and social scene led him to commend the English form of government on two counts: first, because of the Constitution and the law; and, secondly, because the English government, through the Lords and the Commons, exhibited both moderation and virtue, the aristocratic and democratic principles he associated with a republic, instead of the monarchical principle of honour. The English monarchy, therefore, came nearest to Montesquieu's ideal of a 'moderate government'. Despite this conclusion and his critical attitude to the French monarchy as it became corrupt and neared despotism during the latter years of Louis XIV's reign, Montesquieu did not believe that political liberty was impossible in France. For there had long existed in France a body of law which related to the Constitution and to the individual and was based on the monarchical principle of honour. Montesquieu therefore believed that a return to the purity of that principle, and to the rule of law, was imperative for France in order to arrest the descent into despotism. Montesquieu did not maintain that political liberty was exclusive to a republican form of government. As long as a government, whether republican or monarchical, was moderate, political liberty could exist.

It follows then that Montesquieu could not regard freedom as being unlimited. Although his definition of liberty is not free from ambiguity or even contradiction, it is basically in line with Locke's, that liberty is limited only by the law (doc. 5a); but whereas Locke based respect for the law on consent, Montesquieu held that any necessary limitations on freedom were legitimate provided that exercise of power by the government was not arbitrary, or, in other words, provided constitutional

119

checks to the abuse of power operated. Wherever that was the case, and moderate governments existed, there would be no conflict between power and freedom. From this premise Montesquieu seems to have been led to a further definition of political liberty as 'the power of doing what we ought to will, and in not being constrained to do what we ought not to will' (doc. 5a).

Montesquieu's emphasis is on social rather than on individual liberty. He is concerned with the exercise of power rather than with the rights of the individual. Whereas for Locke the end of political society was the preservation of men's 'Lives, Liberties and Estates', Montesquieu less precisely found the political liberty of the individual 'in security, or in the opinion people have of their security' (doc. 5b). As he made a clear distinction between political liberty as it related to the Constitution and political liberty as it related to the individual, Montesquieu regarded the liberty of the individual as being primarily the concern of the civil and criminal law. Further, he pointed out that what constituted freedom in any one country would depend on a number of factors conditioning the general body of law. These factors formed the 'general spirit' which the law should always follow; because

'Mankind are influenced by various causes: by the climate, by the religion, by the laws, by the maxims of government, by precedents, morals, and customs – whence is formed a general spirit of nations.
In proportion as, in every country, any one of these causes acts with more force, the others in the same degree are weakened.'[68]

That statement would suggest that Lockean individualism was not suited to indiscriminate application in all countries and to all peoples. Since laws were, by Montesquieu's definition, 'the necessary relations arising from the nature of things', men had to be governed by several kinds of law, including the law of nature, divine law, ecclesiastical law, the law of nations, general and particular political law, and civil law (doc. 5c). It was therefore essential, as Montesquieu showed, that the connections between each kind of law were recognized and also the limits of each, so that one kind of law did not encroach on the jurisdiction of another. Above all, political law should not invade the area of civil law.[69]

Although at one point Montesquieu seems to suggest that the liberty of the subject (i.e. his security) could be safeguarded without there being political liberty in relation to the constitution, and vice versa,[70] he did in fact see the two kinds of liberty as being dependent on each other. For, in order to ensure the establishment and continuation of both kinds of political liberty, checks to the abuse of power must be instituted, and these of their very nature would be constitutional. Through his observations, Montesquieu found that the English Constitution and government was the most likely to secure political liberty because of the distribution of power. In *The Spirit of the Laws* Montesquieu initially lists the three powers of government as: 'the legislative; the executive in respect to things dependent on the law of nations; and the executive in regard to matters that depend on the civil law' (doc. 5a). Subsequently he broadens his definition by clearly calling the third power a judicial power and including public security and defence against invasion in the second power; and finally he defines the second power as that of 'executing the public resolutions'.[71] Montesquieu's insistence on the judiciary as a separate power is an indication of the importance that he placed on the existence of the *parlements* and the courts of law as independent bodies in the eighteenth-century French monarchy. For this reason, too, he placed most emphasis on the separation of the judicial power from the other two powers; for he saw this as being essential to the rule of law without which there could be no hope of political freedom.

Up to this point, despite differing definitions of the three powers, there is no irreconcilable gulf between Montesquieu and Locke; but the gulf widens when Montesquieu argues that the legislative and executive powers must be exercised separately, whereas Locke had insisted on the supremacy of the legislature. Montesquieu was possibly influenced by English political writers, including his friend, Henry St John Bolingbroke, who emphasized the need for a more distinct separation of the legislative and executive powers in England. In any case, during his visit to England, Montesquieu had soon become well aware of the distinction between the king in Parliament and the executive power which was vested in the king.[72] His main fear remained that the power of the Commons, and not that of the king, would become limitless and encroach on the executive power to the detriment of liberty.[73] Therefore power must limit power:

'The legislative body being composed of two parts, they check one another by the mutual privilege of rejecting. They are both restrained by the executive power, as the executive is by the legislative.
These three powers should naturally form a state of repose or inaction. But as there is a necessity for movement in the course of human affairs, they are forced to move, but still in concert.'[74]

Although Montesquieu's contemporaries in England do not appear to have thought so, the general consensus today is that he misinterpreted the English constitution by deriving from it the doctrine of the separation of powers.[75] Montesquieu never concerned himself with drawing up an ideal constitution for a moderate government. He was content with inquiry into and observation of existing governments which might come nearest to being moderate; and it was from his observations alone that he came to enunciate the theory of the separation of powers. On this point Montesquieu's most recent biographer, Robert Shackleton, has remarked:

'It is from his experience of the English Constitution and of political controversy in England that he empirically formed his theory of the separation of powers . . . It was he who dignified and rationalized the concept, linked it to a theory of liberty, and handed it to posterity as a doctrine far more practical than its proponents had known.' [76]

Those who read and studied Montesquieu's work, and had no first-hand experience of the working of the English Constitution, came to interpret his doctrine of the separation of powers far more literally than the example of the eighteenth-century English Constitution would suggest. This was particularly true of the American colonists in the constitutional debates which preceded the adoption of the United States' Constitution in 1787. Although the checks and balances between the legislative and executive power could be effective in the English form of constitutional monarchy without their being formally defined in a written constitution, a pattern was set in the United States' Constitution for a clear separation and delimitation of each of the three branches of government. Similarly in France, it was recognized in the Declaration of the Rights of Man in 1789 and during the constitutional debates in the Constituent Assembly between 1789 and 1791 that the separation of powers was essential to liberty. Neither in the United States republic nor in the French constitutional monarchy of 1791 was the separation of the three powers linked with a declaration of the supremacy of the legislative power in line with the English practice. Even so, the American and French Constitutions, just as much as the English Constitution which had developed historically, were designed to ensure political liberty through a distribution of power and a system of checks and balances that would prevent any one branch from abusing its power.

---

4. 'Government is a necessary evil': introduction
(Documents 6–7, pp. 195–9)

'I saw an opportunity, in which I thought I could do some good, and I followed exactly what my heart dictated, I neither read books, nor studied other people's opinions. I thought for myself.' [77]

'Government is a necessary evil': introduction

In these words Thomas Paine claimed originality for his ideas on society and government. The opportunity which he utilized was presented to him during the conflict between Great Britain and the American Colonies; and the outcome was the publication in January 1776 of his first important political writing *Common Sense* (doc. 6). Although Paine had had little formal education during his early years in England, his self-education during a life of poverty and a variety of occupations had brought him into contact with a wide range of contemporary political, philosophical and scientific writings. He was well acquainted, for example, with the ideas of Isaac Newton and John Locke. His own career as a writer and journalist began at the age of thirty-seven after his arrival in Philadelphia, in November 1774.

The crisis in the relations between Great Britain and the American Colonies worsened during the early months that Paine was in America until hostilities began with the skirmish at Lexington on 19 April 1775. Yet he always maintained that it was not until the outbreak of hostilities that he gave up any hope of a settlement between the colonies and Great Britain; and then he concluded that the American Colonies must declare their independence immediately rather than wait until they became independent in the fulness of time.[78] As Paine saw the situation, the colonists would have a unique opportunity of creating a new society, free from the evils of tradition and monarchy, once they had declared their independence of Great Britain. In the new society, the equality of natural rights would be recognized, and a representative and democratic government, based on civil rights, would be established. As he explained some years later:

'During the suspension of the old governments in America, both prior to and at the breaking out of hostilities, I was struck with the order and decorum with which everything was conducted; and impressed with the idea, that a little more than what society naturally performed, was all the government that was necessary, and that monarchy and aristocracy were frauds and impositions upon mankind.' [79]

In Paine's view, the simplicity and straightforwardness of colonial society and government contrasted very favourably with the weight and complexity of aristocratic society and monarchical government in Great Britain. Paine therefore regarded American colonial society as being nearest to the original social state when government was first found to be necessary, so that it could deal with the few matters concerning the security of the individual and of society which society itself was unable to handle.

Paine would not have admitted that man was not naturally good, but believed that his moral imperfections, as an individual and as a member of society, made government necessary. So we have his simple and idyllic picture of how the first government came into existence (doc. 6); a North

A. Roots of liberalism: the eighteenth century

American and republican parallel, as it were, of Montesquieu's remark
that the 'beautiful system [of constitutional monarchy] was first invented
in the woods [of Germany]'. According to Paine, who accepted the idea
of a social contract, the only basis necessary for representative and
democratic, i.e. republican, government was the existence of a simple and
happy society in which the equality of natural rights and the exercise of
reason were recognized (doc. 6). In such a society little government
would be needed: its end would be both freedom and security. Society
itself would ensure the exercise of the natural rights 'which appertain to
man in right of his existence. Of this kind are all the intellectual rights, or
rights of the mind, and also all those rights of acting as an individual for
his own comfort and happiness, which are not injurious to the natural
rights of others'.[80] Government would extend no further than to ensure
equality of civil rights, and the security and protection of the individual.

Paine contended that government in its new, representative and
democratic form would be clearly distinguished from the old and defective hereditary system of government; because 'the representative
system takes society and civilization for its basis; nature, reason and experience for its guide.'[81] As simple and direct democracy was possible
only in very small States, representation was the best means of ensuring
good, i.e. republican, government; for 'republican government is no other
than government established and conducted for the interest of the public,
as well individually as collectively'.[82] Paine therefore concluded that the
United States, with a newly created government 'which is wholly on the
system of representation, is the only real republic in character and practice. . . . Its government has no other object than the public business of
the nation, and therefore it is properly a republic. . . . It is representation
ingrafted upon democracy.'[83]

On this ground, Paine and the founding fathers of the United States
were basically in agreement; but on one important point he was at
variance with them. For Paine believed that in a representative and
democratic political framework less and less power would need to be
placed in the hands of an executive. For this reason, he rejected the
theory of the separation of powers which was to be embodied in the
United States' Constitution, and insisted on the supremacy of the
legislature because that was where the people were represented.[84]

As Paine saw the Americans enjoying a unique opportunity of creating
a government for themselves following independence, and because they
could 'begin government at the right end', he believed that the cause of
humanity itself was in their hands as well as that of America. This feeling
for humanity, linked with a belief in the universality of his ideas, gives
continuity to Paine's writings on the American and French revolutions
although they span a period of twenty years. 'My attachment is to all the
world,' he wrote, 'and not to any particular part, and if what I advance is
right, no matter where or who it comes from.'[85] As a citizen of the

world, Paine is himself an example of the unity that can be found in the American and French revolutions, and in the British reform movements of the late eighteenth century, in the form of a 'democratic revolution'. Threads of continuity in Paine's ideas are also to be found in his unchanging view of the natural and civil rights of man, his abhorrence of monarchical and aristocratic government, and his insistence that only a representative, i.e. republican, government is legitimate.

There is no doubt that the arguments Paine put forward in *Common Sense* helped to form and unite public opinion in the American Colonies in favour of separation from Great Britain and the creation of a republican government. For all that, and despite his own claim to originality in his ideas, Paine's main role throughout his political and literary career was that of an influential propagandist of ideas among ordinary men rather than that of a political thinker.

Paine's naive political outlook is most apparent in the sketch of a republican Constitution for the United States which he included in *Common Sense*.[86] He always contended that if the principles on which government was based were in line with man's natural and civil rights, i.e. if there was a written constitution embodying a statement of those rights, then the outward forms of government could vary (doc. 7). The outward form was a 'matter of opinion' and not a matter of principle. As Paine's principles remained constant, his varied political experiences in America, Britain and France had very little effect in modifying his ideas concerning a 'matter of opinion'.

Paine's *Dissertation on First Principles of Government* (doc. 7), written in France in 1795, is a succinct statement of the political ideas he had held since 1776, although it was written for a specific occasion and for the purpose of combatting the inclusion of a property qualification in the French Constitution of 1795. Paine always insisted that representative government must be based on equal representation, i.e. on equal suffrage: 'Every man has a right to one vote, and no more, in the choice of representatives.'[87] Whereas in Great Britain Paine had opposed a reform of Parliament as being insufficient because monarchical institutions would be retained, in France he had viewed the Terror between 1792 and 1794 as exemplifying how autocracy and authoritarianism would arise when the rights of man were suspended.[88] Paine continued to believe that the rights of man had to be recognized as a necessary preliminary to the adoption of a Constitution; but, in accordance with the American precedent, freedom and security had to be preserved as well as won, and so Paine regarded a written constitution as the first and essential means of limiting the powers and functions of government.

'A constitution is not a thing in name only, but in fact. It has not an ideal, but a real existence; and wherever it cannot be produced in a visible form, there is none. A constitution is a thing *antecedent* to a government, and a government is only the creature of a

A. Roots of liberalism: the eighteenth century

constitution. The constitution of a country is not the act of its government, but of the people constituting a government.' [89]

By such reasoning Paine was led to deny that a Constitution existed in Great Britain; and he regarded the Bill of Rights, that charter of English liberties, as an assumption by the 1689 Parliament of the right of 'binding and controlling posterity to the end of time.' [90]

Paine's influence as a political thinker and propagandist reached two peaks, in 1776 in the American Colonies and in 1791–92 in Great Britain following the publication of both parts of *The Rights of Man*. By the time of the *Dissertation on First Principles* his effective influence was declining. There were several reasons for this. The years of political repression in Great Britain during the long war with France had by then already begun; and with the publication of *The Age of Reason* between 1794 and 1796 Paine became associated with atheism. After his return to the United States in 1802 his reputation suffered a further decline there. This was due in part to his reputation as a free-thinker. By the early years of the nineteenth century, the political situation in the United States was very different from that which Paine had utilized so ably in 1776. Then he had skilfully and openly formulated ideas and arguments which many Americans had probably thought about but had not yet put into words. By 1802 his political idealism was out of place in the practical politics of the American republic.

5. Freedom through the general will: introduction
(Documents 8a–e, pp. 200–5)

Throughout his life Jean-Jacques Rousseau, citizen of Geneva, found difficulty in deciding where he belonged, or where he wanted to belong. Although he resided in France, and particularly in Paris, for many years and his literary reputation was established there, he was never fully assimilated as a Frenchman. From the time of his arrival in Paris in the early 1740s onwards, there was a life-long conflict between his marked, and even fierce individualism and his innermost desire to belong, to be accepted by the aristocratic and literary world of Paris. Yet he knew only too well that the world of social privilege could never satisfy his desire to associate on a footing of equality with men and women who would be honest, open and sincere in their dealings with one another.

126

Freedom through the general will: introduction

For all that, Rousseau's political and social ideas must be considered in the context of eighteenth-century France, its government, society and culure, as well as in that of the eighteenth-century Enlightenment. For Rousseau is at one and the same time a part of the Enlightenment and a critic of some of the most cherished assumptions of the *philosophes*. The extent to which his political and social ideas are considered in their contemporary context is very relevant to whether or not Rousseau is regarded as being within the main stream of individualist and liberal thought, or whether the trend of his thought is so noticeably collectivist that he is more rightly regarded as a forerunner of totalitarianism.[91] In attempting to discuss the problem of the relationship between the individual and the community, Rousseau was offering an original approach rather than following on from his individualist predecessors. However, the contradictions in Rousseau's own life find a place in his literary work in the form of an ambivalence between the individualist and the collectivist image.

It has been suggested that the best way of understanding Rousseau's *Social Contract* is 'to contrast its doctrine with the attitudes prevailing at the time it was written, of which one of the most fundamental was that some men must in the nature of things take care of others, that some had the right to govern and others the duty to obey.'[92] But is it sufficient to study the *Social Contract* alone for this purpose? In view of Rousseau's repeated insistence on the unity in his whole literary work, the answer must be in the negative. On the basis of a study of all Rousseau's political writings,[93] C. E. Vaughan found two strands in Rousseau's thought: an individualist strand stemming from Locke and a collectivist strand arising from Rousseau's emphasis on the sovereignty of the State. According to this view, Rousseau does not reconcile these two strands in his thought; he only passes from the former to the latter.[94] Vaughan therefore concludes that Rousseau is 'a collectivist heart and soul'; and, 'so far from being the charter of individualism, the *Contrat social* is a defiant statement of the collectivist ideal'.[95] More recent studies of Rousseau's political and social thought have been based not only on his political writings but also on either the *Discourse on Arts and Sciences* (1750) or the two novels, *La Nouvelle Héloïse* (1761) and *Emile* (1762).[96] To a very large extent, the crux of the problem as to whether Rousseau should be regarded as an individualist or as a collectivist concerns his concept of the general will. In the former case, the general will can be seen as a development of Locke's concept of the freedom of the individual in civil society; but in the latter, the individual will be absorbed into the community to such an extent through the general will that he becomes subject to an all-powerful State.

Rousseau was well acquainted with Locke's political philosophy and also with the French *philosophes'* understanding of Natural Law. The two introductory paragraphs with which the *Social Contract* opens indicate clearly his own intellectual antecedents and his commitment to the

127

freedom of the individual on account of his being a citizen of Geneva who can exercise his vote in the sovereign body of that city (doc. 8*a*). The purpose of Rousseau's inquiry is to establish whether 'a legitimate and stable basis of Government' in civil society can be found by 'considering human beings as they are and laws as they might be'. Then follows what appears to be a clarion and revolutionary call to ordinary men, to all those who form 'the people' and suffer most from the inequality and misery that civilization has brought about: 'Man is born free, and everywhere he is in chains' (doc. 8*a*). The call, however, is less revolutionary than it appears, because Rousseau is not concerned with removing the bonds (the 'chains') of society, but only with seeing how they can be made more legitimate. For men were once led by their needs to agree of their own free will, that is, by convention, to leave the state of nature and enter civil society and so form a people (doc. 8*a*). This was the origin of the social compact. Rousseau does not think of it as a historical event; he regards it as no more than 'a supposition, or assumption, whose function was to justify the existence of government'.[97] Now, although Rousseau accepts the long-standing idea of the social compact between men in order to form civil society, he does not admit that a contract of government is also involved. Even so, according to a new element Rousseau introduces into the social contract theory, man only becomes a moral being with the formation of the social contract: for natural man was only capable of natural (i.e. non-moral) virtue (*bonté naturelle*) which is distinct from the moral virtue (*vertu*) of man in society. Further, when the social contract was formed, man was not only free and naturally good; he was also happy and naturally equal. From this premise comes Rousseau's 'one great principle': 'that nature made men happy and good, but that society depraves him and makes him miserable'. [98] All man's misery and all the inequalities in civil society originated because those who became stronger and wealthier took advantage of the weaker and poorer and enslaved them; and their enslavement became more onerous as civilization advanced and with it greater inequality. At bottom it is the problem of moral freedom, of morality in social life, with which Rousseau is so concerned: 'to deprive man of his free will is to deprive his actions of all moral sanction', he wrote.[99] Further, moral freedom, 'which alone makes a man his own master', is one of the benefits conferred by citizenship.[100] As existing society is evil, Rousseau is in part concerned with moral regeneration in the *Social Contract*; for happiness, which Rousseau accepts as man's right, is inseparable from moral rectitude.

Civil society came into being, then, as the result of 'an agreement reached between individuals'; and that agreement was the foundation of legitimate authority.[101] Since in the state of nature man had enjoyed natural liberty and had relied on his own strength for his self-preservation, how could a man agree to limit his own power and his own freedom

without injuring both his liberty and his security? Rousseau answers this
question by saying that the association which is formed must ensure that
'the whole strength of the community will be enlisted for the protection of
the person and property of each constituent member, in such a way that
each, when united to his fellows, renders obedience to his own will, and
remains as free as he was before'. According to Rousseau, the social contract fulfils this condition because its terms are the same for all. Each
member agrees to the complete alienation of all his rights to the community; but at the same time the rights each thereby acquires are equal to
those surrendered to others, and the power of the community to preserve
those rights is greater than that of each individual on his own (doc. 8a).

This argument raises several problems of interpretation. Rousseau, as
we have already seen, holds that man only becomes a moral being after
the formation of the social contract; and in that case he could not enjoy
any rights while in the state of nature. Yet Rousseau now seems to be
suggesting that man did enjoy rights before he agreed to the social
contract; so it would appear that Rousseau is recognising, at least by
implication, the existence of Natural Law.

Rousseau regarded the institution of private property as the
principal cause of inequality, and consequently of the wickedness
of society and civilization.

In a state of nature men enjoyed natural equality; but when
they entered civil society they exchanged that natural equality
for 'a moral and legal equality'. On account of inequality in bodily
strength, intellect, merit or capacity, it would necessarily follow
that men in society could not be equal in wealth or property.[102] Rousseau
never for one moment believed in equality of wealth and property; but his
ideal society was that of an agrarian and peasant community of small
landowners, such as could be found in the Swiss cantons or in Corsica in
the eighteenth century, where there would be no great inequalities in
wealth and property. Such men would be the citizens of Rousseau's ideal
state, where equality under the law would mean the equal dependence of
each individual on every other member of the community and equal
dependence would safeguard equal freedom.

In Rousseau's community, once it is formed by unanimous agreement,
each individual forms an indivisible part of the whole body politic. 'A
moral and collective body' of all the consenting individuals thus comes
into existence and remains in existence as long as the general will is
recognized. This body is variously called the republic, the body politic, or
the sovereign people. Rousseau then denies the existence of any fundamental law because no natural or positive laws could limit
sovereignty.[103] The outcome of Rousseau's concept is that 'the specific
rights and duties of the individual are determined not by the terms of the
social contract itself, but by the continuing moral consensus of the individuals who are parties to it'.[104] This 'continuing moral consensus' is

the general will; and so the question arises whether or not the idea of the general will 'forms the porch to a collectivism as absolute as the mind of man has ever conceived'.[105]

A noticeable feature of most European countries in the eighteenth century was the lack of a real sense of community. Not only royal absolutism but also the existence of privileged estates prevented the growth of a feeling of unity, a recognition that all the inhabitants of a country formed a people or a nation and identified themselves with the life of that country. Rousseau offered a solution to this problem of identifying the people with the State by making the people sovereign. Through associating the term sovereign with 'the people', Rousseau gives it a new meaning. Traditionally it was associated with the monarch as the head of the body politic; but once the people and the sovereign are one and the same, no contract of government can exist because self-government needs no contract. As members of the sovereign people, men are citizens when they are actively engaged in seeking the general will in the interests of upholding equality; but they 'owe obedience' to the government which they appoint to administer the laws of the State.[106] No contradiction will arise, says Rousseau, because the duty of the citizen will be the same as what each desires to do.

Through their identification with each other, the sovereign people and each citizen assume reciprocal duties towards each other. Further, 'the Sovereign People, having no existence outside that of the individuals who compose it, has, and can have no interest at variance with theirs'.[107] That being so, Rousseau saw no need for the social contract to be limited by any fundamental or constitutional laws in order to secure the rights of each citizen. The sovereign will always fulfil its duty and never injure the people as a whole or even a single individual; but the individual citizen may not always 'observe his duty to the sovereign.'[108] This statement leads directly to one of the most controversial of Rousseau's ideas. Each individual has a particular will concerning his personal interest which may or may not be identical with the general will, and so with the interest of the people as a whole. Therefore, unless the social contract is to be only a 'vain formula', it must include one essential undertaking: 'that whoever shall refuse to obey the general will must be constrained by the whole body of his fellow citizens to do so: which is no more than to say that it may be necessary to compel a man to be free'.[109]

Rousseau's use of the phrase 'to compel a man to be free' is one of the main arguments used by those who detect some of the origins of totalitarian democracy in his political philosophy.[110] On the other hand, those who emphasize Rousseau's concern with individual freedom suggest that an explanation of the phrase is to be found in the continuous moral responsibility and moral participation of each citizen in the political life of the community. And so, 'when Rouseau says that it is only in accordance with the general will that men can be forced to be free, he is maintaining the essentially individualist proposition that a man can only be bound by decisions with which he himself is in moral agreement'.[111] In the light of conditions in eighteenth-century France, and as a more practical explanation of Rousseau's phrase 'to compel a man to be free', it has also been suggested that as the general will can only be enforced through the law, the moral force of society should be used to ensure that all citizens are equally obliged to obey the law which in itself applies equally to all citizens.[112]

The general will, the collective will of the people, has always as its objective the securing of the common interest and the common good of the people as a whole. It must always retain its freedom of action; and it cannot be bound for the future, even to maintain a Constitution unchanged. As sovereignty is inalienable and indivisible, neither the sovereign people nor its collective will can be divided or represented (docs 8b and 8c). It follows then that Rousseau does not accept a separation of powers between the legislature and the executive as two separate parts of the sovereign. Instead he makes a clear distinction between the functions of an assembly of the people and those of a government as different manifestations of the sovereign. The people will meet in assembly to express the general will, that is, to show their sense of community concerning the interests and well-being of all the people collectively; but Rousseau does not envisage that the sovereign people would meet very frequently in order to legislate, because very few laws would be needed as long as the general interest of the community prevailed. The government, on the other hand, is concerned with the application of the general laws, and is subordinate to the sovereign in so far as the sovereign people have entrusted it with power, though the power of governing can be withdrawn by the people at any time if their trust is abused. Government may be placed in the hands of one person, or, as Rousseau thought preferable, entrusted to an elected 'aristocracy'.[113]

When Rousseau is speaking in abstractions, as in the sections of the Social Contract concerning the general will and sovereignty, it is essential to look for the spirit behind his ideas rather than to attempt to interpret them too literally. He is concerned here with finding a means of ensuring that the interests of the community and the interest of each individual are equally secured. He emphasizes that the general will is always right and will always tend to the public advantage, that is, towards securing justice and civil equality, though this is not true of the particular wills of the individual citizens. They inevitably tend towards inequality (doc. 8d). Except in the case of the original social contract, the general will need not be unanimous. Sometimes a majority will be sufficient.[114] Yet the general will is in effect unanimous because every individual who at any given moment gives pride of place to his own interest, and not to that of the community as a whole, is really desirous of acting in accordance with the general will. In this way the consent of an individual may be tacitly acknowledged, even though he appears to be forming part of a minority. Rousseau seems to be suggesting that the minority will always accept the decision of the majority as long as that minority still regards itself as belonging to the same people. Such an interpretation could suggest that Rousseau's argument comes down to nothing more than the practice of constitutionalism, and does not give rise to an incipient totalitarianism. As for the majority, according to Rousseau, it can only be identified with the general will when the will of the majority is in keeping with the true and lasting interests of society as a whole.

The real danger to the general will and the common good lies in the formation of groups and associations. Here Rousseau seems to have in mind the ancient French *parlements*, guilds and corporations which sought to maintain their own privileges and achieve their own ends and advantage instead of seeking the interest of France as a whole. Rousseau's objections to the existence of groups and associations seeking their own ends and advantage are closely connected with his contention that the general will cannot be represented.[115] A reason for his objections may be found in eighteenth-century political practice. Many Englishmen only enjoyed 'virtual representation' (to use Edmund Burke's phrase) in the House of Commons, and Members of Parliament were in no way bound by their constituents. As for the 'estates', which had survived from mediæval times in certain European States, election and representation (whether direct or virtual) were not necessarily the practice in those bodies. Further, a balance of interests and an exchange of views were not part of the political outlook of eighteenth-century Europe. The need was for unity, in contrast to the privileges of the few which marked them off from the many.

As the sovereign and the law are concerned only with the community as a whole what, if anything, does Rousseau say about securing the rights of the individual against the community or State? If the general will always operates for the common good and the citizen in his capacity of subject necessarily owes certain duties to the State at its command, and if at the same time the citizen as an individual does enjoy certain rights, how can both be equally satisfied? If they cannot, must the individual's duties to the State be rendered at the expense of his own rights? Rousseau has far from answered these questions to the satisfaction of all inquirers. He says that each individual alienates to the community just as much of his property and his liberty as will be necessary for the well-being of the community; but it is left to the community to determine what that amount will be. It should be *no more* than the well-being of the community necessitates; and a heavier burden must not be put on one individual than on another because the very essence of the general will is equality before the law.[116] In contrast to this ideal balance between the individual and the community, it has always been man's experience, ever since he entered civil society, that the private interests of both individuals and groups will increasingly prevail over the general interest. Corruption and inequalities will therefore result. Although these undesirable features of society may grow stronger, Rousseau says that the general will is not thereby destroyed; for it is indestructible unless a society is dissolved (doc. 8e). The general will can be disregarded, and then it no longer defends the people from their own destructive impulses or from anarchy or usurpation. In other words, government becomes the agent of inequality and destruction; and the process is inevitable unless means can be found to check it.

The people always desire their own good, but they are easily led away by individual and group interests. Hence they need guidance so that they will recognize the real interests of the community itself and of the individuals who form that community. They need to be led or persuaded through reason, so that each individual becomes community-conscious and identifies his own best interests with those of the community as a whole. This is the particular task of an 'extraordinary figure', whom Rousseau calls the Legislator, in the period of time when the social contract has been made, but the community has not yet adopted any settled law. [117] Rousseau does not believe, however, that the institutions established by the Legislator will continue without becoming corrupt, or that the people will continue of their own accord to follow the law he has given them. Men will still succumb to putting their own interests before those of the community, and inequality will be the result even to the extent of one man proclaiming rule over his fellow citizens.

Few places existed where Rousseau thought an attempt could be made to establish government on the basis of the 'principles of political right' laid down in the Social Contract. The old nations of Europe were too bound by tradition, bad government, private and group interests. The existing States were also too large. As his ideal society was a small, uncorrupted, agrarian people among whom there were no great extremes of wealth or poverty, Corsica alone seemed to fulfil the conditions before it was taken over by France in 1768. Even Geneva, which with Sparta had provided the model for Rousseau's ideal State, was too old and tradition bound; and yet the city-state was the only possible type of State where all the people could meet together in their capacity as citizens, renew their community spirit, and directly elect a government. An elected and 'aristocratic' government, on the Genevan pattern, alone merited Rousseau's approval, seeing that he believed true democracy was suited only to gods. [118] Here Rousseau is giving to democracy and aristocracy meanings which would not have been generally accepted in his own day. The type of government which Rousseau describes as best fulfilling the conditions for legitimate government would have been called democracy by his contemporaries, and democratic representative government in the nineteenth century. If Rousseau's definition of an ideal government is interpreted literally, then it may be said: 'His whole system tended to

133

A. Roots of liberalism: the eighteenth century

imprison man in a small virtuous city, theocratic, poor and with plain, simple needs.' [119]

Although the ideal State, based on the 'principles of political right', was unlikely to be achieved, or, if it was ever achieved, was unlikely to remain uncorrupted, Rousseau thought that it could still be used as a standard for judging existing States. A society in which individual freedom and equality were reconciled would be a society where:

'in the first place, every man is entitled to take part in making decisions which all are required to obey; where, secondly, the persons who make these decisions do so as individual citizens and not as members of organized groups smaller than the State; where, thirdly, citizens make the laws themselves and do not elect representatives to do so for them; and where, fourthly and lastly, the body that makes the laws does *not* administer them.' [120]

During the nineteenth century, liberals found themselves repeatedly and increasingly facing the problem of reconciling individual freedom and authority; but Rousseau did not give them much guidance because he did not recognize that authority, even when exercised legitimately, would limit individual freedom. Further, by concerning himself with reconciling the individual and the community to each other, Rousseau seemed to show little interest in the development of individuality. His concern with the creation and development of the collective self, and his argument that the individual only finds his true self and will in the general will, stands in sharp contrast to the emphasis placed by two nineteenth-century liberals, Wilhelm von Humboldt and John Stuart Mill, on the full development of the individual (see pp. 271–8).

C. E. Vaughan, writing in 1915, concluded that Rousseau's collectivism was so strong as to outweigh his individualism. [121] In considering this judgement we need to bear in mind that in the early years of the present century collectivism and the power of the State over the individual were still regarded by some liberals as being quite alien to their liberal creed. Since then a degree of collectivism and a recognition that the State must make increasing demands on the individual have found a place in the political and social precepts of liberalism; and as a result liberals have come to accept a far greater degree of State authority over the individual. In the light of such a change in liberalism itself, it is possible to reconcile the collectivist and individualist strands in Rousseau's political and social thought without regarding him as an apostle of totalitarianism. Rousseau saw society as the destroyer of man's happiness, innocence and natural equality: but, paradoxically, society, based on the 'principles of political right', might yet be the means of reform and salvation. In the late nineteenth century and during the twentieth century, an ever increasing number of liberals came to believe that it was the role and function of the State, that is, of the community, to reduce inequality and, at the same time, increase every man's happiness and well-being.

---

6. Natural law and the economy – the doctrine of *laissez faire*: introduction
(Documents 9–11, pp. 205–27)

(i) Turgot: The harmony between the economic interests of the individual and those of society .

Two widely held beliefs in the eighteenth century, that man was a 'rational' creature and that he was also 'naturally good', were part of a general concept of a harmonious natural order. If civil society was formed and operated in accordance with the laws of nature, and the rights of man were thereby secured, and if man himself was directed by reason, not only government but also the economy could be guided by natural law and positive law be kept to a minimum. In the same way as natural law and reason brought the individual and civil society into harmony with each other, and enabled each individual to use his faculties to their fullest extent, so too man's economic activity could bring about a natural harmony between the good of the individual and that of the society in which he lived. The harmonious natural order was first of all determined and then regulated by reason itself – or by nature, providence, 'the invisible hand', the 'Author of Nature', the 'all-wise Being' (to name but a few of the euphemisms for God used by eighteenth-century deists).

Although belief in the pre-ordained and uninterrupted progress of man arose in the main from reason – that is, from the acceptance of self-evident truths – it was also an outcome of experience and observation. In economic thought, optimism was as much a characteristic of a pure theorist such as François Quesnay (1694–1774), the founder of the French physiocratic school, as it was of the more empirical French physiocrat Turgot and of the even more pragmatic Adam Smith, the greatest of the eighteenth-century economists. At the same time, reason, coupled with a greater or lesser degree of observation, led Turgot and Adam Smith in particular to test the economic conditions and practices of their own day and to find them wanting. The physiocrats in France and Adam Smith in England were thus led to urge the removal of the restraints which prevented the harmonizing of the interests of the individual and those of society for their mutual benefit. Hence the phrase *laissez faire, laissez passer* was coined as a cry for the removal of government and feudal restraints on the right of each individual to produce, to buy and sell and so trade freely within the whole community.[122]

In the same way as a political society which was guided by natural law would need little positive law, so an economy operating under conditions of perfect freedom would be self-regulating and little or no government interference or regulation would be necessary. The practical outcome of such a belief was that demands for freedom of labour, enterprise and trade became direct attacks on long-established systems of governmental economic control, particularly on mercantilism or the navigation system in England and Colbertism in France. In the case of the former, emphasis had been placed on securing a favourable balance of exports over imports, particularly of manufactures, and trade was directed into certain channels for the purpose of maintaining and expanding the British carrying trade. In France, the granting of monopolies and the continued existence of the guild system prevented freedom of labour; and the artificial encouragement of certain industries in the system introduced by Colbert in the latter part of the seventeenth century under Louis XIV was carried out at the expense of maintaining a wasteful and stagnant feudal structure of agriculture. The economic situations and therefore the economic needs of Britain and France were by no means identical. The domestic system of industry had developed further and was more widespread in England than it was in France; and the contribution made by external trade to the wealth of Great Britain was also greater than in the case of France. There the essential needs were a less wasteful and more productive system of land holding and land usage, and the removal of internal barriers against freedom of trade, freedom of labour and enterprise. Indeed, the French physiocrats wanted to bring French agriculture nearer to the pattern of agriculture in England. Yet there was a sufficiently common basis in the existence of a regulated economic system in both countries, and also in the intellectual climate, for some similarities in the ideas of the French physiocrats and in those of Adam Smith. On this and other grounds, the old contention, that Adam Smith was directly influenced by physiocratic ideas, as a result of the months he spent in Paris in 1765–66, is now rejected.

Both the physiocrats and Adam Smith refuted the long-standing mercantilist view that a country's wealth was marked by an accumulation of bullion. In France, a predominantly agricultural country, even more so than Britain in the eighteenth century, François Quesnay and his disciples regarded land as the sole source of a country's wealth. They believed that land alone produced a 'net product', that is, a surplus or rent, which formed the net income of the nation, and therefore land alone should bear the sole tax. This basic idea led Quesnay to divide men into three classes: first, the proprietors who received the 'net product' and also invested in permanent improvements, such as drainage; secondly, the cultivators of the soil who formed a 'productive' class; and, thirdly, those who were engaged in other pursuits, such as trade and industry, and formed an 'unproductive' or 'sterile' class. From this distinction between the 'productive' and the 'sterile' class Quesnay moved towards the much more valuable theory of the circular flow of wealth. According to Quesnay's *Tableau économique* (1758), this was both self-regulating and self-perpetuating; but it could operate only in conditions of economic freedom. As far as government was concerned, Quesnay and his disciples favoured a form of monarchical but 'legal' despotism. They believed that one of the objects of the State was to maintain order and so guarantee liberty and property.

One of the most notable and influential physiocrats who differed from Quesnay in some respects was Vincent de Gournay, a businessman who became Intendant of Commerce in the 1750s. Gournay is mainly remembered because it was through his business and administrative experience that he exercised an important influence on Turgot (1727–81) before he became Intendant of the *généralité* of Limoges from 1761 to 1774. [123] It was Gournay's ideas that Turgot purported to express in his *Eloge de Gournay*, written in 1759 shortly after Gournay's death; but incidentally it is an expression of Turgot's ideas as much as Gournay's (doc. 9).

The basic tenets shared by Gournay and Turgot were, first, that freedom of labour was essential; secondly, there must be freedom of trade; and, thirdly, the wealth of the State would be increased through a greater rate of industrial production in addition to improved returns from agriculture. In order to realize these beliefs, it was essential that labour should be freed from the restrictions of the guild system and from other government regulations favouring certain industries at the expense of others; land must be freed from feudal conditions of land tenure and wasteful methods of agriculture; and trade, particularly internal trade, must be freed from government regulations and control. In so far as Gournay and Turgot accepted manufactures as being 'a real addition to the mass of wealth of the State', they were departing from the strict physiocratic belief that the real wealth of the State was found solely in the land (doc. 9). This divergence in turn led Turgot to make a slight modification to Quesnay's definition of 'productive' and 'sterile' labour. He preferred to call the artisan class a stipendiary rather than an unproductive or sterile class. [124]

Where agriculture was concerned, Turgot was interested in the development of farming as a large-scale enterprise, as was increasingly becoming the case in eighteenth-century England, in contrast to the fragmentation of agriculture in France. He particularly wanted to see an increase in the 'net product' which derived from land. Capital accumulation could then be used for the improvement of land holdings and for investment in industry and commerce. Hence Turgot could describe the economy he envisaged as 'agriculture animated by commerce', because the latter played and would play an increasingly important role in the circular flow of wealth.[125] Moreover, the economy would be self-regulating: 'The price of food, the nation's wealth, the price of labour, the growth of population are all linked together; they establish themselves in equilibrium according to a natural process of adjustment; and this adjustment is always made when commerce and competition are entirely free.'[126] At the same time both Gournay and Turgot gave some thought to the well-being of the poor because existing conditions in agriculture and industry favoured the rich.[127] Humanitarianism was thus one of the motives behind the edicts of 1776, issued under Turgot as Controller General, which freed the corn trade, and abolished the guilds and the corvée.[128]

At the heart of the physiocratic and *laissez faire* doctrine is the belief that every man knows his own interest better than any other man or the State can know it. The first principle therefore was 'to let things go precisely as they would have gone of themselves, by the simple action of men's interests, influenced by the balance of a free competition' (doc. 10). In a self-regulating economy, the duty of the government would be no more than to protect every man's natural liberty to produce, buy and sell as he pleases. The functions of the State would thus be limited to justice and security. As free competition will not deliberately hurt anyone, there is no need for government regulations to safeguard either the producer or the consumer (docs 9 and 10). Above all Turgot believed that two freedoms were essential in France. The first of these was the establishment of free trade in corn through the removal of internal tariffs and other government restrictions on the transport of corn. As a result of free trade in corn, so Turgot argued, there would be a levelling out of corn prices and, as a result, no rise in the average price of corn.[129] Further, the wider and surer market in corn that free trade would offer to producers was seen by Turgot as a means of improving the yields of French harvests. More large landowners would be willing to invest in capital improvements, and smaller landowners and the *métayers* would be encouraged to improve their holdings and increase their yields. Turgot's ultimate hope was that *métayage* would give way to the English system of tenant farming and disappear altogether.[130]

The second essential freedom was that of labour. As Turgot recognized that manufactures added to 'the mass of wealth of the State', he believed that the guild system and monopolies must be abolished. In his statements on freedom of labour Turgot may be described as holding a middle place between John Locke, who at the end of the seventeenth century maintained that man had a property in his labour, and Louis Blanc in the 1830s and 1840s who demanded not only that man should have freedom in his choice of occupation but also that he had a right to have work provided for him. Turgot claims that it is the sovereign's duty to protect a man's freedom to work; and, according to the edict abolishing the guilds, that protection is owed especially 'to that class of men who, possessing nothing but their labour and industry, above all others have the need and right of employing to the limit of their capacity their sole resources for subsistence'.[131] In order to guarantee freedom of labour, the long-standing restrictions which prevented a man from plying any trade unless he was admitted to a trade guild had to be abolished; and it would follow that restrictions on the numbers practising a trade and the volume of output would be removed also. With more opportunities to practise a trade in France, the emigration of French artisans would be curbed.

With freedom of labour there had to be freedom to buy and sell. Freedom of manufacture and the free movement of manufactured goods were therefore the two main points stressed by Turgot in his letter of 24 December 1773 to the Abbé Terray, then Controller-General, concerning the brand on iron (*la marque des fers*) and the state of ironworks in the *généralité* of Limoges (doc. 10).

Turgot was convinced that once greater opportunities for work and trade in agriculture and industry were enjoyed by more individuals the connections between agriculture and manufactures, which he and other physiocrats saw in the circular flow of wealth, would result in an improvement in the well-being of the individuals concerned and of the country as a whole. This in turn would provide the means of overcoming France's economic weakness which was particularly noticeable in the state of the revenue. When Turgot was appointed Controller-General in August 1774 he laid down three maxims for the royal government to follow: no bankruptcy, no increase of taxes, and no further borrowing.[132] The physiocrats proposed instead the general incidence of a direct single tax on land, including that of the nobility who were exempt from most existing forms of taxation, because those who owned land alone enjoyed an accretion of wealth from what the land yielded.[133] When the *corvée* was abolished, Turgot therefore suggested that forced labour should be replaced by a direct tax on land, payable by all landowners, nobles and peasants alike, which would be assessed, collected and applied locally.[134] In the event Turgot's proposal of such a tax provoked sharp opposition from the court, the nobility, the magistracy and the Church. As a result he lost Louis XVI's favour and was dismissed by the king in May 1776.

According to the nineteenth-century French and English liberal point of view, Turgot was an early champion of liberalism.[135] This interpretation can only be upheld with regard to his belief in freedom of trade and labour and in a minimum of government interference in regulating trade, industry and agriculture. Apart from this, the reforms Turgot envisaged were to be instituted from above because he looked to an enlightened monarch as the agent of reform. He looked to a monarchy that would rule in the interests of the masses and harmonize the interests of the individual and those of the State. He believed in the necessity of maintaining authority in government, and, like other physiocrats, he upheld the continuation of a hierarchical society. Even so, Turgot thought that authority and order should only be exercised as far as was necessary. Governments were often too ready to sacrifice 'the happiness of individuals to certain pretended rights of society. They forget that society is made for individuals.' [136]

In addition to the physiocratic aspects of Turgot's thought there is an element of utility in his view of government and in the connection he saw between good government and the individual's enjoyment of happiness. He wrote:

'The interests of nations and the success of good government reduce themselves to a sacred respect for the liberty of persons and of labour, to the inviolable maintenance of the rights of property, to justice between all, from which conditions necessarily result a greater production of things useful to man, the increase of wealth, and of enjoyment, and of enlightenment and all the means of happiness.' [137]

That was the aspiration; but the reality in France in the 1770s was very different.

(ii) Adam Smith: 'The Wealth of Nations'

Although Adam Smith (1723–90) was not a public man of affairs, he showed a greater propensity than Turgot to allow experience and observation to modify the *a priori* foundations of his thought.

In common with the Scottish intellectuals of his day, he believed in God as a beneficent power, as an 'invisible hand', guiding men towards an order of liberty which would be for their own good both as individuals and as societies. It was a deistic belief, however, rather than a reflection of the religious non-conformism which had been a feature of the commercial and manufacturing classes in England and Scotland before they began to identify themselves too closely with the landed gentry. Providence, according to Adam Smith in *The Theory of Moral Sentiments* (1759), led men to recognize certain qualities or 'sympathies' as a moral basis for seeking their own improvement. [138] From this it followed that men, in striving to enhance their own greater happiness, would incidentally promote that of others. Several writers on Adam Smith have contended, while others have refuted the assertion, that there is an essential difference between the 'sympathies' which led men to seek the betterment of their own condition, and so gain the approval of others, and the 'self-interest' which in *The Wealth of Nations* Smith saw as the guiding force of 'economic man'. [139] Be that as it may, there is a close intellectual link between Smith's two major works.

In the intervening years, from 1759 to 1776, Smith's life passed through varied experiences which are reflected in *The Wealth of Nations* in addition to his vast reading. During that time he was brought into close contact with enterprising merchants in Glasgow and more briefly with members of the government in London. The illustrations and examples he uses in *The Wealth of Nations* give evidence of his wide knowledge of the well-developed domestic system of industry in England. He was also in a position to compare the economic system in England with that which he had observed in France during his visits to that country in the 1760s; and he could consider the English system of trade and industry in relation to what he knew of the ideas of the physiocrats which reflected the less industrial and commercial economy of France. It has been said that 'Smith's theory of the natural economic order differed from that of the physiocrats in being less a theory of an ideal order to be achieved by a rational plan of reform than a theory of an existing order among economic events. *The Wealth of Nations* is a descriptive and explanatory treatise. . . .'[140]

Adam Smith begins *The Wealth of Nations* with two statements that provide the essential key to all that follows:

'The greatest improvement in the productive powers of labour, and the greater part of the skill, dexterity, and judgement with which it is any where directed, or applied, seem to have been the effects of the division of labour. . . .
This division of labour, from which so many advantages are derived, is not originally the effect of any human wisdom, which foresees and intends that general opulence to which it gives occasion. It is the necessary, though very slow and gradual, consequence of a certain propensity in human nature which has in view no such extensive utility; the propensity to truck, barter, and exchange one thing for another. . . .'[141]

From these premises it followed that labour and not land, as the physiocrats believed, was the source of all wealth because man's progress always had been and still would be inescapably based on the further extension of the division of labour. However, 'as it is the power of exchanging that gives occasion to the division of labour, so the extent of this division must always be limited by the extent of that power, or in other words, by the extent of the market.'[142]

From that premise Smith was led to condemn all the policies by which governments in Britain and Europe prevented perfect liberty. He therefore eliminated from the scope of government activity the regulation of trade for the purpose of encouraging exports over imports in order to produce a favourable balance of trade; the forced encouragement of certain industries at the expense of others, or at the expense of agriculture; the granting of exclusive privileges to certain trading companies and also to guilds which restricted the numbers of workmen plying a certain trade; and the passing of legislation restricting the numbers of apprentices or the movement of labour from one village or town to another. To use two very convenient, if misleading rather than specific terms, Adam Smith was denouncing the systems of mercantilism and Colbertism, and also the English laws of settlement and apprenticeship although they were no longer being strictly enforced in the eighteenth century. In agriculture, manufacturing and commerce, Adam Smith saw free competition as the essential basis of a self-regulating economy, of 'a system of natural liberty'. In this he and Turgot were in agreement; but Smith differed in emphasis from most of the physiocrats by being as much concerned with the practice of free competition in manufacturing as in trade and agriculture. Neither did Smith believe, as the physiocrats did with the partial exceptions of Gournay and Turgot, that the source of wealth was only to be found in land, that is, in the annual 'net product'.

Of all the aspects of political economy examined and discussed by Smith in *The Wealth of Nations*, four seem to have had most relevance to the development of economic liberalism and so have exercised most influence. All four are essential aspects of Smith's view of a self-regulating 'system of natural liberty'. First, where there is free competition, Smith tells us, both price and supply will be self-regulating towards the equilibrium of a 'natural price' (doc. 11*a*). Where there is no government interference in the form of regulations and no monopolies exist, the market price of commodities will tend, through the operation of supply and demand, to find their level very close to the natural price: the natural price being a price sufficient 'to pay the rent of the land, the wages of the labour, and the profits of the stock employed in raising, preparing and bringing [that commodity] to market'.[143] Fluctuations in the market price of a commodity, which may arise for various reasons, will have most effect on wages and profit. For example, poor harvests could for a long time keep market prices well above the natural price; but once a good harvest occurs the market price will tend once more to find a level close to the natural price. The natural price is therefore the price arising from the free competition of supply and demand. It contrasts with a market price which is kept well above the natural price through the existence of monopolies and restrictions on the numbers practising a trade or occupation, because such privileges and regulations are designed to restrict both production and competition.

Secondly, Smith maintains that a self-regulating tendency also operates between land and manufactures where there is free competition (doc. 11*b*). Here his argument is more in line with the physiocratic concepts of the circular flow of wealth and of land as the source of wealth. The 'real rent of land', that is, the returns to the landowner, can increase directly from the land itself through improvements, better methods of cultivation, higher prices for cattle and so on, or the rise in rent can come through further extensions of the division of labour, such as when the real price of manufactures is reduced through increasing specialization, technical improvements and the investment of more capital. In following this line of argument, Smith is basically accepting the physiocratic argument that land always receives the increase in wealth, provided both agriculture and manufacturing are maintained and expanded by free competition; but, because labour and not land is the source of wealth, both agriculture and manufactures can contribute to increases 'in the real wealth of the society'. Smith is thus led to discard the physiocratic division of society into productive, sterile (stipendiary) and disposable classes. As the annual product of land and labour naturally divides itself into three parts, that is, into 'the rent of land, the wages of labour and the profits of stock', so there are 'three great, original and constituent orders of every civilized society' made up of those who live by rent (landowners), those who live by wages, and those who live by profit. [144]

Following on from Smith's claim that any increase in real wealth, no matter what its source, raises directly or indirectly the rent of land, is his assertion that only the landowners can promote the interests of society as a whole through looking after their own interests. Unfortunately, so Smith tells us, they do not always know how to promote and look after their own interests effectively. [145] As for the labourers, they are the first to be affected adversely when the real wealth of the nation as a whole is no longer increasing; and, indeed, even when it is growing, the landowners benefit most. Even more so than the landowners, the labourers are not aware of their own interest, and it is their state of ignorance which prevents them from knowing where their interest lies. [146] Smith's picture of the labourer in *The Wealth of Nations* is more realistic than the one he had given in *The Theory of Moral Sentiments*. In the earlier book, Adam Smith's optimistic faith had led him to suggest that there was no real difference in the degree of happiness enjoyed by the rich and the poor. Furthermore, he had then asserted that inequality in the distribution of worldly goods was used by nature for her purpose. Those who were wealthy were 'led by an invisible hand' to advance the interests of society in general. [147] It is necessary to bear in mind, however, that such an idyllic outcome could only be a reality if two conditions operated; first, that the sole aim was not the acquisition of private wealth, because the accumulation of private wealth was not identical with adding to the aggregate wealth of the nation; and, secondly, that a state of perfect freedom, competition and just dealing must be in existence. In those conditions, and even though self-interest and not beneficence was the motivating force, there could still be a natural harmony between the interests of the individual and those of society. [148]

Society, however, as Smith had observed it in Britain and in France, did not fulfil those conditions. He could see, for example, that the division of labour could have stultifying and degrading effects on the intellectual development of the labourers, and therefore it was only just that facilities for their education should be provided by the state. [149] He was sympathetic towards the labourers' uncertain economic position; but because they were politically unaware they could be used on occasions by the landowners in the latter's own interests. Such remarks seem to im-

A. Roots of liberalism: the eighteenth century

ply that despite Smith's contention that the landowners' interests were identified with those of the nation, in practice their 'particular interests' might not always be identical with the interests of society as a whole. Certainly those who sought parliamentary reform in the latter part of the eighteenth and the early nineteenth centuries would have strongly denied that the landed classes, who then exercised political power, did anything more than look after their own interests. The growing manufacturing class increasingly claimed that its interests were being neglected by a 'landed' parliament; but that class, in its turn, was to claim by the mid-nineteenth century that the free trade and *laissez faire* policies, which by then were serving *its* interests, also served the interests of all other classes and the nation as a whole. By then, too, the manufacturers and merchants were making claims directly at variance with Smith's view that the third order of society, 'the employers of stock', had the least identity of interest with society in general. According to Smith, they developed a natural tendency towards monopoly, because their own particular interests (of which they showed far more acute awareness than the landowners of theirs) were centred on widening the market, and on obtaining a higher return of profit by ensuring that the demand was greater than the supply and that prices were higher than the natural price. According to Smith, the necessity for free competition was never more obvious than in this respect.[150]

This brings us to a third aspect of economic liberalism as treated by Adam Smith in *The Wealth of Nations*: that investment will also find its natural direction where there is free competition, and that generally it will tend towards domestic rather than foreign investment (doc. 11c). Smith placed investment in land and agriculture in the first place, followed by manufacturing, the home trade, the foreign trade of consumption and the carrying trade, in that order.[151] Wherever freedom of choice existed that order of preference would spontaneously and naturally arise. In illustrating this natural order, Smith shows that the effect of the higher risks involved in seeking greater profits in foreign trade and in the carrying trade is to direct the greater volume of trade and investment into the import-export trade of the merchant's home country, in addition to domestic manufacturing and commercial enterprises.[152] As self interest is at work here, there is no need for government regulations to stimulate investment in certain chosen trades. Smith also rejects the mercantilist emphasis on increasing exports so as to achieve a favourable balance of trade. Further, the division of labour tends towards the concentration of investment in those products and industries which are best suited to a country; and in addition the self-regulating process of supply and demand, which brings about a market price closest to the natural price, applies in the case of domestic and foreign products of the same commodity.[153] Smith insists on the superiority of domestic trade over foreign trade because to him foreign trade and the exchange of manufactured goods for luxury goods and exotic products is not the most vital form of trade; rather it is the trade which is complementary between town and country. [154]

The fourth aspect of Smith's economic liberalism again concerns the motive of self interest. Behind the operation of self interest and the best utilization of resources, Adam Smith always saw 'the invisible hand' that guided the interests of the individual in consonance with the interests of society as a whole wherever a 'system of natural liberty' existed (doc. 11*d*). Yet Smith sometimes admitted that men do not always act in accordance with 'harmonious nature'. Such is the case, for example, with the 'employers of capital' who always tend towards monopolies. Granted this, and granted also that men are motivated by self interest rather than benevolence and are unconscious that they are directly contributing to the 'harmonious order of nature', it it still essential that their actions should be the result of free choice and freedom of enterprise. [155] As free competition can only operate in conditions of perfect freedom, the functions of government must be clearly limited.

The three areas of government, as defined by Adam Smith, correspond closely to the ideal of minimal government which was to be so dear to English liberals in the first half of the nineteenth century, and was still cherished by an anti-étatist such as Herbert Spencer in the later decades of the century (see p. 583). Smith laid down that the functions of government were limited, first, to providing for the security of the individual and the State; secondly, to protecting the individual from injustice and oppression through the administration of justice; and, thirdly, to the provision of public works and institutions which it would be unprofitable or undesirable for individuals to undertake; but he showed a willingness to admit that circumstances might necessitate an extension of government activity. In the case of the defence of the country, it might be necessary to continue to enforce the Navigation Acts; or, in order to safeguard the livelihood of as many of the inhabitants as possible, it might be wise to introduce the conditions of freedom gradually over a long period. [156] Finally, the emphasis on ethical as well as economic individualism is as strong in Smith as it is in Turgot, and this too was to remain an element in the thought of nineteenth-century English liberals such as John Stuart Mill.

7. The doctrine of the rights of man: introduction
(Documents 12–15, pp. 224–35)

The doctrine of the rights of man, as formally enunciated in the Declaration of Independence of 4 July 1776 by the thirteen British colonies in North America and in the Declaration of the Rights of Man and Citizen adopted by the French National Constituent Assembly on 27 August 1789, was the ultimate expression of ideas arising from the concepts of natural law, natural rights and the social contract. It also derived from concern with the problem of defining the purpose of political society and government and the nature of civil liberty. It marked the climax of the influence of one line of thought at the very time when another, that of utilitarianism, was beginning to take shape in the early writings of Jeremy Bentham.

The Declaration of Independence and the Declaration of the Rights of Man and Citizen fulfilled two distinct but related purposes. They looked backward critically pointing to specific conditions and practices to be rejected or destroyed but they also boldly looked forward indicating the general principles on which political society and government must rest in the future. A European heritage of ideas is common to both declarations, and the American example of following the Declaration of Independence with the institution of a limited, representative and constitutional form of government provided a model for the French National Constituent Assembly in 1789. Some historians, therefore, view the American and French revolutions as part of a much wider democratic, Western or Atlantic revolution of the eighteenth century.[157] Conversely, the common intellectual heritage had less effect in the long run than the way in which the framers of each declaration were primarily concerned with the very different political and social conditions existing in the American colonies and in France. In the same way as the thirteen British colonies in America had enjoyed representative institutions and a large degree of political freedom long before they declared their independence of the British Crown, and knew nothing of the absolute governments which still existed in France and elsewhere in Europe, so their experience of a free society was quite different from the continuing existence of feudal society in Europe.

The particular situation from which the Declaration of Independence ultimately emerged was brought about in the 1760s when the British Parliament tried to exercise supreme authority over the American colonies and the colonial legislatures after a long period of neglect, and also attempted to impose taxes on the colonists. To each attempt by the British Parliament to state the principle of supremacy or to introduce specific measures of control, the spokesmen for the colonies replied with statements of political principles and rights or they appealed to colonial charters and previous constitutional practice. Step by step between 1765 and 1776 the American colonists were brought inexorably to the point where a declaration of their independence from the British Crown was the only way open to them short of recognizing the supremacy of Parliament.[158] When towards the end of 1775, after hostilities had begun, George III declared the colonies to be rebellious and therefore outside his protection, the distinction which the colonists had tried to maintain between loyalty to the king and denial of the legislative supremacy of Parliament could no longer be maintained. In the Declaration of Independence (4 July 1776) no reference was made to Parliament because the link with the Crown was finally broken by attributing to the king himself all the oppressive and evil acts of which the colonists complained (doc. 12).

During the political and constitutional passage from subjection to independence, a consensus of opinion in the colonies was essential if the colonists who spoke as representatives of the American people were truly speaking on their behalf. That consensus was found in the existence of a political theory based on freedom. As the struggle with the British Government continued, it is noticeable that the colonists became less and less concerned with legalistic arguments and far more with universal ideas originating from natural law philosophy. No single source of political ideas, classical, English or European, was more influential than others in shaping the attitudes of American political leaders during the conflict with England; but when claims were made on the basis of the 'rights of Englishmen' and the British Constitution, English political writers of the seventeenth and early eighteenth centuries, including John Locke, were frequently cited in support. They were, however, quoted rather selectively and interpreted in the light of American political and social conditions. Moreover, the foundation of the American colonies and their subsequent history seemed to show that the social contract and the establishment of political institutions by consent was a fact and not an abstraction on which a political theory could be built. The idyllic picture painted by Thomas Paine in *Common Sense* of the initial establishment of government was far more closely related to reality in the early American colonies, as in the Mayflower compact of 1620, for example, than could be the case in Britain or Europe. Given this varied background to the development of American political thought, the Declaration of Independence included statements of universal application rooted in the long tradition of natural law, natural rights and the social contract. At the same time, it was a justification of the action of the thirteen colonies in repudiating their allegiance to George III and setting themselves up as a separate people and as independent states. Beyond that, the Declaration of Independence was an appeal to the world, as the time had passed for appeals to the king and the British people.[159]

A. Roots of liberalism: the eighteenth century

In the same way as Thomas Paine's *Common Sense* had expressed plainly and forcefully in January 1776 the feelings of hostility towards the monarchy that many colonists were experiencing but had not yet expressed, so the Declaration of Independence epitomized what colonists were thinking in July 1776. According to Thomas Jefferson, the chief author of the text of the Declaration, the purpose was:

'Not to find out new principles, or new arguments, never before thought of, not merely to say things which had never been said before; but to place before mankind the common-sense of the subject, in terms so plain and firm as to command their assent. . . . Neither aiming at originality of principle or sentiments, nor yet copied from any particular and previous writing, it was intended to be an expression of the American mind. . . .' [160]

The Declaration speaks first in universal terms in defence of human equality: men are born equal and they all have the same natural rights; and, as men live in society of their own free will, the compact into which they enter with each other is to establish government (doc. 12). Men are naturally good, and therefore government could be good when it was limited in power and when individual rights acted as a restraint on the exercise of power. Men's natural rights of 'Life, Liberty, and the Pursuit of Happiness' were antecedent to the establishment of government; and so those rights could not be surrendered nor could anything else take their place. They were 'unalienable' and distinct from the political, civil and social rights which followed the institution of government. Jefferson's choice of phrase, 'the Pursuit of Happiness', which was by no means original, drew attention to a natural right much broader than the right of 'security' or 'property' which Locke had added to the rights of life and liberty. Through the use of the phrase 'the Pursuit of Happiness' the authors of the Declaration implied that men had the right to take action themselves to improve the quality and condition of their lives. Government was not an end in itself: its purpose was to secure the welfare of each individual. Locke's influence can perhaps be traced most directly in the insistence on the right to resist tyranny.[161] American colonists fully accepted the concept of government as a trust because they believed that each colony had entered of its own free will into a compact with the king after its foundation. In the same way as James II was regarded as having abdicated his trust in November 1688, so the colonists saw George III as abdicating his trust through sanctioning over a period of years actions which they regarded as tyrannous, and finally by declaring the colonies rebellious and outside his protection. The Declaration of Independence does not state explicitly that sovereignty is with the people; but this is clearly implied in the claim that when the people are at length driven to withdraw their trust from the king, they have the right and the duty to establish a new form of government that will secure their liberty, safety and happiness.

As it is the compact with the king that the American people are terminating, all the specific acts of tyranny listed in the Declaration were attributed to the king directly and not to Parliament. The king had deliberately attempted to force an 'absolute tyranny' on the colonies, and had thereby disregarded the rights of the colonists which are no longer claimed as the 'rights of Englishmen' but as the natural and 'unalienable' rights of man. Each charge against the king showed how the rights of freedom of election, no taxation without representation, habeas corpus, trial by jury and other rights had been infringed. As appeals to the British people in 1774 and 1775, in addition to petitions to the king, had fallen on deaf ears, the American people now appealed to the 'Supreme Judge of the world' to establish the rightness of their cause. They absolved themselves from any allegiance to the king and so brought to an end their political connection with Great Britain. They declared themselves to be free and independent states, with all the recognized powers of such states to make war and conclude peace, to trade with all peoples and states, and to conclude alliances with other states.

The Declaration of Independence is in large part a piece of special pleading. Its authors put forward the American case in terms most likely to have a universal appeal far beyond the support that an explanation of their rebellion against the British Crown could have won. The Declaration was also an effective piece of propaganda for winning over the hesitant and the waverers among the colonists by placing all the misfortunes of the colonies squarely on the shoulders of the king. The backward looking part of the Declaration, listing the colonies' grievances against George III, is negative and unconstructive. In 1776 the authors of the Declaration did not see the thirteen United Colonies as having the task of proclaiming principles which would bring about political and social revolutions elsewhere and in vastly different conditions. In general the intention was to preserve in the American 'revolutionary settlement' the political and social conditions already existing in the colonies. At the same time, however, the statement of principles and rights in the first two paragraphs of the Declaration had significance for the future; and the way in which the American people, as the constituent power, established government on the basis of those principles offered something that was both new and constructive. On the basis of those same principles, it would be possible for other peoples to make a new beginning by establishing a political and social order for themselves; but before they could do that the peoples of Europe would have to destroy the age-old institution of absolute and arbitrary monarchical government and the feudal social structure. The principles of government and the rights of man laid down in the Declaration of Independence were sufficiently revolutionary to provide a theoretical justification for such actions; and between 1776 and 1787 the American people also showed how the sovereign and constituent power of the people could be used to establish a limited, representative and democratic form of government. Following

A. Roots of liberalism: the eighteenth century

the American example, whether consciously or unconsciously, a pattern of democratic revolution emerged, a pattern that was transferred to Europe through the French Revolution of 1789. First, the equal rights of each citizen must be defined; and then a Constitution should be drawn up, by the representatives of the people, on the basis of those rights and embodying the principles of representative and democratic government.

In the late eighteenth and early nineteenth centuries the American experiment in Constitution-making probably exercised as great, if not a greater influence on Europe than the Declaration of Independence. For the American example showed how a people could institute new forms of government once absolute and arbitrary power had been overthrown and sovereignty declared to reside in the people.

During the greater part of the nineteenth century the view was widely and persistently held that the French Revolution stemmed directly from the ideas of the Enlightenment. To liberals, in England and in France, this clear connection between ideas and events was praiseworthy; but to conservatives and reactionaries it provided a reason for viewing with hostility the writers and thinkers of the Enlightenment and for condemning the Revolution of 1789 and all that had since derived from it. When this simple and all-embracing interpretation of the Revolution at length came under attack from historians, the political, economic and social factors, to varying degrees, were given far greater emphasis than the spread of ideas in determining the causes of the Revolution in 1789. Although it is now generally accepted that many and very complex factors contributed to the coming of the Revolution and determined the formulation of the Declaration of the Rights of Man and Citizen, the Declaration itself still stands as a summary of eighteenth-century political ideas.

The calling of the Estates General to meet in May 1789 for what appeared to be fairly limited, even if vaguely defined, purposes in the eyes of Louis XVI and his ministers, that is, to establish a more equitable form and incidence of taxation and to advise on the removal of abuses and the introduction of reforms in the administration, opened the way for the Third Estate, as the only true representatives of the French nation, to put forward extensive and far-reaching political, social and economic demands. These demands, all concerned with the exercise of political power, the removal of privileges and the expansion of economic power, were interlinked and conditioned by eighteenth-century ideas in which there was a strong current of political liberalism.[162] As the Commons represented well over ninety per cent of the nation, the Deputies of the Third Estate soon claimed the power to speak and act in its name in consenting to taxation. On 17 June they declared the existence of a National Assembly; and then, believing that it was also their task to provide France with a Constitution so as to limit the absolute power of the Crown, they bound themselves in the famous Tennis Court Oath not

to disband before 'the constitution of the kingdom is established and consolidated upon firm foundations.' [163]

From this it followed almost as a matter of course that the National
Assembly, in keeping with English and American precedents, would
proceed to draw up a declaration of rights as the first step in constitution-making. It was logical that a declaration of rights would be
grounded on modern political ideas and on a condemnation of all the
abuses of the Old Regime. So, on the one hand, the Declaration of the
Rights of Man and Citizen, like the preamble to the American Declaration of Independence, is forward-looking in that it lays down certain
broad political principles of universal and timeless validity on which the
political structure of the future should be based; and, on the other hand,
again like its American counterpart, it lists specific grievances closely
related to existing circumstances. In the French case, however, the circumstances were by no means unique to France. Similar abuses existed
in other European States where an absolute monarchy and a feudal or
semi-feudal social structure still existed. That in part explains the lasting
appeal and influence of the 'Declaration of the Rights of Man and
Citizen'. From the general *cahiers* of the Third Estate it is clear that the
social question was of over-riding importance as the bourgeoisie saw that
their own interests demanded the equality of the three orders in the incidence of taxation, the opening of all careers to talent and complete civil
equality. In order to secure these demands, they wanted an end to
arbitrary government through constitutional limits being placed on the
power of the king; and they insisted that the representatives of the nation
(people) must consent to taxation. There was less unanimity among the
bourgeoisie in demanding the removal of economic restraints and less
still in supporting religious toleration. On all or most of these issues, the
more liberal-minded among the clergy and the nobility held reasonably
similar views.

The National Assembly embarked on its double task of preparing a
declaration of rights and drafting a constitution on 7 July. The debate in
the Assembly, turning on whether a declaration of rights should precede
or follow the drafting of a Constitution, was resolved on the morning of 4
August, following the renunciation of all seigneurial and other rights and
dues, when the decision was taken that the Assembly would work first on
defining the rights of man. In one important respect the renunciation of
all privileges on 4 August greatly simplified the Assembly's task in drawing up a declaration of rights. There was now no barrier in the way of announcing that all Frenchmen were equal in rights and therefore equal
before the law, that public offices were open to all irrespective of birth,
and that all classes must share equally in the incidence of taxation. In
other words, the legal unity of the nation had been established. Further,
two basic rights were no longer in dispute: that sovereignty resided in and
emanated solely from the nation (i.e. the French people); and that all

A. Roots of liberalism: the eighteenth century

Frenchmen were equal in rights.

In the preamble of the 'Declaration of the Rights of Man and Citizen', the members of the National Constituent Assembly underlined the threefold purpose that would be served by setting out the 'natural, inalienable and sacred' rights of man, which they defined as 'liberty, property, security, and resistance to oppression' (doc. 13): first, that all members of the social body should be aware not only of their rights but also of their duties, although the latter, contrary to the wishes of some of the Deputies, were only implied and not defined; secondly, that the acts of both the legislative body and the executive could always be checked against what was stated to be the purpose of political institutions; and, thirdly, that in making demands on the government each citizen should be aware of his rights and of the rights of others so as to uphold the Constitution which ensured the welfare (*bonheur*) of all. By their appeal to natural rights, which were held to antedate the political and historical bases of the monarchy, the members of the Constituent Assembly showed their acceptance of the argument used by Abbé Sieyès in *What is the Third Estate?*, that 'the nation owes its existence to *natural* law alone', whereas the government 'can only be a product of *positive* law'.[164] Such an argument was based on the supposition that the nation had the right to start afresh in constitution-making without paying any attention to the fundamental rights on which the *parlements* had based their case against the absolute monarchy.

The seventeen articles that follow the preamble to the 'Declaration of the Rights of Man and Citizen' (doc. 13) spell out what the members of the Constituent Assembly regarded as the basic rights of the individual. The first six articles are concerned with the more general aspects of freedom and of individual liberty. In these articles in particular a summary of eighteenth-century political thought is to be found. In contrast to the broader wording of the preamble to the American Declaration of Independence, that 'all men are created equal', the French Constituent Assembly declared 'men are born and remain free and equal in rights'. This statement was followed by a reference to the end of the privileges enjoyed under the Old Regime. The 'natural and inalienable rights of man' are stated to be 'liberty, property, security, and resistance to oppression'; and so they stand in contrast to John Locke's definition of those rights as the security of men's 'Lives, Liberties and Estates', and also to the American definition that they are 'Life, Liberty and the pursuit of Happiness'.[165]

Article three of the Declaration proclaims that the source of all sovereignty is to be found only in the nation. This statement too is very much in line with the bold claim Sieyès had made in January 1789: 'The nation is prior to everything. It is the source of everything. Its will is always legal; indeed it is the law itself.'[166] As all power therefore comes from the sovereignty residing in the nation and the nation is indivisible, it

152

is possible to interpret Article 3 of the Declaration in a sense that emphasizes the State rather than the individual. From this point of view, the concept of collectivism and of the unlimited power of the State is allowed for not only in Article 3 but also in parts of Articles 4, 5 and 6; because it is laid down that the natural rights of the individual may be limited by law, law being the expression of the general will, and the law has the right to forbid actions which are injurious to society. When these claims are not interpreted in a collectivist sense, they are still difficult to reconcile with the emphasis on individual liberty in the Declaration. Although in August 1789 many or even most members of the Constituent Assembly were probably unaware of this inherent conflct in interpretation, it is there because they were attempting to combine two different concepts of political freedom: natural rights and popular sovereignty.

Of the seventeen articles in the Declaration of the Rights of Man, Article 3 departs furthest from the political ideas of the French Enlightenment. It also differs markedly from John Locke who had avoided using the term sovereignty in his *Second Treatise on Government* and had insisted that the functions and purpose of the State were limited in scope. From the wording of Article 3 in the Declaration of the Rights of Man, the sovereignty of the nation, in the form of the State, could be regarded as being unlimited; and it would then follow that what the nation, through its representatives, decided was injurious to society, and therefore to the interests of the nation as a whole, might lead to a curtailment of individual liberties. Such restrictions were to be imposed only by law; and a time of war is an obvious case in point where individual liberties may be temporarily restricted. In August 1789 the members of the Constituent Assembly were most unlikely to have thought in terms of the representatives of the nation exercising arbitrary power in any way. They were too much concerned with ending the arbitrary power of the monarchy and establishing individual freedom and the rule of law. At the same time they became caught up in the current mystique of national sovereignty and the general will; yet they could not be expected to foresee the loss of individual liberty and the collectivism to which those concepts would give rise between 1792 and 1794.

The principles on which a programme of legal and social reform could be based are to be found in Articles 6 to 17. In them the general rights already defined are applied to particular areas of human activity, and to the law, employment and administration. In each case, the recognition of the natural and essential rights of man embodies a condemnation of the various practices of the Old Regime. In the new regime, for example, the law is to be uniform in its application to all citizens, merit is to be the only criterion in appointment to public offices and other employments and those holding public office are to be accountable for their acts; freedom of speech and freedom of the press is guaranteed, and there is to

A. Roots of liberalism: the eighteenth century

be uniformity in the incidence of taxation according to means. The Declaration also provided a basis for a thorough reform and codification of civil and criminal law, and for a sweeping reform of the administration and its procedures. The fulfilment of these and of many other tasks was to be the work of the Constituent Assembly during the following months; and citizens would be able to check the Constitution and all other reforms in the light of the guiding principles laid down in the Declaration. For the better security of individual rights, the Declaration clearly stipulated in Article 16 that the legislative, executive and judicial powers of government must be separated. [167] The separation of powers in itself would act as a check on absolute and arbitrary government.

Three articles in the Declaration require some further comment. According to Article 6, law is the expression of the general will. All citizens personally or through their representatives are to take part in determining the general will. The term general will is therefore used in the Declaration in accordance with the more usual meaning given to it, that is, majority decisions taken by the elected representatives of the people in a legislative body. It is employed in the Declaration in a sense very different from Rousseau's concept of the general will. [168]

In Article 10 of the Declaration, the Assembly went no further than to include liberty of conscience as one of the rights of man along with freedom of opinion generally: 'No one is to be disquieted because of his opinions, even religious. . . .' This form was used because it proved impossible to gain a majority in the Assembly for an open declaration of full liberty of public worship; and, indeed, no widespread demand for religious toleration had been found in the *cahiers*. In 1789 the Constituent Assembly had no thought of separating the French State from the Catholic Church; and a good measure of support would probably have been forthcoming from among its members for a declaration that Catholicism was the official religion of the State. The right of liberty of conscience, subject in the Declaration to the proviso that its exercise did not 'disturb the public order established by law', did not go much beyond the position already reached in France in November 1787 when Louis XVI granted civil status to Protestants but did not re-enact the Edict of Nantes. [169]

The inclusion of property as one of the natural, 'sacred and inviolable' rights of man is reiterated in the final article of the Declaration. It appears to have been added as an afterthought, and the reiteration probably seemed necessary to the members of the Assembly after the night of 4 August and before that the weeks of disturbances in the towns and countryside. Bourgeois Deputies had been of one mind with those from the liberal nobility in wishing to see an end to attacks on property and in recognizing that certain dues had a property value and compensation must be paid by the peasants. In view of the economic interests of the French bourgeoisie in 1789, the Deputies in the Constituent

Assembly might well have been expected to show as much interest in asserting certain rights with regard to freedom of enterprise and freedom of labour as they did in removing the social inequalities of the Old Regime. Instead there are two notable omissions in the Declaration of Rights: it does not provide any specific reference to economic liberalism, although freedom of trade and enteprise through the abolition of guilds and the removal of internal customs barriers could be covered by other articles; [170] and there is no reference either to freedom of association. In the case of the latter many members of the Assembly were reluctant to sanction any form of association which could conceivably be taken to cover the continuing existence of the religious congregations. In the 'Chapelier' law of 14 June 1791 the Assembly's attitude was made plain beyond any doubt. Prohibitions already in force against the formation of corporations and guilds (*jurandes*) were now extended to artisans and other workers. They were forbidden the right to organize and they were also forbidden to strike. Workers were left to the mercy of their employers by the 1791 law; but nearly sixty years were to pass before 'the right to work' – that is, that a man had a right to have work provided for him – was widely demanded in 1848 as one of the basic rights of man.

In contrast to the Assembly's decided stand against guaranteeing freedom of association, wide differences of opinion stood in the way of proclaiming freedom of trade and of enterprise; and the divergent views among the Deputies reflected the differences to be found more generally among the supports of the Revolution who came from different social classes and occupations. Bourgeois merchants and manufacturers did not see eye to eye, and their different viewpoints were represented among the members of the Assembly; but the greatest contrast existed between the outlook and interests of the merchants and manufacturers and those of the artisans and small shopkeepers who formed the backbone of the popular revolutionary movement in Paris and other towns. In October 1790 the Assembly proclaimed its belief in a broad principle of economic liberalism: 'that commerce is the source of all agricultural and industrial development and strength, and that it may function effectively only in so far as it enjoys adequate liberty'.[171] However, the measures it adopted were not fully in accord with that principle. In order to satisfy the various and conflicting interests there was to be free trade within France and protection in external trade, and free trade in grain within France and restrictions on its export abroad.

Although the 'Declaration of the Rights of Man and Citizen' was adopted by the Constituent Assembly on 26 August 1789, the Constitution to which it was to be a preamble or a 'direction of intention', to quote Georges Lefebvre's apt phrase,[172] was not completed and adopted until 3 September 1791. During those two years circumstances in France changed and influenced the final form of the Constitution; for example, in

A. Roots of liberalism: the eighteenth century

weakening the powers of the executive in relation to those of the Assembly. Above all, the bourgeoisie felt an increasing need to safeguard and consolidate its own newly-won political, social and economic position. This attitude led, so far as the franchise was concerned, to the division into active and passive citizens. Such a distinction was clearly at variance with the Declaration of Rights which had proclaimed the equal rights of all citizens. In effect, the bourgeoisie saw itself as alone being capable of exercising political and civil rights on behalf of the whole French nation. They did not realize that this lessened the emphasis on freedom which had been such a marked feature of the Declaration of Rights.

The Constitution of 1791 lasted no more than a year, but the Declaration of the Rights of Man has remained as a 'direction of intention' in the drafting of a Constitution or as a yardstick by which political practices may be judged.[173] Further, with the rapid progress of industrialization in Western Europe in the nineteenth century, and with it the widespread acceptance of some if not all of the ideas of economic liberalism, claims were made, for instance in France in 1848, that the rights of the individual should also secure to him greater social justice and greater equality of conditions. This was an adaptation, as a result of changing conditions, of the eighteenth-century belief in welfare or happiness (*bonheur*) as one of the inalienable rights of man; and it was to be secured through political liberty rather than through the beneficent action of an all-powerful State.

The French Revolution came at the end of a decade during which there had been renewed interest in parliamentary reform in England, with demands being made for manhood suffrage, annual parliaments and a redistribution of seats so as to bring about greater equality of representation. Needless to say the movement for parliamentary reform met with strong resistance from most of the aristocracy and from those who benefited by holding sinecure offices and pensions from the Crown. Otherwise there was widespread indifference to parliamentary reform and also to measures designed to bring about more economical government. Among those most interested in reform were the Dissenters. They reformed an educated opposition to the continuance of the existing system and ways of government; and they sought religious as well as political equality. They therefore hailed the events taking place in France because the French National Assembly seemed to be acting on English political principles, and attempting to carry those principles into effect beyond the position reached in England in 1688–89 and since left unchanged.[174]

Most well-informed Englishmen also welcomed the French Revolution, and during the first two years of its course their interest in events in France was, for the most part, enthusiastic and idealistic but also naive.

They saw a new age opening for the French who were about to experience the benefits of constitutional government so long enjoyed by people in Britain. They also believed that Britain and France were moving towards an era of peace and brotherhood. As events in France in 1789 were interpreted in English terms, little or no attempt was made either by the government led by William Pitt or by individuals to understand what was happening in France in the context of French conditions.[175] Dissenters, radicals and others who were interested in reform regarded the revolution in France as a prelude to the achievement of more equitable political representation in England and the removal of the remaining civil disabilities.

Once critical voices did begin to be raised in England, hostility to the French Revolution crystallized rapidly and it had a highly emotional content. When the issue was joined during 1790 and 1791 between the supporters and the opponents of the French Revolution, the bone of contention between them was England and not France; and for the most part the debate was over abstract political principles, though there was also another short-lived period of agitation in favour of parliamentary reform. At the very centre of the debate on political principles were two books: Edmund Burke's *Reflections on the Revolution in France*, published in November 1790, and Thomas Paine's *The Rights of Man*, the first part of which appeared in March 1791 and the second in February 1792.[176]

Burke condemned any application of French revolutionary principles to Britain because he repudiated the doctrine of natural rights. The political principles he expounded in reply subsequently became part of nineteenth-century English conservatism; and therefore, as our study is devoted to liberalism, Jeremy Bentham's criticism of the doctrine of natural rights will be used instead of Burke's to contrast with Thomas Paine's defence of the natural rights of man. Bentham was much better informed than Burke about events in France from 1788 onwards; and he welcomed the revolution as a chance to destroy an unsound political structure and rebuild a sound one. From their very different standpoints of utilitarianism and natural rights, Bentham and Paine were to make important, though very different, contributions to nineteenth-century English liberalism. They were both influenced by eighteenth-century rationalism; and they both proclaimed themselves to be citizens of the world. Both denied that the dead could rule the living, and so they rejected the historic and prescriptive rights that meant so much to Edmund Burke. Both Bentham and Paine believed that the aim of political society should be the increase of human happiness; and in looking at the French Revolution their real concern was with Great Britain and not with France. There the similarities end. Unlike Jeremy Bentham and his utilitarian followers, or the English radicals of the 1780s and 1790s, Thomas Paine was a revolutionary and not a reformer.

In writing *The Rights of Man* Paine deliberately set out to refute

Burke's arguments, but he made use of the opportunity to expound his own political ideas far more fully than he had done during the American revolution. He believed that the political principles he sponsored were valid ones for any country when a corrupt monarchical government was overthrown and replaced by 'republican' government, that is, government based on the sovereignty of the people and representation. According to Paine, the American and French revolutions were founded on a principle and were not the result of mob violence and anarchy; and so he thought it preferable that action should be taken to institute a 'republican' government before violent revolution broke out (doc. 14). He offered no programme for bringing about changes and reforms in the English constitutional monarchy because corrupt institutions, being based on wrong political principles, could not be reformed. Paine contended that the 1688 settlement in England had been no more than a contract between king and people. It had not brought about a change of government, whereas the American and French peoples had gone back to the natural order of things and had acted in the original constitution-making capacity of a people.[177] Through such arguments Paine discounted appeals to tradition and constitutional practice, went back to the doctrine of natural rights and used it to condemn monarchy as a system of government. Monarchy was founded on ignorance, whereas 'the representative system takes society and civilization for its basis; nature, reason, and experience for its guide.'[178]

Paine's concept of natural and civil rights was a very simple one. It was based on the premise that 'men were all of *one degree*'. He defined natural rights as intellectual rights, 'the rights of the mind', such as thinking, speaking and forming an opinion. Civil rights grow out of natural rights, for they are enjoyed by men as members of society and included among them are security, protection and the possession of property.[179] Society is no more than the sum total of individuals, and in society each man still exercises his natural rights with regard to his own comfort and happiness, provided that in so doing he does not injure the equal rights of others. Although the sovereignty of the people is unlimited, government should be both minimal and simple. Here too the emphasis is on the individual. Every man enjoys equal rights, and it is the duty of each citizen to guarantee the exercise of their rights to other citizens; and so 'A Declaration of Rights is, by reciprocity, a Declaration of Duties also. Whatever is my right as a man, is also the right of another; and it becomes my duty to guarantee, as well as to possess.'[180]

Behind Paine's advocacy of minimal and simple government is his belief that man is reasonable and naturally good.[181] 'Man, were he not corrupted by governments, is naturally the friend of man, and . . . human nature is not of itself vicious.'[182] As natural laws are inherently good, so the public good, 'as well individually as collectively', must be the aim of representative government.[183] Paine also subscribed to the idea, widely accepted in the eighteenth century, that man's self-interest would ensure a natural harmony of interests and so lead to the greater good of society being automatically secured.[184] Although Paine insisted on the equality of natural and civil rights enjoyed by each citizen, he recognized that economic equality was impossible; and because he placed such an emphasis on individualism, he upheld the rights of private property.[185] In line, however, with his condemnation of monarchy and aristocracy on political grounds, Paine denied the legitimacy of the power that could be exercised by an aristocracy on the basis of inherited property. As John Locke had done a century earlier, Paine recognized that the labour a man performed was a form of property; and so he included the 'right to work' among the natural and civil rights of man.[186] Further, social justice could be secured by law and should therefore be included among the rights of man, although economic equality was impossible. Paine therefore suggested that a declaration of rights should include the statement: 'Public succours are a sacred debt of society, and it is for the law to determine their extent and application.'[187] The social measures proposed by Paine in the second part of *The Rights of Man*, including a progressive income tax, pensions for the aged poor, assistance for the education of poor children, marriage and childbirth payments to those in need, and the provision of work and shelter for the unemployed, all went far beyond any existing ways and means of social amelioration.[188] The economic and social measures proposed by Paine were widely propagated among the working classes in Britain, and therefore the second part of *The Rights of Man* caused far more concern to Pitt's government than the exposition of abstract political principles and the condemnation of monarchy in the first part.[189] Just as dangerous in the view of governing circles was Paine's contention that the masses must be lifted out of their ignorance by education; for he claimed that education was the right as well as the need of each citizen. Only through education could the citizen exercise his reason in judging whether 'republican' or democratic representative government remained true to the principles on which it was founded.[190]

Although Jeremy Bentham welcomed the overthrow of absolute monarchy in France in 1789 and proffered advice to members of the National Assembly on political tactics and representation, he was immediately critical of the Assembly's decision to adopt a Declaration of the Rights of Man and Citizen. In *Anarchical Fallacies*, probably written about 1796, Bentham examined the Declaration exclusively in terms of abstract principles. He therefore set aside any knowledge or understanding that he had of conditions in France when the Declaration was drawn up. Nor did he show any awareness that the members of the Constituent Assembly were just as much concerned with removing the abuses of the Old Regime as they were with establishing abstract political principles on which to build a new political structure. Bentham's criticism of the Declaration was based on the distinction he made between opinions, which are concerned with things as they *ought* to be, and law which is concerned with things as they *are*. In Bentham's view, therefore, the Constituent Assembly was mistaken in adopting a declaration of general principles before detailed legislation had been drawn up (doc. 15). He began his critique with an examination of the broad principles laid down in the preamble of the Declaration, and then went on to examine each of the seventeen articles separately in order to point out 'the errors it contains in theory' and 'the mischief it is pregnant with in practice'.[191] He concluded with a criticism of the 1795 Declaration of Rights and noted that the rights listed in that document have now become the rights belonging to 'man in society'. Indeed, considering all the changes that had been made since 1789 Bentham thought that the 'inalienable' rights of 'the man or the citizen, or the man in society' had been rather 'unstable'.[192]

First and foremost in Bentham's criticism of the Declaration of Rights is his rejection of the whole concept of natural rights as 'metaphysical nonsense'.[193] Like Burke, he associated the doctrine of natural rights with the armed power of the mob, the end of which was likely to be political anarchy.[194] In such circumstances, natural rights meant rights gained by force and not by law; but as there can be no liberty without security through the law, Bentham insists that rights can only be conferred by law. Further, such rights have corresponding obligations.[195] Bentham denied that man could have had any rights prior to his entry into society. Man is not born free: he is born into subjection.[196] Nor was there a social contract because man has always been social. Further, 'contracts come from government, not government from contracts'.[197] In the Declaration men are opposed to citizens, but Bentham rejects any distinction being made between man in a state of nature and the citizen, that is, man in political society.[198] Man as a citizen is Bentham's concern, irrespective of whether he is to be found in France, or in England where men already had rights defined by law, or elsewhere.[199]

In addition to denying the validity of the principle of natural rights, Bentham criticized the Declaration of Rights on the grounds of procedure. The Constituent Assembly had attempted to draw up a declaration proclaiming general principles before all the particular laws of the constitutional structure had been adopted. According to Bentham's view of the correct procedure, it was only from an examination of the particular laws that general principles, i.e. fundamental laws, could be determined.[200] His own lifelong work of classification was based on that assumption.

In place of the doctrine of natural rights Bentham laid down the principle of utility.[201] Under the guidance of that principle, the aim of political society was the greatest happiness of the greatest number, and the ends of government were subsistence, abundance, security and equality (docs

17–20). Without any need to appeal to the doctrine of natural rights, the end of the Old Regime in France could therefore be justified on the grounds of utility: it had not achieved the greatest happiness of the greatest number and it had not secured the four ends of government that Bentham had defined. His rejection of the doctrine of natural rights epitomizes the dislike of general abstract principles and *a priori* assumptions on which English thinkers often prided themselves. Through the heritage of eighteenth-century rationalism Bentham was led to emphasize the particular and the practical; and so he contended that the principles proclaimed in the Declaration of Rights could not fulfil either the ends of government he had in view or the purposes stated in the preamble of the Declaration. The Declaration was unnecessary as a means of limiting the power of the Assembly, because the people's representatives or the people themselves would always voice their objections to a law that was disagreeable to them irrespective of whether or not it contravened the Declaration of Rights (doc. 15). As for the separation of powers, Bentham rejected that notion and insisted that one branch of government must be supreme; and that branch must be the legislature. With regard to the much vaunted right of resistance to oppression, Bentham did not deny that revolution might be justified in certain circumstances, and if success could be assured; for example, when a government had lost public support so that government and obedience no longer went hand in hand, or when resistance was a lesser mischief than continued submission.[202]

Natural rights *versus* the principle of utility: on the matter of political principles Paine and Bentham were far removed from each other. Yet they had a similar end in view in that they sought greater political and social justice for all men. In their own day they were both disappointed because they made no impact on political ideas and events in France during the revolution; and of the two it was Bentham's reputation as a political reformer that lived on in other European countries, such as Spain, and in South America.[203] In England Paine and Bentham were the sources of two very different radical approaches to parliamentary and other reforms in the early nineteenth century. Paine's simplicity of style, and the over-simplification of his argument at times, contrasts with Bentham's involved style which is often dry and repetitive. In contrast to Bentham, Paine's influence was not due to the originality of his ideas, but rather to his skill as a propagandist.[204] The apt and telling phrases and the pithy statements that Paine used could easily be remembered and repeated by his readers. The influence of Paine's ideas on working-class politics continued into the early nineteenth century in a form of radicalism that emphasized egalitarianism and sought political reform as the way towards achieving social improvement. Yet Paine himself never exclusively directed his attention to the working class; and it so happened that during the reform movements of the early nineteenth century in

England, the two strands of radicalism, working-class radicalism associated in its origins and ideas with Thomas Paine, on the one hand, and that of Jeremy Bentham and the utilitarians, on the other, were more or less complementary.

---

8. The belief in progress: introduction
(Document 16, pp. 236–40)

One major plank in nineteenth-century liberalism was the optimistic belief in the unlimited progress of mankind. It looked forward just as most conservative thought looked back. It was confident that progress would overcome the obstacles in its way furnished by the vested interests of aristocrats and priests. Originating in the earlier writings of Voltaire and Turgot, it maintained an unquestioning faith in the ever wider spread of enlightenment and education. Its foremost pioneer at the end of the eighteenth century was a liberal aristocrat and scientist, Marie-Jean-Antoine-Nicholas de Caritat, Marquis de Condorcet (1743–94). For the last twenty years of his life, which ended tragically in the turmoil of the French Revolution, he was Secretary to the French Academy of Sciences; in 1782 he was elected a member of the renowned *Académie Française*. Condorcet was keenly interested in both scientific enlightenment and social reform. He never doubted that man was 'a sentient being, capable of reasoning, and of acquiring moral ideas'. He was also an ardent champion of the cause of suppressed or restricted social groups like the slaves or the French Protestants.

In 1789 Condorcet became a member of the Commune of Paris, and in 1791 he was elected to the Legislative Assembly which later made him its President. He can be regarded as a Girondist. However, neither his far-reaching schemes on education nor his proposals for a permanent Constitution of the Republic were accepted. When, in a public letter, he ventured to attack the new Constitution of 1793, drawn up by the Jacobins, Condorcet was doomed. While hiding in a friend's house in the country from the wrath of the Jacobins who had ordered his arrest he wrote his famous 'Sketch for a Historical Picture of the Progress of the Human Mind' (*L'Esquisse d'un tableau historique des progrès de l'esprit humain*). This book, his political and ideological testament, was written between July 1793 and March 1794. Soon afterwards Condorcet was arrested, identified as an aristocrat, then a highly pejorative term, detained for being without a passport and imprisoned at Bourg-La-Raine. The next day he was found dead in his cell. The cause of his death has never been clearly established, but it has been aptly said that his last work 'bears the mark of having been written with a great sense of urgency by a man who wished to draw his thought together, and to leave his testament in a summary form in the short time still left to him'.[205]

To Condorcet, belief in progress was a religion. It meant faith in the unlimited perfectability of man. 'This progress', he says confidently in the Introduction, 'will doubtless vary in speed, but it will never be reversed as long as the earth occupies the present place in the system of the universe.' There always were and still are impediments on the road to progress such as human prejudices and great differences in education. In fact Condorcet's sketch of the main phases in the history of mankind is largely a survey of the origins, the triumph and fall of the prejudices which proved obstacles in man's evolution.

Compared with his predecessors, Voltaire and Turgot, Condorcet had one considerable advantage. Taking a more universal view of history he traced progress in many fields, in the political, social, intellectual and artistic life. What mattered to him were not merely some few select individuals but the human race as such. Condorcet distinguished ten stages in the history of mankind. During the first pre-historic period the foundations of morality and of the family were laid; but superstitions were also born, among them the belief in gods. Early the class of the priests established its sinister rule which, according to Condorcet, lasted throughout the ages down to 1789. In the second period agriculture developed; the beginnings of art and science occurred; and institutions and ideas based on authority established themselves, and with them 'the art of deceiving men in order to despoil them'. In the third period property rights became definite and each parcel of land had its owner. There was now a dividing line between the rich and the poor. The alphabet was invented. In the fourth period, the earlier centuries of antiquity, only the Greeks mattered while the Jews, the fathers of monotheistic religion, are not even mentioned. Condorcet admired Socrates, but less so the Greek social system based as it was on slavery. He devoted considerable space to the advance of the human mind in Greece, and to the Greek achievements in science and politics. In the subsequent fifth period Greek civilization declined. Condorcet has no praise for the Romans as he viewed Latin culture simply as a variation of Greek decadence. He is also unsympathetic to the rise of Christianity with its contempt for human knowledge. As Voltaire before him, he paints a grim, black picture of the middle ages which mark the following two periods. They were the days of the triple tyranny of the king, the warrior and the priest who all profited from the general immense belief in authority. In modern times, however, things greatly improved. The eighth period saw the invention of printing which made knowledge 'the object of an active and universal commerce'. This, in its turn, led to the formation of public opinion, a great incentive to progress. Condorcet has high praise for the great and revolutionary

163

A. Roots of liberalism: the eighteenth century

scientists of the sixteenth and seventeenth centuries, for Copernicus, Galileo, Kepler and Descartes; 'through them tradition and authority gave way to universal and natural law and to human reason'.[206] With the eighteenth century the great age of reason had arrived, which was largely, though not entirely, a French affair. The ninth period ranges significantly 'from Descartes to the foundation of the French Republic'. Comparing the American and French revolutions, Condorcet observes that the revolution in North America 'affected the ordinary people or changed the relations between individuals. In France, on the contrary, the revolution was to embrace the entire economy of society, change every social relation and find its way down to the furthest links of the political chain.'[207] The eighteenth century experienced the quick advance of the natural sciences which resulted 'in destroying erroneous views in politics, morals and religion'. But it was only the French Revolution which attacked at the same time royal despotism, political inequality, religious intolerance, the feudal system and aristocratic privilege.

The latest chapter (doc. 16), in which Condorcet ventures to draw the picture of a happier future, has rightly been called 'the most original chapter of the book'.[208] It predicts the future trend of achieving true freedom because human life will be based upon (1) the equality of the nations; (2) the equality of individuals within a nation; (3) the perfectibility of mankind. In many ways Condorcet has proved a realistic visionary, for he visualized 'the outlines of liberal democracy more than a century in advance of his time: universal education, universal suffrage; equality before the law; freedom of thought and expression; the right to freedom and self-determination of colonial peoples; the redistribution of wealth; a system of national insurance; equal rights for women'.[209]

Condorcet's visionary and 'total' liberalism went far beyond the *laissez faire* maxim of Adam Smith or of the later Constitutional liberals in France and Germany. It was a belief in the infinite possibilities of mankind on its march to full self-realization. There is a moving personal note struck at the end of this philosophical testament by this ardent and far-sighted defender of liberty who knew that he might soon become a victim of political prosecution:

'How consoling for the philosopher who laments the errors, the crimes, the injustices which still pollute the earth and of which he is often the victim is this view of the human race, emancipated from its shackles, released from the empire of fate and from that of the enemies of its progress, advancing with a firm and sure step, along the path of truth, virtue and happiness! It is the contemplation of this prospect that rewards him for all his efforts to assist the progress of reason and the defence of liberty.[210]

Condorcet's final work was published posthumously, after the fall of the Jacobins, in Paris in 1795. It assures him a place as a liberal visionary and martyr in the long and winding history of political thought.

164

Notes and references

1. The civil state – representative government

1. J. W. Gough, *The Social Contract. A Critical Study of its Development* (2nd edn), Oxford 1957, p. 145.
2. Peter Laslett dates the beginning of composition as early as 1679–81: cf. P. Laslett (ed.) *Two Treatises of Government,* (2nd edn), Cambridge 1967, pp. 35, 61. 65. This critical edition of Locke's writings is referred to throughout to show the view of modern scholarship.
3. Ibid. p. 78.
4. J. Locke, *Second Treatise,* Ch. 2, §6, in P. Laslett, op. cit. pp. 288–9.
5. Ibid., Ch. 11, §§135, 136, in P. Laslett, p. 376.
6. Ibid., Ch. 2, §§8, 11, in P. Laslett, pp. 290, 292.
7. Ibid., Ch. 7, §87, in P. Laslett, p. 342.
8. Ibid., Ch. 1, §3, in P. Laslett, p. 286.
9. Ibid., Ch. 5, §27, in P. Laslett, pp. 305–6.
10. loc. cit.
11. See J. W. Gough, *John Locke's Political Philosophy,* Oxford 1950, Ch. 4, pp. 73–92; J. Plamenatz, *Man and Society,* London 1963, I, pp. 241–9.
12. Peter Laslett suggests that Ch. 9 (§§123–31) was added by Locke to the text of the *Second Treatise* during 1689. P. Laslett, op. cit., pp. 65, 368.
13. *Second Treatise* Ch. 11, §§138, 140, 143, in P. Laslett, op. cit., pp. 378–9, 380–1
14. Ibid., Ch. 11, §§135–7, in P. Laslett, pp. 375–8.
15. Ibid., Ch. 12, §§149, 156, in P. Laslett, pp. 384–5, 389.
16. Ibid., Ch. 14, §168, in P. Laslett, pp. 397–8.
17. See J. W. Gough, *John Locke's Political Philosophy,* Ch. 3, pp. 47–92; J. Plamenatz, op. cit., I, pp. 220–41.
18. *Two Treatises,* Ch. 19, §211, in P. Laslett, op. cit., pp. 424–5.
19. Ibid., Ch. 13, §149, in P. Laslett, pp. 384–5.
20. Letter to Edward Clarke, 8 February 1689; quoted in M. Cranston, *John Locke. A Biography,* London 1957, p. 309.
21. Ibid., Ch. 19, §213, in P. Laslett, p. 426.
22. Ibid., Ch. 12, §§143, 144, in P. Laslett, pp. 382–3.
23. Ibid., Ch. 13, §§151, 152, 156; Ch. 14, §167. in P. Laslett, pp. 386–7, 389–90, 396.
24. Ibid., Ch. 12, §§143, 144; Ch. 13, §§153, 154, in P. Laslett, pp. 382–3, 387–8.
25. Ibid., Ch. 12, §§145–8, in P. Laslett, pp. 383–4.
26. P. Laslett, op. cit., p. 4.
27. J. W. Gough (ed.), *The Second Treatise of Civil Government and A Letter Concerning Toleration,* Oxford 1946, Introduction, pp. xxix–xxx.
28. John Dunn, 'The Politics of Locke in England and America in the Eighteenth Century', in John W. Yolton (ed.), *John Locke: Problems and Perspectives. A New Collection of Essays,* Cambridge 1969, pp. 59–60.

2. Religious toleration

29. It was first published in Latin in Holland and later in the year in an English translation.
30. John Locke, *A Letter on Toleration* (ed. R. Klibansky), Oxford 1968, pp. 65, 67, 71.
31. Ibid., pp. 67, 69, 71, 93, 95, 99.

A. Roots of liberalism: the eighteenth century

32. A preface added by the translator to the first English edition of the *Letter on Toleration* gave force to such an idea through his use of these words: 'absolute liberty, just and true liberty, equal and impartial liberty, is the thing that we stand in need of.' Ibid., p. 164. The translator was Richard Popple, an English merchant and unitarian. The translation was not authorized or supervised by Locke. R. Klibansky (ed.), op. cit., Preface, pp. xxi–xxii.
33. Ibid., p. 131.
34. Ibid., pp. 133, 135.
35. Ibid., p. 135.
36. Ibid., pp. 59, 65.
37. Bayle's *Philosophical Commentary on these Words of Jesus Christ, Compel Them to Come In* was published in Holland in 1686.
38. Quoted in Kingsley Martin, *French Liberal Thought in the Eighteenth Century*, New York 1963 (reprint), p. 50.
39. Montesquieu, *Lettres persanes* No. LXXXV, in Roger Caillois (ed.), *Oeuvres complètes*, Paris 1949, I, pp. 258–9.
40. Loc. cit. and *The Spirit of the Laws* (trans. T. Nugent) with an introduction by Franz Neumann, New York 1949, II, Bk. xxv, Ch. 9, p. 52.
41. *Lettres persanes*, No. lxxxv, in R. Caillois (ed.) op. cit., pp. 258–9.
42. For differing interpretations of *l'infâme* see Theodore Besterman, *Voltaire*, London 1969, p. 397; Peter Gay, *Voltaire's Politics. The Poet as Realist*, Princeton, New Jersey 1959, p. 239 ff.; René Pomeau, *Politique de Voltaire. Textes choisis et présentés par René Pomeau*, Paris 1963, pp. 36–7.
43. Voltaire, *A Treatise on Religious Toleration*, London 1820, p. 173.
44. Scholars vary in their opinion on Voltaire's religious faith. According to Peter Gay, he was not a Christian but 'a true deist'. After a lengthy examination of the matter, Voltaire's biographer, Theodore Besterman, concludes that Voltaire was only a deist in a very limited sense, if even that. P. Gay, op. cit., pp. 240–3; also P. Gay (ed.), *Voltaire: Philosophical Dictionary*, New York 1962, I, p. 14, and T. Besterman, op. cit., pp. 212–23, 529.
45. Voltaire, *A Treatise on Religious Toleration*, pp. 197–8; and P. Gay, *Voltaire's Politics*, pp. 267–8.
46. See the article 'Tout est bien' in P. Gay (ed.), *Voltaire: Philosophical Dictionary*, I, p. 122.
47. As examples of the widely differing interpretations of Voltaire's famous dictum: 'We must cultivate our garden' see T. Besterman, op. cit., pp. 359–60; T. Besterman, *Voltaire Essays and Others*, London 1962, pp. 40–1; and P. Gay, *The Party of Humanity, Studies in the French Enlightenment*, London 1964, pp. 34–5; in comparison with Kingsley Martin, *French Liberal Thought in the Eighteenth Century*, p. 143.
48. See the articles on 'Fanaticism' and 'Toleration' in P. Gay (ed.), *Voltaire: Philosophical Dictionary*, I, pp. 267–8; II, pp. 482–9.
49. Voltaire, *A Treatise on Religious Toleration*, London 1820, p. 106.
50. The earliest articles for the *Philosophical Dictionary* appear to have been written in 1752. It was first published in 1764, and a second edition with additional articles appeared in 1765.
51. For example 'A Prayer to God' (doc. 3c) could be acceptable to Christians and deists alike.
52. T. Besterman, *Voltaire*, p. 539.
53. T. Besterman, *Voltaire Essays and Others*, p. 152.
54. For example, as in Toulouse. See David D. Bien, *The Calas Affair. Persecution, Toleration, and Heresy in Eighteenth-Century Toulouse*, Princeton, New Jersey 1960, p. 152 ff.
55. Religion, Turgot wrote, 'is the binding together of the several duties of man towards God; duties of worship to be rendered to the Supreme Being, duties of justice and

of benevolence to men; those duties known by the simple light of reason which constitute what we call Natural Religion, and those which the Divinity Himself has taught to men by a supernatural revelation which constitute Revealed Religion.' Turgot's 'Memorial to the King "On Toleration" June 1775' in W. Walker Stephens, *The Life and Writings of Turgot*, London 1895, pp. 257–8.

56. D. Dakin, *Turgot and the Ancien Régime in France*, London 1939, p. 217 ff.

3. 'The spirit of the laws'

57. *The Spirit of the Laws* (trans. T. Nugent) with an introduction by Franz Neumann, New York 1949, Bk. i, Ch. 1.
58. Ibid., Bk. i, Chs. 2, 3.
59. Ibid., Montesquieu's Preface.
60. Ibid., Bk. ii, Ch. 1.
61. Ibid., Bk. ii, Chs. 1 and 5.
62. Ibid., Bk. viii, Ch. 16.
63. Ibid., Bk. iii, Chs. 1 to 2.
64. Ibid., Bk. v, Chs. 2, 3 and 4.
65. Ibid., Bk. v, Ch. 8.
66. Ibid., Bk. ii, Ch. 4; Bk. v, Chs. 9 to 12.
67. Ibid., Bk. ii, Ch. 4.
68. Ibid., Bk. xix, Ch. 4.
69. Ibid., Bk. xxvi, Ch. 15.
70. Ibid., Bk. xii, Ch. 1. Montesquieu uses the paradox: 'The constitution may happen to be free, and the subject not. The subject may be free, and not the constitution. In those cases, the constitution will be free by right, and not in fact; the subject will be free in fact, and not by right.'
71. *The Spirit of the Laws*, Bk. xi, Ch. 6, paras. 1, 2 and 6.
72. As is shown in the travel note quoted in J. Robert Loy, *Montesquieu*, New York 1968, p. 32.
73. *The Spirit of the Laws*, Bk. xi, Ch. 6.
74. Loc. cit.
75. John Plamenatz, however, has contended that on the basis of certain assumptions the legislative and executive powers can be interpreted as being separate in the eighteenth-century Constitution, and are still separate today. What can be said with certainty is that the two powers were separate in England in the eighteenth century in comparison with France. J. Plamenatz, *Man and Society*, London 1963, I, pp. 289–91.
76. R. Shackleton, *Montesquieu. A Critical biography*, Oxford 1961, pp. 300–1.

4. 'Government is a necessary evil'

77. Thomas Paine, *The Rights of Man* (Dolphin ed.), New York 1961, Pt. II, p. 455.
78. Thomas Paine, *Common Sense*, in Moncure D. Conway (ed.), *The Writings of Thomas Paine*, New York 1894, I, p. 93; and *The American Crisis*, No. iii, 19 April 1777, in Hypatia Bradlaugh Bonner (ed.), *Paine's Political Writings During the American and French Revolutions*, London 1909, p. 55.
79. *The Rights of Man*, Pt. II, pp. 455–6.
80. Ibid., Pt. I, pp. 305–6.
81. Ibid., Pt. II, p. 410.
82. Ibid., p. 413.

A. Roots of liberalism: the eighteenth century

83. Ibid., pp. 413–14, 415.
84. Thomas Paine, *Dissertation on First Principles of Government*, in M. D. Conway (ed.), op. cit., New York 1895, III, p. 275.
85. *The American Crisis*, No. vii, in H. B. Bonner (ed.), op. cit., p. 85.
86. *Common Sense* in M. D. Conway (ed.), op. cit., I, p. 97 ff.
87. *Dissertation on First Principles of Government*, in M. D. Conway (ed.), op cit., III, p. 265.
88. *Rights of Man*, Pt. I, pp. 310–11; *Dissertation on First Principles of Government*, in M. D. Conway (ed.), op. cit., III, p. 277.
89. *Rights of Man*, Pt. I, p. 309.
90. Ibid., pp. 277, 309; and *Common Sense*, in M. D. Conway (ed.), op. cit., I, p. 72 ff.

5. Freedom through the general will

91. On this question of whether Rousseau is to be considered in the individualist/liberal or collectivist/totalitarian stream of thought see: Alfred Cobban, *Rousseau and the Modern State* (2nd edn), London 1964; John Plamenatz, *Man and Society*, London 1963, I, pp. 364–442; and John W. Chapman, *Rousseau – Totalitarian or Liberal?*, New York 1956; and compare with: C. E. Vaughan, *The Political Writings of Jean-Jacques Rousseau*, Cambridge 1915, (rp. Oxford 1962); J. L. Talmon, *The Origins of Totalitarian Democracy*, London 1952; and Lester G. Crocker, *Rousseau's Social Contract. An Interpretative Essay*, Cleveland 1968.
92. R. R. Palmer, *The Age of the Democratic Revolution*, Princeton 1959, I, p. 120.
93. That is *Discourse on Inequality* (1755), the article 'Political Economy' (1755) for the *Encyclopedia, Social Contract* (1762), *Lettres de la Montagne* (1763–64), and the projected constitutions for Corsica (1764–65) and Poland (1771–72).
94. C. E. Vaughan, op. cit., I, p. 4.
95. Ibid., p. 111.
96. For example, A. Cobban, op. cit.; Judith N. Shklar, *Men and Citizens. A Study of Rousseau's Social Theory*, Cambridge 1969; Roger D. Masters, *The Political Philosophy of Rousseau*, Princeton, 1968; John McManners, *The Social Contract and Rousseau's Revolt against Society*, Leicester 1967; L. G. Crocker, op. cit.
97. J. W. Gough, *The Social Contract. A Critical Study of its Development* (2nd edn), Oxford 1957, p. 171.
98. *Rousseau juge de Jean-Jacques*, quoted in R. D. Masters, op. cit., p. xiii.
99. *The Social Contract*, Bk. I, ch. iv, in *Social Contract. Essays by Locke, Hume and Rousseau*, with an introduction by Sir Ernest Barker (World's Classics), London 1947, (rp. 1970), p. 248. All subsequent references to Rousseau's *Social Contract* are to this edition.
100. Ibid., Bk. I, ch. viii, p. 263.
101. Ibid., I, iv, p. 246, and I, v, p. 254.
102. Ibid., I, ix, p. 268.
103. Ibid., I, vii, p. 259.
104. Frederick Watkins (ed.), *Rousseau: Political Writings*, Edinburgh 1953, Introduction, p. xxi.
105. C. E. Vaughan, op. cit., I, p. 39.
106. *Social Contract*, I, vi, p. 258.
107. Ibid., I, vii, pp. 259–60.
108. Ibid., I, vii, pp. 260–1.
109. Ibid., I, vii, pp. 261–2.
110. For example J. L. Talmon, op. cit., pp. 43–4.
111. F. W. Watkins, op. cit., p. xxii.

112. A. Cobban, op. cit., p. 75.
113. *Social Contract*, Bk. iii *passim*.
114. Ibid., IV, ii, pp. 388–90.
115. Ibid., III, xv, pp. 372–3.
116. Ibid., II, iv, p. 277.
117. Ibid., II, vii, pp. 290 ff.
118. Ibid., III, iv, pp. 332–5.
119. Jean Guéhenno, *Jean-Jacques Rousseau* (Trans. John and Doreen Weightman), London 1966, II, p. 45.
120. J. Plamenatz, op. cit., I, p. 395.
121. C. E. Vaughan, op. cit., I, p. 111.

6. Natural law and the economy – the doctrine of *laissez faire*

122. The origin of the phrase is often attributed to Vincent de Gournay, one of the French physiocrats.
123. According to Turgot, Gournay 'felt himself to be only developing those principles which experience in business had taught him'. *Eloge de Gournay* (1759), in W. Walker Stephens (ed.), *The Life and Writings of Turgot*, London 1895, p. 235.
124. Turgot, *Reflections on the Formation and Distribution of Riches*, New York, 1898. See paragraphs v, vi, vii, xi, xv, xvii, pp. 7–9, 12, 14–15, 17 for Turgot's classification of society. The book consists of 101 propositions supposedly written for the instruction of two Chinese students in France. Even more so than the *Eloge de Gournay,* it is a distillation of the more doctrinaire theories held by the physiocrats, but modified by Turgot's practical observations in Limoges, then one of the most backward parts of France.
125. Ibid., para. c., p. 96 ff.
126. Turgot's letter to the Abbé Terray on the corn trade, quoted in Douglas Dakin, *Turgot and the Ancien Regime in France*, London 1939, p. 306.
127. *Eloge de Gournay*, W. Stephens (ed.), op. cit., p. 247; Turgot's letter to the Abbé Terray 'sur la marque des fers' (1773), in D. Dakin, ibid., pp. 251–2.
128. Turgot regarded the *corvée* as being particularly unfair as well as being wasteful, because the obligation of forced labour fell on the 'poorest part of our subjects, upon those who have no property other than their hands and their industry, upon the peasants and on the farmers.' Text of the edict suppressing the *corvée*, in Robert Perry Shepherd, *Turgot and the Six Edicts*, New York 1903, p. 151.
129. Declaration on the grain trade (Feb. 1776), quoted in R. Shepherd, op. cit., p. 171. See also Turgot's letters to the Abbé Terray in 1770, and the preamble to the edict of September 1774, quoted in Léon Say, *Turgot*, London 1888, pp. 87–90, 112–13.
130. Turgot, *Reflections on the Formation and Distribution of Riches*, New York 1898, para. lxiv, p. 57; also D. Dakin, op. cit., p. 290.
131. Edict abolishing the guilds (*jurandes*), February 1776, in R. Shepherd, op. cit., p. 182.
132. Turgot's letter to Louis XVI, 24 August 1774, text in D. Dakin, op. cit., pp. 131–4.
133. *Eloge de Gourney,* in W. Stephens (ed.), op. cit., pp. 240–1.
134. Edict suppressing the *corvée*, in R. P. Shepherd, op. cit., p. 152.
135. For example in W. Walker Stephens (ed.), op. cit.; John Morley, 'Turgot' in *Critical Miscellanies*, II, London 1886, p. 152; Léon Say, *Turgot* (trans. Gustave Masson), London 1888, pp. 13–14, 161. Say's study of Turgot was written at a time of controversy over free trade and protection.
136. Turgot, quoted in Léon Say, op. cit., p. 39.
137. Quoted from Turgot's 'Pensées', in W. Walker Stephens (ed.), op. cit., pp. 316–17.

A. Roots of liberalism: the eighteenth century

138. Adam Smith, *The Theory of Moral Sentiments*, London 1853, p. 170.
139. For differing views on this question see, for example, Overton H. Taylor, *Economics and Liberalism. Collected Papers*, Cambridge, Mass. 1955, 'Economics and the Idea of Natural Law', 'Economics and the Idea of *Jus Naturale*'; Jacob Viner, 'Adam Smith and *laissez faire*', and Glenn R. Morrow, 'Adam Smith: Moralist and Philosopher', in J. M. Clark (ed.), *Adam Smith 1776–1926*, Lectures to commemorate the Sesquicentennial of the Publication of *The Wealth of Nations*, New York 1966 (reprint).
140. Overton H. Taylor, 'Economics and the Idea of *Jus Naturale*', op. cit., p. 91.
141. Adam Smith, *The Wealth of Nations* (6th edn, ed. Edwin Cannan), London 1950, Bk. i, Chs. 1 and 2, I, pp. 5, 15.
142. Ibid., Bk. i, 3, I, p. 19.
143. Ibid., Bk. i, Ch. 7, I, p. 57.
144. Ibid., Bk. i, Ch. 11, I, p. 248.
145. Ibid., Bk. i, Ch. 11, I, p. 248.
146. Ibid., Bk. i, Ch. 11, I, pp. 248–9.
147. *The Theory of Moral Sentiments*, pp. 264–5.
148. *The Wealth of Nations*, Bk. i, Ch. 2, I, p. 16; Bk. iv, Ch. 2, I, p. 419.
149. Ibid., Bk. v, Ch. 1, II, pp. 267–70.
150. Ibid., Bk. i, Ch. 11, I, pp. 249–50.
151. Ibid., Bk. ii, Ch. 5, I, pp. 344–52.
152. Ibid., Bk. iv, Ch. 2, I, pp. 419–21.
153. Ibid., Bk. iv, Ch. 2, I, pp. 421–4.
154. Ibid., Bk. iii, Ch. 1, I, pp. 355–6.
155. Ibid., Bk. iv, Ch. 2, I, pp. 419, 421.
156. Ibid., Bk. iv, Ch. 2, I, pp. 427–9, 433.

7. The doctrine of the rights of man

157. R. R. Palmer, *The Age of the Democratic Revolution. A Political History of Europe and America 1760–1800*, Princeton, New Jersey 1959 and 1964; Jacques Godechot, *France and the Atlantic Revolution of the Eighteenth Century, 1770–99*, New York 1965.
158. This very brief indication of the constitutional issues involved in the struggle between Great Britain and the American colonies leaves untouched the many other and varied causes of the American revolution.
159. On 2 July 1776 the Continental Congress resolved that the thirteen United Colonies were free and independent states, absolved from all allegiance to the British Crown. The Declaration of Independence was then formally adopted on 4 July.
160. Quoted in Clinton Rossiter, *Seedtime of the Republic. The Origin of the American Tradition of Political Liberty*, New York 1953, pp. 355–6.
161. There are differences of opinion among historians concerning the extent of Locke's influence. According to Carl Becker (*The Declaration of Independence. A Study in the History of Political Ideas*, New York 1922, pp. 72–3), the colonists found in Locke a reasoned foundation for the kind of government under which they already lived, i.e. a government largely dependent on the consent of the governed and based on a contract between the ruler and the ruled. Clinton Rossiter (op. cit., pp. 358–9) is inclined to see Locke as only the 'most popular source of Revolutionary ideas' because he had 'glorified a rebellion of Englishmen against an English King'.
162. In addition to Sieyès' pamphlet *What is the Third Estate?*, the best indication of the scope and diversity of the Third Estate's demands is to be found in the general *cahiers* of that Estate which were presented in the Estates General in May 1789.

Notes and references

163. 'The Tennis Court Oath (20 June 1789)', in J. H. Stewart, *A Documentary Survey of the French Revolution*, New York 1951, p. 88.
164. Emmanuel Joseph Sieyès, *What is the Third Estate?* (trans. M. Blondel and ed. S. E. Finer), London 1963, p. 126.
165. In the circumstances of peasant attacks on the chateaux between June and August 1789 and grain riots in towns and countryside, it was more than likely that security of life and property was very much in the minds of members of the Assembly. So too was the need to legitimize the popular movements, such as that resulting in the attack on the Bastille on 14 July, which had undoubtedly helped to consolidate the political revolution.
166. E. J. Sieyès, op. cit., p. 124.
167. The separation of powers was defined further in the Decree on the Fundamental Principles of Government (1 October 1789), in J. H. Stewart, op. cit., pp. 115–17.
168. This is not surprising as it has been conclusively demonstrated that Rousseau's political ideas had very little impact in France during the constitution-making period of the Constituent Assembly between 1789 and 1791. Joan McDonald, *Rousseau and the French Revolution 1762–91*, London 1965, especially pp. 87 et seq., 111–12, 158 et seq.
169. The Edict of Nantes (1598) granting freedom of worship to Protestants had been revoked by Louis XIV in 1685.
170. *Inter alia*, a condemnation of the power and practices of the guilds during the Old Regime is included in Article 3; Article 6 stated that employments should be open to all; and Article 17 stipulated that public necessity alone, with the payment of an indemnity, justified the seizure of private property.
171. Decree Providing For a Uniform Tariff (31 October 1790), in J. H. Stewart, op. cit., p. 163.
172. Georges Lefebvre, *The Coming of the French Revolution* (trans. R. R. Palmer), New York 1959, pp. 184–7.
173. For example see doc. 63 in which Adolphe Thiers examines political practice during the Second Empire of Napoleon III in the light of the principles of 1789.
174. This point was emphasized by Dr Richard Price, one of the leading dissenters, in a sermon delivered on 4 November 1789 to mark the anniversary of the 'Glorious Revolution' of 1688. A. Cobban (ed.), *The Debate on the French Revolution 1789–1800*, London 1950, pp. 59–64.
175. Arthur Young, through his travels in France, was the one notable exception.
176. Burke's *Reflections* was in part a direct reply to Dr Richard Price's sermon of 4 November 1789 commemorating the revolution of 1688.
177. Thomas Paine, *The Rights of Man* (Dolphin edn), New York 1961, Pt. I, pp. 277–8, 308–10; Pt. II, p. 422. See also *Dissertation on First Principles of Government*, Moncure D. Conway (ed.), *The Writings of Thomas Paine*, New York 1895, III, pp. 260, 262–4.
178. *The Rights of Man*, Pt. II, p. 410.
179. Ibid., Pt. I, pp. 305–6.
180. Ibid., Pt. I, p. 353.
181. Ibid., Pt. II, pp. 399–400.
182. Ibid. p. 445.
183. Ibid., pp. 413, 434.
184. Ibid., p. 400.
185. *Dissertation on First Principles of Government*, in M. D. Conway (ed.), op. cit., p. 268.
186. Ibid., p. 269. See also Article 20 of the Declaration of Rights drafted by Paine and Condorcet early in 1793, in M. D. Conway, *The Life of Thomas Paine*, New York 1892, II, pp. 39–41.
187. Article 24 in Paine's and Condorcet's draft Declaration of Rights.

A. Roots of liberalism: the eighteenth century

188. *The Rights of Man*, Pt. II, Ch. 5. Paine's proposed social measures are summarized on pp. 494–5.
189. Paine was charged with seditious libel in June 1792, and fled to France before he was tried, convicted and outlawed in December.
190. Article 23 in Paine's and Condorcet's draft Declaration of Rights states: 'Instruction is the need of all, and society owes it equally to all its members.'
191. Jeremy Bentham, *Anarchical Fallacies being an Examination of the Declaration of Rights issued during the French Revolution*, in John Bowring (ed.); *The Works of Jeremy Bentham*, Edinburgh 1843, II, p. 497.
192. Ibid., pp. 524–5.
193. Ibid., pp. 500–1.
194. Ibid., p. 496. Bentham had expressed a similar fear at the time of the American revolution, but later he readily admitted that anarchy had not been the outcome in the American colonies. Mary P. Mack, *Jeremy Bentham: an Odyssey of Ideas 1748–92*, London 1962, pp. 185–7.
195. *The Constitutional Code*, Section VI. Rights and Obligations; extract in Charles W. Everett, *Jeremy Bentham*, London 1966, pp. 243–5.
196. *Anarchical Fallacies*, p. 498.
197. Ibid., p. 502.
198. Ibid., p. 492.
199. Ibid., p. 523.
200. Ibid., pp. 491–3, 522.
201. Bentham had already defined the principle of utility in his *Introduction to the Principles of Morals and Legislation*, completed by 1781 but not published until 1789.
202. D. J. Manning, *The Mind of Jeremy Bentham*, London 1968, pp. 61–2; Mary P. Mack, op. cit., pp. 411–12.
203. In part because some of Bentham's work had first been published in French translations made by Etienne Dumont.
204. Bentham's *Plan for Parliamentary Reform* (1817) was the one work he intended for a mass audience (Mary P. Mack, op. cit., p. 11). It is generally accepted that *The Rights of Man* sold about 200,000 copies in Great Britain between 1791 and 1793; but the number of copies sold is no indication of the numbers who read one or both parts of the book.

8. The belief in progress

205. J. Barraclough (trans.), Marquis de Condorcet, *Sketch for a Historical Picture of the Progress of the Human Mind*; Introduction by Stuart Hampshire, London 1955, p. ix.
206. J. Selwyn Schapiro, *Condorcet and the Rise of Liberalism*, New York 1934, p. 25.
207. Barraclough (trans.), op. cit., p. 146.
208. J. S. Schapiro, op. cit., p. 255.
209. Barraclough (trans.), op. cit., Introduction, p. x.
210. Barraclough (trans.), op. cit., p. 201.

Documents

1. The civil State – representative government: documents

(Introduction, p. 105)

Doc. 1a. JOHN LOCKE: From the Natural State to the Civil State

95. Men being, as has been said, by nature all free, equal, and independent, no one can be put out of this estate and subjected to the political power of another without his own consent, which is done by agreeing with other men, to join and unite into a community for their comfortable, safe, and peaceable living, one amongst another, in a secure enjoyment of their properties, and a greater security against any that are not of it. This any number of men may do, because it injures not the freedom of the rest; they are left, as they were, in the liberty of the state of Nature. When any number of men have so consented to make one community or government, they are thereby presently incorporated, and make one body politic, wherein the majority have a right to act and conclude the rest.

96. For, when any number of men have, by the consent of every individual, made a community, they have thereby made that community one body, with a power to act as one body, which is only by the will and determination of the majority. For that which acts any community, being only the consent of the individuals of it, and it being one body, must move one way, it is necessary the body should move that way whither the greater force carries it, which is the consent of the majority, or else it is impossible it should act or continue one body, one community, which the consent of every individual that united into it agreed that it should; and

so every one is bound by that consent to be concluded by the majority. And therefore we see that in assemblies empowered to act by positive laws where no number is set by that positive law which empowers them, the act of the majority passes for the act of the whole, and of course determines, as having by the law of Nature and reason, the power of the whole.

97. And thus every man, by consenting with others to make one body politic under one government, puts himself under an obligation to every one of that society to submit to the determination of the majority, and to be concluded by it; or else this original compact, whereby he with others incorporates into one society, would signify nothing, and be no compact, if he be left free, and under no other ties than he was in before in the state of Nature. For what appearance would there be of any compact? What new engagement if he were no farther tied by any decrees of the society than he himself thought fit and did actually consent to? This would be still as great a liberty as he himself had before his compact, or any one else in the state of Nature, who may submit himself and consent to any acts of it if he thinks fit.

98. For if the consent of the majority shall not in reason be received as the act of the whole, and conclude every individual; nothing but the consent of every individual can make anything to be the act of the whole, which, considering the infirmities of health and avocations of business, which in a number though much less than that of a commonwealth, will necessarily keep many away from the public assembly; and the variety of opinions and contrariety of interests which unavoidably happen in all collections of men it is next impossible ever to be had. And, therefore, if coming into society be upon such terms, it will be only like Cato's coming into the theatre, *tantum ut exiret.* Such a constitution as this would make the mighty leviathan of a shorter duration than the feeblest creatures, and not let it outlast the day it was born in, which cannot be supposed till we can think that rational creatures should desire and constitute societies only to be dissolved. For where the majority cannot conclude the rest, there they cannot act as one body, and consequently will be immediately dissolved again.

99. Whosoever, therefore, out of a state of Nature unite into a community, must be understood to give up all the power necessary to the ends for which they unite into society to the majority of the community, unless they expressly agreed in any number greater than the majority. And this is done by barely agreeing to unite into one political society, which is all the compact that is, or needs be, between the individuals that enter into or make up a commonwealth. And thus, that which begins and actually constitutes any political society is nothing but the consent of any number of freemen capable of majority, to unite and incorporate into such a society. And this is that, and that only, which did or could give beginning to any lawful government in the world.

[Source: John Locke, *Two Treatises on Civil Government*, London 1884, 'The Second Treatise of Government' (1690), Ch. 8, pp. 240–2.]

Doc. 1*b*. JOHN LOCKE: The Ends of Political Society and Government

123. If man in the state of nature be so free as has been said, if he be absolute lord of his own person and possessions, equal to the greatest and subject to nobody, why will he part with his freedom, this empire, and subject himself to the dominion and control of any other power? To which it is obvious to answer, that though in the state of Nature he hath such a right, yet the enjoyment of it is very uncertain and constantly exposed to the invasion of others; for all being kings as much as he, every man his equal, and the greater part no strict observers of equity and justice, the enjoyment of the property he has in this state is very unsafe, very insecure. This makes him willing to quit this condition which, however free, is full of fears and continual dangers; and it is not without reason that he seeks out and is willing to join in society with others who are already united, or have a mind to unite for the mutual preservation of their lives, liberties and estates, which I call by the general name – property.

124. The great and chief end, therefore, of men uniting into commonwealths, and putting themselves under government, is the preservation of their property, to which in the state of Nature there are many things wanting.

Firstly, there wants an established, settled, known law, received and allowed by common consent to be the standard of right and wrong, and the common measure to decide all controversies between them. For though the law of Nature be plain and intelligible to all rational creatures, yet men, being biased by their interest, as well as ignorant for want of study of it, are not apt to allow of it as a law binding to them in the application of it to their particular cases.

125. Secondly; in the state of Nature there wants a known and indifferent judge, with authority to determine all differences according to the established law. For every one in that state being both judge and executioner of the law of Nature, men being partial to themselves, passion and revenge is very apt to carry them too far, and with too much heat in their own cases, as well as negligence and unconcernedness, make them too remiss in other men's.

126. Thirdly: in the state of Nature there often wants power to back and support the sentence when right, and to give it due execution. They who by any injustice offended will seldom fail where they are able by force to make good their injustice. Such resistance many times makes the punishment dangerous, and frequently destructive to those who attempt it.

A. Roots of liberalism: the eighteenth century

127. Thus mankind, notwithstanding all the privileges of the state of Nature, being but in an ill condition while they remain in it are quickly driven into society. Hence it comes to pass, that we seldom find any number of men live any time together in this state. The inconveniences that they are therein exposed to by the irregular and uncertain exercise of the power every man has of punishing the transgressions of others, make them take sanctuary under the established laws of government, and therein seek the preservation of their property. It is this makes them so willingly give up every one his single power of punishing to be exercised by such alone as shall be appointed to it amongst them, and by such rules as the community, or those authorized by them to that purpose, shall agree on. And in this we have the original right and rise of both the legislative and executive power as well as of the governments and societies themselves.

128. For in the state of Nature to omit the liberty he has of innocent delights, a man has two powers. The first is to do whatsoever he thinks fit for the preservation of himself and others within the permission of the law of Nature; by which law, common to them all, he and all the rest of mankind are one community, make up one society distinct from all other creatures, and were it not for the corruption and viciousness of degenerate men, there would be no need of any other, no necessity that men should separate from this great and natural community, and associate into lesser combinations. The other power a man has in the state of Nature is the power to punish the crimes committed against that law. Both these he gives up when he joins in a private, if I may so call it, or particular political society, and incorporates into any commonwealth separate from the rest of mankind.

129. The first power – viz., of doing whatsoever he thought fit for the preservation of himself and the rest of mankind, he gives up to be regulated by laws made by the society, so far forth as the preservation of himself and the rest of that society shall require; which laws of the society in many things confine the liberty he had by the law of Nature.

130. Secondly. The power of punishing he wholly gives up, and engages his natural force, which he might before employ in the execution of the law of Nature, by his own single authority, as he thought fit, to assist the executive power of the society as the law thereof shall require. For being now in a new state, wherein he is to enjoy many conveniences from the labour, assistance, and society of others in the same community, as well as protection from its whole strength, he is to part also with as much of his natural liberty, in providing for himself, as the good, prosperity, and safety of the society shall require, which is not only necessary, but just, since the other members of the society do the like.

131. But though men when they enter into society give up the equality, liberty, and executive power they had in the state of Nature into

the hands of the society, to be so far disposed of by the legislative as the good of the society shall require, yet it being only with the intention in every one the better to preserve himself, his liberty and property (for no rational creature can be supposed to change his condition with an intention to be worse), the power of the society or legislative constituted by them can never be supposed to extend farther than the common good, but is obliged to secure every one's property by providing against those three defects above mentioned that made the state of Nature so unsafe and uneasy. And so, whoever has the legislative or supreme power of any commonwealth, is bound to govern by established standing laws, promulgated and known to the people, and not by extemporary decrees, by indifferent and upright judges, who are to decide controversies by those laws; and to employ the force of the community at home only in the execution of such laws; or abroad to prevent or redress foreign injuries and secure the community from inroads and invasion. And all this to be directed to no other end but the peace, safety, and public good of the people.

[Source: John Locke, *Two Treatises on Civil Government*, London 1884, 'The Second Treatise of Government' (1690), Ch. 9, pp. 256–9.]

Doc.1c. JOHN LOCKE: Of the Extent of the Legislative Power

134. The great end of men's entering into society being the enjoyment of their properties in peace and safety, and the great instrument and means of that being the laws established in that society, the first and fundamental positive law of all commonwealths is the establishing of the legislative power, as the first and fundamental natural law which is to govern even the legislative. Itself is the preservation of the society and (as far as will consist with the public good) of every person in it. This legislative is not only the supreme power of the commonwealth, but sacred and unalterable in the hands where the community have once placed it. Nor can any edict of anybody else, in what form soever conceived, or by what power soever backed, have the force and obligation of a law which has not its sanction from that legislative which the public has chosen and appointed; for without this the law could not have that which is absolutely necessary to its being a law, the consent of the society, over whom nobody can have a power to make laws but by their own consent and by authority received from them; and therefore all the obedience, which by the most solemn ties any one can be obliged to pay, ultimately terminates in this supreme power, and is directed by those laws which it enacts. Nor can any oaths to any foreign power whatsoever, or any domestic subordinate power, discharge any member of the society from his obedience to the legislative, acting pursuant to their trust, nor oblige him to any obedience contrary to the laws so enacted or farther than they

do allow, it being ridiculous to imagine one can be tied ultimately to obey any power in the society which is not the supreme.

135. Though the legislative, whether placed in one or more, whether it be always in being or only by intervals, though it be the supreme power in every commonwealth; yet, first, it is not, nor can possibly be, absolutely arbitrary over the lives and fortunes of the people. For it being but the joint power of every member of the society given up to that person or assembly which is legislator, it can be no more than those persons had in a state of Nature before they entered into society, and gave it up to the community. For nobody can transfer to another more power than he has in himself, and nobody has an absolute arbitrary power over himself, or over any other, to destroy his own life, or take away the life or property of another. A man, as has been proved, cannot subject himself to the arbitrary power of another; and having, in the state of Nature, no arbitrary power over the life, liberty, or possession of another, but only so much as the law of Nature gave him for the preservation of himself and the rest of mankind, this is all he doth, or can give up to the commonwealth, and by it to the legislative power, so that the legislative can have no more than this. Their power in the utmost bounds of it is limited to the public good of the society. It is a power that hath no other end but preservation, and therefore can never have a right to destroy, enslave, or designedly to impoverish the subjects; the obligations of the law of Nature cease not in society; but only in many cases are drawn closer, and have, by human laws, known penalties annexed to them to enforce their observation. Thus the law of Nature stands as an eternal rule to all men, legislators as well as others. The rules that they make for other men's actions must, as well as their own and other men's actions, be conformable to the law of Nature – i.e., to the will of God, of which that is a declaration, and the fundamental law of Nature being the preservation of mankind, no human sanction can be good or valid against it.

136. Secondly, the legislative or supreme authority cannot assume to itself a power to rule by extemporary arbitrary decrees, but is bound to dispense justice and decide the rights of the subject by promulgated standing laws, and known authorized judges. For the law of Nature being unwritten, and so nowhere to be found but in the minds of men, they who, through passion or interest, shall miscite or misapply it, cannot so easily be convinced of their mistake where there is no established judge; and so it serves not as it ought, to determine the rights and fence the properties of those that live under it, especially where every one is judge, interpreter, and executioner of it too, and that in his own case; and he that has right on his side, having ordinarily but his own single strength, hath not force enough to defend himself from injuries or punish delinquents. To avoid these inconveniences which disorder men's properties in the state of Nature, men unite into societies that they may have the united strength of the whole society to secure and defend their properties, and may have

standing rules to bound it by which every one may know what is his. To this end it is that men give up all their natural power to the society they enter into, and the community put the legislative power into such hands as they think fit, with this trust, that they shall be governed by declared laws, or else their peace, quiet, and property will still be at the same uncertainty as it was in the state of Nature.

137. Absolute arbitrary power, or governing without settled standing laws, can neither of them consist with the ends of society and government, which men would not quit the freedom of the state of Nature for, and tie themselves up under were it not to preserve their lives, liberties, and fortunes; and by stated rules of right and property to secure their peace and quiet. It cannot be supposed that they should intend, had they a power so to do, to give any one or more an absolute arbitrary power over their persons and estates, and put a force into the magistrate's hand to execute his unlimited will arbitrarily upon them; this were to put themselves into a worse condition than the state of Nature, wherein they had a liberty to defend their right against the injuries of others, and were upon equal terms of force to maintain it, whether invaded by a single man or many in combination. Whereas by supposing they have given up themselves to the absolute arbitrary power and will of a legislator, they have disarmed themselves, and armed him to make a prey of them when he pleases; he being in a much worse condition that is exposed to the arbitrary power of one man who has the command of a hundred thousand than he that is exposed to the arbitrary power of a hundred thousand single men, nobody being secure, that his will who has such a command is better than that of other men, though his force be a hundred thousand times stronger. And, therefore, whatever form the commonwealth is under, the ruling power ought to govern by declared and received laws, and not by extemporary dictates and undetermined resolutions, for then mankind will be in a far worse condition than in the state of Nature if they shall have armed one or a few men with the joint power of a multitude, to force them to obey at pleasure the exorbitant and unlimited decrees of their sudden thoughts, or unrestrained, and till that moment, unknown wills, without having any measures set down which may guide and justify their actions. For all the power the government has, being only for the good of the society, as it ought not to be arbitrary and at pleasure, so it ought to be exercised by established and promulgated laws, that both the people may know their duty, and be safe and secure within the limits of the law, and the rulers, too, kept within their due bounds, and not be tempted by the power they have in their hands to employ it to purposes, and by such measures as they would not have known, and own not willingly.

138. Thirdly, the supreme power cannot take from any man any part of his property without his own consent. For the preservation of property being the end of government, and that for which men enter into society, it

necessarily supposes and requires that the people should have property, without which they must be supposed to lose that by entering into society, which was the end for which they entered into it; too gross an absurdity for any man to own. Men, therefore, in society having property, they have such a right to the goods, which by the law of the community are theirs, that nobody hath a right to take them, or any part of them, from them without their own consent, without this they have no property at all. For I have truly no property in that which another can by right take from me when he pleases against my consent. Hence it is a mistake to think that the supreme or legislative power of any commonwealth can do what it will, and dispose of the estates of the subject arbitrarily, or take any part of them at pleasure. This is not much to be feared in governments where the legislative consists wholly or in part in assemblies which are variable, whose members upon the dissolution of the assembly are subjects under the common laws of their country, equally with the rest. But in governments where the legislative is in one lasting assembly, always in being or in one man as in absolute monarchies, there is danger still, that they will think themselves to have a distinct interest from the rest of the community, and so will be apt to increase their own riches and power by taking what they think fit from the people. For a man's property is not at all secure, though there be good and equitable laws to set the bounds of it between him and his fellow-subjects, if he who commands those subjects have power to take from any private man what part he pleases of his property, and use and dispose of it as he thinks good.

139. But government into whosesoever hands it is put, being as I have before showed, entrusted with this condition, and for this end, that men might have and secure their properties, the prince or senate, however it may have power to make laws for the regulating of property between the subjects one amongst another, yet can never have a power to take to themselves the whole, or any part of the subjects' property, without their own consent; for this would be in effect to leave them no property at all. And to let us see that even absolute power, where it is necessary, is not arbitrary by being absolute, but is still limited by that reason, and confined to those ends which required it in some cases to be absolute, we need look no farther than the common practice of martial discipline. For the preservation of the army, and in it of the whole commonwealth, requires an absolute obedience to the command of every superior officer, and it is justly death to disobey or dispute the most dangerous and unreasonable of them; but yet we see that neither the serjeant that could command a soldier to march up to the mouth of a cannon, or stand in a breach where he is almost sure to perish, can command that soldier to give him one penny of his money; nor the general that can condemn him to death for deserting his post, or not obeying the most desperate orders, cannot yet with all his absolute power of life and death dispose of one farthing of that soldier's estate, or seize one jot of his goods; whom yet he can com-

mand anything, and hang for the least disobedience. Because such a blind obedience is necessary to that end for which the commander has his power — viz., the preservation of the rest, but the disposing of his goods has nothing to do with it.

140. It is true governments cannot be supported without great charge, and it is fit every one who enjoys his share of the protection should pay out of his estate his proportion for the maintenance of it. But still it must be with his own consent — i.e., the consent of the majority, giving it either by themselves or their representatives chosen by them; for if any one shall claim a power to lay and levy taxes on the people by his own authority, and without such consent of the people, he thereby invades the fundamental law of property, and subverts the end of government. For what property have I in that which another may by right take when he pleases to himself?

141. Fourthly. The legislative cannot transfer the power of making laws to any other hands, for it being but a delegated power from the people, they who have it cannot pass it over to others. The people alone can appoint the form of the commonwealth, which is by constituting the legislative, and appointing in whose hands that shall be. And when the people have said, 'We will submit, and be governed by laws made by such men, and in such forms,' nobody else can say other men shall make laws for them; nor can they be bound by any laws but such as are enacted by those whom they have chosen and authorized to make laws for them.

142. These are the bounds which the trust that is put in them by the society and the law of God and Nature have set to the legislative power of every commonwealth, in all forms of government. First: They are to govern by promulgated established laws, not to be varied in particular cases, but to have one rule for rich and poor, for the favourite at Court, and the countryman at plough. Secondly: These laws also ought to be designed for no other end ultimately but the good of the people. Thirdly: They must not raise taxes on the property of the people without the consent of the people given by themselves or their deputies. And this properly concerns only such governments where the legislative is always in being, or at least where the people have not reserved any part of the legislative to deputies, to be from time to time chosen by themselves. Fourthly: The legislative neither must nor can transfer the power of making laws to anybody else, or place it anywhere but where the people have.

[Source: John Locke, *Two Treatises on Civil Government*, London 1884, 'The Second Treatise of Government' (1690), Ch. 11, pp. 260–7.]

2. Religious toleration: documents
(Introduction, p. 110)

Doc. 2. JOHN LOCKE: 'A Letter on Toleration' (1689)

Uprightness of conduct, which constitutes not the least part of religion and sincere piety, concerns civil life also, and in it lies the salvation both of men's souls and of the commonwealth. Moral actions belong therefore to the jurisdiction of both the outward and the inner court, and are subject to both dominions, of the civil as well as the domestic governor: I mean both of the magistrate and of conscience. Here, therefore, there is a risk that one of these may infringe the right of the other, and that strife may arise between the guardians of the peace and of the soul. But if what I have said above on the limits of each government be rightly considered, it will easily remove all difficulty in this matter.

Every mortal has an immortal soul, capable of eternal happiness or misery, and as its salvation depends upon his doing and believing those things in this life which are necessary to obtain the favour of the Deity, and are prescribed by God; thence (1) it follows that man is obliged above all else to observe these things, and he must exercise his utmost care, application, and diligence in seeking out and performing them; for nothing belonging to this mortal condition is in any way comparable with eternity. (2) It follows that as a man does not violate anyone's rights by his own wrongful worship, or injure other men by not sharing their correct religious views, and as his perdition does not prejudice the prosperity of others, the care of each man's salvation belongs only to himself. But I would not have this understood as if I meant to rule out all charitable admonitions, and endeavours to refute men's errors, which are indeed a Christian's greatest duty. Anyone may employ as many exhortations and arguments as he pleases for another man's salvation; but all force and compulsion must be forborne, and nothing be done for the sake of dominion. Nobody is obliged in this matter to obey the admonitions or injunctions of another further than he himself chooses. Regarding his salvation every man has the supreme and final power of judging for himself, because he alone is concerned, and nobody else can take any harm from his conduct.

Besides his immortal soul, man has his life in this world. It is precarious and of uncertain duration, and to sustain it he needs earthly conveniences, which he either has obtained, or must obtain, by toil and industry. For the things necessary for living well and happily do not spring up of their own accord, so that on their account man is burdened with additional care. But since men are so dishonest that most of them prefer to enjoy the fruits of other men's labour rather than work to provide for themselves; therefore, to protect their possessions, their wealth and property, and also their liberty and bodily strength, which are their means of livelihood, they are obliged to enter into society with one another, so that by mutual assistance and combined forces each man may have secure and private possession of the things that are useful for life. Meanwhile the care of his eternal salvation is left to each individual, since the attainment of it cannot be assisted by another man's industry, nor can the loss of it turn to another man's prejudice, nor the hope of it be taken from him by any force. But men who unite in civil society by a mutual compact of assistance to defend the things of this life may nevertheless be deprived of their goods, either by the rapine and fraud of their fellow-citizens, or by hostile attack from abroad. For the latter evil a remedy is sought in arms, wealth, and numbers of citizens; for the former, in the laws. The care of all these things, and the power to use them, is entrusted by the society to the magistrates. This is the origin, these are the uses and the bounds of the legislative power, which is the supreme power, in any commonwealth, namely, to provide security for the private possessions of individuals, as also for the whole people and its public interests, so that it may flourish and increase in peace and prosperity, and as far as possible be safe in its own strength against foreign invasion.

This being settled, it is easy to understand the ends that determine the magistrate's prerogative of making laws, that is, the public good in earthly or worldly matters, which is the sole reason for entering society and the sole object of the commonwealth once it is formed; and on the other hand the liberty that is left to private men in matters concerning the life to come: namely that each may do what he believes to be pleasing to God, on whose good pleasure men's salvation depends. For obedience is due first of all to God, and afterwards to the laws. But you will say: What if the magistrate's decree should order something which seems unlawful to the conscience of a private person?; I answer: If the commonwealth is governed in good faith, and the counsels of the magistrate are really directed to the common good of the citizens, this will seldom happen. But if it should chance to happen, I say that such a private person should abstain from the action which his conscience pronounces to be unlawful, but undergo the punishment which it is not unlawful for him to bear. For the private judgement of any person concerning a law enacted in political matters, and for the public good, does not take away the obligation of that law, nor does it deserve toleration. But if the law concerns things which lie outside the magistrate's province, as for example that the people, or any part of it, should be compelled to embrace a strange religion and adopt new rites, those who disagree are not obliged by that law, because political society was instituted only to preserve for each private man his possession of the things of this life, and for no other purpose. The care of his soul and of spiritual matters, which does not belong to the state and could not be subjected to it, is reserved and retained for each in-

A. Roots of liberalism: the eighteenth century

dividual. Thus the safe-guarding of life and of the things that concern this life is the business of the state, and the preservation of them to their owners is the duty of the magistrate. These worldly things cannot therefore be taken away from this man and given to that at the magistrate's pleasure, nor can the private possession of them among fellow-citizens be changed, not even by a law, for a reason which in no way concerns the civil community, I mean for religion; for this, whether true or false, does no injury to the rest of the citizens in their worldly affairs, which alone are subject to the government.

[Source: John Locke, *Epistola de Tolerantia. A Letter on Toleration* ed. Raymond Klibansky, trans. J. W. Gough, Oxford 1968, pp. 123–9.]

Doc. 3a. VOLTAIRE: Whether Intolerance is Consistent with Natural Law

Natural law is that which nature points out to all men. You have brought up your child; he owes you respect as his father, and gratitude as his benefactor. You have a right to the produce of the soil which you have cultivated with your own hands. You have given and received a promise, and it ought to be kept.

Human rights must in every case be founded on natural law; and everywhere the great and universal principle of both is: 'Do not do to others what you would not want them to do to you.' Now, following that principle, it is hard to see how one man can say to another: 'Believe what I believe, and in what you cannot believe, or you shall die.' This is what they say in Portugal, in Spain, and at Goa. In some other countries they are content for the moment to say: 'Believe as I do, or I shall hate you; believe, or I shall do you as much harm as I can. You monster! You do not share my religion; therefore you have no religion. You should be an abomination to your neighbours, your town, and your province.'

If it were in keeping with human rights to behave like this, the Japanese should detest the Chinese, who should abhor the Siamese; the latter pursuing the people of the Ganges, who should fall upon the inhabitants of the Indus; a Mogul should tear out the heart of the first Malabarian he comes across; the Malabarians should slaughter the Persians, who should massacre the Turks; and altogether they should throw themselves upon the Christians, who for so long have been devouring each other.

The law of intolerance is therefore absurd and barbarous. It is the law of tigers; though it is much more horrible, for tigers only kill in order to eat while we destroy each other for paragraphs.

[Source: Voltaire, *Traité sur la Tolérance* (1764), in *Oeuvres complètes de Voltaire* (2nd edn), Paris 1827, tome I, Ch. 6, pp.168–9. Translated by the editors of this volume.]

Doc. 3b. VOLTAIRE: An Account of a Controversial Dispute in China

In the early years of the great Emperor Kang-hi's reign, a mandarin of Canton was in his house when he heard a great commotion going on in the next house. He inquired if anyone was being killed; but he was told that it was only an argument between the almoner of the Danish missionary society, a chaplain from Batavia and a Jesuit. The mandarin made them come to his house, served them with tea and sweetmeats, and asked why they were quarrelling.

The Jesuit replied that it was extremely painful for him, who was always in the right, to have dealings with people who were always in the wrong; that at first he had argued with the greatest restraint; but finally he had lost his patience.

With the utmost discretion, the mandarin impressed on them the need for courtesy in any discussion; he told them that in China people never become offended, and asked what the argument was all about.

The Jesuit replied: My lord, I will make you the judge. These two gentlemen refuse to submit to the decisions of the Council of Trent.

I find that astonishing, said the mandarin. Then, turning to the obstinate pair, he said: It seems to me, gentlemen, that you ought to respect the judgment of a large assembly. I do not know what the Council of Trent is; but several people are always better informed than one. No-one ought to believe that he knows more than all others, and that he alone has any sense. This is the teaching of our great Confucius; and, if you take my opinion, you will do well to abide by the Council of Trent.

The Dane then spoke: Your lordship speaks with the greatest wisdom; we do respect large assemblies, as we should; and we are therefore in complete agreement with the opinion of several assemblies held before the Council of Trent.

Oh! if that is the case, said the mandarin, I beg your pardon; you could well be right. So, you and the Dutchman are of the same opinion against this poor Jesuit?

Not at all, said the Dutchman. This man's opinions are almost as wild as those of the Jesuit, who is being so agreeable to you. I can't stand it.

I do not understand your behaviour, said the mandarin. Are not the three of you Christians? Have not all three of you come to teach Christianity in our empire? Should you not, then, have the same doctrines?

You see, my lord, said the Jesuit, these two persons are mortal enemies, and yet they both argue against me. It is obvious, therefore, that they are both wrong, and that right is on my side alone. That is not so obvious, said the mandarin; it is quite possible that all three of you are wrong. I should be interested to hear you speak one after the other.

The Jesuit then made a rather long speech, during which the Dane and the Dutchman shrugged their shoulders while the mandarin did not un-

A. Roots of liberalism: the eighteenth century

derstand any of it. The Dane spoke next. His two opponents regarded him with pity, and the mandarin still understood nothing. The Dutchman's lot was the same. Finally, all three spoke at the same time and abused each other roundly. The good mandarin had much difficulty in putting a stop to it; and he told them: If you want us to tolerate your doctrine here, you must begin by being neither intolerant nor intolerable.

After the audience had ended, the Jesuit met a Jacobin [i.e. Dominican] missionary. He informed the Jacobin that he had won his point, and assured him that truth always triumphed. But the Jacobin said: If I had been there you would not have prevailed; I would have convicted you of falsehood and idolatry. The quarrel warmed up; and the Jacobin and the Jesuit seized each other by the hair. When the mandarin was informed of the scandal, he sent them both to prison. A deputy mandarin asked the judge: How long does your excellency wish them to be held? Until they agree, replied the judge. Ah! said the deputy mandarin, then they will be in prison for life. Well, then, said the judge, until they forgive each other. They will never forgive one another, said the other; I know them. Very well, then, said the mandarin, until they pretend to forgive each other.

[Source: Voltaire, *Traité sur la Tolérance* (1764), in *Oeuvres complètes de Voltaire* (2nd edn.) Paris 1827, tome I, Ch. 19, pp.271–4. Translated by the editors of this volume.]

Doc. 3c. VOLTAIRE: A Prayer to God

I address myself no longer to men, but to you, God of all beings, all worlds and all ages. If it is permissible for feeble creatures lost in the vastness, and imperceptible to the rest of the universe, to dare to ask something of you, who has given everything, whose decrees are as immutable as they are eternal, deign to look with pity on the errors inherent in our nature, that those errors do not prove calamitous for us. You have not given us a heart so that we can hate, and hands so that we can slaughter each other. Grant that we may mutually help each other to endure the burden of a laborious and transitory life. Let not the small differences between the garments that cover our feeble bodies, between all our inadequate languages, our absurd customs, all our imperfect laws and foolish opinions, between our conditions, so disproportionate in our eyes, and so equal in yours; let not all those little gradations which make distinctions between the atoms called *men* be the signals of hatred and persecution. Let those who light wax candles at mid-day to worship you tolerate those who are content with the light of your sun. Let not those who cover their robe with a white linen cloth to tell us of the necessity to love you, detest those who say the same thing wearing a black woollen cloak. Let it be the same thing to worship you in a jargon taken from an old language or in a more modern jargon. Let those who wear red or purple apparel, who rule over a small part of a little heap of the mud of this world, and who possess a few rounded pieces of a certain metal, enjoy without ostentation what they call greatness and wealth, and that others behold them without envy; for you know that in these vanities there is nothing either for envy or for pride.

May all men remember that they are brothers. May they abominate the exercise of tyranny over souls as they abhor the brigandage which carries off by force the fruits of toil and peaceful industry! If the scourges of war are inevitable, let us not hate each other, let us not vilify each other in the midst of peace; but make use of the moment of our existence to praise on equal terms and in a thousand languages, from Siam to California, your goodness which has given us this moment.

[Source: Voltaire, *Traité sur la Tolérance* (1764), in *Oeuvres complètes de Voltaire* (2nd edn.), Paris 1827, tome I, Ch. 23, pp.295–7. Translated by the editors of this volume.]

Doc. 4. TURGOT: Memorial to the King 'On Toleration' June, 1775

I can conceive that the men who believe all religions to be equally false, and who regard them as inventions of policy in order to govern more easily the people, can make no scruple about compelling them to follow the religion which it is thought most expedient to prescribe for them. . . . But if there is a true religion, if God is to demand account from each man of what he has believed and practised, if an eternity of punishment must be the portion of him who shall reject the true religion, how can we imagine that any power on earth can have the right to order a man to follow another religion than the one which he believes true in his soul and conscience?

If there is a true religion a man must follow it, and profess it in spite of all the powers of the earth, in spite of the edicts of emperors and kings, in spite of the judgment of proconsuls and of the executioner's sword. It is for having had this courage, for having fulfilled this sacred duty, that we have had held up to our veneration the martyrs of the primitive Church. If the martyrs were right in resisting the civil power, and following the voice of their conscience, their conscience, by that fact, did not recognise the civil power as a judge.

All sovereigns have not the same religion, and each religious man feels himself, in his conscience, by his duty and for his salvation, obliged to follow that religion which he believes to be the truth. Sovereigns have not the right to order their subjects to disobey their conscience. God, in judging men, will demand of them whether they have believed and practised true religion; not whether they have believed and practised the religion of their sovereign. How could He demand that of them if all the sovereigns have not the true religion? Cast your eyes, Sire, on the map of the world; and see how few countries there are of which the sovereigns are Catholics. How can it be that with the greatest number of the sovereigns of the world existing in error, they have received from God the right to judge of the true religion? If they have not the right, if they have neither infallibility nor the divine mission which alone could give it them, how dare they take upon themselves to decide the fate of their subjects, of their happiness or their misery during eternity? Every man, by the principles of religion, has his soul to save; he has all the light of reason and of revelation in order to apply these lights — but this conscience is for himself alone. To follow his own conscience is the right and duty of every man, and no man has the right to make his conscience a rule for another. Each one is responsible for himself to God, none is responsible for another.

This principle is so clearly evident, that it would seem a waste of time to prove it, if the illusions opposed to it had not blinded the greater part of the human race, if they had not inundated the earth with blood, if even to-day they did not make millions unhappy.

Will the defenders of intolerance say that the prince has only the right to command when his religion is true and that then he ought to be obeyed? No, even then we cannot and ought not to obey him, for if we ought to follow the religion he prescribes, it is not because he commands it but because it is true, and it is not and it cannot be because the prince commands it that it is true. There is no man so irrational as to believe a religion true for such a reason. The man who submits himself to it in good faith does not obey the prince, he obeys only his conscience, and the order of the prince does not add, and cannot add, any weight to the obligation which conscience alone imposes. Let the prince believe or not believe a certain religion, let him command or not command his subjects to follow it, it is neither more nor less than it is — either true or false. The opinion of the prince is thus absolutely foreign to the truth of a religion, and consequently to the obligation to follow it; the prince then has, as prince, no right to judge, no right to command in this respect; his incompetence is absolute on things of this order, which are beyond his jurisdiction, and in which the conscience of each individual has only, and can have only, God Himself for Judge.

Some theologians say: 'We admit that the prince has not the right to judge of religion, but the Church has this right, and the prince, in submission to the Church, ordains in conformity with its judgments. ... He himself does not judge, but orders his subjects to submit themselves to a legitimate judgment.' As this reasoning has been used and is still used seriously, it has to be answered seriously.

The Church has the right to judge of the things of religion — yes, without doubt; it has the right to exclude from its body, to anathematise, those who refuse to submit to its decisions, its decisions are obligatory [upon those who belong to it, and who believe that] what the Church binds and looses shall be bound and loosed in Heaven. But the Church is not a temporal power, it has neither the right nor the power to punish in this world; its anathemas affect only the penalties which God reserves in the future life for the obstinately refractory. The prince, if he is a Catholic, is the child of the Church; he is subject to her, but only as a man concerned with his personal salvation; as a prince he is independent of the ecclesiastical power. The Church, then, can order him in nothing so far as he is prince, but only so far as he is a man; and as it is only in quality of prince that he could compel his subjects to submit to the judgment of the Church, it follows that the Church cannot make it a duty for him to use his authority to compel his subjects against their conscience. The Church cannot give him the right to do so, because she has it not herself, and besides, because the prince, as prince, not only does not acknowledge the superiority of the Church, but is not competent to judge for others what are the rights of the Church, or whether such a society is the true Church ...

[This doctrine of making the prince the creature of the Church is] the same doctrine, the same spirit, which produced the infernal St. Bartholomew and the detestable League, placing alternately the sword in the king's hand to massacre the people, and in the people's hands to assassinate their Kings. This, Sire, is a subject of meditation which should ever be kept in princes' minds. But, without ascending to those high principles, would the simplest common sense allow it to be imagined that princes could have any right over the conscience and the salvation of their subjects? If the fate of men during eternity could depend upon other men, should there not be a reasonable certitude that these other men should be endowed with natural or acquired enlightenment, superior to those of common men? Without such light – or even with it, without an express mission from the Deity, what man could dare to take upon him the eternal happiness or misery of other men?

The mission of kings is to make the happiness of their people on earth. This mission is noble enough, beautiful enough, and the work it involves is weighty enough for the strength of anyone, whoever he may be. He who has fulfilled with success this sublime and laborious career can die content with himself, and need not fear to render an account of his life. With attention, straightforwardness, and diligence, a prince has every enlightenment and assistance to discover what is really just and truly useful; he has no need to know anything else. He may make mistakes; this is an evil no doubt, but it is an inevitable result of the nature of things. ...

How can religion command sovereigns to use their power to constrain their subjects in matters of religion? Can religion then command, can it permit crimes? To order a crime is to commit one; he who orders to assassinate is regarded by all the world as an assassin. Now the prince who orders some of his subjects to profess a religion they do not believe, or to renounce one they do believe, commands a crime; the subjects who

A. Roots of liberalism: the eighteenth century

obey act a lie, they betray their conscience, they do an act which they believe God forbids . . .

[Source: Turgot, 'Memorial to the King "On Toleration" June 1775'; in *The Life and Writings of Turgot*, ed. W. Walker Stephens, London 1895, pp.258–64.]

3. 'The Spirit of the Laws': documents
(Introduction, p. 117)

Doc. 5a. MONTESQUIEU: Political Liberty with regard to the Constitution and the Separation of Powers

1. A general idea

I make a distinction between the laws that establish political liberty, as it relates to the constitution, and those by which it is established, as it relates to the citizen. The former shall be the subject of this book; the latter I shall examine in the next.

2. Different significations of the word liberty

There is no word that admits of more various significations, and has made more varied impressions on the human mind, than that of Liberty. Some have taken it as a means of deposing a person on whom they had conferred a tyrannical authority; others for the power of choosing a superior whom they are obliged to obey; others for the right of bearing arms, and of being thereby enabled to use violence; others, in fine, for the privilege of being governed by a native of their own country, or by their own laws.* A certain nation for a long time thought liberty consisted in the privilege of wearing a long beard.† Some have annexed this name to one form of government exclusive of others: those who had a republican taste applied it to this species of polity; those who liked a monarchical state gave it to monarchy.‡ Thus they have all applied the name of *liberty* to the government most suitable to their own customs and inclinations:

* 'I have copied', says Cicero, 'Scævola's edict, which permits the Greeks to terminate their difference among themselves according to their own laws; this makes them consider themselves a free people.'
† The Russians could not bear that Czar Peter should make them cut it off.
‡ The Cappadocians refused the condition of a republican state which was offered them by the Romans.

190

and as in republics the people have not so constant and so present a view of the causes of their misery, and as the magistrates seem to act only in confirmity to the laws, hence liberty is generally said to reside in republics, and to be banished from monarchies. In fine, as in democracies, the people seem to act almost as they please, this sort of government has been deemed the most free, and the power of the people has been confounded with their liberty.

3. *In What Liberty consists*

It is true that in democracies the people seem to act as they please; but political liberty does not consist in an unlimited freedom. In governments, that is, in societies directed by laws, liberty can consist only in the power of doing what we ought to will, and in not being constrained to do what we ought not to will.

We must have continually present to our minds the difference between independence and liberty. Liberty is a right of doing whatever the laws permit,* and if a citizen could do what they forbid he would be no longer possessed of liberty, because all his fellow-citizens would have the same power.

4. *The same subject continued*

Democratic and aristocratic states are not in their own nature free. Political liberty is to be found only in moderate governments; and even in these it is not always found. It is there only when there is no abuse of power. But constant experience shows us that every man invested with power is apt to abuse it, and to carry his authority as far as it will go. Is it not strange, though true, to say that virtue itself has need of limits?

To prevent this abuse, it is necessary from the very nature of things that power should be a check to power. A government may be so constituted, as no man shall be compelled to do things to which the law does not oblige him, nor forced to abstain from things which the law permits.

5. *Of the end or view of different governments*

Though all governments have the same general end, which is that of preservation, yet each has another particular object. Increase of dominion was the object of Rome; war, that of Sparta; religion, that of the Jewish laws; commerce, that of Marseilles; public tranquillity, that of the laws of China;† navigation, that of the laws of Rhodes; natural liberty,

* 'Omnes Legum servi sumus ut liberi esse possimus' – Cicero, *pro Cluentio*, 53.
† The natural end of a state that has no foreign enemies, or that thinks itself secured against them by barriers.

that of the policy of the Savages; in general, the pleasures of the prince, that of despotic states; that of monarchies, the prince's and the kingdom's glory; the independence of individuals is the end aimed at by the laws of Poland, thence results the oppression of the whole.*

One nation there is also in the world that has for the direct end of its constitution political liberty. We shall presently examine the principles on which this liberty is founded; if they are sound, liberty will appear in its highest perfection.

To discover political liberty in a constitution, no great labour is requisite. If we are capable of seeing it where it exists, it is soon found, and we need not go far in search of it.

6. Of the Constitution of England

In every government there are three sorts of power: the legislative; the executive in respect to things dependent on the law of nations; and the executive in regard to matters that depend on the civil law.

By virtue of the first, the prince or magistrate enacts temporary or perpetual laws, and amends or abrogates those that have been already enacted. By the second, he makes peace or war, sends or receives embassies, establishes the public security, and provides against invasions. By the third, he punishes criminals, or determines the disputes that arise between individuals. The latter we shall call the judiciary power, and the other simply the executive power of the state.

The political liberty of the subject is a tranquillity of mind arising from the opinion each person has of his safety. In order to have this liberty, it is requisite the government be so constituted as one man need not be afraid of another.

When the legislative and executive powers are united in the same person or in the same body of magistrates, there can be no liberty; because apprehensions may arise, lest the same monarch or senate should enact tyrannical laws, to execute them in a tyrannical manner.

Again, there is no liberty, if the judiciary power be not separated from the legislative and executive. Were it joined with the legislative, the life and liberty of the subject would be exposed to arbitrary control; for the judge would be then the legislator. Were it joined to the executive power, the judge might behave with violence and oppression.

There would be an end of everything, were the same man or the same body, whether of the nobles or of the people, to exercise those three powers, that of enacting laws, that of executing the public resolutions, and of trying the causes of individuals . . .

[Source: Montesquieu, The Spirit of the Laws (1748), trans. Thomas Nugent, London 1878, I, Bk. xi, pp.160–3.]

* Inconvenience of the Liberum veto.

Doc. 5*b*. MONTESQUIEU: Political Liberty in Relation to the Subject

1. *Idea of this Book*

It is not sufficient to have treated of political liberty in relation to the constitution; we must examine it likewise in the relation it bears to the subject.

We have observed that in the former case it arises from a certain distribution of the three powers; but in the latter, we must consider it in another light. It consists in security, or in the opinion people have of their security.

The constitution may happen to be free, and the subject not. The subject may be free, and not the constitution. In those cases, the constitution will be free by right, and not in fact; the subject will be free in fact, and not by right.

It is the disposition only of the laws, and even of the fundamental laws, that constitutes liberty in relation to the constitution. But as it regards the subject: manners, customs, or received examples may give rise to it, and particular civil laws may encourage it, as we shall presently observe.

Further, as in most states liberty is more checked or depressed than their constitution requires, it is proper to treat of the particular laws that in each constitution are apt to assist or check the principle of liberty which each state is capable of receiving.

2. *Of the Liberty of the Subject*

Philosophic liberty consists in the free exercise of the will; or at least, if we must speak agreeably to all systems, in an opinion that we have the free exercise of our will. Political liberty consists in security, or, at least, in the opinion that we enjoy security.

This security is never more dangerously attacked than in public or private accusations. It is, therefore, on the goodness of criminal laws that the liberty of the subject principally depends . . .

[Source: Montesquieu, *The Spirit of the Laws*, trans. Thomas Nugent, London 1878, I, Bk.xii, pp.196–7.]

Doc. 5*c*. MONTESQUIEU: Of Laws in Relation to the order of things which they determine

1. *Idea of this Book*

Men are governed by several kinds of laws; by the law of nature; by the divine law, which is that of religion; by ecclesiastical, otherwise called canon law, which is that of religious polity; by the law of nations, which may be considered as the civil law of the whole globe, in which sense every nation is a citizen; by the general political law, which relates to that human wisdom whence all societies derive their origin; by the particular political law, the object of which is each society; by the law of conquest founded on this, that one nation has been willing and able or has had a right to offer violence to another; by the civil law of every society, by which a citizen may defend his possessions and his life against the attacks of any other citizen; in fine, by domestic law, which proceeds from a society's being divided into several families, all which have need of a particular government.

There are therefore different orders of laws, and the sublimity of human reason consists in perfectly knowing to which of these orders the things that are to be determined ought to have a principal relation, and not to throw into confusion those principles which should govern mankind.

2. *Of Laws Divine and Human*

We ought not to decide by divine laws what should be decided by human laws; nor determine by human what should be determined by divine laws.

These two sorts of laws differ in their origin, in their object and in their nature . . .

15. *That we should not regulate by the Principles of Political Laws those things which depend on the Principles of Civil Law*

As men have given up their natural independence to live under political laws, they have given up the natural community of goods to live under civil laws.

By the first, they acquired liberty; by the second, property. We should not decide by the laws of liberty, which, as we have already said, is only the government of the community, what ought to be decided by the laws concerning property. It is a paralogism to say, that the good of the individual should give way to that of the public; this can never take place, except when the government of the community, or, in other words, the liberty of the subject is concerned; this does not affect such cases as relate to private property, because the public good consists in every one's having his property, which was given him by the civil laws, invariably preserved.

Cicero maintains that the Agrarian laws were unjust; because the community was established with no other view than that every one might be able to preserve his property.

Let us, therefore, lay down a certain maxim, what whenever the public good happens to be the matter in question, it is not for the advantage of the public to deprive an individual of his property, or even to retrench the least part of it by a law, or a political regulation. In this case we should follow the rigour of the civil law, which is the *Palladium* of property.

Thus when the public has occasion for the estate of an individual, it ought never to act by the rigour of political law; it is here that the civil law ought to triumph, which, with the eyes of a mother, regards every individual as the whole community.

If the political magistrate would erect a public edifice, or make a new road, he must indemnify those who are injured by it; the public is in this respect like an individual who treats with an individual. It is fully enough that it can oblige a citizen to sell his inheritance, and that it can strip him of his great privilege which he holds from the civil law, of not being forced to alienate his possessions...

[Source: Montesquieu, *The Spirit of the Laws*, trans. Thomas Nugent, London, 1878, II, Bk.xxvi, pp.144–5, 160–1.]

4. 'Government is a Necessary Evil': documents
(Introduction, p. 122)

Doc. 6. THOMAS PAINE: The Origin and Design of Government

Some writers have so confounded society with government as to leave little or no distinction between them; whereas they are not only different, but have different origins. Society is produced by our wants, and government by our wickedness; the former promotes our happiness *positively* by uniting our affections, the latter *negatively* by restraining our vices. The one encourages intercourse, the other creates distinctions. The first is a patron, the last a punisher.

Society in every state is a blessing, but Government, even in its best state, is but a necessary evil, in its worst state an intolerable one; for when we suffer or are exposed to the same miseries *by a Government* which we might expect in a country *without Government*, our calamity is heightened by reflecting that we furnish the means by which we suffer. Government, like dress, is the badge of lost innocence; the palaces of kings are built on the ruins of the bowers of paradise. For were the impulses of conscience clear, uniform, and irresistibly obeyed, man would need no other lawgiver; but that not being the case, he finds it necessary to surrender up a part of his property to furnish means for the protection of the rest, and this he is induced to do by the same prudence which in every other case advises him out of two evils to choose the least. Wherefore, security being the true design and end of government, it unanswerably follows that whatever form thereof appears most likely to ensure it to us, with the least expense and greatest benefit, is preferable to all others.

In order to gain a clear and just idea of the design and end of government, let us suppose a small number of persons settled in some sequestered part of the earth, unconnected with the rest; they will then represent the first peopling of any country, or of the world. In this state of natural liberty, society will be their first thought. A thousand motives will excite them thereto; the strength of one man is so unequal to his wants, and his mind so unfitted for perpetual solitude that he is soon obliged to seek assistance and relief of another, who in his turn requires the same. Four or five united would be able to raise a tolerable dwelling in the midst of a wilderness, but one man might labor out of the common period of life without accomplishing anything; when he had felled his timber, he could not remove it, nor erect it after it was removed; hunger in the meantime would urge him to quit his work, and every different want would call him a different way. Disease, nay even misfortune, would be death; for though neither might be mortal, yet either would disable him from living and reduce him to a state in which he might rather be said to perish than to die.

Thus necessity, like a gravitating power, would soon form our newly arrived emigrants into society, the reciprocal blessings of which would supersede and render the obligations of law and government unnecessary while they remained perfectly just to each other; but as nothing but Heaven is impregnable to vice, it will unavoidably happen that in proportion as they surmount the first difficulties of emigration, which bound them together in a common cause, they will begin to relax in their duty and attachment to each other; and this remissness will point out the necessity of establishing some form of government to supply the defect of moral virtue.

Some convenient tree will afford them a State House, under the branches of which the whole Colony may assemble to deliberate on public matters. It is more than probable that their first laws will have the title only of Regulations and be enforced by no other penalty than public disesteem. In this first parliament every man by natural right will have a seat.

But as the colony increases, the public concerns will increase likewise, and the distance at which the members may be separated, will render it too inconvenient for all of them to meet on every occasion as at first, when their number was small, their habitations near, and the public concerns few and trifling. This will point out the convenience of their consenting to leave the legislative part to be managed by a select number chosen from the whole body, who are supposed to have the same concerns at stake which those have who appointed them, and who will act in the same manner as the whole body would act were they present. If the colony continue increasing, it will become necessary to augment the number of representatives, and that the interest of every part of the colony may be attended to, it will be found best to divide the whole into convenient parts, each part sending its proper number; and that the *elected* might never form to themselves an interest separate from the *electors*, prudence will point out the propriety of having elections often: because as the *elected* might by that means return and mix again with the general body of the *electors* in a few months, their fidelity to the public will be secured by the prudent reflection of not making a rod for themselves. And as this frequent interchange will establish a common interest with every part of the community, they will mutually and naturally support each other, and on this (not on the unmeaning name of king) depends the *strength of government, and the happiness of the governed.*

Here then is the origin and rise of government; namely, a mode rendered necessary by the inability of moral virtue to govern the world; here too is the design and end of government, viz. Freedom and security. And however our eyes may be dazzled with show or our ears deceived by sound; however prejudice may warp our wills, or interest darken our understanding, the simple voice of nature and reason will say, it is right.

I draw my idea of the form of government from a principle in nature which no art can overturn, viz. that the more simple anything is, the less liable it is to be disordered and the easier repaired when disordered; . . .

[Source: Thomas Paine, *Common Sense* (New Edition, Feb. 1776), in *The Writings of Thomas Paine*, ed. Moncure Daniel Conway, New York 1894, I, pp.69–72.]

Doc. 7. THOMAS PAINE: The First Principles of Government

Hitherto, I have confined myself to matters of principle only. First, that hereditary government has not a right to exist; that it cannot be established on any principle of right; and that it is a violation of all principle. Secondly, that government by election and representation has its origin in the natural and eternal rights of man; for whether a man be his own lawgiver, as he would be in a state of nature; or whether he exercises his portion of legislative sovereignty in his own person, as might be the case in small democracies where all could assemble for the formation of the laws by which they were to be governed; or whether he exercises it in the choice of persons to represent him in a national assembly of representatives, the origin of the right is the same in all cases. The first, as is before observed, is defective in power; the second, is practicable only in democracies of small extent; the third, is the greatest scale upon which human government can be instituted.

Next to matters of *principle* are matters of *opinion*, and it is necessary to distinguish between the two. Whether the rights of men shall be equal is not a matter of opinion but of right, and consequently of principle; for men do not hold their rights as grants from each other, but each one in

197

right of himself. Society is the guardian but not the giver. And as in extensive societies, such as America and France, the right of the individual in matters of government cannot be exercised but by election and representation, it consequently follows that the only system of government consistent with principle, where simple democracy is impracticable, is the representative system. But as to the organical part, or the manner in which the several parts of government shall be arranged and composed, it is altogether *matter of opinion*. It is necessary that all the parts be conformable with the *principle of equal rights*; and so long as this principle be religiously adhered to, no very material error can take place, neither can any error continue long in that part which falls within the province of opinion.

In all matters of opinion, the social compact, or the principle by which society is held together, requires that the majority of opinions becomes the rule for the whole, and that the minority yields practical obedience thereto. This is perfectly conformable to the principle of equal rights: for, in the first place, every man has *a right to give an opinion*, but no man has a right that his opinion should *govern the rest*. In the second place, it is not supposed to be known beforehand on which side of any question, whether for or against, any man's opinion will fall. He may happen to be in a majority upon some questions and in a minority upon others; and by the same rule that he expects obedience in the one case, he must yield it in the other. All the disorders that have arisen in France during the progress of the revolution have had their origin, not in the *principle of equal rights*, but in the violation of that principle. The principle of equal rights has been repeatedly violated, and that not by the majority but by the minority, and *that minority has been composed of men possessing property, as well as of men without property; property, therefore, even upon the experience already had, is no more a criterion of character than it is of rights*. It will sometimes happen that the minority are right, and the majority are wrong, but as soon as experience proves this to be the case, the minority will increase to a majority, and the error will reform itself by the tranquil operation of freedom of opinion and equality of rights. Nothing, therefore, can justify an insurrection, neither can it ever be necessary where rights are equal and opinions free ...

I shall conclude this discourse with offering some observations on the means of *preserving liberty*; for it is not only necessary that we establish it, but that we preserve it.

It is, in the first place, necessary that we distinguish between the means made use of to overthrow despotism, in order to prepare the way for the establishment of liberty, and the means to be used after the despotism is overthrown.

The means made use of in the first case are justified by necessity. Those means are, in general, insurrections; for while the established government of despotism continues in any country, it is scarcely possible that any other means can be used. It is also certain that in the commencement of a revolution, the revolutionary party permit to themselves a *discretionary exercise of power* regulated more by circumstances than by principle, which, were the practice to continue, liberty would never be established, or if established would soon be overthrown. It is never to be expected in a revolution that every man is to change his opinion at the same moment. There never yet was any truth or any principle so irresistibly obvious, that all men believed it at once. Time and reason must cooperate with each other to the final establishment of any principle; and therefore those who may happen to be first convinced have not a right to persecute others, on whom conviction operates more slowly. The moral principle of revolution is to instruct, not to destroy.

Had a constitution been established two years ago (as ought to have been done), the violences that have since desolated France and injured the character of the Revolution would, in my opinion, have been prevented. The nation would then have had a bond of union, and every individual would have known the line of conduct he was to follow. But, instead of this, a revolutionary government, a thing without either principle or authority, was substituted in its place; virtue and crime depended upon accident, and that which was patriotism one day, became treason the next. All these things have followed from the want of a constitution: for it is the nature and intention of a constitution to *prevent governing by party*, by establishing a common principle that shall limit and control the power and impulse of party, and that says to all parties, *thus far shalt thou go and no further*. But in the absence of a constitution, men look entirely to party; and instead of principle governing party, party governs principle.

An avidity to punish is always dangerous to liberty. It leads men to stretch, to misinterpret, and to misapply even the best of laws. He that would make his own liberty secure, must guard even his enemy from oppression; for if he violates this duty, he establishes a precedent that will reach to himself.

[Source: Thomas Paine, *Dissertation on First Principles of Government* (1795) in *The Writings of Thomas Paine*, ed. Moncure Daniel Conway, New York, 1895, III, pp. 272–4, 276–7.]

5. Freedom through the general will: documents
(Introduction, p.126)

Doc. 8a. JEAN-JACQUES ROUSSEAU: The Social Contract

It is my purpose to inquire whether it is possible for there to be any legitimate and certain rule of administration in civil society, taking men as they are and laws as they may be. In this inquiry I shall endeavour at all times to ally the obligation of law and right with the requirements of interest, in order that justice and utility may never be disjoined.

I shall enter upon my subject without demonstrating its importance. It may be asked whether I am a prince or legislator to be writing on politics. I answer that I am not, and that that is the very reason why I am writing on them. If I were a prince or legislator, I should not waste my time saying what ought to be done; I should do it, or be silent.

Since I am by birth the citizen of a free state, and a member of the sovereign, my right to vote in that state, no matter how little influence my voice may have in public affairs, is enough to make it my duty to study them. And whenever I reflect on governments, how happy I am to find that my investigations always give me new reasons for loving that of my own country!

Man is born free, and everywhere he is in chains. One thinks himself master of others, but is himself the greater slave. How did this change take place? I do not know. What can render it legitimate? I believe I can answer this question.

If I were to consider nothing but force and its effects, I should say: 'As long as a people is compelled to obey, and does so, it does well; as soon as it can shake off the yoke, and does so, it does even better; for in recovering its liberty on the same grounds on which it was stolen away, it either is right in resuming it, or was wrongly deprived in the first place.' But the social order is a sacred right which serves as the basis for all others. And yet this right does not come from nature; thus it is founded on conventions. The problem is to know what these conventions are . . .

. . . This problem, in relation to my subject, may be expressed in the following terms: 'To find a form of association which defends and protects the person and property of each member with the whole force of the community, and where each, while joining with all the rest, still obeys no one but himself, and remains as free as before.' This is the fundamental problem to which the social contract provides the answer.

The clauses of this contract . . . rightly understood, can be reduced to the following only: the total alienation of each member, with all his rights, to the community as a whole. For, in the first place, since each gives himself entirely, the condition is equal for all; and since the condition is equal for all, it is in the interest of no one to make it burdensome to the rest.

Furthermore, since the alienation is made without reservations, the union is as perfect as possible, and no member has anything more to ask. For if the individuals retained certain rights, each, in the absence of any common superior capable of judging between him and the public, would be his own judge in certain matters, and would soon claim to be so in all; the state of nature would continue, and the association would necessarily become tyrannical or meaningless.

Finally, each individual, by giving himself to all, gives himself to no one; and since there is no member over whom you do not acquire the same rights that you give him over yourself, you gain the equivalent of all you lose, and greater force to preserve what you have.

If the social compact is stripped to its essentials, therefore, you will find that it can be reduced to the following terms: 'Each of us puts in common his person and all his powers under the supreme direction of the general will; and in our corporate capacity we receive each member as an indivisible part of the whole' . . .

[Source: Jean-Jacques Rousseau, *The Social Contract* (1762), in *Rousseau's Political Writings*, ed./trans. Frederick Watkins, Edinburgh 1953, Bk.i. Ch. 1, pp.3–4, 14–16.]

Doc. 8*b*. JEAN-JACQUES ROUSSEAU: Sovereignty is Inalienable

The first and most important consequence of the principles thus far established is that the general will alone can direct the forces of the state in accordance with the purpose for which it was created, namely, the common good. For if the opposition of private interests made the establishment of societies necessary, it is the agreement of those same interests that made it possible. It is what these several interests have in common that constitutes the social bond; and if there were no point on which all of them were in agreement, there could be no society. Now it is exclusively on the basis of this common interest that society must be governed.

I say, therefore, that since sovereignty is nothing but the exercise of the general will, it can never be alienated; and that the sovereign, which is only a collective being, can be represented by itself only. Power may well be transferred, but will cannot.

As a matter of fact, if it is not impossible for a particular will to agree with the general will on some specific point, at least it is impossible for that agreement to be constant and durable; for the particular will tends by its very nature to partiality, and the general will to equality. Even if this agreement did remain constant, it would be the result not of skill but of chance, and it would be even more impossible to guarantee that it would continue to do so. The sovereign may well say: 'At the present moment I want what that particular individual wants, or at least what he says he wants.' But it cannot say: 'What that individual wants tomorrow,

I too shall want'; since it is absurd for the will to bind itself for the future, and impossible for any willing being to consent to anything contrary to its own welfare. If, therefore, the people promises simply to obey, it dissolves itself by that very act, and ceases to be a people. As soon as there is a master, there is no longer a sovereign; and from that moment the body politic is destroyed.

This does not mean that the commands of rulers may not be taken as expressions of the general will, as long as the sovereign is free to oppose them and fails to do so. In such a case the consent of the people is to be presumed from universal silence ...

[Source: Jean-Jacques Rousseau, *The Social Contract* (1762), in *Rousseau's Political Writings*, ed./trans. Frederick Watkins, Edinburgh 1953, Bk. ii., Ch. 1, pp 25–6.]

Doc. 8c. JEAN-JACQUES ROUSSEAU: Sovereignty is Indivisible

Sovereignty is indivisible for the same reason that it is inalienable. For the will either is or is not general*; it is the will either of the whole body of the people, or of a part only. In the first case, the declaration of that will is an act of sovereignty and constitutes law. In the second, it is only a particular will, or an act of magistracy; at most, it is no more than a decree ...

[Source: Jean-Jacques Rousseau. *The Social Contract* (1762), in *Rousseau's Political Writings*, ed./trans. Frederick Watkins, Edinburgh 1953, Bk. ii, Ch. 2, p.26.]

Doc. 8d. JEAN-JACQUES ROUSSEAU: Whether the General Will is Subject to Error

From the preceding it follows that the general will is always right, and always tends to the public good; but it does not follow that the deliberations of the people will always have the same rectitude. We always desire our own good, but we do not always recognise it. You cannot corrupt the people, but you can often deceive it; and it is then only that it seems to will something bad.

There is often a great difference between the will of all and the general will; the latter looks only to the common interest, while the former looks to private interest, and is simply a sum of particular wills. But if you cancel out from these same wills all the mutually destructive pluses and minuses[+], the general will remains as the sum of the differences.

* For a will to be general it is not always necessary that it should be unanimous; but it is necessary that all the voices should be counted, for any formal exclusion breaks the generality.

[+] 'Each interest,' says the Marquis d'Argenson, 'has different principles. The agreement of two particular interests is created by opposition to the interests of a third party.' He might have added that the agreement of all interests is created by opposition to the interest of each individual. If there were no distinct interests, the common interest would scarcely be felt, since it would never encounter obstacles; everything would go by itself, and politics would cease to be an art.

If the people were sufficiently well-informed, and if in their deliberations the citizens held no communication with one another, the general will would always result from the large number of small differences, and the deliberations would always be good. But when cliques and partial associations are formed at the expense of the whole, the will of each of these associations becomes general with reference to its members, and particular with reference to the state; then it can no longer be said that there are as many voters as there are individuals, but only as many as there are associations. The differences become less numerous, and give a less general result. Finally, when one of these associations becomes large enough to prevail over all the rest, the result is no longer a sum of small differences, but one single difference. Then there is no longer a general will, and the opinion which prevails is only a private opinion.

If the general will is to be well expressed, therefore, it is important that there should be no partial society in the state, and that each citizen should have personal opinions only;* such was the unique and sublime system instituted by the great Lycurgus. And if there are partial societies, their number must be multiplied and provision made against their inequality, as by Solon, Numa and Servius. These precautions are the only effective means of ensuring that the general will always will be enlightened, and that the people will make no mistakes.

[Source: Jean-Jacques Rousseau, *The Social Contract* (1762) in *Rousseau's Political Writings*, ed./trans. Frederick Watkins, Edinburgh 1953, Bk. ii, Ch. 3, pp.28–38.]

Doc. 8e. JEAN-JACQUES ROUSSEAU:
The General Will is Indestructible

In so far as several men conjoined consider themselves as a single body, they have but a single will, which refers to their common conservation and to the general welfare. Then all the motive forces of the state are vigorous and simple, its principles are clear and luminous; it has no quarrelling and contradictory interests; the common good is everywhere clearly evident, and requires no more than common sense to be perceived. Peace, unity and equality are the enemies of political subtlety. Upright and simple men are hard to deceive because of their simplicity; they are in no way imposed upon by wiles and subtle pleadings; they are not even clever enough to be dupes. When, among the happiest people on earth, you see crowds of peasants deciding affairs of state under an oak-

---

* 'It is a fact,' says Machiavelli, 'that some divisions are harmful and some beneficial to republics; the harmful ones are those which are accompanied by sects and partisanship, the beneficial those which are accompanied by neither. Since the founder of a republic cannot provide that there will be no enmities within it, he must therefore provide at least that there will be no sects.' *History of Florence*, Book VII.

203

tree, and behaving with uniform wisdom, how can you help despising the subtleties of other nations, which devote so much skill and mystification to making themselves famous and wretched?

A state thus governed has need of very few laws; and as soon as it becomes necessary to promulgate new ones, this necessity is universally recognised. The first to propose them does no more than to say what all have already felt; and it requires neither intrigue nor eloquence to secure the enactment of that which each has already decided to do, as soon as he is sure that the others will do likewise.

What deceives the theorists is the fact that, seeing nothing but states badly constituted from the beginning, they are impressed with the impossibility of maintaining such a polity among them. They laugh at the thought of all the stupidities that an adroit rascal, an insinuating talker, could persuade the people of Paris or London to commit. They fail to realise that Cromwell would have been drummed out of town by the people of Berne, and the Duc de Beaufort given the cat-o'-nine-tails by the Genevans.

But when the social bond begins to loosen and the state to grow weak, when particular interests begin to make themselves felt and lesser associations to influence the whole, then the common interest deteriorates and encounters opposition; unanimity no longer prevails in voting; the general will ceases to be the will of all; contradictions and debates arise; and the best opinion does not go by any means undisputed.

Finally, when the state, on the brink of ruin, maintains no more than a vain and illusory existence, when the social bond is broken in every heart, when the basest interest brazenly flaunts the sacred name of public good, then the general will falls silent; guided by secret motives, no one thinks as a citizen any more than as if the state had never existed; and under the guise of laws are enacted iniquitous decrees whose only purpose is to further private interests.

Does this mean that the general will is annihilated or corrupted? No, it is always constant, unalterable and pure; but it is subordinated to other interests which prevail over it. Each individual, when he detaches his interest from that of the community, is clearly aware that the two are not entirely separable; but his share of the common misfortune is as nothing to him in comparison with the exclusive benefit he hopes to appropriate to himself. Apart from this particular benefit, he seeks the general benefit, in his own interest, as vigorously as anyone else. Even when he sells his vote for money, he does not extinguish, but eludes, the general will within him. His fault lies in changing the terms of the question, and in answering one different from the one he has been asked; with the result that, instead of saying with his vote, 'It is advantageous to the state,' he says, 'It is advantageous to a certain individual or to a certain party that a certain proposal should be enacted.' Thus the maintenance of public order in assemblies depends not so much on maintaining the general will as on ensuring that it will always be interrogated, and that it will always answer.

There are many reflexions which I might make at this point on the mere right to vote in any act of sovereignty, a right of which the citizens can in no circumstances be deprived; and on the right to express an opinion, to initiate, to separate and to discuss, which government is always at great pains to confine to its own members. But this important subject would need a treatise in itself; I cannot deal with everything here.

[Source: Jean-Jacques Rousseau, *The Social Contract* (1762), in *Rousseau's Political Writings*, ed./trans. Frederick Watkins, Edinburgh 1953, Bk. iv, Ch. 1, pp.113–15.]

6. Natural law and the economy: the doctrine of *laissez faire*: documents

(Introduction, p. 135)

(i) The harmony between the economic interests of the individual and those of society

Doc. 9. TURGOT: 'Eloge de Gournay' (1759)

[M. de Gournay] was astonished to see that a citizen could neither make nor sell anything without having bought the right to do so at a great expense in a corporation, and that, after having bought it, it was still sometimes necessary for him to sustain an action at law to determine whether by entering into such or such corporation he really had acquired the right to make or sell precisely this or that article. He imagined that a workman who had manufactured a piece of stuff had made a real addition to the mass of wealth of the State; that if this stuff happened to be inferior to others, there might yet be found among consumers some one to whom this inferiority might be more suitable than a more costly perfection. He was far from imagining that this piece of stuff, for not being conformable to certain regulations, might be cut up into fragments of three ells length, and that the unfortunate man who had made it must be condemned to pay a penalty, enough to bring him and his family to beggary. He could not see the necessity that a workman in making a piece of stuff should be exposed to risks and expenses from which an idle man was exempt. He could not see it to be useful to society that a manufactured piece of stuff should involve legal procedures and tedious discussions in order to ascertain whether it was conformable to a complicated system of

A. Roots of liberalism: the eighteenth century

regulations, often difficult to understand, nor that such discussions ought
to be held between a poor manufacturer, who perhaps could not read,
and an inspector who could not manufacture, nor that this inspector
should be the final judge of the unlucky man. . . . M. de Gournay could
not see the propriety of the Government regulating by express laws the
length and breadth of each piece of stuff, the number of threads it was to
contain, and to stamp with the seal of the executive power four volumes
in quarto filled with these important details, nor could he see the need of
innumerable statutes dictated by the spirit of monopoly, the whole effect
of which is to discourage industry, to concentrate trade within a limited
number of persons by the multiplication of formalities and expenses, by
the subjecting of industry to apprenticeships and journeymanships (*com-
pagnonnages*) of ten years for some trades which might be learned almost
in ten days, by the exclusion of those not being the sons of 'masters,' or
of those born beyond certain bounds, and by the prohibition of employing women in manufacture.

He had not imagined that in a kingdom under the same monarch all
the towns should reciprocally regard themselves as enemies, should
arrogate the right to prohibit work within their precincts to Frenchmen
(described under the name of *étrangers*), to set themselves in opposition
to the sale or the free transit of commodities of a neighbouring province –
thus, for a slender interest of their own town, to contend against the
general interest of the State.

He was not less astonished to see the Government concern itself in
regulating the course of each commodity, in proscribing one kind of industry in order to encourage another, in subjecting to special restraints
the sale of provisions the most necessary to life, in forbidding stores to be
made of a product, the crop of which varies from year to year and the
consumption of which is nearly always equal, in forbidding the export of
an article subject to deteriorate, in expecting to insure the abundance of
corn by rendering the condition of the labourer more uncertain and more
unhappy than that of other men.

[In condemning these anomalies M. de Gournay] felt himself to be
only developing those principles which experience in business had taught
him, and which he saw were unanimously recognised by the enlightened
merchants with whom he had associated. Those principles appeared to
him as only the maxims of simple common sense . . . that in general a
man knows his own interest better than another man can know it for him.
Hence he concluded that as the interest of individuals is, on the whole,
precisely the same as the general interest, we should leave every man free
to manufacture whatever he considers desirable, because, with industry
and commerce left free, it would be impossible for the aggregate
individual interests not to concur with the general interest.

Commerce can be related to the general interest, or, which is the same
thing, the State can interest itself in commerce only under two points of

view. As protector of the individuals who compose it, it is its interest that no one should in the course of business suffer any wrong from another against which he cannot secure himself. Next as being a political body, having to defend itself against exterior invasions, it is the interest of the State that the mass of the wealth of the community and the yearly productions of the land and of industry should be the greatest that is possible. Under each point of view it has a special interest in insuring the value of necessaries of life against those sudden shocks which, by plunging the people into the horrors of famine, endanger public tranquillity and the safety of citizens and magistrates. Now, it is clear that the interest of all the individuals, kept free from restraints of all kinds, necessarily fulfils all these conditions of general utility.

As for the first object, that in trade none should be injured by others, it is evidently sufficient that the Government should always protect the natural liberty of the buyer to buy and of the seller to sell. For the buyer being always the master to buy or not to buy, it is certain that he will select among the sellers the man who will give him at the best bargain the merchandise that suits him best. It is not less certain that every seller, it being his chief interest to merit the preference over his competitors, will sell in general the best merchandise and at the lowest price profitable, in order to attract customers. It is not true therefore that a merchant has an interest to deceive – unless at least he has some exclusive privilege. But if the Government limits the number of sellers by exclusive privileges or otherwise, it is certain that the consumer will be wronged and that the seller, made sure of selling, will compel him to buy dearly bad articles. If, on the other hand, it is the number of buyers which is diminished by the exclusion of foreigners or of certain persons, then the seller is wronged, and if the injury be carried to the point when the price cannot cover his expenses and risks, he will cease to produce the commodity, its regular supply will thus be endangered, and a famine may be the consequence. The general liberty of buying and selling is therefore the only means to insure on the one side to the seller a price sufficient to encourage production; on the other side to the consumer the best merchandise at the lowest price. If we descend to particular cases, we may indeed find a merchant who is a cheat and a consumer a dupe, but the cheated customer will instruct himself and will cease to frequent the cheating merchant, who will become discredited and punished for his knavery; but that will never happen very frequently, because in general men will be enlightened upon their evident self-interest . . .

As for the second object of Government in this connection, that there should be the greatest possible production of wealth by the nation, is it not evident that the only real wealth of the State being the yearly productions of its land and the industry of its inhabitants, its wealth will be at its greatest when the produce of each acre of land and the industry of each individual shall be carried to the highest possible point? and is it not evi-

A. Roots of liberalism: the eighteenth century

dent that each proprietor has more interest than any other person to draw from his land the greatest possible return, that each labourer and artisan has the same interest to gain by his work all the wages he can get?

... To imagine that there are commodities which the State ought to favour, in order that the land may produce more of them than of others, that it ought to favour certain manufactures more than others, and consequently to prohibit certain productions and encourage others, to interdict certain kinds of industry from fear of injuring other kinds, to attempt to sustain manufactures at the expense of agriculture by forcing the price of provisions to be under what it would naturally be, to establish certain manufactures at the cost of the Treasury, to accumulate on them privileges, favours, exclusions of all other manufactures of the same kind, for the object of procuring for the privileged manufacturers a profit which it is assumed their productions could not obtain naturally – all this is to misapprehend greatly the real advantages of commerce, it is to forget that no operation of commerce can be otherwise than reciprocal, for to desire to sell everything to foreigners and to buy nothing from them is absurd.

... The market value of each commodity, all expenses on it paid, is the only rule by which to judge of the advantage which the State derives from a certain class of productions; consequently every manufacture whose natural market value does not compensate the manufacturer with profit after the expenses of production is of no advantage to the State; the sum spent on sustaining it against the natural course of commerce is a charge made on the nation, to its absolute loss.

M. de Gournay concluded that the only end the administration should propose to itself was:– 1. To render to all branches of commerce that precious liberty which the prejudice of ignorant ages, the facility of the Government to lend itself to particular interests, and the desire for an ill-understood perfection in workmanship had caused them to lose. 2. To free the road for work to all members of the State, for the purpose of exciting the greatest competition in the market, from which would necessarily result the greatest perfection in manufacture and a price most advantageous to the *buyer*. 3. To give at the same time to the buyer the greatest possible number of competitors by opening for the *seller* all the outlets for his commodity – the true means of assuring to labour its recompense and of developing production.

He held, besides, that the Government ought to remove those obstacles which retard the progress of industry by diminishing the measure or the extent of its profits. He considered the chief of these obstacles to be the high interest of money, which, offering to all possessors of capital the means of living without working, encourages luxury and idleness, withdraws from commerce and renders unproductive for the State the riches and industry of a multitude of citizens; which excludes the nation from all branches of commerce not yielding one or two per cent above the actual rate of interest; which consequently gives to foreigners the exclusive privilege of all these branches of commerce, and enables them to gain the preference over us in almost all other countries by selling at a price which would be unremunerative to us; which gives to the inhabitants of our colonies a powerful interest to carry on contraband trade with the foreigner, and through that to weaken the natural affection they ought to have for the mother-country; which secures for the Duke and for the Hanse Towns the coasting trade of Europe, including France itself; which renders us yearly tributaries to the foreigners by the high rate on their loans to us; which, finally, condemns to be left uncultivated all the land of the kingdom that cannot yield more than five per cent., since with the same capital one could, without working, procure the same return. But he believed also that the commerce of capital itself, whose price is the interest of money, can only be led to attain this price equitably and with all necessary economy, as in the case of every other commerce, by competition and by reciprocal liberty, and that the Government could assist towards this end only, on the one hand, by abstaining from making laws for its rate while agreements can accomplish this much better, and, on the other hand, by the Government avoiding to swell the number of debtors and consumers of capital in contracting loans, or in not paying its obligations with exactitude ...

[Gournay also saw the multiplicity of taxes (and the onerous modes of collection) as an obstacle to the progress of industry.]

Fiscal finance is necessary, for the State has need of revenues, but agriculture and commerce are, or rather agriculture animated by commerce is, the ultimate source of their revenues.* If State finance is injurious to commerce, it is injurious to itself. These two interests are essentially united, and if they have appeared opposed to each other it is perhaps because we have confounded the interests of finance in relation to the State, which always exists, with the interests of the *financiers*, who being charged with the collection of revenues only for a certain time, think more of increasing these for the moment than of conserving the source which produces them.

He considered that the Board of Commerce was less useful for the management of commerce (which ought to go its own way) than for defending it against the enterprises of State finance. He would have desired that the financial arrangements of the State could permit it to free commerce from duties of all kinds. He believed that a nation fortunate enough to have arrived at this point would necessarily draw to itself the greatest part of the commerce of Europe. He believed that all taxes, of whatever kind they may be, are in the last analysis paid by the proprietor of the land, who sells by so much the less the produce of his land, and

---

* There can be little doubt that Turgot here uses the term 'agriculture' in the philosophical meaning of the 'physiocratic' school, as including the whole productions of the earth.

that if all the taxes were assessed on landed property the proprietors and the kingdom would thereby gain all that was absorbed in the cost of administration, the unproductive employment of men wasted in collecting the various taxes, or engaged in contraband trade, or in preventing it, and without reckoning the natural gain from the immense increase of capital and of income that would result from the increase of commerce.

He did not absolutely limit the duties of Government towards commerce to removing the obstacles that oppose the mere march of industry. He was quite convinced of the utility of the encouragements that could be given to industry either by recompensing the authors of useful inventions, or by exciting by prizes or gratuities the emulation of artists aiming at perfection ...

[Source: 'Eloge de Gourney' (1759), in *The Life and Writings of Turgot*, ed. W. Walker Stephens, London 1895, pp.233–41.]

Doc. 10. TURGOT: Letter to the Abbé Terray 'sur la marque des fers' (Limoges, 24 December 1773)

I know of no means of stimulating any trade or industry whatever but that of giving to it the greatest liberty, and of freeing it from all those burdens which the ill-understood interest of the revenue has multiplied to excess upon all kinds of merchandise, and particularly upon the manufactures in iron ...

If, after complete liberty has been obtained by the relief from all taxes on the fabrication, the transport, the sale and the consumption of commodities, there remains to the Government any means of favouring a branch of trade, that can only be by the means of instruction; that is to say, by encouraging those researches of scientific men and artists which tend to perfect art, and, above all, by extending the knowledge of practical processes which it is in the interest of cupidity to keep as so many secrets. It would be advisable for the Government to incur some expense by sending young men to foreign countries in order to instruct themselves in processes of manufacture unknown in France, and for the Government to publish the result of these researches. These means are good; but liberty of movement and freedom from taxes are much more efficacious and much more necessary.

You appear, in the letters with which you have honoured me on this subject, to believe that certain obstacles which might be placed to the import of foreign irons would act as an encouragement to our national trade. You intimate even that you have received from different provinces several representations to the effect that the demand which these foreign irons obtain acts to the prejudice of commerce in manufacture of the native iron. I believe, indeed, that iron-masters, who think only of their own iron, imagine that they would gain more if they had fewer competitors. It is not the merchant only who wishes to be the sole seller of his commodity. There is no department in commerce in which those who exercise it do not seek to escape from competition, and who do not find sophisms to make the State believe that it is interested, at least, to exclude the rivalry of foreigners, whom they easily represent to be the enemies of national commerce. If we listen to them, and we have listened to them too often, all branches of commerce would be infected by this spirit of monopoly. These foolish men do not see that this same monopoly is not, as they would have it believed, to the advantage of the State, against foreigners, but is directed against their own fellow-subjects, consumers of the commodity, and is retaliated upon themselves by these fellow-subjects − sellers in their turn − in all other branches of trade. They do not see that all associations of men engaged in a particular trade need only to arm themselves with the same pretexts in order to obtain from the misled Government the same exclusion of foreigners, they do not see that in this balancing of vexation and injustice between all kinds of industry, in which the artisans and the merchants of each kind oppress as sellers, and are oppressed as buyers, there is no advantage to any party; but that there is real loss on the total of the national commerce, or rather a loss to the State, which, buying less from the foreigner, must consequently sell him less. This forced increase of price for all buyers necessarily diminishes the sum of enjoyments, the sum of disposable revenues, the wealth of the proprietors and of the sovereign, and the sum of the wages to be distributed among the people.*

Again, this loss is doubled, because in this war of reciprocal oppression, in which the Government lends its strength to all against all, the only one left outside excepted is the small cultivator of the soil, whom all oppress in concert by their monopolies, and who, far from being able to oppress anyone, cannot even enjoy the natural right to sell his commodity, either to foreigners or to those of his fellow-subjects who would buy it; so that he remains the only one who suffers from monopoly as buyer, and at the same time as seller. There is only he who cannot buy freely from foreigners the things of which he has need; there is only he who cannot sell to foreigners the commodity he produces, while the cloth-merchant or any other buys as much wheat as he wants from the foreigner and sells to him as much as he can of his cloth.

Whatever sophisms the self-interests of some commercial classes may heap up, the truth is that *all* branches of commerce ought to be free,

---

* Here Turgot puts his finger on the evil. Let A be the body of the privileged; B the rest of the nation; 100,000,000 the yearly gain to the monopolisers. This sum must evidently come out of the pocket of B, to enter the pocket of A. But B, again, evidently represents the non-privileged capitalist, the proprietors, and the mass of simple workmen. Now, if the tithe levied by A strikes these three classes without distinction, it is clear that it takes from the two first but a portion of their superfluities, while it attacks the third in its circumscribed means of subsistence, represented in the *sum of wages* of which Turgot speaks.' (E. Daire, *Oeuvres de Turgot*, i, 381, *note*.)

equally free, *entirely* free; that the system of some modern politicians who imagine they favour national commerce by prohibiting the import of foreign merchandise is a pure illusion; that this system results only in rendering all branches of commerce enemies one to another, in nourishing among nations a germ of hatred and of wars, even the most feeble effects of which are a thousand times more costly to the people, more destructive of its wealth, of population and of happiness, than all those paltry mercantile profits imaginable *to individuals* can be advantageous to their nations. The truth is, that in wishing to hurt others we hurt only ourselves, not only because the reprisal for these prohibitions is so easy that other nations do not fail in their turn to make it, but still more because we deprive our own nation of the incalculable advantages of a free commerce – advantages such, that if a great state like France would but make experience of them, the rapid advancement of her commerce would soon compel other nations to imitate her in order not to be impoverished by the loss of their own.

But supposing these principles not to be perfectly demonstrated, supposing even that we admit the expediency of prohibition in some branches of commerce, then I contend that the article of iron ought to be excepted, for a particular and decisive reason. This reason is, that iron is not merely a commodity of itself useful for the different purposes of life; the iron employed in household utensils, in ornaments and in armour, is not the most considerable portion of the metal worked and sold. It is principally as an article necessary in the practice of all the arts, without exception, that this metal is so precious and is so important in commerce. It is the chief material employed in all the different manufactures – in agriculture even, to which it furnishes the greater part of its instruments. For this reason it is a commodity of the first necessity. For this reason, even were we to adopt the idea of favouring manufactures by prohibitions, iron ought never to be subject to them, because these prohibitions, in the opinion even of their partisans, ought to be placed only on an article manufactured for consumption, and not on the necessary materials used in manufactures. According to this very policy, the buyer of instruments of iron, of service to his manufacture or to his land culture, ought to enjoy the advantages which the policy gives to the seller over the consumer. To prohibit the import of foreign iron is therefore to favour the ironmasters, not only, as in the ordinary cases of prohibition, at the cost of the home consumers of the simple article; it is to favour them at the cost of all manufactures, of all branches of industry, at the cost of agriculture, and of the production of all foodstuffs.

I feel convinced that this reflection, which doubtless has occurred also to yourself, will restrain you from yielding to the indiscreet solicitations of the ironmasters and all those who look upon this branch of commerce as one by itself, and isolated from all the other branches with which it has connections of the first necessity. . . .

Our true policy consists in following the course of Nature and the course of commerce (not less necessary, not less irresistible than the course of Nature), and without pretending to direct the course. Because, in order to direct it without deranging it, and without injuring ourselves, it would be necessary for us to be able to follow all the changes in the needs, the interests, and the industry of mankind. It would be necessary to know these in such detail as it would be physically impossible to arrive at; in such a study the Government the most able, the most active, the most painstaking, would risk always to be wrong in half the cases.... Even if we had in all these particulars that mass of knowledge impossible to be gathered, the result would only be to let things go precisely as they would have gone of themselves, by the simple action of men's interests, influenced by the balance of a free competition.

But, if we ought not to drive away the foreign irons of which we have need, it does not follow that we should burden our own irons by taxes on their fabrication or on their transport. Quite the contrary, the fabrication and transport of French irons should be left perfectly free, in order that the contractors may work our mines and our forests to the best advantage, and may by their competition supply to our agriculture and to our arts, as cheaply as possible, the instruments they require...

[Source: 'Letter to the Abbé Terray "sur la marque des fers"' (1773), in *The Life and Writings of Turgot*, ed. W. Walker Stephens, London 1895, pp.249–55.]

(ii) 'The Wealth of Nations'

Doc. 11a. ADAM SMITH:
Of the Natural and Market Price of Commodities

There is in every society or neighbourhood an ordinary or average rate both of wages and profit in every different employment of labour and stock. This rate is naturally regulated, as I shall show hereafter, partly by the general circumstances of the society, their riches or poverty, their advancing, stationary, or declining condition; and partly by the particular nature of each employment.

There is likewise in every society or neighbourhood an ordinary or average rate of rent, which is regulated too, as I shall show hereafter, partly by the general circumstances of the society or neighbourhood in which the land is situated, and partly by the natural or improved fertility of the land.

These ordinary or average rates may be called the natural rates of wages, profit, and rent, at the time and place in which they commonly prevail.

When the price of any commodity is neither more nor less than what is

213

sufficient to pay the rent of the land, the wages of labour, and the profits of the stock employed in raising, preparing, and bringing it to market, according to their natural rates, the commodity is then sold for what may be called its natural price ...

The actual price at which any commodity is commonly sold is called its market price. It may either be above, or below, or exactly the same with its natural price.

The market price of every particular commodity is regulated by the proportion between the quantity which is actually brought to market, and the demand of those who are willing to pay the natural price of the commodity, or the whole value of the rent, labour, and profit, which must be paid in order to bring it thither. Such people may be called the effectual demanders, and their demand the effectual demand; since it may be sufficient to effectuate the bringing of the commodity to market ...

When the quantity of any commodity which is brought to market falls short of the effectual demand, all those who are willing to pay the whole value of the rent, wages, and profit, which must be paid in order to bring it thither, cannot be supplied with the quantity which they want. Rather than want it altogether, some of them will be willing to give more. A competition will immediately begin among them, and the market price will rise more or less above the natural price, according as either the greatness of the deficiency, or the wealth and wanton luxury of the competitors, happen to animate more or less the eagerness of the competition. Among competitors of equal wealth and luxury the same deficiency will generally occasion a more or less eager competition, according as the acquisition of the commodity happens to be of more or less importance to them. Hence the exorbitant price of the necessaries of life during the blockade of a town or in a famine.

When the quantity brought to market exceeds the effectual demand, it cannot be all sold to those who are willing to pay the whole value of the rent, wages, and profit, which must be paid in order to bring it thither. Some part must be sold to those who are willing to pay less, and the low price which they give for it must reduce the price of the whole. The market price will sink more or less below the natural price, according as the greatness of the excess increases more or less the competition of the sellers, or according as it happens to be more or less important to them to get immediately rid of the commodity. The same excess in the importation of perishable, will occasion a much greater competition than in that of durable commodities; in the importation of oranges, for example, than in that of old iron.

When the quantity brought to market is just sufficient to supply the effectual demand and no more, the market price naturally comes to be either exactly, or as nearly as can be judged of, the same with the natural price. The whole quantity upon hand can be disposed of for this price, and cannot be disposed of for more. The competition of the different dealers obliges them all to accept this price, but does not oblige them to accept of less.

The quantity of every commodity brought to market naturally suits itself to the effectual demand. It is the interest of all those who employ their land, labour, or stock, in bringing any commodity to market, that the quantity never should exceed the effectual demand; and it is the interest of all other people that it never should fall short of that demand.

If at any time it exceeds the effectual demand, some of the component parts of its price must be paid below their natural rate. If it is rent, the interest of the landlords will immediately prompt them to withdraw a part of their land; and if it is wages or profit, the interest of the labourers in the one case, and of their employers in the other, will prompt them to withdraw a part of their labour or stock from this employment. The quantity brought to market will soon be no more than sufficient to supply the effectual demand. All the different parts of its price will rise to their natural rate, and the whole price to its natural price.

If, on the contrary, the quantity brought to market should at any time fall short of the effectual demand, some of the component parts of its price must rise above their natural rate. If it is rent, the interest of all other landlords will naturally prompt them to prepare more land for the raising of this commodity; if it is wages or profit, the interest of all other labourers and dealers will soon prompt them to employ more labour and stock in preparing and bringing it to market. The quantity brought thither will soon be sufficient to supply the effectual demand. All the different parts of its price will soon sink to their natural rate, and the whole price to its natural price.

The natural price, therefore, is, as it were, the central price, to which the prices of all commodities are continually gravitating. Different accidents may sometimes keep them suspended a good deal above it, and sometimes force them down even somewhat below it. But whatever may be the obstacles which hinder them from settling in this centre of repose and continuance, they are constantly tending towards it.

The whole quantity of industry annually employed in order to bring any commodity to market, naturally suits itself in this manner to the effectual demand. It naturally aims at bringing always that precise quantity thither which may be sufficient to supply, and no more than supply, that demand.

But in some employments the same quantity of industry will in different years produce very different quantities of commodities; while in others it will produce always the same, or very nearly the same...

The occasional and temporary fluctuations in the market price of any commodity will fall chiefly upon those parts of its price which resolve themselves into wages and profit. That part which resolves itself into rent is less affected by them...

Such fluctuations affect both the value and the rate either of wages or

A. Roots of liberalism: the eighteenth century

of profit, according as the market happens to be either over-stocked or understocked with commodities or with labour; with work done, or with work to be done...

But though the market price of every particular commodity is in this manner continually gravitating, if one may say so, towards the natural price, yet sometimes particular accidents, sometimes natural causes, and sometimes particular regulations of police, may in many commodities, keep up the market price, for a long time together, a good deal above the natural price...

A monopoly granted either to an individual or to a trading company has the same effect as a secret in trade or manufactures. The monopolists, by keeping the market constantly under-stocked, by never fully supplying the effectual demand, sell their commodities much above the natural price, and raise their emoluments, whether they consist in wages or profit, greatly above their natural rate.

The price of monopoly is upon every occasion the highest which can be got. The natural price, or the price of free competition, on the contrary, is the lowest which can be taken, not upon every occasion indeed, but for any considerable time together. The one is upon every occasion the highest which can be squeezed out of the buyers, or which, it is supposed, they will consent to give: The other is the lowest which the sellers can commonly afford to take, and at the same time continue their business.

The exclusive privileges of corporations, statutes of apprenticeship, and all those laws which restrain, in particular employments, the competition to a smaller number than might otherwise go into them, have the same tendency, though in a less degree. They are a sort of enlarged monopolies, and may frequently, for ages together, and in whole classes of employments, keep up the market price of particular commodities above the natural price, and maintain both the wages of the labour and the profits of the stock employed about them somewhat above their natural rate...

The market price of any particular commodity, though it may continue long above, can seldom continue long below, its natural price. Whatever part of it was paid below the natural rate, the persons whose interest it affected would immediately feel the loss, and would immediately withdraw either so much land, or so much labour or so much stock, from being employed about it, that the quantity brought to market would soon be no more than sufficient to supply the effectual demand. Its market price, therefore, would soon rise to the natural price. This at least would be the case where there was perfect liberty...

[Source: Adam Smith, *An Inquiry into the Nature and Causes of the Wealth of Nations*, ed. Edwin Cannan, New York 1937, Bk i, Ch. 7, pp.55–62.]

Doc. 11*b*. ADAM SMITH: Of the Rent of Land

Every improvement in the circumstances of the society tends either directly or indirectly to raise the real rent of land, to increase the real wealth of the landlord, his power of purchasing the labour, or the produce of the labour of other people.

The extension of improvement and cultivation tends to raise it directly. The landlord's share of the produce necessarily increases with the increase of the produce.

That rise in the real price of those parts of the rude produce of land, which is first the effect of extended improvement and cultivation, and afterwards the cause of their being still further extended, the rise in the price of cattle, for example, tends to raise the rent of land directly, and in a still greater proportion. The real value of the landlord's share, his real command of the labour of other people, not only rises with the real value of the produce, but the proportion of his share to the whole produce rises with it. That produce, after the rise in its real price, requires no more labour to collect it than before. A smaller proportion of it will, therefore, be sufficient to replace, with the ordinary profit, the stock which employs that labour. A greater proportion of it must, consequently, belong to the landlord.

All those improvements in the productive powers of labour, which tend directly to reduce the real price of manufactures, tend indirectly to raise the real rent of land. The landlord exchanges that part of his rude produce, which is over and above his own consumption, or what comes to the same thing, the price of that part of it, for manufactured produce. Whatever reduces the real price of the latter, raises that of the former. An equal quantity of the former becomes thereby equivalent to a greater quantity of the latter; and the landlord is enabled to purchase a greater quantity of the conveniences, ornaments, or luxuries, which he has occasion for.

Every increase in the real wealth of the society, every increase in the quantity of useful labour employed within it, tends indirectly to raise the real rent of land. A certain proportion of this labour naturally goes to the land. A greater number of men and cattle are employed in its cultivation, the produce increases with the increase of the stock which is thus employed in raising it, and the rent increases with the produce.

The contrary circumstances, the neglect of cultivation and improvement, the fall in the real price of any part of the rude produce of land, the rise in the real price of manufactures from the decay of the manufacturing art and industry, the declension of the real wealth of the society, all tend, on the other hand, to lower the real rent of land, to reduce the real wealth of the landlord, to diminish his power of purchasing either the labour, or the produce of the labour of other people.

The whole annual produce of the land and labour of every country, or what comes to the same thing, the whole price of that annual produce, naturally divides itself, it has already been observed, into three parts; the rent of land, the wages of labour, and the profits of stock; and constitutes a revenue to three different orders of people; to those who live by rent, to those who live by wages, and to those who live by profit. These are the three great, original and constituent orders of every civilized society, from whose revenue that of every other order is ultimately derived.

The interest of the first of those three great orders, it appears from what has been just now said, is strictly and inseparably connected with the general interest of the society. Whatever either promotes or obstructs the one, necessarily promotes or obstructs the other. When the public deliberates concerning any regulation of commerce or police, the proprietors of land never can mislead it, with a view to promote the interest of their own particular order; at least if they have any tolerable knowledge of that interest. They are, indeed, too often defective in this tolerable knowledge. They are the only one of the three orders whose revenue costs them neither labour nor care, but comes to them, as it were, of its own accord, and independent of any plan or project of their own. That indolence, which is the natural effect of the ease and security of their situation, renders them too often, not only ignorant, but incapable of that application of mind which is necessary in order to foresee and understand the consequences of any public regulation.

The interest of the second order, that of those who live by wages, is as strictly connected with the interest of the society as that of the first. The wages of the labourer, it has already been shown, are never so high as when the demand for labour is continually rising, or when the quantity employed is every year increasing considerably. When this real wealth of society becomes stationary, his wages are soon reduced to what is barely enough to enable him to bring up a family, or to continue the race of labourers. When the society declines, they fall even below this. The order of proprietors, may, perhaps, gain more by the prosperity of the society than that of the labourers; but there is no order that suffers so cruelly from its decline. But though the interest of the labourer is strictly connected with that of society, he is incapable either of comprehending that interest, or of understanding its connexion with his own. His condition leaves him no time to receive the necessary information, and his education and habits are commonly such as to render him unfit to judge even though he was fully informed. In the public deliberations, therefore, his voice is little heard and less regarded, except upon some particular occasions, when his clamour is animated, set on, and supported by his employers, not for his, but for their own particular purposes.

His employers constitute the third order, that of those who live by profit. It is the stock that is employed for the sake of profit, which puts into motion the greater part of the useful labour of every society. The plans and projects of the employers of stock regulate and direct all the most important operations of labour, and profit is the end proposed by all those plans and projects. But the rate of profit does not, like rent and wages, rise with the prosperity, and fall with the declension, of the society. On the contrary, it is naturally low in rich, and high in poor countries, and it is always highest in the countries which are going fastest to ruin. The interest of this third order, therefore, has not the same connexion with the general interest of the society as that of the other two. Merchants and master manufacturers are, in this order, the two classes of people who commonly employ the largest capitals, and who by their wealth draw to themselves the greatest share of the public consideration. As during their whole lives they are engaged in plans and projects, they have frequently more acuteness of understanding than the greater part of country gentlemen. As their thoughts, however, are commonly exercised rather about the interest of their own particular branch of business, than about that of the society, their judgment, even when given with the greatest candour (which it has not been upon every occasion), is much more to be depended upon with regard to the former of those two objects, than with regard to the latter. Their superiority over the country gentleman is, not so much in their knowledge of the public interest, as in their having a better knowledge of their own interest than he has of his. It is by this superior knowledge of their own interest that they have frequently imposed upon his generosity, and persuaded him to give up both his own interest and that of the public, from a very simple but honest conviction, that their interest, and not his, was the interest of the public. The interest of the dealers, however, in any particular branch of trade or manufactures, is always in some respects different from, and even opposite to, that of the public. To widen the market and to narrow the competition, is always the interest of the dealers. To widen the market may frequently be agreeable enough to the interest of the public; but to narrow the competition must always be against it, and can serve only to enable the dealers, by raising their profits above what they naturally would be, to levy, for their own benefit, an absurd tax upon the rest of their fellow-citizens. The proposal of any new law or regulation of commerce which comes from this order, ought always to be listened to with great precaution, and ought never to be adopted till after having been long and carefully examined, not only with the most scrupulous, but with the most suspicious attention. It comes from an order of men, whose interest is never exactly the same with that of the public; who have generally an interest to deceive and even to oppress the public, and who accordingly have, upon many occasions, both deceived and oppressed it.

[Source: Adam Smith, *An Inquiry into the Nature and Causes of the Wealth of Nations*, ed. Edwin Cannan, New York 1937, Bk i, Ch. 11, pp.247–50.]

Doc. 11c. ADAM SMITH: Of Restraints Upon the Importation from Foreign Countries of Such Goods as Can be Produced at Home

By restraining, either by high duties, or by absolute prohibitions, the importation of such goods from foreign countries as can be produced at home, the monopoly of the home market is more or less secured to the domestic industry employed in producing them . . .

That this monopoly of the home market frequently gives great encouragement to that particular species of industry which enjoys it, and frequently turns towards that employment a greater share of both the labour and stock of the society than would otherwise have gone to it, cannot be doubted. But whether it tends either to increase the general industry of the society, or to give it the most advantageous direction, is not, perhaps, altogether so evident.

The general industry of the society never can exceed what the capital of the society can employ. As the number of workmen that can be kept in employment by any particular person must bear a certain proportion to his capital, so the number of those that can be continually employed by all the members of a great society, must bear a certain proportion to the whole capital of that society, and can never exceed that proportion. No regulation of commerce can increase the quantity of industry in any society beyond what its capital can maintain. It can only divert a part of it into a direction into which it might not otherwise have gone; and it is by no means certain that this artificial direction is likely to be more advantageous to the society than that into which it would have gone of its own accord.

Every individual is continually exerting himself to find out the most advantageous employment for whatever capital he can command. It is his own advantage, indeed, and not that of society, which he has in view. But the study of his own advantage naturally, or rather necessarily, leads him to prefer that employment, which is most advantageous to the society.

First, every individual endeavours to employ his capital as near home as he can, and consequently as much as he can in the support of domestic industry; provided always that he can thereby obtain the ordinary, and not a great deal less than the ordinary profits of stock.

Thus, upon equal or nearly equal profits, every wholesale merchant naturally prefers the home-trade to the foreign trade of consumption, and the foreign trade of consumption to the carrying trade. In the home-trade his capital is never so long out of his sight as it frequently is in the foreign trade of consumption. He can know better the character and situation of the persons whom he trusts, or if he should happen to be deceived, he knows better the laws of the country from which he must seek redress. In the carrying trade, the capital of the merchant is, as it were, divided between two foreign countries, and no part of it is ever necessarily brought home, or placed under his own immediate view and command.

The capital which an Amsterdam merchant employs in carrying corn from Konnigsberg to Lisbon, and fruit and wine from Lisbon to Konnigsberg, must generally be the one-half of it at Konnigsberg and the other half at Lisbon. No part of it need ever come to Amsterdam. The natural residence of such a merchant should either be at Konnigsberg or Lisbon, and it can only be some very particular circumstances which can make him prefer the residence of Amsterdam. The uneasiness, however, which he feels at being separated so far from his capital, generally determines him to bring part both of the Konnigsberg goods which he destines for the market of Lisbon, and of the Lisbon goods which he destines for that of Konnigsberg, to Amsterdam: and though this necessarily subjects him to a double charge of loading and unloading, as well as to the payment of some duties and customs, yet for the sake of having some part of his capital always under his own view and command, he willingly submits to this extraordinary charge; and it is in this manner that every country which has any considerable share of the carrying trade, becomes always the emporium, or general market, for the goods of all the different countries whose trade it carries on. The merchant, in order to save a second loading and unloading, endeavours always to sell in the home market as much of the goods of all those different countries as he can, and thus, so far as he can, to convert his carrying trade into a foreign trade of consumption. A merchant, in the same manner, who is engaged in the foreign trade of consumption, when he collects goods for foreign markets, will always be glad, upon equal or nearly equal profits, to sell as great a part of them at home as he can. He saves himself the risk and trouble of exportation, when, so far as he can, he thus converts his foreign trade of consumption into a home-trade. Home is in this manner the centre, if I may say so, round which the capitals of the inhabitants of every country are continually circulating, and towards which they are always tending, though by particular causes they may sometimes be driven off and repelled from it towards more distant employments. But a capital employed in the home-trade ... necessarily puts into motion a greater quantity of domestic industry, and gives revenue and employment to a greater number of the inhabitants of the country, than an equal capital employed in the foreign trade of consumption: and one employed in the foreign trade of consumption has the same advantage over an equal capital employed in the carrying trade. Upon equal, or only nearly equal profits, therefore, every individual naturally inclines to employ his capital in the manner in which it is likely to afford the greatest support to domestic industry, and to give revenue and employment to the greatest number of people of his own country.

Secondly, every individual who employs his capital in the support of domestic industry, necessarily endeavours so to direct that industry, that its produce may be of the greatest possible value.

The produce of industry is what it adds to the subject or materials upon which it is employed. In proportion as the value of this produce is great or small, so will likewise be the profits of the employer. But it is only for the sake of profit that any man employs a capital in the support of industry; and he will always, therefore, endeavour to employ it in the support of that industry of which the produce is likely to be of the greatest value, or to exchange for the greatest quantity either of money or of other goods.

But the annual revenue of every society is always precisely equal to the exchangeable value of the whole annual produce of its industry, or rather is precisely the same thing with that exchangeable value. As every individual, therefore, endeavours as much as he can both to employ his capital in the support of domestic industry, and so to direct that industry that its produce may be of the greatest value; every individual necessarily labours to render the annual revenue of the society as great as he can. He generally, indeed, neither intends to promote the public interest, nor knows how much he is promoting it. By preferring the support of domestic to that of foreign industry, he intends only his own security; and by directing that industry in such a manner as its produce may be of the greatest value, he intends only his own gain, and he is in this, as in many other cases, led by an invisible hand to promote an end which was no part of his intention. Nor is it always the worse for the society that it was no part of it. By pursuing his own interest he frequently promotes that of the society more effectually than when he really intends to promote it. I have never known much good done by those who affected to trade for the public good. It is an affectation, indeed, not very common among merchants, and very few words need be employed in dissuading them from it.

What is the species of domestic industry which his capital can employ, and of which the produce is likely to be of the greatest value, every individual, it is evident, can in his local situation, judge much better than any statesman or lawgiver can do for him. The statesman, who should attempt to direct private people in what manner they ought to employ their capitals, would not only load himself with a most unnecessary attention, but assume an authority which could safely be trusted, not only to no single person, but to no council or senate whatever, and which would nowhere be so dangerous as in the hands of a man who had folly and presumption enough to fancy himself fit to exercise it.

To give the monopoly of the home market to the produce of domestic industry, in any particular art or manufacture, is in some measure to direct private people in what manner they ought to employ their capitals, and must, in almost all cases, be either a useless or a hurtful regulation. If the produce of domestic can be bought there as cheap as that of foreign industry, the regulation is evidently useless. If it cannot, it must generally be hurtful . . .

[Source: Adam Smith, *An Inquiry into the Nature and Causes of the Wealth of Nations*, ed. Edwin Cannan, New York, 1937, Bk iv, Ch. 2, pp.420–4.]

Doc. 11*d*. ADAM SMITH: The System of Natural Liberty

The greatest and most important branch of the commerce of every nation, it has already been observed, is that which is carried on between the inhabitants of the town and those of the country. The inhabitants of the town draw from the country the rude produce which constitutes both the materials of their work and the fund of their subsistence; and they pay for this rude produce by sending back to the country a certain portion of it manufactured and prepared for immediate use. The trade which is carried on between these two different sets of people consists ultimately in a certain quantity of rude produce exchanged for a certain quantity of manufactured produce. The dearer the latter, therefore, the cheaper the former; and whatever tends in any country to raise the price of manufactured produce tends to lower that of the rude produce of the land, and thereby to discourage agriculture. The smaller the quantity of manufactured produce which any given quantity of rude produce, or, what comes to the same thing, which the price of any given quantity of rude produce is capable of purchasing, the smaller the exchangeable value of that given quantity of rude produce, the smaller the encouragement which either the landlord has to increase its quantity by improving or the farmer by cultivating the land. Whatever, besides, tends to diminish in any country the number of artificers and manufacturers, tends to diminish the home market, the most important of all markets for the rude produce of the land, and thereby still further to discourage agriculture.

These systems, therefore, which, preferring agriculture to all other employments, in order to promote it, impose restraints upon manufactures and foreign trade, act contrary to the very ends which they propose, and indirectly discourage that very species of industry which they mean to promote. They are, so far perhaps, more inconsistent than even the mercantile system. That system, by encouraging manufactures and foreign trade more than agriculture, turns a certain portion of the capital of the society from supporting a more advantageous, to support a less advantageous species of industry. But still it really and in the end encourages that species of industry which it means to promote. Those agricultural systems, on the contrary, really and in the end discourage their own favourite species of industry.

It is thus that every system which endeavours, either by extraordinary encouragements to draw towards a particular species of industry a greater share of the capital of the society than would naturally go to it, or, by extraordinary restraints, force from a particular species of industry some share of the capital which would otherwise be employed in it, is in reality subversive of the great purpose which it means to promote. It retards, instead of accelerating, the progress of society towards real wealth and greatness; and diminishes, instead of increasing, the real value of the annual produce of its land and labours.

All systems either of preference or of restraint, therefore, being thus completely taken away, the obvious and simple system of natural liberty establishes itself of its own accord. Every man, as long as he does not violate the laws of justice, is left perfectly free to pursue his own interest his own way, and to bring both his industry and capital into competition with those of any other man, or order of men. The sovereign is completely discharged from a duty, in the attempting to perform which he must always be exposed to innumerable delusions, and for the proper performance of which no human wisdom or knowledge could ever be sufficient; the duty of superintending the industry of private people and of directing it towards the employments most suitable to the interests of the society. According to the system of natural liberty, the sovereign has only three duties to attend to; three duties of great importance, indeed, but plain and intelligible to common understandings: first, the duty of protecting the society from the violence and invasion of other independent societies; secondly, the duty of protecting, as far as possible, every member of the society from the injustice or oppression of every other member of it, or the duty of establishing an exact administration of justice; and, thirdly, the duty of erecting and maintaining certain public works and certain public institutions, which it can never be for the interest of any individual, or small number of individuals, to erect and maintain; because the profit could never repay the expense to any individual or small number of individuals, though it may frequently do much more than repay it to a great society.

[Source: Adam Smith, *An Inquiry into the Nature and Causes of the Wealth of Nations*, ed. Edwin Cannan, New York 1937, Bk iv, Ch. 9, pp.649–51.]

7. The doctrine of the rights of man: documents
(Introduction, p. 146)

Doc. 12. The Declaration of Independence, 4 July 1776

The Unanimous Declaration of the Thirteen United States of America

When in the Course of human events, it becomes necessary for one people to dissolve the political bonds which have connected them with another, and to assume among the Powers of the earth, the separate and equal station to which the Laws of Nature and of Nature's God entitle them, a decent respect to the opinions of mankind requires that they should declare the causes which impel them to the separation.

We hold these truths to be self-evident, that all men are created equal, that they are endowed by their Creator with certain unalienable Rights, that among these are Life, Liberty, and the pursuit of Happiness. That to secure these rights, Governments are instituted among Men, deriving their just powers from the consent of the governed, – That whenever any Form of Government becomes destructive of these ends, it is the Right of the People to alter or abolish it, and to institute new Government, laying its foundation on such principles and organizing its powers in such form, as to them shall seem most likely to effect their Safety and Happiness. Prudence, indeed, will dictate that Governments long established should not be changed for light and transient causes; and accordingly all experience hath shown, that mankind are more disposed to suffer, while evils are sufferable, than to right themselves by abolishing the forms to which they are accustomed. But when a long train of abuses and usurpations, pursuing invariably the same Object evinces a design to reduce them under absolute Despotism, it is their right, it is their duty, to throw off such Government, and to provide new Guards for their future security. – Such has been the patient sufferance of these Colonies; and such is now the necessity which constrains them to alter their former Systems of Government. The history of the present King of Britain is a history of repeated injuries and usurpations, all having in direct object the establishment of an absolute Tyranny over these States. To prove this, let Facts be submitted to a candid world.

He has refused his Assent to laws, the most wholesome and necessary for the public good.

He has forbidden his Governors to pass Laws of immediate and pressing importance, unless suspended in their operation till his Assent should be obtained; and when so suspended, he has utterly neglected to attend to them.

He has refused to pass other Laws for the accommodation of large districts of people, unless those people would relinquish the right of Representation in the Legislature, a right inestimable to them and formidable to tyrants only.

He has called together legislative bodies at places unusual, uncomfortable, and distant from the depository of their Public Records, for the sole purpose of fatiguing them into compliance with his measures.

He has dissolved Representative Houses repeatedly, for opposing with manly firmness his invasions on the rights of the people. He has refused for a long time, after such dissolutions, to cause others to be elected; whereby the Legislative powers, incapable of Annihilation, have returned to the People at large for their exercise; the State remaining in the meantime exposed to all the dangers of invasion from without, and convulsions within.

He has endeavoured to prevent the population of these States; for that purpose obstructing the Laws of Naturalization of Foreigners; refusing to pass others to encourage their migration hither, and raising the conditions of new Appropriations of Lands.

He has obstructed the Administration of Justice, by refusing his Assent to Laws for establishing Judiciary Powers.

He has made Judges dependent on his Will alone, for the tenure of their offices, and the amount and payment of their salaries.

He has erected a multitude of New Offices, and sent hither swarms of Officers to harass our People, and eat out their substance.

He has kept among us, in times of peace, Standing Armies without the Consent of our legislatures.

He has affected to render the Military independent of and superior to the Civil Power.

He has combined with others to subject us to a jurisdiction foreign to our constitution, and unacknowledged by our laws; giving his Assent to their Acts of pretended Legislation:

For quartering large bodies of armed troops among us:

For protecting them, by a mock Trial, from punishment for any Murders which they should commit on the Inhabitants of these States:

For cutting off our Trade with all parts of the world:

For imposing Taxes on us without our Consent:

For depriving us in many cases, of the benefits of Trial by Jury:

For transporting us beyond Seas to be tried for pretended offences:

For abolishing the free System of English Laws in a neighbouring Province, establishing therein an Arbitrary government, and enlarging its Boundaries so as to render it at once an example and fit instrument for introducing the same absolute rule into these Colonies:

For taking away our Charters, abolishing our most valuable Laws, and altering fundamentally the Forms of our Governments:

For suspending our own Legislature, and declaring themselves invested with power to legislate for us in all cases whatsoever.

He has abdicated Government here, by declaring us out of his Protection and waging War against us.

He has plundered our seas, ravaged our Coasts, burnt our towns, and destroyed the Lives of our people.

He is at this time transporting large armies of foreign mercenaries to compleat the works of death, desolation and tyranny, already begun with circumstances of Cruelty and perfidy scarcely paralleled in the most barbarous ages, and totally unworthy the Head of a civilized nation.

He has constrained our fellow Citizens taken Captive on the high Seas to bear Arms against their Country, to become the executioners of their friends and Brethren, or to fall themselves by their Hands.

He has excited domestic insurrections amongst us, and has endeavoured to bring on the inhabitants of our frontiers, the merciless Indian Savages, whose rule of warfare, is an undistinguished destruction of all ages, sexes and conditions.

In every stage of these Oppressions We have Petitioned for Redress in the most humble terms: Our repeated Petitions have been answered only by repeated injury. A Prince, whose character is thus marked by every act which may define a Tyrant, is unfit to be the ruler of a free people.

Nor have We been wanting in attention to our British brethren. We have warned them from time to time of attempts by their legislature to extend an unwarrantable jurisdiction over us. We have reminded them of the circumstances of our emigration and settlement here. We have appealed to their native justice and magnanimity, and we have conjured them by the ties of our common kindred to disavow these usurpations, which, would inevitably interrupt our connections and correspondence. They too have been deaf to the voice of justice and of consanguinity. We must, therefore, acquiesce in the necessity, which denounces our separation, and hold them, as we hold the rest of mankind, Enemies in War, in Peace Friends.

We therefore, the Representatives of the United States of America in General Congress, Assembled, appealing to the Supreme Judge of the world for the rectitude of our intentions, do, in the Name, and by the authority of the good People of these Colonies, solemnly publish and declare, That these United Colonies are, and of Right ought to be Free and Independent States; that they are Absolved from all Allegiance to the British Crown, and that all political connection between them and the State of Great Britain, is and ought to be totally dissolved; and that as Free and Independent States; they have full Power to levy War, conclude Peace, contract Alliances, establish Commerce, and to do all other Acts and Things which Independent States may of right do. And for the support of this Declaration, with a firm reliance on the Protection of Divine Providence, we mutually pledge to each other our Lives, our Fortunes, and our sacred Honor.

[Source: Henry Steele Commager (ed.), *Documents of American History*, New York 1958, pp.100–2.]

Doc. 13. Declaration of the Rights of Man and Citizen, 27 August 1789

The representatives of the French people, constituted as a National Assembly, considering that ignorance, neglect or contempt for the rights of man are the sole cause of public misfortunes and the corruption of governments, have resolved to set forth in a solemn declaration the natural, inalienable and sacred rights of man in order that this declaration, constantly before all members of the social body, may ever remind them of their rights and duties; in order that the acts of the legislative power and those of the executive power can be compared at every moment with the aims of all political institutions and be the more respected; and in order that the demands of citizens, based henceforth on simple and incontestable principles, shall always be directed towards the maintenance of the constitution and the happiness of all.

Accordingly, the National Assembly recognizes and declares, in the presence and under the auspices of the Supreme Being, the following rights of man and of the citizen:

Article I. Men are born and remain free and equal in rights. Social distinctions can only be based on common utility.

II. The aim of every political association is the preservation of the natural and imprescriptible rights of man. These rights are liberty, property, security and resistance to oppression.

III. The source of all sovereignty is to be found essentially in the nation. No group, no individual can exercise any authority that does not expressly emanate from it.

IV. Liberty consists in being able to do everything which does not harm others. Thus the exercise of the natural rights of every man has no other limits than those which assure to other members of society the enjoyment of those same rights. These limits can only be determined by law.

V. The law has the right to forbid only those actions which are harmful to society. All that is not forbidden by law cannot be prevented, and no-one can be forced to do what it does not prescribe.

VI. The law is the expression of the general will. All citizens have the right to concur in person or through their representatives in its formation. It must be the same for all whether it protects or punishes. All citizens, being equal before it, are equally admissible to all public offices, positions and employment according to their ability, and without any distinctions other than those of their virtues and their talents.

VII. No man can be accused, arrested or detained except in cases determined by the law, and according to the forms that it prescribes. Those who incite, expedite or carry out, arbitrary orders must be punished; but every citizen summoned or seized by virtue of the law must obey immediately; he renders himself culpable by resistance.

VIII. The law should establish only those penalties which are strictly and obviously necessary, and no-one can be punished except by virtue of a law established and promulgated prior to the offence and legally applied.

IX. Since every man is presumed innocent until he has been declared guilty, when it is judged indispensable to arrest him, all unnecessary severity to secure his person should be severely repressed by law.

X. No-one should be disturbed on account of his opinions, even those on religion, provided that their expression does not disturb the public order established by law.

XI. The free expression of thought and opinion is one of the most precious rights of man: every citizen can then speak, write and publish freely, subject to his responsibility for the abuse of this liberty in cases determined by law.

XII. The guaranteeing of the rights of man and of the citizen necessitates a public force: this force is then established for the advantage of all, and not for the special benefit of those to whom it is entrusted.

XIII. For the maintenance of the public force and for the expenses of administration, a general tax is indispensable; it must be assessed equally among all citizens in proportion to their means.

XIV. All citizens have the right of ascertaining themselves or through their representatives the necessity of the public tax, to consent to it freely, to supervise its use, and to determine the quota, assessment, payment and duration.

XV. Society has the right to demand from every public agent an account of his administration.

XVI. Every society in which the guarantee of rights is not assured, nor the separation of powers laid down, has no constitution at all.

XVII. Since property is an inviolable and sacred right, no-one can be deprived of it unless public necessity, legally established, obviously requires it and with the condition of the award of a just and previous indemnity.

[Source: *Archives Parlementaires de 1787 à 1860,* ed. M. J. Mavidal, M. E. Laurent, M. E. Clavel, Première série (1787 à 1799), Paris 1877, tome IX, pp.236–7. Translated by the editors of this volume.]

Doc. 14. THOMAS PAINE: The Voice of an English Supporter

Reason and Ignorance, the opposite to each other, influence the great bulk of mankind. If either of these can be rendered sufficiently extensive in a country, the machinery of Government goes easily on. Reason obeys itself; and Ignorance submits to whatever is dictated to it.

The two modes of Government which prevail in the world, are –

First, Government by election and representation.

Secondly, Government by hereditary succession.

The former is generally known by the name of Republic; the latter by that of Monarchy and Aristocracy.

Those two distinct and opposite forms erect themselves on the two distinct and opposite bases of Reason and Ignorance.

As the exercise of Government requires talents and abilities, and as talents and abilities cannot have hereditary descent, it is evident that hereditary succession requires a belief from man to which his reason cannot subscribe, and which can only be established upon his ignorance; and the more ignorant any country is, the better it is fitted for this species of Government.

A. Roots of liberalism: the eighteenth century

On the contrary, Government, in a well-constituted Republic, requires no belief from man beyond that his reason can give.

He sees the *rationale* of the whole system, its origin and its operation; and as it is best supported when best understood, the human faculties act with boldness, and acquire under this form of Government a gigantic manliness . . .

When we survey the wretched condition of Man, under the monarchical and hereditary systems of Government, dragged from his home by one power, or driven by another, and impoverished by taxes more than by enemies, it becomes evident that those systems are bad, and that a general Revolution in the principle and construction of Governments is necessary.

What is Government more than the management of the affairs of a Nation? It is not, and from its nature cannot be, the property of any particular man or family, but of the whole community, at whose expense it is supported; and though by force and contrivance it has been usurped into an inheritance, the usurpation cannot alter the right of things. Sovereignty, as a matter of right, appertains to the Nation only, and not to any individual; and a Nation has at all times an inherent, indefeasible right to abolish any form of Government it finds inconvenient, and to establish such as accords with its interest, disposition, and happiness. The romantic and barbarous distinction of men into Kings and subjects, though it may suit the conditions of courtiers, cannot that of citizens; and is exploded by the principle upon which Governments are now founded. Every citizen is a member of the sovereignty, and, as such, can acknowledge no personal subjection: and his obedience can be only to the laws.

When men think of what Government is, they must necessarily suppose it to possess a knowledge of all the objects and matters upon which its authority is to be exercised. In this view of Government, the Republican system, as established by America and France, operates to embrace the whole of a Nation; and the knowledge necessary to the interests of all the parts, is to be found in the centre, which the parts by representation form; but the old Governments are on a construction that excludes knowledge as well as happiness; Government by monks, who know nothing of the world beyond the walls of a convent, is as inconsistent as Government by Kings.

What we formerly called Revolutions, were little more than a change of persons, or an alteration of local circumstances. They rose and fell like things of course, and had nothing in their existence or their fate that could influence beyond the spot that produced them. But what we now see in the world, from the Revolutions of America and France, are a renovation of the natural order of things, a system of principles as universal as truth and the existence of man, and combining moral with political happiness and national prosperity.

I. *Men are born, and always continue, free and equal in respect of their rights. Civil distinctions, therefore, can be founded only on public utility.*

II. *The end of all political associations is the preservation of the natural and imprescriptable rights of man; and these rights are liberty, property, security, and resistance of oppression.*

III. *The Nation is essentially the source of all sovereignty; nor can ANY INDIVIDUAL, or ANY BODY OF MEN, be entitled to any authority which is not expressly derived from it.*

In these principles there is nothing to throw a Nation into confusion by inflaming ambition. They are calculated to call forth wisdom and abilities, and to exercise them for the public good, and not for the emolument or aggrandisement of particular descriptions of men or families. Monarchical sovereignty, the enemy of mankind, and the source of misery, is abolished; and sovereignty itself is restored to its natural and original place, the Nation . . .

As it is not difficult to perceive, from the enlightened state of mankind, that hereditary Governments are verging to their decline, and that Revolutions on the broad basis of national sovereignty and Government by representation, are making their way in Europe, it would be an act of wisdom to anticipate their approach, and produce Revolutions by reason and accommodation, rather than commit them to the issue of convulsions.

From what we now see, nothing of reform in the political world ought to be held improbable. It is an age of Revolutions, in which everything may be looked for.

[Source: Thomas Paine, *The Rights of Man*, Part One (1791), London (Everyman's Library) 1954, pp.130, 134–5, 138.]

Doc. 15. JEREMY BENTHAM: The Voice of an English Critic

It concerns me to see so respectable an Assembly hold out expectations, which, according to my conception, cannot in the nature of things be fulfilled.

An enterprise of this sort, instead of preceding the formation of a complete body of laws, supposes such a work to be already existing in every particular except that of its obligatory force.

No laws are ever to receive the sanction of the Assembly that shall be contrary in any point to these principles. What does this suppose? It supposes that the several articles of detail that require to be enacted, to have been drawn up, to have been passed in review, to have been confronted with these fundamental articles, and to have been found in no respect repugnant to them. In a word, to be sufficiently assured that the several

A. Roots of liberalism: the eighteenth century

laws of detail will bear this trying comparison, one thing is necessary: The comparison must have been made.

To know the several laws which the exigencies of mankind call for, a view of all these several exigencies must be obtained. But to obtain this view, there is but one possible means, which is, to take a view of the laws that have already been framed, and of the exigencies which have given birth to them.

To frame a composition which shall in any tolerable degree answer this requisition, two endowments, it is evident, are absolutely necessary: – an acquaintance with the law as it is, and the perspicacity and genius of the metaphysician: and these endowments must unite in the same person.

I can conceive but four purposes which a discourse, of the kind proposed under the name of a Declaration of Rights, can be intended to answer:– the setting bounds to the authority of the crown – the setting bounds to the authority of the supreme legislative power, that of the National Assembly; – the serving as a general guide or set of instructions to the National Assembly itself, in the task of executing their function in detail, by the establishment of particular laws; – and the affording a satisfaction to the people.

These four purposes seem, if I apprehend right, to be all of them avowed by the same or different advocates of this measure.

Of the fourth and last of these purposes I shall say nothing: it is a question merely logical – dependent upon the humour of the spot and of the day, of which no one at a distance can be a judge. Of the fitness of the end, there can be but one opinion: the only question is about the fitness of the means.

In the other three points of view, the expediency of the measure is more than I can perceive.

The description of the persons, of whose rights it is to contain the declaration, is remarkable. Who are they? The French nation? No; not they only, but all citizens, and all men. By citizens, it seems we are to understand men engaged in political society: by men, persons not yet engaged in political society – persons as yet in a state of nature.

The word men, as opposed to citizens, I had rather not have seen. In this sense, a declaration of the rights of men is a declaration of the rights which human creatures, it is supposed, would possess, were they in a state in which the French nation certainly are not, nor perhaps any other; certainly no other into whose hands this declaration could ever come.

This instrument is the more worthy of attention, especially of the attention of a foreigner, inasmuch as the rights which it is to declare are the rights which it is supposed belong to the members of every nation in the globe. As a member of a nation which with relation to the French comes under the name of a foreign one, I feel the stronger call to examine this declaration, inasmuch as in this instrument I am invited to read a list of rights which belong as much to me as to the people for whose more particular use it has been framed.

The word men, I observe to be all along coupled in the language of the Assembly itself, with the word citizen. I lay it, therefore, out of the question, and consider the declaration . . . as that of a declaration of the rights of all men in a state of citizenship or political society.

I proceed, then, to consider it in the three points of view above announced:–

1. Can it be of use for the purpose of setting bounds to the power of the crown? No; for that is to be the particular object of the Constitutional Code itself, from which this preliminary part is detached in advance.

2. Can it be of use for the purpose of setting bounds to the power of the several legislative bodies established or to be established? I answer, No.

(1) Not of any subordinate ones: for of their authority, the natural and necessary limit is that of the supreme legislature, the National Assembly.

(2) Not of the National Assembly itself:– Why? Such limitation is unnecessary. It is proposed, and very wisely and honestly, to call in the body of the people, and give it as much power and influence as in its nature it is capable of: by enabling it to declare its sentiments whenever it thinks proper, whether immediately, or through the channel of the subordinate assemblies. Is a law enacted or proposed in the National Assembly, which happens not to be agreeable to the body of the people? It will be equally censured by them, whether it be conceived, or not, to bear marks of a repugnancy to this declaration of rights. Is a law disagreeable to them? They will hardly think themselves precluded from expressing their disapprobation, by the circumstance of its not being to be convicted of repugnancy to that instrument; and though it should be repugnant to that instrument, they will see little need to resort to that instrument for the ground of their repugnancy; they will find a much nearer ground in some particular real or imaginary inconvenience.

In short, when you have made such provision, that the supreme legislature can never carry any point against the general and persevering opinion of the people, what would you have more? What use in their attempting to bind themselves by a set of phrases of their own contrivance? The people's pleasure: that is the only check to which no other can add anything, and which no other can supersede.

In regard to the rights thus declared, mention will either be made of the exceptions and modifications that may be made to them by the laws themselves, or there will not. In the former case, the observance of the declaration will be impracticable; nor can the law in its details stir a step without flying in the face of it. In the other case, it fails thereby altogether of its only other object, the setting limits to the exercise of the legislative power. Suppose a declaration to this effect:– no man's liberty shall be abridged in any point. This, it is evident, would be a useless extravagance, which must be contradicted by every law that came to be made. Suppose it to say – no man's liberty shall be abridged, but in such points as it shall be abridged in, by the law. This, we see, is saying nothing: it leaves the law just as free and unfettered as it found it.

Between these two rocks lies the only choice which an instrument destined to this purpose can have. Is an instrument of this sort produced? We shall see it striking against one or other of them in every line. The first is what the framers will most guard against, in proportion to their reach of thought, and to their knowledge in this line: when they hit against the other, it will be by accident and unawares.

Lastly, it cannot with any good effect answer the only remaining intention, viz. that of a check to restrain as well as to guide the legislature itself, in the penning of the laws of detail that are to follow.

The mistake has its source in the current logic, and in the want of attention to the distinction between what is first in the order of demonstration, and what is first in the order of invention. Principles, it is said, ought to precede consequences; and the first being established, the others will follow of course. What are the principles here meant? General propositions, and those of the widest extent. What by consequences? Particular propositions, included under those general ones.

That this order is favourable to demonstration, if by demonstration be meant personal debate and argumentation, is true enough. Why? Because, if you can once get a man to admit the general proposition, he cannot, without incurring the reproach of inconsistency, reject a particular proposition that is included in it.

But, that this order is not the order of conception, of investigation, of invention, is equally undeniable. In this order, particular propositions always precede general ones. The assent to the latter is preceded by and grounded on the assent to the former.

If we prove the consequences from the principle, it is only from the consequences that we learn the principle.

Apply this to laws. The first business, according to the plan I am combating, is to find and declare the principles: the laws of a fundamental nature: that done, it is by their means that we shall be enabled to find the proper laws of detail. I say, no: it is only in proportion as we have formed and compared with one another the laws of detail, that our fundamental laws will be exact and fit for service. Is a general proposition true? It is because all the particular propositions that are included under it are true. How, then, are we to satisfy ourselves of the truth of the general one? By having under our eye all the included particular ones. What, then, is the order of investigation by which true general propositions are formed? We take a number of less extensive – of particular propositions; find some points in which they agree, and from the observation of these points form a more extensive one, a general one in which they are all included. In this way, we proceed upon sure grounds, and understand ourselves as we go: in the opposite way, we proceed at random, and danger attends every step.

No law is good which does not add more to the general mass of felicity than it takes from it. No law ought to be made that does not add more to the general mass of felicity than it takes from it. No law can be made that does not take something from liberty; those excepted which take away, in the whole or in part those laws which take from liberty. Propositions to the first effect I see are true without any exception: propositions to the latter effect I see are not true till after the particular propositions intimated by the exceptions are taken out of it . . .

What follows? That the proper order is − first to digest the laws of detail, and when they are settled and found to be fit for use, then, and not till then, to select and frame *in terminis*, by abstraction, such propositions as may be capable of being given without self-contradiction as fundamental laws.

What is the source of this premature anxiety to establish fundamental laws? It is the old conceit of being wiser than all posterity − wiser than those who will have had more experience, − the old desire of ruling over posterity, − the old recipe for enabling the dead to chain down the living . . .

Such indigested and premature establishments betoken two things:− the weakness of the understanding, and the violence of the passions: the weakness of the understanding, in not seeing the insuperable incongruities which have been above stated − the violence of the passions, which betake themselves to such weapons for subduing opposition at any rate, and giving to the will of every man who embraces the proposition imported by the article in question, a weight beyond what is its just and intrinsic due.

[Source: Jeremy Bentham, *Anarchical Fallacies being an Examination of the Declaration of Rights issued during the French Revolution* (1824) in *The Works of Jeremy Bentham*, ed. John Bowring, Edinburgh 1843, II, pp.491–4.]

8. The belief in progress: document
(Introduction, p. 162)

Doc. 16. THE MARQUIS DE CONDORCET: The Future Progress of the Human Mind

Our hopes for the future condition of the human race can be subsumed under three important heads: the abolition of inequality between nations, the progress of equality within each nation, and the true perfection of mankind. Will all nations one day attain that state of civilization which the most enlightened, the freest and the least burdened by prejudices, such as the French and the Anglo-Americans, have attained already? Will the vast gulf that separates these peoples from the slavery of nations under the rule of monarchs, from the barbarism of African tribes, from the ignorance of savages, little by little disappear?

Is there on the face of the earth a nation whose inhabitants have been debarred by nature herself from the enjoyment of freedom and the exercise of reason?

Are those differences which have hitherto been seen in every civilized country in respect of the enlightenment, the resources, and the wealth enjoyed by the different classes into which it is divided, is that inequality between men which was aggravated or perhaps produced by the earliest progress of society, are these parts of civilization itself, or are they due to the present imperfections of the social art? Will they necessarily decrease and ultimately make way for a real equality, the final end of the social art, in which even the effects of the natural differences between men will be mitigated and the only kind of inequality to persist will be that which is in the interests of all and which favours the progress of civilization, of education, and of industry, without entailing either poverty, humiliation, or dependence? In other words, will men approach a condition in which everyone will have the knowledge necessary to conduct himself in the ordinary affairs of life, according to the light of his own reason, to preserve his mind free from prejudice, to understand his rights and to exercise them in accordance with his conscience and his creed; in which everyone will become able, through the development of his faculties, to find the means of providing for his needs; and in which at last misery and folly will be the exception, and no longer the habitual lot of a section of society?

Is the human race to better itself, either by discoveries in the sciences and the arts, and so on in the means to individual welfare and general prosperity; or by progress in the principles of conduct or practical morality; or by a true perfection of the intellectual, moral, or physical faculties of man, an improvement which may result from a perfection either of the instruments used to heighten the intensity of these faculties and to direct their use or of the natural constitution of man? In answering these three questions we shall find in the experience of the past, in the observation of the progress that the sciences and civilization have already made, in the analysis of the progress of the human mind and of the development of its faculties, the strongest reasons for believing that nature has set no limit to the realization of our hopes . . .

In looking at the history of societies we shall have had occasion to observe that there is often a great difference between the rights that the law allows its citizens and the rights that they actually enjoy, and again, between the equality established by political codes and that which in fact exists amongst individuals: and we shall have noticed that these differences were one of the principal causes of the destruction of freedom in the Ancient republics, of the storms that troubled them, and of the weakness that delivered them over to foreign tyrants.

These differences have three main causes: inequality in wealth; inequality in status between the man whose means of subsistence are hereditary and the man whose means are dependent on the length of his life, or, rather, on that part of his life in which he is capable of work; and, finally, inequality in education.

We therefore need to show that these three sorts of real inequality must constantly diminish without however disappearing altogether: for they are the result of natural and necessary causes which it would be foolish and dangerous to wish to eradicate; and one could not even attempt to bring about the entire disappearance of their effects without introducing even more fecund sources of inequality, without striking more direct and more fatal blows at the rights of man.

It is easy to prove that wealth has a natural tendency to equality, and that any excessive disproportion could not exist or at least would rapidly disappear if civil laws did not provide artificial ways of perpetuating and uniting fortunes; if free trade and industry were allowed to remove the advantages that accrued wealth derives from any restrictive law or fiscal privilege; if taxes on covenants, the restrictions placed on their free employment, their subjection to tiresome formalities and the uncertainty and inevitable expense involved in implementing them did not hamper the activity of the poor man and swallow up his meagre capital, if the administration of the country did not afford some men ways of making their fortune that were closed to other citizens; if prejudice and avarice, so common in old age, did not preside over the making of marriages; and if, in a society enjoying simpler manners and more sensible institutions, wealth ceased to be a means of satisfying vanity and ambition, and if the equally misguided notions of austerity, which condemn spending money in the cultivation of the more delicate pleasures, no longer insisted on the hoarding of all one's earnings.

Let us turn to the enlightened nations of Europe, and observe the size of their present populations in relation to the size of their territories. Let us consider, in agriculture and industry the proportion that holds between labour and the means of subsistence, and we shall see that it would be impossible for those means to be kept at their present level and consequently for population to be kept at its present size if a great number of individuals were not almost entirely dependent for the maintenance of themselves and their family either on their own labour or on the interest from capital invested so as to make their labour more productive. Now both these sources of income depend on the life and even on the health of the head of the family. They provide what is rather like a life annuity, save that it is more dependent on chance; and in consequence there is a very real difference between people living like this and those whose resources are not at all subject to the same risks, who live either on revenue from land, or on the interest on capital which is almost independent of their own labour.

Here then is a necessary cause of inequality, of dependence and even of misery, which ceaselessly threatens the most numerous and most active class in our society.

We shall point out how it can be in great part eradicated by guaranteeing people in old age a means of livelihood produced partly by their own savings and partly by the savings of others who make the same outlay, but who die before they need to reap the reward; or, again, on the same principle of compensation, by securing for widows and orphans an income which is the same and costs the same for those families which suffer an early loss and for those which suffer it later; or again by providing all children with the capital necessary for the full use of their labour, available at the age when they start work and found a family, a capital which increases at the expense of those whom premature death prevents from reaching this age. It is to the application of the calculus to the probabilities of life and the investment of money that we owe the idea of these methods which have already been successful, although they have not been applied in a sufficiently comprehensive and exhaustive fashion to render them really useful, not merely to a few individuals, but to society as a whole, by making it possible to prevent those periodic disasters which strike at so many families and which are such a recurrent source of misery and suffering.

We shall point out that schemes of this nature, which can be organized in the name of the social authority and become one of its greatest benefits, can also be the work of private associations, which will be formed without any real risk, once the principles for the proper working of these schemes have been widely diffused and the mistakes which have been the undoing of a large number of these associations no longer hold terrors for us.

(We shall reveal other methods of ensuring this equality, either by seeing that credit is no longer the exclusive privilege of great wealth, but that it has another and no less sound foundation; or by making industrial progress and commercial activity more independent of the existence of the great capitalists. And once again, it is to the application of the calculus that we shall be indebted for such methods.)

The degree of equality in education that we can reasonably hope to attain, but that should be adequate, is that which excludes all dependence, either forced or voluntary. We shall show how this condition can be easily attained in the present state of human knowledge even by those who can study only for a small number of years in childhood, and then during the rest of their life in their few hours of leisure. We shall prove that, by a suitable choice of syllabus and of methods of education, we can teach the citizen everything that he needs to know in order to be able to manage his household, administer his affairs and employ his labour and his faculties in freedom; and to know his rights and to be able to exercise them; to be acquainted with his duties and fulfil them satisfactorily; to judge his own and other men's actions according to his own lights and to be a stranger to none of the high and delicate feelings which honour human nature; not to be in a state of blind dependence upon those to whom he must entrust his affairs or the exercise of his rights; to be in a proper condition to choose and supervise them; to be no longer the dupe of those popular errors which torment man with superstitious fears and chimerical hopes; to defend himself against prejudice by the strength of his reason alone; and finally, to escape the deceits of charlatans who would lay snares for his fortune, his health, his freedom of thought and his conscience under the pretext of granting him health, wealth and salvation . . .

These various causes of equality do not act in isolation; they unite, combine and support each other and so their cumulative effects are stronger, surer and more constant. With greater equality of education there will be greater equality in industry and so in wealth; equality in wealth necessarily leads to equality in education; and equality between the nations and equality within a single nation are mutually dependent.

So we might say that a well directed system of education rectifies natural inequality in ability instead of strengthening it, just as good laws remedy natural inequality in the means of subsistence, and just as in societies where laws have brought about this same equality, liberty, though subject to a regular constitution, will be more widespread, more complete than in the total independence of savage life. Then the social art will have fulfilled its aim, that of assuring and extending to all men enjoyment of the common rights to which they are called by nature.

The real advantages that should result from this progress, of which we can entertain a hope that is almost a certainty, can have no other term than that of the absolute perfection of the human race; since, as the various kinds of equality come to work in its favour by producing ampler sources of supply, more extensive education, more complete liberty, so

239

A. Roots of liberalism: the eighteenth century

equality will be the more real and will embrace everything which is really of importance for the happiness of human beings.

[Source: Marie-Jean-Antoine-Nicolas Caritat, Marquis de Condorcet, *Sketch for a Historical Picture of the Progress of the Human Mind* (1795), trans. June Barraclough, Introduction by Stuart Hampshire, London 1955, pp.173–5, 179–83.]

Section B

Classical liberalism

1. The utilitarian approach to government: Introduction
(Documents 17–22, pp. 294–309)

Bentham objected to a reform of existing institutions being based on a Declaration of Rights. In the American Declaration of Independence with its claim that all men are created equal and that they are endowed by their creator with certain inalienable rights he saw nothing but 'a hodgepot of confusion and absurdity'. In a letter to the French Deputy Brissot he rejected the French Declaration of Man and Citizen of 1789 as 'a metaphysical work, the *ne plus ultra* of metaphysics. It may have been a necessary evil, but is nevertheless an evil' [1] He was also averse to the universal claim of the Declaration to refer to man and citizen in the abstract and to apply it to human beings in all countries.

Completely unhistorically, Bentham denied that all men were born free. All rights were derivative, none of them could be anterior to the State as every right presupposed a sanctioning authority. There was, however one principle which forms the foundation of any State or society: *Self-Interest*. 'The cell of moral and political society is for him not man as the possessor of rights but *homo economicus*. Every man is the best judge of his own interest and is best able to secure and provide for it.' [2]

But what is the position when the self-interests of people clash? There is the problem of reconciliation. Bentham solves this problem 'by the logic of self-interest itself, which demonstrates in concrete facts that the interests of individuals so harmonize with each other that each man, in attending to his own business creates one element in a common utility, the sum of utilities.' [3]

Unfortunately the individual is not always consistent in developing the logic of his own interest. He sometimes acts against his own true interest and then infringes the interest of others. Here the work of the government comes in representing the logic of truth as against the anti-logic of errors. The government should be led by the interest of the greatest number and not by the 'sinister interest' of some specific section in society. All institutions, juridicial, economic, social and political had to be tested and judged by the extent to which they answered the interest of the greatest number and ensured their happiness. They had to provide both security, a term which to Bentham was identical with liberty, and equality. In the event of a conflict between them, security was to be given pride of place. Nevertheless, seen in historic perspective Bentham's insistence that 'Every man is to count for one and no man for more than one' formed a democratic basis of the utilitarian philosophy, a basis subsequently to be developed by James Mill and J. S. Mill.

Bentham's teachings were a battle-cry against the existing privileges of the landed aristocracy and the interference by the government. If the proper end in every community was the creation and preservation of the greatest happiness of the greatest number, the false end was by contrast the greatest quantity of happiness enjoyed by the privileged few. Bentham had no illusions about the role of power in society. 'The greater the quantity of power possessed, the greater the facility and the incitement to the abuse of it.' (doc. 20) As power and wealth were regarded as interrelated the same truth applied to wealth. The maximum of inequality, conditioned by the combination of power and wealth, was to be found in the monarchy.

All law is in Bentham's eyes an evil, as it interferes with the liberty of the individual. Government which issues and enforces laws is thus an evil, too, unfortunately an indispensable one. If every function of the government is an evil it has to be reduced to a minimum; and of two evils the lesser one has to be chosen. Some limitations of freedom are unavoidable. 'It is impossible to create rights, impose obligations, or protect person, life, reputation, property, subsistence, and even liberty, except by a sacrifice of liberty.' [4] However this sacrifice is worthwhile if by creating good laws we help to produce conditions which guarantee liberty and equality.

The government must be obeyed and at the same time anxiously watched if and when it usurped more power than required for carrying out its limited legitimate functions. In a society based on the rule of law the good citizen had the double obligation, 'to obey punctually and to censure freely'. He had to test the utility or mischievousness of individual laws in order that they could be modified if necessary. To Bentham the abstract maximum of utility was in practically all cases a sufficient guide for judging institutions and laws.

This vigorous critic of existing institutions did not idealize man. He maintained that everyone is largely selfish but hard and painful experience tells him 'that he has one great interest in common with all other men: the existence of a government that seeks to promote the greatest happiness of the greatest number and can be trusted to do so only if it is responsible to all the people and jealously watched by them.' [5]

Influenced by the Austrian reformer of penal law, the Marquis de Beccaria and his *Treatise of Crime and Punishment* (1764), Bentham argued that it was the task of government to promote the happiness of society by punishing and rewarding. In his major work *The Introduction to the Principles of Morals and Legislation* (1789) he took the very modern line that 'all punishment is mischief, all punishment in itself is evil'. Upon the principle of utility if it ought at all to be admitted, it ought only to be admitted in as far as it promises 'to exclude some greater evil'. [6]

Trusting in his 'felicific calculus', Bentham was oddly concerned only with the amount but not with the quality of human happiness. Pushpin was to him as good an instrument of happiness as poetry. Bentham also failed to realize that not all men are always motivated in their actions and views by clearly understood self-interest. Though Bentham felt urged to

The utilitarian approach to government: introduction

make all things new, he was far from being a champion of 'political messianism' in the sense of Professor J. L. Talmon's term. 'He did not propose ... to regulate by positive law the education, the work, the amusements, the domestic life and the social intercourse of his fellow citizens.'[7]

His qualified *laissez faire* approach was eminently suited to assist the rising self-made men of industry and commerce in England at the turn of the century. As J. S. Mill observed in 1838, a few years after Bentham's death, 'Bentham's idea of the world' was 'that of a collection of persons pursuing each his separate interest and pleasure'.[8] Such a philosophy was, of necessity, limited in range and vision. What it could do was to 'teach the means of organizing and regulating the merely *business* part of the social arrangement'. Bentham 'committed the mistake of supposing that the business part of human affairs was the whole of them; all at least that the legislator and the moralist had to deal with'.[9]

But whilst there were whole areas of human nature outside the grasp and understanding of the father of political radicalism in England, he had an astute insight into what he called the 'interest-begotten prejudice', the often hypocritical inclination of man to make a duty and a virtue out of pursuing his self-interest. If this was so, it was imperative to make sure that the self-interest of the privileged few forming the establishment, did not prevail. Instead the majority of the people should decisively participate in political power.

Compared with Bentham his pupil James Mill was less systematic but equally vigorous. His diction was less ponderous and more concise. Mill was not concerned in the first instance with reform and modification of law but with reform of government. This determined radical in his turn influenced Bentham, who from 1808 onward took a greater interest in politics and turned to the making of constitutional codes. Basing his *Essay on Government* of 1820 on Bentham's hedonist utility principle James Mill declared it the end of government to promote the greatest happiness of the greatest number. The task of government was 'to increase to the utmost the pleasures and diminish to the utmost the pains' of the citizens. Government's main concern was with those pleasures and pains that men derive from one another. Men must work to produce the means of happiness which were not naturally abundant. Human beings were inclined to let others do the unpleasant work for them, to take advantage of their labour and to make their persons and properties subservient to their own pleasures. The only way to prevent this and to ensure that every man should retain as much as possible of the fruits of his labour was self-protection by joining with others. This object could be 'best attained when a great number of men combine and delegate to a small number the powers necessary for protecting them all. This is Government'.[10]

B. Classical liberalism

James Mill was even more conscious of the dangers of abuse of power than was Bentham. What guarantee, he asked, was there that the few selected to protect the many would not abuse their power for their own purposes? Systems of government had to be judged according to the degree of diminuation of the misuse of power by those who held it. None of the known systems of government seemed safe in this respect. The Democratic system was not workable, because 'a community in mass was ill adapted for the business of government'. [11]

In the aristocratic system a comparatively small number of people enjoyed excessive power. This made them inclined 'to take from the rest of the community as much as they please of the objects they desire.' [12] Moreover an aristocracy was without the necessary intellectual qualifications for ruling over others, as it lacked a strong incentive to work. The same was true of the monarchical system. Kings, too, aimed at obtaining a maximum of power in order to take from every man as much as they pleased.

The only chance of avoiding the abuse of power lay in a representative system which could make the government responsible to the governed. Its success depended on two conditions. First the representatives had to possess sufficient checking power to keep an adequate check on the government. Secondly the representative body must 'have an identity of interest with the community; otherwise it will make mischievous use of its power'. [13] A reformed House of Commons should, as a checking body, have sufficient power to match the combined power of the King and the House of Lords.

The House of Commons could not become more representative by selecting its members as Lord Liverpool had suggested in 1793, on the basis of status and occupation, including besides the landholding gentry, merchants and manufacturers, officers of the army and the navy, practitioners of law, even literary men. Such procedure would simply lead to 'the formation of a number of fraternities', each of them with a 'sinister interest', with its own *esprit de corps*. On the contrary what was required was a wider suffrage which would make impossible the predominance of such 'fraternities'.

Though James Mill did not insist on universal manhood suffrage whilst approving of it in principle, he wanted to see the franchise extended to the 'middle rank', the numerous members of the middle classes. The 'middle rank' more than deserve the vote as it 'gives to science, to art and to legislation itself their most distinguished ornaments, all that has exalted and refined human nature'. [14] Mill presupposed an identity of interest between the 'middle rank' and the uneducated masses, as 'the great majority of the people never cease to be guided by that rank'. [15]

James Mill did not want any class of people to remain unrepresented whose interest was not obviously included in that of other people. As he saw it, the interests of the 'middle rank' and of the uneducated masses of labourers did not basically diverge and the latter would obviously fare better if the middle classes were given the vote. He did not consider a vote for women was necessary as he regarded the interest of almost all of them 'involved either in that of their fathers or in that of their husbands'. In this point James Mill, the political radical, remained conventional. What mattered to him was the extension of the franchise to the (male) members of the middle classes in order that their opinion 'would ultimately decide'. A limited period for each parliament with elections at regular intervals would be an additional factor in securing a true identity of the interests of the electors with those of the representatives and a safeguard against the forming of interest cliques.[16]

Although Mill's approach was somewhat narrow and much coloured by his dislike of the Aristocratic Establishment, his criticism did not stop at its misrule at home. 'An English gentleman', he observed acidly, 'may be taken as a favourable specimen of civilization, of knowledge, of humanity, of all the qualities in short that make human nature estimable.'[17] Yet this had not prevented English gentlemen in the West Indies, until fairly recently, from a deplorable abuse of their power over negro slaves, from depriving them of their property and treating them cruelly. Such behaviour was equally wrong abroad as at home, and ways and means had to be found to stop this flagrant abuse of power.

John Stuart Mill testified that in politics his father had 'an almost unbounded confidence in the efficacy of two things: representative government, and complete freedom of discussion. . . . He thought that when the legislation no longer represented a class interest, it would aim at the general interest, honestly and with adequate wisdom; since the people would be sufficiently under the guidance of educated intelligence, to make in general a good choice of persons to represent them, and having done so, to leave to those whom they had chosen a liberal discretion.'[18] It was the long-term optimism of an honest though perhaps not very sophisticated rationalist inclined to underestimate the obstacles in the path of a gradual amelioration of mankind.

Compared with his teachers Bentham and James Mill, John Stuart Mill had a much subtler mind and more diversified intellectual interests. Lacking the vigour and resolute radicalism of his predecessors he modified and refined their doctrines to a point where his own views were not seldom inclined to contradict them. He agreed with the creed of Utility, the Greatest Happiness principle according to which actions were 'right in proportion as they tended to promote happiness i.e. pleasure and avoided unhappiness or the privation of pleasure'. But he was not satisfied with the mere quantitative concept of pleasure and pain. He found it 'quite compatible with the principle of utility to recognize the fact that some *kinds* of pleasure are more desirable than others.'[19] As Mill said in a classic passage: 'It is better to be a human being dissatisfied than a pig satisfied; better to be a Socrates dissatisfied than a fool satisfied.' [20] In other words he allowed for a qualitative approach which differed greatly from Bentham's 'felicific calculus'. J. S. Mill saw a plurality of phenomena, the complexity of situations where Bentham had only noticed a single phenomenon or a clear-cut situation. A thinker who insisted on the impact of historical, geographical and institutional factors on society was bound to see the problems of representative government in a wider context. If less forceful, his comparative insights into political attitudes or institutions are more profound than those of the earlier utilitarians.

In his ideas on government, J. S. Mill favoured universal suffrage, a vote for every man and woman. He championed the female vote and he advocated the extension of the suffrage to the working classes. This accorded with his concept of 'the ideally best form of government' in which the supreme controlling power was 'in the last resort vested in the entire aggregate of the community'. [21] Citizens should not only have a voice in the exercise of that ultimate sovereignty, but also at least occasionally be able to discharge some public function. It was therefore wrong that the working classes were still excluded from any direct participation in government. Mill denied that the classes participating in government had at the time 'in general any intention of sacrificing the working classes to themselves'. [22] On the contrary, they willingly made 'considerable sacrifices, especially of their pecuniary interest for the benefit of the working classes', and erred 'rather by too lavish and indiscriminating beneficence'. But this was not the decisive point. The fact remained that Parliament or nearly all its members did not look 'at any question with the eyes of a working man'. [23] Although Mill did not identify himself with the working-class man's point of view, he insisted that it should be represented in Parliament. A case in point was the question of strikes. The members of the House of Commons then all favoured the employers' point of view rejecting strikes and the viewpoint of the striking workers remained unrepresented.

However, Mill's insistence on universal suffrage for men and women was not without one qualification. The special achievements of the educated, he argued, should not be ignored. 'Though everyone ought to have a voice – that everyone should have an equal voice' was 'a totally different proposition.' [24] In fact as Mill explained in his *Thoughts on Parliamentary Reform,* an electoral system was 'perfect only when each person has a vote, and the well-educated have more than a vote'. [25] Such a suggestion corresponded with the additional vote first granted to fellows and later also to graduates of the old English and Scottish universities.

In common with the earlier utilitarians J. S. Mill had no clear concept of class. He looked at class not as a sociologist but as a moralizing reformer. To him a class was 'politically speaking, any number of persons

The utilitarian approach to government: introduction

who have the same sinister interest – that is, whose direct and apparent interest points to towards the same description of bad measures'.[26] Yet Mill was confident that although in the existing division in British society between the labourers and the employers, the majority of each class would in any conflict 'be mainly governed by their class interests', a minority of each would subordinate that consideration 'to reason, justice and the good of the whole'.[27] Mill was convinced that the enlightened and public-spirited minority of, say, class A would vote on a controversial issue with the entire class B. On other occasions conversely a coalition would be formed between a minority of class B and the entire class A again ensuring that the general interest would prevail. If Mill was rather too optimistic in such casuistic constructions he soberly realized that in a democracy as with all other forms of government 'the sinister interest' of the power-holders represents a constant danger. Yet he remained confident that 'in any tolerably constituted society', justice and the general interest in most cases won in the end because of the almost always existing division between the various separate selfish interests of mankind. The representative system was not as simply arrived at as Bentham and James Mill had presumed. In J. S. Mill's considered opinion it ought 'not to allow any of the various sectional interests to be so powerful as to be capable of prevailing against truth and justice and the other sectional interests combined'.[28]

Mill not only favoured representative government, he also thought it could not flourish without an active, self-reliant and enterprising personality. He maintained that 'inactivity, unaspiringness, absence of desire' were 'a more fatal hindrance to improvement than any misdirection of energy'.[29] He favoured 'the active, self-helping type of man' required in a democracy as against 'the passive type of character', preferred by the government of a monarchy or aristocracy. Subjection to the will of others and the virtues of self-help and self-government were incompatible. It was 'the striving, go-ahead character of England and the United States' which laid 'the foundation of the best hopes for the general improvement of mankind'.[30] There was an intimate connection between Mill's ideas on representative government and his emphasis on the energetic and original individuality, between his political democracy and his cultural élitism. Each determined the other, and his qualified emphasis on democracy and his aesthetic individualism were two sides of the same medal. The many had to have a vote and a voice in representative government, but the few active, original individuals were 'the salt of the earth, without them human life would become a stagnant pool'.[31] Both in his ideas on government and his aesthetic individualism* J. S. Mill had in the end travelled farther from the earlier utilitarians than he was inclined to concede.

* For a discussion of Mill's aesthetic individualism see pp. 271–8.

2. Economic liberalism – introduction

(i) Free trade and *laissez faire* in Britain
(Documents 23–6, pp. 310–26)

During the first half of the nineteenth century Great Britain went through a remarkable period of change, economically and socially as well as politically. Readjustment to peacetime conditions, after the long wars with revolutionary France and Napoleon, brought to the fore serious difficulties concerning the financial situation, agriculture and trade at the same time as the country faced new problems arising from the rapidly rising population, increasing industrialization and urbanization. The pervasive economic theories during this period were those of the classical economists, notably Ricardo, James Mill, J. R. McCulloch, Nassau Senior and later John Stuart Mill, who re-stated and refined or developed ideas already well-known through Adam Smith's *Wealth of Nations*. Although classical economic theory should not (any more than Benthamism) be wholly identified with *laissez faire*, it was a liberal doctrine and involved a basic commitment to the principle of free trade.

In the same way as Bentham and the utilitarians attacked aristocratic government, the classical economists attacked monopoly, and especially the protection given to the large landowners, the greatest monopolists of all. The economists' concept of a free market economy led them first and foremost to an attack on the corn laws, and from there to an advocacy of free trade. Although their theories might be constructed largely on an agricultural system, they did not regard land as the only productive element in the economy. They clearly recognized that with Great Britain's rapid advance as a manufacturing country, and on the basis of the principle of comparative costs as well as on the principle of the division of labour, which was by then well established, freedom of trade in corn and manufactured goods provided the key to a prosperous and healthy post-war economy. Beyond that broad area of agreement on basic theoretical principles, there were important differences among the classical economists concerning the policies that governments should follow, including whether the corn laws should be abolished at once or the restrictions on the importation of foreign corn be removed by gradual stages.

When the classical economists, acting as advisers to the government or as practical men with experience in finance or in public administration, turned their attention to the means through which a free market economy could be created, their economic theories were likely to touch on areas of possible government action in the social sphere. It is in relation to government policy and intervention in areas such as factory reform, Poor

Law reform, public health and education that the long-standing identification of classical economic liberalism with *laissez faire* has been most seriously and effectively questioned: and, as a result, the association between the two bodies of doctrine has now been qualified in many important respects.[32]

David Ricardo (1772–1823), the most influential of the classical economists, was born into a successful stockbroking family of Dutch-Jewish origin; and later he enjoyed a very successful career on his own as a dealer in government securities. He was also a wealthy landowner and a respected writer on economic and financial matters by the time he entered politics in 1819 as the member for an Irish pocket borough.

Ricardo first entered the public arena of financial and economic controversy in 1809–10 when he wrote a pamphlet on the currency policy of the Bank of England in a wartime period of inflation. Then, between 1814 and 1815 he took part in the economic controversies set off by the corn laws. Indeed, it was his interest in the corn laws that initially led him to attempt an abstract analysis of value and distribution.[33] The two main bases of Ricardo's economic theories were then formed: he built up a theory of distribution and formulated a law of diminishing returns; and he demonstrated that Great Britain's economic policy should be firmly based on the principle of free trade. His major treatise, *On the Principles of Political Economy and Taxation,* was published in 1817, and the practical influence of that work is apparent during the first half of the nineteenth century, not only on his disciples and those who popularized his arguments but also on Parliament's handling of financial and economic matters.

There was, according to Ricardo, a need to 'determine the laws' which regulated distribution between 'the proprietor of the land, the owner of the stock or capital necessary for its cultivation, and the labourers by whose industry it is cultivated'; that is, between 'rent, profit, and wages.'[34]

According to his analysis, in a country which produced its own food and had only a limited supply of land, there was a tendency, as population grew, for rents to increase and for money wages (though not real wages) to rise, while profits fell. He argued that as more and more land, of a progressively less fertile nature, was brought into cultivation to feed a growing population, the rents payable to owners of the more fertile land would steadily increase, while the application of increased amounts of labour and capital to land would (after a certain point) be subject to diminishing returns. The price of food would rise as its costs of production rose, and money wages would have to be raised to ensure the continued subsistence of the labourer. At the same time the profits of farmers and capitalists would steadily decline. If this trend were allowed to continue, it would lead in the end to a stagnant economy in which incentives for investment no longer existed.

The solution for Britain, in Ricardo's view, was that she should exchange manufactured goods for imports of cheaply-produced foreign grain; and to make this possible the level of agricultural protection would have to be very much reduced. He did not demand an immediate repeal of the corn laws, which would have caused a sudden upheaval in British agriculture, but he suggested a gradual reduction of duties over a ten-year period. He recommended greater freedom of trade on the general grounds that it would enable each country to specialize in the types of production for which it was best suited. Moreover, he reinforced the theoretical case for the desirability of international trade by his theory of comparative advantage. Adam Smith had taken the view that trade was advantageous where the country exchanged goods which it could produce more efficiently than another country for goods which the other country could produce more efficiently. Ricardo showed that even when one country had an absolute advantage in respect of both products, if it could produce one of them more efficiently than the other it would profit from concentrating its resources on that product and obtaining the other through an exchange with the less efficient country. He was confident that increased specialization and international division of labour would contribute to the good of all, and would bind together 'by one common tie of interest and intercourse, the universal society of nations throughout the civilized world'. [35] At home the effect of free trade would be to check the rise in rent and in the price of corn, and the downward tendency of profits. His analysis of trends within an economy dependent on its own food production had resulted in a seemingly gloomy view of economic laws whose operation would produce in the end a stationary state. But his pessimism was 'entirely dependent upon the maintenance of the tariff on raw produce'[36]; its abandonment would open a much more hopeful prospect.

Ricardo's arguments in favour of free trade, propagated in a simplified and more readily digestible form than in his *Principles of Political Economy and Taxation*, provided the gist of the case put forward for the repeal of the corn laws in the late 1830s and the 1840s. To a very large extent, it was the reiteration of these arguments by Cobden and Bright that led to the close identification of the classical economists with the Manchester School and its advocacy of free trade and *laissez faire*.

Richard Cobden (1804–65), a successful Manchester manufacturer, became the political leader of the free trade movement after the Anti-Corn Law Association, formed in Manchester in October 1838, had turned into a national league in March 1839. The Anti-Corn Law League gained its early support from middle-class businessmen like Cobden and his close associate John Bright; and it was through Cobden's influence that the League adopted the political tactic of concentrating exclusively on one issue, the repeal of the corn laws, rather than dispersing its energies over several political and social issues on which it would be impossible for members of the League to speak with one voice. Further, provided the League concerned itself exclusively with agitating for the repeal of the corn laws, and given the distress in urban and rural areas from a depression in trade and poor harvests in some years during the 1830s and 1840s, working-class support could well be harnessed in support of the League and its middle-class membership.

In their campaign for the repeal of the corn laws, Cobden and Bright saw the economic monopoly exercised by the landowners as an inseparable part of the landlords' 'political despotism'; and both could therefore be attacked at the same time.[37] Cobden, moreover, deliberately associated free trade with the middle class in order to distinguish it from the protectionism of the landowning aristocracy and gentry. According to him in 'the middle and industrious classes' were to be found the 'wealth, intelligence and productive industry' which had already led England to become the envy of the world. So, by implication, acceptance of the middle-class values of thrift and economy, in association with a policy of tariff reform, would ensure the continued material and moral progress of the country. No wonder later commentators have found a strong element of nationalism in free trade.[38]

The popular appeal of the case against the corn laws and the way in which it was possible to interpret economic theories in human terms, apart from the gifts of public oratory demonstrated by Cobden and even more so by Bright, were shown on innumerable occasions during the campaign before the corn laws were repealed in 1846. A typical example of Cobden's style of oratory, with its mixture of popularized economic arguments and its expectation of social harmony in Britain and among the nations of the world, is found in his address in London on 8 February 1844 at a mass meeting organized by the League (doc. 24). Cobden denied that there was any evidence in the manufacturing areas that a reduction in the price of corn, consequent on the repeal of the corn laws, would lead to a fall in profits or a fall in wages. As for the conditions of the rural labourers, Cobden maintained that with free trade in corn and the increased demand for British manufactures abroad, there would be a greater need for more industrial workers to be drawn from the rural areas and poverty and destitution would be very greatly reduced if not eliminated altogether. Cheaper and more abundant food would then be assured to the working classes, while manufacturers could look forward to larger markets abroad. Even tenant farmers would benefit in the long run from corn being able to find its natural price rather than being held at an artificially high one; and, indeed, the favourable conditions for British agriculture in the 1850s and 1860s seemed to confirm the truth of Cobden's argument.

253

B. Classical liberalism

To the economic and moral arguments in favour of repeal and free trade, as so far mentioned, Cobden added another moral one. The national interests of Great Britain which demanded economic expansion through manufacturing industry and trade would lead in turn to international amity: free trade means 'breaking down the barriers that separate nations; those barriers, behind which nestle the feelings of pride, revenge, hatred, and jealousy, which every now and then burst their bounds, and deluge whole countries with blood. . .' [39]The conclusion of treaties of commercial reciprocity, such as the Cobden–Chevalier Treaty of 1860 between Great Britain and France, would mark important stages on the way from free trade to international harmony, because the lowering of duties would lead to increased trade and other contacts between the countries concerned.

Several of the arguments used in support of the repeal of the corn laws remained an essential element in economic thinking during the long period of liberal political ascendancy in the 1850s and 1860s. Indeed, very similar arguments were used by Gladstone in his masterly expositions of the nation's housekeeping in his budget speeches of 1853 and the early 1860s. Under the banner of free trade, protection and discrimination in all their various forms were attacked. Now, although free trade was by far the most important element in *laissez faire*, it has been argued that *laissez faire* as a policy was not also triumphant, even if the application of the term is restricted to the socio-economic field. [40] Indeed, one historian has gone so far as to contend that by the 1850s the *laissez faire* movement 'had been finally routed by new techniques of government control of the economy which had their own built-in tendency to develop, grow and multiply'.[41] Such a conclusion seemingly stands in marked contrast to the dogmatic assertion John Stuart Mill made in 1848, and to which he continued to hold in subsequent years: 'Letting alone [*laissez faire*], in short, should be the general practice: every departure from it, unless required by some great good, is a certain evil.' [42]

John Stuart Mill (1806–73) had early been schooled by his father, James Mill, in Ricardo's economic theories. His *Principles of Political Economy*, published early in 1848, was the first comprehensive and systematic statement of classical economic policy.[43] Somewhat paradoxically perhaps, it can also be described as 'the last great statement of classical economy.'[44] It added to the stature of Ricardian economics at a time when administrative centralization and government interference, in relation to certain social issues, were publicly being discussed.[45]

Mill did not set out to be an originator. For the most part, he re-stated the orthodox principles of classical political economy, including those of Ricardo and his father, despite some doubts and qualifications; but, in contrast to Ricardo, Mill was also concerned with the application of

254

those principles. By the time he published his treatise, economic and social conditions in Great Britain were far more obviously those of an industrial rather than an agricultural society.[46] Mill, therefore, was only concerned in part, albeit a large part, with elaborating theories of production, distribution and exchange, and indicating the likely influence a progressing society would have on the various aspects of production and exchange. On these matters, and especially with regard to international trade, his conclusions were not so very different from those of Ricardo, except that Mill did not necessarily regard a stationary state as undesirable. In addition, Comte's concept of social science influenced Mill in his approach to political economy. In the preface to his treatise he stated quite clearly: 'For practical purposes, Political Economy is inseparably intertwined with many other branches of social philosophy.' Few or no questions could therefore be 'decided on economical premises alone'.[47] This appreciation led Mill to include a detailed consideration of the influence and functions of government; and on these matters he modified his ideas to some extent between the publication of the first edition of the *Principles* in 1848 and the third edition in 1852. By the time of the latter edition, collectivist elements, particularly with regard to cooperation, had become more readily acceptable to him. Mill's own explanation of this change is given in his *Autobiography*, where he writes:[48]

The social problem of the future we considered to be, how to unite the greatest individual liberty of action, with a common ownership in the raw materials of the globe, and an equal participation of all in the benefits of combined labour ... [Employers and the labouring masses] must learn by practice to labour and combine for generous, or at all events for public and social purposes, and not, as hitherto, solely for narrowly interested ones.

The extent to which Mill was prepared by the early 1850s to countenance government interference is shown in the final chapter of his *Principles of Political Economy* (doc. 25). He saw government intervention taking either of two forms: it could be authoritative, and therefore in his view unacceptable, when a government controlled the free agency of individuals by saying that they should not do this or that action; or it could be non-authoritative when a government only helped to create the conditions in which individuals could then make the best of themselves.[49] Mill then went on to examine some of the general objections to government interference of any kind: its compulsory nature, the need for taxes to be levied in support of such intervention, the increase in the power and influence, the functions and responsibilities of government, and the exercise of such power being at variance with the 'importance of cultivating habits of collective action in the people'.[50] All of these objections had been debated at length in the 1830s and 1840s; and in general Mill's conclusions were in line with the utilitarian doctrines which by and large he still supported. The self-interest of individuals and the ultimate harmony

255

of interests would ensure that many things would be done better privately than they would by governments. In short, the onus was on those who recommended government interference to make out a strong case that 'some great good' required it.

The importance of Mill's restatement of the principle of *laissez faire* lies, however, not in its dogmatic assertion but in the qualification. The necessity of 'some great good' had provided the justification for the factory acts prohibiting child labour and limiting the number of hours for women and young persons, and for the introduction of the Poor Law Amendment Act of 1834 and the Public Health Act of 1848. For the continuance of the existing situation in each case would have been a greater evil than the introduction of new legislation and regulations. So, in the concluding pages of his *Principles*, Mill looked at certain areas where he believed that non-authoritative government interference might be justified: first, in the area of education, where 'Those who most need to be made wiser and better, usually desire it least, and if they desired it, would be incapable of finding the way to it by their own lights.' The government 'should therefore be capable of offering better education and better instruction to the people, than the greater number of them would spontaneously demand'.[51] Secondly, Mill recognized that some individuals or classes of individuals, such as children and the mentally handicapped, could not be the best judge of their own interests; and, on that ground, children should be protected from excessively long hours of work because the general condition of not interfering with freedom of contract could not apply in their case.[52]

Among other possible exceptions to the general principle of *laissez faire*, Mill was willing to include acts done through public charity. On this ground, he accepted the principle of 'less eligibility' on which the 1834 Poor Law Amendment Act had been based, but he refused to countenance the State making any distinction between the deserving and the undeserving poor.[53] Lastly, Mill admitted that in the general interest governments could undertake to provide certain works that were desirable, but could not be undertaken by private agencies because of lack of resources or technical knowledge. In the case of backward nations, in particular, governments should give whatever aid was necessary; but it 'should be so given as to be as far as possible a course of education for the people in the art of accomplishing great objects by individual energy and voluntary cooperation.'[54]

The several exceptions to non-interference that Mill was prepared to accept were based solely on expediency. He did not think that a 'universal rule' for government intervention was at all possible.[55] Even so, the exceptions opened up a very large area for government intervention. One historian has argued[56] that Mill was making an attempt to combine

'two sets of ideas − one came from the classic liberalism of the seventeenth century and directed policy toward increasing the freedom of the individual and protecting his rights;

the other came from utilitarianism and directed policy towards improving the individual
... Mill tried to make policy serve both freedom and improvement, but in the end he
made the latter, the utilitarian, objective, the more important'.

In his *Principles of Political Economy,* Mill also restated and
elaborated certain principles of taxation in the tradition of Ricardo. The
first and foremost of these was equality of taxation: 'Equality of taxation,
as a maxim of politics, means equality of sacrifice. It means apportioning
the contribution of each person towards the expenses of government, so
that he shall feel neither more nor less inconvenience from his share of
the payment than every other person experiences from his.' [57] However,
the application of the principle of equality in taxation did not mean that
the classical economists necessarily favoured direct as against indirect
taxation. For, as Mill declared, 'people should be taxed, not in proportion
to what they have, but to what they can afford to spend.' [58]

William Ewart Gladstone (1809–98), Chancellor of the Exchequer
from 1852 to 1855 and again between 1859 and 1866, based his famous
budgets of 1853 and the early 1860s on that same principle of the
classical economists:[59] of ensuring fiscal equality by taxing all classes in
the community at the same rate, while continuing to implement a general
policy of economical government founded on the twin pillars of retrenchment and the removal of the last vestiges of a protective tariff. Good and
economic government meant that revenue and expenditure must be
balanced; that public spending should be kept to the essential minimum,
despite the increasing need for the government to satisfy 'the real permanent wants of the country'; that taxation must be kept as low as possible;
and that Great Britain should follow a policy of peace abroad (doc. 26a).
Between direct and indirect taxation Gladstone would make no choice;
and he compared the two means of taxation open to him as displaying
the equal charms of two very attractive but very different sisters.[60]

The building up of armaments to support national ambitions abroad
was frowned on by Gladstone just as much as an expansion of the functions of government and administration at home. Both showed an unwelcome 'spirit of expenditure' by government departments, parliament
and the public at large.[61] In contrast to that 'spirit of expenditure',
Gladstone associated retrenchment with reform (doc. 26b). To Gladstone
the Crimean War between 1854 and 1856 had been an unwelcome
interlude. It had broken the long period of peace, the steady economic
progress and increase in national wealth; and instead it had helped to encourage an irresponsible spirit of expenditure. Between 1860 and 1866
Gladstone successfully, although temporarily, renewed the classical
liberal budgets for which his budget of 1853 had set the desirable pattern.
They included further reductions in the tariff; reductions in the rate of income tax with the intention of discontinuing it altogether, because
Gladstone feared that its use would lead to extravagance in government

expenditure; provisions for regularly reducing the National Debt; and ending the year with a very small surplus of revenue over expenditure. By the mid 1860s, as a result of Gladstone's budgets, indirect taxation was being raised from only a few articles, the consumption of which had shown a marked increase and on which taxes could be collected easily and cheaply.

The basis of Gladstone's fiscal policy was, therefore, the extension of trade abroad and of industry at home; with taxation being imposed for revenue purposes only, while free and unrestricted play was given to capital and enterprise.[62] Moreover, according to 'the principle of a sound political economy applicable to commercial legislation', the working classes would benefit most, not by reducing taxes on articles consumed by them, but by giving them the maximum of employment; so that 'it is the enhanced price their labour thus brings, even more than the cheapened price of commodities, that forms the main benefit they receive'.[63] Gladstone, 'a rigid economist' to borrow the phrase he once used to describe Sir Robert Peel, saw himself as directly continuing that statesman's work in implementing free trade; and by the early 1860s there was no longer any controversy in British politics over free trade or protection. Beyond that, Gladstone's financial orthodoxy was in line with both the utilitarian idea of cheap and efficient government and the Ricardian belief in the necessity of making provision for the elimination of the National Debt.

By the 1860s the national wealth and taxable income of the country had increased several fold;[64] and the increasing prosperity of the middle classes and rising wages for the skilled workers provided the economic background to a further extension of the franchise in 1867. Apart from the Lancashire 'cotton famine' of 1864–5, there were few indications that the long period of rapid economic growth was not going to continue indefinitely. For all that, the era of *laissez faire* was at most short lived; and by the 1870s the theories of the classical economists were no longer generally held to be valid. There was an increasing acceptance of State intervention in those areas where economic policy and social policy could not be kept separate. In the long run, it was in the field of government finance that classical economics held sway most firmly and pervasively. Through Gladstone's tenure of office as Chancellor of the Exchequer, increasing Treasury control over other government departments had been established in practice by the 1860s; and it continued under subsequent chancellors no matter whether they were liberal or conservative. For by the 1850s and 1860s an increased sense of responsibility had developed among government ministers and civil servants concerning the use of public funds; and under Gladstone's tutelage the Treasury came to epitomize the Victorian virtues of probity and financial orthodoxy with an abhorrence of public waste.

(ii) Some trends on the Continent
(Documents 27–30, pp. 326–34)

It was only three years after the publication of *The Wealth of Nations* in 1776 that the first translation of the work was published on the Continent; and altogether four translations of the book appeared in France and elsewhere in Europe between 1779 and 1802. By the beginning of the reform era in Prussia in 1807, for example, Adam Smith's ideas were well known in that country. *The Wealth of Nations* exercised a two-fold influence on the Continent: first, through the use of Smith's tools of analysis by French and German economists; and, secondly, when France and to a lesser extent Prussia after 1815 began to experience the industrial changes through which Britain had already been passing at the time of the publication of Smith's treatise in 1776, his observations and analysis were more pertinent to that situation than the theories of the French physiocrats. For all that, Smith's style, with its diffuseness and lack of unity, did not lend itself to a ready assimilation and propagation of his ideas. There was an obvious need for the economic principles embedded in *The Wealth of Nations* to be systematized; and that task was ably performed by the French economist Jean Baptiste Say. On the other hand, as the nineteenth century advanced and with it the growth of industrialization, economists such as Friedrich List found it less easy to share Smith's faith in the self-regulating mechanism of the natural order where national interests were concerned.

In contrast to England, there was never a group of classical economists on the Continent who could clearly be identified as such. Something of the variety in French and German economic thought, its links with Adam Smith and the English classical economists, and in some cases the rejection of certain elements of classical economic thought while still retaining a belief in political liberalism, can be seen in four representative thinkers: Jean Baptiste Say, Frédéric Bastiat, Friedrich List and John Prince Smith.

France

Jean Baptiste Say (1767–1832) came from a Protestant merchant family in Lyons. During his career he was in turn a journalist, a member of the Tribunate, a cotton manufacturer and a celebrated professor of political economy. He made two visits to England, one immediately before the Revolution and the other just after the Restoration when he had ceased to be a manufacturer. He first read *The Wealth of Nations* in 1789; and when he realized the need in France for a treatise on political economy, Say, as a disciple of Adam Smith, set himself the task of systematically formulating the principles contained in the master's work. When his

B. Classical liberalism

Traité d'économie politique first appeared in 1803, it met with considerable success; but a second edition did not come out before 1814.[65] The new edition had been revised in the light of Say's own experience as a cotton manufacturer. From 1815 onwards he became the first academic teacher of economics in France and in 1830 was appointed as the first professor of political economy at the Collège de France.[66] Say's model was Newton and he saw economics as a science. The task of the political economist was to observe, analyse and describe. He corresponded with Malthus and Ricardo but his conclusions proved very different from theirs.

Although Say systematized and thereby popularized Adam Smith's ideas on the Continent, he also revised and developed Smith's work and added some important contributions of his own. His prime aim was to continue the distinction Smith had made of an investigation of wealth, i.e. of the manner in which it 'is produced, distributed and consumed', from a study of political organisation. 'Political economy, from facts always carefully observed, makes known to us the nature of wealth; from the knowledge of its nature deduces the means of its creation, unfolds the order of its distribution, and the phenomena attending its destruction.' [67]

In following out this aim, Say was concerned solely with general facts, 'the results of the nature of things'.

'General facts, or, if you please, the general laws which facts follow, are styled *principles*, whenever it relates to their application. . . . [68]

Political economy, in the same manner as the exact sciences, is composed of a few fundamental principles, and of a great number of corollaries or conclusions, drawn from these principles. . . .' [69]

Political economy, therefore, is 'purely theoretical and descriptive'. As a rationalist Say could also declare that as the general facts or principles on which political economy is based are to be derived from nature, they should never be violated. Furthermore, the principles of political economy were associated with the liberty which every human being ought to possess, of disposing of his person, fortune and talents, according to the bent of his inclination; without which, indeed, individual happiness and national prosperity are but empty and unmeaning sounds.[70] Although Say believed that it was important for princes, ministers and statesmen to be acquainted with 'the principles upon which national prosperity is founded', it was especially important in countries enjoying representative government for the middle classes to have the same knowledge. And why? Because

'It is in the middling classes of society, equally secure from the intoxication of power, and the compulsory labour of indigence, in which are found moderate fortunes, leisure united with habits of industry, the free intercourse of friendship, a taste for literature, and the ability to travel, that knowledge originates, and is disseminated amongst the highest and lowest orders of the people.' [71]

260

An investigation of the production, distribution and consumption of wealth forms the subject matter of Say's *Treatise*. He refuted the theories of the physiocrats who had claimed that land was the only productive element; and, on the basis of his own manufacturing experience, he went much further than Adam Smith, who had still put agriculture in the first place, in defining what were the productive forces. For he regarded agriculture, industry and commerce as being equal in that respect; and whereas Smith had only viewed material products from agriculture and industry as productive forces, Say also included immaterial products, such as the services provided by managers and technicians as well as the professional services of doctors and lawyers.[72]

From these two premises Say made two important contributions to economic theory: first, he rejected Adam Smith's acceptance of labour as the measure of value, and replaced it with the principle of utility as the measure of value. Since the value of objects depends on the use that can be made of them 'to create objects which have any kind of utility, is to create wealth; for the utility of things is the ground-work of their value, and their value constitutes wealth.'[73] As utility determines demand, so demand interacts with supply; and supply is then determined by the cost of production. Goods are always exchanged for goods, and so money is only an intermediary in the exchange: 'Money performs but a momentary function in this double exchange; and when the transaction is finally closed, it will always be found, that one kind of commodity has been exchanged for another. . . . A product is no sooner created, than it, from that instant, affords a market for other products to the full extent of its own value.'[74] Price is thus based only on the utility of the goods offered for exchange.

On the basis of Say's understanding of the productive forces and of value, he was led to differ in an important respect from Ricardo as well as from Smith. Whereas Ricardo had emphasized the role of the capitalist in utilizing the three factors of production – land, capital and labour – Say introduced a new figure. This was the entrepreneur whom he put into first place in an industrial society because he was the intermediary in relation to landowner, farmer, capitalist, labourer and consumer.[75] Say therefore developed a new theory of distribution, which separates him from Ricardo, because he saw that it was necessary to distinguish profit, that is, the entrepreneur's surplus over interest, from rent, interest, his salary and wages.[76]

Say's second major contribution to economic theory was his formulation of the 'law of markets'. Total supply and demand would naturally equal each other in a free economy; and, although there might be a temporary over-supply in one commodity, this would be adjusted naturally such as through a fall in price creating a greater demand.[77] Say denied that in a free economy there would ever be a general glut from overproduction; and he did not alter this view despite the occurrence of

261

B. Classical liberalism

short-term economic crises in the early nineteenth century.

To achieve natural harmony in the production, distribution and consumption of wealth meant doing away with all forms of protection (see doc. 27). As State interference ruined the natural order, freedom of production and freedom of trade must be allowed by governments, apart from their exercise of such limited functions as ensuring the existence of adequate professional qualifications, the absence of fraud in business dealings and certifying gold and silver. The criterion for government interference must always be whether or not such intervention would 'cramp any branch of industry':[78] because the prosperity of one industry or one nation was dependent on the prosperity of other industries and other nations.

Although through his lectures Say hoped to reach statesmen, landowners, capitalists, manufacturers and other men of affairs, he lacked the true spirit of propaganda. In his hands political economy became a purely theoretical and descriptive science, a science which, it is true, had gathered momentum by the advance of industry in contemporary France. As he wrote to Malthus in 1820, the economist 'must be content to remain an impartial spectator'.[79]

As a young man Say's pupil, Frédéric Bastiat (1801–50) had been inspired by Say's boundless belief in free trade and in the beneficial effects of competition. He, too, rejected the pessimism of Ricardo and Malthus and believed in the 'natural harmony' of economic and social life as long as it was not interfered with. But in contrast to Say, Bastiat was not primarily a thinker, but a brilliant economic journalist. Bastiat's amusing and hard-hitting parables in *Sophismes économiques* (Paris 1846) did more to bring the message of free trade to a wider public in France than any learned treatise. They exposed the follies of protectionism with biting satire and ridicule. In those pre-electric days he wrote his famous 'Candlemakers' Petition', to wit 'the petition of the Manufacturers of Dips, Candles, Lamps, Snuffers, Extinguishers, and of the Producers of Tallow, Oil, Resin, Spirit, and, generally, of everything connected with Lighting, to the Members of the Chambers of Deputies'. The latter were urgently asked to take measures to prevent the sunlight from entering houses. The petitioners complained:

'We are suffering from the intolerable competition of a foreign rival, placed, it appears, in circumstances so far superior to ours for the production of light that he *inundates our national market* with it at a fabulously reduced price. As soon as he shows himself our sales cease, all consumers apply to him, and a branch of French industry, with countless ramifications, is abruptly reduced to a state of complete stagnation. This rival, who is no other than the sun, wages war against us so relentlessly that we suspect that it has been put up to it by *perfidious Albion*. This suspicion is supported by the fact that he displays towards that haughty isle a consideration which he does not show where we are concerned.'[80]

262

The Deputies of the Chamber were solemnly exhorted to safeguard the interests of the producers rather than those of the consumers. They had always favoured the producer. 'When you were told "The consumer is interested in the free importation of iron, coal, sesame, wheat, textile fabrics", "Yes", you replied "but the producer is interested in their exclusion".'[81]

Although Bastiat published his pamphlets and articles only during the last five years of his life his fertile pen succeeded in transforming the issue of free trade from a merely academic matter into one of practical politics. He founded a Free Trade Association in Paris which brought tradesmen, journalists and deputies together and had many leading free-traders as speakers including Cobden from England. Different from the earlier days of propagating free trade, Bastiat and his friends fought on two fronts simultaneously, against protectionism and against socialism (doc. 28). Both were devoid of individual responsibility and efficiency. The producer calls in the State to protect him as otherwise he feels he cannot make a profit. Socialism on its side takes refuge in the collective and is a tool of exploitation. 'In support of the principle of *laissez faire*, Bastiat introduced the concept of service to the consumer as the explanation of every kind of income.'[82] At the same time he shared the anti-étatism of his predecessors. Bastiat once called the State 'the great fiction by means of which everybody contrives to live at the expense of everybody else'.[83]

The dividing line between the school of Political Economy and that of the various camps of contemporary French socialism was a difference in emphasis, between Justice on the one hand and Fraternity on the other. As Bastiat saw it, the political economist 'asks *of the law* nothing but universal justice', whilst socialism 'demands of the law, in addition, the realization of the principles of fraternity'.[84] Both schools desired harmony. The free-traders believed harmony was imminent in the nature of men and things. The socialists, however, 'seek it in the innumerable schemes they want the law to impose on men'.

Where the socialist sees only the part, the free-trade economist sees the whole.[85] When reflecting on competition the socialists stop at the producer whereas the political economists follow the economic process to the end, that is to the consumer. They thus arrive at the conclusion that competition 'is the most powerful agent for equality and progress, whether at home or abroad'.[86]

Yet with all his dogmatic belief in the natural and ultimate harmony of things Bastiat was not blind to the ills and hardships in society. In one of his most graphic and penetrating essays entitled 'The Physiology of Plunder' he argued that plunder is practised in the world on too vast a scale to be ignored by political economy.[87] War, slavery, theocracy, monopolies were seen and described by him as forms of plunder, which prohibit freedom of exchange. The 'true and just rule for mankind is the voluntary exchange of service for service'. Plunder prohibits this freedom of exchange by force or fraud. It means receiving a service without rendering one in return.[88] War has always been waged in the interest of the few at the expense of the many. Sharing the traditional anti-clericalism of French liberal thought Bastiat was critical of the divergency between theory and practice in Christianity. But he was free of a Voltairian wrath against the Church. To him the priest has an alternative: if he is the instrument of religion, his work is regarded as beneficial. If, however, religion is the instrument of the priest, and he gets involved in intrigues and makes a pact with the Establishment, he can become a veritable scourge to society. Commercial fraud, too, offers an immense field for plunder. Governing on the other hand is so pleasurable a profession that throughout history unscrupulous elements have taken advantage of it. One has only to reflect what services were performed *for the people* and *by the people* from antiquity to modern times, from Assyria and ancient Egypt to modern Spain, France and England to realize that 'the enormous disparity between the one and the other in each case staggers the imagination.'[89] It was true, recently representative government had been introduced. If it has not yet worked properly, there is some hope that it will succeed ultimately. The trouble was that so far governments have had too much discernment and the people too little. Governments are very adroit. They study men and their passions and make use of them. Plunder, both in the form of commercial fraud and of governmental Macchiavellism, was an undeniable fact, but in the long run it was unable to remove the harmony inherent in the economic processes of society.[90]

Neither very astute nor systematic as a thinker, Bastiat was perhaps the most lively and imaginative propagandist in the service of economic liberalism.

Germany

Can Friedrich List (1789–1846), the German economist and pamphleteer be regarded as a liberal? The answer must be both affirmed and denied. In 1819 List, then a professor of political science at the university of Tübingen in Württemberg, was the eloquent spokesman of German manufacturers and merchants. In their name he petitioned the Confederal Diet, the organization of the German states at Frankfurt, to allow free trade between the 38 separate states by the abolition of the existing custom barriers and tariffs (doc. 29). There should be no restrictions on trade within the territories of the German states.[91] Though in 1819 List's persistent efforts to achieve the abolition of the custom barriers within Germany remained unsuccessful, fifteen years later when the *Zollverein* – the German Customs Union between Prussia and some South German states – came into operation, the road was clear for the gradual economic integration of the German states apart from Austria.

This economic unification was later followed by political unification under Bismarck, an event which List would doubtless have welcomed. At a time of incipient industrialization in his country he saw in national freedom 'the first condition of all German development'. List favoured not only economic freedom within the German states but also the Western liberal demands of representative government, freedom of the press and of speech, freedom of association. He shrewdly realized that 'the constitutional State and the industrial machine belonged together'.[92] Through his pleas for constitutional rights of the citizens he became suspect to the powerful conservative forces of the Establishment in Württemberg and was twice imprisoned and deprived of his Chair. Prince Metternich, the opponent of any liberalizing movement regarded List as a sinister figure, 'a Jacobin, a rioter, an heroic swindler and a revolutionary'.[93]

Yet while List desired economic and political liberalization within the German states, he strongly objected to free trade between them and foreign countries. He saw in it a serious danger to the growth of German industry and commerce. After the end of the Napoleonic Continental blockade, Western and Central Europe were flooded with British goods at prices with which the native industries could not compete. The competition had proved particularly ruinous to the German textile industry. Impressed by the effect of protectionism in both post-Napoleonic France and the United States – two countries of which List had first-hand experience – List argued that German industrial production and commerce would be crippled by free trade with the outside world. In 1841 he produced his major work 'The National System of Political Economy'. In the Introduction he emphasized that society can be regarded from two different points of view, 'the cosmopolitan which considers mankind as a whole and the political which pays attention to particular interests and conditions'. Similarly the economy of the individual and of society can be seen under two different aspects, 'as we look at the personal, social and material forces by which wealth is produced, or the exchange value of material goods'. There is 'a cosmopolitan and a political economy, a theory of exchange values and a theory of productive powers, two doctrines which are essentially distinct and which must be developed independently'.[94]

Different from Adam Smith and J. B. Say, List regarded 'the power of producing wealth' as 'infinitely more important than wealth itself'. The prosperity of a nation was not, as Say believed, growing in the proportion to its amassing of wealth. List's concept of 'the productive forces' was rather comprehensive. He argued that 'the balance of the productive forces' within a nation, agriculture, industry and commerce had all to be developed. The 'productive forces' included moral and political institutions and the freedoms, stressed at the time by all Western liberalism, such as freedom of thought, freedom of conscience, liberty of the press,

B. Classical liberalism

trial by jury, publicity of justice, control of administration and representative government. These 'productive forces' developed best within the framework of the nation. 'However industrious, thrifty, enterprising, moral and intelligent the individuals may be, without national unity, national division of labour, national cooperation of productive powers the nation will never reach a high level of prosperity and power or ensure to itself the lasting possession of its intellectual social and material goods.'[95] In List's view the principle of the division of labour, so much emphasized by Adam Smith and his followers, had not yet been fully grasped for it had to be supplemented by the other principle of cooperation. Productivity depended 'not only on the division of various manufacturing operations among many individuals, but still more on the moral and physical cooperation of the individuals for a common end'.[96]

In this context manufactures had high priority among the productive forces, for List believed that they greatly developed the moral strength of a nation. A nation that neglected manufacture and the new means of transport, such as the railway and the steamship, would progress very little and even its agriculture would suffer.[97] However, a progressive regime favouring manufacture and commerce was bound to lead to greater freedom. As List put it: 'the spirit of striving for a steady increase in mental and bodily requirements, of emulation, and of liberty, characterize, on the contrary, a state devoted to manufacture and commerce.'[98] In this way List's pro-industrial bias was matched by his belief in liberty.

He did not demand protectionism or condemn free trade without qualifications. Protection would be indispensable for Germany until she would have achieved the same level of productivity as England. In attempting to match the competition of this superior manufacturing rival Germany was in an unequal position. The reason why she could not succeed was, in List's graphic language 'the same as that why a child or a boy wrestling with a strong man can scarcely be victorious or even offer steady resistance'.[99] It is perhaps significant that List preferred the term 'educational tariffs' to that of 'protective tariffs'. Freedom of trade for manufacture and commerce could only operate naturally after the less advanced nations had been raised 'by artificial measures to the stage of cultivation to which the English nation has been artificially elevated'.[100] List, whose book carried the motto 'la patrie et L'humanité', emphasized that protection 'was not a universal remedy which may be indifferently applied to every country at any period or for all its products', but rather 'a particular process which can only be used in certain cases and under certain conditions'.[101] It was for instance not to be extended to German agriculture.

By and large, however, List favoured political liberalism whilst remaining opposed to classical economic liberalism. Thirty years after his death his protectionist ideas were adopted in the Second German Empire and then extended to agriculture as well. However until 1878 the German liberals believed in free trade. Considering List's critical attitude to the industrial might of Great Britain it is not without some irony that one of the most determined and enthusiastic apostles of the gospel of free trade in Germany was a naturalized Englishman, John Prince Smith.

Unlike Friedrich List John Prince Smith (1809–74) was not an academic.[102] The son of a London barrister and one-time Governor of the West Indies, he had been forced by the early death of his father to leave Eton prematurely and to earn a living the hard way, first as a clerk with a London warehouse, then in a bank and later as a journalist. In 1830 he left London for Hamburg and after a year there went to Elbing, a commercial town in East Prussia, teaching modern languages at a secondary school. He soon made useful contacts with local merchants, exporters of grain and timber who bought manufactured goods from England and were thus keenly interested in free trade. Prince Smith expressed his ardent belief in free trade in articles in German newspapers and pamphlets. Although not an original thinker, he proved an adroit pragmatist tirelessly spreading the doctrines of Adam Smith in his adopted country.

In contrast to List, Prince Smith's liberalism was one without reservation. Smith entered fully into the spirit of the industrial age with its striking technological inventions and the advance of physics and chemistry. He favoured the bold productivity and keen endeavour of the new individualistic entrepreneur; he predicted that 'heroes of industry' would arise on the Continent and compete with those in England and America. Their task required 'the highest development of courage, strength and intelligence in a people and the best instrument to achieve it was political independence'. When Prince Smith protested against *Handelsfeindseligkeit*, hostility to free trade, he must have realized that self-made German industrial entrepreneurs like Alfred Krupp, August Borsig and Werner von Siemens were pushing forward the advance of the steel and iron, the locomotive and other machine industries in their country. Prince Smith felt that the traditional paternalistic attitudes of so many German state governments could only hinder the industrial development. On the other hand he argued that it could be stimulated by 'a popular constitution which transforms subjects into citizens by giving them a share in the government of the state and widens the outlook from the narrow circle of individual activity to the larger movements of the general interest' (doc. 30).

Compared with List's far-ranging reflections Prince Smith appears rather as a lightweight, but he was deeply convinced that freedom of trade and political freedom conditioned each other. Without free trade and liberty for the entrepreneur there could be no true political freedom and without the latter large-scale business could not prosper. Social progress meant simply expansion of industry and trade. Its requirements

267

dictated by 'the eternally valid laws of nature', had to be fulfilled. While List never gained the ear of the powers-that-be Prince Smith managed in the 1850s and 1860s to influence the decision-makers and to pave the way for the rule of free trade with foreign countries characteristic of the German scene in the 1860s and 1870s.

---

3. The superiority of the middle classes – introduction
(Documents 31–3, pp. 334–39)

During the economic and political advance of the middle classes in the first half of the nineteenth century there was no shortage of voices from their ranks raised in self-praise. The middle classes were presented as the embodiment of virtue, hard work and prosperity. The emphasis was more on the upper than on the lower strata of the middle classes, a concept which was seldom clearly defined. The middle classes often meant simply a large section of the property-owners. Neither the old oligarchy nor the propertyless multitude were regarded as fit to rule, whereas the property-owners were considered the natural governing class. 'For Macauley it was not by numbers that the country should be governed but by wealth and intelligence, for Brougham it was the middle classes who were "the genuine depositaries of sober, rational, intelligent and honest English feeling".'[103] In France the position was similar, the owning of property seemed the best safeguard and insurance against a return of the pre-1789 feudal order or the threat from the potentially revolutionary ignorant multitude. Men like James Mill in England and François Guizot in France shared the proud assumption that morally as well as economically the middle classes were the backbone of their country. Both emphasized equality before the law and some form of representative government. James Mill went further than Guizot in his belief that the best form of government was a representative democracy. Whilst not proposing universal suffrage he favoured a franchise which would prevent the predominance of sinister interests.[104] Mill realized that it was not politic to demand the abolition of the monarchy or of the aristocracy but he was strongly opposed to the rule of an oligarchy, which would never promote the Benthamite goal of 'the greatest happiness of the greatest number'. Mill was more benevolent towards the masses; if they were ignorant this could be remedied. Moreover in his opinion, the lower orders enjoyed a splendid mentor and guide in the middle classes, that 'wisest and most virtuous part of the community'. Their contribution to science and legislature had been outstanding. The middle classes were described in Mill's *Essay on Government* (1820) simply as 'the chief source of all that has exalted and refined human nature'. In fact James Mill, that sober and vigorous radical, was inclined to become lyrical when he spoke of the middle classes. They were a guide-post, a loadstar for the lower orders. The superiority of the middle classes lay not only in their prudence and thrift, but also in their function as a shining example for the less fortunately placed people below. Even granted that not all sections of the people follow the path of 'the wisdom of the middle rank', 'the great majority of the people never cease to be guided by that rank', (doc. 31) a somewhat sweeping generalization rather than a true piece of evidence. Outbursts of mob behaviour and occasional turbulence were for Mill only an indirect confirmation of his theory of the beneficial influence of the middle classes, because these aberrations happened in manufacturing districts which suffered 'from a very great deficiency of the middle rank'. There the poor proletarians missed that helpful model and source of sympathy which middle-class families meant for them in other areas. There the gulf between rich manufacturers and poor workmen remained therefore unbridged.

James Mill was a theorist and philosopher; Guizot, a politician and statesman. Both regarded the middle classes as the essence of society, but Guizot did not entirely share Mill's unqualified admiration of them. Guizot even admitted that the middle classes had 'their faults, their illusions, their share in lacking foresight and in showing obstinacy, vanity and egoism'. However, these faults counted for little when Guizot reflected on their merits and achievements. Their influence has been both beneficial and indispensable. The middle class possessed a universal function as it had 'in the name of all and for the profit of all . . . conquered the rights which it possesses and it has established the principles which prevail in our social order' (doc. 32). It was not an exclusive, but an inclusive class. Like the British aristocracy it constantly regenerated itself through capable and aspiring newcomers from outside. Trustees of independent property and of education, the middle classes did not prevent outsiders from reaching a degree of intelligence and independence which made them capable and worthy of participating in the exercise of political power. They could become members of the very limited *pays légal* of the voter, differing from the propertyless and voteless millions of the *pays réel*. There was no intention on Guizot's part to extend the very limited franchise. Whereas equality before the law, that precious legacy of 1789, was a shibboleth with him, political and economic equality were out of the question.

Guizot's views on parliamentary government were based on his concept of the middle classes which – as we have seen (p. 58) – he viewed not in economic but in political and historical terms. The middle classes were the true representatives of the general interests of society. They fought on a double front: against the men of yesterday, who would have liked to restore the privileges of the old feudal order, and against the democrats and socialists who aimed at a levelling down in favour of social equality. The austere calvinist Guizot could not imagine a society without an élite. He hoped it would originate from the upper bourgeoisie. There could evolve a new aristocracy formed by groups 'whose fortune was already made who were stable and less absorbed by private interests than the vast majority of Frenchmen'. In 1842 Guizot said to Saint-Aulaire that he greatly favoured 'la race des country-gentlemen'; [105] in his eyes they were the best guarantors of stability, liberty and progress. Filled with sinister memories of Jacobin terror and of the costly Napoleonic despotism, he shared with many men and women of his generation a craving for stability which, he argued, a democratic government could never satisfy. Guizot conceived liberty only in conjunction with order while anarchy and mob rule were the deadly enemies of both.

The upper layers of the middle classes participated in political power in England from 1832 onward and in France from 1830. The position was quite different in Prussia. There existed no Prussian State parliament and the government, responsible only to the monarch, relied heavily on the prerogatives of the crown and the devotion to duty of the State bureaucracy. There was a striking discrepancy between the economic and cultural prestige of the bourgeoisie and its political impotence. David Hansemann noted in 1830 that the middle classes preferred to be non-political and did not care for (political) freedom (doc. 33). They were interested only in material advancement, in acquisitions and comfort. When Hansemann complained that in the middle classes as well as in the aristocracy the spirit of freedom was missing, he identified it with a progressive patriotism. Although compared with the middle classes there were proportionately more men among the aristocrats with a noble and high-minded spirit, the majority lacked a true spirit of patriotism. Yet a much greater threat to the welfare of Prussia came from what Hansemann dubbed 'the democratic element'. It aspired to revolution. In contrast to Guizot, Hansemann shrewdly tried to explain this repellent phenomenon, as the result of economic and technological factors (doc. 33). He saw it as a by-product of the new role of the machine, that great equalizer which diminished the social distance between the classes as well as the traditional distinction between higher and lower qualities in behaviour and dress. Progress in food production and quicker and cheaper means of transport made for greater social mobility and circulation of ideas. The democratic element was further strengthened by conscription in the army which made the lower classes conscious of their strength, by the universal extent of education, the loosening of religious ties, the general trend towards the seeking of pleasure and the decline of old customs and habits. Finally the philanthropic spirit in the State bureaucracy was to be blamed. According to Hansemann it increased the carelessness and the shirking of work of the lower classes.

Like his contemporary F. C. Dahlmann, Hansemann can be described as a 'conservative liberal'. He was as little inclined to take up a philanthropic attitude towards the propertyless masses as was Guizot. His desire was to lay the spectre of democracy by 'granting freedom to the not entirely propertyless section of the lower classes'. If allowed a legitimate and proper political influence, they would become useful and conservative at the same time.

James Mill saw in the middle classes the very core of the strength of the nation. Their relationship with the lower classes was to him beneficial because the latter could only profit from the wise councils and guidance of the former. Danger came only from the old ruling class, the aristocracy. Guizot, on the other hand, was equally opposed to a return of the privileges of the former First Estate and to an advance of the propertyless masses. Hansemann, in his turn, desired that more political freedom should be granted in order to vitalize and strengthen the middle classes and to put them into a position 'to keep a too great and harmful influence of democracy with bounds'. Hansemann wanted to strike a new balance between the forces of order and freedom. In his opinion the Prussian State relied too much on the strength of the police and the bureaucracy. He was prepared to take risks in order to establish a more meaningful society. He favoured a middle position between tradition and renovation, an attitude sober, realistic, without any Utopian enthusiasm. In some ways he proved a forerunner of the later National Liberals by asking the searching question:

'Shall the lack of freedom be preserved for the maintenance of order strictly based on the police in spite of the considerable dangers and defects connected with it? Or shall freedom be granted as a lasting safeguard of the splendour of the throne and the greatness of the nation in spite of the inconveniences and deficiencies which are invariably connected with it?' (doc. 33).

It was an unheroic but realistic approach.

4. Aesthetic individualism:
'The object of all mankind should be individuality'
– introduction
(Documents 34–5, pp. 340–52)

Though the philosophy of aesthetic individualism originated in the period of classicism in Germany at the end of the eighteenth century it only reached wider circles half a century later through the work of John

B. Classical liberalism

Stuart Mill. Mill was much stimulated by an early essay from the pen of Wilhelm von Humboldt, [106] (1767–1835), published in part in 1792 and in full only in 1851.

Philosopher and diplomat, educationist and statesman in different phases of his life, Wilhelm von Humboldt's attitude was greatly influenced by his early association with Goethe and Schiller. This group of Philhellenists regarded an idealized picture of the ancient Greeks as a model for the fully rounded and harmonious human character. They saw the essence and meaning of life in the cultured individual and believed in reason as a creative faculty, sharing a belief in *Bildung* as a main value. *Bildung*, a term difficult to translate, meant both the process of education and the state of mind arrived at through it. In Humboldt's concept of the individual who for his own good exposes himself to a variety of situations, the influence of Kant's philosophy is also discernible. Reflected in it is 'the Kantian assertion of the absolute claims of the moral law, and the Kantian insistence that each individual must be treated as an end and never simply as a means'. [107] Wilhelm von Humboldt and his brother, the great geographer and naturalist Alexander von Humboldt (1769–1859), were the sons of a Prussian court official in Berlin. Different from Alexander, Wilhelm was basically an introvert whose strength lay less in action and empirical research than in introspection and idealistic speculation. The main trend of his thought is clearly expressed in a letter to Georg Forster written in 1792: 'My aim, that which I have always had before my mind, has been the highest and most proportionate development of all human forces into a whole.' [108] Allied with this classical idea was his conviction that the essential force in man was his spontaneity. *Bildung* remained the focal point of his philosophy and it was from it that he viewed the place and function of the State. As the young Humboldt once expressed it: 'The State is nothing but a means to the furtherance of *Bildung* or rather to the removal of hindrances which would be in its way in a social state.' [109] He was anything but an admirer of the absolute State, its fetters having been still noticeable in Prussia during the days of Frederick the Great [1740–86].

As our extracts illustrate (docs 34a and b) Humboldt's essay of 1792 is concerned with both the purpose of man and the purpose of the State; but it is the former which in his opinion should mould the latter and not the other way round. The purpose of man is central, that of the State only derivative. To achieve the purpose of man, 'the highest and most truly proportionate formation of his potentialities to an integrated whole', two pre-conditions are essential: liberty and a variety of situations. For the individual cannot develop if he is fettered or confined to monotony. Just as Humboldt values the diversity of individuals so he stresses the need for a variety of situations to be experienced by each individual in order to bring out the powers latent in him. Creative potentialities can only turn into realities through the challenge of situations which may differ widely with different human beings. Obviously in this context the State is viewed as being only of secondary importance. As Humboldt sees it, the State can have a maximum or a minimum purpose. Its minimum purpose is the provision of security for its citizens, both internally and externally. In fact it confines itself to security from foreign attack and to justice at home. A State with a maximum purpose undertakes in addition to promote 'positive prosperity' or 'the positive welfare of the nation'. Humboldt's idea of a 'welfare state' was less comprehensive than that with which we are familiar in the second half of the twentieth century. His State promotes welfare either directly by caring for the poor or (and) indirectly by furthering agriculture, industry and trade. Altogether it concerns itself with 'the preservation or furtherance of the physical welfare of the nation'.

Humboldt rejects such a Welfare State entirely. His arguments against it are characteristic. Firstly he finds that it 'produces uniformity and an alien mode of behaviour in the nation'. Like J. S. Mill after him he feared for the diversity of human beings; this is 'certainly invariably forfeited to the degree in which the State interferes'. If the State is granted a maximum purpose, a relationship is bound to develop 'in which, from the outset, the superior power of the State inhibits the free interplay of the forces'. It is this interplay which Humboldt takes as much for granted as did Adam Smith, though for different reasons. Secondly State intervention weakens the nation. It makes man dependent upon external guidance and assistance and weakens his power 'to think a way out for himself'. Humboldt was the first, but not the last, liberal theorist who feared that the excessive care of the Welfare State stifles the spirit of initiative and self-reliance. Man's happiness can only be obtained by his own exertions. If on the road to it he is bound to run into obstacles they will sharpen his mind and strengthen his character. Conversely welfare states 'only too frequently resemble the doctors who nurse diseases and stave off death'.

Humboldt's idea of the State limits its functions radically to those of a nightwatchman; it 'should refrain from all care for the welfare of the citizens'. The only justification for restricting their liberty is the maintenance of internal and external security. Behind this position lies a specific concept of freedom, one 'closely connected with his concept of culture'. For Humboldt freedom 'means the possibility for an indefinite and multiple activity which forms the indispensable basis for the development of the human forces and therefore for that of culture.' [110] Whenever he reflected Humboldt placed the creative individual in the centre of his philosophy. The private sphere of the individual was sacrosanct to him and the state had only the right to interfere with it when 'the violation of the right of one person by another' was involved.

Humboldt's complete belief in the 'free play of the forces' may seem to us unrealistic, but it should be remembered that he was much more concerned with cultural than with social forces in a country in which industrialization was still in its infancy. His basic concern was not sociological but aesthetic. He was much afraid of the monotony which prevents man from developing into a meaningful whole, into a work of art. '... Nothing could have been further from the utilitarian concepts of Bentham.' He 'was convinced that men and nations develop themselves organically, like plants, that they "grow" since they are part of nature. And just as it is best to leave plants to themselves and to trust the forces which nature has given them, man should be left to himself and his own initiative as much as possible.' [111]

Like many individualists, the young Humboldt had a profound dread of the State bureaucracy. He sensed its trend toward self-multiplication, and in his way he anticipated Parkinson's Law. 'In most States', he complained, 'the personnel of the officials and the extent of the offices increases from decade to decade and the liberty of the subjects decreases in proportion.' [112]

It is ironic that the man who in 1792 had denied the State the right to regulate the system of education twenty-seven years later, after the Napoleon's defeat of his country, was to reform the educational system of Prussia and to found the University of Berlin controlled by the State. Yet there was less contradiction than one might suppose. For the aim of Humboldt's new type of university, centred on 'the creation of perfection in the individual and the means was *Wissenschaft*, the scholarly and scientific approach to learning'. The basic idea was the unlimited freedom of research. 'Both students and professor now became seekers after truth, and it became essential that both should have complete academic freedom.' [113]

Though in later years he modified his views on the State his insistence on the value of the individual and on the need to grant him almost unlimited freedom was maintained to the end. Throughout his life his liberalism was accompanied by 'cultural experimentalism'. 'Self-education through a creative acceptance of experience is in fact the master concept of Humboldt's political theory.' [114] The need of self-realization through a variety of experiences meant more to him than to any other liberal thinker with the exception of his pupil J. S. Mill.

J. S. Mill's essay *On Liberty* (1859) extended the earlier concepts of English liberals by two new dimensions. Firstly, while maintaining the traditional emphasis on political freedom, that is freedom from the pressure of the State, he added a new and ardent plea for social freedom, for freedom from the 'tyranny of the majority', from the pressure of society and its insistence on conformity of behaviour and *mores*. Secondly, he gave the concept of the individual a much richer meaning. Refined and articulate, he was not only concerned with *freedom from*, but also with *freedom for*, a freedom which would make for greater spontaneity, originality and a better chance of progressive development (doc. 35).

While maintaining the utilitarianism of Bentham and of his father James Mill, he modified it considerably if not altogether logically in his essay *Utilitarianism* (1861). He maintained the utility of the Greatest Happiness Principle according to which actions are right in proportion as they tend to produce happiness, wrong as they tend to produce the reverse of happiness'. Yet he gave the principle a new qualitative angle by arguing 'that some *kinds* of pleasure are more desirable and valuable than others'. Mill professed a preference for the pleasures based on 'the higher faculties of man' and he tried to justify this qualitative distinction by talking of 'utility in the largest sense grounded in the permanent interests of man as a progressive being'.

To J. S. Mill man can be spontaneous; for what distinguishes him is man's capacity for choice. He desired that people should make their own choices and express their own preferences instead of being moulded by the experience of others, by customs and traditions. 'Though the customs may be both good as customs and suitable to him', – he argued, 'yet to conform to custom, merely *as* custom, does not educate or develop in him any of the qualities which are the distinctive endowment of a human being'[115]

Mill with his cultural élitism saw people divided into the multitude of mere imitators allowing their entourage, their social milieu to determine the pattern of living for them, and a select minority of strong and capable characters who insist on making their own choices and on developing their own preferences; 'These few are the salt of the earth. Without them, human life would become a stagnant pool.'[116] Mill's emphasis on these dynamic men with their strong impulses and predilections must be seen against the background of the growing monotony of customs and attitudes in the urbanized and industrialized Britain of the middle of the nineteenth century. There was then an often sub-conscious passion for *social* conformity in England comparable with the passion of *political* conformity in the totalitarian systems of our own century. Like Tocqueville, J. S. Mill was deeply conscious of the phenomenon of crowd behaviour. 'Even in what people do for pleasure, conformity is the first thing thought of', he observed. 'They like being in crowds; they exercise choice only among things commonly done: peculiarity of taste, eccentricity of conduct, are shunned equally with crimes.' The multitude is, in fact, a feeble lot: 'They become incapable of any strong wishes or native pleasures, and are generally without either opinions or feelings of home growth, or properly their own.'[117] The times of the buccanneers, of the men seeking adventure for its own sake, of the strong, wilful and passionate individuals have passed. What now sets the tone is an undistinguished and undistinguishable mediocrity.

Like Wilhelm von Humboldt, Mill was impressed by the Greek idea of self-development and it is in this context that he made his plea for a pluralism of value-systems in society which is one of his major con-

B. Classical liberalism

tributions to the advance of liberal thought. He argued that Calvinism and Greek paganism should both have their place in our intellectual universe. To him 'pagan self-assertion' was one of the elements of human worth just as 'Christian self-denial' was another. He did not conceal his bias in favour of Greek civilization.[118] He was influenced to some extent by Goethe and the German Romantics when arguing in favour of an organic concept of man, an idea utterly alien to the utilitarians. Man is conceived as an organism rather than as a machine and compared with 'a tree that requires to grow and develop itself on all sides, according to the tendency of the inward forces which make it a living thing'.[119]

Mill also defines the realms of liberty more fully than the thinkers before him. It comprises three layers; first, what is called 'the inward domain of consciousness' demanding 'liberty of conscience in the most comprehensive sense; liberty of thought and feeling'. This demand for freedom of thought does not allow any exceptions; it is radical: 'absolute freedom of opinions and sentiment on all subjects, practical or speculative, scientific, moral or theological'. The second layer pursues 'liberty of tastes and pursuits; of framing the plan of our life to suit our own character'. We should have the liberty of 'doing as we like, subject to such consequences as may follow'. The only limit is that we should do no harm to others. The possibility that others 'should think our conduct foolish, perverse or wrong' is no reason for interfering with our freedom. Thirdly, there should be full liberty of association among individuals so long as they are not forced or deceived, and again, do no harm to others.

Mill discerned a contemporary trend towards changes which 'strengthen society and diminish the power of the individual'. He therefore thought it necessary to make a strong plea for the rights and the chances of self development of the individual. Mill argued that an increase of the power of the State was prejudicial to liberty, and further that a distinction can be drawn between the part of human life 'in which it is chiefly the individual that is interested and the part which chiefly interests society'. Liberty is infringed if the State interferes with the first part. Finally Mill regards spontaneous choice as the most valuable element in human life; everything that is done by compulsion diminishes the scope of that choice and thus infringes liberty.

Perhaps Mill was too suspicious of the power of the majority to force the minority to abide by its desires (see doc. 103) to be called a democrat, although as a liberal he was much concerned with the rights of minorities, with black people (an attitude unusual at that time), or with women. He was particularly critical of the fact that in spite of their substantial contribution to society, women were still underprivileged, had no vote and remained economically and socially dependent on their husbands or other male members of the family.

A balanced and even-tempered thinker, Mill argued the need for freedom of expression with consummate skill. There is feeling behind his dictum in *On Liberty*: 'If all mankind minus one were of the opinion, and only one person were of the contrary opinion, mankind would be no more justified in silencing that one person, than he, if he had the power, would be justified in silencing mankind.' [120] This passionate upholder of the right to non-conformity maintains that even the most absurd and perverted view should be allowed expression. A major reason for this approach was his conviction that man is not infallible. To silence discussion implies an assumption of infallibility. On the other hand the misuse of judgement is no argument against using it. If man is fallible, he is at the same time capable of rectifying his mistakes by discussion and experience. Truth can only be established properly by discussion and argument.

Another aspect of Mill's plea for unfettered expression of opinion is what one might call his 'collision theory'. Since truth and error are often mixed up with each other and 'since the general or prevailing opinion on any subject is rarely or never the whole truth, it is only by the collision of adverse opinions that the remainder of the truth has any chance of being supplied'.[121] Even where a received opinion comprises the whole truth, unless it is vigorously and earnestly contested, it will function as a mere prejudice with little comprehension and rationality towards its meaning. Moreover Mill seems to imply, though he does not use the term, that the pursuit of truth is a dialectical process, and that all good arguments are seldom on one side. He makes the point that 'even the most intolerant of churches, the Roman Catholic Church, even at the canonization of a saint, admits and listens patiently to a "devil's advocate".' [122]

It is not surprising that J. S. Mill, 'the Saint of Rationalism', cites the fates of Socrates and of Jesus as superb examples of the miscarriage of justice towards champions of minority views unacceptable to their judges. On the other hand he regards the persecution of Christianity under the Roman Emperor Marcus Aurelius as 'one of the most tragical facts in all history'.[123]

History teaches us that oppression of opinions is always a serious mistake. For 'if the opinion is right, they (mankind) are deprived of the opportunity of exchanging error for truth, and if wrong they lose what is almost as great a benefit, the clearer perception and livelier impression of truth, produced by its collision with error'.[124]

The search for truth brings us back to Mill's accent on individualism. Although he acknowledges that truth concerns all mankind, he insists that the individual has to arrive at it by his own efforts. In this context a letter from Mill to Carlyle in 1834 – twenty-five years before he completed *On Liberty* – is revealing, as it throws light on his aim of a synthesis of collective utilitarianism and belief in the individual: 'Though I hold the good of the species (or rather of its several units) to be the *ultimate* end (which is the alpha and omega of my utilitarianism), I believe with the fullest belief that this end can in no other way be forwar-

B. Classical liberalism

ded but by the means you speak of, namely each taking for his exclusive aim the development of what is best in *himself*.' [125]

5. The belief in international harmony — introduction
(Documents 36–44, pp. 352–83)

(i) Through free trade and non-intervention

An important aspect of the liberal ideology in the nineteenth century was the belief in the harmony of the interests of the nations. There existed, it suggested, a natural order on an international scale just as there was one within each society. This faith was closely allied with a belief in the productive function of commerce as an instrument for bringing the nations together more closely.

If freedom of trade from government interference was the magic formula for peace and prosperity at home, its corollary in foreign affairs was the non-intervention of one State in the affairs of another. It meant the application of *laissez faire* in a different field, the belief that growing trade interchange and prosperity made the traditional methods of diplomacy with their resort to war in the last instance unnecessary. In future war should only be permissible in clear cases of national self-defence and even then only when all means to end a conflict by way of arbitration had failed. Considering the leading role Great Britain played in commerce and industry it is not surprising that the pioneers of the doctrine of international harmony were mainly Englishmen, but, as we shall see, by the middle of the century the movement had also acquired some vocal champions on the Continent.

In England the earnest plea of the Radicals from Bentham to Bright for international harmony through commerce went hand in hand with a deep distrust of the privileged position of the aristocracy. They opposed its traditional diplomacy and took a very different view of what should be regarded as 'the vital interests of the nation'. The liberals' distrust of the actions of any government extended to the game of international diplomacy. It was Jeremy Bentham who set the tone. His advice to governments 'to be quiet' did not stop at the doors of the Foreign Office. Already in his startling *Plan for a Universal and Perpetual Peace*, one of four essays written between 1786 and 1789, he demanded that 'secrecy

278

in the operations of the Foreign Department ought not to be endured in England' as it was 'altogether useless and equally repugnant to the interests of liberty and to those of peace'.[126] He also declared himself in favour of the emancipation of colonies which to him were a source of much conflict between the nations and of little or no use to their mother country. Bentham was convinced that struggles for 'distant dependencies' and 'secrecy in the operation of the Foreign Department' 'were the only serious causes of war and that public opinion could be educated to the truth of this'.[127]

In later years he was even more drastic, denouncing all conquest and control of other nations 'as no better than an instrument, a device for the accumulation of patronage and oppressive power in the hands of the dominating, at the expense, and by the sacrifice, of the interest and felicity, of the subject many, in both States' (doc. 36). Bentham expressly rejected war except in the case of national self-defence or to enforce the receiving of compensation for financial damage suffered by a nation, and even then only if all efforts to settle the conflict by arbitration had proved unsuccessful.

In some ways Bentham's approach proved rather more negative than positive; it was directed against any 'recognition of superiority' on the part of Britain in relation to any other State, against its seeking 'to procure or consent to receive' any 'factitious honour or dignity' for itself or for any of its citizens 'at the hands of any other State' (doc. 36). On the eve of the French Revolution Bentham made a strong plea for the reduction of military and naval forces and recommended the establishment of an International Court of Judicature for the settlement of disputes between States, although the Court should not have any coercive powers.

As the secrecy of the actions of government was, in Bentham's eyes, a major evil it was necessary to mobilise reason and public opinion against it. His dislike and distrust of governments were somewhat pathological. As he put it bluntly in one of his earlier pamphlets: 'There are properly no other criminals than the heads of nations: the subjects are always honest.'[128]

Thirty years later, with English commercial capacity and political influence further advanced, the idea of non-intervention found new spokesmen in two English politicians of the Anti-Corn League, both champions of middle-class radicalism. Richard Cobden (doc. 43), and John Bright (doc. 39) deeply distrusted Lord Palmerston's assertive foreign policy rooted, as they saw it, in the vested interests of the old ruling class. In a speech delivered in 1858 John Bright described British foreign policy as 'nothing more or less than a gigantic system of outdoor relief for the aristocracy of Great Britain'. In his eyes the large diplomatic service and an 'inflamed' army and navy had the function of providing employment for members of the aristocracy, while British foreign policy

B. Classical liberalism

had the purpose of 'justifying overgrown establishments'.[129] Bright therefore demanded that the abolition of the corn laws should be followed by that of the equally outdated and unsuccessful system of foreign policy which provided posts for the sons, brothers and cousins of the discredited landlords.[130] In 1865, Bright declared the theory of the balance of power, so dear to the Establishment, 'to be pretty nearly dead and buried'. He called it 'a ghastly phantom' and 'this foul idol' which had during the last 170 years led to the sacrifice of 'the lives of hundreds and thousands of Englishmen'.[131]

Cobden, who possessed a wider vision and less aggressive instincts than John Bright, had already in 1835 expressed his belief that 'the progress of freedom depends more upon the maintenance of peace and the spread of commerce and the diffusion of education than upon the labour of Cabinets or Foreign Offices'.[132] They should therefore reduce international contacts through diplomatic channels and increase them through commercial channels under a system of free trade.[133] With this conviction to which he stuck for the rest of his life Cobden conjured up the vision of a better world 'with commerce as the great panacea which like a beneficial medical discovery' (a tribute to the growing power of medical science) would 'serve and innoculate with the healthy and saving taste for civilization all the nations of the world'.[134]

Cobden was both a realistic businessman and a visionary who resented the criticism that he had stressed the material interests too much in his fight for free trade. Taking a long-range view of the next 1,000 years in a speech at Manchester in 1846, he speculated on the consequences of the triumph of the free-trade doctrine and predicted that the desire and the motives for large and powerful empires, for gigantic armies and navies would disappear and a system of world government would then prevail. Mankind would become one united family and man would freely exchange 'the fruits of his labour with his brother.'[135] Indeed a pretty picture, yet Cobden did not conceal from his listeners that the realization of this dream was left to the dim future. As a factory owner and canvassing politician he was well aware of what was expedient in his own age. He realized, as did his opponent Lord Palmerston, that the belief in free trade 'conveniently suited the moral temper and the commercial supremacy of Great Britain in mid-century.'[136]

The gospel of free trade and of non-intervention, passionately preached by Cobden (doc. 37), led him at regular intervals to put forward positive proposals to lessen the danger of armed conflict between States through arbitration.[137] Cobden's aim in this context was moderate. Whilst he favoured arbitration in disputes between two States, he was not for an International Court of Arbitration. As he wrote in a letter to George Combe in April 1849: 'My plan does not embrace the scheme of a congress of nations or imply the belief in the millenium or demand your homage to the principle of non-resistance.' What he proposed was simply

280

that 'England should offer to enter into an agreement with other coun- tries – France for instance – binding them to refer any disputes that may arise to arbitration.' His political experience had taught Cobden 'a degree of cynicism: permanency for him went hand in hand with intrigue and corruption in international affairs.' [138] His plea for arbitration between States meant 'to bind them to do before a war what nations always virtually do after it'. [139]

For some years Cobden had taken an interest in the International Peace Movement, active in USA and England and mainly directed by Quakers. He began to regard peace and free trade as 'one and the same cause'. [140] Soon Cobden and other free traders, both English and French, played a prominent part at the international Peace Congresses, the first held in Brussels in 1848, the second in Paris in 1849, the third in Frankfurt on Main in 1850. Cobden was a Vice-President at the Paris and Frankfurt congresses. At the second Congress in Paris, described by a historian recently 'as the peak of the International Peace Movement during the first half of the century', [141] a number of eminent French economists took part. [142]

The Paris Congress was presided over by Victor Hugo, the author, who in his brilliant opening address coined the phrase 'the United States of Europe'. Two other leading French congress members were the politicians Francisque Bouvet and Emile de Girardin. [143] The fervent plea for international arbitration and universal peace put forward in Bouvet's speech at the National Assembly in November 1848 is characteristic of his approach (doc. 42). All his life he was a pacifist who believed in arbitration as the best solution of international conflicts. Though an ideal- ist like Cobden, Bouvet also used practical arguments for propagating his cause, stressing the heavy burden on the budgets of many States through the expenses for armaments. In the revolutionary enthusiasm of 1848, he expressed his conviction that 'to be consistent with its own Constitution, the new French Republic ought henceforth to aim at suppressing the military system and replacing it with an international jurisdiction'.

In his articles and speeches, Emile Girardin declared himself strictly for a policy of non-intervention in foreign affairs. He rejected war under all circumstances and even disapproved of any attempt to intervene in order to enforce non-intervention (doc. 40). As he put it bluntly in an arti- cle in *La Presse* in 1849, France 'wants to keep an industrial society in an equilibrium on a bayonet; she will not succeed. She wants to be knightly and mercantile, a double pretence which Britain has never entertained.'[144] He favoured the abandonment of conscription and a serious reduction of the military forces. Girardin and Cobden were not pacifists at any price, but wanted to put pressure on the governments to disarm because their military commitments placed a heavy tax burden on the peoples. [145]

B. Classical liberalism

There followed a few more Peace Congresses, 1851 in London, coupled with the International Exhibition at the Crystal Palace, 1853 in Manchester and Edinburgh, but the 1850s were not favourable to the cause after the revolutionary *élan* had spent itself and nationalism had become a growing force on the Continent. However, interest in free trade caught on even in France, reaching its climax in the conclusion of the Anglo-French Treaty of Commerce in 1860, negotiated for Palmerston's Government by Cobden and in France by Michael Chevalier with the blessing of Emperor Napoleon III. In Germany the free trade doctrine was energetically propagated in the 1840s and 1850s by John Prince Smith. [146] As mentioned above, Smith, too, saw in free trade not only an economic necessity but also a first-rate instrument for promoting international peace and understanding. In 1846 he became known to a wider German public as sponsor of an address to Sir Robert Peel by Elbing merchants, congratulating him on the abolition of the corn laws in Britain. In his reply Peel assured them protectionism had no hope of victory as it was proved that only free trade would benefit the nation. The Elbing declaration and Peel's reply turned free trade in Germany into a national issue. In 1847 Prince Smith with others founded the Free Trade Union in Berlin where he then lived. Soon similar societies sprang up in other major German towns. In the same year on a triumphant Continental tour Cobden visited Berlin, talked with leading Prussian officials and was honoured at a dinner by 180 free-traders. Although Prince Smith lacked Cobden's demagogic qualities, he was a skilful tactician who gradually succeeded in 'identifying economic with political and parliamentary liberalism'. [147] He linked the free-traders with other progressive movements among the German middle classes enjoying a greater appeal. Supporters of the various groups, which included the Cooperative Movement of Hermann Schulze-Delitzsch, combined to inaugurate the 'Congress of German Economists' which began its sessions at Gotha in 1858 and reached a peak at Cologne in 1860. These congresses had some political significance as the majority of their members were Deputies in various State parliamentary bodies who influenced new legislation. Decision-makers in Germany, that is, the various governments and the civil servants, had to take note of the Congress speeches and resolutions. In Cologne the free-traders under Prince Smith 'were successful and secured adoption by the Congress of plans for a thorough reform of the *Zollverein* Tariff'. This programme, which was particularly concerned with the existing duties on pig-iron, was 'virtually adopted by the Prussian Government and was carried out by the Zollverein in the 1860s'. [148] During his last few years Prince Smith had the satisfaction of having become 'the intellectual leader of powerful commercial interests in Prussia' [149] and of seeing the free trade doctrine established as a determining policy factor in the early years of the Second German Empire. Yet only a few years after his death in 1874 the principle was abandoned by Bismarck and replaced by a rigorous protectionism.

Our extract (doc. 38) from Prince Smith's address at the Congress of Cologne shows clearly that like Cobden he used both idealist and realistic arguments in favour of the free-trade panacea. He regarded the strengthening of peaceful international relations through free trade as much more important than the immediate economic gain through a cheaper supply of goods.

It seems appropriate to end the selection of voices emphasizing the close ties between free trade and international arbitration with a piece by the Belgian economist and sociologist Emile de Laveleye (1822–92). A year before his death he said of his unorthodox position: 'On the one hand I belong to the extreme left of the 'Socialism of the Chair' [a term coined by non-Marxist social reformers in Germany in the 1880s], on the other hand I have remained in the camp of liberalism, even in its doctrinaire form.' [150]

Laveleye can hardly be called a liberal Utopian. Like Bentham he was convinced that man's self-interest ruled his actions and was 'the great moving power of the whole living world'. While it was wrong to expect too much altruism from people, he believed that the self-interest of individuals and of nations could be made to work for peaceful purposes, for cooperation. What was required was a tribunal to dispense justice between the nations. 'Self-interest which ushered war into the world, ends its evolutions in universal peace' (doc. 44).

Different from other free-traders Laveleye acknowledged the strong power of national prejudices and passions which could only disappear gradually 'with the progress of enlightenment and trade'. Pointing to the Zollverein and to the Anglo-French Treaty of Commerce he insisted that commerce was cementing better international relations. In Laveleye's view the two measures needed to improve international relations generally were the establishing of a Code of International Law and of an International Court of Justice to settle disputes between the States by arbitration. Laveleye followed in Cobden's footsteps with his demand that the Court should have no military force at its disposal to enforce its decisions. The danger of a Concert of Powers, of another Holy Alliance had to be avoided. He therefore suggested that the Court should be placed in a small country. In fact, this happened with the Court of International Arbitration established in The Hague after the Conference of May 1899 convened by the Tsar in the same city. The governments of all the European States as well as of the United States, China, Japan, Siam and Mexico were represented. Although the limitations on the efficiency and scope of the Hague Court[151] would have disappointed Laveleye, the fact that the Court depended on the good will of the disputants, before being called into action, and that it lacked any means of enforcing its decisions was in line with his thought. However, he hoped that public opinion would gradually compel every State to submit disputes with other States to the Court. Laveleye realized that questions arousing strong nationalist passions such as the demand for the return of Metz to France, the Polish question, and what he called 'the Slav question', could never be settled by an arbitration court. Yet its existence would at last mean a great step forward on the road to international peace.

(ii) Non-intervention and the image of the British abroad

There was another aspect of the belief in international harmony, which occupied some of the subtler and less doctrinaire minds among the Liberals in England. How, they asked themselves, did other nations see Britain and the role of the British abroad? Why was there so much anti-British prejudice on the Continent? Gladstone's speech on non-intervention in the House of Commons on 27 June 1850 is a good example of this concern.[152] While English travellers abroad were generally found 'to be upright, high-minded, brave, liberal and true' he remarked, they had too high an opinion of themselves and 'too little disposition to regard the feelings, the habits and the ideas of others'. Gladstone argued that Palmerston's determined interventionist policy contributed to this deplorable stereotype. The remedy was clear. Britain should in future 'refrain from all gratuitous and arbitrary meddling in the internal concerns of other States', just as the British would resent the same sort of interference practised by others to themselves.

If here Gladstone only touched on the problem of England's national image abroad, J. S. Mill considered it continuously, and on a wider canvass, with all the subtlety of his penetrating mind.[153] In his discussion of non-intervention in 1859 (doc. 41), he was puzzled by the discrepancy between the actual attitudes and motives of the English and their misinterpretation abroad. 'Far exceeding any other (country) in wealth, and in the power that wealth bestows', Britain's 'declared policy' was 'to let other nations alone'. She was free from any aggressive designs on other countries. If other nations did not meddle with her, she would not meddle with them. British attempts to exert influence over other nations 'even by persuasion', were 'rather in the service of others than of itself'. Britain aimed at mediation in the quarrels between foreign States, at arresting civil wars and reconciling belligerents. She procured 'the abandonment of some national crime and scandal to humanity, such as the slave-trade'. She desired 'no benefit' to herself 'at the expense of others' even none in which all others do not 'as freely participate'. She concluded 'no treaties stipulating for separate commercial advantages'. All her 'own ports and commerce were free as the air and the sky' and all her neighbours were at liberty to use them. It did not concern her that other nations, on their part, kept all to themselves, and persisted 'in the most jealous and narrow-minded exclusion of its merchants and goods'. [154]

A nation like the British pursuing such a policy was 'a novelty in this world'. Mill felt that this was perhaps the reason that many were 'unable to believe it when they see it'. For the estimate of English foreign policy, widespread on the Continent, was far from flattering. Britain appeared as the very embodiment 'of egoism and selfishness, as a nation which thought of nothing but of out-witting and out-generalling its neighbours'. [155] To Mill such a distortion was a surprising specimen of 'the depths of human prejudice'.

Yet this picture of the British nation as 'crafty and hypocritical' could not be simply ignored; it required some searching self-analysis. How could such a distortion have arisen? At the present critical moment 'when the whole turn of European events, and the course of European history for a long time to come' might 'depend on the conduct and the estimation of England', [156] British statesmen were by their sins of speech or action most effectively playing into the hands of Britain's enemies and thus seemed to justify 'injurious misconceptions of the British character and people'. At the time of the Italian crisis and the brief Franco-Austrian war, Mill was obviously as critical of the argument of the needs of Britain's 'vital interests' as were Cobden and Bright. Mill denounced what we might call in retrospect the negative theory of non-intervention, 'the eternal repetition of the shabby *refrain*' of the Establishment 'we did not interfere because no English interest was involved'. 'We ought not to interfere where no English interest is concerned.' [157] The corollary of this view was that Britain would profess that 'it interferes only when it can serve its objects by it'.

Mill introduced another novel element in the discussion of war and of non-intervention. To him the question of armed conflict was not only one of distinguishing between aggressive or defensive wars, but it had also an anthropological background. There existed, he argued, 'rational' rules of warfare between nations of the same, or at least a similar degree, of civilization, but these hardly applied in the relations between civilized nations and primitive nations or barbarians. He called it 'a grave error', to suppose that the same international customs, and the same rules of international morality 'can apply between one civilized nation and another, and between civilized nations and barbarians'. [158]

Mill was not free from a somewhat priggish feeling of the white man's superiority. Barbarians, he insisted, could not be 'depended upon for observing any rules'. They had not yet arrived 'beyond the period during which it is likely to be for their benefit that they should be conquered and held in subjection by foreigners'. Mill obviously regarded independence and nationality as a sign of advanced civilization, of which the barbarians were not yet capable. At the same time he stressed that the only moral law for the civilized and barbarous governments were 'the universal rules of morality between men and men'.[159] These do not seem to have excluded the propriety of warfare then conducted by 'civilized' nations against primitive barbarians.

However 'among civilized peoples, members of an equal community of nations, like Christian Europe', the question of the legitimacy of war had to 'be decided on totally different principles'. The immorality of wars of conquest, or of conquest, 'even as the consequence of lawful war was beyond even the need for debate'. The annexation of any civilized people to be controlled by another was unacceptable unless it was done 'by their own spontaneous election' (doc. 41).

Another problem was the permissibility of intervention in taking part in the civil wars of another nation. The big question which concerned Mill, as many other English liberals at the time, was whether one country might 'justifiably aid the people of another country in struggling for liberty'. Mill would answer, that it all depended on the specific case. If the contest was with native rulers and their followers, in other words, if it was a contest without any foreign support, then no country had the right to intervene. If a progressive faction in say Russia or Hungary was fighting its government for greater national liberty, a foreign country, enjoying a free government could only give its moral support, but the position was different if that country was itself threatened by a coalition of Continental despots. In that case England, for instance, 'ought to consider the popular party in every nation of the Continent as its natural ally: the Liberals should be to it, what the Protestants of Europe were to the Government of Queen Elizabeth'.[160]

Mill insisted that 'the doctrine of non-intervention to be a legitimate principle of morality', had to be accepted by all governments. 'Despotic regimes' (i.e. Russia) must be bound by it as much as 'free governments' (i.e. Great Britain). He therefore came to the conclusion which went far beyond the less sophisticated formulae of Bentham or Cobden that 'intervention to enforce non-intervention is always rightful, always moral, if not always prudent'.[161] It was all a question of subtle distinctions. Hungary's fate during the revolution of 1848–49 served Mill as a test case. When Hungarians revolted against the yoke imposed on them by Vienna, it might not have been right for England to have intervened for Hungary, but later when the Russian Czar sent his troops into that country to join those of Austria, England should have regarded this as a challenge and 'have declared that this should not be, and that if Russia gave assistance to the wrong side, England would aid the right'.[162]

Here Mill was in marked contrast to Cobden. In a very characteristic letter in September 1853 to Louis Kossuth, the Hungarian freedom fighter, Cobden rejected the idea that England should engage in hostilities against despotic Russia. Despite his sympathy with the cause of the Hungarian patriots he maintained that he had the duty of consulting English interests and did not consider himself 'justified in plunging my

The belief in international harmony: introduction

country into war to rectify the wrongs of other nations'.[163]

Differing from most English Radicals, Mill also did not reject the idea of the balance of power, on which, he declared, 'the permanent maintenance of freedom in a country depended'. Assisting a foreign country that was kept down meant to him 'to redress that balance when it is already unfairly and violently disturbed'.

In the context of a brief Introduction it is not possible to consider British liberal foreign policy in action as different from liberal thought on international issues. The divergent views of Cobden and Mill on the question of British intervention in Hungary illustrate the diversity of liberal positions. While most liberals were in theory impressed by the *fata morgana* of harmony and balance in international affairs, the practice of liberal politicians and statesmen in this field was seldom systematic and often contradictory. On the whole British liberalism proved much less effective in foreign affairs than in the realm of domestic and constitutional issues. However, in the nineteenth century the Anglo-Saxon ideology of society and State remained fairly consistent in its approach to international affairs. Since the days of Bentham the liberal attitude to war and peace, intervention and non-intervention was to a large extent fashioned by

'the rise of the emphasis on material and economic, as opposed to political, ends; the rise of the conceptions of nation and society in antithesis to the conceptions of the government and the state; and the rise of the conviction that, whereas there was a natural disharmony between governments and states, there was a natural harmony between nations and societies.'[164]

Notes and references

1. The utilitarian approach to government

1. Quoted in A. V. Dicey, *Lectures on the Relations between Law and Public Opinion*, London 1924, p. 145.
2. Guido de Ruggiero, *The History of European Liberalism*, London 1927, p. 101.
3. Ibid.
4. Ibid., pp. 99–100.
5. John Plamenatz, *The English Utilitarians*, Oxford 1958, p. 84.
6. Jeremy Bentham, *A Fragment on Government* and *The Introduction to the Principle of Morals and Legislation*, ed. Wilfred Harrison, Oxford 1948, p. 281.
7. F. C. Montague in his introduction to Bentham's *Fragment on Government*, Oxford 1891, p. 41.
8. J. S. Mill in his essay on Bentham, reprinted in *Mill and Coleridge*, introduction by F. R. Leavis, London 1950, p. 70.
9. Op. cit., pp. 73–4.
10. James Mill, *An Essay on Government*, ed. Ernest Barker, Cambridge 1937, p. 5.
11. Ibid., p. 9.
12. Ibid., p. 12.
13. Ibid., p. 35.
14. Ibid., p. 72.
15. Ibid., p. 73.
16. Bentham, too in his later years favoured 'a system of representation, with annual parliaments, universal suffrage and a secret ballot, to check the selfishness of governments and secure the common interest'. Ernest Barker in his introduction to James Mill's *Essay on Government*, p. xiii.
17. Ibid., p. 23.
18. J. S. Mill, *Autobiography* (The World's Classics), Oxford 1952, p. 89.
19. J. S. Mill, *Utilitarianism* (Everyman's Library) London 1948, p. 7.
20. Ibid., p. 9.
21. *Considerations on Representative Government.* The essay first appeared in 1861 and was reprinted in *Utilitarianism, Liberty, and Representative Government*, London 1948 (Everyman's Library), p. 207.
22. Ibid., p. 209. However Mill admitted that 'once they had that intention; witness the persevering attempts so long made to keep down the wages by law'.
23. Ibid., p. 211.
24. Ibid., p. 282.
25. Quoted in J. M. Robson, *The Improvement of Mankind*, London 1968, p. 226.
26. J. S. Mill, *Representative Government*, p. 255.
27. Ibid.
28. Ibid., p. 256.
29. Ibid., p. 214–15.
30. Ibid.
31. J. S. Mill, *On Liberty* (Everyman's Library), p. 122.

2. Economic liberalism

32. A summary of some of the arguments for and against is included in Arthur J. Taylor, *Laissez Faire and State Intervention in Nineteenth Century Britain*, Lon-

don 1972, Chs. 2, 7, 8. Lionel Robbins, *The Theory of Economic Policy in English Classical Political Economy,* London 1952, is an important statement of the revisionist point of view; see also John B. Brebner, 'Laissez-Faire and State Intervention in Nineteenth Century Britain', *Journal of Economic History,* vii (1948) Supplement viii.

33. See Ricardo's *Essay on the Influence of a Low Price of Corn on the Profits of Stock,* February 1815.
34. David Ricardo, *Principles of Political Economy and Taxation,* ed. R. M. Hartwell, London 1971, preface p. 49.
35. Ibid., p. 152.
36. Mark Blaug, *Ricardian Economics,* New Haven 1958, p. 32.
37. Richard Cobden, speeches in London on 28 Sept. 1843 and 3 July 1844; *Speeches on Questions of Public Policy by Richard Cobden M.P.,* ed. John Bright and James E. Thorold Rogers, London 1880, pp. 36–7, 105–6. John Bright, speech at the Covent Garden Theatre, 19 Dec. 1845, in Francis W. Hirst, *Free Trade and Other Fundamental Doctrines of the Manchester School,* London, 1903, pp. 211–12.
38. For example Lionel Robbins. op. cit., pp. 10–11. William Grampp, *Economic Liberalism* (2 vols), II, *The Classical View* New York 1965, pp. 61–5.
39. Cobden, speech in London 28 Sept. 1843; in *Speeches on Questions of Public Policy by Richard Cobden M.P.,* ed. John Bright and James E. Thorold Rogers, London 1880, p. 40. Liberal ideas on international harmony are further illustrated in 'Belief in International Harmony', above 278.
40. It has less validity when applied to the social and administrative field. See Arthur J. Taylor, op. cit., Chs. 5 & 6; David Roberts, *Victorian Origins of the British Welfare State,* New Haven 1960.
41. Phyllis Deane, *The First Industrial Revolution,* Cambridge 1965, p. 345.
42. John Stuart Mill, *Principles of Political Economy* (6th edn.), London, 1867, p. 573.
43. W. Grampp, op. cit., p. 75.
44. W. Grampp, *The Manchester School of Economics,* Stanford 1960, p. 33.
45. For example concerning the Ten Hours Act 1847 and the Public Health Act 1848.
46. In 1800 agriculture had formed $33\frac{1}{3}$% of the gross national product; but by 1850 it had fallen to 20%. Although by 1850 agricultural production had increased in absolute terms, the rate of increase had been nowhere near as great as that in manufacturing industry. Donald Read, *Cobden and Bright. A Victorian Political Partnership,* London 1967, p. 20.
47. J. S. Mill, op. cit., Preface p. v.
48. J. S. Mill, *Autobiography,* ed. Max Lerner, New York 1961, p. 137.
49. J. S. Mill, *Principles of Political Economy,* 6th edition, p. 568.
50. Ibid., pp. 569–73.
51. Ibid., p. 575.
52. Ibid., p. 578.
53. Ibid., p. 585.
54. Ibid., p. 591.
55. Ibid., p. 482.
56. W. Grampp, *Economic Liberalism,* II, p. 76.
57. J. S. Mill, *Principles of Political Economy,* p. 484.
58. Ibid., p. 492.
59. According to F. W. Hirst, 'Gladstone's budgets were his own. His was not only the master mind which decided the main features of the Budget; he also went into the minutest details and scrutinised all the available figures as eagerly and closely as a great businessman on entering a new venture.' Francis W. Hirst, *Gladstone as Financier and Economist,* London 1931, pp. 275–6.
60. W. E. Gladstone, budget speech in the House of Commons, 15 April 1861. *The Financial Statements of 1853, 1860–63,* London 1863, pp. 241–2. Gladstone's budget speeches have been described as perorations in which he 'dramatized the an-

B. Classical liberalism

nual statement in his five-hour meditations upon the nation's economy, conveying in them an extraordinary intensity of moral and intellectual deliberation'. Henry Roseveare, *The Treasury. The Evolution of a British Institution*, London 1969, pp. 192–3.

61. W. E. Gladstone, budget speech in the House of Commons, 16 April 1863. *Financial Statements*, pp. 334–5. National expenditure rose and fell as follows: it rose from £50 mill. to £51 mill. between 1850 to 1853, to £72 mill. for the year ending 31 March 1861; and then fell to £71 mill. in 1862, £69 mill. in 1863, £67 mill. in 1864 and £66 mill. in 1865. Public expenditure increased $4\frac{1}{2}$ per cent between 1843 and 1853, and $22\frac{1}{2}$ per cent between 1853 and 1860. F. W. Hirst, op. cit., pp. 184, 211.

62. Sydney Buxton, *Mr Gladstone as Chancellor of the Exchequer*, London 1901, pp. 101–2.

63. W. E. Gladstone budget speech 10 Feb. 1860; *The Financial Statements of 1853, 1860–63*, p. 129.

64. The national wealth increased 12 per cent between 1843 and 1853, and $16\frac{1}{2}$ per cent between 1853 and 1866. Taxable income increased approximately 6 per cent between 1842 and 1852, and 20 per cent between 1853 and 1861. Income tax was progressively reduced from 9d. in the pound in 1861 to 4d. in 1865–66. At the same time the total value of imports into Great Britain rose from £179 mill. to £295 mill. between 1859 and 1866, while the value of British exports rose from £155 mill. to £238 mill. F. W. Hirst, op. cit., pp. 184, 211.

65. Further editions of Say's *Traité d'économie politique* appearing during his life time were in 1817, 1819 and 1826. The English translation by C. R. Prinsep, *Treatise on Political Economy*, published 1821, is of the 4th edition of 1819.

66. Two of his courses of lectures were published: the *Catechisme d'économie politique* in 1815, and the lengthy *Cours complet d'économie politique pratique* in 1828–29.

67. J. B. Say, *A Treatise on Political Economy* (trans C. R. Prinsep) (Reprints of Economic Classics) New York 1964, preface, p. xviii.

68. Ibid. p. xxv.

69. Ibid. p. xxvi.

70. Ibid. p. xxxv.

71. Ibid. p. liv.

72. Ibid. Bk. i, Ch. 13 'Of immaterial products, or values consumed at the moment of production', p. 119ff.

73. Ibid. p. 62.

74. Ibid. Bk. i, Ch. 15, 'Of the demand or market for products', p. 134.

75. See Say's definition of the entrepreneur in Ibid. pp. 330–1.

76. 'The power of industrial *entrepreneurs* exercises a most notable influence upon the distribution of wealth. In the same kind of industry one *entrepreneur*, who is judicious, active, methodical, and willing makes his fortune, while another who is devoid of these qualities or who meets with very different circumstances would be ruined.' *Ouevres diverses*, p. 274, quoted in Charles Gide and Charles Rist, *A History of Economic Doctrines* (2nd English edn) London 1948, p. 128.

77. Ibid, p. 135.

78. J. B. Say, *Treatise on Political Economy*, p. 182.

79. C. Gide and C. Rist, op. cit., p. 123.

80. *Bastiat and the ABC of Free Trade*. Translated from the writings of F. Bastiat and edited by Lorenza Garreau, London 1926, p. 39.

81. Ibid., p. 41.

82. Eduard Heimann, *History of Economic Doctrines*, London 1945, p. 124.

83. Quoted in Alexander Gray, *The Development of Economic Doctrines*, London 1931, pp. 261.

84. Essay 'Justice and Fraternity', F. Bastiat, in *Selected Essays on Political Economy*, ed. George B. Huozar, Princeton 1964, p. 116.

Notes and references

85. See Bastiat's *Les Harmonies économiques, Oeuvres Completes,* I. (1850).
86. G. B. Huozar (ed.), op. cit., p. 138.
87. F. Bastiat, *Economic Sophisms,* translated from the French and edited by Potter Goddard, New York 1964, p. 129.
88. Ibid., p. 132.
89. Ibid., p. 141.
90. It was his 'belief that evil, far from being antagonistic to the good, in some mysterious ways promotes it while the good can never end in evil. In the final reckoning the good must triumph.' (*Les Harmonies économiques,* op. cit. p. 21.)
91. C. Gide and C. Rist, *A History of Economic Doctrines* (2nd English edn), London 1948, p. 276.
92. Franz Schnabel, *Deutsche Geschichte des 19. Jahrhunderts* (2nd edn.), Freiburg i. Br. 1949, vol. 3, p. 340.
93. Friedrich Lenz, *Friedrich Lists Staats- und Gesellschaftslehre,* Neuwied 1967, p. 20.
94. Introduction to the 'National System of Political Economy'. See, Margaret E. Hirst, *Life of Friedrich List and Selections from his Writings,* London 1909, p. 306.
95. Introduction to the *National System of Political Economy* op. cit., pp. 306–307.
96. Ibid.
97. In a country devoted to mere agriculture 'dullness of mind, awkwardness of body, obstinate adherence to old notions, customs, methods and processes, want of culture, of prosperity, and of liberty, would prevail'. *The National System of Political Economy,* English trans. S. S. Lloyd, London 1904, Ch. xvii, p. 159.
98. Ibid.
99. Ibid., p. 240.
100. Ibid., p. 107.
101. C. Gide and C. Rist, op. cit., pp. 283–4.
102. On John Prince Smith see W. O. Henderson 'Prince-Smith and Free Trade in Germany' in his book *Britain and Industrial Europe 1750–1850,* Liverpool 1954, pp. 167–8, and Donald G. Rohr, *The Origins of Social Liberalism in Germany,* Chicago 1963, pp. 85–91.

3. The superiority of the middle classes

103. Douglas Johnson, *Guizot,* London 1963, p. 75.
104. John Plamenatz, *The English Utilitarians,* Oxford 1958, p. 106.
105. D. Johnson, op. cit., p. 78.

4. Aesthetic individualism

106. *Ideen zu einem Versuch, die Grenzen der Wirksamkeit des Staates zu bestimmen.* The title of the English translation used by J. S. Mill is less cumbersome: *The Sphere and Duties of Government,* London 1854.
107. J. W. Burrow in his editorial introduction to Wilhelm von Humboldt, *The Limits of State Action,* Cambridge 1969, p. xi.
108. Quoted in R. Aris, *History of Political Thought in Germany 1789–1815,* London 1960, p. 143.
109. Ibid., p. 144.
110. Ibid., p. 147.
111. Ibid., p. 151.
112. Quoted, ibid., p. 153.

B. Classical liberalism

113. D. F. S. Scott, *Wilhelm von Humboldt and the Idea of a University*, Inaugural Lecture, University of Durham 1960, pp. 12–13.
114. J. W. Burrow, op. cit., p. xviii.
115. J. S. Mill, *On Liberty* (Everyman edn) Ch. 3, p. 116.
116. Ibid., p. 122.
117. Ibid., p. 119.
118. Ibid., p. 120.
119. Ibid., p. 117.
120. Op. cit., p. 79.
121. Ibid., p. 111.
122. Ibid., p. 83.
123. Ibid., p. 88.
124. Ibid., p. 79.
125. Quoted in John M. Robson, *The Improvement of Mankind. The Social and Political Thought of John Stuart Mill.* Toronto 1968, p. 127. The biographical roots of Mill's essay *On Liberty* as well as the legacy of its ideas have been ably discussed by Gertrude Himmelfarb in Parts Two and Three of her book *On Liberty and Liberalism. The Case of John Stuart Mill*, New York 1974.

5. The belief in international harmony

126. Jeremy Bentham's *Plan for a Universal and Perpetual Peace* (Grotius Society Publications No. 6), London 1927, p. 13.
127. F. H. Hinsley, *Power and the Pursuit of Peace*, Cambridge 1963, p. 84.
128. Quoted ibid., p. 86.
129. Donald Reid, *Cobden and Bright*, London 1967, p. 11.
130. Some years earlier, when travelling abroad, Cobden had advised Bright to 'oppose yourself to the Palmerston system and try to prevent the foreign office from undoing the good which the Board of Trade has done to the people'. Ibid.
131. *Speeches on Questions of Public Policy* by John Bright, London 1869, pp. 331–2.
132. D. Read, *Cobden and Bright*, pp. 109–10. See also doc. 37.
133. Ibid.
134. Richard Cobden, *England, Ireland and America*, see doc. 37.
135. *Speeches on Questions of Public Policy* by Richard Cobden, M.P., ed. John Bright and James. E. Thorold Rogers, London, 1880, p. 187.
136. Kenneth Bourne, *The Foreign Policy of Victorian England 1830–1902*, London 1970, p. 84.
137. See Maureen M. Robson, 'Liberals and vital interests, the debate on international arbitration, 1815–72', *Bulletin of the Institute of Historical Research*, xxxii (1959), p. 4.
138. Ibid., p. 47.
139. Quoted in John Morley, *Life of Richard Cobden*, London 1881, II, p. 44.
140. Ibid., I, p. 230.
141. F. S. L. Lyons, *Internationalism in Europe 1815–1914*, Leyden 1963, p. 315.
142. They included Frédéric Bastiat and Michael Chevalier.
143. Bouvet, who had been to the first Congress at Brussels in 1848, was a member of both the French Constituent Assembly and its successor the Legislative Assembly of 1848–49. Girardin, too, was a Deputy of the Legislative Assembly and Director of the popular mass paper *La Presse*.
144. *La Presse*, 2 April 1849 quoted in August Schon, *Histoire de L'Internationalisme*, III, Oslo 1963, p. 159.

145. Although Girardin, basically a journalist, was a great admirer of Cobden and published a handsome eulogy of him after his death in 1865, he regarded Cobden as inconsistent in his actions. See J. A. Hobson, *Richard Cobden, The International Man* (2nd ed.), London 1968, pp. 75 and 79.
146. See pp. 266–8 and also doc. 30. W. O. Henderson 'Prince Smith and Free Trade in Germany' in *Britain and Industrial Europe 1750–1850*, Liverpool 1954, pp. 167–78 and Donald G. Rohr, *The Origins of Social Liberalism in Germany*, Chicago 1963, pp. 85–91.
147. W. H. Dawson, *Protection in Germany* (1904) quoted in W. O. Henderson, op. cit., p. 171.
148. W. O. Henderson, op. cit., p. 175.
149. D. G. Rohr, op. cit., p. 87.
150. Quoted in Maurice Wilmotte, *Trois Semineurs d'Idées*, Paris 1907, p. 179.
151. See F. H. Hinsley, *Power and the Pursuit of Peace*, pp. 268–9 and F. S. L. Lyons, *Internationalism in Europe 1815–1914*, pp. 348–9.
152. See W. E. Gladstone, on the 'Spirit of Interference' in Palmerston's Foreign Policy, *Gladstone's Speeches*, ed. Arthur Tilney Bassett, London 1916, pp. 146–54.
153. Earlier Mill had fully shared the belief that 'commerce first taught nations to see with goodwill the wealth and prosperity of one another' and that commerce was 'rapidly rendering war obsolete'. J. S. Mill, *Political Economy* (1848), II, p. 120.
154. J. S. Mill, 'A Few Words on Non-Intervention' (1859) in *Dissertations and Discussions, Political, Philosophical and Historical*, London 1867, III, pp. 153–4.
155. Ibid.
156. Ibid., p. 158.
157. Ibid., p. 158.
158. Ibid., p. 167.
159. Ibid., p. 168.
160. Ibid., p. 175.
161. Ibid., p. 176.
162. Ibid., p. 177.
163. J. A. Hobson, *Richard Cobden*, Appendix, pp. 410–11.
164. F. H. Hinsley, op. cit., p. 111.

Documents

1. The utilitarian approach to government: documents
(Introduction, p. 243)

Doc. 17. JEREMY BENTHAM: The End of Legislation – the Greatest Happiness to the Greatest Number

In matters of law – in matters of legislation at least – reason is an instrument by which *means* are employed and directed to the attainment of an *end*. Of legislation the proper end may, it is hoped, without much presumption, be stated as being, – not but there are those who will deny it, – in every community, *the creation and preservation of the greatest happiness to the greatest number* – or, in one word, *happiness*: a *false* end, the creation and preservation of the greatest quantity of happiness to a few, to the prejudice, and in diminution of the happiness of the greatest number:– to a few, and those few naturally and usually the possessors of the several powers of government, with their official subordinates, and their associates and connexions:– and this, in proportion as the machinery of government is looked into, will almost everywhere be seen to be the end, principally at least, if not exclusively, aimed at and pursued.

[Source: Jeremy Bentham, *An Introductory View of the Rationale of Evidence; for the Use of Non-Lawyers as well as Lawyers. The Works of Jeremy Bentham*, ed. John Bowring, Edinburgh 1843, VI, pp. 5–6.]

Doc. 18. JEREMY BENTHAM: The Principle of Utility

Nature has placed mankind under the governance of two sovereign masters, *pain* and *pleasure*. It is for them alone to point out what we ought to do, as well as to determine what we shall do. On the one hand the standard of right and wrong, on the other the chain of causes and effects, are fastened to their throne. They govern us in all we do, in all we say, in all we think: every effort we can make to throw off our subjection, will serve but to demonstrate and confirm it. In words a man may pretend to abjure their empire: but in reality he will remain subject to it all the while. The *principle of utility** recognizes this subjection, and assumes it for the foundation of that system, the object of which is to rear the fabric of felicity by the hands of reason and of law. Systems which attempt to question it, deal in sounds instead of sense, in caprice instead of reason, in darkness instead of light. . . .

By the principle of utility is meant that principle which approves or disapproves of every action whatsoever, according to the tendency which it appears to have to augment or diminish the happiness of the party whose interest is in question: or, what is the same thing in other words, to promote or to oppose that happiness. I say of every action whatsoever; and therefore not only of every action of a private individual, but of every measure of government.

By utility is meant that property in any object, whereby it tends to produce benefit, advantage, pleasure, good, or happiness, (all this in the present case comes to the same thing) or (what comes again to the same thing) to prevent the happening of mischief, pain, evil, or unhappiness to the party whose interest is considered: if that party be the community in general, then the happiness of the community: if a particular individual, then the happiness of that individual . . . The community is a fictitious *body*, composed of the individual persons who are considered as constituting as it were its *members*. The interest of the community then is, what? – the sum of the interests of the several members who compose it . . .

An action then may be said to be conformable to the principle of utility, or, for shortness sake, to utility, (meaning with respect to the community at large) when the tendency it has to augment the happiness of the community is greater than any it has to diminish it.

A measure of government (which is but a particular kind of action, performed by a particular person or persons) may be said to be conformable to or dictated by the principle of utility, when in like manner the tendency which it has to augment the happiness of the community is greater than any which it has to diminish it.

---

* Note by the Author, July 1822.

To this denomination has of late been added, or substituted, the *greatest happiness or greatest felicity* principle: this for shortness, instead of saying at length *that principle* which states the greatest happiness of all those whose interest is in question, as being the

B. Classical liberalism

right and proper, and only right and proper and universally desirable, end of human action: of human action in every situation, and in particular in that of a functionary or set of functionaries exercising the power of Government. The word utility does not so clearly point to the ideas of *pleasure* and *pain* as the words *happiness* and *felicity* do: nor does it lead us to the consideration of the *number* of the interests affected: to the *number*, as being the circumstance, which contributes, in the largest proportion, to the formation of the standard here in question; the *standard of right and wrong*, by which alone the propriety of human conduct, in every situation, can with propriety be tried. This want of a sufficiently manifest connexion between the ideas of *happiness* and *pleasure* on the one hand, and the idea of *utility* on the other, I have every now and then found operating, and with but too much efficiency, as a bar to the acceptance that might otherwise have been given to this principle.

[Source: Jeremy Bentham, *An Introduction to the Principles of Morals and Legislation. The Works of Jeremy Bentham,* ed. John Bowring, Edinburgh 1843, I, pp.1–2.]

Doc. 19. JEREMY BENTHAM: The Duties of a Citizen – to Obey and Censure

Under a government of laws, what is the motto of a good citizen? *To obey punctually; to censure freely.*

Thus much is certain; that a system that is never to be censured, will never be improved; that if nothing is ever to be found fault with, nothing will ever be mended: and that a resolution to justify every thing at any rate, and to disapprove of nothing, is a resolution which, pursued in future, must stand as an effectual bar to all the *additional* happiness we can ever hope for; pursued hitherto, would have robbed us of that share of happiness which we can enjoy already.

Nor is a disposition to find 'every thing as it should be,' less at variance with itself, than with reason and utility. The commonplace arguments in which it vents itself justify not what is established, in effect, any more than they condemn it; since whatever *now* is establishment, *once* was innovation.

Precipitate censure, cast on a political institution, does but recoil on the head of him who casts it. From such an attack it is not the institution itself, if well grounded, that can suffer. What a man says against it either makes impression or makes none. If none, it is just as if nothing had been said about the matter; if it *does* make an impression, it naturally calls up some one or other in defence. For if the institution is in truth a beneficial one to the community in general, it cannot but have given an interest in its preservation to a number of individuals. By their industry, then, the reasons on which it is grounded are brought to light; from the observation of which, those who acquiesced in it before upon trust, now embrace it upon conviction. Censure, therefore, though ill-founded, has no other effect upon an institution than to bring it to that test, by which the value of those, indeed, on which prejudice alone has stamped a currency, is

296

cried down, but by which the credit of those of sterling utility is confirmed.

Nor is it by any means from passion and ill-humour, that censure, passed upon legal institutions, is apt to take its birth. When it is from passion and ill-humour that men speak, it is with *men* that they are in ill-humour, not with laws ... The Law is no man's enemy: the Law is no man's rival. Ask the clamorous and unruly multitude – it is never the Law itself that is in the wrong: it is always some wicked interpreter of the Law that has corrupted and abused it ...

Now then, with respect to actions in general, there is no property in them that is calculated so readily to engage, and so firmly to fix the attention of an observer, as the *tendency* they may have *to*, or *divergency* (if one may so say) *from*, that which may be styled the common *end* of all of them. The end I mean is *Happiness*: and this *tendency* in any act is what we style its *utility*: as this *divergency* is that to which we give the name of *mischievousness*. With respect, then, to such actions in particular as are among the objects of the Law, to point out to a man the *utility* of them or the mischievousness, is the only way to make him see *clearly* that property of them which every man is in search of; the only way, in short, to give him *satisfaction*.

From *utility*, then, we may denominate a *principle*, that may serve to preside over and govern, as it were, such arrangement as shall be made of the several institutions, or combinations of institutions, that compose the matter of this science: and it is this principle that, by putting its stamp upon the several names given to those combinations, can alone render *satisfactory* and *clear* any arrangement that can be made of them.

Governed in this manner by a principle that is recognised by all men, the same arrangements that would serve for the jurisprudence of any one country, would serve with little variation for that of any other.

Yet more. The mischievousness of a bad Law would be detected, at least the utility of it would be rendered suspicious, by the difficulty of finding a place for it in such an arrangement:. . .

That this advantage may be possessed by a natural arrangement, is not difficult to conceive. Institutions would be characterized by it in the only universal way in which they can be characterized; by the nature of the several *modes* of *conduct* which, by prohibiting, they constitute *offences*.

These offences would be collected into classes denominated by the various modes of their *divergency* from the common *end*; that is, as we have said, by their various forms and degrees of mischievousness: in a word, by those properties which are *reasons* for their being made *offences*: and whether any such mode of conduct possesses any such property is a question of experience. Now, a bad Law is that which prohibits a mode of conduct that is *not* mischievous. Thus would it be found impracticable to place the mode of conduct prohibited by a bad Law under any denomination of offence, without asserting such a matter

B. Classical liberalism

of fact as is contradicted by experience. Thus cultivated, in short, the soil of Jurisprudence would be found to repel in a manner every evil institution; . . .

The consequences of any Law, or of any act which is made the object of the Law — the only consequences that men are at all interested in — what are they but *pain* and *pleasure*?

[Source: Jeremy Bentham, *A Fragment on Government or a Comment on the Commentaries*: being an examination of what is delivered, on the subject of government in general, in the Introduction to Sir William Blackstone's *Commentaries* with a Preface in which is given a Critique on the Work at Large. *The Works of Jeremy Bentham*, ed. John Bowring, Edinburgh 1843, I, pp.230–1, 237.]

Doc. 20. JEREMY BENTHAM: The Leading Principles of a Constitutional Code

1. This Constitution has for its general end in view, the greatest happiness of the greatest number; namely, of the members of this political state: in other words, the promoting or advancement of their interests. By the *universal interest*, understand the aggregate of those same interests. This is the all-comprehensive end, to the accomplishment of which, the several arrangements contained in the ensuing code are all of them directed.

2. Government cannot be exercised without coercion; nor coercion, without producing unhappiness. Of the happiness produced by the government, the net amount will be — what remains of the happiness, deduction made of the unhappiness.

3. Of the unhappiness thus produced, is composed, in the account of happiness, the *expense* of government, the gross amount being given, the net amount will be inversely as this expense.

4. Of the members of this, as of other states in general, the great majority will naturally, at each given point of time, be composed of the several persons who, having been born in some part or other of the territory belonging to the state, have all along remained inhabitants of it. But, to these, for the purposes of benefit, of burden, or of both, will have to be added sundry other classes of persons, of whom designation is made in an appropriate part of the ensuing code.

5. Immediately specific, and jointly all-comprehensive, ends of this constitution are — subsistence, abundance, security, and equality; each maximized, in so far as is compatible with the maximization of the rest . . .

9. Security against evil, is either against evil from calamity, or against evil from hostility . . .

12. Of calamity, the principal sources are — inundation, conflagration, collapsion, explosion, pestilence, and famine.

13. The evil-doers, against whose hostility, that is to say, against

298

whose evil agency, security is requisite, are either external or internal. By the external, understand those adversaries who are commonly called *enemies*.

14. Internal adversaries, against whose evil agency security is requisite, are the *unofficial* and the *official*.

15. By the *unofficial* adversaries, understand those evil-doers who are ordinarily termed *offenders, criminals, malefactors*. These are resistible, everywhere resisted, and mostly with success.

16. The *official* are those evil-doers whose means of evil-doing are derived from the share they respectively possess in the aggregate of the powers of government. Among these, those of the highest grade, and in so far as supported by those of the highest, those of every inferior grade, are everywhere irresistible.

17. To provide, in favour of the rest of the community, security against evil in all its shapes, at the hands of the above-mentioned internal, and, so long as they continue in such their situation, irresistible adversaries, – is the appropriate business of the constitutional branch of law, and accordingly of this code.

18. As in difficulty so in importance, this part of the business of law far surpasses every other. Of the danger to which an assemblage of individuals stand exposed, the *magnitude* will be in the joint ratio of the *intensity* of the evil in question on the part of each, the *duration* of it, the *propinquity* of it, the *probability* of it; and, on the part of all, the *extent* of it; the extent, as measured by the *number* of those who stand exposed to it. Measuring it in every one of these *dimensions*, taking into account every one of these *elements of value* in both cases, – minute will be seen to be the danger to which the other members of the community stand exposed at the hands of those their resistible, in comparison with that to which they stand exposed at the hands of these their irresistible, adversaries. In the first case, it has place on no other than an individual scale; in the other, on a national scale.

19. Inferior even is the danger to which they stand exposed at the hands of foreign and declared enemies, in comparison with that to which they stand exposed at the hands of their everywhere professed protectors . . .

20. On the texture of the *constitutional* branch of law, will depend that of every other. For on this branch of law depends, in all its branches, the *relative* and *appropriate* aptitude of those functionaries, on whose will depends, at all times, the texture of every other branch of law. If, in the framing of this branch of law, the greatest happiness of the greatest number is taken for the end in view, and that object pursued with corresponding success, so will it be in the framing of those other branches: if not, not . . .

22. In the case of *equality*, that of *distribution* is implied. Distribution is either of *benefits* or of *burdens*: under one or other of these names, may

B. Classical liberalism

every possible subject-matter of the operation be comprised. Benefits are distributed by *collation* made of the instruments of felicity [i.e. subsistence, abundance, security] − burdens by the *oblation* of them, or by the *imposition* of positive hardship.

23. In proportion as equality is departed from, inequality has place: and in proportion as inequality has place, evil has place. First, as to inequality, − in the case where it is in the *collation* made of these same instruments that it has place. In this case, it is pregnant with two distinguishable evils: the one may be styled the *domestic* or *civil*; the other, the *national* or *constitutional*.

24. The *domestic* evil is that which has place in so far as the subject-matter of the distribution is the matter of wealth − matter of subsistence and abundance. It has place in this way: − The more remote from equality are the shares possessed by the individuals in question, in the mass of the instruments of felicity, − the less is the sum of the felicity produced by the sum of those same shares.

25. The national or constitutional evil is that which has place, in so far as the subject-matter of the distribution is *power*. It has place in this way: − The greater the quantity of power possessed, the greater the facility and the incitement to the abuse of it. In a direct way, this position applies only to *power*. But, between *power* and *wealth* such is the connexion, that each is an instrument for the acquisition of the other; in this way, therefore, the position applies to *wealth* likewise.

26. Of inequality as applied to both subjects, − and of the evil with which, in both the above shapes, it is pregnant, − the case of monarchy may serve for exemplification: for exemplification, and thereby for proof.

27. Of the maximum of inequality, every monarchy affords an example. Of the matter of wealth, to the monarch is allotted a mass as great as suffices for the subsistence of from 10,000 to 100,000 of the individuals from whom, amongst others, after being produced by their labour, it is extorted. Yet does it still remain a matter of doubt, whether the quantity of felicity thus produced in the breast of that one, be greater than that which has place in the breast of one of these same labourers taken on an average, − has place, or at least would have had, but for the extortion thus committed . . .

29. True it is, that if, *per contra*, by a monarch maintained at an expense such as the above, good is, by means of that same expense, produced in greater quantity than by a commonwealth chief whose maintenance will not be a hundredth part of the monarch's; − true it is, that on this supposition, the excess of expense, vast as it is, may not be ill-bestowed. But, by whomsoever the existence of any such excess of good is asserted, upon him does it rest to prove or probabilize it.

30. If in the case of those whose share in the *instruments* of felicity is *greatest*, the excess of *felicity itself* is, on an average, so small. − and, in some individuals out of the small number belonging to this class, the non-

existence of any such excess certain – still less and less will be the probable amount of the excess of felicity, in the case of those whose share in the instruments of felicity is *less* and *less*. And thus it is, that as, in a pure *monarchy*, the distribution made of the external instruments of felicity is in the highest degree – so, in a pure *aristocracy*, is it in the next highest degree – unfavourable to the maximization of felicity itself.

31. Hence, throughout the whole population of a state, the less the inequality is between individual and individual, in respect of the share possessed by them in the aggregate mass or stock, of the instruments of felicity, – the greater is the aggregate mass of felicity itself: provided always, that by nothing that is done towards the removal of the inequality, any shock be given to security, – namely, in respect of the several subjects of possession above mentioned . . .

[Source: Jeremy Bentham, *Leading Principles of a Constitutional Code for any State* (1823). *The Works of Jeremy Bentham*, ed. John Bowring, Edinburgh 1843, II, pp.269–72.]

Doc. 21. JAMES MILL: Good Government

In the Representative System alone the Securities for good Government are to be found.

What then is to be done? For, according to this reasoning, we may be told that good government appears to be impossible. The people, as a body, cannot perform the business of government for themselves. If the powers of government are entrusted to one man, or a few men, and a monarchy or governing aristocracy is formed, the results are fatal: and it appears that a combination of the simple forms is impossible.

Notwithstanding the truth of these propositions, it is not yet proved that good government is unattainable. For though the people, who cannot exercise the powers of government themselves, must entrust them to some one individual or set of individuals, and such individuals will infallibly have the strongest motives to make a bad use of them, it is possible that checks may be found sufficient to prevent them. . . . It is sufficiently conformable to the established and fashionable opinions to say, that, upon the right constitution of checks, all goodness of government depends . . . For as there is no individual, or combination of individuals, except the community itself, who would not have an interest in bad government if entrusted with its powers; and as the community itself is incapable of exercising those powers, and must entrust them to some individual or combination of individuals, the conclusion is obvious: the community itself must check those individuals, else they will follow their interest and produce bad government.

B. Classical liberalism

But how is it the community can check? The community can act only when assembled: and then it is incapable of acting.

The community, however, can choose representatives: and the question is, whether the representatives of the community can operate as a check?

What is required in a Representative Body to make it a Security for good Government?

We may begin by laying down two propositions, which appear to involve a great portion of the inquiry; and about which it is unlikely that there will be any dispute.

I. The checking body must have a degree of power sufficient for the business of checking.

II. It must have an identity of interest with the community; otherwise it will make a mischievous use of its power.

I. To measure the degree of power which is requisite upon any occasion, we must consider the degree of power which is necessary to be overcome. Just as much as suffices for that purpose is requisite, and no more. We have then to inquire what power it is which the representatives of the community, acting as a check, need power to overcome. The answer here is easily given. It is all that power, wheresoever lodged, which they, in whose hands it is lodged, have an interest in misusing. We have already seen, that to whomsoever the community entrusts the powers of government, whether one, or a few, they have an interest in misusing them. All the power, therefore, which the one or the few, or which the one and the few combined, can apply to insure the accomplishment of their sinister ends, the checking body must have power to overcome, otherwise its check will be unavailing. In other words, there will be no check ...

These conclusions are not only indisputable, but the very theory of the British Constitution is erected upon them. The House of Commons, according to that theory, is the checking body. It is also an admitted doctrine, that if the King had the power of bearing down any opposition to his will that could be made by the House of Commons; or if the King and the House of Lords combined had the power of bearing down its opposition to their joint will, it would cease to have the power of checking them; it must, therefore, have a power sufficient to overcome the united power of both.

II. All the questions which relate to the degree of power necessary to be given to that checking body, on the perfection of whose operations all the goodness of government depends, are thus pretty easily solved. The grand difficulty consists in finding the means of constituting a checking body, the powers of which shall not be turned against the community for whose protection it is created.

There can be no doubt, that, if power is granted to a body of men, called representatives, they, like any other men, will use their power, not for the advantage of the community, but for their own advantage, if they can. The only question is, therefore, how they can be prevented? In other words, how are the interests of the representatives to be identified with those of the community?

Each representative may be considered in two capacities; in his capacity of representative, in which he has the exercise of power over others, and in his capacity of member of the community, in which others have the exercise of power over him.

If things were so arranged, that, in his capacity of representative, it would be impossible for him to do himself so much good by misgovernment, as he would do himself harm in his capacity of member of the community, the object would be accomplished. We have already seen, that the amount of power assigned to the checking body cannot be diminished beyond a certain amount. It must be sufficient to overcome all resistance on the part of all those in whose hands the powers of government are lodged. But if the power assigned to the representative cannot be diminished in amount, there is only one other way in which it can be diminished, and that is, in duration.

This, then, is the instrument; lessening of duration is the instrument by which, if by anything, the object is to be attained. The smaller the period of time during which any man retains his capacity of representative, as compared with the time in which he is simply a member of the community, the more difficult it will be to compensate the sacrifice of the interests of the longer period, by the profits of misgovernment during the shorter.

[Source: James Mill, *Essay on Government* (1820), reprinted from the Supplement to the *Encyclopaedia Britannica*, London 1828, pp.16–17, 18.]

Doc. 22. JOHN STUART MILL: 'That the Ideally Best Form of Government is Representative Government'

There is no difficulty in showing that the ideally best form of government is that in which the sovereignty, or supreme controlling power in the last resort, is vested in the entire aggregate of the community; every citizen not only having a voice in the exercise of that ultimate sovereignty, but being, at least occasionally, called on to take an actual part in the government, by the personal discharge of some public function, local or general.

To test this proposition, it has to be examined in reference to the two branches into which, as pointed out in the last chapter, the inquiry into the goodness of a government conveniently divides itself, namely, how far it promotes the good management of the affairs of society by means of the existing faculties, moral, intellectual, and active, of its various members, and what is its effect in improving or deteriorating those faculties.

The ideally best form of government, it is scarcely necessary to say,

B. Classical liberalism

does not mean one which is practicable or eligible in all states of civilisation, but the one which, in the circumstances in which it is practicable and eligible, is attended with the greatest amount of beneficial consequences, immediate and prospective. A completely popular government is the only polity which can make out any claim to this character. It is pre-eminent in both the departments between which the excellence of a political constitution is divided. It is both more favourable to present good government, and promotes a better and higher form of national character, than any other polity whatsoever.

Its superiority in reference to present well-being rests upon two principles, of as universal truth and applicability as any general propositions which can be laid down respecting human affairs. The first is, that the rights and interests of every or any person are only secure from being disregarded when the person interested is himself able, and habitually disposed, to stand up for them. The second is, that the general prosperity attains a greater height, and is more widely diffused, in proportion to the amount and variety of the personal energies enlisted in promoting it.

Putting these two propositions into a shape more special to their present application; human beings are only secure from evil at the hands of others in proportion as they have the power of being, and are, self-*protecting*; and they only achieve a high degree of success in their struggle with Nature in proportion as they are self-*dependent*, relying on what they themselves can do, either separately or in concert, rather than on what others do for them.

The former proposition − that each is the only safe guardian of his own rights and interests − is one of those elementary maxims of prudence, which every person, capable of conducting his own affairs, implicitly acts upon, wherever he himself is interested. Many, indeed, have a great dislike to it as a political doctrine, and are fond of holding it up to obloquy, as a doctrine of universal selfishness. To which we may answer, that whenever it ceases to be true that mankind, as a rule, prefer themselves to others, and those nearest to them to those more remote, from that moment Communism is not only practicable, but the only defensible form of society; and will, when that time arrives, be assuredly carried into effect. For my own part, not believing in universal selfishness, I have no difficulty in admitting that Communism would even now be practicable among the *élite* of mankind, and may become so among the rest. But as this opinion is anything but popular with those defenders of existing institutions who find fault with the doctrine of the general predominance of self-interest, I am inclined to think they do in reality believe that most men consider themselves before other people. It is not, however, necessary to affirm even thus much in order to support the claim of all to participate in the sovereign power. We need not suppose that when power resides in an exclusive class, that class will knowingly and deliberately sacrifice the other classes to themselves: it

304

suffices that, in the absence of its natural defenders, the interest of the excluded is always in danger of being overlooked; and, when looked at, is seen with very different eyes from those of the persons whom it directly concerns. In this country, for example, what are called the working classes may be considered as excluded from all direct participation in the government. I do not believe that the classes who do participate in it have in general any intention of sacrificing the working classes to themselves. They once had that intention; witness the persevering attempts so long made to keep down wages by law. But in the present day their ordinary disposition is the very opposite: they willingly make considerable sacrifices, especially of their pecuniary interest, for the benefit of the working classes, and err rather by too lavish and indiscriminating beneficence; nor do I believe that any rulers in history have been actuated by a more sincere desire to do their duty towards the poorer portion of their countrymen. Yet does Parliament, or almost any of the members composing it, ever for an instant look at any question with the eyes of a working man? When a subject arises in which the labourers as such have an interest, is it regarded from any point of view but that of the employers of labour? I do not say that the working men's view of these questions is in general nearer to the truth than the other: but it is sometimes quite as near; and in any case it ought to be respectfully listened to, instead of being, as it is, not merely turned away from, but ignored. On the question of strikes, for instance, it is doubtful if there is so much as one among the leading members of either House who is not firmly convinced that the reason of the matter is unqualifiedly on the side of the masters, and that the men's view of it is simply absurd. Those who have studied the question know well how far this is from being the case; and in how different, and how infinitely less superficial a manner the point would have to be argued, if the classes who strike were able to make themselves heard in Parliament.

It is an adherent condition of human affairs that no intention, however sincere, of protecting the interests of others can make it safe or salutary to tie up their own hands. Still more obviously true is it, that by their own hands only can any positive and durable improvement of their circumstances in life be worked out. Through the joint influence of these two principles, all free communities have both been more exempt from social injustice and crime, and have attained more brilliant prosperity, than any others, or than they themselves after they lost their freedom. Contrast the free states of the world, while their freedom lasted, with the contemporary subjects of monarchical or oligarchical despotism: the Greek cities with the Persian satrapies; the Italian republics and the free towns of Flanders and Germany, with the feudal monarchies of Europe; Switzerland, Holland, and England, with Austria or ante-revolutionary France. Their superior prosperity was too obvious ever to have been gainsaid: while their superiority in good government and social relations is proved by the prosperity, and is manifest besides in every page of history. If we compare, not one age with another, but the different governments which co-existed in the same age, no amount of disorder which exaggeration itself can pretend to have existed amidst the publicity of the free states can be compared for a moment with the contemptuous trampling upon the mass of the people which pervaded the whole life of the monarchical countries, or the disgusting individual tyranny which was of more than daily occurrence under the systems of plunder which they called fiscal arrangements, and in the secrecy of their frightful courts of justice.

It must be acknowledged that the benefits of freedom, so far as they have hitherto been enjoyed, were obtained by the extension of its privileges to a part only of the community; and that a government in which they are extended impartially to all is a desideratum still unrealised. But though every approach to this has an independent value, and in many cases more than an approach could not, in the existing state of general improvement, be made, the participation of all in these benefits is the ideally perfect conception of free government. In proportion as any, no matter who, are excluded from it, the interests of the excluded are left without the guarantee accorded to the rest, and they themselves have less scope and encouragement than they might otherwise have to that exertion of their energies for the good of themselves and of the community, to which the general prosperity is always proportioned.

Thus stands the case as regards present well-being; the good management of the affairs of the existing generation. If we now pass to the influence of the form of government upon character, we shall find the superiority of popular government over every other to be, if possible, still more decided and indisputable.

This question really depends upon a still more fundamental one, viz., which of two common types of character, for the general good of humanity, it is most desirable should predominate – the active, or the passive type; that which struggles against evils, or that which endures them; that which bends to circumstances, or that which endeavours to make circumstances bend to itself.

The commonplace of moralists, and the general sympathies of mankind, are in favour of the passive type. Energetic characters may be admired, but the acquiescent and submissive are those which most men personally prefer. The passiveness of our neighbours increases our sense of security, and plays into the hands of our wilfulness. Passive characters, if we do not happen to need their activity, seem an obstruction the less in our own path. A contented character is not a dangerous rival. Yet nothing is more certain than that improvement in human affairs is wholly the work of the uncontented characters; and, moreover, that it is much easier for an active mind to acquire the virtues of patience than for a passive one to assume those of energy.

Of the three varieties of mental excellence, intellectual, practical and moral, there never could be any doubt in regard to the first two which side had the advantage. All intellectual superiority is the fruit of active effort. Enterprise, the desire to keep moving, to be trying and accomplishing new things for our own benefit or that of others, is the parent even of speculative, and much more of practical talent. The intellectual culture compatible with the other type is of that feeble and vague description which belongs to a mind that stops at amusement, or at simple contemplation. The test of real and vigorous thinking, the thinking which ascertains truths instead of dreaming dreams, is successful application to practice. Where that purpose does not exist, to give definiteness, precision, and an intelligible meaning to thought, it generates nothing better than the mystical metaphysics of the Pythagoreans or the Vedas. With respect to practical improvement, the case is still more evident. The character which improves human life is that which struggles with natural powers and tendencies, not that which gives way to them. The self-benefiting qualities are all on the side of the active and energetic character: and the habits and conduct which promote the advantage of each individual member of the community must be at least a part of those which conduce most in the end to the advancement of the community as a whole . . .

Now there can be no kind of doubt that the passive type of character is favoured by the government of one or a few, and the active self-helping type by that of the Many. Irresponsible rulers need the quiescence of the ruled more than they need any activity but that which they can compel. Submissiveness to the prescriptions of men as necessities of nature is the lesson inculcated by all governments upon those who are wholly without participation in them. The will of superiors, and the law as the will of superiors, must be passively yielded to. But no men are mere instruments or materials in the hands of their rulers who have will or spirit or a spring of internal activity in the rest of their proceedings: and any manifestation of these qualities, instead of receiving encouragement from despots, has to get itself forgiven by them. Even when irresponsible rulers are not sufficiently conscious of danger from the mental activity of their subjects to be desirous of repressing it, the position itself is a repression. Endeavour is even more effectually restrained by the certainty of its importance than by any positive discouragement. Between subjection to the will of others, and the virtues of self-help and self-government, there is a natural incompatibility. This is more or less complete, according as the bondage is strained or relaxed. Rulers differ very much in the length to which they carry the control of the free agency of their subjects, or the supersession of it by managing their business for them. But the difference is in degree, not in principle; and the best despots often go the greatest lengths in chaining up the free agency of their subjects. A bad despot, when his own personal indulgences have been provided for, may sometimes be willing to let the people alone; but a good despot insists on doing them good, by making them do their own business in a better way than they themselves know of. The regulations which restricted to fixed processes all the leading branches of French manufactures were the work of the Great Colbert.

Very different is that state of the human faculties where a human being feels himself under no other external restraint than the necessities of nature, or mandates of society which he has his share in imposing, and which it is open to him, if he thinks them wrong, publicly to dissent from, and exert himself actively to get altered. No doubt, under a government partially popular, this freedom may be exercised even by those who are not partakers in the full privileges of citizenship. But it is a great additional stimulus to any one's self-help and self-reliance when he starts from even ground, and has not to feel that his success depends on the impression he can make upon the sentiments and dispositions of a body of whom he is not one. It is a great discouragement to an individual, and a still greater one to a class, to be left out of the constitution; to be reduced to plead from outside the door to the arbiters of their destiny, not taken into consultation within. The maximum of the invigorating effect of freedom upon the character is only obtained when the person acted on either is, or is looking forward to becoming, a citizen as fully privileged as any other. What is still more important than even this matter of feeling is the practical discipline which the character obtains from the occasional demand made upon the citizens to exercise, for a time and in their turn, some social function. It is not sufficiently considered how little there is in most men's ordinary life to give any largeness either to their conceptions or to their sentiments. Their work is a routine; not a labour of love, but of self-interest in the most elementary form, the satisfaction of daily wants; neither the thing done, nor the process of doing it, introduces the mind to thoughts or feelings extending beyond individuals; if instructive books are within their reach, there is no stimulus to read them; and in most cases the individual has no access to any person of cultivation much superior to his own. Giving him something to do for the public, supplies, in a measure, all these deficiencies. If circumstances allow the amount of public duty assigned him to be considerable, it makes him an educated man. Notwithstanding the defects of the social system and moral ideas of antiquity, the practice of the dicastery and the ecclesia raised the intellectual standard of an average Athenian citizen far beyond anything of which there is yet an example in any other mass of men, ancient or modern. The proofs of this are apparent in every page of our great historian of Greece; but we need scarcely look further than to the high quality of the addresses which their great orators deemed best calculated to act with effect on their understanding and will. A benefit of the same kind, though far less in degree, is produced on Englishmen of the lower middle class by their liability to be placed on juries and to serve parish offices; which, though it does not occur to so many, nor is so continuous, nor introduces them to so great a variety of elevated considerations, as to admit of comparison with the public education which every citizen of Athens obtained from her democratic institutions, must make them nevertheless very different beings, in range of ideas and development of faculties, from those who have done nothing in their lives but drive a quill, or sell goods over a counter. Still more salutary is the moral part of the instruction afforded by the participation of the private citizen, if even rarely, in public functions. He is called upon, while so engaged, to weigh interests not his own; to be guided, in case of conflicting claims, by another rule than his private partialities; to apply, at every turn, principles and maxims which have for their reason of existence the common good: and he usually finds associated with him in the same work minds more familiarised than his own with these ideas and operations, whose study it will be to supply reasons to his understanding, and stimulation to his feeling for the general interest. He is made to feel himself one of the public, and whatever is for their benefit to be for his benefit. Where this school of public spirit does not exist, scarcely any sense is entertained that private persons, in no eminent social situation, owe any duties to society, except to obey the laws and submit to the government. There is no unselfish sentiment of identification with the public. Every thought or feeling, either of interest or of duty, is absorbed in the individual and in the family. The man never thinks of any collective interest, of any objects to be pursued jointly with others, but only in competition with them, and in some measure at their expense. A neighbour, not being an ally or an associate, since he is never engaged in any common undertaking for joint benefit, is therefore only a rival. Thus even private morality suffers, while public is actually extinct. Were this the universal and only possible state of things, the utmost aspirations of the lawgiver or the moralist could only stretch to make the bulk of the community a flock of sheep innocently nibbling the grass side by side.

From these accumulated considerations it is evident that the only government which can fully satisfy all the exigencies of the social state is one in which the whole people participate; that any participation even in the smallest public function, is useful; that the participation should everywhere be as great as the general degree of improvement of the community will allow; and that nothing less can be ultimately desirable than the admission of all to a share in the sovereign power of the state. But since all cannot, in a community exceeding a single small town, participate personally in any but some very minor portions of the public business, it follows that the ideal type of a perfect government must be representative.

[Source: John Stuart Mill, *Representative Government* in the Everyman's Library edition of *Utilitarianism, Liberty and Representative Government*, London 1948, Ch. 3, pp. 207–12, 215–18.]

---

2. Economic liberalism: documents
(Introduction, p. 250)

(i) Free trade and *laissez faire* in Britain

Doc. 23. DAVID RICARDO: On Foreign Trade and the Benefits to be Derived from Free Trade

No extension of foreign trade will immediately increase the amount of value in a country, although it will very powerfully contribute to increase the mass of commodities, and therefore the sum of enjoyments. As the value of all foreign goods is measured by the quantity of the produce of our land and labour, which is given in exchange for them, we should have no greater value, if by the discovery of new markets, we obtained double the quantity of foreign goods in exchange for a given quantity of our's . . .

It is not, therefore, in consequence of the extension of the market that the rate of profit is raised, although such extension may be equally efficacious in increasing the mass of commodities, and may thereby enable us to augment the funds destined for the maintenance of labour, and the materials on which labour may be employed. It is quite as important to the happiness of mankind, that our enjoyments should be increased by the better distribution of labour, by each country producing those commodities for which by its situation, its climate, and its other natural or artificial advantages it is adapted, and by their exchanging them for the commodities of other countries, as that they should be augmented by a rise in the rate of profits.

It has been my endeavour to show throughout this work, that the rate of profits can never be increased but by a fall in wages, and that there can be no permanent fall of wages but in consequence of a fall of the necessaries on which wages are expended. If, therefore, by the extension of foreign trade, or by improvements in machinery, the food and necessaries of the labourer can be brought to market at a reduced price, profits will rise. If, instead of growing our own corn, or manufacturing the clothing and other necessaries of the labourer, we discover a new market from which we can supply ourselves with these commodities at a cheaper price, wages will fall and profits rise; but if the commodities obtained at a cheaper rate, by the extension of foreign commerce, or by the improvement of machinery, be exclusively the commodities consumed by the rich, no alteration will take place in the rate of profits. The rate of wages would not be affected, although wine, velvets, silks, and other expensive commodities, should fall 50 per cent., and consequently profits would continue unaltered.

Foreign trade, then, though highly beneficial to a country, as it increases the amount and variety of the objects on which revenue may be expended, and affords, by the abundance and cheapness of commodities incentives to saving, and to the accumulation of capital, has no tendency to raise the profits of stock, unless the commodities imported be of that description on which the wages of labour are expended.

The remarks which have been made respecting foreign trade, apply equally to home trade. The rate of profits is never increased by a better distribution of labour, by the invention of machinery, by the establishment of roads and canals, or by any means of abridging labour either in the manufacture or in the conveyance of goods. These are causes which operate on price, and never fail to be highly beneficial to consumers; since they enable them with the same labour, or with the value of the produce of the same labour, to obtain in exchange a greater quantity of the commodity to which the improvement is applied; but they have no effect whatever on profit. On the other hand, every diminution in the wages of labour raises profits, but produces no effect on the price of commodities. One is advantageous to all classes, for all classes are consumers; the other is beneficial only to producers; they gain more, but every thing remains at its former price. In the first case, they get the same as before; but every thing on which their gains are expended, is diminished in exchangeable value.

The same rule which regulates the relative value of commodities in one country, does not regulate the relative value of the commodities exchanged between two or more countries.

Under a system of perfectly free commerce, each country naturally devotes its capital and labour to such employments as are most beneficial to each. This pursuit of individual advantage is admirably connected with the universal good of the whole. By stimulating industry, by rewarding ingenuity, and by using most efficaciously the peculiar powers bestowed by nature, it distributes labour most effectively and most economically: while, by increasing the general mass of productions, it diffuses general benefit, and binds together by one common tie of interest and intercourse, the universal society of nations throughout the civilized world. It is this principle which determines that wine shall be made in France and Portugal, that corn shall be grown in America and Poland, and that hardware and other goods shall be manufactured in England.

In one and the same country, profits are, generally speaking, always on the same level; or differ only as the employment of capital may be more or less secure and agreeable. It is not so between different countries. If the profits of capital employed in Yorkshire, should exceed those of capital employed in London, capital would speedily move from London to Yorkshire, and an equality of profits would be effected; but if in consequence of the diminished rate of production in the lands of England, from the increase of capital and population, wages should rise, and profits fall, it would not follow that capital and population would

B. Classical liberalism

necessarily move from England to Holland, or Spain, or Russia, where
profits might be higher.

If Portugal had no commercial connexion with other countries, instead
of employing a great part of her capital and industry in the production of
wines, with which she purchases for her own use the cloth and hardware
of other countries, she would be obliged to devote a part of that capital to
the manufacture of those commodities, which she would thus obtain
probably inferior in quality as well as quantity.

The quantity of wine which she shall give in exchange for the cloth of
England, is not determined by the respective quantities of labour devoted
to the production of each, as it would be, if both commodities were
manufactured in England, or both in Portugal . . .

. . . The labour of 100 Englishmen cannot be given for that of 80
Englishmen, but the produce of the labour of 100 Englishmen may be
given for the produce of the labour of 80 Portuguese, 60 Russians, or 120
East Indians. The difference in this respect, between a single country and
many, is easily accounted for, by considering the difficulty with which
capital moves from one country to another, to seek a more profitable
employment, and the activity with which it invariably passes from one
province to another in the same country.

It would undoubtedly be advantageous to the capitalists of England,
and to the consumers in both countries, that under such circumstances,
the wine and the cloth should both be made in Portugal, and therefore
that the capital and labour of England employed in making cloth, should
be removed to Portugal for that purpose. In that case, the relative value
of these commodities would be regulated by the same principle, as if one
were the produce of Yorkshire, and the other of London; and in every
other case, if capital freely flowed towards these countries where it could
be most profitably employed, there could be no difference in the rate of
profit, and no other difference in the real or labour price of commodities,
than the additional quantity of labour required to convey them to the
various markets where they were to be sold.

Experience, however, shews that the fancied or real insecurity of
capital, when not under the immediate control of its owner, together with
the natural disinclination which every man has to quit the country of his
birth and connexions, and intrust himself with all his habits fixed, to a
strange government and new laws, check the emigration of capital. These
feelings, which I should be sorry to see weakened, induce most men of
property to be satisfied with a low rate of profits in their own country,
rather than seek a more advantageous employment for their wealth in
foreign nations.

Gold and silver having been chosen for the general medium of circulation, they are, by the competition of commerce, distributed in such
proportions amongst the different countries of the world, as to accommodate themselves to the natural traffic which would take place if no

312

such metals existed, and the trade between countries were purely a trade of barter.

Thus, cloth cannot be imported into Portugal, unless it sell there for more gold than it cost in the country from which it was imported; and wine cannot be imported into England, unless it will sell for more than it cost in Portugal. If the trade were purely a trade of barter, it could only continue whilst England could make cloth so cheap as to obtain a greater quantity of wine with a given quantity of labour, by manufacturing cloth than by growing vines; and also whilst the industry of Portugal were attended by the reverse effects . . .

It is thus that the money of each country is apportioned to it in such quantities only as may be necessary to regulate a profitable trade of barter. England exported cloth in exchange for wine, because by so doing, her industry was rendered more productive to her; she had more cloth and wine than if she had manufactured both for herself; and Portugal imported cloth, and exported wine, because the industry of Portugal could be more beneficially employed for both countries in producing wine. Let there be more difficulty in England in producing cloth, or in Portugal in producing wine, or let there be more facility in England in producing wine, or in Portugal in producing cloth, and the trade must immediately cease.

No change whatever takes place in the circumstances of Portugal; but England finds that she can employ her labour more productively in the manufacture of wine, and instantly the trade of barter between the two countries changes. Not only is the exportation of wine from Portugal stopped, but a new distribution of the precious metals takes place, and her importation of cloth is also prevented.

Both countries would probably find it their interest to make their own wine and their own cloth; but this singular result would take place: in England, though wine would be cheaper, cloth would be elevated in price, more would be paid for it by the consumer; while in Portugal the consumers, both of cloth and wine, would be able to purchase those commodities cheaper. In the country where the improvement was made, prices would be enhanced; in that where no change had taken place, but where they had been deprived of a profitable branch of foreign trade, prices would fall.

This, however, is only a seeming advantage to Portugal, for the quantity of cloth and wine together produced in that country would be diminished, while the quantity produced in England would be increased. Money would in some degree have changed its value in the two countries – it would be lowered in England, and raised in Portugal. Estimated in money, the whole revenue of Portugal would be diminished; estimated in the same medium, the whole revenue of England would be increased.

Thus then it appears, that the improvement of a manufacture in any country tends to alter the distribution of the precious metals amongst the

313

B. Classical liberalism

nations of the world: it tends to increase the quantity of commodities, at the same time that it raises general prices in the country where the improvement takes place.

To simplify the question, I have been supposing the trade between two countries to be confined to two commodities, to wine and cloth, but it is well known that many and various articles enter into the list of exports and imports. By the abstraction of money from one country, and the accumulation of it in another, all commodities are affected in price, and consequently encouragement is given to the exportation of many more commodities besides money, which will therefore prevent so great an effect from taking place on the value of money in the two countries, as might otherwise be expected.

Besides the improvements in arts and machinery, there are various other causes which are constantly operating on the natural course of trade, and which interfere with the equilibrium, and the relative value of money. Bounties on exportation or importation, new taxes on commodities, sometimes by their direct, and at other times by their indirect operation, disturb the natural trade of barter, and produce a consequent necessity of importing or exporting money, in order that prices may be accommodated to the natural course of commerce; and this effect is produced not only in the country where the disturbing cause takes place, but, in a greater or less degree, in every country of the commercial world.

This will in some measure account for the different value of money in different countries; it will explain to us why the prices of home commodities, and those of great bulk, though of comparatively small value, are, independently of other causes, higher in those countries where manufactures flourish. Of two countries having precisely the same population, and the same quantity of land of equal fertility in cultivation, with the same knowledge too of agriculture, the prices of raw produce will be highest in that where the greater skill, and the better machinery is used in the manufacture of exportable commodities. The rate of profits will probably differ but little; for wages, or the real reward of the labourer, may be the same in both; but those wages, as well as raw produce, will be rated higher in money in that country, into which, from the advantages attending their skill and machinery, an abundance of money is imported in exchange for their goods.

Of these two countries, if one had the advantage in the manufacture of goods of one quality, and the other in the manufacture of goods of another quality, there would be no decided influx of the precious metals into either; but if the advantage very heavily preponderated in favour of either, that effect would be inevitable.

[Source: David Ricardo, *On the Principles of Political Economy and Taxation. The Works and Correspondence of David Ricardo*, ed. Piero Sraffa with the collaboration of M. H. Dobb, Cambridge 1953, I, pp. 128, 132–7, 140–2.]

314

Doc. 24. RICHARD COBDEN: Free Trade and the Argument against the Corn Laws (Speech in London, 8 February, 1844)

Now, we are 'Free Traders,' and what is Free Trade? Not the pulling down of all custom houses, as some of our wise opponents the dukes and earls have lately been trying to persuade the agricultural labourers; ... By Free Trade we mean the abolition of all protective duties. It is very possible that our children, or at all events their offspring, may be wise enough to dispense with custom-houses altogether. They may think it prudent and economical to raise their revenues by direct taxation, without circumventing their foreign trade. We do not propose that; ...

Now, what are the objections alleged against the adoption of Free-trade principles? First of all, take the most numerous body – the working class – by far the most important in the consideration of this question: for probably nine-tenths of all the population of this country are dependent on labour, either the hard work of hands, or the equally hard toil of heads. I say, take their case first. We are told this system of restriction is for the benefit of the labourers. We are informed by the earls, dukes, and the squires, that the price of corn regulates the rate of wages; and that, if we reduce the price of corn by a free trade in that article, we shall only bring down the rate of wages. Now, I see a good many working people in this assembly, and would ask them whether, in any bargain ever made for labour in London, the question of corn or its price was ever made an element in that agreement? ...

Now, the first and greatest count in my indictment against the Corn-law is, that it is an injustice to the labourers of this and every other country. My next charge is, that it is a fraud against every man of capital engaged in any pursuit, and every person of fixed income not derived from land ...

Why, then, do you look at this monopoly of corn with such complacency? Simply because you and I and the rest of us have a superstitious reverence for the owners of those sluggish acres, and have a very small respect for ourselves and our own vocation ...

What are the grounds on which this system is maintained? The farmer is put forward – the interests of the farmer and the farm-labourer are put forward – as the pretext for maintaining this monopoly. I have heard the admission made at agricultural meetings by landlords themselves, that there are twenty farmers bidding for every farm, and that they excuse themselves to the farmers at these very meetings that they let their land at the full value, and they cannot help it. It is not their fault because there are these twenty farmers bidding for every farm that is vacant. Now, I would ask you, or the merest tyro in this question, if there be twenty farmers bidding for every farm, and the law can raise the price of the produce of that farm, do you think that one out of those twenty farmers will get the benefit of that rise in price? Will not the other nineteen take

315

care that it is brought down by competition to the ordinary profit of trade in this country? The farmers have been too long deluded by the mere cry of 'protection' ... It is destruction to the farmers ...·

With respect to the farm-labourers, our opponents tell us that our object in bringing about the repeal of the Corn-law is, by reducing the price of corn, to lower the rate of their wages. I can only answer upon this point for the manufacturing districts; but, as far as they are concerned, I state it most emphatically as a truth, that, for the last twenty years, whenever corn has been cheap wages have been high in Lancashire; and, on the other hand, when bread has been dear wages have been greatly reduced. Now, I distinctly put this statement on record, and challenge anyone to controvert it. Wages may possibly be affected by the price of food in the agricultural districts, and rise and fall in proportion; but if they do, it is simply for this reason – that they have reached their minimum, on the point at which they verge towards what you might call slave labour, when a man gets in the best of times only as much as will keep him in health ... Now, let me be fully understood as to what Free Traders really do want. We do not want cheap corn merely in order that we may have low money prices. What we desire is plenty of corn, and we are utterly careless what its price is, provided we obtain it at the natural price. All we ask is this, that corn shall follow the same law which the monopolists in food admit that labour must follow; that 'it shall find its natural level in the markets of the world.'

And now, what would be the process of this equalisation of prices? I think I can give you the rationale of it. The effect of free trade in corn will be this. It would increase the demand for agricultural produce in Poland, Germany, and America. That increase in the demand for agricultural produce would give rise to an increased demand for labour in those countries, which would tend to raise the wages of the agricultural labourers. The effect of that would be to draw away labourers from manufactures in all those places. To pay for that corn, more manufactures would be required from this country; this would lead to an increased demand for labour in the manufacturing districts, which would necessarily be attended with a rise in wages, in order that the goods might be made for the purpose of exchanging for the corn brought from abroad. Whether prices would be equalised, ... by a rise in the price of bread abroad to the level at which it is here, or whether it would be by a fall in the prices here to the level at which they now exist on the Continent, would not make the least earthly difference to the Free Traders; all they ask is, that they shall be put in the same position with others, and that there should be no bar or hindrance to the admission of food from any quarter into this country ...

I would ask you, if you can set more people to work at better wages – if you can clear your streets of those spectres which are now haunting your thoroughfares begging their daily bread – if you can depopulate your workhouses, and clear off the two millions of paupers which now exist in the land, and put them to work at productive industry – do you not think that they would consume some of the wheat as well as you; and may not they be, as we are now, consumers of wheaten bread by millions, instead of existing on their present miserable dietary? ...

[Source: *Speeches on Questions of Public Policy by Richard Cobden M.P.*, ed. John Bright and James E. Thorold Rogers, London 1880, pp.58–62.]

Doc. 25. JOHN STUART MILL: The Grounds and Limits of the Laisser-faire or Non-Interference Principle

1. We must set out by distinguishing between two kinds of intervention by the government, which, though they may relate to the same subject, differ widely in their nature and effects, and require, for their justification, motives of a very different degree of urgency. The intervention may extend to controlling the free agency of individuals. Government may interdict all persons from doing certain things; or from doing them without its authorization; or may prescribe to them certain things to be done, or a certain manner of doing things which is left optional with them to do or to abstain from. This is the *authoritative* interference of government. There is another kind of intervention which is not authoritative: when a government, instead of issuing a command and enforcing it by penalties, adopts the course so seldom resorted to by governments, and of which such important use might be made, that of giving advice, and promulgating information; or when, leaving individuals free to use their own means of pursuing any objective of general interest, the government, not meddling with them, but not trusting the object solely to their care, establishes, side by side with their arrangements, an agency of its own for a like purpose. Thus, it is one thing to maintain a Church Establishment, and another to refuse toleration to other religions, or to persons professing no religion. It is one thing to provide schools or colleges, and another to require that no person shall act as an instructor of youth without a government license. There might be a national bank, or a government manufactory, without any monopoly against private banks and manufactories. There might be a post-office, without penalties against the conveyance of letters by other means. There may be a corps of government engineers for civil purposes, while the profession of a civil engineer is free to be adopted by every one. There may be public hospitals, without any restriction upon private medical or surgical practice.

2. It is evident, even at first sight, that the authoritative form of government intervention has a much more limited sphere of legitimate action than the other. It requires a much stronger necessity to justify it in

any case; while there are large departments of human life from which it must be unreservedly and imperiously excluded. Whatever theory we adopt respecting the foundation of the social union, and under whatever political institutions we live, there is a circle around every individual human being, which no government, be it that of one, of a few, or of the many, ought to be permitted to overstep: there is a part of the life of every person who has come to the years of discretion, within which the individuality of that person ought to reign uncontrolled either by any other individual or by the public collectively. That there is, or ought to be, some space in human existence thus entrenched around, and sacred from authoritative intrusion, no one who professes the smallest regard to human freedom or dignity will call in question: the point to be determined is, where the limit should be placed; how large a province of human life this reserved territory should include. I apprehend that it ought to include all that part which concerns only the life, whether inward or outward, of the individual, and does not affect the interests of others, or affects them only through the moral influence of example. With respect to the domain of the inward consciousness, the thoughts and feelings, and as much of external conduct as is personal only, involving no consequences, none at least of a painful or injurious kind, to other people; I hold that it is allowable in all, and in the more thoughtful and cultivated often a duty, to assert and promulgate, with all the force they are capable of, their opinion of what is good or bad, admirable or contemptible, but not to compel others to conform to that opinion; whether the force used is that of extra-legal coercion, or exerts itself by means of the law.

Even in those portions of conduct which do not affect the interest of others, the onus of making out a case always lies on the defenders of legal prohibitions. It is not a merely constructive or presumptive injury to others which will justify the interference of law with individual freedom. To be prevented from doing what one is inclined to, or from acting according to one's own judgment of what is desirable, is not only always irksome, but always tends, *pro tanto*, to starve the development of some portion of the bodily or mental faculties, either sensitive or active; and unless the conscience of the individual goes freely with the legal restraint, it partakes, either in a great or in a small degree, of the degradation of slavery. Scarcely any degree of utility, short of absolute necessity, will justify a prohibitory regulation, unless it can also be made to recommend itself to the general conscience; unless persons of ordinary good intentions either believe already, or can be induced to believe, that the thing prohibited is a thing which they ought not to wish to do.

It is otherwise with governmental interferences which do not restrain individual free agency. When a government provides means for fulfilling a certain end, leaving individuals free to avail themselves of different means if in their opinion preferable, there is no infringement of liberty, no irksome or degrading restraint. One of the principal objections to government interference is then absent. There is however, in almost all forms of government agency, one thing which is compulsory; the provision of the pecuniary means. These are derived from taxation; or, if existing in the form of an endowment derived from public property, they are still the cause of as much compulsory taxation as the sale or the annual proceeds of the property would enable to be dispensed with.* And the objection necessarily attaching to compulsory contributions, is almost always greatly aggravated by the expensive precautions and onerous restrictions which are indispensable to prevent evasion of a compulsory tax.

3. A second general objection to government agency is that every increase of the functions devolving on the government is an increase of its power, both in the form of authority, and still more, in the indirect form of influence. The importance of this consideration, in respect to political freedom, has in general been quite sufficiently recognized, at least in England; but many, in latter times, have been prone to think that limitation of the powers of the government is only essential when the government itself is badly constituted; when it does not represent the people, but is the organ of a class, or coalition of classes: and that a government of sufficiently popular constitution might be trusted with any amount of power over the nation, since its power would be only that of the nation over itself. This might be true, if the nation, in such cases, did not practically mean a mere majority of the nation, and if minorities were only capable of oppressing, but not of being oppressed. Experience, however, proves that the depositaries of power who are mere delegates of the people, that is of a majority, are quite as ready (when they think they can count on popular support) as any organs of oligarchy, to assume arbitrary power, and encroach unduly on the liberty of private life. The public collectively is abundantly ready to impose, not only its generally narrow views of its interests, but its abstract opinions, and even its tastes, as laws binding upon individuals. And the present civilization tends so strongly to make the power of persons acting in masses the only substantial power in society, that there never was more necessity for surrounding individual independence of thought, speech, and conduct, with the most powerful defences, in order to maintain that originality of mind and individuality of character, which are the only source of any real progress, and of most of the qualities which make the human race much superior to any herd of animals. Hence it is no less important in a democratic than in any other government, that all tendency on the part of public

---

* The only cases in which government agency involves nothing of a compulsory nature, are the rare cases in which, without any artificial monopoly, it pays its own expenses. A bridge built with public money, on which tolls are collected, sufficient to pay not only all current expenses, but the interest of the original outlay, is one case in point. The government railways in Belgium and Germany are another example. The Post Office, if its monopoly were abolished, and it still paid its expenses, would be another.

authorities to stretch their interference, and assume a power of any sort which can easily be dispensed with, should be regarded with unremitting jealousy. Perhaps this is even more important in a democracy than in any other form of political society; because, where public opinion is sovereign, an individual who is oppressed by the sovereign does not, as in most other states of things, find a rival power to which he can appeal for relief, or, at all events for sympathy.

4. A third general objection to government agency rests on the principle of the division of labour. Every additional function undertaken by the government, is a fresh occupation imposed upon a body already overcharged with duties. A natural consequence is that most things are ill done; much not done at all, because the government is not able to do it without delays which are fatal to its purpose; that the more troublesome, and less showy, of the functions undertaken, are postponed or neglected, and an excuse is always ready for the neglect; while the heads of the administration have their minds so fully taken up with official details, in however perfunctory a manner superintended, that they have no time or thought to spare for the great interests of the state, and the preparation of enlarged measures of social improvement...

5. But though a better organization of governments would greatly diminish the force of the objection to the mere multiplication of their duties, it would still remain true that in all the more advanced communities, the great majority of things are worse done by the intervention of government, than the individuals most interested in the matter would do them, or cause them to be done, if left to themselves. The grounds of this truth are expressed with tolerable exactness in the popular dictum, that people understand their own business and their own interests better, and care for them more, than the government does, or can be expected to do. This maxim holds true throughout the greatest part of the business of life, and wherever it is true we ought to condemn every kind of government intervention that conflicts with it. The inferiority of government agency, for example, in any of the common operations of industry or commerce, is proved by the fact, that it is hardly ever able to maintain itself in equal competition with individual agency, where the individuals possess the requisite degree of industrial enterprise, and can command the necessary assemblage of means. All the facilities which a government enjoys of access to information; all the means which it possesses of remunerating and therefore of commanding, the best available talent in the market – are not an equivalent for the one great disadvantage of an inferior interest in the result...

6. I have reserved for the last place one of the strongest of the reasons against the extension of government agency. Even if the government could comprehend within itself, in each department, all the most eminent intellectual capacity and active talent of the nation, it would not be the less desirable that the conduct of a large portion of the affairs of the

society should be left in the hands of the persons immediately interested in them. The business of life is an essential part of the practical education of a people; without which, book and school instruction, though most necessary and salutary, does not suffice to qualify them for conduct, and for the adaptation of means to ends ...

In proportion as the people are accustomed to manage their affairs by their own active intervention, instead of leaving them to the government, their desires will turn to repelling tyranny, rather than to tyrannizing: while in proportion as all real initiative and direction resides in the government, and individuals habitually feel and act as under its perpetual tutelage, popular institutions develop in them not the desire of freedom, but an unmeasured appetite for place and power; diverting the intelligence and activity of the country from its principal business to a wretched competition for the selfish prizes and the petty vanities of office.

7. The preceding are the principal reasons, of a general character, in favour of restricting to the narrowest compass the intervention of a public authority in the business of the community: and few will dispute the more than sufficiency of these reasons, to throw, in every instance, the burthen of making out a strong case, not on those who resist, but on those who recommend, government interference. *Laisser-faire*, in short, should be the general practice: every departure from it, unless required by some great good, is a certain evil.

[Source: John Stuart Mill, *Principles of Political Economy* (1848), ed. Sir W. J. Ashley, London 1929, Book V, Ch. 11, pp.942–5, 947–8, 950.]

Doc. 26. W. E. GLADSTONE: On Economical Government

(a) On Increasing Public Expenditure

1. An impression prevails that the public expenditure of the country is growing. That, I am glad to say, is not true at the moment when I speak ... While, however, I do not hesitate to make this statement, I am bound to say that the present high level of our expenditure is still such a level, as ought to attract the serious and careful consideration of the House. It is a higher level than can be borne by the people, even in their present state, with comfort and satisfaction. It has been borne with exemplary patience; but it is too high to be borne with comfort. It is plainly higher than is compatible with perfect health and soundness in a financial point of view; for, if it were compatible with perfect health and soundness, I should be asking you to let me begin the year with a sensible surplus, and not with a barely equalized income and expenditure. Whether there is a fault chargeable on anyone in the state of things which I am describing, and to whom that fault belongs, are matters which it is entirely un-

B. Classical liberalism

necessary at the present moment to examine. But, as to the causes, I take them to be the following. In the first place, the greatness of our expenditure is due in some considerable degree to the growth of the real permanent wants of the country: of wants, which it is desirable to supply, and to which if you were to deny fitting satisfaction, you would be doing great public mischief. In the second place, it has been due to apprehensions prevailing with respect to the security of the country, and to a natural anxiety to make full provision for placing that security beyond doubt. In the third place, it is impossible that there should not be some description of relation between the state of establishments and of expenditure in other countries generally, and the state of establishments, and of expenditure, in this country. In the fourth place – and this is the point to which of all I am most anxious to call the attention of the Committee – it is due to special demands, which are in substance, and in everything except the name, war demands of such extent as to give them great significance, and lying altogether and entirely outside of the ordinary demands and exigencies of the public service[1]... With respect to the state of establishments and expenditure abroad, I do not know whether hon. Members ... have fully comprehended what a race the Governments of the world are running, and at what a fearful pace, outside of England, national obligations, in other words national deficits and national debts, are now in the course of accumulation ... This is not a matter, I admit, which will afford a justification for any folly of ours. It is of secondary moment in our discussions; but still it is of considerable weight and interest. We do not deserve any sort of credit for not having made a similar addition to our debt. We have sown our wild oats long ago. The state of this country with reference to its disposition to bear taxation has long warned and admonished us, for all time coming, that pranks like these, here at least, must not be played by legislatures or by statesmen.

(Speech in the House of Commons, 3 April 1862)

2. All these causes of increase in the public expenditure were definite in their character, and easily traceable in their effects: but I should not do full justice to the elucidation of the case if I failed to add, that together with these causes another cause came into operation, which is less easy to follow and detect, but which is pretty certain to exercise a powerful influence at periods when, from whatever reason, a vast and sudden increase of public expenditure may occur. I mean this – that together with the called-for increase of expenditure there grows up what may be termed a spirit of expenditure; a desire, a tendency prevailing in the country, which, insensibly and unconsciously perhaps, but really, affects the spirit of the people, the spirit of Parliament, the spirit of the public Departments, and perhaps, even the spirit of those, whose duty it is to submit the Estimates to Parliament, and who are most specially and directly responsible for the disbursements of the State. When this spirit of

expenditure is in action, we must expect to find some relaxation of the old principles of prudence and rules for thrift, which direct and require, that whatever service is to be performed for the public should be executed in the most efficient manner, but likewise at the lowest practicable cost.

(Speech in the House of Commons, 16 April 1863)

(b) National Wealth and Public Expenditure

3. We have at our command a tolerably accurate and tolerably complete comparison, between the rate of growth in the wealth of the country and the increase in its expenditure. Between the years 1842 and 1853 the increase in her wealth was apparently at the rate of 12 per cent; and the growth of her expenditure at the rate of $8\frac{3}{4}$ per cent; while between 1853 and 1859 the natural wealth grew at the rate of $16\frac{1}{2}$; but the public expenditure, so far as it was optional and subject to the action of public opinion, rose upwards at the rate of 58 per cent.

I have troubled the Committee with these particulars, because I deemed it right to invite their attention to what is a subject of vital importance. Without stopping to inquire into the distinction between certain objects to be attained, and carelessness of cost in the methods of attaining them, I will only say the country may be right in the course which she is now taking; but, at all events, that course ought not to be taken blindfold. We ought, on the contrary, to carry along with us a clear knowledge of the proportion which our wealth bears to our expenditure, in order that we may be able to take from time to time a comprehensive view of our financial position, and have full means of measuring the policy which we ought to adopt...

I may at once venture to state frankly that I am not satified with the state of the public expenditure, and the too rapid rate of its growth. I trust, therefore, that we mean in a great degree to retrace our steps by watching for, and by turning to account, every opportunity for retrenchment. The process of retracing our steps in such a matter, however, even were it resolved upon and begun, is one which must necessarily be gradual; for, if it be not pursued with circumspection and with caution, it will serve but to aggravate the very evils which it may be intended to remove. I assume, therefore, whether the Committee concurs with the Government in the expediency of the Estimates which they have submitted, or are about to submit to the House, with a due regard to the present demands of the public service and of the national feeling, or whether it does not, still that you in either case can effect no radical change in the scale of that expenditure on which you have now, for a series of years embarked – no radical change, I mean applicable to the operations of the present year, or to the provision you will have to make for filling up the gap which yawns before you, ... and which is represented by the figures £9,400,000. There is a further question with which we have to deal; it is, whether we ought upon this occasion to say our necessities are too great, our means too narrow, to enable us to effect any commercial reforms. Such reforms are all very well, it may be contended, for seasons of fine weather, but they do not suit a period of pressure, perhaps even of alarm. That is, I know, a favourite doctrine with some classes; but against the justice of that doctrine I, for one, protest. It was not at a period of financial ease that they were commenced in 1842.[2] And upon the part of the Government I do not hesitate to say that, at an epoch so marked and signal in our financial history as the year 1860, it is their opinion that it is the duty of Parliament to take some onward steps in that career of commercial improvement which, perhaps more than any other cause, has contributed to confirm the prosperity of the country, and the security of its institutions. . . .

We must take it for granted that for the present we have attained to what may be called a high level of public expenditure, and that we are likely to remain on that high level for some time at least. Is that a reason, or is it not, why we should arrest the process of reforming the commercial legislation of the country? I say that is no reason for stopping – I say more, it is a distinct reason for persevering in that process, and for carrying it boldly and steadily to its completion. Let us, however, glance for a moment at our position. If we were, in the year 1860, to hold our hands, let us consider what aspect our procedure would bear. For seven years, under the pressure of war and of demands for increased expenditure, we have intermitted the course of commercial improvement on which we had entered with such advantage. We have now arrived at a year of unexampled financial relief as regards the charge of the public Debt, a year of which the ways and means will be enlarged by special resources, and a year which obliges us to reconsider the existing duties on tea and sugar. If, after such a period of years, on a review of a juncture like the present, we stop in 1860, will it not be supposed that our work is in our view at an end, and that we stop for ever? In truth, if this be not a fitting opportunity for endeavouring to give increased effect to the beneficial principles of your legislation, I for one, must frankly own I know not when such an opportunity will arise. But I come now to the broader view of the truth of the case. Our high taxation is not a reason for stopping short in our commercial reforms; it is, when largely viewed, rather a reason why we should persevere in them. For it is by means of these very reforms that we are enabled to bear high taxation . . .

But I do not hesitate to say that it is a mistake to suppose that the best mode of giving benefit to the labouring classes is simply to operate on the articles consumed by them. If you want to do them the *maximum* of good, you should rather operate on the articles which give them the *maximum* of employment. What is it that has brought about the great change in their position of late years? Not the mere fact that you have legislated here and there for the purpose of taking off 1d. or 2d. in the pound from some article consumed by the labouring classes. This is good as far as it goes; but it is not this which has been mainly operative in bettering their condition as it has been bettered during the last 10 or 15 years. It is that you have set more free the general course of trade; it is that you have put in action the emancipating process, that gives them the widest field and the highest rate of remuneration for their labour. Take the great change in the corn laws; it may even possibly be doubted whether, up to this time, you have given them cheaper bread; at best it has been but a trifle cheaper than before; that change, however, is a material one indeed, yet, it may almost be said, comparatively immaterial; but you have created a regular and steady trade in corn, which may be stated at £15,000,000 a year; by that trade you have created a corresponding demand for the commodities of which they are the producers, their labour being an essential and principal element in their production, and it is the enhanced price their labour thus brings, even more than the cheapened price of commodities, that forms the main benefit they receive. That is the principle of a sound political economy applicable to commercial legislation. . . .

(Speech in the House of Commons, 10 February 1860)

4. In ten years from 1842 to 1852 inclusive, the taxable income of the country, as nearly as we can make out, increased by 6 per cent; but in eight years, from 1853 to 1861, the income of the country again increased, upon the basis taken, by 20 per cent . . .

If I may presume to refer to the causes of this vast increase of wealth, I would suggest two in particular. First of all the enormous constant, rapid, and diversified development of mechanical power, and the consequent saving of labour in so many forms, and to too vast an extent, by the extension of machinery; in this, I of course include the modern means of locomotion. But the extension of machinery, by steam power and otherwise, has, speaking generally, been in active operation, together with the economy of labour it begets, for the last hundred years. There is another cause, which has been more or less actively at work during the lifetime of our generation, and which especially belongs to the history of the last twenty years. I mean the wise legislation of Parliament, which has sought for every opportunity of abolishing restrictions upon the application of capital, and the exercise of industry and skill; and has made it a principal object of its policy to give full and free scope to the energies of the British nation. To this special cause appears especially to belong most of what is peculiar in the experience of the period I have named, as far as regards the increase of the national wealth.

(Speech in the House of Commons, 16 April 1863)

[Source: W. E. Gladstone, *The Financial Statements of 1853, 1860–63*, London 1863, (a) pp.314–17; 334–35; (b) pp.120–2, 124–5, 128–9; 403–4.]

B. Classical liberalism

Editors' Notes
1 i.e. expenditure on account of the China War and the Maori War in New Zealand.
2 In his budget of 1842 Peel reduced the tariff on a large number of articles.

(ii) Some trends on the Continent
(Introduction, p. 259)

Doc. 27. JEAN BAPTISTE SAY: On the Limits of Government Interference

If the measures of authority, levelled against the free disposition of each man's respective talents and capital, are criminal in the eye of sound policy, it is still more difficult to justify them upon the principles of natural right. 'The patrimony of a poor man', says the author of the *Wealth of Nations*, 'lies in the strength and dexterity of his hands; and to hinder him from employing this strength and dexterity in what manner he thinks proper, without injury to his neighbour, is a plain violation of his most sacred property.'

However, as society is possessed of a natural right to regulate the exercise of any class of industry, that without regulation might prejudice the rest of the community, physicians, surgeons, and apothecaries, are with perfect justice subjected to an examination into their professional ability. The lives of their fellow-citizens are dependent on their skill, and a test of that skill may fairly be established; but it does not seem advisable to limit the number of practitioners nor the plan of their education. Society has no interest, further than to ascertain their qualification.

On the same grounds, regulation is useful and proper, when aimed at the prevention of fraud or contrivance, manifestly injurious to other kinds of production, or to the public safety, and not at prescribing the nature of products and the methods of fabrication. Thus, a manufacturer must not be allowed to advertise his goods to the public as of better than their actual quality: the home consumer is entitled to the public protection against such a breach of faith; and so, indeed, is the mercantile character of the nation, which must suffer in the estimation and demand of foreign customers from such practices. And this is an exemption to the general rule, that the best of all guarantees is the personal interest of the manufacturer. For, possibly, when about to give up business, he may find

326

it answer to increase his profit by breach of faith, and sacrifice a future object he is about to relinquish for a present benefit.

Hence we may form an opinion of the extent, to which government may carry its interference with benefit. The correspondence with the sample or conditions, express or implied, must be rigidly enforced, and government should meddle with the production no further. I would wish to impress upon my readers, that the mere interference is itself an evil, even where it is of use: first, because it harasses and distresses individuals; and, secondly, because it costs money, either to the nation, if it be defrayed by government, that is to say, charged upon the public purse, or to the consumer, if it be charged upon the specific article; in the latter case, the charge must of course enhance the price, thereby laying an additional tax upon the home consumer, and *pro tanto* discouraging the foreign demand.

If interference be an evil, a paternal government will be most sparing of its exercise. It will not trouble itself about the certification of such commodities, as the purchaser must understand better than itself; or of such as cannot well be certified by its agents; for, unfortunately, a government must always reckon upon the negligence, incapacity, and misconduct of its retainers. But some articles may well admit of certification; as gold and silver, the standard of which can only be ascertained by a complex operation of chemistry, which few purchasers know how to execute, and which, if they did, would cost them infinitely more, than it can be executed for by the government in their stead.

In Great Britain, the individual inventor of a new product or of a new process may obtain the exclusive right to it, by obtaining what is called, a patent. While the patent remains in force, the absence of competitors enables him to raise his price far above the ordinary return of his outlay with interest, and the wages of his own industry. Thus he receives a premium from the government, charged upon the consumers of the new article; and this premium is often very large, as may be supposed in a country so immensely productive as Great Britain, where there are consequently abundance of affluent individuals, even on the lookout for some new object of enjoyment . . .

Privileges of this kind no one can reasonably object to; for they neither interfere with, nor cramp any branch of industry, previously in operation. Moreover, the expense incurred is purely voluntary; and those, who choose to incur it, are not obliged to renounce the satisfaction of any previous wants, either of necessity or of amusement.

However, as it is the duty of every government to aim at the constant amelioration of its subjects' condition, it cannot deprive other producers to eternity of the right to employ part of their industry and capital in this particular channel, which perhaps they might sooner or later have themselves discovered, or preclude the consumer for a very long period from the advantages of a competition-price.

[Source: Jean Baptiste Say, *A Treatise on Political Economy;* or *The Production, Distribution and Consumption of Wealth* trans. from the fourth edn. of the French by C. R. Prinsep, London 1821, I, pp.265–9.]

Doc. 28. FREDERIC BASTIAT: Free Trade and Competition

There is not in the whole vocabulary of Political Economy a word which has roused the fury of modern reformers so much as the word *Competition,* which, in order to render it the more odious, they never fail to couple with the epithet *anarchical.*

What is the meaning of *anarchical competition?* I really don't know. What could we substitute for it? I am equally ignorant.

I hear people, indeed, calling out *Organization! Association!* What does that mean? Let us come to an understanding, once for all. I desire to know what sort of authority these writers intend to exercise over me, and all other living men; for I acknowledge only one species of authority, that of reason, if indeed they have it on their side. Is it their wish then to deprive me of the right of exercising my judgment on what concerns my own subsistence? Is their object to take from me the power of comparing the services which I render with those which I receive? Do they mean that I should act under the influence of restraint, exerted over me by them, and not by my own intelligence? If they leave me my liberty, Competition remains. If they deprive me of freedom, I am their slave. Association will be free and voluntary, they say. Be it so. But then each group of associates will, as regards all other groups, be just what individuals now are in relation to each other, and we shall still have *Competition.* The association will be *integral.* A good joke truly. What! Anarchical Competition is now desolating society, and we must wait for a remedy, until, by dint of your persuasion, all the nations of the earth — Frenchmen, Englishmen, Chinese, Japanese, Caffres, Hottentots, Laplanders, Cossacks, Patagonians — make up their minds to unite in one of the forms of association which you have devised? Why, this is just to avow that competition is indestructible; and will you venture to say that a phenomenon which is indestructible and consequently providential, can be mischievous?

After all, what is Competition? Is it a thing which exists and is self-acting like the cholera? No, Competition is only the absence of constraint. In what concerns my own interest, I desire to choose for myself, not that another should choose for me, or in spite of me — that is all. And if any one pretends to substitute his judgment for mine in what concerns me, I should ask to substitute mine for his in what concerns him. What guarantee have we that things would go on better in this way? It is evident that Competition is Liberty. To take away the liberty of acting is to destroy the possibility, and consequently the power, of choosing, of judging, of comparing; it is to annihilate intelligence. To annihilate thought, to annihilate man. From whatever quarter they set out, to this point all modern reformers tend – to ameliorate society they begin by annihilating the individual, under the pretext that all evils come from this source – as if all good did not come from it too.

We have seen that services are exchanged for services. In reality, every man comes into the world charged with the responsibility of providing for his satisfaction by his efforts. When another man saves us an effort, we ought to save him an effort in return. He imparts to us a satisfaction resulting from his effort; we ought to do the same for him.

But who is to make the comparison? For between these efforts, these pains, these services exchanged, there is necessarily a comparison to be made, in order to arrive at equivalence, at justice; – unless indeed injustice, inequality, chance, is to be our rule, which would just be another way of putting human intelligence *hors de cause*. We must, then, have a judge; and who is this judge to be? Is it not quite natural that in every case wants should be judged of by those who experience them, satisfactions by those who seek them, efforts by those who exchange them? And is it seriously proposed to substitute for this universal vigilance of the parties interested, a social authority (suppose that of the reformer himself), charged with determining in all parts of the world the delicate conditions of these countless acts of interchange? Do you not see that this would be to set up the most fallible, the most universal, the most arbitrary, the most inquisitorial, the most insupportable – we are fortunately able to add, the most impossible – of all despotisms ever conceived in the brain of pasha or mufti?

It is sufficient to know that Competition is nothing else than the absence of an arbitrary authority as judge of exchanges, in order to be satisfied that it is indestructible. Illegitimate force may no doubt restrain, counteract, trammel the liberty of exchanging, as it may the liberty of walking; but it can annihilate neither the one nor the other without annihilating man. This being so, it remains for us to inquire whether Competition tends to the happiness or misery of mankind; a question which amounts to this, – Is the human race naturally progressive, or are its tendencies fatally retrograde?

I hesitate not to say that Competition, which, indeed, we might denominate Liberty, despite the revulsion which it excites, despite the declamations to which it has given rise, is a law which is democratical in its essence. Of all the laws to which Providence has confided the progress of human society, it is the most progressive, levelling, and *communautaire*. It is this law which brings successively into the *common* domain the use and enjoyment of commodities which nature has accorded gratuitously only to certain countries. It is this law, again, which brings into the *common* domain all the conquests which the genius of each age bequeaths to succeeding generations, leaving them only supplementary labours to execute, which last they continue to exchange with one another, without succeeding, as they desire, in obtaining a recompense for the co-operation of natural agents; and if these labours, as happens always in the beginning, possess a value which is not proportionate to their intensity, it is still Competition which, by its incessant but unperceived action, restores an equilibrium which is sanctioned by justice, and which is more exact than any that the fallible sagacity of a human magistracy could by possibility establish. Far from Competition leading to inequality, as has been erroneously alleged, we may assert that all *factitious* inequality is imputable to its absence; and if the gulf between the Grand Lama and a Paria is more profound than that which separates the President from an artisan of the United States the reason is this, that Competition (or Liberty), which is curbed and put down in Asia, is not so in America. This is the reason why, whilst the Socialists see in Competition the source of all that is evil, we trace to the attacks which have been made upon it the disturbance of all that is good. Although this great law has been misunderstood by the Socialists and their adepts; although it is frequently harsh in its operation, no law is more fertile in social harmonies, more beneficent in general results; no law attests more brilliantly the measureless superiority of the designs of God over the vain and powerless combinations of men.

[Source: Frédéric Bastiat, *Harmonies of Political Economy* (1850), trans. from the third edn. of the French by Patrick James Stirling, Edinburgh (Second edn., n.d.), Ch. 10, pp. 288–90.]

Doc. 29. FRIEDRICH LIST: Petition on behalf of the *Handelsverein* to the Federal Assembly (April, 1819)

The humble petition of the German merchants and manufacturers, met together at Frankfort-on-Main for the Easter Fair of 1819, for the removal of all custom-duties and tolls in the interior of Germany, and the establishment of a universal German system founded on the principle of retaliation against foreign states. Presented by Professor List of Tübingen as agent for the petitioners.

Worshipful Federal Assembly.* We, the undersigned German merchants and manufacturers met together at the Fair in Frankfort, approach with deep respect this the highest representative assembly of the German nation in order to set forth the causes of our suffering and to beg for help. In a country where it is common knowledge that the majority of manufacturers are either entirely ruined or drag on a precarious and

---

* *Federal Assembly.* It consisted of delegates from the Governments of the various states belonging to the German Confederation (founded 1814), under the Presidency of Austria. It soon became a mere tool in the hands of the reactionary rulers.

burdensome existence, where the fairs and markets are filled with foreign wares, where merchants have almost lost their occupation, there is little need of detailed proof to show the intensity of the evil. The ruinous condition of German trade and manufactures must be due either to individuals or to the conditions of society. But who can reproach the German with lack of talent or industry? Is he not proverbial for these qualities among all the nations of Europe? Who can deny his enterprise? Did not these towns which now serve as the instruments of foreign competition once conduct the trade of the world?[†] It is only in the faults of the social organization that we can find the cause of the evil.

National freedom is the first condition of all human development, whether physical or mental. As the individual mind is hampered by restrictions on the exchange of ideas, so the prosperity of nations is impaired by the fetters which are placed on the production and exchange of material goods. Not until universal, free, and unrestricted commercial intercourse is established among the nations of the world will they reach the highest degree of material well-being. If, on the other hand, they wish to become irrevocably weak, then let each not only impede, but entirely destroy the import, export, and transport of goods by means of prohibitions, duties, and embargoes. A certain opinion has become a dogma among statesmen, although all experienced merchants and manufacturers are convinced of its error. It is that internal industry can be created by taxes and dues.

Such imports, on the one hand, act as premiums for the smuggler who can simultaneously defeat the main and the secondary aim of the statesman – the advancement of home industry and the raising of revenue. On the other hand, they recoil on the home industry, because the taxed country can lay similar restrictions on the products of the taxing country. Of course, when the other state does not retaliate, but suffers itself to be stripped and ruined by prohibitions or high duties, then the policy may be advantageous. This is the case among our neighbours; encircled by the custom barriers of England, France, and Holland, Germany can do nothing effective to help the cause of universal free trade, by means of which alone Europe can reach the highest stage of civilization. But the German people impose still narrower restrictions upon themselves. Thirty-eight customs boundaries cripple inland trade, and produce much the same effect as ligatures which prevent the free circulation of the blood. The merchant trading between Hamburg and Austria, or Berlin and Switzerland must traverse ten states, must learn ten customs-tariffs, must pay ten successive transit dues. Any one who is so unfortunate as to live on the boundary-line between three or four states spends his days among hostile tax-gatherers and custom-house officials; he is a man without a country.

[†] *These towns,* i.e., the Hanse towns.

B. Classical liberalism

This is a miserable condition of things for men of business and merchants. They cast envious glances across the Rhine where, from the Channel to the Mediterranean, from the Rhine to the Pyrenees, from the Dutch to the Italian borders, a great nation carries on its trade over free rivers and free roads without ever meeting a custom-house official. Customs and tolls, like war, can only be justified as a means of defence. But the smaller the country which imposes a duty, the greater is the loss, the more harmful the effect on national enterprises, the heavier the cost of collection; for small countries are all boundary. Hence our thirty-eight customs boundaries are incomparably more injurious than a line of custom-houses on the external boundary of Germany, even if in the latter case the imposts are three times as heavy. And so the power of the very nation which in the time of the Hansa carried on the world's trade under the protection of its own fleet, is now ruined by the thirty-eight lines of customs.

We think that we have brought forward sufficient reasons to prove to your august assembly that only the remission of the internal customs, and the erection of a general tariff for the whole Federation, can restore national trade and industry or help the working classes . . .

[Source: Margaret M. Hirst, *Life of Friedrich List and Selections from his Writings*, London 1909, pp.137–40.]

Doc. 30. JOHN PRINCE SMITH: On Freedom of Trade in Relationship to Political Freedom

This publication has been given the task to prove:
1. that armed diplomacy was a result of antagonism among the nations;
2. that antagonism between the nations is now sustained only by misunderstanding of the interests of intercourse;
3. that an absolutist government is indispensable for supporting armed diplomacy;
4. therefore, to demand at the same time from a government both freedom from restrictions for the citizen and restrictions on the earnings of the foreigners means desiring the end without the means;
5. that, in fact, the nations have no antagonistic interests in business intercourse;
6. that perfect freedom of trade is going to remove the last remnants of international antagonism, that is, the field of armed diplomacy; and with it also the need for absolutist and centralising government;
7. that the most secure way of attaining the freedom of the citizen is through peace between the nations fortified for all time by free trade.

The unequivocal tendency of this publication is thus to support civic freedom through freedom of trade . . .

Just as freedom of trade is bound to further political freedom, so will the latter strengthen and intensify the former. In recent times industry has been furnished with bigger instruments by means of the steam engine, the steam-boat, the railway and innumerable other mechanical inventions, as well as through the development and spread of the physical and technical sciences. These means are already demonstrating their power as levers for the transformation of life. A transition is going on and everyone who does not want to be pushed aside and suppressed has to advance with it. The task for our time is a bold productivity, a mighty endeavour. This task requires the highest development of courage, strength and intelligence in a people. The first and most effective means for it is political independence. A popular constitution, which transforms subjects into citizens, by giving them a share in the government of the state, raises the outlook from the narrow circle of individual activity to the larger movements of the general interest; it strengthens the mind and removes that timidity in action which is inseparable from restricted conditions. It also allows full scope for efficiency; it forms important personalities and acknowledges individuality. Where new things are to be created, great things to be done, new movements to be coped with and directed, there is need for independent personalities. Systems are of no use there or else they are dangerous through their rigidity. The slogan, 'Everything for the people, nothing through the people,' applies only if the one thing which alone can always be done through the people, that is, production itself, makes smaller demands and can be done with tied hands and in the dark. But to-day the merchant and the factory-owner must step forward with magnificent creativity and interfere to a greater extent with the conditions of their fellow-citizens and even in distant regions in order to obtain a power commensurate with their enterprises and a prestige commensurate with their responsibility. You have only to look into the matter to see how every industrial upsurge stems from important personalities among the management. Under the blessings of civic freedom, heroes of industry will rise on the Continent and compete with those of England and America. One has no idea how much potential greatness there is in man so long as he is not allowed to develop a feeling of his strength through complete independence. And this is the worst aspect of tutelage in industry. Through its protective tariffs the government undertakes to open a path for business forces. It sets an aim for them; it furnishes them with its insight. The path may be good, the goal desirable and the insight very great. But who can say what path would have been opened or what goal would have been reached, if those forces could have followed that natural destiny in complete freedom based on the arrangements of providence for human progress in those world laws that we can only recognise from their results? We cannot obtain criteria for the harmfulness of protective tariffs by calculating the capital destroyed through them. For one cannot calculate what wonderful successes of free development might have been hindered by them. To

restrain the freedom of creative activity is to hinder the rule of the work
of divine creation by depriving it of freedom in order to control and lead
it. It is to desire the replacement of providence by human insight.

Just as freedom of trade is necessary in order to make political
freedom possible, so is political freedom necessary in order to develop
business, and the latter in its turn is necessary to promote social progress.
To effect social progress is the great destiny of the eternally valid laws of
the life of nature. What is required for that purpose must be fulfilled.
[Source: J. Prince Smith: *Über Handelsfeindseligkeit,* Königsberg, 1843, pp.84–7. Translated by the editors of this volume.]

3. The superiority of the middle classes: documents
(Introduction, p. 268)

Doc. 31. JAMES MILL: On the Superior Wisdom and Virtue of the
Middle Class

That there is not only as great a proportion of wise men in that part of
the community which is not the aristocracy, as in that which is; but that,
under the present state of education, and the diffusion of knowledge,
there is a much greater, we presume, there are few persons who will be
disposed to dispute. It is to be observed, that the class which is universally described as both the most wise and the most virtuous part of the community, the middle rank, are wholly included in that part of the community which is not the aristocratical. It is also not disputed, that in
Great Britain the middle rank are numerous, and form a large proportion
of the whole body of the people. Another proposition may be stated, with
a perfect confidence of the concurrence of all those men who have attentively considered the formation of opinion in the great body of society,
or, indeed, the principles of human nature in general. It is, that the
opinions of that class of the people, who are below the middle rank, are
formed, and their minds are directed by that intelligent, that virtuous
rank who come the most immediately in contact with them, who are in
the constant habit of intimate communication with them, to whom they
fly for advice or assistance in all their numerous difficulties, upon whom
they feel an immediate and daily dependence in health and in sickness, in
infancy and in old age, to whom their children look up as models for their
imitation, whose opinions they hear daily repeated, and account it their
honour to adopt. There can be no doubt that the middle rank, which
gives to science, to art, and to legislation itself, their most distinguished
ornaments, and is the chief source of all that has exalted and refined

human nature, is that portion of the community of which, if the basis of representation were ever so far extended, the opinion would ultimately decide. Of the people beneath them a vast majority would be sure to be guided by their advice and example.

The incidents which have been urged as exceptions to this general rule, and even as reasons for rejecting it, may be considered as contributing to its proof. What signify the irregularities of a mob, more than half composed, in the great number of instances, of boys and women, and disturbing, for a few hours or days, a particular town? What signifies the occasional turbulence of a manufacturing district, perculiarly unhappy from a very great deficiency of a middle rank, as there the population almost wholly consists of rich manufacturers and poor workmen; with those whose minds no pains are taken by anybody, with whose afflictions there is no virtuous family of the middle rank to sympathize; whose children have no good example of such a family to see and to admire; and who are placed in the highly unfavourable situation of fluctuating between very high wages in one year, and very low wages in another?It is altogether futile with regard to the foundation of good government to say that this or the other portion of the people may, at this, or the other time, depart from the wisdom of the middle rank. It is enough that the great majority of the people never cease to be guided by that rank; and we may, with some confidence, challenge the adversaries of the people to produce a single instance to the contrary in the history of the world.

[Source: James Mill, *Essay on Government* (1820), reprinted from the Supplement to the *Encyclopaedia Britannica*, London 1828, pp.31–2.]

Doc. 32. FRANCOIS GUIZOT: On the Middle Class as the Basis of the New Society

I support with fervour the cause of the new society which is the outcome of the Revolution. It has equality before the law as its first principle and the middle classes as its fundamental element ...

Undoubtedly it should be the aim and it is the natural result of good social institutions to raise progressively more and more people to that degree of intelligence and independence which makes them capable and worthy of participating in the exercise of political power. But what a gulf exists between this principle of free government and that of universal manhood suffrage which is given as the first and fundamental law in human societies! What an ignoring of innumerable facts, rights and truths that justly claim their place and share in the social organisation.

Nothing is more evident or sacred than the duty of the government to come to the assistance of the classes less favoured by fate, to ease their wretchedness and to assist them in their endeavour to rise towards the blessings of civilisation. But to maintain that it is through the defects in the social organisation that all the misery of so many human beings originates, and to impose on the government the task of guaranteeing and distributing equally the good things of life, is to ignore absolutely the human condition, abolish the responsibility inherent in human liberty and excite bad passions through false hopes . . .

To conclude that democracy is now the sole element, the only master of society, that no power is legitimate or beneficial if it does not emanate from it, and that democracy has always the right to unmake in the same way as it has the sole right to make governments, is to misunderstand frivolously the diversity of conditions and rights which naturally co-exist, although in unequal degrees, in every society. It is to substitute the insolence and tyranny of the many for the insolence and tyranny of privilege; it is to enthrone sometimes anarchy and sometimes despotism in the name of and under the cloak of democracy.

As with all human associations in a similar situation, the middle classes have their faults, their illusions, their share in lacking foresight and in showing obstinacy, vanity and egoism; and it is easy to point them out. But it is slanderous to attribute to these imperfections a significance that they do not have and to magnify them beyond measure so that there may arise between the bourgeoisie and the people a rivalry, an active and profound hostility, analogous to that which has existed for a long time between the bourgeoisie and the nobility. The modern bourgeoisie does not deny its history at all. It is in the name of all and for the profit of all that it has conquered the rights which it possesses and has established the principles which prevail in our social order. It does not exercise or claim any class rule, any exclusive privilege. In the vast space it fills in the midst of society, the doors are always open and places are never lacking for those who understand this and want to enter. It is often said, and with good reason, that the English aristocracy has had the merit of knowing how to expand and rejuvenate itself by finding recruits from other classes in the same proportion as those classes increase. This merit belongs still more completely and infallibly to the French bourgeoisie; it is its very essence and its public right. Born from the people, it draws on and feeds incessantly from that same source which rises and flows without ceasing. Different conditions and whims of passion exist and will always exist; they are the natural product of social movement and of liberty. But it is a gross error to take advantage of these moral observations on nature and human society in order to infer from them a political war between the bourgeoisie and the people that is without either serious or legitimate motives.

[François Guizot, *Mémoires pour servir à l'histoire de mon temps*, Paris 1872, I, p.296; VI pp.346–9. Translated by the editors of this volume.]

Doc. 33. DAVID HANSEMANN: The Middle Class in Prussia

§25. The middle class (*der Mittelstand*) is in Prussia, as in many other countries, unquestionably the most propertied class; that means in a certain, though only limited context the more powerful class. Yet how weak they are in the political field! Given to gain, to the enjoyment of what they acquire, only a few of their members have not yet lost the feeling of the value of freedom; generally they are indifferent to the highest interests and the State, as long as they are not disturbed in their acquisitive activities and comfort. The latter has so much become part of their nature that they are not even inclined to timely patriotic sacrifices from fear of a violation of their interests. They let things come and go without thinking of intervention and vigorous co-operation, and they console themselves with the idea that the passing time will produce some advice. They are satisfied with a bit of external honour, a title, an order or some other high acts of favour, no matter where they originate from as long as they have only some customary prestige. Truly this attitude of so powerful a class deprives the State in times of danger of a great part of its strength. Only freedom is capable of shaking up such phlegm, and of imbuing a numerous, propertied class of politically indifferent inhabitants with a genuine and effective patriotism.

§26. As an excuse for the middle classes it can be argued that they largely originate from the old class of the completely unfree people; and thus the present situation, compared with that of former centuries, is a great progress in freedom; one might say that their plebeian origin was sticking to them, and therefore they have no sense of higher values. But where is then the old spirit of freedom and independence of the nobility? One now finds little of it. Instead of that spirit, nurtured by the memories of glorious ancestors, instead of the demand to participate in legislation, instead of a lively patriotism ready for sacrifices for the general good of the country, the great majority of this class is quite satisfied with a lack of political freedom, is servile and values external honours greatly. They strive for maintenance through State service; and seek their political prestige by preserving or regaining tedious privileges over fellow citizens below them, and partly to shun the burdens of the state. This is not the true love of the fatherland, nor the means of being its vigorous support. On the contrary, it is an unfortunate, pernicious tendency which in the long run would be bound to complete the destruction of the nobility, even if only in the case of a great political crisis.

To prevent the annihilation of the nobility, to make it again noble, to utilise fully its influence for the welfare of the fatherland, there is only one means: It should be one of the main supports of full freedom. By the way, in order to do justice to the nobility, I should like to mention that there is a higher proportion of high and noble-minded people amongst it than amongst the middle classes . . .

B. Classical liberalism

§32. The greatest concern is felt by every Prussian statesman about the strong and extraordinary increase of the democratic element, all the more as experience shows that this very element bases its absolute or partial domination easily on revolution. With a few words we might sketch here the most prominent causes, which are bound to contribute to the development and strengthening of the democratic element as well as to its dangerousness:

(1) The role of machines. On the one hand, it increases the number of propertyless people, who only live from day to day. On the other hand, it reduces the price of manufactured goods, and decreases the striking differences between their more refined and more inferior qualities in such a way that dress or external appearance already contributes to the equalisation of, or to a rapprochement between the classes (*Stände*).

(2) The progress in food production, particularly in that of the potato.

(3) The appearance of cheaper and quicker means of transport. By it a great number of people are offered a means that had not existed previously, not only of finding jobs far from one's place of birth or habitation, but also of absorbing plenty of new ideas, views and wants through travelling.

(4) The system of the Prussian Army which gradually makes the lower classes conscious of their strength. The basis of this system, the arming of the people, cannot be given up, for without it a powerful Prussia cannot be imagined.

(5) The loosening of religious ties, particularly with the Protestants.

(6) The general attitude favouring quick and changing enjoyment.

(7) The universal character of education.

(8) The decline of old customs and habits.

(9) The philanthropy, or the nursing spirit, in the State administration which increases the carelessness, and the shirking of work by the lower classes through legal regulations and the furthering of certain institutions. The idea may sound strange, at first, that the granting of freedom should be a means of avoiding the danger resulting from the present development of democracy. Yet this is my conviction. By granting freedom to the not entirely propertyless section of the lower classes a tie exists that connects them with the state. They obtain then a legitimate and proper political influence, and this is useful and conservative at the same time. They become a safeguard vis-à-vis the dangerous democratic elements further below. Also, only through freedom can the forces of the middle classes and of the nobility be so vitalised and strengthened that they are able to keep a too great and harmful influence of democracy within bounds.

§33. While fully acknowledging the good brought about by the philosophy of the 18th century, particularly its wholesome effect on humanitarian attitudes and recognition of the dignity of man, it cannot be overlooked that the principle of equality, which this philosophy tries generally to apply to life, brings about not only triteness and vulgarisation of ideas, but also the danger of revolution by its final success. This has been conceded by the most thoughtful and distinguished statesmen; and quite the most liberal among them are therefore against equality of freedom in order that the latter does not perish through itself.

34. However, the masses do not recognise this and philosophical ideas continue to affect them. The danger gradually being spread through this is not diminished, but rather increased, by the circumstance that in Prussia there does exist one equality, so to speak, that of a lack of freedom (*Unfreiheit*). This ought to increase the danger, as in that way the conserving forces within the people do not develop freely; and the government, relying on the regime of the bureaucracy, has isolated itself.

Thus let freedom protect us in good time from dangerous effects of that philosophy! . .

§39. Freedom is incompatible with order – thus runs an argument. However, this does not apply to order as it exists in Prussia today. For this order is *Unfreiheit*, a lack of freedom. If the government decides to grant freedom, admittedly it must accustom itself to regard some things as order which seem to be the opposite according to its present concepts. Fully conscious of its strength, based on the main forces of the nation, it must even regard the excesses of freedom, the improprieties that sometimes occur, as being less dangerous and threatening than present concepts would suggest. No human institution is absolutely perfect and good; each of them has its weaknesses and dangers. The question remains only on which side are the greatest advantages, and, in proportion to them, the smallest defects? That means in this case: Shall the lack of freedom (*Unfreiheit*) be continued for the preservation of order strictly based on the police, in spite of the considerable dangers and defects connected with it? Or shall freedom be granted as a lasting safeguard of the splendour of the throne and the greatness of the nation, in spite of the inconveniences and deficiencies which are invariably connected with it?

[Source: David Hansemann, '*Memorandum on Prussia's Position and Politics, August, September 1840*'. J. Hansen (ed.) *Rheinische Briefe und Akten zur Geschichte der politischen Bewegung, 1830–1850*. Band I, 1830–1845, Essen 1919, pp.218–25. Translated by the editors of this volume.]

4. Aesthetic individualism –
'The object of all mankind should be individuality': documents
(Introduction, p. 271)

Doc. 34*a*. WILHELM VON HUMBOLDT: The Purpose of Man

The true end of man, or that which is prescribed by the eternal and immutable dictates of reason, and not suggested by transient desires, is the highest and most truly proportionate development of his powers to a complete whole. For such formation, freedom is the foremost and indispensable condition. Nevertheless, besides freedom, the development of human potentialities requires yet something else which is closely related to freedom: that is, a variety of situations. Even the freest and most independent of men develops himself to a lesser degree when placed in a monotonous situation. It is true, on the one hand, that this variety is always a result of freedom; but, on the other hand, there exists a kind of oppression which, instead of restricting man, endows the things around him with an arbitrary shape so that both, man and his surroundings, are to a certain extent identical. However, it serves the clarity of these ideas better to keep them still apart.

Every man can act at any one time only with one dominant faculty; or rather, his whole being is simultaneously attuned to one single activity. Therefore man would appear to be destined to be one-sided, since he weakens his energies as soon as he directs them to several objectives. Yet he can avoid this one-sidedness if he strives to unite his separate and often separately exercised faculties, and to permit the dying sparks of one activity together with that, the bright radiance of which the future will kindle, to play a simultaneous role at every stage of his life; and also if he further endeavours to increase and diversify the forces with which he works by harmoniously combining them instead of aiming at a mere variety of objects for their separate exercise. What here, as it were, produces in the individual the interconnection of the past and the future with the present is brought about in society by association with others. For, in the course of all the phases of his life, each individual can only achieve one of the perfections which, so to speak, represents the character of all mankind. Through the associations, therefore, which emanate from the inner selves of its members, each one must appropriate to himself the inner wealth of the others. According to the general experience – even of the most primitive of nations – the relationship between the sexes is an example of such a character-forming relationship. Although in this case the expression of the difference, as well as of the yearning for union, is, so to speak, the stronger; nevertheless, both trends are no less strong, only more difficult to discern, in other kinds of association where there is no difference of sex. Studied more closely and expounded more precisely, these ideas might lead us to a better explanation of certain relationships among the ancients, and particularly the Greeks, which even the legislators practised. These are often referred to rather ignobly as 'common love' (*gewöhnliche Liebe*) and always incorrectly by the label of mere 'friendship'. The formative effectiveness of such relations rests always upon the extent to which the independence of people thus associated is combined with the intimacy of the relationship. For, if without such intimacy the one is not capable of sufficiently understanding the other, an independent attitude is also necessary in order to assimilate what has been apprehended, as it were, to become a part of one's own being. But both require strength on the part of the individuals; and yet also a difference which is neither too great to prevent the one being able to comprehend the other nor too small as to allow admiration of what the other possesses and so awaken the desire to assimilate it into one's own character. This individual vigour and this manifold diversity unite to form originality. It is on this originality, therefore, that the whole greatness of man ultimately rests and towards which every human being must ceaselessly strive; and of which those who want to influence their fellow-beings must never lose sight: in other words, the individuality of one's strength and self-cultivation (*Eigentümlichkeit der Kraft und Bildung*). Just as this individuality is brought about by freedom of action and by the diversity of its agents; so it, in its turn, reproduces both. Even inanimate nature, in accordance with eternal, unchangeable laws, advances by regular steps and appears more truly individual to the self-cultivated person. He will, as it were, project himself into nature itself; and so it is true in the highest sense that everyone always realises the variety and beauty of the outer world to the extent to which he harbours both within himself. How much closer, surely, must this correspondence between effect and cause become when man not only feels and comprehends external impressions, but becomes active himself?

[Source: Wilhelm von Humboldt, *Ideen zu einem Versuch, die Grenzen der Wirksamkeit des Staates zu bestimmen* (1792); *Werke*, Berlin 1903, Band I, pp.106–8. Translated by the editors of this volume.]

Doc. 34*b*. WILHELM VON HUMBOLDT: The Purpose of the State

The purpose of the State can be twofold; it can seek to promote happiness, or merely to prevent evil; and, in the latter case, evils caused either by nature or by human beings. If it confines itself to the second of these objectives, it seeks security only, so may I be permitted to set this security, for once, against all the other possible purposes of state agency and combine them under the heading of 'positive welfare'? . . .

B. Classical liberalism

It will, meanwhile, be best to begin by examining whether the State should concern itself also with the positive welfare of the nation or merely with its security; whether in all its institutions it should consider purely what are their chief objectives and consequences; and, in the case of both these aims, at the same time, to examine the means which the State may properly use to accomplish them.

I am, therefore, considering here the entire endeavour of the State to increase the positive welfare of the nation, all its care for the country's population and the maintenance of its inhabitants, either directly through institutions for the poor or indirectly by promoting agriculture, industry, and trade – all finance and money operations, import and export restrictions etc. (in so far as they have this purpose), and, lastly, all the measures taken to prevent or remedy the ravages of nature – in short, every measure taken by the State which has for its purpose to preserve or further the physical welfare of the nation. For since morality is fostered less readily for its own sake than for the purpose of security, I shall come to this subject later.

All these institutions, so I maintain, have harmful consequences, and are incompatible with true policies which stem from the highest, though always from humane points of view.

1. The spirit of the Government prevails in all such institutions, and however wise and salutary such a spirit may be, it nevertheless produces uniformity and an alien mode of behaviour in the nation. Instead of people entering into social life in order to strengthen their powers, even if need be at the price of thereby diminishing their exclusive possessions and enjoyments, they acquire possessions at the expense of their powers. The greatest gift society can bestow lies just in the very diversity arising out of such an association of several people; and this diversity is invariably forfeited in proportion to the degree of State interference. It is, in point of fact, no longer a matter of the members of a nation living together in community, but rather one of individual subjects who have entered into relationship with the State, or rather with the spirit prevailing in the government of that State. In this relationship, from the outset, the preponderance of the State inhibits the free interplay of individual forces. Similar causes bring about similar effects. Thus, the greater the influence the State contributes, the greater will be the resemblance not only between all the agents but also between their products. This is the very intention of states. They aim at prosperity and peace. Both of which are ever easily attainable in proportion to the extent to which individual conflict is diminished. Yet what man does propose and what he ought to propose is something quite different: it is diversity and activity. This alone is conducive to the formation of many-sided and vigorous characters; and surely no human being has yet sunk so deep as to choose for himself prosperity and enjoyment in preference to greatness. But he who reasons thus in the case of others may be justly suspected of mis-

judging mankind and of seeking to turn men into machines.

2. This would be the second harmful effect: that these institutions of the State weaken the strength of the nation. Just as form burgeons out of spontaneous matter, matter itself thereby receives more variety and beauty – for what is form other than the combination of that which was erstwhile in conflict? – a combination resulting from the discovery of fresh points of contact, and therefore necessitating a whole multitude of fresh discoveries, ever increasing proportionately with the degree of previous difference. So, in the same way, matter is destroyed by the form superimposed upon it from without. For there the naught (*Nichts*) will suppress the aught (*Etwas*). Everything in man is organisation. Whatever is to thrive in him must first have been germinated in him ... Man's mind, like all his other faculties, is shaped only by his own active efforts, his own inventiveness, or his own use of the inventions of others. Measures of the State, on the other hand, always involve some degree of compulsion; and, even where this is not the case, they accustom man too much to rely more and more upon external tuition, external guidance, and external assistance rather than to think of a way out for himself. Almost the sole means that the State has of being able to instruct its citizens consists in setting up what it pronounces to be the best for them, the end product, as it were, of its investigations, and making it compulsory – either directly by law or recommending it indirectly by some institution binding upon the citizens – or by seeking to move them towards it by its prestige and proffered rewards or other inducements, or, lastly, merely recommending it by giving reasons. But whichever of these methods a State may choose to follow, it always falls far short of the best way of instruction. For this undeniably consists in presenting, as it were, all possible solutions to the problem in question, solely in order to prepare the people for selecting the most appropriate one of their own accord; or, better still, for discovering this solution independently themselves out of an adequate presentation of all the obstacles in the way. In the case of its adult citizens the State can practise this method of teaching only in a negative manner, by according freedom which both lets obstacles arise and gives strength and ability to clear them away; and in a positive manner only by way of a truly national education of those who are still in the process of formation...

Yet what suffers even more through a too intensive care of the State, is the spirit of initiative and man's moral character. This should scarcely require further argument. The person, who is guided frequently and firmly may easily reach the point where, as it were, he voluntarily surrenders what remains of his capacity for acting independently. He believes himself released from all the worries, which he sees operating in the case of others, and thinks it will suffice if he awaits their guidance and then follows it. This distorts his noticing merit and guilt. The idea of the former does not spur him on, and the torturing feeling of the latter assails him less frequently and less effectively, since he can much more easily attribute it to his position and push the blame on to those whom he regards as responsible for making it what it is . . .

If men were left to their own deeds and devices, deprived of all outside help that they did not manage to obtain themselves, they would also frequently run into difficulty and misfortune whether through their own fault or not. But the happiness for which man is destined is none other than that which he achieves by his own energies. And it is these very situations which sharpen a man's mind and develop his character. Do you think that such evils do not arise wherever the State impedes such initiative by too specific interference? They do arise there too; and then they leave the person accustomed to lean on external aid to a far more harrowing fate. Because, just as misfortune is alleviated by struggle and hard work, so too, only ten times more so, is it aggravated by hopeless and perhaps deluded expectations. Even in the best case, States, like those to which I refer, only too frequently resemble the physicians who nurse diseases and stave off death. Before there were doctors, man knew only health or death.

3. Everything that occupies man's mind is very closely bound up with his internal sensations, even though the purpose may only be the direct or indirect gratification of physical needs or the achievement of some external object. Besides the external object there is sometimes also an inner impulse; and at times this latter is the one properly intended, and the other, either of necessity or by chance, is merely connected with it. The more unity a man possesses, the more freely the outward activity which he chooses will originate in his inner being; and, conversely, where the inner purpose was not freely chosen, the more frequently and firmly will it be shackled to the outward one. That is why the interesting person is interesting in all situations and in all affairs; that is why he unfolds to an entrancing beauty only in a way of living which is in harmony with his character . . .

Yet freedom is undoubtedly the essential condition without which even the most congenial activity cannot bring about salutary effects of this kind. Whatever is not freely chosen by man of his own accord, but is merely the product of restriction and guidance, does not merge with his being; it always remains alien to him, and he does not perform it out of his own human energies, but rather with merely mechanical ability . . .

5. . . . All the aspects of his being which man is able to cultivate coexist in a wonderful interdependence; and if their coherence, even in the sphere of the intellect, is perhaps not more intimate — it is at least more distinct and noticeable than in the physical sphere. How much more so is this the case in the moral sphere. Therefore, human beings have to associate not in order to diminish their specific character, but rather in order to lessen some of the exclusiveness of their isolation. The union ought not to transform one being into the other; but, as it were, open up

channels of communication between them. Each must compare what he essentially is himself with that which he receives from others, and use the latter to modify but not suppress his own individuality. For, as in the realm of the intellect, truth is never torn by conflict, so, in the sphere of morality, there is no rivalry between things worthy of man; and close and manifold unions of individual characters with one another are therefore necessary in order to destroy what cannot co-exist in proximity and does not of itself conduce to greatness and beauty while they preserve, cherish, and stimulate to yet more marvellous formation the qualities which can co-exist undisturbed. Therefore the highest principle in the art of social intercourse appears to be the need for an incessant effort to comprehend the innermost uniqueness of the other person and to avail oneself of it; and then, filled by the most sincere respect for this uniqueness as the very individuality of a free being, to exert an influence upon it – an influence in which that respect will reveal one's own self, and, as it were, compare that self with the other in its full view. This art has been badly neglected so far. And though this neglect might easily borrow some sort of excuse from the fact that social intercourse should be a wholesome recreation and not a tedious labour, and that unfortunately in the case of very many people it is hardly possible to discover any interesting facets peculiar to them, nevertheless everyone should surely have too much self-respect to seek recreation in something other than the change between interesting activities, let alone choose one which leaves his noblest capacities inactive; and he should have too great a respect for humanity to regard even a single human as being entirely useless and insensitive. At least he who makes it his business to manage and influence human beings must not overlook this aspect; and it then follows that the State, in catering for the positive welfare of the external and physical well-being of each person which is inseparably linked with the inner being, cannot well avoid becoming an obstacle to the development of individuality. This is yet another reason for never sanctioning such welfare intervention except in the case of the most absolute necessity.

These then may be the main negative effects resulting from the planned solicitude of the State for the welfare of its citizens...

7. To bring this part of our enquiry to a close with a general reflection from the highest standpoint: man is neglected in favour of things, and creative forces are neglected in favour of results. In such a system a State resembles more closely an accumulation of lifeless and living tools of production and of pleasures than an assembly of forces for work and enjoyment. The aim seems to have been mere happiness and pleasure to the neglect of the initiative of active human beings. Even if this calculation were found to be correct – since alone subjective experience is capable of the right assessment of happiness and pleasure – it would still underestimate human dignity. For how else could it be explained that this system – concerned as it is with the goal of tranquillity – is willing to

forego the highest human satisfaction, as it were, from the very fear of turbulence? Man derives his greatest joy from those moments in which he becomes aware, to the highest degree, of his creative energy and of his inner unity. Yet at that moment he is also closest to the profoundest misery. For the moment of such intensity can only be followed by a similar intensity, and the trend towards enjoyment or utter deprivation lies in the hand of unconquered fate. Only if man's feeling of the most sublime alone deserves the term 'bliss', will pain and suffering too gain a changed meaning. Man in his inner self then becomes the seat of happiness and unhappiness, and does not vacillate with every changing tide that carries him. That other system leads, in my opinion, to a fruitless effort to avoid pain. He who truly understands enjoyment will tolerate pain – which is bound to overtake those who flee from it – and rejoice unceasingly at the quiet course of fate. The very sight of grandeur fascinates him, whether it is in the course of creation or destruction. And thus man arrives rarely – (except for the ecstatic person) – at the sensation that the moment of feeling his own destruction is a moment of delight . . .

In attempting to draw the final conclusion from the whole argument presented here, the first principle of this part of the present enquiry must be that the State should abstain from all solicitude for the positive welfare of its citizens, and should not proceed a step further than is necessary for their mutual security and protection against foreign enemies. For no other purpose should it restrain their freedom.

[Source: Wilhelm von Humboldt, *Ideen zu einem Versuch, die Grenzen der Wirksamkeit des Staates zu bestimmen* (1792); *Werke*, Berlin, 1903, Band I, pp.111–29. Translated by the editors of this volume.]

Doc. 35. JOHN STUART MILL: Of Individuality, as One of the Elements of Well-Being

It is desirable, in short, that in things which do not primarily concern others, individuality should assert itself. Where, not the person's own character, but the traditions or customs of other people are the rule of conduct, there is wanting one of the principal ingredients of human happiness, and quite the chief ingredient of individual and social progress.

In maintaining this principle, the greatest difficulty to be encountered does not lie in the appreciation of means towards an acknowledged end, but in the indifference of persons in general to the end itself. If it were felt that the free development of individuality is one of the leading essentials of well-being; that it is not only a co-ordinate element with all that is designated by the terms civilisation, instruction, education, culture, but is itself a necessary part and condition of all those things; there would be no danger that liberty should be undervalued, and the adjustment of the boundaries between it and social control would present no extraordinary difficulty. But the evil is, that individual spontaneity is hardly recognised by the common modes of thinking as having any intrinsic worth, or deserving any regard on its own account. The majority, being satisfied with the ways of mankind as they now are (for it is they who make them what they are), cannot comprehend why those ways should not be good enough for everybody; and what is more, spontaneity forms no part of the ideal of the majority of moral and social reformers, but is rather looked on with jealousy, as a troublesome and perhaps rebellious obstruction to the general acceptance of what these reformers, in their own judgment, think would be best for mankind. Few persons, out of Germany, even comprehend the meaning of the doctrine which Wilhelm von Humboldt, so eminent both as a *savant* and as a politician, made the text of a treatise – that 'the end of man, or that which is prescribed by the eternal or immutable dictates of reason, and not suggested by vague and transient desires, is the highest and most harmonious development of his powers to a complete and consistent whole;' that, therefore, the object 'towards which every human being must ceaselessly direct his efforts, and on which especially those who design to influence their fellow-men must ever keep their eyes, is the individuality of power and development;' that for this there are two requisites, 'freedom, and variety of situations;' and that from the union of these arise 'individual vigour and manifold diversity,' which combine themselves in 'originality.'*

Little, however, as people are accustomed to a doctrine like that of Von Humboldt, and surprising as it may be to them to find so high a value attached to individuality, the question, one must nevertheless think, can only be one of degree. No one's idea of excellence in conduct is that people should do absolutely nothing but copy one another. No one would assert that people ought not to put into their mode of life, and into the conduct of their concerns, any impress whatever of their own judgment, or of their own individual character. On the other hand, it would be absurd to pretend that people ought to live as if nothing whatever had been known in the world before they came into it; as if experience had as yet done nothing towards showing that one mode of existence, or of conduct, is preferable to another. Nobody denies that people should be so taught and trained in youth as to know and benefit by the ascertained results of human experience. But it is the privilege and proper condition of a human being, arrived at the maturity of his faculties, to use and interpret experience in his own way. It is for him to find out what part of recorded experience is properly applicable to his own circumstances and character. The traditions and customs of other people are, to a certain extent, evidence of what their experience has taught *them*; presumptive evidence, and as such, have a claim to his deference: but, in the first place, their experience may be too narrow; or they may not have inter-

* *The Sphere and Duties of Government*, from the German of Baron Wilhelm von Humboldt, pp.11–13.

preted it rightly. Secondly, their interpretation of experience may be correct, but unsuitable to him. Customs are made for customary circumstances and customary characters; and his circumstances or his character may be uncustomary. Thirdly, though the customs be both good as customs, and suitable to him, yet to conform to custom, merely *as* custom, does not educate or develop in him any of the qualities which are the distinctive endowment of a human being. The human faculties of perception, judgment, discriminative feeling, mental activity, and even moral preference, are exercised only in making a choice. He who does anything because it is the custom makes no choice. He gains no practice either in discerning or in desiring what is best. The mental and moral, like the muscular powers, are improved only by being used. The faculties are called into no exercise by doing a thing merely because others do it, no more than by believing a thing only because others believe it. If the grounds of an opinion are not conclusive to the person's own reason, his reason cannot be strengthened, but is likely to be weakened, by his adopting it: and if the inducements to an act are not such as are consentaneous to his own feelings and character (where affection, or the rights of others, are not concerned) it is so much done towards rendering his feelings and character inert and torpid, instead of active and energetic.

He who lets the world, or his own portion of it, choose his plan of life for him, has no need of any other faculty than the ape-like one of imitation. He who chooses his plan for himself, employs all his faculties. He must use observation to see, reasoning and judgment to foresee, activity to gather materials for decision, discrimination to decide, and when he has decided, firmness and self-control to hold to his deliberate decision. And these qualities he requires and exercises exactly in proportion as the part of his conduct which he determines according to his own judgment and feelings is a large one. It is possible that he might be guided in some good path, and kept out of harm's way, without any of these things. But what will be his comparative worth as a human being? It really is of importance, not only what men do, but also what manner of men they are that do it. Among the works of man, which human life is rightly employed in perfecting and beautifying, the first in importance surely is man himself. Supposing it were possible to get houses built, corn grown, battles fought, causes tried, and even churches erected and prayers said, by machinery — by automatons in human form — it would be a considerable loss to exchange for these automatons even the men and women who at present inhabit the more civilised parts of the world, and who assuredly are but starved specimens of what nature can and will produce. Human nature is not a machine to be built after a model, and set to do exactly the work prescribed for it, but a tree, which requires to grow and develop itself on all sides, according to the tendency of the inward forces which make it a living thing . . .

It is not by wearing down into uniformity all that is individual in themselves, but by cultivating it, and calling it forth, within the limits imposed by the rights and interests of others, that human beings become a noble and beautiful object of contemplation; and as the works partake the character of those who do them, by the same process human life also becomes rich, diversified, and animating, furnishing more abundant aliment to high thoughts and elevating feelings, and strengthening the tie which binds every individual to the race, by making the race infinitely better worth belonging to. In proportion to the development of his individuality, each person becomes more valuable to himself, and is therefore capable of being more valuable to others. There is a greater fulness of life about his own existence, and when there is more life in the units there is more in the mass which is composed of them. As much compression as is necessary to prevent the stronger specimens of human nature from encroaching on the rights of others cannot be dispensed with; but for this there is ample compensation even in the point of view of human development. The means of development which the individual loses by being prevented from gratifying his inclinations to the injury of others, are chiefly obtained at the expense of the development of other people. And even to himself there is a full equivalent in the better development of the social part of his nature, rendered possible by the restraint put upon the selfish part. To be held to rigid rules of justice for the sake of others, develops the feelings and capacities which have the good of others for their object. But to be restrained in things not affecting their good, by their mere displeasure, develops nothing valuable, except such force of character as may unfold itself in resisting the restraint. If acquiesced in, it dulls and blunts the whole nature. To give any fair play to the nature of each, it is essential that different persons should be allowed to lead different lives. In proportion as this latitude has been exercised in any age, has that age been noteworthy to posterity. Even despotism does not produce its worst effects, so long as individuality exists under it; and whatever crushes individuality is depotism, by whatever name it may be called, and whether it professes to be enforcing the will of God or the injunctions of men.

Having said that the individuality is the same thing with development, and that it is only the cultivation of individuality which produces, or can produce, well-developed human beings, I might here close the argument: for what more or better can be said of any condition of human affairs than that it brings human beings themselves nearer to the best thing they can be? or what worse can be said of any obstruction to good than that it prevents this? Doubtless, however, these considerations will not suffice to convince those who most need convincing; and it is necessary further to show, that these developed human beings are of some use to the undeveloped – to point out to those who do not desire liberty, and would not avail themselves of it, that they may be in some intelligible manner rewarded for allowing other people to make use of it without hindrance.

B. Classical liberalism

In the first place, then, I would suggest that they might possibly learn something from them. It will not be denied by anybody, that originality is a valuable element in human affairs. There is always need of persons not only to discover new truths, and point out when what were once truths are true no longer, but also to commence new practices, and set the example of more enlightened conduct, and better taste and sense in human life. This cannot well be gainsaid by anybody who does not believe that the world has already attained perfection in all its ways and practices. It is true that this benefit is not capable of being rendered by everybody alike: there are but few persons, in comparison with the whole of mankind, whose experiments, if adopted by others, would be likely to be any improvement on established practice. But these few are the salt of the earth; without them, human life would become a stagnant pool. Not only is it they who introduce good things which did not before exist; it is they who keep the life in those which already exist. If there were nothing new to be done, would human intellect cease to be necessary? Would it be a reason why those who do the old things should forget why they are done, and do them like cattle, not like human beings? There is only too great a tendency in the best beliefs and practices to degenerate into the mechanical; and unless there were a succession of persons whose ever-recurring originality prevents the grounds of those beliefs and practices from becoming merely traditional, such dead matter would not resist the smallest shock from anything really alive, and there would be no reason why civilisation should not die out, as in the Byzantine Empire. Persons of genius, it is true, are, and are always likely to be, a small minority; but in order to have them, it is necessary to preserve the soil in which they grow. Genius can only breathe freely in an *atmosphere* of freedom. Persons of genius are, *ex vi termini*, more individual than any other people – less capable, consequently, of fitting themselves, without hurtful compression, into any of the small number of moulds which society provides in order to save its members the trouble of forming their own character. If from timidity they consent to be forced into one of these moulds, and to let all that part of themselves which cannot expand under the pressure remain unexpanded, society will be little the better for their genius. If they are of a strong character, and break their fetters, they become a mark for the society which has not succeeded in reducing them to commonplace, to point out with solemn warning as 'wild,' 'erratic,' and the like; much as if one should complain of the Niagara river for not flowing smoothly between its banks like a Dutch canal.

I insist thus emphatically on the importance of genius, and the necessity of allowing it to unfold itself freely both in thought and in practice, being well aware that no one will deny the position in theory, but knowing also that almost every one, in reality, is totally indifferent to it. People think genius a fine thing if it enables a man to write an exciting poem, or paint a picture. But in its true sense, that of originality in thought and action, though no one says that it is not a thing to be admired, nearly all, at heart, think that they can do very well without it. Unhappily this is too natural to be wondered at. Originality is the one thing which unoriginal minds cannot feel the use of. They cannot see what it is to do for them: how should they? If they could see what it would do for them, it would not be originality. The first service which originality has to render them, is that of opening their eyes: which being once fully done, they would have a chance of being themselves original. Meanwhile, recollecting that nothing was ever yet done which some one was not the first to do, and that all good things which exist are the fruits of originality, let them be modest enough to believe that there is something still left for it to accomplish, and assure themselves that they are more in need of originality, the less they are conscious of the want.

In sober truth, whatever homage may be professed, or even paid, to real or supposed mental superiority, the general tendency of things throughout the world is to render mediocrity the ascendant power among mankind. In ancient history, in the Middle Ages, and in a diminishing degree through the long transition from feudality to the present time, the individual was a power in himself; and if he had either great talents or a high social position, he was a considerable power. At present individuals are lost in the crowd. In politics it is almost a triviality to say that public opinion now rules the world. The only power deserving the name is that of masses, and of governments while they make themselves the organ of the tendencies and instincts of masses. This is as true in the moral and social relations of private life as in public transactions. Those whose opinions go by the name of public opinion are not always the same sort of public: in America they are the whole white population; in England, chiefly the middle class. But they are always a mass, that is to say, collective mediocrity. And what is a still greater novelty, the mass do not now take their opinions from dignitaries in Church or State, from ostensible leaders, or from books. Their thinking is done for them by men much like themselves, addressing them or speaking in their name, on the spur of the moment, through the newspapers. I am not complaining of all this. I do not assert that anything better is compatible, as a general rule, with the present low state of the human mind. But that does not hinder the government of mediocrity from being mediocre government. No government by a democracy or a numerous aristocracy, either in its political acts or in the opinions, qualities, and tone of mind which it fosters, ever did or could rise above mediocrity, except in so far as the sovereign Many have let themselves be guided (which in their best times they always have done) by the counsels and influence of a more highly gifted and instructed One or Few. The initiation of all wise or noble things comes and must come from individuals; generally at first from some one individual. The honour and glory of the average man is that he is capable of following that initiative; that he can respond internally to wise and noble things, and be led to them with his eyes open. I am not countenancing the sort of 'hero-worship' which applauds the strong man of genius for forcibly seizing on the government of the world and making it do his bidding in spite of itself. All he can claim is, freedom to point out the way. The power of compelling others into it is not only inconsistent with the freedom and development of all the rest, but corrupting to the strong man himself. It does seem, however, that when the opinions of masses of merely average men are everywhere become or becoming the dominant power, the counterpoise and corrective to that tendency would be the more and more pronounced individuality of those who stand on the higher eminences of thought. It is in these circumstances most especially, that exceptional individuals, instead of being deterred, should be encouraged in acting differently from the mass. In other times there was no advantage in their doing so, unless they acted not only differently but better. In this age, the mere example of non-conformity, the mere refusal to bend the knee to custom, is itself a service. Precisely because the tyranny of opinion is such as to make eccentricity a reproach, it is desirable, in order to break through that tyranny, that people should be eccentric. Eccentricity has always abounded when and where strength of character has abounded; and the amount of eccentricity in a society has generally been proportional to the amount of genius, mental vigour, and moral courage it contained. That so few now dare to be eccentric marks the chief danger of the time.

[Source; John Stuart Mill, *On Liberty* (1859), Everyman's Library, reprint, London 1962, Ch. 3, pp.115–17, 120–5.]

5. The belief in international harmony: documents
(Introduction, p. 278)

Doc. 36. JEREMY BENTHAM: In International Dealings, Justice and Beneficence

On the occasion of the dealings of this our State with any other States – sincerely and constantly shall my endeavours be directed to the observance of the same strict justice and impartiality, as on the occasion of the dealings of the Legislature with its Constituents, and other its fellow-countrymen, of this our State.

Never will I seek to add, to the opulence or power of this our State, at the expense of the opulence or power of any other State, any otherwise than, in the competition between individual and individual, each may, without injury seek to advance his own prosperity in preference to that of the other.

All profit, by conquest in every shape, I acknowledge to be no more than robbery: robbery, having murder for its instrument; both operating upon the largest possible scale: robbery, committed by the ruling few in the conquering nation, on the subject many in both nations: robbery, of which by the expense of armament, the people of the conquering nation are the first victims: robbery and murder, the guilt of which, as much exceeds the guilt of the crimes commonly called by those names, as the quantity of suffering produced in the one case exceeds the quantity produced in the other.

Seeing, that in all war, it is only through the sides of the unoffending many that the guilty few can ever receive a wound, – never will I, for any other purpose than that of national self-defence, or receipt of compensation for pecuniary damage actually sustained, consent to make war on any other State: nor yet for pecuniary damage, till all endeavours for the obtainment of compensation, in the way of arbitration or other means less destructive than general war, are hopeless: nor unless, if not prevented by war, future injury from the same source as the past, is actually apprehended by me.

Never will I consent to the receiving, under the dominion of this our State – even though it were at the desire of the inhabitants, – any portion of territory, situate at any such distance from the territory of this State, as to prevent any of the wants of the inhabitants of such other territory, from receiving, at the hands of the Supreme Legislature of this our State, relief as effectual, as that which they could receive, were their places of habitation situated within the pristine limits of the territory of this our State: regarding, as I do, all such dominion, as no better than an instrument, a device, for the accumulation of patronage and oppressive power, in the hands of the ruling few in the dominating State, at the expense, and by the sacrifice, of the interest and felicity, of the subject many, in both States.

No recognition of superiority, on the part of this our State, in relation to any other State, will I ever seek to procure, or consent to receive: no factitious honour or dignity will I seek to procure, or consent to receive, for this my own State, or any of its citizens, at the hands of any other State.

I acknowledge all honour to be false honour, all glory to be false glory, all dignity false dignity, – which is sought to be advanced, or maintained, at the expense of justice, probity, self-regarding prudence, or effective benevolence: I acknowledge all such words to be words of delusion, employed by rulers, for the purpose of engaging subject citizens to consent, or submit, to be led, for the purpose of depredation, to the commission of murder upon the largest scale: words, which, as often as they are employed, will, in proportion as the eyes of men are open to their true interests, reflect dishonour, more and more intense and extensive, on all those by whom they are thus employed.

On every favourable occasion, – my endeavours shall be employed to the rendering, to the subjects, and for their sake to the constituted Authorities, of every foreign State, all such positive good offices, as can be rendered thereto, without its being at the expense of some other State or States, or against the rightly presumable inclination, as well as at the expense, of the majority of my fellow-countrymen, in this our State.

Never, by force or intimidation, never by prohibition or obstruction, will I use any endeavour to prevent my fellow-countrymen, or any of them, from seeking to better their condition in any other part, inhabited or uninhabited, of this globe. In the territory of this State, I behold an asylum to all: a prison to none.

[Source: Jeremy Bentham, *The Constitutional Code. The Works of Jeremy Bentham*, ed. John Bowring, Edinburgh 1843, IX, pp.202–3.]

Doc. 37. RICHARD COBDEN: 'Commerce is the Grand Panacea'

To protect Turkey against her neighbour, Russia – to defend the Turks against their own government – to force on the latter a constitution, we suppose – to redress all internal grievances in a state where there is no law but despotism! Here then, in a word, is the *'trifling succour'* which we are called on to render our ancient ally; and if the people of Great Britain desired to add another couple of hundreds of millions to their debt, we think a scheme is discovered by which they may be gratified, without seeking for quarrels in any other quarter.

If such propositions as these are, however, to be received gravely, it might be suggested to inquire, would Russia, would Austria, remain passive, whilst another power sent her squadrons and her armies from ports a thousand miles distant to take possession of the capital and supersede the government of their adjoining neighbour? Would there be no such thing as Russian or Austrian jealousy of British aggrandisement, and might not our Quixotic labours in behalf of Mahometan regeneration be possibly perplexed by the co-operation of those Powers? These questions present to us the full extent of the dilemma in which we must be placed, if we ever attempt an internal interference with the Ottoman territory. *Without* the consent and assistance of Russia and Austria, we should not be allowed to land an army in that country. We might, it is true, blockade the Dardanelles, and thus at any time annihilate the trade of Constantinople and the Black Sea. But our interests would suffer by such a step; and the object of intermeddling at all is, of course, to benefit, and not destroy our trade. We must, then, if we would remodel Turkey, act in conjunction with Russia, Austria, and France. Would the two former of these powers be likely to lend a very sincere and disinterested co-operation, or must we prepare for a game of intrigues and protocols?

These are the probable consequences of our interposing in the case of Turkey; and, from the danger of which, the only alternative lies in a strict neutrality. We are aware that it would be a novel case for England to remain passive, whilst a struggle was going on between two European powers; and we know, also, that there is a predilection for continental politics amongst the majority of our countrymen, that would render it extremely difficult for any administration to preserve peace under such circumstances. Public opinion must undergo a change; our ministers must no longer be held responsible for the everyday political quarrels all over Europe; nor, when an opposition journalist, wishes to assail a foreign secretary, must he be suffered to taunt him with neglect of the honour of Great Britain, if he should prudently abstain from involving her in the dissensions that afflict distant communities.

There is no remedy for this but in the wholesome exercise of the people's opinion in behalf of their own interests. The middle and industrious classes of England can have no interest apart from the preservation of peace. The honours, the fame, the emoluments of war belong not to them; the battle-plain is the harvest-field of the aristocracy, watered with the blood of the people.

We know of no means by which a body of members in the reformed House of Commons could so fairly achieve for itself the patriotic title of a national party, as by associating for the common object of deprecating all intervention on our part in continental politics. Such a party might well comprise every representative of our manufacturing and commercial districts, and would, we doubt not, very soon embrace the majority of a powerful House of Commons. At some future election, we may probably see the test of 'no foreign politics' applied to those who offer to become the representatives of free constituencies. Happy would it have been for us, and well for our posterity, had such a feeling predominated in this country fifty years ago! But although, since the peace, we have profited so little by the experience of the revolutionary wars as to seek a participation in all the subsequent continental squabbles, and though we are bound by treaties, or involved in guarantees, with almost every state of Europe; still the coming moment is only the more proper for adopting the true path of national policy, which always lies open to us.

We say the coming moment is only the more fit for withdrawing ourselves from foreign politics; and surely there are signs in Europe that fully justify the sentiment. With France, still in the throes of her last revolution, containing a generation of young and ardent spirits, without the resources of commerce, and therefore burning for the excitement and employment of war; with Germany, Prussia, Hungary, Austria, and Italy, all dependent for tranquillity upon the fragile bond of attachment of their subjects to a couple of aged paternal monarchs; with Holland and Belgium, each sword in hand; and with Turkey, not so much yielding to the pressure of Russia, as sinking beneath an inevitable religious and political destiny — surely, with such elements of discord as these fermenting all over Europe, it becomes more than ever our duty to take natural shelter from a storm, from entering into which we could hope for no benefits, but might justly dread renewed sacrifices.

Nor do we think it would tend less to promote the ulterior benefit of our continental neighbours than our own, were Great Britain to refrain from participating in the conflicts that may arise around her. An onward movement of constitutional liberty must continue to be made by the less advanced nations of Europe, so long as one of its greatest families holds out the example of liberal and enlightened freedom. England, by calmly directing her undivided energies to the purifying of her own internal institutions, to the emancipation of her commerce — above all, to the unfettering of her press from its excise bonds — would, by thus serving as it were for the beacon of other nations, aid more effectually the cause of political progression all over the continent than she could possibly do by plunging herself into the strife of European wars.

For, let it never be forgotten, that it is not by means of war that states are rendered fit for the enjoyment of constitutional freedom; on the contrary, whilst terror and bloodshed reign in the land, involving men's minds in the extremities of hopes and fears, there can be no process of thought, no education going on, by which alone can a people be prepared for the enjoyment of rational liberty. Hence, after a struggle of twenty years, *begun in behalf of freedom*, no sooner had the wars of the French revolution terminated, than all the nations of the continent fell back again into their previous state of political servitude, and from which they have, ever since the peace, been *qualifying* to rescue themselves, by the gradual process of intellectual advancement. Those who, from an eager desire to aid civilisation, wish that Great Britain should interpose in the dissensions of neighbouring states, would do wisely to study, in the history of their own country, how well a people can, by the force and virtue of native elements, and without external assistance of any kind, work out their own political regeneration: they might learn too, by their own annals, that it is only when at peace with other states that a nation finds the leisure for looking within itself, and discovering the means to accomplish great domestic ameliorations.

To those generous spirits we would urge, that, in the present day, commerce is the grand panacea, which, like a beneficent medical discovery, will serve to inoculate with the healthy and saving taste for civilisation all the nations of the world. Not a bale of merchandise leaves our shores, but it bears the seeds of intelligence and fruitful thought to the members of some less enlightened community; not a merchant visits our seats of manufacturing industry, but he returns to his own country the missionary of freedom, peace, and good government — whilst our steam boats, that now visit every port of Europe, and our miraculous railroads, that are the

talk of all nations, are the advertisements and vouchers for the value of our enlightened institutions.
[Source: Richard Cobden, *England, Ireland, and America* (1835). *The Political Writings of Richard Cobden*, London 1886, pp.31–6.]

Doc. 38. JOHN PRINCE SMITH: On the Significance of Freedom of Trade in World Politics

Sometimes it is admitted that freedom of trade alone is economical for the nation but should only be introduced if all states proclaim it simultaneously. One knows quite well that this is unobtainable. But the inability of obtaining entire freedom of trade at one stroke is no reason for not enjoying as much of it as one can give to oneself. If there is not yet full freedom of selling abroad when one wants to sell, this is no reason for denying oneself at least the freedom of buying from abroad what one desires. The removal of import tariffs is an economic concession which we grant primarily to ourselves and not merely to foreign countries.

Freedom of trade can only be implemented when every state ceases to demand concessions from others and decides to make them in its own favour. It can only become general through a unilateral procedure. It is also said that one has to produce everything in one's own country in order to be supplied safely in times of war. In other words, one should in times of peace voluntarily impose on oneself the calamities arising from disrupted trade and dearer consumption which are the greatest evils of war. On the contrary, in times of peace one has to seek supplies as cheaply as possible in order to have the means to bear the dearness in times of war. Moreover, the international interconnection of the interests resulting from freedom of trade is the most effective means for the prevention of wars. Had we advanced so far as to see a good customer in every foreigner, there would be much less inclination to shoot at him . . .

Now, gentlemen, it is the especial aim and intention of the Free Traders, who have understood the importance of this principle, to moderate national antipathies and deprive reason of the servitude of blind passions, and to teach the nations that they should recognise their joint economic interests and thus blunt the fierceness of the wretched antagonisms between the states. They aim to strengthen the interest of the national economy, in unity and peace, as a counter-weight to the divisive and hostile principle of the state, and make it into a force for the co-operation of civilised nations. They want to regulate and strengthen the relations between enlightened neighbouring nations in such a way that they cannot frivolously be torn asunder at any moment. Further, they want to deliver the civilised world, as far as is possible, from the pressure of permanent armaments which is being intensified without any

357

B. Classical liberalism

limitation, and to overcome conditions in world affairs that are now as intolerable as they are untenable in the long run. For obviously, gentlemen, in the present state of affairs, the political powers are moving further and further away from their objective. Instead of guaranteeing security, on the contrary they provoke attack through their mutual antagonism against which their institutions offer only unreliable protection. Instead of guaranteeing to the economic community under their control the tranquillity which is indispensable for its prosperity, they surrender it to paralysing worry. They absorb the capital and the working force to an ever growing extent; and they demand sacrifices from the economic community which would be excessive even if they could make possible the purpose for which the state really exists, that is, to establish peaceful order and freedom for the protection of the economic community.

The strengthening of peaceful international relations through freedom of trade is much more important than the immediate economic gain of a cheaper supply of goods to satisfy our needs. World-wide political reform, much more than mere economic reform, is the great aim for which the leading Free Traders are also striving, and for which they would like to create enthusiasm in public-spirited people. The greatness of the goal raises their courage despite the difficulty of how to attain it. This goal is not unattainable for it lies on the road of necessary progress. Its realisation also will take place in a not very remote time. For its recognition is spreading with a strength that grows daily. Like everything great, it only requires persistent efforts rooted in deep conviction.

We are well aware that in the present perverse relations between the states, a transformation could only be brought about by a quite extraordinary motive force; and that a quite extraordinary lever would be needed in order to direct the state powers into another channel. What, then, I ask, is the power that shapes human institutions? It is human opinion. And what is the lever which transforms even the most powerful institution? It is a general change in opinion. Well, then, gentlemen, let us work for a change in the general view of the position between the nations which are separated from each other by states. Let us work in order to spread a general clear view of the economic world community, the unity of which must not be divided by state frontiers if the economic welfare of every individual and of civilisation in general is not to be impaired. Let us spread the view that nations competing in economic production under a system of free intercourse can only be helpful to each other, and that by its very nature the advantage derived from exchange is never one-sided; and, further, that by way of free trade one nation can never enrich itself at the expense of another, and that even the gain is always relatively most important for the economically weaker nation, that is, for the nation least advanced in industry. If we spread this view, we gain a strong counterweight against national antipathies; we destroy many a passionate prejudice and bring the nations to a point from which they see

358

each other with different eyes, with the eyes of reason; and so they have a more correct appreciation of the common economic interests as compared with the alleged particular interests of the states.

Let us thus raise the spirit of the people to the height of our economic principle. From there we offer a wide and free view. From the heights the world looks more beautiful, richer and more peaceful. The view from an elevated position clears the eye and purifies the mood.

(From an Address delivered at a Congress of German Economists in Cologne, 1860.)

[Source: John Prince Smith, *Uber die weltpolitische Bedeutung der Handelsfreiheit*, (Rede auf dem dritten Kongress deutscher Volkswirthe zu Köln am 13 September, 1860), Leipzig: 1860, pp.8–12. Translated by the editors of this volume.]

Doc. 39. JOHN BRIGHT: On Non-Intervention as a Principle of Foreign Policy

We are against intervention. Now, this question of intervention is a most important one, for this reason, that it comes before us sometimes in a form so attractive that it invites us to embrace it, and asks us by all our love of freedom, by all our respect for men struggling for their rights, to interfere in the affairs of some other country. And we find now in this country that a great number of those who are calling out loudest for interference are those who, being very liberal in their politics, are bitterly hostile to the despotism and exclusiveness of the Russian Government. But I should like to ask this meeting what sort of intervention we are to have? There are three kinds – one for despotism, one for liberty; and you may have an intervention like that now proposed, from a vague sense of danger which cannot be accurately described. What have our interventions been up to this time? I will come to that of which Admiral Napier spoke by-and-by. It is not long since we intervened in the case of Spain. The foreign enlistment laws were suspended; and English soldiers went to join the Spanish legion, and the Government of Spain was fixed in the present Queen of that country; and yet Spain has the most exclusive tariff against this country in the world, and a dead Englishman is there reckoned little better than a dead dog. Then take the case of Portugal. We interfered, and Admiral Napier was one of those employed in that interference, to place the Queen of Portugal on the throne, and yet she has violated every clause of the charter which she had sworn to the people; and in 1849, under the Government of Lord John Russell, and with Lord Palmerston in the Foreign Office, our fleet entered the Tagus and destroyed the Liberal party, by allowing the Queen to escape from their hands, when they would have driven her to give additional guarantees for liberty; and from that time to this she has still continued to violate every clause of the charter of the country. Now let us come to Syria; what has

Admiral Napier said about the Syrian war? He told us that the English fleet was scattered all about the Mediterranean, and that if the French fleet had come to Cherbourg, and had taken on board 50,000 men and landed them on our coasts, all sorts of things would have befallen us. But how happened it that Admiral Napier and his friends'got up the quarrel with the French? Because we interfered in the Syrian question when we had no business to interfere whatever. The Egyptian Pasha, the vassal of the Sultan, became more powerful than the Sultan, and threatened to depose him and place himself as monarch upon the throne of Constantinople; and but for England, he would assuredly have done it. Why did we interfere? What advantage was it to have a feeble monarch in Constantinople, when you might have had an energetic and powerful one in Mehemet Ali? We interfered, however, and quarrelled with France, although she neither declared war nor landed men upon our coast. France is not a country of savages and banditti. The Admiral's whole theory goes upon this, that there is a total want of public morality in France, and that something which no nation in Europe would dare to do, or think of doing, which even Russia would scorn to do, would be done without any warning by the polished, civilised, and intelligent nation across the Channel.

But if they are the friends of freedom who think we ought to go to war with Russia because Russia is a despotic country, what do you say to the interference with the Roman Republic three or four years ago? What do you say to Lord John Russell's Government, – Lord Palmerston with his own hand writing the despatch, declaring that the Government of her Majesty, the Queen of England, entirely concurred with the Government of the French Republic in believing that it was desirable and necessary to re-establish the Pope upon his throne? The French army, with the full concurrence of the English Government, crossed over to Italy, invaded Rome, destroyed the Republic, banished its leading men, and restored the Pope; and on that throne he sits still, maintained only by the army of France.

My hon. Friend has referred to the time when Russia crossed through the very Principalities we hear so much about, and entered Hungary. I myself heard Lord Palmerston in the House of Commons go out of his way needlessly, but intentionally, to express a sort of approbation of the intervention of Russia in the case of Hungary. I heard him say, in a most unnecessary parenthesis, that it was not contrary to international law, or to the law of Europe, for Russia to send an army into Hungary to assist Austria in putting down the Hungarian insurrection. I should like to know whether Hungary had not constitutional rights as sacred as ever any country had – as sacred, surely as the Sovereign of Turkey can have upon his throne. If it were not contrary to international law and to the law of Europe for a Russian army to invade Hungary, to suppress there a struggle which called for, and obtained too, the sympathy of every man in favour of freedom in every part of the world, I say, how can it be contrary to international law and the law of Europe for Russia to threaten the Sultan of Turkey, and to endeavour to annex Turkey to the Russian Empire?

I want our policy to be consistent. Do not let us interfere now, or concur in or encourage the interference of anybody else, and then get up a hypocritical pretence on some other occasion that we are against interference. If you want war, let it be for something that has at least the features of grandeur and of nobility about it, but not for the miserable, decrepit, moribund Government which is now enthroned, but which cannot long last, in the city of Constantinople.

(*Speech at Edinburgh, 13 October 1853.*)

[Source: *Speeches on Questions of Public Policy by John Bright, M.P.*, ed. James E. Thorold Rogers, London 1883, pp.461–2.]

Doc. 40. EMILE DE GIRARDIN: On the Principle of Non-Intervention

In coming on to this platform, to which I am called, I do not hide from myself that I am going to offend certain susceptibilities that I respect, because I have come to support the principle of non-intervention in the most absolute terms. In my judgment, every principle which is not absolute ceases to be a principle. I am not one of those who think that the exception confirms the rule; on the contrary, I think that it destroys it. Every rule which admits an exception ceases to be of value as a rule. . . .

As soon as we admit a single exception to the principle of non-intervention, forthwith we inevitably return, by way of consequence, to the system of armed peace, that system which costs Europe a thousand million francs per annum. As soon as we suppose a single case where a state ought to intervene, were it only to make the principle of non-intervention respected, that supposition, transforming itself into foresight requires that a state should not expose itself to be caught unawares by the eventuality. I defy anyone to answer to the contrary. Well, then, to admit one single exception to the principle of non-intervention, is to acquiesce indirectly in the maintenance of the present system:– ruinous armies, crushing budgets, taxes without number, restricted consumption, and increasing misery. That is what I do not want; is that what you do want?

I know the side from which the opinion I uphold can be assailed; for more than once I have had to defend it against opponents who said to me: Would you allow, then, a foreign government to intervene in the affairs of a nation, without interposing yourself to prevent it? Whatever it may cost me, I do not hesitate to answer affirmatively, for if one state does not begin by giving the most scrupulous example of the most absolute respect for the principle of non-intervention, how shall we succeed in introducing that principle into the new law of nations? I have more confidence in the force of law and the right of peoples than those who place the defence of liberty under the protection of the sword. Examine the past! How many wars have been started in the name of liberty! Have they not always ended by turning against it?

Was it not by appealing to the sentiment of liberty among all nations that we succeeded, in 1814 and 1815, in rousing and uniting them in a coalition against France? Alas! What has been gained? Mention to me, one single intervention on which people and government have had to congratulate themselves. I know one recent one; that also assumed the most generous sentiments in saying that it went to protect all legitimate rights. And how has it protected them? By starting with a bombardment which lasted thirty days; by overturning an established government; and by re-establishing a government which had been overthrown. That intervention, which has dragged on for a year, knows not how to remain or how to depart, for, after the occupation comes the evacuation: this is the snag, the stumbling-block of all interventions.

Every intervention necessarily supposes two parties in conflict; every intervention, then, is forced to hoist the flag of one party; if that party be the weaker, if it be unfit to defend itself, what will become of it when it no longer has the intervening power for its support? Will not the intervention withdraw periodically only to return for an indefinite time?

If the intervention is not a general war, and one to the death, of all peoples against all kings, or of all kings against all peoples, it is an absurd action; but after all the peoples have conquered all the kings, who will preserve the peoples from the victorious generals? Who will guarantee to me that the European war to the death will not end only in a change of masters, who will begin by calling themselves consuls and end by calling themselves emperors? I utterly distrust war, for I do not see that it has ever benefited the liberty of any nation. On the contrary, wherever peace has lasted, liberty has gained ground, however slowly it may have been, arbitrary power has lost it, and peoples have become more enlightened, united and strong. I have confidence only in peace. But in that my confidence is complete. Let us hope that it will resume its course, disturbed for a moment by the revolution of 1848, and, by peace, let us doubt not, will be resolved not only all the questions of unity which trouble Germany and Italy, but also all the problems of well-being which agitate industrial Europe. The more the duration of peace shall be prolonged, the more shall the number of bayonets be reduced; this is the end at which we must constantly and patiently aim, for when bayonets disappear, ideas show themselves.

I return to the objection that is put forward against my opinion [i.e. of interposing in order to prevent another foreign power from intervening in the internal affairs of a nation]. One of two things must then follow:

either the government which intervened by force of arms will make itself odious by the excesses it will have committed, or, on the contrary, it will prudently endeavour to avoid them. If it does not fall into any excess, shall it not be congratulated for having spared the blood that would have been shed in war? If, on the contrary, it has only known how to make itself odious, however great the number of victims we may suppose it to have made, this number will always be less considerable than that of the victims which a war would have made, and wherever there exists a free platform and a free press, that press and that platform will unite to brand its unworthy conduct. Do we believe this is nothing? That would be to deceive ourselves strangely, and, in order to justify war, to calumniate liberty.

Peace establishes, extends and draws closer the solidarity of peoples; it makes the cause of each one of them the cause of all. But as soon as war breaks out, that solidarity is broken, rivalries are awakened, enmities are revived, a people and its government, which were two, draw together and make but one; the peoples, on the contrary, which were but one, are divided ... In the general interest of the peoples, even though the liberty of one of them were to suffer for a short time, it is of importance, therefore, that they shut themselves up hermetically in the principle of non-intervention, and do not leave that shelter under any pretext, led away by any consideration. If it is possible to introduce into the law of nations, into international law, the absolute principle of non-intervention, let us be sure that it will be only in this way. There is no other way. Certain organs of democracy may think and pretend the contrary; but, they must allow me to tell them, that to show so much confidence in war, is to show too little in liberty. Let England, the United States and France, proclaim loudly and in agreement, by the voice of their statesmen, their diplomats, their orators and their writers, the absolute principle of non-intervention, and, of all the principles on which the law of nations rests, there will be none held in more respect. Who, then, will dare to attempt it? I put the question, and I shall wait for a reply.

(*Speech at the Peace Congress, Frankfurt-on-Main, 24 August 1850.*)

[Source: Emile de Girardin, *Questions de mon temps 1836 à 1856. Questions politiques,* tome IX, *Politique extérieure de la France – Politique de l'Europe – Des Armées permanentes,* Paris 1858 pp.707–10. Translated by the editors of this volume.]

Doc. 41. JOHN STUART MILL: Non-Intervention as a Legitimate Principle of Morality

There is a country in Europe, equal to the greatest in extent of dominion, far exceeding any other in wealth, and in the power that wealth bestows, the declared principle of whose foreign policy is, to let other nations alone. No country apprehends or affects to apprehend from it any aggressive designs. Power, from of old, is wont to encroach upon the weak, and to quarrel for ascendancy with those who are as strong as itself. Not so this nation. It will hold its own, it will not submit to encroachment, but if other nations do not meddle with it, it will not meddle with them. Any attempt it makes to exert influence over them, even by persuasion, is rather in the service of others, than of itself: to mediate in the quarrels which break out between foreign States, to arrest obstinate civil wars, to reconcile belligerents, to intercede for mild treatment of the vanquished, or finally, to procure the abandonment of some national crime and scandal to humanity, such as the slave-trade. Not only does this nation desire no benefit to itself at the expense of others, it desires none in which all others do not as freely participate. It makes no treaties stipulating for separate commercial advantages. If the aggressions of barbarians force it to a successful war, and its victorious arms put it in a position to command liberty of trade, whatever it demands for itself it demands for all mankind. The cost of the war is its own; the fruits it shares in fraternal equality with the whole human race. Its own ports and commerce are free as the air and the sky: all its neighbours have full liberty to resort to it, paying either no duties, or, if any, generally a mere equivalent for what is paid by its own citizens; nor does it concern itself though they, on their part, keep all to themselves, and persist in the most jealous and narrow-minded exclusion of its merchants and goods.

A nation adopting this policy is a novelty in the world; so much so, it would appear, that many are unable to believe it when they see it. By one of the practical paradoxes which often meet us in human affairs, it is this nation which finds itself, in respect of its foreign policy, held up to obloquy as the type of egoism and selfishness; as a nation which thinks of nothing but of out-witting and out-generalling its neighbours. An enemy, or a self-fancied rival who had been distanced in the race, might be conceived to give vent to such an accusation in a moment of illtemper. But that it should be accepted by lookers-on, and should pass into a popular doctrine, is enough to surprise even those who have best sounded the depths of human prejudice. Such, however, is the estimate of the foreign policy of England most widely current on the Continent ...

It is foolish attempting to despise all this – persuading ourselves that it is not our fault, and that those who disbelieve *us* would not believe though one should rise from the dead. Nations, like individuals, ought to suspect some fault in themselves when they find they are generally worse thought of than they think they deserve; and they may well know that they are somehow in fault when almost everybody but themselves thinks them crafty and hypocritical ...

All, therefore, who either speak or act in the name of England, are bound by the strongest obligations, both of prudence and of duty ... to put a severe restraint upon the mania of professing to act from meaner motives than those by which we are really actuated, and to beware of perversely or capriciously singling out some particular instance in which to act on a worse principle than that by which we are ordinarily guided. Both these salutary cautions our practical statesmen are, at the present time, flagrantly disregarding.

We are now in one of those critical moments, which do not occur once in a generation, when the whole turn of European events, and the course of European history for a long time to come, may depend on the conduct and on the estimation of England. At such a moment, it is difficult to say whether by their sins of speech or of action our statesmen are most effectually playing into the hands of our enemies, and giving most colour of justice to injurious misconception of our character and policy as a people.

To take the sins of speech first: What is the sort of language held in every oration which, during the present European crisis, any English minister, or almost any considerable public man, addresses to parliament or to his constituents? The eternal repetition of this shabby *refrein* – 'We did not interfere, because no English interest was involved;' 'We ought not to interfere where no English interest is concerned.' England is thus exhibited as a country whose most distinguished men are not ashamed to profess, as politicians, a rule of action which no one, not utterly base, could endure to be accused of as the maxim by which he guides his private life; not to move a finger for others unless he sees his private advantage in it. There is much to be said for the doctrine that a nation should be willing to assist its neighbours in throwing off oppression and gaining free institutions. Much also may be said by those who maintain that one nation is incompetent to judge and act for another, and that each should be left to help itself, and seek advantage or submit to disadvantage as it can and will. But of all attitudes which a nation can take up on the subject of intervention, the meanest and worst is to profess that it interferes only when it can serve its own objects by it. Every other nation is entitled to say, 'It seems, then, that non-interference is not a matter of principle with you. When you abstain from interference, it is not because you think it wrong. You have no objection to interfere, only it must not be for the sake of those you interfere with; they must not suppose that you have any regard for their good. The good of others is not one of the things you care for; but you are willing to meddle, if by meddling you can gain anything for yourselves.' Such is the obvious interpretation of the language used.

There is scarcely any necessity to say, writing to Englishmen, that this is not what our rulers and politicians really mean. Their language is not a correct exponent of their thoughts. They mean a part only of what they seem to say. They do mean to disclaim interference for the sake of doing good to foreign nations. They are quite sincere and in earnest in repudiating this. But the other half of what their words express, a willingness to meddle if by doing so they can promote any interest of

England, they do not mean. The thought they have in their minds, is not the interest of England, but her security. What they would say, is, that they are ready to act when England's safety is threatened, or any of her interests hostilely or unfairly endangered. This is no more than what all nations, sufficiently powerful for their own protection, do, and no one questions their right to do. It is the common right of self-defence. But if we mean this, why, in Heaven's name, do we take every possible opportunity of saying, instead of this, something exceedingly different? Not self-defence, but aggrandizement, is the sense which foreign listeners put upon our words...

Why should we abnegate the character we might with truth lay claim to, of being incomparably the most conscientious of all nations in our national acts? Of all countries which are sufficiently powerful to be capable of being dangerous to their neighbours, we are perhaps the only one whom mere scruples of conscience would suffice to deter from it. We are the only people among whom, by no class whatever of society, is the interest or glory of the nation considered to be any sufficient excuse for an unjust act; the only one which regards with jealousy and suspicion, and a proneness to hostile criticism, precisely those acts of its Government which in other countries are sure to be hailed with applause, those by which territory has been acquired, or political influence extended. Being in reality better than other nations, in at least the negative part of international morality, let us cease, by the language we use, to give ourselves out as worse.

But if we ought to be careful of our language, a thousand times more obligatory is it upon us to be careful of our deeds, and not suffer ourselves to be betrayed by any of our leading men into a line of conduct on some isolated point, utterly opposed to our habitual principles of action – conduct such that if it were a fair specimen of us, it would verify the calumnies of our worst enemies, and justify them in representing not only that we have no regard for the good of other nations, but that we actually think their good and our own incompatible, and will go all lengths to prevent others from realizing even an advantage in which we ourselves are to share...

There seems to be no little need that the whole doctrine of non-interference with foreign nations should be reconsidered, if it can be said to have as yet been considered as a really moral question at all. We have heard something lately about being willing to go to war for an idea. To go to war for an idea, if the war is aggressive, not defensive, is as criminal as to go to war for territory or revenue; for it is as little justifiable to force our ideas on other people, as to compel them to submit to our will in any other respect. But there assuredly are cases in which it is allowable to go to war, without having been ourselves attacked, or threatened with attack; and it is very important that nations should make up their minds in time, as to what these cases are. There are few questions which more require to be taken in hand by ethical and political philosophers, with a view to establish some rule or criterion whereby the justifiableness of intervening in the affairs of other countries, and (what is sometimes fully as questionable) the justifiableness of refraining from intervention, may be brought to a definite and rational test. Whoever attempts this, will be led to recognise more than one fundamental distinction, not yet by any means familiar to the public mind, and in general quite lost sight of by those who write in strains of indignant morality on the subject. There is a great difference (for example) between the case in which the nations concerned are of the same, or something like the same, degree of civilization, and that in which one of the parties to the situation is of a high, and the other of a very low, grade of social improvement. To suppose that the same international customs, and the same rules of international morality, can obtain between one civilized nation and another, and between civilized nations and barbarians, is a grave error, and one which no statesman can fall into, however it may be with those who, from a safe and unresponsible position, criticise statesmen. Among many reasons why the same rules cannot be applicable to situations so different, the two following are among the most important. In the first place, the rules of ordinary international morality imply reciprocity. But barbarians will not reciprocate. They cannot be depended on for observing any rules. Their minds are not capable of so great an effort, nor their will sufficiently under the influence of distant motives. In the next place, nations which are still barbarous have not got beyond the period during which it is likely to be for their benefit that they should be conquered and held in subjection by foreigners. Independence and nationality, so essential to the due growth and development of a people further advanced in improvement, are generally impediments to theirs. The sacred duties which civilized nations owe to the independence and nationality of each other, are not binding towards those to whom nationality and independence are either a certain evil, or at best a questionable good. The Romans were not the most clean-handed of conquerors, yet would it have been better for Gaul and Spain, Numidia and Dacia, never to have formed part of the Roman Empire? To characterize any conduct whatever towards a barbarous people as a violation of the law of nations, only shows that he who so speaks has never considered the subject. A violation of great principles of morality it may easily be; but barbarians have no rights as a nation, except a right to such treatment as may, at the earliest possible period, fit them for becoming one. The only moral laws for the relation between a civilized and a barbarous government, are the universal rules of morality between man and man.

The criticisms, therefore, which are so often made upon the conduct of the French in Algeria, or of the English in India, proceed, it would seem, mostly on a wrong principle. The true standard by which to judge their proceedings never having been laid down, they escape such comment and censure as might really have an improving effect, while they are tried by a standard which can have no influence on those practically engaged in such transactions, knowing as they do that it cannot, and if it could, ought not to be observed, because no human being would be the better, and many much the worse, for its observance . . .

But among civilized peoples, members of an equal community of nations, like Christian Europe, the question assumes another aspect, and must be decided on totally different principles. It would be an affront to the reader to discuss the immorality of wars of conquest, or of conquest even as the consequence of lawful war; the annexation of any civilized people to the dominion of another, unless by their own spontaneous election. Up to this point, there is no difference of opinion among honest people; nor on the wickedness of commencing an aggressive war for any interest of our own, except when necessary to avert from ourselves an obviously impending wrong. The disputed question is that of interfering in the regulation of another country's internal concerns; the question whether a nation is justified in taking part, on either side, in the civil wars or party contests of another; and chiefly, whether it may justifiably aid the people of another country in struggling for liberty; or may impose on a country any particular government or institutions, either as being best for the country itself, or as necessary for the security of its neighbours.

Of these cases, that of a people in arms for liberty is the only one of any nicety, or which, theoretically at least, is likely to present conflicting moral considerations . . .

With respect to the question, whether one country is justified in helping the people of another in a struggle against their government for free institutions, the answer will be different, according as the yoke which the people are attempting to throw off is that of a purely native government, or of foreigners; considering as one of foreigners, every government which maintains itself by foreign support. When the contest is only with native rulers, and with such native strength as those rulers can enlist in their defence, the answer I should give to the question of the legitimacy of intervention is, as a general rule, No. The reason is, that there can seldom be anything approaching to assurance that intervention, even if successful, would be for the good of the people themselves. The only test possessing any real value, of a people's having become fit for popular institutions, is that they, or a sufficient portion of them to prevail in the contest, are willing to brave labour and danger for their liberation . . . When a people has had the misfortune to be ruled by a government under which the feelings and the virtues needful for maintaining freedom could not develop themselves, it is during an arduous struggle to become free by their own efforts that these feelings and virtues have the best chance of springing up. Men become attached to that which they have long fought for and made sacrifices for; they learn to appreciate that on which their thoughts have been much engaged; and a contest in which many have been called on to devote themselves for their country, is a school in which they learn to value their country's interest above their own.

It can seldom, therefore — I will not go so far as to say never — be either judicious or right, in a country which has a free government, to assist, otherwise than by the moral support of its opinion, the endeavours of another to extort the same blessing from its native rulers. We must except, of course, any case in which such assistance is a measure of legitimate self-defence. If (a contingency by no means unlikely to occur) this country, on account of its freedom, which is a standing reproach to despotism everywhere, and an encouragement to throw it off, should find itself menaced with attack by a coalition of Continental despots, it ought to consider the popular party in every nation of the Continent as its natural ally: the Liberals should be to it, what the Protestants of Europe were to the Government of Queen Elizabeth. So, again, when a nation, in her own defence, has gone to war with a despot, and has had the rare good fortune not only to succeed in her resistance, but to hold the conditions of peace in her own hands, she is entitled to say that she will make no treaty, unless with some other ruler than the one whose existence as such may be a perpetual menace to her safety and freedom. These exceptions do but set in a clearer light the reasons of the rule; because they do not depend on any failure of those reasons, but on considerations paramount to them, and coming under a different principle.

But the case of a people struggling against a foreign yoke, or against a native tyranny upheld by foreign arms, illustrates the reasons for non-intervention in an opposite way; for in this case the reasons themselves do not exist. A people the most attached to freedom, the most capable of defending and of making a good use of free institutions, may be unable to contend successfully for them against the military strength of another nation much more powerful. To assist a people thus kept down, is not to disturb the balance of forces on which the permanent maintenance of freedom in a country depends, but to redress that balance when it is already unfairly and violently disturbed. The doctrine of non-intervention, to be a legitimate principle of morality, must be accepted by all governments. The despots must consent to be bound by it as well as the free States. Unless they do, the profession of it by free countries comes but to this miserable issue, that the wrong side may help the wrong, but the right must not help the right. Intervention to enforce non-intervention is always rightful, always moral, if not always prudent. Though it be a mistake to *give* freedom to a people who do not value the boon, it cannot but be right to insist that if they do value it, they shall not be hindered from the pursuit of it by foreign coercion. It might not have been right for England (even apart from the question of prudence) to have taken part with Hungary in its noble struggle against Austria; although the Austrian Government in Hungary was in some sense a foreign yoke. But when, the Hungarians having shown themselves likely to prevail in this struggle, the

Russian despot interposed, and joining his force to that of Austria, delivered back the Hungarians, bound hand and foot, to their exasperated oppressors, it would have been an honourable and virtuous act on the part of England to have declared that this should not be, and that if Russia gave assistance to the wrong side, England would aid the right. It might not have been consistent with the regard which every nation is bound to pay to its own safety, for England to have taken up this position single-handed. But England and France together could have done it; and if they had, the Russian armed intervention would never have taken place, or would have been disastrous to Russia alone: while all that those powers gained by not doing it, was that they had to fight Russia five years afterwards, under more difficult circumstances, and without Hungary for an ally. The first nation which, being powerful enough to make its voice effectual, has the spirit and courage to say that not a gun shall be fired in Europe by the soldiers of one Power against the revolted subjects of another, will be the idol of the friends of freedom throughout Europe. That declaration alone will ensure the almost immediate emancipation of every people which desires liberty sufficiently to be capable of maintaining it: and the nation which gives the word will soon find itself at the head of an alliance of free peoples, so strong as to defy the efforts of any number of confederated despots to bring it down. The prize is too glorious not to be snatched sooner or later by some free country; and the time may not be distant when England, if she does not take this heroic part because of its heroism, will be compelled to take it from consideration for her own safety.

[Source: John Stuart Mill, 'A Few Words on Non-Intervention' (1859), in *Dissertations and Discussions. Political, Philosophical, and Historical*, London 1867, III, pp.153–61, 166–8, 171–8]

Doc. 42. FRANCISQUE BOUVET: International Arbitration and Universal Peace

On the day when I attack the War Budget, I shall do so radically. It will not be a trifling reduction that I shall call for; it will be the suppression of three-quarters of this enormous budget.

But that day has not yet come, and you will understand that it is connected in my thought with a new military organisation, with a transformation of the aggressive force of the nation into a purely defensive force; for I think, along with Kant, that right lies solely in defence. No, I am not attacking your War Budget; do not disorganise your armies, do not deprive the Republic of its active forces; that would be to deliver it to its enemies.

But you must do something with that army; and what you now have to do with it, I told you a few days ago: make your army the support of a policy of peace; so that it serves you in raising France to the noble role of enforcing justice and liberty in the world; so that for you it is the fatherly hand of the great human family, the *compelle intrare*[1] of the political faith of nations.

I am afraid, citizens, of speaking a language which is little appreciated by most of you. I have not forgotten the harshness with which the Assembly received, some three months ago, the proposal which I made to inscribe in the preamble of the constitution a simple wish, the expression of which might have been the foundation of the only foreign policy suited to a country placed, as France is, at the head of civilisation. I have not forgotten either that this wish, which was stifled by the opposition within these walls, reached England and Germany, and, to my great astonishment, was heard there, and the European press re-echoed it with words of encouragement.

(*On the left.* Hear, hear!)

And that is what sustains my courage here, and strengthens in me the conviction of a possible and permanent peace among the governments of the nations.

Allow me, citizens, to speak to you for a moment on a subject which, I assure you, is worthy of your attention.

It is a dream, you say; a dream of the moralist and the philosopher! I admit it; but the fraternity written on your walls has been a dream also, a dream coming from the hard pillow of Calvary. How does it happen, then, that you yourselves have inscribed it in your constitution and on your public monuments as the foundation of the right of citizenship? And if you have been brought to recognise fraternity as the moral basis of the rights of man in the city, why should you not be disposed to recognise it as the base of international right, and that, by a necessary analogy, international right must some day be transformed into positive institutions, into institutions of universal peace?

But, even now, citizens, the friends of peace are no longer reduced to speaking only in the fleeting language of abstractions. The governments themselves, having constantly evaded the principles of religion and philosophy, after having sported for ages with the blood of their peoples, are now forced, for want of the resources of war, to resign themselves to peace.

Indeed, it is not only France which sees the military system absorb, in enormous proportions, the resources which would be better devoted to means of securing public prosperity. Most of the states of Europe view their budgets in a situation which is no less abnormal. In Austria, for example, the war budget takes more than a third of general expenditure; in England nearly a quarter; in Prussia, half; in Russia, seven-tenths. Note, at the same time, that all these states are overburdened with debts created with a view to war, and the military system precludes them from ever paying off those debts.

How have the states of Europe been reduced to so deplorable a financial situation? It is through the system of a balance of power which is opposed to the policy of fraternal association; it is by the reciprocal augmentation of their armies which, for nearly a century, has tended continually to the common ruin of nations.

Montesquieu has already pointed out this fatal tendency: 'A new disease,' said he, 'is spreading through Europe; it has seized our princes, and makes them maintain an excessive number of soldiers. As soon as one state augments what it calls its troops, the others suddenly augment theirs, so that they gain nothing thereby but ruin.'

Yes, it is thus that governments, reputed as the wisest and ablest, have proceeded. It is thus that they have drawn their peoples into an abyss of misery, and have themselves plunged into it.

War! War! Do you know how much it cost England alone in her struggles against the Republic and the Empire? The fabulous sum of 33 billion francs, of which there still remains nearly 20 billions to discharge.

The disposition of the peoples, however, does not naturally have this tendency towards hatred and antipathy; for, at the same time as we see the expansion of the military system of the princes, we see also the manifestation of the peaceful sympathies of the peoples; we hear, from beyond our frontiers, their voices calling to each other in mutual distress, their groans intermingling and their hands succouring each other after the occurrence of great calamities.

Recall the deep and universal emotion which was awakened, in the last century, by the catastrophe at Lisbon; see, in our own day, the peoples of Great Britain, and those of the Hanseatic towns and Germany, initiating subscriptions on behalf of the victims of the floods at Lyons; and the whole of Europe coming to the assistance of the city of Hamburg when it was devastated by a terrible fire.

In France, in Prussia, in Belgium, you continually see the appearance of reciprocal fellow-feeling among the peoples, and likewise the banks of various countries help each other through mutual loans.

I can name other recent events of great significance. I may mention the congress of the friends of peace, which lately brought together in Brussels a considerable number of eminent men of all nations; I can refer to the visit which the National Guards from Paris made to London, where the English people received them with the most cordial fraternity. But the peoples are not satisfied with setting their inclinations in opposition to the warlike system of their governments. They do much more; they bring against it their intelligence, their labour, their literature, their industrial inventions, and their fine arts. They break through the frontiers, they build bridges over the rivers which separate them, and fly to each other on the wings of vehicles propelled by steam. (*Hear, hear!*)

Observe, I beg you, how in the present epoch, the commerce between the different nations has risen to not less than 7 or 8 billion francs. How then, I ask, can war still be possible in the face of such mutual sympathies and such important transactions between the peoples?

No, citizens, war, properly speaking, war as a system and as a right, is no longer possible between peoples. And, therefore, without doubt you will not want to continue the armed peace which ruins you.

All the states of Europe must now disarm to a considerable degree. French diplomacy must actively pursue this aim; and, by every means, by coercive and revolutionary force, if necessary, France must make prevail the system of congresses of representative jurisdiction. I do not mean by that the decrees of some great states being forced on small states with all the weight of a despotic coalition; I mean general congresses of the small as well as the great states to discuss their interests on an equal footing, so as to 'unite under the same law,' as Massillon said, 'every tribe and every nation.'

Citizens, I have just conceded that the idea of permanent peace, by means of the institution of a system of arbitration, was the dream of the philosopher and moralist. I feel no embarrassment in making this concession, for all progress comes from imagination and intelligence before it takes the form of facts. Allow me, however, to say: not only have philosphers and moralists, such as Kant, Rousseau, Pascal, Fénelon, Massillon, Saint-Pierre, Fourrier and Pecqueur, or even myself, become convinced of the idea of the pacification of the world; there are also various learned men, political writers, military men and statesmen of the highest standing, such as Grotius, Vattel, Montesquieu, Leibnitz, de Maistre, William Penn, Ancillon, Arago, Tyler, Adams, Bentham, and even Napoleon, the man who pressed the abuse of war to such an extent.

Yes, citizens, Napoleon Bonaparte himself, the ambitious commander, who, having betrayed the Republic to place an imperial crown on his own head, dragged France and the whole of Europe through the human slaughter house of war, has left, as the fruit of one moment's remorse, a word in favour of universal peace (*Sensation*), and here, in a report to Bonald, is what he said: 'I wish (the expression *I wish* was familiar to this great man), I wish that the prevalence of philanthropic and generous ideas should be the characteristic of this age; such sentiments cannot be imputed to me as weakness. It is for the most amiable, the most enlightened, the most humane nation (he pointed to France), to suggest to the civilised nations of Europe that they form themselves into one family' . . .

This array of unquestionably valuable authorities ought at least to be sufficient, citizens, to persuade you that the idea of permanent peace and of international jurisdiction is not only the ideal of a few persons devoted to metaphysical contemplation.

There are, as I have told you, military men, statesmen and diplomats of the highest distinction. For my own part, I wonder at the way in which force of circumstances and the understanding of men, though often spur-ning the trends of philosophy and morality, yet arrive at the same final results in their own proper way.

I wonder at the way in which material necessity reduces the states to take refuge in a system of peace, their sole retreat at the present time . . .

Citizens, these are my conclusions, and I set them down in the presence of the fundamental principles of our democratic constitution: war, arising from force and restraint, is contrary to *liberty*; war, imposing the strong on the weak, is contrary to *equality*; war, shattering violently the laws of love which unite individuals and peoples, is contrary to *fraternity*.

Thus, the Republic, to be consistent with its own constitution, ought henceforth to aim at suppressing the military system and replacing it with an international jurisdiction.

Such an object is too honest, too generous and too beneficial to the welfare of nations, for France to blush in making it the principal aim of her external policy.

Peace, justice, liberty, labour: such is the motto that the French Republic ought to present to mankind. (*Hear, hear! Hear, hear!*)
(*Speech on the War Budget in the French National Assembly, 28 November 1848.*)

[Source: *Compte Rendu des Séances de l'Assemblée Nationale*, tome V, (21 octobre au 30 novembre 1848), Paris, 1850, pp.886–9. Translated by the editors of this volume.]

Editors' Note

1. The phrase from the Vulgate refers to the parable in which the Kingdom of heaven is likened to a wedding feast. The English Authorised Version reads: 'Go out into the highways and hedges and compel them to come in.' *St. Luke* 14:23.

Doc. 43. RICHARD COBDEN: International Arbitration

I think there is nothing unreasonable in our seeking to take another step towards consolidating the peace of nations, and securing us against the recurrence of the greatest calamity that can afflict mankind.

I stand here the humble representative of two distinct bodies, both of some importance in the community. In the first place, I represent on this occasion, and for this specific motion alone, that influential body of Christians who repudiate war in any case, whether offensive or defensive; I also represent that numerous portion of the middle classes of this country, with the great bulk of the working classes, who have an abhorrence of war, greater than at any former period of our history, and who desire that we should take some new precautions, and, if possible, obtain some guarantees, against the recurrence of war in future. Those two classes have found in the motion which I am about to submit a common ground – and I rejoice at it – on which they can unite without compromising their principles, on one side or the other. It is not necessary that any one in this House, or out of it, who accedes to this motion, should be of opinion that we are not justified, under any circumstances, in resorting to war, even in self-defence. It is only necessary that you should be agreed that war is a great calamity, which it is desirable we should avoid if possible. If you feel that the plan proposed is calculated to attain the object sought, you may vote for it without compromising yourselves on the extreme principle of defensive war. I assume that every one in this House would only sanction war, in case it was imperatively demanded on our part, in defence of our honour, or our just interests. I take it that every one here would repudiate war, unless it were called for by such motives. I assume, moreover, that there is not a man in this House who would not repudiate war, if those objects – the just interests and honour of the country – could be preserved by any other means. My object is to see if we cannot devise some better method than war for attaining those ends; and my plan is, simply and solely, that we should resort to that mode of settling disputes, which individuals resort to in private life. I only want you to go one step farther, to carry out in another instance the principle which you recognise in other cases – that the intercourse between communities is nothing more than the intercourse of individuals in the aggregate. I want to know why there may not be an agreement between this country and France, or between this country and America, by which the nations should respectively bind themselves, in case of any misunderstanding arising, which could not be settled by mutual representation or diplomacy, to refer the dispute to the decision of arbitrators. By arbitrators I do not mean necessarily crowned heads, or neutral states; ... I should prefer to see these disputes referred to individuals, whether designated commissioners, or plenipotentiaries, or arbitrators, appointed from one country to meet men appointed from another country to inquire into the matter and decide upon it; or, if they cannot do so, to have the power of calling in an umpire, as is done in all arbitrations. I propose that these individuals should have absolute power to dispose of the question submitted to them ... It appears that what I propose is no novelty, no innovation; it has been practised, and practised with success; I only want you to carry the principle a little farther, and resort to it, in anticipation, as a mode of arranging all quarrels.

For this reason, I propose an address to the Crown, praying that Her Majesty will instruct her Foreign Secretary to propose to foreign Powers to enter into treaties, providing that, in any case of future misunderstanding, which cannot be settled by amicable negotiation, an arbitration, such as I have described, shall be resorted to ... Now, I shall be met with this objection – I have heard it already – and I know there are Members of this House who purpose to vote against the motion on this ground: they say, 'What is the use of a treaty of this sort, between France and England, for instance; the parties would not observe the treaty; it would be a piece of waste paper; they would go to war, as before, in spite of any treaty.' It would be a sufficient answer to this objection to say, 'What is the use of any treaty? What is the use of the Foreign Office? What is the use of your diplomacy?' You might shut up the one and cashier the other. I maintain, that a treaty binding two countries to refer their disputes to arbitration, is just as likely to be observed as any other treaty. Nay, I question very much whether it is not more likely to be observed; because, I think there is no object which other countries will be less likely to seek than that of having a war with a country so powerful as England. Therefore, if any provision were made by which you might honourably avoid a war, that provision would be as gladly sought by your opponents as by yourselves. But I deny that, as a rule, treaties are violated; as a rule, they are respected and observed. I do not find that wars, generally, arise out of the violation of any specific treaty – they more commonly arise out of accidental collisions; and, as a rule, treaties are observed by powerful States against the weak, just as well as by weak States against the powerful. I, therefore, see no difficulty specially applying to a treaty of this kind, greater than exists with other treaties. There would be this advantage, at all events, in having a treaty binding another country to refer all disputes to arbitration. If that country did not fulfil its engagement, it would enter into war with the brand of infamy stamped upon its banners. It could not proclaim to the world that it was engaged in a just and necessary war. On the contrary, all the world would point to that nation as violating a treaty, by going to war with a country with whom they had engaged to enter into arbitration. I anticipate another objection which I have heard made: they say, 'You cannot entrust the great interests of England to individuals or commissioners.' That difficulty springs out of the assumption, that the quarrels with foreign countries are about questions involving the whole existence of the empire. On the contrary, whenever these quarrels take place, it is generally upon the most minute and absurd pretexts – so trivial that it is almost impossible, on looking back for the last hundred years, to tell precisely what any war was about . . .

But, to return to the point whether or not commissioners might be entrusted with the grave matters which form the subjects of dispute between nations, I would draw the attention of the House to the fact, that already you do virtually entrust these matters to individuals. Treaties of peace, made after war, are entrusted to individuals to negotiate and carry out. Take the case of Lord Castlereagh, representing the British power at the Congress of Vienna. He had full power to bind this country to the Treaty of Vienna . . . I want to know, whether as good men as Lord Castlereagh could not be found to settle these matters before, as after, a twenty years' war? Why not depute to a plenipotentiary the same powers before a conflict as you give him after? . . .

Probably I shall be told that there are signs of a pacific tendency on the part of the Government and the country; it will be said that we are carrying out a pacific policy, and that there is no necessity for passing any resolution to impose on the Government the obligation of giving us this guarantee. But I do not see that this is in process of being done. I do not see any proof, in the last five or six years, that the Government has been increasing in its confidence of peace being preserved, or gaining security for its preservation. In the last ten years we have increased our armed forces by 60,000; in the army, navy, and ordnance, the expenditure has been augmented sixty to seventy per cent. From 1836, down to last year, there is no proof of the Government having any confidence in the duration of peace, or possessing increased security against war ...

What are we to deduce from these facts? That instead of making the progress of civilisation subservient to the welfare of mankind – instead of making the arts of civilisation available for increasing the enjoyments of life – you are constantly bringing these improvements in science to bear upon the deadly contrivances of war, and thus are making the arts of peace and the discoveries of science contribute to the barbarism of the age. But will anybody presume to answer me by the declaration that we want no further guarantee for the preservation of peace? Will any one tell me that I am not strictly justified and warranted in trying, at all events, to bring to bear the opinion of this House, of the country, and of the civilised world, upon some better mode of preserving peace than that which imposes upon us almost all the burdens which war formerly used to entail? ...

But I wish to know where this system is to end. I have sat on the army, navy, and ordnance committees, and I see no limit to the increase of our armaments under the existing system. Unless you can adopt some such plan as I propose, unless you can approach foreign countries in a conciliatory spirit, and offer to them some kind of assurance that you do not wish to attack them, and receive the assurance that you are not going to be assailed by them, I see no necessary or logical end to the increase of our establishments. For the progress of scientific knowledge will lead to a constant increase of expenditure. There is no limit but the limit of taxation, and that, I believe, you have nearly reached. I shall probably be told that my plan would not suit all cases. I think it would suit all cases a great deal better than the plan which is now resorted to. At all events, arbitration is more rational, just, and humane than the resort to the sword ...

I may be told that, even if you make treaties of this kind, you cannot enforce the award. I admit it. I am no party to the plan which some advocate – no doubt with the best intentions – of having a Congress of nations, with a code of laws – a supreme court of appeal, with an army to support its decisions. I am no party to any such plan. I believe it might lead to more armed interference than takes place at present ... I have no plan for compelling the fulfilment of treaties of arbitration. I have no idea of enforcing treaties in any other way than that now resorted to. I do not, myself, advocate an appeal to arms; but that which follows the violation of a treaty, under the present system, may follow the violation of a treaty of arbitration, if adopted. What I say, however, is, if you make a treaty with another country, binding it to refer any dispute to arbitration, and if that country violates that treaty, when the dispute arises, then you will place it in a worse position before the world – you will place it in so infamous a position, that I doubt if any country would enter into a war on such bad grounds as that country must occupy ...

I shall be quite satisfied, as a beginning, if I see the noble Lord [Palmerston], or any one filling his place, trying to negotiate an arbitration treaty with the United States, or with France. But I should like to bind ourselves to the same principle with the weakest and smallest States. I should be as willing to see it done with Tuscany, Belgium, or Holland, as with France or America, because I am anxious to prove to the world that we are prepared to submit our misunderstandings, in all cases, to a purer and more just arbitrament than that of brute force. Whilst I do not agree with those who are in favour of a Congress of nations, I do think that if the larger and more civilised Powers were to enter into treaties of this kind, their decisions would become precedents, and you would in this way, in the course of time, establish a kind of common law amongst nations, which would save the time and trouble of arbitration in each individual case.

I do not anticipate any sudden or great change in the character of mankind, nor do I expect a complete extinction of those passions which form part of our nature. But I do not think there is anything very irrational in expecting that nations may see that the present system of settling disputes is barbarous, demoralising, and unjust; that it wars against the best interests of society, and that it ought to give place to a mode more consonant with the dictates of reason and humanity. I do not see anything in the present state of European society to prevent us from discussing this matter, and hoping that it may be brought to a satisfactory conclusion ... All I want is, that we should enter into mutual engagements with other countries, binding ourselves with them, in all future cases of dispute which cannot be otherwise arranged, to refer the matter to arbitration. No possible harm can arise from the failure of my plan. The worst that can be said of it is, that it will not effect its object – that of averting war. We shall then remain in that unsatisfactory state in which we now find ourselves. I put it to any person having a desire to avert war, whether, when he sees that the adoption of this plan can do no harm, it is not just and wise to try whether it may not effect good.

(*Speech in the House of Commons, 12 June 1849.*)

[Source: *Speeches on Questions of Public Policy by Richard Cobden*, M.P., ed. John Bright and James E. Thorold Rogers, London 1880, pp.390–8.]

Doc. 44. EMILE DE LAVELEYE: On the Causes of War, and the Means of Reducing Their Number

Mankind is drawing more and more away from the state of war, and getting nearer and nearer to a state of peace; but the progress is slow, and interrupted by many periods of apparent retrogression ... The heart of man does not change, but his ideas do; his passions remain the same, but as the institutions in the midst of which they work undergo modification, the actions to which they give rise will vary in like manner. Man is before all things selfish ... Self-interest is the great moving power of the whole living world ... Hence you will never transform men into heroes of self-devotion, but you may make it their interest to be just by punishing injustice and crime ... The savage slays the man who disputes his possession; the civilised human being summons him to a court of justice. Each follows his interest in the manner that seems to himself most advantageous. Nations act like savages, because there is no tribunal to do justice between them. Establish the tribunal, and it becomes their interest to submit their differences to it, instead of slaughtering one another ... Self-interest, which ushered war into the world, ends its evolutions in universal peace ...

Every country that seeks military success renounces liberty. In the strength of passive obedience and discipline lies the strength of armies; criticism, discussion, and the assertion of lawful rights are the mainsprings of free institutions. In a country at war, or preparing for war, authority must be absolute; its proper sovereign is a general and a dictator. The spirit of conquest and the spirit of freedom are therefore incompatible. Force reigns with the one, reason with the other. And the war ended, victory ordinarily seals the subjugation of the victorious people; for Bonapartes are much more common than Washingtons. Seeing, therefore, that in every war nations must stake both their prosperity and their freedom, it is obvious that, if they have their eyes open, they cannot wish for it. But if no nation will enter on an aggressive war, none will have to stand on the defensive.

To ensure peace, then, only two conditions are requisite; that nations should understand their own interest in the matter, and that means should be found of settling unavoidable differences without resort to arms.

As regards the first point, nations have begun to understand how injurious war and preparations for war are to them; but many causes ... historical grudges, race hostilities, colonial interests, revindication of natural boundaries, defective political institutions – cloud this perception, or render it inefficacious, save in America and England. These prejudices, passions, and false ideas can only disappear by degrees, with the progress of enlightenment and international trade. To further the movement, everything ought to be done to foster community of views and identity of interests among nations ... What insulates men disposes to war, whatever brings them into relation with each other inclines them to peace. And nothing tends to secure such intimate relations between nations as commerce ... It was by the Zollverein, i.e., by the suppression of the custom-house barriers, that the unity of Germany was founded ... Nothing could show more clearly how commercial relations soften down feuds between nations than the effects of the Anglo-French Treaty of Commerce; ancient prejudices have been dissipated, antipathies have disappeared as it were by enchantment ...

Independently of the measures ... [which] would have a general tendency to incline nations towards peace, there are means of preventing, not indeed all wars, as some enthusiasts hope, but certain wars.

1st. – The settlement of a code of international law, defining the reciprocal rights and duties of nations in time both of peace and war.

2nd. – The institution of a system of arbitration, to arrange such international differences as may arise ...

Most disputes arise from the fact of there being no generally recognised rules. Were there such rules, the differences themselves would be forestalled, and the necessity even for arbitration would rarely arise.

It is therefore indispensable that the problems of international law should be promptly elucidated, and civilised nations induced to adopt the solutions arrived at. In this the governments of Great Britain and the United States ought to take the initiative, being the countries in which these problems have been most discussed. They ought to propose a congress of diplomatists and jurists, to which they should invite all other powers to send representatives, and which would have for its object to frame an international code. In the event of there being any difference of opinion, the majority should decide, each country having no more than one vote. In lieu of a *veto*, each of the participant powers should have the right to repudiate at once the obligation of any principle voted by the majority ...

The urgency of an understanding taking place among civilised nations with reference to these matters is becoming more and more apparent ... The method most dignified, and least likely to clash with the *amour-propre* of the different states, is to submit such questions to a Joint High Commission of International Law, for examination and settlement. By such a commission the independence of no power would be jeopardised, inasmuch as its decisions would be binding only upon such of these as should acquiesce in them; yet the meeting of such an areopagus would form a landmark in history. It would be a great step towards the realisation of the brotherhood of nations ...

But it would not be enough to have a code of international law; there should also be a court of arbitration, to settle future differences between governments that may have accepted the code. It may be said that all Europe, horrified by the dreadful wars that have of late years sprung up without any real cause, demands the adoption of some means of rendering the recurrence of such calamities impossible; and the means clearly pointed out by public opinion is a system of international arbitration.

The first point to be kept in view is that the Court of Arbitration would have no military force at its disposal for the execution of its decision . . . Otherwise nations would cease to be independent; and a universal right of intervention, even in the most trifling differences between any two states, might give rise to a general war. We should find ourselves once more in the presence of a Holy Alliance on an enlarged scale – a very poor guarantee for the progress of liberty. Besides, no state is willing to be absolutely bound by the judgment of a court, whose decisions might imperil its prosperity and its very existence . . .

The High Court of Nations ought to be composed of the diplomatic representatives of the concurring powers, assisted in their labours by jurists versed in the international law. To prevent the susceptibilities of any great state from being hurt, it should have its seat in the capital of some small neutral country, such as Belgium or Switzerland. It should be permanent, as regards its formation, although it would sit only in the event of there being a difference to be settled. The court would be established by virtue of the special treaty promulgating the code of international law. It is important that it should hold a lofty position, to attract the attention and respect of the world; so that the pressure of the public opinion of nations might be brought to bear upon any state that should seek to evade the obligation of submitting a difference to it.

The principle of non-intervention in domestic affairs having been laid down in the most absolute terms, the court might take cognisance of all international differences, and give judgment upon the merits of each case; no other proviso being necessary than that its sentences should not be carried into execution by force . . .

The establishment of an International High Court, with the restrictions indicated above, would be in keeping with the wants of our age; it would soon be recognised by the majority of civilised nations; and it would be an immense boon to mankind at large, and actually mark, as it were, the dawn of that era of peace of which all right-minded men are dreaming, and which is, in truth, the destiny of our race . . .

There are doubtless, certain questions which cannot at present be settled by arbitration, because they bring all the passions of a nation into play; such as, for instance, the revindication of Metz by France, the Polish question, or the Slav question. Were the people wise, or possessed of a clear understanding of their own interests, all these difficulties might be removed without conflict or war; in the barbarous condition in which we are still groping, we cannot, unfortunately, hope for such a situation . . .

In most quarrels the matter at stake is not worth the cost of one day's mobilisation of the armies; but the state which might otherwise give way fears the loss of authority, and exposure to future insults. Thus each is led to carry every difference to the last extremity. International arbitration, on the contrary, would leave the honour of both parties safe, and thus ensure peace, while in no way affecting the dignity of either litigant...

States dreaming of future conquests, and sovereigns anxious for war in order to govern at home, may with difficulty be led to adopt the principle of arbitration. But to nations like the English or Americans, which have everything to lose and nothing to gain by mutual slaughter, arbitration is an institution easily invested with practical authority, because public opinion rules, and public opinion, as well as the real interest of both countries, would be on its side...

Were there a regular known, and approved means of obtaining satisfaction without resort to arms, the public opinion of the world would brand with infamy the state which insisted on war. The institution of an International Court of Arbitration would produce at once this effect... Let the International Court of Arbitration be established, and public opinion will compel all states to submit to it. Nay, public opinion exerts more influence upon governments than upon individuals; all their acts being public and open to general comment, and their authority being dependent upon opinion. Therefore, states will not demur the decisions of the Court of Arbitration, unless they be manifestly unjust, and opposed to interests of the highest order...

It is certain that nations will one day adopt this system; the whole course of history proves it. The fact of mediation, arbitration, and conferences becoming more and more frequent shows that nations aspire towards the adjustment of their differences by a less barbarous process than war. Were England, were her present Prime Minister [Gladstone] ... to propose to the other states the appointment of a commission for settling disputed points of international law and establishing a system of international arbitration, more than one government would agree at once to the proposal, and the public opinion of the entire world would acclaim him as the benefactor of the human race. The question is fully ripe... The United States, to whom the first idea of the arbitration system is due, would not repel it... The Treaty of Washington, by virtue of which the principal differences between England and the United States have been referred to arbitration, might form the stepping-stone to a general measure, in which all nations could concur, with no fear for their independence...

But if no government will take the initiative towards realising the magnificent idea conceived by American philanthropists, and advocated by Cobden before the Parliament of Great Britain, it is then for the public itself to take up this noble cause. A vast international association ought, in that case, to be founded, having for its sole object to make the system of international arbitration prevail...

[Source: Emile de Laveleye: 'On the Causes of War, and the Means of Reducing Their Number, in *Cobden Club Essays,* Second Series, 1871–2, London 1872, pp.26–37, 46–52.]

Section C

Major aspects of Continental liberalism in the nineteenth century

Attitudes and ideas in France, Germany, Italy and Spain (1815–1881)

Introductory

Nineteenth-century liberalism on the European continent, being largely based on and supported by the middle classes, was a complex affair. European liberals everywhere desired a constitution, political representation in an elected parliament and a clearly defined voting system. They insisted on limiting the powers of the monarch and resented the privileges of the old ruling classes, the aristocracy and the higher clergy. In a progressively industrialized society life was to be based on the rule of law. After the Napoleonic Wars a liberal constitution was largely visualized on the British pattern. To a lesser extent the French Charters of 1814 and 1830 as well as the Belgian Constitution of 1831 served as models east of the Rhine. Everywhere equality of the citizens before the law and their security from arbitrary interference by the authorities were regarded as essential.

During the first half of the century ideology appeared more relevant than liberal organization. In fact, only after the revolutions of 1848–49 did party groupings develop, and liberal associations come into existence in Germany, Austria and Italy. Liberal ideas were however also fermenting in other associations and parties which did not use the label 'liberal'. This is particularly striking in France where no organized party ever called itself 'liberal', though the term 'parti libéral' sometimes appeared in the title of books. .

Freedom of opinion, of the press, of association were throughout key issues in the liberal ideology and so was freedom of religion. Liberals were generally opposed to the authoritarian attitude and to the privileges of the Churches, particularly those of the Roman Catholic Church. They objected to the existing close affinity between throne and altar and many of them came to favour the separation of Church and State. Although not all liberals were anti-clerical, a Voltairian dislike and distrust of the activities of the ruling Church was widespread among them.

The desire for creating a nation-state was another problem besetting liberals in Germany and Italy. While they were mostly anti-étatist, wanting to curtail the powers and the sphere of activity of the State, this attitude changed frequently after the formation of the nation-state which they had supported so fervently. Liberal opposition to State power often diminished when liberals were able to participate directly or indirectly in it. The term 'national liberal', used by dissidents in Germany who in 1866 had broken away from the more intransigent Progressive Party in Prussia and had made their peace with the authoritarian Chancellor Bismarck, clearly illustrates this change of attitude.

1. The constitutional state: introduction
(Documents 45–57, pp. 431–69)

(i) Limitation of power – the role of the monarch

After 1814 French liberals desired above all a constitutional monarchy in which the spheres of the legislative, executive and judicial powers were clearly defined and separated. There evolved a new interest in the work of Montesquieu, which was not only reflected in the intensive contemporary commentary on the *Spirit of the Laws*, by Destutt de Tracy (doc. 45), but also in Benjamin Constant's acceptance of Montesquieu's belief that as all power, particularly if unlimited, tends to corrupt, a system of checks and balances was essential for any healthy body politic.

Constant wished to reduce the rights of the State to a minimum. To him the State had no other raison d'être than the protection of the rights and the freedom of the individual. Individual liberty was the primary aim of all human association. On it public and private ethics were based and on it rested even the calculations of industry. Without it there could be no dignity or human happiness. Like other French liberals Constant saw history as a continuous struggle between the sovereignty of man and the sovereignty of the State, a struggle in which the aim was a constant reduction of State-power.

Different from his contemporary Hegel and the German historical school, Constant viewed the State not as an organism in its own right, but only as a derivative instrumentality to be used to guarantee the rights of the individual. As he put it neatly: 'Les droits individuels c'est la liberté, les droits sociaux, c'est la guarantie.' The State was not to concern itself with cultural or economic tasks; its only function was to protect the rights of the individual against undue interference by others. Political liberty of the individual meant above all the right to say what he thought, the right to criticize and to protest.

Constant's originality in the plea for a constitutional State lies in his concept of the monarchy as a 'neutral power'. He saw it as a fourth arm which would serve to keep the other three arms of political power in check. It was a concept much in line with the limited monarchy of Louis Philippe which Constant helped to found in February 1830, a few months before his death. The monarch as 'pouvoir neutre' stands in the centre of the political system in which the four powers of the executive, the representative power of permanence (Hereditary Chamber), the representative power of opinion (Lower Chamber) and the judiciary tend to cross, challenge and impeach each other. While each of the powers has its special function the king represents the focal point of the system, 'a neutral and intermediary authority without a definite interest in upsetting the equilibrium, but on the contrary being fully interested in its preservation' (doc. 46). Across the Channel the monarch was unable to abuse his strictly limited power nor could any of the other powers do so.

It was in South Germany that the ideas of Benjamin Constant and of other French liberals found an echo between 1830 and the March Revolution of 1848. The constitutions granted by the monarchs in the South German States soon after 1815 had been largely modelled on the Charter of Louis XVIII, but they were at least a step forward towards some political participation of the propertied classes, still denied to them in Prussia and Austria.

While the influence of the Diets of Baden and Hessen under the new regime was modest, at least they formed a platform for the public airing of important political issues. Some of the South-West German progressive deputies were impressed by French liberal thought. Though the position in Germany was different – as there the old feudal powers were by no means eradicated and the power of the bureaucracy was strong – Constant's middle of the road liberalism had a natural appeal to the South German liberals. They too were opposed both to a return of the old feudal powers and to the aspirations of the uneducated masses. Additionally they shared Constant's desire for a constitutional monarchy with responsible ministers and an effective parliament. The main difference between them and Constant was one of national background. The Germans had not experienced a revolution and the power and prestige of the old ruling class were still little impaired. Therefore the South German liberals fought negatively for the right to stop reactionary measures of the government rather than positively for political power and for a basic change of the political system.

The most indefatigable and widely known champions of moderate constitutional liberalism in South Germany were Karl von Rotteck and Karl Theodor Welcker (docs 48 and 49). The fact that, like nearly all spokesmen of German liberalism, they were professors – Friedrich Dahlmann, Robert von Mohl, Georg Gervinus and Heinrich von Treitschke, are other examples – was not always a blessing, for they were inclined to write and speak in an over-abstract and didactic manner and lacked the lucidity and analytical finesse so characteristic of the style of John Stuart Mill or Alexis de Tocqueville. (Only Treitschke, who was active after 1848, expressed his thoughts in a forceful and attractive manner.)

Rotteck and Welcker were filled with a quasi-missionary spirit in their zeal to spread the gospel of constitutionalism. They were also to some extent political martyrs as they both lost their university chairs for some time on account of their active role in Baden's Second Chamber. They became widely known as editors of the first political encyclopedia in Germany, the *Staatslexikon*, published in nineteen volumes between 1834–48. It functioned as a kind of political bible to two generations of

C. Aspects of continental liberalism in the nineteenth century

the middle classes in Germany. Rotteck and Welcker were rationalists. Rotteck followed the French ideas of natural rights and social contract, whereas Welcker was closer to the English model in regarding the British Constitution as exemplary. Both desired the people's sovereignty and with it a Republic. But this was only in theory. In practice they did not object to the role of the monarch in Baden à la Louis Philippe. In their opinion government should be conducted 'by friendly contact with the spirit of the people, by respect for the voices of the people and of the people's representatives, through frankness and through loyalty, sticking to the Constitution and to all the rights guaranteed to the citizen by it and to all the rights to which they are reasonably entitled.' [1]

The Constitution visualized in the *Staatslexikon* provided for a distribution of power between the territorial or people's representatives and the government, in a way which assured 'as far as possible the predominance of the true, considered and enduring collective will.' There was to be the usual division of powers between the legislative, the administrative and the judiciary powers. There was also a strong demand for free and unhindered access of the people to information on public affairs and for 'the free expression of their opinions and judgments on the process of their administration'. Freedom of the press and the need for giving publicity to the decisions of the government and of the representatives of the people were regarded as 'essential factors in a constitutional system'. Among the other rights of the people, freedom of divine worship and freedom to emigrate were especially emphasized. A key feature in the constitutional system was the principle of responsibility of all persons holding executive power, after the British model.[2] Responsible to the king, the ministers and top civil servants were also declared responsible to the people's representatives.

When Heinrich von Treitschke wrote his remarkable essay on 'Freedom' (*Die Freiheit*, 1861), he was professor of history at the University of Freiburg where earlier Rotteck and Welcker had taught. Their ideal was the constitutional, rather than the national, State and individual freedom rather than national unity. Treitschke in his turn was an ardent champion for German unity under Prussian leadership. French ideas of liberty were anathema to him and so was the ideology of the social contract. He took up a middle position between old-fashioned étatism and modern individualism, between what he regarded as the extremes of conservatism and of liberal radicalism. In discussing the problems of freedom in his essay (see doc. 51) he was critical of the aesthetic individualism of J. S. Mill and Laboulaye. For Treitschke freedom was not freedom from the State, but *within* the State. From Hegel he took over 'the conception of the State as a transpersonalistic national individuality and organism whose essence is *Macht* (power)'.[3] At the same time the State ought to be a *Rechtsstaat*, based on the rule of law. He argued that the French had never experienced liberty but only equality and that it

390

was 'Teutonic' to insist on the definite right of the individual. There existed no personal freedom without political freedom, a term significantly defined by him as 'politically limited freedom'. For Treitschke the State evoked an emotional response. 'The State's honour', he proclaimed, 'is our honour and he who cannot regard his State with enthusiastic pride, innately lacks one of the supreme emotions a man can experience.' Treitschke utterly rejected the individualistic view of the State as a nightwatchman. To him the State was 'an end in itself as are all living things'. It was easy for Mill and Laboulaye who lived 'in powerful, respected States', to take the blessings of the State for granted and to keep a sharp watch on its possible trespasses. The Germans, on the other hand, with their *Kleinstaaterei* had their 'appreciation of the dignity of the State sharpened by painful deprivation'. In other words, they were inclined to overcompensate the role and power of the State from a marked inferiority complex. Treitschke emphasized the tasks of social justice and education which, he claimed, only the State can tackle satisfactorily. In reverse the citizen was obliged to 'make every personal sacrifice' for the State 'which the preservation of the collective whole requires, even the sacrifice of his life' (doc. 51).

Treitschke was then by no means in favour of a tyrannical or authoritarian regime but welcomed citizens with individuality and initiative in an age of entrepreneurs like the Krupps and Borsigs. To him 'every part of the government' was 'beneficial which evokes, promotes and purifies the initiative of individuals'. While he was in agreement with J. S. Mill and Laboulaye in their desire for the highest possible degree of personal freedom, he definitely rejected their denigration of the State as an alleged hindrance to personal freedom.

(ii) The English model

Between 1814 and 1848 the British political system was regarded as a model by many advanced thinkers and politicians on the Continent. Britain had, it seemed, established a limited monarchy painlessly, once and for all. In the wake of Montesquieu, the French writers on politics admired and overrated the division of powers, the position of the king in England who ruled but did not govern, and the role of the English aristocracy. An open caste, its strength was not based on military prowess and its sons were not ashamed to become barristers and even successful businessmen. A generation which in their youth had experienced the nightmare of Jacobin terror and the ruthlessness of Napoleonic autocracy viewed Britain as a balanced, stable and prosperous political country in which the citizens enjoyed equality before the law and safeguards from arbitrary arrest. These anglophils looked to England as to a political eldorado, comparable with the way in which some Western

C. Aspects of continental liberalism in the nineteenth century

intellectuals were a century later viewing the new political system of the Soviet Union.

Madame de Staël was impressed by the universal validity of the law in Britain, equally binding as it seemed on aristocrats and commoners (doc. 52). Yet to her relief equality before the law did not mean social equality but was compatible with a 'separation of ranks'. England was a differentiated society with an unchallenged common basis. Influenced by Montesquieu, she did not doubt that countries differed in their administrative, financial, commercial and military aspects according to varying local conditions, but 'the fundamental parts of a constitution were identical everywhere' (doc. 53).

Friedrich C. Dahlmann, the German historian and political scientist, was another anglophil. As an empiricist he appreciated that the English system was the outcome of traditional practical wisdom and not the outcome of theory. The future constitutions in Europe should be based on the English model, which to Dahlmann was 'most perfectly shaped and preserved' (doc. 54). The German professor also recommended the English two-chamber system as it presented a neat balance between tradition and innovation. In the British parliament the big national issues could be discussed reasonably and effectively, while the monarch remained 'sacrosanct and immune, but without responsibility' (doc. 55). Dahlmann too, maintained a middle of the road position. The people's voice, he argued, must be heard, but mob rule was to be avoided. At a time when Prussia still had provincial Diets only, but no nationwide representation, he desired a national parliament with more than an advisory function.

Dahlmann's fellow-countryman David Hansemann, a pushing and self-confident Rhenish industrialist, struck a new note in the debate. In his Memorandum of 1830 for King Frederick William III (doc. 56) he argued that the English Constitution was *not* a model for Prussia. He gave two reasons for this: firstly, Prussia had not an aristocracy of the 'open type'; secondly she lacked that degree of freedom which was higher in England than in any other country. This very freedom enabled the aristocracy constantly to renew itself through 'the excellent talents of the middle classes'.

Like Dahlmann, Hansemann was afraid of mob rule and of a weakening of the power of the State. He regarded it as unwise and impractical to reduce the power of the Crown to the extent that had been done in Britain and to allow more de-centralization of State power. In England parliament and the local authorities fulfilled many administrative functions which in Prussia had to be retained by the Crown, if the central power of the State on which the position of the Crown depended was not to be weakened. Although Hansemann was often critical of the Prussian bureaucracy he obviously did not want to diminish its strength which he conceived as an arm of the power of the Crown (doc. 50).

During the turmoil of the revolutions of 1848 Britain surprised many Continental observers by the fact that she managed to pull through without a revolution. It Italy Camillo di Cavour, later the leader of the *risorgimento*, was impressed by the manner in which the British Government was able to combine freedom and order and so avoid any large-scale social upheaval (doc. 57). In fact, it acknowledged the right of minorities to voice their grievances without allowing them to endanger law and order. The occasion for Cavour's reflections was the Chartist demonstration at Kennington Common, London, on 10 April 1848. Although a serious challenge to the existing regime, the government mastered it by combining firmness with a prudent lack of violence. Whereas the mass meeting itself was not interfered with, the planned procession of the Chartists to Westminster to present a mammoth petition to the House of Commons was disallowed. The petition, however, was handed in without the intervention of the troops who had been ready. While, as Cavour put it, the mass orators at Kennington Common were permitted to 'pronounce the most violent and incendiary discourses', the Chartist leaders had to give way in the end thus avoiding an 'open and violent conflict'. The reason was that the government had on its side not only the troops and 'all the property owners, the shopkeepers of London, but even the workers, being friends of order as well as of liberty'. It was this union of liberty with order which impressed the Italian reformer most. On the Continent there was talk of granting liberties and rights, which in fact were 'little respected by various parties', whereas on the other side of the Channel they were regarded 'as unshakable dogmas of political faith'. Through the centuries England had remained 'the jealous and faithful custodian' of 'the great principles of liberty on which the institutions of modern peoples rest'. In Britain individual liberty, the liberty of the press, the rights of assembly and of petition had on the whole been successfully maintained against both usurpers of power and popular violence. To Cavour England compared favourably with France. The attitude of the British government towards obstreperous minorities, and towards outspoken critics in the newspapers in London and Dublin and the general way in which religious worship was regulated by the State were much to be preferred to the handling of these things in France. Chartist socialism and Irish nationalism could be voiced in Westminster with a belligerent vehemence which would not be tolerated on the Continent, and yet this did not affect the basic stability of the British system. To most continental liberals England remained 'the classic country of liberalism', a shining example that liberty and order could be harmonized and the rights of minorities safeguarded.

2. Freedom and the individual: introduction
(Documents 58–71, pp. 469–511)

(i) The rights of the individual

The ardent pleas for greater freedom of the individual that emerged in Western Europe during the years after the Napoleonic Wars indicate the impact of the trauma of twenty-five years of revolution and dictatorship. The contours of the Restoration and the memories of past terror forced the pioneers of liberalism to tread warily and to make their ideas acceptable to a 'burnt' generation which preferred peace to political experiments and moderation to bold innovation. Yet by 1830 the problem of liberty for everyone had proved more complex than the idealistic Madame de Staël or the cautiously pragmatic Guizot realized. The Revolution of 1830 in France did not enlarge greatly the number of people entitled to vote and Guizot continued to praise the virtues of the middle classes only. Madame de Staël had defended the friends of freedom against the accusation that they were enemies of religion. She had refuted the doctrine that 'one has to be an atheist in order to love freedom' (doc. 58). A decade later a significant attempt was made to bridge the traditional antagonism between Liberals and Catholics in France. 'We are afraid of Liberalism', declared Abbé Felicité de Lamennais, 'Catholicize it and it will be born again.' Although Lamennais' newspaper *L'Avenir* was short-lived because it incurred the displeasure of the Vatican and of the higher French clergy, its slogan *Dieu et la Liberté* was never forgotton.[4]

In his earlier writings Lamennais had been an uncompromising Ultramontane; later he drew a sharp line of distinction between the old intolerant and opportunistic anti-clerical liberals and the young liberals in favour of a constructive separation of Church and State. Accepting the revised Charter of 1830 Lamennais made a passionate plea for 'the liberty which belongs to us, equal for all, complete for all.' *L'Avenir* claimed to be integrally catholic and sincerely liberal – integrally catholic in its unshakeable attachment to the centre of unity in Rome; sincerely liberal in its determination to defend the liberties of all individuals and communities within the State whatever their opinions – for as the newspaper put it, 'true liberalism understands ... that liberty must be equal for all or it is secure for no-one'.[5]

It was only logical that among the six freedoms, proclaimed by *L'Avenir* (doc. 67) 'freedom of conscience or freedom of religion, full and universal, without distinction as well as without privileges' took pride of place. The State should cease to subsidize the Church but also stop interfering with the appointment of bishops and other internal matters.

Separation of Church and State was judged better than the concordat between them. Closely connected with this demand was the other one for freedom of education. There should be no monopoly of education. Freedom of education would, in Lamennais' opinion, increase the number of Church schools. Lamennais also enthusiastically emphasized the need for freedom of the press, 'the most effective instrument' by which to hasten 'the progress of the general intelligence'. Equally important was the liberty of association, a natural right particularly relevant in a democratic society. Further Lamennais pleaded for a vast extension of the suffrage 'in such a way that it reaches right into the heart of the masses'. This Christian democrat desired universal suffrage as an ultimate goal. Finally Lamennais and his colleagues insisted on decentralization. They desired a large measure of self-government, of local and provincial autonomy; for what was required was unity in diversity, not unity imposed from above.

Although Lamennais was mainly concerned with the liberalization of his own country, he thought to some extent also in terms of a Liberal International; he sympathized with the struggle for independence by Catholic liberals in Belgium and in Poland. In 1831 Lamennais and his friends Montalembert and Lacordaire suspended the publication of *L'Avenir* after having received clear indications of the opposition of the Vatican to their ideas. They visited Rome hoping to persuade the Pope and his advisers of the value of liberal Catholicism, but the Vatican remained hostile. After Pope Gregory XVI had expressly condemned liberal Catholicism in an encyclical, Montalembert and Lacordaire submitted. Abbé Lamennais himself became alienated from the Church and in 1834 ceased to fulfil his functions as a priest, though he was never excommunicated. He then sent out his message in a more fervent key. His book *Paroles d'un Croyant* (*Words of a Believer*, 1835), from which a characteristic passage has been translated here (doc. 59) became a best-seller and was translated into many languages. Lamennais regarded himself as the people's prophet and there was now a growing egalitarian emphasis in his ideas of liberty. His sympathy was with the dispossessed and half-starving masses. He warned against the hypocrites, the false 'friends of the people' who professed (as then indeed did most educated persons) that the people were incapable of understanding their own interests and were therefore in need of guardianship. Against that smug argument Lamennais set his mystical doctrine of gaining freedom by sacrifice. By then his liberal stance was anti-authoritarian, egalitarian and mystical. To obtain liberty for the masses meant a fight for social justice, a fight with mystical Christian overtones. Deeply aware of the plight of many men, women and children during those early days of industrialization in France, Lamennais was not a revolutionary concerned with the class struggle, but a prophetic reformer in apocalyptic terms, a Christian liberal populist.

C. Aspects of continental liberalism in the nineteenth century

It was not by chance that some twenty years later Guiseppe Mazzini, the Italian radical and fighter for national unity, in his pages on Liberty (see doc. 61) expressly referred to Lamennais' doctrine. Both men shared a sense of idealistic mission, an emotional rather than a strictly rational language and a belief in the freedom of human association for the benefit of mankind. In his own way each wanted to see the City of God erected on earth and each believed that what mattered was general cooperation and harmony rather than the efforts of isolated individuals.

Unlike the liberal lawyers and professors of their generation Lamennais and Mazzini were not concerned primarily with technical questions such as the extension of the franchise or the allocation of seats in parliament. They viewed liberty in the wider compass of national and religious regeneration. A country was to Mazzini not a mere aggregation but an association. This concept ruled out any privilege or other form of inequality. Visualizing a united Italy based on the individuality of her great cities he declared: 'In your City you have need of *liberty* as in your Country you have need of *association*'. [6]

Yet liberty was only a means and not an end. Liberty must not be identical with unreal egotism or exclusive liberation. Mazzini argued that the tendency of such doctrines was to convert liberty into anarchy. Freedom was not a purpose for its own sake. Mazzini wanted 'the free and educated man' to be 'a prophet of future progress'. Individualism in the sense of stubborn self-centredness was taboo to him. 'He who withdraws himself even for a moment in his actions, from the general line of thought, and the national aim, is acting apart from the vital conditions of Association, and this must not be.' [7]

Although Mazzini allowed the individual to think for himself and to push his own heresy, he had to obey the will of the majority as legally known.[8] Such reservation did not prevent him from sponsoring a long list of individual freedoms, such as freedom of movement, of religious belief, of opinion and the right to express it in print or by any other pacific means, freedom of association and freedom of trade.[9] But even when he talked of freedom of trade he did so with a view to the welfare of the country. 'No one has a right to forbid free trade. Your country is your lawful market which no one may limit or restrain.'

Both Lamennais and Mazzini fought the establishment of 'throne and altar', though the latter did so with much greater vehemence. Both appealed to the masses and both held strong views on religion and Christianity. Mazzini was a moralist who stressed the duties of man as much as his rights. 'Without liberty', he argued, 'man cannot fulfil any of his duties.' Therefore he had both 'a right to liberty and a duty towards it'. Liberty was thus conceived as a precondition of true morality and genuine society. It has an equalizing function. 'Liberty must be for all men, and in the face of all men.'

(ii) Freedom of speech, of the press and of association

Freedom of association was as essential to Mazzini as it was to Lamennais. The right of association was pronounced as sacred as religion itself, which is called 'the association of souls. You are all the sons of God; you are therefore brothers. Who then may without guilt set limits to association, the communion of brothers?' These solemn words of Mazzini might have come straight from Lamennais' *Words of a Believer*. Lamennais and Mazzini based their demand for freedom of association on idealistic principles. Professor Karl Theodor Welcker, on the other hand, was far removed from such an emotional approach. He coolly examined the advantages and dangers of free associations and gave reasons why they were to be regarded as indispensable (doc. 68). Yet Welcker also saw the other side of the medal. He remarked, not without a whimsical touch, that 'associations have this in common with all that is good, with religion, with the power of the king and that of the government and particularly that of the police (*sic*), with language, with fire, and with iron, with arms and legs and their free use: the more a thing is good, important and effective, the more terribly it lends itself to abuse.' Never mind, Welcker added, raising his finger solemnly to heaven, 'able statesmen and governments will tolerate along with liberty, its unavoidable dangers also, just as God tolerates them too.' An odd comparison, but characteristic of the half-hearted attitude of a German liberal in the *Obrigkeitsstaat* (a State based on respect for the authorities). There must be, he conceded, legally fixed possibilities of preventing an abuse of the freedom of association. The government must have 'the right to exercise repressive measures against unlawful uses of the freedom of association'. Welcker's concern for liberty was certainly not excessive. In the days of the German *Vormärz*, the period before the March Revolution of 1848, a moderate constitutionalism appeared safer to him than the insistence of the radicals on complete freedom of association.

Welcker as well as Dahlmann played a role in the Committee of the National Assembly at Frankfurt which in 1848 prepared the Constitution of the German Empire. Although this Constitution like the entire work of the Assembly, proved abortive, its Catalogue of 'Fundamental Rights of the German People' (doc. 60) contained items of considerable significance for the evolution of German liberalism. It clearly reflects the juxtaposition of the demand for individual liberty with the urge towards national liberty and unification. The synthetical character of the Constitution is reflected in the statements that 'the German people consists of the states forming the German Empire' (art.I, 131) and that, 'every German possesses German Reich citizenship. He can exercise the rights to which he is entitled in every German state' (art.I, 132). Equality

397

C. Aspects of continental liberalism in the nineteenth century

before the law, expressly laid down (in art.II, 137) meant that every German could exercise his citizenship rights in any of the thirty-nine German states and that there were no more distinctions between the Estates (Stände). None of them would have any privileges; those of the nobility were expressly abolished[10] (art.II, 137). German citizens of one German state could no longer be regarded as 'foreigners' in other German states. They had the right to unimpeded mobility within the Reich but also the right to emigrate from it. There was a significant emphasis on the right of every German to express his opinion freely, on freedom of science and teaching, on freedom of the citizen to select his own occupation and training, on the right of Germans to assemble peacefully with the characteristic reservation that 'assemblies of the people in the open can be forbidden in case of urgent danger for public order and security' (art.VIII, 161). On the other hand it was unambiguously stated that the right of Germans to form associations 'shall not be restricted by any preventive measure' (art.VIII, 162).[11]

The concern for national freedom was not confined to Germans. Though it may well have appeared utopian to many contemporaries and unacceptable to some German nationalists, provision was made for the rights of national minorities in Germany, such as the Poles, Danes, etc., who were 'guaranteed their national development, particularly the equal right of their languages in their respective regions'. This right was extended to their Churches, education and internal administration (art.XIII, 188). Seen in historical perspective the article anticipated the national minority rights, established seventy-five years later by the League of Nations.

During most years of the Second Empire liberalism in France was uneasily on the defensive. This was partly due to the regime of plebiscitarian Caesarism which gave the masses that universal manhood suffrage which the liberals had opposed between 1815 and 1848. It also resulted from the competition of various socialist theories ranging from the belligerent anti-capitalism of Proudhon to the more systematic efforts of class-warfare of the First International. What the spokesmen of liberalism attempted was to bring the attitude of their forerunners of 1789 and 1830 up to date. They took pains to explain that they were not revolutionary Jacobins set upon an overthrow of society but moderate reformers eager to seek an implementation of liberties which, they asserted, by no means ran counter to the Constitution of the Second Empire. They presented themselves largely as rather conservative liberals, eager to insist upon the basic rights of the individual, frequently violated by the existing regime. Among them Edouard Laboulaye (doc. 62) and Adolphe Thiers (doc. 63) were representative: the one as an academic theorist (Laboulaye was Professor of Comparative Legislation at the

Collège de France), the other as an adroit and resourceful parliamentary tactician.

Laboulaye observed that the 'liberal party' – a term not used in the sense of an existing party organisation – seemed to have risen from the soil in 1863 as it had done before in 1795 and 1814, each time sustained and pushed forward by public opinion. Yet he also emphasized that the regimes overthrown in 1830 and 1848 would not come back and that the eternal demand for freedom must now find forms of its own. [12] The Emperor's Constitution of 1852, he argued, recognized and guaranteed the great principles of 1789 which were still the basis of the life of the nation. Yet in fact these constitutional guarantees did not go very far and proved an empty shell without really protecting human rights. What was required was 'justice replacing administration and responsibility the tutelage by the State'. Each citizen should be master of his own thoughts and actions (within the jurisdiction of the courts). He should be given a role in the business of the community and his representatives should exercise effective control over public affairs. These demands, rooted in the history of constitutionalism from Mirabeau to Royer-Collard and Benjamin Constant[13] had remained on paper in the Second Empire. 'With us', Laboulaye lamented, 'politics is still armed and it seems that the State is in a constant duel with the parties.'

Like some other liberal and 'radical' publicists of the period, such as Jules Simon and Prevost Paradol, Laboulaye was cautiously critical of democratic Caesarism. These writers shared 'a tendency, favoured by the necessity of conducting their guerilla warfare with circumspection, to ignore the forms of government and to represent the conflict in a purely impersonal way, as a conflict between the individual and the State'.[14] Laboulaye desired neither the minimum nor the maximum State. 'The State, as representing nationality and justice', he observed, 'is the greatest and most august of human institutions; it is the country itself in visible form, but if it oversteps its own domain, it is a tyrant. Its limit is the freedom of the citizen, the principles of 1789. But to secure that freedom, constitutions are not enough.' [15]

Different from the theorist Laboulaye, Adolphe Thiers scored as an experienced man of affairs, an old hand in the political game. Although he often changed his arguments he continued to adhere to his earlier doctrine of the constitutional monarchy according to which the king reigned but did not govern.

Elected as a deputy to the Corps Législatif in 1863, Thiers spoke for the middle classes by propagating a cautious type of liberalism. At a time when many new republicans were returned by the voters he organized 'Conservative opposition, known as the "Third Party", distinct from that of the republicans, but likewise committed to an unremitting resistance to the policies of the Government'. [16]

C. Aspects of continental liberalism in the nineteenth century

During the 1860s when Napoleon III was inclined to 'liberalize' his regime to some extent, Thiers developed the theory of the five 'Indispensable Liberties' which he claimed were in line with the main doctrines of 1789. In a speech before the French Chamber, the 'legislative body', in January 1864 (doc. 70), with a somewhat cynical realism Thiers observed that the word 'Liberty' left nobody unmoved. It aroused 'unlimited desires in some, fantastic fears in others'. The way out of the dilemma was a sober pragmatic approach which determined his survey of the five indispensable conditions of freedom, presented with an eye on the shortcomings of the regime in power.

In February 1866 Thiers reiterated his plea for the five freedoms in Parliament (doc. 63). This time he based his demands on the traditional principles of 1789, and on the two declarations preceding the Constitution of 1791. But such convenient flashbacks to the early years of the Revolution were to this restless and adroit mind rather a means to an end than an end in itself. Thiers argued that the nation had 'the right to follow the government step by step and to insist that public opinion, which represents its will, is the guide of all the acts of that government'. It was by no means enough to speak of 'freedom of election' through which public opinion expressed itself in general terms. The citizen 'must have the inviolability of his preferences', when called upon to choose his representatives in parliament. In other words the electors should be able to make their own choice of candidates and not, as was then often the case in France, have it made for them by the government which unblushingly pushed the candidates it favoured with the support of the prefects and other organs of the State bureaucracy.[17] Another important point: when the representatives of the nation assemble in parliament they should enjoy complete freedom. But did they do so in fact? Again Thiers hinted at existing abuses. During his almost forty years in parliament he had always found that it was able to assert its authority sufficiently. But there had been one real difficulty: 'to find a majority which respects the minority when the latter says what it thinks', clearly a reflection on the Emperor's Yes men who disliked the voice of the opposition. Thiers pointed here to a basic problem in any liberal and democratic approach, the tyranny of the majority over the minority. The same problem has been seen in a wider social framework and more profoundly analysed by de Tocqueville and Lord Acton.[18]

Compared with the cautious, aged Thiers, the youthful lawyer-orator Léon Gambetta struck a more daring note. In his 'Belleville Manifesto' of 1869 (doc. 71) he interpreted the principles of 1789 in a different way. For him they pointed to the idea of a 'radical democracy', particularly with reference to the universal suffrage. In addition to the usual liberal freedoms Gambetta demanded the separation of the Church from the State. After his election as a Deputy the future Republican leader

400

Gambetta visualized a division on the Left. He and his followers insisted 'that the People were the one lawful sovereign and must really exercise power'. To them 'mere responsibility of ministers to parliament' was not enough. There was a need for checking all office-holders, particularly the head of the executive. On the other hand, according to Gambetta the mere liberals believed with Thiers that universal suffrage could be fitted with the essential liberties, granted by limited monarchy. While a definite division of the Left would avoid confusion for the future, 'good neighbourly relations, momentary cooperation' between the two camps were not excluded. [19]

France

At the time of the Congress of Vienna when political parties were still unknown on the Continent, freedom of the press was a demand uppermost in the minds of progressive writers. Both the German publicist Joseph Goerres, the romantic editor of the anti-Napoleonic *Rheinischer Merkur*, and the unromantic French 'doctrinnaire' Guizot pressed for it but thought it politic to do so with some caution. Steering a middle course between the extremes of oppression and licence they argued that basically society had nothing to fear from freedom of the press. It was a privilege, said Goerres, and the State had ample means at its disposal against its abuse. He demanded complete press freedom 'within the boundaries of what is morally permissible' (doc. 64). On the other hand, the austere Guizot argued that the advisable degree of freedom of the press depended on the state of the society in which it operated. In the present state of affairs restrictions on the press must be regarded as inevitable. They might never become a danger if 'in establishing a barrier against licence, a door is always left open for liberty (doc. 65). In this matter as in others Guizot was a gradualist with an aversion to taking any unnecessary risks. He differed from Goerres who in 1814 was willing to run risks, convinced that society and its members could only profit from allowing far-reaching freedom to the press.

As French politicians and writers had sinister recollections of the wild language of some Jacobin papers and of the subsequent severe control of the press under Napoleon, they welcomed article 8 of the Charter of 1814 which declared: 'The French people have the right to publish and to have their opinions in unison with the laws which should repress the abuses of this liberty.'

Both Guizot and Royer-Collard took a hand in drafting the Press Law of 1814 during the First Restoration of the Bourbons. Guizot, who was then Secretary to the Minister of the Interior, regarded some form of press control as desirable.[20] His attitude to the press issue remained somewhat ambiguous. As our extract shows (doc. 65) he expressed

C. Aspects of continental liberalism in the nineteenth century

himself at the time in favour of a reasonable freedom of the press, recommending the adoption of 'a system of liberty and frankness'. Truth should 'circulate freely from the throne to the people, and from the people to the throne'. Yet he was convinced that after the bitter experiences of the recent past, 'a certain restraint in the liberty of the press was unavoidable'. Liberty, he felt, was a tender plant, uneasily placed between suppression and licence.

Although in 1814 Royer-Collard, perhaps the most authoritative figure among the *'doctrinaires'*, had shared Guizot's lukewarm attitude to the freedom of the press, he soon began to take both freedom of speech and of writing more seriously. He declared himself against the advance censorship of newspapers, introduced by the Press Law of 1814. Editors, he suggested, should have to account for the content of their newspapers *after* and not before publication. Frenchmen had now under the Charter the right to publish and to have their opinions printed. While abuse of that freedom had to be punished, a system of prevention in advance was out of the question. In some of his most eloquent speeches in the Chamber Royer-Collard took a stand against repressive press laws and measures of the government (doc. 66). Liberty of the press was to him at the same time an essential 'individual right and a limiting force.' [21] In the Chamber Royer-Collard enjoyed great prestige. 'His independence, his eloquence as well as his slightly rude character and his irony made his authority stronger and more formidable.[22] His interventions in the debates on the press in 1822 and later in 1835 were incisive. In 1822 under Minister Villèlle the press laws were tightened up with all press offences being referred to a correctional tribunal without a jury. A journal in which the general tendency seemed injurious to public peace or to the respect due to the king and to the constitution, could be cited before the royal courts, suspended for a first or second offence and suppressed for a third.[23] Royer-Collard compared this clause with the methods of the Revolutionary Tribunal in the days of the Jacobins. In both cases an extraordinary organ of justice struck against alleged delicts which were irreproachable when judged by ordinary law. He protested that the proposed articles would destroy the liberty of the press and that the amendments put forward by a special commission would destroy it altogether.[24]

Thirteen years later under the regime of Louis Philippe a savage attempt on the king's life by Fiesci led to the introduction of several bills in the Chamber curtailing the liberty of the press. Although they met with a hostile reception in the Chamber of Deputies, in the end they were passed owing to a strong feeling that some newspapers had contributed to fostering the state of mind which had caused a fanatic to try to assassinate the king. But even some friends of the monarchy in the Chamber condemned the severe Press Law of September 1835 as useless against sedition and dangerous to liberty. Royer-Collard pointed out that definite insights into the task of the press had emerged from their long discussion, which had more and more penetrated the mind of the general public. There was now recognition that 'the good and the evil of the press are inseparable. There is no liberty without some licence. The delict escapes definition, the interpretation remains arbitrary. The delict itself is not constant; what is a delict in one period, is none in another.' [25]

Germany

As long as Goerres' forceful visionary language had been directed against Napoleon's dictatorship, his paper, the *Rheinischer Merkur* was tolerated by the Prussian authorities. But when in 1816 King Frederick William III took exception to Goerres' independent language and to his plea for liberal and national reform, it was suppressed. [26] In the following year the Carlsbad Decrees of the German Confederation, inspired by Prince Metternich, established censorship over all publications of twenty sheets of paper and thereby prohibited any free discussions of political issues in the daily or weekly press. Some oppositional writers tried to circumvent this restriction by writing for periodicals or by trying to influence public opinion in Germany from abroad, as the irreverent Heinrich Heine and the more radical Ludwig Boerne did in their articles and books from Paris, but their efforts reached only a very limited German public. After the French Revolution of 1830, which had repercussions in several German states, the Deputies Welcker and Rotteck made a strong plea in the Chamber of Baden for an end to the oppressive censorship. In a tract on freedom of the press, K. T. Welcker called the censorship 'a continuous betrayal of the princes and of the people, as it had been a shame for Germany'. In March 1832 Rotteck and Welcker persuaded a majority in the Baden Diet to accept a progressive press law, which was in the end approved by the Baden Government. It abolished all censorship over printed matter published or distributed in the Grand Duchy of Baden. But only a few months afterwards the law was withdrawn after the German Confederation had complained about it and put pressure on the Baden Government. [27] In Prussia the censorship reached a peak in the 1830s when no fewer than 312 *Verbote* of the suppression of newspapers and periodicals were enforced, 55 of them alone by 1844.

On the other hand in the 1840s some new, progressive newspapers made their bow. In 1847 there appeared at Heidelberg the *Deutsche Zeitung* which voiced the views of moderate liberals like Gervinus, Häusser and other professors in favour of a constitutional monarchy. [28] In 1848 it expressed the views of the majority of the members of the Frankfurt National Assembly. In the Rhineland, where liberal-minded merchants like Mevissen and Hansemann had considerable influence, the

C. Aspects of continental liberalism in the nineteenth century

left-liberal *Rheinische Zeitung* in the early 1840s published a series of critical articles on the debates about the freedom of the press which were then taking place in the Rhenish Provincial Diet. The author of these articles was no other than Karl Marx, who in October 1842 became the editor of the paper. Six months later the *Rheinische Zeitung* was forbidden for good after it had dared to argue that 'censorship meant the deepest immorality'.[29]

In the debates on the Constitution in the Frankfurt Assembly of 1848 freedom of the press was a major issue. The result was Article IV of the Constitution which gave every German 'the right of expressing freely his views in speech, in writing, in print and in pictorial presentation'. There was added a characteristic, if indirect, reference to the many restrictive measures against the press which had previously been in operation in the German states. The freedom of the press, Article IV declared, was 'under no circumstances and in no manner to be restricted, suspended or abolished by preventive measures such as censorship, licensing, security orders, impositions by the State, restrictions of the printers or booksellers, postal prohibitions or other hindrances of free communication' (doc. 60).

While in 1848 the censorship of the press was abolished all over Germany, the proclaimed freedom of the press was shortlived. With the return of the old powers, particularly in Austria and Prussia, many restrictive measures of press control came back. In 1854 the revived German Federation issued a decree on the abuses of the press which forced publishers to obtain a permit from their government before issuing publications concerned with social and political questions. In Prussia, where censorship had been officially abolished in March 1848, the Constitution of January 1850 reintroduced restrictions on the press, but the censorship and the power of the State to prevent new publications did not return. However, both in Prussia and Bavaria the requirement of caution money for every newspaper or periodical was reinstated.[30] Yet in spite of new petty restrictions the trend towards greater freedom of the press made itself felt and continued to form a major point in liberal propaganda. Moreover, both political and technological factors worked in favour of greater freedom for the newspaper industry. In an age of advancing industrialization, largely improved methods of communication and the formation of political parties, the government found it less profitable to restrict the newspapers. The fact that the Prussian Conservatives had now their own daily, the *Kreuzzeitung,* indirectly helped the non-conservative press. The latter was also assisted by the formation of liberal organizations like the *Nationalverein*, the German Progressive Party and later the National Liberal Party.[31] In spite of the split among the liberals they agreed in demanding a *Rechtsstaat*, a State based on the rule of law. In the programme of the National Liberal Party of June 1867 the abolition of all caution money and taxes on newspapers and periodicals was called for (doc. 90). Liberals in the Reichstag of the Second Empire also managed to improve the Bill on the Press eventually issued by Bismarck as the Reich Press Law of 7 May 1874. Although Bismarck was never in principle against freedom of the press, he was also not at any moment its friend.[32]

The Reich Press Law can be regarded as a considerable step forward towards a more liberalized position of the German press. At least there could now be no arbitrary repressive measures by the authorities. The fundamental freedom of the press from preventative measures by the authorities such as censorship was expressly acknowledged. Every newspaper or periodical had to carry the name and address of the publisher and also that of the responsible editor who would be accountable for any infringement of the laws. The possible confiscation of a newspaper issue was restricted to a number of clearly defined cases such as omission to give the names of the publisher and responsible editor, immoral (pornographic) publications, information on troop-movements in times of war.[33] Punishable was further incitement to treason or high treason, the crime of lèse-majesté, incitement to disobey the laws and to class-hatred.[34] All these offences were laid down in the general penal code.

Seen in historical perspective, the uniform Reich Press Law of 1874 which took the place of the former twenty-seven different German State Laws was, in spite of its drawbacks emanating from Bismarck's authoritarian attitude, an important step forward to the liberalization of the German press. Notwithstanding its limitations it allowed the editors and contributors of newspapers a much greater margin of freedom than had existed before, and it proved no obstacle to spirited political satire as expressed in such weeklies as *Kladderadatsch* and *Simplizissimus*.

France again

In France the long expected coup d'état of July 1830 had been provoked by the heavy-handed ordinances of King Charles X, the first of which suspended the liberty of the press. The July Revolution was thus set in motion by a protest organized in the office of the newspaper *National* by the young Thiers and signed by representatives of nearly all the liberal newspapers in Paris. Under the new regime censorship was not reintroduced, but from 1835 the government of Louis Philippe attempted to silence the oppositional newspapers of the pro-Bourbon legitimists and the Republican factions. Yet these measures were on a small scale compared with the later large-scale repressive measures in force for sixteen years under the dictatorship of Napoleon III. For his Press Law of 1852 'required founders and publishers of journals to seek authorization from

405

the government and to submit all changes of personnel for the government's approval'.[35]

Moreover prefects and ministers had power to enforce warnings, suspensions and suppressions of newspapers, a system which reached a climax under Eugene Rouher's supervision. It is not surprising that, different from contemporary Germany, between 1852 and 1868 very few new French journals were founded. With the 'liberalization' of the regime in the 1860s this state of affairs was modified. In 1868 a less forbidding Press Law appeared. As a result new journals sprang up, among them Henri Rochefort's cheeky and provocative *Lanterne*. As its amusing fun spared no one, not even the Emperor himself, it was a huge success. *Lanterne* sold 500,000 copies each in June and July 1868. Not surprisingly after three months the paper was suppressed by the irate Rouher.[36]

Throughout the 1860s French liberals and radicals never tired of pressing for freedom of the press. Liberal professors such as Laboulaye, Vacherot and Jules Simon emphasized it while Thiers supported it with some qualifications. The liberty of the press was essential, he declared, but it was not identical with impunity. Press liberty existed 'on condition that the writer does not insult the honour of the citizens or disturb the peace of the country' (see doc. 70). Gambetta on the other hand had no such reservations. His Belleville Manifesto of 1869 demanded 'liberty of the press in every way, freedom from stamp duty and caution money and suppression of licencing for printers and publishers' (doc. 71).

When, after the fall of the Emperor in the autumn of 1870, the government of National Defence was founded it abolished stamp duty and caution money for the press and declared the professions of printing and publishing free. A year later Gambetta himself and some of his friends commenced a new daily, the *République Française*. Yet under the presidencies of Thiers and MacMahon repressive measures against the press returned if on a smaller scale. Since 1873 it became government policy to prevent anyone from founding a new newspaper. However, the overall trend towards greater press freedom could not be halted. After five years of preparatory work by a committee of the Chamber of Deputies, a constructive and comprehensive Press Law emerged in July 1881 which did away with all government interference with, or demands on, the press and guaranteed full freedom of printing and of distribution of newspapers and periodicals.[37] It has been characterized as 'a fine example of liberal legislation in a field where liberty had long given pride of place to security, stability and often to downright tyranny'.[38]

3. Freedom from the Church and freedom for the Church: introduction
(Documents 72–80a, pp. 512–35)

Freedom of conscience and freedom of religious (and non-religious) belief were heavily charged major issues in Continental liberal thought during the nineteenth century. In political terms religious freedom meant freedom from the Churches or freedom from 'clericalism' which has been defined as 'the intervention of the Church in the formulation and direction of public policies through the exercise of special powers conferred on its clergy by the State'.[39] Liberals everywhere resented and feared the close alliance between Church and State as it had existed in France before 1789 and had returned under the Bourbons between 1814 and 1830. The Catholic Church also remained a powerful factor in most of the Italian states, in the Austrian Empire and in Spain. On the other hand, there existed on the Protestant side from 1817 onward the Union of the Reformed and the Lutheran Church in Prussia with the king as supreme bishop (*summus episcopus*). Liberals were sharply opposed to such close ties between throne and altar and demanded constitutional safeguards against them. Although not all liberals favoured the complete separation of Church and State, it was the logical outcome of the anti-clerical attitude in itself strengthened by the advance of science and by the structure of a new industrial society. The alleged secret machinations of the 'ultramontanes' and of the Jesuit Order worried many liberals in Western and Southern Europe. The clash between secularized liberalism and the Catholic Church reached its height under Pope Pius IX, with his *Syllabus Errorum* (1864) and the Dogma of Papal Infallibility (1870). The Kulturkampf of the 1870s against Roman Catholicism, enthusiastically supported by liberals in Germany, Austria and Switzerland, was the climax in the efforts to free the modern State from interference by the 'foreign' power of the Catholic Church.

'Freedom from the Churches', with its important corollary, freedom from control of education by the Church, culminated in the demand for separation of Church and State, a long-standing battle-cry of French radicalism, which became a reality in France under Emile Combes in 1905.

Not all liberals were anti-clericals. Madame de Staël deplored the chasm between the French revolution and organized religion. Half a century after her a liberal thinker like E. Laboulaye declared liberalism and religion compatible. He even argued that anti-etatism had its source in Christ. 'You will only find modern liberty with the Christians, for only Christianity has separated religion from politics and distinguished between the believer and the citizen.'[40]

C. Aspects of continental liberalism in the nineteenth century

Yet freedom of religion, liberals soon maintained, was not exhausted by demanding freedom from the Churches; the doctrine behind it also supported the plea for freedom for the Churches. People could claim the right to regulate their own affairs without interference by the State or organized pressure groups. Seen in retrospect it is significant that the formula 'A Free Church in a Free State' was used and supported simultaneously by Cavour, the liberal architect of Italian unification, and by Montalambert, the spokesman of Catholicism in France.

France

During the 1820s when the close interconnection between the Church and the Bourbon monarchy was strikingly demonstrated under the bigoted Charles X, two different voices caused a sensation by criticizing the Establishment and the close ties between throne and altar. Both Count Montlosier and the Abbé de Lamennais demanded greater freedom for the Church but they did so from very different points of view. Montlosier, an eccentric, an emigré from revolutionary France and later an officer under Napoleon, showed no sympathy for eighteenth-century liberals in his challenging book *Mémoire à consulter sur un systême religieux et politique* (1826). Whereas deism, rationalism and individualism were taboo to him, his main attack was directed against the ultramontane policies then prevailing in France. Montlosier alleged the existence of a vast conspiracy against the king and against religion (doc. 72). He branded the nefarious elements within the Establishment which 'as religious men, as royalists and citizens' conspired 'to destroy everything'. As a staunch Gallican he denounced the 'Congrégation' as the clandestine channel of the Ultramontanes, the friends of Rome, and above all the Jesuits, seen as a sinister hand behind the face of public affairs. He maintained that 'if they were allowed to continue, the hatred they were arousing would destroy the monarchy and ruin the Church.'[41]

What Montlosier aimed at was true freedom for the monarchy and the Church from such ruinous powers. Though this knight-errant caused a tremendous stir with his book, in the end it satisfied neither the authoritarian royalists nor the liberals in the French Chamber.

On the other hand, the fierce Abbé de Lamennais was then strongly opposed to Gallicanism, the belief in the autonomy of the Catholic church in France. As an ardent champion of ultramontanism he insisted in 1825 that there was 'without the Pope no Church, without the Church no Christianity, without Christianity no religion for any people which would be Christian and therefore no society'. Lamennais was equally hostile to Gallicans, Royalists and Liberals, centring all his hopes on the Vatican. Yet by 1828 his position had changed profoundly. As pointed out earlier (see p. 394), Lamennais then pioneered an alliance between

408

Catholicism and Liberalism. The clergy, he suggested, should leave the field of politics altogether. 'Be bishops, be priests and nothing more', he advised them. Lamennais, the visionary, was thrilled by the revolution of 1830, but he also felt that without Christianity the people's just desire for liberty and equality would come to nought. He wanted both freedom for the Church and freedom for the people (docs 73 and 74). As he put it in a letter to a friend in May 1830,[42] 'Liberty which has been called for in the name of atheism must now be demanded in the name of God.' The young liberalism which was growing and which would finish by supplanting the earlier anti-religious liberalism of the eighteenth century 'here confines itself, in regard to religion, to demanding the separation of Church and State, necessary for the liberty of the Church, and equally desired by all enlightened catholics'.[43]

Although Lamennais, disowned by the Church, later gave up his functions as a priest, liberal Catholicism was not dead. Its main spokesman for the next thirty-five years, Charles de Montalembert, was much more of a politician and diplomat than the rather unsophisticated Lamennais. Montalembert continued to maintain that educational liberty was in the best interest of Catholics and that the Church could only gain under a pluralistic system. In 1852 he argued that Liberal Catholics could welcome both reason and freedom.[44] He also took a somewhat qualified stand in favour of liberty of conscience: 'That principle so long invoked by the enemies of religion' was 'now turning everywhere to its profit'. In the States where it had been once legally introduced, Catholics should 'be careful not to efface it, for it becomes therein the safeguard of the faith and the bulwark of the Church'.[45] Liberty had two enemies, he declared, revolution on the one hand and despotism on the other, while religion was liberty's 'safeguard, its natural and legitimate counterpoise'.[46]

A decade later the confrontation in France between the ultramontane supporters of the intransigent Pope Pius IX and the liberal Catholics, led by Montalembert, had grown more acute. It reached a climax at a meeting at Malines in Belgium in June 1863 during which Montalembert delivered two celebrated addresses on 'The Free Church in the Free State'.[47] Montalembert readopted this formula, originally devised by him, after it had gained wider publicity through the eloquence of Cavour (doc. 75). In fact in an additional note to the printed addresses Montalembert explained his interpretation of the formula which, he maintained, was by no means identical with Cavour's. 'A free Church in a free State' was the only one of the possible relationships between Church and State of which a liberal Catholic could approve. It was pointless for Catholics to hanker after the impossible return of the ancien régime. The age of privileges for the Church had passed. Now universal suffrage, equality of the law, liberty of association, of education and of the press were in the interest of the Catholics. Freedom of conscience should be granted to all with the exception of declared atheists or people who desired to

C. Aspects of continental liberalism in the nineteenth century

destroy society. 'You cannot claim liberty for yourself and deny it to others.'[48] Common law was the only refuge of religious freedom. Although Pope Pius IX confined himself to expressing his disapproval of this challenge to the ultramontanes in a private letter to Montalembert, a much more drastic reply came a few months afterwards with his momentous *Syllabus Errorum* (doc. 78).

Italy

For centuries the Roman Catholic Church had been both *the* spiritual authority and a temporal power. Could the Church be liberalized? In the euphoria of the dawn of the revolution of 1848 many Italians thought it possible. There was much hope that the new Pope Pius IX, suspected of progressive ideas by Prince Metternich, would prove a liberal Pontiff and take the lead towards the unification of Italy. Count Camillo di Cavour was, in those days of promising change, equally sanguine. A prominent Deputy in the Turin parliament, he felt confident that the Church and the striving for liberty were not incompatible and that many priests in Italy would follow the line of liberal Catholicism prevailing in Belgium and shared by Montalembert in France. Cavour's outlook was patterned on France under Louis Philippe and on Britain after the Reform Bill. Equally opposed to clericalism and democratic radicalism, Cavour, a cool Western rationalist and economic reformer, dreamed of establishing harmony between the Church and a unified national State of Italy. He was also well aware that most moderate liberals in Italy remained devout Catholics. In 1848 Cavour still believed that the great majority of the Catholic clergy in Italy had embraced the cause of liberty, considering it to be closely connected with that of religion itself. Was not Catholicism in other European countries, in Belgium, in Poland, in Ireland, siding with the oppressed against the oppressors? Everywhere, Cavour wrote in May 1848, it had 'made itself a supporter of popular liberty' and had 'inscribed on its banner *religious liberty*' (doc. 76). Yet in Italy, too, the high hopes of the noontide of 1848 were soon to prove an illusion. As Prime Minister, Cavour had to face a Pope bitterly opposed to any compromise with the new liberal and national State. The Curia rejected liberal Catholicism without the slightest concession.

By 1860 the formula 'A free Church in a free State', originally used by Montalembert, then adopted by Cavour and even repeated by him on his deathbed, summed up his hope of reconciling the Church and liberty, Catholicism and the nineteenth century, the rights of the nation and the freedom of the Pope, while simultaneously disarming the hostility of foreign Catholics to Italy. 'When the Church had renounced political power then the State could safely renounce its control over the Church and allow it to order its own affairs without either the privileges or the restrictions of a Concordat.'[49]

Cavour was as much concerned to see the Church free from the shackles of control by the State as to establish freedom of conscience and fair play for all creeds. As a Macchiavellian tactician, Cavour favoured both freedom from the Church as well as freedom for the Church. He regarded 'the freedom of the Church supreme among all political and civil liberties';[50] but he was equally convinced of the need for a full separation of the temporal and the religious spheres. On the other hand, Joseph Mazzini, the radical democrat, wanted to do away with the Church altogether while proclaiming at the same time his passionate belief in 'God and the People'. He was as much opposed to the diplomatic ruses of Cavour as to the existence of the Papacy as both a temporal and a spiritual power. He was also often critical of Western rationalism, materialism and *laissez faire*. Mazzini distrusted Voltairian free-thinkers as much as nefarious clericals. Anti-authoritarian and anti-clerical, he was yet religious, a Populist, profoundly steeped in a somewhat abstract religious humanitarianism. Mazzini's ideology was fervent but vague (doc. 77). 'We all demand a common faith, a common pact, an interpreter of God's Law', he declared in 1849, and he was to stick to this line for the rest of his life. Mazzini was never more hopeful than in 1849 during his short spell as one of the triumvirs of the Roman Republic, when he believed that the old order, based on the intertwining of throne and altar, was disappearing altogether. 'The Constituent Assembly and the Council', he wrote in September 1849, 'these are the princes and the pope of the future.' In the end this tireless prophet of 'God and the People' achieved little in concrete terms and his direct influence on the destinies of the new Italy proved negligible. Yet his liberal-radical slogans and formulas became part of the intellectual Italian tradition. They seemed so simple, so alluring. 'One sole master God, one sole law, progress, one sole interpreter of that law on earth, the people, with genius and virtue for its guides.'[51]

There was something of Condorcet's touching belief in progress and emancipation in this creed. The Roman triumvir of 1849 was as confident and convinced that the course of the future would take the path he predicted, as Condorcet had been more than fifty years earlier. The existing evil government was 'an alliance in order to oppress'. Let the people, Mazzini demanded, challenge it by 'an alliance to emancipate', by a new democratic and universally religious order.

The *Syllabus of Errors* (1864)

If liberalism in Western and Southern Europe was traditionally inclined to identify itself with anti-clericalism, the identity became more sharply accentuated after the publication of the *Syllabus Errorum* issued by Pius IX in December 1864 (doc. 78). It listed not only theological and philosophical doctrines, unacceptable to the Church, but also 'Errors concerning the Civil Society, considered by itself and in relation to the Church'. These 'errors' included views in favour of the separation of Church and State, the placing of public schools under exclusive State control and the abolition of the temporal powers of the Papacy. Yet it was less these detailed points however far-reaching, which shook the non-Catholic world, but the all embracing denunciation of modern civilization pronounced in the last section of the document. Under the heading 'Errors which refer to Contemporary Liberalism', it declared it to be an error that the Catholic religion should no longer be regarded as the only State religion, but also that conversely all other forms of religious worship should be tolerated. It condemned the idea of a pluralism of tolerated religious creeds as this was said 'to be conducive to the easier corruption of the morals and minds of people' and to 'the spread of the pest of indifference'. It was an error to think that 'the Church ought to be separated from the State and the State from the Church' (art. 55). The whole document reached its dramatic climax in the final paragraph 80 which altogether denounced the view that 'the Roman Pontiff can and should reconcile himself to and reach agreement with progress, liberalism and civilization as lately introduced'.

Though unambiguous in its wording, the document was in fact interpreted very differently by devout Catholics and by others. In France, England and the United States it was seen by many as a declaration of war by the Papacy on the modern world of scientific progress and on a liberal attitude of mind. Today when the hot passions engendered by the *Syllabus* have long receded it can above all be seen as a product of the contemporary Italian scene. Shortly before its publication Cavour had established the new United Italy free from Church control and had propagated his line of 'a free Church in a free State'. In its origin the *Syllabus* was 'almost a cri-de-coeur against the Turin government, and its religious and political works, but it was a cri-de-coeur, too, against Mazzini, "the liberal radical".' [52] The progress Protestantism had lately made in Piedmont and Tuscany and the increased influence of freemasonry weighed heavily with a Pope who at the beginning of his pontificate had been erroneously welcomed as a liberal. The reception of the *Syllabus* is an interesting example of the possible variety in the interpretation of political slogans such as 'progress, liberalism and recent civilization'. To many Italians these terms meant simply 'the closure of the convents and monasteries and the imposition of secular education'. [53] They pointed to secularism and anti-clericalism. In England, however, progress was an almost sacred word, positively used by most members of the political and the scientific elites. In America 'progress' and 'liberalism' had even more sacred overtones.

It is to some extent understandable that, incensed by the loss of his temporal power, the Pope should generalize in his denunciation of major trends of the age; nevertheless it showed a marked lack of insight on his part and that of his advisers as they ignored the different meanings which concepts like 'progress' and 'liberalism' had in Rome and Naples and in London and New York.

Six years later the occupation of Rome by troops of the new Kingdom of Italy made the Pope a virtual prisoner in the Vatican and intensified the anti-liberal stand of orthodox Catholics. In spite of strong efforts by the King to meet the Pope halfway through concessions in the Law of Guarantees the Pope refused to be reconciled. Everywhere the confrontation between Church and State, between the traditional claims of Church authority and those of modern secularism became intensified. In the new Kingdom of Italy and in the new German Empire there was a growing alienation between these two powers. Their confrontation in the German *Kulturkampf* (struggle for civilization) in the 1870s was a complex phenomenon. Though largely a tussle for power and mind-control between Church and State, it was also a clash between different ideologies of religious freedom put forward on the one hand by the Vatican and on the other by determined liberal anti-clericals in an odd coalition with the conservative étatist Bismarck. [54]

Germany

Whereas in France and Italy only one Church mattered, Germany had three established Churches, all of them closely connected with the State. The Catholics, Lutherans and members of the Reformed (Calvinist) Churches enjoyed a privileged position and received financial assistance from the State. In Prussia the king was the head of the Evangelical Union which combined Lutherans and the Reformed Church. It was in the wake of the revolution of 1848 that the question of religious freedom and the issue of the relations between State and Church attracted much attention. The debate on it in the National Assembly at Frankfurt showed clearly that few Deputies were happy with the status quo. At a time when everything in society was in a flux, the ideas of the supporters and opponents of organized religion were voiced with keen intensity. The debate on Church and State became 'the climax of the first phase of the discussions of the Assembly'. [55] Orthodox Christians, both Catholics and Protestants, pressed for the freedom of the Church from the State, while conversely free-thinkers and the spokesmen of religious minorities stressed the need for freedom of the State from the Church. There were few attempts to justify and defend the old order and the tradition-honoured concept of a 'Christian State' was 'buried with almost indecent haste'. [56]

C. Aspects of continental liberalism in the nineteenth century

Both the State and the Churches came under sharp criticism and some speakers tended 'to blame the State and government interference for the troubles of the Christian Church, even for the often strained relations between the two religions'.[57] A great desire for independence prevailed on all sides, but the area it should cover varied a good deal. The defenders and the critics of organized religion agreed on one point: the Churches would be better off without State protection. The possibilities of a new relationship between State and Church attracted most speakers, however different their positions. A few anti-clerical deputies preferred separation between State and Church to independence, but the majority did not favour such a drastic solution. To Sylvester Jordan, by birth and upbringing a Catholic but later alienated from the Church, that Church was largely a part of the Establishment, of the police state under the grip of which he had suffered (doc. 79). Jordan did not believe in a peaceful co-existence of State and Church, even if separated. There should be only one power, that of the State. The Churches as such should disappear altogether and be replaced by religious societies.

On the other hand, Ignaz von Döllinger, a prominent Catholic theologian and professor of Church history at the University of Munich, was a strong champion of the freedom of the Church from the State. In his speech to the National Assembly in August 1848 (doc. 80) he demanded that 'the Church should be in a position where she was no longer forced to be a machine of the police state and at the same time an object and a tool of the administrative bureaucracy'.[58] Döllinger was impressed by the situation in Belgium with the Church enjoying complete freedom, and in the United States with complete separation of the Churches from the State. However, he did not go so far as to recommend a similar solution for Germany. Although he admitted that religious freedom also implied the right not to belong to any Church, he did not favour the liberty of professing atheism openly. In his view freedom of conscience did not extend to the liberty to destroy all religion, as the atheistic deputy Vogt, a professor of zoology, had maintained in his address, when he demanded liberty not only for belief but also for unbelief.[59] Against this Döllinger argued that 'even in the United States of America which went furthest in granting religious freedom everybody had to declare his belief in the existence of a Deity.'[60] He also suggested that the false relations between Church and State in the past had prevented a rapprochement between German Catholics and Protestants, which he was confident the independence of the Churches would promote. Only then would the two Christian denominations be able to live amicably side by side.

On the whole the debate reached a high level. There was little animosity. 'Even the extremists displayed the will to remain together, the desire for unity and reconciliation, at least in the state of the future.' The traditional formula of a 'Christian State' was abolished. According to the

Constitution accepted (doc. 60) there would be no State Church and no religious community would enjoy special privileges.[61] All religious communities could order their affairs independently, but they would remain subject to the general State laws.

Yet the failure of the Frankfurt experiment and of the Constitution came as a great relief to leading circles of the Protestant Church in Prussia, who had been disturbed by the discussions on a possible separation of Church and State. The negative attitude of the Protestant Church to the revolution caused the victorious reaction to regard the Church as its ally. 'This meant that it was discredited in the eyes of the rest of the people and the path was set for an alienation of the liberal bourgeoisie as well as of the socialist workers from the Church'. [62]

Spain

The liberal fight for religious freedom, for freedom of conscience differed greatly in Spain from that in other Western European countries. In Spain for many centuries the Catholic religion and Church had been a major part of the civilization and social fabric to an extent unknown in almost all other European countries. There is much truth in the observation that 'concepts like liberalism, Church, parliament' have had 'quite other meanings there to what they have in France or England'.[63] The Reformation never had a foothold in Spain. Protestant denominations were taboo and for a long time modern rationalism was unable to take root in a highly traditionalist society. Yet in the nineteenth and twentieth centuries not only clericalism but also anti-clericalism played a major role. The fanaticism of the Spanish Church evoked an equal fanaticism among many anti-clericals. For a long time Spain was an uncompromising country of 'the either-or'; 'either the religion of authority or that of the solitary individual, the religion of absolute certainty or that of isolated search'.[64]

While religious toleration was slowly and grudgingly conceded in the course of the nineteenth century, full religious freedom remained practically unknown in Spain until 1931, the year of the abolition of the monarchy. The Spanish Church was fiercely antagonistic to modernization and religious freedom, a stance only to be matched by the angry intolerance of the anti-clericals. The attitude of the working class and of the petite bourgeoisie in the towns towards the priests and monks 'was not one of indifference but of hatred'. [65]

Liberal ideas were first proclaimed in the aftermath of the revolt against Napoleonic rule by the Constitution of the Cortes of 1812 (doc. 47). It proclaimed freedom of the press and other civil freedoms and abolished the Inquisition. The Cortes issued laws suppressing monasteries and convents with fewer than twelve inmates, confiscating

C. Aspects of continental liberalism in the nineteenth century

some church property and expelling the Papal Nuncio. Yet the Constitution did not provide for freedom of religion. Article 12 declared that 'the religion of the Spanish nation is and shall be perpetually Apostolic Roman Catholic, the only true religion. The nation protects it by wise and just laws and prohibits the exercise of any other, whatsoever.' (doc. 47.)

In the prolonged upheavals during the Carlist wars in the 1830s the Carlists were sharply opposed to any liberal concessions, including that of religious tolerance. Their adversaries consisted of the Progressives, at times anti-clerical, and the moderates, averse to liberal ideas and in favour of enforced Catholic unity. While the government suppressed some monasteries and convents and sold church property, the State nevertheless felt obliged to support the Church and the clergy, an attitude which was to serve 'as the basis of all subsequent claims of the Church to financial support from the government.' [66] According to the Constitution of 1837 which became a model for the structure of most subsequent constitutions in the same century the nation was obliged 'to maintain the cult and the ministers of the Catholic religion which Spaniards profess (doc. 80a). The Church regained some ground in the Constitution of 1845, when the moderates were in control. It proclaimed 'the Apostolic Roman Catholic religion' as 'the religion of the Spanish nation', adding that 'the State binds itself to maintain the cult and its ministers' (doc. 80a).

The position changed with the revolution of 1858 which was accompanied by a fierce anti-clerical wave. The next Constitution of 1869 was therefore a democratic and radical version of the model of 1837. While it confirmed that the nation bound itself 'to maintain the cult and the ministers of the Catholic religion', it added significantly that 'the public or private observance of any other cult' was 'guaranteed to all foreigners in Spain without any further limitation than the universal rules of morality and right' (doc. 80a). The same applied to Spaniards 'who profess religion other than Catholicism'. The idea of religious freedom was advanced during the shortlived (first) republic of 1873. Its 'republican project' insisted that 'the observance of all cults shall be free in Spain' (doc. 80a) and even pronounced the separation of Church and State (doc. 80a). It also forbade 'the direct or indirect subsidizing of any cult' (doc. 80a), and declared all titles of nobility abolished (doc. 80a). Such liberalization soon proved an Utopian dream, but the restoration of the monarchy under Alfonso XII in the following year meant no full return to the old system of religious intolerance. The next Constitution (1876), which remained in force for 55 years, granted religious tolerance but not religious freedom. Its article 11 – which, by the way, was condemned by Pius IX – was unambiguous: 'The apostolic Catholic Religion', it stated, 'is the religion of the State. The nation binds itself to maintain this cult and its ministers. No one in Spanish territory shall be molested for his religious opinion, or for the observation of his particular form of worship provided that he shows proper respect to Christian morality. Public manifestations and ceremonies other than those of the religion of the State shall not be permitted' (doc. 80*a*). In other words services of Protestant and other non-Catholic denominations could not be held in public but only in the privacy of the home.

Between 1876 and the end of the century clericalism as well as anti-clericalism made their impact. 'Court, universities, press and indeed a large part of the governing class went down before a wave of clericalism the leaders of which were the Jesuits.' Education became a main target of conflict between the Church and liberal and other progressive forces. [67] The hostility of the Church to any form of liberalism was reflected in the 'Complete Church Catechism' taught in schools controlled by the Church. It rejected the view that the State was independent of the Church and argued that 'the State must be subject to the Church as the body to the soul, as the temporal to the eternal'. [68] It condemned the false liberties of conscience, of education, of propaganda, of meetings and particularly of the press. It denounced liberalism altogether as 'a most grievous sin against faith and the casting of a vote for a liberal generally as a mortal sin'. [69] Liberal Catholics were rationalists and therefore no better than freethinkers.

Such crude and fanatical clericalism was met by an equally crude and fanatical anti-clericalism. Each side believed in the sinister machinations of the other side. The clericals were deeply suspicious of the freemasons while the anti-clericals distrusted the machinations of the monks and the Jesuits. By the end of the nineteenth century an anti-clerical play like *Electra* by Galdos sold 10,000 copies in two days and became extremely popular. It was 'regarded as an appeal to the youth of Spain to join battle against clericalism'. [70]

The abolition of the monarchy in 1931 and the setting up of a republic marked a radical change in the relations between Church and State. A basic article in the Constitution of December 1931 laid down that the Spanish State had 'no official religion' (doc. 80*a*); Church and State were completely separated. On the other hand the Constitution positively affirmed religious freedom. 'Liberty of conscience and the right to profess and practice any religion freely' were guaranteed 'save for due respect to demands of public morality' (doc. 80*a*).

The changed position of the Church was in line with the general trend towards democracy and egalitarianism characteristic of that Constitution. The fact that in 1930 two-thirds of the secondary schools were in the hands of teaching orders accounts perhaps for the violent reaction of the men of the Constituent Cortes of the Republic to the educational privileges of the Church.

The radical character of the new regime was clearly expressed in the 1931 constitution; 'None of the following may be the foundation of

417

C. Aspects of continental liberalism in the nineteenth century

juridical privilege: place of birth, descent, sex, social class, wealth, political ideas or religious beliefs' (doc. 80*a*). Simultaneously with the abolition of all distinctions and titles of nobility all religious denominations were put on the same footing, being considered associations subject to the same laws (doc. 80*a*). State subsidies to the Church were terminated and religious orders, such as that of the Jesuits which imposed a 'special vow of obedience to an authority other than the State', were dissolved (doc. 80*a*). 'Their property was to be nationalized and used for charitable and educational purposes' (doc. 80*a*).[71]

The basic ideology of the Constitution of 1931 was clearly stated in its 'preliminary article' which described Spain as 'a democratic Republic of workers of all classes which is organized as a regime of liberty and justice'.[72] Although the Constitution aimed at both freedom from the Church, so long extremely powerful, and freedom for the Churches to regulate their own affairs, in the practice of the Republic the former aim played the greater role. The clerical bias of the former rulers was now replaced by an anti-clerical bias which was to display itself in the burning down of churches and in other acts of organized fury before and during the Spanish Civil War.

Seen in retrospect, it remains paradoxical that the country which provided the concepts 'liberal' and 'Liberalism' proved in practice to be among the least liberal of the countries during the period discussed in this book.

4. Freedom, power and the nation-state: Germany 1814–1881: introduction
(Documents 81–95, pp. 535–65)

One of the major differences between German and English liberalism was that the latter was not burdened by the problem of the nation and national unity. Between 1800 and 1871 German liberals not only concerned themselves with the safeguarding of human rights and the claims of the individual, but also at the same time with the problem of the unification of Germany, and with introducing liberal institutions in a national State. The Whigs and Liberals in England might have to press for parliamentary reform, but at least they could take the existence of a national government and parliament for granted. The German liberals, however, were faced with the multiplicity of German states and with the

418

task of reaching national unity on a constitutional basis. The fact that in the end this new Empire was founded not by the liberals but by a master of non-liberal power-politics made a deep imprint on the subsequent history of Germany.

Although in this volume we are not primarily concerned with the problems of German nationhood and nationalism it seems necessary at least to indicate the role played by the image (or trauma) of national freedom and unity in the liberal debate and thought during most of the nineteenth century. If the liberals pressed much more for a united Germany than did the conservatives, this resulted from their belief in a synthesis of individual and national freedom. The desire for liberal institutions in an up-to-date national State goes back to the war of liberation against Napoleon. The need to rebuild the badly battered Prussian State forced its reformers to reduce the barriers between the Estates and to allow for greater participation of the educated and propertied citizens in municipal affairs. The Stein-Hardenberg reforms of 1807 marked not only the passing of the age of feudalism, but also the indispensable need for a measure of liberalization which would make for greater coherence and cooperation among the people. The often untidy mixture of liberal and nationalist thought to be found in Germany during the nineteenth century was characteristic of the long career of Ernst Moritz Arndt (1769–1860). It remained with him from his youth as a passionate pamphleteer against Napoleon and his foreign yoke to his final role as a revered father-figure at the Frankfurt National Assembly of 1848–49.

Born a Swede on the Baltic island of Rügen, he later identified himself completely with German politics and culture. He never understood foreign nations nor did he discard his prejudices, especially against the French and the English. In his youth he was critical of the regime of bad princes. A son of a former serf he wrote a searching book on the history of serfdom in Sweden which led to its abolition. As our extract shows, he later pleaded as resolutely for the emancipation of peasants in Germany (doc. 82).

Freedom of the nation and freedom of the individual were complementary to Arndt. As he once put it, 'Without the nation there is no humanity and without the free citizen there is no free man. The noblest spirits are only born from the whole nation. Where there is nothing free and high-flying in the group then it is no longer produced in the individuals.' [73]

To Arndt freedom did not mean the right of the individual to live as it suited him, it merely meant that he was able to live according to the customs, the *mores* and laws of his ancestors in a fatherland free from foreign rule (doc. 81). Freedom was impregnated with the corporate spirit of the mediaeval town or even of the ancient Germans. Arndt did not acknowledge the right of the people to reform, although in 1815 he favoured public representation 'from all classes of the inhabitants' and 'particularly from the peasants and the burghers, that greatest and most honourable part of the people'. In his own frank way he had a vision, though by no means lucid, of a German national State, identical with the nation and based on 'an expanded political order allowing room for legitimate monarchical rule, political and social hierarchy and popular liberty'.[74] With his almost neurotic aversion to Western Enlightenment, Arndt had little in common with the more articulate liberalism of younger men like Dahlmann and Hansemann.

Friedrich Christoph Dahlmann was less dramatic and more precise. It was his great merit that 'unlike the turbulent nationalists and equally unlike the basically unpolitical romanticists, he accorded priority to the constitutional movement over the slogans about national unity'.[75] As the title of his major work of 1835 (*Politik auf den Grund und das Maass der gegebenen Zustände zurückgeführt*) indicates, he tried to explain 'politics reduced to the foundations and the measure of given conditions'. To him politics was a science based on empirical investigation. Although theoretically Dahlmann's system of politics distinguished between the monarchy, the aristocracy and the democracy, in fact he only considered the monarchies – there existed no republics in Europe in the 1830s. As we saw earlier (see p. 392), he favoured the English monarchy, and the British political system with its balance between the king, the aristocracy and the commoners, making for preservation rather than for radical change. In a good constitution *conservation* was 'more important than the easy making of quick improvements'. However, in other respects Dahlmann was a liberal: in his emphasis on the need for the division of power and the right of the individual to resist unconstitutional actions of the ruler. Although Dahlmann did not favour resistance at any price, in principle he acknowledged the right to it, an attitude rare in German political thought. [76] The people were not obliged to obey every government order which was unconstitutional, for this would mean acquiescence in what was wrong and assistance in carrying it out. Dahlmann was equally opposed to unlawful revolution and reaction. While the revolutionary mentality remained taboo to him, in the second edition of his work *Politik,* published in 1847, he put more emphasis on the right of resistance (doc. 83). [77]

In the 1830s Dahlmann taught history at the University of Goettingen in Hanover which had been granted a Constitution in 1833. When four years later Queen Victoria's uncle, Duke Ernst August became King of Hanover, he quickly annulled the Constitution and requested all officials and university professors to pay homage to himself. Most civil servants and university professors complied. However, seven professors at Goettingen, including Dahlmann and Jacob and Wilhelm Grimm, protested and upheld the Constitution. The king dismissed them at once and forced them to leave the country. The professors were then invited and feted by the South German liberals. During this period, 'around 1840, the leadership of liberalism was in the hands of the respected stratum of the educated Germans, the scholars'. [78]

By 1848 Dahlmann's position had changed. As a Deputy to the National Assembly at Frankfurt he was more inclined to press for German national unity than for individual freedom. 'The course of power', he declared in a speech in the Assembly on 22 January 1849, 'is the only one which will satisfy and appease the fermenting impulse of freedom, that has so far not recognized itself'. [79] On the other hand, for Karl von Rotteck individual liberty came before national unity. He preferred an independent constitutional State like Baden to a united but reactionary Germany. [80] As he put it in a speech in 1832, 'I do not desire [national] unity in any other way than with freedom and I prefer freedom without unity to unity without freedom. I do not want any unity under the wings of the Prussian and Austrian eagles.' [81]

David Hansemann was not an academic, but a pushing entrepreneur, a self-confident man of affairs from the Rhenish bourgeoisie. In his plea for political representation of the educated and propertied classes he remained conscious of the advanced character of the Rhineland, which had only been incorporated in Prussia in 1815. Through its flourishing industry and commerce the Rhineland was far superior to the still semi-feudal Eastern provinces of Prussia to which it showed the path their development should take. [82] In a memorandum to King Frederick William at the end of 1830 Hansemann argued that the former military State of Prussia could now be more properly called an industrial State (doc. 56). Prussia should increase her strength by the introduction of a liberal constitution valid for her entire realm.

Hansemann rejected the privileges of the nobility. He talked scornfully of 'a few thousand individuals desiring to form an Estate, the political significance of which had expired'. [83] Though in the 1830s he still thought in terms of a reformed Prussia, he felt the need for modernizing and liberalizing it sufficiently in order to enable it later to take the lead towards a united Germany. As has been shown (see p. 392), Hansemann favoured cooperation between the crown and a national parliament in Prussia, based on qualifications of property and education. Equality before the law and representation of the citizens, although without a universal manhood suffrage, was his recipe for a progressive State. [84]

He thought that by accepting a proper constitutional political system Prussia would qualify as the leading power among the German states and might even extend this lead to the other smaller States in Central Europe, thus giving all of them a greater degree of independence from the major European powers. [85] Ten years later Hansemann expressed similar ideas even more clearly and forcefully in another memorandum (doc. 84). He wanted to see Prussia strong and powerful in order to safeguard Prussian and German independence against dangerous enemies, i.e. acquisitive Tsarist Russia in the East and excitable chauvinist France in the West.

Such strength could only derive from a patriotism of the Prussian people based on freedom. Freedom in this context meant to him a 'legitimate and proper political influence' of the people, guaranteed by a Constitution and combined with a sense of order. Although critical of the feudalist interests of the nobility and of tutelage by the bureaucracy, however well-meaning, Hansemann still maintained in 1840 that freedom was not identical with equality of rights.[86] Like Arndt and Dahlmann, Hansemann was a conservative liberal, but he saw with greater clarity than they had done the connection between greater participation of the people in the State, however limited, and the attraction Prussia would have as a leader within the Germanies.

Hansemann's ideas on reform were laid down in memoranda destined for the King of Prussia or his advisers, in other words for members of the Establishment. Two political programmes published seven years later in South-west Germany were of a different kind. They were the outcome of meetings of two sets of liberal politicians – one radical, the other moderate – in the autumn of 1847. Both wished to influence public opinion and anticipate a national movement for reform. The group of radicals who met in September 1847 at Offenburg (see p. 83), laid stress on 'our inalienable human rights' which included protection from arbitrary arrest by the police, the right of association with others and the right of the individual to move freely 'on the soil of the German fatherland' (doc. 85).

To the men of Offenburg liberalization meant above all participation of the people in the affairs of an overall German State. Freedom within Germany and national prestige abroad were seen as the two sides of the same coin. 'Justice and freedom in our internal life, a firm position vis-à-vis foreign countries' were declared 'due to us as a nation'.

In October 1847 a number of middle-of-the-road oppositional liberal Deputies and notables from Baden, Württemberg and Hessen met at Heppenheim near Frankfurt and discussed their plans for a nationwide reform. The Rhinelander Hansemann was present.[87] Though more cautious in their formulations, the gathering of Heppenheim, too, saw freedom and national unification as complementary. German unity, they felt, could not be achieved by the rule of force (*Gewaltherrschaft*), but only 'through and together with freedom' (doc. 86).

It was the moderate Heppenheim rather than the radical Offenburg line which was pursued by the majority at the Frankfurt National Assembly in 1848–49. Although that Assembly spent much time on the formulation of a long catalogue of human rights it concerned itself even more with the character and structure of a united German Empire. Was it to be unitary or federalist? Was a lesser Germany without the German provinces of the Austrian Empire preferable to a Greater Germany with them? These were major issues in the lengthy and all too academic debates in the Paul's Church at Frankfurt.

When in the end King Frederick William IV of Prussia refused the Imperial Crown offered to him by a delegation from the Frankfurt Assembly, the dream of a united liberal nation vanished into thin air. However, although the old powers returned and a radical like Friedrich Hecker had to emigrate to the New World, the clock could not simply be put back. Even in Prussia a Diet was elected, however heavily loaded in favour of the Establishment, the old forces of aristocracy, bureaucracy and the army. Conservative and liberal party organizations began to develop. The bourgeoisie could be restricted, but different from the workers it could not be ignored. Yet 'the modern constitutional movement was now in a position of impotence'. It was unable to initiate the overdue measures of liberalization in time or to deal with the issues of power-politics.[88]

A dozen years later, in the early 1860s the liberal movement in Prussia received a new impetus. In part this was due to the founding of the *Nationalverein* at Eisenach in August 1859, 'the first political organization of Germany transcending the borders of the individual states and attempting to fuse all the liberals and democrats into one national party'.[89] The image of the future Empire in the minds of these liberals was clearly expressed by Ludwig August von Rochau, the editor of the journal of the *Nationalverein*, who coined the phrase *Realpolitik*. It was

'the concentration of all military and democratic power in one single hand, the restoration of a general representative assembly for the nation, alert protection of all true German interests against . . foreign nations . . . the supplanting of an illegal bureaucratic and police regime by a rationally constituted system of self-government in province, community, and association.'[90]

While the influence of the *Nationalverein* must not be exaggerated, the association did fulfil a double function. It tried to persuade the liberals and the middle classes in general all over Germany to back Prussian leadership in the struggle for unification. At the same time it supported the appeal of the Prussian liberals to make their State more progressive and constitutional. When the liberal majority in the Prussian Diet came into conflict with the conservative government and King William, the liberals formed the German Progressive Party which issued its Programme in June 1861 (doc. 89). It took a similar line to that pursued by the *Nationalverein*, arguing that only liberal reforms inside Prussia would qualify her for moral leadership on the road to a united German Empire. The customary liberal institutions and safeguards were asked for, the rule of the law, the responsibility of the ministers, an administrative reorganization based on the equality of rights and of self-administration, an unequivocal separation of Church and State and so on. Yet these and similar demands were not so much presented as a goal in themselves but as a means *ad majorem gloriam patriae*, to the greater glory of a future German Empire.

C. Aspects of continental liberalism in the nineteenth century

A year after the publication of this Programme, Otto von Bismarck, the staunch opponent of the liberals, was appointed Prime Minister of Prussia by the anxious King William after the government's plans for the reform and extension of army service had been repeatedly rejected by the Prussian Diet. The subsequent bitter conflict over the budget between Bismarck's government and the liberal majority of the Diet was not solved by parliamentary methods – Bismarck simply ignored the repeated majority votes against him – but by the success of his policy of 'blood and iron'. The Prussian victories in the wars against Denmark and Austria together with Bismarck's astute diplomacy in the 1860s soon evoked second thoughts in many of his liberal opponents. By adroitly asking the Chamber for indemnity for financial measures taken previously by the State without the required approval of parliament, Bismarck caused a split in the ranks of the liberals. Some of them remained his intransigent adversaries; others, filled with admiration for his statesmanship and political acumen, were now prepared to cooperate with him. They included even such bitter former opponents as Max von Forckenbeck and Karl Twesten. Breaking away from the Progressive Party they formed the new National Liberal Party. As its Programme neatly put it (doc. 90), the Party aimed at the unification of Germany, 'a unity tending towards Power and Freedom'. The National Liberals believed that freedom and national unity were determining each other. They argued with some sophistry that 'without the active and driving power of national unity the freedom of the German people' could 'not be satisfied'. After the decisive victory of the Prussian army at Königgrätz and after Bismarck's concessions to the Prussian Diet the identification of liberalism and the national State, the association of a liberal Constitution with a unified Empire seemed plausible and attractive to them. They now argued that 'the German State and German freedom must be achieved simultaneously by the same means'. In their opinion not only were the days of the old cabinet policy past, but also those of a doctrinaire liberalism which would soon find itself in a ghetto of its own making. If it was necessary to 'Bismarckize' the liberal ideals, it might also be possible to liberalize Bismarck's policies. If 'to harmonize a monarchichal Federal State with the conditions of constitutional law' was 'a difficult task, so far not yet achieved in history', the Prussian National Liberals were willing and confident enough to attempt it.

The remaining deputies of the Progressive Party who did not trust Bismarck were less optimistic. Their leader in the Reichstag, Eugen Richter, expressed his misgivings in looking back some years later to the fateful year 1866. As Richter put it in 1874: 'Whereas there was then the least danger that liberalism was practised unaccompanied by the national idea, in reverse the worry was close at hand that the national idea would prevail unaccompanied by liberalism' (doc. 94).

In the elections to the Constituent North German Reichstag in 1867 the liberals fared badly, particularly in the old provinces of Prussia. The Progressivists were pushed on to the defensive, but did their best to stand up for liberal rights. Viewed from their stalwart liberalism the trouble came from the National Liberals who had been elected in the new provinces such as the former Kingdom of Hanover acquired by the might of Prussian arms. These men who had formerly opposed the dynasties now deposed, felt attracted by Bismarck's strong and triumphant government. They were much less prepared to stand up for the rights of the individual. The right of parliament to decide about the budget, the question of the responsibility of the ministers to parliament were issues of lesser importance to the new Prussian deputies than they were to some of the old liberals, who had previously clashed bitterly with Bismarck and now resented his annexations in North Germany (doc. 92).

Among the many liberals who experienced a change of heart was the South German historian Hermann Baumgarten. During Bismarck's early years as Prussian Prime Minister, Baumgarten shared with many other prominent liberals, including his fellow-historians Heinrich von Treitschke and Heinrich von Sybel, a profound distrust of the Macchiavellian Junker. In his letters from Karlsruhe in Baden, Baumgarten critized the attitude of the liberal deputies in Prussia in their conflict with Bismarck as being too tame (doc. 87a). 'People who despise the Constitution, reason and the law like naughty boys must be made to tremble', he wrote to von Sybel in Berlin; 'A permanent rule by Bismarck would mean revolution.' The permanence of his illiberal regime would also finish Prussia's position in Germany and in Europe.

Yet by 1866 Baumgarten was much more inclined to see the good points in the extraordinary Junker (doc. 87c and d). Having had no sympathy for Austria he now desired an alliance between the German liberals and Prussia. An Austrian victory would mean, anyway, the end of liberalism; but should Prussia win a war against her without the support of the German liberals, the people would turn away from liberalism. The Fatherland must stand above the Party and the liberals should, therefore, back Prussia in a war with Austria.

After the quick resounding victory of the Prussian troops at Königgrätz, Baumgarten was able 'to be proud of Prussia for the first time'. She had fulfilled his hopes and exceeded his expectations. It was in the same year that Baumgarten published a searching self-criticism of liberalism (doc. 88). Its conclusions were severe. Liberalism had failed in its opposition to the forces of the Old Order in Prussia, including the Junkers. Nearly all the assertions of the liberal ideology had proved wrong. Instead of losing itself in unproductive opposition, liberalism must now join the Establishment and become capable of governing. Baumgarten hoped for an alternation between liberal and conservative governments after the British model, and now favoured an alliance between the old Prussian landed aristocracy and the middle-class

C. Aspects of continental liberalism in the nineteenth century

strata of industry, commerce and the professions. Yet when the Second Empire was dominated by the towering figure of the Iron Chancellor, Baumgarten unlike other National Liberals, became very independent and critical of the new regime. Bismarck's domestic policies did not fulfil the earlier high expectations of his critic.

By then a professor at Strassburg in Alsace-Lorraine which the French had been forced to cede to Germany in 1871, Baumgarten disliked its first German governor (*Statthalter*), Edwin von Manteuffel. But his main worry was Bismarck's domestic policy. In a letter to von Sybel in January 1881 he disagreed with Sybel's description of Bismarck as 'the greatest statesman of the century' and maintained that ten years hence he would only be regarded as its 'greatest diplomat' (doc. 93*d*). By 1881 Bismarck had given up his fight against the Catholic Church to the intense discomfort of Baumgarten who saw in the Vatican the source of all evil. Again he made the liberals responsible for the present trend and predicted that Bismarck would 'leave behind a horrible chaos and we shall have to atone horribly for our blindness'.

Heinrich von Sybel did not concur with that sinister prediction, nor did he find Baumgarten's verdict on Bismarck just, although he admitted that fault could be found with his political style and his brusque manner (doc. 93*c*). Sybel defended Bismarck's legislation on Church matters, and he denied any sell-out to Rome by the government. If Bismarck's liberal opponents in the Reichstag deplored his sudden volte-face in 1878 from free trade to protective tariffs, from cooperation with the National Liberals to an alliance with the conservatives and the Centre Party, Sybel did not equate this change with a triumph of political reaction. He quite approved of Bismarck's opportunism; as a statesman was bound to work with the parties which granted him the means to carry out his sound financial policies.

Baumgarten, however, continued to argue that the domestic policy of the Chancellor was 'becoming more and more pernicious' whereas 'his foreign policy was, and is, magnificent and admirable'. He now saw in Bismarck 'a truly Caesarian demagogue' appealing to the passions of the masses (doc. 93*f*).

The masses had come to the fore, he argued, because Bismarck had granted universal manhood suffrage. The advance of socialism, abhorred by that stubborn Strassburg liberal, was to him an effect of Bismarck's unlimited power. Most Germans then bowed before him and his opportunistic policies. But what would come after Bismarck? Baumgarten feared a wave of radicalism: owing to Bismarck's enmity and its own weakness the liberal bourgeoisie would disappear as a political factor and there would be a sharp confrontation 'between big property and the greedy masses'.

In the end, Baumgarten not only became frightened by Bismarck's ruthless power politics which he had so much admired earlier, he also displayed a complete lack of understanding of the big social issues of the time, a telling commentary on the limits of his brand of German liberalism.

Notes and references

1. The constitutional State

1. Foreword to the *Staatslexikon*, I, 1834.
2. In his article 'The Responsibility of Princes and Ministers of State' Welcker discussed the position in England.
3. K. S. Pinson, *Modern Germany. Its History and Civilisation*, New York 1954, p. 115.

2. Freedom and the individual

4. It was revived a century later after the Second World War in the Christian Democratic parties in Western Europe.
5. Alec R. Vidler, *Prophecy and Papacy*, London 1959, p. 163.
6. Mazzini, *The Duties of Man* (Everyman edn.), London 1934, p. 56.
7. Quoted in G. Salvemini, *Mazzini*, London 1956, pp. 92–3.
8. Salvemini, op. cit., p. 92.
9. Significant omissions on his list were individual freedom of education and academic freedom.
10. The proposal to abolish the nobility as an institution altogether was rejected by the National Assembly against a substantial minority. See Frank Eyck, *The Frankfurt Parliament 1848–1849*, London 1968, p. 223.
11. For the articles on freedom of religion and on the relations between Church and State see p. 413.
12. E. Laboulaye, *Le Parti libéral*, Paris 1864, p. 3.
13. It is significant that Laboulaye took a great interest in the work of Benjamin Constant and in 1861 introduced and annotated a new edition of Constant's *Cours de politique constitutionnelle*.
14. Guido de Ruggiero, *The History of European Liberalism*, London 1927, p. 199.
15. E. Laboulaye, *L'Etat et ses limites*, Paris 1863, p. 96.
16. *New Cambridge Modern History*, vol. 10 (*The Zenith of European Power, 1830–70*) 1960, p. 456.
17. Thiers realised that it was not practical politics to ask the government to abstain from favouring some candidates. He conceded realistically that 'practical men ... have reduced demands of this kind to a minimum: they have only asked that the government, if it has any preferences, confines itself to propriety and honesty'. In other words, the government may have its favourites, but it must not push them unscrupulously.
18. See below, Section D, docs 102 and 104.
19. See J. P. T. Bury, *Gambetta and the National Defence*, London 1936, p. 24.

C. Aspects of continental liberalism in the nineteenth century

20. Irene Collins, *The Government and the Newspaper Press in France, 1814–1881*, London 1959, p. 8.
21. Gabriel Remond, *Royer-Collard. Son essai d'un système politique*, Paris 1933, p. 96.
22. Roger Langernon, *Un Conseiller Secrèt de Louis XVIII, Royer-Collard*. Paris 1956, p. 130.
23. Irene Collins, op. cit., pp. 37–8.
24. M. de Barante, *La vie politique de Royer-Collard. Ses Discours et Ses Ecrits*, II, Paris 1861, pp. 138, 146.
25. Ibid., II, pp. 500, 505.
26. See Franz Schneider, *Pressefreiheit und politische Offentlichkeit*, Neuwied 1966, pp. 196–8.
27. K. Koszyk, *Deutsche Presse im 19. Jahrhundert*, Berlin 1966, p. 71.
28. On the *Deutsche Zeitung* see R. Hinton Thomas, *Liberalism, Nationalism and the German Intellectuals*, Cambridge 1951, p. 125.
29. K. Koszyk, op. cit., p. 99.
30. Caution money indicated the obligation of the founder or the subsequent owner of a newspaper or periodical to deposit a considerable sum of money with the Government as a guarantee for the payment of fines. In France caution money remained obligatory from 1819 to 1881. See Irene Collins, op. cit., p. 24.
31. After 1870 Catholic newspapers and Socialist newspapers each catered for a specific public.
32. See Irene Fischer-Frauendienst, *Bismarcks Pressepolitik*, Münster 1965.
33. See Schwarz-Appelius-Wulffen, *Reichs Pressegesetz*, Munich 1914, p. 14, and K. Koszyk, op. cit., p. 243.
34. Bismarck's repressive measures against the Social Democratic press 1878–90 were based on a special emergency law, passed by a majority in the Reichstag.
35. Irene Collins, op. cit., p. 116.
36. Rochefort fled to Brussels but the reappearance of his paper there with copies smuggled into France was not a success.
37. The journals were obliged to give the name and address of an editor responsible for the contents of the issue (*le gérant*) and of the printer to the authorities. Both could be prosecuted in certain cases.
38. Irene Collins, op. cit., p. 181.

3. Freedom from the Church and freedom for the Church

39. J. Salwyn Schapiro, *Anticlericalism*, Princeton 1964, p. 25. For the origins and use of the terms 'clericalism' and 'anticlericalism' see Owen Chadwick, *The Secularization of The European Mind in the Nineteenth Century*, Cambridge 1975, ch. 5, pp. 107–39.
40. E. Laboulaye, *L'Etat et ses limites*, p. 112.
41. F. B. Artz, *Reaction and Revolution 1814–1832*, New York 1945, p. 71.
42. A. R. Vidler, *Prophecy and Papacy*. A study of Lamennais, the Church and the Revolution, London 1954, p. 153.
43. Ibid., p. 161.
44. In *Des Interêts catholiques au Dix-neuvième Siècle*, Paris 1852. An English translation was published in the same year. The quotations here are from the English edition, *Catholic Interests in the Nineteenth Century*, London 1852. Chapter VI entitled 'Religion stands in need of liberty; liberty stands in need of religion'.
45. Op. cit., p. 66.
46. Op. cit., p. 72.
47. Comte Charles de Montalembert, *L'Eglise libre dans L'Etat libre*. Discours prononcé au Congrès catholique de Malines. Paris 1863.

48. Montalembert's plea for tolerance applied to all religious beliefs. He declared, 'the Spanish inquisitor who says to the heretic "The truth or death!" ' is 'as odious as the French terrorists who said to my grandfather "Liberty, fraternity or death".' *L'Eglise libre dans L'Etat libre*, p. 135.
49. Christopher Seton Watson, *Italy from Liberalism to Fascism 1870–1925*, London 1967, p. 9.
50. S. William Halperin, *The Separation of Church and State in Italian Thought from Cavour to Mussolini*, Chicago 1937, p. 9.
51. See the article 'The Holy Alliance of the Peoples' (1848), in Joseph Mazzini, *Life and Writings*, V, p. 281.
52 and 53. E. E. Hales, *Pio Nono*, London 1954, p. 259.
54. For the *Kulturkampf* attitude of German liberals see doc. 95.
55. Veit Valentin, *Geschichte der deutschen Revolution 1848–49*, Berlin 1931, vol. 2, p. 131.
56. Frank Eyck, *The Frankfurt Parliament, 1848–1849*, London 1968, p. 229.
57. Ibid., p. 230.
58. Fritz Vigener, *3 Gestalten aus dem modernen Katholizismus*, München 1926, p. 132.
59. F. Eyck, op. cit., p. 237.
60. Ibid., p. 238.
61. Veit Valentin, op. cit., vol. 2, p. 133.
62. Fritz Fischer, 'Der deutsche Protestantismus und die Politik im 19. Jahrhundert', *Historische Zeitschrift*, Band 171, 1951, p. 489.
63. Gerald Brenan, *The Spanish Labyrinth*, London 1943, p. viii.
64. Salvador de Madariaga, *Spain*, London 1942, p. 128, and Brenan, op. cit., p. 53.
65. G. Brenan, op. cit., p. 59.
66. John David Highey, jr. *Religious Freedon in Spain. The Ebb and Flow*, London 1955, p. 20.
67. In 1876 about 60 per cent of the population were still illiterate and only in 1901 did education come under State control, although the amount allocated to it in the budget was still 'scandalously small'. G. Brenan, op. cit., p. 51.
68. R. Carr, *Spain, 1808–1939*, Oxford 1966, p. 467.
69. G. Brenan, op. cit., pp. 51–2, and J. B. Trend, *The Origin of Modern Spain*, London 1934, p. 61.
70. R. Carr, op. cit., p. 467.
71. Arnold R. Verduin, *Manual of Spanish Constitutions 1808–1931*, Michigan 1941, p. 89. A special law by the Constituent Cortes also decreed the dissolution of other orders 'which by their activities constitute a menace to the safety of the State'.
72. Ibid., p. 85.

4. Freedom, power and the nation-state: Germany 1814–1881

73. E. M. Arndt, *Geist der Zeit I,* quoted in Leonard Krieger, *The German Idea of Freedom*, Boston 1957, p. 496.
74. L. Krieger, op. cit., p. 194.
75. K. D. Bracher in his essay on Dahlmann, in *The German Dilemma*, London 1974, p. 32.
76. In modern terminology Dahlmann favoured not active, but passive resistance, at least in certain cases. When laws and taxes were not in accordance with the Constitution, they should not be accepted and ministers who signed such laws or order should be impeached.
77. There was a new meaningful passage on 'the right of subjects, which the courts are obliged to respect, to regard the rule of a prince, who refuses to acknowledge the

C. Aspects of continental liberalism in the nineteenth century

country's constitution, as never having begun'. The reason for this insertion was that 'between the first and the second edition this theorist, suspected of conservatism, had become a martyr of liberalism'. Friedrich C. Sell, *Die Tragödie des deutschen Liberalismus*, p. 129.

78. Ibid., p. 131.
79. Ibid., p. 153.
80. Ibid., p. 125.
81. Ibid., p. 125. The opposite view was put by another South German, P. A. Pfizer, about the same time in his *Briefwechsel zweier Deutschen* (1831). He declared 'it is questionable whether constitutional states would advance the cause of unity. On the other hand, once unity was achieved, freedom would follow. The preservation of liberty requires the protection of a strong unified state.' Quoted in Georg G. Iggers *The German Conception of History*, Middletown, Connecticut 1968, p. 99.
82. J. Hansen, *Rheinische Briefe und Akten zur Geschichte der politischen Bewegung 1830–1850*, I, p. 17.
83. Ibid., p. 39. Like Dahlmann he appreciated the political importance of the English nobility, but unlike him he regarded the role played by the German nobility as out of date.
84. In a memorandum of December 1830 Hansemann declared it 'Prussia's noble calling and at the same time her existential interest, to promote the power and welfare of Germany vigorously and therefore to unite the German states in a joint confederation tied together firmly by their true interests'. Hansen, op. cit., p. 39.
85. Ibid., pp. 71, 75.
86. Ibid., pp. 228, 237–8.
87. In 1848 David Hansemann was not a deputy to the National Assembly at Frankfurt, but for some months a leading liberal Cabinet Minister in Prussia. It is interesting that in this capacity he became more concerned with the rights of the Prussian State as a constitutional monarchy than with the national unity of Germany. See Frank Eyck, *The Frankfurt Parliament, 1848–1849*, London 1968, p. 171.
88. K. D. Bracher, *The German Dilemma*, p. 45.
89. Koppel S. Pinson, *Modern Germany. Its History and Civilisation*, New York 1954, p. 122.
90. Ibid., p. 122.

1. The constitutional state: documents
(Introduction, p. 388)

(i) Limitation of power – the role of the monarch

France

Doc. 45. DESTUTT DE TRACY: A Commentary on Montesquieu's 'Spirit of the Laws'

Book XII. Of the Laws which Constitute Political Freedom in Relation to the Citizen
Political freedom would not know how to exist without individual freedom and freedom of the press, and these in their turn without trial by jury.

Montesquieu entitled the preceding book [Book XI]: *Of the laws which constitute political freedom in relation to the constitution.* We saw that under this title he deals with the effects on man's freedom of the laws which make up the constitution of the state, that is to say, of the laws which determine the distribution of political powers. These are, in effect, the main laws of those who rule over the general interests of society; and by joining to them the laws which regulate the administration and the public economy, that is, those which direct the creation and distribution of wealth, there would be a complete system of laws governing the interests of the body politic, taken as a whole, and influencing the happiness and freedom of each person by the effect it produces on the happiness and freedom of all.

In this book [Book XII] it is a question of the laws which bear directly upon the private interests of every citizen. It is no longer public and political freedom which they attack or protect directly; it is individual and private freedom. It is felt that this second kind of freedom is very necessary to the first, and is intimately bound up with it. For, in order to be able to uphold public liberty, every citizen must be safeguarded against oppression of his person and his property; and it is obvious enough that if, for example, any authority whatsoever was invested with the right to order arbitrarily imprisonment, banishment or other penalties, it would be impossible to contain that authority within limits which could be prescribed by the constitution, even though the state had a very precise and formal one. Montesquieu also says that under the relationship in question *freedom* consists in *safety*, and that the constitution could be free (that is, possess arrangements favourable to freedom) and the citizen not be free; and he adds, with good reason, that in the majority of states (he would say in all) individual freedom is *more constrained, struck at or beaten down* than their constitution demands. The reason for this is that the authorities, wanting always to go beyond the rights conceded to them, need to lean heavily on that kind of freedom in order to oppress the other.

Just as there are laws which are mainly constitutional, followed by administrative laws, which influence general liberty; so there are criminal laws, and, subsidiary to them, civil laws which deal with individual freedom. The subject we have to discuss is treated almost entirely in Book VI, where Montesquieu proposed to survey *the consequences of the principles of the different governments in regard to the simplicity of the civil and criminal laws, the form of judgement and the fixing of penalties.* A better order in the arrangement and connection of his ideas would have been to join that book with this, and even with the twenty-ninth which treats *of the way to fashion laws* and at the same time of the way to appraise their results. But we have tied ourselves to following the order adopted by our author. It will be to everyone's advantage to improve and remould his work and ours, in order to create a consistent and complete system of principles.

At the beginning of the sixth book, we agreed that, despite the great and noble views it includes, we did not find in it all the learning we would have expected. We are bound to make the same admission about this. It ought naturally to include a discussion and an assessment of the chief institutions which are the most favourable or the most prejudicial to the safety of the citizen and to the free exercise of his natural civil and political rights. Now, this is not what we find. Montesquieu, in his usual way, in a multitude of short unconnected chapters surveys all times and all countries, and ancient times and little known countries most of all. Granted, he draws from all these facts inferences which most often are very sound. But so much research and intelligence are not needed in order to inform us that the accusation of magic is absurd; that purely religious errors ought to be repressed by purely religious punishments also; that under monarchies the crime of high treason has often been abused to the point of being barbarous and ridiculous; that it is tyrannical to punish satirical writings, unguarded words, and even thoughts; that judgements by commissioners, espionage, and information given anonymously are cruel and repugnant things, etc. If Montesquieu was compelled to have recourse to artfulness in order to dare to tell such truths, and if it was impossible for him to go any further, he must be pitied; but we do not have to stop there.

In the midst of all this, I find only one profound reflection. It is this: *That it is of the greatest danger for republics to pile up punishments for the crime of high treason against the king or the nation.* Under the *pretext of avenging the republic*, says Montesquieu, *the tyranny of the avengers will be set up. It is not a question of destroying those who have the mastery, but of destroying the domination itself. As soon as possible, the manner of government must be resumed in which the laws protect all and do not take up arms against anyone.* These are admirable words. The testimony drawn from examples is unanswerable. Among the Greeks, in order not to have acted thus, *exile or the return of exiles always marked the periods indicating the changing of the constitution.* How modern events would support this, if need be!

But, beside these very wise conclusions, I find in it one rather dangerous one, which is contrary to the stated opinion of Cicero. It is that there are times when a law can be made expressly against one man; and that *there are cases when, for a moment, a veil must be drawn over liberty, just as the statues of the gods are hidden.* (*The Spirit of the Laws*, Book 12, ch. 19.) Thus far has Anglomania led this great man.

Although this is so, but seeing that our author has not considered it appropriate to penetrate deeper into his subject, we shall limit ourselves to repeating here that political freedom would not know how to exist without individual freedom and freedom of the press, and that, in order to maintain these, it is absolutely essential to proscribe all arbitrary imprisonment and follow the practice of trial by jury, at least for the criminal. Thus we shall refer the reader to what we have said on this matter in earlier books, and particularly in the fourth, sixth and eleventh books where we have indicated how and why these principles are favoured or opposed by the nature and spirit of every type of government.

[Source: Destutt de Tracy, 'Commentaire sur L'ésprit des Lois de Montesquieu'; in *Oeuvres de Montesquieu*, avec éloges, analyses, commentaires, remarques, notes, réfutations, imitations par M. Destutt de Tracy, Paris 1827, VI, pp. 211–16. Translated by the editors of this volume.]

Doc. 46. BENJAMIN CONSTANT: On Constitutional Powers and Political Rights

Constitutional Powers
The constitutional powers are: the royal power, the executive power, the power of the representative assembly, the judiciary power and the municipal power.

Observations
It will cause surprise that I distinguish the royal power from the executive power. This distinction, which is always misunderstood, is very important. It is, perhaps, the key to the entire political organisation. I do not claim the honour of finding it: for the concept is to be found in the writings of a very enlightened mind* who perished in the days of our troubles, as did nearly all the enlightened men.

'Two distinct powers,' he says, 'are contained in the power of the monarch: the executive power, which is invested with positive prerogatives, and the royal power which is maintained by historical memories and by religious traditions.' In pondering over this idea, I am convinced of its correctness. The subject is sufficiently novel to warrant some discussion.

The three political powers which are usually distinguished, that is, the executive, the legislative, and the judiciary powers, are three spheres which should co-operate, each in its turn, in a general movement; but when these spheres become deranged, they cross, challenge and impede each other, and a force is required to put them in their respective places. This force cannot be found in any one of these spheres, for it will serve its own interests by destroying the others. It must be found outside, and be neutral in some way, so that its action can be applied wherever it is necessary. Without being hostile, it must be protective and restorative.

Constitutional monarchy has the great advantage in that it has created that neutral power in the person of a king, who is already surrounded by traditions and memories and invested with a prestige which serves as a basis for his political power. It is by no means in the true interest of the king that one of the powers should overthrow the other, but rather that all of them should maintain themselves, understand each other and act in concert.

The legislative power resides in the assemblies, with the sanction of the king; the executive power in the ministers, and the judiciary power in the courts. The first of these makes the laws, the second supervises their general implementation, and the third applies them in specific cases. The king stands in the centre of these three powers, a neutral and in-

* M. de Clermont-Tonnère.

termediary authority without any definite interest in upsetting the equilibrium, but, on the contrary, being fully interested in its preservation.

Undoubtedly, as men do not always obey their true interest, it is necessary to take the precaution of making the royal power unable to act in place of the other powers. This is what marks the difference between absolute monarchy and constitutional monarchy. As it is always useful to illustrate abstractions by facts, we refer to the English constitution.* No law can be made without the consent of parliament; no decree can be put into practice without the signature of a minister (of the Crown); and judgement can be pronounced only by independent courts. But this precaution having been taken, see how the English constitution uses the royal power to put an end to all dangerous struggles, and to re-establish harmony among the other powers. If the action of the executive power, that is to say, the action of the ministers, is irregular, the king dismisses the executive power. If the action of the representative power becomes detrimental, the king dissolves the representative body. Finally, where the action of even the judiciary is grievous, because it applies to individual actions punishments which are too severe, the king can mitigate this action through his right of royal pardon.

The vice of nearly all constitutions has consisted in not having created a neutral power, but of having placed in one of the active powers instead the sum total of the authority with which it should be invested. When this sum total of authority finds itself joined to the legislative power, the law, which should only extend to clearly defined matters, is extended to everything. It becomes an arbitrary and unlimited tyranny. From thence came the excesses of the assemblies of the people in the Italian republics, and those of the Long Parliament during some periods of its existence. When the sum total of authority finds itself joined with the executive power there is despotism, from them came the usurpation which resulted in the Roman dictatorship ...

As I have said, constitutional monarchy offers us this neutral power which is so indispensable for every regular freedom. But this immense advantage is lost either by reducing the royal power to the level of the executive power, or by raising the executive power to the level of the royal power. Then a thousand questions become insoluble: for instance, that of responsibility. When the ministers are considered simply as agents of the executive power, it seems absurd to make the instrument responsible and declare the arm inviolable which uses it. But if the

* I ought to remark that it is a fact of the right established by the English constitution as the neutrality of the royal power. This neutrality was introduced into the English constitution by the force of events, and because it is an indispensable condition, a necessary outcome of all constitutional monarchy. In the English constitution there are also certain royal prerogatives which are incompatible with this neutrality, and therefore cannot serve as a model to peoples called to enjoy the benefit of liberty under a monarchy.

executive power, that is to say, the ministers, is considered as a separate power which the royal power is intended to restrain by dismissing it, just as it restrains the representative assemblies by dissolving them, then the responsibility of the executive power becomes reasonable and the inviolability of the royal power is assured.

Can it be said that the executive power emanates from the king? Undoubtedly this is so; but, although it emanates from the king, it is no longer the king, just as the representative power is not the people, although it emanates from the people.

Whilst the citizens, who are divided among themselves by their interests, do harm to each other, a neutral authority separates them, pronounces judgement on their pretensions and preserves them from each other. This authority is the judiciary power. In the same way, when the public powers are divided and prone to do each other harm, a neutral power is required which can do with respect to them what the judiciary power does in the case of individuals. In a constitutional monarchy this authority is the royal power. The royal power is to some extent the judiciary power as far as the other powers are concerned.

We shall come back to this question and throw more light on it when discussing the dismissal of the executive power. We shall show that the possibility of doing so is indispensable; but, nevertheless, when the executive power is not distinguished from the royal power, it is a source of confusion in theory and a danger in practice.

Political Rights

1. Political rights consist in being a member of the various national authorities, in being a member of the local authorities in the Departments, and in taking part in the election of these various authorities.

2. All Frenchmen, if they possess landed property or industrial property,* and pay a fixed amount in taxes, are entitled to exercise political rights; or if they have leasehold property on the basis of a sufficiently long and non-revocable lease and, through this holding, exist without the help of a wage which makes them dependent on others.

Observations

No nation has regarded as members of the State all the individuals who in one way or another reside in its territory. It is not a question here of

---

* I had intended in my *Principles of Politics* to accord the rights of citizenship only to landed proprietors, but experience has enlightened me. I saw that in our century industrial property was even more substantial (real), and above all more powerful than that of the soil. So, recognising my error, I have corrected my work.

436

the distinctions with which the ancient peoples separated the slaves from the free men, and which in modern times separate the nobles from the commoners. The most absolute democracy establishes two classes. Into one class are relegated foreigners and those who have not yet reached the age prescribed by law which enables them to exercise the rights of citizenship. The other class is composed of men who have reached that age and were born in the country. Thus there exists a principle, according to which, there are among the individuals living in a territory those who are members of the State and those who are not.

This principle evidently is, that, in order to be a member of an association, a certain degree of intelligence and an interest in common with other members of that association is necessary. Men below the legal age are not regarded as having that degree of intelligence; and foreigners are not regarded as being guided by that common interest. As proof of this, the former on reaching the age laid down by law become members of the political association, and the latter become members through residence and the possession of property or relations. It is presumed that these things give insight to the one and the requisite interest to the other.

But this principle needs a further extension. In our existing societies, birth in the country and maturity of age do not suffice to confer on men the proper qualities for exercising the rights of citizenship. Those whom poverty keeps in eternal dependence and condemns to day labour have no more understanding of public affairs than children, or more interest than foreigners in the national prosperity of which they do not know the elements and in the advantages of which they share only indirectly.

I do not want to wrong the working class. That class is no less patriotic than other classes. It is often ready to make the most heroic sacrifices, and its devotion, which is recompensed neither by fortune nor by glory, is the more admirable. But I think that the patriotism which gives a man courage to die for his country is one thing, and that which makes him capable of knowing its interests well is another. Consequently there must be a condition besides birth or the age prescribed by law. This condition is the leisure which is indispensable for acquiring knowledge and rectitude of judgement. Property alone assures that leisure, and property alone makes men capable of exercising political rights ...

In all countries where there are representative assemblies, it is essential that these assemblies, whatever be their subsequent organisation in other respects, should be composed of property-owners. An individual, by striking merit, can captivate the crowd; but representative bodies, in order to gain confidence, need to have interests which are obviously conformable to their duties. A nation always presumes that men assembled together are guided by their interests. It believes without any doubt that love of order, justice and preservation will have the majority among property-owners, who are useful, therefore, not only on account of the qualities which are proper to them, but also because of the qualities

437

attributed to them, through the prudence which they are supposed to have and the favourable prejudices which they inspire. But place some who are not property-owners, however well-intentioned they be, among the legislators, and the disquietude of those who do own property will hinder all their measures. The wisest of laws will be suspect, and consequently disobeyed, whilst the opposite organisation would have reconciled popular feeling, even to a government which was defective in some respects.

It is true that during our revolution property-owners joined with non-proprietors to make foolish and despoiling laws for fear that the latter would assume power. They wanted to be pardoned for their property. Fear of losing what they have makes men faint-hearted, and then they imitate the fury of those who want to obtain what they do not have. The faults or the crimes of the property-owners resulted from the influence of the non-proprietors.

But what are the conditions of property that it is equitable to establish?

Property can be so restricted that those who possess it are property-owners in appearance only. Whoever does not receive from it in income, says a writer who has discussed this matter fully,* an adequate amount on which to live during the year, without working for others, is not entirely a property-owner. He finds himself, respecting the amount of property which he lacks, in the class of wage-earners. Property-owners are masters of his existence, for they can refuse him work. Those who possess the income necessary for existing independently of any unknown will, can, therefore, alone exercise the rights of citizenship. A condition of lower property is illusory; a condition of higher property is unjust.

I do not believe that I am very far from these principles in recognising as property-owners those who hold on a long lease a farm which yields an adequate income. In the existing state of property in France, the tenant-farmer who cannot be turned out is in reality a property-owner more than the citizen who apparently is one only from an estate which he rents. It is just, therefore, to grant to the one the same rights as the other. If it is objected that at the end of the lease the farmer loses his title of property-owner, I shall reply that through a thousand accidents every property-owner may lose his property some day or another.

[Source: Benjamin Constant, *Cours de Politique constitutionelle*, ed. M. J-P. Pagès, Paris 1836, I, pp. 1–5, 6–7, 116–23. Translated by the editors of this volume.]

Spain

Doc. 47. Political Constitution of the Spanish Nation (Proclaimed in Cadiz, 19 March 1812 [Extracts]

* Count Garnier.

Preamble
In the name of God Almighty, Father, Son, and Holy Ghost, Creator and Supreme Legislator of society:

The general and extraordinary Cortes of the Spanish nation, well convinced, after very close examination and mature deliberation, that the ancient fundamental laws of the monarchy, accompanied by the opportune provisions and precautions which assure their entire fulfillment in a stable and permanent manner, will worthily achieve the great object of promoting the glory, prosperity, and welfare of the entire nation, decree the following political constitution for the good government and just administration of the state.

TITLE I. The Spanish Nation and the Spaniards

Chapter I. The Spanish Nation
Art. 1. The Spanish nation consists of all Spaniards in both hemispheres.
Art. 2. The Spanish nation is free and independent, and is not, nor can it be, the patrimony of any family or person.
Art. 3. Sovereignty resides essentially in the nation, and therefore the right of establishing its fundamental laws belongs to it exclusively.
Art. 4. The nation is obliged to preserve and protect by just and wise laws, the civil liberty, the property, and the other legitimate rights of all individuals belonging to it.

Chapter II. Spaniards
Art. 5. The following are Spaniards:
 1. All free men born and resident in Spanish dominions and their children;
 2. Foreigners who have obtained certificates of naturalization from the Cortes;
 3. Foreigners who, without such certificate, reside ten years in a district, may obtain it, according to law, in any town of the monarchy;
 4. Freedmen as soon as they obtain their liberty in Spain.
Art. 6. Love of his country is one of the principal obligations of all Spaniards, as well as justice and beneficence.
Art. 7. Every Spaniard is bound to be faithful to the constitution, to obey the laws, and to respect established authorities.
Art. 8. Every Spaniard is likewise bound, without any distinction, to contribute in proportion to his means, to the expenses of the state.
Art. 9. Every Spaniard is also bound to defend his fatherland by bearing arms when called upon by law.

C. Aspects of continental liberalism in the nineteenth century

TITLE II.   The Territory of Spain, Its Religion and Government, and Spanish Citizens

Chapter II.   Religion
Art. 12.   The religion of the Spanish nation is, and shall be perpetually, Apostolic Roman Catholic, the only true religion. The nation protects it by wise and just laws and prohibits the exercise of any other, whatsoever.

Chapter III.   Government
Art. 13.   The object of the government is the happiness of the nation since the end of all political society is only the well being of the individuals who compose it.
Art. 14.   The government of the Spanish nation is a limited, hereditary monarchy.
Art. 15.   The power of making laws resides in the Cortes and the King.
Art. 16.   The power of executing laws resides in the King.
Art. 17.   The power of applying laws in civil and criminal cases resides in the courts established by law.

TITLE III.   The Cortes

Chapter I.   The Manner of Forming the Cortes
Art. 27.   The Cortes is the assembly of all the Deputies who represent the nation, elected by the citizens in the manner given below.
Art. 28.   The basis for national representation is the same in both hemispheres.
Art. 29.   This basis is the population consisting of the natives who, on both sides, have originated in Spanish dominions and of those who have received a certificate of citizenship from the Cortes as well as those comprehended in art. 21.
Art. 31.   There shall be a Deputy to the Cortes for every 70,000 souls of population, composed according to the explanation in art. 29.

Chapter VII.   The Powers of the Cortes
Art. 131.   The Cortes has the following powers:
1. To propose and decree laws and to interpret and alter them when necessary;
2. To receive the oath from the King, the Prince of Asturias, and the regency as provided in their places;
3. To settle any doubt of fact or right occurring in the order of succession to the crown;
4. To elect a regency or regent of the kingdom, as provided by the constitution and to designate the limits within which the regency or regent may exercise the royal authority;

440

5. To recognize publicly the Prince of Asturias;
6. To appoint a guardian for the minor King as provided by the constitution;
7. To approve before ratification, treaties of offensive alliance, of subsidies, and special treaties of commerce;
8. To grant or refuse the admission of foreign troops in the kingdom;
9. To decree the creation and suppression of offices in the courts established by the constitution and also the creation and suppression of public offices;
10. To fix annually upon royal proposal, the forces on land and sea, determining the establishment in time of peace, and the increase in time of war;
11. To issue ordinances to the army, navy, and national militia in all their branches;
12. To fix the expenses of the public administration;
13. To establish annually the taxes and imposts;
14. To obtain loans, in cases of necessity, on national credit;
15. To approve the division of taxes among the provinces;
16. To examine and approve the accounts of the inversion of public funds;
17. To establish customs-houses and the duties paid therein;
18. To order what is expedient for the administration, preservation, and alienation of national property.
19. To determine the value, weight, standard, type, and denomination of money;
20. To adopt the system of weights and measures that it considers most suitable and just;
21. To promote and encourage all kinds of industry and to remove obstacles impeding it;
22. To establish a general plan of public instruction in all the monarchy, and to approve what is planned for the education of the Prince of Asturias;
23. To approve the general regulation for the police and sanitation of the kingdom;
24. To protect the political liberty of the press;
25. To render effective the responsibility of the secretaries of state and other public employees;
26. To grant or refuse its consent in all those cases and acts which the constitution prescribes as necessary.

TITLE IV. The King

Chapter I. The Inviolability of the King and His Authority.
Art. 168. The person of the King is sacred and inviolable and he is not subject to responsibility.

Art. 169. The King shall bear the title of Catholic Majesty.

Art. 170. The power of executing the laws rests exclusively in the King, and his authority extends to everything that conduces to the preservation of public order at home and to the security of the state abroad, in conformity with the constitution and the laws.

Art. 173. The King upon his accession to the throne, or if he has been under age, upon his assumption of the government of the kingdom, shall take the following oath before the Cortes:

'N (here his name) by the grace of God, and the Constitution of the Spanish Monarchy, King of Spain: I swear by God and the Holy Gospels that I shall protect and preserve the Apostolic Roman Catholic religion without permitting any other in the kingdom; that I shall defend and cause to be supported, the political constitution and the laws of the Spanish monarchy and that all my actions shall be directed to its good and welfare; that I shall not alienate, grant, or dismember any part of the kingdom; that I shall not exact any produce, money, or anything else which has not been decreed by the Cortes; that I shall never deprive anyone of his property and that I shall respect, above all, the political liberty of the nation and the personal liberty of the individual; if I shall act in opposition to what I have sworn, or any part thereof, I ought not to be obeyed, and such acts shall be null and void. May God help me and defend me if I keep my oath; otherwise, may He call me to account.'

Chapter VI. The Ministers of State

Art. 222. There shall be seven ministers of state.

Art. 226. The ministers of state shall be responsible to the Cortes for the orders that they authorize contrary to the constitution and the laws, and their having been ordered to do so by the King shall not serve as an excuse.

Art. 227. The ministers of state shall every year produce an estimate of the expense of their respective departments of the public administrations, and shall render accounts of their expenditures, according to the manner prescribed.

Art. 228. In order to enforce the responsibility of the ministers, the Cortes shall first decree that there is cause for accusation.

Art. 229. After this decree has been given, the minister of state shall be suspended, and the Cortes shall send to the Supreme Court of Justice all the documents concerning the case. That court shall have cognizance of the case and shall decide it according to the laws.

Art. 230. The Cortes shall assign the salaries that the ministers of state shall receive during their actual service.

Chapter VII. The Council of State

Art. 231. The Council of State shall be composed of forty persons who are citizens in the full exercise of their rights; foreigners, although they possess a certificate of citizenship, are excluded.

Art. 232. The Councillors shall be precisely of the following description, to wit: only four ecclesiastics of acknowledged and distinguished talent and merit, of which number two shall be bishops; only four grandees of Spain of reputed virtue, talent, and necessary knowledge; and the remainder shall be chosen from those subjects who have distinguished themselves most by their brilliance and attainments, or by their signal service in one of the principal branches of the administration and government of the state . . .

Art. 233. All the Councillors of State shall be appointed by the King upon the proposal of the Cortes.

Art. 236. The Council of State is the only council of the King; he shall consult it in grave affairs of state and especially in granting or refusing his sanction to laws, and in declaring war and making peace treaties.

Art. 241. Upon taking office the Councillors of State shall take oath before the King to support the constitution, to be faithful to the King, and to advise him, looking to the best interests of the nation, without regard to personal interests or private views.

| Source: Arnold R. Verduin, *Manual of Spanish Constitutions 1808–1931*, Michigan 1941.|

Germany

Doc. 48. KARL VON ROTTECK: 'Constitution'

The constitutional system as it has evolved since the beginning of the American Revolution, and from the French Revolution with its more direct influence on Europe, corresponds completely in theory and at least approximately in practice to a system of constitutional law based on pure reason as is applicable to conditions prevalent everywhere or resulting from historical circumstances.

1. The principal proposition in this system runs as follows: The sovereignty of the State is the sovereignty of the whole society. Thus it follows that it is a sovereignty emanating from the whole of the people and theoretically belonging uninterruptedly to it. That is to say, it is nothing but the effective collective will of the participants constituting such a society, as defined by the social contract. Therefore this power is not autocratic; nor is it derived from any property rights, nor does it originate directly from any divine or patriarchal source, nor any title of privilege whatever other than what is founded upon the social contract; or, at the very least, every power, even though arising originally out of some other title and now upheld by historically legitimate right, must be adapted and modified in content and in form in such a manner as to

further the rule of the true consensus of the collective will as faithfully and reliably as possible.

2. To this end the chief and most indispensable condition is the effective expression by means of the vote of the wishes of the totality of the people to be governed; that is to say, that since we are here considering mainly, if not exclusively, States which cannot gather all their citizens into a single national assembly because of their greater size, there has to be reliance on a representative body able to express fairly and truly the consensus of the wishes of the entire people by way of free elections.

3. Between the territorial or people's representatives and the established government of the country there should be such a distribution of powers, or such a relationship between the forces of movement and those of resistance, as to assure as far as possible the predominance of the true, considered and enduring collective will of the people; and to prevent the rule of any private interests, as well as that of any temporarily misguided interpretation or only a seemingly genuine expression of the collective will.

4. The most reliable method of achieving this aim is to transfer or delegate to the national representatives the major portion of the legislative powers, including the power to levy taxation; and, on the other hand, to entrust the existing government with the powers of administration. This does not preclude the necessity for both bodies to carry out their respective functions of acting both in confrontation and in co-operation with one another in exercising their controlling, checking and law-enforcing authority.

5. Besides the legislative and administrative authorities, there should exist completely independent of all other holders of power an authority which pronounces on what is law in certain cases which appear to be controversial or doubtful. That is to say, it should pronounce upon the purely theoretical aspects of law and the aspects to be considered by unprejudiced reason as to what is constitutionally legal or illegal according to the prevailing laws, and what should, therefore, be carried out and executed as such by the established authorities. The formation of independent and, as far as possible, reliable courts of law is therefore another main article in a valid constitution.

6. For the preservation of the integrity of the people's representatives and for the guidance of the government in keeping with its avowed purpose, the people as a whole, and each of its individual members in particular, should have free and unhindered means of obtaining information on public affairs; and the free expression of their opinions and judgements on the process of their administration should also be assured. Public opinion, which is practically synonymous with the rational general will, should be universally allowed to develop and express itself without hindrance. The facts upon which public opinion has the right and the duty to pronounce should be brought to the people's notice without con-

cealment or distortion. The publication of the decisions of the government and of the deliberations of the bodies representing the estates or the people (*der landständischen oder Volksvertretungsverhandlungen*), and the freedom of the press are, therefore, essential factors in a constitutional system.

7. The concept of social association and of its inherent, vital collective will implies the further concept of the equality and the liberty of every participant in this association. Accordingly, the constitutional system also stipulates an equal right to participate in the benefits of such a state association, the equal legal and judicial guarantee of personal liberty and of the right to own and acquire property, the equal claim of all qualified persons to positions of office and to resultant honours; and, on the other hand, the same obligations to the law, the same submission to the legitimately constituted authorities, with an equal share in the burden of the State, that is to say, a share commensurate to the individual protection of property and its acquisition.

8. Among the rights of every individual citizen of a constitutional State, as postulated by liberty and equality, there belong also the freedom of divine worship (so long as this does not comprise actions which in themselves are contrary to law, morality, public order or security), and the freedom to emigrate, i.e., to withdraw from allegiance to the State, since the constitutional citizen is a free member and not a serf.

9. State property may only be used for purposes sanctioned by the collective will, and its administration is further subject to the supervisory joint control of Parliament. The property belonging to the Sovereign (in general, that belonging to ruling personages and their families) and which is theirs by civil law, remains, of course, free from such control. Besides this, provision is also made for the worthy maintenance of the Monarch and of his House by an adequate civil list allowance provided for out of State funds.

10. The constitutional monarch is not held responsible in person. On the other hand, all persons holding executive power (civil servants and state servants together) are answerable for the faithful and constitutional exercise of the power entrusted to them, not only each person towards his superior authorities immediate or remote and in the last instance to the King himself; but they, and in particular the Ministers or the highest civil servants are also answerable to the people's representatives. A special State Court of Justice created specifically for this purpose has to pronounce upon relevant crimes and transgressions. The members of the Diet of the people's representatives, however, in their representative function, are not to be held responsible since in this capacity they are obliged merely to express opinions but to wield no actual power; and the same applies to the people itself, in whose name the elected representatives act and whose opinions, wishes and desires they are entitled and obliged to express following their own free conviction ...

[Source: Karl von Rotteck, 'Konstitution', in *Staatslexikon*, Altona 1843, III, pp. 766–8. Translated by the editors of this volume.]

Doc. 49. KARL THEODOR WELCKER: The Responsibility of Princes and the Ministers of State

As a wonderful fruit of English political wisdom and of our constitutions patterned on the English model, we recognise the non-responsibility of our princes. However, this can only exist because the ministers who have to sign all government decrees are responsible for all the actions of the government. Only if this responsibility is a true fact, only then is the crown really safe from attacks on that most precious attribute of the princes, that non-responsibility, and safe from wild storms that tear the crowns along with them. But there can be no doubt that such a sufficient responsibility [of the ministers] is lacking in Germany.

The mere parliamentary responsibility of the proceedings in the Diets, and even refusing to pay taxes and making declarations of indignity, cannot be sufficient. They sometimes have too partisan a character and obtain their true effect and true importance only when responsibility before the courts of law is in the background. Arbitration courts will never suffice in bad cases; and if formed by foreigners they are contrary to the independence and freedom of the state organism. Even more so is the appeal for foreign aid, guarantee and mediation which ruined the Poles.

Thus, there remains in the end only the responsibility of the ministers with a view to punishment by the courts as the indispensable final part of a free constitution. Even the non-responsible sovereign Athenian people punished those who, as public orators, had advised them to do bad things. This responsibility of their advisers can only be odious to despotic princes, but not to those with a sense of law, as it protects their lawful dignity instead of endangering it. It alone implements the legal dictum, the juridical fiction that 'the king can do no wrong'. That means that juridically, and regarding responsibility, the view is taken and maintained that the responsibility for the wrongfulness of a government measure can only be attributed to the minister who puts his signature to it.

For the legal execution of this responsibility requires the proper clauses in penal law, a sufficient stipulation on the right of accusation, a good court and a practical public procedure for trials. It is hardly necessary to say more in order to show that only a genuinely implemented responsibility of the highest public servants before the penal laws is able, in a truly admirable fashion, to solve the puzzle of how, on the one hand, the prince himself can remain non-responsible and in a position as secure as possible, and how, on the other, sovereignty is possible before the law; and, further, how at the same time all the duties of the government can be reinforced through punishment, how every wrongful government action can be punished, or how the lawful freedom of the people is compatible with the sovereignty of the prince.

For this, however, the clause is indispensable that no government action as such is valid, or is in the form valid before the law, unless it is signed by a responsible minister or a top-ranking public servant.

It is no less clear that no wrong is being done to the minister through his responsibility. For in doubtful cases, he is not merely guilty of evil through his influence and advice, or through sins of omission. He makes them his own by his signature. Instead of signing, he can at any time give up his office, although admittedly this is often difficult in the case of German ministers. If the prince is well-intended, he will find another minister to sign; and if not, he will be taught a lesson and no longer desire the evil.

It is equally clear that for a good minister, let alone for the prince and the people, a strictly enforced responsibility of the ministers is salutary. The minister is protected by it from intrigues and mere caprices and obtains the necessary strength to do good, while the prince and the people are preserved from rottenness.

[Source: Karl Theodor Welcker, 'Verantwortlichkeit der Fürsten und der Minister', in *Staatslexikon*, Altona 1843, XV, pp. 640–1. Translated by the editors of this volume.]

Doc. 50. DAVID HANSEMANN: The Formation of the Constitution in Prussia[1] (1840)

During the last twenty years it has become more and more obscure which course the State Government actually wants to pursue in the formation of the Constitution. It seems, therefore, it is itself not in unison on this matter. This is quite understandable because the influences which determine the will of the State vary a great deal. On the one hand, you have the civil servants. They, and particularly the ablest men among them, put the idea of the State before everything, and want to obtain a harmonious rule of this idea in such a way that the various conditions and relations should subordinate themselves to this idea with small modifications.

On the whole, the Civil Servants whom we have in mind favour liberal views as far as the civil rights of the subjects and the development of the State are concerned. They do this, however, in such a way that they do not desire a constitutional representative form of government and they are partly very averse to it. On the other hand, they wish to implement liberal views through an enlightened Civil Service. The mental attitude of the inhabitants of the Rhenish provinces comes closest to such views. It is characteristic of the great majority of the Rhenish Prussians that they share the attitude, usually attributed to the French, of putting equality higher than liberty.

On the other hand, there is a party which wants to counter the destructive ideas of the philosophy of the eighteenth century, particularly that of

C. Aspects of continental liberalism in the nineteenth century

levelling everything, or the democratic principle. This party does not mind sometimes to pronounce the word 'freedom', if only shyly. It not only desires to secure permanence of what is characteristic (*eigentümlich*), where it has been preserved, but also wants to revive it when the omnipotence of conditions and the ideas of the century have already undermined it. The nobility in particular is active in this party. Only a few men among them are able to comprehend the higher ideas which could develop through this trend. Most of them are only concerned with avoiding the payment of state burdens to the detriment of their other fellow-citizens, and to maintain the patrimonial privileges of the Middle Ages or, if they have been lost, to regain them. By the way, they are pliable and obedient to the powers above them. According to the evidence from the debates of the *Landstände* (Estates) in the province of Brandenburg, the views of this party are most noticeable there. The fact that the nobility of this province is, owing to its geographical position, closest to the seat of the State Government may have had some influence on the attitude of the Government on various occasions.

So far there has been no struggle between the two parties about freedom, but only about the question whether, with the most unrestricted sovereignty of the state (*Landeshoheit*), the idea of the most profitable economic system, which most raises the material forces in the state, shall be implemented. Or whether, contrary to that idea, again with unlimited state sovereignty, the right shall be granted to a single and not very numerous class (*Stand*), to shirk part of the financial burden of the State, and, to a certain extent, exercise a direct or indirect control over other classes in the nation; or, of preferentially securing higher or lower positions in the State, in order to obtain greater influence, while at the same time the specific character of other associations (*Genossenschaften*) would be preserved or restructured.

To a certain extent this struggle between the two parties can also be viewed as a struggle between democracy and aristocracy. It is characteristic of it that the latter party has for a considerable time been on the offensive, with the result that the activities of the other party have been more directed towards the prevention of legal regulations and institutions, which are contrary to its views, rather than to make them clearly visible by issuing new laws. If the discussions on legislation would take place in public, this characteristic attitude would be seen more clearly than is now the case.

[Source: David Hansemann, 'Memorandum on Prussia's Position and Politics, August-September 1840', in J. Hansen, *Rheinische Briefe und Akten zur Geschichte der politischen Bewegung, 1830–1850*, Essen 1919, I, 1830–45, pp. 200–2. Translated by the editors of this volume.]

Editors' Note

1. Prussia was then still without a Constitution. It was only granted by the king in 1848 owing to the pressures of the Revolution.

Doc. 51. HEINRICH VON TREITSCHKE: Political Freedom and its Limitation

Political freedom is freedom politically limited – this dictum, still decried as servile a few decades ago, is to-day accepted by everyone capable of political judgement. How relentlessly bitter experience has destroyed all those delusions which hid under the cloak of the great name of freedom! The ideas of freedom which prevailed during the French Revolution were a vague blend of Montesquieu's ideas and Rousseau's semi-classical concepts. The construction of political freedom was believed to be complete, provided the legislative power was separated from the executive and the judiciary, and every citizen was equally entitled to assist in electing the deputies of the national parliament. Those demands were fulfilled, fulfilled in every way, and what was achieved? The most monstrous despotism that Europe has ever experienced. The idolatry which our radicals carried on all too long a time for the horrors of the Convention is at last beginning to fall silent through a trifling consideration: If an omnipotent state-power stops my mouth, compels me to deny my faith, and guillotines me the moment I defy this arbitrariness, it is quite immaterial whether this despotism is exercised by a hereditary prince or by a Convention; the one means just as much servitude as the other. The fallacy in Rousseau's dictum, that where all are equal each one obeys himself, is all too obvious. It is rather that he obeys the majority; and what is there to prevent this majority from acting just as tyrannically as an unscrupulous monarch?

When we consider the feverish convulsions which for the past seventy years have shaken the nation beyond the Rhine (which is, despite all, a great nation), we are dismayed to discover that the French, despite all their enthusiasm for liberty, have only experienced equality and never liberty. Equality, however, is a vague concept which can as readily mean 'equal servitude for all' as 'equal freedom for all'. And it certainly signifies the former when it is desired by a nation as the sole, supreme political good. The highest imaginable degree of equality, communism, constitutes the highest imaginable degree of servitude, because it presupposes the suppression of all natural inclinations. It is, surely, no mere accident that the passionate urge for equality emerges especially from that nation, whose Celtic strain has time and again found pleasure in rallying in blind submissiveness around some great Caesarean figure, no matter whether his name be Vercingetorix, Louis XIV, or Napoleon. We Teutons insist too stubbornly on the infinite right of the individual for us to be able to discover freedom in universal suffrage; we recall to mind that even in many religious orders the superiors are elected by universal suffrage; yet who on earth has ever sought for freedom in a convent? It is certainly not the spirit of freedom which speaks to us from Lamartine's declaration in 1848: 'Every Frenchman is an elector, and therefore is a ruler in his own right; no Frenchman can say to his neighbour, "You are more a ruler than I." ' Which of man's instincts is gratified by such words? None other than the basest of them all – envy! Even Rousseau's enthusiasm for the citizenship of antiquity does not stand up to serious examination. The glory of the citizens of Athens rested on the broad basis of slavery, of contempt for all menial occupations; whilst we in our day find glory in having respect for every man, in recognising the nobility of every form of honest labour. The most die-hard aristocrat of our modern world seems like a democrat beside Aristotle who ingenuously uttered words of such terrible hardheartedness as: 'It is not possible for virtuous actions to be performed by those leading the life of a manual worker.'

Such reflections have long since caused the more thoughtful to examine carefully on what principles the much-envied freedom of the British was established. They discovered that over there no omnipotent state-power determines the destinies of the most remote community, but rather that even the smallest county administers its own affairs. This recognition of the blessings of self-government was an immense advance; for the paralysing effect on the citizens of a state that keeps everything in tutelage can hardly be described in sufficiently dismal terms; and it is all the more sinister because a morbid state of the nation only reveals itself in its full extent in a later generation. As long as the eye of the great Frederick watched over his Prussians, even humble souls were raised above their natural stature by the sight of their hero, and sluggards were prodded onward by his vigilance. But at his death he left behind him a spineless generation, accustomed – as Napoleon III proudly claims of his French subjects – to expect every initiative for action to come from the state, inclined towards that vainglory which is the very opposite of true national pride, and capable of a momentary enthusiasm for the idea of unity of the state, but incapable of self-government, that is, incapable of the greatest task which is imposed on modern nations. The work of colonisation, of carrying the blessings of European civilisation to primitive peoples, can only be done by citizens who have learnt, through self-government, to act like statesmen in an emergency. It may be technically more perfect and more in keeping with the principle of the division of labour to have municipal affairs looked after by salaried state officials; yet a state which allows its citizens to look voluntarily after county and municipal affairs in an honorary capacity gains moral strength through the self-esteem, and the active, practical patriotism of the citizens – a strength which an omnipotent civil service could never evoke ...

In order to understand to what extent society should exercise control over the individual, let us start by throwing nonchalantly overboard a question over which political thinkers have needlessly worried for many anxious hours: Is the state merely a means for the promotion of the vital aims of the citizens? Or does the welfare of the citizens only serve the purpose of bringing about a fair and pleasant collective life? Humboldt, Mill and Laboulaye, and the entire liberal school of Rotteck and Welcker, are in favour of the former; the Ancients, as we know, were in favour of the latter. To me it would appear that the one view is as worthless as the other. As Falstaff says, the controversy concerns a question which should never be raised. For all the world admits that a relationship of mutual rights and obligations exists between the state and its citizens. Between entities, however, whose relationship is solely one of means and ends, reciprocity is out of the question. The state is an end itself, as are all living things. For who can deny that the state leads quite as real a life as each of its citizens? How anomalous it seems that we Germans, in the midst of our conglomeration of petty principalities (*Kleinstaaterei*), must admonish a Frenchman and an Englishman to think more highly of the state! Both Mill and Laboulaye live in powerful, respected states; they take that rich blessing for granted, and see in the state only the frightening power which threatens the freedom of man. We Germans have had our appreciation of the dignity of the state sharpened by painful privation. When abroad we are asked to name our 'specific' country and a mocking smile passes across the faces of the listeners at such names as 'Reuss junior branch' or 'Sovereignty of Schwarzburg-Sonderhausen', then we certainly feel that the state is something greater than a means for making our private life easier. The state's honour is our honour, and he who cannot regard his state with enthusiastic pride, innately lacks one of the supreme emotions a man can experience. If to-day our best men are striving to create for this nation a state which is deserving of respect, they are not impelled merely by the wish to lead their personal lives henceforth in greater security; they are also conscious that they are fulfilling a moral obligation which devolves upon every nation.

The state that protected our forbears with its laws, which our fathers defended with their bodies, and which the living are called upon to build up further and to pass on more highly developed to their children and their children's children, thus forms a sacred bond linking many generations; it is an integral structure which lives according to its own laws. The views of the governors and the governed can never coincide completely; in a free and mature state they will certainly reach the same goal, but they will do so along vastly different ways. The citizen demands from the state the greatest possible measure of personal freedom, because he wants to live his life to the full and to develop all his capacities. The state accedes to this, not because it wants to oblige the individual citizen, but because it views itself in its wholeness. The state must rely for support upon its citizens; but in the moral world only that which is free, and which can also offer resistance, affords support. Indeed, the respect which the state pays to the individual and to personal liberty gives the most reliable measure of its culture; but it pays that respect primarily because political freedom, which the state itself needs, is impossible with citizens who do not themselves conduct their own affairs without hindrance.

The indissoluble connection between political and personal freedom — especially the nature of freedom as a firmly coherent system of noble rights — was not properly understood by either Mill or Laboulaye. The former, in full enjoyment of English rights of citizenship, tacitly takes political freedom for granted; the latter, under the pressure of Bonapartism, dares not for the time being to give it a thought. And yet personal freedom without political freedom leads to the dissolution of the state. Those who see the state solely as a means for realizing the vital aims of the citizen must, in accord with the good old mediæval tradition, logically demand freedom *from* the state, not freedom *within* the state. The modern world has outgrown this error. Still less, however, may a generation that devotes itself in the main to private ends, and can spare only a small part of its time for the state, succumb to the opposite error of the Ancients. For this present age is called upon to absorb and develop further the imperishable fruits of the cultural and also of the political work of antiquity and of the Middle Ages. It thus arrives at the correlating and yet independent conclusion that there is a physical necessity and a moral obligation for the state to promote everything that serves the individual development (*Ausbildung*) of its citizens. On the other hand, the individual is faced with the physical necessity and the moral obligation to participate actively in the state to make every personal sacrifice for it which the preservation of the collective whole requires, even the sacrifice of his life. And, indeed, man is subject to this obligation, not merely because it is only as a citizen that he can become an integrated being, but also because it is a historical imperative that mankind should form states, fair and worthy states. The world of history is more than well endowed with examples of such relationships of mutual rights and mutual interdependence; everything that is determined appears in it at the same time as its own determining factor. It is that fact which often makes the understanding of political matters more difficult for precise mathematical minds, which, like Mill, prefer to cut the Gordian knot by means of a radical law.

Thus Mill tries to define the permissible limits of the operation of society with the statement: The interference of society with the personal freedom of the individual is only justified when it is necessary to protect the community itself or to prevent harm to other individuals. We do not wish to contradict this statement — if only it were not so utterly devoid of meaning! How little is achieved by such vague abstractions of natural law in a historical science! For is not the 'self-protection of the community' historically variable? Is not a theocratic state obliged, in the interest of self-preservation, to interfere autocratically even with the thoughts of its citizens? And do not those common labours, said to be

452

'indispensable to the community as a whole', which the citizen has to be compelled to carry out, differ widely according to time and place? There is no such thing as an absolute limit to the power of the state, and it is the greatest merit of modern science that it has taught politicians to think only in terms of relationships. Every advance of civilisation, every extension of natural education, necessarily makes the activities of the state more varied. North America, too, is experiencing that truth; states and municipalities in the big cities there are also being forced to develop various activities which were not needed in the primeval forest.

The much-vaunted voluntarism, the activity of free private associations, is by no means sufficient everywhere to satisfy the needs of our society. The net of our system of social intercourse has such a close mesh that thousands of clashes of rights and interests are bound to occur; the state has the duty in both cases to intervene in a conciliatory and prophylactic way as an impartial force. Likewise, in every highly civilised nation there exist strong private forces which, in fact, exclude free competition. The state has to curb their selfishness, even if they do not infringe any rights of third parties. A few years ago the British Parliament ordered the railway companies not only to provide for the safety of passengers, but also to schedule a specified number of so-called 'parliamentary' trains with carriages of each class at normal fares. No one can see in this law, which enables the lower classes to travel, a transgression of the reasonable limits of the power of the state. But those who look upon the state merely as an institution for safety can only defend this measure with the help of very artificial and untenable arguments: for who has a right to demand to be transported from point A to point B for three shillings? The railway company, after all, possesses no monopoly by law, and it is free to anyone to build a rival line! No, the modern state is not permitted to renounce extensive positive activities for the welfare of the people. In every nation there are spiritual and material resources, without which the state cannot exist. A constitutional state presupposes a high average standard of national education; it can never leave it to parents to please themselves whether they want to give their children the most elementary instruction; it has to make school attendance compulsory. The range of these resources, which are necessary for the life of the community (*Gesamtheit*) is inevitably widened with the growth of civilisation. Who would seriously wish to close the treasured art galleries of our states? We old, civilised nations will surely not relapse into the crude idea which regards art as a luxury; art is like daily bread to us. Indeed, the demand for the utmost restriction of state activity is being raised to-day ever more loudly in theory, the more it is contradicted in practice, even in free countries. The school of Tocqueville, Laboulaye and [Charles] Dollfuss grew in the Second Empire during the struggle with an all-embracing state power which does not want to lead but rather to replace society. In its turn, that school becomes excessive, and sees in the state only a barrier, an oppressive power. Even Mill is dominated by the notion that the greater the power of the state, the smaller is freedom. But the state is not the enemy of the citizen. England is free, and yet the English police have a very considerable discretionary power, and must have it; and it suffices that the citizen can call every civil servant to account before the courts.

Fortunately, another historical law operates counter to the growing extension of the power of the state. To the same extent as the citizens progress towards mature self-government, the state is obliged − nay, is actually compelled − to moderate its manner of approach even though its fields of activity are widening. Just as the immature state acted as a guardian for single branches of the activities of the nation, so the guardianship of a highly developed state comprises the entire life of the nation; but the state acts as far as possible only in an encouraging, educative and path-clearing capacity. A mature people must therefore make these demands of the state for the guarantee of personal freedom. The most fruitful result of the metaphysical struggles for freedom during the past century, that is, the truth that the citizen must never be utilised by the state merely as a means, must be recognised as a basic principle of justice. Further, every activity on the part of the government is beneficial which evokes, promotes and purifies the individual initiative of the citizens; every activity is evil which suppresses this initiative; for the whole dignity of the state rests ultimately in the personal worth of its citizens, and that state is the most ethical which combines the efforts of the citizens in achieving the greatest number of works beneficial to the community, and yet allows each one, uprightly and independently, to further his personal development unaffected by pressure on the part of the state and public opinion. Thus we agree with Mill and Laboulaye in the final result − in the desire for the highest possible degree of personal freedom − while we do not share their view of the state as a barrier to freedom.

[Source: Heinrich von Treitschke, 'Die Freiheit' (1861), in *Historische und politische Aufsätze*, Leipzig 1867, pp. 615 ff. Translated by the editors of this volume.]

(ii) The English model

(Introduction, p. 391)

France

Doc. 52. MME DE STAEL: On Liberty and Public Spirit among the English

The particular characteristic of England is a mixture of the chivalrous spirit with an enthusiasm for liberty, the two most noble sentiments of which the human heart is capable. Circumstances have brought about this happy result, and it must be admitted that new institutions would not suffice to produce it: remembrance of the past is necessary to consecrate the aristocratic ranks; for, if they were all of the creation of power, they would be a part of the inconveniences experienced in France under Bonaparte. But what can be done in a country where the nobility should be hostile to all liberty? The third estate could not form a union with the nobility; and, as the third estate is the stronger, it would always threaten the nobility until it had submitted to the progress of reason.

The English aristocracy is more fixed than that of France in the eyes of a genealogist; but the English nation appears, it may be said, a whole body of gentlemen. You see in every English citizen what he may become one day, since any rank is accessible to talent, and these ranks have always preserved their ancient splendour. It is true that what above all makes nobility, in the view of an elevated mind, is being free. An English noble or gentleman (the word gentleman signifying an independent property owner) performs some useful employment in the county, to which no salary is attached: such as, justice of the peace, sheriff or lord lieutenant of the county in which his property is situated; he influences elections in a suitable manner, and that adds to his credit in the minds of the people; as a peer or member of parliament, he serves in a political capacity, and his importance is real. This is not the idle aristocracy of a French noble, who was of no importance in the state after he lost the king's favour; it is a distinction founded on all the interests of the nation; and it is amazing that French gentlemen preferred their existence as courtiers on the road from Versailles to Paris to the majestic stability of an English peer on his estate surrounded by men to whom he can do a thousand acts of kindness, but over whom he cannot exercise any arbitrary power. The authority of the law prevails over all the powers of the state in England, like Fate in ancient mythology over the authority of the gods themselves.

To the political miracle of respect for the rights of everyone, founded on the sentiment of justice, there must be added the skilful and equally happy union of equality before the law with the advantages attached to the separation of ranks. Everyone in England has need of others for his happiness, and yet everyone is independent of all by his rights. This third estate, which has grown so prodigiously in France and in the rest of Europe, this third estate, the increase of which gives rise to successive changes in all the old institutions, is united to the nobility in England, because the nobility itself is identified with the nation. A great number of peers originally owed their dignity to the law, some to commerce, others to the career of arms, and others to political eloquence; there is not a virtue or a talent which does not have its place or may not flatter itself with attaining it; and in the social edifice all contribute to the glory of that constitution which is as dear to the Duke of Norfolk as to the meanest porter in England, because it equally protects the one and the other . . .

All men are more or less attached to their country; the recollections of childhood, and the habits of youth, form that inexpressible love of the native land which must be acknowledged as a virtue, for all true feelings are its source. But in a great State, liberty and the happiness that this liberty gives, alone can inspire a true patriotism: therefore nothing is comparable to the public spirit in England. The English are accused of selfishness, and it is true that their way of life is so well-regulated, that they generally confine themselves within the circle of their domestic affection and their habits; but what sacrifice is too costly for them, when the question of their country arises? And among what people in the world are services rendered felt and rewarded with more enthusiasm? . . .

In a country governed like England and enlightened moreover by the torch without which all is darkness – the liberty of the press, men and things are judged with more equity. Truth is submitted to the view of all, while the various restraints which are the practice elsewhere are necessarily the cause of great uncertainty in judgements. A libel which steals across the silence enforced on the press, can change public opinion in regard to anyone, for the praise or censure ordered by the government is always suspect. Nothing can be established soundly and firmly in the minds of men except by free discussion.

'Do you pretend,' it may be said, 'that there is no fickleness in the judgement of the English people, and that they do not flatter today those whom they will perhaps tear in pieces tomorrow?' No doubt the leaders of the government ought to be in danger of losing the people's favour if they are not successful in the conduct of public affairs. The depositaries of authority have to be fortunate; it is one of the conditions of the advantages granted to them. Besides, as power nearly always corrupts those who possess it, it is very desirable in a free country that the same men do not remain too long in office; and it is right to change ministers, if only for the change. But reputation when once acquired is very lasting in England, and public opinion can be regarded as the conscience of the state.

If anything can seduce the equity of the English nation, it is misfortune. An individual persecuted by any power might inspire an unmerited and consequently a passing interest; but this noble error belongs, on the one hand, to the generosity of the English character, and, on the other, to that sentiment of liberty which wants to prove to all the necessity of mutually defending themselves against oppression, for it is in that respect especially that in politics one must treat one's neighbour as oneself.

The understanding and energy of public spirit more than suffices to answer those who pretend that the army would overcome the liberty of England, if England were a continental power. No doubt it is an advantage for the English that their strength lies in the navy rather than in land forces. More knowledge is required to be the captain of a ship than to be a colonel, and none of the habits acquired at sea lead to a desire to interfere in the internal affairs of the country. But when nature, becoming prodigal, should give birth to ten Lord Wellingtons, and when the world should again see ten battles of Waterloo, it would not enter the heads of those who so easily give their lives for their country to turn their forces against it, or, at the very least, they would encounter an invincible obstacle among men as brave as themselves, and more enlightened, who detest the military spirit although they can admire and practise the warlike virtues.

The sort of prejudice which persuaded the French nobility that they could only serve their country in the career of arms, does not exist at all in England. Many sons of peers are barristers; the Bar shares in the respect that exists for the law, and in all careers civil occupations are well regarded. In such a country, there is no fear up to the present of a takeover by the military power; only ignorant nations have a blind admiration for the sword. Bravery is a magnificent thing when a life dear to his family is imperilled, and, with a mind full of virtue and understanding, a citizen becomes a soldier to uphold his civic rights. But when men fight only because they do not want to take the trouble to occupy their minds and their time with any employment, they cannot for long be admired in a nation where labour and thought hold the first place. The henchmen of Cromwell overthrew a civil power which had neither strength nor dignity; but, since the existence of the constitution, and of public opinion which is its life and soul, princes or generals would only give rise to a feeling of pity in the whole nation for their folly should they dream one day of enslaving their country.

[Source: Mme. de Staël, *Considérations sur les principaux évènements de la Révolution française*, London, 2nd edn, 1819, III, part vi, ch. iv, pp. 258–63, 265–9. Translated by the editors of this volume.]

Doc. 53. MME DE STAEL: Can a Limited Monarchy have other Foundations than those of the English Constitution?

It seems to me that up to the present time thinkers have not been able to find other principles of monarchical and constitutional liberty than those which are admitted in England.

Democrats will say that there should be a king without an aristocracy, or that there should be neither; but experience has demonstrated the impossibility of that system. Of the three powers, the aristocrats contest only that of the people; so, when they pretend that the English constitution cannot be adapted to France, they are simply saying that there should be no representatives of the people, for it is certainly not the nobility or hereditary kingship they are contesting. Hence it is evident that we cannot deviate from the English constitution without establishing either a republic by cutting out hereditary succession; or a despotism by suppressing the commoners: for one of the three powers cannot be taken away without producing the one or the other of these two extremes.

After a revolution such as that in France, constitutional monarchy is the sole peace, the only treaty of Westphalia, so to speak, that can be concluded between the enlightenment of present times and hereditary interests, between almost the whole nation and privileged persons supported by the European powers.

The king of England enjoys power that more than suffices for a man who wants to do good, and I find it hard to conceive how religion itself does not inspire princes with scruples on the use of unlimited authority; but in this case pride prevails over virtue. As for the well-worn argument of the impossibility of being free in a continental state, where a large army of the line must be maintained, the same people who repeat it unceasingly are ready to quote England in the opposite sense and say that there a standing army is not dangerous to liberty. The diversity in the arguments of those who renounce all principles is an extraordinary thing: they make use of circumstances when theory is against them, and theory when circumstances demonstrate their errors; in short, they twist and turn with a pliability which could not escape in the broad light of discussion, but may mislead public feeling, when it is not lawful either to silence the sophists or reply to them. If a standing army gives more power to the kings of France than to those of England, the ultra-royalists, according to their way of thinking, will enjoy that excess of strength, and the friends of liberty do not fear it, if representative government and its guarantees are established in France genuinely and without exception. It is true that the existence of a chamber of peers must reduce the number of noble families: but will the public interest suffer through this change? Should ancient families complain of seeing associated with them in the peerage new men whom the king and public opinion think worthy of it? Should the nobility, which has most to do to reconcile itself with the nation, be the most obstinately attached to inadmissible pretensions? We have the advantage, we French, of being more spirited, but also more foolish, than any other people in Europe; I do not think that we should boast of it.

Arguments deserving more serious consideration, because they are not solely inspired by frivolous pretensions, were renewed against the chamber of peers with regard to Bonaparte's constitution. People said that human reason had made too great progress in France to support any hereditary distinction ... [but] it seems to me that all thinkers recognise that the esteem with which a conservative element surrounds a government is advantageous to liberty as well as to order, and makes the use of force less necessary. What obstacle would there then be in France rather than in England to the existence of a chamber of peers, large in numbers, imposing and enlightened? The elements of it exist, and already we see how easy it would be to combine them happily.

What! people will still say, for all political maxims are worth the trouble of being combatted on account of the multitude of common minds who repeat them, you want France to be only a copy, and a bad copy, of the government of England? In truth, I do not see why the French, or any other nation, should reject using the compass because the Italians discovered it. In the administration of a country, in its finances, its commerce and its armies, there are many things appertaining to local districts, and necessarily differing according to the localities; but the foundations of a constitution are the same everywhere. The republican or monarchical form is prescribed by the extent and situation of the state; but there are always three elements given by nature: deliberation, execution and preservation. These three elements are necessary to guarantee to the citizens their liberty and their fortune, the peaceful development of their abilities and the due rewards of their labour. What nation is there to whom such rights are not necessary, and by what other principles than those of England can their lasting enjoyment be obtained? Can all the failings which people so readily attribute to the French serve as a pretext for refusing them such rights? In truth, even if the French were rebellious children, as their European grandparents pretend, I would all the more advise giving them a constitution which was in their eyes a guarantee of equity in those who govern them; for rebellious children, when they are in so great a number, can be corrected more easily by reason than repressed by force.

Time will be needed before a patriotic aristocracy can be created in France; for, the revolution having been directed against the privileges of the nobles more than against the royal authority, the nobles even now support despotism as their safeguard. It could be said with reason that this state of things is an argument against the creation of a chamber of peers, as being too favourable to the power of the crown. But, first of all, it is, generally speaking, in the nature of an upper chamber to support the throne; and the opposition of the great nobles in England is almost always in a minority. Besides, there can be introduced into a chamber of peers many nobles who are friends of liberty; and those who may not be so today will become so, by the mere fact that the exercise of a high magistracy alienates them from the life of the court, and attaches them to the interests of the state. I shall not fear to profess a sentiment that many persons will call aristocratic, but with which all the circumstances of the French revolution have imbued me: it is that the nobles who have adopted the cause of representative government, and consequently of equality before the law, are generally the most virtuous and the most enlightened Frenchmen of whom we may as yet boast. Like the English, they unite the spirit of chivalry with the spirit of liberty; they have besides the appreciable advantage of basing their opinion on their sacrifices, while the third estate must necessarily find its particular interest in the general interest. Lastly, they have to endure every day the enmity of their class, and sometimes even that of their family. They are told that they are traitors to their order, because they are loyal to their country; whereas men of the opposite extreme, democrats uncurbed by reason or morality, have persecuted them as enemies of liberty by considering only their privileges, and by not believing, although very unjustly, in the sincerity of their renunciation. These illustrious citizens who have voluntarily exposed themselves to so many trials, are the best guardians of liberty on which a state may rely; and a chamber of peers ought to be created for them, even if the necessity of such an institution in a constitutional monarchy should not be recognised even to the demonstration ...

It must be stated quite frankly that constitutional government cannot be established if, from the outset, the enemies of the constitution itself are introduced into all places, either as deputies or as agents of the executive power. The first condition for making representative government work is that elections should be free; for then they will produce men who in good faith desire to see the success of the institutions of which they will be part. A deputy, so it is said, remarked in company: 'People accuse me of not being for the constitutional charter, they are wrong, I am always mounted on this charter; true, it is to ride it to death.' After this charming proposal, it is likely that this deputy would nevertheless think it very amiss that his good faith in politics was suspect; but it is too much to want to unite the pleasure of revealing his secrets with the advantage of keeping them. Do people think that with these hidden, or rather too well-known, intentions the experiment of representative government is being made in France? A minister recently declared in the chamber of deputies that, of all the powers, the one on which the royal authority must exercise most influence is the electoral power; which is to say, in other words, that the representatives of the people ought to be named by the king. In that case, the royal chamberlains ought to be named by the people.

Let the French nation elect the men it will believe worthy of its confidence; let not representatives be imposed on it, and especially representatives chosen from the constant enemies of all representative government; for then and only then, will the political problem be solved in France. We may, I believe, regard it as a true maxim that, when free institutions have lasted for twenty years in a country, it is on them that the blame must be put, if every day there cannot be seen an improvement in the morality, the intelligence and the happiness of the nation that possesses them. It is for these institutions, having reached a certain age, so to speak, to answer for men; but, in the first days of a new political set-up, it is for men to answer for the institutions; for the strength of the citadel cannot be judged in any way if the commanding officers open the gates, or seek to undermine the foundations.

[Source: Mme de Staël, *Considérations sur les principaux évènements de la Révolution française*, London, 2nd edn, 1819, III, part vi, ch. ix, pp. 364–76. Translated by the editors of this volume.]

Germany

Doc. 54. FRIEDRICH CHRISTOPH DAHLMANN: 'On Constitution' (1815)

The State is a sacred cause. The Bible is right when it declares that monarchs and authorities are appointed by God; but they are so only to the same extent as the people are. The good prince of his own accord solely desires the welfare of the people. He does not seek any other power than that which is conducive to this finest of all purposes, nor has he any claim to it unless one were to assume that the Deity had granted rights to the rulers to practise injustice. In order to render justice to the people, their voice must necessarily be heard – not the wild clamour of the mob which ignorantly runs after any immediate advantage – but their speech in which reason and distinctiveness are reflected. Every constitution, even the most primitive, wants to reflect the language of the people; to express the nobler part (*besseren Teil*) of the people. Therein lies the skill of constitution-making. Yet because this better and reasonable element is not distributed evenly everywhere, different means in different States will often lead to equal ends, though they will in no way be so divergent as to prevent the recognition of a common basis of procedure.

Despite all the differences between the individual nations, modern Europe has a common, basic character and is, therefore capable of producing similar constitutions. Moreover, all those who in any way acknowledge the idea of an adequate structure of the State are unanimous that the foundations of a constitution, such as every European State aspires to, are most perfectly shaped and preserved in England.

C. Aspects of continental liberalism in the nineteenth century

There you have two Chambers, of essentially different and yet of identical interest, as far as the preservation of the whole is concerned – those, on the one hand, bound to the preservation of tradition and custom by inherited status, length of ancestry and extensive landed property; and those, on the other, who are qualified by their varied insights, their learning and practical experience to assess clearly the trend of the age and the necessary requirements of the moment. At their head is a monarch, who, sacrosanct and immune as he is, is never burdened even by a shadow of responsibility since he subjects his principal advisers to responsibility and even to have to face impeachment by the people; a monarch upon whom nothing can be imposed by the Chambers, and who only consents to what he deems to be in keeping with the common weal, and, in short, who is only limited to the same extent as a wise man would set limits to himself. The king cannot do all that he might desire to do; but he is not forced to do anything he does not wish to do. This is the limitation: and, in exceeding this, whatever the French Constitution of the year 1791 or the more recent one by the Spanish Cortes laid down for the limitation of the royal prerogative proves in practice to be confusing to the State, it breaks the strength of the government and is essentially untenable.

But it is equally evident that any constitutional act which is carried out is nothing more than empty pretence in States where every whim can be imposed upon the people, and where the opinion of the people's elected representatives is allowed to be despised in the most vital matters of legislation and the national economy. A purely advisory function for the representatives, such as is envisaged by many a modern political artist (*Staatskünstler*), contains no automatic assurance of its permanence, and it must diminish in strength from year to year because it is not supported by law and power. Although the added right of initiative may be welcome to the restless and the loud-mouthed, the better element will soon become weary of propositions which lead nowhere.

The most perilous form, however, is to be found in Provincial or District Estates which never come together in a general assembly. Such an institution destroys community spirit most terribly; it degrades the interest of the State to a purely local and regional level. Instead of a strong co-operative spirit, each provincial assembly in the end merely hastens to outdo the others, whose steadfastness it has no means of assessing, in the virtue of blind obedience. If the highest power in the State now even places presidents at the head of each provincial assembly, there will be no end to submissiveness and meanness. If, on the other hand, these disparate representative bodies were urged on some day by dire necessity to unite to form one body, a total overthrow of the government would have to be feared because of such an immense revolution; a catastrophe which the well-intentioned will in most cases shun even more than a certain curtailment of his liberty. Rulers are imperilled by half and quarter measure

462

constitutions, whereas in true and complete ones they find their surest support.

Therefore, the malicious assumption generally put forward by the enemies of constitutions, i.e. that those who desire the freedom of the people were impairing the prerogative of the Prince and opposing him, is utterly dishonest and false. If this were so, the now universal demand for constitutions would be less favoured among the nations. For, in the case of all of them, to have a Prince and to hold him in affection is the same. For the generations of hereditary monarchs are mild; and at all times there has been only a few who would have preferred to destroy autocratically rather than hand on a happy realm to a beloved heir. Moreover, it is not avarice that prompts the subjects to this demand; nor is it mean possessiveness that seeks to rid itself of the burden imposed by the State. What Prince is there alive who had reason thus to complain of his people? Yet the nations follow a twofold law: one of reason and one of the law of nature. Though both of them place supreme power and glory in a privileged hand, nevertheless they do not regard any human being as being utterly worthless and devoid of rights.

That a worthy nation has rights, and ought to have them, is an ancient tradition which the whole of past history sanctions. Although during the past hundred years scores of lifeless theorists have been querying it, today it is ingrained in the hearts of the better elements more deeply than ever before. For even the most uninhibited liberty of the people never brought in its wake in Europe such dire misery as in recent years the tyranny of one individual did; and never before have the most determined rulers, vested with unlimited power, effected such a miraculous redemption of the world as did those nations recently when they awakened to a consciousness of their national identity while adhering with free affection to their kind sovereigns. Only maniacs and the insane have to be constrained. To other human beings a certain right is due upon which they can rely and in which they can take pride, though varying according to their individual nature and education. A nation which neglects, sacrifices or forfeits its rights may for a while remain ignorant of the value of what it has lost; it may even rejoice loudly and congratulate itself because, in place of the bustling life and the competition between the various forces prevailing in a State in which the people are free, a sort of tepid quiescence and comfortable ease sets in. But it is from this very placidity that there gradually evolves that narrowness of horizon, a dull falling silent of public opinion and an indifference towards the welfare of the nation, as the individual now participates in it only as a tiny particle of the crowd. And since in the final analysis the individual cannot help exercising some power, this principle of domineering control manifests itself in the internal relations between the citizens. Offices are administered arrogantly and without care; a host of petty tyrants comes forward, each of whom allows himself to be treated disdainfully by his superior because he in turn can mete out the same treatment to a subordinate. A patient subject, however, sighs and cannot understand why he must put up with so many hardships at the hand of a benevolent Prince, and why the fine human relationship between government and subjects is vanishing more and more.

If some great tempest from outside hits such a State, or if great disasters or perilous complications eventuate, then such a nation presents a most pitiful spectacle. Everywhere there is distrust and despondency, and nowhere is there any firm coherence; the echo of individual voices dies away unheard, and the honourable, conscientious and noble qualities, which are not alien to any European nation, bear no useful fruit in the hour of peril; until ultimately, perhaps, a plethora of ills brings about clear insight, but without necessarily producing any improvement in the condition. Thus it is not distrust of the Princes which renders liberal constitutions so desirable, but rather the fear of a condition of ignominious weakness with which even the best of Princes cannot cope, as well as fear of control by irresponsible ministers and the petty tyrannies of the authorities; and, in addition to this, the longing to see the lost internal prosperity re-established.

The finances of all European States, without exception, are in distress; the most stringent necessity requires that their system be simplified and returned to its natural foundation. At the same time a reduction of the levies must be aimed at, so that whoever is still solvent among the people should cease to be an object of envy. Yet almost more important still is a concern for an adequate assessment and distribution of taxes ... 'The most oppressive manner of imposing dues,' says Hume, 'is open piracy.' To what extent some governments have approximated to this 'ideal' in recent times, and what atrocities of this kind have been committed, cannot be gone into here. But this much is pertinent to the matter and must be stated: the miracle-worker has not yet been found, nor ever will be, who, by means of a mathematical sleight of hand and tricks, would be able to retrieve the national economy from the brink of the abyss and return to the people that security of property which it truly deserves, without re-establishing the goodwill of the State. But whereby does it obtain this goodwill, since the original innocent trust has gone once and for all? By one means only: that henceforth the property of the nation shall be decided upon with the consent and knowledge of the people. What strange times these are in which such things can be said as though they were something new, and perhaps be interpreted as an unheard-of demand!
...[1]

Everything that has been said here in praise of constitutions should not, by the way, be taken to mean that a good constitution of necessity suffices to make the State happy, or that it would unfailingly prevent great political crimes and mistakes. But it makes the happiness of a people likely, and raises that people in every respect to a higher level in the scale of values than a people without a constitution could ever attain. A constitution is like that legendary spear which in turn is able to heal the wounds that it has inflicted.

[Source: Friedrich Christoph Dahlmann, 'Ein Wort über Verfassung', from *Kleine Schriften und Reden*, Stuttgart 1886, pp. 18–23. Translated by the editors of this volume.]

Editors' Note

1. Dahlmann goes on to quote a passage from Montesquieu on the different attitudes of a nation which determines its own taxes and another which has no say in their fixation and distribution.

Doc. 55. FRIEDRICH CHRISTOPH DAHLMANN: On Discussions in Parliament (1835)

The wisdom of these forms of discussion [in Parliament], the stages of development of which emerge very clearly from the dry folios of John Hatsell,[1] and the high degree of their general validity has also been proved outside their home country and not only in the free states of North America. Mirabeau tried to make use of them for his National Assembly, and the best standing orders of the German assemblies of the Estates know no other source. It is true that discussion in parliament has for a very long time taken place in the full public limelight in spite of the old regulation which forbids access to strangers and prohibits the deliberations from being printed. Owing to the strength of public participation, a great parliamentary moment is retained forthwith in such a way that its significance finds an echo everywhere. Yet the long deepened river-bed of the debates, which discreetly moves towards its goal, is only seldom flooded by the magnificence of theatrical speech at a place where men, who, on their part, have to keep a great fatherland great, speak without an orator's platform and without costumes, but simply from their seats. None of them is so immense that he was not faced by a great figure. In recent times, the weight of the issues pressing for a solution lets the splendour of the speech and even its elegance fade away more and more. The Asian profusion, even of an Edmund Burke, would now no longer have its former effect. He would not lack his Phocion, of whom even a Demosthenes had to be afraid as 'the axe of his speeches'. The trained ear, penetrating through the mere appearance of words, is open to the arguments only, and puts them into the order of a conviction. Shorter speeches lead to more lasting victories; and the resignation of the majority, which prefers to co-operate silently rather than disturb national affairs by loquacious inquisitiveness, meets with deserved recognition.

C. Aspects of continental liberalism in the nineteenth century

[Source: F. C. Dahlmann, *Die Politik auf den Grund und das Maass der gegebenen Zustaende zurueckgefuehrt*, Leipzig, 2nd edn, 1847, pp. 78–9. Translated by the editors of this volume.]

Editors' Note

1. Dahlmann refers to John Hatsall, *Precedents of Proceedings in the House of Commons*, London, second ed. 1785, p. 92.

Doc. 56. DAVID HANSEMANN: England as a Model for the Formation of a Constitution (1830)

Several men, meaning well and some of them with merits, desire to seek in England the type of constitutional government which is commensurate with the new age. A few remarks will suffice to show the error of these men.

Where are the rich and influential landed proprietors in Prussia who could form an aristocracy like that in England? They are thoroughly lacking. The position of many Prussian landed proprietors, provided they are not really *rentiers* who own the estates in order to obtain interest from them, is deplorable according to the information of the mortgage books. 'But one could try to make them rich and influential through institutions and laws.' They can only become rich if they use the same means as other honest people. They can be given influence, but not such as is contrary to the formation of political forces; and that does not mean an influence as it exists in England, where a large section of the deputies in the House of Commons are appointed through it; otherwise we would arrive at chaos or revolution.

It is understandable, to a large degree, that in England the extraordinary aristocratic system has maintained itself so long only because there existed simultaneously such a high degree of freedom as exists in no other country, and which would very likely be unfeasible for us in Prussia; and also because, owing to the freedom there, the aristocracy renewed itself through the excellent talents of the middle classes that are raised automatically in the public life of the nation. Does not any enlightened Englishman, whose insight is not barred through his own participation in privileges detrimental to the common weal, realise completely that those privileges are largely the cause of the immense debt under which the country is sighing, and that only a gradual abolition of these privileges, for which a moderate reform of parliament is the beginning, can lead the country out of its misery without a revolution? Should anyone so close his eyes to the evidence, and not recognize from the example of England that elections in which the propertyless masses compete are, therefore, most dangerous for the throne, particularly in a country where public opinion has not yet, as in England, been purified and strengthened; for the throne can be in danger if the lawful organ of the

466

nation does not express its true mental attitude. Can it occur to any practical man to restrict the executive power of the crown to a degree like that
in England? Parliament and the local authorities there carry out many
administrative actions which in Prussia must remain a necessary function
of the crown, if the central power of the state, which largely determines
the power of the crown, is not to be weakened.

[Source: David Hansemann, 'Memorandum for King Frederick William of Prussia,
Aachen, 31 December 1830;' in J. Hansen (ed.), *Rheinische Briefe und Akten zur
Geschichte der politischen Bewegung*, Essen 1919, I, *1830–1850*, pp. 36–8.
Translated by the editors of this volume.]

Italy

Doc. 57. CAMILLO DI CAVOUR: 'The Chartist Revolution and the
British Government' (17 April 1848)

The great Chartist demonstration in London, proclaimed by many
writers and journalists, who are more inspired by passions than furnished
with exact knowledge on the state of England, as the prelude of a terrible
civil war between the workers and the other classes of society, had the
most peaceful outcome possible, order being maintained without the
necessity, we will not say of the intervention but even of the presence, of
armed force.

The cabinet, taking advantage of a power given to it by an ancient
statute decreed in the stormy times of Charles II, prohibited not the great
assembly convened by the Chartists in the fields of Kennington but the
planned procession to the palace of Westminster to present to Parliament
the petition signed by all the Chartists in the kingdom. On the eve of the
meeting, the Chartists were still threatening to have recourse to force in
order to effect their plans, and so were threatening revolution and
violence. The cabinet was not upset by this; and, respecting the right of
citizens to come together freely to discuss their common interests, did not
seek to impede the meeting at Kennington. It contented itself with
publishing a proclamation announcing that the procession would be impeded by regular troops, by the municipal police and by citizens who, in
immense numbers, had offered their services to the magistrates to
co-operate in the maintenance of order and the triumph of the laws.

The Chartists, having assembled without obstacle in a much smaller
number than their chief orators had predicted, had a free hand to
pronounce the most violent and incendiary discourses. Except for one
commissioner, who announced that the approaches to the bridges over
the Thames would be manned by armed guards who would drive back
the procession if an attempt was made to cross them, the police were not
to be seen.

C. Aspects of continental liberalism in the nineteenth century

This declaration, the only open act of authority, was enough to induce the assembly to break up peacefully. The Chartist leaders judged with reason that it would be extreme folly to enter into open and violent conflict with the government, for which not only the troops were ready to fight, but also all the property owners, all the shopkeepers of London and even a good number of workers, being friends of order as much as of liberty.

From the bottom of the heart we applaud this simple outcome of the popular crisis which appeared to menace England; since such a revolution as that promised by the Chartists would be one of the most terrible events which could strike humanity. For it would have changed not only the political order of the country, but might perhaps have ruined the foundation of that social edifice which, if not the most regular, is certainly the most splendid of which the history of the world can boast. We are not followers of England, and still less are we passionate admirers of the politics of the Court of St. James, as is testified by several of our articles; but we are convinced that the preservation of English society is necessary to the cause of progress and liberty. The cause of civilisation in the entire world is involved in the means by which the English people proceed in the way of political and social improvements, as it has done resolutely for some years not having fallen among revolutionary storms that might produce final ruin.

For many centuries, while the rest of Europe still groaned under the yoke of absolutism, England was the jealous and faithful custodian of those great principles of liberty on which the institutions of modern peoples rest. Except for a few, brief exceptional periods, she knew how to keep safe from usurpations of power and from popular violence individual liberty, the liberty of the press, the right of assembly and that of petition: in short, all those liberties and rights which are so little respected on the Continent by victorious parties, but are held there on the other side of the Channel as unshakable dogmas of political faith.

The French revolutions did much for the popular cause; in the past they promised equality, and now they promise fraternity. But until now, the cause of true liberty has not been greatly favoured by them, and as yet England is still the freest country in Europe.

If one compares, in fact, the conduct of the English Government towards both the Chartist party and the supporters of ending the union with Ireland with that of the French Government towards conquered parties; if one compares the tolerance towards the press in London and Dublin with the violence of the people of Paris against the newspaper *La Presse*; and finally, if one considers the method by which every kind of worship is regulated in the two countries, one will not deny to England the boast of being the classic land of liberty in Europe.

Until experience has proved that there is in Europe another land in which the principles of liberty are held equally sacred and are equally safeguarded from any violence or insult, we will not cease to proclaim Great Britain as a great source of blazing light which illuminates the way travelled by modern peoples on the trail of better fortunes.

When we see another Government, of whatever kind, republican or monarchical, tolerate manifestations so hostile and acts so threatening as those allowed every day to the Irish Separatists and the English Chartists; when we see meeting elsewhere assemblies similar to the Chartist convention in London, or to that which sat in the famous Conciliation Hall in Dublin; when in a parliament on the Continent is heard incitement to rebellion and civil war equal to that hurled with complete impunity in Parliament by the Chartist O'Connor and the Irishman O'Brien, then we will concede to the enemies of England that her humanitarian mission is finished, and that it can be overturned by revolutions without the cause of liberty running the risk of not having any secure refuge in our old continent.

[Source: Camillo di Cavour, *Scritti Politici*. Nuovamente raccolti e publicati da Giovanni Gentile, Rome 1925, XXVIII, pp. 142–4. Translated by Dr Roslyn Pesman.]

2. Freedom and the individual: documents

(i) The rights of the individual
(Introduction, p. 394)

Doc. 58. MME DE STAEL: On the Love of Freedom

Examine the adversaries of freedom in all countries and you will find among them some deserters from the camp of intelligent men, but in general you will see that the enemies of freedom are the enemies of knowledge and enlightenment. They are proud of their deficiency in this respect, and it must be admitted that such a negative triumph is easily gained.

The secret has been found of presenting the friends of freedom as the enemies of religion. There are two pretexts for the singular injustice which would forbid the noblest sentiment on this earth to enter into an alliance with Heaven. The first is the revolution: as this was made in the name of philosophy, the conclusion has been drawn that one has to be an atheist in order to love freedom. To be sure, it is because the French did not unite religion with freedom that their revolution deviated so soon from its early course. There might be certain dogmas of the Catholic Church which did not accord with the principles of freedom; passive obedience to the Pope was as little tenable as passive obedience to the king. Yet Christianity has truly brought freedom upon this earh, justice to the oppressed, respect for the unfortunate, and, above all, equality before God, of which equality before the law is only an imperfect image. It is through an intentional confusion of thought with some, and blindness with others, that people have tried to regard the privileges of the nobility and the absolute power of the throne as religious dogmas. The forms of social organization can only concern religion by their influence on the maintenance of justice for all, and on the morals of everybody. The rest belongs to the science of this world.

It is time that twenty-five years, of which fifteen belong to military despotism, should no longer place themselves as a phantom between history and us, and deprive us of all the lessons and all the examples which it offers us. Should we no longer remember Aristides, Phocion and Epaminondas in Greece; Regulus, Cato and Brutus in Rome; Tell in Switzerland; Egmont and Nassau in Holland; Sidney and Russell in England; because a country that had for a long time been governed by arbitrary power, saw itself handed over during a revolution to men who had been perverted by the arbitrary regime itself? Is there anything so extraordinary in such an event, as to change the course of the stars, that is, to make truth go backwards, although it was advancing with history in order to enlighten the human race? By what public sentiment shall we be moved henceforth, if we are to reject the love of freedom? The old prejudices no longer affect men except from calculation; they are upheld only by those who have a personal interest in defending them. Who in France wants absolute power out of pure love, that is, for its own sake? Apprise yourself of the personal situation of each of its defenders and you will very quickly know the motives behind their doctrine. On what then would the fraternity of human associations be based, were it not for some enthusiasm developing in people's hearts? Who would be proud of being French, after having seen freedom destroyed by tyranny, tyranny broken by foreign armies, and the laurels of war not at least made honourable by the conquest of liberty? There would be nothing more to see than a struggle between the selfishness of those privileged by birth and the selfishness of others privileged by events. But where would France be? Who could boast of having served her, seeing that nothing would remain in people's hearts, either of the past or of the new reform?

Freedom! Let us repeat its name with all the more vigour, because the men who should pronounce it at least as an apology, keep it at a distance by their flattery; let us repeat it without fear of hurting any power worthy of respect; for everything we love, everything we honour, is contained in it. Nothing but freedom can arouse the soul in the interests of the social order. Assemblies of men would only be associations for commerce or agriculture if the life of patriotism did not encourage individuals to sacrifice themselves for their fellow-men. Knighthood was a brotherhood of warriors that satisfied the need for self-sacrifice which is felt by all generous hearts. The nobles were comrades in arms, bound together by honour and duty; but since the progress of the human spirit has created nations, that is to say, since all men participate in some way in the same advantages, what would become of mankind without the feeling of freedom? Why should French patriotism begin at this frontier and stop at that, if there did not exist within these bounds the hopes and joys, an emulation and a security, which make the country of one's birth loved as much by the soul as through mere habit? Why should the name of France evoke an invincible emotion, if there were no other ties among the inhabitants of this beautiful country than the privileges of some and the enslavement of the others?

Wherever you meet with respect for human nature, affection for one's fellow-men, and that force of independence which can resist everything on earth, and prostrates itself only before God; there you see man in the image of his Creator, there you feel in the depths of the soul such an intimate tenderness that it cannot deceive you about the truth. And you, noble Frenchmen, for whom honour was freedom; you who, through a long history of heroic deeds and greatness, should regard yourselves as the élite of mankind, allow the nation to raise itself to your level; it also has the rights of conquest now, and today every Frenchman can call himself a gentleman, even if everyone of gentle birth does not want to call himself a citizen.

It is indeed remarkable that among all men, at a certain depth of thought, there does not exist an enemy of freedom. In the same way as the famous Humboldt has traced upon the mountains of the New World the different degrees of height which permit the development of this or that plant, men could foretell to what extent, what height, the human spirit can conceive the great interests of humanity in their entirety and in their truth. The evidence of these opinions is such, that those who have once admitted them can never renounce them, and from one end of the world to the other, the friends of freedom communicate with each other through reason just as religious men do through their feelings; or, to express it better, reason and feelings are united in the love of freedom as in that of the Supreme Being. When it is a question of the abolition of the slave trade, of the freedom of the press, or religious toleration, Jefferson thinks like La Fayette, and La Fayette like Wilberforce; and those who are no longer alive count also in the holy league. Is it then from calculation, or from bad motives, that men so superior, in such different situations and countries, are so much in harmony through their political opinions? Undoubtedly reason is needed to raise oneself above prejudices; but it is in the soul also that the principles of liberty are rooted: they make the heart beat, like love and friendship; they originate in nature, they ennoble the character. The whole order of virtues and ideas seems to form that golden chain described by Homer, which, in linking man with Heaven, frees him from all the chains of tyranny.

[Source: Mme de Staël, *Considérations sur les principaux événements de la Révolution française*, London, 2nd edn, 1819, III, part vi, ch. xii, pp. 423–30. Translated by the editors of this volume.]

Doc. 59. FELICITE DE LAMENNAIS: The Conditions of Liberty

XIX

You have only one father, who is God, and one master, who is Christ.

So, when they say to you of those who possess great power on earth, 'Those are your masters', do not believe them. If they are just, they are your servants; if they are not, they are tyrants.

All are born equal; no one, coming into the world, brings with him the right to command.

I have seen a child crying and dribbling in its cradle, and around it were old men who said to it, 'Lord,' and who, falling on their knees, worshipped it. Then I understood all the misery of man.

It is sin which has made princes; because instead of loving and helping one another like brothers, men began to injure one another.

Then from among themselves, they chose one or more, whom they believed the most just, in order to protect the good against the wicked, and so that the weak might live in peace.

And the power that they exercised was a legitimate power, for it was the power of God, who desires that justice reigns, and the power of the people who had elected them.

And this is why each man was in conscience bound to obey them.

But before very long it happened that there were those who wished to rule for their own sake, as if they were of a higher nature than that of their brothers.

The power of those is not legitimate, for it is the power of Satan, and their domination is that of pride and covetousness.

And that is why, when there need be no fear that worse might result, everyone can, and sometimes ought in conscience to resist them.

In the balance of eternal right, your will weighs more heavily than the will of kings; for it is the people who make kings; and kings are made for the people, not the people for kings.

The heavenly Father has not formed the limbs of his children that they should be broken by fetters, nor their souls that they should be killed by servitude.

He has united them in families, and all families are sisters; he has united them in nations, and all nations are sisters; and whoever separates families from families, and nations from nations, divides that which God has joined; he does the work of Satan.

472

And that which unites families to families, and nations to nations, is firstly the law of God, the law of justice and charity, and then the law of liberty, which is also the law of God.

For without liberty what union could exist among men? They would be united as the horse is united to him who rides it, or the master's whip to the skin of the slave.

If, then, someone comes and says, 'You are mine'; reply, 'No; we are of God, who is our Father, and of Christ, who is our only master.'

XX

Do not let yourselves be deceived by vain words. Some seek to persuade you that you are truly free, because they have written the word 'liberty' on a piece of paper, and stuck it up in all the public places.

Liberty is not a placard to be read at the corner of the street. It is a living force to be felt within and around us, the protecting genius of the domestic hearth, the guarantee of social rights, and the first of those rights.

The oppressor who covers himself with its name is the worst of oppressors. He joins falsehood to tyranny, and profanity to injustice; for the name of liberty is sacred.

So guard yourselves from those who say, 'Liberty, liberty', and destroy it by their works.

Is it you who choose those who govern and command you to do this and not to do that, who tax your goods, your industry, your work? And if it is not, how are you free?

Can you provide for your children as you think best, and confide to whom you please the task of instructing them and forming their ways? And if you cannot, how are you free?

The birds of the air, and even the insects, gather to do in common that which they cannot do alone. Can you assemble to discuss your interests, to defend your rights, to obtain alleviation of your wrongs? And if you cannot, how are you free?

Can you go from one place to another without permission, make use of the fruits of the earth and the produce of your labour, dip your finger in the water of the sea and let a drop fall into the poor earthen vessel in which your food is cooking without running the risk of paying a fine and being dragged off to prison? And if you cannot, how are you free?

Can you, when lying down at night, be certain that no one can possibly come, during your sleep, to ransack the most secret places of your house, tear you from the bosom of your family and throw you into the depths of prison, because authority, in its fear, is distrustful of you? And if you cannot, how are you free?

Liberty will shine upon you, when, by means of courage and per-

C. Aspects of continental liberalism in the nineteenth century

severance, you are freed from all this servitude.

Liberty will shine upon you when you can say, from the bottom of your heart: 'We want to be free'; when, to gain freedom, you are ready to sacrifice all and to suffer all.

Liberty will shine upon you when, at the foot of the cross on which Christ died for you, you have sworn to die for one another.

XXI

'The people are incapable of understanding their interests; for their own good, they should be held in tutelage. Is it not for those who have lamps to guide those who are in need of light?'

Thus speaks a crowd of hypocrites who want to look after the people's affairs, so as to grow fat on the people's substance.

'You are incapable,' they say, 'of understanding your own interests'; and thereupon they will not even let you dispose of something which you judge to be useful; but they will dispose of it against your will, for some other object which displeases you and is repugnant to you.

You are incapable of looking after a small common property, incapable of knowing what is good or bad for you, of recognising your needs and providing for them; and so they send, at your expense, well-paid men who manage your property according to their fancy, prevent you from doing what you will, and force you to do that which you do not wish to do.

You are incapable of discerning what education is appropriate for your children; and out of tenderness for your children, they throw them into cess-pools of ungodliness and bad habits, unless you prefer them to be deprived of any education at all.

You are incapable of judging whether you can live, you and your family, on the wages they give you for your work; and you are forbidden, under severe penalties, to join together in order to obtain an increase of wages so that you can live, you and your wives and your children.

If what this hypocritical and greedy race said were true, you would indeed be less than the brute beast, for the beast knows all that they say you do not know, and only needs instinct to know it.

God did not make you to be the herd belonging to a few other men. He made you to live freely in society like brothers. For a brother has nothing to command of his brother. Brothers are bound to one another by mutual agreements, and these agreements are the law, and the law should be respected, and all should join together to prevent it from being violated, because it is the safeguard of all, the will and the interest of all.

Be men! No one is powerful enough to put a yoke upon you in spite of yourselves; but you can put your own head into the collar if you wish.

There are stupid animals which are shut up in a stall, and fed so that

474

they may work; and then, when they grow old, they are fattened, so that their flesh may be eaten.

There are others living in the fields of liberty, which cannot be brought to servitude, and do not allow themselves to be seduced by false caresses or vanquished by threats and ill-treatment.

Courageous men resemble these; cowards are like the former.

XXII

Now, understand how to make yourselves free.

To be free, it is needful above all to love God, for if you love God you will do his will, and the will of God is justice and charity, without which there is no liberty.

When, by violence or guile, that which is another's is taken away; when his person is attacked; when he is prevented from doing as he wishes in lawful matters, or is forced to do what he does not wish; or when his rights are violated in any way; what is that? Injustice. It is injustice, then, which destroys liberty.

If each loved no one but himself and thought only of himself, without coming to the aid of others, the poor man would often be obliged to steal what is another's to enable him and his to live; the weak man would be oppressed by someone stronger, and the latter by someone stronger still. Injustice would reign everywhere. It is charity, then, which sustains liberty.

Love God above all things, and your neighbour as yourself, and servitude will disappear from the earth.

Nevertheless, those who profit by their brothers' servitude will do all they can to prolong it. For that they will use lying and force.

They will say that arbitrary rule by some and the slavery of all the others is the order established by God; and, to preserve their tyranny, they will have no fear of blaspheming Providence.

Answer them that their god is Satan, the enemy of the human race, and that yours is he who has vanquished Satan.

After that, they will let loose their satellites against you; they will build prisons without number in which to incarcerate you; they will pursue you with the sword and with fire; they will torture you and pour out your blood like fountains.

If, then, you are not resolved to fight without respite, to endure all without flinching, never to weary, never to yield, keep your chains and renounce the liberty of which you are not worthy.

Liberty is like the kingdom of God; it suffers violence and is outraged by wicked men.

The force that puts you in possession of liberty is not the ferocious violence of robbers and brigands, of injustice, vengeance and cruelty; but a strong, inflexible will, a calm and generous courage.

The most sacred cause becomes an impious and execrable one when crime is used to sustain it. From being a slave, the criminal may become a tyrant, but he will never become free.

XXXVI

Young soldier, where are you going?

I go to fight for God and the altars of the fatherland.

May your arms be blessed, young soldier.

Young soldier, where are you going?

I go to fight for justice, for the sacred cause of the people, for the sacred rights of the human race.

I go to fight to deliver my brothers from oppression, to break their chains and the chains of the world.

I go to fight against wicked men for those whom they throw down and trample underfoot, against the masters for the slaves, against the tyrants for liberty.

I go to fight so that all may no longer be the prey of a few, to raise up bowed heads and to support sagging knees.

I go to fight so that fathers may no longer curse the day when they were told, 'A son is born to you', nor mothers curse the day when they pressed him to their breast for the first time.

I go to fight so that a brother may no longer grow sad at seeing his sister wither like the grass which the earth refuses to nourish; that the sister may no longer gaze weeping at her brother when he goes away never to return.

I go to fight so that everyone may eat in peace the fruit of his labour; to dry the tears of little children who ask for bread, and who are given the reply 'There is no more bread; they have taken from us all that was left.'

I go to fight for the poor man, so that he may no longer be deprived of his share of the common heritage.

I go to fight to drive hunger from the cottage, to bring back abundance, security, and joy.

I go to fight to give back to those whom the oppressors have cast into the depths of prison the air which their lungs are lacking and the light which their eyes are seeking.

I go to fight to throw down the barriers which divide the peoples and keep them apart, as sons of the same Father, destined to live united in the same love.

I go to fight to free from tyranny the thoughts, words, and conscience of man.

I go to fight for the eternal laws descended from on high, for the justice which protects the right, for the charity which sweetens inevitable ills.

Young soldier, where are you going?

I go to fight so that all may have a God in heaven and a fatherland upon earth.

May your arms be blessed, young soldier.

[Source: Félicité de Lamennais, *Paroles d'un Croyant*, Paris, new edn, 1858, pp. 50–9, 95–6. Translated by the editors of this volume.]

Doc. 60. The Fundamental Rights of the German People

(Section VI of the Constitution for the German Empire, accepted by the National Assembly in Frankfurt, 1849)

130. The following fundamental rights shall be guaranteed to the German people. They shall serve as a norm for the constitutions of the individual German States, and no constitution or legislation of an individual German State shall ever be able to suspend or confirm them.

Article I
131. The German people consists of the people of the States which form the German Empire.
132. Every German possesses German Reich citizenship. He can exercise the rights to which he is entitled by it in every German State ...
133. Every German has the right to stay and reside in any part of the Reich territory, to buy and dispose of property of any kind there, to exercise any occupation and to acquire the right of local citizenship.
134. No German State is allowed to distinguish between its own citizens and other Germans in civil law, penal law and litigation which would discriminate against the latter as foreigners ...
136. The freedom to emigrate is not restricted by the State. No payments may be extracted from those who depart from the country.

Article II
137. There is no distinction between the estates (*Stände*) before the law. Nobility as an estate (*Stand*) has been abolished. Germans are equal before the law. Unless connected with the holding of office, all titles are abolished and must never be re-introduced. Public office is open equally to all qualified persons. Service in the army is the same for all. To send a substitute is not allowed.

Article III
138. The freedom of the person is inviolable.
139. The death sentence, except when it is prescribed by martial law or is admissible in maritime law in the case of mutiny, all punishment by pillory or stigmatisation and corporal punishment are abolished.

140. The home is inviolable . . . The inviolability of the home is no hindrance to the arrest of a person wanted by the Courts.
142. The privacy of letters is guaranteed . . .

Article IV
143. Every German has the right to express his opinion freely by word, in writing, in print and in pictorial representation.

Freedom of the press must under no circumstances and in no manner be restricted, suspended or terminated by preventive measures such as censorship, concessions, security orders, state directives to print, restrictions on printers or booksellers, being forbidden to be posted and other hindrances in free traffic.

Article V
144. Every German has full freedom of belief and conscience. No one is obliged to reveal his religious convictions.
147. Every religious community orders and administers its affairs independently, but is subject to the general State laws. No religious community enjoys any privileges from the State compared with others. There exists no State church. New religious communities may be formed. They do not require any acknowledgment of their denomination by the State.
149. The form of the oath in future shall be: 'The truth, so help me God.'

Article VI
152. Science and its teaching are free.
153. The system of schools and of education is under the supervision of the State; and, apart from religious instruction, is not supervised by the clergy . . .
158. Everyone is free to select his occupation and to train for it how and where he desires . . .

Article VIII
161. Germans have the right to assemble peacefully and without arms. No special permission is required. Assemblies of people in the open can be forbidden in case of urgent danger for public order and security.
162. Germans have the right to form associations. This right shall not be restricted by any preventive measure . . .

Article IX
164. Property is inviolable . . .
166. Any relationship of submission and serfdom ceases forever.

Article X
174. All jurisdiction is exercised by the State. There must be no patrimonial courts. [These existed in the eastern provinces of Prussia

with the aristocratic landowners exercising jurisdiction.]
175. The judicial power is exercised by the Courts. Justice by way of the Cabinet or the military is inadmissible ...
176. There shall be no privileged persons or goods as far as the Courts are concerned. Valid judgements are equally effective and are to be implemented in all the German States ...

Article XII
186. Every German State shall have a constitution and representation of the people. The ministers are responsible to the people's representatives. The people's representatives have a decisive voice on legislation, taxation and the determination of the State budget. They also have the rights of proposing laws, of complaint, of formulating addresses as well as of impeaching ministers. (Where there are two Chambers, each Chamber exercises the right separately.) Sessions of the Diet are generally public ...

Article XIII
188. The non-German national groups in Germany are guaranteed their national development, particularly the equal right of their languages in their respective regions, and of their churches, education, internal administration and jurisdiction.

Article XIV
189. Every German citizen abroad is under the protection of the Empire.
[Source: *Deutsche Reichsverfassung*, Amtliche Ausgabe 1849. Translated by the editors of this volume.]

Doc. 61. GIUSEPPE MAZZINI: Liberty (1858)

You live. The life which is in you is not the work of chance; the word chance is void of meaning, and was invented to express the ignorance of mankind in certain things. The life which is in you comes from God, and in its progressive development it reveals an intelligent design. Your life, then, has necessarily a scope, an aim.

The *ultimate* aim for which we were created is still unknown to us: it cannot be otherwise, but this is no reason why we should deny its existence. Does the infant know the aim towards which it must tend through the family, the country, and humanity? No; but this aim exists, and we are beginning to comprehend it for him. Humanity is the infant of God: He knows the end and aim towards which it must develop itself.

Humanity is only now beginning to comprehend that progress is the law. It is beginning vaguely to comprehend somewhat of the universe by which it is surrounded; but the majority of the individuals that compose it are still incapable, through barbarism, slavery, or the absolute absence of

479

all education, of studying that law and obtaining a knowledge of that universe; both of which it is necessary to comprehend before we can truly know ourselves.

Only a minority of the men who people our little Europe is as yet capable of developing itself towards the right use and understanding of its own intellectual faculties.

Amongst yourselves, deprived as the greater number of you are of instruction, and bowed down beneath the necessity of an ill-organised physical labour, those faculties lie dormant, and are unable to bring their tribute to raise the pyramid of science.

How then should we pretend as yet to understand that which will require the associate labour of the whole? Wherefore rebel against our not having already achieved that which will constitute the last stage of progress, while, few in number, and still disunited, we are but learning to lisp its sacred name?

Let us resign ourselves then to our ignorance of those things which must yet a long while remain inaccessible to us, and let us not in childish anger abandon the study of the truths we may discover. Impatience and human pride have destroyed or misled more souls than deliberate wickedness. This is the truth which the ancients sought to express when they told us how the despot who strove to scale the heavens succeeded only in building up a Babel of confusion, and how the giants who attacked Olympus were cast down by the thunderbolt, and buried beneath our volcanic mountains.

That of which it is important to be convinced is this, that whatever be the end and aim towards which we are created, we can only reach it through the progressive development and exercise of our intellectual faculties. Our faculties are the instruments of labour given to us by God. It is therefore a necessity that their development be aided and promoted, and their exercise protected and free.

Without liberty you cannot fulfil any of your duties. Therefore have you a right to liberty and a duty to wrest it at all risks from whatsoever Power shall seek to withhold or deny it.

Without liberty there is no true Morality, because if there be not free choice between good and evil, between devotion to the common progress and the spirit of egotism, there can be no responsibility.

Without liberty there is no true Society, because association between free men and slaves is impossible; there can only exist the rule of the one over the others.

Liberty is sacred, as the individual, of whose life it is the reflex, is sacred.

Where liberty is not, life is reduced to a mere organic function, and when man allows the violation of his liberty, he is false to his own nature, and rebels against the decree of God.

There is no true liberty whenever a Caste, a Family, or a Man, assumes to rule over others in virtue of a pretended right divine, or from any privilege of birth or riches. Liberty must be for all men, and in the face of all men.

God does not delegate the Sovereign power to any individual. That degree of Sovereign Power which can be justly represented on this earth, has been entrusted by God to Humanity, to the Nations, to Society. And even that ceases, and is withdrawn from those collective fractions of Humanity, whensoever they cease to wield it for good, and in accordance with the Providential Design. The Sovereign rule therefore exists *of right* in none, the true Sovereignty being in the *Aim*, and in those acts which bring us nearer to that. These acts, and the aim towards which we are advancing, must be submitted to the judgement of all. There is not, therefore, there cannot be, any permanent Sovereignty.

The institution which we term Government is merely a Direction, a mission confided to a few in order more speedily to attain the National Intent or Aim; and should that mission be betrayed, the power of Direction confided to those few must cease.

Every man called to the Government is an Administrator of the Common Thought. He should be elected, and be subject to have his election revoked whensoever he misconceives or deliberately opposes that Thought.

Therefore, I repeat, there can exist neither Family nor Caste possessing the Governing Power in its own right, without a violation of your liberty. How could you call yourselves free in the face of men possessing the power to command you without your consent? The Republic is then the only logical and truly legitimate form of Government.

You have no master save God in heaven, and the People on earth. Whensoever you discover a line of the Law, of the will of God, you are bound to bless and obey it. Whensoever the people, the Collective Unity of your brother men, shall declare that such is their belief, you are bound to bow the head, and abstain from any act of rebellion.

But there are certain things constituting your own individuality, and which are essential elements of human life. Over these not even the People has any right. No majority may decree tyranny, or destroy or alienate its own freedom. You cannot employ force against the People that should commit this suicidal act, but there exists and lives eternally in each of you a right of protest, in the manner circumstances may suggest.

You must have liberty in all that is indispensable to the moral and material aliment of life: personal liberty, liberty of locomotion, liberty of religious faith; liberty of opinion upon all subjects, liberty of expressing that opinion through the Press, or by any other peaceful means; liberty of association in order to render that opinion fruitful by cultivation and contact with the thoughts and opinions of others; liberty of labour, and of trade and commerce with its produce; all these are things which may not be taken from you (save in a few exceptional cases which it is unnecessary here to enumerate) without your having a right to protest.

No one has any right to imprison you, or subject you to personal espionage or restraint in the name of Society, without telling you wherefore, telling it you with the least possible delay, and immediately conducting you before the judicial power of the Country.

No one has any right of persecution, intolerance, or exclusive legislation as to your religious opinions: no voice, save the grand peaceful voice of Humanity, has any right to interpose itself between God and your conscience.

God has given you the faculty of Thought: no one has a right to suppress or restrain its expression, which is the act of communion between your soul and the souls of your brother men, and is our one sole means of progress.

The Press must be absolutely free. The rights of intellect are inviolable, and every *preventive* censorship is tyranny. Society may, however, punish the errors of the Press, or the teaching of crime or immorality, just as it may punish any other description of error. This right of punishment (decreed in virtue of a solemn public judgement) is a consequence of our human responsibility; but every anterior intervention is a negation of liberty.

The right of peaceful association is as sacred as thought itself. God gave us the tendency to association as a perennial means of progress, and as a pledge of that Unity which the human family is destined one day to attain.

No power then has a right to limit or impede Association.

It is the duty of each of you to employ the life given him by God, to preserve it, and to develop it: each of you then is bound to labour as the sole means of its material support. Labour is sacred. No one has a right to impede it, forbid it, or render it impossible by arbitrary regulations. No one has any right to forbid free trade in its productions. Your Country is your lawful market, which no one may limit or restrain.

But when all these various forms of liberty shall be held sacred, when the State shall be constituted according to the universal will, and in such wise that each individual shall have every path towards the free development of his faculties thrown open before him – forget not that high above each and every individual stands the Intent and *Aim* which it is your duty to achieve, your own moral perfectibility, and that of others through an ever more intimate and extended communion between all the members of the human family, so that the day may come when all shall recognise one sole Law.

'Your task is to found the Universal Family, to build up the City of God, and unremittingly to labour towards the active progressive fulfilment of His great work in Humanity.

'When each of you, loving all men as brothers, shall reciprocally act like brothers; when each of you, seeking his own wellbeing in the wellbeing of all, shall identify his own life with the life of all, and his own interest with the interest of all; when each shall be ever ready to sacrifice himself for all the members of the Common Family, equally ready to sacrifice themselves for him; most of the evils which now weigh upon the human race will disappear, as the gathering vapours of the horizon vanish on the rising of the sun; and the will of God will be fulfilled, for it is His will that love shall gradually unite the scattered members of Humanity and organise them into a single whole, so that Humanity may be One, even as he is One.' *

Let not these words, the words of a man whose life and death were holy, and who loved the people and their future with an immense love, ever be forgotten by you, my brothers. Liberty is but a *means*. Woe unto you and to your future should you ever accustom yourselves to regard it as the *end*! Your own individuality has its rights and duties, which may not be yielded up to any; but woe unto you and to your future, should the respect you owe unto that which constitutes your individual life ever degenerate into the fatal crime of egotism.

Liberty is not the negation of all authority: it is the negation of every authority that fails to represent the Collective Aim of the Nation, or that presumes to impose or maintain itself upon any other basis than that of your free consent.

In these later days the sacred idea of Liberty has been perverted by sophistical doctrines. Some have reduced it to a narrow and immoral egotism, have made *self* everything, and have declared the aim of all social organisation to be the satisfaction of its desires. Others have declared that all government and all authority is a necessary evil, to be restricted and restrained as far as possible; that liberty has no limit, and that the aim of all society is that of indefinitely promoting liberty, which man has the right of using or abusing, provided his doing so result in no direct evil to others, and that government has no other mission than that of preventing one individual from injuring another.

Reject these false doctrines, my brothers! The first has generated the egotism of class: the second makes of society – which, well organised, would be the representation of your collective life and aim – naught better than the soldier or police-officer commissioned to maintain an external and apparent peace.

The tendency of all such doctrines is to convert liberty into anarchy; to cancel the idea of collective moral improvement, and that mission of Progress which society ought to assume. If you should understand liberty thus, you would deserve to lose it, and sooner or later you would lose it.

Your liberty will be sacred so long as it shall be governed by and evolved beneath an idea of duty, of faith in the common perfectibility.

Your liberty will flourish, protected by God and man, so long as you hold it – not as the right to use or abuse your faculties in the direction it

* Lamennais, *Livre du Peuple, iii.*

C. Aspects of continental liberalism in the nineteenth century

may please you to select – but as the right of free choice, according to your separate tendencies – of the means of doing good.

[Source: Giuseppe Mazzini, 'On the Duties of Man' (1858); in *The Life and Writings of Joseph Mazzini*, IV, Critical and Literary, London 1867, ch. viii, pp. 305–15.]

Doc. 62. EDOUARD LABOULAYE: Freedom, Ancient and Modern (1863)

The principles of 1789 reappeared with the Charter; Benjamin Constant and Mme de Staël being its most enlightened and ablest supporters; but, without saying anything about the memories and the passions which were to disturb the reign of the Bourbons, it is evident that from the first day the battle was joined between the traditions of the past and modern freedom, between the individual who wants to govern himself and the administration which wants to take over and control everything.

For fifty years this war has continued with changing fortunes. Commerce and industry have spread more and more widely the taste for individual action; on the other hand, the government has cast its net more and more widely. If we measure the ground gained by centralisation, it seems that very little would remain to be done in order to restore the ancient state in a milder form. The government gathers and concentrates in itself all sovereignty, all political life: it is itself the nation.

Were it not for the energetic resistance of private interest, if industry, by its very nature did not escape from the Government's control, and above all, if people listened to a school which regards itself as national because it lives by old prejudices, the State, which is the personification of the nation and the representative of the French people, would very soon be master of everything. As protector of the recognised churches, it would when the need arose eliminate schism and heresy as causes of disturbance and agitation; charged with education, it would teach our children, and form their minds to a triumphant uniformity; as the organiser of charity, it would give us alms and replace free association with a regulated administration; as the protector of the communes, it would look after all local interests; as the sole guardian of order, it would organise a universal police which would watch over us, guiding us like children, charge itself with our happiness and only ask us to live and obey in peace and quietness.

This form of government has an attraction for classical liberals, who, at bottom, have little regard for freedom. They are persuaded that not only is it a system which suits the temperament of France, but also that this system is the last word of civilisation. I know of very honest men who reckon indeed that before long England, renouncing her feudal barbarity, and America, its wild anarchy, will come to the school of France, and borrow its centralisation. This is turning their back to the light, and not seeing that the Christian idea, derived from dogma, has passed into morality; that the reign of the individual is drawing near, and that all political effort must be to further this new progress of humanity.

In industry and commerce the revolution is already accomplished. To the individual and to free association we leave the care of our bodies and our life. The last barriers of protection have been broken down, but has the State suffered? Is it less peaceful or less wealthy? To speak only of bread, the principal food of the French, has the supply ever been more plentiful, more regular and more certain than it has since the government was forced in spite of itself to abdicate its role of providence, and abandoned everything to the anarchy of private interests? What a denial of Colbert's wisdom and the knowledge of his heirs!

Is this an isolated phenomenon? Is what is true of industry untrue of religion or politics? No, all liberties hold together; for, under different names, all liberties are only the play of our activity, the effort of our mind more than of our arms. Religious freedom, freedom of education, freedom of association, communal freedom, freedom of the press, all these phantoms which alarm the so-called wise men, will be beneficent forces on the day when an intelligent political policy will open to them a full career. Not only will they elevate the mind, they will also purify it; far from being a danger to the State, they will be a cause of its security. By dividing human activity, and regularly giving it occupation, by creating new and considerable interests for the individual, they will ward off those kinds of political epidemics, which at a given moment sweep down on a people that is weary of its repose and corrupted by its leisure.

This gives proof of the example of all the peoples who, instead of fighting against and hindering liberty, find that it is simpler to live with it, and demand of it good fortune, happiness and peace. What country is more thoroughly peaceful and stronger than England! The thunderstorm can rumble outside, but confidence is in all hearts. Even when they quarrel, the area of the conflict is limited; it is a new right that they want to win; it is not a government that they want to overthrow.

France, so it is said, has neither the spirit nor the habits of liberty. I am not so modest as those statesmen who generously issue us with a certificate of incapacity; I regard that harsh judgement as a prejudice. Whenever have we been allowed to enjoy liberty, to declare us incapable of using it? Can people at this moment believe that if it were legally permissible to speak, to assemble, and to form committees, France would know less well how to relieve misery than free England does? What people are better born for associating than the pre-eminently sociable people? Before declaring us incapable, why not allow us to make use of one or two months of association?

All liberty, so it is said, is an education; it truly exists only when the practice and habit of liberty have passed into the customs of a country. I acknowledge the truth of that saying, but I draw a very different conclusion from it than that which is usually drawn. If all liberty is an education, what other means are there of elevating and instructing France than letting us live in freedom? Although we have been kept in leading-strings for half a century or more, will we be more capable of walking? Does not practice make perfect? Does one become a soldier by remaining by the fireside?

It would be good to finish with these sophisms and understand at last one's own times and one's own country. In the middle of the nineteenth century in Europe, among Christian peoples, freedom is not a question of race; it is a question of civilisation, that is to say, of practice and education. The better instructed, the more intelligent, and the more daring make use of that wonderful tool, and advance at the head of the nations; the more ignorant or the more timid mistrust that marvellous power, and lag behind. Power, wealth, intelligence, morality, faith, everything is in proportion to individual liberty. To tell France that she does not have sufficient moderation, prudence or spirit to aspire to the first rank, is a peculiar kind of wisdom or a strange patriotism. You will allow me to appeal against those decisions given by judges who are more idle than competent. England preceded us by half a century in the course of industrial freedom; do you not see that with our French fury we are regaining the lost ground by big steps? Then why should we be incapable on the day when it will be a question of religion, education, or self-sacrifice?

People often suppose that this grand name of freedom is one of those magic words which charm youth and seduce it like many other illusions. Mature age, so it is said, cures us of these first and misleading loves. This again is a prejudice; people can be old and liberal; I even add that perhaps it is necessary to have lived for a long time in order to comprehend the powerlessness of all administrative machinery, and the productive energy of freedom. When we are young, systems have something which attracts us, we love the symmetry and the unity; it seems good to create the happiness of peoples with a wave of the wand; such is the dream. The life of peoples, like that of man, is the reign of diversity; freedom alone can satisfy those many and varied needs which arise and succeed each other every hour. It is not folly to understand and love freedom; but it is folly to believe in sterile formulae, and in a powerless and fatal uniformity.

Only yesterday people were crying out to us that France was lost if we lowered our frontiers before commercial freedom. The test is being made; France has not perished. In the same way, a day will come when people will understand that the rights and interests of the least important citizen have their supreme guarantee in those journals which it is good form to curse today; the more ignorant, taught and reassured by experience, will know that without freedom of the press there is neither complete justice, nor productive administration, prosperous finances, certain peace, or really strong government; people will laugh at those oracles who have frightened us too long. On that day, perhaps, they will feel that our mistakes came from this political concept which we were wrong to borrow from antiquity; they will restore the problem to its true foundations; and, instead of some being afraid of Christianity and others of liberty, they will see clearly that both have the same origin, and if the individual today has a right to be sovereign, it is because Christ has freed our spirit and broken forever the despotism of the State.

[Source: Edouard Laboulaye, 'La liberté antique et la liberté moderne' (January 1863), in *L'état et ses limites*, Paris, 2nd ed, 1863, pp. 132–7. Translated by the editors of this volume.]

Doc. 63. ADOLPHE THIERS: On the Principles of 1789

(*Speech to the Legislative Body, 26 February 1866*)
The aim that we pursue is the restoration of liberty in France, this aim alone, and we know that every new revolution would be a new postponement of liberty, and a great difficulty besides, for what makes liberty so difficult in France are the numerous revolutions which we have passed through. (*True! – Hear, hear!*) ...

Are the principles of 1789 obscure and difficult to rediscover, like those texts, mutilated by time, which can only be re-established through great efforts of historical criticism? No, gentlemen, these principles are what is most certain in the world. Their spirit is in the *cahiers* that France drew up on the eve of the Estates-General and which included all its desires; their invincible demonstration is found in the debate in our immortal Constituent Assembly. As for the text of these principles, I have it here: it is contained in two declarations which precede the Constitution of 1791, and are, the one, the declaration of the rights of man, and, the other, the declaration of the guarantees granted by the constitution to all French citizens. ...

The French Revolution had two aims: the first, a social aim; the second, a political aim.

Here is the social aim ...

The French Revolution wanted to give to all Frenchmen, not that chimerical equality of socialism, but the sacred equality which is called equality before the law. (*Hear, hear!*) And the revolution gave it not only to the French, but to all men on the face of the earth, for, as someone once magnificently declared, its principles have gone round the world in the train of the tricolour flag.

From that day onwards, I shall not say all Frenchmen, but nearly all

C. Aspects of continental liberalism in the nineteenth century

men have been placed under the same law; all citizens of the same country have to pay the same taxes, perform military service, appear before the same judges for the application of the same laws, and, when they have gloriously served their country, they can obtain, the same rewards.

That is the social aim.

There is another which is at least equally incontestable: it is the political aim. What did the French Revolution really desire in following the second aim? It wished to change the form of government; and the government which was to be changed was not that which is called absolute monarchy ...

It was a government under which the monarch was obliged to listen sometimes to the advice of the nation, but without any obligation to follow it.

The French Revolution wished to place France under a monarchy where the king not only listened to the advice of the country, but was also obliged to follow it. (*Various movements.*)

This is what the principles of 1789 established in twice defining national sovereignty in terms which I need not recall to you, but of which I should like to quote the most important, and which states: 'Sovereignty is one, indivisible, and inalienable; it appertains to the nation; no portion of the people nor any individual can claim to exercise it.'

Thus, gentlemen, the two aims of the French Revolution: to establish equality before the law, and to make France free.

I address myself to the minds which are the most inclined to deny the right of France, and I demand of them if we should dare today to challenge one of these two aims, if we should admit only the social aim, if we should deny the political aim, if we should dare to say that the French Revolution, in making all French citizens equal, did not also wish to make them free? In that case, we would have to create in the universe, which knows our history as well as we do, the greatest of surprises, and persuade it to obliterate its memory of the Revolution. (*Applause around the speaker.*)

No, gentlemen, the French Revolution wished to make the French equal; it wished to make them free in founding their government on the great principle of national sovereignty. (*New applause from the same benches.*) I know very well that there are some who think that homage has been sufficiently rendered to national sovereignty when the reigning dynasty founds its right on that sovereignty. But would it be true that national sovereignty is an exhausted right when the nation is given a dynasty? No, gentlemen, otherwise the exercise of sovereignty would reduce itself, do you know to what? to an act of abdication. If the French Revolution had only done that, do you know what it would have done? It would have founded only one thing: the legitimacy of despotism. (*Signs of agreement from several benches.*)

When the nation gives itself to a dynasty, it does well to carry on; but its right is not exhausted: it has the right to follow its government step by step and to insist that public opinion, which represents its will, is the guide of all the acts of that government.

So, gentlemen, either we deny half, and not the least important, of the principles of '89, or else we must recognise that every monarchy of our day, and in France especially, is founded on the principle of the sovereignty of public opinion.

The forms in the meantime have altered, they have changed after three-quarters of a century. The constitution of '91 has been swept away by events; but something remains and will always remain; it is, the aim.

Well! gentlemen, the aim dictates the means; and the aim is to see that the opinion of the country inspires the thoughts and acts of the government. For that, it is necessary that public opinion can be formed; after it has taken form, it is necessary that it can be propagated, can be communicated to the holders of public authority, in order to inspire their thoughts and their acts. From that results the indispensable freedoms, which I am going to enumerate to you once more, although that has already been done by others and by me in particular. It will not have the interest of novelty, but we cannot, in this matter, create new truths so as to procure for ourselves the literary pleasure of novelty ...

The aim, therefore, is the supremacy of public opinion. In order to attain that aim, it is necessary first of all that this opinion can be formed. For it to take form, there must be individual freedom, that is to say, that every citizen, whatever side he takes in the affairs of the country, is protected from the arbitrariness of power. When I say 'whatever side he takes', I do not mean that the citizen can conspire against and disturb the established order: all freedom has its limit in the law administered by the courts; I mean by these words which I have just used, that the citizen must, whatever opinion he professes, whatever use he makes of his influence to make that opinion prevail, be protected from every arbitrary act.

That is the individual freedom which is expressly sanctioned in the declaration of principles of '89, and with an essential guarantee, formally expressed, which does not exist today, the right to proceed against any agent who co-operates in an arbitrary act. (*Hear, hear! from several benches.*)

The second freedom is the following.

It is not enough that a citizen can think in private, he must be able to express his thought, and publish it if he believes he should do so; and that is what constitutes the freedom of the press, also formally enunciated in the principles of '89, and twice defined with this condition that the expression of the writer's opinion may not be submitted, either to a preliminary authorisation or to censorship. You will find these provisions formally specified in the declaration of the principles of '89.

Can it really be said that the press is free, when, in the case of a periodical work, we are obliged to apply to the authority so as to obtain the preliminary authorisation to publish it, and we are submitted besides to the censorship of the government even when we have criticised?

On this subject, I shall only say one word about a matter on which volumes have been written.

Yes, I recognise the disadvantages of the freedom of the press, I recognise them in all their seriousness. I know that legal repression, which is essential for giving a just satisfaction sometimes to honest, indignant men, I know that legal repression is not enough to prevent the abuses of the press. What is the real, the only means revealed by experience? It is the use of freedom. Yes, when one gives freedom to the press, it abuses it, that is true. I, speaking here for it, would not be treated better than those who want to keep it shackled, but that is of little matter. The press abuses freedom, but when it abuses that freedom, it soon incurs public censure, and with time – (*ironical exclamations from several benches.*)

If I had been allowed to finish expressing my thought, you would have seen that what I was going on to say was not so strange, it rested on some indisputable experiences.

Yes, the press always begins by abusing; but very soon it feels public censure arising around it, and then it recognises its mistake. (*A new interruption.*)

That is what all the publicists who are interested in this question have recognised, and all sincere observers with them. Now, I think I am one of these sincere observers, when, recognising the abuses of the press, as honestly as I can, I add that it reforms itself, and that the right means of repression is use. It then reforms itself, and instead of seeking to agitate and pervert public opinion, in time it becomes its obedient and faithful mouthpiece. (*Exclamation from several benches. – approval from several others.*) ...

Volumes can be written on this subject, but the truth is reduced to these few words: we cannot reach the true form of repression otherwise than by use. It is a test to go through; but as long as the test is not made, it remains to be done ...

Now, I ask all men of good faith, when will you resolve to begin the test? Do you then want to condemn France eternally to that humiliating state of infancy in which she is kept today? Will you never want to give her what is the first sign of real freedom, that is to say, freedom to think and to write? ... Well then! I repeat it, when do you want to begin the test? Do you prefer to begin under a feeble government or under a strong government? ...

Let me have your answer! (*Signs of assent from several benches. – Murmuring from several others.*)

Now, it is not enough that the citizen is protected from every arbitrary act, that he enjoys the inviolability of his person and the inviolability of his thought; he must have the inviolability of his preferences, when he is called on to choose those who have to represent his opinion and support it in the counsels of the nation.

That is the freedom of elections.

This freedom rests in the first place on a right: that of assembling and acting together. If we could not act together, every one being committed to his individual preferences, it would take years to reach a vote which would determine the opinion of all the electors on two candidates, one for the minority, one for the majority; and this right of assembly that I apply here only to the electoral right, is also sanctioned formally by the declaration of principles of '89, because it says there: 'Citizens can assemble peaceably without arms.'

The second condition for electoral freedom is that the citizen can, without his interests suffering, choose the person he prefers.

A question arises on which I shall only say a word, and on which I shall be all the more brief if I am interrupted less.

If we take our stand on absolute principles, the government has no right to take part in an election; it does not have that right, for in that election it is not a question of giving representatives to the government, but indeed of giving them to the country.

However, practical men, recognising the difficulty of imposing on a government an absolute impassiveness when it is a matter of similar interest, practical men, not wishing to ask something so difficult from human nature, have reduced demands of this kind to a minimum: they have only asked that the government, if it has any preferences, confines itself to propriety and honesty. (*Murmuring from a great number of benches.*)

Baron de Geiger. That is what the government always does.

M. Thiers. When a government designates a candidate as its candidate, it commits a great impropriety. (*Murmuring from the same benches. – approval around the speaker.*)

Baron de Geiger. That is never done, it is the first time that such an accusation is made.

M. Thiers. You deny it, gentlemen, very well! but you must indeed be devoid of foresight, or else you must recognise that what I am asking for here is the minimum of what you will insist on one day in effecting electoral freedom. (*Faint murmuring. – approval from several benches.*)

Thanks to electoral freedom, the representatives of the nation, freely chosen, assemble in parliament, and there they should enjoy complete freedom.

C. Aspects of continental liberalism in the nineteenth century

I said just now that freedom always had its limits in the law administered by the courts. Well then! the freedom which we need to enjoy here, what can be the law, what can be the tribunal which limits it? You, gentlemen, are the law, the tribunal.

You have not found it otherwise, and, as for me, after sitting in French assemblies for nearly forty years, I have always found that authority sufficient.

I do not recall an occasion when an assembly has not shown how to make itself, the law and the government respected. And in recognising that authority, do you know what is the only real difficulty? It is to find a majority which respects the minority when the latter says what it thinks. (*Commotion.*)

[Source: Adolphe Thiers, *Discours de M. Thiers député de la Seine sur les principes de 1789 prononcé le 26 février 1866 au corps legislatif dans la discussion de l'addresse*, Paris 1866, pp. 9–19. Translated by the editors of this volume.]

(ii) Freedom of Speech, of the Press, and of Association
(Introduction, p. 397)

Doc. 64. JOSEPH GOERRES: Freedom of Speech

Whatever fermentation and upheaval goes on in the realm of ideas of a people must be able to find an outlet for expression as well: there can be no greater folly than to believe that it is possible to smother the smouldering conflagration of a highly agitated period of turmoil by covering it over with a handful of cinders. To some extent certain excesses may even be disregarded; because for one thing – particularly in the case of the Germans – it is a far cry from words to deeds. Moreover, free discussion quickly provokes a countering antithesis to any extremist point of view, and this in its turn is conducive to the finding of a happy mean. And this middle course will always be the attitude to which the German nation is bound to return, because of the innate fairness and good nature which are its essential characteristics, even if temporarily it has permitted itself to be sidetracked by some act of audacity. Only some individuals, who have taken their abode in an out of the way corner in order to shelter a shady existence, will shun the freedom of the press; but society as a whole has nothing whatever to fear from it. The state has adequate safeguards against a presumptuous abuse of this privilege, so long as he who has acted irresponsibly is aware that he will be called to account. Within the limits of the morally permissible, there should be complete freedom of speech. Nothing could be more ill-advised than to believe that what is truly just and great should require the dubious protection of a false, petty cleverness. Nowhere is the press more free than in England; and right in the midst of the revolution we witnessed no ill resulting from that freedom. Moreover, among all the nations, none more closely approximates to the British than the Germans, since both originated from the same roots.

[Source: Joseph Goerres, 'Freiheit der Meinungsäusserung' from the *Rheinischer Merkur*, 1 May 1814, in *Auswahl*, München 1921, I, *Rheinischer Merkur*, pp. 207–8. Translated by the editors of this volume.]

Doc. 65. FRANCOIS GUIZOT: Thoughts upon the Liberty of the Press (1815)

When the truth is openly manifested, when a Government displays a noble confidence in its own sentiments and in the good feeling of its subjects, this confidence excites theirs in return, and calls up all their zeal . . . The French, certain to understand, and quick to utter truth, will soon abandon that injurious tendency to suspicion which leads them from all esteem for their head, and all devotion to the State. The most indifferent spirits will resume an interest in public affairs, when they discover that they can take a part in them; the most apprehensive will cease their fears when they cease to live in clouds; they will no longer be continually occupied in calculating how much they should reject out of the speeches that are addressed to them, the recitals delivered and the portions presented for investigation; or how much artifice, dangerous intention, or afterthought remains hidden in all that proceeds from the throne . . . An extended liberty of the press can alone, while restoring confidence, give back that energy to the King and the people which neither can dispense with: it is the life of the soul that requires to be revived in the nation in which it has been extinguished by despotism; that life lies in the free action of the press, and thought can only expand and develop itself in full publicity . . .

Let us . . . adopt a system of liberty and frankness; let truth circulate freely from the throne to the people, and from the people to the throne; let the paths be opened to those who ought to speak freely, and to others who desire to learn; we shall then see apathy dissipate, suspicion vanish, and loyalty become general and spontaneous, from the certainty of its necessity and usefulness . . .

For twenty-five years the nation has been so utterly a stranger to habits of true liberty, it has passed through so many different forms of despotism, and the last was felt to be so oppressive, that, in restoring freedom, we may dread inexperience more than impetuosity; it would not dream of attack, but it might prove unequal to defence; in the midst of the necessity for order and peace which is universally felt, in the midst of a collision of opposing interests which must be carefully dealt with, Government may wish, and with reason, to avoid the appearance of clashing and disturbance, which might probably be without importance, but the danger of which would be exaggerated by imagination.

The question then reduces itself to this: – What are, under existing circumstances, the causes which call for a certain restraint in the liberty of the press? and by what restrictions, conformable to the nature of these causes, can we modify without destroying its freedom? and how shall we gradually remove these qualifications, for the present considered necessary?

All liberty is placed between oppression and license: the liberty of man in the social state is necessarily restrained by certain laws, the abuse or oblivion of which are equally dangerous; but the circumstances which expose society to either of these perils are different. In a well-established government, solidly constituted, the danger against which the friends of liberty have to contend is oppression: all is there combined for the maintenance of law; all tends to support vigorous discipline, against which every individual labours to retain the share of freedom which is his due; the function of government is to support order; that of the governed to watch over liberty.

The state of things is entirely different in a government only commencing. If it follows a period of misfortune and disturbance, during which morality and reason have been equally perverted, – when passions have been indulged without curb, when private interests have been paraded without shame, – then oppression falls within the number of dangers which are only to be anticipated, while license is that which must be directly opposed. Our Government has not yet attained its full strength; it is not yet possessed of all the means which are to be placed at its disposal to maintain order and rule: before acquiring all, it will be careful not to abuse any; and the governed, who are still without some of the advantages of order, wish to possess all those of confusion. They are not yet sufficiently sure of their own tranquillity, to abstain from attacking that of others. Every one is ready to inflict the blow he is exposed to receive; we offend with impunity the laws which have not yet foreseen all the methods that may be adopted to elude them; we brave without danger the authorities which cannot yet appeal, in their own support, to the experience of the happiness enjoyed under their auspices. It is, then, against particular attempts that constant watch should be kept; thus it becomes necessary to protect liberty from the outrages of license, and sometimes to prevent a strong government from being reduced to defence when uncertain of commanding obedience.

Thus, unrestricted liberty of the press, without detrimental consequences in a state of government free, happy, and strongly constituted, might prove injurious under a system only commencing, and in which the citizens have still to acquire liberty and prosperity. In the first case there

494

is no danger in allowing freedom of thought and utterance to all, because, if the order of things is good, the great majority of the members of society will be disposed to support it, and also because the nation, enlightened by its actual happiness, will not be easily drawn to the pursuit of something always represented as better, but ever uncertain of acquirement. In the second case, on the contrary, the passions and interests of many individuals, differing in themselves, and all, more or less, abstracted from any feeling for the public good, are neither instructed by prosperity nor enlightened by experience; there exist therefore in the nation very few barriers against the plotters of evil, while in the government there are many gaps through which disorder may introduce itself: every species of ambition revives, and none can tell on what point to settle; all seek their place, without being sure of finding it; common sense, which invents nothing, but knows how to select, has no fixed rule upon which to act; the bewildered multitude, who are directed by nothing and have not yet learned to direct themselves, know not what guide to follow; and in the midst of so many contradictory ideas, and incapable of separating truth from falsehood, the least evil that can happen is, that they may determine to remain in their ignorance and stupidity. While information is still so sparingly disseminated, the license of the press becomes an important obstacle to its progress; men, little accustomed to reason upon certain matters, and poor in positive knowledge, adopt too readily the errors which are propagated from every quarter, and find it difficult to distinguish readily the truth when presented to them; thence originate a host of false and crude notions, a multiplicity of judgements adopted without examination, and a pretended acquirement, the more mischievous as, occupying the place which reason alone should hold, it for a long time interdicts her approach ...

Regarded in this point of view, the restrictions which may be applied will less startle the friends of truth and justice; they will see in them nothing more than a concession to existing circumstances, dictated solely by the interest of the nation; and if care is taken to limit this concession so that it may never become dangerous; if, in establishing a barrier against license, a door is always left open for liberty; if the object of these restrictions is evidently to prepare the French people to dispense with them, and to arrive hereafter at perfect freedom; if they are so combined and modified that the liberty may go on increasing until the nation becomes more capable of enjoying it profitably; – finally, if, instead of impeding the progress of the human mind, they are only calculated to assure it, and to direct the course of the most enlightened spirits; – so far from considering them as an attack upon the principles of justice, we shall see in them a measure of prudence, a guarantee for public order, and a new motive for hoping that the overthrow of that order will never again occur to disturb or retard the French nation in the career of truth and reason.

C. Aspects of continental liberalism in the nineteenth century

[Source: F. Guizot: *Memoirs to Illustrate the History of my Time*, transl. J. W. Cole, London 1858, I, pp. 392–3, 394–7.]

Doc. 66. PIERRE PAUL ROYER-COLLARD: On Freedom of Speech and Publication

(*Speech in the Chamber of Deputies, 1819*)
[In the Chamber of Deputies] an article of law was formulated as follows: 'Speeches delivered within the two Chambers, like reports and all other documents printed by order of one of the two Chambers, will not give an opening to any action for defamation or slander.' This article stirred up a discussion. M. Laîné had added the word 'opinion', in order to include in the privilege the opinions that a deputy would not have uttered on the rostrum, but would make known by way of print.

M. de Serre had opposed this amendment, and had asked that the words 'defamation' and 'slander' be struck out.

M. Manuel attacked the principle of the article. He saw in it the prohibition to every member of the Chamber of having his speeches printed, unless the printing had been expressly ordered or permitted by the Chamber; he asked that the deputy be prosecuted only if the Chamber authorised the action. It was a notable debate. M. Laîné, M. de Serre, M. Manuel, had never spoken with such ability and animation. After them, M. Royer-Collard mounted the rostrum.

'I shall certainly not go into the depths of the question; I have no hope of penetrating any further into it. I am only going to endeavour to find, in the reason for the article which is proposed to you, the grounds for adopting or rejecting the amendments.

'Here, I believe, is the reason that speeches delivered in one of the Chambers cannot open the way to an action for defamation.

'The *speeches delivered* are the elements of the discussion. Discussion is the means of coming to a resolution. Therefore, if the speeches delivered in the Chambers were submitted to any sort of external action, the Chambers' resolution would not be independent. Now, the existence of the Chambers is conditional on their complete and perfect independence. This is why it is an axiom of representative government that the rostrum only comes under the jurisdiction of the Chamber.

'It follows from this that speeches delivered in the Chambers cannot open the way to an action for defamation; but it does not follow, as could perhaps be concluded from some of the principles which have been put forward, that defamation is permitted on the rostrum. All that this article establishes is that defamation in this case can be restrained and punished only by the Chamber, the sole judge of what exceeds the freedom of debate. If it did happen, I mean defamation which was gratuitous and quite foreign to the object of the discussion, what would the Chamber do? I do not know; I am obliged to answer as, on a similar occasion, an orator in the British Parliament did: "God only knows!". But it is a certainty that the Chamber would do something, and whatever it did, it alone would have had the right to do it. Its jurisdiction over its members, although not as yet determined, is not the less certain because of that, and it exercises it over every speech delivered inside it.

'Therefore, it seems to me an established fact that the many times that a speech has been delivered in the Chamber without incurring disapprobation in any way, represent an act of the Chamber, an actual, though tacit, judgement; from which it follows that this speech, whatever it is, is merely a legitimate exercise of the deputy's functions.

'Granting this, M. Manuel's amendment is superfluous and ought to be rejected as such. A legislative provision is not needed to authorise publication, and this provision would always allow the question of fact to stand, which is to know whether the speech has been delivered just as it is published. Now, the debate on this question is, of course, set aside from any publisher whatsoever, be he deputy or journalist.

'It is now easy to judge M. Laîné's amendment. This is the question to decide: should the relative inviolability accorded by the law to *speeches delivered* be extended to those which have not been delivered? What is a speech which has not been delivered? I beg you to tell me. It seems to me that here we are not dealing with a speech, that actually this is a written work in a dramatic form. Now, do the written works of deputies belong to the deliberation of the Chamber? This is a question of fact. What is the Chamber doing when it deliberates? Are you reading me, gentlemen, or do you deign to listen to me? My words are submitted to your jurisdiction; but written works are not, since you do not hear them. Not hearing them, you cannot judge whether they are worthy of censure.

'The Chamber is responsible, in some respects, for what we have said there; and it is solely because the Chamber is responsible, that we are not responsible to anyone. But the Chamber cannot be responsible, in the same way, for our written works, because it is not obliged to read them as it is obliged to listen to us.

'This being granted, the result of M. Laîné's amendment would be that in relation to defamation, the deputy who is not irresponsible when he speaks, and can be punished by the Chamber if he takes advantage of speech, would be relieved of all responsibility if he wrote instead of speaking. Under these circumstances, he would have the privilege of defamation, he would be inviolable on that point. An arrogant privilege, which we ought to be eager to abdicate, if we were unfortunate enough to be endowed with it! Personally, I refuse it. I do not believe that a man of honour should be allowed to accept this claim to the life or death of the reputation of his fellow-citizens.

'People will come and tell you that it is in the common interest; do not believe it, gentlemen. Privilege has always presented itself in the guise of good; it wants nothing for itself; it is simply self-denial, a sacrifice; but let it grow larger, and harden, and you will soon see it oppress all rights, because that is its unchangeable nature. Privilege is active, industrious, indefatigable; it thinks of everything. Open to it the door on which it is knocking just now, and you will be excused from making a law about newspapers; the newspapers will be for it: defamation will be privileged under the title of *Speeches which have not been delivered in the Chambers*. Again, you will be told that the privilege in question is a weapon of freedom against power. I confess that I cannot admire enough the facility with which words are misused. What are we doing here, if not exercising power? Are we not making our demands in the capacity of members of a power? And against whom are we making them? Against everyone. What is this actually all about? That we should be above the law, that there should be no justice against us, that the entire public belong to us, that every citizen be amenable to us in regard to his reputation and honour. There are, certainly, people who stand on the soil of freedom and repulse this intolerable domination with all their strength.

'Who doubts that the intentions are pure? The justification to which the previous speaker is about to give himself up is superfluous. What the keeper of the seals merely wanted to say, and what I repeat with the same conviction, is that all these proposals are stamped with the great, constant mistake of the revolution, a mistake which led, perhaps, to the majority of its crimes: that of wanting to bring forth freedom along with despotism, equality beside privilege, and, too often, justice beside violence and cruelty. It is time, after thirty years, to realise: freedom is only made along with freedom, equality beside equality, justice beside justice.

'No privilege, gentlemen; it is our honour to live under the common law. Aspire to remain there; no inviolability against our fellow citizens. And, as a last reply to our opponents, I will say to you: if you want to be inviolable, at least have responsible ministers; I would not lower your position by comparing it with the King's.

'I vote against all the amendments.'

A general movement of agreement showed itself, and all the amendments were rejected.

[Source: M. de Barante, *La Vie politique de M. Royer-Collard, ses discours et ses écrits*, Paris 1861, 'Loi sur la Police de la Presse', I, pp. 467–71. Translated by the editors of this volume.]

Doc. 67. FELICITE DE LAMENNAIS: The Doctrines of *L'Avenir* (7 December 1830)

As some persons have not understood, and others have affected not to understand, what are the doctrines of *L'Avenir*, we think it useful to set them out again as clearly as we can, and in an order which allows them to be grasped easily in their entirety. We have nothing to conceal, nothing to dissemble: what we are, we state openly ...

We recognise the present government of France, as set down in the Charter, and will obey it, and support it as long as it is obedient to the Charter which has formed it, and it respects the rights given to us by that same Charter. In short, we want the faithful and complete execution of the Charter; being determined not to put up with any one deluding us with empty promises, and ready, if necessary, to fight and die, in order to wrest from the blind power which would dare to be false to its oaths, the liberty which belongs to us, equal for all, complete for all.

And so that no cloud remains on our thought, we demand, firstly, freedom of conscience or freedom of religion, full and universal, without distinction as well as without privilege; and consequently, as far as concerns us, we who are Catholics, the complete separation of Church and State, separation which is written in the Charter and which the State and the Church ought equally to desire, for the reasons set out several times already in *L'Avenir*. This necessary separation, without which there would exist no religious freedom for Catholics, implies, on the one hand, the suppression of the ecclesiastical budget, as we have openly acknowledged; and, on the other, the complete independence of the clergy in spiritual matters: the priest, however, remaining subject to the laws of the country, like other citizens and to the same extent. Accordingly, the Charter being the first law, and freedom of conscience the first right of Frenchmen, we hold as annulled and of no force every special law which is inconsistent with the Charter and incompatible with the rights and liberties it proclaims; and therefore we believe that it is the duty of the government to come to an understanding with the Pope, and without any delay, in order to terminate the Concordat which has become legally inexecutable since, thank God, the Catholic religion has ceased to be the religion of the State. The power which is set apart from all the religious faiths, has no authority over any of them, and equally protects them all. They must be entirely free in their doctrines, teaching, worship and internal administration, otherwise the Charter, instead of being a *true fact*, would be the most hateful delusion. Therefore we cannot consent, in any way, to the government's exercising an unconstitutional influence over the choice of our bishops, which rightly disturbs us, since it follows, among other consequences, that our chief pastors would be given us by men whose faith may be opposed to ours or by men who may not even be Christians. We protest with all our might against a claim of that nature, which would create an exceptional servitude for us, and in general against any intervention whatever by the government in matters of religion, because from now on a similar intervention could only be illegal and tyrannical. In the same way that nowadays there must be nothing of religion in politics, there should be nothing of politics in religion. It is the desire and interest of all; it is the Charter.

In the second place, we demand freedom of instruction, because it comes from natural right, and, so to speak, is the first freedom of the family; because without it there exists neither religious freedom nor freedom of opinions; in fine, because it is expressly stipulated in the Charter. Consequently we regard the university monopoly as a violation of that same Charter, and, moreover, we reject it as illegal, the privileges of the university, odious in themselves, not resting on the law, as the government has several times recognised. True to the principles of our public law, such as have sanctioned the solemn declarations made to France in August last, ... we do not want to be put back under the system of regulations; and for this reason we urge the heads of establishments, against which some would like to put into effect the regulations of June 1828, to defend themselves energetically before the tribunals, being persuaded that in thus legally resisting the illegal acts, they will deserve the approbation of all true Frenchmen and very usefully serve the glorious cause of our common freedom.

In the third place, we demand the freedom of the press, that is to say, that it may be freed from the numerous fetters which still hinder its development, and in particular from the fiscal shackles by which some appear to have wanted above all to obstruct the periodical press. We think that too great a fear of the misuse that can be made of this freedom engenders a certain touchy susceptibility which leads to licence, through the obstacles which that fear sets against the legitimate manifestation of opinions, and sometimes to the defence of the most sacred rights. In our eyes, the press is not only an extension of the spoken word; but like the spoken word it is also a divine blessing, a powerful and universal means of communication between men, and the most effective instrument which has been given them for hastening the progress of the general intelligence. No doubt it can be abused; and who is not aware of that? but the spoken word is also abused, and, whatever people may say, the former of these abuses is not to be dreaded more than the latter, and perhaps even less. Have faith in the truth, in its eternal power, and we will considerably reduce those suspicious precautions and retributions against thought, which have never suppressed any error and have often lost the power to do so, by lulling it into a foolish confidence and a false security.

In the fourth place, we demand freedom of association, because wherever there may be interests, opinions or common beliefs, it is human nature to draw closer and associate; because it is besides a natural right; because only through association can anything be done, to such a degree is man feeble, poor and wretched while he is alone: *Voe soli*! because where all classes, all corporations have been dissolved, so that only individuals remain, no defence is possible to any of them, if the law isolates them from one another and does not let them unite for an action in common. Arbitrariness can reach them in turn or all at once with an ease which will soon lead to the complete destruction of rights; for there is

500

always in authority, even the most just and moderate, a tendency to encroachment, and liberty preserves itself only by a perpetual struggle. Today, however, when governments have to follow public opinion, public opinion must have apart from the governments a means of forming and showing itself in a powerful manner which does not in any case allow it to be despised or disregarded; and that in itself is a guarantee, and the strongest guarantee, in the present state of Europe, of the stability of governments.

In the fifth place, we demand that the principle of election is developed and extended, in such a way that it reaches right into the heart of the masses, in order to put our institutions in harmony with them, and at the same time to strengthen authority and public order. For the desire, the need for order exists nowhere as much as in the masses, and nothing creates such a great number of enemies for the government as the actual places it distributes, seeing that among the thousands of applicants who contend for the same employment, it is forced, in satisfying one to dissatisfy all the others. If great and little ambitions are left to distinguish it from their quarrels with other people, the government will gain some repose, and what is better still, a disinterested respect which also belongs to power.

In the sixth place, we demand the abolition of the disastrous policy of centralisation, the deplorable and shameful remains of the imperial despotism. According to our principles, every restricted interest has the right to manage its own affairs, and the State could no more rightfully interfere in the proper concerns of the parish [*commune*], the department or the province, than in those of the father of a family. It should only supervise the whole, so as to prevent the clashes which could take place between the various interests. We pray for the coming of a law which organises parochial and provincial administrations on such a broad foundation of freedom. And as we distrust intensely all uniform and *a priori* institutions; as the differences in situation, habits and customs very often require similar differences in special institutions of this kind, in order to effect the general good that is intended, we think it would be far better to leave it, at least to a great extent, to the parishes [*communes*] and provinces to become organised administratively. The variety which would result would only convey more fully the political unity of the State; for the arbitrary similarity, which is contrary to freedom because it is contrary to nature, forms only an apparent and material unity, and destroys the true, essential unity which arises from the proper, inward and energetic life of each part of the social body.

Such are the doctrines of *L'Avenir*, and we have the steadfast hope that they will gradually disperse many prejudices, quieten many passions, and draw together hearts long divided which only need to understand one another, only to believe in one another, in order to love each other. We never forget, union alone will save us, the union which springs from con-

501

fidence, as confidence itself comes from respect for mutual rights. Blessed if our efforts, which nothing will discourage because they have their source in feelings which are our very soul, could contribute to hastening that fraternal union and establishing, in an unshakeable manner, order and freedom in our fair country.

[Source: Félicité de Lamennais, 'Articles publiés dans le journal *L'Avenir*' in *Oeuvres complètes*, Paris 1836–7, X, pp. 196, 198–205. Translated by the editors of this volume.]

Doc. 68. KARL THEODOR WELCKER: On the Political Salutariness and the Danger of Free Associations

What has been said up to now inevitably contained already the most important proofs of the salutariness of free associations and in particular of political associations. First and foremost, they are essential to the growth and strength of States; they are the strongest source of the patriotic sense of community, and the most powerful lever for all efforts in the whole sphere of culture, whether superior or more primitive. They are the most fruitful means of satisfying all the needs of the citizens, and the strongest incentive for them to work everywhere in cooperation with the State. There are three things *par excellence* by means of which it is possible to spur on the forces and instincts of human beings for what is effective and great: freedom, free association, and the joy in things of one's own, in one's own work and property. That man has adopted the right course as an educationist and as a guide of youth and of the people who, above all things else, leaves them as much as possible of the exhilarating feeling of liberty, and makes their task and their ambition towards the realization of their freedom the basis of a noble *amour-propre*; who urges them on to a sincere interchange of views and association with others of the same mentality; and, lastly, who awakens and encourages in them the sentiment that the goal they cherish and protect, and towards which they are to work, strive and sacrifice, is also, in part, their own property and their own work. When the citizens have the free right of association, and particularly that of petition, these three things act jointly in order to unite their energetic striving for the tasks of the political community, and to preserve it through a fresh and cheerful vitality.

Secondly, free associations are of immeasurable importance for the maintenance of the constitution of the State, i.e. of the universal, all-comprehending association. They provide the most lively guardians and the most reliable support for the preservation of liberty and civil order, both of which concern none more closely than the citizens themselves.

Thirdly, for culture and also for the constitution, these special local, free organs of the community, in accordance with the requirements of place and time, are ever in the course of new formation and reformation; and they are, therefore, doubly essential because they reflect the true, contemporary and local opinions, sentiments, needs and efforts of the people more faithfully, thoroughly and immediately than the authorities alone. They bring these opinions to the notice of the government and the legislature, and in a lawful manner they obtain for them such effect and satisfaction as is in keeping with the common weal.

As we have shown, political associations as such are the most important associations. Moreover, as has been demonstrated they cannot be distinguished from non-political associations by any recognizable demarcation line. The entire freedom, therefore, to form associations which do not infringe the law, thus stands as an essential and beneficial element of human liberty, equally as much under the protection of political wisdom as under that of justice and the free constitution.

Even to make the formation of associations conditional upon prior permission from the State would, from a strictly legal point of view, destroy the right of free association, and particularly its most essential and important part, just as the right of freedom of the press would be destroyed by the obligation to secure the permission of the censorship. Here too, of course, the arbitrariness of the authorities would assert itself, and would be able to destroy all the combined efforts which had sought to assert themselves in the name of beneficial vigilance for liberty and against deceptions and malpractices on the part of the government, the ministers, the authorities for proper elections, and as a salutary influence in the Estates (*Stände*). A natural timidity displayed by some authorities, their natural hesitation possibly to tie or compromise the government by the granting of official permission, and the annoyance of the citizens perhaps at seeing themselves put under tutelage and restrained in their most innocent and worthy efforts, would easily have detrimental effects. Added to this, there would be real danger for the government in that an association it has authorized might immediately compromise it by pursuing some bad trend; and also danger for the citizens that in carrying out the most insignificant everyday actions, perhaps in taking a walk with acquaintances or a meal in company, they might be exposed to the danger of the offence of constituting an unauthorized association or of being unpleasantly disturbed by the police. On the other hand, it has to be the immediate goal of the citizens themselves and of their governments to introduce such forms and procedures as will not essentially restrict legitimate liberty in itself, and yet are suitable for removing abuses and malpractices. Thus, for instance, it can probably only be explained by the novelty of large political gatherings in Germany that, though to a certain extent people tried to copy the English pattern of mass political gatherings, they nevertheless completely ignored the beneficial English provisions for the preservation of public propriety, such as the election of a president and a committee from among the most respected citizens of the region with a view to maintaining order and propriety, particularly

C. Aspects of continental liberalism in the nineteenth century

in the case of political discussions; and thereby they brought about open public scandals.

But is there no danger whatever in the right of free association? And cannot some associations at times become dangerous and harmful? And does not it require some special means of protecting society against such dangers? Yes, one can and must, after all, acknowledge a certain general danger in the right of free association. Some associations can pursue a very bad course, serving the ambition and the selfishness of individual members to the detriment of fellow-members or the rest of society, and thus strengthening the power for evil as well as for good. But associations have this in common with all that is good, with religion, with the power of the king and that of the government and particularly that of the police, with language, with fire, and with iron, with arms and legs and their free use: the more a thing is good, important and effective, the more terribly it lends itself to abuse. But wise, just and courageous men, who are able to assess and appreciate the permanent value of these benefits as against isolated and passing interruptions here and there, and the danger of possible injustice caused by their unlawful suppression, will not want to sacrifice liberty itself because of possible individual cases of its abuse. They will not deem themselves called upon to correct the plan of divine Providence which gave liberty to man. Able statesmen and governments will tolerate along with liberty its unavoidable dangers also, just as God tolerates them too. They will bear with them because justice and human improvement are unthinkable without liberty. But if the commandments of justice are respected, if liberty is really respected, one must, of course, also permit the quite universal principles of justice to prevail, as they do in the case of freedom of speech, or the use of one's hands or one's property for which the granting of a permit, to be granted or rejected at whim, cannot be required. In general, the government has, therefore, merely the right to those beneficent measures which do not in themselves limit liberty and to such preventive measures as do not restrict rightful liberty itself, such as, for instance, through supervision, through the threat of lawful penalties, and through legitimate self-defence against the direct perpetration of a provable injustice; besides this, it also has the right to exercise repressive measures against unlawful uses of the freedom of association, viz., the right to suppress associations which contravene the law, and to take legal action against them. Also, in the case of use of this particular lawful freedom, the government thus has for its guidance the same legitimate safeguards against its misuse as in all other cases of lawful freedom. It could only have occurred to a modern type of excessive German jurisprudence to derive a quite contrary ruling from a so-called supervisory power.

Yet, as shown above, we are far from denying ... the legality of all preventive measures against associations. On the contrary, in addition to all the regular measures of prevention and repression mentioned above, in emergency cases we would declare, as with all other rights and freedoms, that even those preventions are permissible which really contravene or suspend lawful freedom in order to avoid dangers. These may consist of the prohibition of a specified association, as happened on several occasions in England; or of the suspension of a whole class of associations until a permit from the State has been applied for and granted, as under the new French law; or of giving the government the power to dissolve, under threat of punishment, those associations which it regards as being harmful or dangerous, as in the case of the new Baden law of 1833 ...

[Source: Karl Theodor Welcker, 'Uber die politische Heilsamkeit oder Gefährlichkeit der freien Vereine' in *Staatslexikon*, Altona 1843, II, pp. 41–4. Translated by the editors of this volume.]

Doc. 69. GIUSEPPE MAZZINI: Association – Progress (1858)

God has created you social and progressive beings. It is therefore your duty to associate yourselves, and to progress as far as the sphere of activity in which circumstances have placed you will permit. You have a right to demand that the society to which you belong shall in no way impede your work of association and progress, but, on the contrary, shall assist you, and furnish you with the means of association and progress of which you stand in need.

Liberty gives you the power of choosing between good and evil; that is to say, between duty and egotism. Education will teach you to choose rightly. Association will give you the means of reducing your choice to action. Progress, the *Aim* by which you must be guided in your choice, is, at the same time, when visibly achieved, the proof that your choice was not mistaken.

Whenever any one of these conditions is neglected or betrayed, the man and the citizen either do not exist, or exist in a state of imperfection and impeded development.

You have therefore to strive to realise all these conditions, and above all, the right of association, without which both liberty and education are useless.

The right of association is as sacred as Religion itself, which is the association of souls. You are all the sons of God: you are therefore brothers. Who then may without guilt set limits to association, the communion among brothers?

This word *communion*, which I have written advisedly, was taught us by Christianity, which the men of the past declared to be an immutable Religion, but which is in fact a step in the scale of the religious manifestations of Humanity.

And it is a sacred word. It taught mankind that they were a single family of equals before God, and united master and servant in a single

C. Aspects of continental liberalism in the nineteenth century

thought of salvation, of love, and of hope in Heaven.

It was an immense advance upon the preceding ages, when both philosophers and people believed the souls of citizens and the souls of slaves to be of different nature and race. And this mission alone would have sufficed to stamp the greatness of Christianity. The Communion was the symbol of the equality and fraternity of souls, and it rested with Humanity to amplify and develop the truth hidden under that symbol . . .

The religious association of souls carries with it the association of intellect and of action, which converts thought into reality.

Consider association, therefore, both your duty and your right.

There are those who seek to put a limit to the rights of the citizen by telling you that the true association is the State, the Nation: that you ought all to be members of that association, but that every partial association amongst yourselves is either adverse to the state or superfluous.

But the State, the Nation, only represents the association of the citizens in those matters and in those tendencies which are common to *all* the men who compose it. There are tendencies and aims which do not embrace *all* the citizens, but only a certain number of them. And precisely as the tendencies and the aims which are common to all constitute the Nation; so the tendencies and aims which are common to a portion of the citizens should constitute special associations.

Moreover – and this is the fundamental basis of the right of association – association is a security for progress. The State represents a certain sum or mass of *principles*, in which the universality of the citizens are agreed at the time of its foundation. Suppose that a new and true principle, a new and rational development of the truths that have given vitality to the State, should be discovered by a few among its citizens. How shall they diffuse the knowledge of this principle except by association?

Suppose that in consequence of scientific discovery, or of new means of communication opened up between peoples and peoples, or from any other cause, a new *interest* should arise among a certain number of the individuals composing the State. How shall they who first perceive this make their way among the various interests of long standing, unless by uniting their efforts and their means?

Inertia, and a disposition to rest satisfied with the order of things long existing, and sanctioned by the common consent, are habits too powerful over the minds of most men to allow a single individual to overcome them by his solitary word. The association of a daily-increasing minority can do this. Association is the method of the future. Without it, the State would remain motionless, enchained to the degree of civilisation already reached.

Association should be progressive in the scope it endeavours to attain, and not contrary to those truths which have been conquered for ever by the universal consent of Humanity and of the Nation.

506

An association founded for the purpose of facilitating theft of the property of others; an association obliging its members to polygamy; an association which should preach the dissolution of the Nation or the establishment of Despotism, would be illegal. The Nation has the right of declaring to its members: *We cannot tolerate the diffusion amongst us of doctrines in violation of that which constitutes Human Nature, Morality, or the Country. Go forth, and establish amongst yourselves, beyond our frontiers, the associations which your tendencies suggest.*

Association must be peaceful. It may not use other weapons than the apostolate of the spoken and written word. Its object must be to persuade, not to compel.

Association must be public. Secret associations – which are a legitimate weapon of defence where there exists neither liberty nor Nation – are illegal, and ought to be dissolved, wherever Liberty and the inviolability of thought are rights recognised and protected by the country.

As the scope and intent of association is to open the paths of progress, it must be submitted to the examination and judgement of all.

And finally, association is bound to respect in others those rights which spring from the essential characteristics of human nature. An association which, like the corporations of the middle ages, should violate the rights of labour, or which should tend directly to restrict liberty of conscience, ought to be repressed by the government of the nation.

With these exceptions, liberty of association among the citizens is as sacred and inviolable as that progress of which it is the life.

Every government which attempts to restrain them betrays its social mission, and it becomes the duty of the people first to admonish it, and – all peaceful means being exhausted – to overthrow it.

[Source: Giuseppi Mazzini, 'On the Duties of Man' (1858), in *The Life and Writings of Joseph Mazzini*, London 1867, IV, pp. 325–7, 329–32.]

Doc. 70. ADOLPHE THIERS: The 'Indispensable Liberties' *(Speech to the Legislative Body, 11 January 1864)*

For me, gentlemen, there are five conditions which constitute what is indispensable as regards liberty. The first is the condition which ensures the security of the citizen. The citizen should be able to live quietly in his home, and travel all over the State without being exposed to any arbitrary action. Why do human beings combine in society? In order to ensure their security. But when they are sheltered from individual violence, they will have missed their aim if they are subjected to the arbitrary actions of the power designed to protect them. The citizen must have guarantees against individual violence and against all arbitrary action from those in power. Thus I shall say no more about what is called in-

C. Aspects of continental liberalism in the nineteenth century

dividual liberty; it is good that it deserves to be regarded as incontestable and indispensable.

But when citizens have obtained that security, this is not enough. If it falls into the sleep of quiet indolence, then that security will not be maintained for long. The citizen must keep a watch on public affairs. To do so, he must think about them; but he must not do so alone, for then he would arrive at a single opinion. His fellow citizens must also think about them. Together they must exchange their ideas and arrive at that joint thought which is called public opinion. This is only possible through the press. Thus it is necessary that the press should be free; but if I say freedom I do not mean impunity. Just as individual liberty, where the liberty of the citizen exists on condition that he does not provoke prosecution under the law, so the liberty of the press exists on condition that the writer does not insult the honour of the citizens or disturb the peace of the country. (*Signs of Approval*)

Thus for me the second indispensable liberty is that liberty of the exchange of ideas which creates public opinion. But when this opinion comes forward it must not be a vain noise but must produce a result. For that men must be selected to express it here in the centre of the State. This presupposes freedom of elections. By freedom of elections, I do not mean that the government, which is responsible for the laws, should not play a role; nor do I mean that the government, which consists of citizens, should not have an opinion. I simply want to say that it must not be able to dictate who is chosen and impose its will in the elections. This is what I call electoral freedom.

Yet, gentlemen, this is not all. When these elected men come here as representatives of public opinion, they must be able in time – will you, gentlemen, please, appreciate, the implications of what I say – they must be able in time to exert real control over all actions of the men in power. This control need not come too late, and there are only irretrievable mistakes to deplore. It is the liberty of national representation, which I shall discuss later, and this liberty is the fourth of the indispensable liberties.

Finally, there remains the fifth liberty – I shall not say the most important one – they are all equally important – but the last one which has the following aim: to ensure that public opinion, as duly shown here by the majority actually guides the actions of the government. (*Noise*)

Gentlemen, in order to achieve this liberty, complete liberty, as one may say, men have conceived two instruments, the Republic and the Monarchy. In a republic the method is quite simple. The Head of the State is changed every four, six or eight years, according to the wording of the constitution.

Now the supporters of a monarchy, too, want to be as free as under a republic. And what is the system they have thought out? Instead of bringing the pressure of public opinion on the Head of the State, they bring pressure on the agents of his authority, to establish the debate not with the sovereign but with the agents of his authority. In this manner the sovereignty does not change and the permanence of power is ensured; but something else changes, and that is, politics. Thus the beautiful phenomenon is achieved of a country under a monarch who remains above our discussions, of a country which governs itself according to its own ideas and its own opinion. (*Prolonged but varied commotion*)

Well, these are the five conditions of liberty which I consider necessary, incontestable and indispensable. Which of these five conditions have we already obtained? And which still remain to be obtained? Which can we have? Which can we have without overturning our constitution? I repeat, all of them. (*Noise*)

[Source: *Discours prononcés par M. Thiers dans la Session 1863–64*, Paris 1864, pp. 41–5. Translated by the editors of this volume.]

Doc. 71. LEON GAMBETTA: The Belleville Manifesto (1869) [1]

Memorandum From My Electors [2]

Citizens,

In the name of universal suffrage, the basis of all political and social organisation, let us give a mandate to our deputy to reaffirm the principles of radical democracy and to demand rigorously:

The most radical application of universal suffrage in the elections of mayors and of municipal councillors without any local distinction as well as in the election of deputies;

The repartition of the existing constituencies according to the actual number of electors entitled to vote and not according to the number of voters registered;

The liberty of the individual from now on to be placed under the shield of law and not left to the convenience and arbitrariness of the administration;

The repeal of the Law on General Security;

The suppression of Article 75 of the constitution of the year VIII [3] and the direct responsibility of all public servants;

Trial by jury for political offences of every kind;

Liberty of the press in every way, freed from stamp-duty and caution-money;

Suppression of licensing for printers and publishers;

Freedom of meetings without impediments and traps, with the right to discuss all religious, philosophical, political and social questions;

The repeal of article 291 of the Penal Code; [4]

Full and complete freedom of association;

The suppression of the ecclesiastical budget and the separation of the Churches and the State;

Free and compulsory secular primary education with competitive examinations for selected highly intelligent children for admission to higher education, also to be free;

The abolition of town tolls, the abolition of high salaries and pluralities and the modification of our taxation system;

The appointment of all public servants by election;

The abolition of standing armies, the cause of the ruin of the finances and the business of the nation, the source of hatred between the peoples and of distrust at home;

Abolition of privileges and monopolies which we define by the words: *a bonus for idleness.*

The economic reforms touch on the social problem the solution of which, although subordinated to political change, should be constantly studied and investigated in the name of the principle of justice and social equality. In fact this principle, generalised and applied, can alone bring about the disappearance of social antagonism and completely implement our slogan: Liberty, Equality, Fraternity.

Answer to the Memorandum From My Electors[5]
Citizen Electors,

I accept the mandate. Under these conditions I shall be particularly proud to represent you, for this election will take place in conformity with the true principles of universal suffrage.

The electors will have freely chosen their candidate. The electors will have determined the political program of their delegate.

This method seems to me to conform both with the law and with the tradition of the early days of the French Revolution. Therefore on my part I adhere freely to the declaration of the principles and the claim of the rights which you commissioned me to demand from the tribune. Like you, I think there is no other sovereign than the people and that universal suffrage, the instrument of this sovereignty, has only value, has only a basis and only binds if it is radically free.

The most urgent reform should therefore be to free it from every tutelage, from every fetter, from every corruption.

Like you, I think that universal suffrage, once made the master, would suffice to carry out the entire destruction which your program demands and to establish all the liberties, all the institutions which together we are seeking to bring about.

Like you, I think that France, the home of an indestructible democracy, will encounter liberty, peace, order, justice, material prosperity and moral grandeur only through the triumph of the principles of the French Revolution.

Like you, I think that a legal and loyal democracy is above all the system which implements the moral and material emancipation of the greatest number most promptly and most definitely, and best ensures social equality in the laws, actions and customs.

But like you, I, too, am of the opinion that the progressive achievement of these social reforms depends absolutely on the political regime and on political reform, and it is for me axiomatic in these matters that the form involves and determines the substance. It is furthermore this sequence and order of priority which our fathers have pointed out and established in the profound and comprehensive slogan: Liberty, Equality, Fraternity. We are therefore in mutual agreement. Our contract is complete. I am at once your delegate and your agent.

I go further than to signify agreement. I give you my vow. I swear obedience to the present contract and faithfulness to the sovereign people.

[Source: *L'Avenir National*, 15 May 1869, reprinted in E. Cahm, *Politics and Society in Contemporary France (1789–1971)*, London 1972, pp. 82–3. Translated by the editors of this volume.]

Editors' Notes

1. This is the text of the radical Program for the elections in 1869 to the Legislative Body in the constituency of Belleville. Gambetta was elected at Belleville as well as at Marseilles.
2. The title in French is 'Cahier de mes Electeurs'.
3. This read: 'Apart from the Ministers, the agents of the Government cannot be prosecuted for deeds in connection with their functions except by a decision of the Council of State. In this case the prosecution takes place before the ordinary Tribunals.'
4. This had been introduced by Napoleon I in 1810. It forbade the formation of associations of more than twenty people for religious, literary, political and other purposes without the consent of the Government. It thus prevented workers' organisations.
5. The title in French is 'Réponse au Cahier de mes Electeurs'.

3. Freedom from the Church and freedom for the Church: documents
(Introduction, p. 407)

France
(Introduction, p. 408)

Doc. 72. COUNT DE MONTLOSIER: Concerning a Religious and Political System tending to overthrow Religion, Society and the Throne

I am going to accuse virtue of crime. I am going to show piety driving us to irreligion. I shall accuse fidelity of leading us to revolt ...

Those who have given us the congregations, the Jesuits, ultramontanism and the domination of priests, have, as a marvellous thing, imagined commanding the same respect for these inventions as for religion. This stupidity, exploited with a great deal of talent, has gained its ends; consequently for a great part of religious France, religion and the congregations, religion and the Jesuits, religion and ultramontanism, religion and refusals of Christian burial have been one and the same thing ...

The revolution having first of all overthrown the head [i.e. the king], and then ravaged the heart of our organisation, the result of this was as it were a great, untenanted space which has been offered to the first occupier. First, it is the common people, under the name of sans-culotte; in the next place, men following the profession of arms, and then the middle class. This situation aroused the hopes of the clergy, and carried them thither in the mass with their Jesuits and ultramontanes, and the members of the congregations. In this way we have arrived, after many sovereignties, at the sovereignty of the priests.

Constantly faithful to the true and legitimate sovereignty, I shall oppose that of the priests today, as I fought against those that preceded it ...

My opposition, far from being anti-religious, is, on the contrary, favourable in every way to religion; far from being directed against the priests, it is all for them, and they are and always will be, in spite of their errors, the object of my affections ...

I am going to show that the system of the congregations, taken separately, and those of the Jesuits, ultramontanism and the spirit of encroachment in the priests, each considered individually, would be sufficient to overthrow an empire ...

If these three classes of power [the Jesuits, the ultramontanes and the priests] have some points of disagreement, which weaken them, they also have a common, central point of doctrine by which they are becoming very strong. It consists of establishing as an axiom: 1. that morality is necessary for society; 2. that religion is necessary for morality; and as the priest is necessary for religion and morality, he must have in society the importance which belongs to the one and the other.

We are about to see how inference by inference drawn from this principle and skilfully spun, we are succeeding in bringing about social servitude ...

It is far from being enough that the authors of the system which I am indicating see real calamities in those to which I have drawn attention. The reefs appear a haven to them; the dangers, a means of safety. They never deny the reality of their conspiracy, they glory in it; religion, society and the throne, which they are overthrowing, they believe they are strengthening: it is as religious men, as royalists and citizens, that they conspire to destroy everything which can be dear to a religious man, a royalist and a citizen.

At the same time, though their intention is pure, their plan of defence is clever. They ask us to consider in what state they find society, religion and the king at this moment? Society, they tell us, has been destroyed by the revolution, religion by impiety. That is enough to give an idea of the situation of the king. What authority has he but that which is undermined on all sides by doctrines and precedents, and is more and more admitted by some as a convenience, and tolerated by others as a necessity; such an authority, having lost all its supports, is going to fall at the slightest breath, if our zeal does not manage to sustain it ...

We have seen, 1. the existence of a congregation the system of which, at one time religious, at another time political, and sometimes mixing these two characters, at one time mysterious, at another time open, sometimes strengthening itself in the shadows, sometimes appearing in broad daylight, has ended by embracing the whole of France; or, at the least, it is spread like a net over all the bodies, the combinations and movements that it seeks to envelop.

We have seen, 2. the existence of a monastic society founded, according to some, to prevent or to destroy protestantism, which it has neither prevented nor destroyed; according to others, to prevent or to destroy, through education, an irreligious philosophical system which, on the contrary, has sprung from its schools and from its bosom; a society rejected from its birth by the Sorbonne which, after having examined its rules, declared it *better formed for destruction than for edification* (*magis ad destructionem quam ad aedificationem*); a society which was the scourge of France and of Europe for several centuries, through its doctrine, its intrigues and its outrages; a society which all the sovereigns and all the magistrates at the time were united in excluding from well-organised states.

We have seen, 3. the existence of a sect openly seditious and disloyal, occupied in assigning, through all the means of doctrine which are in its power, to a foreign sovereign established beyond the mountains, from

513

which it has been called ultramontane, all or part of the rights of sovereignty vested in his majesty Charles X our good king, and in his successors.

We have seen, 4. the existence of a system strongly woven together and persistently pursued by a considerable part of the clergy, for the purpose of claiming, sometimes in opposition to the royal authority and sometimes contrary to our social freedoms, a domination which does not appertain to it in any way. Intermediary between God and us, when our love comes and brings to Him in church our worship and our respects, intermediary also between God and us, when our grief comes and brings to Him our repentance and our troubles, the priest grieves at this double ministry which seems small and insignificant to him; he lays claim to the province of youth through education, and to that of the rest of society through all the rules which it will suit him to lay down: it is not enough for him to be called, like an angel of benediction, to baptisms, marriages and burials, he claims to be the organiser and the arbitrator ...

The complaints and griefs exposed in the present statement can be reduced to the following principal points:

1. The four great calamities to which I have drawn attention, namely: the congregation, Jesuitism, ultramontanism and the system of encroachment by the priests, threaten the security of the State, and the safety of society and religion.

2. These four great calamities are not in a new form which could have escaped the vigilance or the preciseness of the legislator: they are noted in our ancient laws and charged with their anathema.

3. These ancient laws are neither abrogated nor fallen into abeyance; they are in their full and complete vigour: they are confirmed in several instances by new laws.

4. The breach of these laws constitutes an offence.

5. Whereas this offence menaces the safety of the throne, and of society and religion, it is classed with the crimes of lèse-majesty.

6. By its character of offence against the security of the State, action by civic accusation is not only open, it is commanded.

[Source: Le Comte de Montlosier, *Mémoire à consulter sur un système religieux et politique tendant à renverser la religion, la société et la trône,* Paris 1826, pp. 2, 6, 13–14, 77, 98, 165, 289–92, 313. Translated by the editors of this volume.]

Doc. 73. FELICITE DE LAMENNAIS: Freedom for the Church

The Church is oppressed by governments everywhere; it would perish if this state of affairs lasted. The Church must therefore be liberated, and today that can only be done by separating it entirely from the State. Its health and life depend on that, and I do not doubt for one moment that, in these great catastrophes of which we are and will continue to be witnesses, the ultimate aim of Providence is to effect this necessary liberation.

In regard to France, I have no doubt at all that we have to go through very bad and difficult times; I have said nothing about this that I do not still believe. But every situation has its own obligations, and all the obligations of our present situation are, in my opinion, concentrated in one only: that of being united in order to stop, if possible, the anarchy menacing us, and consequently of supporting without hesitation the present government for as long as it defends us, by defending itself, against the frenzies of Jacobinism. And if Jacobinism triumphs, what will it do? It will persecute religion, abolish all Christian education, and violently attack people, property and all rights. And what will have to be demanded them? Freedom of religion and education, of person and property, that is, enjoyment of the rights without which we cannot even imagine society; namely, what I have never ceased to claim for fifteen years. And how can these claims continue to be made without freedom of the press? Destroy that, and there is nothing left but to bend one's head beneath all the tyrannies.

For the future, as for the present, salvation is thus only possible with freedom and through freedom.

It would need a volume to cover everything on this subject; nevertheless, I believe that these few words will suffice to enable the present questions to be considered at a new and more proper day. Personally, I could not see them otherwise, and this is becoming a general way of thinking in France. They are opposing principles. Charles X was undone by royalist and gallican servility; he would still be on the throne if those who called themselves his friends, and were merely his flatterers, had been willing to offer him some resistance.

In two words: in epochs of social dissolution, there is safety only for all of those who combine in order to defend their rights, which are general liberties, as I have said above. This does not prevent the disorders, which are inevitable in these great upheavals, but it curtails and weakens them.

[Souce: F. de Lamennais, Letter to the Countess Louise de Senfft, 5 September 1830; in *Oeuvres Posthumes: Correspondance*, ed. E. D. Forgues, Paris 1859, II, pp. 165–7, Translated by the editors of this volume.]

Doc. 74. FELICITE DE LAMENNAIS: On the Separation of Church and State (*L'Avenir*, 18 October 1830)

It has been said many times that without common beliefs from which common duties are derived, there can be no stable society and even no society at all: for true society exists only among intelligent beings; and if interests can draw men together temporarily, the bond which unites them should, to use Pascal's expression, have its innermost recesses in something good which is more profound, in what lies hidden in their nature at one and the same time and is more intimate and nobler. It is that union of minds, that law which, in ruling thoughts and wills, restores the individual to social unity, and all peoples call religion; and all peoples also have seen in religion the first foundation, the essential condition of every society; and that society of which the proper object is to regulate political and civil relations or the external relations between men, is only the extension, the complement of the original society of minds.

By nature religious and civil society, Church and State, are therefore inseparable; they should be united as soul and body: that is the order. But it may happen that, beliefs dividing them, several spiritual societies are formed in some manner in the same State; and from the moment that the State cannot identify itself with one without breaking with the others and treating them as enemies, it follows, first, that each of them wanting, as it were, to institute itself outwardly, or to create a state within the State, the war of beliefs or opinions becomes a permanent political and civil war, and, secondly, that every opinion or every belief prevailing in turn, they end by all being oppressed in succession. Force takes the place of discussion, instead of becoming enlightened, people become angry; passions are inflamed, people do not even listen to themselves any more; anarchy becomes never ending.

The remedy, the sole remedy for so great an evil is to let that spiritual war be carried on and come to an end by means of purely spiritual weapons. Truth is all-powerful. What delays its triumph the most is the support that material force attempts to lend it; it is the very appearance of compulsion in the essentially free domain of the conscience and of reason: it is the brutal act of violence which violates and profanes the sanctuary of the soul where God alone has the right to enter. No man should account to human power for his faith, and the opposite principle, directly opposed to Catholicism and of which it destroys the foundation, has never, all the times that it has appeared in the world, brought about anything but bloody divisions, and calamities and crimes without number; it has conjured up from hell Dukes of Alba and Henry VIIIs.

We firmly believe that the growth of modern enlightenment will one day bring back, not only France, but also the whole of Europe, to Catholic unity, which, subsequently and by a continuing progress, will attract the rest of the human race, and by means of one law will form it into one spiritual society: *Et fiet unum ovile et unus pastor*. But, for the reasons set out above, we believe at the same time that religion today must be totally separated from the State and the priest from politics: that Catholicism, exposed everywhere to the defiance of peoples and too often to the persecution of governments, would ever grow weaker if it did not hasten to shake off the yoke of their burdensome protection; and that Catholicism can only revive through freedom. In the false position in

516

which it is placed through its connections with the temporal power, Catholicism is presented to men in a human guise which alienates them from it, while it is hampered and burdened with a thousand times which deprive it of its proper action; it languishes of itself, pressed down under the weight of an abject servitude. The time has come for Catholicism to get rid of its fetters. By degrees it was as good as imprisoned in the State; and now God himself, preparing its liberation in wonderful ways, the secret of which cannot yet be well understood, strikes with redoubled blows and breaks down the doors of the prison in which the Church has been groaning for centuries: for, have no doubt, all that we are seeing has, in the designs of Heaven, as its principal aim to restore to the Church, along with her independence, the action she has lost and which will save the world.

The instinct of peoples, guided perhaps by a vague presentiment of the future that Providence destines for them, demands this total separation of Church and State, a separation intended by the new Fundamental Law, and involving the solemnly sanctified principle of freedom of conscience; a separation, in fact, which alone can draw Church and State from a position as equally violent and fatal for the one as for the other.

To speak first of the State: in what relations can the government be placed with regard to the Church? Clearly it must either protect the Church or oppress her: there is no middle course.

If the State protects the Church, at the very same moment it stirs up against itself an opposition similar to that which contributed so greatly to overthrowing the ancient power. The same reproaches will be addressed to it, it will be exposed to the same attacks. When it is forced to account for its acts, and to justify them continually, people will not believe its protestations, or will pretend not to believe them. Public opinion will rise like the waves of the sea and sweep away the feeble dikes that the State tries to put in its way.

Frightened by this unquestionable danger, will the State oppress the Church? No power today is strong enough to attempt to do so with success. Such an attempt would rouse at once the vast body of Catholics, and those who, otherwise, sincerely desire freedom. The time for violence is past; there are rights that cannot from now on be attacked with impunity. Anyone who tries to disturb them will be powerless against them. To be sure, it would be a fine thing to see a government, in the present age, and under the rule of the general principles and laws which govern us, come and interpose itself between God and the conscience of a single Frenchman!

Suppose, in its basely contradictory conduct, a government shows itself, as it did not long ago, hostile and benevolent alternatively; if it strikes and indulges according to its fears, swinging, it may be said, like the pendulum of cowardliness, between the protection of the previous day and the persecution of the morrow, what fruit will it gather from these odious vacillations, except universal hatred and contempt?

Let us consider, on the other hand, what in present circumstances, circumstances which will not change for a long time, will be the situation of the Church, supposing she retains her ties with the State.

The past, in this respect, teaches us about the future. If the Church, dependent on the government, resigns herself to endure its domination, if the Church yields to its influence, is obedient to its orders or is only suspected of obeying them, all political opposition will become religious opposition; we shall see again what has been seen before: the priest, discredited in public opinion, and the perpetual object of the suspicion and animosity of the political parties, will be represented as the venal tool of the administration, as the abettor of despotism and the natural supporter of tyranny; he will be accused of servility, intrigue, avarice and wordly ambition. If, on the contrary, he ventures to resist the government and its orders, even when his conscience obliges him the most strictly to do so, and when the sayings of the evangelist and the canons of the Church make it a stern duty; listen to those voices which are raised and call loudly for public animadversion and acts of violence by authority against the rebel, the fanatic, the man of agitation and disorder who refuses to submit to the laws.

Between these two equally dangerous alternatives, what will the Church do? What security can she expect? Where will she find a few minutes rest? How will she exist?

And this is not all. Behold the inevitable results of the Church's subjection; calculate, if possible, the future consequences of the prolongation of a situation which has already brought about such fatal results: religion administered like customs and tolls, the priesthood degraded, discipline destroyed, teaching oppressed, the Church, in a word, deprived of her necessary independence, communicating every day with greater difficulty with her Head, and also subjected more severely every day to the caprices of the temporal power; formed by it in all the practices, receiving everything from it, its pastors, its laws, even its doctrine: what is that, if it is not death?

Catholics, let it be well understood, we have to save our faith; and we shall save it by means of freedom. It has been promised us; let us loudly demand, and demand without ceasing the fulfilment of that promise: it constitutes our right, and that right is sacred, and no one will deprive us of it if we claim it, if we defend it with courage and perseverance. Henceforth the State must have nothing to do with the choice of bishops and parish priests; it belongs to the Pope alone to determine their manner of election or presentation. The government must no longer interfere with what concerns worship, instruction and discipline; the spiritual order must be separate, completely separate from the temporal order: without that the Fundamental Law will be shamefully broken in the letter and in its spirit. And if ever it is allowed to be broken in one point, who will prevent its being broken before long in all the others? All Frenchmen, whatever the diversity of their opinions, therefore have the same interest in maintaining the free and full execution of that Law; and moreover it is a question here of the first of freedoms, that of religious freedom, and of the consequence of that freedom, desired not only by Catholics, but by the whole of France.

However, we must state, and state boldly, there can be no freedom for the Church except on one condition, which no doubt will hinder it very little, that is, the discontinuance of the stipend which the State grants annually to the clergy. Anyone who is paid is dependent on whoever pays him. It is what Irish Catholics have rightly felt, and they have always rejected this servitude that the English Government has attempted several times to impose on them. As long as we do not follow their example, Catholicism will only have a precarious and feeble existence among us. The morsel of bread that is thrown to the clergy will be the title to their oppression: free by law, the clergy will, whatever they do, be slaves through the stipend; and is it not already the means that some prefects use in order to obtain what they are pleased to exact illegally from the clergy? It is time, high time that the priest recovers his independence, and his dignity: no advantage can ever compensate him for the loss. He has to live, it is true: but above all the Church must live; and her life, we repeat, is bound up with the sacrifice which will restore his freedom. Then the political hatreds, of which the Church has become the object, will die away; then, being renewed through discipline and knowledge, the Church will appear in the eyes of the people as she is, as God has created her, raised above the earth in order to shed over it the enlightenment and the consolation of Heaven, rich in her poverty, and strong in the only power, that of virtue, which does not arouse envy and give rise to opposition.

And let us not be deterred by the disadvantages which, at the first glance, the suppression of the stipend seems as if it could entail; real though they may be, we would still have to resign ourselves to them without hesitation, since the safety of the Church depends on her separation from the State. But, in fact, the disadvantages will be much less serious than we cannot help fearing. Providence does not forsake those who put their trust in Him. Zeal will create boundless resources. The more the priest shows of disinterestedness and self-denial, the more will the offerings of charity come to meet his needs, and first of all, those to alleviate distress the secret of which is deposited in his bosom every day. What Catholic would refuse to contribute to the repairs of the church in which the sacred mysteries of his faith are celebrated, and to the upkeep of the institutions devoted to perpetuating the priesthood? Of all the Catholic populations in Europe, the most poverty-stricken is that in Ireland, and nowhere is religion more substantially endowed; for it is the poor who endow it. I know that in France there are districts where the faith is nearly extinguished and which will offer few resources of this kind;

but these districts are small in number, and this weakening of the faith is due in part, we say it with sorrow, to the lack of zeal and the absence of the true priestly spirit among the pastors. Wherever they are what they ought to be, necessaries will not be lacking for them. There are so many blessings in religion, it is so strong in the heart of man, that hardly ever is it religion itself that he spurns, but only the false and unworthy image that he has been shown.

The time has come to put religion back in a position which removes any pretext for hatred and mistrust; the time has come for the Church to be put in possession again of the freedom belonging to her, the freedom that our Fundamental Law guarantees to her. The public resolve will support it. Let the bishops, weary from a long oppression, lift up their heads and behold even in the revolutions which disturb society, the dawn of their deliverance; let them desire what the peoples desire, the full enjoyment of their rights, and they will obtain it. But for that reason, let them not be mistaken, they must help themselves, they must accomplish, by a unanimous and decisive act, the separation which will set them free; they must, in a word, say to the State: We renounce the stipend that you grant us, and we regain our independence. Subject like all Frenchmen to the political and civil laws of the country insofar as they do not injure the sacred rights of conscience, we do not recognize your authority in anything concerning religion, our worship, our discipline and our instruction. In this purely spiritual order, we are free in virtue of the law; we owe obedience only to the spiritual head that Jesus Christ has given us; he alone must determine our beliefs, direct and superintend our administration, and provide for the perpetuation of the divine ministry. And do not think that this resolve, irrevocable on our part, is inspired by any view, any feeling of opposition against you: on the contrary, it has for its motive only an eager desire to remove the lamentable causes of division; to end a struggle against nature, the results of which are incalculable; to effect, through what depends on us, the reconciliation of the parties and the union of all Frenchmen which alone will strengthen order: in short, the resolve is inspired in us by the stern duty of preserving Christianity, and raising it above human passions and the storms of politics.

Ministers of Jesus Christ, who was born in a manger and died upon a cross, go back to your beginning, voluntarily acquire new strength through poverty and suffering, and, patient and poor, the word of God will resume on your lips its former effectiveness. Without any support other than that divine word, go down, like the twelve fishermen, into the midst of the people, and again begin the conquest of the world. A new era of triumph and glory is preparing for Christianity. See on the horizon the precursory signs of the rising of the star, and, messengers of hope, begin to sing the canticle of life on the ruins of empires and on the remains of all that passes away.

[Source: Félicité de Lamennais, 'Articles publiés dans le journal *L'Avenir*' in *Oeuvres complètes*, X, Paris 1836–37, pp. 149–59. Translated by the editors of this volume.]

Doc. 75. COUNT CHARLES DE MONTALEMBERT: 'An explanatory note on the formula "A Free Church in a Free State" ' (1863)

Those who do not desire freedom either for the Church or for the State, like those who only desire freedom for themselves, must naturally reject our formula. But those who, on the other hand, espouse religious freedom and political freedom or only one of the two shall perhaps have fewer scruples in accepting it if they reflect well on the only reasonable meaning it has ...

In order to determine its value it is well to remember its origins. Count Cavour, the Prime Minister of King Victor Emmanuel, has permitted himself to appeal to the accord between religion and liberty in a speech on 12 October 1860 designed to excuse the invasion of the Papal States and the crime of Castelfidardo. He did me the very unexpected honour of quoting me as having '*in a lucid moment*' shown to Europe through a famous book that liberty had been very useful to lift up the religious spirit. On the 25th of that month I answered him in a letter published in *le Correspondant*. In it I protested entirely against a policy that had had no equal in the history of our century other than the ambush of Bayonne, and proved completely to him that Catholics would never accept a freedom that begins with the suppression of the independence of the Head of the Church. I defined the guarantees and the conditions of religious freedom, and I said: *A Free Church in the midst of a Free State: this is my ideal.*

In his speeches of 27 March and 9 April 1861, always on the Roman Question, M. de Cavour returned to the matter. He quoted me again as one of the forerunners of the liberalism he desired for Catholics. After declaring that the spiritual independence of the Church was a vital problem for 300 million Catholics, he stated that once in possession of Rome, 'Italy would proclaim that great principle: *A Free Church in a Free State.*'

It is in this way that this formula has entered history and from which it will never disappear.

This being so, which is the best course to take? To abandon it entirely and simply to our enemies? Or to claim it well and accept it resolutely by turning against the successors, the complices and the admirers of him who had caught it from us?

In the manner I had worded it, it signified, and could not signify anything else, but the liberty of the church based on public liberties. I owe it in justice to M. de Cavour that he tried by no means to give it another meaning. But one comes to me with the objection that *a Free*

State could be interpreted as a State that grants itself the liberty of spoiling and oppressing whatever seems appropriate to it.

This confusion of ideas has as a pretext the double meaning that is attached in our language to the word *State*. In fact it means simultaneously the government of a country and that country itself with the people who inhabit it, but that country entirely considered from the point of view of its legal aspects, of its constitution.

Thus the State, improperly and by taking the part for the whole, is the Government. But it was the governments which invented that quite modern meaning. It goes back to Louis XVI; it pleases our ministers and our sub-prefects. For, on the lips of the gentlemen of the Civil Service, the State is these gentlemen themselves. The State is still and better the whole of the laws and the institutions of a country whoever may be its chiefs. The State is finally and above all the country, and the people. But anyone who knows French knows that the word 'State', followed by an adjective, always indicates a country or a people and never a government.

Thus if one says *The Church and the State*, one understands by the State the government which treats or fights with the Church. But if one says the *United States* or the *Confederate States* one cannot mean anything else but the peoples of Virginia, Pennsylvania, etc. When one says the *State of the Church* or even in Italian *lo Stato pontificio* (the Papal State) one does not mean the government of the Pope but actually the country and the people whose sovereign he is.

A *Free State*, therefore, never signifies a government in a position to do what it wants. On the contrary, a State is all the more free as its Government is less so. No one would dare to say that Russia is a free State, just because the Emperor of Russia disposes there freely of the lives, the goods and the honour of his unfortunate subjects. On the other hand, the entire world recognises that England is a free State, precisely because the Government there has its hands tied more than anywhere else.

Thus the term 'a free State' will not and cannot mean anything else but '*a free country*'. Certainly I should have done better to say 'A free Church in a free country'. I would then have avoided the appearance of a certainly involuntary complicity with those who pretend that the Church should be in the State and not the State in the Church. For it is as wrong that the Church should be in the State as it is that the State should be in the Church. They are merely two societies that co-exist in the same country which can be composed of the same people, but which nevertheless remain no less subject to separate laws and emanate from different sources. There is also the difference that the State can only comprise one country, whereas the Church comprises all countries and all centuries.

However, in the end, the formula used by M. de Cavour, nearly the same as that which had been used in writing (by Montalembert) and to which he gave publicity, is an *accomplished fact*. One can and one should rectify its meaning, but one will not change its words.

I listened one day to a German scholar in Berlin explaining at full length to a French scholar that for all sorts of reasons, historical, philosophical and political, the Prussians ought to call themselves Brandenburgers. 'This is perfectly true', answered the Frenchman, 'but you will have to admit: Prussia will never call herself anything but Prussia.'

So much for the formal side. As for the subject-matter, we know well that it is not a question of a dogma, nor of a symbol, nor of a rule of conscience, but of a word intended to sum up a situation, what is called in law, a *modus vivendi*. And after having said this, let us ask ourselves whether there exists a means in the real world (and even in Rome where a sacerdotal government can by no means be incompatible with true liberty), let us ask ourselves whether there is a means by which to imagine a situation other than the following four:

a free Church in a free country;
an enslaved Church in an enslaved country;
an enslaved Church in a free country;
a free Church in an enslaved country.

A free Church in an enslaved country. One can dream of it; but one cannot find it anywhere. It has never been seen and, I add with happiness, for the honour of the Church, it never will be seen. *An enslaved Church in a free country*. This could long be found in England, and this is still the position in Sweden, Portugal and Piedmont. This would be the position in Belgium, if the Belgian Constitution were not an obstacle to it. This is the ideal of the false liberals in Italy, in Spain, in France and everywhere. But there is not one among us who does not reject this ideal with horror. *An enslaved Church in an enslaved country*. This is to be found in Russia and elsewhere. Whatever the depraved taste for absolute power of too many Catholics might be, I do not know of any one of them who would dare to declare himself prepared to buy the happiness of suppressing public liberty at the price of the liberty of the Church.

There thus remains *a free Church in a free country*. I have said that this was my ideal. I can add that it is a happy reality not only in England and in America, not only in Belgium, but further and above all in Austria since the Concordat [1855] and the liberal regeneration of that Empire.

Should the day come when France will return to public life, when she will take again the too long interrupted course of her intellectual and moral, Catholic and liberal mission, let us hope that she will then not prove backward compared with Austria.

In the meantime I maintain our formula. I maintain it as the safeguard of the Catholics and as the touchstone of the Liberals. I claim it for the liberal Catholics. It serves to distinguish them neatly from the intolerant Catholics who do not want a liberal State, and from the illogical liberals who do not want a free Church. We, who want both liberties frankly, resolutely and forever, should know how to prove it by our words and still better by our deeds.

[Source: Comte Charles de Montalembert, *L'Eglise libre dans l'Etat libre*. Discours prononcé au Congrès Catholique de Malines, Paris 1863, pp. 177–87. Translated by the editors of this volume.]

Italy
(Introduction, p. 410)

Doc. 76. CAMILLO DI CAVOUR: For Liberty of Conscience and of Worship (18 May 1848)

Among the major, the more important, conquests of modern civilisation is certainly to be counted liberty of conscience, and hence the liberty of worship that derives from it as a logical consequence. This great principle has not yet been proclaimed in our constitution. The legislator, perhaps in order not to precipitate an irrevocable definition in so grave a matter, believed it more opportune not to make any particular mention of it, reserving to himself the introduction in practice with special laws.

In fact, at the publication of the constitution, the sovereign measures that caused the most serious infractions of the principle of liberty of conscience to disappear from our legislation, by emancipating the Protestants and Jews, were held back. We do not doubt it to be the view of the legislator to progress in this practical way, and to amend successively all the dispositions contained in our penal and civil codes which are opposed at present.

But this is not enough. A principle such as that of liberty of worship cannot be introduced into the constitution of a highly civilised people by indirect means: it must be proclaimed as one of the fundamental foundations of the social agreement.

Therefore, we do not doubt in asserting that when the epoch predicted in the Address from the Throne has arrived, in which *the desired fusion of the various parts of the peninsula* with our States will render opportune *the promotion of those changes in the laws that are valuable in making the destinies of the country rise* to greatness, in that time the declaration, in the most explicit way, that every conscience is an inviolable sanctuary and that complete liberty must be accorded to all cults, can no longer be omitted from the Italian Magna Carta.

This modification, or better, this explanation of our constitution, will certainly not be opposed by any man who is enlightened and zealous in religious matters. In Italy, thanks be to God, the Catholic clergy including the more elect part, even if not unanimously, but at least in a great majority, had embraced the cause of liberty, considering it to be closely connected with that of religion itself. Therefore, one can likewise applaud a disposition that by this time is a part of the constitution of all free and civilised peoples.

The Catholic clergy, convinced of the truth of the dogmas it professes, of the sublimity of the cult of which it is minister, cannot seek protection for the cause of religion in power, in privileges, or in restrictions.

In almost all Europe, Catholicism, moved by that divine instinct which drives it to knot again around itself the living forces of society, makes common cause with the peoples. In Ireland, in Belgium, in Poland, it has fought, and fights, for the oppressed against the oppressors. Everywhere it has made itself a supporter of popular liberty, everywhere it has inscribed on its banner *religious liberty*.

That liberty, for which the clergy asks with such energy and reason in the countries in which the Catholic principle predominates, should not be denied in all its fullness to Catholics in those countries in which it exercises so just an influence. If the Italian clergy should fall into such a contradiction, if, in not listening to the voice of the great Gioberti, we should attempt to retain in our political and civil codes any traces of the religious despotism of past centuries, it would cause greater damage to Catholicism than that which can be done to it by its most fiery persecutors. By giving proof to the suspicion of the sincerity of its proclaimed alliance with the cause of liberty, it would diminish the authority that it has re-acquired over the peoples; it would deliver terrible weapons to those who still fight it before that tribunal which now decides all questions, that of public opinion.

Secure in the adherence of the enlightened clergy, in the sympathies of all men of progress, of all those who in their affections join the cause of religion with that of liberty, we are certain that it will suffice to pronounce in the first Parliament of Alta, Italy, the great principle of liberty of worship, whence it will be acclaimed the fundamental law of our redeemed country.

[Source: Camillo di Cavour, *Scritti Politici*. Nuovamente raccolti e publicati da Giovanni Gentile, Rome 1925, XL, pp. 188–9. Translated by Dr Roslyn Pesman.]

Doc. 77. GIUSEPPE MAZZINI: Humanity and the Papacy (1849)

Humanity and the Papacy — these are the two extreme terms of a controversy which is an integral part of the Providential progressive education of the human soul, and which has visibly agitated Europe for now four centuries. The substitution of the words *Liberty* and *Authority* for these two words leads to a misconception of the terms of the problem, falsifies the elements by which the question should be decided, and

C. Aspects of continental liberalism in the nineteenth century

assigns to Humanity a character of *opposition* tending to a negation of its very essence ...

[The programme of the Catholic party] is a solemn confirmation of our own convictions: Liberty is irreconcilable with the Papacy. The absolute authority of the Catholic church must remain what it was in the time of Gregory XVI, must derive inspiration solely from its own conscience, unfettered by any institutions, unrestrained by any compact or bond whatsoever. So says the orator of the Catholic party [Montalembert], and in order to render his statement as true in the future as it is in the present, he has only to cancel one thing – the conscience of the human race.

The conscience of the human race, superior to the Papacy, and to far higher than it – the conscience of the human race, which by its consent constituted the power and right of the Popes for many centuries, protests at the present day – not in the name of Liberty, but of true Authority, against that institution ...

We are no followers of the eighteenth century and Voltaire. They denied and destroyed: where they destroyed, we seek to found; where they denied, we affirm. Humanity is, now as ever, deeply, inevitably religious, and because it is religious it makes war upon the Papacy, which is not religion, but the form or phantasm of religion.

The accusation of irreligion, of mere negation of *all* authority, which is cast against democracy, is unworthy of any who take the trouble to study its most important and most potent manifestations in a spirit of impartiality. We are combating to gain a true Authority for the world; we all desire the termination of this period of crisis, in which one only of the two human criterions of truth – the conscience of Humanity and the conscience of the individual is left to us. We all demand a common faith, a common pact, an interpreter of God's Law.

The cry for liberty which bursts forth from the peoples, is in fact a cry for emancipation from the corpse of a dead authority, which usurps the place of the new. But before this pact can be indeed religious, and our souls be security for its observance, it must first be freely accepted by our conscience; before this authority can indeed govern and direct our life, it must have faith in itself, and the world have faith in it; it is necessary that it should be to us a Word of unity, of progress, and of the unceasing revelation of the truth. And we assert that not one of these essential characteristics of authority is possessed by the Papacy.

[Source: Giuseppe Mazzini, 'Rome and the French Government' (1849) in *The Life and Writings of Joseph Mazzini*, London 1869, V. Autobiographical and Political, pp. 257–60.]

Doc. 78. POPE PIUS IX: *Syllabus Errorum* (8 December 1864)

The Syllabus of the principal errors of our time, which are stigmatized in the Consistorial Allocutions, Encyclicals, and other Apostolical Letters of our Most Holy Lord, Pope Pius IX ...

VI. *Errors concerning the Civil Society, considered by itself and in relation to the Church*

39. The commonwealth, since it is the origin and source of all laws, is possessed of a type of law which can be circumscribed by no limits.
40. The doctrine of the Catholic Church is inimic to the good and well-being of human society.
41. To the civil power, even when exercised by an unbelieving ruler, belongs an indirect negative authority in religious matters; so that there belongs to it not only the right known as 'exequatur', but also the right known as 'appeal from abuse'.
42. In a legal conflict between the two powers, civil law ought to prevail.
43. The secular power has authority to rescind and declare and render void solemn undertakings (commonly called *Concordats*) concluded with the Apostolic See concerning the functioning of laws dealing with the immunity of the Church, without the consent of that See; or even in spite of its protests against such action.
44. The civil authority can intervene in matters relating to religion, morals and spiritual discipline. Hence, it can decide concerning the instructions which the clergy of the Church issue, as part of their duty, for the regulation of consciences. It can reach decisions on the administration of the divine sacraments and the dispositions necessary for their reception.
45. The whole administration of public schools, in which the youth of Christian States is educated, can and should be placed in the hands of the civil authority, with the sole exception, for a good reason, of episcopal seminaries; it should be so placed in the hands of the authority, that there may be recognised to no other authority whatever any right of intervention in the discipline of the schools, the arrangement of the studies, the conferring of degrees, or the choice or approval of the teachers.
46. Even in clerical seminaries, the method of study to be adopted is subject to the civil authority.
47. The best interest of civil society requires that the popular schools, which are open to the children from all classes and all public institutes, intended for instruction in letters and philosophy and for conducting the education of the young, should be freed from any control, directive power or supervision of the Church; and being at the complete discretion of the civil and political authority, they may be fully subjected to the civil and political power according to the prevalent opinions of the age.
48. For Catholic men, concerned with the education of youth, reason

C. Aspects of continental liberalism in the nineteenth century

can approve of what may be separated from the Catholic faith and the authority of the Church, and of those things which pertain merely to the knowledge of natural things and the ends of temporal social life either wholly or at least primarily.

49. The civil authority can impose restrictions in order that the clergy and faithful laity may not freely and mutually communicate with the Roman Pontiff.

50. The secular authority has in itself the right of 'presenting' bishops and may insist that they enter upon the administration of their dioceses before receiving canonical institution and the Apostolic Letters from the Holy See.

51. Furthermore, the secular government has the right to depose bishops from the exercise of their pastoral ministry, and it is not bound to obey the Roman Pontiff in those things which concern the institution of bishops and bishoprics.

52. The government can, by its own law, change the age prescribed by the Church for religious profession of men and women, and can direct all religious congregations not to admit anyone to the taking of solemn vows without the Government's permission.

53. The laws for the protection of religious establishments and for securing their rights and functions are to be abolished; in addition, the civil government can furnish aid to all those who wish to give up the religious life they have undertaken and to break their solemn vows; equally it can also completely suppress religious congregations, collegiate churches and simple benefices, even those belonging to private patronage, and claim their goods and revenues to be subject to the administration and disposal of the civil power.

54. Not only are kings and princes exempt from the jurisdiction of the Church, but they are even superior to the Church in deciding questions of jurisdiction.

55. The Church should be separated from the State and the State from the Church.

VII. *Errors concerning Natural and Christian Ethics*
56. Moral laws do not require Divine sanction, and there is no need for human laws to conform to the Natural Law or to receive obligatory force from God.

57. The knowledge of philosophical matters, ethics and civil laws can and should be divorced from Divine and ecclesiastical authority.

58. No forces other than material ones are to be recognized and all moral discipline and moral excellency ought to aim at the enlargement and increase of wealth by every possible means and at the enjoyment of pleasure.

59. Law consists in material fact; all human duties are only vain words and all human acts have the force of law.

60. Authority is nothing other than the result of numerical superiority and material force.
61. An unjust act, being successful, does not detract from the binding sanctity of laws.
62. The principle known as that of 'non-intervention' (i.e. of the Church in political affairs) ought to be proclaimed and observed.
63. It is lawful to refuse obedience to legitimate princes and even to rebel against them.
64. The violation of the most solemn oath or the commission of the most sinful and depraved action imaginable is not only free from blame but is even to be regarded as lawful and extremely praiseworthy in every way, when it is performed for the sake of one's country.

IX. *Errors concerning the Civil Government of the Roman Pontiff*
75. The children of the Christian and Catholic Church may differ in their opinions about the compatibility of the temporal with the spiritual power.
76. The abolition of the temporal power possessed by the Apostolic See would contribute in the highest degree, to the liberty and happiness of the Church.

X. *Errors which refer to Contemporary Liberalism*
77. In this age of ours it is no longer expedient that the Catholic religion should be treated as the sole State religion and that all other forms of religious worship should be excluded.
78. Hence certain States, called Catholic, who have provided by law that immigrants be permitted to have free exercise of their own particular religion, are to be praised.
79. Similarly, it is not true that civil liberty for any religious cult whatever and the granting to all of the full power to express any kind of opinion and thought whatever, openly and publicly, conduces to the easier corruption of the morals and minds of peoples and the spread of the pest of indifferentism.
80. The Roman Pontiff can and should reconcile himself and reach agreement with progress, liberalism and civilization, as lately introduced.

[Source: William E. Gladstone and Philip Schaff, *The Vatican Decrees in Their Bearing on Civil Allegiance*, New York 1875, pp. 118–27. Translated from the Latin text.]

Germany
(Introduction, p. 413)

Doc. 79. SYLVESTER JORDAN: On the Freedom of Faith and the Separation of Church and State
(*Speech in the National Assembly, Frankfurt-on-Main, 21 August 1848*)

Gentlemen! It gives me satisfaction that there is now a discussion in the National Assembly on the realization of the principles which I put forward and fought for already twenty years ago, and which could not be included in the specific constitution of a state (*Land*) before now. The real issue at stake is the emancipation of man, for this is the essential question. In former times man was, so to speak, submerged in two institutions, in his being a citizen and a member of the Church in earlier days. As a citizen man perished, because his religious convictions, his convictions altogether, his intellectual life were subordinated to the external laws. The first thing was to be a citizen, the second to be a human being. In the Church man perished, as he was there forbidden to think and thinking was made a crime, a crime against the Church. It was pronounced there that you shall believe what is prescribed to you, no matter whether or not in writing, and reason and man had there to subordinate themselves. The Reformation was truly opposed to this principle; it liberated man first from the pressure on his thoughts. But after the Reformation, too, man remained in the Church and under Church pressure; the Church was only partly liberated from the power of Rome and then handed over to the power of the State. It was rescued from Scylla in order to be thrown to Charybdis.

Now the relations between the Church and the State are in question. I should like, however, to put the question differently. Is it at all possible to conceive a peaceful relationship between Church and State, if both co-exist in the *old* manner, that means in their old inner essence? ... Now we are discussing the question of the separation of the Church from the State. Gentlemen! The question is whether the two heads which have so far been in conflict, shall now be separated from each other. Do you believe, gentlemen, that peace will be established when the separation is carried out? Look at individual countries of the Catholic or the Protestant creed, have they been liberated from the fetters of the Church? Has freedom of thought been restored to them or will the Church, separated from the State – I mention here only the Catholic Church – set free its co-religionists? Will it then press less hard with its dogmas on its own or on other co-religionists? Will peace last so long as dogmas are being put forward that only one Church can provide salvation?

As long as there exist two powers in the State, no matter whether they are equal or one is subordinated to the other, there will always be quarrels ... There must be only *one* power in the State, for, gentlemen, the State is an external society, in the first instance destined for temporal interests in order that man can simultaneously pursue and realise his higher spiritual objectives. That power, I say, is the State – and therefore everybody fulfils the duties of the State in order to be able to shape and develop his humanity (*Menschentum*), and thus be in a position to pursue his spiritual interests: there can only be this one power because it must be supreme; only the supreme power can rule and this is the State ... Two things are always necessary; a positive condition, that the citizen (*Untertan*) is brought up in a denomination, that means on a religious basis; and, secondly, the passive condition, that a religious organisation or the religion should never be misused or used to circumvent one's duties to the State or to hurt the feelings of others. But, as I said before, all the propositions do not mean much, and particularly not the proposition that the Church be separated from the State. My principle is that the Church must be changed into religious societies without any external Church power in the present sense ...

I had a friend who said: 'What do I bother about religion? I stick to what I learnt until my seventh year. I go to Church, I leave the remainder to the clergy.' In that manner religion is a rather indifferent matter of convention; one conforms to it in order not to be decried as a heretic, in a word, one just goes along in the company of others. There is no inner conviction; in the Catholic Church one is not allowed to secure it, for that is tabooed. (*Unrest on the Right.*) In the Protestant Church, too, one loses all desire to arrive at such a conviction and to profess it openly. However, if religion is truly free, so that everyone can follow his conviction, unimpeded by external force, he will soon convince himself of the sanctity and the importance of religion. He will convince himself of the sanctity and the importance of religion. He will enquire and reflect himself, he will join others who are of the same opinion; people of the same mind will group together; and then a type of church association will be formed which has not merely an external but a truly inner character. Religion will lose the mere external facade, which it has usually formed until now, and become an inner component of man. Only in this way, with religion receiving an inner, true consecration, can man become free as an inwardly religious person. Then no Church power will be able any longer to shake his conviction. Only then will he be freed, then only is the State protected from an attempt by an alien power to divert it from its high purpose and to incite people against the State.

Therefore, gentlemen, in order to sum up in a few words, I argue that the separation of the Church from the State, the Churches being what they are now, does not lead to any goal, because it is practically sterile, even dangerous; because the Church power would then be able to manipulate things for its private and special purposes more freely than has hitherto been the case. What matters is that the power of the Church as such should perish, and that then, in this manner, the State would exist as an independent and free power, as a true power, and also be able to protect the individual, as far as true freedom of conscience is concerned, from any interference from outside. (*Lively, continuous applause in the Assembly and from the gallery.*)

[Source: *Stenographischer Bericht über die Verhandlungen der deutschen constituierenden Nationalversammlung zu Frankfurt-am-Main*, Franz Wigard (ed.), Leipzig 1848–50, III, pp. 1646–8. Translated by the editors of this volume.]

Doc. 80. IGNAZ VON DOLLINGER: On the Freedom of Belief and the Separation of State and Church
(*Speech in the National Assembly, Frankfurt-on-Main, 22 August 1848*)

If striving for the independence of the Churches should at the same time mean striving for control of the State or a desire to interfere with the field of politics and the State, the position of the State would be bound to be much simpler and the rejection of such interference much easier. For the State would have the adversary it has to fight outside of itself instead, as is now the case, of being mixed up with it and being involved in it, having grown jointly into it in all the relations of life. As we know, this is the case to a still higher degree with the Protestant Church than with the Catholic Church at present. In Belgium there has not occurred until today a single conflict between the Church and the State power since 1831 when the principle of the freedom of the Church was proclaimed in the constitution. In North America, no one knows anything of a conflict between the State power and the individual religious societies. Further, can we deceive ourselves over the fact that the bitterness which unfortunately has developed between Catholics and Protestants in Germany has its main cause in the interference of the State? ... I believe, too, that the State power will be all the stronger, firmer and more determined to reject any intervention and interference by a Church or the clergy of any denomination in an alien, non-confessional field once the conditions, which until now have been detrimental and burdensome to all sides and parties, have ceased to exist or have improved.

In the end no German will give up the hope that we in Germany (I am referring to the two big Churches) will gradually come closer to each other; the hope that perhaps Germany, which has been fragmented for three centuries, will once more be reunited. Every German entertains this hope in one or another fashion. I should like to say that it has cost us too much of our best blood for us not to entertain the hope that one day things in Germany will again become what they once were ... When I remarked that 'things might become again in Germany what they once were', I only wanted to convey by that remark that discord would be healed one day and that reunification could take place once more.

532

Everyone is free to formulate the condition of that reunion as he likes, and to think of it in one shape or another ... I will not discuss that topic here. However, let us confess: Do we not have that hope? Do we think this state of affairs, as it is to-day, this state of separation and fragmentation will have to continue for the entire future? If we entertain that hope, and if it is impossible for us to shut our eyes to the striking experience we meet everywhere that it is just these relations between State and Church, as we said, that have so far been the main cause of the lasting, I shall not say separation, but of the frictions, of the religious animosity that has flared up again and again; then we must wish from this patriotic viewpoint, out of a regard for the welfare of Germany, that a state of affairs should be ended ... from which all parts suffer equally.

[Source: *Reden aus der ersten deutschen Nationalversammlung in der Paulskirche zu Frankfurt 1848–49*, Herman Struck (ed.), Leipzig (n.d.), pp. 37–8. Translated by the editors of this volume.]

Spain
(Introduction, p. 415)

Doc. 80a: Articles on Religion and Religious Cults in the Constitutions of Spain 1837–1931*

1. *The Constitution of 1837*
Art. 11.   The nation is obliged to maintain the cult and the ministers of the Catholic religion which Spaniards profess.

2. *The Constitution of 1845*
Art. 11.   The religion of the Spanish nation is the Apostolic Roman Catholic religion. The State binds itself to maintain the cult and its ministers.

3. *The Constitution of 1869*
Art. 21.   The nation binds itself to maintain the cult and the ministers of the Catholic religion.

   The public or private observance of any other cult is guaranteed to all foreigners resident in Spain, without any further limitations than the universal rules of morality and right.

4. *Project of the Federal Constitution of the Spanish Republic (1873)*
Art. 34.   The observance of all cults shall be free in Spain.
Art. 35.   The church is separated from the State.
Art. 36.   The direct or indirect subsidizing of any cult is forbidden to the nation or federal State and to regional states, and municipalities.
Art. 37.   Records of birth, marriage and death shall be registered by the civil authorities.

C. Aspects of continental liberalism in the nineteenth century

5. *The Constitution of 1876*

Art. 11. The Apostolic Roman Catholic religion is the religion of the State. The nation binds itself to maintain this cult and its ministers.

No one in Spanish territory shall be molested for his religious opinions, or for his observation of his particular form of worship, provided that he shows proper respect to Christian morality.

Public manifestations and ceremonies other than those of the religion of the State, however, shall not be permitted.

6. *The Constitution of the Spanish Republic, 9 December 1931*

Art. 3. The Spanish State has no official religion.

Art. 25. None of the following may be the foundation of juridical privilege: place of birth, descent, sex, social class, wealth, political ideas, or religious beliefs.

The state recognizes no distinction or titles of nobility.

Art. 26. All religious denominations shall be considered associations subject to special laws.

The State, regions, provinces, and municipalities may not maintain, favour, or subsidize financially churches and institutions.

A special law shall provide for the total extinction within two years of the State subsidy to the Church.

Those religious orders which impose by rule, in addition to the three canonical vows, the special vow of obedience to an authority other than the State, are dissolved. Their property shall be nationalized and employed for charitable and educational purposes.

The other religious orders shall be subject to a special law voted by this constitutional Cortes established on the following bases:

1. Dissolution of those orders, which, by their activities, constitute a menace to the safety of the State;
2. Registration of those which are to remain, in a special registry under the care of the ministry of justice;
3. Inability to acquire and hold, either by themselves or through an agent, any more property than that assigned, after previous justification, for their support or for the direct attainment of their particular aims;
4. Prohibition of their participation in industry, commerce, or teaching;
5. Submission to all tax laws of the country;
6. Obligation of rendering annual accounts to the State of the inversion of their funds in relation to the purposes of their association.

The property of the religious orders may be nationalised.

Art. 27. Liberty of conscience and the right to profess and practise any religion freely are guaranteed in Spanish territory, save for the respect of public morality.

Cemeteries shall be subject exclusively to civil jurisdiction. There may not be a separation of districts therein for religious reasons.

All denominations may observe their rites privately. Public manifestations of the cults must be authorised, in any case by the government.

No one may be compelled to declare officially his religious beliefs.

Religious beliefs may not affect the civil or political status of a person, except for the provisions in this constitution for the election of the President of the Republic and the selection of the president of the council of ministers.

[Source: Arnold R. Verduin, *Manual of Spanish Constitutions 1808–1931*, Michigan 1941, pp. 41, 46, 60, 70, 78, 88–9.]

---

4. Freedom, power and the nation-state: Germany 1814–1881
(Introduction, p. 418)

Doc. 81. ERNST MORITZ ARNDT: On Freedom and Fatherland (1814)

Wretched and cold wiseacres have come forward nowadays, who say in the emptiness of their hearts: Fatherland and Freedom, empty names without a meaning, beautiful sounds, with which to befool the simpletons! Where man prospers, there is his fatherland; where he is least troubled, there flourishes his freedom.

Like stupid cattle they are only motivated by the stomach and its desires, and they perceive nothing of the breeze of the divine spirit.

Like cattle they graze only to secure food for the day, and what offers them gratification of the senses seems the only certainty to them. An animal loves too; but such people do not love who carry God's image and the seal of divine reason only externally on them. But man shall love unto death and never give up his love or separate from it.

No animal is able to do this, for it forgets easily; nor can an animal-like human being do so because only indulgence suits him.

Therefore, oh man, you have a fatherland, a holy land, a loved land, a soil of which your longing always dreams and to which it aspires forever.

Where God's sun shone first on you, where his lightning first manifested his all-powerfulness to you and his stormy winds first raged through your soul with sacred fear, there is your fatherland.

Where the first pair of human eyes bent lovingly over your cradle, where your mother first carried you joyfully in her lap and your father instilled the lessons of wisdom in your heart, there is your love, there is your fatherland.

535

C. Aspects of continental liberalism in the nineteenth century

Even if it consisted of nothing but bare rocks and desolate islands, and if poverty and toil dwell there with you, you must love the land forever; for you are a human being and shall not forget but remember it in your heart.

Freedom is also no empty dream and no wild folly; but in it live your courage and your pride and the certitude that your origin is in heaven.

Freedom is where you may live as it pleases a brave heart; where you may live in accordance with the customs and ways and laws of your fathers; where what makes you happy already made your great-grandfather happy; where no foreign tyrants boss you and no foreign drivers drive you on, as one drives the cattle on with the stick.

This fatherland and this freedom are the most sacred things on earth, a treasure in which are hidden infinite love and faithfulness, the noblest possession that a good human being has and desired to have.

And therefore they are an illusion and a folly in the eyes of the vulgar, to all who live for the moment.

However, they raise the brave to the sky and achieve miracles in the hearts of the simple.

Onward then, you honest German! Pray to God every day that he may fill your heart with strength and kindle your soul with confidence and courage.

That no love should be more sacred to you than the love of the fatherland and no joy sweeter to you than the joy of freedom.

That you may regain that of which traitors cheated you, and obtain by blood what fools let slip.

For the serf is a cunning and avaricious animal, and the man without a fatherland the most wretched of all men.

[Source: 'Katechismus für den deutschen Kriegs-und Wehrmann' (1814) reprinted in E. M. Arndt, *Staat und Vaterland. Eine Auswahl aus seinen politischen Schriften*, ed. Ernst Müsebeck, Munich 1921, pp. 13–14. Translated by the editors of this volume.]

Doc. 82. ERNST MORITZ ARNDT: The Constitution and the Peasants (1815)

They turned round the old things and refurbished them a little; they gave them a few new colours and titles; and we are now asked to believe that the things have really become something new. However, we cannot be misled by individual trifles; we must call this constitution* one made by

* Hanover which had been raised to a Kingdom at the Congress of Vienna in 1814 was given a General Assembly of Estates (*Allgemeine Ständeversammlung*) in the same year. The emancipation of the peasants was carried out there after the Prussian models between 1831 and 1833. A proper constitution was granted in 1833 which provided for a limited participation of the townspeople and the peasants in the affairs of the state. However, when in 1837 Ernest August, Duke of Cumberland, became King of Hanover (on the accession of Queen Victoria to the throne in Britain), one of his first steps was to suspend the constitution.

the aristocracy and for the aristocracy and to its advantage; we must call it an aristocratic constitution. With this we come at the same time to the conclusion that it is a constitution unsuited for this age, an age more easily compatible with anything than the aristocracy.

We had expected that the Government of Hanover would begin to give the towns a freer (municipal) constitution as has been done in Prussia since 1807, in order to awaken civic spirit and pride and courage towards freedom and law, and to prepare for the dignified fight for the noblest values in life among the various classes in society.

We had also hoped that the peasants, the largest and most respectable section of the people, would be allowed to send their delegates to the public sessions. Yet this has not happened. In its draft the Government had forgotten those who in most states of Germany have far too long been regarded and treated as deaf and dumb. Instead the nobility of Hanover declared very innocently: as they (the nobility) were above all appearing in the Diets in their capacity as landowners, the peasants did not need any special representatives, as the latter were adequately represented by them. It was just as if at a Reich assembly of the animals, the dogs declared: the hares need not send any delegates, we will run and bark for them. At home and abroad all people of good faith were bound to dislike that this Estate (*Stand*), which in fact carries the state more than all the others, has been so completely excluded. Fortunately, the time has passed when, as Lichtenberg remarks somewhere, the rich and the noble were allowed to speculate whether or not a farmer-general would one day invent an ointment with which to grease the peasants so that they could produce wool and be shorn in June.

But enough of such jokes and especially with this joke that might appear as a mockery. If one honours the nobility as something that is to take a necessary place in the state and is to be respected as such, one may say the same, if not with greater right, of the peasantry. I need not prove here how the nobility opposes the latter as an Estate, although both have this in common that they own country property and cultivate it and have it cultivated. History proves this best, as it showed during long centuries and still shows it to this day, that when laws did not bind the nobility and when very small landowners as an independent Estate did not confront it, it has always endeavoured to make the peasants its serfs and in this it has usually succeeded only too well. As history proves this, it can rightly be said that the peasants are represented worst and most unnaturally by those whose advantage is in many respects contrary to their own and whose Estate and purpose of Estate have hardly anything in common with theirs. When speaking here for the peasant, one has in mind the old worthy dictum: To everyone his own.

If anyone should try to excuse the worthy delegates (*die Herren Landboten*), it would not be easy. They have well realised that they have acted against the spirit of the age and against the opinion of their own people

C. Aspects of continental liberalism in the nineteenth century

and of the German people, and that they have not done or organised what they should have done or organised if they had regarded the honour and the advantage of all more sacred than that of individuals. The question has been raised whether the sessions and deliberations (of the delegates) should be made public, and their uneasy conscience has been shocked by this cheeky and admittedly somewhat English question. Yes, the greatest issue has been regarded in such a ridiculous and wretched fashion by many, as if a ball or a club was at stake.

Realizing that our age, and altogether that the idea of a proper constitution and administration, demanded the frankest and most complete publicity, they proposed that each member of the Assembly of the Estates** should be granted a free admission ticket to bring along one listener. (It was understood that the member was held responsible for the true and undangerous mentality of his guest.) In the end most members found this too clumsy, and it was decided that they would keep their secrets to themselves and would bar all troublesome and curious listeners and critics.

[Source: Article by E. M. Arndt in *Der Wächter*, a periodical published in Cologne in 1815. Third issue *Die Aristokratie*. Reprinted in F. Federici, *Der Deutsche Liberalismus*, Zürich 1946, pp. 64–6. Translated by the editors of this volume.]

Doc. 83. FRIEDRICH CHRISTOPH DAHLMANN: On the Right of Resistance (1835)

Yet what justifies or excuses the deed of revolution does not eliminate its consequences. Any revolution is not only proof of an immense misfortune which has befallen the state and of a guilt, by no means only one-sided, but is in itself a misfortune, burdened itself by guilt. Therefore wise and conscientious men will neither present the success of a revolution as its justification, because it guarantees them freedom of punishment, nor raise their hesitant hand to acts of resistance as if there remained no other means of escaping the general degradation. For what is intended alone against the ruler of the dynasty, easily becomes excessive as a revolution of the entire social order; and even if the better will of the new regime could be safe-guarded, will it be able to establish itself? For that reason, can a revolution once established also be adhered to worthily by the patriot, by the same man who had disapproved of its outbreak, because a state of affairs must not last in which the government is nowhere because it is everywhere. It has always been regarded as unworthy of a good citizen to emigrate or to shun one's obligations at a time when all the good elements in the state should come closer together.

Even the revolution which has the best intentions is a serious crisis,

** Of the Kingdom of Hanover.

confusing the conscience of the people, interrupting inner security and no less endangering all state treaties, for these are based on an undisputed government which is therefore capable of being recognised. There are, it is true, some cases where the destruction inevitably connected with every revolution has disappeared at the time of restoration; or where it happened more as an occurrence than according to a thought out plan, as was the case when Gustav Vasa became king;* and in even more rare cases, the strength of the part of the Constitution which continues without violation to supplement the impaired state body and to confine the unruly chaos without a ruler to a very short period, as in England in 1689, where then the best thing possible happened, the question does not arise whether what happened was according to the law.

The revolutionary mentality which calculates revolutions, like a public entertainment, for which one should not have to wait too long, is much more remote from patriotism than is the indolent adoration of all the traditional country *mores* about which it feels so very much superior. Patriotism has its roots in the places which surrounded the cradle of a human being. Perhaps it sticks to them and shuts its eye on a provincial basis to the development of nation and state in their large-scale dimensions. However, the more restricted mind remains loyal to the most human desires which keep together the 24 hours of every day until perhaps the hour of emergency forces him to look further afield. The revolutionary mentality has its shallow roots in the intellect, is without family ties, without a home country. Only the large scale relations count for it. It would like to transform the century no matter if the nearest home country with its happiness and its contours becomes a victim of the revolution. It is true posterity will not grant honour to political quietism, which it bestows on itself extravagantly; but he who administers the realm well in which everyone is a born king, has the control of his own soul and produces an image of the good state in the family, improves the public morals which are the carrier of all progressive institutions and preserves one inviolable realm of freedom even under despotism.

[Source: Friedrich Christoph Dahlmann, *Die Politick auf den Grund und das Maass der gegebenen Zustände zurückgeführt*, 2nd edn, Leipzig 1847, pp. 202–4. Translated by the editors of this volume.]

Doc. 84. DAVID HANSEMANN: Freedom and Patriotism. The Necessity of Freedom (1840)

You who believe that in Prussia tutelage of a people and its lack of freedom (*Unfreiheit*) could be a permanent, normal state of affairs, if only a mild and humane regime caring for material welfare is connected with it and at most some scant freedom in local affairs is granted, you

* Gustav I. G. Ericson Vasa became King of Sweden in 1523.

C. Aspects of continental liberalism in the nineteenth century

will not argue that you possess sufficient guarantees of a strong, powerful Prussian Empire (*Reich*) without a general, lively, national patriotism. Powerful and strong the Empire must be for the preservation of Prussian and German independence, for we have dangerous neighbours in the East and in the West. There (in the East) the most tenaciously conquering State since the days of the Romans, which, while already deeply penetrating into the Prussian provinces, has taken up a threatening position and in the nature of things regards the acquisition of the country lying between this position and the Baltic Sea as its further aim – a goal against the obtaining of which ties of blood relationship and friendship among the monarchs cannot provide a lasting security. Here, in the West, is a State dangerous through the concentration of its forces, the bellicose and excitable mentality of its inhabitants and the fatal fixed idea that they must sooner or later possess the frontier of the Rhine to its mouth. And let us not hide our weak spots! The danger is still amplified through other circumstances. Prussia's provinces do not lie in a concentrated position, but there are large distances between their furthest frontier points. And the patriotism of the people must be lively, general and national. It must not only awaken to enthusiasm and to devoted sacrifice when the foreigner presses us hard with burdens and shame (as was unfortunately the case in former days), but it must do so as soon as our national independence and honour are in danger. Only freedom can create such patriotism in Prussia.

Social conditions differ greatly in the provinces of Prussia. Her inhabitants even differ in their racial origins; one province gives the impression of a withering nationality, has few Germanic elements and is averse to ties with the state for certain political reasons. National feeling has so little penetrated the essence of the people that the majority of the inhabitants of the Western provinces do not shudder at the idea of ceding part of the Easternmost provinces as if it were a national calamity. On the other hand, in the Eastern provinces, the view is often expressed without a feeling of shame that the *Rheinland* is a burden for Prussia and her loss would by no means be lamentable. Such a state of affairs and such attitudes can lead the Empire to an abyss, once the time of danger has come.

Only freedom can raise the national feeling so much that compared with it provincial differences disappear, and, in particular, that a certain fading nationality sincerely joins the new fatherland with which it is connected.[1]

Belgium is an example of how quickly national feeling develops through political freedom where it had not existed earlier or had been pushed into the background through the differences of views and interests. Although after only ten years of the existence of this freedom the work of national amalgamation cannot yet be regarded as complete, even a biased observer must admit that great progress has been made in this field. Alsace and the pro-French mentality prevailing there can also be quoted as an instructive example.

[Source: David Hansemann, 'Memorandum on Prussia's Position and Politics, August-September 1840' in J. Hansen (ed.) *Rheinische Briefe und Akten zur Geschichte der politischen Bewegung*, (1830–1850), Essen 1919, I, 1830–1845, pp. 216–18. Translated by the editors of this volume.]

Editors' Note

1. In a footnote Hansemann makes it clear that he refers here to the Polish element in the Eastern Provinces of Prussia.

Doc. 85. The Offenburg Programme of the South-West German Democrats (10 September 1847)

Art. 1. We demand that our State Government should renounce the Carlsbad Decrees of 1819, the Frankfurt Decrees of 1831 and 1832 and the Vienna Decrees of 1834. These Decrees equally violate our inalienable human rights as do the Acts of the German Confederation and our State Constitution.

Art. 2. We demand freedom of the press: We must not be deprived any longer of the inalienable right of the human mind to communicate his ideas without mutilation.

Art. 3. We demand freedom of conscience and of teaching. The relationship between man and his God belongs to man's most intimate sphere and no exterior power must presume to determine it at its discretion. Every religious creed can therefore claim to have equal rights in the state. No power should interfere between the teachers and those who learn. Teaching should not be divided by any religious creed.

Art. 4. We demand that the military should take an oath on the Constitution. The citizen, who is given arms by the state, should, like the other citizens, confirm his loyalty to the Constitution by oath.

Art. 5. We demand personal freedom. The police should cease to tutor and to torment the citizen. The right of association, a spontaneous communal life, the right of the people to assemble and to talk, the right of the individual to move about and to do so freely on the soil of the German fatherland should be undisturbed from now on.

Art. 6. We demand representation of the people at the German Confederation. The German should be given a fatherland and a voice in its affairs. Justice and freedom in our domestic life, and a firm position vis-à-vis foreign countries are due to us as a nation.

Art. 7. We demand a people's militia. The citizen trained in the handling of arms, and armed, alone can protect the state. The people should be given arms and be relieved from the intolerable burden imposed on them by standing armies.

C. Aspects of continental liberalism in the nineteenth century

Art. 8. We demand just taxation. Everyone should contribute to meet the charges of the state according to his ability. The present tax should be replaced by a progressive income tax.

Art. 9. We demand that education through teaching should be equally accessible to all. The means for it have to be provided by all people in just proportions.

Art. 10. We demand a re-adjustment in the disparity between labour and capital. Society has the obligation to raise and protect labour.

Art. 11. We demand laws worthy of free citizens and which are applied by juries. The citizen should be judged by his fellow-citizens. The system of justice should be a matter of the people.

Art. 12. We demand an administration of the state by the people. The spontaneous life of a people needs free organs. The forces cannot be regulated and fixed by bureaucratic offices. The place of the multiple regime of officials should be taken by self-government of the people.

Art. 13. We demand the abolition of all privileges. For everybody the respect of his free fellow-citizens should be his only privilege and reward.

[Source: *Dokumente zur deutschen Verfassungsgeschichte*, ed. E. R. Huber, Stuttgart 1961, I, pp. 260–1. Translated by the editors of this volume.]

Doc. 86. The Heppenheim Programme of the South-West German Liberals (19 October 1847)

The meeting expressed itself in favour of enlarging the German Customs Union to an overall German Association, a step which would promote the 'aim of uniting Germany through a German policy and a joint direction of national interests.'* The meeting also decided to press in all existing German diets for liberal reforms. These included: 'the liberation of the press, so that Germans can participate in the unfettered impact of this most powerful means of culture (*Bildung*) and be freed from the shame so often thrown in their faces by foreigners because they have not yet achieved one of the highest goods of free nations that has been promised to them; further public and oral procedure at the courts with juries; separation of the administration from the judiciary; the transfer of all branches of the judiciary, of administrative justices and the police power of punishment to the courts, and formulation of relevant police punitive laws; liberation of the soil and of its cultivation from mediaeval burdens; independence for the communities in the administration of their affairs; a decrease in expenses for the standing army, and the introduction of a

* It was declared 'undoubtable that in the course of development of the century and of Germany, unification by the rule of force was impossible and was only to be obtained through and with freedom'.

people's militia were fully discussed. So too were the constitutional means which are suited to push forward the just demands of the people. Above all, the means against impoverishment and misery, as well as the taxation system connected with them, took up the time and attention of the meeting. As, however, such important and comprehensive themes could not be brought in a few hours to a joint decision on certain proposals, as were frequently put forward on the direction of the poor and of education, on income tax etc., a committee was formed by deputies from various countries. It will report systematically next year about the taxation system and the conditions of the poorer classes, and make proposals in this context with special emphasis on a just distribution of the public taxes for the alleviation of the lower middle classes and of the workers.'

[Source: *Deutsche Zeitung*, Heidelberg, 15 October 1847, reprinted in *Dokumente zur deutschen Verfassungsgeschichte*, ed. E. R. Huber, Stuttgart 1961, I, pp. 262–4. Translated by the editors of this volume.]

Doc. 87. German liberals at the Crossroads – For or Against Bismarck, 1863–1866

(a) Hermann Baumgarten to Heinrich von Sybel, Karlsruhe, 22 May 1863

Prussia has presumably a bad future if her fate remains dependent on the insight and the will-power of the Hohenzollern, if the people themselves do not take the matter into their own hands. Human beings who are as narrow-minded as they are conceited have to be compelled to become reasonable or one has to get rid of them altogether. I would, of course, prefer the former and, owing to experiences made elsewhere, not despair of success. But, of course, one has really to mean business and to bring about in the persons concerned the very definite feeling that for them everything is at stake, if they do not become reasonable very soon. For that purpose the speeches in the House of Representatives do not seem to me to suffice; no, the entire country must make a stand and express its will very decidedly. It seems to me and to us that the struggle in Prussia has been so far waged too tamely. People who despise the Constitution, reason and the law like naughty boys must be made to tremble. You have to produce a lively concern in them that they might be beaten to death one day like mad dogs. You have to impress on them a strong passionate determination to go to extremes in the worst case. Such a way of fighting certainly does not appeal to the taste of civilised men. Yet it is not our taste that matters but what is necessary. If you allow Bismarck to rule the roost, even if only for the time being, revolution seems to me inevitable. If Prussia puts up with such a regime permanently, her position in Germany and Europe would be finished. The question is therefore how

C. Aspects of continental liberalism in the nineteenth century

to prevent such terrible dangers. Let just indignation express itself fully and energetically! Send combined deputations from all the towns and districts to Berlin! Let them go to the castle, accompanied by thousands of the most respected citizens and let them use very serious and very determined language! They do by this only what the English among other things did against North's ministry in 1770. It is possible that you will disturb the peace by doing this. But, on the other hand, you have the certitude of a terrible revolution or a deep humiliation ...

(b) Heinrich von Sybel to Hermann Baumgarten, Berlin, 26 May 1863
The plan [of mass deputations to the King] which you suggest has often been discussed here since December. I have always been in its favour for I believe, too, that if the thing succeeds it would make a certain impression in the highest quarters. But the leaders of the Progressive Party have until now been of the opinion that it would be difficult to get the people moving for this very purpose. It would be highly unpopular still now to petition that man [Bismarck]. And it would be a great defeat if the demonstration should turn out to be thin. On the other hand, should it succeed the gain would be smaller than you imagine.

If 40,000 deputies should come for one day, they would be given a polite refusal as a reply and would go home. Certainly it would be another chapter of agitation and indignation, but I can assure you we are having already an abundance of these things in Prussia. Thus I cannot very much contradict that calculation of the chances made by the Progressive Party. Our powers-that-be have long ago given up trembling before the addresses, the deputations and the mood of the people. They know very well how categorically they are condemned by the latter. Their only question is: have we sufficient money and reliable soldiers? They tremble before every non-commissioned officer who reads the *Volkszeitung* and before any word in parliament which might attract the soldiers, but not before anything else. From their point of view they are right; as long as the army is reliable, the people *cannot* use material force. Their regime will continue until the army declares itself in favour of the constitution or until it is broken in a foreign war ... These circumstances are to us who live here mercilessly clear, and I must therefore also protect the Prussian people against your remark that they would be exposed to just contempt in Germany by a long duration of the regime. Should Germany condemn us for this she would in my opinion pass an overhasty judgement against herself. As long as a disciplined army of 200,000 men keeps together in obedience and discipline a people has never achieved anything by violence. In 1789 the army revolted together with the people; in 1830 Charles had hardly 12,000 soldiers in Paris under the weakest leadership. In 1848 half the Government there was in favour of the revolt, and so also was a large section of the officer corps. Whether a *coup de main* would be possible today, as was the case with us in 1848, is doubtful to all sensible people and revolutionaries here. I have had no practical experience in this field, but I can assure you that I have not heard a different opinion from anybody, and I know very well how Bismarck is longing more strongly for a revolt (*émeute*) than Napoleon [III] did on 2 December [1851].

(c) Hermann Baumgarten to Heinrich von Sybel, Karlsruhe, 11 May 1866

... I am happy that on the whole you view the situation as we do. Our friend* was called to Berlin to advise and help. He found Bismarck as we can only want him to be: determined, forceful, clever and fully aware that the situation is demanding a different home policy. But he is hard pressed by two difficulties: above him and beside him. Above him one does not yet want to realize such a necessity, one wants to stand or fall with the ministry, one does not recognise the foreign situation clearly either. One thinks more or less only of waging a defensive war. One desires the annexation of the Duchies [of Schleswig-Holstein], but neither its preconditions nor its consequences. Beside him [Bismarck] they are incapable, lame, stupid. Despite this, and his own illness, he has directed politics with a skill and a quick-wittedness which you will also find unusual ...

We regard it as our duty to do everything possible in order to draw the attention of the liberals in North Germany and Prussia to the immense danger and significance of the present moment, and to tell you that if you seize the given fact of the war energetically and throw the entire strength of the people on to the Prussian side, Prussia will of necessity have to take the line of the people. If Bismarck wins with the vigorous support of the popular forces, a liberal Prussia will win: If he wins while the liberals share the lament of the *Kölnische Zeitung* and of the Jewish *Volkszeitung* then the Prussian people will turn their backs on liberalism. If Austria wins the fate of the liberals is a matter of course. You can also in the end bring Prussia into a position of having to beg for the assistance of Napoleon [III]. In this serious situation we direct our urgent request to you to raise your weighty voice in order to show to the people that the fatherland stands above the Party ...

Prussia should certainly realize what superiority Bismarck is creating for her in Europe, and how suicidal it is if she turns her fury blindly against the man before whom all the enemies of Prussia tremble. One should recall to the memories of the people that in 1859 the fury of South Germany against the Prussia of the liberal era was infinitely greater than it is today against the Prussia of Bismarck, and that there is only one way, if Prussia really wants to ease the burden of her army; the effective usage of German forces, and, further, that these cannot be utilised

---

* Franz Freiherr von Roggenbach (1825–1907), a liberal statesman in Baden, who had changed from a critic to an admirer of Bismarck's policies.

C. Aspects of continental liberalism in the nineteenth century

without a war against Austria. A liberal ministry would hardly get the
dynasty, the nobility and the military party to accept the war, and it
would perhaps shirk the responsibility of doing so. But, as someone else
has taken it upon himself, we should accept the bitter necessity and use a
chance which could hardly have better offered itself to us.

*(d) Hermann Baumgarten to Heinrich von Sybel, Karlsruhe, 23 June
1866*
I need not say that the events of the last eight days have not failed to
make an impression here too. The South German newspapers had
nothing to report but Prussian victories for eight days, and the
*Schwäbischer Merkur** registers them in a manner which is highly amusing. Blind confidence in the Austrian brothers is seriously shaken and the
non-arrival of the revolution in Prussia is a highly sore spot. Nobody
knows what Bavaria is doing. Should you be victorious in Bohemia, Herr
von der Pfordten† will become very neutral. I suppose that Napoleon's
attitude makes a strong impact on Munich. He is furious with the
medium-sized states. He will never concede a victory to Austria. You can
regard this at least for the present as positive.

As far as I am concerned you can imagine that my position is highly
painful. To have to be an onlooker with tied hands at this moment which
is decisive for the future! I would be happy if, like Treitschke, I could
resign with a good conscience and go North.‡ As things are, I shall wait
for the time being. If Prussia continues to be victorious I shall be redun-
dant in the North. But should she suffer a heavy defeat, I don't believe
anything could retain me here. This is a time like 1813 where everyone
has to bring sacrifices. Meanwhile I am in a position to be proud of
Prussia for the first time. How Bismarck is fulfilling our hopes, how the
Prussian people exceed all our expectations!

However, I fear liberalism has badly lost the game. Had the good men
in Berlin listened to my warning at the end of May a rescue would still
have been possible. Now, I fear, it will come as I predicted: the people
will turn their backs on liberalism. These are, however, minor worries.
First a great state, then we can wait and see about the other things.

[Source: *Deutscher Liberalismus im Zeitalter Bismarcks. Eine politische Briefsammlung.*
Band I, *Die Sturmjahre der preussisch-deutschen Einigung 1859–1870 Politische Briefe
aus dem Nachlass liberaler Parteiführer.* Ausgewählt und bearbeitet von Julius
Heyderhoff, Osnabrück 1967, pp. 151–3, 281–4 and 313–5. Translated by the editors of
this volume.]

* A daily newspaper, published in Stuttgart.
† Ludwig Freiherr von der Pfordten, Prime Minister of Bavaria from 1849 to 1859 and
again from December 1864 to December 1866.
‡ Heinrich von Treitschke gave up his Chair in History at the University of Freiburg in
Baden when that country sided with Austria during the Prussian-Austrian war in 1866.

Doc. 88. HERMANN BAUMGARTEN: German Liberalism: A Self Criticism (1866)

Today the doubts about what is possible in Germany have been dissolved not only in thinking people but even more so in nearly the entire mass of the nation. They touch the existing German power with their hands. They saw and felt its deeds and these deeds are of such irresistible force after the long, sad misery of our powerlessness that the mentality of the Germans has experienced changes during a few months for which we could not have hoped for decades. All the insoluble problems with which we were troubled for eighteen years suddenly disappeared from our horizon. Only a single problem has remained which, it is true, will still require much work, but we can hope for its solution, as the existing conditions and efforts now lead all to the same point while formerly they tore them asunder in all directions.

Now it is only the question of how the small states can find a healthy relationship with the undeniably dominating Prussia. It is a fact about which only the most obstinate Swabian democrat can fool himself in doubting that Prussia is the German power and that all the other countries are only unsteady fragments, only able to secure their existence through a close and honest connection (*Anschluss*) with her. This beneficial simplification of our situation, this happiness we feel that at last we have firm soil under our feet, is certainly going shortly to push back our political bad habits and let the sturdy health which we, thank God, enjoy in other fields become profitable in our politics too. The chatterboxes who until now occupied the bulk of our political stage will have no more luck in the sharp, clear air in which we are now moving. After having experienced on the largest scale what action means, we shall no longer enjoy having our ears tickled by high faluting phrases. As the work of the political dilettantes has so completely failed, we shall demand that, in the large political structure through which we have entered the life of the world, the whole seriousness and virile efficiency, which in all other fields have long been taken for granted by us, should prove themselves. After we experienced that in a monarchical state the nobility forms an indispensable element, and after we saw that these much maligned Junkers know how to fight and to die for the fatherland in spite of the best liberal, we shall limit our bourgeois conceit a little and be modest enough to maintain an honourable place beside the nobility. We thought to turn the German world fundamentally upside down by our agitation; in fact we were about to get rid of ourselves. I think we shall take the experience to heart. We have realized through the greatest events that our eyes have seen how extremely fickle those hypotheses were on which we had built, as if on rocks, our national and liberal policies during the last few years.

C. Aspects of continental liberalism in the nineteenth century

The facts have proved nearly all the elements of our political system erroneous.

We need only to look back a short while in order to realize the infinite wealth of the blessings accorded to us. Certainly such a salvation will be the beginning of quite a new development, in which all its parts will co-operate, for a people that erred for centuries in the desert of statelessness and was so long a nobody among the nations and whose best forces degenerated.

We have experienced in the case of Prussia what such facts are capable of doing. Whether we look at the crown, the ministers, the nobility, the military or at the deputies, the magistrates, the newspapers, they all have changed, they all have learned great things. And this process of learning has its strength not only in the ideas of reason but also in the inclinations of the heart. They do not only think differently, they also feel differently. Three months ago the call: 'Party or Fatherland?' was answered from all sides by 'Party!' Today they all pay homage to the fatherland.

Truly, it has become a pleasure to work for the public interest. Until now it was a harsh, sad service only carried out from duty. Now the finest reward makes it attractive and we have only to do one task, that is, to overcome certain prejudices, to do away with certain weaknesses which cling to us in our unfortunate past. As soon as German Liberalism stands up for the great facts which it acknowledges, with full devotion and unaffected by minor misgivings, there can be no doubt that the next decade will bring us the German state that has become as much a compulsory need for our science, art and morals as it has for our political development and position of national power. Only we can hinder this wholesome process, only we could push ourselves back into the old misery . . .

In concluding these reflections I am again troubled by the doubt which made me refrain from the task for so long and which during its execution was so often a handicap, the doubt whether a self-criticism, as I dare to carry it out, should not be based on a better personal calling than that I can claim for myself . . . I have the feeling of having carried out a hard, thankless, but necessary duty. I am prepared to be blamed by many, perhaps to be violently attacked by some. I will gladly put up with the discomfort connected with the task, if it only can be of some advantage to the fatherland and to the party to which it is dedicated . . .

There will probably be no lack of people who will call a betrayal of the Party that which only loyal devotion to the Party could cause me to do. Did I not care for liberalism, well, I would not have bothered so much about it. I am of the firm conviction that a satisfactory solution of our political tasks will only succeed if liberalism ceases to be primarily in opposition, if it manages to satisfy certain important interests of the nation for which it only has a full and sincere understanding, and by its own activity in the government when we shall obtain a beneficial and refreshing alternative between liberal and conservative governments. *Liberalism must become capable of governing (regierungsfähig)*. Admittedly I cannot help those who see a degeneration of liberal greatness in the idea that instead of making unlimited demands in opposition, it should do a minimum as a government. However, I trust that no-one will dare to call a defection from liberalism, the demand that liberalism should at last become a power which implements its own ideas. I am far from drawing a line beyond which liberalism should not exercise this power; it should be exercised by it with full vigour as far as its power really stretches. I only wish it would cease to lose all its real power through illusions about the extent of its strength.

I did not want to write a history of liberalism nor a sketch, however slight, of the development of our most recent German politics, but only a self-criticism. I had, therefore, to dwell on the weaknesses of liberal politics with full emphasis, untroubled by the worry that other parties might profit from the candid straightforwardness of my judgements ... The others have known and used our weaknesses for a long time, and nothing will be easier than to counter their arrogance when we have freed ourselves from the fetters which we have carried until now. The political position held by us at the moment can only gain through earnest self-criticism. If we kept to the political method pursued by us until the beginning of August, we would destroy ourselves very soon. But if we listen to the serious lessons of the most recent past, we shall regain the importance due to us.

In conclusion, I must add a short remark about another point. Hardly anything will give greater offence to my party friends than what I said about the necessary position of the nobility in the constitutional monarchy. And yet nothing is more irrefutable to me. Our future will essentially depend on the attitude of the nobility in the new state that has been granted to us. If the nobility continues on the unfortunate course that the Prussian House of Lords and nearly all the Upper Chambers in Germany have so far pursued, we shall have every reason to fear for the monarchy or for freedom. But might we not hope that the perverse situation of our public life until recently was mainly responsible for this bad attitude of our nobility just as it was for the errors of liberalism – and further, that the beneficial role of a real state, in which alone there is room for a real aristocracy, will quickly separate truly noble views and efforts from the wretched ways of the Junkers, the sick product of thoroughly unhealthy political conditions? I think the new German state will no longer be too small for the Peers in order to serve it in an outstanding way. I even hope that some of our princes will learn the feeling that it is more glorious and honourable to be a Peer in this German state than to continue the disagreeable embarrassments of territorial sovereignty, divested of all real power. It seems to me that the German way (*die deutsche Art*) which is completely different from the envious egalitarianism of the French, would in every way facilitate a return of our higher nobility, from the false position into which the unfortunate course of our Imperial policy lured it, to the infinitely honourable and blessed calling of a true aristocracy. In any case, it is the duty·of an enlightened liberal policy in every way to assist this transformation of our nobility. However, the decisive steps can be taken only by the nobility itself, and by a royalty which has risen too high to show still any favour to the petty desires of a needy pseudo-nobility.

[Source: *Der Deutsche Liberalismus. Eine Selbstkritik* (1866), reprinted in Hermann Baumgarten, *Historische und Politische Aufsätze und Reden*, ed. Erich Marcks, Strassburg 1894, pp. 210–16. Translated by the editors of this volume.]

Doc. 89. Programme of the Progressive Party in Prussia (6 June 1861)

In November of this year the legislative period of the present Diet comes to an end. Thus still in the course of the year the entire nation will be called upon to a new election of its deputies. The pressing seriousness of our time, the uncertain position of the external relations of our fatherland, the domestic difficulties which the present Diet was unable to face, oblige every Prussian entitled to vote more than ever to express his political conviction diligently and fearlessly by exercising his right to vote. In order to fulfil this duty and to provide a firm focal point for the fellow citizens who share our conviction at the forthcoming elections, we express already the political principles guiding us for them, in the following election programme.

'We are united in our loyalty to the King and in our firm conviction that the Constitution is the insoluble tie which keeps princes and people together. However, with a view to the big and far-reaching changes in the states' system of Europe, we have arrived also at the clear realisation that the existence and greatness of Prussia depends on the firm unification of Germany which cannot be imagined without a strong, central power in the hands of Prussia and without a joint German people's representation.

As for our internal institutions, we demand a firm, liberal Government which sees its strength in the respect for the constitutional rights of the citizens, which knows how to enforce ruthlessly their principles with all sections of the Public Servants, and in this way creates and maintains the respect of the other German tribes (*Stämme*) for us.

In the field of legislation a strong and consistent implementation of the constitutional state based on law seems to us to be the first and absolute necessity. We particularly demand, therefore, protection of the law through really independent judges and that this protection should be equally accessible to everybody ...

We demand further that the decree of the law on the responsibility of the ministers, promised in article 61 of the Constitution, will at last be issued. In the interests of Prussia's honour, and for an extension of the Constitution, it appears no less necessary to bring about a constitutional organisation of the municipalities, districts, and provinces based on the principles of equality of rights and of self-administration, and to eliminate the Estate principle and the police function of the lord of the manor.

The equality of all religious associations guaranteed in article 12 of the Constitution must emphatically be preserved.

The improvement of education in the elementary as well as in the secondary schools can only be carried by at least the issuing of a Law on Education, and by the abolition of the existing ministerial directives and orders contrary to the Constitution. In this Law on Education, as well as in the urgent legislation on marriage, the separation of the Church from the State must be maintained and completed – in the case of the laws on marriage, through the acceptance of obligatory civil marriage.

For the honour and power prestige of our Fatherland sacrifices will never be too great for us should these values have to be preserved or achieved by war. However, in the interest of effective warfare, the greatest economy in the military Budget seems to us imperative in times of peace. We are convinced that the maintenance of the Army Reserve (*Landwehr*), the general introduction of the physical training of youth, the increased call-up of men capable of military service, with a two-year period of service, guarantee the complete effectiveness of the Prussian people under arms in times of war.

The obtaining of these aims, however, and this must be absolutely clear to the most stupid person after the history of the last three years, will remain a pious wish as long as there is no thorough reform of the present House of Lords (*Herrenhaus*). This above all has therefore to be aimed at energetically as the beginning of all reform.

We now ask all people with the same views to elect men who carry these principles, the principles of the German Progressive Party, deep in their hearts, and whose character and external position are guarantees that they will profess these principles frankly and unimpeded by considerations of any kind in the House of Deputies.

Finally, we regard it as the duty of every person who shares these opinions, and whom his fellow-citizens want to elect as a deputy, to put aside all his own interests and to respond to the confidence of his fellow citizens by accepting the mandate. In a constitutional state goals can only be achieved by exercising constitutional rights fearlessly as well as consequently and tenaciously ...'

[Source: *Die deutschen Parteiprogramme*, ed. Felix Salomon, Leipzig-Berlin 1907, I, pp. 44. Translated by the editors of this volume.]

Doc. 90. Programme of the National Liberal Party (12 June 1867)

When last year the old Confederation collapsed and the Prussian Government expressed its serious desire to preserve the national tie and to put German unity on a firmer foundation, we had no doubt that the liberal forces of the nation had to co-operate if the work of unification was to succeed and was at the same time to satisfy the need for freedom in our nation. For the sake of that purpose, we were prepared to co-operate. This was only made possible when the Government gave up the violation of the Law of the Constitution, and acknowledged the principles so strongly defended by the Liberal Party by asking for an indemnity which was granted. In order to secure that co-operation, the groupings within the Party caused by the quarrel over the Constitution were not sufficient. The new need was met by the formation of the National Liberal Party with the purpose of bringing about the unity of Germany on the given fundaments, a unity tending towards Power and Freedom.

We have never underestimated the difficulty of the task of furthering the development towards freedom with imperfect constitutional weapons, and in co-operation with a Government that had maintained the constitutional conflict for years and had ruled without a lawful budget. But we entered upon this task with the firm will to overcome the difficulty by continuous, serious work, and with the confidence that the greatness of the goal will strengthen the energy of the people. For we are animated and united by the idea that national unity cannot be satisfied and achieved, and permanently preserved, without full satisfaction of the liberal claims of the people; and that without the active and driving power of national unity, the sense of freedom of the German people cannot be satisfied. Therefore our motto is: the German State and German Freedom must be achieved simultaneously by the same means. It would be a pernicious error to believe that a nation, its speakers and representatives only have to look after the interests of freedom, and, on the other hand, that unification can be achieved without us by the Government through cabinet policy.

The unification of the entire Germany under one and the same Constitution is *to us the highest task of the present time.*

To harmonize a monarchical Federal State with the conditions of constitutional law is a difficult task, so far not yet achieved in history. The Constitution of the North German Federation has not solved it completely either in its extent or in a finally satisfactory manner. But we regard the new work as the first step on the road to the German State consolidated in freedom and power. The adherence of South Germany provided for in the Constitution has to be furthered urgently and with all our strength.

The joining of South Germany, which is left open in the Constitution, must be promoted intensively and urgently, but under no circumstances should it impair or weaken the central authority ...

We regard parliament as the place for combining the lively and effective forces of the nation. With our co-operation universal, direct and secret suffrage has been made the basis of our public life. We do not conceal from ourselves the dangers that it carries with it as long as freedom of the press, of the right of assembly and of association are curtailed, the elementary schools are under paralyzing regulations, and elections are subjected to interference by the bureaucracy. However, as we could not secure any guarantees, the dangers have not been a deterrent for us. It is now up to the people to make a stand for the integrity of the elections. Strenuous efforts will succeed in expressing their voice faithfully, and then universal suffrage itself will be the strongest bulwark of freedom. It will remove the ruins of the Estate system and at last implement the promised equality before the law ...

We do not entertain the hope of supplying all the many wants at once; but we do not close our eyes to any of them and give preference to the one or other of them according to favouring circumstances. But at all times we regard an administration that corresponds to the laws and respects the rights and the freedom of individual political bodies, like those of the general public, as inviolable and as the indispensable condition of a harmonious co-operation between the government and the people's representatives. A relapse into a different practice of the administration must be resisted unreservedly, notwithstanding any risks. We can only co-operate with a government faithful to the laws. We are prepared to seek the right methods jointly with such a government.

Intense experience has taught us that one cannot fight for the same tasks with the same weapons at all times. When one has to aspire to such meaningful and serious aims simultaneously, as is the case in Germany and Prussia at present, then it does not suffice only to stick to traditional propositions and to ignore new and manifold needs in favour of a simple and comfortable tradition. It requires hard and circumspect work to do justice to the diverse claims, to watch the course of events and to take advantage of the given situation. The final aims of Liberalism are constant, but its demands and ways are not separated from life and do not exhaust themselves in fixed formulae. Its very essence consists in taking notice of the signs of the present time and in satisfying their claims. The present age makes it quite clear that in our Fatherland every step towards constitutional unity means at the same time progress in the sphere of freedom or carries the stimulus for this in it.

We are not prepared to oppose other parliamentary groups of the Liberal Party, for we feel united with them in the service of freedom. But regarding the great question of our time, and being responsibly aware of how much depends on the right choice of means, we endeavour and hope to enforce the afore-mentioned principles within the Party.

C. Aspects of continental liberalism in the nineteenth century

[Source: Oskar Stillich, *Die politischen Parteien in Deutschland*, II, *Der Liberalismus*, Leipzig 1911, pp. 270–5. Translated by the editors of this volume.]

Doc. 91. KARL TWESTEN: Draft of the Foundation Programme of the National Liberal Party (1867)

Until the great events of the year 1866, the liberal majority of the Prussian people and of the people's representatives were solidly opposed to the Government in order to maintain the right and freedom of the country against unconstitutional theories and measures. The war and its results have changed the position of our fatherland. For after the immense successes in the war, with the increased tasks in foreign affairs and the tense problems of the re-building of Germany, the existing army institutions and the heavy burden for them could no longer be questioned. The Government gave up the interpretation and handling of the Constitution, which were the outcome of the original dispute and which had cancelled the legal influence of the representatives of the people. Through the statements in the speech from the throne of 5 August 1866, through the Indemnity Bill and through the budget agreed upon, the constitutional position was restored in time and thus co-operation between the Government and the deputies became possible. In addition to the immediate enlargement of our state, the unification of Germany under a parliamentary constitution was put forward as the historical task; by its solution, the national and liberal hopes of the past should at last be fulfilled. The steps of the Government reflected the insight that the power of the state and national unity cannot be safely founded without pacifying the liberal parties. The co-operation of Government and People appeared more than ever imperative in order to reach the high aims.

One part of the Opposition, nevertheless, believed it must maintain its previous position and refuse its consent. Some members of the House of Representatives voted against the Law of Indemnity, some against the annexations, some against the Budget, and some against the Constitution of the North German Federation. They thought to be able to preserve freedom through continued conflict with the Government and to leave the bringing about of unification entirely to the Government.

The National Liberal Party in the House of Representatives and in the North German Reichstag regarded this as a dangerous error. A party, that has not the power to force the Government into its course, loses all influence if it unwisely puts itself aside and in fact gives up participation in the tasks of the state. As long as it remains active, the liberal party has to be considered as a weighty and indispensable element in the life of the state.

Instead of a mere negation on principle, we therefore regard earnest and positive participation in public affairs as necessary in order to further

554

the nation and the state in the fields of legislation and administration. In this sense, while fully preserving the principles of progress and freedom, the members of the Party took an outstanding and successful share in the important laws of the last period of the legislature. They raised their voices everywhere against abuses, illegalities and neglect; they supported the foreign policy of the Government strongly, and finally succeeded in obtaining numerous and essential improvements in the original draft of the Constitution of the North German Confederation.

This Constitution has been completed. The Government and the majority of the liberal parties equally regarded it as their duty to seek agreement, without which a great part of the efforts and the successes of last year would have been lost. Mutual hostility and the memories of former discords were not allowed to endanger a work on which the hope of German unification is based.

The difficult task of a monarchical confederation reached a solution in the North German Constitution which undoubtedly does not fulfil all just demands, but it puts future development into the hands of the German people through the parliament based on universal manhood suffrage. The entry of the South [of Germany], without a weakening of the central power, and the firmer formation of the unity of the state will be the most essential task that requires the joint work of Government and the representatives of the people. It guarantees a strong influence to the latter, if put forward by an independent liberal majority. The national unification will not be achieved and be permanently secured without the sincere co-operation of the liberal parties in Germany. Equally for the education (*Bildung*) and welfare of the people, as for its political activity and for a wholesome usage of the general equal suffrage, we are demanding that full personal and civic liberty, the raising of the elementary schools and the free movement of the press and associations be safeguarded for all parts of Germany by juries for political delicts. The establishment of free movement and of freedom of trade, liberated from the bondage of antiquated laws and from the coercion of the system of licences, will be one of the first tasks of the [North German] Reichstag.

Equally urgent is the further development of the German and Prussian Constitutions, expressly reserved in the latter, but so far without effect. To it belong, above all, district and community decrees, the regulating of relations between Church and School and the political laws, which, whilst eliminating the conflicts of competency and the monopoly of accusation by the public prosecutor, must fully make the responsibility not only of ministers but also of civil servants a fact and must separate the courts of the administration from the administration proper.

The fixation of the structure of the army by law and the lowering of the expenses for the military will have to be left to politically more quiet times, when the interim period laid down in the Federal Constitution comes to an end . . .

C. Aspects of continental liberalism in the nineteenth century

Just as uniform legislation and particularly far-reaching reforms in penal law and procedure have become a pressing need, so we put the highest emphasis on the development of social and political life on the basis of true independence and self-administration in local communities and districts. We reject bureaucratic centralisation and wish to see eliminated the estate-basis of our district regulations (*Kreisordnung*), as well as the police functions of the lord of the manor (*gutsherrlich Polizei*). As a precondition of large-scale organic legislation, a reform of the House of Lords has to be visualised.

An energetically reformatory legislation, which has been delayed all too long under the rule of the Conservative Party, is now required all the more urgently through the necessary amalgamation of the old and the new parts of the country; for the new provinces enjoy some advantages in the fields of justice and administration that should by no means be replaced by the more defective institutions of old Prussia.

The tasks and the position of the liberals in the [Prussian] House of Representatives and in the [North German] Reichstag will be essentially the same. The Reichstag now to be elected for three years will have the task of laying new fundaments for the material and political development of the German people, of bringing about the unity of the entire fatherland and of giving the decisive lead to the efficacy of the new Constitution.

It is certainly more difficult to gain attention towards and the participation of the people in positive (day to day) affairs than in the excitement of great political conflicts. Yet it is of the greatest importance for the entire future of our new political life that its beginnings are not in fact handed over to the ruling party by blind confidence in the Government or by pessimistic depression.

To judge by its past, it seems doubtful whether the Government will be moved to energetic reforms by the great impulses of our time. It can be taken for granted that its activity will not voluntarily correspond to liberal requests everywhere. It is all the more necessary that the Prussian and German people demonstrate tenaciously on which side they perceive the interests and the salvation of their future to lie. The persistent will of the decisive majority cannot fail to achieve final success. The need for true harmony between the people and the Government must in the end direct the latter to the course demanded by the people.

The indispensable condition for co-operation between the Government and the representatives of the people, and for the avoidance of new conflicts, is an administration in accordance with the laws and one which respects the rights and freedom of individual citizens and those of the community as inviolable. Relapses into a different practice of the past must be resisted unreservedly in spite of any possible risk.

[Source: Julius Heyderhoff (ed.), *Deutscher Liberalismus im Zeitalter Bismarcks. Eine politische Briefsammlung*, Osnabrück 1967, I, pp. 500–3. Translated by the editors of this volume.]

Doc. 92. G. G. GERVINUS: A Warning Voice in Times of National Victory. Memorandum for the Peace: To the Royal House of Prussia (1870)[1]

... Prussia has led Germany's entire military forces in a glorious fight against France. The French nation which one was accustomed to regard as an hereditary enemy against whom one had to be armed to the teeth at all times, has been rendered innocuous for the time being. Experience has shown that Prussia, when attacked by a foreign enemy, has the support of the whole German nation freely and willingly, even on an occasion when the alliance obligation was more than dubious for the South German states and when in any case only dynastic interest was involved. She (Prussia) has the right and the chance of strengthening her power anew in this respect. In the West the old frontiers of Germany have been restored.

No matter whether one regards it as more suitable to incorporate Alsace and Lorraine in the Prussian state, or in the German Confederation as a direct federal territory, the entire increase in power will essentially benefit the German protector ... South Germany will join the German Confederation and with her forces will be chained to the common German cause more securely than by any treaty. Yet a last thing is still missing in order to give a full range and a most reliable solidity to this great and inspiring German Power: that she should restore independence to the German territories and people annexed in 1866,[2] in order that no internal enemy should remain when now no external enemy has to be feared. Prussia's monarchy should arrive at this great unselfish and noble decision so that the exultation of Germany over the war, the victory and the peace is everywhere the same and is not disturbed by any dissonance, even if only subdued.

Just now, at this very moment, the King of Prussia can take this step by his own freest will, as an act of the most genuine strength without in any way giving in to any exterior influences. He might take this step at this moment as an act of recognition and gratitude for the patriotic loyalty shown to him by the people of the subjected territories. He should take this step as an act of the wisest statesmanship. For Germany does not wholly belong to herself as long as these suppressed tribes do not belong once more to themselves. The superabundantly strong body of the German people, the admirable vigour of which the world has come to know, carries a cancerous sore in itself as long as that wound nearest the heart of North Germany has not been cured with only a scar remaining.

For the violated rights in these territories – whatever frivolous advisers may whisper in the ears of the Prussian royalty – will not be silenced even by the most brilliant glory of the present days and by the most intensified exterior power of the Prussian state. Even if they could be suppressed and killed in the annexed territories, together with the tribes and their own tribal life, they would continue to testify in history and leave a dark blot on the shield of honour of the Hohenzollerns, a blot which cannot adorn and further their future. This truth, however much it might resound as a shrill dissonance in the joint eulogies of the German peoples, this truth should not be concealed, especially not now at this solemn moment. It requires courage to make it vocal particularly at this very moment. But truth must have the courage to confess ...

... Yet at the foundation of the Bogus Confederation (*Scheinbund*) for Half-Germany[3] only the victor's dictate, issued by the unapproachable Prussian Government, was listened to. Its former small group of supporters and the former formidable Opposition in Old Prussia, as well as the voluntary and enforced supporters of success in New Prussia and in the federal states, all simply submitted to it. The large respectable core of the entire people was neither heard nor considered; it was also not listened to subsequently cither in the Reichstag or in the Diets, in which it was only fragmentarily represented by men who were and are determined by onesided and moreover highly contradictory party motives, with which the simple needs of the people have usually nothing in common at all. Thus freedom and the influence of the written word were almost exclusively with the ruling party which behind its voices relied on the levers of power. It was that party which practically alone put and answered all questions in the newspapers with the largest circulation. In this way the voice of public opinion was falsified; and owing to this unnatural state of affairs more than one government or political system in Europe has unexpectedly perished during the last half-century ...

[Source: G. G. Gervinus, *Hinterlassene Schriften*, Vienna 1872, pp. 4–6 and p. 16. Translated by the editors of this volume.]

Editors' Notes
1. This Memorandum, composed under the impact of the German victories in the Franco-Prussian War of 1870–71 was written shortly before the author's death in 1871.
2. Following the Prussian victory over Austria in 1866 the states of Hanover, Hesse-Kassel, Nassau, together with Schleswig-Holstein and the Free City of Frankfurt were annexed by Prussia.
3. A reference to the North German Confederation under Prussian leadership, formed by Bismarck in 1866–67.

Doc. 93. The Liberals and the New Empire 1871–1881

(a) Hermann Baumgarten to Max Weber, Strassburg (Alsace) 30 May 1878*

I cannot say that the last developments have surprised me very much; for years I have not expected much good. We are an unpolitical nation as we always have been. Twelve years ago we came a few years too late.[+] This has taken a bitter revenge. As far as a correct appraisal of Bismarck's role in domestic affairs is concerned, we are in my opinion a few years too late. May we not be punished for it too severely! With him we shall not advance these matters. Without him it will now be more difficult than it was formerly. But better today than still later. As the years pass one views these things more quietly. The gloomiest view must become more cheerful when looking back twenty five years. Only in one respect have we receded badly: the moral foundations of national life have been so badly shaken that one is bound to get frightened. The Reichstag has recently talked much about the Church. It is true that it alone could restore some things, but where does it stand? Even in the distance I cannot see forces for its rejuvenation. For the time being all spiritual movements are forced to proceed in the quite opposite direction. I am, therefore, by no means so desperate that I should like to submit to a stupid orthodoxy or even allow it to do its work in silence. As I fear perhaps the greatest evil to come from it, I would know how to console myself should a revered head move towards the well-deserved rest.[‡]

* Max Weber, a National Liberal Member of the Reichstag. Not identical with the famous economist of the same name.
† In 1866 the Liberals approved of Bismarck's policies only after his successes in foreign affairs.
‡ This is an allusion to the aged Emperor William I who was close to Protestant orthodoxy. He died in 1888.

(b) Hermann Baumgarten to Heinrich von Sybel, Strassburg, 27 December 1879
I should like to know how you judge our domestic situation. To me it seems as miserable as the foreign one is brilliant and I can never think without deep regret of the Crown Prince* who will have to suffer for all the domestic sins in this glorious time. Your neighbour[†] has become quite incomprehensible to me. To write in this way on the General Synod! I will have nothing to do any more with these blue journals, which surrender everything for the maintenance of which they were created; and, as I react, so do many of the oldest and most faithful friends of the *Jahrbücher*.[‡]

* Crown Prince Frederick, later Emperor Frederick III.
† Heinrich von Treitschke.
‡ The *Preussische Jahrbücher*, then the organ of Treitschke and his friends.

(c) Hermann Baumgarten to Heinrich von Sybel, Strassburg, 21 July 1880
The world outside, I am afraid, is becoming more and more sick. How could it be otherwise as the all-powerful physician, to whom we have entrusted everything,* is himself so sick? I am, therefore, sincerely glad that you gave up active politics for good and want to devote yourself entirely to your studies ...
[Baumgarten suggests to Sybel to write a book on the history of 1848.]
I now regard such a history as being indeed very necessary. At first I fear a repetition of the conservative follies of 1840–48 and then

559

an infinitely worse version of the radical follies for which Bismarck properly has paved the way by his violent and absolutely unscrupulous policies. It is true, that a good history of 1848 cannot now prevent but only mitigate this, as far as books are at all able to do so. (The main thing, however, will have to be achieved through a hard time of trial, which we shall certainly not be spared.) Who could write this history better than you can?

Perhaps you will laugh about the repetition of the follies of 1840–48. Now we are in the midst of it. Herr von Manteuffel [†] shows himself at every opportunity as an admiring disciple of the policy of Frederick William IV, [‡] beside the Emperor William only a non-commissioned officer. He is equally fantastic and does as much mischief on a small scale as his admired model on a larger scale. How this gentleman could achieve anything as a diplomat is incomprehensible to me. For he sins against the simplest tact even more than against political intelligence.

* An allusion to Bismarck.
† Edwin von Manteuffel, Governor of Alsace-Lorraine.
‡ King Frederick William IV of Prussia (1840–1861).

(d) Hermann Baumgarten to Heinrich von Sybel, Strassburg, January 1881

... What we have to fear most are the conservative inclinations towards Rome.* Also now the desire is very great in Berlin to seek a prop for the throne in Rome. Nothing, therefore, seems to me more urgent than to show that this prop has successively ruined all the thrones. The follies thought by the liberals on relations with the Curia seem to me at present rather irrelevant. For Bismarck will really have achieved that the liberals will be ruined for a long time at the price of throwing Germany into the disaster of the Latin world, of the fight between extremes. I very much fear, therefore, that in ten years' time your verdict that he is the greatest stateman of the century will meet with strong opposition, and that it will then suffice to call him the greatest diplomat. It is entirely our fault that he has impaired the incomparable glory of 1866 and 1870 so sadly by his regime in domestic affairs. He will leave behind a terrible chaos for us and we shall have to atone terribly for our blindness. I know that I am nearly alone in this view among my old friends. I wish nothing more than that my folly should appear still worse in five or ten years' time. But I shall then have the sad consolation that the entire German and Prussian developments of the last hundred years will appear absurd ...

* 'Rome' stands here for the Vatican.

(e) Heinrich von Sybel to Hermann Baumgarten, Berlin, 8 January 1881

Your outlook seems to me to be somewhat more sombre than fair and your judgement on Bismarck not just. The strong man could make it easier by his form and manner for the world to accept his views. This is certain. If he would produce his motions more cautiously, would contact the party leaders earlier, would treat his colleagues and his officials more humanely and so on, he would avoid much confusion and misunderstanding. But where has he sinned in the subject matter?

... I have never in my life been an admirer of protective tariffs, but I find it absurd when Bamberger, Rickert, Richter* now rub it in that protective tariffs are equal with political reaction. But has not Bismarck allied himself with conservatives and clericals in order to obtain the tariffs? Well, I think that when a minister needs money and one party refuses it, whereas the other pushes it on to him, he would never prove a statesman who says that he refuses the money because he did not want to take it from those hands. And where is there a shadow of evidence that our ministry is otherwise reactionary, now when Eulenburg[†] has put forward three super-liberal district regulations, Stolberg[‡] is maintaining the emancipation of the Jews and the judges (*Amts- und Landrichter*) are made more independent than ever ...

I deplore as you do that the middle of the road parties are suffering; but if the liberal electors allow themselves to be hoodwinked by the Manchester men I cannot reproach Bismarck for it, but only see in it an occasion for a new 'Self-Criticism of Liberalism'.

* Left-wing liberal deputies in the Reichstag.
† Count Eulenburg, Prussian Minister of the Interior, submitted these regulations to the Prussian Diet on 8 January 1881.
‡ Count Otto zur Stolberg-Wernigerode, Vice-President of the Prussian State Ministry and Deputy of Bismarck.

(f) Hermann Baumgarten to Heinrich von Sybel, 29 March 1881
(In reply to Sybel's letter of 8 January 1881)
... You misjudge me in thinking that it is my main criticism of Bismarck that he is ruining liberalism. I have conservative as well as liberal doubts as regards him; I do not at all look at things from a party point of view, but only look at our German development as a whole. There I am bound to find that his domestic policy, always dubious in some respects, is becoming more and more pernicious, just as his foreign policy was and is magnificent and admirable. He has also bestowed on us the curse of universal manhood suffrage, which admittedly he knows how to manipulate as a truly Caesarian demagogue but which must cause the greatest disaster in the hands of his successors. You agreed, at least formerly, with me on the perniciousness of this institution. Had Bismarck not been there, the mood of the summer of 1878 could have been used, I believe, to liberate us from the worst evil, whereas in fact not even an attempt has been made. We also owe our second misfortune, the misfortune of ultramontanism, essentially to Bismarck. That he took up the fight with Rome in 1871 was just as necessary as the passionate, vehement way with which he opened it was ruinous for us. Only his method has enabled the Catholic priests (*Pfaffen*) to awaken the fanaticism of the masses, and

only the universal manhood suffrage granted by him has given them the power to acquire the imposing position in politics which they possess today and which they will keep during our life-time. You will say that these are very old complaints of mine. During the last seven years I have thought of Bismarck's influence similarly as I do today, only that every year has strengthened my view.

I would not have thought that you would approve of Bismarck's economic policies as you always were a zealous Free Trader . . . Where is coolest calm more necessary than in the treatment of these questions? Bismarck, however, has tackled them from the beginning with such vehemence, has appealed so much to the passions of the masses that we are more torn by economic antagonism than we have ever been before. And far from realizing the doubtfulness of such a situation and working towards calming down the passions with the superiority of the all-powerful statesman, he blows into the flames ever more strongly and exaggerates his one-sided tendencies ever more without any sense of measure. It seems he cannot touch anything in a different manner.

What we have experienced during the last few weeks represents the extreme of violence, a violence which has also no longer any scruples about injuring the crown directly and by this endangering monarchial prestige. Violent, yes, crude and brutal does the character of our domestic politics become more and more, and for no nation this seems to me more dangerous than for the German one. If we become a prey to the fate of the Latin people to be thrown hither and thither between extremes, the worst thing that exists at all, we shall owe this essentially to Bismarck.

I feel the pernicious effects of his unlimited power everywhere, particularly in the incredible socialism that has come over us. As it gradually becomes a certainty for everyone that nothing can shake his power, and as this power makes the strongest and most direct impact on all relations, all the clever calculators bow to it unconditionally. In a few years' time many of them will follow a radical flag equally joyfully, if it promises success; and I fear it will promise success, for it seems to me that everything is driving us towards radicalism. When Bismarck's enmity and its own weakness of political thought will have destroyed the liberal bourgeoisie as a political factor and only big property and the greedy masses will then confront each other, it would, considering the political and spiritual impotence and the uneconomic inclinations of our nobility, need a miracle for demagoguery not to become the master, at least for a transitory period, with the tools prepared by Bismarck. Our modern orthodoxy strives to bring about the same radical turn in the ecclesiastical field . . .

[Source: Paul Wentzke (ed.), *Deutscher Liberalismus im Zeitalter Bismarcks. Eine politische Briefsammlung*, II, Osnabrück 1967, pp. 194–5, 285, 332–3, 373–4, 377–9. Translated by the editors of this volume.]

Doc. 94. EUGEN RICHTER: Liberalism and National Unity. The Split Within the Liberal Camp (1874)

Whereas there was then [1866] the least danger that liberalism was practised unaccompanied by the national idea, in reverse the worry was close at hand that the national idea would prevail unaccompanied by liberalism. For the national policy lay in the hands of a man who in previous years had proved to be the most decisive adversary of liberalism. The brilliant successes of the army and of diplomacy just then made liberal and parliamentary institutions appear of lesser value. One should form new parties in times of an upward movement, as was the case in 1861 when the Progressive Party was formed. In the autumn of 1866, on the other hand, liberalism was on the decline. In such times the alteration of old party formations only too easily becomes the signal of desertion, of the dissolution of the party. The split caused by the foundation of the National Liberal Party was to a large extent responsible for the fact that at the elections to the first constituting North German Reichstag the liberals in the old province of Prussia suffered such a big defeat.

With a half-broken strength the liberal party then entered the Reichstag. We were then by no means under the illusion that the time had come to implement liberal ideals, that also the connection with the Reich Constitution of 1849 would have any success. But we believed that we had to defend the freedom rights already acquired under all circumstances to the last moment. There was no reason for giving up anything of parliamentary rights at the transfer of constitutional regulations from the single states to the North German Confederation.

At first it seemed as if the National Liberal Party would fight with us on the same lines. For their address, previously mentioned, had declared: 'Without the safeguarding and developing of the constitutional rights of the people we shall not be allowed to count on the homage of the minds and hearts in Germany that alone provides power with durability and permanence.' Also, the declaration of the national liberal candidates before the electors in the old provinces took the same line.

Meanwhile in the Reichstag a right wing from the new provinces had been added to the National Liberals from the old provinces. In the new provinces so far, liberal endeavours had only been pursued by way of opposition to the dynasties now expelled. These people were quite absorbed by the consciousness of now belonging to a larger state. They failed to recognise that the contrast of liberal or conservative was also valid in the larger state, and they viewed the conflict which had lasted in Prussia for several years as almost a big misunderstanding. It soon turned out that this section of the National Liberal Party was less determined to defend liberal rights than the section which had formerly belonged to the Progressive Party. The right wing even did not mind strengthening the Conservative Party and outvoting their own party fellows with its help,

C. Aspects of continental liberalism in the nineteenth century

as in the question of the parliamentary daily allowances.

At the end, we were thus faced with a constitution which in essential points restricted the liberal rights that had until then been valid in the single states of North Germany. I mention only the refusal to grant daily allowances to the deputies; and the restrictions on the budget right, involving the weakening of the principle of the responsibility of Ministers.

[Source: *Die deutsche Fortschrittspartei und die nationalliberale Partei.* Vortrag der Abgeordneten Eugen Richter gehalten am 23 Oktober 1874, Berlin 1874, pp. 5–7. Translated by the editors of this volume.]

Doc. 95. The Anti-Clerical Reaction of the German Liberals. The Slogan of the 'Kulturkampf' against the Catholic Church
(*From the Programme of the Progressive Party for the Reichstag elections in the spring of 1873*)

... Voters! The great goals for which the German Progressive Party has striven since its foundation [in 1861] have by no means been attained. Meanwhile some of them have been implemented more quickly than we had ever dared to hope. Whoever compares the state of public affairs today with that of twelve years ago will have to admit that the changes sponsored by the state are more in line with our programme than with those of our opponents.

[The programme then points out which of the demands of the Party had been accomplished; and goes on:]

Lastly, in the field of human and individual development, too, several great steps forward have been taken. The school regulations were abolished, and, with the decisive co-operation of our Party, the Government put through the law on the authorities concerned with the inspection of schools. In the long list of laws concerning the Churches, there will be confirmation of the definite break with that reprehensible system of mutual insurance between the domination of the Civil Servants in the State and the domination of the priests in the Church which has so long hindered our development.

Few of these measures could be supported by our Party without reservations. At the time it tried to obtain those amendments to the laws which it regarded as desirable. However, if it has indeed been all too often unsuccessful, it has nevertheless recognised the necessity, in accord with the other liberal parties, to support the Government in a struggle which every day is taking on more the character of a great struggle for the civilisation of mankind.*

It is for this reason that the Progressive Party has not become a Government party. It is a party of independent men who have no

*... *der mit jedem Tage mehr den Charakter eines grossen Kulturkampfes der Menschheit annimmt.*

obligations to the Government or to its individual members. Its programme was and is purely objective. Great decisions are imminent in the fields of school and church affairs. Especially a decision will be made for a long time to come on whether the parish will be granted its rightful place in the future constitution. Make sure therefore, by electing independent and genuinely free-thinking men, that the decision does not turn against freedom, against education, against the more noble aims of mankind.

[Source: Felix Salomon (ed.) *Die deutschen Parteiprogramme*, Leipzig and Berlin 1907), II, pp. 12–14. Translated by the editors of this volume.]

Section D

Liberty and Democracy

Introductory

The documents in this section reflect the debate on the relations between liberty and equality, liberalism and democracy from a variety of angles. Among them are the right to non-conformity and the tensions between the majority and the minorities in a society, as analysed by Tocqueville and J. S. Mill. During the second half of the nineteenth century, the scope of the State and its limitations were re-examined, one liberal school in England and France intensifying its anti-étatism, another in England pleading for moderate State intervention. The antagonism between freedom and power as stressed by Acton and later by Alain contrasted markedly with the optimistic belief in the harmony of interests which had been felt by earlier liberals. There was a similar abandonment by liberal economists of the belief that national income and national welfare would be automatically maximized if every individual were allowed or encouraged to maximize his own private income.

1. Are liberty and democracy compatible?: introduction
(Documents 96–101, pp. 605–23)

Most liberals in Western Europe between 1814 and 1848 favoured a limited franchise, based on qualifications of property and education. Liberty for them involved equality of all before the law, but not equality in any other sense. They therefore took up a defensive position against the champions of democracy, who insisted on universal manhood suffrage. Despite differences of emphasis on other points men like Royer-Collard, Benjamin Constant and François Guizot all desired a constitutional monarchy and a restricted vote preventing any mass participation in the affairs of the State. They were inclined to regard such mass-participation as a scheme by cranky and subversive extremists who might endanger the safety of society as their predecessors had tried to do in 1793–94. Their *annus mirabilis* was 1688 and not 1789. They were hardly aware that the demand for democracy was a by-product of the process towards the growing industrialization and urbanization of the country. François Guizot insisted more than anyone that the zest for democracy was incompatible with the thirst for freedom. For him the principles of representative government and those of Rousseau's Sovereignty of the People were irreconcilable (doc. 97). Though both

D. Liberty and democracy

were founded on the principle of the majority, the majority had a different meaning in each case. To the champions of democracy it had a quantitative meaning, to those of representative government a qualitative one. The possession of the vote was to depend on the possession of the qualities allegedly needed for its exercise. Representative government was based 'on a majority of those who are qualified to govern'. Abstract rights or public opinion were not sufficient to produce this capacity. The French Revolution had allegedly demonstrated that such a qualification could only be one of property. Guizot often explained that 'from the time of the electoral law of 1817, political power had been placed in the most independent, enlightened and çapable part of society'. This power of the middle classes had, in his view, 'descended as far down as possible, to the limit at which political capacity stopped'.[1] There might be variations of this limit when both property and education spread, but 'the principle remained that political rights were attached to capacity, in accordance with the sovereignty of reason'. And this capacity was counted in terms of the amount of tax paid by those aspiring to the vote.

Yet with all his conviction that a stable government in France could only be based on the middle classes, Guizot was in many ways an élitist who — as we have seen — admired the role of the aristocracy in Britain. After 1848 he was even less sure that the middle classes were *a priori* the depositories of political sagacity. They were 'apt to be attracted towards new ideas, contrary to their interests; they were also inclined to become disgusted with politics'.[2]

With his Calvinist background Guizot did not share Rousseau's optimism about the potentialities in human nature. Representative government, he observed, 'renders homage to the dignity of our nature, without ignoring its frailty, and recognizes its frailty, without outrage to its dignity' (doc. 97). To the end Guizot desired to erect a dam against the flood of democracy, the springs of which he failed to understand. Alexis de Tocqueville on the other hand regarded the trend to democracy as inevitable, even as ordained by Providence. Yet he cared deeply, even passionately for the maintenance of freedom which he too saw seriously threatened by that development. At the same time his detached sociological analysis made him realize that the chances of freedom were much conditioned by the type of society in which it would exist or vanish. With great lucidity he saw that Western society was passing through a period of transition from the older type of feudal and aristocratic society, the break up of which had set in long before 1789, to a new type of social democracy with still vague and uncertain contours. When visiting the United States of America, then still little known in Europe, Tocqueville was not only concerned with studying the structure and the *mores* of the New World. As he confessed in the introduction to his *Democracy in America*, he saw in the United States 'more than America'. He 'sought the image of democracy itself, with its inclinations, its character, its prejudices, and its passions, in order to learn what we have to fear or hope from its progress'. [3]

Tocqueville discovered the democratic principle at work in the United States everywhere, (doc. 96) in all spheres of society, not only in politics, law and warfare, but also in social relationships, in the attitudes between parents and children, masters and servants and in the position of art, literature and religion. He looked back to the old type of society in Europe and constantly drew comparisons with it. In that society unity and uniformity were conspicuously absent, whereas the private rights of the privileged individuals, the 'liberties' of the first two estates, had been respected. Great men counted for much while the multitude counted for little. On the other hand, in the democratic society the emphasis was more on things and tools than on men; the individuals were weak and therefore did not make a strong nation. Variety and inequality were characteristic features of the old society just as equality and uniformity were those of the new. There everything threatened to become so much alike that any specific individuality would soon be entirely lost in the general aspect of the world.

Two possible extremes were to be found in a democratic society as far as freedom was concerned. On the one hand it could degenerate into anarchy, on the other hand be stifled by servitude under the strong collective. Yet Tocqueville was no one-sided prophet of gloom. If new dangers and social ills were bound to occur in that type of society, there were also new remedies for them, and Tocqueville thought he saw both in the New World across the Atlantic. There the good things and the evils of life were more equally spread, each individual stood apart in solitary weakness, but society as a whole was 'active, provident and powerful'. Extremes of wealth and poverty, of great insight and complete ignorance were less marked; rank, race and country counted far less and 'the great bond of humanity' far more. Altogether life moved on in a way 'at once less lofty and less low, less brilliant and less obscure than that which existed in the (old) World'. If Tocqueville had by birth and upbringing a bias towards the old order, as a Christian he felt obliged to regard the trend towards a democratic society as pre-ordained. Quality might suffer but justice would gain. God, the Creator and Preserver of men, was not concerned with the singular prosperity of the few but with the greater well-being of all. 'A state of equality is perhaps less elevated, but it is more just; and its justness constitutes its greatness and beauty.' (doc. 96).

Tocqueville saw the inevitable trend towards equality in historical perspective. Since the eleventh century the aristocrat had gone down the ladder and the commoner up until they were shortly to meet. In his penetrating essay 'France before the Revolution' [4] he makes the point that the seeds of equality and integration were laid long before 1789 in the age of Absolutism. The levelling of the subjects then paved the way

D. Liberty and democracy

for the equality of the citizens under the Revolution. Contemporary Western Europe, as Tocqueville saw it, lived in a state of transition. The old order was receding but the new one had not yet fully arrived. The position was quite different in the United States. There men were seen 'on a greater equality in point of fortune and intellect, or, in other words, more equal in their strength, than in any other country of the world, or in any age of what history has preserved the remembrance.' [5]

Tocqueville did not argue that freedom and equality were, of necessity, incompatible with each other in such a society. The problem proved more complex. For equality had a positive and a negative aspect. On the one side there existed 'a manly and lawful passion for equality which excites men to wish all to be powerful and honoured', tending 'to elevate the humble to the rank of the great'. But there was also 'a perverse taste for equality which impels the weak to attempt to lower the powerful to their own level, and reduces men to prefer equality in slavery to inequality with freedom'.[6]

Though democratic nations did not despise liberty, unfortunately it was not liberty but equality which was their idol. To them liberty was a secondary aim, but equality a primary one. 'They make rapid and sudden efforts to obtain liberty, and if they miss their aim resign themselves to their disappointment; but nothing can satisfy them except equality, and rather than lose it they resolve to perish.' [7]

Yet the picture had a brighter side. For Tocqueville discovered that in the USA liberty flourished in fields where it was constantly attacked in France. There, the friends of religion were the enemies of liberty, while the friends of liberty were hostile to religion. In America, on the other hand, State and Churches were separated and there was a multiplicity of churches and creeds. The clergy had no influence on the affairs of the State or on its servants. Religion remained 'a distinct sphere, in which the priest is sovereign but out of which he takes care never to go'.[8] He saw no reason why religion, in accommodating itself to the democratic tendencies, should not be in a rather advantageous position with 'that spirit of individual independence' which is characteristic of a liberal society.

Other aspects of liberty in America impressed the foreign observer equally. The Press was not subject to any restrictions. The State did not interfere with it and American editors, different from those in France, did not find themselves in prison from time to time. And the same was true of the liberty of associations, political as well as non-political. They flourished everywhere in the USA and their unfettered existence had several advantages. They often brought together critics of the existing Government majority and frequently helped a political minority to supplant the existing regime. It was also characteristic that America knew no secret and clandestine societies of the type frequent in France at the time. The independence of the political associations in America reflected the general opinion in the country that Government was not ordained by God but was a necessary evil. There was no cult of the State, but a 'manly independence of the citizens who respect the office more than the officer'.[9]

At the end of the nineteenth century the question of the compatability of democracy and liberty was posed once more in another national context by the English historian, W. E. H. Lecky, well known for his works on the history of Ireland and on the advance of rationalism in Europe. In his earlier work 'he set out to show that the advancing power of reason must inevitably break down the power of sacerdotalism, and that the advance of civilisation proceeded step by step with enfranchisement from ecclesiastical shackles'.[10] His later major work *Democracy and Liberty* (1896) is not confined to that problem but offers a kind of guide-book to a wide range of political issues occupying the minds of the English at the end of the Victorian age. In our context Lecky is relevant for two reasons (doc. 100). Firstly, he reformulated the view, earlier put forward by Tocqueville, that democracy and liberty were not identical. Whereas according to Lecky democracy was here to stay, liberty was fighting a rear-guard action. Modern democracy in the Western industrialized nations led to an increase of State power, which meant 'a multiplication of restrictions imposed on various forms of human action' and with it the constant growth of bureaucracy. It equally signified a continuous increase of taxation, another serious interference with the liberty of the individual. Lecky conceded that many of these taxes had a positive value serving purposes which greatly benefited the property-owner. They gave him the 'necessary security of life, property and industry' and thus added 'in countless ways to his enjoyments' – words which might have come from the pen of François Guizot. Yet they vitiated 'the old fundamental principle of English freedom that no one should be taxed except by his consent'.

Lecky was also much worried by what he dubbed 'the love of democracy for authoritative regulations'. He lamented that two features of true liberty, free contract and free trade, were discredited. He also deplored a new trend towards restrictive practices enforced by the trade unions, which desired to 'introduce the principle of legal compulsion into every branch of industry, to give the trade union an absolute coercive power over its members, to obtain a high average (of work), but to permit no superiorities'. It was a trend far removed from the ideals of Cobden. Liberty in other spheres was unlikely to prove very secure, if power was 'mainly placed in the hands of the men who, in their own sphere, value it so little'.[11]

Like de Tocqueville and Guizot, Lecky saw the future of constitutional liberty threatened by the lower classes. Referring to the plebiscitary 'democracy' of Napoleon III in France he argued that democracy favoured the ignorant masses while it tended to dethrone 'the upper and middle classes who have chiefly valued constitutional liberty'. Indeed,

D. Liberty and democracy

'Lecky rated liberty far above democracy, and though he realized their deep interpenetration, he was completely untouched by those arguments which asserted the essential equality of mankind'.[12] Lecky emphasized that liberty was not everything to everybody on this globe. Nor did politics matter to the millions outside the western orbit. In some Western, and in nearly all Eastern nations, good administration was far more valued than representation. The repeated extension of the franchise in Britain increased his pessimistic outlook on British democracy.

Yet such pessimism did not prevent him from gladly asserting that 'one most important form of liberty' which in his generation 'had been almost completely achieved, both in England and in most foreign countries', was 'religious liberty'. At least in this sphere democracy and liberty had not proved incompatible.

Michel Chevalier, the prominent French economist and with Cobden joint author of the Anglo-French Commercial Treaty of 1860, was more optimistic, though he shared Lecky's concern about the tyrannical practices of British trade unions. This one-time supporter of Saint Simonism and successor to J. B. Say at the Collège de France had later become a balanced supporter of the classic economic school. Whilst he defended the right of the State to undertake certain works of a public character, his main concern was with freedom of labour. He saw the entire modern development in its terms. Chevalier was confident that the progress of Western civilization spread in all directions. Basically an optimist, he felt that 'liberty reasonably interpreted leads to equality and carries it in its bosom' (doc. 98). Writing in 1869, he argued that 'the indissoluble union between liberty and equality exists visibly, especially in the domain of political economy, in the sphere of labour'. Freedom of labour was the cause of the rise of modern industry. Under its auspices an improvement of the conditions of the working class had taken place which still continued. But this precious freedom of labour was now threatened by a new form of violence abroad which might spread to France. Unlike Lecky, Chevalier was not opposed to trade unions on principle. He acknowledged the legitimate aims of the workers and saw in the forming of trade unions 'the legitimate happy exercise of the right of association', which was in his eyes 'honest, humane and worthy'. But recent developments in the British trade unions, he felt, had deviated from such a legitimate aim. The unions had become a sinister pressure group, employing 'threats, everything up to and including violence'. They coerced workers who desired to stay outside their ranks. The workmen lost their freedom, obliged to submit to the orders of trade union committees and to commence a strike when the signal was given. This unfortunate tendency was by no means confined to Britain. In Europe, too, there was a trend urging 'a part of the working population to seek their enfranchisement and the improvement of their lot by means contrary to the freedom of others' (doc. 98). This was a bad misunderstanding of the freedom of labour and

574

of its auxiliary, the freedom of capital.

Although Chevalier ended his criticism on an optimistic note of confidence in 'the patriotism and the good sense of his fellow-citizens', he took seriously the threat to individual freedom by a misuse of the collective bargaining power of the trade unions as it had its partisans in France too. Like most French liberals and radicals he harked back in his admonitions to the French Revolution, to the exemplary attitude of an unnamed member of the Constituent Assembly of 1789, who, when a proposal was made contrary to justice, had criticized his fellow deputies by exclaiming: 'you wish to be free and you do not know how to be just'. [13]

Léon Gambetta, that flamboyant and eloquent spokesman of Republicanism after the fall of the Second Empire, did not share Chevalier's misgivings over the threat to individual liberty by the organized collectivism of the trade unions which were still small in France. The lower classes, he felt, had all too long been kept silent by the old monarchical Establishment. In his major speech at Grenoble in September 1872 Gambetta addressed himself to 'the deep layers of society' until recently untouched by politics (doc. 99). These strata should now, under the universal manhood suffrage, be encouraged to voice their opinions. For the new democracy was not 'government by uniformity' but 'the government by freedom of thought, of freedom of action'. It seemed a far cry from Guizot's one-sided concern for the well-to-do middle classes. After the disappearance first of 'the legitimate monarchy' and then 'the parliamentary monarchy', the path was now open for the forming of a republic, in which the peasants and small shopkeepers 'the workers of town and country would participate'. Gambetta skilfully welcomed 'the arrival of a new, energetic, although restrained generation, intelligent, united for public affairs, in love with the country, anxious about general rights.'

It was a fighting speech by a new radical leader, striking an emotional note and unburdened by any doubts about the compatibility of freedom and equality. Gambetta harked back to the tradition of 1789 by proclaiming the 'need for a perpetual communication between all the citizens among themselves when and how they desire it', deliberating 'peacefully as the first legislators of the French Revolution formulated it'.

If Gambetta was keen to integrate the lower strata in the reconstructed Third Republic, a similar effort met with much greater obstacles in the contemporary German Empire. For in that monarchic confederation, founded by Bismarck's iron will, democracy remained at a discount both under Bismarck and Emperor William II. The pact between the old aristocracy and the successful industrialists kept the working classes continuously out of power. Shortly before the First World War, Friedrich Naumann, a former Protestant parson and a left-wing liberal with a social conscience, longingly looked to Britain as a model democracy with a constitutional monarch. There liberty and democracy had proved compatible. Until very recently a member of the Reichstag for the 'Progressive People's Party', Naumann in 1912 desired a rapprochement between a modernized monarchy and the industrial masses who were at last to be given a stake in the political system. His article 'Democracy and Monarchy' (doc. 101) was published a few weeks after the Social Democrats had won more seats than any other party in the Reichstag elections. [14]

Naumann put his finger on the weak spot of the existing semi-feudal and authoritarian regime, burdened with a considerable variety of voting rights in the individual German states. Although Germany was a *Rechtsstaat*, a country based on the rule of law, its largest component, Prussia, still had a franchise favouring the rich and well-to-do and depriving the lower classes of any political influence. A grotesque situation arose when the Social Democrats had become the strongest party in the Reichstag while holding only a dozen seats in the Prussian Diet owing to the antiquated election system detrimental to the poor and propertyless. It was then that the seven million voters of the German Left, in the words of Naumann, demanded 'progress in the self-determination of the people' (doc. 101). He argued convincingly that the German Constitution of 1871 had been too much of a half-way house. Bismarck's Empire was a compromise as a 'Federation of the Princes and the People' and suffered from the uneasy contradictions of two political systems, the one monarchical, the other parliamentary. The Federal Council functioned as the symbol of the former, the Reichstag, based on universal manhood suffrage, as that of the latter. Altogether the situation in Germany was complicated, and Naumann's problem was not how to make democracy and liberty compatible but rather how to make democracy at last a reality by the participation of a large majority of the voters in the political process.

As things were, Chancellor von Bethmann-Hollweg tried in vain to be 'above the parties'. He had to implement his policies with changing majorities and remained 'unable to enforce real political leadership by a genuine Government of the parties of the Left'. [15]

There was a refreshingly unacademic note in Naumann's appeal. He knew that simple imitation of foreign models would be unacceptable. But the monarch himself could not wish to be permanently the monarch of a minority. He should in future choose his ministers from the ranks of the majority parties, a practice which then existed to some extent in some of the South German states, but not in Prussia, and above all not in the Empire. In 1912 such a suggestion sounded rather adventurous in a country where obedience to the *Obrigkeit*, the powers that be, was deeply ingrained. Naumann argued that the position had been similar in England three or four generations earlier, yet there a parliamentary monarchy had evolved over the years. In Britain personal liberty and parliamentary

The tyranny of majority and the right to non-conformity: introduction

democracy had proved compatible. Naumann thought this combination could and should come in Germany too, without a revolution, by allowing the millions of voters on the left to exercise a rightful influence, and by the Kaiser becoming a popular leader of the nation. It was an illusionary hope soon to prove pointless. When during the war in 1917 the first Chancellor was chosen from the ranks of the Reichstag parties, the measure came too late. A year afterwards the reformed monarchy was swept away by the unexpected tides of national defeat and of revolution.

2. The tyranny of the majority and the right to non-conformity: introduction
(Documents 102–4, pp. 624–33)

In the 1830s Alexis de Tocqueville and twenty years later John Stuart Mill added a new dimension to the political philosophy of liberalism. They both realized that in an age of industrialization and increased urbanization it was not sufficient to take liberty for granted by proclaiming human rights, a limited monarchy, ministerial responsibility, the freedom of the press and of religion in the traditional manner. They felt that in their time the advance of democracy was inevitable. Whilst Mill welcomed it more warmly than the French liberal aristocrat, he too was filled with pessimistic forebodings and with a clear insight into the tyranny of the majority and of social democracy as an inevitable corollary to political democracy. De Tocqueville and his admirer Mill combined a high regard for liberty of the individual with an extraordinary analytical power which threw light on the conditions, problems and dangers of contemporary society. Both realized that while political democracy was inevitable and, at least for Mill, was desirable, social democracy, the other side of the medal, could seriously threaten the liberty of the individual and the free and fair play for minorities.

Alexis de Tocqueville's classic *Democracy in America* (1835–40) remains outstanding, for two reasons. Firstly it does not confine its analysis to the political structure, but traces the impact of democratic thought and behaviour through all sectors and products of American society. Secondly, as we have seen and as the author said himself, in America he saw 'more than America'; he 'sought the image of democracy itself'. [16] His work therefore examines both the facts and the potentialities of democracy.

D. Liberty and democracy

In the United States he found that the multitude was ruled by public opinion which was ready made and uniform and spared the individual the necessity of thinking for himself (doc. 102). He regarded it as inevitable that in a society which from the beginning had lacked an aristocracy, 'faith in public opinion will become a species of religion there and the majority its ministering prophet'. [17] The rights of the majority, clearly written into the American Constitution, form more than a recognized political habit. In France before 1789 the king could do no wrong; if he did wrong his advisers had to take the blame. In the American democracy a similar attitude prevailed with respect to the recognition of the rights of the majority. In politics all parties were willing to recognize the rights of the majority simply because they all hoped 'to turn those rights to their own advantage at some future time'. [18]

If in all political systems abuse of power was inherent, the danger signal in modern democracy – as exemplified by the United States – lay in the unlimited power of the majority. The question which troubled this French visitor was where and how the individual or a minority group could obtain redress, if they felt wronged.

'If to public opinion, public opinion constitutes the majority; if to the legislature it represents the majority, and implicitly obeys its injunctions; if to the executive power, it is appointed by the majority, and remains a passive tool in its hands; the public troops consist of the majority under arms; the jury is the majority invested with the right of hearing judicial cases; and in certain States even the judges are elected by the majority.' [19]

In fact the immense prestige of the majority in the United States erected 'very formidable barriers to the liberty of opinion'. For it did not only mean that the non-conformist became a prey of social ostracism, it also evoked a mental cowardice in most people who conformed from sheer habit. 'By sacrificing their opinions, they prostitute themselves'. [20] What suffered was individuality, the willingness to follow one's own mental bent and preferences. 'I confess,' declared Tocqueville, 'I fear boldness much less than the mediocrity of desires in democratic societies', [21] a remark which could have come from the pen of J. S. Mill. If these authors were so much concerned about the tyranny of the majority, rooted in social attitudes, the reason was that they deeply cared for the free display of the creative individual threatened by it.

Tocqueville knew of no other country with 'so little true independence of mind and freedom of discussion as in America'. [22] Yet, though the tyranny of the majority was a formidable barrier to the liberty of opinion, it was not complete. Several institutions and factors helped to hold it in bounds. Owing to the federal structure of the country the United States of America had a centralized Government but lacked a centralized administration. It was thus able 'to combine the power of a great Empire with the security of a small state'. Another positive feature were the municipal institutions 'which limit the despotism of the majority and at the same time impart a taste of freedom and a knowledge of the art of being free to the people'.[23] The constitution of the judicial powers worked in the same direction. The courts of justice were in a position to counteract the excesses of democracy and "to check and direct the impulses of the majority without stopping its activity".[24] In the USA lawyers formed a kind of semi-aristocracy. The authority enjoyed 'by members of the legal profession and the influence which these individuals exercise in the Government' were seen by Tocqueville as 'the most powerful existing security against the excesses of democracy'. The advantageous position of the profession of lawyers in a democracy like the United States was largely due to the absence of a nobility and of men of letters. They therefore formed the most powerful counterpoise to the democratic element and were eminently suited 'to neutralize the vices which are inherent in popular government'.[25]

Though Tocqueville rejected the assumptions of European radicals that a democratic electorate would choose able men and that a democratic government would be more economical than any other, when writing *Democracy in America* he did not doubt that in the balance of advantage the 'good which political democracy could produce outweighed the evil', largely because 'its general tendency was to attend to the interests of the majority'.[26] Aristocratic government of the kind Europe had experienced for centuries, he thought, had often produced abler leaders, but they had acted only in the interests of a minority. On the other hand, a majority in a democracy, whatever its faults and those of its leaders, at least 'was in a position to bend them to their wishes'. Moreover, to de Tocqueville the notion of liberty was closely connected with the idea of rights, not as an abstract doctrine, but in a practical way. The possession of property or political rights developed the respect for them. He found in America that there 'the lowest class have a very high respect for political rights, because they exercise these rights, and they refrain from attacking those of others to save their own from attack'.[27]

Unlike Tocqueville, John Stuart Mill was not concerned with the antithesis between the European aristocratic and the North American democratic societies. The contrast stressed by Mill was one between a stagnant monolithic society and a progressive pluralistic society. 'The progressive principle ... whether as the love of liberty or of improvement', observed Mill, 'is antagonistic to the sway of Custom, involving at least emancipation from that yoke; and the contest between the two constitutes the chief interest of the history of mankind.' [28] Yet if Mill favoured movement and progress he did not share the naivety which Condorcet had displayed in this respect sixty years earlier. In the East, Mill observed, China had long become a sad specimen of mental stagnation as the result of a once excellent but now petrified wisdom, now the trend in the West was one making for stagnation, too. For there 'the modern *régime* of public opinion', is in an unorganized form, what the

D. Liberty and democracy

Chinese educational and political systems are in an organized; and unless individuality shall be able successfully to assert itself against this yoke, Europe will tend to become another China.' [29]

Individuality presupposes a healthy pluralism. Hitherto Europe had been distinguished for her 'remarkable diversity of character and culture. Individuals, classes, nations, have been extremely unlike another'. The progressive and many-sided development, characteristic of Europe in the past, was largely due to her plurality of paths. Now it was threatened by a growing trend to uniformity. Tocqueville had noted how much more the Frenchmen of the present generation resembled one another. Mill thought that the same applied to Englishmen to a far greater extent. Where formerly different ranks, neighbourhoods, trades and professions had created a welcome diversity of worlds, now the currents of politics, of economic change, of new and quicker means of transport and of a greater spread of education were bringing about a degree of assimilation and conformity unknown before. As Mill observed grimly, 'comparatively speaking, they now read the same things, listen to the same things, see the same things, go to the same places, have their hopes and fears directed to the same objects, have the same rights and liberties and the same means of asserting them'.[30] Fortunately this enforced assimilation was not yet complete, there was still a chance to emphasize the rights of the individual and of the minorities to make a stand for a plurality of paths and attitudes.

As Mill saw it, the tyranny of the majority raised its ugly head everywhere (doc. 103). The original and perhaps eccentric individual was as much threatened by it as were political, religious, racial minorities who desired to maintain their own views and attitudes. The wielding of power, Mill felt, made a big difference to the behaviour of individuals as well as of groups. He was hardly less aware of the corrupting impact of power as Tocqueville had been before him and Lord Acton was to be after him. The powerful rule of public opinion was the rule of the majority which aimed at utter uniformity. As Mill put it neatly: 'One God, one France, one King, one Chamber' was the exclamation of a member of the first Constituent Assembly (in France in 1789). [31] Sir Walter Scott appended to it an appropriate commentary 'one mouth, one nose, one ear, one eye', while the twentieth-century version of the formula was the German Socialist slogan 'ein Volk, ein Reich, ein Führer'.

Most societies have their minorities. In Mill's own days there was conflict between the whites and the negroes, the Catholics and the Protestants, the English and the Irish, between skilled and unskilled labour. The actual minority in some cases and the underprivileged in others were at a vast disadvantage. Different from Bentham, J. S. Mill clearly realized that it was not enough to uphold representative democracy; one had also to face its dangers. One was the possible low grade of intelligence of the deputies. Another was the class legislation on the part of the numerical majority. A restricted suffrage à la Guizot would certainly not combat the latter though it might alleviate the former obstacle. Mill was in favour of the representation of minorities, both for reasons of democratic justice and for the sake of cultural productivity. If justice demanded that the voice of minorities should be heard in politics, his élitist belief in the genius of the few also demanded free play for them in the cause of cultural progress. 'These few', he insisted, 'are the salt of the earth, and without them human life would become a stagnant pool.' [32]

In principle Mill favoured universal manhood suffrage, but with two modifications. He realized that a decision by a simple majority vote left minorities unrepresented, thus wasting their votes. The voice of the minority had as much right to be heard as that of the majority. He was therefore an enthusiastic supporter of the idea of proportional representation, as put forward in a scheme by Thomas Hare. Yet he also felt that with the vast ignorance of the masses at a time when primary education was not yet compulsory in England the educated should be granted an additional vote. This in fact was the practice in the case of the graduates of some English and Scottish universities. Whilst favouring representative democracy as his father and Bentham had done, he was also deeply aware that 'many men are democrats, but few are thoughtful and careful democrats'. Bentham had still somewhat naively maintained that 'in truth, representation requires only four things to be perfect – Secrecy, Annuality, Equality, Universality'. J. S. Mill in the end modified or rejected all four provisions. 'Secrecy gives way to publicity of vote, one year term to five years, equality of votes to plurality voting, and universality which is retained as an ideal, is postponed until the electorate can be properly educated.' [33]

Today with the vast extension of education at all stages Mill would have no hesitation to plead for universal suffrage, and would probably even more emphatically insist on the benefits of proportional representation. The tragedy of Northern Ireland in recent years has driven home the point that a mere representation by majority vote runs the danger of alienating minorities and of acerbating the existing social and religious tensions.

It was not by chance that both Mill and Tocqueville emphasized the importance of local government in safeguarding a political system in which liberty matters. Its great advantage over central government is that the people are able to participate in many of their affairs. 'Town-meetings are to liberty', Tocqueville observed, 'what primary schools are to science; they bring it within the people's reach, they teach men how to use and how to enjoy it. A nation may establish a system of free government, but without the spirit of municipal institutions it cannot have the spirit of liberty.' [34] Mill took a similar line by calling municipal institutions the best 'normal school' to fit a people for representative government. 'The only democracy which can work, in fact, is one based on a broad inclusion of the people in their own government, whether through municipal institutions or voluntary agencies.' [35] Through such participation men can obtain better insight into social and political reality. Moreover they are 'progressively moralized' and learn to see other people's points of view. On the other hand, the big concentration in the central government is detrimental to moral progress 'not only by removing self-dependence and rational foresight but by preventing all but the selfish interests from developing'. Mill has repeatedly argued in his writings that the prejudice against overactive centralization was 'really one of the great sources of the superiority of English over French representative institutions'.[36] Over-organization can be a threat to liberty. For the actual position in the nineteenth century Mill's remark is very revealing. 'In England there has always been more liberty, but worse organization, while in other countries there is better organization but less liberty.' [37]

Lord Acton (doc. 104) shared the fear of the tyranny of the majority with Tocqueville and J. S. Mill. On the whole he had more in common with the former than with the latter. Tocqueville and Acton were both loyal Catholics. Both approved of the aristocracy and had an unmistakable distaste for democracy. Tocqueville might have agreed with Acton's emphatic statement that the idea of liberty is 'the unity, the only unity of the history of the world and the one principle of a philosophy of history'. Like Mill, and even more so, Acton saw the individual in constant danger of being swamped and checkmated by strong collective powers. Thus follows Acton's characteristic definition of liberty: liberty meant to him 'the assurance that every man shall be protected in doing what he believes his duty against the influence of authority and majorities, custom and opinion' (doc. 111). What was the criterion by which to judge the freedom prevailing in a country? Acton gave the characteristic answer; 'the most certain test . . . is the amount of security enjoyed by minorities' (doc. 111).

It was for this reason that Acton, too, favoured the replacing of the existing voting system in Great Britain, by which the candidate obtaining the highest vote was elected, by a system of proportional representation. He felt it would be more just to both majorities and minorities. He also was sympathetic towards a federal system of state organization, although in the past it had not always proved a success.[38]

3. The limitations and the scope of the State: introduction

(i) Anti-étatism intensified

(Documents 105–7, pp. 634–52)

England: Herbert Spencer

Herbert Spencer (1820–1903), sociologist and writer on politics, was perhaps the most outspoken and widely read critic of the power of the State and of Government in the nineteenth century.

Brought up in circles of Wesleyan dissent without much formal education and originally a railway engineer by occupation, Spencer came to combine a tenacious, old-fashioned political radicalism with reliance on the findings of modern science, first of physics and later of biology. He used the theory of evolution, the ideas of Lamarck and later of Charles Darwin, for his own sociological constructions. At a time of growing collectivism in English political life Spencer strongly upheld the doctrines of *laissez faire* stressing them in the economic field as well as in politics. His own brand of political utilitarianism differed from the older Benthamite school. He rejected the principle of 'the greatest happiness of the greatest number', declaring its calculation as 'a task beyond the ability of any finite mind'; and he also objected to Benthamite ideas of legal and political measures to be carried out by a reformed Government. He disagreed with Bentham's contention that the Government was creating rights of the individual which had not existed previously, but instead maintained a theory of *a priori* natural rights of the individual. When man entered into society these rights were regulated in such a way that they did not clash with the equal claims to freedom of others. They then became *ethical* rights. Freedom in society must mean equal freedom and with it self-restraint for all.

As a young man Spencer emphasized in the articles he wrote that society could greatly gain from the repeal of government restrictions on trade, such as the Corn Laws, and that all governmental power should be reduced to a minimum required to maintain order against external and internal enemies of the society. Yet, when later the trend towards collectivism was making itself felt in England, the State, even under a liberal Prime Minister like Gladstone, increased its intervention in many fields ranging from public health and education to the protection of working men, women and children in the factories. In the 1880s Spencer condemned the attitude of Liberals who had unfortunately betrayed the old liberal tradition of insisting on strict limitations of the scope of the State. In such latter-day liberals Spencer saw nothing but new tories. He went even further. If the Benthamites had rightly challenged the divine rights

D. Liberty and democracy

of kings and of an aristocratic oligarchy to rule, Spencer found it necessary to challenge the divine right of Parliament and the rule by parliamentary majority.

He did so with a stern puritan rectitude and with a propagandist's repetition. Influenced in his younger days by the doctrines of William Godwin, the doyen of British anarchists, Spencer regarded Government as a transitory evil, which would eventually disappear. In his first major work *Social Statics* (1851) he maintained that as 'civilization advances, governments decay'. If until recently the history of the people had been identical with the history of government, this was no longer the case. Mankind was moving from the old pre-industrial *Kriegsstaat*, the military State, in which war prevailed and the Government controlled the lives of its subjects as means to its ends, to the *Handelsstaat*, the State entirely based on industry and commerce in which all men were ends in themselves and joined each other by voluntary association. While democracy prevailed in politics, in religion a State church was replaced by a number of free churches and both education and charity were run on a voluntary basis. Progress in the industrial State came through constant competition resulting in the survival of the fittest, a process which involved suffering by the unfit and the unadaptable. The biological categories of Lamarck were translated into the sociological 'concepts' of Spencer. The result was a somewhat confused ideology of a process both benevolent and harsh. As Spencer put it in a passage first written in 1851 and republished by him in 1884 in the proud conviction that its truth had stood the test of time:

'The well-being of existing humanity, and the unfolding of it into this ultimate perfection, are both secured by that same beneficent, though severe discipline, to which the animate creation at large is subjecc: a discipline which is pitiless in the working out of good: a felicity-pursuing law which never swerves for the avoidance of partial and temporary suffering. The poverty of the incapable, the distresses that come upon the imprudent, the starvation of the idle, and those shoulderings aside of the weak by the strong, which leave so many 'in shallows and in miseries' are the decrees of a large, far-seeking benevolence. ...' [39]

To Spencer the State was nothing but a 'joint protecting company for mutual assurance' or a 'committee of management'. Although it had a duty to protect the individual against attacks from others, it did not possess the right or duty to protect the individual against himself. It was 'one thing to secure to each man the unhindered power to pursue his own good', it was 'a widely different thing to pursue the good for him'. To fulfil the former task efficiently, the State had 'merely to look on while its citizens act; to forbid unfairness; to adjudicate when called on; and to enforce restitution for injuries'. To carry out the second task efficiently, it had to 'become an ubiquitous worker − must know each man's needs

584

better than he knows them himself – must in short, possess superhuman power and intelligence' [40] (doc. 105). Indeed an impossible demand!

Spencer was a relentless critic of the faults and misdeeds of the State, of its double sins of commission and omission. By ever extending the circle of its functions, he argued, the Government fulfilled all of them badly. As Spencer put it acidly in a whale of a sentence:

'If an Institution undertakes not two functions, but a score – if a government, whose office it is to defend citizens against aggressors, foreign and domestic, engages also to disseminate Christianity, to administer charity, to teach children their lessons, to adjust prices of food, to inspect coalmines, to regulate railways, to superintend house-building, to arrange cab-fares, to look into people's stink-traps, to vaccinate their children, to send out emigrants, to prescribe hours of labour, to examine lodging houses, to test the knowledge of mercantile captains, to provide public libraries, to read and authorize dramas, to inspect passenger-ships, to see that small dwellings are supplied with water, to regulate endless things from a banker's issue down to the boat-fares on the Serpentine [was] it not manifest that its primary duty must be ill discharged in proportion to the multiplicity of affairs it busies itself with?' [41]

Spencer took great pride in the advance of English technology; it had set an example for the Continent, where English experts had been called in to establish water-supplies, steam navigation, railway lines and gas companies from Sweden to Italy and from Germany to Russia. To Spencer this was evidence of 'the progressiveness of a self-dependent race and the torpitude of paternally-governed ones'. Even the 'great fact, the overspreading of the Earth by the Anglo-Saxons' was seen by this honest doctrinaire as the outcome of the greater discipline and the 'habitual self-dependence' of the English race. [42]

Spencer's sympathies were unmistakably with the strong, the enterprising, the self-dependent. Spencer also maintained the individual's right of withdrawal from the state. 'If every man has his freedom to do all that he wills, provided he infringes not the equal freedom of any other man, he is free to drop connection with the state – to relinquish its protection and to refuse paying towards its support.' [43] This view was the logical outcome of extreme Victorian radical individualism. More than any other contemporary writer on politics, Spencer suffered from a compulsive neurotic aversion towards the State and a fear of its blunders. He constantly exposed the mistakes, the stupidity and ineffectiveness, even the corruption of the bureaucracy. Officialdom was 'habitually slow, lazy, extravagant, and unadaptable'. Worse, Government was corrupt. 'As we once heard said by a State Official of twenty years standing – "Wherever there is government there is villainy".' Spencer even alleged that 'in State organizations ... corruption is unavoidable', whereas 'in trading organizations it rarely makes its appearance; and when it does, the instinct of self-preservation soon provides a remedy'. [44]

In a later essay 'The Coming Slavery' (1884) Spencer was still much obsessed by the spectacle of the State taking over more and more fields from private enterprise. Municipal authorities turned to the building of houses with the result that 'they inevitably lower the values of houses otherwise built, and check the supply of more'. Builders were likely to resent dictation by the State on 'modes of building and conveniences to be provided', because these diminished their profits and forced them to use their capital in other fields. The municipal authorities would have to build more and more houses or to purchase houses rendered unsaleable to private persons. After the urban houses it would be the turn of the rural ones. The trend was manifestly 'to approach the socialistic ideal in which the community is sole house-owner'. [45]

Another threatening ogre was State-ownership of railways, which existed then to a large extent on the Continent. The outlook was grim. 'Already exclusive letter-carrier, exclusive transmitter of telegrams, and on the way to become exclusive carrier of parcels, the State will not only be exclusive carrier of passengers, goods and minerals, but will add to its present various trades many other trades.' [46]

The changes in progress and those urged, would, Spencer gloomily predicted, carry the country 'not only towards State-ownership of land and dwellings and means of communication, all to be administered and worked by State-agents, but towards State-usurpation of all industries'. [47] The desired ideal of the socialists and also of those 'so-called Liberals' who prepared the path for them would be implemented. But these 'pioneers' suffered from a delusion. They believed 'that by due skill an ill-working humanity may be framed into well-working institutions'. In fact 'the defective natures of citizens will show themselves in the bad acting of whatever social structure they are arranged into'. There was 'no political alchemy by which you can get golden conduct out of leaden instincts'. [48] Spencer, a kind of George Orwell of mid-Victorian individualism, blamed 'the great political superstition' of his age, the thoughtless belief in Government based on a majority in Parliament, for such flagrant political mismanagement. It was, he insisted, 'the function of true Liberalism in the future' to put 'a limit to the powers of Parliament'. [49] Earlier he had consoled himself with the sociological observation that the faith in governments was 'a subtle form of fetishism ... as natural to the present phase of human evolution as its grosser prototype (the belief in the divine rights of kings) was to an earlier phase...' As all superstitions died hard, Spencer feared 'that this belief in government omnipotence will form no exception'. [50]

Herbert Spencer's perpetual warnings, his indignant protests that the State was a tyrant when it should have played the protector were perhaps salutary and his exposure of the sins of bureaucracy, though exaggerated, had some basis in fact. However, with his unmitigated dogmatism he was unable to comprehend the excesses of the harsh competitive struggle in an evolutionary society in which only the fit could succeed while thousands of less well-equipped or fortunate people might be trampled on and even be destroyed. Spencer replaced one superstition by another: the belief in the wisdom and efficiency of governments by the faith in the constructive leadership of private enterprise. In the last analysis, his political philosophy, though reflecting much of the self-confidence of the Victorian bourgeoisie and of its distrust of the State, appears fundamentally confused. This confusion was largely due 'to the fact that *a priori* conceptions with which he starts do not and cannot accord with the organic and evolutionary concepts of the State which he attains through the use of natural science. His philosophy consequently begins and ends as "an incongruous mixture of Natural Rights and physiological metaphor".' [51]

France: Emile Faguet and Paul Leroy-Beaulieu

The criticism of the State by these two contemporary French theorists lacked the acidity and savage indignation of Spencer's anti-étatism. To them the State was a necessary evil and its basic functions beyond dispute. The fact of human coexistence, they argued, made the State indispensable but the constant attempts of the bureaucracy to increase its functions had to be resisted. Faguet did not regard it as the task of what he dubbed 'intelligent liberalism' to weaken the power of the State 'as much as possible and on all points'. Yet he drew firmly 'the limit up to which the central power should be strong and beyond which it should be nothing at all' (doc. 106).

In characteristic fashion Faguet first considered the small, the minimum State which, as it is not involved in international affairs, needs only good courts of justice and a good police. The big State, on the other hand, he viewed as constantly threatened by power-conscious rivals, thus making the need for defence, for military forces imperative. If to the anarchists the State was an evil that had to be fought and destroyed, to Faguet it meant 'the result of a voluntary association for the defence of common interests', a remedy to avert 'the dangers of combative mankind'. The paradox of such liberal thought in an age of imperialist power-politics is reflected in his words: 'The State is a necessary evil, it is respectable and we owe gratitude to it. It is not something good in itself.' The modern nation-state, 'the big fatherland' was ambiguous, 'in part genuine, in part factitious and artificial'.

Compared with Faguet's subtle but rather academic distinctions, Paul Leroy-Beaulieu, the successor of Michel Chevalier in the Chair of Economics at the Collège de France and also active as a lively journalist, was much closer to the political and social realities of his country (doc. 107). He has been called 'one of the most brilliant of those "notables" who were the godfathers of the Third Republic and who set themselves to

587

D. Liberty and democracy

surround it with as much prestige and dignity as had the monarchies of the rest of Europe'.[52] He shared the resentment towards the daily pretensions of the Government, with its arrogant claim 'the country, that is me'. Both critics protested against 'the cult of impotence', of the ever-increasing bureaucracy; both argued that private enterprise, the skilled professional men outside the Government were much more effective than the anonymous work of arrogant public servants.

Leroy-Beaulieu was equally averse to the veneration of the State, as German thinkers from Hegel to Lorenz von Stein had proclaimed it, and to the utopian belief of his fellow-liberal Jules Simon that the State 'ought to strive to render itself useless and to prepare for its own decease'. To Leroy-Beaulieu the State was essential for the protection of the nation, 'to keep its life, preserve its frontiers, be subject to no oppression and no tribute from abroad'. In this respect after 1870 the European powers found themselves in a position very different from that of non-European countries like the USA or the Australian Colonies which were without any near neighbours and thus need not worry about defence.

Leroy-Beaulieu's élitist criticism of the State was mainly two-fold. Firstly, the State was without any creative force, it was a mere copier. The State bureaucracy had much in common with the human mass, both were naturally inert. The State can invent nothing. It is simply a complicated machine with numerous systems of wheels. The contrast between the cumbersome apparatus of the State and the productive world of the business and banking world is striking. While private initiative has set the model, the State in imitating it makes more mistakes than the original. Like Spencer, Leroy-Beaulieu was biased against civil servants. They are unlikely to be as strongly involved in their work as the men who work on their own or in any other private enterprise. Lacking both the stimulus and the restraint of personal interest, public servants often misunderstand 'the real character of their mission'. Their attitude towards community projects such as the construction of highways, roads and schools is more motivated by aesthetic than by practical considerations. Altogether individual action, based on competition is bound to be superior and 'should *a priori* be preferred to that of the State for all enterprises susceptible of renumeration' (doc. 107).

A second weakness of étatism was that in the Third Republic the Government of the day reflected a mere majority at the date of election. It was in Leroy-Beaulieu's eyes in fact the result of a passing infatuation of the electorate. Its dependence on changing parliamentary majorities gave some underlying instability to the work of the Government which could well be overthrown at the next election. On the other hand in recent years the realm of the State, the range of its operations had alarmingly grown. The State had become 'the greatest consumer, the greatest executor of works, the greatest employer of labour', for this economist a worrying fact, particularly as actions on such a scale were likely 'to have

The limitations and the scope of the State: introduction

an enormous weight with the nation at large'.

One cannot overlook that this severe critic of State power and champion of private enterprise was at the same time 'France's most determined, tireless and ardent protagonist for the cause of colonial expansion'.[53] At the age of 31 he published a standard work on colonisation in which he drew a sharp distinction between colonies of settlers (like the British white dominions) and colonies of capital which he regarded as much preferable.[54] He argued that 'emigration needed to be directed to an area (like Tunisia or Egypt) where capital could be invested for the greater benefit of the inhabitants and of investors'.

Later in the 1890s Leroy-Beaulieu became a prominent member of the 'Comité de l'Afrique Francaise', which claimed that owing to 'the veritable partition of an unknown continent (Africa) by certain European countries' France was 'entitled to the largest share'.[55] The intense propaganda of the Comité was successful. 'Public opinion accepted the policy of expansion, even when it criticized colonialism for its faults.'[56]

Thus Leroy-Beaulieu's liberal anti-étatism and criticism of the Government went hand in hand with a colonial nationalism based on a strong belief in the virtues of private enterprise and on the desire to profit from colonial investment so as to increase the strength of the nation against its enemies.

(ii) The case for moderate State intervention
(Documents 108–10, pp. 652–69)

Despite the confidence and dogmatism with which Herbert Spencer expressed his anti-étatist beliefs in the 1850s and 1860s, and the widespread acceptance of his and similar ideas in English political and social thought, these did not hold the field unchallenged. Doubts about utilitarianism, such as those already being felt by John Stuart Mill,[57] were to grow in strength and intensity in the 1870s and 1880s.

Following the passage of the Second Reform Bill in 1867, liberals first felt the need to reconsider the tenets of utilitarianism and *laissez faire* in relation to the new political situation. In the interests of democracy and of good government, it seemed very necessary to ensure that the new working-class electors in the towns would exercise the franchise responsibly and preferably in support of Gladstone and those who acknowledged his political leadership. The immediate concern was the provision of elementary education which ideally should be compulsory and free. Liberals, and radicals especially, soon concentrated their attention on the passage of Forster's Elementary Education Act of 1870. It was in connection with this issue that liberals and radicals began to build up effective local political organizations in several parts of the country, and

D. Liberty and democracy

notably so in Birmingham under Joseph Chamberlain's active leadership and guidance. Yet the changing political fortunes of liberalism and radicalism in the 1880s were not by any means due solely to the active and effective political organisation of the electorate.

During the mid 1870s Britain experienced the first serious economic depression since the 1840s. Recovery was under way by the 1880s, but the old optimism concerning the future had been shaken and there were unmistakable signs of industrial rivalry and foreign competition, particularly where Germany was concerned. The depression of the 1870s also raised serious social questions and radicals in particular realized that the pressing but different problems of both the large towns and the rural areas could not be met solely through concentrating, as in the early 1870s, on educating the working-class electorate. Even so, liberals and radicals looked on the problem as being primarily a political one: the problem of freedom versus authority. The creed of individual liberty still stood at the heart of liberalism and radicalism; but in practice, from the 1840s onwards, parliamentary legislation on a number of specific issues had clearly shown that there were certain areas where the State must necessarily intervene, either in the interests of justice or in providing safeguards against the exercise of unfettered freedom by some at the expense of many others.

The prospect of increasing State interference ran contrary to two pervasive theories, utilitarianism with the Manchester School emphasis on *laissez faire* and the belief in social evolution derived from Darwinism. Both these creeds encouraged the optimism which had been such a marked characteristic of the mid-nineteenth century. Liberals, and radicals in particular, had long accepted the utilitarian argument that the moral and intellectual capacity of the working classes would develop naturally, given the opportunity of education and better economic conditions, and in time they would become a responsible element of society. They would then exercise the franchise responsibly while remaining docile and willing to accept middle-class political, economic and social leadership. At the same time, continuing economic expansion and prosperity would encourage the middle classes to improve their own conditions of life and those of the working classes through the provision of parks, libraries, art galleries and so on. 'However, the foundations of such beliefs were seriously undermined in the 1870s and 1880s. When the long run of unchecked expansion received a serious setback during the depression of the mid 1870s, the subsequent social investigations of Charles Booth, followed by those of Joseph Rowntree and others, showed beyond any shadow of doubt that the social and economic conditions of thousands of the urban working class, let alone the impoverished rural workers, would not improve of their own accord. The theory and practice of the doctrine of self-help, restraint and hard work, along with the mid-century economic prosperity, had helped to produce a working-class

590

élite; but it would not and could not lift to a better life the masses of un-skilled and impoverished workers. In order to reduce the inequalities of working-class life and raise the economic and social conditions of the masses, the State would have to intervene directly and either supplement or take over from private and voluntary charity organisations, unless the government was prepared to accept the full implications of Social Darwinism and leave the poor to their misery if they could not help themselves.

Undiluted utilitarianism had never in practice formed the theoretical basis of the policy followed by whig and liberal governments any more than it had that of tory governments. For the policy of very limited State interference in matters of health and sanitation, or in relations between employers and the employed through the Factory Acts, had not been the preserve of any one party. Furthermore, the provision of gas, water and other public utilities by municipal authorities, instead of by private com-panies, was regarded as a matter of justice and of cheapness, rather than an interference with private enterprise.

The strictly limited aim and object of State interference was to es-tablish the conditions in which self-help, self-improvement and the moral and intellectual development of all citizens could operate more extensive-ly than before. It was a matter of justice to equalise opportunities; and the need for such justice became the more urgent with the further exten-sion of the franchise to near universal manhood suffrage in 1884. In the political and social situation of the 1880s, a general identity of purpose was to be found among political thinkers and radical liberal politicians in that they concentrated their attention on three main areas where they saw that government could best play an active, although strictly limited role: in education, temperance and land reform. T. H. Green and his school provided a philosophical political basis for a reinterpretation of certain aspects of utilitarian individualism in the light of idealist concepts; and, on a more practical level, some of those who were directly influenc-ed by Green, such as Arnold Toynbee, went out among the working classes to establish means for the improvement of their conditions. For Green's teachings brought a new element into English radicalism. Men from privileged middle-class backgrounds were led to adopt a creed of citizenship and a life of service through which they could help to bring about the moral improvement and fuller development of those much less fortunate than themselves.

In contrast to Green and those who were directly influenced by him, Joseph Chamberlain's radicalism derived from an older middle-class, non-conformist tradition, though the end to be achieved was very similar: social justice through legislation in the interests of all and not deliberately or incidentally in the interests of a few. However, following the split in the liberal party in 1886 when Gladstone adopted Home Rule for Ireland, the strand of radicalism of which Chamberlain was representative soon

D. Liberty and democracy

ceased to be a constructive and dynamic political force.[58] After the long period of conservative and unionist ascendancy in English politics between 1895 and 1905, the 'New Liberalism', of which L. T. Hobhouse was representative, provided the intellectual basis of the active programme of social legislation introduced by the liberal governments of Campbell-Bannerman and Asquith between 1906 and 1914. There was, however, no clear break between the *laissez faire* liberalism of the mid-nineteenth century and the 'New Liberalism' of the early twentieth century, although governments were willing to play a more direct role in bringing about a greater degree of social justice and an equalization of opportunities.

Thomas Hill Green (1836–82), fellow and tutor at Balliol, Oxford, and later Professor of Moral Philosophy, combined in his career the roles of philosopher and political thinker. At the same time, he had practical experience in local politics through being elected as one of the town councillors for Oxford. In the 1860s he had given active support to the Reform League in pressing for the extension of the franchise; and subsequently he had been a supporter of the National Education League and of plans to extend and improve secondary and adult education in Oxford. In addition he was very active in the temperance movement and supported the adoption of legislation as a means of curbing drunkenness among the working classes. Green regarded these and other measures as practical ways through which the condition of life among the working classes could be improved, and individual self-development thereby encouraged.

Green was very careful to distinguish between the old paternalism and the moderate State intervention that he proposed: 'The true ground of objection to "paternal government" is not that it violates the *laissez faire* principle and conceives that its office is to make people good, to promote morality, but that it rests on a misconception of morality. The real function of government being to maintain the conditions of life in which morality shall be possible. . . .'[59] The end result of this process, in Green's view, would be the development of a sense of citizenship among working-class people and their full participation in the national political life. They would then be able to ensure that their own interests were taken into account when parliament was considering legislation that would affect them. Further, Green hoped that the active and informed participation of the working classes in political life would lead to the recognition of an identity of interests between the middle classes and the working classes, and so bring to an end middle-class tutelage of the working class. Conversely, the acceptance of an ideal of citizenship provided a means whereby men from the wealthy, educated middle classes could directly aid in removing some of the barriers that divided the middle class and the working class, and in leading working-class men and women towards

592

moral improvement and fuller self development. In that way, citizenship, as a social and secular religion, would in some measure provide a substitute faith for the evangelicalism in which Green and others of his generation had been brought up, but which seemed to them less and less able to provide an answer to the problems of late nineteenth-century society.

The philosophical basis of Green's political thinking was his rejection of both the older utilitarianism and the newer Social Darwinism for an idealism based on certain aspects of the philosophy of Kant and Hegel. Two ideas in particular influenced Green: the idea of moral and individual self-realization and that of progress. Green's idealist philosophy, as well as his rejection of evangelicalism, were therefore essential elements in determining his political philosophy.[60] In brief, the principle of 'positive freedom' meant the removal, through legislation, of the obstacles that prevented 'the liberation of the powers of all men equally for contributions to a common good' (doc. 108). In its most basic form this entailed the intervention of the State to protect from exploitation those who were least able to look after their own interests. Having laid down this principle, Green remained over-optimistic concerning both the capacity and the desire of the working classes for moral as well as material improvement, once the State had removed what were regarded as the barriers to such development.

Although the term 'collectivism' has been applied to Green's concept of 'positive freedom', it is not truly applicable; because to him the end result of state intervention in certain clearly defined and limited directions was to uphold the right of the citizen to the full development of the individual as a member of society.[61] Active citizenship would then represent the awareness of 'an idea of common good, which each member of the society can make his own so far as he is rational'.[62] Citizens, therefore, must have a sense of duty as well as an understanding of their rights; and, conversely, a citizen's right to disobey the law would depend on whether or not such disobedience would be in the interests of the common good. State intervention, then, was no more and no less than 'the removal of all obstructions which the law can remove to the free development of English citizens'.[63] The precedent had already been established by existing legislation relating to some forms of labour, as well as to health and education; and Green advocated the extension of the principle to the disposition, sale and letting of land and to liquor licensing.[64]

Green's political influence in the early 1880s was not widespread beyond Oxford. His radical liberalism had most effect on men, such as Asquith, who entered politics after being taught by him at Balliol. In that way, Green's ideas became very influential between 1890 and 1914 in forming a bridge between utilitarianism and the older radicalism of the nineteenth century, on the one side, and, on the other, the 'Progressive

D. Liberty and democracy

Movement' of the 1890s, the 'New Liberalism' of the early twentieth century and the social legislation of the liberal government between 1906 and 1914.

In contrast to Green's limited scope of appeal, popular radicalism in the 1880s was associated with Joseph Chamberlain (1836–1914). Chamberlain had first been active in radical and non-conformist politics in Birmingham in the late 1860s. Following the election of 1868, which resulted in a liberal victory, and given the strength of radicalism and non-conformity in Birmingham, Chamberlain saw in the agitation preceding and following the Elementary Education Act of 1870 an opportunity of ensuring that the newly enfranchised urban working class would become an active force in British politics. In 1869 Chamberlain had taken the lead in creating the National Education League; and four years later his activities in the fight to take the control of education in Birmingham out of the hands of the conservatives and the Church of England brought him to the mayoralty. At the same time Chamberlain recognized that on the national political level radicalism, and therefore non-conformity, had to find a wider field of action than education, and hence his call in 1873–74 for the four freedoms of 'Free Church, Free Schools, Free Land and Free Labour'. His drive in establishing the Birmingham municipal gas and water supplies on a firm financial basis showed that publicly controlled enterprises could be profitable and efficient, and, in the case of water, provided cheaply as well. The principle on which Chamberlain saw such enterprises resting, that private individuals or companies should not exercise a monopolistic control of those enterprises which provided essential public necessities, later formed the basis of one of his arguments in favour of State intervention on a national level in connection with land ownership, slum clearance, the safety of merchant shipping, and free education.

As a radical, Chamberlain accepted the arguments that the weak should be protected against the strong, and that all men had a right to equal opportunities in conditions in which they could make the best of themselves.[65] This was only justice in the 1880s when government was no longer that of a particular class but that of the people as a whole; for, as Chamberlain pointed out, 'Politics is the science of human happiness, and the business of a statesman and of politicians is to find out how they can raise the general condition of the people; how they can increase the happiness of those who are less fortunate among them.'[66] By the time Chamberlain made those remarks he was trying to reach a wider audience to win support for radicalism from among the working classes as well as middle-class support for social reform.

With Chamberlain's appointment to the Board of Trade with Cabinet rank in 1880, the strength of the radical wing in the liberal party seemed to have been recognized; but political and social reform moved more slowly than Chamberlain wished. With the passage of the 1884 Reform Act, which extended the franchise to near manhood suffrage and established single-member constituencies for the most part, Chamberlain recognized the pressing need for a social programme that would win the new rural as well as the urban working-class voters for liberalism and establish beyond all doubt that 'government is only the organization of the whole people for the benefit of all its members'. [67] This belief was the basis of the 'state socialism', proclaimed by Chamberlain in his 'unauthorized programme' during the 1885 election campaign − a programme that differed somewhat in content and emphasis from *The Radical Programme* which had been in preparation under Chamberlain's guidance during the past two years. As the majority of the nation would then be represented in the House of Commons, 'ideas and wants and claims which have been hitherto ignored in legislation will find a voice in Parliament, and will compel the attention of statesmen'.[68] Chamberlain therefore proclaimed that liberalism and radicalism must turn from clearing the ground to undertaking 'constructive legislation'.

Chamberlain frequently used the term 'socialism' in his speeches; and on one occasion, when he attempted to define his meaning, he said: 'The Poor Law is Socialism; the Education Act is Socialism; the greater part of municipal work is Socialism; and every kindly act of legislation by which the community has sought to discharge its responsibilities and obligations to the poor is Socialism.' [69] On another occasion Chamberlain spoke of the 'ransom' that might be required of the landed classes;[70] but in each case what he was calling for was no more than moderate intervention on the part of the State, in the interests of justice, so that the working classes, when they had been politically educated, would be drawn into cooperation and not into antagonism with the Government. In his electoral campaign in the autumn of 1885 Chamberlain therefore concentrated on three major issues: land reform, through local authorities having the power to acquire land for allotments or for small holdings in order to bring into existence a class of small landowners; free education; and a system of graduated taxation whereby the wealthy would pay a fairer share than they did at present in comparison with the poorer classes (doc. 109). However, he was in no sense attacking property as such or preaching confiscation. His concern rather was to lessen inequalities by providing the legislative framework in which excessive inequalities in the distribution of wealth could be corrected and the general condition of the people raised.[71]

Despite the great liberal and radical electoral victory of 1885, the political force of radicalism was quickly dissipated when Gladstone took up the issue of Irish Home Rule in 1886 instead of social reform; and Chamberlain's subsequent resignation from the Cabinet split the liberal party. There was little hope of advance in the direction of social reform as long as Gladstone was determined to concentrate on Irish Home Rule.

D. Liberty and democracy

This was one of the reasons for the development in the 1890s of the 'Progressive Movement' among radicals and others, such as the Webbs. As a political thinker, L. T. Hobhouse contributed decisively to the ideas on social policy fostered by the 'Progressive Movement'. For the most part its supporters were younger men then entering political life, men who had to a greater or lesser extent been influenced by T. H. Green rather than by the political radicalism of the 1880s, of which John Morley remained representative in the liberal party.

Leonard Trelawney Hobhouse (1864–1929), after being educated at Marlborough and Corpus Christi, Oxford, began his career teaching philosophy at Oxford. In the late 1880s and early 1890s his interest in philosophy, sociology and politics led him to be active in supporting trade unionism, particularly the organization of unskilled workers in the 'New Unions' which were then rapidly expanding, and also in extending the scope of adult and worker education. Although Hobhouse did not by any means fully accept T. H. Green's idealistic philosophy, he was, like Green, greatly concerned about social and economic justice for the working classes and the improvement of their conditions of life in the interests of human betterment. In the early 1890s, Hobhouse's interest in the development of the labour movement led him to advocate closer relations between the trade union movement and the cooperative movement; and he regarded the extension of government intervention, at both the national and the municipal level, as the best means of lessening the inequalities and removing the injustices which adversely affected the working classes and stunted the opportunities for betterment that were open to them.

This was the theme of *The Labour Movement* which was published in 1893 with a foreword by R. B. Haldane. In political terms, both Hobhouse and Haldane were aware by the 1890s that unless the liberals and radicals could put forward a social and economic programme which offered the means of improving their conditions, the trend among the urban working classes to support the conservatives and unionists would continue. As in Green's case, Hobhouse and Haldane were still assuming that the working classes were interested in their own moral improvement as well as their material improvement.[72] His aim was to bring about 'a good and full life for all members of the community'.[73] Hobhouse was particularly concerned about 'the relation of liberty to collective control because it lies at the root of the harmonic conception of society'. For 'the collective effort, which has already been in progress in this country for a generation or more, is not adverse to the freedom, the responsibility, or the dignity of the individual'.[74] It was on this basis that Hobhouse advocated going much further than Green had done in the direction of State intervention in order to bring about 'a better distribution of wealth'. When that had been achieved, there would be a better distribution of duties: 'We have to work towards a healthier state of social organisation in which each man will find his place in society and will recognize it. The "social organism" is a perfect organism only when its members feel that they depend on one another.' [75] It was, therefore, through the progressive achievement of social justice that Hobhouse could ascribe to the liberal belief in progress.

In the middle stage of his career between 1897 and 1902, Hobhouse combined philosophy and sociology with political and social journalism on the staff of the radical liberal and anti-imperialist *Manchester Guardian*, then under C. P. Scott's control. [76] In 1907 Hobhouse entered the final stage of his career when he was appointed Martin White Professor of Sociology at the London School of Economics. He then wrote his two most mature statements on political thought published in 1911: *Social Evolution and Political Theory*, the text of a series of lectures given at Columbia University, and *Liberalism*, a succinct, but clear, theoretical statement of the liberal doctrines which had provided the basis for the social legislation introduced by the liberal government since 1906.

Hobhouse always maintained that there was no essential break between the mid nineteenth century liberalism of Cobden and the 'New Liberalism' of the early twentieth century. [77] The difference between them concerned means and not ends, because the State only stepped in where the conditions of true freedom did not apply: 'Rightly understood, therefore, this kind of socialistic legislation appears not as an infringement of the two distinctive ideals of the older Liberalism, "Liberty and Equality". It appears rather as a necessary means to their fulfilment. It comes not to destroy but to fulfil.' [78] Government by the end of the nineteenth century was no longer 'an alien power' but 'the organ of the governed';[79] and so, once there is no longer any antagonism between democracy and governmental action: 'In its place there arises a stronger sense of collective responsibility and a keener desire for the use of the collective resources and organized powers of the community for public needs.'[80] Further, the object of the community, through government action, 'is to secure certain conditions which it believes necessary for the welfare of its members, and which can be secured only by an enforced uniformity' (doc. 110a).

In 1911, following on from the liberal government's social legislation providing for old-age pensions, health and unemployment insurance, Hobhouse felt that the prevailing economic conditions, especially with regard to land ownership and the industrial situation, were most in need of change through government action in the direction of bringing about greater economic equality in the interests of the working classes (doc. 110b).[81] That was an end which he had long believed could not be achieved by increased production, but only through a more equitable distribution of wealth. [82] However, the liberal governments of Campbell-Bannerman and Asquith were far more hesitant to enter these areas of reform even at the risk of alienating working-class support.

Hobhouse, again like T. H. Green, was far too optimistic that the labour movement would always work in harmony with the middle classes and would not pursue its own separate interests and seek political power for itself.[83] In the event, the First World War hastened the process that Hobhouse had hoped to avoid; and liberalism was left in the post-war world to face the almost impossible task of finding a new political and economic programme in order to ensure its survival. As for Hobhouse, he refused to join the Labour Party, and in the 1920s he attempted, though unsuccessfully, to rebuild the foundations of liberal and working-class cooperation.

4. Freedom and power: introduction

(Documents 111–12, pp. 669–73)

Lord Acton was a thinker and historian *sui generis*, with a complex dialectical approach of his own. Like Tocqueville he differed sharply from the run-of-the-mill liberals who in the wake of the Enlightenment believed in the automatic march towards progress and in the perfectibility of man. Often enigmatic and sometimes self-contradictory, he was never satisfied with convenient stereotypes. 'When you perceive a truth', he wrote, 'look out for the balancing truth.'

In an age of advancing industrial organization which also saw the rise of new nationalities, Acton was not the only historical thinker vexed by the problems of Power. He did not go as far as his Swiss contemporary Jacob Burckhardt who maintained that 'power is in itself evil.' [84] Burckhardt was inclined to escape from the study of that insatiable powerdrive into the realm of aesthetic contemplation. Acton, on the other hand, saw history largely as a tug-of-war between the corrupting effect of power and the striving of the conscience of individuals for liberty. His insistence that 'power tends to corrupt and absolute power corrupts absolutely' led him to suspect all authority. Yet he seems to have believed that authority can be redeemed, if it serves the cause of liberty. 'Authority that does not exist for liberty', he wrote, 'is not authority, but force. It has no sanction.' [85] If Acton had a bias it was anti-authoritarian. In a passage in his Correspondence with Creighton, he sharply rejected a favourable, indulgent attitude towards popes and kings, the Establishment of the past. He insisted they must be judged like other men. For their temptations were greater than those of other men. History was 'not a web woven with innocent hands. Among all the causes which degrade and demoralise men, power is the most constant and the most active'. [86] Yet such pessimism was not unmitigated. For Acton believed in the redeeming strength of the individual conscience which 'exists in each of us. It is limited by the consciences of others. ... It tends to restrict authority and to enlarge liberty. It is the law of self-government.' [87]

Though his planned 'History of Freedom' was unfortunately never completed, the fragments we have clearly indicate that the relationship between authority and liberty was a focal point of his interest. A State, Acton declared, has to possess some authority, but a reasonable modicum is seldom to be found. In antiquity the State intruded on the domain of personal freedom. In the Middle Ages it possessed too little authority and suffered others to intrude. Modern states were plagued by both excesses.

Acton views the role of liberty in history without trying to idealize it (doc. 111). As he sees it, in history liberty next to religion bears man's Janus face. 'Liberty has been the motive of good deeds and the common pretext of crime, from the sowing of the seed at Athens' in the fifth century B. C. 'until the ripened harvest was gathered' by men of the British race. Liberty has fought an uphill struggle against formidable odds, against ignorance and superstition, lust of conquest and love of ease against 'the strong man's craving for power and the poor man's craving for food'. Like Mill, Acton was convinced that progress was a matter of small élites. 'At all times sincere friends of freedom have been rare and its triumphs have been due to minorities', though the latter sometimes imperilled their cause by an association with auxiliaries pursuing very different interests. To survey the uneasy struggle in which the zest for freedom was pursued through the centuries was the task of the historian; to offer a valid formulation of liberty was that of the moralist. In the struggle for liberty there were gains and losses. Acton was too realistic as well as too pessimistic to accept the belief in constant and irrepressible progress voiced by Condorcet and later by the nationalistic liberals. It is significant that in his definition of liberty, quoted earlier (see p. 582); Acton bracketed authority and majorities together as the powers by which the freedom of the individual was threatened. He emphasized that religious liberty and civil liberty condition each other, a discovery made in the seventeenth century. It was then found in England that religious liberty 'is possible only where the co-existence of different religions is admitted, with an equal right to govern themselves according to their own several principles'. Only in communities where rights are sacred and where law is supreme can religious and civil liberty flourish.

'If the first duty is held to be obedience to authority and the preservation of order, as in the case of aristocracies and monarchies of the patriarchal type, there is no safety for the liberties either of individuals or of religion. Where the highest consideration is the public good and the popular will, as in democracies, and in constitutional monarchies after the French pattern, majority takes the place of authority, an irresistible power is substituted for an idolatrous principle, and all private rights are equally insecure.' [88]

D. Liberty and democracy

In his contemplation of the pressures exercised by various forms of power throughout history Acton was indeed a pessimist.

As he put it, history could become 'a school of liberalism' for it showed 'that three great things are not what they seem — Fame, antiquity and power'. He argued that 'history undermines respect. Very little looking up to persons ... wherein history is liberal, teaches disrespect. Shows up horrors, error, follies, crimes of the ablest and the best'. [89] Yet Acton's pessimism never impaired or dimmed his vision. To him liberty remained 'the highest ideal of man, the reflection of his divinity'. In the words of Gertrude Himmelfarb, 'Acton had the highest of ideals and the most modest of expectations.' [90]

This indefatigable critic of the aberrations of power and believer in an absolute morality was proud of the prominent share his own country had in the relative advance towards a more liberalized society. Surveying the struggle between the power holders and the champions of religious and civil liberty, he dwelt on 'the impressive fact that so much of the hard fighting, the thinking, the enduring that has contributed to the deliverance of man from the power of man' had been the work of the British and of their descendants abroad. Acton praised the British 'qualities of perseverance, moderation, individuality and manly sense of duty' which had enabled people of their stock 'to thrive as no other can on inhospitable shores'. In the heyday of the British Empire this austere historian of power-politics displayed a mild glow of optimism as far as his own nation was concerned. As he put it in the conclusion of the essay on 'The History of Freedom in Christianity' (1877): 'If there is reason for pride in the past, there is more for hope in the time to come. Our advantages increase while other nations fear their neighbours or covet their neighbour's goods. Anomalies and defects there are, fewer and less intolerable, if not less flagrant than of old.' [91] Acton firmly believed that a liberal approach to life had been more fully developed in England than abroad.

Acton, the historian, surveyed and judged 3,000 years of history from the summit of his political philosophy and the vast resources of his knowledge. He was convinced that great men were 'almost always bad men, even when they exercise influence and not authority: still more, when you super-add the tendency or the certainty of corruption by authority.' As he saw it there was 'no worse heresy than that the office sanctifies the holder of it'. [92]

Alain, [93] in his own way a moralist too, was full of scepticism and distrust towards the power-holders. A humanist with a classical background, he was concerned with contemporary France, with the current affairs and political practices of the Third Republic. His argument that one should not allow oneself to be deceived by the façade of politics and Government appealed to innumerable Frenchmen in the years before and after the First World War. They felt vaguely what Alain expressed in his eloquent diction that there were hidden flaws in the parliamentary and governmental system, that reality and presentation, the facts and their image seemed to differ greatly and that power-holders often tended to take an inflated view of their importance. In Alain's eyes power did not so much corrupt as inflate the egos of the men who exercised it (doc. 112a and b). That state of affairs should not be allowed to continue. Ways must be found of making all office holders directly or indirectly accountable to the citizens. Imperative was the permanent control of the elected by the elector, of the minister by the elected (deputies) and of the administrative apparatus by the minister who technically was in charge of it. This minister should live up to his true function, that of 'a People's Tribune'. Alain had few illusions about the power-game played by the military and the bureaucracy, setting the pace for other sections of the Establishment: 'Every diplomat loves his schemes; every police commissioner loves order; every senior clerk works towards the extension of his right of control and of his prerogatives ... Altogether the abuse of power is a natural fruit of power; and so it follows that all people who fall asleep in liberty will wake up in servitude.' [94] It is the army which sets the model for the exercise of power. A colonel knows how to persuade and how to punish. The subordinate ranks let his orders circulate to the farthest points of the army corps. The power of the police differs little from this model. Other power-holders, such as the judge or the industrialist, depend on these two and follow suit. As a result the citizens are more governed than is necessary. While the army extends and establishes itself by its very nature, all the power-holders imitate it from the President who demands new powers downward. People who call themselves democrats are naive enough not to see through this power-game. 'In their eyes it is sufficient that the people are consulted from time to time, in such a way that they could choose other masters or confirm the present ones.'[95] Meanwhile deputies and ministers are trapped by the official machinery.

Alain proposed a different concept of leadership. The people should not elect chiefs, but *controllers*. The Head of State should not be seen 'as the head of all the State offices but as the delegate of the people, the model citizen who has the task to discover all abuses of power, and to put an end to them', a gigantic Ombudsman, as we would say today, fifty years after Alain.[96] Only in this way he thought, could the power of the Establishment be deflated and the freedom of millions of ordinary citizens be safeguarded.

With the growing pressure of collectivism and of the exposure of minorities in the present century vigilance in the face of the concentration and abuse of power has become an essential feature of the liberal legacy.

Notes and references

1. Are liberty and democracy compatible?

1. Douglas Johnson, *Guizot*, London 1963, p. 77.
2. Ibid., p. 78.
3. Preface to Part I, *Democracy in America*, trans. H. Reeve, ed. H. S. Commager, (World's Classics) Oxford 1946, p. 16.
4. Reprinted in A. de Tocqueville, *Memoir, Letters and Remains*, London 1861, I, pp. 253–62.
5. Tocqueville, *Democracy in America*, p. 48.
6, 7. Ibid., p. 49.
8. Ibid., p. 307.
9. Ibid., p. 143.
10. J. J. Auchmuty, *Lecky: A Biographical and Critical Essay*, Dublin and London 1945, p. 3.
11. Lecky, *Democracy and Liberty*, I, p. 213.
12. J. J. Auchmuty, op. cit., p. 82.
13. M. Chevalier, *History of Political Economy Taught by the History of Labour*, London 1869, p. 43.
14. The article appeared 1912 in Naumann's weekly journal *Die Hilfe*, vol. 18, No. 6. It has been recently reprinted in Friedrich Naumann, *Politische Schriften*, ed. Theodor Schieder, II, Köln 1964, II, 439–44.
15. Wolfgang J. Mommsen in his introduction to Friedrich Naumann, *Politische Schriften*, II, Köln 1964, p. 15.

2. The tyranny of the majority and the right to non-conformity

16. Tocqueville, *Democracy in America*, trans. H. Reeve, ed. H. S. Commager (World's Classics) Oxford 1946, p. 16.
17. Ibid., p. 299.
18. Ibid., p. 185.
19. Ibid., pp. 189–90.
20. Ibid., p. 196.
21. Quoted in Jack Lively, *The Social and Political Thought of Alexis de Tocqueville*, Oxford 1962, p. 102.
22. *Democracy in America*, p. 192.
23, 24. Ibid., p. 228.
25. Ibid., p. 205.
26. J. Lively, op. cit., p. 109.
27. Quoted in J. Lively, op. cit., p. 110.
28. *On Liberty*, (Everyman's Library edn.), Ch. 3, p. 128.
29. J. S. Mill, op. cit., p. 129.
30. Ibid., p. 130.
31. J. S. Mill in his article 'Centralisation', *Edinburgh Review* (1862) p. 358. Quoted in John M. Robson, *The Improvement of Mankind*, Toronto and London 1968, p. 222.
32. *On Liberty*, Ch. 7, p. 122.
33. John M. Robson, op. cit., p. 244.
34. *Democracy in America*, Ch. 4, p. 57.
35. Quoted in John M. Robson, op. cit., p. 221.

36. Ibid., p. 222.
37. *Representative Government*, Ch. 10, p. 347.
38. For Acton's concept of power see p. 598, below.

3. The limitations and the scope of the State

39. First published in *Social Statics* (1851), reprinted in the essay 'The Sins of Legislators', *The Man versus the State*, (1884) London 1909, p. 67.
40. 'Over-Legislation', in *Essays: Scientific, Political and Speculative*, London 1868, pp. 54–5.
41. 'Over-Legislation', op. cit., pp. 93–4.
42. 'Over-Legislation', op. cit., pp. 102–3.
43. *Social Statics*, 1868 edn, p. 229.
44. 'Over-Legislation', op. cit., p. 72.
45. 'The Coming Slavery' in *The Man Versus the State*, pp. 35–6.
46. 'The Coming Slavery', op. cit., p. 38.
47. 'The Coming Slavery', op. cit., p. 39.
48. 'The Coming Slavery', op. cit., p. 43.
49. 'The Coming Slavery', op. cit., p. 107.
50. 'Over-Legislation', op. cit., pp. 105–6.
51. Ernest Barker, *Political Thought in England 1878–1914*, London 1928, p. 71.
52. Henri Brunschwig, *French Colonialism 1871–1914. Myths and Realities*, London 1966, p. 27.
53. Agnes Murphy, *The Ideology of French Imperialism 1871–1881*, Washington 1948, p. 105.
54. *De la colonisation chez les peuples modernes*, Paris 1874.
55. Quoted from the Comité's *Bulletin* in H. Brunschwig, op. cit., p. 111.
56. H. Brunschwig, op. cit., p. 117.
57. J. S. Mill, *Autobiography* ed. Max Lerner, New York 1961, pp. 136–9.
58. The Newcastle Programme of 1891 was little more than a diluted form of the Radical Programme of 1885.
59. T. H. Green, *Lectures on the Principles of Political Obligation*, London 1895, pp. 39–40.
60. This is particularly the case with regard to his *Lectures on the Principles of Political Obligation*, delivered in Oxford between 1879 and 1880 but not published until after his death. However, the essence of his concept of 'positive freedom' and his advocacy of some practical applications of that idea can be found in a somewhat later lecture on 'Liberal Legislation and Freedom of Contract'. This was given to the Liberal Association at Leicester early in 1881, in support of legislation to be introduced by the Gladstone administration. T. H. Green, *Works*, ed. R. L. Nettleship, London 1891, III, pp. 365–86.
61. *Ibid.*, pp. 371, 374.
62. R. L. Nettleship, 'Memoir'; in T. H. Green, *Works*, III, p. cl.
63. *Ibid.*, p. cxxx; quoting from a speech by Green in Oxford, 10 January 1882.
64. 'Liberal Legislation and Freedom of Contract', *Works*, III, pp. 377–84.
65. For example see Chamberlain's speech to the Eighty Club, 28 April 1885. *Speeches of the Right Hon. Joseph Chamberlain M.P.*, ed. Henry W. Lucy, London 1885, pp. 130–1, 132.
66. Speech at Glasgow, 15 September 1885. Ibid., p. 198.
67. Speech to the Eighty Club, 28 April 1885. Ibid., p. 131.
68. Chamberlain's preface to *The Radical Programme*, dated July 1885. *The Radical Programme*, ed. with an Introduction by D. A. Hamer, Brighton 1971.

D. Liberty and democracy

69. Speech at Warrington, 8 September 1885. *Speeches* ed. Lucy, p. 189.
70. Speech at Birmingham, 5 January 1885. Ibid., p. 104.
71. Apart from Gladstone's attempt to deal with the Irish land question, the control of land as a political issue had been forcefully raised by the publication of Henry George's *Progress and Poverty* (1879).
72. L. T. Hobhouse, *The Labour Movement* with a preface by R. B. Haldane, London 1893, pp. xi, 92–3.
73. *Ibid.*, p. 3.
74. L. T. Hobhouse, *Social Evolution and Political Theory*, London 1911, pp. 203–4.
75. L. T. Hobhouse, *The Labour Movement*, p. 4.
76. Hobhouse's next major political work, *Democracy and Reaction* (published in 1904) arose out of his experience in opposition to the South African War and his belief that the masses had been drawn away from liberal democracy by imperialism. It was necessary therefore, if liberalism was to survive, to provide it with a programme that would bring the middle classes and the new political labour movement together by lessening economic and social inequalities and providing a sense of community.
77. L. T. Hobhouse, *Democracy and Reaction*, ed. with an Introduction by P. F. Clarke, Brighton 1972, pp. 214, 217.
78. *Ibid.*, p. 217.
79. *Ibid.*, p. 220.
80. *Ibid*, pp. 221–2.
81. Hobhouse was particularly concerned that the State should have power to acquire land bordering on the new towns. Ibid., pp. 230–1.
82. *The Labour Movement*, p. 3.
83. Preface to 1909 edition of *Democracy and Reaction*, p. 271.

4. Freedom and power

84. Jakob Burckhardt, *Reflections on History*, London 1943, p. 38.
85. Quoted in L. Kochan, *Acton on History*, London 1957, p. 119.
86. *Add. MSS* University Library, Cambridge, 5011.
87. *Add. MSS.*, University Library, Cambridge, 4091.
88. 'The Protestant Theory of Persecution' in *Lord Acton, Essays on Freedom and Power*, selected by G. Himmelfarb, London 1956, pp. 115–16.
89. Quoted in Lionel Kochan, *Acton on History*, London 1954, p. 134.
90. Gertrude Himmelfarb, *Lord Acton. A Study in Conscience and Politics*, London 1952, p. 241.
91. Lord Acton, *The History of Freedom in Christianity*. An address delivered to the members of the Bridgnorth Institute on 28 May 1877, Bridgnorth 1877, p. 12.
92. 'Acton-Creighton Correspondence', reprinted in *Essays on Freedom and Power*, selected by Gertrude Himmelfarb, p. 364.
93. On Alain as a French Radical see pp. 78–9.
94. Alain, *Politiques*, Paris 1952, pp. 7–8.
95. Alain, essay 'Le Tribun', *Elements d'une doctrine radicale*, Paris 1925, p. 14.
96. Ibid., this essay appeared first on 15 May 1924.

Documents

1. Are liberty and democracy compatible?: documents
(Introduction, p. 569)

Doc. 96. ALEXIS DE TOCQUEVILLE: The Influence of Democratic Opinions and Sentiments on Political Society

The principle of equality, which makes men independent of each other, gives them a habit and a taste for following, in their private actions, no other guide but their own will. This complete independence, which they constantly enjoy toward their equals and in the intercourse of private life, tends to make them look upon all authority with a jealous eye, and speedily suggests to them the notion and the love of political freedom. Men living at such times have a natural bias to free institutions. Take any one of them at a venture, and search if you can his most deep-seated instincts; you will find that of all governments he will soonest conceive and most highly value that government whose head he has himself elected, and whose administration he may control. Of all the political effects produced by the equality of conditions, this love of independence is the first to strike the observing, and to alarm the timid; nor can it be said that their alarm is wholly misplaced, for anarchy has a more formidable aspect in democratic countries than elsewhere. As the citizens have no direct influence on each other, as soon as the supreme power of the nation fails, which kept them all in their several stations, it would seem that disorder must instantly reach its utmost pitch, and that, every man drawing aside in a different direction, the fabric of society must at once crumble away.

I am, however, persuaded that anarchy is not the principal evil that democratic ages have to fear, but the least. For the principle of equality begets two tendencies: the one leads men straight to independence, and may suddenly drive them into anarchy; the other conducts them by a longer, more secret, but more certain road, to servitude. Nations readily discern the former tendency, and are prepared to resist it; they are led away by the latter, without perceiving its drift; hence it is peculiarly important to point it out ...

On reflecting upon what has already been said, the reader will be startled and alarmed to find that in Europe everything seems to conduce to the indefinite extension of the prerogatives of government, and to render all that enjoyed the rights of private independence more weak, more subordinate, and more precarious. The democratic nations of Europe have all the general and permanent tendencies which urge the Americans to the centralization of government, and they are, moreover, exposed to a number of secondary and incidental causes with which the Americans are unacquainted. It would seem as if every step they make toward equality brings them nearer to despotism. And, indeed, if we do but cast our looks around, we shall be convinced that such is the fact. During the aristocratic ages which preceded the present time, the sovereigns of Europe had been deprived of, or had relinquished, many of the rights inherent in their power. Not a hundred years ago, among the greater part of European nations, numerous private persons and corporations were sufficiently independent to administer justice, to raise and maintain troops, to levy taxes, and frequently even to make or interpret the law. The State has everywhere resumed to itself alone these natural attributes of sovereign power; in all matters of government the State tolerates no intermediate agent between itself and the people, and in general business it directs the people by its own immediate influence. I am far from blaming this concentration of powers, I simply point it out.

At the same period a great number of secondary powers existed in Europe, which represented local interests and administered local affairs. Most of these local authorities have already disappeared; all are speedily tending to disappear, or fall into the most complete dependence. From one end of Europe to the other the privileges of the nobility, the liberties of cities, and the powers of provincial bodies, are either destroyed or upon the verge of destruction. Europe has endured, in the course of the last half century, many revolutions and counter-revolutions which have agitated it in opposite directions: but all these perturbations resemble each other in one respect – they have all shaken or destroyed the secondary powers of government. The local privileges which the French did not abolish in the countries they conquered, have finally succumbed to the policy of the princes who conquered the French. Those princes rejected all the innovations of the French Revolution except centralization: that is the only principle they consented to receive from such a source. My object is to remark, that all these various rights, which have been successively wrested, in our time, from classes, corporations, and individuals, have not served to raise new secondary powers on a more democratic basis, but have uniformly been concentrated in the hands of the sovereign. Everywhere the State acquires more and more direct control over the humblest members of the community, and a more exclusive power of governing each of them in his smallest concerns. Almost all the charitable establishments of Europe were formerly in the hands of private persons or of corporations; they are now almost all dependent on the supreme government, and in many countries are actually administered by that power. The State almost exclusively undertakes to supply bread to the hungry, assistance and shelter to the sick, work to the idle, and to act as the sole reliever of all kinds of misery. Education, as well as charity, is become in most countries at the present day a national concern. The State receives, and often takes, the child from the arms of the mother, to hand it over to official agents: the State undertakes to train the heart and to instruct the mind of each generation. Uniformity prevails in the courses of public instruction as in everything else; diversity, as well as freedom, are disappearing day by day. Nor do I hesitate to affirm that among almost all the Christian nations of our days, Catholic as well as Protestant, religion is in danger of falling into the hands of the government. Not that rulers are over-jealous of the right of settling points of doctrine, but they get more and more hold upon the will of those by whom doctrines are expounded; they deprive the clergy of their property, and pay them by salaries; they divert to their own use the influence of the priesthood, they make them their own ministers – often their own servants – and by this alliance with religion they reach the inner depths of the soul of man ...

The authority of government has not only spread ... throughout the sphere of all existing powers, till that sphere can no longer contain it, but it goes further, and invades the domain heretofore reserved to private independence. A multitude of actions, which were formerly entirely beyond the control of the public administration, have been subjected to that control in our time, and the number of them is constantly increasing. Among aristocratic nations the supreme government usually contented itself with managing and superintending the community in whatever directly and ostensibly concerned the national honour; but in all other respects the people were left to work out their own free will. Among these nations the government often seemed to forget that there is a point at which the faults and the sufferings of private persons involve the general prosperity, and that to prevent the ruin of a private individual must sometimes be a matter of public importance. The democratic nations of our time lean to the opposite extreme. It is evident that most of our rulers will not content themselves with governing the people collectively: it would seem as if they thought themselves responsible for the actions and private condition of their subjects – as if they had undertaken to guide and to instruct each

D. Liberty and democracy

of them in the various incidents of life, and to secure their happiness quite independently of their own consent. On the other hand, private individuals grow more and more apt to look upon the supreme power in the same light; they invoke its assistance in all their necessities, and they fix their eyes upon the administration as their mentor or their guide....

In the ages of aristocracy which preceded our own, there were private persons of great power, and a social authority of extreme weakness. The outline of society itself was not easily discernible, and constantly confounded with the different powers by which the community was ruled. The principal efforts of the men of those times were required to strengthen, aggrandize, and secure the supreme power; and, on the other hand, to circumscribe individual independence within narrower limits, and to subject private interests to the interests of the public. Other perils and other cares await the men of our age. Among the greater part of modern nations, the government, whatever may be its origin, its constitution, or its name, has become almost omnipotent, and private persons are falling, more and more, into the lowest stage of weakness and dependence. In olden society everything was different; unity and uniformity were nowhere to be met with. In modern society everything threatens to become so much alike, that the peculiar characteristics of each individual will soon be entirely lost in the general aspect of the world. Our forefathers were ever prone to make an improper use of the notion that private rights ought to be respected; and we are naturally prone, on the other hand, to exaggerate the idea that the interest of a private individual ought always to bend to the interest of the many. The political world is metamorphosed: new remedies must henceforth be sought for new disorders. To lay down extensive, but distinct and settled limits, to the action of the government; to confer certain rights on private persons, and to secure to them the undisputed enjoyment of those rights; to enable individual man to maintain whatever independence, strength, and original power he still possesses; to raise him by the side of society at large, and uphold him in that position – these appear to me the main objects of legislators in the ages upon which we are now entering. It would seem as if the rulers of our time sought only to use men in order to make things great; I wish that they would try a little more to make great men; that they would set less value on the work, and more upon the workman; that they would never forget that a nation cannot long remain strong when every man belonging to it is individually weak, and that no form or combination of social polity has yet been devised to make an energetic people out of a community of pusillanimous and enfeebled citizens.

I trace among our contemporaries two contrary notions which are equally injurious. One set of men can perceive nothing in the principle of equality but the anarchical tendencies which it engenders: they dread their own free agency – they fear themselves. Other thinkers, less numerous but more enlightened, take a different view: beside that track which starts from the principle of equality to terminate in anarchy, they have at last discovered the road which seems to lead men to inevitable servitude. They shape their souls beforehand to this necessary condition; and, despairing of remaining free, they already do obeisance in their hearts to the master who is soon to appear. The former abandon freedom, because they think it dangerous; the latter, because they hold it to be impossible. If I had entertained the latter conviction, I should not have written this book, but I should have confined myself to deploring in secret the destiny of mankind. I have sought to point out the dangers to which the principle of equality exposes the independence of man, because I firmly believe that these dangers are the most formidable, as well as the least foreseen, of all those which futurity holds in store: but I do not think that they are insurmountable. The men who live in the democratic ages upon which we are entering have naturally a taste for independence: they are naturally impatient of regulation, and they are wearied by the permanence even of the condition they themselves prefer. They are fond of power; but they are prone to despise and hate those who wield it, and they easily elude its grasp by their own mobility and insignificance. These propensities will always manifest themselves, because they originate in the groundwork of society, which will undergo no change: for a long time they will prevent the establishment of any despotism, and they will furnish fresh weapons to each succeeding generation which shall struggle in favour of the liberty of mankind. Let us then look forward to the future with that salutary fear which makes men keep watch and ward for freedom, not with that faint and idle terror which depresses and enervates the heart.

[Source: Alexis de Tocqueville, *Democracy in America*, trans. H. Reeve, ed. H. S. Commager, (World's Classics) Oxford 1946, Ch. 24, pp. 549–50, 564–7, 592–4.]

Doc. 97. FRANCOIS GUIZOT: On the Government of the Majority and the True Doctrine of Representation

It has been often said, that representative government is the government of the majority, and there is some truth in the assertion; but it must not be thought that this government of the majority is the same as that involved in the sovereignty of the people. The principle of the sovereignty of the people applies to all individuals, merely because they exist, without demanding of them anything more. Thus, it takes the majority of these individuals and says, – Here is reason, here is law. Representative government proceeds in another way; it considers what is the kind of action to which individuals are called; it examines into the amount of capacity requisite for this action; it then summons those individuals who are supposed to possess this capacity, – all such, and such only. Then it seeks for a majority among those who are capable.

D. Liberty and democracy

It is in this way, in fact, that men have everywhere proceeded, even when they have been supposed to act according to the idea of the sovereignty of the people. Never have they been entirely faithful to it; they have always demanded for political actions certain conditions, that is to say, indications of a certain capacity. They have been mistaken, more or less, and have excluded the capable, or invited the inefficient, and the error is a serious one. But they have followed the principle which measures right by capacity, even when they have professed the principle that right is derived from the simple fact of possessing a human nature. Representative government, then, is not purely and simply the government of the numerical majority, it is government by the majority of those who are qualified to govern; sometimes assuming the existence of the qualification beforehand, sometimes requiring that it should be proved and exemplified. The peerage, the right to elect and to be elected, the royal power itself, are attached to a capacity presumed to exist, not only after certain conditions have been complied with, but by reason of the position occupied by those men in whom the capacity is presumed, in their relations to other powers, and in the limits of the functions assigned to them. No one is recognised as possessing an inherent right to an office or a function. Nor is this all; representative government does not content itself with demanding capacity before it confers power; as soon as the capacity is presumed or proved, it is placed in a position where it is open to a kind of legal suspicion, and where it must necessarily continue to legitimize itself, in order to retain its power. According to the principle of the sovereignty of the people, absolute right resides with the majority; true sovereignty exists wherever this force is manifested; from this follows necessarily the oppression of the minority, and such has, in fact, generally been the result. The representative form of government, never forgetting that reason and justice, and consequently a right to sovereignty, do not reside fully and constantly in any part of the earth, presumes that they are to be found in the majority, but does not attribute them to it as their certain and abiding qualities. At the very moment when it presumes that the majority is right, it does not forget that it may be wrong, and its concern is to give full opportunity to the minority of proving that it is in fact right, and of becoming in its turn the majority. Electoral precautions, the debates in the deliberative assemblies, the publication of these debates, the liberty of the press, the responsibility of ministers, all these arrangements have for their object to insure that a majority shall be declared only after it has well authenticated itself, to compel it ever to legitimatize itself, in order to its own preservation, and to place the minority in such a position as that it may contest the power and right of the majority . . .

The true doctrine of representation is more philosophical and more sincere. Starting from the principle that truth, reason and justice, – in one word, the divine law, – alone possess rightful power, its reasoning is

610

somewhat as follows: – Every society according to its interior organization, its antecedents, and the aggregate of influences which have or do
still modify it, is placed to a certain extent in a position to apprehend
truth and justice as the divine law, and is in a measure disposed to conform itself to this law. Employing less general terms: – there exists in
every society a certain number of just ideas and wills in harmony with
those ideas, which respect the reciprocal rights of men and social
relations with their results. This sum of just ideas and loyal wills is dispersed among the individuals who compose society, and unequally diffused among them on account of the infinitely varied causes which influence the moral and intellectual development of men. The grand concern, therefore, of society is – that, so far as either abiding infirmity or
the existing condition of human affairs will allow, this power of reason,
justice, and truth, which alone has an inherent legitimacy, and alone has
the right to demand obedience, may become prevalent in the community.
The problem evidently is to collect from all sides the scattered and incomplete fragments of this power that exist in society, to concentrate
them, and from them, to constitute a government. In other words, it is
required to discover all the elements of legitimate power that are disseminated throughout society, and to organize them into an actual
power; that is to say, to collect into one focus, and to realize, public
reason and public morality, and to call them to the occupation of power.

What we call *representation* is nothing else than a means to arrive at
this result: – it is not an arithmetical machine employed to collect and
count individual wills, but a natural process by which public reason,
which alone has a right to govern society, may be extracted from the
bosom of society itself. No reason has in fact a right to say beforehand
for itself that it is the reason of the community. If it claims to be such, it
must prove that it is so, that is to say, it must accredit itself to other individual reasons which are capable of judging it. If we look at facts, we
shall find that all institutions, all conditions of the representative system,
flow from and return to this point. Election, publicity, and responsibility,
are so many tests applied to individual reasons, which in the search for,
or the exercise of, power, assume to be interpreters of the reason of the
community; so many means of bringing to light the elements of legitimate
power, and preventing usurpation.

In this system, it is true, – and the fact arises from the necessity of
liberty as actual in the world – that truth and error, perverse and loyal
wills, in one word, the good and evil which co-exist and contend in society as in the individual, will most probably express themselves; this is the
condition of the world; it is the necessary result of liberty. But against the
evil of this there are two guarantees: one is found in the publicity of the
struggle, which always gives the right the best chance of success, for it
has been recognized in all ages of the world that good is in friendship
with the light, while evil ever shelters itself in darkness; this idea, which is

common to all the religions of the world, symbolizes and indicates the first of all truths. The second guarantee consists in the determination of a certain amount of capacity to be possessed by those who aspire to exercise any branch of power. In the system of representing wills, nothing could justify such a limitation, for the will exists full and entire in all men, and confers on all an equal right; but the limitation flows necessarily from the principle which attributes power to reason, and not to will.

[Source: François Guizot, *History of the Origin of Representative Government in Europe*, trans. Andrew R. Scoble, London 1852, pp. 72–3, 347–9.]

Doc. 98. MICHEL CHEVALIER: Association as a Danger to Liberty

Observe all the nations of Western civilization, I mean that civilization which peoples Europe and the New World, and which, by unexampled expansion, is now spread in all directions, and takes the direction of the affairs of the human race. They all gravitate towards a social and political type of constitution uniform in its general features. This is why modern political economy is uniform, at least among the numerous groups of nations which together compose Western civilization, whose populousness, whose enlightenment, and the surface over which their empire is acknowledged, cause them to be constantly increasing in power.

That which gives their civilization its own stamp is, that it acknowledges and affirms, to the profit of all the members of the nation, the great principle of freedom. This affirmation, which now resounds throughout so vast a space, is the marvel, the honour, and sometimes the torment of our age. It has made it a great age, one of the greatest in history, in spite of the littleness by which it is marked.

Under this generic name of freedom are ranged a multitude of rights, which may be summed up in regard to each individual, as the rights of exercising in his degree his personal activity, his intelligence, his feelings, all his faculties in short, in all the spheres accessible to civilized man: religion, politics, science, literature, industry. The only limit which may be assigned to the liberty of each, is that he should not attempt the liberty of another, and that he should not compromise public order which a philosopher has perfectly defined as the collective liberty of the nation.

It is equally, the right of each to act in concert freely with a number, however great, however limited, of his fellow citizens under broad conditions and the same for all . . .

By the side of the general principle of liberty, which is the distinctive sign of nations which have adopted an advanced civilization, we observe another principle, which is parallel with it, that of equality which likewise receives successive development as civilization advances. But it may be said that liberty reasonably interpreted leads to equality and carries it in its bosom. This indissoluble union between liberty and equality exists visibly, especially in the domain of political economy, in the sphere of labour . . .

Freedom of labour has two aspects, very distinct, and both essential: the one is the freedom of the labourer, the fact in virtue of which he has personal freedom, enjoys citizenship of right, and exercises the different attributes of father of a family and citizen; the other is that liberty which is relative to the very mode of labour, and in virtue of which each exercises the profession for which he has, or thinks he has aptitude, and practises it in the manner which he judges best, by processes to his mind, with materials which he supposes most advantageous, and then, once the work of production is terminated, exchanges with his like the products which he has obtained for those which are the result of labour and genius different from his own. This second form of the freedom of labour comprehends and implies the freedom of transaction . . .

Thus freedom of labour is absolutely necessary to facilitate and permit the growth of the productive power of society, a growth which is indispensable to give prosperity to that very considerable part of the population which devotes itself to agricultural or manufacturing labour. In modern times we should never forget that this prosperity is one of the conditions of social tranquillity . . .

Freedom of labour is the power by which the regeneration of modern industry is undertaken and followed up. It is under the auspices of freedom of labour that the classes formerly enslaved or disinherited have already greatly modified the conditions of their existence and will continue to change them for the better.

Therefore let the working populations, impatient as they are to ameliorate their condition, cling to this flag with a loving grasp and never let it go! Let them demand that it shall float over mankind, that it cover them entirely with its resplendent folds! Let them never forget that all classes without exception, ought to be admitted under its tutelary shade. We have far better foundation for claiming advancement for ourselves when we claim it in the interest of all.

Here, contemporary events lead me to speak to you of a danger which freedom of labour is running from a particular kind of violence to which it is subjected, and the affecting picture of which is offered, in a neighbouring country; French soil is unstained by it at this moment. I speak of the acts which have been committed by many of the associations of working men existing in Great Britain, which have acquired the respectability which attaches to long establishment, under the name of Trades Unions. They are formed of workmen of a particular trade, in a town or even in a more extensive district. Their end is to secure, by the power of voluntary individual association, the interests of the workmen of the trade. Originally they proposed principally or solely to organize resistance in cases where the masters or heads of establishments wanted to lower wages. Thus they came to use pressure to

613

D. Liberty and democracy

increase wages when circumstances gave them a favourable opportunity. From time to time the delegates of the unions have conferences with the delegates of the masters and agree upon a tariff for workmanship in the different operations of the trade. By means of a weekly or monthly payment, help is given to the sick, and to widows and orphans; sometimes they go so far as to give pensions to workmen whom age or infirmity renders incapable of working. Up to this point all is honest, humane and worthy. We see in the Trades Unions only the legitimate and happy exercise of the right of association. The moralist and the administrator, as a guardian of public order, can but applaud them.

But, under the influence of angry passions, this state of things has been entirely altered. From protecting institutions for the workmen, the Trades Unions have become instruments of tyranny directed not only against the masters, but against the very numerous part of the working classes which wished to keep its freedom and remain outside the associations in order to escape the subscriptions which had become onerous, or engagements incompatible with personal independence. Instead of confining themselves to free discussion, and, in extreme cases, to a peaceful strike to oblige the masters to increase wages which might be influenced by the great activity of trade and the abundance of capital, they employed threats, violence, everything in fact, up to and including assassination. Instead of seeking to rally to themselves by conviction the workmen who, remaining outside the association, did not observe their laws or injunctions, and who intended to work in their own way, they overwhelmed them with ill-usage, molested them from morning to night, insulted them, beat them, and shot them down like wild beasts. They arrogated to themselves the right of interdicting a solitary manufacturer, or compelling him to discharge a foreman or workman who did not belong to their body. They attempted even to silence the journalists who had blamed their association and pointed them out by acts and gestures when they found out the guilty. The penalty of disobedience, of which they warned independent writers, was the same which they enforced against masters and workmen who showed themselves recalcitrant; a committee of directors condemned them to death and let loose upon them hired assassins ... The unionist workmen themselves were obliged to give up their arbitrary freedom. They were obliged to submit to the orders of the committee without discussing them, to commence a strike when the signal was given them, and conform without a word to regulations vexatious to a good workman, such as not to work by the piece but only by the day, to work only for the master pointed out by the office, instead of choosing one for himself and leaving him when he liked. Workmen once enrolled in the Union were like the soldiers of the centurion in Scripture: they no longer had any concerns of their own; they had nothing to do but to obey passively.[1]

In a word a system of terror was thus created which was a protest

614

against the pretensions of the age to have liberal manners, against the pretension of England to be by its intelligent practice of liberty in civil as well as political life, a model which the nations of Europe might set themselves to imitate . . .

But let us not delude ourselves: among the winds which now blow over Europe, there is an air, not the weakest or the least obeyed, which urges a part of the working population to seek their enfranchisement and the improvement of their lot by means contrary to the freedom of others. In most civilized countries they try to attain this freedom by claiming to limit the number of apprentices, by setting themselves against task-work, by opposing female labour in certain manufactures. Thus is misunderstood, in the name of the interests of the workman, freedom of labour, which is their palladium. They do not less understand freedom of capital, which is the indispensable auxiliary of labour. In France these tendencies have their partisans, and they show themselves in the face of day; the law has ceased to oppose them . . .

I hold it to be certain that discussion will enlighten every one, because every one has goodwill. Let us have confidence in the patriotism and the good sense of our fellow-citizens. The perilous sophisms of which a part of the working population are the dupes, will be reduced to their just value in the workmen's own eyes. The French are not exclusive, and here is an opportunity of showing it. One of the orators of the illustrious Constituent Assembly of 1789, upon a proposition which was contrary to justice, uttered these fine words, which remain as a warning which it may be often useful to repeat: 'You wish to be free,' said he, 'and you know not how to be just.' And, in fact, he who refuses justice to others, turns his back on freedom in his own behalf. The people of our workshops should take care not to forget this.

[Source: Michel Chevalier, *The History of Political Economy Taught by the History of the Freedom of Labour*, trans. William Bellingham, London 1869, pp. 8–10, 38, 39–43.]

Editors' Note

1. In this passage Chevalier refers to the Sheffield saw-grinders and their leaders. Following a number of outrages in Sheffield, a royal commission of inquiry was appointed to investigate unionist activities and make recommendations for new legislation concerning the legal position of the unions.

Doc. 99. LEON GAMBETTA: Speech at Grenoble, September 1872

Speaking of the two types of monarchy, legitimate and parliamentary monarchy, experienced by France before 1871, Gambetta continued:

'As we lived, I say, under either of these monarchies, I understand that both these regimes are afraid of the people, for they do not know them and are neither willing nor able to appreciate them. They have found only one means of governing them; and that is to shut them up and detain them illegally. (*Laughter of approval, applause*) But, gentlemen, that is not a regime, a political system, like the present democracy, a world which is still new, the origins, birth and model of which date from 1789. On the whole, it has set foot among us ånd has had a grip on affairs and has been equipped with the means of protecting its sovereignty and has been given its full right only in 1848 by universal suffrage. It is not, I say, this new world of French democracy which can flatter itself to govern, regulate, lead and teach by the conduct and the practices of the fifteen to twenty skilful talkers who governed and led the parliamentary monarchy. (*No! No! Bravo*)

'Today one must go down to the deep strata and layers of society. One must understand that public opinion can only be formed out of open, contradictory discussion which encounters positive as well as negative statements. For democracy is not government by uniformity, nor by that passive discipline of which they dream in other parts and in other sects. It is the government of freedom of thought and of freedom of action. From this there follows the need for a perpetual communication between all citizens among themselves, when they desire it and how they desire it, and under one condition only, a unique condition, that they deliberate peacefully, without arms, just as the first legislators of the French Revolution formulated it in order not to provide the temptation for some people to violate the right of others. (*That is so! Very good, very good*) ...

'What do you want? In France people in certain classes of society have not been able during the last forty-five years to get used to siding not only with the French Revolution, but also with its consequences, its results. They cannot confess that the monarchy is finished, that all the regimes which, with different modifications, can represent the monarchy stand equally condemned. And it is to that lack of revolution, of courage in a notable part of the French bourgeoisie that I trace the origin, the explanation of all our misfortunes, of all our shortcomings, of everything that is still uncertain, doubtful and demoralising in current politics. One wonders, indeed, from where such obstinacy can come; one wonders whether these people have well reflected on what is going on. One wonders how they have not realized the errors they commit and how much longer they can preserve in good faith the ideas on which they pretend to rely, how they can close their eyes to a sight that should affect them. Have they not since the fall of the Empire witnessed the arrival of a new, energetic, though restrained generation, which is intelligent, suited for public affairs, in love with the country, and anxious about general rights? Have they not seen it enter the Municipal Councils, raise itself gradually in the other elective Councils of the country, and claim and secure its place more and more on a large scale in electoral contests? Have we not seen the arrival all over the country – and I emphasize

616

strongly the viewing in perspective of this new generation of democracy – of a new political and electoral personnel, the new personnel of universal suffrage? Have they not noticed the workers of the towns and of the country, that working world, to whom the future belongs, making its entry into political affairs? Did not their entry indicate that, after having tried many forms of government the country wants in the end to turn to another social stratum in order to experiment with the Republican form? (*Yes, yes! Prolonged sensation*) Yes, I foresee, I feel, I announce the arrival and the presence in politics of a new social stratum which has been playing its part in politics; a new social stratum which has played its part in politics for some eighteen months and which, to be sure, is far from being inferior to its predecessors.' (*Bravo*)

Gambetta then discussed the reaction to this new stratum 'in the camp of our adversaries'. 'They have screamed about triumphant radicalism. They have said that radicalism was before the gate with the procession of ghosts, misfortunes and catastrophes that must of necessity follow it. They have thus tried to alarm the country, this unhappy country which for seventy-five years the reactionary parties have ruled and exploited through fear. For fear, political fear, gentlemen, is the chronic illness of France. In fact, as much as France is brave, generous, energetic, heroic, disinterested on the battlefields, she is just as timid, hesitant, easy to disturb, deceive, bewitch and frighten in the political sphere.'

Gambetta then pointed out that the reactionaries of 1800, 1813, 1831 and 1849 had drawn on evoking fear. It has been 'a miserable and odious calculation on the part of our adversaries always to count on the eternal fear of France. And, as fear has become the expedient and the resource of our enemies, it follows that the Republican party, the Radical party, which finds its satisfaction below the general interest, sets itself the task of curing France of this malady. For what is the remedy, the means to use for this purpose? Oh, it is always the same and it is always the victor: it is prudence (*la sagesse*).' (*Very good! rounds of applause, prolonged interruption. The commotion of the audience prevents the speaker from continuing for some minutes.*)

[Source: Léon Gambetta, *Discours prononcé à Grenoble le 26 Septembre 1872*, Paris 1872, pp. 15–23. Translated by the editors of this volume.]

Doc. 100. WILLIAM EDWARD HARTPOLE LECKY: Democracy does not Harmonise well with Liberty

I do not think that any one who seriously considers the force and universality of the movement of our generation in the direction of democracy can doubt that this conception of government will necessarily, at least for a considerable time, dominate in all civilised countries, and the real question for politicians is the form it is likely to take, and the means by which

D. Liberty and democracy

its characteristic evils can be best mitigated. As we have, I think, abundantly seen, a tendency to democracy does not mean a tendency to parliamentary government, or even a tendency towards greater liberty. On the contrary, strong arguments may be adduced, both from history and from the nature of things, to show that democracy may often prove the direct opposite of liberty. In ancient Rome the old aristocratic republic was gradually transformed into a democracy, and it then passed speedily into an imperial despotism. In France a corresponding change has more than once taken place. A despotism resting on a plebiscite is quite as natural a form of democracy as a republic, and some of the strongest democratic tendencies are distinctly adverse to liberty. Equality is the idol of democracy, but, with the infinitely various capacities and energies of men, this can only be attained by a constant, systematic, stringent repression of their natural development. Whenever natural forces have unrestricted play, inequality is certain to ensue. Democracy destroys the balance of opinions, interests, and classes, on which constitutional liberty mainly depends, and its constant tendency is to impair the efficiency and authority of parliaments, which have hitherto proved the chief organs of political liberty . . .

In our own day, no fact is more incontestable than the love of democracy for authoritarian regulation. The two things that men in middle age have seen most discredited among their contemporaries are probably free contract and free trade. The great majority of the democracies of the world are now frankly protectionist, and even in free-trade countries the multiplication of laws regulating, restricting, and interfering with industry in all its departments is one of the most marked characteristics of our time. Nor are these regulations solely due to sanitary or humanitarian motives. Among large classes of those who advocate them another motive is very perceptible. A school has arisen among popular working-class leaders which no longer desires that superior skill, or industry, or providence should reap extraordinary rewards. Their ideal is to restrict by the strongest trade-union regulations the amount of work and the amount of the produce of work, to introduce the principle of legal compulsion into every branch of industry, to give the trade-union an absolute coercive power over its members, to attain a high average, but to permit no superiorities. The industrial organisation to which they aspire approaches far more nearly to that of the Middle Ages or of the Tudors than to the ideal of Jefferson or Cobden. I do not here argue whether this tendency is good or bad. No one at least can suppose that it is in the direction of freedom. It may be permitted to doubt whether liberty in other forms is likely to be very secure if power is mainly placed in the hands of men who, in their own sphere, value it so little.

The expansion of the authority and the multiplication of the functions of the State in other fields, and especially in the field of social regulation, is an equally apparent accompaniment of modern democracy. This increase of State power means a multiplication of restrictions imposed upon the various forms of human action. It means an increase of bureaucracy, or, in other words, of the number and power of State officials. It means also a constant increase of taxation, which is in reality a constant restriction of liberty. One of the first forms of liberty is the right of every man to dispose of his own property and earnings, and every tax is a portion of this money taken from him by the force and authority of the law. Many of these taxes are, no doubt, for purposes in which he has the highest interest. They give him the necessary security of life, property, and industry, and they add in countless ways to his enjoyment. But if taxes are multiplied for carrying out a crowd of objects in which he has no interest, and with many of which he has no sympathy, his liberty is proportionately restricted. His money is more and more taken from him by force for purposes of which he does not approve. The question of taxation is in the highest degree a question of liberty, and taxation under a democracy is likely to take forms that are peculiarly hostile to liberty. I have already pointed out how the old fundamental principle of English freedom, that no one should be taxed except by his consent, is being gradually discarded; and how we are steadily advancing to a state in which one class will impose the taxes, while another class will be mainly compelled to pay them. It is obvious that taxation is more and more employed for objects that are not common interests of the whole community, and that there is a growing tendency to look upon it as a possible means of confiscation; to make use of it to break down the power, influence, and wealth of particular classes; to form a new social type; to obtain the means of class bribery.

There are other ways in which democracy does not harmonise well with liberty. To place the chief power in the most ignorant classes is to place it in the hands of those who naturally care least for political liberty, and who are most likely to follow with an absolute devotion some strong leader. The sentiment of nationality penetrates very deeply into all classes; but in all countries and ages it is the upper and middle classes who have chiefly valued constitutional liberty, and those classes it is the work of democracy to dethrone. At the same time democracy does much to weaken among these also the love of liberty. The instability and insecurity of democratic politics; the spectacle of dishonest and predatory adventurers climbing by popular suffrage into positions of great power in the State; the alarm which attacks on property seldom fail to produce among those who have something to lose, may easily scare to the side of despotism large classes who, under other circumstances, would have been steady supporters of liberty. A despotism which secures order, property, and industry, which leaves the liberty of religion and of private life unimpaired, and which enables quiet and industrious men to pass through life untroubled and unmolested, will always appear to many very preferable to a democratic republic which is constantly menacing, disturbing, or plundering them. It would be a great mistake to suppose that the French despotic Empire after 1852 rested on bayonets alone. It rested partly on the genuine consent of those large agricultural classes who cared greatly for material prosperity and very little for constitutional liberty, and partly on the panic produced among the middle classes by the socialist preaching of 1848.

The dangers to be apprehended from democracy are enormously increased when the transformation is effected by sudden bounds. Governments or societies may be fundamentally changed, without producing any great convulsion or catastrophe, if the continuity of habit is preserved, if the changes are made by slow, gradual, and almost imperceptible steps. As I have already said, it is one of the evils of our present party system that it greatly accelerates this progress. Very few constitutional changes are the result of a genuine, spontaneous, unforced development. They are mainly, or at least largely, due to rival leaders bidding against each other for popularity; to agitators seeking for party purposes to raise a cry; to defeated statesmen trying, when they are condemned by existing constituencies, to regain power by creating new ones. The true origin of some of the most far-reaching changes of our day is, probably, simply a desire so to shuffle cards or combine votes as to win an election. With a powerful Upper Chamber and a strong organisation of property in the electorate, the conservative influences are sufficient to prevent a too rapid change. But when these checks are weakened and destroyed, and when there are no constitutional provisions to take their place, the influences working in the direction of change acquire an enormously augmented force, the dangers of the process are incalculably increased, and the new wine is very likely to burst the old bottles.

[Source: W. E. H. Lecky, *Democracy and Liberty* (1896), London 1899, Vol. I, pp. 256–61.]

Doc. 101. FRIEDRICH NAUMANN: Democracy and Monarchy [1]

In Germany every third voter (34.8%) is a Social Democrat. Even if Social Democratic voters often do not adhere strictly to their party programme, they have to be counted without exception under the heading of democracy for it was just this fact which drove them away and separated them from the other parties: that they were in search of something still more radical and more red. A text-book perception of what democracy, republic and government by the people are and how they can be introduced is, of course, lacking in many Social Democratic voters, and is also not very easy; but what the masses can offer altogether in politics is not by any means a political theory, but a mood. This mood is quite clear: 4,200,000 votes for the Social Democrats!

To them 3,300,000 Liberals have to be added. With these, radicalism is thinner and towards the right wing gets lost in a mere touch of liberalism-from-memory [*Erinnerungsliberalismus*]. However, it is a fact that these 3,300,000 voters do not wish to be governed on conservative lines. If they wanted that, they would not vote for liberals ... The fact remains that over seven million voters want a different Government ...

What is it the seven million want? It is approximately called progress in the self-determination of the people. Some expect more from it than others, but in spite of all the differences of temperament and of social position there is a certain unity of direction. All liberalism and all democracy draw on the ideas of the Western powers which had developed earlier. Eyes are directed to France, England and North America. None of the foreign constitutions will be or can be simply copied by us; but we, too, want to have a people's representation which is not only a stock-exchange for secondary gains but also rises to the heights of a power leading the state. The aim is the ability of the majority of the people to govern.

The idea of government by a majority forms an immense problem for Germany as our Constitution is more involved and more complicated than that of any other State. Our constitutional law is so confused and difficult that usually foreigners do not understand it and Germans only do so after having studied it intensively. We have not arrived at a unitary State [*Einheitsstaat*], but have stopped in the middle of the road. Bismarck's Constitution of the Empire was magnificent because it created a durable Empire, but now we are suffering from it because it was and had to be a compromise. Germany is a 'Federation of Princes and Peoples' which means that it has two co-existing systems of government, one monarchical, the other parliamentary: the Federal Council and the Reichstag. The monarchical system is in itself impaired by the parliamentarism of the individual states which in turn is not uniform, but differs extraordinarily from Mecklenburg to Baden. Nowhere are there pure forms, but everywhere in some spots the stream is frozen in its flow and curious blocks of ice pile up fantastically.

To this one has to add that the federation of the half-broken monarchies is also again a pseudo-federation because Prussia alone possesses two-thirds of the forces. One has thus retained kings and grand dukes with honours and dignities, but has left them very little of their sovereignty. Over them lords the King of Prussia who concluded military agreements with them, but now allows himself to depend on the consent of the majority in the Reichstag as far as his soldiers are concerned. As a military monarch he is sovereign through treaties; but as a civilian Emperor he is commissioned by the Federal Council whose first member he is, and as financial head he is dependent on the Reichstag ... The English and the French have had their great revolutions, and the Americans started anew on fresh soil. We, however, have only had a semi-revolution and a small one at that; and no one has taken the burden

D. Liberty and democracy

of the centuries from us. Therefore everything is so heavily involved and inter-connected. Whom do you face if you face the Reich Chancellor? Is he the Commissioner of the Kaiser or of the Federal Council; is he the Prussian Premier Minister; is he the servant of the Government [of Prussia] based on a three class suffrage? He can wear very different jackets; but one only he does not wear, that of Commissioner of the majority [of the voters]. Prince Bülow held this jacket in his hands [1907–9], yet he did not wear it. Now, when the seven million voters aim at a majority government, it is as if they had to ride into a dark wood. If we still lived in the age of the revolutions, one might think that we Germans belatedly now had to do what the English and the French did in the 17th and 18th centuries. But that age has passed for good and completely, for our modern life does not bear such disturbances for the sake of changes in the constitution. This has clearly been shown by the debates of the Social Democrats on the general strike. The working class, too, does not stand any weakening of the security of the State. All the reasons it has put forward against war are valid to a still higher degree against revolution. Therefore, for the seven million voters, only a programme of lawful progress is possible. Even occasional, stupid leading articles in the *Leipziger Volkszeitung* [the organ of the left wing of the Social Democrats] can no longer change this. The problem is how to translate the will of the majority into governmental energy if it has neither the intention nor the chance of paralysing first the entire mechanism of the State. How does a non-revolutionary democracy look?

The best model for this process is to be found in English history from 1830 to the present day. We must study it much more intensively than we have done so far. The modern English development is based on the idea that one can well leave old paragraphs intact, provided the real power relations change. Formally no changes have been made in England in the rights of the monarch. Today Ministers are still the servants of His Majesty and the laws are proclaimed in the name of the king. The king himself has not really lost anything, for earlier he already could not do anything himself but depended on organized groups of his entourage. These groups have been democratized in the course of the decades. The place of court cliques has been taken by party associations. This is the change; its legal expression is only in the extension of the right to vote. The proper parliamentary system is unwritten law. There would be little purpose in decreeing it solemnly, for it exists so long as there are majorities which regard this law as their law. If, in England, history has already taken this course, the same or a similar procedure will be more necessary still for Germany as our monarchic system is so incomparably more complicated. We cannot erect any normal, academic constitutional structure. For that there exist no seven million voters. But there are seven millions in favour of the formation of a majority [government], of reform of the standing orders, of responsibility of ministers and of equality in the

622

franchise. We do not want general debates on monarchy or republic. This does not make any practical sense! What we want is the removal of obstacles which stand in the path of a successful participation of the majority in the business of government. It is also not necessary to think in terms of all the future ages. They will do that themselves; and the monarchy will remain with us, as well as with England, as far as and because it is necessary in order to have an unchangeable central power between the changing parties. Of course, the bloc of the Blacks and the Blues[2] will try to hide behind the king and push the question of the monarchy forward. However, this can only have a transitory effect, for the king himself cannot wish to be permanently the king of a minority. Monarchs require majorities. They exist because they are regarded as necessary. If this belief is ended, then even the oldest hereditary law is of no use ... It is their aim to strengthen this belief. The preservation of the dynasty is based on it ... It is, therefore, quite improbable that a contemporary or a future monarch would seriously and after careful consideration resist the majority principle. He is going to defend any position as well as he is able to do so, but he will make concessions in small things in order to remain what he is in the big things. This the English kings have done and have not fared badly with it, and the policies of their country have scored brilliant successes with it. If today a servant of His Majesty would want to advise the Emperor to take on principle a hostile attitude to the seven million voters, he would do the worst thing imaginable for him. The king should be 'above the parties' because this is the royal attitude. However, he should obtain his ministers from the hands of the parties. This sounds rather adventurous in Germany, but it was the same three or four generations ago in England. The world is round and it rotates, and just now one has noticed the rotation quite strongly. And even if all the Heydebrandts[3] and Hertlings[4] could command a standstill, the slogan still applies, as it did in ancient days: yet it is moving!

[Source: Friedrich Naumann, *Demokratie und Monarchie* (1912); reprinted in F. Naumann, *Werke. Politische Schriften*, ed. Th. Schieder, Köln 1966, Band 2, pp. 439–44. Translated by the editors of this volume.]

Editors' Notes

1. The article appeared in Naumann's weekly journal *Die Hilfe*, vol. 18, no. 6. In the general election to the Reichstag in 1912 the Social Democrats increased their strength from 29 to 110 seats and became the strongest party. The left-wing Liberals (*Fortschrittliche Volkspartei*) achieved a moderate increase, polling 12.3% of the total vote. It is ironic that Naumann himself lost his seat at Heilbronn in Württemberg in the 1912 election to a Social Democrat.
2. The cooperation of the 'Blacks' (Centre Party) and the 'Blues' (German Conservatives) provided a majority in the Reichstag for Chancellor Bülow in 1907. In 1909 both parties joined again on the question of financial reform and formed the 'Black-Blue Bloc'.
3. Ernst von der Heydebrandt und der Lasa (1851–1924) was the leader of the Conservative Party in the Prussian Diet and a diehard conservative.

4. Freiherr Carl von Hertling was at the time the leader of the Centre Party and Prime Minister of Bavaria. He became Reich Chancellor at the end of 1917. Hertling was known as a conservative traditionalist.

---

2. The tyranny of the majority and the right to non-conformity: documents

(Introduction, p. 577)

Doc. 102. ALEXIS DE TOCQUEVILLE: The Unlimited Power of the Majority in the United States and its Consequence

In the United States the unbounded power of the majority, which is favorable to the legal despotism of the legislature, is likewise favorable to the arbitrary authority of the magistrate. The majority has an entire control over the law when it is made and when it is executed; and as it possesses an equal authority over those who are in power and the community at large, it considers public officers as its passive agents, and readily confides the task of serving its designs to their vigilance. The details of their office and the privileges which they are to enjoy are rarely defined beforehand; but the majority treats them as a master does his servants when they are always at work in his sight, and he has the power of directing or reprimanding them at every instant.

In general the American functionaries are far more independent than the French civil officers within the sphere which is prescribed to them. Sometimes, even, they are allowed by the popular authority to exceed those bounds; and as they are protected by the opinion, and backed by the co-operation, of the majority, they venture upon such manifestations of their power as astonish a European. By this means habits are formed in the heart of a free country which may some day prove fatal to its liberties.

It is in the examination of the display of public opinion in the United States that we clearly perceive how far the power of the majority surpasses all the powers with which we are acquainted in Europe. Intellectual principles exercise an influence which is so invisible, and often so inappreciable, that they baffle the toils of oppression. At the present time the most absolute monarchs in Europe are unable to prevent certain notions, which are opposed to their authority, from circulating in secret throughout their dominions, and even in their courts. Such is not the case in America; as long as the majority is still undecided, discussion is carried on; but as soon as its decision is irrevocably pronounced, a submissive silence is observed, and the friends, as well as the opponents, of the measure unite in assenting to its propriety. The reason of this is perfectly clear: no monarch is so absolute as to combine all the powers of society in his own hands, and to conquer all opposition with the energy of a majority which is invested with the right of making and of executing the laws.

The authority of a king is purely physical, and it controls the actions of the subject without subduing his private will; but the majority possesses a power which is physical and moral at the same time; it acts upon the will as well as upon the actions of men, and it represses not only all contest, but all controversy.

I know of no country in which there is so little true independence of mind and freedom of discussion as in America. In any constitutional State in Europe every sort of religious and political theory may be advocated and propagated abroad; for there is no country in Europe so subdued by any single authority as not to contain citizens who are ready to protect the man who raises his voice in the cause of truth from the consequences of his hardihood. If he is unfortunate enough to live under an absolute government, the people is upon his side; if he inhabits a free country, he may find a shelter behind the authority of the throne, if he requires one. The aristocratic part of society supports him in some countries, and the democracy in others. But in a nation where democratic institutions exist, organized like those in the United States, there is but one sole authority, one single element of strength and of success, with nothing beyond it.

In America, the majority raises very formidable barriers to the liberty of opinion: within these barriers an author may write whatever he pleases, but he will repent it if he ever steps beyond them. Not that he is exposed to the terrors of an *auto-da-fé*, but he is tormented by the slights and persecutions of daily obloquy. His political career is closed for ever, since he has offended the only authority which is able to promote his success. Every sort of compensation, even that of celebrity, is refused to him. Before he published his opinions he imagined that he held them in common with many others; but no sooner has he declared them openly than he is loudly censured by his overbearing opponents, while those who think like him, without having the courage to speak, abandon him in silence. He yields at length, oppressed by the daily efforts he has been making, and he subsides into silence, as if he was tormented by remorse for having spoken the truth.

Fetters and headsmen were the coarse instruments which tyranny formerly employed; but the civilization of our age has refined the arts of despotism, which seemed, however, to have been sufficiently perfected before. The excesses of monarchical power had devised a variety of physical means of oppression: the democratic republics of the present day have rendered it as entirely an affair of the mind as that will which it is intended to coerce. Under the absolute sway of an individual despot the body was attacked in order to subdue the soul, and the soul escaped the blows which were directed against it and rose superior to the attempt; but such is not the course adopted by tyranny in democratic republics; there the body is left free and the soul is enslaved. The sovereign can no longer say, 'You shall think as I do on pain of death'; but he says: 'You are free to think differently from me, and to retain your life, your property, and all that you possess; but if such be your determination, you are henceforth an alien among your people. You may retain your civil rights, but they will be useless to you, for you will never be chosen by your fellow-citizens if you solicit their suffrages, and they will affect to scorn you if you solicit their esteem. You will remain among men, but you will be deprived of the rights of mankind. Your fellow-creatures will shun you like an impure being, and those who are most persuaded of your innocence will abandon you too, lest they should be shunned in their turn. Go in peace! I have given you your life, but it is an existence incomparably worse than death.'

Monarchical institutions have thrown an odium upon despotism; let us beware lest democratic republics should restore oppression, and should render it less odious and less degrading in the eyes of the many, by making it still more onerous to the few ...

The tendencies to which I have just alluded are as yet very slightly perceptible in political society, but they already begin to exercise an unfavorable influence upon the national character of the Americans. I am inclined to attribute the singular paucity of distinguished political characters to the ever-increasing activity of the despotism of the majority in the United States. When the American Revolution broke out they arose in great numbers, for public opinion then served, not to tyrannize over, but to direct the exertions of individuals. Those celebrated men took a full part in the general agitation of mind common at that period, and they attained a high degree of personal fame, which was reflected back upon the nation, but which was by no means borrowed from it ...

In free countries, where every one is more or less called upon to give his opinion in the affairs of state; in democratic republics, where public life is incessantly commingled with domestic affairs, where the sovereign authority is accessible on every side, and where its attention can almost always be attracted by vociferation, more persons are to be met with who speculate upon its foibles and live at the cost of its passions than in absolute monarchies. Not because men are naturally worse in these States than elsewhere, but the temptation is stronger, and of easier access at the same time. The result is a far more extensive debasement of the characters of citizens.

Democratic republics extend the practice of currying favour with the many, and they introduce it into a greater number of classes at once: this is one of the most serious reproaches that can be addressed to them. In democratic States organized on the principles of the American republics, this is more especially the case, where the authority of the majority is so absolute and so irresistible that a man must give up his rights as a citizen, and almost abjure his quality as a human being, if he intends to stray from the track which it lays down.

In that immense crowd which throngs the avenues to power in the United States I found very few men who displayed any of that manly candour and that masculine independence of opinion which frequently distinguished the Americans in former times, and which constitutes the leading feature in distinguished characters, wheresoever they may be found. It seems, at first sight, as if all the minds of the Americans were formed upon one model, so accurately do they correspond in their manner of judging. A stranger does, indeed, sometimes meet with Americans who dissent from these rigorous formularies; with men who deplore the defects of the laws, the mutability and the ignorance of democracy; who even go so far as to observe the evil tendencies which impair the national character, and to point out such remedies as it might be possible to apply; but no one is there to hear these things besides yourself, and you, to whom these secret reflections are confided, are a stranger and a bird of passage. They are very ready to communicate truths which are useless to you, but they continue to hold a different language in public ...

Despotism debases the oppressed much more than the oppressor: in absolute monarchies the king has often great virtues, but the courtiers are invariably servile. It is true that the American courtiers do not say 'Sire', or 'Your Majesty' − a distinction without a difference. They are forever talking of the natural intelligence of the populace they serve; they do not debate the question as to which of the virtues of their master is pre-eminently worthy of admiration, for they assure him that he possessed all the virtues under heaven without having acquired them, or without caring to acquire them; they do not give him their daughters and their wives to be raised at his pleasure to the rank of his concubines, but, by sacrificing their opinions, they prostitute themselves. Moralists and philosophers in America are not obliged to conceal their opinions under the veil of allegory; but, before they venture upon a harsh truth, they say: 'We are aware that the people which we are addressing is too superior to all the weaknesses of human nature to lose the command of its temper for an instant; and we should not hold this language if we were not speaking to men whom their virtues and their intelligence render more worthy of freedom than all the rest of the world.' It would have been impossible for the sycophants of Louis XIV to flatter more dexterously. For my part, I am persuaded that in all governments, whatever their nature may be, servility will cower to force, and adulation will cling to power. The only means of preventing men from degrading themselves is to invest no one with that unlimited authority which is the surest method of debasing them.

Governments usually fall a sacrifice to impotence or to tyranny. In the former case their power escapes from them; it is wrested from their grasp in the latter. Many observers, who have witnessed the anarchy of democratic States, have imagined that the government of those States was naturally weak and impotent. The truth is, that when once hostilities are begun between parties, the government loses its control over society. But I do not think that a democratic power is naturally without force or without resources: say, rather, that it is almost always by the abuse of its force and the misemployment of its resources that a democratic government fails. Anarchy is almost always produced by its tyranny or its mistakes, but not by its want of strength.

It is important not to confound stability with force, or the greatness of a thing with its duration. In democratic republics, the power which directs society is not stable; for it often changes hands and assumes a new direction. But whichever way it turns, its force is almost irresistible. The governments of the American republics appear to me to be as much centralized as those of the absolute monarchies of Europe, and more energetic than they are. I do not, therefore, imagine that they will perish from weakness.

[Source: Alexis de Tocqueville, *Democracy in America* trans. H. Reeve, ed. H. S. Commager (World's Classics), Oxford 1946, Ch. 14, pp. 190–7.]

Doc. 103. JOHN STUART MILL: On the Dangers Arising from the Rule of the Numerical Majority

Looking at democracy in the way in which it is commonly conceived, as the rule of the numerical majority, it is surely possible that the ruling power may be under the dominion of sectional or class interests, pointing to conduct different from that which would be dictated by impartial regard for the interest of all. Suppose the majority to be whites, the minority negroes, or *vice versa*: is it likely that the majority would allow equal justice to the minority? Suppose the majority Catholics, the minority Protestants, or the reverse; will there not be the same danger? Or let the majority be English, the minority Irish, or the contrary: is there not a great probability of similar evil? In all countries there is a majority of poor, a minority who, in contradistinction, may be called rich. Between these two classes, on many questions, there is complete opposition of apparent interest. We will suppose the majority sufficiently intelligent to be aware that it is not for their advantage to weaken the security of property, and that it would be weakened by any act of arbitrary spoliation. But is there not a considerable danger lest they should throw upon the possessors of what is called realized property, and upon the larger incomes, an unfair share, or even the whole, of the burden of taxation; and having done so, add to the amount without scruple, expending the proceeds in modes supposed to conduce to the profit and advantage of the labouring class? Suppose, again, a minority of skilled labourers, a majority of unskilled: the experience of many trade unions, unless they are greatly calumniated, justifies the apprehension that equality of earnings might be imposed as an obligation, and that piecework, payment by the hour, and all practices which enable superior industry or abilities to gain a superior reward might be put down. Legislative attempts to raise wages, limitation of competition in the labour market, taxes or restrictions on machinery, and on improvements of all kinds tending to dispense with any of the existing labour – even, perhaps, protection of the home producer against foreign industry – are very natural (I do not venture to say whether probable) results of a feeling of class interest in a governing majority of manual labourers.

It will be said that none of these things are for the *real* interest of the most numerous class: to which I answer, that if the conduct of human beings was determined by no other interested considerations than those which constitute their 'real' interest, neither monarchy nor oligarchy would be such bad governments as they are; for assuredly very strong arguments may be, and often have been, adduced to show that either a king or a governing senate are in much the most enviable position, when ruling justly and vigilantly over an active, wealthy, enlightened, and high-minded people. But a king only now and then, and an oligarchy in no known instance, have taken this exalted view of their self-interest: and why should we expect a loftier mode of thinking from the labouring classes? It is not what their interest is, but what they suppose it to be, that is the important consideration with respect to their conduct: and it is quite conclusive against any theory of government that it assumes the numerical majority to do habitually what is never done, nor expected to be done, save in very exceptional cases, by any other depositaries of power – namely, to direct their conduct by their real ultimate interest, in opposition to their immediate and apparent interest . . .

Now it is a universally observed fact, that the two evil dispositions in question, the disposition to prefer a man's selfish interests to those which he shares with other people, and his immediate and direct interests to those which are indirect and remote, are characteristics most especially called forth and fostered by the possession of power. The moment a man, or a class of men, find themselves with power in their hands, the man's individual interest, or the class's separate interest, acquires an entirely new degree of importance in their eyes. Finding themselves worshipped by others, they become worshippers of themselves, and think themselves entitled to be counted at a hundred times the value of other people; while the facility they acquire of doing as they like without regard to consequences insensibly weakens the habits which make men look forward even to such consequences as affect themselves. This is the meaning of the universal tradition, grounded on universal experience, of men's being corrupted by power. Every one knows how absurd it would be to infer from what a man is or does when in a private station, that he will be and do exactly the like when a despot on a throne; where the bad parts of his human nature, instead of being restrained and kept in subordination by every circumstance of his life and by every person surrounding him, are courted by all persons, and ministered to by all circumstances. It would be quite as absurd to entertain a similar expectation in regard to a class of men; the Demos, or any other. Let them be ever so modest and amenable to reason while there is a power over them stronger than they, we ought to expect a total change in this respect when they themselves become the strongest power.

Governments must be made for human beings as they are, or as they are capable of speedily becoming: and in any state of cultivation which mankind, or any class among them, have yet attained, or are likely soon to attain, the interests by which they will be led, when they are thinking only of self-interest, will be almost exclusively those which are obvious at first sight, and which operate on their present condition. It is only a disinterested regard for others, and especially for what comes after them, for the idea of posterity, of their country, or of mankind, whether grounded on sympathy or on a conscientious feeling, which ever directs the minds and purposes of classes or bodies of men towards distant or unobvious interests. And it cannot be maintained that any form of government would be rational which required as a condition that these exalted principles of action should be the guiding and master motives in the conduct of average human beings. A certain amount of conscience, and of disinterested public spirit, may fairly be calculated on in the citizens of any community ripe for representative government. But it would be ridiculous to expect such a degree of it, combined with such intellectual discernment, as would be proof against any plausible fallacy tending to make that which was for their class interest appear the dictate of justice and of the general good . . .

One of the greatest dangers, therefore, of democracy, as of all other forms of government, lies in the sinister interest of the holders of power: it is the danger of class legislation; of government intended for (whether really effecting it or not) the immediate benefit of the dominant class, to the lasting detriment of the whole. And one of the most important questions demanding consideration, in determining the best constitution of a representative government, is how to provide efficacious securities against this evil.

If we consider as a class, politically speaking, any number of persons who have the same sinister interest, – that is, whose direct and apparent interest points towards the same description of bad measures; the desirable object would be that no class, and no combination of classes likely to combine, should be able to exercise a preponderant influence in the government. A modern community, not divided within itself by strong antipathies of race, language, or nationality, may be considered as in the main divisible into two sections, which, in spite of partial variations, correspond on the whole with two divergent directions of apparent interest. Let us call them (in brief general terms) labourers on the one hand, employers of labour on the other: including however along with employers of labour, not only retired capitalists, and the possessors of inherited wealth, but all that highly paid description of labourers (such as the professions) whose education and way of life assimilate them with the rich, and whose prospect and ambition it is to raise themselves into that class. With the labourers, on the other hand, may be ranked those smaller employers of labour, who by interests, habits, and educational impressions are assimilated in wishes, tastes, and objects to the labouring classes; comprehending a large proportion of petty tradesmen. In a state of society thus composed, if the representative system could be made ideally perfect, and if it were possible to maintain it in that state, its organization must be such that these two classes, manual labourers and their affinities on the one side, employers of labour and their affinities on the other, should be, in the arrangement of the representative system, equally balanced, each influencing about an equal number of votes in Parliament: since, assuming that the majority of each class, in any difference between them, would be mainly governed by their class interests, there would be a minority of each in whom that consideration would be subordinate to reason, justice, and the good of the whole; and this minority of either, joining with the whole of the other, would turn the scale against any demands of their own majority which were not such as ought to prevail. The reason why, in any tolerably constituted society, justice and the general interest mostly in the end carry their point, is that the separate and selfish interests of mankind are almost always divided; some are interested in what is wrong, but some, also, have their private interest on the side of what is right: and those who are governed by higher considerations, though too few and weak to prevail against the whole of the others, usually after sufficient discussion and agitation become strong enough to turn the balance in favour of the body of private interests which is on the same side with them. The representative system ought to be so constituted as to maintain this state of things: it ought not to allow any of the various sectional interests to be so powerful as to be capable of prevailing against truth and justice and the other sectional interests combined. There ought always to be such a balance preserved among personal interests, as may render any one of them dependent for its successes on carrying with it at least a large proportion of those who act on higher motives and more comprehensive and distant views.

631

D. Liberty and democracy

[Source: John Stuart Mill, *Considerations on Representative Government;* in *Utilitarianism, Liberty and Representative Government* (Everyman's Library) London 1906, Ch. 6, pp. 249–56.]

Doc. 104. LORD ACTON: On the Will of the Majority

The manifest, the avowed difficulty is that democracy, no less than monarchy or aristocracy, sacrifices everything to maintain itself and strives, with an energy and a plausibility that kings and nobles cannot attain, to override representation, to annul all the forces of resistance and deviation, and to secure, by Plebiscite, Referendum, or Caucus, free play for the will of the majority. The true democratic principle, that none shall have power over the people, is taken to mean that none shall be able to restrain or to elude its power. The true democratic principle, that the people shall not be made to do what it does not like, is taken to mean that it shall never be required to tolerate what it does not like. The true democratic principle, that every man's free will shall be as unfettered as possible, is taken to mean that the free will of the collective people shall be fettered in nothing. Religious toleration, judicial independence, dread of centralization, jealousy of State interference, become obstacles to freedom instead of safeguards, when the centralized force of the State is wielded by the hands of the people. Democracy claims to be not only supreme, without authority above, but absolute, without independence below; to be its own master, not a trustee. The old sovereigns of the world are exchanged for a new one, who may be flattered and deceived but whom it is impossible to corrupt or to resist, and to whom must be rendered the things that are Caesar's and also the things that are God's. The enemy to be overcome is no longer the absolutism of the State, but the liberty of the subject . . .

For the old notions of civil liberty and of social order did not benefit the masses of the people. Wealth increased, without relieving their wants. The progress of knowledge left them in abject ignorance. Religion flourished, but failed to reach them. Society, whose laws were made by the upper class alone, announced that the best thing for the poor is not to be born, and the next best, to die in childhood, and suffered them to live in misery and crime and pain. As surely as the long reign of the rich has been employed in promoting the accumulation of wealth, the advent of the poor to power will be followed by schemes for diffusing it. Seeing how little was done by the wisdom of former times for education and public health, for insurance, association, and savings, for the protection of labour against the law of self-interest, and how much has been accomplished in this generation, there is reason in the fixed belief that a great change was needed, and that democracy has not striven in vain. Liberty, for the mass, is not happiness; and institutions are not an end but a means. The thing they seek is a force sufficient to sweep away scruples and the obstacles of rival interests, and, in some degree, to better their condition. They mean that the strong hand that heretofore has formed great States, protected religions, and defended the independence of nations, shall help them by preserving life, and endowing it for them with some, at least, of the things men live for. That is the notorious danger of modern democracy. That is also its purpose and its strength. And against this threatening power the weapons that struck down other despots do not avail. The greatest happiness principle positively confirms it. The principle of equality, besides being as easily applied to property as to power, opposes the existence of persons or groups of persons exempt from the common law, and independent of the common will; and the principle, that authority is a matter of contract, may hold good against kings, but not against the sovereign people, because a contract implies two parties . . .

The one pervading evil of democracy is the tyranny of the majority, or rather of that party, not always the majority, that succeeds, by force or fraud, in carrying elections. To break off that point is to avert the danger. The common system of representation perpetuates the danger. Unequal electorates afford no security to majorities. Equal electorates give none to minorities. Thirty-five years ago it was pointed out that the remedy is proportional representation. It is profoundly democratic, for it increases the influence of thousands who would otherwise have no voice in the government; and it brings men more near an equality by so contriving that no vote shall be wasted, and that every voter shall contribute to bring into Parliament a member of his own opinions . . .

Of all checks on democracy, federalism has been the most efficacious and the most congenial; but, becoming associated with the Red Republic, with feudalism, with the Jesuits, and with slavery, it has fallen into disrepute, and is giving way to centralism. The federal system limits and restrains the sovereign power by dividing it, and by assigning to Government only certain defined rights. It is the only method of curbing not only the majority but the power of the whole people, and it affords the strongest basis for a second chamber, which has been found the essential security for freedom in every genuine democracy.

[Source: John Emerich Edward Dalberg-Acton (Lord Acton), 'Sir Erskine May's *Democracy in Europe*'; in *Essays on Freedom and Power*, ed. Gertrude Himmelfarb, Glencoe, Ill. 1949, pp. 159–63.]

3. The limitations and the scope of the State: documents
(Introduction, p. 583)

(i) Anti-étatism intensified

Doc. 105. HERBERT SPENCER: Over-Legislation

Though we no longer presume to coerce men for their *spiritual* good, we still think ourselves called upon to coerce them for their *material good* – not seeing that the one is as useless and unwarrantable as the other. Innumerable failures seem, so far, powerless to teach this. Take up a daily paper, and you will probably find a leader exposing the corruption, negligence, or mismanagement of some State department. Cast your eye down the next column, and it is not unlikely that you will read proposals for an extension of State-supervision ... Ever since society existed Disappointment has been preaching – 'Put not your trust in legislation'; and yet the trust in legislation seems scarcely diminished.

Did the State fulfil efficiently its unquestionable duties, there would be some excuse for this eagerness to assign it further ones. Were there no complaints of its faulty administration of justice; of its endless delays and untold expenses; of its bringing ruin in place of restitution; of its playing the tyrant where it should have been the protector – did we never hear of its complicated stupidities; its 20,000 statutes, which it assumes all Englishmen to know, and which not one Englishman does know; its multiplied forms, which, in the effort to meet every contingency, open far more loopholes than they provide against – had it not shown its folly in the system of making every petty alteration by a new act, variously affecting innumerable preceding acts ... had we, in short, proved its efficiency as judge and defender, instead of having found it treacherous, cruel and anxiously to be shunned, there would be some encouragement to hope other benefits at its hands.

Or if, while failing in its judicial functions, the State had proved itself a capable agent in some other department – the military for example – there would have been some show of reason for extending its sphere of action ... Even though it had bungled in everything else, yet had it in one case done well – had its naval management alone been efficient – the sanguine would have had a colourable excuse for expecting success in a new field ...

As it is, however, they seem to have read backwards the parable of the talents. Not to the agent of proved efficiency do they consign further duties, but to the negligent and blundering agent. Private enterprise has done much, and done it well. Private enterprise has cleared, drained, and fertilized the country, and built the towns – has excavated mines, laid out roads, dug canals, and embanked railways – has invented, and brought to perfection, ploughs, looms, steam-engines, printing-presses, and machines innumerable – has built our ships, our vast manufactories, our docks – has established banks, insurance societies, and the newspaper press – has covered the sea with lines of steam-vessels, and the land with electric telegraphs. Private enterprise has brought agriculture, manufactures, and commerce to their present height, and is now developing them with increasing rapidity. Therefore, do not trust private enterprise. On the other hand, the State so fulfils its protective function as to ruin many, delude others, and frighten away those who most need succour; its national defences are so extravagantly and yet inefficiently administered, as to call forth almost daily complaint, expostulation, or ridicule; and as the nation's steward, it obtains from some of our vast public estates a minus revenue. Therefore, trust the State. Slight the good and faithful servant, and promote the unprofitable one from one talent to ten.

Seriously, the case, while it may not, in some respects, warrant this parallel, is, in one respect, even stronger. For the new work is not of the same order as the old, but of a more difficult order. Badly as government discharges its true duties, any other duties committed to it are likely to be still worse discharged. To guard its subjects against aggression, either individual or national, is a straightforward and tolerably simple matter; to regulate, directly or indirectly, the personal actions of those subjects is an infinitely complicated matter. It is one thing to secure to each man the unhindered power to pursue his own good; it is a widely different thing to pursue the good for him. To do the first efficiently, the State has merely to look on while its citizens act; to forbid unfairness; to adjudicate when called on; and to enforce restitution for injuries. To do the last efficiently, it must become an ubiquitous worker – must know each man's needs better than he knows them himself – must, in short, possess superhuman power and intelligence. Even, therefore, had the State done well in its proper sphere, no sufficient warrant would have existed for extending that sphere; but seeing how ill it has discharged those simple offices which we cannot help consigning to it, small indeed is the probability of its discharging well offices of a more complicated nature.

Change the point of view however we may, and this conclusion still presents itself. If we define the primary State-duty to be, protecting each individual against others; then, all other State action comes under the definition of protecting each individual against himself – against his own stupidity, his own idleness, his own improvidence, rashness, or other defect – his own incapacity for doing something or other which should be done. There is no questioning this classification. For manifestly all the obstacles that lie between a man's desires and the satisfaction of them, are either obstacles arising from other men's counter desires, or obstacles arising from inability in himself. Such of these counter desires as are just, have as much claim to satisfaction as his; and may not, therefore, be thwarted. Such of them as are unjust, it is the State's duty to hold in check. The only other possible sphere for it, therefore, is saving the individual from the results of his own weakness, apathy, or foolishness — warding off the consequences of his nature; or, as we say — protecting him against himself. Making no comment, at present, on the policy of this, and confining ourselves solely to the practicability of it, let us inquire how the proposal looks when reduced to its simplest form. Here are men endowed with instincts, and sentiments, and perceptions, all conspiring to self-preservation. Each of these faculties has some relationship, direct or indirect, to personal well-being. The due action of each brings its quantum of pleasure; the inaction, its more or less of pain. Those provided with these faculties in due proportions, prosper and multiply; those ill-provided, increasingly tend to die out. And the general success of this scheme of human organisation is seen in the fact that under it the world has been peopled, and by it the complicated appliances and arrangements of civilized life have been developed.

It is complained, however, that there are certain directions in which this apparatus of motive works but imperfectly. While it is admitted that men are duly prompted by it to bodily sustenance, to the obtainment of clothing and shelter, to marriage and the care of offspring, and to the establishment of the more important industrial and commercial agencies; it is yet argued that there are many desiderata, as pure air, more knowledge, good water, safe travelling, and so forth, which it does not duly achieve. And these short-comings being assumed permanent, and not temporary, it is urged that some supplementary means must be employed. It is therefore proposed that out of the mass of men thus imperfectly endowed, a certain number, constituting the legislature, shall be instructed to secure these various objects. The legislatures thus instructed (all characterized, on the average, by the same defects in this apparatus of motives as men in general), being unable personally to fulfil their tasks, must fulfil them by deputy — must appoint commissions, boards, councils, and staffs of officers; and must construct their agencies of this same defective humanity that acts so ill. Why now should this system of complex deputation succeed where the system of simple deputation does not? The industrial, commercial, and philanthropic agencies, which citizens form spontaneously, are directly deputed agencies; these governmental agencies made by electing legislators who appoint officers, are indirectly deputed ones. And it is hoped that, by this process of double deputation, things may be achieved which the process of single deputation will not achieve. What, now, is the rationale of this hope? Is it that legislators, and their employés, are made to feel more intensely than the rest these evils they are ready to remedy, these wants they are to satisfy? Hardly, for by position they are mostly relieved from such evils and wants. Is it, then, that they are to have the primary motive replaced by a secondary motive — the fear of public displeasure, and ultimate removal from office? Why, scarcely; for the minor benefits which citizens will not organize to secure *directly*, they will not organize to secure *indirectly*, by turning out inefficient servants: especially if they cannot readily get efficient ones. Is it, then, that these State-agents are to do, from a sense of duty, what they would not do from any other motive? Evidently this is the only possibility remaining. The proposition on which the advocates of much government have to fall back, is, that things which the people will not unite to effect for personal benefit, a law-appointed portion of them will unite to effect for the benefit of the rest. Public men and functionaries love their neighbours better than themselves! The philanthropy of statesmen is stronger than the selfishness of citizens!

No wonder, then, that every day adds to the list of legislative miscarriages. If colliery explosions increase, notwithstanding the appointment of coal-mine inspectors, why it is but a natural moral to these false hypotheses. If Sunderland shipowners complain that, as far as tried, 'the Mercantile Marine Act has proved a total failure'; and if, meanwhile, the other class affected by it – the sailors – show their disapprobation by extensive strikes; why it does but exemplify the folly of trusting a theorizing benevolence rather than an experienced self-interest. On all sides we may expect such facts; and on all sides we find them . . .

'Well, let the State fail. It can but do its best. If it succeed, so much the better; if it do not, where is the harm? Surely it is wiser to act, and take the chance of success, than to do nothing.' To this plea the rejoinder is, that unfortunately the results of legislative intervention are not only negatively bad, but often positively so. Acts of Parliament do not simply fail; they frequently make worse. The familiar truth that persecution aids rather than hinders proscribed doctrines . . . is a part of the general truth that legislation often does indirectly, the reverse of that which it directly aims to do . . .

Moreover, when these topical remedies applied by statesmen do not exacerbate the evils they were meant to cure, they constantly – we believe invariably – induce collateral evils; and these often graver than the original ones. It is the vice of this empirical school of politicians that they never look beyond proximate causes and immediate effects. In common with the uneducated masses they habitually regard each phenomenon as involving but one antecedent and one consequent. They do not bear in mind that each phenomenon is a link in an infinite series – is the result of myriads of preceding phenomena, and will have a share in producing myriads of succeeding ones. Hence they overlook the fact, that, in disturbing any natural chain of sequences, they are not only modifying the result next in succession, but all the future results into which this will enter as a part cause. The serial genesis of phenomena, and the interaction of each series upon every other series, produces a complexity utterly beyond human grasp. Even in the simplest cases this is so. A servant who mends the fire sees but few effects from the burning of a lump of coal.

D. Liberty and democracy

The man of science, however, knows that there are very many effects ...

If now from a simple inorganic change such complex results arise, how infinitely multiplied, how utterly incalculable must be the ultimate consequences of any force brought to bear upon society. Wonderfully constructed as it is – mutually dependent as are its members for the satisfaction of their wants – affected as each unit of it is by his fellows, not only as to his safety and prosperity, but in his health, his temper, his culture; the social organism cannot be dealt with in any one part, without all other parts being influenced in ways that cannot be foreseen ... In every case, you perceive, on careful inquiry, that besides acting upon that which you sought to act upon, you have acted upon many other things, and each of these again on many others; and so have propagated a multitude of changes more or less appreciable in all directions.

We need feel no surprise, then, that in their efforts to cure specific evils, legislators have continually caused collateral evils they never looked for. No Carlyle's wisest man, nor any body of such, could avoid causing them. Though their production is explicable enough after it has occurred, it is never anticipated. When, under the New Poor-law, provision was made for the accommodation of vagrants in the Union-houses, it was hardly expected that a body of tramps would be thereby called into existence, who would spend their time in walking from Union to Union throughout the kingdom ... Thus on all sides are well-meant measures producing unforeseen mischiefs – a licensing law that promotes the adulteration of beer; a ticket-of-leave system that encourages men to commit crime; a police regulation that forces street-hucksters into the workhouse. And then, in addition to the obvious and proximate evils, come the remote and less distinguishable ones, which, could we estimate their accumulated result, we should probably find even more serious.

[Source: Herbert Spencer, 'Over-Legislation' (1853), in *Essays: Scientific, Political, and Speculative*, London, 1868, II, pp. 50–8, 60, 62–5.]

Doc. 106. EMILE FAGUET: The Rights of the State

It is therefore not necessary to say precisely: the big State has two superimposed aims, that of the small State and that of the big State. It is necessary to say, the big State has two aims, that of the small State, but this *reduced to its minimum*, and then that of the big State.

For what is the aim of a small State, not menaced by any neighbour? To exist, nothing else, to be undisturbed. What is necessarily regarded as concern of the State is an apparatus of courts and of police so that order prevails in the streets and the quarrels between the citizens do not last for ever and become bitter. This is there in a small State, *the minimum aim* of the State. It could set itself five or six other aims without danger and even with some advantage. It could have the intention of 'seeing the arts flourish'; it could wish to educate; it could desire to regulate religious matters; it could want to watch over good domestic behaviour, insist on the father and mother of the family being accountable for the manner in which they live together and in which they educate their children and regulate matters of domestic hygiene. By God, yes. In the *fratrie*, such things would not be very offensive or painful indiscretions. But in a big State they would perhaps be. Let us reduce the aim of the small State to its minimum in order to know what the big State should preserve of it. The minimum aim of the State in a small country unthreatened by neighbours is to assure order and peace through good courts of justice and good police. Police and the courts, these are the 'matters of State' in a small country. What are they in a big one? In a big one they remain these at first. They join those which have become necessary through the causes which have made it a big State instead of a small one. Why does this big State exist? Because it has neighbours which are also big and which menace it incessantly. Therefore, it has the following aims: first, peace and order, like any State; then defence because it is a big State. Thus, in this big State, the concerns of the State should include one useful addition: the police, the courts of justice, and the military forces.

And what then? Then nothing else except the money necessary for all these things. Thus a State budget, a State police, a State army. And what further? Then nothing further. Everything else goes beyond the purpose of the State, and therefore exceeds its right, if I may express it so.

I will recognize that the State possesses all rights; but one can say that it is against the right of using right for the simple pleasure of using it and when it is not at all necessary. I have the right of legitimate self-defence. I am a very honourable person and I make use of it in the last extremity. If I use it very quickly, when I am hardly threatened, with zeal and with a secret satisfaction that the man I do not love has given me a chance through a slight threat to get rid of him, then I am not an honourable person and it is said of me: 'He had not the right of making use of his right.' I have not exceeded my right, but I have not acted with propriety.

The same is true of the State which, because it is impossible to contest seriously that it has all rights, uses those which are not formally agreed upon by the very necessities of its tasks. Such a State does not exceed its right, if you like; but it goes beyond its natural limitation. It gives itself a satisfaction which can be disagreeable, painful, offensive or harsh to others, instead of confining itself to carrying out its job and its duty. It has not exceeded its right; but it is a State dishonourable person. 'It had not the right of using its right.'

For, take note of it, in order not to depart from this moral viewpoint, take note, should not the State above all, if it knows how to examine its conscience, tell itself *that it is an evil*? It is very much so, just because it is a remedy. A remedy is a small evil that one invents in order to get rid of a big one. The State is an evil which mankind has invented in order to avert the dangers of combative mankind; but it is certainly an evil. It inconveniences the individual, it impedes him, it weighs upon him. It demands money from him which the individual would have no idea of giving or even of earning. It imposes the obligation of becoming a soldier on a very peaceful citizen. All this is very grievous. The State is a necessary evil, it is respectable and we owe gratitude to it. It is not something good in itself. It is an evil like a cuirasse or a sword. Arms are something destined to bring evil to him who receives their blows, but they begin to bring evil to him who wears them.

If the State knew how to tell these things to itself, it would consider that as one is an evil, one should logically endeavour to be the least possible one.

I know well that it reasons inversely. It tells itself that as it is inconvenient through many of its functions, it is nice for it to compensate for that evil-doing by being, on the other hand, beneficent, magnificent, sumptuous and paternal, by pouring out to the citizens the benefices, the cares, the considerations and the munificences. Only it should tell itself that one can be mistaken, that one can deceive oneself, that the works of necessity are very precisely designed and defined by their necessity itself, and that the works of beneficence are very much subject to being undertaken with a wrongness and contrary to the object they pursue.

This applies above all to the works of general and common benevolence. Vis-à-vis an individual there is a rather, if not completely, certain means of getting to know the good or the pleasure one can give him, and that is to ask him what he wants. He can be mistaken, but there is still a good chance that he is not absolutely mistaken. Vis-à-vis a nation it is rather difficult to know what beneficial deeds should suitably be showered upon it. It is rather difficult no matter whether one consults it or not. If you do not consult it you need pretty big and sharp eyes in order to see very correctly what suits it, and, guided mainly by your own taste, you could make immense errors. If you consult it, you know very well that you will always get several different replies, and which of them should you then choose? That which will obtain a majority. It is hard, if by satisfying a lot of people, one displeases a still considerable number of others who could, by the way, be the most enlightened people simply by following the needs of the greatest number. That which conforms most with your own taste? That is always what will happen, and you take always the necessary and easy precautions with a view to seeing that what is demanded from you should be what you wish to grant. But then you return to the first possibility, and to the considerable mistakes which I said result in this case.

It seems to me, therefore, a good thing that the State should employ its integrity, its loyalty, and also its moderation, to regard itself as a salutary remedy, as a necessary evil. Consequently, and in this capacity, it should restrain its natural functions, that means only to those of them for which it was established, only for what it alone can do, only for what is of such a character that if the State would not do it, the country would disappear tomorrow. These natural functions are the police, the courts of justice and defence. Everything else is a pretence of the State, not a function of the State. If the State does any of those other things, then it is no longer a good official, a good public servant of the fatherland, it is a dilettante. It occupies itself with things with which I recognize it has the right of occupying itself, but which do not concern it. It can do them well accidentally, but there are chances that it will do them badly as they are not within its game; and in any case, there is too much solicitude. One does not demand so much of it. This is an excessive zeal, and any excess of zeal entails troublesome habits of annoyance and of officiousness, which are painful for everyone.

This conception of the State which I have just sketched will make certain philosophers, who are full, if I may say so, of administrative mysticism, smile with pity. To them the State is by no means an evil. It is by no means a necessary evil, by no means a salutary evil. For them it is good, it is the sovereign good. For them the individual does not exist. He only exists enshrined in the State, thrown into gear by the State, integrated in the State, animated by the State. It is the State which gives him a soul . . .

The truth is that human society is in principle a natural fact; and in its development, which becomes voluntary, a fact still natural. It is in principle a natural and non-voluntary fact: human beings do not associate themselves; they are associated; they are born associated through family ties which extend to the clan, and through the ties of habit, common language, common customs, common memories, common traditions, common cults and common rituals. That is the true society, in which we suppose there interferes no conquest, no suppression of one class by another. This is the natural society.

The need for self-defence creates the big fatherland which is still natural, as it is only an agglomoration of clans; but it also is voluntary, for these clans have no natural reason to agglomorate; no natural instinct pushing them into association. They had to associate not for natural but for historical reasons. I maintain that this association, natural enough in its origins, is above all voluntary . . .

The big fatherland is thus an association, natural in its distant origins, voluntary in its development and considered in the actual condition in which one finds it. It has as distant cause the natural sociability of man, as less distant cause the necessity of defence. It is thus in part *genuine*, in part *factitious* and artificial. As far as it is genuine it is entitled to our respect and to our veneration. As far as it is factitious it is only entitled to our obedience. It should remember that as its only claim lies in the necessity of defence, its true right, its honourable right, to use this phrase, is defined by its principle and does not extend further than is required by defence. You, primitive clan, I revere you and I love you. You are my roots; you are the ashes of my ancestors. You, present society, I love you and I revere you as representing the primitive clan and finally as being its extension; but yet remember that you are *above all* only an expedient, only an instrument of defence, adopted owing to the lack of something better and to the fear of something worse. Remember that what is not true of the primitive clan, that is, contract and treaty and trade, is nevertheless a bit true of you. You are definitely the result of a voluntary association for the defence of common interests. Consequently, if you go beyond the function for which you have been made, you do doubtlessly not violate any formal contract, but exceed a 'quasi-contract'; you trespass, you go rather further than the point which was understood, because it was reasonable that you would stop. You misused a tacit confidence. If one has created you or supported you (this amounts actually to the same), so as to be able to defend oneself against the external enemy, you have been told that your function reached its limit there. Anything which you do beyond that point, you will be wrong in doing because it is not demanded from you. You are not exactly violating the contract because the contract has never existed; but you are an unfaithful mandatory ...

The core of the mentality of every government is expressed in this thought: 'The country, that is me.' It is, therefore, in the nature of any government not to tolerate contradiction. If it tolerates it, you may be sure, it is because it cannot react differently. This is true of all possible governments. It is true of monarchy; it is true of aristocracy; needless for me to say that it is even still truer of democracy; for in this case the government, emerging by delegation from the people themselves, has to all appearances more than any other the right of saying: 'The country, that is me', and of refusing to tolerate not only any contradiction, but even any velleity of thinking differently from it. We shall see this in much greater detail when we come to deal with parliamentary government.

What lies meanwhile at the bottom of these astonishing pretensions? What is it that makes this government boast of being the entire country? It is a civil servant who has been charged, or whom circumstances have charged, which is the same to a sociologist, with ensuring order in the country and with defending the country against the foreigner. It is nothing more. What power shall one therefore give to him? The necessary force to make order prevail in the country: the necessary force in order to defend the country against the foreigner; obedience with reference to what he regards as his function of ensuring order in the country, obedience and devotion to what he regards as his function of defending the country against the foreigner. What else? Nothing. Absolutely nothing. Where his function stops, there stops, if not his right, then at least the legitimate and reasonable use of his right. Beyond that limit he is perhaps within his right, but he is unreasonable, he is troublesome, he is vexatious and he is stupid.

Intelligent liberalism, therefore, does not consist in weakening power as much as possible and on all points – this too, would be stupid; but in drawing firmly the limit up to which the central power should be very strong and beyond which it should be nothing at all. About this, nothing better has ever been said than the dictum of Benjamin Constant: 'Outside its realm the government should not have any power; within its sphere it should not have too much.' It is thus a matter of tracing the contours of this sphere. It is exactly what we have done in broad outline and by way of general principles. What now remains for us to do is to consider the details; for in the details, this does not cease to be a delicate matter.

[Source: Emile Faguet, *Le libéralisme*, Paris 1903, Ch. 2, pp. 20–5, 35–7, 42–3. Translated by the editors of this volume.]

Doc. 107. PAUL LEROY-BEAULIEU: The Functions and Limitations of the State

For since most of the prerogatives which are today considered as essential to the State did not belong to it primarily, but long remained in the hands of individuals or of free associations, and only devolved upon the State gradually, through the slow application of the principle of division of labour, and the recognition of the fact that a great collective organ, armed with the power of constraint, is more capable of generalizing them than a number of small collective organs, spontaneous and variable, possessing little more than the power of persuasion – how then are we to fix, either for the present or the future, the limits of the domain of the State? This same historical account will, however, give us some assistance by enabling us better to recognise the general characteristics of the State.

The first point which forces itself upon our notice is, that the State is absolutely devoid of inventive genius.

The State is a rigid collective organ, which can only act by means of a complicated apparatus, composed of numerous wheels and systems of wheels, subordinated one to another; the State is a hierarchy either aristocratic, or bureaucratic, or elective, in which spontaneous thought is by the very nature of things subjected to a prodigious number of controlling and hampering checks. Such a machine can invent nothing.

The State, as a matter of fact, invents nothing, and never has invented anything. The whole or almost the whole of human progress is traceable to particular names, to those exceptional men whom the principal Minister of the Second Empire called 'individualities without a mandate'.

It is through and by these 'individualities without a mandate' that the world advances and develops itself. These are the prophets and inspired teachers who represent the fermentation of the human mass, which is naturally inert . . .

I have no wish to contest the services which in some directions the State undoubtedly renders, or to overlook the perfecting in detail which many of its engineers or experts introduce or disseminate. I do not deny that the State has in its service some eminent and distinguished men; I maintain, however, that most of them, when they have the opportunity, prefer to leave the official administration, where advancement is slow and pedantically managed, and is subject to nepotism or senile incapacity, that they may enter the ranks of private enterprise where men are at once admitted to the rank which their talents and their merit mark out for them.

How could it be otherwise? 'The spirit', says the Scripture, like the wind, 'bloweth where it listeth.' Modern philosophy has rendered this great thought by another formula, 'Tout le monde a plus d'esprit que Voltaire.' (Everyone has more wit than Voltaire.) It is not within regular limits, prudently and deliberately designed, that the spirit of invention will work; it chooses its *élite* freely from among the crowd.

When we say that the State is essentially lacking in the faculty of invention and in the faculty of promptly applying new discoveries, we have no intention of blackening its character, or laying it open to damaging sarcasms. We are simply portraying its nature, which has different and opposing merits.

From the social point of view again, the State can discover nothing. Bills of exchange, demand drafts, cheques, the multifarious operations of banks, the clearing-house, assurance, savings banks, ingenious methods of payment by profit-sharing, co-operative societies – not one of all these improvements is traceable to the thought or the action of the State. All these ingenious contrivances have sprung out of the free social medium.

What, then, is the State? It is not a creative organ, by any means. It is an organ of criticism, an organ of generalization, coordination, vulgarization. It is, above all, an organ of conservation.

The State is a copyist, an enlarger, an exaggerator even. In its copies and adaptations from private enterprise, it runs many chances of making mistakes, or of multiplying indefinitely whatever mistakes it finds in the original from which it is borrowing.

It intervenes after discoveries have been made, and it may then give them a certain amount of assistance. But it may also stifle them: with the intervention of the State – which may, in many cases, be beneficent – we have always this element of caprice to fear, this brutal, monopolizing tendency, this *quia nominor leo*. It possesses, in fact, a double power, which it can wield with terrible force, legal constraint and fiscal restraint.

From this very fact that the State is so absolutely destitute of the faculty of invention, that it possesses only the capacity of assimilation and of co-operation, and that in a very variable measure, it follows that the State cannot be the first agent, the primary cause of progress in human society: is it not in a position to do more than to play the part of an auxiliary, an agent of propagation, which, moreover, runs the risk of transforming itself, by an injudicious presumption, into an agent of perturbation.

It must, therefore, descend from the throne on which some have attempted to place it.

It follows, further, that the State is not the highest form of personality, as M. von Stein maintains. It is the largest, no doubt, but not the highest, since it is devoid of that most marvellous of human attributes – the power of invention.

Before entering in detail into the tasks undertaken by the trinity of State-powers – the central, provincial, and communal power – we have thought it desirable to refute these errors, and to lay down these principles. The mission of the State will by this means become all the clearer . . .

Since the Modern State is constituted from out of the mass of its citizens by delegation of authority for short periods, it is not only not in its essence more intelligent than they – especially than the more enlightened among them – but also it is subject to all the successive prejudices which dominate and which lead astray the human kind: it is a prey to all kinds of infatuations one after another.

But more than this, it is in itself always in some sort the *résumé*, the accentuation, the intensification of the special kind of infatuation prevalent in the country at the last renewal of the public authorities, that is, at the last general election.

This characteristic of the Modern State has not been sufficiently insisted on. The Modern State expresses for four or five years at a time the will not of the whole nation, but of a mere majority, and often of a majority that is more apparent than real: and further, it expresses this will as it was manifested at a period of excitement and of fever. Elections are not preceded by retreats, by fasting, and by prayer; they are not conducted in silence and meditation. But even if this were the case, they would still be defective, since it is incidental to human nature that the elections should always be influenced by intrigue, and by the prestige which professional politicians and all turbulent, excited, and ambitious persons know how to win among those yielding and timid souls who practically form the great bulk of the electorate. The elections take place amid noise and uproar and confusion.

The modern elector is like the poor wretch whom the recruiting sergeant of former days caught in the public thoroughfare, and whom, when he had turned his head with wine and promises, he would get to sign an engagement for the army. The same methods of procedure are employed in both cases. Thus the Modern State in general represents the highest triumph of the momentary infatuation of the majority of the nation.

For there is no time or season which has not its dominant infatuations: the infatuation for force and repression, or, on the other hand, for unlimited individual liberty; the infatuation for public works, or for some special form of public works, railroads, canals, monuments; the infatuation for or against religion; the infatuation for public instruction in all its forms; the infatuation for tutelage and excess of regulation; the infatuation for freedom of exchange, or for restricted exchange and for protection etc. There are a thousand different forms of infatuation to which in their turn a nation is ready to yield.

Each of these infatuations, that is to say, each of these incomplete or exaggerated conceptions, entails perils for the society, perils of every kind. The duty of the State is to endeavour seriously to resist being so carried away, and to dominate and restrain these caprices. But so far from doing this, the Modern State by the very circumstances of its origin must in a sense multiply and prolong for four or five years the infatuation of a moment.

The Modern State represents the nation much as the instantaneous photograph represents the horse which it takes in the act of galloping, and which, as far as it is concerned, remains at a gallop for ever.

Legislation in Modern States, therefore, almost always goes further than public opinion would desire, when it has subsided after the excitement induced by the elections. Thus it frequently happens that one Chamber or House is followed by another animated by an absolutely contrary spirit; and this also explains the frequent contradiction, the almost immediate reversal which is given to the general election by succeeding bye-elections.

The legislation of Modern States is of necessity almost always extreme, either in the direction of action or of reaction. One legislature spends three parts of its time in undoing what the one or two preceding legislatures have done. There are two remedies possible for this intemperence, this excess in legislation: the one is obstruction working within the Parliament itself, the other is the *referendum*, or ratification by the entire electorate of any important laws which have just been voted by the Chambers.

It is not likely that society will ever fully appreciate the enormous services which parliamentary obstruction renders to the nation. It ensures repose and continuity in the conditions of existence. For one good measure whose adoption it may retard, there are nine bad or useless measures which it casts into the limbo of forgotten things. The celebrated 'massacre of innocents', to which the English Parliament sets itself in the last days of the session, is often the best piece of work it does in the whole session. For the same reasons, it would be a mistake to lay aside in France, as it has been proposed to do, the practice of allowing all proposals to lapse which by the expiration of the life of a Parliament have only been voted by one Chamber.

A great deal has been said about educational 'over-pressure', but not enough about parliamentary 'over-pressure', which is much more real and more dangerous. Against educational 'over-pressure' there is some guarantee, some refuge, in the children's happy faculty of inattention: their body is present at the class, but their mind is often far away. Against parliamentary 'over-pressure' there is some slight refuge and guarantee in that same useful but much calumniated weapon of obstruction just referred to, with all its methods of procedure, some ingenious, some naive. But for a really serious democratic society yet another check is needed – the *referendum*, or popular sanction of the most important laws. The *referendum* is a defensive weapon which societies should always keep in reserve against the too hasty impulses of their irrevocable mandatories.

The first and greatest vice of the Modern State, namely, that it intensifies and prolongs through many consecutive years the particular infatuation or enthusiasm which prevailed in the country for a few days, leads us to speak of a second weakness which springs out of the first. The Modern State never has a complete sequence of ideas, nor yet of *personale*.

We think it will be enough to enunciate this proposition without its being necessary to demonstrate it. Since all governing power springs from elections which take place often, the *personale* which represents the State is very variable. The more the elective principle has play in a State, the more this instability becomes apparent. Formerly only ministers and certain very high and very well remunerated functions were affected by it, but now it shows a tendency to penetrate the entire administrative body. Since political struggles in most countries go on not only between two conflicting bodies of doctrine, but also between two bodies of greedy politicians, most of them without resources or other means of subsistence, it follows that the triumph of either camp means a general clearance throughout . . .

The instability of the *personale* in the Modern State – outside those monarchies which stand on a firm basis of authority – results in a certain incoherence in the action of the State, or at least in a difficulty in making the machine work with regularity and precision, with flexibility and caution, in order that it may produce its full effect without disturbance or injury to anyone. For clearness and precision of will and for intelligent continuity of effort the Modern State lags far behind gifted individuals, or even behind well-conducted corporations.

This leads us to a third defect, which is in some respects the greatest of all, and which working in and with the other two contributes to their development and renders them still more harmful. In theory the State represents the whole body of citizens: the State is therefore theoretically the impartial being *par excellence*. Now, in the Modern State this impartiality is entirely illusory: it does not, and cannot exist. Absolute and undisputed monarchies may pretend to this ideal of sovereign impartiality. It is scarcely possible that even they should attain it completely, but there is nothing in their actual constitution to disqualify them for it. The Modern State, on the contrary, the State based upon election, cannot by its very constitution be impartial: it runs counter to its very definition, since it is government by a party.

The State, as conceived by the Western nations today, is the actual mandatory, not of the whole number of citizens, but simply of the majority, and generally a weak majority, instantaneous, momentary, precarious, variable. Not only is there a party in power, but it is a party always threatened by a rival party, and in constant fear of losing this power which it has with such difficulty conquered. Moreover, there are not only ideas and sentiments, but there are also solid interests which in our greedy societies of today may be favoured by the possession of power . . .

We have not yet exhausted the enumeration of all the special features which characterize the Modern State and exert an influence on all its actions. One of the least recognized of its features, but which is productive of the most serious consequences, is the general conception which the modern elective State forms of the interests of society, and hence of the means by which they are to be satisfied.

In consequence of its origin, which is by incessant election, always disputed and often indecisive, the Modern State hardly ever conceives of social interests in a synthetic form: it sees them only parcelled out into small portions, and in a condition of antagonism towards each other. It has never, so to say, more than particular interests in view: the absolute collective interest of the whole entirely escapes it. It shares the very common notion that the general interest of the whole is the sum of the various particular interests of its parts, a proposition which holds good in ordinary cases, but which cannot always be admitted without reserve. Take one of the most debatable questions of our time – that of custom-house relations with foreign countries. The Modern State will be much more struck with the number of particular interests, concerned in protection, or, at least, who think themselves concerned in it (for these particular interests often deceive themselves and are the dupes of appearances), than with the general stimulus, the gradual increase of vitality which a liberal commercial *régime* would secure to the whole country. It is the same with public works, with education, and with the national forces.

As well as being more concerned with particular interests than with the synthetic interest of the nation, the Modern State, for the same reasons of origin and precarious tenure, is also more sensible of immediate and present interests than of larger interests which are deferred or distant. Hence it runs counter to one of the most important missions of the State, which is to preserve the future, even the far-distant future.

There are still two more weaknesses, which are peculiar to all States, not only to the modern elective State. From the strictly professional point of view, in the technical works which they direct, public functionaries have neither the stimulus nor the restraint of personal interest.

By the habitual conditions under which they work they find themselves, as it were, in some measure detached from their work, or, at least, from some of the consequences of their work. No doubt they may be animated by lofty sentiments and zeal for the public good. But this zeal has not the sanction of the natural rebound of the practical results of their work upon themselves. Even the sentiment of honour, which is the highest and most potent of all by which they are inspired, may sometimes lead them astray. They often allow themselves to be deceived as to the real character of their mission; they strive after the great instead of the useful, they work for ends which may bring them honour and distinction, instead of fulfilling the humble and common-place tasks which appertain to the daily round. Even in enterprises which they undertake for the community they adopt an aesthetic point of view which involves them in a great waste of force. We see this in the construction of highways, roads, and schools.

I now have to notice the last of the State's weaknesses, whether it be ancient or modern, republican or monarchial, moderate or despotic. The State is debarred from the action of competition, the most energetic of all the social forces, and the one which most actively subserves the improvement of individuals and of society.

With this double power of legal and fiscal constraint which has devolved upon it, the State, when acting within the territory of the nation, has no fear of being supplanted, annulled or suppressed. Being a personality without a rival, the only one of its species, it is secure from the danger of eviction or annihilation which besets individuals or free associations which fulfil their task indifferently or badly . . .

By virtue of its superiority from the point of view of conception, invention, and aptitude for frequent modifications, or varied experiments, individual action should *à priori* be preferred to that of the State for all enterprises susceptible of remuneration . . .

Face to face with a State administration, the private individual is constantly coming into collision with an arrogant bureaucracy, more or less irresponsible, with laws that derogate from the common right, with special and more or less partial legal jurisdiction. Thus we cannot be too chary of admitting exceptions to the rule that all services of whatever kind, which are susceptible to remuneration, should be left in the hands of individual action.

Therefore, voluntary associations, free societies, in any shape or form, by virtue of the flexibility they enjoy, of the rapidity of their successive adaptations, of the greater play they allow to personal interest, and to innovation, of their better-defined responsibility towards their customers, and of the competition they have to face, and which acts as a stimulus to them, ought to be preferred to the State for all services which admit of being fulfilled either by the one or by the other.

Since the State is an organ of authority which uses the weapon of constraint or the threat of it, wherever equivalent results, or nearly so, can be attained by the method of liberty, this method ought to have the preference.

Even if we conceive that the State might, under certain circumstances, for the moment organize a service in a more general, perhaps even a more complete, manner than free societies, this would not be a sufficient reason for pronouncing in favour of State action. It is here, in fact, that we find the importance of rising to a synthetic view of society, instead of considering isolated parties, and examining things as it were with a microscope. Liberty, private enterprise, voluntary habits of collective action, hold, in fact, the very germs of life and progress; and these germs have a general importance for the entire social medium which is vastly greater than the mere technical perfection of such and such a secondary detail.

We should not only be concerned to attain in the present, and as rapidly as possible, such and such material results with reference, say, to insurance, or the assistance of the poor, we have also to think of the conservation of a certain energy and spontaneity of movement among all the social forces. A man has not only the execution of his daily task to consider; he ought also to take care that all his organs, all his muscles, and all his nerves, are well at his service, and capable of acting, that none of them should go to waste, but that they are in such a condition that he can resume the use of them at any moment should the necessity arise.

It is the same with human societies. It is better that life and initiative should be diffused throughout the social body than that it should be concentrated in a single organ which wields an unlimited power of constraint and an limited power of taxation.

Besides the method of legislative constraint and taxation, which is but another form of constraint, the State has a third method of influencing society – namely, by way of example. This method is subject to less criticism than the other two. But it is none the less insidious, or likely, if the State does not use extreme discretion in exercising it, to cause a fatal disturbance of social relations.

The force of the example set by the State increases every day. The indirect action of the State, altogether apart from its legal injunctions or from the levying of its taxes, is in some respects more felt in modern societies than it was among the ancients. Man has always been prone to imitation: the crowd keeps its eyes uplifted towards those who occupy prominent positions, and seeks to reproduce in its common everyday life some of the features of their conduct.

But it is not in this that the secret of the new power lies which the example set by the State exercises today. It arises from the fact that the State is the greatest consumer, the greatest executor of works, the greatest 'employer of labour' in the nation. For the requirements of national defence, that is, for those two formidable and progressive industries, the naval and military services: for the gigantic public works with which it has over-laden its trinity of powers, the central, provincial and municipal authorities: for all the services which it has more or less monopolized – the post, the telegraph, education, etc. – the State spends annually in ordinary and extraordinary (an extraordinary which is, however, permanent) from forty to fifty millions sterling, after deducting the interest on the national and local debts. This amounts to certainly more than a tenth of the entire expenditure, both public and private, of all the citizens put together, and they are the most ostentatious forms of expenditure, and the ones that most immediately strike the eye. If, therefore, the State should make up its mind to declare that in its workshops no one should work more than eight or nine hours in the day, and if it imposed on its purveyors the observance of the same length of working-day: if by means of simple internal regulations it were pleased to decree that certain combinations, more or less new and more or less contested, such as co-operation, or profit-sharing, should be practised by all the industrial houses with which it has relations; if it should fix for the labourers in its employ, or in that of the food purveyors to whom it gives orders, a different rate of pay from that which is in ordinary use: it is clear that this example being set by so gigantic a consumer, so preponderating a customer, will have an enormous weight with the nation at large.

The fancies and caprices of the State, even when they do not take the form of general injunctions or laws, reverberate for these reasons far and wide throughout the whole social domain. Such examples set by the State may often prove useful if they are undertaken with extreme discretion and careful consideration: but there is on the whole more likelihood of their being pernicious and disturbing.

When the State thus undertakes to furnish models to private individuals, and to encourage types of organization which it believes to be progression, it assumes, often all too lightly, a very grave responsibility. For, first, it does not act with the resources which are its own property, but with derived resources taken from others, so that even if at first in appearance lacking, fiscal constraint ultimately becomes a necessity. And next, the State does not enjoy entire liberty, or absolute independence or judgment, because the electoral yoke and all the mental servitude it involves weighs without a single moment's intermission constantly upon the shoulders of those who represent the Modern State. Lastly, being

D. Liberty and democracy

obliged to act always uniformly and on a large scale, it multiplies the errors that are so frequent in all human endeavours.

[Source: Paul Leroy-Beaulieu, *The Modern State in Relation to Society and the Individual*, trans. A. C. Morant, London 1891, pp. 81–3, 88–91, 103–9, 112–14, 118–21 and 147–54.]

(ii) The case for moderate State intervention

Doc. 108. THOMAS HILL GREEN: Liberal Legislation and Freedom of Contract

We shall probably all agree that freedom, rightly understood, is the greatest of all blessings; that its attainment is the true end of all our efforts as citizens. But when we thus speak of freedom, we should consider carefully what we mean by it. We do not mean merely freedom from restraint or compulsion. We do not mean merely freedom to do as we like irrespectively of what it is that we like. We do not mean a freedom that can be enjoyed by one man or one set of men at the cost of a loss of freedom to others. When we speak of freedom as something to be so highly prized, we mean a positive power or capacity of doing or enjoying, and that, too, something that we do or enjoy in common with others. We mean by it a power which each man exercises through the help or security given him by his fellow-men, and which he in turn helps to secure for them. When we measure the progress of a society by its growth in freedom, we measure it by the increasing development and exercise on the whole of those powers of contributing to social good with which we believe the members of the society to be endowed; in short, by the greater power on the part of the citizens as a body to make the most and best of themselves. Thus, though of course there can be no freedom among men who act not willingly but under compulsion, yet on the other hand the mere removal of compulsion, the mere enabling a man to do as he likes, is in itself no contribution to true freedom. In one sense no man is so well able to do as he likes as the wandering savage. He has no master. There is no one to say him nay. Yet we do not count him really free, because the freedom of savagery is not strength, but weakness. The actual powers of the noblest savage do not admit of comparison with those of the humblest citizen of a law-abiding state. He is not the slave of man, but he is the slave of nature. Of compulsion by natural necessity he has plenty of experience, though of restraint by society none at all. Nor can he deliver himself from that compulsion except by submitting to this restraint. So to submit is the first step in true freedom, because it is the first step towards the full exercise of the faculties with which man is en-

652

dowed. But we rightly refuse to recognize the highest development on the part of an exceptional individual or exceptional class, as an advance towards the true freedom of man, if it is founded on a refusal of the same opportunity to other men. The powers of the human mind have probably never attained such force and keenness, the proof of what society can do for the individual has never been so strikingly exhibited, as among the small groups of men who possessed civil privileges in the small republics of antiquity. The whole framework of our political ideas, to say nothing of our philosophy, is derived from them. But in them this extraordinary efflorescence of the privileged class was accompanied by the slavery of the multitude. That slavery was the condition on which it depended, and for that reason it was doomed to decay. There is no clearer ordinance of that supreme reason, often dark to us, which governs the course of man's affairs, than that no body of men should in the long run be able to strengthen itself at the cost of others' weakness. The civilization and freedom of the ancient world were shortlived because they were partial and exceptional. If the ideal of true freedom is the maximum of power for all members of human society alike to make the best of themselves, we are right in refusing to ascribe the glory of freedom to a state in which the apparent elevation of the few is founded on the degradation of the many, and in ranking modern society, founded as it is on free industry, with all its confusion and ignorant licence and waste of effort, above the most splendid of ancient republics.

If I have given a true account of that freedom which forms the goal of social effort, we shall see that freedom of contract, freedom in all the forms of doing what one will with one's own, is valuable only as a means to an end. That end is what I call freedom in the positive sense: in other words, the liberation of the powers of all men equally for contributions to a common good. No one has a right to do what he will with his own in such a way as to contravene this end. It is only through the guarantee which society gives him that he has property at all, or strictly speaking, any right to his possessions. This guarantee is founded on a sense of common interest. Every one has an interest in securing to every one else the free use and enjoyment and disposal of his possessions, so long as that freedom on the part of the one does not interfere with a like freedom on the part of others, because such freedom contributes to that equal development of the faculties of all which is the highest good for all. This is the true and the only justification of rights of property. Rights of property, however, have been and are claimed which cannot be thus justified. We are all now agreed that men cannot rightly be the property of men. The institution of property being only justifiable as a means to the free exercise of the social capabilities of all, there can be no true right to property of a kind which debars one class of men from such free exercise altogether. We condemn slavery no less when it arises out of a voluntary agreement on the part of the enslaved person. A contract by which

D. Liberty and democracy

any one agreed for a certain consideration to become the slave of another we should reckon a void contract. Here then, is a limitation upon freedom of contract which we all recognise as rightful. No contract is valid in which human persons, willingly or unwillingly, are dealt with as commodities, because such contracts of necessity defeat the end for which alone society enforces contracts at all.

Are there no other contracts which, less obviously perhaps but really, are open to the same objection? In the first place, let us consider contracts affecting labour. Labour, the economist tells us, is a commodity exchangeable like other commodities. This is in a certain sense true, but it is a commodity which is attached in a peculiar manner to the person of man. Hence restrictions may need to be placed on the sale of this commodity which would be unnecessary in other cases, in order to prevent labour from being sold under conditions which make it impossible for the person selling it ever to become a free contributor to social good in any form. This is most plainly the case when a man bargains to work under conditions fatal to health, *e.g.* in an unventilated factory. Every injury to the health of the individual is, so far as it goes, a public injury. It is an impediment to the general freedom; so much deduction from our power, as members of society, to make the best of ourselves. Society is, therefore, plainly within its right when it limits freedom of contract for the sale of labour, so far as is done by our laws for the sanitary regulations of factories, workshops, and mines. It is equally within its right in prohibiting the labour of women and young persons beyond certain hours. If they work beyond those hours, the result is demonstrably physical deterioration; which, as demonstrably, carries with it a lowering of the moral forces of society. For the sake of that general freedom of its members to make the best of themselves, which it is the object of civil society to secure, a prohibition should be put by law, which is the deliberate voice of society, on all such contracts of service as in a general way yield such a result. The purchase or hire of unwholesome dwellings is properly forbidden on the same principle. Its application to compulsory education may not be quite so obvious, but it will appear on a little reflection. Without a command of certain elementary arts and knowledge, the individual in modern society is as effectually crippled as by the loss of a limb or a broken constitution. He is not free to develop his faculties. With a view to securing such freedom among its members it is as certainly within the province of the state to prevent children from growing up in that kind of ignorance which practically excludes them from a free career in life, as it is within its province to require the sort of building and drainage necessary for public health.

Our modern legislation then with reference to labour, and education, and health, involving as it does manifold interference with freedom of contract, is justified on the ground that it is the business of the state, not indeed directly to promote moral goodness, for that, from the very nature of moral goodness, it cannot do, but to maintain the conditions without which a free exercise of the human faculties is impossible. It does not indeed follow that it is advisable for the state to do all which it is justified in doing. We are often warned nowadays against the danger of over-legislation; or, as I heard it put in a speech of the present home secretary [Sir William Harcourt] in days when he was sowing his political wild oats, of 'grandmotherly government'. There may be good ground for the warning, but at any rate we should be quite clear what we mean by it. The outcry against state interference is often raised by men whose real objection is not to state interference but to centralisation, to the constant aggression of the central executive upon local authorities . . . But centralization is one thing; over-legislation, or the improper exercise of the power of the state, quite another. It is one question whether of late the central government has been unduly trenching on local government, and another question whether the law of the state, either as administered by central or by provincial authorities, has been unduly interfering with the discretion of individuals. We may object most strongly to advancing centralisation, and yet wish that the law should put rather more than less restraint on those liberties of the individual which are a social nuisance. But there are some political speculators whose objection is not merely to centralisation, but to the extended action of the law altogether. They think that the individual ought to be left much more to himself than has of late been the case. Might not our people, they ask, have been trusted to learn in time for themselves to eschew unhealthy dwellings, to refuse dangerous and degrading employment, to get their children the schooling necessary for making their way in the world? Would they not for their own comfort, if not from more chivalrous feeling, keep their wives and daughters from overwork? Or, failing this, ought not women, like men, to learn to protect themselves? Might not all the rules, in short, which legislation of the kind we have been discussing is intended to attain, have been attained without it; not so quickly, perhaps, but without tampering so dangerously with the independence and self-reliance of the people?

Now, we shall probably all agree that a society in which the public health was duly protected, and necessary education duly provided for, by the spontaneous action of individuals, was in a higher condition than one in which the compulsion of law was needed to secure these ends. But we must take men as we find them. Until such a condition of society is reached, it is the business of the state to take the best security it can for the young citizen's growing up in such health and with so much knowledge as is necessary for their real freedom. In doing so it need not at all interfere with the independence and self-reliance of those whom it requires to do what they would otherwise do for themselves . . . But it was not their case that the laws we are considering were especially meant to meet. It was the overworked women, the ill-housed and untaught families, for whose benefit they were intended. And the question is whether without these laws the suffering classes could have been delivered quickly or slowly from the condition they were in. Could the enlightened self-interest or benevolence of individuals, working under a system of unlimited freedom of contract, have ever brought them into a state compatible with the free development of the human faculties? No one considering the facts can have any doubt as to the answer to this question. Left to itself, or to the operation of casual benevolence, a degraded population perpetuates and increases itself. Read any of the authorized accounts, given before royal or parliamentary commissions, of the state of the labourers, especially of the women and children, as they were in our great industries before the law was first brought to bear on them, and before freedom of contract was first interfered with in them. Ask yourself what chance there was of a generation, born and bred under such conditions, ever contracting itself out of them. Given a certain standard of moral and material well-being, people may be trusted not to sell their labour, or the labour of their children, on terms which would not allow that standard to be maintained. But with large masses of our population, until the laws we have been considering took effect, there was no such standard. There was nothing on their part, in the way either of self-respect or established demand for comforts, to prevent them from working and living, or from putting their children to work and live, in a way which no one who is to be a healthy and free citizen can work and live. No doubt there were many high-minded employers who did their best for their workpeople before the days of state-interference, but they could not prevent less scrupulous hirers of labour from hiring it on the cheapest terms. It is true that cheap labour is in the long run dear labour, but it is so only in the long run, and eager traders do not think of the long run. If labour is to be had under conditions incompatible with the health or decent housing or education of the labourer, there will always be plenty of people to buy it under those conditions, careless of the burden in the shape of rates and taxes which they may be laying up for posterity. Either the standard of well-being on the part of the sellers of labour must prevent them from selling their labour under those conditions, or the law must prevent it. With a population such as ours was forty years ago, and still largely is, the law must prevent it and continue the prevention for some generations, before the sellers will be in a state to prevent it for themselves.

[Source: Thomas Hill Green, 'Liberal Legislation and Freedom of Contract' (1881), *The Works of Thomas Hill Green*, ed. R. L. Nettleship, London 1889, III, pp. 370–5.]

Doc. 109. JOSEPH CHAMBERLAIN: The Main Lines of Liberal Progress (*Speech at Hull, 5 August 1885*)

It is not desirable, even if it were possible, that all Liberals should think exactly alike, and that every candidate should be cut to precisely the same pattern. In the Liberal army there must be pioneers to clear the way, and there must be men who watch the rear. Some may always be in advance, others may occasionally lag behind; but the only thing we have a right to demand is, that no one shall stand still, and that all should be willing to follow the main lines of Liberal progress to which the whole party are committed. I do not conceal from you my own opinion that the pace will be a little faster in the future than it has been in the past . . .

The Liberal party has always seemed to me the great agency of progress and reform, and by the changes which have recently taken place it has secured a vantage ground which I myself had hardly ever dared to anticipate. I had looked forward with hope to the future, but I had not supposed in my time so great a change could have been successfully effected. But now that my wildest expectations have been surpassed, I am not willing to be silent as to the uses to which I believe the people ought to put the new power and the privileges which have been conferred upon them. I had already a deep conviction that when the people came·to govern themselves, and when the clamour of vested interests and class privileges were overborne by the powerful voice of the whole nation, that then the social evils which disgrace our civilization and the wrongs which have cried vainly for redress would at last find a hearing and a remedy. And if that be not so it will be no longer statesmen or governments that you will have to blame. It will not be the fault of parties or of individuals; it will be the apathy or the ignorance, the indifference or the folly of the people themselves which alone can hinder their progress and their prosperity . . .

I do not want you to think that I suggest to you that legislation can accomplish all that we desire, and, above all, I would not lead you into wild and revolutionary projects, which would upset unnecessarily the existing order of things. But, on the other hand, I do not want you to accept as final or as perfect, arrangements under which hundreds of thousands, nay, millions, of your fellow countrymen are subjected to untold privations and misery, with the evidence all around them of accumulated wealth and unbounded luxury. The extremes of wealth and of poverty are alike the sources of great temptation. I believe that the great evil with which we have to deal is the excessive inequality in the distribution of riches. Ignorance, intemperance, immorality, and disease – these things are all interdependent and closely connected; and although they are often the cause of poverty, they are still more frequently the consequence of destitution, and if we can do anything to raise the condition of the poor in this country, to elevate the masses of the people, and give them the means of enjoyment and recreation, to afford to them opportunities of improvement, we should do more for the prosperity, ay, for the morality of this country than anything we can do by laws, however stringent, for the prevention of excess, or the prevention of crime. I want you to make this the first object in the Liberal programme for the reformed Parliament. It is not our duty, it is not our wish, to pull down and abase the rich, although I do not think that the aggregation of wealth in a few hands is any advantage to anybody; but our object is to raise the general condition of the people ... Our ideal, I think, should be that in this rich country, where everything seems to be in profusion, an honest, a decent, and an industrious man should be able to earn a livelihood for himself and his family, should have access to some means of self-improvement and enjoyment, and should be able to lay aside something for sickness and old age ...

Let us consider what are the practical means by which we can accomplish such an object. I am not a Communist, although some people will have it that I am. Considering the difference in the character and the capacity of men, I do not believe that there can ever be an absolute equality of conditions, and I think that nothing would be more undesirable than that we should remove the stimulus to industry and thrift and exertion which is afforded by the security given to every man in the enjoyment of the fruits of his own individual exertions. I am opposed to confiscation in every shape or form, because I believe that it would destroy that security and lessen that stimulus. But on the other hand, I am in favour of accompanying the protection which is afforded to property with a large and stringent interpretation of the obligations of property. It seems to me that there are three main directions in which we may seek for help in the task which I think we ought to set ourselves. In the first place, I look for great results from the development of local government amongst us. The experience of the great towns is very encouraging in this respect. By their wise and liberal use of the powers entrusted to them, they have, in the majority of cases, protected the health of the community; they have provided means of recreation and enjoyment and instruction, and they have done a great deal to equalize social advantages, and to secure for all the members of the community the enjoyments which, without their aid and assistance, would have been monopolized by the rich alone. You have, in connection with the great municipal corporations, hospitals, schools, museums, free libraries, art galleries, baths, parks. All these things which a generation ago could only have been obtained by the well-to-do, are now, in many large towns, placed at the service of every citizen by the action of the municipalities. I desire that this opportunity should be afforded to the whole country, and I think that, having regard to what has been done in the past, we may show great confidence in the work of popular representative bodies, and be contented to extend their functions and increase their powers and authority. Closely connected with this subject there is another question, which I think of urgent importance. I have spoken of education. I think the time has come when education ought to be free. I have always held that the exaction of fees in our primary schools was unjust and un-economical, and prejudicial to the best interests of education . . .

I believe that nothing has done more to tend to the unpopularity of our education system than the exaction of these miserable fees. It is un-economical, because the cost of collection is in excessive proportion to the amount collected; and it is unjust because it lays upon the shoulders of the poor man a burden which is proportioned, not to his means, but to his necessities and his wants . . . I hope that one of the first acts of the new Parliament will be to see that this anomaly shall cease, and that education, suited to the capacity of every child, which is the indispens-able instrument for any progress in life, shall be conferred on all, for the benefit of all, at the cost of all.

In the second place, we have to consider the question of taxation. Now, I have been criticized a good deal for saying that the rich pay too little, and the poor pay too much. Well, I have given the matter further and careful consideration, and I maintain the statement . . . Twenty-six and a half millions of working people have between them incomes available for taxation of £203,000,000. Upon that the taxation which they pay amounts to $13\frac{1}{2}$ per cent. On the other hand, nine and a half millions belonging to the upper and middle classes have an income available for taxation of £639,000,000, upon which the taxation which they actually pay amounts to 6 per cent, so that, to put the matter in another way, at the present time the working classes are paying upon their available incomes more than double the rate which is paid by the upper and the middle classes.

In my opinion there is only one way in which this injustice can proper-ly be remedied, and that is by some scheme of graduated taxation – of taxation which increases in proportion to the amount of the property tax-ed. It need not necessarily be a graduated income-tax. It might be more convenient to levy it in the shape of a graduated death-tax or house-tax. I care nothing at all about the method. All I want to bring before you for your earnest and serious consideration is the principle of such taxation . . . In my opinion it is the only principle of taxation fair and just to all classes of the community.

I will go on to what is the last but also the most important of the reforms to which I wish to call your attention, and that is the reform of the land laws. This is a question which lies at the root of the whole matter that we have been discussing. Agriculture is the greatest of all of our in-dustries. When it is depressed every employment follows suit, and when work is scanty in the counties and the wages are low, the agricultural labourers are driven into the towns to compete with you for employment, and to reduce the rates of your remuneration. Anything which could

D. Liberty and democracy

bring about a revival of prosperity in agriculture, anything which would increase the production of the land and give better prospects to the agricultural labourer, would do an immense deal towards raising the general condition of the whole country and would procure a market for our manufactures far surpassing any that can possibly be expected from foreign countries and even from our own colonies. The evils of the present land system are apparent to everybody ... Our laws and practice seem to have been designed over a long course of years in order to build up and maintain vast estates, until at the present moment something less than one thousand persons hold one-third of the land of the United Kingdom. In the meantime the rights of property have been so much extended that the rights of the community have almost altogether disappeared, and it is hardly too much to say that the prosperity and the comfort and the liberties of a great proportion of the population have been laid at the feet of a small number of proprietors who 'neither toil nor spin'. The soil of every country originally belonged to its inhabitants, and if it has been thought expedient to create private ownership in place of common rights, at least that private ownership must be considered as a trust and subject to the conditions of a trust. Land must be owned so as to give the greatest employment to the largest number of persons, and so as to secure the greatest possible return in the produce of the soil. The land was not created – and it must not be used as a mere machine for exacting the highest possible rent from the cultivators of the soil – for the benefit of those who own it ... I am in favour of Free Trade in land. That includes the registration of titles, the cheapening of transfer, the abolition of settlements and entails and of the customs of primogeniture in cases of intestacy. Upon all that, I think, we are pretty well agreed. It would do something. It would tend no doubt to the dispersion of those great estates. It would bring more landed property into the market, but I do not think it would do much for the labourers of Wiltshire, or for the crofters of the Highlands of Scotland. We must go further if we want to go to the root of the matter. Well, what can we do for the farmer? If we want to revive agriculture, the farmer must become prosperous ...

There is only one thing that can benefit the farmer, and that is a fair rent fixed by an impartial tribunal – with the right of free sale of the good will of his undertaking. He would be required, of course, to find a fit and proper person, and his landlord might object if the person was not satisfactory in character or means. Subject to that the farmer should have the same liberty of sale which is enjoyed by other persons. I am told that the farmers do not care about fair rent or free sale. All I can say is, that as long as that is their position they are not likely to get it. Nobody will impose upon them a benefit that they do not want ... But when we come to the labourers the task is easier. They know what they want, which is the first condition for getting it. They require that facilities shall be afforded to them for having decent cottages and fair allotments at

660

reasonable rent and with security of tenure. Why should they not have it? Who would be injured if they did have it? The produce of the land would be increased, the respectability and character of the labourers would be raised, and the happiness of their families would be secured. Who would be injured? For my part, I confess I see no injustice at all in the case of the great landlords, many of whom have driven the labourers off their properties, and have pulled down their cottages, partly in order to escape responsibilities in connection with them, partly in order to throw the land into immense farms, and partly for other reasons – I see no objection in such cases as these to compelling the landlords to repair the wrongs they have done. I do not see why you should not enforce upon them the duty of providing in every case a sufficient number of decent cottages with land attached for all the men who are required for the cultivation of the particular estate. I would leave the supervision of this duty to the local authorities, and in order to meet every case which may arise, I would give to the local authorities power to acquire land on their own behalf, and to let it out in allotments for labourers and small farms.

I believe that this would meet the cases to which I have called your attention. Where the landlord will not do his duty to the land the local authority would have power to step in and restore it to production . . . All these things could be done, and only one other condition is absolutely necessary, and that is that when the local authority acquires land for this or any other public purpose, it should not be called upon to pay an extravagant or unnatural price, that it should be able to obtain it at the fair market value – at the value which the willing purchaser would pay to the willing seller – without any addition for compulsory sale. I believe that if these additional powers were conferred upon local authorities, if these additional obligations were enforced upon landlords, that at all events, so far as labourers are concerned, the land difficulty will disappear. Then I would go a step further, and I would revise the taxation upon land. I would equalize the death duties, as the government recently proposed to do. To that extent, at all events, I would invade the sanctity of landed property, and in addition I would tax all unoccupied and sporting land at its full value. I believe that that would put an end to much of the abuse of which we now complain. And lastly, I would insist upon the restitution of the property of the community where it has been wrongfully appropriated. I would insist upon the restitution of the endowments which have been diverted to improper uses, of enclosures which have been illegally made, of rights which have been improperly disregarded and ignored. I cannot allow that there should be a prescription for such arbitrary acts as these, or that a man should be able to allege a long enjoyment of profits as a reason for immunity and a bar to all redress on the part of the people who have suffered . . .

The sanctity of private property is no doubt an important principle, but the public good is a greater and higher object than any private in-

D. Liberty and democracy

terest, and the comfort and happiness of the people and the prosperity of
the country must never be sacrificed to the exaggerated claims of a
privileged class who are now the exclusive possessors of the great gift of
the Almighty to the human race.

[Source: *Speeches of the Right Hon. Joseph Chamberlain, M.P.,* ed. Henry W. Lucy
(London, 1885), pp. 161–172.]

Doc. 110a. Leonard T. HOBHOUSE: The State and the Individual

Let us first observe that, as Mill pointed out long ago, there are many
forms of collective action which do not involve coercion. The State may
provide for certain objects which it deems good without compelling any
one to make use of them. Thus it may maintain hospitals, though any one
who can pay for them remains free to employ his own doctors and
nurses. It may and does maintain a great educational system, while leaving every one free to maintain or to attend a private school ... It is true
that for the support of these objects rates and taxes are compulsorily
levied, but this form of compulsion raises a set of questions of which we
shall have to speak in another connection, and does not concern us here.
For the moment we have to deal only with those actions of State which
compel all citizens, or all whom they concern, to fall in with them and
allow of no divergence. This kind of coercion tends to increase. Is its extension necessarily an encroachment upon liberty, or are the elements of
value secured by collective control distinct from the elements of value
secured by individual choice, so that within due limits each may develop
side by side?

We have already declined to solve the problem by applying Mill's distinction between self-regarding and other-regarding actions, first because
there are no actions which may not directly or indirectly affect others,
secondly because even if there were they would not cease to be matter of
concern to others. The common good includes the good of every member
of the community, and the injury which a man inflicts upon himself is
matter of common concern, even apart from any ulterior effect upon
others. If we refrain from coercing a man for his own good, it is not
because his good is indifferent to us, but because it cannot be furthered
by coercion. The difficulty is founded on the nature of the good itself,
which on its personal side depends on the spontaneous flow of feeling
checked and guided not by external restraint but by rational self-control.
To try to form character by coercion is to destroy it in the making. Personality is not built up from without but grows from within, and the function of the outer order is not to create it, but to provide for it the most
suitable conditions of growth. Thus, to the common question whether it is
possible to make men good by Act of Parliament, the reply is that it is
not possible to compel morality because morality is the act or character

662

of a free agent, but that it is possible to create the conditions under which morality can develop, and among these not the least important is freedom from compulsion by others . . .

Where, then, is the sphere of compulsion, and what is its value? The reply is that compulsion is of value where outward conformity is of value, and this may be in any case where the non-conformity of one wrecks the purpose of others. We have already remarked that liberty itself only rests upon restraint. Thus a religious body is not, properly speaking, free to march in procession through the streets unless people of a different religion are restrained from pelting the procession with stones and pursuing it with insolence. We restrain them from disorder not to teach them the genuine spirit of religion, which they will not learn in the police court, but to secure to the other party the right of worship unmolested. The enforced restraint has its value in the action that it sets free. But we may not only restrain one man from obstructing another – and the extent to which we do this is the measure of the freedom that we maintain – but we may also restrain him from obstructing the general will; and this we have to do whenever uniformity is necessary to the end which the general will has in view. The majority of employers in a trade we may suppose would be willing to adopt certain precautions for the health or safety of their workers, to lower hours or to raise the rate of wages. They are unable to do so, however, so long as a minority, perhaps as long as a single employer, stands out. He would beat them in competition if they were voluntarily to undertake expenses from which he is free. In this case, the will of a minority, possibly the will of one man, thwarts that of the remainder. It coerces them, indirectly, but quite as effectively as if he were their master. If they, by combination, can coerce him no principle of liberty is violated. It is coercion against coercion, differing possibly in form and method, but not in principle or in spirit. Further, if the community as a whole sympathizes with the one side rather than the other, it can reasonably bring the law into play. Its object is not the moral education of the recusant individuals. Its object is to secure certain conditions which it believes necessary for the welfare of its members, and which can only be secured by an enforced uniformity.

It appears, then, that the true distinction is not between self-regarding and other-regarding actions, but between coercive and non-coercive actions. The function of State coercion is to override individual coercion, and, of course, coercion exercised by any association of individuals within the State. It is by this means that it maintains liberty of expression, security of person and property, genuine freedom of contract, the rights of public meeting and association, and finally its own power to carry out common objects undefeated by the recalcitrance of individual members. Undoubtedly it endows both individuals and associations with powers as well as with rights. But over these powers it must exercise supervision in the interests of equal justice. Just as compulsion failed in the sphere of

D. Liberty and democracy

liberty, the sphere of spiritual growth, so liberty fails in the external order wherever, by the mere absence of supervisory restriction, men are able directly or indirectly to put constraint on one another. This is why there is no intrinsic and inevitable conflict between liberty and compulsion, but at bottom a mutual need. The object of compulsion is to secure the most favourable external conditions of inward growth and happiness so far as these conditions depend on combined action and uniform observance. The sphere of liberty is the sphere of growth itself. There is no true opposition between liberty as such and control as such, for every liberty rests on a corresponding act of control. The true opposition is between the control that cramps the personal life and the spiritual order, and the control that is aimed at securing the external and material conditions of their free and unimpeded development . . .

So far we have been considering what the State compels the individual to do. If we pass to the question what the State is to do for the individual, a different but parallel question arises, and we have to note a corresponding movement of opinion. If the State does for the individual what he ought to do for himself what will be the effect on character, initiative, enterprise? It is a question now not of freedom, but of responsibility, and it is one that has caused many searchings of heart, and in respect of which opinion has undergone a remarkable change. Thus, in relation to poverty the older view was that the first thing needful was self-help. It was the business of every man to provide for himself and his family. If, indeed, he utterly failed, neither he nor they could be left to starve, and there was the Poor Law machinery to deal with his case . . .

These views no longer command the same measure of assent. On all sides we find the State making active provision for the poorer classes and not by any means for the destitute alone. We find it educating the children, providing medical inspection, authorizing the feeding of the necessitous at the expense of the rate-payers, helping them to obtain employment through free Labour Exchanges, seeking to organize the labour market with a view to the mitigation of unemployment, and providing old-age pensions for all whose incomes fall below thirteen shillings a week, without exacting any contribution. Now, in all this, we may well ask, is the State going forward blindly on the paths of broad and generous but unconsidered charity? Is it and can it remain indifferent to the effect on individual initiative and personal or parental responsibility? Or may we suppose that the wiser heads are well aware of what they are about, have looked at the matter on all sides, and are guided by a reasonable conception of the duty of the State and the responsibilities of the individual? Are we, in fact – for this is really the question – seeking charity or justice?

We said above that it was the function of the State to secure the conditions upon which the mind and character may develop themselves. Similarly we may say now that the function of the State is to secure conditions upon which its citizens are able to win by their own efforts all that is necessary to a full civic efficiency. It is not for the State to feed, house, or clothe them. It is for the State to take care that the economic conditions are such that the normal man who is not defective in mind or body or will can by useful labour feed, house, and clothe himself and his family. The 'right to work' and the right to a 'living wage' are just as valid as the rights of person or property. That is to say, they are integral conditions of a good social order. A society in which a single honest man of normal capacity is definitely unable to find the means of maintaining himself by useful work is to that extent suffering from malorganization. There is somewhere a defect in the social system, a hitch in the economic machine. Now, the individual workman cannot put the machine straight. He is the last person to have any say in the control of the market. It is not his fault if there is over-production in his industry, or if a new and cheaper process has been introduced which makes his particular skill, perhaps the product of years of application, a drug in the market. He does not direct or regulate industry. He is not responsible for its ups and downs, but he has to pay for them. That is why it is not charity but justice for which he is asking. Now, it may be infinitely difficult to meet his demand. To do so may involve a far-reaching economic reconstruction. The industrial questions involved may be so little understood that we may easily make matters worse in the attempt to make them better. All this shows the difficulty in finding means of meeting this particular claim of justice, but it does not shake its position as a claim of justice. A right is a right none the less though the means of securing it be imperfectly known; and the workman who is unemployed or underpaid through economic malorganization will remain a reproach not to the charity but to the justice of society as long as he is to be seen in the land.

If this view of the duty of the State and the right of the workman is coming to prevail, it is owing partly to an enhanced sense of common responsibility, and partly to the teaching of experience. In the earlier days of the Free Trade era, it was permissible to hope that self-help would be an adequate solvent, and that with cheap food and expanding commerce the average workman would be able by the exercise of prudence and thrift not only to maintain himself in good times, but to lay by for sickness, unemployment and old age. The actual course of events has in large measure disappointed these hopes. It is true that the standard of living in England has progressively advanced throughout the nineteenth century. It is true, in particular, that, since the disastrous period that preceded the Repeal of the Corn Laws and the passing of the Ten Hours' Act, social improvement has been real and marked. Trade Unionism and co-operation have grown, wages upon the whole have increased, the cost of living has diminished, housing and sanitation have improved, the death rate has fallen from about twenty-two to less than fifteen per thousand. But with all this improvement the prospect of a complete and lifelong economic independence for the average workman upon the lines of individual competition, even when supplemented and guarded by the collective bargaining of the Trade Union, appears exceedingly remote. The increase of wages does not appear to be by any means proportionate to the general growth of wealth. The whole standard of living has risen; the very provision of education has brought with it new needs and has almost compelled a higher standard of life in order to satisfy them. As a whole, the working classes of England, though less thrifty than those of some Continental countries, cannot be accused of undue negligence with regard to the future. The accumulation of savings in Friendly Societies, Trade Unions, Co-operative Societies, and Savings Banks shows an increase which has more than kept pace with the rise in the level of wages; yet there appears no likelihood that the average manual worker will attain the goal of that full independence, covering all the risks of life for self and family, which can alone render the competitive system really adequate to the demands of a civilized conscience ... It is this belief slowly penetrating the public mind which has turned it to new thoughts of social regeneration. The sum and substance of the changes that I have mentioned may be expressed in the principle that the individual cannot stand alone, but that between him and the State there is a reciprocal obligation. He owes the State the duty of industriously working for himself and his family. He is not to exploit the labour of his young children, but to submit to the public requirements for their education, health, cleanliness and general well-being. On the other side society owes to him the means of maintaining a civilized standard of life, and this debt is not adequately discharged by leaving him to secure such wages as he can in the higgling of the market.

This view of social obligation lays increased stress on public but by no means ignores private responsibility. It is a simple principle of applied ethics that responsibility should be commensurate with power. Now, given the opportunity of adequately remunerated work, a man has the power to earn his living. It is his right and his duty to make the best use of his opportunity, and if he fails he may fairly suffer the penalty of being treated as a pauper or even, in an extreme case, as a criminal. But the opportunity itself he cannot command with the same freedom. It is only within narrow limits that it comes within the sphere of his control. The opportunities of work and the remuneration for work are determined by a complex mass of social forces which no individual, certainly no individual workman, can shape. They can be controlled, if at all, by the organized action of the community, and therefore, by a just apportionment of responsibility, it is for the community to deal with them.

But this, it will be said, is not Liberalism but Socialism. Pursuing the economic rights of the individual we have been led to contemplate a Socialistic organization of industry. But a word like Socialism has many meanings, and it is possible that there should be a Liberal Socialism, as

Document 110

well as a Socialism that is illiberal. Let us, then, without sticking at a word, seek to follow out the Liberal view of the State in the sphere of economics. Let us try to determine in very general terms what is involved in realizing those primary conditions of industrial well-being which have been laid down, and how they consort with the rights of property and the claims of free industrial enterprise.

[Source: Leonard T. Hobhouse, *Liberalism* (1911), New York 1964, pp. 75–8, 82, 83–5, 86–7.]

Doc. 110*b*. Leonard T. HOBHOUSE: Social Service and Reward

The ground problem in economics is not to destroy property, but to restore the social conception of property to its right place under conditions suitable to modern needs. This is not to be done by crude measures of redistribution, such as those of which we hear in ancient history. It is to be done by distinguishing the social from the individual factors in wealth, by bringing the elements of social wealth into the public coffers, and by holding it at the disposal of society to administer to the prime needs of its members.

The basis of property is social, and that in two senses. On the one hand, it is the organized force of society that maintains the rights of owners by protecting them against thieves and depredators. In spite of all criticism many people still seem to speak of the rights of property as though they were conferred by Nature or by Providence upon certain fortunate individuals, and as though these individuals had an unlimited right to command the State, as their servant, to secure them by the free use of the machinery of law in the undisturbed enjoyment of their possessions. They forget that without the organized force of society their rights are not worth a week's purchase . . .

This brings us to the second sense in which property is social. There is a social element in value and a social element in production. In modern industry there is very little that the individual can do by his unaided efforts. Labour is minutely divided; and in proportion as it is divided it is forced to be co-operative. Men produce goods to sell, and the rate of exchange, that is, price, is fixed by relations of demand and supply the rates of which are determined by complex social forces. In the methods of production every man makes use, to the best of his ability, of the whole available means of civilization, of the machinery which the brains of other men have devised, of the human apparatus which is the gift of acquired civilization. Society thus provides conditions or opportunities of which one man will make much better use than another, and the use to which they are put is the individual or personal element in production which is the basis of the personal claim to reward. To maintain and stimulate this personal effort is a necessity of good economic organiza-

667

tion, and without asking here whether any particular conception of Socialism would or would not meet this need we may lay down with confidence that no form of Socialism which should ignore it could possibly enjoy enduring success. On the other hand, an individualism which ignores the social factor in wealth will deplete the national resources, deprive the community of its just share in the fruits of industry and so result in a one-sided and inequitable distribution of wealth. Economic justice is to render what is due not only to each individual but to each function, social or personal, that is engaged in the performance of useful service, and this due is measured by the amount necessary to stimulate and maintain the efficient exercise of that useful function. This equation between function and sustenance is the true meaning of economic equality . . .

But we can go further. We said at the outset that the function of society was to secure to all normal adult members the means of earning by useful work the material necessaries of a healthy and efficient life. We can see now that this is one case and, properly understood, the largest and most far-reaching case falling under the general principle of economic justice. This principle lays down that every social function must receive the reward that is sufficient to stimulate and maintain it through the life of the individual. Now, how much this reward may be in any case it is probably impossible to determine otherwise than by specific experiment. But if we grant, in accordance with the idea with which we have been working all along, that it is demanded of all sane adult men and women that they should live as civilized beings, as industrious workers, as good parents, as orderly and efficient citizens, it is, on the other side, the function of the economic organization of society to secure them the material means of living such a life, and the immediate duty of society is to mark the points at which such means fail and to make good the deficiency. Thus the conditions of social efficiency mark the minimum of industrial remuneration, and if they are not secured without the deliberate action of the State they must be secured by means of the deliberate action of the State. If it is the business of good economic organization to secure the equation between function and maintainance, the first and greatest application of this principle is to the primary needs. These fix the minimum standard of remuneration beyond which we require detailed experiment to tell us at what rate increased value of service rendered necessitates corresponding increase of reward . . .

The central point of Liberal economics, then, is the equation of social service and reward. This is the principle that every function of social value requires such remuneration as serves to stimulate and maintain its effective performance; that every one who performs such a function has the right, in the strict ethical sense of that term, to such remuneration and to no more; that the residue of existing wealth should be at the disposal of the community for social purposes. Further, it is the right, in the same sense, of every person capable of performing some useful social function that he should have the opportunity of so doing, and it is his right that the remuneration that he receives for it should be his property, *i.e.* that it should stand at his free disposal enabling him to direct his personal concerns according to his own preferences. These are rights in the sense that they are conditions of the welfare of its members which a well-ordered State will seek by every means to fulfil. But it is not suggested that the way of such fulfilment is plain, or that it could be achieved at a stroke by a revolutionary change in the tenure of property or the system of industry. It is, indeed, implied that the State is vested with a certain overlordship over property in general and a supervisory power over industry in general, and this principle of economic sovereignty may be set side by side with that of economic justice as a no less fundamental conception of economic Liberalism. For here, as elsewhere, liberty implies control. But the manner in which the State is to exercise its controlling power is to be learnt by experience and even in large measure by cautious experiment. We have sought to determine the principle which should guide its action, the ends at which it is to aim. The systematic study of the means lies rather within the province of economics; and the teaching of history seems to be that progress is more continuous and secure when men are content to deal with problems piecemeal than when they seek to destroy root and branch in order to erect a complete system which has captured the imagination.

[Source: L. T. Hobhouse, *Liberalism* (1911), New York 1964, pp. 98–9, 105–6, 107–8.]

4. Freedom and power: documents
(Introduction, p. 598)

Doc. 111. LORD ACTON: 'The History of Freedom in Antiquity' (1877)

Liberty, next to Religion has been the motive of good deeds and the common pretext of crime, from the sowing of the seed at Athens, 2,460 years ago, until the ripened harvest was gathered by men of our race. It is the delicate fruit of a mature civilization; and scarcely a century has passed since nations, that knew the meaning of the term, resolved to be free. In every age its progress has been beset by its natural enemies, by ignorance and superstition, by lust of conquest and by love of ease, by the strong man's craving for power, and the poor man's craving for food. During

D. Liberty and democracy

long intervals it has been utterly arrested, when nations were being rescued from barbarism and from the grasp of strangers, and when the perpetual struggle for existence, depriving men of all interest and understanding in politics, has made them eager to sell their birthright for a mess of pottage, and ignorant of the treasure they resigned. At all times sincere friends of freedom have been rare, and its triumphs have been due to minorities, that have prevailed by associating themselves with auxiliaries whose objects often differed from their own; and this association, which is always dangerous, has sometimes been disastrous, by giving to opponents just ground of opposition, and by kindling dispute over the spoils in the hour of success. No obstacle has been so constant, or so difficult to overcome as uncertainty and confusion touching the nature of true liberty. If hostile interests have wrought much injury, false ideas have wrought still more; and its advance is recorded in the increase of knowledge as much as in the improvement of laws. The history of institutions is often a history of deception and illusions; for their virtue depends on the ideas that produce and on the spirit that preserves them, and the form may remain unaltered when the substance has passed away . . .

By Liberty I mean the assurance that every man shall be protected in doing what he believes his duty, against the influence of authority and majorities, custom and opinion. The state is competent to assign duties and draw the line between good and evil only in its immediate sphere. Beyond the limit of things necessary for its wellbeing, it can only give indirect help to fight the battle of life, by promoting the influences which avail against temptation, – Religion, Education, and the distribution of Wealth. In ancient times the state absorbed authorities not its own, and intruded on the domain of personal freedom. In the middle ages it possessed too little authority, and suffered others to intrude. Modern states fall habitually into both excesses. The most certain test by which we judge whether a country is really free is the amount of security enjoyed by minorities . . .

Now Liberty and good government do not exclude each other; and there are excellent reasons why they should go together; but they do not necessarily go together. Liberty is not a means to a higher political end. It is itself the highest political end. It is not for the sake of a good public administration that it is required, but for security in the pursuit of the highest objects of civil society, and of private life. Increase of freedom in the state may sometimes promote mediocrity, and give vitality to prejudice; it may even retard useful legislation, diminish the capacity for war, and restrict the boundaries of Empire. It might be plausibly argued that, if many things would be worse in England or Ireland under an intelligent despotism, some things would be managed better; that the Roman government was more enlightened under Augustus and Antoninus than under the Senate, in the days of Marius or of Pompey. A generous spirit prefers that his country should be poor, and weak, and of no account, but free, rather than powerful, prosperous, and enslaved. It is better to be the citizen of a humble commonwealth in the Alps, without a prospect of influence beyond the narrow frontier, than a subject of the superb autocracy that overshadows half of Asia and of Europe. But it may be urged on the other side that liberty is not the sum or the substitute of all the things men ought to live for; that to be real it must be circumscribed, and that the limits of circumscription vary; that advancing civilization invests the state with increased rights and duties and imposes increased burdens and constraint on the subject; that a highly instructed and intelligent community may perceive the benefit of compulsory obligations which, at a lower stage would be thought unbearable; that liberal progress is not vague or indefinite, but aims at a point where the public is subject to no restrictions but those of which it feels the advantage; that a free country may be less capable of doing much for the advancement of religion, the prevention of vice, or the relief of suffering, than one that does not shrink from confronting great emergencies by some sacrifice of individual rights, and some concentration of power; and that the supreme political object ought to be sometimes postponed to still higher moral objects. My argument involves no collision with these qualifying reflections. We are dealing not with the effects of freedom, but with its causes. We are seeking out the influences which brought arbitrary government under control, either by the diffusion of power, or by the appeal to an authority which transcends all government; and among those influences the greatest philosophers of Greece have no claim to be reckoned. It is the Stoics who emancipated mankind from its subjection to despotic rule, and whose enlightened and elevated views bridged the chasm that separates the ancient from the Christian state, and led the way to Freedom. Seeing how little security there is that the laws of any land shall be wise or just, and that the unanimous will of a people and the assent of nations are liable to err, the Stoics looked beyond those narrow barriers, and above those inferior sanctions for the principles that ought to regulate the lives of men and the existence of society. They made it known that there is a will superior to the collective will of man, and a law that overrules those of Solon and Lycurgus. Their test of good government is its conformity to principles that can be traced to a higher legislator. That which we must obey, that to which we are bound to reduce all civil authorities, and to sacrifice every earthly interest, is that immutable law which is perfect and eternal as God Himself, which proceeds from His nature, and reigns over heaven and earth and over all the nations.

[Source: John Emerich Edward Dalberg-Acton (Lord Acton) *The History of Freedom in Antiquity*. An Address delivered to the members of the Bridgnorth Institute, 26 February 1877, Bridgnorth 1877.]

D. Liberty and democracy

Doc. 112a. ALAIN: Traps for a Minister

As soon as a man becomes a minister, traps are set for him. At the first moment he always resembles a snake which has changed its skin. He was a deputy, always ready to resist and threaten the powers-that-be. He now takes over power, sees all questions from another angle and the nation differently grouped. Only the idea, that one has to live first and then to act if one can, imposes itself on him without his having any doubts about it, and suddenly turns him into an opportunist. He cannot escape that malady of a change of skin, which leaves him a bit weak afterwards and without the power of resistance to external actions. It is from this critical moment onward that a thousand envoys press him and push him, all of them talking in the name of the people and acting for the privileged. In the front rank one must employ the general staff of the bureaucrats which has friendships, habits, kinships and alliances with all who drive in a car and ingeniously get pleasure out of the work of somebody else. It is a strange thing, which should have been foreseen, that the same interests which opposed the radical candidate in his constituency are identical with those which, without having been invited, are making friends in Paris with the radical who has become a Minister.

[Source: Alain (pen-name for Emile August Chartier), *Eléments d'une doctrine radicale*, Paris 1925, p. 80. The essay was first published on 7 March, 1911. Translated by the editors of this volume.]

Doc. 112b. ALAIN: Politics of the Citizen

'Do not bother about politics; reserve your time and your strength for the things of the mind which are rather your business.' This counsel was given to me more than once, and on one occasion by a profound and venerable scholar. But I have never paid attention to it either at that time or at others. It always requires some passion to put the pen into your hand. I have always lacked the true ambition of the writer. Probably I would never have written at all had not the occasion offered itself two or three times through radical newspapers which lacked money and people of the Establishment wanted to ignore. This is the way whereby I find writing to my taste, and perhaps an urge to write. And equally, when, for a long time, I talked and held discussions in courses for Adult Education [*les Universités populaires*] it was done less in order to teach the people than to establish my friendship with them very clearly against the Castles, the Academics and the Important Persons whom I do not love. An Important Person who has become a failure and been humiliated is the most beautiful spectacle for my taste. For instance, when Senator Ribot, a great preacher of Importance, offered a new Ministry to a new Chamber of Deputies, I recognised one good opportunity among many others. True, the Important Persons have since put their feet on our heads. If you prove to me that there is no remedy for this, and that we shall not see again what we have seen, I will go for a stroll to an ivory tower.

Truly, this eloquent idea that one should leave politics to the politicians is old-fashioned, like the small tie, the frock-coat or the boots with elastic bands. The people who gave me this advice, as I mentioned, have never known the compulsory military service which makes us into politicians despite ourselves. The reality of the Prince was in their eyes like a reality of nature, before which they get out of the way in the same way as they do from in front of a carriage as a superior force. But now one has to run over or be run over. If one is not an officer, one has to be member of the other ranks. It is the officers moreover, who always write of *Grandeur and Servitude*. The dream of the Important Person is to serve in order to Command. And I understand well that only real politics, the politics of resistance and criticism, is to them without any meaning or interest. For this reason, I say that the majority of the politicians misunderstands politics; and they count instead upon the reality of the Prince and adore it in the same way as a commander of Light Infantry prepares for war and the reality of his complete Importance without paying the slightest attention to the causes; and, as we saw, he bathes freely in this favourable *milieu* and in its politics. What, then, remains to be done by those who never seek power under any form? To insist on real politics, which means a sustained effort against military despotism and against political despotism. What remains is to transform all power into civil power, which makes out of a minister a higher official comparable to a carriage attendant or a railway porter. Such power impedes no one. But Self Importance troubles everyone, as soon as one allows it to spread itself. We have had experience of it.

[Source: Alain, *Eléments d'une doctrine radicale* (Paris, 1925) pp. 17–18. The essay was first published on 24 January 1923. Translated by the editors of this volume.]

Section E

Epilogue: Liberalism challenged, revised, maintained 1900–1950

Introductory

(Documents 113–23, pp. 700–47)

While the labels of centuries often do not fit the changing tide of political and social thought, it can be said safely that the mental climate of the twentieth century has been far less favourable than that of the nineteenth to liberal ideas. Even before 1900 the belief in automatic progress had lost much of its strength. Astute observers realized that the impact of changing conditions – industrial, technological and military – had made its advance more complicated. It became clear that the favourite instrumentalities of the liberal faith in progress – education and rationalist propaganda – were often inadequate to remove the obstacles in its path. Nevertheless for a long time the original liberal message 'continued in its various forms to exercise an almost universal spell'.[1] Yet in the twentieth century humanitarian liberalism has seemed pale and ineffective to many people. Groups who regarded themselves as underprivileged expected little from the mild zeal of liberal reformers and much more from radical socialist or communist methods. After 1918 it was not liberal individualism but the belief in a collective – whether class or nation – which seemed to carry the day. Most liberal thinkers were prepared to admit that the tide of the *Zeitgeist* ran against liberalism forcing it on to the defensive. They became more or less affected by the strong trend away from and antagonistic to liberalism. In any case the trend forced them to rethink and reformulate the liberal position in a critical age.

In England J. M. Keynes and William Beveridge added new dimensions to the liberal doctrine, the former by his more up-to-date version of individuality in a free economy, the latter by pointing the way to the modern welfare State. Quite different was the approach of prominent Continental emigrés like Thomas Mann and Karl Mannheim, who, distressed by the brutal advance of fascism, pleaded for a new synthesis of liberty and equality, of freedom and democratic planning. Planning was sharply rejected as 'utopian' by the economist F. A. Hayek, a stubborn defender of the tradition of *laissez faire*. What was to Mannheim the road to greater freedom, meant to Hayek the road to certain serfdom.

Benedetto Croce

Only Benedetto Croce (1866–1952), the Italian philosopher and historian, and perhaps the most significant liberal thinker of the period, remained little affected by the receding tide. The reason for his adamant attitude was that he saw liberty basically as the result of a constant and never-ending process of liberation against heavy odds; for him it meant a continuous struggle between the forces of suppression and violence, on the one hand, and, on the other, those of liberation raising mankind again and again to a higher level.

To Croce, man was a microcosm not in the sense of nature but in the sense of history; and he was, so to speak, a compendium of universal history receiving meaning only through the basic categories of truth, beauty, goodness and freedom. Croce has often been called a neo-Hegelian and indeed he always took a keen interest in Hegel, carefully distinguishing between living and dead elements in Hegel's philosophy. But Croce gave Hegel's well-known dictum that 'history is the history of liberty' a different interpretation (doc. 113). [2] He rejected Hegel's intention 'to assign to history the task of creating a liberty which did not exist in the past but will exist in the future'. To him liberty has its own dialectics and the relationship between history and liberty is a dual one. 'Liberty is the eternal creator of history and itself the subject of every history.' It is, on the one hand, 'the explanatory principle of the course of history', and, on the other, 'the moral ideal of humanity'. [3]

Croce's liberalism does not express itself in nineteenth-century style as a demand for this or that individual freedom or in a plea for aesthetic individualism; it takes an overall view of life as a process of liberation. The emphasis is not on the individual and his uniqueness but on the often harsh struggle in which he is involved. For Croce liberty has no libertarian undertones; freedom is correlated with sacrifice; not with the senseless slaughter of thousands on the altar of autocratic rule, but with 'the sacrifice of well-being and even of life itself which good men make in order to do their duty and preserve their human worth'. Croce does not subscribe to the belief in automatic progress. As he expressed it on the eve of the Second World War: 'All history still gives evidence of an unquiet, uncertain and disordered liberty with brief intervals of unrest, rare and lightning moments of a happiness perceived rather than possessed, mere pauses in the tumult of oppressions, barbarian invasions, plunderings, secular and ecclesistical tyrannies, wars between peoples, persecutions, exiles and gallows.' [4]To fight and live for liberty does not provide certainty, it is done with continual risk. A liberal order is never established once and for all, for 'the more it is established and undisputed, the more surely (it) decays into habit' gradually loosening 'its vigilant self-awareness and readiness for defence'. Thus the philosopher 'observes with serenity how periods of increased or reduced liberty follow upon each other'. Liberty can become lost or emasculated.

After 1918 the influence of liberalism remained stronger in Britain and in the Scandinavian countries than in the rest of Europe. A liberal approach to political and social affairs was still an important factor in English life although the Liberal Party itself declined sharply after the First World War. In 1914 it had 261 members in the House of Commons, by 1935 their number had dwindled to 21. [5] In Germany, the liberal Democrats, one of the three coalition parties forming the Weimar Government in 1919 sank to complete insignificance in the last years of the hapless Republic with only a handful of seats in the Reichstag. During the first 'total' world war, in which millions fought each other, the individual counted for little and the national collective for everything. Admittedly the aftermath of the war saw a brief new emphasis on 'human rights' and in, the message of President Woodrow Wilson, on 'the rights of national self determination' which, like the idea of the League of Nations, was very much in the liberal tradition. However, different from America,[6] in Europe the new dream soon lost its attraction and the idea of national determination became an instrument in the hands of a new nationalism which rejected the universalist claims of liberalism. The idea of democratic parliamentarism, so closely allied with liberal concepts, also weakened in many countries. The emphasis was now on integration, not on freedom, on the collective not on human rights, on the claims of nation or class and not on those of the individual. Many young people regarded liberalism as a thing of the past. By the middle of the century Gilbert Murray admitted resignedly that liberalism had 'become largely a fruitless longing in the hearts of specially conscientious or thoughtful people for something lost or unattainable' (doc. 122).

Among the writers or politicians reflecting mainly in English on the liberal position between 1918 and 1950, three main attitudes can be distinguished. First there were those who favoured a fundamental change, a move 'Forward from Liberalism'. A second group less drastically pleaded only for a modification of the liberal platform. Liberalism, their spokesmen argued, should become more self-disciplined and the demand for liberty should be reconciled with that for equality. They felt that a basic re-interpretation of liberalism was required for its survival. The place of constructive freedom had to be reconsidered within a new planned society. Thirdly, there was the attitude of 'the unrepentant liberals', deeply suspicious of all forms of planning and dismissing socialism, communism and fascism as equal threats of Organization Man. They wanted to move 'Back to Liberalism', at least to the fundamental ideas, if not to the detail of the doctrines of the nineteenth-century classical school.

A characteristic spokesman of the first group was Stephen Spender, the young eloquent literateur of the 1930s. He regarded liberal political parties and institutions simply as obsolete and doomed to failure. Although not condemning liberal ideas outright, he maintained that everything political freedom implied, the right to vote, the right to a good education, rights of assembly, equality before the law etc., was only meaningful in a classless society. In the contemporary Western set-up with its mixture of oligarchy and democracy, these rights were to him in fact 'ironic abstractions for the poor and legal instruments of ascendancy for the rich'. 'Forward from Liberalism'[7] meant to move from an unjust and obsolete type of society, in which democratic institutions were paralysed by the power of capitalism, to an egalitarian society where political freedom was truly possible. Spender had a genuine appreciation of individualism but he maintained that the West, threatened by the danger of fascist regimes, only possessed a chance of survival through a transformation into a classless communist society.

Other writers on liberalism held less drastic views. Pressing for a modification of the liberal approach, they were ready to discard all traits of the earlier *laissez faire* brand of liberalism. While liberalism was not to be exchanged for communism, only as social liberalism or radical liberalism could it become a true bridge builder to a better society. As pointed out earlier this view was first put forward in the writings of L. T. Hobhouse (see above, p. 596). When he published his book *Liberalism* in 1911, the Liberal Party was still a major political factor in Britain. Fifteen years later, J. M. Keynes entertained no illusions about its severely reduced strength. Yet by discarding out-dated *laissez faire* policies and by boldly facing the issues of the day, liberalism, as Keynes interpreted it, would still have a useful role to play.

John Maynard Keynes and William Beveridge

It has rightly been said of J. M. Keynes (later Lord Keynes) that 'by temperament and conviction he was certainly a Liberal throughout his life'. [8] He had a great antipathy towards the conservatives. 'They offer me neither food nor drink', he complained in a spirited address to a Liberal Summer School at Cambridge in 1925. Their mentality, he felt, promoted neither his self-interest nor the common good. He was no less critical of, though less severe towards the Labour Party. Keynes rejected State socialism as well as the class war. When it was a question of pursuing sectional interests, he would pursue his own. He could be influenced, he declared, 'by what seems to me justice and good sense'; but the class war would find him 'on the side of the educated bourgeoisie'. [9] Admittedly a sense of social justice was strong in the Labour Party and it included valuable intellectual elements but they would, he feared, never exercise adequate control. It would fall into the hands of the extreme left wing which he dubbed 'the Party of Catastrophe'. These people were, in their own way, the opposite number to the die-hards, the right wing of the Tories. Keynes acknowledged the value of the left wing of the conservatives, embracing 'the best type' of educated, humane, conservative free traders as well as that of the right wing of the Labour Party, 'the best type' of educated, human socialist reformers. However, he insisted that there was still room for a third party without a class commitment and determined 'to spoil the constructions' of the two major parties. Yet it was an illusion to deny that the Liberal Party was in decline at a time when 'the liberals found themselves uncertainly placed between the forces of right and left, and afflicted by internal struggles over vital issues of policy which invariably ended in deadlock or ineffectual compromise'.[10] Keynes did not believe that the Liberal Party could ever become a great party again, but it might operate as a lever and a filter *vis-à-vis* the changes which the Labour Party would try to bring about. These changes could only be fruitful after they had passed the test of 'the criticism and the precaution of the liberals'. On their part the liberals had to give up old-fashioned liberalism and *laissez faire* attitudes and show awareness of today's questions 'of living interest and importance'.

In his forceful essay 'The End of Laissez Faire' (doc. 115) Keynes denied the assumption of classical economic liberalism that private and social interests coincide and that self-interest is generally enlightened. He regarded it as the chief task of the government to distinguish between what, in Benthamite language, was its *Agenda* and its *Non-Agenda*, between what it should and what it should not do. It should encourage the formation, growth and recognition of semi-autonomous bodies within the State, in other words, of public corporations, autonomous in their field, but subject to ultimate control by Parliament. The Bank of England and, later, the British Broadcasting Corporation were specimens of this type. In Keynesian terms, governments 'must not do things which individuals are doing already and to do them a bit better and a bit worse', but must 'do things which at present are not done at all'.

With his varied talents and wide interests Keynes was basically an élitist in the sense of J. M. Mill's notion that 'the few are the salt of the earth'. Keynes was never an egalitarian. 'If he wanted to improve the lot of the poor ... that was not for the sake of equality, but in order to make their lives happier and better ... The idea of destroying anything good in itself in the interest of equality was anathema to him.'[11] He was basically not a party man. It was largely 'his regard for the middle classes, for artists, brain workers and scientists of all kinds' that made State socialism unacceptable to Keynes.[12] At the same time he felt that liberalism should face squarely the new issues and problems of contemporary society in all fields; it had to come to grips with major questions, not only concerning Peace, Government and Economics but also comprising sex problems and the use of drugs. With his fine sense of perception Keynes was one of the first to raise the problems of a new 'permissive society'. He questioned traditional taboos with their hypocrisy and he pleaded for a liberalisation of out-of-date attitudes towards birth control and the use of contraceptives, marriage laws, the treatment of sexual offenders and abnormalities, and last but not least the economic position of women and of the family.[13] Though he saw all these questions as being interrelated with economic issues, he judged them as an independent humanist. In the question of the use and misuse of drugs, too, he saw further than the great majority. Though expecting that the prohibition of alcoholic spirits and of bookmakers would do good, Keynes felt that

E. Epilogue: Liberalism challenged, revised, maintained

it would by no means settle the problem. How far, he asked searchingly, was 'bored and suffering humanity to be allowed, from time to time an escape, an excitement, a stimulus, a possibility of change?' [14]

Essentially Keynes' liberalism was a basic attitude to life and society. Although he believed that the State would have to intervene at many points, yet 'the structure of a free economy with its scope for individual initiative was to be preserved'. In the last analysis 'Keynes remained essentially an individualist', [15] who thought that after the turmoil of the First World War and the challenge of mass-unemployment afterwards, mankind required a new combination of three ideals, of Economic Efficiency, Social Justice and Individual Liberty (doc. 116). The first and third, he felt, were championed by the Liberal Party and the second by the Labour Party.

Looking back, one wonders, if with all his impressive brilliance, J. M. Keynes, the liberal élitist, did not in the end vainly endeavour to achieve the squaring of the circle in these matters of social philosophy.

Two reports, *Report on Social Insurance and Allied Services* (1941–42) and *Full Employment in a Free Society* (1944) by William Beveridge, both published during the Second World War, profoundly changed Britain's social fabric. At a time when millions of people were involved in a common war effort risking their lives for the survival of their country, it seemed imperative to Beveridge that the State should generally extend its activities in order to achieve greater social security for the individual. Freedom from want thus became an important aspect of the revised Liberal programme, and together with freedom from enforced idleness or unemployment, it formed a basic concept in Beveridge's security system. The State was to provide a scheme for full employment which would make a return of pre-war mass unemployment practically impossible. In 1944 Beveridge, who described himself as a Liberal Radical, visualized the Liberal Party as 'above all, the party of the citizens at large, as consumers'. Its Radical Programme, he assured his electors, was 'a programme of putting first things first, bread and health for all before cake and circuses for anybody' (doc. 117).

Like Keynes, Beveridge (later Lord Beveridge), was a distinguished economist with wide journalistic and administrative experience. Before 1914 a Director of the Labour Exchange in the Board of Trade and later (1919–37) heading the London School of Economics as Director, Beveridge did important work in Whitehall during both World Wars. In 1944 he won a by-election to the House of Commons as a Liberal, only to be defeated several months later in the General Election by a Conservative. By then his name had become a household word in Britain through the 'Report on Social Security' which he wrote for the Churchill government. Its recommendations were, with some modifications, carried out by it. It was followed by a second Report on 'Full Employment in a

Free Society' published by Beveridge in 1944.[16]
Beveridge set out to readjust traditional liberalism to a changed social climate. He became convinced that man desired and required both individual freedom and social security; or, to express it in the language of the Anglo-Saxon freedom ideology current during the Second World War and shared by Beveridge and President Franklin D. Roosevelt, man needed 'freedom from want, freedom from enforced idleness or unemployment and, last but not least, freedom from war'. Different from Keynes, Beveridge emphasized that man had to be protected as well as be set free. This meant new responsibility for the State. Individual freedom in a welfare State corresponded to the democratic vision behind the Beveridge Plan. Its nucleus was a government-sponsored contributory insurance scheme comprising all workers and employees for sickness, accidents, unemployment and old age.

In his report on full employment and in his essay 'Why I am a Liberal' (London 1945), Beveridge drew a significant distinction between 'essential liberties' and 'lesser liberties' (doc. 117). Whereas the former were regarded as indispensable, the latter, although desirable, could be discarded under certain circumstances. To the 'essential liberties' belong 'the intimate personal liberties' and 'the political liberties'. Besides such customary 'liberties' from the catalogue of the nineteenth century as freedom of worship, of speech, of writing, of study and teaching, the 'personal liberties' also included some novel features like 'freedom in spending one's personal income and in the choice of one's occupation'. On the other hand, 'the political liberties' repeated postulates of earlier generations, 'freedom of assembly and of association for industrial and political purposes'. In the 1940s Beveridge neither conceived the State as a mere nightwatchman à la Humboldt nor did he approve of the étatism of some German and French liberals before 1914. While he fully maintained that the State existed for the sake of the individual, he demanded an increase of the responsibilities and functions of the State in order to fulfil this task more adequately in a changing society. Above all the State should facilitate the life of the individual in society by making full employment possible. It had to provide opportunities of service and earning in accordance with the capabilities of the individuals, and to give them the chance of a life free from the indignities and iniquities of mere relief for the poor. The bitter shadows of mass unemployment during the inter-war period had to be banished. Though the essential·liberties of the individual were to be safeguarded under all circumstances, this need not be the case with 'secondary' or 'lesser' liberties. Beveridge did not provide a clear-cut list, but only some examples of them. 'Secondary liberties' were only to be preserved as far as they were consistent with 'social justice' and 'social progress'. If they endangered these, then they had to be discarded. For instance, in criticizing the anti-collectivist views of Professor F. A. Hayek, put forward in The Road to Serfdom (doc. 121),

E. Epilogue: Liberalism challenged, revised, maintained

Beveridge argued that investment of capital was a 'secondary liberty'. Investment of capital was 'desirable in itself' but only as long as its exercise did 'not harm others'. If it was practised by ruthless individuals at the expense of the community causing grave social ills, then the community had to be protected. The reformer pointed to the slums in Britain's industrial towns which had proved so detrimental to many lives. The freedom of businessmen to place their factories wherever they wanted had led to the arbitrary growth of congested areas in cities with their squalor, pollution, lack of space and unhealthy living conditions for the multitude. A continuation of this trend would make human beings unfree, 'forcing squalor and unemployment on them'. Therefore it was necessary to stabilize the process of investment, 'by interfering so far as necessary with businessmen' as 'the only alternative to destroying human beings in unemployment and subjecting them to the misery of a dole, with or without the means test' (doc. 117). The social injustice and misery experienced by numerous unemployed men and their families in Britain in the 1920s and 1930s caused Beveridge to recommend restrictions in the 'secondary liberty' of the few in order to ensure a more dignified existence of the many. As he put it, it was necessary to sacrifice 'some of the less important liberties of the past' in order to 'preserve the essential liberties and increase their effective enjoyment by all'. As Beveridge was a reformer and not a revolutionary he did not wish to go too far. Although private enterprise and the practice of collective bargaining were not regarded by him as 'essential liberties', he argued that they 'should be left to be exercised responsibly as long as they do not block the way to full employment'.

However successful Beveridge can be deemed as a very influential liberal pioneer for social security, in other fields of aspiration he confessed his disillusionment towards the end of his life – a disillusionment rather typical of many liberal and progressive minds of his generation. 'Fading of Dreams 1933–1937' is the heading of a chapter in his autobiography *Power and Influence*.[17] He admitted in retrospect that three of the dreams of his younger days had not come true: 'the dream of ever-widening justice and liberty', 'the dream of settled peace' and the 'dream of economics as a science'.

One feature of the fascist dictatorships in the 1930s, particularly odious to convinced liberals, was the suppression of the freedom of teaching and research. Beveridge joined with other leading British scholars in 1933 in founding the 'Academic Assistance Council' in London, an organization with the purpose of helping academic emigrés from Central and Southern Europe financially and by finding posts for them in British and other countries. As its president for some years he later wrote an interesting and careful account of the work of this body.[18] By their practical help and solidarity Beveridge and his colleagues showed not only a strong belief in the liberty of thought and research, they also

684

testified to the existence of an unchartered liberal International, ready to give effective help to victims of totalitarian oppression.

Liberty and equality

In a different way a revision of the liberal outlook was demanded by two Continental writers who had both experienced the collapse of liberalism and democracy in Germany. Thomas Mann, the famous novelist and essayist, and Karl Mannheim, the pioneer sociologist, were impressed and worried by the advance of fascism. They thought largely in terms of an inquest: Why, they asked, had the forces supporting individual freedom failed and those savagely suppressing it succeeded? They examined the errors and blunders of a liberalism which had ignored the need for a synthesis of liberty and equality. In their opinion the atomized individual who had undergone harsh experiences in war and under inflation desired economic and social security above all. Democracy in Europe was in deadly peril. If it was to survive a different balance between liberty and equality was indispensable.

Thomas Mann

In the 1930s Thomas Mann looked at the traditional conventions of liberalism with a critical eye. He regarded the *laissez faire* concept of liberalism as dated and inadequate and was anxiously aware that the threat of fascism to Western culture required a more up-to-date intellectual approach and platform. In so far as Mann wanted to move 'Forward from Liberalism' he could be called a Social Democrat rather than a Liberal. He saw Western civilization equally threatened by the two totalitarian systems, though he conceded that communism was an idea, whilst fascism was not. Although after 1918 Thomas Mann supported the Weimar Republic he became much more politically minded in exile after 1933 as one of the most distinguished German emigrés. Before 1918 an 'un-political' writer, conservative in his outlook but liberal in his basic attitude, a defender of German 'Kultur' against the mere civilization of the West, he had gradually learned to appreciate liberal democracy without becoming blind to its shortcomings.

Although not a very precise thinker on matters of politics, he was much concerned with the problems of freedom and democracy in his addresses to American audiences before the Second World War and in his broadcasts to Germany for the BBC during it. He saw freedom not as a mere freedom *from* coercion but as being involved in a dialectical relationship with equality. One without the other did not make sense. Both were closely connected with the concept of democracy. Democracy aimed at a reconciliation between the claims of freedom and equality, the former sponsoring the claims of individuality, the latter those of society. A balance between liberty and equality was desirable, a balance which, however, can never be fully reached. But whilst Mann acknowledged the right and the necessity of both factors, he thought it necessary to put more emphasis on equality and favoured a system in which freedom recognized its social obligations.

Unlike the Liberals of the nineteenth century he thought liberty should be seen as one of the fundaments of social democracy. Liberty must discipline itself and be wary of false friends who tried to decry the need for freedom to stand up for itself and who confused sloppy toleration of the most illiberal dictatorship with true freedom. These false friends had taken the idea of tolerance to the extreme of a self-surrender of freedom to its deadly totalitarian enemies. Mann's definition of freedom must be viewed against the background of the totalitarian menace to the West. Basically he was a moralizing humanist, keen to make sure that the private sphere of the individual should survive. Thus his somewhat surprising definition of freedom as 'the just and reasonable emphasis on the individual and the social elements in the human make-up (*im Menschlichen*), the limiting of the political and social factors to their natural proportions in humanity and life'. Conversely, he regarded 'the total dictatorship of politics over everything human' as 'the death of freedom as destructive in our view as is anarchy' (doc. 118). The contrast to anarchy on the one hand and to totalitarian compulsion on the other indicates Mann's position of self-disciplined freedom. Whereas the old liberalism was obsolete, the urge for freedom and the need to safeguard it remained as part of the idea of man which expressed itself equally in the striving for freedom and for truth and justice. While he was not concerned with the splitting of terminological hairs, Thomas Mann wanted to see democracy and the individual survive. This was only feasible if by concessions to equality, by a move towards social democracy, liberty would save the individual values, so indispensable for the future of civilization. How to resist the onslaught of totalitarian violence and to make freedom viable through self-discipline and social justice was the problem discussed by Mann again and again during the years when Western democracy was in deadly peril.

Mann emphasized that the traditional forms of liberalism were not the same as liberty; to maintain this was the gross deception of fascism. With an overall humanist philosophy – the precision of which leaves much to be desired – Thomas Mann detached himself from 'bourgeois liberalism', 'the liberalism of our fathers and grandfathers'. Through the pressure of atomistic mass society and of fascism 'freedom', he argued, had been 'driven out of liberalism by the deepest anguish' (doc. 119). Now social democracy instead of liberal democracy alone could restore freedom. If justice was to prevail, individual freedom must have its place in a planned society. Although such a demand might sound revolutionary, in fact its implications, Mann insisted, were conservative, for it was a question of the survival of the cultural traditions of the West from the onslaught of the alien philosophies of fascism and bolshevism.

Karl Mannheim

What the essayist Thomas Mann only indicated aphoristically, Karl Mannheim, the sociological thinker, developed more fully and cogently, if not always lucidly. Whereas Mann was inclined to acquiesce in vague terms such as a demand for greater self-discipline of freedom, Mannheim considered freedom and discipline as functions of the social group organisation. Freedom had to be seen in the social context in which it was supposed to be meaningful. Mannheim argued that at the time class distinctions interfered with a full enjoyment of freedom. Many members of the lower classes, when compared with those in the upper classes, were in fact so much handicapped by circumstances that terms like political freedom, freedom of expression, of occupation and of consumer choice became rather meaningless to them. Only in a more egalitarian society with a fairer distribution of the goods now produced on a larger scale, could freedom become meaningful for all. Karl Mannheim, the distinguished sociologist who, after losing his chair at the University of Frankfurt in 1933 when Hitler came to power, had found refuge in England, reflected in retrospect on 'the failure of the liberal democratic machinery in the Weimar Republic'. As he put it a few years later, he had noticed 'its impotence to solve the problems of modern mass democracy'. He had observed how the planning of the liberal order 'had turned into anarchy, how the principle of *laissez faire* which once maintained the balance of the social process' had at that stage of development 'resulted in chaos, both in political and cultural life'.[19] Mannheim was also aware of the widespread 'fear of freedom' (Erich Fromm) in a society of mass unemployment and unstable or non-existing majorities in Parliament.

This experience had convinced him of the necessity of some form of planning. He had shared 'involuntarily the feeling then prevalent in Central Europe that the democratic system had already run its course'. [20]Yet he gradually changed his mind after settling down in England, that is in a country where, as he discovered, 'liberal democracy functions almost undisturbed'.

Mannheim's posthumous work *Freedom, Power and Democratic Planning*[21] from which we include a significant passage (doc. 120), clearly reflects the impact of his experiences in Germany and England. Unlike Hayek, his former colleague at the London School of Economics, Mannheim was not inclined to talk of freedom in the abstract; he saw it and its counter-part, discipline, as existing in various social contexts. Both freedom and discipline were to be viewed in the institutional frame-work. They meant different things to members of a football team or to soldiers in an army. Freedom was further differently interpreted in four competing concepts, the anarchist, the totalitarian, the liberal and the plutocratic. Mannheim had some sympathy and understanding for the anarchist viewpoint with its belief in a kind of self-regulating power in human nature. In his opinion it did in fact operate as the creative power of small groups, but did not become effective in large-scale organizations which are unavoidable in modern mass society. Yet 'vital social interaction is generated primarily in small groups; real understanding of life, new ideas, originate in them; without their vital energy society would become anaemic'. In the totalitarian system freedom was replaced by tyranny, the creative tension between freedom and discipline by an over-organization based on absolute command and obedience. The liberal concept of freedom and discipline was inadequate in modern mass society. Its optimistic belief in an *a priori* harmony between the free choices of the individual and the self-regulating processes of society was groundless in the present era of big enterprise and organized pressure groups. The modern extreme of liberalism was the plutocratic view of freedom and discipline, the by-product of 'a stage in society when a limited class of wealthy people applies the liberal ideology in disregard of social change'. It stressed 'the investor's right to invest and speculate freely and the owner's right to use his property without restraint' which is bound to lead to freedom only for the few.

Mannheim was critical of both, the plutocratic and the liberal views; their emphasis on freedom was sociologically blind, as in fact the freedoms they propagated, such as political freedom, freedom of expression, of occupation and of consumer choice, 'primarily concerned educated people in fairly secure positions'. They meant 'less to the lower income levels' and were 'frequently not available to low-income groups'. Here Mannheim sided with the socialist critics of liberalism. Free choice of consumer goods or of occupation must remain academic for people who 'cannot afford to buy certain goods or acquire the prerequisite skills for higher occupations'.

If in these concepts freedom had become an illusory term, this did not mean that it was a reality in a more egalitarian society which produced goods on a large scale and distributes them more fairly. It would be a mistake to exchange cultural and political freedom for greater equality of income and education. For Mannheim's aim remained throughout 'the full development of personality which cannot take place without suitable material fundaments and cultural chances'.

Mannheim saw the need for the new forms of individual freedom to be built into a planned society, but he did not convincingly show how the traditional liberties of the individual which he wished to see preserved could be effectively safeguarded in such a society. He was aware that man needs both freedom and security, that the freedom of groups is as important as that of individuals. If, on the one hand, he maintained that 'the forms of freedom can only be formulated in reference to a given society and to the social techniques existing in it', on the other, Mannheim was again and again haunted by the 'fundamental philosophical question: was not an ideally planned society a prison?' or, in other words, 'a strait-jacket, even compared with the almost intolerable life led by many classes in an unplanned society?' For while in such an unplanned society many people might be threatened with insecurity, the individual was 'still (potentially at least) a free agent and could cope with his difficulties himself'. Might not 'the continual development of social techniques' lead to 'the complete enslavement of the individual?' [22] It was a decisive question requiring a definite answer.

Unfortunately, Mannheim died before he could fully work out his solution of the problem, but he remained convinced that a mixture of planning combined with the maintenance of the Anglo-Saxon tradition of self-supporting institutions would be a big step towards such a solution. He thought primarily in functional terms; therefore his very important query, not raised by previous liberal thinkers: 'What use is the freedom to choose our own philosophy of life, to form our own opinions, if the sociological mechanisms of our society create insecurity, anxiety, neuroses which prevent us from making sound and rational decisions?' [23]

Mannheim by no means discarded the liberal ideology completely. There was, he argued, 'undeniable wisdom in the idea of liberalism. Our Third Way will incorporate some of its elements.' As a system, however, liberalism was 'no longer applicable. In the bewildering complexity of institutional pressures the individual no longer sees his way to meaningful contributions to the common end.' Mannheim viewed history as a dialectical process when arguing that 'from the thesis of *laissez faire* and the anti-thesis of rigid regimentation, the idea of Democratic Planning gradually evolves in the cultural sphere'. [24]

Back to Liberalism

F. A. Hayek

If Stephen Spender with youthful nonchalance proclaimed the slogan 'Forward from Liberalism', the opposite battle-cry of 'Back to Liberalism' was raised a few years afterwards midst the turmoil of the Second World War by F. A. von Hayek, a leading Austrian economist who, like Mannheim, taught at the London School of Economics. Having experienced the collapse of liberalism and of the *Rechtsstaat* in Central Europe, he blamed the rise of collectivism for it. In his polemical book *The Road to Serfdom* (1944) he saw great danger for humanity in the advance and possible triumph of socialist planning. Favouring a return to the true principles of nineteenth-century liberalism, he did not deny that the earlier Liberals had made mistakes or that there were inherent dangers in monopolies, but to him the great threat to a survival of individual freedom came from a different quarter. As he saw it, all collectivists, the socialists and communists on the left and the fascists and national socialists on the right, shared the fierce opposition to the liberal traditions of competition and individualism. By lumping fascism and Marxist socialism together Hayek painted a grim picture of a society with a progressing lack of freedom as a serious threat to the West. He quoted with approval the German economic writer Peter Drucker, then in exile, who had argued that 'the complete collapse of the belief in the attainability of freedom and equality through Marxism' had 'forced Russia to travel the same road towards a totalitarian, purely negative, noneconomic society of unfreedom and inequality which Germany had been following' (doc. 121). Hayek also made much of the fact that a number of prominent fascists such as Mussolini and Quisling had at one time been socialists and that Oswald Spengler, the gloomy prophet of the *Decline of the West*, had recommended a synthesis of prussianism and socialism. During the 1930s English and American students had returned from the Continent 'uncertain whether they were communists or nazis and certain only that they hated Western liberal civilization' (doc. 121). To both communists and fascists, the real enemy was 'the liberal of the old type'. In fact 'freedom and organization' were, according to a dictum by Elie Halévy, 'absolutely different, perhaps even contradictory'. Long before the advent of Hitler the Germans had experienced the *Beamtenstaat*, with its authoritarian pattern which saw to it that 'not only in the Civil Service proper but in almost all spheres of life income and status were assigned and guaranteed by some authority'. [25]

Although Hayek agreed that 'political freedom is meaningless without economic freedom', he insisted that this was true 'in a sense almost opposite from that used by the planners'. It could not mean the 'freedom from economic care', promised by the socialists, which relieved 'the individual at the same time of the necessity and the power of choice'. It must be 'the freedom of our economic activity which, with the right of choice, inevitably carries the risk and the responsibility of that right'. [26] Particularly important was the freedom of choice of one's work which Hayek regarded as probably more important for our happiness than freedom to spend our income during the hours of leisure. Whilst admitting that in Western society choice of occupation was limited, nevertheless it remained imperative that there should be some choice at least.

Hayek's attitude to the need for the security of the individual was somewhat ambiguous. If economic security was 'often represented as an indispensable condition of real liberty', he conceded that this was 'in a sense both true and important'. Yet he deplored the vagueness of the term, which he feared might turn the general demand for security into a 'Danger for Liberty'. Some security was essential if freedom was to be preserved, he argued, 'because most people are willing to bear the risk which freedom invariably involves only as long as this risk is not too great'; however it was characteristic of his approach that he quoted 'against the present fashion of extolling security at the expense of freedom' the contemptuous words by Benjamin Franklin, that 'those who would give up essential liberty to purchase a little temporary safety deserve neither liberty nor safety'.[27]

Hayek drew a characteristic distinction between 'limited' and 'absolute' security. Limited security could be 'achieved for all' and was 'therefore no privilege but a legitimate object of desire' . . . while absolute security – a rather inadequate term – could not 'in a free society be achieved for all and ought not to be given as a privilege except in a few instances such as that of the judges where complete independence is of permanent importance'.

As regards 'limited security', even Hayek could not but make concessions to social liberalism as being different from the classical liberal ideology. He felt that 'for security against severe privation the certainty of a given minimum of sustenance for all' was advisable. He took it for granted that 'some minimum of food, shelter and clothing sufficient to preserve health and the capacity to work, can be assured to everybody'.[28] The State should help to organize a comprehensive insurance system to provide for the individual in case of sickness, accident etc. However, there were definite limits beyond which assistance by the state should not go. It could not be a universal provider for the unfortunate person who by the force of technological and economic changes suddenly suffers 'a great diminution of his income and bitter disappointment of all his hopes through no fault of his own, and despite hard work and exceptional skill'.[29] He simply will have to grin and bear it. If executives are no longer wanted in their 'fifties or early 'sixties, this is regrettable, but the State cannot be expected to look after them or other groups of people who have become the victims of adverse social circumstances. Hayek sharply disagreed with a statement by his colleague, Harold Laski, that 'without economic security, liberty' was 'not worth having'. To Hayek it was always worthwhile.

In retrospect it is easier to ascertain what Hayek stood against than what he stood for. He was opposed to the socialist concept of freedom which he regarded only as another term for equal distribution of wealth. He feared a New Order on a collectivist basis, either of the type proclaimed by Hitler during the war, or the socialist-communist version propagated by Laski, Stephen Spender and others. Hayek should be seen in the wake of liberal dissent, finding new formulae for it in a changing world. In a way he followed the half assertive, half sceptical line of J. S. Mill when remarking that 'in any society freedom of thought will be

E. Epilogue: Liberalism challenged, revised, maintained

probably of direct significance only for a small minority. But this does not mean that anyone is competent, or ought to have power, to select those to whom this freedom is to be reserved'. In an age of ever growing and often totalitarian planning it seemed imperative that the voice of dissent could still be heard. 'So long as dissent is not suppressed, there will always be some who will query the ideas ruling their contemporaries and put new ideas to the test of argument and propaganda.' [30] Individualism and 'the demand for comprehensive direction of the social process' were incompatible.

In his own way Hayek raised again the question of how far liberty and democracy are compatible, which had occupied the minds of Tocqueville and J. S. Mill. To Hayek the idea of liberty had priority before that of democracy. He argued, it could not be claimed of democracy as 'Lord Acton had truly said of liberty, that it "is not a means to a higher political end. It is in itself the highest political end" '. Hayek saw in democracy 'essentially a means, a utilitarian device for safeguarding internal peace and individual freedom', for safeguarding, in other words, an instrument 'by no means infallible and certain'.[31] The threat to liberty came now from those who regarded the trends towards socialism and planning as the high road to freedom while in fact it might well prove the low road to serfdom.

The idea that socialism would obtain greater economic freedom – Hayek claimed – was based on a confusion of freedom with power and wealth. The promise of economic freedom through an equal distribution of wealth had led many younger liberals astray to the socialist camp. If it was true that 'political freedom is meaningless without economic freedom', it was so 'in a sense almost opposite from which it is used by our planners'. [32] To a genuine liberal, economic freedom could not mean 'the freedom from economic care', as promised by the socialists, for this would deprive the individual at the same time 'of the necessity and power of choice'. Economic freedom must mean 'the freedom of our economic activity, which with the right of choice, inevitably also carries the risk and the responsibility of that right'. For a planner like Karl Mannheim man's need for security, economic, social and psychological, was of paramount importance. Hayek, on the other hand, distinguished a limited and an absolute kind of security, accepting the former and rejecting the latter. Like many of his forerunners in the nineteenth century, Hayek was not concerned with human beings *en masse* but as individuals. Although the planners professed it as their aim 'that man should cease to be a mere means', in fact in the planned society, where individual likes and dislikes could not be considered, the individual would become a mere instrument in the hands of the authorities. He would be used in the service of such abstractions as 'the social welfare' or 'the good of the community'.[33] We can see the sinister shadow of George Orwell's prophecy of a totalitarian England in *1984* rise behind the less dramatic

692

but equally disquieting Hayek portrait of the planned welfare State in 1944.[34]

Gilbert Murray and Croce

Compared with younger men like Mannheim and Hayek, Gilbert Murray and Benedetto Croce appear in retrospect rather as 'die-hard' liberals, little affected by the search for a balance of liberty and equality, individual freedom and planning. Murray, an Australian by birth but an Englishman by domicile and affinity, shared an indefatigable faith in the value of liberty and a high degree of intellectual refinement with Croce. Both stuck to their liberal principles in adverse times.

For many years professor of Greek at the University of Oxford, Murray played an active role in the work of the League of Nations at Geneva and was for some years Chairman of the League of Nations Union in Britain. His profound understanding of Greek civilization and his devotion to liberalism were inter-twined. In the words of his friend Arnold Toynbee, Murray 'interpreted the achievements and ordeals of the modern Western world in the terms of the experience of ancient Greece as he saw it'. This picture of Greek civilization as 'a light shining in the darkness of a surrounding barbarism that did not appreciate it', 'not only reinforced his sympathy for liberal causes; it moved him to devote himself to them and to do hard labour for them to the end of his long life'.[35] Like Sir Edward Grey and Lord Robert Cecil (later Viscount Cecil), Murray saw the society of his time divided into 'the weak, who suffered oppression and needed succour, and the strong, who had a choice being oppressors of the weak or champions of them'.[36]

Retaining a benevolent, often paternalistic attitude to oppressed minorities, Murray was little pleased when after the First World War the oppressed began to refuse to be patronized any longer, but organized themselves and acquired strength. One result was that in his later years Murray jibbed 'at the spectacle of certain under-dogs' once 'a liberal's protegés now championing their own cause, sometimes rather aggressively and turning against top-dog and all his works and values'.[37]

Unlike some other English Liberals who exchanged their liberal radicalism for membership of the Labour Party, Murray always remained a Liberal. In fact he fought a gallant ideological rearguard action for liberalism when in England the party of Gladstone and Asquith was practically destroyed after 1914. Again and again Murray was baffled and shocked by liberalism's fading appeal. In this respect his two addresses of 1937 and 1949 – from the second of which extracts are here reprinted (doc. 122) – are highly significant.[38] While European dictators became stronger and stronger, Murray agreed with the view of a very distinguished Continental historian who told him, about 1937, 'If Europe as

693

a whole does not adopt liberal policies, we feel that it may be the end of civilization'. In 1949 Murray sadly confessed that liberalism had 'become largely a fruitless longing in the hearts of specially conscientious or thoughtful people for something lost or unattainable' (doc. 122). Yet paradoxically 'most people in most countries' recognized 'this crash of Liberalism in the world as a disaster'.

But if liberalism was practically extinguished, the zest for liberty was not. One had to see beyond the changing party labels and diagnose the roots of the contemporary ills. What mattered was a spirit of liberality, a quality recently lost in Europe. 'Liberality' – a term which in 1937 Murray preferred to the devalued and misunderstood word 'liberalism' – was to him not an abstract doctrine or a dogma, but 'a spirit or attitude of mind'. The man filled with liberality 'befriends not the strong, but the weak, those who cannot help themselves or him'. In practical terms this meant in the 1930s that he would help 'the voteless natives in Africa, the Jews in Germany and Poland, the racial minorities in Eastern Europe'.[39] He tried to keep aloof from class and national interest and thus constantly ran the risk of being right but unpopular.

Salvador de Madariaga, who saw much of Cecil and Murray during their time at Geneva, in retrospect described them as two 'civic monks' working ceaselessly for a better world of international cooperation and understanding.[40] Murray was particularly active in the realm of intellectual co-operation.

'If the great majority of the nations want peace', Murray argued still hopefully in 1937, 'let them cooperate with one another in the things of peace; let them refuse absolutely to cooperate with the makers of war, and war presently will be impossible.'[41]

After the holocaust of what he called, a 'Thirty Years' War' of mass-destruction, mass-unemployment and collectivist dictatorships, Murray looked at the liberalism of the past with a more critical eye. In the nineteenth century when nations in Central, Eastern and Southern Europe struggled to achieve identity and self-realization, liberalism, he realized, had encouraged nationalism and its watchwords had been 'independence, nationality and to some extent even (sic) rebellion'. Nationalism had soon proved a plaything of irrational emotions and aggressive instincts. In his old age, Murray, like any old-fashioned conservative, deplored the excesses of the urge for national independence. What was required was cooperation between nations, not their independence. He regretted that India and even Burma then regarded independence as essential and that the British, Dutch and French empires were threatened with disintegration.

Liberals of the Murray type were fundamentally reformers, not rebels. 'Reform, constant reform and vigilant criticism' were certainly needed, but their function was 'to save, not to destroy'. Eventually Murray was even doubtful whether Freedom and Peace were 'entirely a positive thing'. He now felt that in the last analysis the struggle for freedom and the vigilance needed to make it possible were more important and more inspiring than its mere possession. Faced with the growing complexities of modern society the octogenarian, half with pride and half with resignation, still vigorously insisted that liberalism was 'a spirit. Not a dogma, a process, not an end' (doc. 122). Benedetto Croce might have agreed with him.

Croce, who perhaps had lesser expectations of a steady improvement of mankind than Murray, maintained a similar stoic serenity. As a neo-Hegelian he had never believed that conflict and war would cease. A liberal regime could not be established permanently. In his view periods of increased or reduced liberty alternated in history. Having been from 1922 till January 1925 'a conditional supporter of fascism', Croce turned into 'the leading anti-fascist among those Italians who did not go into exile'. [42] In 1939 he admitted: 'not only have liberal institutions in many countries where they seemed to stand four-square tumbled to the ground, but on every hand there is a coolness, a distrust, a detachment in respect of that ideal, which no longer seems to be able to inspire the heart or inform the will of men'. [43]

But as the liberal ideal was 'a moral ideal of humanity and civilization', it would have to be replaced by 'a new and victorious ideal, the ideal of a new, more vigorous, more profound humanity and civilisation'. No such valid successor was in sight. For 'the one party which in practice offers its candidature for the succession', was 'devoid of moral character, of creative force for the development of civil and human life'. Croce labelled this party with broad comprehension 'the party of regimentation, of constraint' and rejected its claim, no matter if it came from the extreme left or right, no matter if the constraint was 'exercised in the name of the race, or of the State, or of the dictatorship of the proletariat'. [44] As there was no other, more worthy ideal being offered, he defiantly concluded that 'in spite of all the "din of arms and shouting", and in spite of all "this scorn and mockery" directed against it', 'the ideal of liberty remains substantially untouched and invulnerable.'

Both as a moralist and a philosopher of history Croce remained confident that a revival of true liberalism was to be expected.

'One should keep up one's courage' – he commented sternly – 'in the first place because it is the duty of man to work and fight, and in the second place because human society has passed through other ages of moral weariness and choking materialism, and has always emerged from them through a spontaneous rekindling of enthusiasm and ideals, a return of spiritual springtime, the word and example of religious and apostolic genius, which in due course, whether quickly or slowly, gains the assent of the peoples.' [45]

Even at the height of the fascist and National Socialist regimes, Croce had thus little doubt that the banishment of political freedom could only

E. Epilogue: Liberalism challenged, revised, maintained

be temporary but never permanent. He remained convinced that after 'a period of long and turbid travail', sooner or later 'liberty, that is humanity' would 'spring forth, once more'.[46]

Croce and Madariaga

As early as 1930, in spite of the then strong rule of fascism Croce proclaimed a strikingly strong belief in a democratic European Union to come. At a time when outside Italy the first ideas of a "Pan Europe" were expressed by Count Coudenhove-Kalergie and sympathetically considered by the French statesman Aristide Briand, Croce anticipated the trend towards future European integration. In the Epilogue of his *History of Europe in the Nineteenth Century* he expressed his belief in new pacts between the nations, that would save 'if not the political and economic supremacy' of the European nations, 'at least their supremacy as creators and promotors of civilisation'. A new Europe would be born. The process of integration which in the great days of the *Risorgimento* had turned Piedmontese and Neapolitans into Italians would be repeated on a larger scale. Now Italians, Frenchmen, Germans would turn into Europeans, the First World War having assisted in bringing the nations together despite of their deep divisions. National competition and the whole psychology connected with it would come to an end. 'And if this happens, or when it happens, the liberal ideal will be fully restored in men's minds and will resume its rule' (doc. 114).

Twenty years later, after the devastation of the Second World War and the obliteration of Hitler's totalitarian 'New Order' for Europe, another prominent liberal writer, Salvador de Madariaga, journalist, diplomat and author, who from 1933 to 1936 had represented the Spanish Republic at the League of Nations, took up this idea of European Union against the background of a revitalized liberalism. By itself European Union, he found, was insufficient, for it might appear under a fascist or communist banner. The idea made sense only if the nations and the individuals would be genuinely free in a United Europe. It was the task of the liberals to achieve this. Europe, Madariaga insisted, 'will be liberal or will not be' (doc. 123). Like Croce he put the emphasis on variety as against uniformity, on quality as against quantity, on individuality as against mass. Two traditional postulates of European liberalism were restated: the demand for free research and the respect for the human personality.

At the end of the 1920s Croce had been rather inclined to underestimate communism as a deadly adversary of liberalism. In 1948, the year of the first major crisis over Berlin, and of the communist coup in Prague, Madariaga was not prepared to do so. He expressly rejected the 'doctrinaire idea of equality' and warned against 'the hankering after the left', which he thought characteristic of many good liberals. This

696

weakness explained why 'so many and distinguished liberals remained faithful – and deceived – friends of communism, the anti-liberal doctrine *par excellence*' (doc. 123). Madariaga was worried by the 'cold-war' and the machinations of Moscow. He saw in the 'neutralists' assistants of Moscow, he warned of the miracle belief that international conferences could solve all problems. However on the positive side he believed in the cooperation of the nations of Western, Central and Southern Europe. In his book *Portrait of Europe* [47] he paid tribute to the individual and the common features of the major European nations; he contrasted Hamlet and Don Quixote, Faust and Don Juan as symbols and displayed a remarkable insight into the variety and uniformity of the European mind. Madariaga, who at the time played an active role in the work of the new European College at Bruges, was a lively essayist rather than a master of historical analysis and dialectics of the calibre of Croce. With all his realistic warnings he was a liberal idealist. 'Man is body and mind (*Geist*)', he wrote in 1948, 'but it is the mind, by the strength of which he is a human being. This is in the last analysis of all things the most profound of the liberal principles.' (doc. 123.) Gilbert Murray and Benedetto Croce would have concurred.

Yet Croce was highly critical of an 'empirical' and 'Utilitarian' thinker such as J. S. Mill. In the chapter on 'The Liberal Age' in his *History of Europe in the Nineteenth Century*, Croce deplored the decline of philosophical speculation and the prevailing hollow positivism and revolutionism. 'Even when liberty was defended and theorized over, the defence and the theory were empirical and superficial, as they were in the famous book on this argument by John Stuart Mill.' [48] An acid comment which reveals in a flash the conflicting diversity in two majo. inter-pretations of liberty and liberalism during the last 150 years.

Notes and references

1. Isaiah Berlin, *Four Essays on Liberty*, London 1969, p. 9.
2. Hegel had conceived the process of liberty in stages, from its birth in the Orient ('one free') growing in the world of the Greeks ('some free') to its maturity in the Germanic world ('all free'), when it reached its peak in the conservative regime of Prussia during Hegel's time.
3. B. Croce, *History as the Story of Liberty*, London 1941, p. 59.
4. Ibid., p. 60.
5. See Trevor Wilson, *The Downfall of the Liberal Party 1914–1935*, London 1964, Appendix.

E. Epilogue: Liberalism challenged, revised, maintained

6. 'The events of 1918 preyed on the American conscience for twenty-five years whereas in Europe the *exalté* atmosphere of 1918–19 was soon dissipated.' I. Berlin, op. cit., p. 31.
7. See Stephen Spender, *Forward from Liberalism*, London 1937.
8. R. F. Harrod, *The Life of John Maynard Keynes*, London 1963, p. 331.
9. J. M. Keynes, 'Am I a Liberal?', *Essays in Persuasion*, London 1947, p. 324.
10. Trevor Wilson, *The Downfall of the Liberal Party 1914–1935*, London 1968, p. 235.
11 and 12. R. F. Harrod, op. cit., p. 333.
13. In these matters, Keynes observed that 'the existing state of the Law and of orthodoxy is still mediaeval – altogether out of touch with civilized opinion and civilized practice and with what individuals educated and uneducated alike, say to another in private. 'Am I a Liberal?', *Essays in Persuasion,* p. 332.
14. *Essays in Persuasion*, p. 333.
15. R. F. Harrod, op. cit., p. 334.
16. See *Full Employment in a Free Society* (2nd edn), London 1953.
17. Lord Beveridge, *Power and Influence*, London 1959, ch. XI.
18. Lord Beveridge, *Defence of Freedom*, London 1957.
19. Karl Mannheim, *Man and Society in an Age of Reconstruction*, London 1940, pp. 3–5.
20. Op. cit.
21. Edited by H. Gerth and E. K. Bramsted, London 1951 and New York 1950.
22. Karl Mannheim, *Man and Society in an Age of Reconstruction*, p. 369.
23. Ibid., p. 371.
24. *Freedom, Power and Democratic Planning*, p. 77.
25. F. A. Hayek, *The Road to Serfdom*, London 1944, p. 98.
26 and 27. Ibid., p. 99.
28. Ibid., p. 90.
29. Ibid., p. 91.
30. Ibid., p. 122. For an immediate sharp rejoinder from a socialist point of view see the book by Herman Finer, *The Road to Reaction*, London 1946.
31. Hayek, op. cit., p. 52.
32. Ibid, p. 75.
33. In his criticism of a 'centralized or collectivist' economy of excessive planning Hayek was supported by K. R. Popper in his influential work *The Open Society and its Enemies*, London 1945, 2 vols. See the Foreword and vol. I, p. 242. Conversely, Popper was critical of K. Mannheim's arguments in favour of 'planning for freedom' (vol. II, p. 319).
34. There was a good deal of scepticism in Hayek's thought. See 'The Road to Serfdom', p. 122.
35. Arnold Toynbee in *Gilbert Murray, An Unfinished Autobiography*, London 1960, pp. 213–14.
36. Ibid., p. 215.
37. Ibid., p. 216.
38. For the address of 1937 see *Liberality and Civilisation*, London 1938. The book contains lectures given at three English universities in the autumn of 1937.
39. Gilbert Murray, *Liberality and Civilisation*, pp. 37–8.
40. Salvador de Madariaga in his essay 'Gilbert Murray and the League of Nations' in *Gilbert Murray. An Unfinished Autobiography*, pp. 184–5.
41. Gilbert Murray, op. cit., p. 91.
42. Denis Mack Smith, 'Benedetto Croce', in *History and Politics*, ed. W. Laqueur and G. L. Mosse, London 1974, p. 156.
43. 'The Principle, the Ideal and the Theory of Liberty' in *Benedetto Croce Philosophy Poetry, History. An Anthology of Essays*, ed. Cecil Sprigge, London 1966, p. 704.
44. *Ibid.*

45. Ibid., p. 706.
46. B. Croce, *History of Europe in the Nineteenth Century*, London 1934, p. 358.
47. London 1952.
48. *History of Europe in the Nineteenth Century*, p. 318.

Documents

Doc. 113. BENEDETTO CROCE: History as the History of Liberty

Hegel's famous statement that history is the history of liberty was repeated without being altogether understood and then spread throughout Europe by Cousin, Michelet and other French writers. But Hegel and his disciples used it with the significance which we have criticized above, of a history of the first birth of liberty, of its growth, of its maturity and of its stable permanence in the definite era in which it is incapable of further development. (The formula was: Orient, Classic World, Germanic World = one free, some free, all free.) The statement is adduced in this place with a different intention and content, not in order to assign to history the task of creating a liberty which did not exist in the past but will exist in the future, but to maintain that liberty is the eternal creator and itself the subject of every history. As such it is on the one hand the explanatory principle of the course of history, and on the other the moral ideal of humanity.

Jubilant announcements, resigned admissions or desperate lamentations that liberty has now deserted the world are frequently heard nowadays; the ideal of liberty is said to have set on the horizon of history in a sunset without promise of sunrise. Those who talk or write or print this deserve the pardon pronounced by Jesus, for they know not what they say. If they knew or reflected they would be aware that to assert that liberty is dead is the same as saying that life is dead, that its mainspring is broken. And as for the ideal, they would be greatly embarrassed if invited to state the ideal which has taken, or ever could take, the place of the ideal of liberty. Then they would find that there is no other like it, none which makes the heart of man, in his human quality, so beat, none other which responds better to the very law of life which is history: and that this calls for an ideal in which liberty is accepted and respected and so placed as to produce ever greater achievements.

Certainly when we meet the legions of those who think or speak differently with these self-evident propositions, we are conscious that they may well be of the kind to raise laughter or derision about philosophers who seem to have tumbled on the earth from another world ignorant of what reality is, blind and deaf to its voice, to its cries, and to its hard features. Even if we omit to consider contemporary events and conditions in many countries, owing to which a liberal order which seemed to be the great and lasting achievement of the nineteenth century has crumbled, while in other countries the desire for this collapse is spreading, all history still gives evidence of an unquiet, uncertain and disordered liberty with brief intervals of unrest, rare and lightning moments of a happiness perceived rather than possessed, mere pauses in the tumult of oppressions, barbarian invasions, plunderings, secular and ecclesiastical tyrannies, wars between peoples, persecutions, exiles and gallows. With this prospect in view the statement that history is the history of liberty sounds like irony, or, if it is seriously maintained, like stupidity.

But philosophy is not there just to be overwhelmed by the kind of reality which is apprehended by unbalanced and confused imaginings. Thus philosophy, when it inquires and interprets, knowing well that the man who enslaves another wakes in him awareness of himself and enlivens him to seek for liberty, observes with serenity how periods of increased or reduced liberty follow upon each other and how a liberal order, the more it is established and undisputed, the more surely decays into habit, and thereby its vigilant self-awareness and readiness for defence is weakened, which opens the way for a 'recourse', as Vico termed it, to all of those things which seemed to have vanished from the world, and which themselves, in their turn, open a new 'course'. Philosophy considers, for example, the democracies and the republics like those of Greece in the fourth century, or of Rome in the first, in which liberty was still preserved in the institutional forms but no longer in the soul or the customs of the people, and then lost even those forms, much as a man who has not known how to help himself but has in vain for a time received ministrations of good advice is finally abandoned to the hard school of life. Or philosophy looks at Italy, exhausted and defeated, entombed by barbarians in all her pompous Imperial array rising again, as the poet said, 'in her Tyrrhenian and Adriatic republics' like an agile sailor. Or philosophy contemplates the absolute monarchs who beat down the liberty of the barons and the clergy once they had become privileged, and superimposed on all men their own form of government, exercised by their own bureaucracy, and sustained by their own army, thus preparing a far greater and more useful participation of the people in political liberty. A Napoleon destroys a merely apparent and nominal liberty, he removes its appearance and its name, levels down the peoples under his rule and leaves those same people with a thirst for liberty and a new awareness of what it really was and a keenness to set up, as they did shortly afterwards in all Europe, institutions of liberty. Even in the darkest and crassest times liberty trembles in the lines of poets and affirms itself in the pages of thinkers and burns, solitary and magnificent, in some men who cannot be assimilated by the world around them, as Vittoria Alfieri discovered in the eighteenth century grand-ducal Siena, where he found a friend, 'freest of spirits', born 'in hard prison', and abiding there 'like a sleeping lion', for whom he wrote the dialogue in his *Virtue Unrecognized*. Yes, to the eye of philosophy, whether the age is propitious or unfavourable, liberty appears as abiding purely and invincibly and consciously only in a few spirits; but these alone are those which count historically, just as great philosophers, great poets, great men and every kind of great work have a real message only to the few, even though crowds may acclaim and deify them, ever ready to abandon them in order noisily to acclaim other idols and to exercise, under whatever slogan or flag, a natural disposition for courtisanship and servility. And on account of this, and through experience and meditation, the philosopher thinks and tells himself that if in liberal times one enjoys the welcome illusion of belonging to a great company, while in illiberal times one has the opposite and unwelcome illusion of being alone or almost alone, the first optimistic view was surely illusory, but maybe the second pessimistic view was illusory also. He sees this and he sees so many other things and he draws the conclusion that if history is not an idyll, neither is it a 'tragedy of horrors' but a drama in which all the actions, all the actors, and all the members of the chorus are, in the Aristotelian sense 'middling', guilty-non-guilty, a mixture of good and bad, yet ruled always by a governing thought which is good and to which evil ends by acting as a stimulus and that this achievement is the work of liberty which always strives to re-establish and always does re-establish the social and political conditions of a more intense liberty. If anyone needs persuading that liberty cannot exist differently from the way it has lived and always will live in history, a perilous and fighting life, let him for a moment consider a world of liberty without obstacles, without menaces and without oppressions of any kind; immediately he will look away from this picture with horror as being something worse than death, an infinite boredom.

Having said this, what is then the anguish that men feel for liberty that has been lost, the invocations, the lost hopes, the words of love and anger which come from the hearts of men in certain moments and in certain ages of history? We have already said it in examining a similar case: these are not philosophical nor historical truths, nor are they errors or dreams; they are movements of moral conscience; they are history in the making.

[Source: Benedetto Croce, *History as the Story of Liberty*, translated by Sylvia Sprigge, London 1941, Ch. XII, pp. 59–62.]

Doc. 114. BENEDETTO CROCE: Towards a Liberalised Europe

Because this [liberty that is humanity] is the sole ideal that has the solidity once owned by Catholicism and the flexibility that this was never able to have, the only one that can always face the future and does not claim to determine it in any particular and contingent form, the only one that can resist criticism and represent for human society the point around which, in its frequent upheavals, in its continual oscillations, equilibrium is perpetually restored. So that when the question is heard whether liberty will enjoy what is known as the future, the answer must be that it has something better still; it has eternity. And today too, notwithstanding the coldness and the contempt and the scorn that liberty meets, it is in so many of our institutions and customs and our spiritual attitudes, and operates beneficently within them. What is more important, it lives in many noble intellects in all parts of the world, which, no matter how they are dispersed and isolated and reduced almost to an aristocratic but tiny *respublica literaria*, yet remain faithful to it and surround it with greater reverence and pursue it with more ardent love than in the times when there was no one to offend it or to question its absolute lordship, and the crowd surged around it hailing it by name, and in the very act contaminated its name with vulgarity, of which it has now been cleansed.

Nor does liberty live only in these men, nor does it exist and resist only in the government of many of the major states and in institutions and customs, but its virtue operates even in things themselves, it opens a path for itself with more or less slowness through the rudest difficulties. This can be seen principally in the sentiment and the idea that is arousing general solicitude, of a truce and a diminution of 'preparedness' and armaments, of a peace and alliance between the states of Europe, of an agreement of intentions and efforts between her nations that shall save in the world and for the good of the world, if not their economic and political supremacy, at least their supremacy as creators and promoters of civilization, their acquired aptitude for this unceasing task. This is the only political project that, among all those formed since the war, has not been lost or dissipated but on the contrary gains ground from year to year and converts to itself minds that were hostile to it or displayed incredulity or would have liked to but did not dare to believe in it; and it is pleasant to hope that it will not be allowed to drop and that it will reach achievement, despite all opposition, overcoming and outflanking all obstacles, thanks to the arts of statesmen, thanks to the will of nations. The World War – which perhaps future historians will consider as the *reductio ad absurdum* of all nationalism – may have embittered certain relations between states because of the iniquitous and stupid treaty of peace that ended it, but it has brought into intimate communion the nations who have felt themselves, and will always more and more feel themselves, equal in their virtues and their errors, in their strength and their weakness, subject to the same fate, troubled by the same loves, saddened by the same sorrows, proud of the same ideal heritage. Meanwhile, in all parts of Europe we are watching the growth of a new consciousness, of a new nationality (because, as we have already remarked, nations are not natural data, but historical states of consciousness and historical formations). And just as, seventy years ago, a Neapolitan of the old kingdom or a Piedmontese of the subalpine kingdom became an Italian without becoming false to his earlier quality but raising it and resolving it into this new quality, so the French and the Germans and the Italians and all the others will raise themselves into Europeans and their thoughts will be directed towards Europe and their hearts will beat for her as they once did for their smaller countries, not forgotten now but loved all the better.

This process of European union, which is directly opposed to nationalist competition and has already set itself up against it and one day will be able to liberate Europe from it altogether, tends at the same time to liberate her from the whole psychology that clings to this nationalism and supports it and generates kindred manners, habits, and actions. And if this thing happens, or when it happens, the liberal ideal will be fully restored in men's minds and will resume its rule. But we must not imagine the restoration of this ideal as a return to the conditions of another day, as one of those returns to the past which romanticism sometimes dreamed of, cradling itself in a sweet idyll. All that has happened, and all that will have happened in the meanwhile, cannot have happened in vain; several institutions of the old liberalism will have to be modified in greater or lesser measure, or replaced by others that are better adapted, and ruling and political classes of quite a different composition from the former ones will arise; and the experience of the past will produce other concepts and give a different direction to the will.

With this mental and moral disposition the problems will have to be taken up again that are called social, which certainly were not born today, over which thinkers and statesmen have laboured throughout the centuries, solving them from time to time according to the age, and which in the course of the nineteenth century formed the object of the most passionate attention and the most ardent care. And even then they were solved from time to time so far as they could be and with such results as greatly to change the conditions of the workers, to improve their tenor of life and elevate their juridical and moral status. Nor is 'rationalized economy', as the phrase runs, which has now come into the forefront in discussion, anything intrinsically new, nor can the discussion turn on the replacement that it imposes of individual economics or of free initiative,

704

which are indispensable to human life and even to economic progress, but only on the greater or lesser proportion to be attributed to the one with respect to the other, according to materials, places, times, and other circumstances. This is an argument for experts and statesmen, upon whom it is incumbent to solve it from time to time in such a way as may be most advantageous for the increase of production and most equitable for the distribution of wealth. But experts and statesmen will never be able to fulfil their function, nor to hope for an actuation of their proposals that is not fictitious, unless liberty prepares and maintains the intellectual and moral atmosphere necessary for so great a task, and guarantees the juridical order in which the actuation is to be accomplished.

All this, rapidly outlined, is not prophecy, for that is forbidden to us and to everyone for the simple reason that it would be vain, but a suggestion of what paths moral consciousness and the observation of the present may outline for those who in their guiding concepts and in their interpretation of the events of the nineteenth century agree with the narrative given of them in this history. Others, with a different mind, different concepts, a different quality of culture, and a different temperament, will choose other paths, and if they do so with a pure mind, in obedience to an inner command, they too will be preparing the future well. A history inspired by the liberal idea cannot, even in its practical and moral corollary, end with the absolute rejection and condemnation of those who feel and think differently. It simply says to those who agree with it: "Work according to the line that is here laid down for you, with your whole self, every day, every hour, in your every act; and trust in divine Providence, which knows more than we individuals do and works with us, inside us and over us." Words like these, which we have often heard and uttered in our Christian education and life, have their place, like others from the same source, in the 'religion of liberty.'

[Source: Benedetto Croce, *History of Europe in the Nineteenth Century*, translated by Henry Furst 1934, London, pp. 358–362.]

Doc. 115. JOHN MAYNARD KEYNES: The Liberal Position Redefined (1926)

Let us clear from the ground the metaphysical or general principles upon which, from time to time, *laissez faire* has been founded. It is *not* true that individuals possess a prescriptive 'natural liberty' in their economic activities. There is *no* 'compact' conferring perpetual rights on those who Have or on those who Acquire. The world is *not* so governed from above that private and social interest always coincide. It is *not* so managed here

E. Epilogue: Liberalism challenged, revised, maintained

below that in practice they coincide. It is *not* a correct deduction from the Principles of Economics that enlightened self-interest always operates in the public interest. Nor is it true that self-interest generally *is* enlightened; more often individuals acting separately to promote their own ends are too ignorant or too weak to attain even these. Experience does *not* show that individuals, when they make up a social unit, are always less clear-sighted than when they act separately.

We cannot therefore settle on abstract grounds, but must handle on its merits in detail what Burke termed 'one of the finest problems in legislation, namely, to determine what the State ought to take upon itself to direct by the public wisdom, and what it ought to leave, with as little interference as possible, to individual exertion.'* We have to discriminate between what Bentham, in his forgotten but useful nomenclature, used to term *Agenda* and *Non-Agenda*, and to do this without Bentham's prior presumption that interference is, at the same time, 'generally needless' and 'generally pernicious'.** Perhaps the chief task of Economists at this hour is to distinguish afresh the *Agenda* of Government from the *Non-Agenda*; and the companion task of Politics is to devise forms of Government within a Democracy which shall be capable of accomplishing the *Agenda*. I will illustrate what I have in mind by two examples.

(1) I believe that in many cases the ideal size for the unit of control and organisation lies somewhere between the individual and the modern State. I suggest, therefore, that progress lies in the growth and the recognition of semi-autonomous bodies within the State – bodies whose criterion of action within their own field is solely the public good as they understand it, and from whose deliberations motives of private advantage are excluded, though some place it may still be necessary to leave, until the ambit of men's altruism grows wider, to the separate advantage of particular groups, classes, or faculties – bodies which in the ordinary course of affairs are mainly autonomous within their prescribed limitations, but are subject in the last resort to the sovereignty of the democracy expressed through Parliament.

I propose a return, it may be said, towards mediaeval conceptions of separate autonomies. But, in England at any rate, corporations are a mode of government which has never ceased to be important and is sympathetic to our institutions. It is easy to give examples, from what already exists, of separate autonomies which have attained or are approaching the mode I designate – the Universities, the Bank of England, the Port of London Authority, even perhaps the Railway Companies. In Germany there are doubtless analogous instances.

But more interesting than these is the trend of Joint Stock Institutions,

* Quoted by M'Culloch in his *Principles of Political Economy*.
** Bentham's *Manual of Political Economy*, published posthumously, in Bowring's edition (1843).

706

when they have reached a certain age and size, to approximate to the status of public corporations rather than that of individualistic private enterprise. One of the most interesting and unnoticed developments of recent decades has been the tendency of big enterprise to socialise itself. A point arrives in the growth of a big institution – particularly a big railway or big public utility enterprise, but also a big bank or a big insurance company – at which the owners of the capital, *i.e.* the shareholders, are almost entirely dissociated from the management, with the result that the direct personal interest of the latter in the making of great profit becomes quite secondary. When this stage is reached, the general stability and reputation of the institution are more considered by the management than the maximum of profit for the shareholders. The shareholders must be satisfied by conventionally adequate dividends; but once this is secured, the direct interest of the management often consists in avoiding criticism from the public and from the customers of the concern. This is particularly the case if their great size or semi-monopolistic position renders them conspicuous in the public eye and vulnerable to public attack. The extreme instance, perhaps, of this tendency in the case of an institution, theoretically the unrestricted property of private persons, is the Bank of England. It is almost true to say that there is no class of persons in the Kingdom of whom the Governor of the Bank of England thinks less when he decides on his policy than of his shareholders. Their rights, in excess of their conventional dividend, have already sunk to the neighbourhood of zero. But the same thing is partly true of many other big institutions. They are, as time goes on, socialising themselves.

Not that this is unmixed gain. The same causes promote conservatism and a waning of enterprise. In fact, we already have in these cases many of the faults as well as the advantages of State Socialism. Nevertheless we see here, I think, a natural line of evolution. The battle of Socialism against unlimited private profit is being won in detail hour by hour. In these particular fields – it remains acute elsewhere – this is no longer the pressing problem. There is, for instance, no so-called important political question so really unimportant, so irrelevant to the re-organisation of the economic life of Great Britain, as the Nationalisation of the Railways.

It is true that many big undertakings, particularly Public Utility enterprises and other business requiring a large fixed capital, still need to be semi-socialised. But we must keep our minds flexible regarding the forms of this semi-socialism. We must take full advantage of the natural tendencies of the day, and we must probably prefer semi-autonomous corporations to organs of the Central Government for which Ministers of State are directly responsible.

I criticize doctrinaire State Socialism, not because it seeks to engage men's altruistic impulses in the service of Society, or because it departs from *laissez faire*, or because it takes away from man's natural liberty to make a million, or because it has courage for bold experiments. All these

E. Epilogue: Liberalism challenged, revised, maintained

things I applaud. I criticise it because it misses the significance of what is actually happening; because it is, in fact, little better than a dusty survival of a plan to meet the problems of fifty years ago, based on a misunderstanding of what someone said a hundred years ago. Nineteenth-century State Socialism sprang from Bentham, free competition, etc., and is in some respects a clearer, in some respects a more muddled version of just the same philosophy as underlies nineteenth-century individualism. Both equally laid all their stress on freedom, the one negatively to avoid limitations on existing freedom, the other positively to destroy natural or acquired monopolies. They are different reactions to the same intellectual atmosphere.

(2) I come next to a criterion of *Agenda* which is particularly relevant to what it is urgent and desirable to do in the near future. We must aim at separating those services which are *technically social* from those which are *technically individual*. The most important *Agenda* of the State relate not to those activities which private individuals are already fulfilling, but to those functions which fall outside the sphere of the individual, to those decisions which are made by *no one* if the State does not make them. The important thing for Government is not to do things which individuals are doing already, and to do them a little better or a little worse; but to do those things which at present are not done at all ...

Many of the greatest economic evils of our time are the fruits of risk, uncertainty, and ignorance. It is because particular individuals, fortunate in situation or in abilities, are able to take advantage of uncertainty and ignorance, and also because for the same reason big business is often a lottery, that great inequalities of wealth come about; and these same factors are also the cause of the Unemployment of Labour, or the disappointment of reasonable business expectations, and of the impairment of efficiency and production. Yet the cure lies outside the operations of individuals; it may even be to the interest of individuals to aggravate the disease. I believe that the cure for these things is partly to be sought in the deliberate control of the currency and of credit by a central institution, and partly in the collection and dissemination on a great scale of data relating to the business situation, including the full publicity, by law if necessary, of all business facts which it is useful to know. These measures would involve Society in exercising directive intelligence through some appropriate organ of action over many of the inner intricacies of private business, yet it would leave private initiative and enterprise unhindered. Even if these measures prove insufficient, nevertheless they will furnish us with better knowledge than we have now for taking the next step.

My second example relates to Saving and Investment. I believe that some co-ordinated act of intelligent judgment is required as to the scale on which it is desirable that the community as a whole should save, the scale on which these savings should go abroad in the form of foreign investments, and whether the present organisation of the investment

708

market distributes savings along the most nationally productive channels. I do not think that these matters should be left entirely to the chance of private judgment and private profits, as they are at present.

My third example concerns Population. The time has already come when each country needs a considered national policy about what size of Population, whether larger or smaller than at present or the same, is most expedient. And having settled this policy, we must take steps to carry it into operation. The time may arrive a little later when the community as a whole must pay attention to the innate quality as well as to the mere numbers of its future members.

[Source: John Maynard Keynes, *The End of Laissez-Faire*, London 1927 (3rd impression) pp. 39–49.]

Doc. 116. JOHN MAYNARD KEYNES: Liberalism and Labour*

I do not wish to live under a Conservative Government for the next twenty years. I believe that the progressive forces of the country are hopelessly divided between the Liberal Party and the Labour Party. I do not believe that the Liberal Party will win *one-third* of the seats in the House of Commons in any probable or foreseeable circumstances. Unless in course of time the mistakes of the Conservative Government produce an economic catastrophe – which is not impossible – I do not believe that the Labour Party will win *one-half* of the seats in the House of Commons. Yet it is not desirable that the Labour Party should depend for their chances of office on the occurrence of a national misfortune; for this will only strengthen the influence of the party of catastrophe which is already an important element in their ranks. As things are now, we have nothing to look forward to except a continuance of Conservative Governments, not merely until they have made mistakes in the tolerable degree which would have caused a swing of the pendulum in former days, but until their mistakes have mounted up to the height of a disaster. I do not like this choice of alternatives.

That is the practical political problem which confronts all those, in whichever party they are ranged, who want to see progressive principles put into effect, and believe that too long a delay in doing so may find the country confronted with extreme alternatives.

The conventional retort by Labour orators is to call upon Liberals to close down their own Party and to come over. Now it is evident that the virtual extinction of the Liberal Party is a practical possibility to be reckoned with. A time may come when any one in active politics will have only two choices before him and not three. But I believe that it would be bad politics and bad behaviour to promote this end; and that it

* The substance of a speech delivered at the Manchester Reform Club, 9 February 1926.

is good politics and good behaviour to resist it.

Good politics to resist it, because the progressive cause in the constituencies would be weakened, and not strengthened, by the disappearance of the Liberal Party. There are many sections of the country, and many classes of voters, which for many years to come will never vote Labour in numbers, or with enthusiasm, sufficient for victory; but which will readily vote Liberal as soon as the weather changes. Labour leaders who deny this are not looking at the facts of politics with unclouded eyes.

Good behaviour to resist it, because most present-day active Liberals, whilst ready on occasion to vote Labour and to act with Labour, would not feel comfortable, or sincere, or in place, as full members of the Labour Party. Take my own case. I am sure that I am less conservative in my inclinations than the average Labour voter; I fancy that I have played in my mind with the possibilities of greater social changes than come within the present philosophies of, let us say, Mr Sidney Webb, Mr Thomas, or Mr Wheatley. The Republic of my imagination lies on the extreme left of celestial space. Yet – all the same – I feel that my true home, so long as they offer a roof and a floor, is still with the Liberals.

Why, though fallen upon such evil days, does the tradition of Liberalism hold so much attraction? The Labour Party contains three elements. There are the *Trade-Unionists*, once the oppressed, now the tyrants, whose selfish and sectional pretensions need to be bravely opposed. There are the advocates of the methods of violence and sudden change, by an abuse of language called *Communists*, who are committed by their creed to produce evil that good may come, and, since they dare not concoct disaster openly, are forced to play with plot and subterfuge. There are the *Socialists*, who believe that the economic foundations of modern society are evil, yet might be good.

The company and conversation of this third element, whom I have called Socialists, many Liberals to-day would not find uncongenial. But we cannot march with them until we know along what path, and towards what goal, they mean to move. I do not believe that their historic creed of State Socialism, and its newer gloss of Guild Socialism, now interest them much more than they interest us. These doctrines no longer inspire any one. Constructive thinkers in the Labour Party, and constructive thinkers in the Liberal Party, are trying to replace them with something better and more serviceable. The notions on both sides are a bit foggy as yet, but there is much sympathy between them, and a similar tendency of ideas. I believe that the two sections will become more and more friends and colleagues in construction as time goes on. But the progressive Liberal has this great advantage. He can work out his policies without having to do lip-service to Trade-Unionist tyrannies, to the beauties of the class war, or to doctrinaire State Socialism – in none of which he believes.

In the realm of practical politics, two things must happen – both of which are likely. There must be one more General Election to disillusion Labour optimists as to the measure of their political strength, standing by themselves. But equally on our side there must be a certain change. The Liberal Party is divided between those who, if the choice is forced upon them, would vote Conservative, and those who, in the same circumstances, would vote Labour. Historically, and on grounds of past service, each section has an equal claim to call itself Liberal. Nevertheless, I think that it would be for the health of the party if all those who believe, with Mr Winston Churchill and Sir Alfred Mond, that the coming political struggle is best described as Capitalism *versus* Socialism, and, thinking in these terms, mean to die in the last ditch for Capitalism, were to leave us. The brains and character of the Conservative Party have always been recruited from Liberals, and we must not grudge them the excellent material with which, in accordance with our historic mission, we are now preserving them from intellectual starvation. It is much better that the Conservative Party should be run by honest and intelligent ex-Liberals, who have grown too old and tough for us, than by Die-Hards. Possibly the Liberal Party cannot serve the State in any better way than by supplying Conservative Governments with Cabinets, and Labour Governments with ideas.

At any rate, I sympathise with Labour in rejecting the idea of co-operation with a party which included, until the other day, Mr Churchill and Sir Alfred Mond, and still contains several of the same kidney. But this difficulty is rapidly solving itself. When it is solved, the relations between Liberalism and Labour, at Westminster and in the constituencies, will, without any compacts, bargains, or formalities, become much more nearly what some of us would like them to be.

It is right and proper that the Conservative Party should be recruited from the Liberals of the previous generation. But there is no place in the world for a Liberal Party which is merely the home of out-of-date or watery Labour men. The Liberal Party should be not less progressive than Labour, not less open to new ideas, not behindhand in constructing the new world. I do not believe that Liberalism will ever again be a great party machine in the way in which Conservatism and Labour are great party machines. But it may play, nevertheless, the predominant part in moulding the future. Great changes will not be carried out except with the active aid of Labour. But they will not be sound or enduring unless they have first satisfied the criticism and precaution of Liberals. A certain coolness of temper, such as Lord Oxford has, seems to me at the same time peculiarly *Liberal* in flavour, and also a much bolder and more desirable and more valuable political possession and endowment than sentimental ardours.

The political problem of mankind is to combine three things; Economic Efficiency, Social Justice, and Individual Liberty. The first

711

needs criticism, precaution and technical knowledge; the second, an unselfish and enthusiastic spirit which loves the ordinary man; the third, tolerance, breadth, appreciation of the excellencies of variety and independence, which prefers, above everything, to give unhindered opportunity to the exceptional and to the aspiring. The second ingredient is the best possession of the great party of the Proletariat. But the first and third require the qualities of the party which, by its traditions and ancient sympathies, has been the home of Economic Individualism and Social Liberty.

[Source: J. M. Keynes, *Essays in Persuasion* (1931), London 1947, pp. 339–45.]

Doc. 117. SIR WILLIAM BEVERIDGE: Liberal Radicalism and Liberty

I believe that the things that I most desire to see done are essentially Liberal things – a carrying forward into the new world of the great living traditions of Liberalism.

What are the things that most need doing? To my mind there are three things above all that every citizen of this country and, indeed, of the world needs as conditions of a happy and useful life after the war. He needs freedom from Want and fear of Want; freedom from Idleness and fear of Idleness enforced by unemployment; freedom from War and fear of War.

The first of these freedoms is the aim of the Report on Social Insurance and Allied Services which I made to H.M. Government nearly two years ago. That Report sets out a plan for Social Security to ensure that every citizen of the country, on condition of working and contributing while he can, has an income to keep him above want when for any reason – of sickness, accident, unemployment, or old age – he cannot work and earn an income sufficient for the honourable subsistence of himself and all who depend on him, an income sufficient though he has nothing else of his own and not cut down by any means test if he has anything of his own.

Freedom from Idleness enforced by unemployment is the subject of a second Report on Full Employment in a Free Society, which I have just written . . . setting out a plan by which Full Employment at all times can be maintained without interfering with any of the essential British liberties. That plan is designed to make impossible any return to the mass unemployment which marked the interval between the wars.

Freedom from War and fear of War is the most important and the most difficult of the three freedoms to attain. It depends on the kind of peace that we make and the organisation that we set up to establish the rule of law between nations instead of the rule of force and violence. This task is difficult, but not impossible; it is absurd to say that wars are inevitable; wars are man-made, and by man they can be prevented . . .

In regard to each of these three problems, it is to me obvious that the action required is essentially Liberal. To win Freedom from Want means building on the structure of Social Insurance begun in 1911 by Mr Lloyd George in the great Liberal administration of that time. Freedom from Idleness means prevention of unemployment. In the bad period between the two wars, the Liberal Party in 1929 was the only party which made serious proposals for dealing with unemployment. They didn't get the chance of trying those proposals and, to-day, we shall have to go beyond them: but when these proposals were made, they were far ahead of anything contemplated by the other parties: they went at least as far as the Unemployment Policy of the Government of to-day. As regards freedom from War, that cannot be obtained either by pacifism or by nationalism; it depends upon carrying into the international field essentially Liberal ideas of the rule of law, and of making the world safe for the small nations by justice and the policeman.

I have mentioned these three general problems, because they show why I stand as a Liberal. That does not mean that I have no interest in other problems. I have that interest, in housing and town planning and education; and above all in the making of a prosperous agriculture. The last is an essential part of my Plan for Full Employment of all our resources in meeting human needs.

Full Employment is defined there as a state of affairs in which there are always more vacant jobs than men and women looking for jobs, in which jobs rather than men have to wait. A Free Society is defined as one which preserves all the essential liberties . . .

The way to full employment lies not in waiting until people are unemployed and trying to make work for them, but in determined collective pursuit of a common objective, in deciding that certain things should be done and setting ourselves to do them. We abolish unemployment in war because we decide that it is so essential to defeat the enemy that we will spend ourselves and our money for that purpose. We can abolish unemployment in peace on the same principle by deciding that there are things to be done sufficient to use all our energies. The things to be done are, on the one hand, the abolition of the giant evils of Want, Disease, Ignorance and Squalor and, on the other hand, the raising of our output per head by extending and rejuvenating the capital needs of our industries . . .

Full employment in a Free Society, as proposed in my Second Report, though in due course it may, like social insurance be accepted by all parties, is in essence a radical plan, profoundly different from anything that would occur naturally to the Conservative or the Labour Parties. The Conservative attitude, at is best and most progressive, is represented by the Government's White Paper on Employment Policy – a paper which treats private enterprise as master in the economic field, and proposes

E. Epilogue: Liberalism challenged, revised, maintained

public works to compensate for the instabilities of private work. The Labour Party is Socialist — tied to the formula of nationalisation of the means of production, distribution and exchange, desiring state enterprise for its own sake. The line of my second Report is a new line, of social demand rather than socialised production, of keeping private enterprise as servant not as master, of finding full employment for ourselves by planned raising of our standard of living. If you want a new line, you must rebuild a party that welcomes new ideas and knows how to put them into action ...

The Liberal Party has no hampering connections of privilege; while it presses for social justice and security for producers, it is above all the party of the citizens at large, as consumers. Its Radical Programme is a programme of putting first things first, bread and health for all before cake and circuses for anybody ...

In taking as our objective the making of a strong Liberal Party with a Radical Programme, we reconcile the good of the past with the new measures needed for the future. The ultimate aims of Liberalism are unchanged — equal enjoyment of all essential liberties secured by the rule of law, material progress for the sake of increasing spiritual life, toleration for variety of opinion, the common interests of all citizens over-riding every sectional privilege at home, peace and goodwill and international trade abroad. These aims endure. To-day they must be pursued by new methods, by positive radical methods based on experience, suited to changed conditions. Liberalism is a faith, not a formula.

The execution of a Radical Programme involves an extension of the responsibilities and functions of the State. It means at the same time more individual liberty, not less. That is because Liberal radicalism avoids the errors both of the so-called individualists, who treat every liberty as equally important and of the collectivists who desire extension of state activity for its own sake.

Liberal radicalism in relation to liberty may be defined by three propositions:

1. Certain citizen liberties are essential, and must be preserved at all costs. These are, on the one hand, the intimate personal liberties (worship, speech, writing, study, teaching; spending of personal income; choice of occupation) and on the other hand, the political liberties (assembly and association for industrial and political purposes) which are necessary to prevent the establishing of arbitrary power.

2. Subject to preservation of these essential liberties, the power of the State should be used so far as necessary to protect citizens against the social evils of Want, Disease, Ignorance, Squalor and Idleness, as it is used to protect them against robbery and violence at home and against attack from abroad.

3. The power of the State should not be used except for purposes which cannot be accomplished without it. That is to say, liberties outside

the list of essential liberties can and should be allowed to continue, so long as they are exercised responsibly and in such a way as not to hurt others.

All liberties are not equally important. The error of the individualists is to treat them as if they were. The essence of Liberalism is to distinguish between essential liberties to be preserved at all costs and lesser liberties which should be preserved only so far as they are consistent with social justice and social progress.

The error of the individualists can be illustrated by a passage in a recent book – the *Road to Serfdom*, by Professor Hayek. This passage is the opening of Chapter V on page 42. The chapter is headed by a quotation from Adam Smith, saying that for any Government to interfere with individuals in the application of the capitals would be presumptuous and tyrannous. Professor Hayek then proceeds as follows:

'The various kinds of collectivism, communism, fascism, etc., differ between themselves in the nature of the goal towards which they want to direct the efforts of society. But they all differ from liberalism and individualism in wanting to organise the whole of society and all its resources for this unitary end, and in refusing to recognise autonomous spheres in which the ends of the individual are supreme.'

The simple answer to this is that Liberal radicalism, as defined above, does recognise autonomous spheres in which the ends of the individual are supreme, but that it does not recognise among these spheres, as Professor Hayek does, the investment of capital. That is a secondary liberty, desirable in itself but only so long as its exercise does not harm others. In fact, investment of capital, as it has been practised by individuals in the past without guidance in the general interest has resulted in grave social evils.

(1) The allowing of business men before the war to place their factories just where they thought best for themselves has led to the endless harmful growth of great cities, with congestion, squalor, a cramped home for the housewife, and interminable journeys for the worker. Between 1932 and 1936 five-sixths of the new factories built in Britain were placed in the London area, that is to say, the area of greatest congestion and strategic danger. To allow business men to go on like this, means forcing squalor and unemployment on others; control of business men in the location of their factories is the alternative to direction of labour and creation of depressed areas.

(2) To allow business men freely to order factories, machines, raw materials when they want and not when they do not want, has meant in the past, and will continue to mean in the future, perpetual fluctuation in the demand for labour ... To stabilise the process of investment, by interfering so far as necessary with business men, is the only alternative to destroying human beings in unemployment and subjecting them to the

misery of a dole, with or without means test. Only by sacrificing some of the less important liberties of the past can we preserve the essential liberties and increase their effective enjoyment by all.

Those who talk most of liberties have seldom taken the trouble to define these liberties. If they did, their case would fall to the ground in ridicule. Professor Hayek's argument, at this point, leads to one or other of two conclusions, each of which is ridiculous. Either he must assert that the liberty of a business man to place his factory where he likes or to order machinery just when he likes is as essential as any of the intimate personal liberties (which it obviously is not). Or he must assert that though liberty of investment may not be essential in itself, it is impossible to interfere with it without going on to interfere with essential liberties. That is like saying that no one can walk one mile without going on to walk a hundred miles.*

Let us get back to common sense. To interfere with the quite unimportant freedom of a few business men in the location of factories or the ordering of investment is the way to preserve the essentials of healthy, self-respecting life for thousands of others. We cannot end the social evils and injustices which have marred Britain in the past unless we are prepared to substitute a planned economy guided by social purpose for an unplanned market economy driven hither and thither by pursuit of individual interests. But planning must be planning for freedom. Planning can and should increase freedom, not diminish it. We increase liberty by use of the organised power of the community to stop crime by establishing the rule of law. We can increase enjoyment of liberty no less certainly by using the organised power of the community to put an end to Want, Disease, Squalor, Ignorance and mass-unemployment.

We can and should use the organised power of the community to increase the rights of individuals. Take one example: by having compulsory social insurance with benefits adequate for a subsistence, we can assure to all men the right to adequate care in youth, and to an honoured old age without dependence on the young, without charity, without subjection to a means test.

Take another example – of full employment. The liberal radical doctrine is that the State exists for the individual. Therefore, 'a State which fails in respect of many millions of individuals to ensure them any opportunity of service and earning in accordance to their powers or the

---

* Professor Hayek's book contains, of course, many arguments more valid than the one that is criticised here. It includes a useful criticism of totalitarianism, and a recognition of the need for some social measures to deal with social evils. But, in so far as it lends support to the view that 'liberty is indivisible', and that you cannot interfere anywhere without interfering everywhere, it gives support to anarchy and privilege. As was pointed out by John Stuart Mill in his classic work *On Liberty* more than eighty years ago: 'All that makes existence valuable to any one depends on the enforcement of restraints upon the actions of other people.'

possibility of a life free from the indignities and inquisitions of relief is a State which has failed in a primary duty. Acceptance by the State of responsibility for full employment is the final necessary demonstration that the State exists for the citizens – for all the citizens – and not for itself or for a privileged class.'

In pursuance of full employment, the State may and should do anything necessary for that end, except interfere with essential liberties. But it should not do anything that is not yet proved to be necessary for that purpose, such as suppression of private enterprise in industry or of the practice of collective bargaining. These liberties – though not essential – should be left, to be exercised responsibly, so long as they do not block the way to full employment.

We cannot overcome social evils without an extension of the responsibilities of the State. That is a prospect which alarms some people. But it is defeatist for a democracy as experienced as ours to be afraid of the State.

[Source: Sir William Beveridge, *Why I am a Liberal*, London 1945, pp. 16–20, 26–7, 31–8.]

Doc. 118. THOMAS MANN: The Problem of Freedom

The just and reasonable emphasis on the individual and the social elements in the human make-up [*im Menschlichen*], the limiting of political and social factors to their natural proportions in humanity and life – this is freedom. To make politics absolute, its dictatorship total over everything human, this is the death of freedom, as destructive in our view as is anarchy. In their will to do this Fascism and Bolshevism find a common denominator. The essential contrast between Bolshevism and what we call social democracy, *a conscientious liberty*, cannot be stressed clearly enough today ... A militant democracy is required today that gives up doubting itself, that knows what it wants, namely victory; that is, the victory of civilisation over barbarism, which is not being paid for too dearly by the sacrifice of the luxury of humanitarianism, namely, of a tolerance that is extended to everything, including the determination to put a stop to all humanitarianism. A humanitarian attitude must never reach this excess of tolerance. It must do so least in times of emergency and struggle like our own. If I say that the freedom concept of democracy must not grant free speech and action to the deadly enemies of democracy, you will then denounce me and say that this is the self-surrender of liberty. No, I reply, it is its self-preservation.

The fact that one can have different opinions on this shows that liberty has become a subject of controversy, a problem, or rather it has become evident that it has always been one. The crisis of democracy is in truth

717

the crisis of freedom; and the rescue of democracy from a hostile onslaught threatening it today is only possible through a solution of the problem of freedom which does justice to life. Anyone who speaks of conditions which freedom should impose on itself for its own sake, who speaks of voluntary self-restrictions, of a social self-discipline of freedom, must be prepared to be accused of its betrayal and of that of democracy. And yet I believe, it is not the most valuable and unselfish supporters of freedom who raise this reproach most quickly and most loudly.

The solution of the freedom problem is made more difficult as there exists a threefold relationship with freedom. It has genuine enemies – we can manage them. It has genuine friends, to which all of us would like to belong. But between them it has also *false friends*, because consciously or unconsciously they confuse its life with interest, *their* interest in it, and they proclaim that democracy is in danger as soon as one advises freedom to put itself under a wholesome discipline.

To say that the two, liberalism and liberty are identical, that the one falls with the other, is a deception of fascism, one among many, but one of the most evil of them. We do not want to succumb to it. Liberalism in the intellectual and economic spheres is the content of an epoch; it is a *Zeitgeist* (spirit of the age) and epochs change. But freedom is an immortal idea, which does not age and perish with the *Zeitgeist*, and he is not its true friend who claims that freedom is perishing with its liberal forms. One does not help it, one does harm to it and one is, consciously or unconsciously, about to play the game of its enemies, if one, apparently in its name, resists the recognition that today stricter and more socially binding forms are suited to it than they were in the days of our fathers and grandfathers when its slogan was '*Laissez faire, laissez aller*'. We have attempted to realise what democracy is: it is the human balance between logical contrast, the reconciliation of liberty and equality, of the values of the individual with the claims of society.

This balance is never completed and finally achieved. It remains a humanitarian task to be solved again and again. We feel that today in the combination of liberty and equality the chief emphasis has moved to the side of equality, to economic justice. Today *social democracy* is the order of the day. Only in this intellectual form and shape as a liberty matured in the social sphere, which, particularly by its friendly concessions to equality, saves individual values, and as justice in the economic sphere that ties all its children more firmly to itself, will democracy be able to resist the onslaught of a dehumanising spirit of violence and to fulfil its great conservative task, i.e. to be the safeguard of the Christian fundaments of life in the West, of civilisation itself against barbarism.

[Source: Thomas Mann, 'Das Problem der Freiheit', address delivered at the 17th International Pen Congress at Stockholm in September 1939. Reprinted in Thomas Mann, *Gesammelte Werke*, vol. XI, Frankfurt 1960, pp. 964–71. Translated by the editors of this volume.]

Doc. 119. THOMAS MANN: The Social Renewal of Democracy

I called democracy timelessly human and fascism, its opponent, which today is so triumphantly asserting itself, a transitory manifestation. In doing so I am not forgetting that fascism also has deep and perhaps indestructible roots in human nature; for its essence is force. It is in physical and mental oppression that fascism believes; this is what it practises, loves, honours, and glorifies. Oppression is not the ultimate goal but the first principle of fascism, and we know only too well that force as a principle is just as eternally human as its opposite, the idea of justice ...

For it is a singular thing, this human nature, and distinguished from the rest of nature by the very fact that it has been endowed with the idea, is dominated by the idea, and cannot exist without it, since human nature is what it is because of the idea. The idea is a specific and essential attribute of man, that which makes him human. It is within him a real and natural fact, so impossible of neglect that those who do not respect human nature's participation in the idea – as force certainly does not – commit the clumsiest and, in the long run, the most disastrous mistakes. But the word 'justice' is only one name for the idea – only one; there are other names which can be substituted that are equally strong, by no means lacking in vitality; on the contrary, even rather terrifying – for example, freedom and truth. It is impossible to decide which one should take precedence, which is the greatest. Each one expresses the idea in its totality, and one stands for the others. If we say *truth*, we also say *freedom* and *justice*; if we speak of freedom and justice,we mean truth. It is a complex of an indivisible kind, freighted with spiritually and elementary dynamic force. We call it the absolute. To man has been given the absolute – be it a curse or a blessing, it is a fact. He is pledged to it, his inner being is conditioned by it, and in the human sphere a force which is opposed to truth, hostile to freedom, and lacking in justice, acts in so low and contemptible a manner because it is devoid of feeling and understanding for the relationship between man and the absolute and without comprehension of the inviolable human dignity which grows out of this relationship ...

We must define democracy as that form of government and society which is inspired above every other with the feeling and consciousness of the dignity of man ...

This dignity which the mysterious confers upon man, democracy recognises and honours; democracy's understanding and respect for this quality, it calls 'humanity' ... For all men of violence, tyrants, those who seek to stupefy and stultify the masses, and all those who are intent upon turning a nation into an unthinking war-machine in order to control free and thinking citizens – these necessarily despise humanity ...

Democracy, whatever may be its conception of humanity, has only the best of intentions towards it. Democracy wishes to elevate mankind, to teach it to think, to set it free. It seeks to remove from culture that stamp of privilege and disseminate it among the people – in a word, it aims at education. Education is an optimistic and humane concept; and respect for humanity is inseparable from it. Hostile to mankind and contemptuous of it is the opposing concept called propaganda, which tries to stultify, stupefy, level, or regiment men for the purpose of military efficiency and, above all, to keep the dictatorial system in power. I do not wish to imply that propaganda could not be used in the sense of education – that is, in the democratic sense. It may be that all over the world and even in this country [USA] democracy has heretofore made too little use of it in its own educational sense. But certainly in the hands of the dictators propaganda is an instrument of cynical contempt for humanity . . .

Let me try to state simply what is needed. A reform of freedom is necessary which will make of it something very different from the freedom that existed and could exist in the times of our fathers and grandfathers, the epoch of bourgeois liberalism. Now we need something different from '*laissez faire, laissez aller,*' for freedom cannot survive on such a basis. It is no longer adequate. The reform I have in mind must be a social reform, a reform in the social sense. Only in this way can democracy take the wind out of the sails of fascism and also of bolshevism and overcome the merely temporary and deceptive advantages which the charm of novelty gives the dictatorships. Moreover, this social reform must aim at spiritual as well as economic freedom. In both directions the times of Manchesterism and of passive liberalism are gone forever. Freedom has been driven out of liberalism – driven out by the deepest anguish. But liberalism has learned its lesson. Humanity will no longer mean a tolerance that endures everything – even the determination to destroy humanity. Face to face with fanaticism incarnate, a freedom which through sheer goodness and human sceptism no longer believes in itself will be irrevocably lost. It is not the sort of humanity which is weak and patient to the point of self-doubt that freedom needs today. Such an attitude makes freedom look pathetic and contemptible in the face of a power-concept which is not in the least sicklied o'er with the pale cast of thought. What is needed is a humanity strong in will and firm in the determination to preserve itself. Freedom must discover its virility. It must learn to walk in armour and to defend itself against its deadly enemies. And after the most bitter experiences, it must finally understand that a pacifism which admits it will not wage war under any circumstances will surely bring about war instead of banishing it . . .

If democracy wishes to make its undoubted moral superiority over fascism effective and challenge its pseudo-socialism, it must adopt in the economic as well as the spiritual domain as much of socialistic morality as the times make imperative and indispensable. Here, likewise, freedom must be restored through social discipline. Democracy must continue to develop the bourgeois revolution not only politically, but also economically. For justice is the dominant idea of this epoch, and its realisation, as far as is humanly possible, has become a matter of world conscience, from which there is no escape and which can no longer be neglected ... Everybody who would consider it a great human disaster, if, in this historical struggle of the world philosophies, democracy should succumb for lack of adaptability, must desire as one desires a necessity that liberal democracy will develop into social democracy, from the economic as well as the spiritual point of view.

Is this demand alarming because it sounds revolutionary? Its revolutionary nature must be taken in a relative sense. In reality its implications are conservative, for it aims to preserve our Occidental cultural traditions, to defend them against barbarism and political outrage of every sort ...

The social renewal of democracy is the presupposition and the guarantee of its victory. This renewal will create a national unity which will prove itself far superior to the tissue of falsehoods which fascism calls by that name. In democracy this communal spirit is already a living force. For this is the aim of all political action – the community of nations – and this eventually will abolish politics itself.

[Source: Thomas Mann, *The Coming Victory of Democracy*. Lecture given during a tour of the USA, February – May 1938. Translated from the German by Agnes E. Meyer, London 1938, pp. 16–19, 22, 26–7, 30–1, 70–5, 78.]

Doc. 120. KARL MANNHEIM: The Discipline of Freedom

I. Freedom and discipline in group organization
There is neither freedom nor discipline in the abstract, but only in concrete forms that depend on the cultural context. Among the determining factors we intend to deal with are the impact of group organization and aims.

C. H. Cooley, in comparing the structure of the play group and the Army, made some suggestive remarks.* These social organizations demonstrate that freedom and discipline are functions of group organization and have no meaning apart from it. Robinson Crusoe was not free, as there was no social discipline or organization that could shape his freedom. Nature poses obstacles, but no one would be called unfree because illness hampered his activities. The football team and the Army not only pursue different aims, but they differ in organizational means. As the movements of the ball can hardly be foreseen and the variety of

* C. H. Cooley, *Social Organization*, New York 1929.

situations is considerable, the organization of a football team must be extremely flexible. A great many choices and decisions have to be left to individual players. More important than the few rules of the game is the unwritten law of team spirit which forbids the individual to dominate at the expense of the team.

Army organization, on the other hand, requires the main decisions to be made at the top; therefore real choices and decisions are beyond the scope of the lower ranks; their choices derive from systematic delegation of initiative, responsibility, and freedom. If freedom means the power of making over-all decisions and choices, there is little scope for it in the lower echelons of the Army. Still on every level down to the individual soldier in the platoon relevant decisions have to be made from time to time. Thus every private has certain freedom compatible with army organization, or, more precisely, with a given type of army organization.

Similar considerations apply, of course, to discipline, the reverse of freedom. Discipline means to establish social restrictions on initiative and choices for the sake of organizational routines. Just as the football team allows for greater individual initiative, its discipline evolves only during the game by constant redefining of rules. In contrast army discipline is rigid, most of its conduct patterns are preconceived, standardized, and thoroughly inculcated, enabling army personnel to operate predictably under long chains of commands. Similar is the discipline of a centralized bureaucracy, and it might be said that the Army is a bureaucratized fighting unit.

The Army and the football team may be seen as two extreme types in a series of social organizations. The most rigid organization would seek to extend the army pattern to all spheres of life, whereas the most elastic organization might conceive of society and its subgroups more or less as a team. Needless to say, the Third Way will try to combine the two techniques by allowing for rigid organization where efficiency demands it, and by pleading for the flexible pattern wherever feasible. Progress toward freedom consists in a steady advance toward flexibility.

II. Contemporary concepts of freedom

This measuring rod can help us to place the different concepts of freedom in present-day discussion. Disagreement springs mainly from different and unclarified meanings of the same word. As in our discussion of power, the prevailing currents of thought can best be classified under the headings 'anarchist,' 'totalitarian,' 'liberal,' and 'plutocratic.'

1. *The anarchist view* holds that there is something in human nature, a kind of self-regulating power, which, if allowed complete freedom, will lead to spontaneous self-discipline. One of the basic convictions of this school of thought is that the more we use repressive devices for enforcing discipline, the more we foster what is called 'negativism' in the individual. We pay for repression by blocking human spontaneity and

722

readiness to co-operate under good working self-restraint. Anarchists are not simply individualists against any and all forms of discipline, but they believe 'real freedom' to result from spontaneous submission to the rules of group life. Statements like 'Der Gegenpol von Zwang ist nicht Freiheit sondern Verbundenheit' ('The opposite to coercion is not freedom, but fellowship') and 'Certain forms of freedom can only be realized in group life' may serve to make the point.

The anarchist idea of freedom contains a great deal of truth but lacks sociological qualification. Certainly, such self-regulating powers exist, but only in small groups. The larger an organization becomes, the less one can expect or wait for the self-imposed discipline of the whole to emerge out of a lengthy process of minor adjustments. The Greeks realized this and established new social units when the old ones reached the prescribed limits. Today this is impracticable, for modern economic and social techniques are efficiently geared to large-scale operations.

The anarchist idea suggests, however, to the Third Way – the mobilization of self-regulating powers of small groups wherever possible. Vital social interaction is generated primarily in small groups; real understanding of life, new ideas, originate in them; when they lose vital energy, society is apt to become anemic.

2. *The totalitarian approach to discipline and freedom* realizes that the idea of a spontaneously emerging discipline is inapplicable in a large-scale society. Accordingly, a discipline of command and obedience is hailed under the *Führer* principle, which represents a universal scheme of strictly militarized central organization. The Army and bureaucracy serve as models. Two factors foster this spirit of over-organization. On the one hand, herdlike masses, which have never known or cherished real civic freedom, accept the dictatorial structure readily after a panic that makes them crave order. On the other hand, minorities, skilled in mass management, may grow power-drunk in expanding their military organizations. They no longer offer freedom, but tyranny and mass regimentation, drilling the community by shouted slogans: 'Leader, command – we follow.'

3. *The liberal view of freedom and discipline* is in many ways the rash application of the anarchist idea of emerging freedom and spontaneous self-discipline to mass society. It also presupposes that out of individual freedom of choice will result mysterious harmony by self-regulating powers of society. What the anarchists observe only in small groups, the liberals apply to an ever-growing society. There was some reason in their expectations under a prevailing handicraft and peasant economy before the days of big enterprise and organized pressure groups. Liberalism worked fairly well in the former setting, but has lost its validity and applicability under modern conditions. By insisting on their idea of freedom and discipline in disregard of the changed social structure, the liberals deliberately block the invention of adequate controls. To them,

any freedom differing from their own will seem to be the opposite of freedom.

4. *The plutocratic concept of freedom and discipline* emerges at a stage in society when a limited class of wealthy people apply the liberal ideology in disregard of social change. The plutocratic concept of freedom and discipline upholds basically the investor's right to invest and speculate freely, and the owner's right to use his property without restraints. Whenever these freedoms are endangered, the plutocrats bewail the loss of all freedom, complaining of regimentation and bureaucracy. This narrow idea of freedom overlooks the fact that private property, free enterprise, competition, occupational and consumer choice have new meaning in an age of corporate big business. As Tawney rightly has pointed out, freedom of property originally meant ensuring the legitimate use of his tools to the craftsman or farmer in a society antedating large-scale industrial techniques. Needless to say, 'free' private investment and enterprise even if intrinsically desirable, would mean freedom only for the few.

The liberals likewise disregard the number of those who can actually use certain freedoms. They emphasize freedom in the political sphere, freedom of expression, freedom of occupation and consumer choice – all freedoms that primarily concern educated people in fairly secure positions. These freedoms mean less on lower economic levels, and are frequently not available to low-income groups. Money, being the one indispensable means for acquiring goods and skills, limits freedom of choice for many who legally and politically enjoy these nominal choices. Consumer and occupational free choice are illusory for men who cannot afford to buy certain goods or acquire the prerequisite skills for higher occupations. This objection has rightly been raised by the socialists against the liberals, and applies even more in a plutocratic society with its disproportionate accumulation of wealth.

On the other hand, it is equally short-sighted to say that freedom prevails if a society produces goods and services on a sufficiently large scale and distributes them more or less fairly, but leaves the regulation of discipline and freedom in the political and cultural spheres to a bureaucratic or political elite. A society that sacrifices cultural and political freedom for greater equality of income and education demonstrates its low appreciation of the former values. The issue is not that political and cultural freedoms are less relevant than material welfare, but how to extend self-determination to all spheres of life for the full development of personality, which requires both material and cultural opportunities.

III. Freedom and discipline under democratic planning
These reflections on the social setting of the various concepts of freedom and discipline may reveal their one-sidedness and serve to combine their

desirable features in a system of democratic planning. Freedom and discipline under democratic planning will be defined by the nature of groups, sub-groups, and their purposes.

A democratically planned society will have a personal concept of freedom in social relationships, i.e. it will foster flexibility, afford maximum opportunities for choice, and favour self-expression in small groups and private relationships.

In large groups and mass organizations, the Third Way will make use of the insight and wisdom of both the syndicalist movement and certain tendencies in corporatism. These movements emphasized that in mass society the liberty of small and large corporate associations is more important than that of the individual to pursue his advantage regardless. In an age of mass action, the individual can often be protected only by his group organization.

Liberalism, by juxtaposing the individual to society or the State, disregards the significance of intermediary and functional groups. The sacred claim, 'Rights of Man,' needs to be translated into the Age of Planning. A planned Democracy has to look after the individual's right to personal development. Sociologically speaking, the man who prefers free-lancing to work in professional and other organizations should not go unprotected, but should have opportunities to follow his bent. But in an age of mass organization it is not enough to guarantee rights to individuals, it is equally important to protect the liberties of groups and associations.

The right of groups to propagate their ideas, to defend their way of life is no less sacrosanct than that of the individual. Thus, freedom and self-discipline apply also to groups. Group self-discipline demands the same self-restraint in intergroup relations as we expect in personal relations. If the State's main function is to control intergroup relations, it will have to control group egoism, which is more dangerous than individual egoism ... Attempts of groups to usurp a monopoly position must be checked; many forms of discipline and freedom derive not from life in small, self-adjusting units, but from the regulated interplay of organized groups. Such rules of intergroup life differ from primary group disciplines as the anarchist conceives of it. They affect the individual only segmentally and are experienced as 'organized' rather than 'spontaneous' relations, as you might compare behavior toward an official or toward a friend.

The State will partly guarantee existing intergroup relations and their freedoms, and partly initiate change, if existing patterns prove to be unsatisfactory. As in all other cases, such external control of group discipline by the State must, of course, be exercised in constitutional forms. The support of an existing group equilibrium and/or its gradual transformation has to be agreed upon and sanctioned by the electorate and carried out by publicly accountable officials. These examples should make clear that it is folly to accuse all manipulation from a center of being despotism. Manipulation is democratic as long as it is based upon consent and carried out in a spirit that guarantees freedom among groups, even if the planning controls concern themselves with all activities of the group. If a group is as large and powerful as in the case of economic corporations, for instance, we must control not only their external relationships, but also their internal organization, in favor of industrial democracy.

IV. Freedom of choice in an age of planning
Behind the ambiguous use of words such as 'freedom' and 'discipline' and the failure to relate them to different societies, a fundamental transformation is silently in the making. This has not yet been recognized and clarified sufficiently.

One of the striking changes in modern society is the increase in the number of deliberate choices. The chief reason for this is that, in the past, natural scarcity and poverty automatically limited opportunities for choice; these now increase automatically with the increasing capacity to produce. Another factor, which works in the same direction, is the rising volume and efficiency of means of communication, distribution, and of advertising, which spreads knowledge about desirable things far and wide. A third factor formerly restricting choice resulted from habits and customs of self-restraint. These often prevented wishes and desires from coming to the fore, whereas they are now allowed much wider scope. Fourth, even where wealth was present and luxury goods existed, the tacit or open exclusion of certain social classes from their use reduced the number of relevant choices in society.

This striking change has come about because the choice-restricting factors have largely been reduced to price–income relationships. Therefore the generally raised level of aspirations and wants fosters intense and widespread desire to rise in the social scale. If not accompanied by a general rise in mass income, the new aspiration must result in a resentful yearning to equalize wealth and income opportunities. An unplanned, unlimited expansion of aspirations, continuously outdistancing available means, readily produces dissatisfaction in the midst of plenty. We must realize that scarcity is only one source of dissatisfaction. The disparity between wants and their possible satisfaction is no less powerful a source. Formerly people accepted the impersonal mechanism of supply, prices, and income differentials that ruled the distribution of purchasing power as natural processes, not amenable to conscious regulation. Now we realize that the creation of such equilibrium lies more or less in our own hands. New methods of distributing goods at differential prices – cheap milk for school children, reduced movie tickets for the unemployed or for soldiers, reduced railroad fares, and so on – or the wartime experience of combining price controls with rationing in order to give low-income groups a better diet for efficiency's sake, have raised the problems of free consumers' choices and of planned intervention in the price mechanism to a new level of social awareness.

In a planned society the freedom of the individual will operate on two planes: The individual will still have maximum opportunities for free choice compatible with the organization of society; but he will also have to decide whether by planning and central co-ordination consumers' choices should be stimulated and in which direction. Whereas formerly profit-motivated advertising, price policies, and income distribution determined what should be consumed in what quantities by whom, central planning allows for the guidance of consumers' choices under dietary and social welfare considerations by means of price privileges, consumer credit, subsidized consumption, low-cost public housing, educational campaigns and – if need be – rationing and price controls. The yardstick for freedom and discipline cannot be the freedom of the well-to-do to monopolize high-priced goods, but the common good.

We are at the beginning of a process in which a dualism of attitudes that formerly occurred only occasionally will become permanent. Owing to this dualism, the individual in one context is compelled to follow his self-interest, and in another he will curb his egoism by institutions in the interest of the community. He will, e.g. accept heavy taxation if he feels it necessary for the maintenance of Society, yet make every legitimate effort to keep his own contribution as low as possible. Egotistic and communal attitudes formerly fluctuated; there was a kind of confusion, the situations alternatively provoking self-assertive and altruistic reactions. Now, such a dualism is built into the structure of the Self. In a planned society a citizen can only behave adequately if he clearly distinguishes between the field where planning – and, therefore, collective discipline and collective freedom – must prevail, and the other areas in which self-centered reactions are evoked by the circumstances.

With these formulae in mind, we can see that many of the old demands for freedom cannot be realized in the old way in the new planned society. In an unplanned society freedom of occupational choice was largely theoretical for those without money, educational opportunities, and information. Many young people chose a job because it was the only one within their reach. People still believed in freedom of occupational choice, because the limitations seemed to be caused by unseen natural forces and were not recognized as by-products of the social order, which was accorded tacit support.

If a man living in a planned society were sent back to such conditions of freedom, he would feel unhappy and restricted to an intolerable degree: unhappy if he should realize that in an unplanned society his occupational choice might be determined primarily by chance factors; that many young people may find themselves in blind-alley jobs, and that in a world of free competition it may take years to find a satisfactory place in society. As compared with this old unregulated freedom, he may praise his new type of freedom, which, in spite of the increase of bureaucracy and, if necessary, of State guidance, leads him to a job required by society that, fitting into the pattern of future development, is promising and no blind alley. He can find his job by consulting agencies for occupational guidance, which may co-operate with the schools; by turning to the respective services of vocational associations and public agencies devoted to the management of the labor market. Provided these agencies pay sufficient attention to his specific aptitudes and preferences, their broad scope of operation and central co-ordination of information may offer the individual actually wider and sounder occupational choices and career opportunities than he could find on his own. Disparities between planning goals, available opportunities, and possibly irrational vocational aspirations — as often found today under the influence of mass fiction and screen images of heroes — could be reduced, if not gradually eliminated, by educational effort. Although writers on social and political affairs make highly individualized choices, most people, however, have no strictly formulated occupational preferences to begin with and thus may be amenable to and even grateful for expert advice and tactful suggestions shifting them from less promising to more promising occupational pursuits in line with economic plans and predictable developments. Furthermore, labor turnover in the Soviet Union as well as in the United States shows that millions of modern men acquire with relative ease the ability to adjust to a great variety of occupational demands. By placing special premiums, pecuniary and/or honorific, upon possibly less desirable pursuits one can attract the required number of job applicants.

Thus, freedom in a planned society should not be judged in terms of the absence or presence of bureaucracy and regulation, but in terms of the common good and the best use of individual potentialities. Intelligence tests, interviews, expert observation of physical and mental development and dispositions, and expert guidance of vocational choices in agreement with planned and predictable developments — and at the same time provision of unplanned sectors which give scope to people of specific gifts or aspirations — may serve man's quest for freedom in a planned world.

[Source: Karl Mannheim, *Freedom, Power and Democratic Planning*, London 1951 (3rd impression 1968) Ch. 12, pp. 275–84.]

Doc. 121. F. A. HAYEK: The Great Utopia

That socialism has displaced liberalism as the doctrine held by the great majority of progressives does not simply mean that people had forgotten the warnings of the great liberal thinkers of the past about the consequences of collectivism. It has happened because they were persuaded of the very opposite of what these men had predicted. The extraordinary thing is that the same socialism that was not only early recognised as the gravest threat to freedom, but quite openly began as a reaction against the liberalism of the French Revolution, gained general acceptance under the flag of liberty. It is rarely remembered now that socialism in its beginnings was frankly authoritarian. The French writers who laid the foundations of modern socialism had no doubt that their ideas could be put into practice only by a strong dictatorial government. To them socialism meant an attempt to 'terminate the revolution' by a deliberate reorganisation of society on hierarchical lines, and the imposition of a coercive 'spiritual power'. Where freedom was concerned, the founders of socialism made no bones about their intentions. Freedom of thought they regarded as the root-evil of nineteenth-century society, and the first of modern planners, Saint-Simon, even predicted that those who did not obey his proposed planning boards would be 'treated as cattle'.

Only under the influence of the strong democratic currents preceding the revolution of 1848 did socialism begin to ally itself with the forces of freedom. But it took the new 'democratic socialism' a long time to live down the suspicions aroused by its antecedents. Nobody saw more clearly than de Tocqueville that democracy as an essentially individualist institution stood in an irreconcilable conflict with Socialism:

'Democracy extends the sphere of individual freedom [he said in 1848], socialism restricts it. Democracy attaches all possible value to each man; socialism makes each man a mere agent, a mere number. Democracy and socialism have nothing in common but one word: equality. But notice the difference: while democracy seeks equality in liberty, socialism seeks equality in restraint and servitude.'*

To allay these suspicions and to harness to its cart the strongest of all political motives, the craving for freedom, socialism began increasingly to make use of the promise of a 'new freedom'. The coming of socialism was to be the leap from the realm of necessity to the realm of freedom. It was to bring 'economic freedom', without which the political freedom already gained was 'not worth having'. Only socialism was capable of effecting the consummation of the agelong struggle for freedom in which the attainment of political freedom was but a first step.

The subtle change in meaning to which the word freedom was subjected in order that this argument should sound plausible is important. To the great apostles of political freedom the word had meant freedom from coercion, freedom from the arbitrary power of other men, release from the ties which left the individual no choice but obedience to the orders of a superior to whom he was attached. The new freedom promised,

---

* Discours prononcé à l'assemblée constituante le 12 Septembre 1848 sur la question de droit au travail. *Oeuvres complètes d'Alexis de Tocqueville*, vol. IX, 1866, p. 546.

however, was to be freedom from necessity, release from the compulsion of the circumstances which inevitably limit the range of choice of all of us, although for some very much more than for others. Before man could be truly free, the 'despotism of physical want' had to be broken, the 'restraints of the economic system' relaxed.

Freedom in this sense is, of course, merely another name for power* or wealth. Yet, although the promises of this new freedom were often coupled with irresponsible promises of a great increase in material wealth in a socialist society, it was not from such an absolute conquest of the niggardliness of nature that economic freedom was expected. What the promise really amounted to was that the great existing disparities in the range of choice of different people were to disappear. The demand for the new freedom was thus only another name for the old demand for an equal distribution of wealth. But the new name gave the socialists another word in common with the liberals and they exploited it to the full. And although the word was used in a different sense by the two groups, few people noticed this and still fewer asked themselves whether the two kinds of freedom promised really could be combined.

There can be no doubt that the promise of greater freedom has become one of the most effective weapons of socialist propaganda and that the belief that socialism would bring freedom is genuine and sincere. But this would only heighten the tragedy if it should prove that what was promised to us as the Road to Freedom was in fact the High Road to Servitude. Unquestionably the promise of more freedom was responsible for luring more and more liberals along the socialist road, for blinding them to the conflict which exists between the basic principles of socialism and liberalism, and for often enabling socialists to usurp the very name of the old party of freedom. Socialism was embraced by the greater part of the intelligentsia as the apparent heir of the liberal tradition: therefore it is not surprising that to them the idea should appear inconceivable of socialism leading to the opposite of liberty.

In recent years, however, the old apprehensions of the unforeseen consequences of socialism have once more been strongly voiced from the most unexpected quarters. Observer after observer, in spite of the contrary expectation with which he approached his subject, has been im-

---

* The characteristic confusion of freedom with power, which we shall meet again and again throughout this discussion, is too big a subject to be thoroughly examined here. As old as socialism itself, it is so closely allied with it that almost seventy years ago a French scholar, discussing its Saint-Simonian origins, was led to say that this theory of liberty 'est à elle seule tout le socialisme' (P. Janet, *Saint-Simon et le Saint-Simonisme*, 1878, p. 26, note). The most explicit defender of this confusion is, significantly, the leading philosopher of American left-wingism, John Dewey, according to whom 'liberty is the effective power to do specific things' so that 'the demand for liberty is demand for power' ('Liberty and Social Control', *The Social Frontier*, November 1935, p. 41).

pressed with the extraordinary similarity in many respects of the conditions under 'fascism' and 'communism'. While 'progressives' in this country and elsewhere were still deluding themselves that communism and fascism represented opposite poles, more and more people began to ask themselves whether these new tyrannies were not the outcome of the same tendencies. Even communists must have been somewhat shaken by such testimonies as that of Mr Max Eastman, Lenin's old friend, who found himself compelled to admit that 'instead of being better, Stalinism is worse than fascism, more ruthless, barbarous, unjust, immoral, antidemocratic, unredeemed by any hope or scruple', and that it is 'better described as superfascist'; and when we find the same author recognising that 'Stalinism *is* socialism, in the sense of being an inevitable although unforeseen political accompaniment of the nationalisation and collectivisation which he had relied upon as part of his plan for erecting a classless society',* his conclusion clearly achieves wider significance.

Mr Eastman's case is perhaps the most remarkable, yet he is by no means the first or the only sympathetic observer of the Russian experiment to form similar conclusions. Some years earlier Mr W. H. Chamberlin, who in twelve years in Russia as an American correspondent had seen all his ideals shattered, summed up the conclusions of his studies there and in Germany and Italy in the statement that 'Socialism is certain to prove, in the beginning at least, the road NOT to freedom, but to dictatorship and counter-dictatorships, to civil war of the fiercest kind. Socialism achieved and maintained by democratic means seems definitely to belong to the world of utopias'** Similarly a British writer, Mr F. A. Voigt, after many years of close observation of developments in Europe as a foreign correspondent, concludes that 'Marxism has led to Fascism and National-Socialism, because, in all essentials, it is Fascism and National Socialism.' † And Dr Walter Lippmann has arrived at the conviction that

'the generation to which we belong is now learning from experience what happens when men retreat from freedom to a coercive organisation of their affairs. Though they promise themselves a more abundant life, they must in practice renounce it; as the organised direction increases, the variety of ends must give way to uniformity. That is the nemesis of the planned society and the authoritarian principle in human affairs' ‡

Many more similar statements from people in a position to judge might be selected from publications of recent years, particularly from those by men who as citizens of the now totalitarian countries have lived

* Max Eastman, *Stalin's Russia and the Crisis of Socialism*, 1940, p. 82.
** W. H. Chamberlin, *A False Utopia*, 1937, pp. 202–3.
† F. A. Voigt, *Unto Caesar*, 1939, p. 95.
‡ *Atlantic Monthly*, November 1936, p. 552.

through the transformation and have been forced by their experience to revise many cherished beliefs. We shall quote as one more example a German writer who expresses the same conclusion perhaps more justly than those already quoted.

'The complete collapse of the belief in the attainability of freedom and equality through Marxism [writes Mr Peter Drucker]* has forced Russia to travel the same road towards a totalitarian, purely negative, non-economic society of unfreedom and inequality which Germany has been following. Not that communism and fascism are essentially the same. Fascism is the stage reached after communism has proved an illusion, and it has proved as much an illusion in Stalinist Russia as in pre-Hitler Germany.'

No less significant is the intellectual history of many of the Nazi and Fascist leaders. Everybody who has watched the growth of these movements in Italy[†] or Germany has been struck by the number of leading men, from Mussolini downwards (and not excluding Laval and Quisling), who began as socialists and ended as Fascists or Nazis. And what is true of the leaders is even more true of the rank and file of the movement. The relative ease with which a young communist could be converted into a Nazi or *vice versa* was generally known in Germany, best of all to the propagandists of the two parties. Many a University teacher in this country during the 1930s has seen English and American students return from the Continent, uncertain whether they were communists or Nazis and certain only that they hated Western liberal civilisation.

It is true, of course, that in Germany before 1933 and in Italy before 1922 communists and Nazis or Fascists clashed more frequently with each other than with other parties. They competed for the support of the same type of mind and reserved for each other the hatred of the heretic. But their practice showed how closely they are related. To both, the real enemy, the man with whom they had nothing in common and whom they could not hope to convince, is the liberal of the old type. While to the Nazi the communist, and to the communist the Nazi, and to both the socialist, are potential recruits who are made of the right timber, although they have listened to false prophets, they both know that there can be no compromise between them and those who really believe in individual freedom.

Lest this be doubted by people misled by official propaganda from either side, let me quote one more statement from an authority that ought not to be suspect. In an article under the significant title of 'The Rediscovery of Liberalism', Professor Eduard Heimann, one of the leaders of German religious socialism, writes:

* *The End of Economic Man*, 1939, p. 230.
† An illuminating account of the intellectual history of many of the Fascist leaders will be found in R. Michels (himself an ex-Marxist Fascist), *Sozialismus und Faszismus*, Munich 1925, vol. II, pp. 264–6 and 311–12.

'Hitlerism proclaims itself as both true democracy and true socialism, and the terrible truth is that there is a grain of truth for such claims – an infinitesimal grain, to be sure, but at any rate enough to serve as a basis for such fantastic distortions. Hitlerism even goes so far as to claim the rôle of protector of Christianity, and the terrible truth is that even this gross misinterpretation is able to make some impression. But one fact stands out with perfect clarity in all the fog: Hitler has never claimed to represent true liberalism. Liberalism then has the distinction of being the doctrine most hated by Hitler.*'

It should be added that this hatred had little occasion to show itself in practice merely because, by the time Hitler came to power, liberalism was to all intents and purposes dead in Germany. And it was socialism that had killed it.

While to many who have watched the transition from socialism to fascism at close quarters the connection between the two systems has become increasingly obvious, in this country the majority of people still believe that socialism and freedom can be combined. There can be no doubt that most socialists here still believe profoundly in the liberal ideal of freedom, and that they would recoil if they became convinced that the realisation of their programme would mean the destruction of freedom. So little is the problem yet seen, so easily do the most irreconcilable ideals still live together, that we can still hear such contradictions in terms as 'individualist socialism' seriously discussed. If this is the state of mind which makes us drift into a new world, nothing can be more urgent than that we should seriously examine the real significance of the evolution that has taken place elsewhere. Although our conclusions will only confirm the apprehensions which others have already expressed, the reasons why this development cannot be regarded as accidental will not appear without a rather full examination of the main aspects of this transformation of social life. That democratic socialism, the great utopia of the last few generations, is not only unachievable, but that to strive for it produces something so utterly different that few of those who now wish it would be prepared to accept the consequences, many will not believe till the connection has been laid bare in all its aspects . . .

Conclusion

The purpose of this book has not been to sketch a detailed programme of a desirable future order of society. If with regard to international affairs we have gone a little beyond its essentially critical task, it was because in this field we may soon be called upon to create a framework within which

* *Social Research* (New York), vol. VIII, no. 4, November 1941. It deserves to be recalled in this connection that, whatever may have been his reasons, Hitler thought it expedient to declare in one of his public speeches as late as February 1941 that 'basically National Socialism and Marxism are the same' (cf. *The Bulletin of International News* published by the Royal Institute of International Affairs, vol. XVIII, no. 5, p. 269).

E. Epilogue: Liberalism challenged, revised, maintained

future growth may have to proceed for a long time to come. A great deal will depend on how we use the opportunity we shall then have. But whatever we do, it can only be the beginning of a new, long, and arduous process in which we all hope we shall gradually create a world very different from that which we knew during the last quarter of a century. It is at least doubtful whether at this stage a detailed blueprint of a desirable internal order of society would be of much use – or whether anyone is competent to furnish it. The important thing now is that we shall come to agree on certain principles and free ourselves from some of the errors which have governed us in the recent past. However distasteful such an admission may be, we must recognise that we had before this war once again reached a stage where it is more important to clear away the obstacles with which human folly has encumbered our path and to release the creative energy of individuals than to devise further machinery for 'guiding' and 'directing' them – to create conditions favourable to progress rather than to 'plan progress'. The first need is to free ourselves of that worst form of contemporary obscurantism which tries to persuade us that what we have done in the recent past was all either wise or inevitable. We shall not grow wiser before we learn that much that we have done was very foolish.

If we are to build a better world we must have the courage to make a new start – even if that means some *reculer pour mieux sauter*. It is not those who believe in inevitable tendencies who show this courage, not those who preach a 'New Order' which is no more than a projection of the tendencies of the last forty years, and who can think of nothing better than to imitate Hitler. It is indeed those who cry loudest for the New Order who are most completely under the sway of the ideas which have created this war and most of the evils from which we suffer. The young are right if they have little confidence in the ideas which rule most of their elders. But they are mistaken or misled when they believe that these are still the liberal ideas of the nineteenth century, which in fact the younger generation hardly knows. Though we neither can wish, nor possess the power, to go back to the reality of the nineteenth century, we have the opportunity to realise its ideals – and they were not mean. We have little right to feel in this respect superior to our grandfathers; and we should never forget that it is we, the twentieth century, and not they, who have made a mess of things. If they had not yet fully learnt what was necessary to create the world they wanted, the experience we have since gained ought to have equipped us better for the task. If in the first attempt to create a world of free men we have failed, we must try again. The guiding principle, that a policy of freedom for the individual is the only truly progressive policy, remains as true to-day as it was in the nineteenth century.

[Source: F. A. Hayek, *The Road to Serfdom*, London 1944, pp. 18–23, 177–8.]

734

Doc. 122. GILBERT MURRAY: The Meaning of Freedom

Before attempting any analysis of the meaning of Liberalism as it appeals to me and the essential appeal which it makes in varying forms to different persons, I should like to consider some of the obvious external facts affecting our cause. At the beginning of this century Liberalism was the dominant political force in Europe, and not merely dominant for the time being in practical politics but steadily on the increase in most departments of life. In religion, in education, in international relations, in social ideas, Liberty seemed to be the rising tide. Now it has sunk with a crash. In history and philosophy Liberal ideas are unfashionable. Humane studies are on the downgrade. In European politics the Liberal Parties have in country after country almost been pushed out of existence and seen the establishment of despotic governments, illiberal beyond the worst dreams of my generation.

Why is this? Mainly of course it is due to our Thirty Years of War. A very large part of Liberalism consists in extending goodwill to your opponents, trusting their sincerity, leaving them free, understanding their point of view and eradicating one's own prejudices. The main effort of war – that is, the concentration of the whole power of the nation on saving itself by doing harm to other human beings – is the direct contrary of Liberality. Even the splendid idealisms of war are not exactly Liberal. And the necessity of winning the war becomes such an overwhelmingly strong motive that all other considerations give way to it. It produces the party that calls itself Nazi, Fascist or Communist according to circumstances, but is at heart the same, a party absorbed by unbridled lust of power. Liberalism has become largely a fruitless longing in the hearts of specially conscientious or thoughtful people for something lost or unattainable. Yet to most people in most countries, I think this crash of Liberalism in the world is recognised as a disaster. Not so, of course, to real revolutionaries; nor yet to those who pin their faith to some cut-and-dried system for dealing with the ever-changing stream of human affairs, as if politics were an exact science like logic. Sidney Webb once said to me that what he hoped for most was the extinction of the Liberal Party, which would leave a purely Socialist Party confronting one that was purely Conservative and upper class. The working class would no longer be led astray by sympathetic Radicals. I said that such an extinction might well lead to War; at which he smiled and said, 'A heavy price, but not too much to pay'. It was a shock to find in a man so reasonable and well-informed and disinterested this touch of fanaticism; it shows the effect of a devotion to dogma in regions where dogma is not applicable. This fanaticism, now so widespread in Europe, is both generated and fostered by war, and also is one of the causes which make it so difficult to reach an atmosphere of peace. It is perhaps the main reason why the almost universal longing for peace has not taken the form of any general

E. Epilogue: Liberalism challenged, revised, maintained

effort towards toleration and mutual understanding. Of course War is not the only cause of our trouble; there must be others.

One is fairly simple. Liberalism in practice in the nineteenth century had two chief tasks. It stood for Enlightenment as against prejudice and obscurantism, and it stood generally for the cause of the oppressed. But its essence was really Enlightenment, inner freedom, the search for truth. It stood for justice to all oppressed classes; but it was never for unconditional support of any of them. Mr Gladstone used to speak strongly on the need of making principle and not class interest the dividing line between parties. The great stream of beneficent democratic legislation which was the glory of the nineteenth century from the first Reform Bill onwards, consisted very largely in a progressive resignation of privileges by those who possessed them for the benefit of the unprivileged – Christians for Jews, Churchmen for Nonconformists, Protestants for Catholics, the well-to-do classes for the workers and so on. But it would be absurd to speak of the Liberals as a class party ...

Principle, not class interest, must be the dividing line between parties in a really healthy community. But owing to a number of strains which I will not stop to analyse, it seems clear that the dividing line of late years has shifted greatly from principle to sheer economic class interest. It tends to be poor against rich, employed against employer, even the inefficient and unsuccessful against the efficient and successful. Both sides give a general approval to Liberal principles, but when plain economic self-interest takes the field a reasoned concern for high principles seems rather a bloodless thing. A friend of mine who wished to stand as a Labour candidate for a great industrial town was told: 'We don't want your damned bourgeois idealism.'

On this issue, in general, Liberals were right though no doubt like all parties in power the old Liberal Party sometimes had blind spots.

But is there no point where we were wrong? In every political movement, indeed in every living movement, political, social or intellectual, there are sure to be two classes of principles; some that are permanently true and some that are specially called forth or over-emphasised by the needs of the time but prove no longer useful or applicable when circumstances change. The mid-nineteenth century found many nations in Europe held down and stifled by great foreign Empires; the Balkan nations by the Turks, Italy by the Austrians and so on. Consequently the Liberal watchwords were Independence, Nationality and to some extent even Rebellion. When I was a boy in Australia, our national hope for the future was simply to 'cut the painter' which bound us to Britain and stand on our own feet. Under present conditions it is clear that this emotion of Nationality needs toning down; nationalism is recognised as one of the chief dangers to the world. Co-operation is the great need, not Independence; Australian statesmen are proud of the unity of the British Commonwealth and wish to play their full part in it, contribute to its strength and share in its security. The new need is almost the opposite of the old need; yet the old watchwords, by mere force of tradition, retain much of their old magic. India and even Burma prefer the pride of independence to the strength of unity. The United States indeed has sloughed off its old pride of independence and isolation; for itself it accepts a very high degree of co-operation. But for the rest of the world it is still charmed by the old ideal. It wants Independence and Nationality for everything that forms part of the great Empires, British or Dutch or French. But it is worth noticing that in America, as in Europe, it is on the whole the Liberal and intellectual forces, just those which in the eighteenth century formulated the ideal of isolation and independence, which have moved most firmly away towards the new ideal of large free units with close organised co-operation between them, and it is much to our credit that on the whole we Liberals have been the first to recognise it though it means that many of our old watchwords no longer work . . .

Again, we all know how much Liberalism has to fight against the mere inertia of human nature and its acquiescence in what is customary and usual. A code of custom is necessary to the life of any human group. Yet such a code has its dangers because habits and institutions, when not watched, have a tendency to slip downwards and lose their meaning or their usefulness. They become dead and form a sort of hard crust hindering freedom and making thought difficult. People cling to horrible things like the old English Criminal Law, or the torturing of Chinese ladies' feet, or slavery, or disease and hunger among the poor because they are accustomed to them and at home with them. A large part of the work of Liberalism in normal times lies here. The Liberal must be ready to make the effort of criticism, and, if necessary, the courage to break the crust. But it needs an effort, and always a fresh effort. And here, of course, he comes into conflict with his proper complement the Conservative, who is slower to move, believes less in abstract reasoning, and emphasises the immense part that mere unconscious custom plays in keeping human societies together in peace. The points of view are different, but there is no absolute contradiction. A Liberal does not advocate change for the sake of change; he must only be free to think.

Lastly, there is something we have to learn from the Conservatives (Liberals are people who can learn). There is a subject on which not only political Liberals but the great mass of intellectuals and literary England stands in some need of repentance – or at least what Paul Valéry calls *un nouveau rhombe*, a change of direction. All through the nineteenth century our civilisation seemed to all of us so strong and secure, and above all so complacent, that we rather liked throwing stones at it. Not only socialist orators and revolutionaries, but all the chief writers, from Byron and Shelley, through Carlyle and Ruskin, Dickens, Thackeray and Trollope, on to H. G. Wells and Bernard Shaw, have been satirists, mockers of the existing social order and its conventions and particularly the Empire. We all enjoyed this satire. Other nations enjoyed it even more. I am told that Dickens' description of Dotheboys Hall is popularly used in Russia as a realistic account of the present English educational system, while the popularity of Galsworthy in Germany before 1914 was partly due to his picture of our hopeless decadence. Now, I think, we are rather sorry that we have provided the enemy with so much useful ammunition. People are so slow in unlearning things. We see that our civilisation is in mortal danger and feel at last what a precious thing it is. We can understand what Mr Gladstone meant when he said he 'felt in every fibre of his being the nobleness of the inheritance that has come down to us and the sacredness of the duty of maintaining it'. Like Lord Grey of the Reform Bill we want Reform, constant reform, and vigilant criticism, but we want it in order to save, not to destroy. Liberalism is an essential part of civilisation, the great Hellenic or Christian tradition on which the civilisation of Europe is based.

If Liberal policies are to change like this, what, it may well be asked, is their fundamental principle? It is, I think, Freedom. And it is worth noting that the idealisation of Freedom is somewhat peculiar to the Hellenic or European tradition. You do not find much about it in, for instance, the Hebrew or Egyptian or Chinese tradition. The word *Liberalis* is of course derived from *Liber*, a free man, and means 'like a free man', or 'with the qualities of a free man'. The Greek ideal from which it was taken used simply the word ... 'free'. It is an ancient word and has, I freely admit, certain ancient, aristocratic associations about it. A Free Man must not stoop to certain ways of behaviour, such as cowardice, lying, meanness, stupidity. They are beneath him, slavish. Of course he must resist all tyranny, whether foreign or home-grown. That is obvious. But the ideal of Freedom was specially taken up and developed in another sense by the Greek philosophers, who were fond of pointing out how few men are really free. Is a drunkard or a madman free? Obviously not; he is the slave of his craving or his delusion. A tyrant? No, he is always the slave of his passions or his fears. Men are constantly slaves of their passions, customs, most of all perhaps of their greed, self-love and the like. All these things prevent a man from thinking freely, seeing freely. They make him so that he cannot see the truth; he cannot even wish for the right things, and choose good in preference to evil. The man who would be really *Liberalis* has a great many bondages to guard against.

Love of power, above all; is it not true that in all governments there is a tendency to extend their power, a hidden and unconscious hankering after absolute power? The Liberal will always be on the look out to see that individuals or unrepresented groups are not oppressed, are if necessary defended against their governments. The strong, in general, have a temptation to abuse their strength, especially after a conflict. Now the great protection of the weak against the strong, the subject against his rulers, is Law. The Liberal will vigilantly support the rule of Law against the will of rulers who tend to break it; whether they be rich or poor, majorities or minorities; but of course the existing Law itself may be oppressive, and the Liberal must be vigilant to see it brought nearer to true justice.

Presumably this desire for power is merely one form of a primitive vital instinct, the urge to grow, to be greater, pleonexia, the instinct 'to have more', as the Greeks put it, more than you have got, or more than your share, taking sometimes the form of greed and avarice, sometimes of ambition. An old and epigrammatic Labour leader once said of politics, 'It is quite simple. We want your money and you want ours – or at least our work without paying for it.' He did himself a great injustice, by the way, in saying that, but it does represent the part that one great human instinct plays in checking our freedom and distorting our vision. The true attitude of the Free Man is not to get more but to see that the *res publica* is, as far as possible, governed justly. It has been quite simply expressed by ... Field Marshal Smuts: a true Liberal goes into public life thinking what he can contribute rather than what he can get. As a Free Man he is the possessor of a great privilege, and that constitutes an obligation. Noblesse oblige ...

Sir Arthur Keith in his *New Theory of Evolution*, published in 1949, makes things much clearer than Plato by starting, not with the individual, but with the small primitive human group, and finds it guided to survival and to higher development by one instinct for life and power which takes shape in two instinctive codes; a code of Amity or Mutual Help inside the group, and a code of Enmity, Pugnacity, Plato's Fight, towards all outside. Both are necessary for survival and development; both the competitive struggle for life which was often over-emphasised by some early Darwinians, and the instinct of Mutual Help, perhaps equally over-emphasised in Kropotkin's famous and attractive book with that title. The two are the same Life Instinct in different forms, both of which run to excess.

It is a great advance to start with the group rather than the individual, who hardly emerges at all till a much later stage of development. The group explains both the love and the hate, the self-sacrifice and the pugnacity. The group must be able to defend itself and its territory. It must not let itself be robbed or conquered or enslaved. It must fight with much tough endurance against the numberless perils that surround primitive man ...

This code of amity within the group takes various forms ... We like our own way of behaving because it is our own, and tend to hate other competing ways. A difference in table manners, a difference in pronunciation, begins to remove the author of it from our own Group, and put him under the Enmity Code. In uneducated or uncritical people this produces a violent instinctive intolerance of people who are in any way strange. It is largely a question of the degree of competition. English people are apt to be shocked by the colour feeling in South Africa or the United States, but as soon as they settle in a place where they are outnumbered by the blacks, fear and a sort of repulsion begin to show themselves. The same with anti-semitism; where there are few Jews and those few have the same habits as the rest of the country, there is no anti-semitism; where they are great and increasing in numbers, and especially if they have foreign manners, the Group Instinct is roused to fear and dislike; the more dangerous because it is based on a primeval unreasoning instinct.

Now obviously the essence of Liberalism here is not democracy; popular prejudices, popular passions, popular customs are just what we have most to be critical about. In order to be free we need Thought, Conscience, Enlightenment. The Liberal applies reasoned criticism to these movements of group instinct. He makes a definite effort to overcome prejudice, and no doubt, as our critics tell us, he is apt at times to 'lean over backwards'. Most Englishmen did so in the reaction after the first World War. We always have in England, and to some extent I think in all civilised countries, groups or whole parties who are anxious to adopt the outsider or enemy into the Amity Code, to be pro-Boer, pro-German, pro-Indian, pro-Russian, as the case may be. Liberals have often been called 'anti-British' or 'friends of every country but their own', and occasionally may have deserved the title. Still, the correction of the code of Enmity is one of Liberalism's greatest tasks. That code has enormous influence, and is always in need of vigilant supervision. Every community is far more thrilled by a great fighter than by a great philosopher or philanthropist ... The Liberal applies his critical reason to this militarist enthusiasm, and is apt to agree with Voltaire that statues are generally erected to the most conspicuous enemies of the human race because militarism implies an appeal to the Rule of Force, and the Rule of Force is the denial of Freedom. He naturally becomes anti-militarist.

The progress of civilisation is, we may fairly say, the progress of Liberality. Liberal criticism has continually been limiting and reducing the Fighting Instinct, except when it was a fight in defence of freedom against tyranny and from the times of the Stoics onward has looked forward to a time when the Code of Enmity may no longer be needed, and the Universe may be indeed 'one great city of Gods and Men'.

Sir Arthur Keith will have none of this. He holds both instincts, of Amity and of Enmity, to be equally necessary, and even maintains that both are still growing stronger. He points out that wars are growing larger and worse, their preparation more absorbing, their methods more destructive, the general dread of them more pervasive. War has become a bigger thing, nor can you say that it is more rare. That is true; yet I think there is a general feeling that this 'time of troubles' is somehow abnormal, as dangerous as the interim between a time of increasing peace in the nineteenth century and more established peace hereafter. And I think it is noteworthy that, if the recent wars were more cruel the reaction after them was also greater than ever before. I do not know of any parallel to the great efforts of charity put forth in this country and the USA to heal the effects of war in allied and enemy countries alike.

Many critics too insist that it is only hate of our enemies that generates love of our friends. If nations had no neighbours, says Paul Valèry, they would spend their time in civil wars. There is some force in this view that hate comes first and friendship is a mere subsequent derivative. Yet the evidence on the whole does not support it. The countries that have mostly lived in security, like the USA or like Great Britain before aviation, did not break out into more violent feuds and seditions than others: quite the contrary. They have tended to be peaceful and to take their politics easily. Their party feeling, like their patriotism, tended to become less passionate. We do, most of us, envisage a time when nations will have ceased to regard neighbours as enemies, and organised war will no longer have a place in the scheme of things. Mankind will go on becoming more Liberal ...

The constant struggle for freedom, the vigilance, the determination never to forget the duty of keeping the soul of man free, is perhaps more important, and certainly far more inspiring, than the mere possession of freedom itself. To be merely free is not much. To be able to do whatever you want to do does not in itself produce a good life or a fine character. All you can say is that without freedom the real problem of a good life cannot even begin.

Liberalism is that struggle, that vigilance, the constant remembrance of that duty. It is a spirit, not a dogma, a process, not an end. Many people, I know, are not content with this. How can we Liberals contend on equal terms, they say, against tyrants, Chauvinists, Fascists, Communists, religious fanatics, without offering the world some dogma as sharp, some vision of bliss as fascinating as theirs? Well, we must; and if Liberalism clings to truth and sanity, it possesses in the long run more effective weapons than the maddening delusions of group egoism or the dazzling promises of advertisement. True Liberalism is not crazy, it does not lie, it does not make apocalyptic promises. Such promises are, I believe, indeed as Yeats calls them, 'the world's bane'. They are all the lust for power in disguise. They lead easily to the belief that any expense, any crime, any cruelty is justified if it hastens the coming of the promised heaven on earth; and, of course, when all the crimes are committed, the heaven you have promised is not there, but the law that you have broken is. The Liberal takes Society as a growing organism, helps it to grow, corrects bit by bit what is wrong, and is vigilant to deal with the new wrongs or oppressions that will arise as conditions alter. That is one of the criticisms I would make against all forms of Socialism except the most carefully Fabian kind. It proposes a dogma; it promises a reign of bliss; whereas in the ever-shifting stream of politics, where all ideas have cloudy edges, and all words mean different things to different speakers, no absolute dogmas are ever true and no reign of bliss ever arrives. I always think it significant that the most philosophic and influential leaders of the Socialist movement in England, leaders universally admired and respected, the Webbs and Mr Shaw, were all led logically in their old age to belief in Russian Communism. There must have been something wrong in their premisses.

No doubt the special needs of this post-war time require more public controls of private freedom, no doubt, as the State acquires increased knowledge of the facts it deals with, its interferences become less blundering and more apt to bring real organised help for those in special need of help. All these points Liberals have seen as well, and perhaps as quickly, as Socialists, but they have considered each case on its merits, not decided them all on an a priori principle. I think it is true also that the Free Man takes into account various elements in a problem which the dogmatic Socialist ignores. It does not expect, as a Scottish Socialist once told me he intended, to lay on happiness with a pipe as one lays on gas and water. For example, it seems to be agreed now that the whole plan of sending children from unsatisfactory homes to large well-inspected institutions is open to very grave drawbacks which those who wished the State to be a parent never thought of. The fact is, a dogma soon tends to become a tyranny, an abuse of power; and that is the special evil against which the Free Man has always fought. There are no political parties without myths; but the Free Man tries not to mistake his myth for fact.

More than this. In the present 'Time of Trouble' surely the task of Liberalism is not to establish some particular detailed form of constitution but to unite the freedom-loving and law-abiding elements in Europe to overthrow a hideous and almost incredible growth of tyranny ...

How are we to resist? I read with some scepticism the Declarations of Human Rights and Covenants of Human Rights drawn up by Committees of UNO and by other bodies. Partly because they are stated in abstract principles which always need some exceptions and derogations, partly because I feel it is not so much some new philosophy that we have to define and create but an old familiar freedom that we have to recover. I do not of course mean that the social or political condition of any European country before the world wars was perfect and that we ought simply to go back to it. I mean that we have a great tradition of Law and Freedom, a tradition of Hellenism or of Christendom, which was, granted due vigilance and a Liberal spirit, leading steadily towards a Good Life for man, that Good Life which Aristotle laid down long ago as the aim for which all our walls and armies and constitutions exist. We have not to discover a new panacea for human ills. In the main we already know what is right and have to unite in doing it. The first necessity of civilisation, I think, is the rule of Law, Law based either on formal consent, or, more often perhaps, and more fundamentally, on an unspoken recognition of what is by nature right. That, after all, was the principle at the back of Roman Law, the only law that has given general peace to Europe. The essential error, the first false step, which sets everything after it wrong, is to make the law simply an instrument of the government in power, and the judge not a minister of justice but an agent for 'liquidating the enemies or rivals of the ruling clique'.

I was moved the other day by reading the experience of a Polish woman, Karolina Lanckononska, a University lecturer, imprisoned by the Gestapo in solitary confinement in Ravensbruck. For a long time she was allowed no books. She speaks of the sharpening of her thoughts and her sense of spiritual values both by long meditation in the lack of all human contacts and more positively by the continual proximity of death. At last she was allowed to have three books, and she asked for three very old best-sellers, Homer, Shakespeare and Thucydides, a striking choice. She tries to express the intensity of the effect which, coming at last to her starved spirit, these great minds had upon her. She speaks particularly of one passage she had never read before, that famous speech which Thucydides, writing after the downfall of Athens, puts into the mouth of Pericles, to describe what the beloved city once was. One can imagine how some of those old sentences of practical Liberalism came home to a victim of the NKVD and the Gestapo. 'Easy and unsuspicious in our private lives', says Pericles, 'we take pride in obedience to the law – especially to those laws which are made for the protection of the oppressed, and those unwritten laws which have no sanction but a man's own sense of honour.' (No spite, no underground conspiracy, no rule of terror.) 'We are called a democracy because in private differences all have equality before the law, but in estimation each man is valued for his quality in whatever work he distinguishes himself.' (No levelling downwards.) 'We do not shut out foreigners from seeing or learning what they can in our country on the ground that, if revealed, it might be of use to an enemy.' (No Iron Curtain.) 'We seek beauty in a simple life; we seek intellectual culture without loss of manliness.' 'There is no shame in a man's confessing to poverty; there is some in not escaping poverty by work.' 'We gain friends by giving help to other nations, and we help them not from a subtle calculation of interest, but fearlessly with the trustfulness of free men.' The difficult phrases of attempted political analysis go on, sometimes hard to understand, always hard to translate, sometimes no doubt with blind spots or with an idealization that is pardonable in the memory of a lost greatness, till at last the speaker urges his hearers to look at the City, see what she might be, and became her lovers. 'Realise', he says, 'how this City that you possess was made by men who dared; who saw what ought to be done, and did it.

'They gave themselves to their City, as the best contribution they could make. Be like them, knowing that the secret of happiness is freedom, and the secret of freedom courage.' With what magic, what appositeness, that message came, still fresh after two thousand five hundred years, to that woman in her solitary prison cell! What a message it brings to the Liberal Exiles . . . and to the prisoners of all Europe! What a message to us Britons of all parties on whom the prison walls have never closed, and who still can lead in the struggle for human freedom!

[Source: *The Meaning of Freedom*, Foreword by Lord Samuel, London 1957 pp. 5–20. The volume contains a number of addresses delivered by prominent Liberals in London in 1949.]

Doc. 123. SALVADOR DE MADARIAGA: 'Europe and the Liberal Principles' (1948)

It is significant and not only incidental that the Congress of the Liberal World Union assembles this year at Zurich, the city in which Winston Churchill delivered his famous address on the necessity of a European Union. For, on the one hand, Zurich is a liberal city *par excellence* and has in this newspaper* an organ of liberal thought, worthy of the *Manchester Guardian*; and, on the other hand, the movements for a *revival of liberalism* and for a *union of the free nations of Europe* aim at the same goal and supplement each other. Truly the second of these movements, which must fatefully lead Europe to constitute herself, is conditioned by economic facts and by the mechanical apparatus of the formation of opinion to such a high degree that this development is very much exposed to the danger of implementing itself under the sign of totalitarianism. The masses which have become uniform in the material field through trade and serial production and psychologically through radio and cinema, themselves demand nothing apart from their integration; and the dictator, no matter whether he is red or black, is always ready to mould all of them in the same form, no matter what degree of sufferings individuals have to put up with in this. Hitler dreamt of a single Europe, Moscow tries to enforce it. And in fact was not a single Europe also the dream of Napoleon?

If one preaches the gospel of a united Europe only, then this is merely fragmentary and not the whole thing. In this context, the unambiguous explanation is required that it is a question of a Europe in which *the nations* and *human beings* shall remain *free*. I am told, perhaps, that it is a matter of 'federation'. My answer to this must be that such words are excellent labels, but they by no means guarantee the quality of the wine contained in the bottle. We all know of a big 'federation' in which the freedom of human beings is as illusory as that of the 'federated' nations. We should create Europe, agreed – but let us create her as a free Europe! This is *the task of the liberals* and therefore a renewal of the

* *Neue Züricher Zeitung*

liberal spirit is indispensable if the future European federation is to be real progress and not a historical regression. The Socialists, or at least an important group of that party, have proclaimed the view that European federalism has to be created under the sign of socialism. But this view is only valid as far as the Socialists themselves are liberals, and the proof of this is to be found in the fact that Western socialism, after by far too long a delay and hesitation, has at last had to make a stand against communism, that is, against the totalitarian variation [*Abart*] of its own doctrine. This confirms the political axiom of our time: Europe will be liberal or she will not be.

This axiom results from the character of Europe and from the character of liberalism. He who says 'Europe', says variety and not uniformity, quality and not quantity, individuality and not mass. He who says 'Europe', says originality. In order to be able to develop its full strength, the European mind needs an atmosphere of freedom, as only in freedom can originality with full spontaneity produce all that which constitutes its individuality and quality and, in the end, its variety.

There are *two fundamental principles* which liberalism has to affirm if it wishes to be worthy of Europe: the principle of free research and the principle of the sacred character of human personality. Owing to *free research,* which from time immemorial has represented a human tradition and was first personified by Socrates and took visible shape in him, Europe has achieved the high degree of her culture. Thanks to free research she has become the pioneer in the sciences, in law, in the field of discoveries and inventions. Liberalism has to give the top position in its outlook to this principle, and has to grant it logical priority before any other tenet or point in its programme. Therefore liberalism must not admit economic or social reforms which would threaten this essential principle. If, for instance, it could be proven from a purely economic or social stand-point that the nationalisation of the press or of publishing firms would present a useful reform, the very fact, by itself, that such a measure would destroy the freedom of opinion, would condemn it in the eyes of liberals. It is worthwhile to emphasize this point especially; for only too often, from fear of being regarded as reactionaries, liberals have given in to measures which could be debatable, or even worth being considered from a purely economic point of view, but were disastrous for spiritual life.

The second essential principle, with reference to which liberals never must give in, is the principle of respect for the human personality. Unfortunately the humiliating fact has to be admitted that in this respect the conscience of Europe has receded during the last thirty years. There are still with us one or two generations of those people who experienced how the whole of Europe trembled with indignation in face of the injustice suffered by Dreyfus or Ferrer. Since then we have witnessed incomparably much harsher cases and are continuing to witness them – and unfortunately Europe no longer trembles over them. I would even like to say that until today we, the liberals, have not given to Europe the signal of moral protest, of disgust and indignation in face of the judicial murders, the kidnappings, the disappearance of so-called 'witness' who, in the darkness of prisons, sign documents the authenticity of which nobody can prove; in other words, in face of a total series of horrors which our fathers would not have tolerated and which we let pass with indifference or resignation.

European liberalism must above all recognise its obligations when facing these fundamental problems. It would enter on a wrong path if it should want to undertake either to revive the absolute and limited capitalism of the nineteenth century or, conversely, try to catch the masses in competition with the socialists. The materialist politics of the capitalists and the materialist politics of the masses are the two abysses on the right and on the left of which European liberalism must beware. European liberals must have courage to be the movement of an elite which allows itself to be led by moral and political principles commanding respect, and to be inspired by the welfare of all. Liberalism alone can speak in the name of the entire nation. But if they have to rely on a class, then it should be the middle classes and the elite of the workers; that is, on the part of the society from which everything has emerged that makes life valuable, beautiful and worth living, but also, it must be admitted, the social stratum which is nearly being sacrificed by demagogy. Politics of the masses irresistibly lead to a mechanical concept of the State; liberalism must, on the contrary, feel committed to an organic concept according to which the community out of itself produces the best elements in a spontaneous development in order to place them in leading positions. Liberalism also must have the courage to revolt against *the doctrinaire idea of equality* in our time which stifles initiative, devalues true merit, punishes legitimate success, kills inventive vigour and creative leisure, and in the long run is levelling the social landscape so much until only a desolate flatness of concrete remains on which one could put up machines for the serial production of human beings. It is up to liberalism to liberate Europe from these horrors which so much contradict the European spirit.

The task is not easy as traditionally European liberalism inclines towards the Left, and this has practically become a firm bias with liberals. This hankering after the Left explains why so many and so excellent liberals have remained, until the last moment, loyal – and deceived – friends of communism, of the anti-liberal doctrine *par excellence*. It is time to put things right and to revise the course, not according to the somewhat naive concepts of 'Right' and 'Left', but by orientating oneself like sailors according to the unchangeable stars in the world of ideas, according to the eternal principles which hover above human conduct.

The hope that this revival of liberalism becomes a reality is in vain, if the liberals do not boldly re-adopt that intellectual attitude without which every liberal doctrine lacks a basis: man is both body and spirit, but it is the spirit alone through the strength of which he is a human being. In the last analysis, this is the most profound of liberal principles.

[Source: Essay first published in the *Neue Züricher Zeitung* 23 May 1948; and republished in *Rettet die Freiheit. Ausgewählte Aufsätze von S. de Madariaga in der Neuen Zürcher Zeitung 1948 bis 1957*, Bern, 1958, pp. 232–236. Translated by the editors of this volume.]

Biographical List

JOHN EMERICH EDWARD DALBERG-ACTON, LORD ACTON (1834–1902) belonged to an aristocratic Catholic family with important European connections. He studied in Munich for seven years under Ignaz von Döllinger, the leading Catholic Church historian, and also travelled widely in Europe during that time. He entered the House of Commons in 1859 and was made a peer by Gladstone in 1869. In the 1860s Acton attempted to publicize a liberal Catholic point of view in two short-lived periodicals. He was deeply troubled by the declaration of papal infallibility in 1870; but he did not leave the Church. Original and trenchant in his approach, he intended to write a vast history of liberty. Although he gathered much material for this purpose, the direction which this work might have taken can only be surmised from his two essays on the history of freedom, written in the 1870s, and from his inaugural lecture on the study of history delivered after he was appointed Regius Professor of Modern History at Cambridge in 1895. His great influence on British historical writing came in part from his essays and lectures, but far more so from his advocacy of German historical methods and his independent view of the progress of mankind.

'ALAIN', pseudonym for Emile Auguste Chartier (1868–1951). As a political writer and philosopher 'Alain' was the voice of French Radicalism *par excellence* during the first three decades of the twentieth century. As Professor Emile Chartier his academic career included appointments in Rouen and at the Lycée Henri IV in Paris. He sided with the Dreyfusards in the 1890s, and he saw active service during the First World War. Afterwards he became critical of the war. In his political writings 'Alain' strongly upheld radical individualism and the need to

749

keep the power of government in check. Like many members of the Radical Party, 'Alain' was hostile to and suspicious of the deputies elected to the French Chamber. The most important statement of his political ideas is found in *Eléments d'une doctrine radicale* (1925). Other writings include: *La Guerre jugée* (1921); *Le citoyen contre les pouvoirs* (1926); and *Propos d'économique* (1935).

ERNST MORITZ ARNDT (1769–1860) was born in Swedish Pomerania but for the greater part of his long life he identified himself with German politics ardently preaching German patriotism. Although he welcomed Napoleon's early victories, he turned against the First Consul in 1801. By that time Arndt had travelled widely in Germany, Italy and France, and had become aware of the diversity of languages, cultures and nationalities in Europe. As a publicist he set out to encourage German awareness of a distinctive national character and to work for political unity. In 1803 in his *Germanien und Europa,* he attacked French expansion; and after the defeat of Prussia in 1806 he was one of those who called most strongly for a national German struggle against the French. His major nationalist statement, *Geist der Zeit,* was published between 1806 and 1809. Arndt was in contact with the Prussian reformers, and in 1812 went to St Petersburg to assist Stein in making plans to defeat Napoleon. After 1815 he appeared to be too radical for the Prussian Government. Although appointed Professor of History at the University of Bonn in 1818, he was dismissed two years later not to be reinstated until 1840; but by that time he appeared rather conservative in comparison with the new generation of German liberals. A veteran delegate at the Frankfurt National Assembly in 1848, his hopes for German unity under Prussia's leadership were disappointed.

FREDERIC BASTIAT (1801–50), the son of a merchant, was born at Bayonne. While working in a family business concern he began to take an interest in the works of Adam Smith and J. B. Say and in free trade. His earliest writings in 1844 and 1845 were on tariffs and free trade. Bastiat was active in the formation of the French Free Trade Association and its weekly journal *Libre-Echange*. By that time he had met Cobden and Bright in England. As a pamphleteer Bastiat showed great talent in ridiculing the protectionist arguments of his opponents, e.g. in the 'Petition from the Manufacturers of Candles' (1845). He was also strongly opposed to Proudhon's socialistic ideas. Bastiat firmly believed in the virtues of competition, in individualism and in progress. He had a considerable influence on French economists and others who supported free trade, including his contemporary Michel Chevalier and later French liberals like Paul Leroy-Beaulieu. In 1848 he was elected to the Constituent Assembly and subsequently to the Legislative Assembly. His most important writings are included in *L'Etat* (1849) which is an attack on Proudhonism, *Sophisms of Protection* and *Harmonies of Political Economy*.

HERMANN BAUMGARTEN (1825–93) came from South Germany. As a historian he had been a student of G. G. Gervinus; in the 1860s he taught at the University of Karlsruhe in Baden. He was a specialist in Spanish history and published in this field. As a moderate liberal he took an active part in politics in Baden, and in the early 1860s he emphasized the role of the middle class in the Progressive Party. In 1866 he turned pro-Prussian; and from then until after the victory over France in 1870 he was very close in outlook to his fellow historian Treitschke. His critique of German liberalism, *Der deutsche Liberalismus. Eine Selbstkritik,* was published towards the end of 1866. He publicly supported the war against France in 1870; but in the new Empire he became disillusioned with the spirit of monarchism, militarism and nationalism. In the 1880s he was critical of Bismarck's domestic policies; he also sharply criticized the second volume of Treitschke's *History of Germany in the Nineteenth Century* (1882). Baumgarten taught as Professor of History at the University of Strassburg from 1872 to 1889.

JEREMY BENTHAM (1748–1832), the son of a prosperous London attorney, was educated at Westminster School and Queen's College, Oxford. In addition to studying law, he undertook a wide-ranging study of philosophy and science. He also travelled in France, visited Turkey and spent two years in Russia. He was the friend and correspondent of influential men ranging from Lord Shelburne to Mirabeau and John Quincy Adams. In the early nineteenth century his influence was exerted more from behind the political scene, through a group of friends and disciples who included James Mill, rather than through his vast output of works on legislation and reform. Bentham's utilitarian philosophy was first set forth in *An Introduction to the Principles of Morals and Legislation,* published in 1789. His lifelong task was the formulation of a Constitutional Code; but from time to time he also concerned himself with parliamentary reform, prison reform, education, and the construction of an ideal prison system in the Panopticon scheme. In 1824 he founded the *Westminster Review* as a forum for the radicals and utilitarians. Through Bentham's acquaintance with Etienne Dumont and the consequent publication of some of his works in French from 1802 onwards, his ideas on legislation and constitutional issues were better known in several European countries than in Britain.

WILLIAM H. BEVERIDGE (1879–1963). After his education at Oxford, Beveridge was interested in civic service. He became sub-warden of Toynbee Hall, the social settlement house in East London. A period as a civil servant followed from 1909 to 1916 when Beveridge was the Director of the Labour Exchanges established under the Board of Trade. From 1919 to 1937 he was an outstanding Director of the London School of Economics. As an economist his interests were closely connected with employment and insurance; and his early writings include *Unemployment* (1909) and *Insurance for All* (1924). In 1925, when a general strike was threatening, he was appointed a member of the (Samuel) Royal Commission on the Coal Industry. In 1944 he won a by-election to the House of Commons as a liberal, but was defeated in the general election of 1945. His name became a household word in Britain in the 1940s after the publication of the report of the committee, of which he was president, on *Social Insurance and Allied Services* (1942), and of the later report on *Full Employment in a Free Society* (1944). In the Beveridge Plan he attempted to provide for both individual liberty and social security. The proposals in the two reports became the basis of the National Insurance Scheme introduced by the Attlee Government. Beveridge's autobiography *Power and Influence* was published in 1959.

FRANCOIS JOSEPH FRANCISQUE BOUVET (1799–1871), the son of a former officer, came from the department of the Ain. He studied medicine, but did not practise. In 1828 he went to Greece during the Greek War of Independence and returned to France in 1830 in time to take part in the July Revolution. He was soon discontented with the new regime and wrote liberal pamphlets against it. In 1840 he became interested in the Eastern Question and proposed the creation of a permanent international congress at Constantinople. He also wrote on religious questions in the 1840s. In 1848 he was elected to the French Constituent Assembly and the following year to the Legislative Assembly. As a Deputy he supported the left; and among other proposals he urged the calling of a disarmament conference. During the Second Empire he entered the French consular service. Throughout his life he advocated pacifism and the international arbitration of disputes, Cf. *La guerre et la civilisation* (1855) and *Introduction à l'etablissement d'un droit public européen* (1856).

JOHN BRIGHT (1811–89), the son of a mill owner, was born in Rochdale. His political liberalism was closely related to his faith as a Quaker, while his economic and social ideas were shaped by his own business experience. His political friendship with Cobden dates from

1836–37. In 1841 Bright became prominent in the agitation for the repeal of the Corn Laws. A skilful orator, he was able to popularize free-trade doctrines. He was first elected to Parliament in 1843. In the 1850s and 1860s Bright took up other issues including internationalism, and his opposition to Britain's involvement in the Crimean War temporarily cost him his seat in Parliament. He supported the North during the American Civil War, and he was a prominent advocate of parliamentary reform; but his *laissez faire* principles led him to reject State intervention in the form of factory legislation. Despite his long parliamentary career, he never consistently held high Cabinet office, although he was appointed to the Board of Trade in Gladstone's first administration in 1868. In the 1870s and 1880s he supported Gladstone's Irish land reforms, but in 1886 he opposed Home Rule.

COUNT CAMILLO DI CAVOUR (1810–61), the younger son of a Piedmontese aristocrat, was expected to follow a career in the army, but resigned from it in 1831 at a time when Liberal ideas were suspect in Piedmont-Sardinia. He travelled widely in England and France; and then interested himself in introducing new methods of farming on the family estates. He also took up a new career as an industrialist and banker. In the 1840s he acquired a reputation as both a Piedmontese patriot and a supporter of liberalism on the English model. He founded the newspaper *Il Risorgimento* in 1847. With the new constitution of 1849 he was elected to the Piedmontese parliament. In 1851 he was appointed the minister in charge of agriculture, industry and commerce. He became Prime Minister in 1852. A pragmatist in politics, he sought to build up a liberal-conservative political alliance. Between 1850 and 1857 he concentrated on the economic development of the small and backward kingdom. In foreign affairs he was an opportunist as well as a pragmatist. In view of the failure of the attempts to expel the Austrians from Italy in 1848–49, he recognized that foreign support was essential. For political reasons Piedmont took part in the Crimean War on the British and French side; and in 1858 Cavour entered into the Pact of Plombières with Napoleon III. He resigned from office in protest after the armistice of Villafranca in July 1859 but returned in January 1860 and arranged with Napoleon III for Piedmont to annex the Romagna, Tuscany, Parma and Modena in return for the cession of Nice and Savoy to France. Cavour's last diplomatic successes were to turn the tide of the radical Garibaldi's progress in southern and central Italy in 1860 and, shortly before his untimely death, to secure the union of all Italy under the Piedmontese crown with the exception of Rome and Venetia.

Biographical List

JOSEPH CHAMBERLAIN (1836–1914) was born in London. His family, Unitarians by religion, were engaged in manufacturing. Joseph settled in Birmingham as a young man when his father went into partnership with Nettlefold's screw-making firm; he succeeded in building up the fortunes of the firm. He entered politics at the age of 32 at a time when the education issue became important for non-conformists. In 1870 he joined the Birmingham School Board; and his long friendship with Sir Charles Dilke and John Morley began in the same year. Elected Mayor of Birmingham in 1873, he inaugurated a period of 'municipal socialism'. In 1874 he sold his shares in Nettlefold-Chamberlain in order to follow a political career. He was elected to Parliament for one of the Birmingham seats in 1876, and in the following year he was instrumental in forming the National Liberal Federation. In 1880 he was appointed to office as President of the Board of Trade in Gladstone's Liberal administration. Dissatisfied with the slowness with which the government was introducing reforms, he announced an 'Unauthorised Programme' of radical measures for the 1885 general election. In 1886 his opposition to Gladstone's Home Rule Bill helped to split the Liberal Party. Chamberlain remained in the political wilderness until 1895 when he joined Salisbury's Unionist Government as Colonial Secretary. He was keenly interested in maintaining the unity of the Empire, and his support for Milner's policy in South Africa helped to bring about the Boer War in 1899. In 1903 he took up the cause of tariff reform; but his active political career came to an end in 1906 when he suffered a paralytic stroke.

MICHEL CHEVALIER (1806–79) was born in Limoges and educated at the *Ecole Polytechnique* and then at the *Ecole des Mines*. His first appointment was as a mining engineer in the department of the Nord. He became connected with Enfantin and the Saint-Simonians in the early 1830s, and he brought success to their journal, the *Globe*, as its editor (1831). In the following year he served a six months' prison sentence as a result of his editorship and on his release he broke with the Saint-Simonians. Following a suggestion by Thiers, he went on a mission to the United States for two years. He also visited Canada, Mexico and Cuba. After his return to France he published *Lettres sur l'Amerique* (1836). In that year he was sent to England to observe conditions during an industrial depression. Soon afterwards he was made a Chevalier of the Legion of Honour and held official posts including that of Councillor of State. He was elected to the Chamber of Deputies in 1845. Following the publication of *Des intérêts materiels en France* in 1838, in which he considered the improvements that could be brought about through roads,

754

canals and railways, he was appointed to the Chair of Political Economy at the *Collège de France* in 1840. He retained it until his death (with a short break in 1848 when he opposed the national workshops and the socialist ideas of Louis Blanc). His lectures at the Collège de France were first published in 1842–44 as *Cours d'économie politique*. Chevalier applauded Louis Napoleon's *coup d'état* in December 1851 because he thought it would bring about internal peace and material progress. He was a convinced supporter of free trade and with Napoleon III's encouragement he negotiated and signed the Treaty of Commerce with England in 1860. He became president of the *Ligue internationale de la paix* in 1869. In the Senate (of which he had been a member since 1860), he voted against war with Prussia in 1870. After the end of the Second Empire he retired from politics.

RICHARD COBDEN (1804–65), born in Midhurst, Sussex, was the son of a small farmer. After some commercial experience in London, the young Cobden set up his own business in Manchester in 1828 and three years later became a master calico printer. In the 1830s and 1840s he travelled widely in Europe and also visited the United States. His knowledge of Europe stood him in good stead in his advocacy of internationalism and the international arbitration of disputes. Cobden's belief in free trade and *laissez faire* was closely connected with his view of international politics. His major political writings were *England, Ireland and America* (1835) and *Russia* (1836). Cobden was active in Manchester politics before he took up the Anti-Corn Law cause in 1838. He entered the House of Commons in 1841. His political activities concentrated on a few well-defined areas: the repeal of the Corn Laws in the early 1840s; the peace movement and international arbitration in the late 1840s and early 1850s; on the free-trade treaty with France in 1860 and parliamentary reform up to the time of his death. Despite the esteem with which he was regarded by Whigs and Liberals, Cobden did not hold Cabinet office.

ANTOINE-NICOLAS CARITAT, MARQUIS DE CONDORCET (1743–94) was educated at the Jesuit school in Rheims and the *Collège de Navarre* in Paris. As a mathematician he was elected to the Academy of Sciences while still in his twenties, and a few years later was appointed its Secretary. His major scientific publication was *The Theory of Probability*. He was the friend and correspondent of D'Alembert, Voltaire and Turgot; and on the basis of his scientific reputation he was made a member of several other academies, including the Royal Society in London. Like many of the *philosophes,* he believed in the perfectibility of man. He was also particularly interested in education. Critical of the *ancien régime,* he became a member of the Paris *Commune* in 1789. By the time he was elected to the Legislative Assembly in 1791 he was no longer in favour of a constitutional monarchy, but he voted against the death penalty for Louis XVI. He was a member of the Legislative Assembly's committee on education and drew up its report. As a member of the Convention, Condorcet, with Thomas Paine, produced a draft of a new Declaration of Rights in 1793. Although he was not a Girondist, Condorcet came under suspicion when the Jacobins eliminated their rivals. He went into hiding in order to avoid arrest; and between July 1793 and March 1794 he used his enforced leisure to write his *Sketch for a Historical Picture of the Progress of the Human Mind.* Shortly after he was arrested and imprisoned, he was found dead, but the cause of his death has never been finally determined.

BENJAMIN CONSTANT DE REBECQUE (1767–1830) was born in Lausanne (Switzerland) to a Protestant émigré family from France. Educated in different parts of Europe and finally in Paris, he observed the French Revolution while holding an appointment at the Court of Brunswick. In July 1794 he returned to Switzerland where his long and stormy association with Germaine de Staël began. In May 1795 when he and Mme de Staël went to Paris, Constant supported the *Directoire* and wrote political pamphlets in its support. Following the establishment of the *Consulat* in November 1799, Constant became a member of the *Tribunat* until February 1802. By that time he was dissatisfied with the loss of political liberty in France. Between 1804 and 1814 Constant visited Germany several times, and during that period established his reputation as a writer and publicist. Despite his opposition to Napoleon's despotism, he was made a Councillor of State during the Hundred Days in 1815, and he drew up the *Acte additionnel* for Napoleon – which would have established a liberal and parliamentary empire. His *Principes de politique applicables à tous les gouvernements,* published in May 1815, is an able plea for a liberal, parliamentary monarchy. His lively novel *Alphonse,* written in 1807, was published in London in 1816. After he had again returned to France he pursued a political career as writer and deputy, being first elected to the Chamber in March 1819. He personified the liberal constitutional opposition in the Chamber by defending liberal principles and speaking against all reactionary laws. His classical exposition of French liberalism in the *Cours de politique constitutionnelle* was published between 1818 and 1820. In July 1830 he supported Louis Philippe as a constitutional monarch, but still defended the right and liberty of criticism at the same time. Constant's last speech in the Chamber was in support of the freedom of the press.

BENEDETTO CROCE (1866–1952), the eminent Italian philosopher, critic and historian, was born in the Abruzzi but lived most of his life in Naples. One of his earliest interests was in Neapolitan history. He had some contact with socialist ideas before 1900 and was influenced by Hegel. His major works began to be published in 1902 with *Aesthetic*, followed by *Logic, Philosophy of Conduct* and *Theory and History of Historiography* (1912–13). He established the periodical *La Critica* in 1903. He became a senator in 1910. He was pro-German in 1914 but later supported Salandra's decision for Italy to join Britain and France. Croce was Minister of Education in Giolitti's moderate liberal government from 1920 to 1921. At first he gave conditional support to Mussolini after the fascist seizure of power in October 1922, but from 1925 onwards he voiced his opposition to fascism. His three major historical works were published in the late 1920s and the 1930s, *viz. History of Italy* (1928), *History of Europe in the Nineteenth Century* based on a series of lectures given in Naples in 1931 (1932), and *History as the Story of Liberty* (completed in 1938). With the fall of fascism in 1943 he refounded the Liberal Party. He acted as the leader of the Liberals between 1944 and 1947, and for a while was Minister without Portfolio.

FRIEDRICH CHRISTOPH DAHLMANN (1785–1860) was born in the Baltic city of Wismar which was then part of Sweden. He studied classics at the universities of Copenhagen and Halle. In 1812 he was appointed to the Chair of History at the University of Kiel (then in Denmark). While in Kiel he was active in agitating for the constitutional rights of Schleswig-Holstein. In 1814 he devised proposals for the future political order in Germany. He was appointed to a Chair in the University of Göttingen in 1829. Dahlmann had a large share in the drawing up of the Hanoverian constitution of 1833, and when King Ernst August withdrew it in 1837 he was one of the seven professors who protested and were therefore dismissed. His important political work *Die Politik auf den Grund und das Maass der gegebenen Zustände zurückgeführt*, a plea for moderate liberalism, first appeared in Göttingen in 1835. Dahlmann was appointed to a Chair at the University of Bonn in 1842. Large audiences attended his lectures on politics in which he linked constitutional and historical themes. In 1848 he was elected to the Frankfurt National Assembly and became a member of the Assembly's commission on the Constitution. In the following year he belonged to the deputation that offered the German crown to Frederick William IV of Prussia. Dahlmann's major historical works dealt with the English Revolution (1844) and the French Revolution (1845).

ANTOINE LOUIS CLAUDE, COMTE DESTUTT DE TRACY

(1754–1836) was born and died in Paris. In 1789 he was a liberal-minded representative of the nobility in the Estates-General. He took an active part in political affairs until 1792 when he went into exile. After his return to France he was made a senator under Napoleon. As one of the leading *idéologues*, whom Napoleon came to dislike, Destutt de Tracy was later out of favour. During the Restoration, he was given a peerage by Louis XVIII. A thinker of distinction, his most notable work *Commentaire sur l'esprit des lois de Montesquieu*, written during the Napoleonic regime (1806), was banned at that time. In this work he analyses Montesquieu's treatise book by book, considering its moral as well as its political aspects. An English translation of the *Commentaire* appeared first in the United States in 1811; but an authorized French text was not published in France until 1828.

IGNAZ VON DOLLINGER

(1799–1890) was the outstanding Catholic ecclesiastical historian in Germany in the nineteenth century. Influenced by the French thinker Joseph de Maistre, young Döllinger was an out-spoken champion of the Papacy. In 1826 he was appointed Professor of Canon Law and Ecclesiastical History in the University of Munich. As a member of the Bavarian *Landtag* and then of the Frankfurt National Assembly in 1848 he developed more liberal political views. During the debates in the Assembly he emphasized the need for freedom for the Church from the State. A series of lectures in which Döllinger argued in favour of the Papacy giving up its temporal power was published in 1861 (*The Church and the Churches, or the Papacy and Temporal Power*). From his criticism of the history of the papal territories since the sixteenth century, Döllinger was led on to criticize the papal authority itself under Pius IX. In his articles he then voiced opposition to the declaration of papal infallibility in matters of faith. These articles were republished as *The Pope and the Council* (1869) and the book was translated into several languages. Following a letter to the Archbishop of Munich in which he definitely refused to accept the doctrine of infallibility, Döllinger was excommunicated in 1871. He and others holding similar views published a statement of their position in the *Munich Declaration of Whitsuntide 1871*, which marked the beginning of the 'Old Catholic' movement in Germany. A powerful writer, Döllinger greatly influenced Lord Acton.

EMILE FAGUET

(1847–1916) was educated at the *Ecole Normale*. In 1890 he became Professor of French Literature at the Sorbonne; and in 1900 he was elected a member of the *Académie Française*. He dis-

Biographical List

tinguished himself as a literary critic and as a historian. In 1902 he founded his own journal *Revue Latine*. His moderate, dispassionate and empirical attitude towards liberalism was stated in *Le libéralisme* (1903), whereas his literary reputation rests mainly on the three volumes of *Politiques et Moralistes du dix-neuvième siècle* (1891–99). His other works include *Problèmes politiques du temps présent* (1899) and *Questions politiques* (1902), also *Le Culte de l'incompétence* (1910) and *L'Horreur des responsibilités* (1911) in which he criticized the parliamentary system of the Third Republic.

LEON GAMBETTA (1838–82), the son of an Italian immigrant, came from the *petite bourgeoisie* whose rising political power he was to emphasize in the early years of the Third Republic. As a law student and later as a barrister, Gambetta identified himself with the republican opposition to Napoleon III. His skill as an orator served him well in the 1860s when he forcefully restated the radical republican creed, the essentials of which were laid down in 1869 in the 'Belleville Manifesto'. He was first elected to the Legislative Body in the same year. Following the military disaster at Sedan and the proclamation of a republic in September 1870, Gambetta became Minister of the Interior in the Government of National Defence. He then attempted to raise the provinces to continue the war against Prussia. In January and February 1871 he opposed the armistice and temporarily retired from politics. He therefore took no part in the Paris *Commune* nor in the royalist and conservative National Assembly until after the elections in July 1871. As a radical republican he was politically influential in the 1870s, and he was also interested in electoral reform. After 1875 he began to move from the left towards the centre to become one of the leaders of the Opportunists, i.e. of those republicans who were sharply anti-clerical but at the same time conservative in matters of social policy. Gambetta encountered the hostility of President Grévy, and although he was president of the parliamentary commission on finance (1877–81) and held high ministerial office he did not become Prime Minister until after the fall of Jules Ferry in November 1881. His cabinet lasted little more than two months. Gambetta had failed to achieve his objective of republican unity.

GEORG GOTTFRIED GERVINUS (1805–71) was born in Darmstadt, Hesse, but most of his life was spent in Heidelberg. He was a journalist as well as a literary historian. Between 1835 and 1842 he published the five volumes of his *History of the Political National Literature of the Germans*. In 1837 he was one of the seven professors expelled from Göttingen University for political reasons. Between 1847 and 1850 he edited the liberal *Deutsche Zeitung* at Heidelberg. Gervinus

759

had a good understanding of liberal constitutional ideas and practice in Britain and in the United States. Disappointed with the terms under which Frederick William IV called the Prussian Landtag in 1847, Gervinus participated in the planning of a national parliament at Frankfurt. As a member first of the Pre-Parliament and then of the National Assembly, he was active in the moderate constitutional and democratic movement. In July 1848 he became disillusioned with the work of the Assembly, lost hope for a regenerated Prussia and went to Italy. In 1853 he published an *Introduction to the History of the Nineteenth Century*. After 1862 he opposed Prussian militarism under Bismarck and wanted to see the Prussian royal house abandon the concept of divine right. Gervinus continued to support liberal federalism as well as national unity. Between 1866 and 1870 he expressed himself in favour of German unification through federalism and against the annexation of other German states by Prussia.

EMILE DE GIRARDIN (1806–81) was born in Paris. Early in his career he discovered a talent for journalism and became aware of the influence the Press could exercise. He was capable of tremendous activity, had a prodigious memory and easily assimilated information on a wide variety of subjects. With the foundation of *La Presse* in 1836 he helped to create the new type of cheap and popular press. Yet Girardin believed that a newspaper should be serious in purpose and politically committed. He encouraged advertisements, a practice then not common in Paris, but which helped to ensure profits for the paper. During his career as a writer, journalist and newspaper owner, Girardin amassed a considerable fortune. In December 1848 he supported Louis Napoleon Bonaparte's candidacy for the French presidency, but afterwards he moved towards the left. During the 1860s he advocated a 'liberal empire'. In the last years of the Second Empire he was disappointed not to be given political office; and he continued both to support and to attack the government of Napoleon III up to its fall in September 1870. He opposed the Government of National Defence. In 1872 he bought the *Journal Officiel*, in 1873 *Le Petit Journal* and in 1874 *La France*. By 1877 Girardin had become a republican. Elected to the Chamber of Deputies in December 1877, he proved ineffective as a parliamentarian. His more serious works include *La politique universelle. Décrets de l'avenir* (1852) with its emphasis on permanent peace and international arbitration.

WILLIAM EWART GLADSTONE (1809–98) was born in Liverpool into a mercantile family of Scottish descent. He was educated at Eton and Christ Church, Oxford. In 1833 entered the House of Commons and between 1834 and 1835 he held a junior ministerial post in Peel's

Cabinet. The publication of *The State in its Relation with the Church* (1838) reflected Gladstone's interest in religious issues and his High Church outlook. In Peel's 1841–46 cabinet he was first President of the Board of Trade and then Colonial Secretary. After Peel's death in 1850 Gladstone began to move towards the Whigs and in 1852 he was appointed Chancellor of the Exchequer in Aberdeen's Government. He presented his first budget in 1853, and resigned in 1855 after Palmerston became Prime Minister. In 1859 Gladstone again became Chancellor of the Exchequer in Palmerston's cabinet. He supported the Cobden-Chevalier Free Trade Treaty with France in 1860. His sympathies were with the South during the American Civil War. Gladstone became Prime Minister for the first time in 1868 and major measures secured by his government included the Disestablishment of the Irish Church and the Irish Land Act of 1870. In 1875 he temporarily retired from politics but returned to agitate against the Bulgarian massacres in 1876. The 'Midlothian campaign' of 1880 returned Gladstone to power at the head of a liberal and radical cabinet. In 1886 he split the Liberal Party by the introduction of an Irish Home Rule Bill. He became Prime Minister for the last time in 1892 and resigned from office in 1894. His last major speech in 1896 was a denunciation of the massacres in Armenia.

JOSEPH GOERRES (1776–1848) originated from a Roman Catholic middle-class family in the Rhineland. During his early years as a publicist, he was a rationalist, supported the French Revolution and favoured the union of the Rhineland with France. By 1800 after visiting Paris, he was disillusioned with Napoleon and also with French military rule in the Rhineland. He became a German nationalist and a defender of historic rights, although he still supported popular rights against absolutism. His interests also turned to the Middle Ages and to German romanticism. In 1806 he settled in Heidelberg; his *Reflections on the Fall of Germany and its Rebirth* were published in 1810. After the battle of Leipzig he turned to political journalism. The first issue of the newspaper *Rheinischer Merkur* appeared in Koblenz on 23 January 1814. It soon became politically influential and an issue came out every other day until 3 January 1816 when it was suppressed by the Prussian Government because of its criticism of the Establishment. In 1817 Goerres was expelled from the Prussian Rhineland (owing to his polemical tract *Germany and the Revolution*) and took refuge in Strasbourg (France). By that time his attitude was anti-Prussian, pro-Habsburg and more conservative. He now stressed the Catholic faith. In 1821, while he was in exile in Switzerland, he completed *Europa und die Revolution*. In 1827 he was appointed professor of history in the University of Munich. In 1838 he founded and edited *Historisch – politische Blätter* as a prominent organ of conservative political catholicism, which favoured a 'Greater Germany'.

THOMAS HILL GREEN (1836–82), the son of an Anglican clergyman, was born in Yorkshire. He was educated at Rugby School and at Balliol College, Oxford, from 1855 to 1859. Green began teaching ancient and modern history and the New Testament at Oxford in 1860 and later he also taught philosophy. He was appointed a Fellow of Balliol in 1861 and tutor in 1866. In 1878 he was elected Whyte Professor of Moral Philosophy. Stemming from his interest in neo-Hegelianism, Green became the influential founder of the Idealist school of philosophy at Oxford. His one major philosophical work, *Prologomena to Ethics,* left incomplete at his death, was published in 1883. During his academic career Green was actively concerned with secondary education, being a member of a Royal Commission inquiring into middle-class schools (1865–66). He was also closely associated with liberal politics in Oxford. In 1876 he was elected to the Oxford Town Council. Green was an advocate of positive State action, an attitude expressed in his *Lectures on the Principles of Political Obligation* only published after his death. It was through Green's teachings that some of his pupils adopted a religion of citizenship to replace their former evangelical religious creed.

FRANCOIS GUIZOT (1787–1874) combined the careers of statesman and historian. He was a Protestant. His father was executed during the Revolution. While still a law student in Paris, François Guizot opposed the Napoleonic Empire. After the Restoration he became one of the academic liberals known as the *'Doctrinaires'*. The moderation of their liberalism was shown in their support for the electoral law of 1817 and the press law of 1819. For a short period between 1814 and 1816 Guizot held ministerial office, but then returned to teaching and historical research. His *Essai sur l'histoire de France* appeared in 1824; he also published the course of lectures on modern history which he gave at the Sorbonne in the late 1820s. An admirer of English political institutions and practice, he particularly appreciated the economic and political role of the middle class in England. Owing to some mild criticism of the regimes of Louis XVIII and Charles X, he was forced for a time to leave his university post. When elected to the Chamber of Deputies in 1830, Guizot opposed Charles X. After the July Revolution King Louis Philippe made him Minister of the Interior. From 1832 to 1839 Guizot was Minister of Education, a period during which French primary school education was reorganized. In 1840 he became Minister for Foreign Affairs, and was in fact Louis Philippe's chief minister until the revolution of 1848. He remained the personification of the 'Party of Order'. After the fall of the July Monarchy he returned to historical and political writing. His later works include *De la Démocratie en France* (1849), *Histoire des origines du gouvernement représentatif* (1851) and *Memoires pour servir à l'Histoire de mon temps* (1856–64).

DAVID HANSEMANN (1790–1864) was a self-made businessman with little formal education. As a successful Rhineland merchant with international connections, he had definite ideas on the role and position of the middle class. Although a sober thinker, a realist and a practical man, Hansemann was also a lively orator; both these aspects of his personality helped to make him influential in advocating a liberal constitution for Prussia, in establishing self-help organizations and in urging State assistance in the promotion of commerce and modernised industry. Advocating the political union of the Crown and the middle classes, he favoured the type of constitutional government established by Louis Philippe in France (cf. Hansemann's *Preussen und Frankreich* published in 1833). He was anxious that Prussia should not become isolated in European politics. Hansemann's political ideas are clearly expressed in the memoranda he addressed to King Frederick William III of Prussia in 1830 and later to his successor Frederick William IV in 1840. Following the revolution in Prussia, Hansemann was appointed Prussian Minister of Finance in March 1848, but resigned in July. After the failure of the 1848 revolutions he remained interested in the formation of a parliament for the *Zollverein*. In 1861 he became chairman of the first German businessmen's convention (*Handelstag*).

FRIEDRICH A. VON HAYEK (1899–   ), the son of a university professor, was born in Vienna. He studied at the University of Vienna after the First World War and obtained doctorates in law and political science. After a period in the civil service he became the first director of the Austrian Institute for Economic Research (*Konjunkturforschung*). He came to the notice of economists in 1928 when he put forward his *Monetary Theory of the Trade Cycle* (published in 1929, English translation in 1933). In 1931 he was appointed Professor of Economic Science and Statistics at London University. Hayek held this appointment at the London School of Economics until 1950. From 1952 to 1962 he was Professor of Social and Moral Sciences at the University of Chicago, and later Professor of Economics at the University of Freiburg (1962 to 1970). In the 1930s Hayek was a critic of Keynesian economic theories.Towards the end of the Second World War he strongly criticized what he regarded as the trend away from liberalism and towards socialism in Britain and the United States in his book *The Road to Serfdom* (1944). Hayek, who was awarded the Nobel Prize for

763

Biographical List

Economics in 1974, has exercised an important influence on economic studies in Austria, Britain, the United States, Germany and Japan. His works include *Prices and Production* (1931), *The Pure Theory of Capital* (1941), *Individualism and Economic Order* (1948), *The Constitution of Liberty* (1960), and *Law, Legislation and Liberty* (1973).

LEONARD T. HOBHOUSE (1864–1929), the son of an Anglican clergyman, was born in Cornwall and educated at Marlborough and Corpus Christi, Oxford. He taught philosophy at Oxford in the late 1880s and early 1890s, and in 1894 was elected a Fellow of Corpus Christi College. Interested in sociology and politics, he was active in supporting trade unionism and particularly the organization of unskilled workers; and he also energetically supported adult and worker education, cooperatives and settlements such as Toynbee Hall. In *The Labour Movement* (1893), Hobhouse advocated a new social-economic policy designed to bring about closer cooperation between the Liberal Party, the trade unions, the cooperative movement and local government. Between 1897 and 1902 he was a leader writer for the *Manchester Guardian*. The political views which he held during this period of his career, in which he opposed British policy and the war in South Africa, are presented in *Democracy and Reaction* (1904). During his years in journalism, Hobhouse's academic standing was maintained through the publication of *The Theory of Knowledge* (1896) and *Mind in Evolution* (1901). In 1907 he was appointed Martin Whyte Professor of Sociology at the London School of Economics. The two most mature statements of his political thought are *Social Evolution and Political Theory* and *Liberalism,* both published in 1911.

WILHELM VON HUMBOLDT (1767–1835) was the elder brother of Alexander von Humboldt the famous explorer, geographer and anthropologist. Wilhelm, educated in the classics and in linguistics, was influenced by the Enlightenment and particularly by Leibnitz. During the years that were devoted to study, Wilhelm von Humboldt also travelled in Europe. In 1802 he was appointed Prussian Envoy to the Holy See, but returned to Berlin after Prussia was defeated by Napoleon in 1806. In 1808 Humboldt became a member of the Prussian State Council and was the author of far-reaching reforms in primary and secondary education. He was instrumental in the founding of the University of Berlin in 1809, but he resigned in April 1810 before the new university was opened. Between 1812 and 1817 Humboldt served as Prussian Ambassador in Vienna and was a member of the Prussian delegation at the Congress of Vienna 1814–15. He also attended the Congress of Aix-la-Chapelle in 1818. Humboldt favoured a stronger form of federalism for Germany

764

than the loose confederation established in 1815. He also believed that a representative assembly should be set up in Prussia. In 1819 he resigned and gave up political life when it became clear that Frederick William III would not create such an assembly. His main contribution to liberal thought is found in his *Ideen zu einem Versuch die Grenzen der Wirksamkeit des Staates zu bestimmen.* The book was written in 1792 but only published in full in 1851; English translation *The Limits of State Action* (1969).

SYLVESTER JORDAN (1792–1861) a South Tyrolean of humble origins, owed his early education to the interest of the local Catholic clergy. Later he was a pupil and disciple of Rotteck. He studied law in Munich and Vienna and after a spell as a lawyer became Professor of Law at Marburg in 1821 and the author of some important works on constitutional law. In 1830 he was the representative of the university in the Diet of Hesse-Cassel when it was summoned by the Elector; and in the following year Jordan became one of the fathers of the Hesse-Cassel constitution. During the years of reaction in this state he was charged with treasonable activities and arrested in 1839. Held in prison for a long time, he was eventually sentenced to fifteen years' imprisonment in 1843; but he was subsequently acquitted in 1845. Three years later Jordan was appointed Envoy for the Elector of Hesse at the Diet of the German Confederation in Frankfurt; and in 1848 he was a member first of the Pre-Parliament and then of the National Assembly in Frankfurt. An orthodox Catholic and a champion of freedom of conscience, he attacked the Church and opposed its independence during the debates on the religious question in the National Assembly.

JOHN MAYNARD KEYNES (1883–1946) was educated at King's College, Cambridge. During his career as civil servant and economist, he also played an active role in liberal politics. In 1906 he entered the civil service working in the India Office; and his first book, published in 1913, was on the Indian financial system. In 1908 Keynes became a lecturer in economics at Cambridge. He returned to the civil service in 1915 and worked for the Treasury with responsibility for external financial matters. He was the principal Treasury representative at the Paris Peace Conference in 1919. Although not a member of the Reparations Commission, Keynes sharply criticized the reparations clauses in the Treaty of Versailles, and as a consequence he resigned from his appointment in June 1919. He attacked the reparations policy in his polemical book *The Economic Consequences of the Peace,* first published in December 1919. Later he criticized the return to the gold standard in *The Economic Consequences of Mr. Churchill* (1925). During the Depression Keynes' reputation as an unorthodox economist was enhanced when he advocated policies designed to bring about the encouragement and resumption of investment in his major work, *The General Theory of Employment, Interest and Money* (1936). He was principal Treasury adviser 1940–46; and at the end of the Second World War Keynes pioneered the creation of an International Monetary Fund and of an International Bank. He was created a baron in 1942.

EDOUARD LABOULAYE (1811–83), who was born and died in Paris, was a publicist and political theorist as well as a lawyer. He became Professor of Comparative Legislation at the *Collège de France* in 1849. During the Second Empire he became one of its inveterate critics. Laboulaye's opposition to the Empire was expressed in a satirical vein in *Paris en Amerique* (1863). Although a stimulating lecturer, Laboulaye was not an original political thinker. In his writings he expounded the orthodox liberal programme of the 1860s, cf.: *La Liberté religieuse* (1858); *La liberté antique et la liberté moderne* (1863); *L'Etat et ses limites* (1863); and *Parti libéral: son programme et son avenir* (1863). He was elected to the National Assembly in 1871 as a Deputy for Paris and became a Senator for life in 1875.

FELICITE ROBERT DE LAMENNAIS (1782–1854) was born in St Malo, the son of an ennobled wealthy shipowner. He attended the *Collège de France* and St Sulpice, and taught briefly in St Malo. In 1809 he and his brother Jean published *De l'Etat et de l'Eglise au 18e siècle et à l'heure*, a defence of ultramontanism. Following his brother, Lamennais was ordained in 1816. His first major religious work, *Essai sur l'indifférence en matière de religion*, appeared between 1818 and 1823. Towards the end of the 1820s he turned against Charles X and the Legitimists for their use of the Church for political purposes. Lamennais then advocated freedom for the Church. From 1830 onwards he became an anti-royalist, attempting to reconcile liberalism and catholicism. With Lacordaire and Montalembert, he was a founder of French liberal catholicism. After the July Revolution of 1830 they collaborated in producing the newspaper *L'Avenir*; it gained a wide following but soon liberal catholicism was condemned by Pope Gregory XVI in the encyclical *Mirari vos* (1832). Lamennais was excommunicated in June 1834 after he had refused to renounce the liberal principles he had proclaimed in his widely read book *Paroles d'un Croyant*. In contrast to Lamennais, Lacordaire and Montalembert submitted to the Church. While Lamennais ceased to practise his religion, he continued to emphasize democratic principles, cf. *Le Livre du Peuple* (1837) and *De l'Esclavage moderne* (1839). In 1848 he was elected a member of the

766

National Constituent Assembly. He died excommunicated and in obscurity.

EMILE DE LAVELEYE (1822–92) was a Belgian political economist and sociologist. Educated in Paris, he studied law at the University of Ghent. He was appointed Professor of Political Economy in the University of Liège in 1864. To some extent Laveleye was a more dogmatic liberal than some of his fellow liberals in England, including his friend Richard Cobden, cf. *Le gouvernement dans la démocratie* (1891). Laveleye believed that the State could play a positive role in ensuring progress. In addition to works on monetary questions, his economic writings include *Elements of Political Economy* (1882), and *The Socialism of Today* (1884). He was also interested in aspects of political catholicism, e.g. in *De l'Avenir des Peuples Catholiques. Etude d'économie sociale* (1875). Although a free trader, Laveleye did not expect international peace to come of its own accord. He advocated the drawing up of a Code of International Law and the creation of an International Court of Justice.

WILLIAM EDWARD HARTPOLE LECKY (1838–1903), historian and essayist, was born in Ireland; he completed his education at Trinity College, Dublin. His first success as a writer came in 1865 with the publication of *The History of the Rise and Influence of the Spirit of Rationalism in Europe*. Although a liberal, Lecky opposed the adoption of a democratic franchise, and therefore also the Reform Bill of 1867, as he feared that the ultimate outcome would be illiberalism. In 1886 he opposed the Irish Home Rule Bill, and later he became a supporter of the Unionist Party. Lecky was Unionist M.P. for Dublin University from 1896 to 1903. He declined to accept the Regius chair of modern history at Oxford in 1892. He was a member of the British Academy and one of the first recipients of the Order of Merit in 1902. His major historical study, *History of England in the Eighteenth Century* (published in 8 volumes between 1878 and 1890) was long regarded as the standard work on that period. Lecky's other writings include: *Leaders of Public Opinion in Ireland* (first published 1861); *European Morals from Augustus to Charlemagne* (1869); *Democracy and Liberty* (1896); and *The Map of Life: Conduct and Character* (1899). He also published a collection of *Historical and Political Essays* (1908).

PAUL LEROY-BEAULIEU (1843–1916), an influential French economist and political journalist, came from a family of well-known writers. He was educated in France and at universities in Germany. An

Biographical List

early work, *L'Influence d'état moral et intellectuel des populations ouvrières* (1868) received recognition from the Academy of Moral and Political Sciences. In 1872 Leroy-Beaulieu was appointed Professor at the School of Political Studies *[Ecole libre des sciences politiques]* which he had helped to found. In 1880 he became Professor of Political Economy at the *Collège de France*. It was through him that the journal *L'économiste française* was established in 1873. His most famous work *La colonisation chez les peuples modernes*, first published in 1874, ran through many subsequent editions. In it Leroy-Beaulieu justified colonization in economic terms so that France would remain a great power. In his *Essai sur la repartition des richesses et sur la tendance à une moindre inégalité des conditions* (1881) Leroy-Beaulieu advocated the export of capital in order to prevent a declining rate of profit. His other writings on economics include *Précis d'économie politique* (1888) and *Traité theorique et pratique d'économie politique* (1895). His liberalism always rejected State intervention, cf. *L'Etat moderne et ses fonctions* (1890).

FRIEDRICH LIST (1789–1846) was born at Reutlingen (later part of Württemberg). His early career as a civil servant was followed by a short period as Professor of Political Science at Tübingen University. He was elected as a Deputy to the Württemberg Diet in 1820. In the following year, after he had put forward radical proposals for a reform of the administration, he was expelled from the Diet. He first became more widely known in Germany when he founded an association of merchants and industrialists for the purpose of seeking the removal of the existing tariff barriers and the formation of a Customs Union. In 1825 List emigrated to the United States where he made a fortune from railways and coalmines. From his observations in that country List became firmly convinced of the need to protect infant industries. After his return to Germany in 1832 as an American citizen, he became United States' consul in Leipzig in 1834. He was active in drawing up plans for railways in France and Germany and in seeking financial backing for them. List encouraged Rotteck and Welcker to edit the *Staatslexikon* to which he contributed. His *National System of Political Economy* (1841) met with much interest. In 1841 he commenced the weekly *Zollvereinsblatt* to encourage national protection of industry; and by 1845 he wanted to see a German parliament evolve from the Zollverein. In the late 1830s and early 1840s, List spent some considerable time in Austria and Hungary; he also visited Brussels and Paris and later London just after the repeal of the Corn Laws. Although he opposed free trade, he admired England's political system. In 1846 List committed suicide during a period of mental depression at Kufstein (Austria).

JOHN LOCKE (1632–1704) was born at Wrington (near Bristol), the son of a country lawyer who followed and supported the parliamentary cause during the Civil War. He was educated at Westminster School and at Christ Church, Oxford. In 1659 he obtained a fellowship at Oxford and he taught Greek and rhetoric while studying medicine and science. He became a member of the Royal Society and was a friend of Robert Boyle. Locke's association with Lord Ashley, later the first Earl of Shaftesbury, began in 1666 when he became tutor to Ashley's son. He held some minor official appointments in the late 1660s and early 1670s; but in 1675 when Ashley was out of favour with Charles II, Locke went to France and spent five years there. He resumed his political association with Ashley on his return to England. After Shaftesbury's final fall from political power, when the Whigs failed to exclude Charles II's brother, the Duke of York, from the succession, Locke was forced to flee to Holland in 1683. In the following year Charles II deprived him of his Oxford fellowship. In Holland Locke found a congenial atmosphere of religious freedom and he associated with others who were close to his own 'unitarian' religious faith. The fruits of Locke's years of study and contemplation in England, his long discussions with Shaftesbury and his experiences in Holland are contained in the publication of three major works which appeared after his return to England in February 1689 following the 'Glorious Revolution' of 1688. Locke's persuasive argument in favour of religious toleration and freedom of thought first came out in Latin in 1689 followed by an English translation later in the same year. His *Two Treatises on Civil Government* was first published in 1690, and so was his *Essay concerning Human Understanding* in which his philosophical and ethical ideas are expounded. Locke was shown favour by the new government under William and Mary. Appointed Commissioner of Appeals, he later became a member of the Board of Trade and Plantations.

SALVADOR DE MADARIAGA Y ROYO (1886–   ) diplomat, man of letters and 'liberal European parliamentarian' (to use his own phrase), was educated in Paris at the Ecole Polytechnique and then at the School of Mines; but he was not interested in engineering as a career. While in Paris he associated with British and Americans living there; and having determined on a literary career he settled in London in 1916. His first book *Shelley and Calderón* was published in 1920. His diplomatic career began in Barcelona in 1921 when he was a Spanish delegate to the League of Nations Transit Conference. This led to his joining the League Secretariat in Geneva in August 1921; and in the following year he became chief of the disarmament section. He remained with the Secretariat until 1927, during which time he published a book on disarmament. He was then appointed to a new chair of Spanish Studies at Oxford which he held from 1928 until 1931 when he became Spanish Ambassador in Washington, following the establishment of the Republic in Spain. He was also a Vice-President of the Spanish Constituent Assembly. In 1932 he was appointed Spanish Ambassador in Paris. Salvador de Madariaga was also the Spanish delegate to the League of Nations between 1931 and 1935. For a few weeks he was Minister of Education in the Lerroux Cabinet in 1934. He left Spain for England in August 1936 after the beginning of the Spanish Civil War and remained in opposition to the Franco regime. His works include: *Englishmen, Frenchmen and Spaniards* (1930); *Anarchy or Hierarchy* (1936); *Histoire de l'Empire espagnol d'Amerique* (1955); and *L'Amerique Latine entre l'ours et l'aigle* (1936). He published a volume of memoirs, *Morning without Noon,* in 1974.

THOMAS MANN (1875–1955) was born into a prosperous merchant family in Lübeck; his father was twice mayor of that city. The Lübeck milieu formed the background for his first major novel *Buddenbrooks,* published in 1901. He studied art and literature in Munich, and then decided to concentrate on writing. Other important works published before the First World War include: *Tonio Kröger* (1903); *Royal Highness* (1909); and *Death in Venice* (1912). Until the fall of the German Empire in November 1918 Mann had been conservative and critical of Western civilization, although he had stood aside from politics. This phase in Mann's development is expressed in his long essay *Reflections of a Non-Political Man.* After the war he became a supporter of the Weimar Republic. His ironic novel *The Magic Mountain* (1924) throws much light on attitudes in contemporary Europe. By the end of the 1920s Mann was pointing clearly to the fascist danger in works such as *Mario and the Magician* (1929). He was awarded the Nobel Prize for Literature in 1929. Mann left Germany in 1933 and lived first in Switzerland and then in the United States. During these years Mann became an outspoken champion of freedom and democracy. He actively supported the war effort, writing scripts for the B.B.C. He also wrote several major novels including the tetralogy *Joseph and his Brothers* (1933–44) and *Lotte in Weimar* (1939). Although he visited Germany in 1949 he did not settle there. He remained in the United States until 1952 when he returned once more to Switzerland. Major works belonging to the latter years of his life include *Doctor Faustus* (1947); *The Holy Sinner* (1951); and *The Confessions of Felix Krull* (1954).

770

Biographical List

KARL MANNHEIM (1893–1947) was born in Budapest of Hungarian-German parentage. He studied in Budapest, Freiburg, Heidelberg and Paris and was influenced by Georg Lukács. His early interest in philosophy later changed to the social sciences. In 1925 he became *Privatdozent* in Heidelberg and from 1929 until his dismissal by the National Socialists he was professor of sociology at Frankfurt-am-Main. In 1933 he went to England and became a lecturer in sociology at the London School of Economics. He was appointed to a new chair in the sociology of education at the University of London in 1946, and was nominated director of UNESCO shortly before his death. During his years in England Karl Mannheim made an important contribution to the development of sociology as an academic discipline. His works include: *Ideology and Utopia* (first published in German in 1929) perhaps his most influential piece of writing; *Man and Society in an Age of Reconstruction: Studies in Modern Social Structure* (1940); *Diagnosis of our Time* (1940); and *Freedom, Power and Democratic Planning* (1950).

GIUSEPPE MAZZINI (1805–72), the son of a professor of anatomy, was born and educated in Genoa. Soon after he completed his studies in 1827 he joined the Carbonari. From then onwards as an Italian patriot, humanitarian idealist and republican revolutionary, Mazzini led a life of conspiracy and agitation. He was imprisoned for a while in 1830 and then forced into exile, first to France and eventually to England after a sojourn in Switzerland. The programme of 'Young Italy', aimed at organizing middle-class Italian youth, was formulated by Mazzini in Marseilles in 1831. It became the pattern for the similar organizations in other countries which together formed 'Young Europe'. Their common ideology stressed national unity, liberty, democracy and social justice. While in Switzerland in 1834 Mazzini organized an unsuccessful attempt to invade Piedmont from Savoy. Mazzini played an important role in the revolutionary year of 1848–49; first in Milan, when the Austrians were driven from Lombardy, and later in Rome. In February 1849, when the Roman Republic was declared, Mazzini became chief Triumvir. With Garibaldi he led the resistance to the French occupation of Rome. As Mazzini the republican and Cavour the liberal monarchist were unable to work in harmony in the 1850s, the unification of Italy under the crown of Piedmont-Sardinia took place without Mazzini's direct participation. For the rest of his life he remained unacceptable to the new Italian Government. Mazzini, the romantic revolutionary, was also a prolific writer. Among the best known and most typical of his writings is *The Duties of Man* (1860), which he addressed to working men.

771

JAMES MILL (1773–1836), the son of a Forfarshire shoemaker, took advantage of the educational opportunities available in Scotland for those who did not belong to wealthy families. From Montrose Academy, he was assisted by Sir John Stuart M.P. to go to Edinburgh University where he studied Greek and philosophy. He then trained for the ministry, but in 1802 he became a journalist and literary editor in London. Although he gradually lost his religious beliefs, Mill remained upright, self-disciplined, doctrinaire and uncompromising throughout his life. He first met Jeremy Bentham in 1808 and from 1814 onwards became closely associated with him in London. Mill was not only Bentham's disciple, he also helped to edit for publication some of Bentham's work on evidence and the penal code. After meeting David Ricardo in 1807, Mill later played an important role in encouraging Ricardo to persevere with the writing of his *Principles of Political Economy and Taxation.* Among many others holding a radical viewpoint in politics with whom Mill associated was Francis Place. Mill's three volume *History of British India,* which he had begun writing in 1806, was published in 1818; and this led to an appointment at East India House (1819). Through his position in the office of the East India Company and through the Political Economy Club, founded in the year in which Mill published his *Elements of Political Economy* (1821), he met many men influential in politics or in the commercial world. Between 1816 and 1823 Mill wrote several outstanding articles, including those on 'Government' and 'Colonies', for the Supplement to the *Encyclopaedia Britannica.* In 1824 Mill supported the launching of the *Westminster Review* as an organ for radical and utilitarian ideas; and between 1824 and 1828 he was with others instrumental in founding the institution which was later to become the University of London. The latter years of his association with the East India Company saw him defending the Company's charter and suggesting changes in the government of India before the 1833 Act renewed the charter and initiated changes in company rule.

JOHN STUART MILL (1806–73), the eldest son of James Mill, received a unique but rigorous education from his father which included learning Greek at the age of three and thoroughly studying political economy at eleven. By the age of eighteen he was writing Benthamite articles on economic matters for the *Westminster Review.* Between 1820 and 1821 he spent some months in France where he came to know the French economist Jean Baptiste Say. In 1823 he became a clerk in East India House. He remained with the Company and progressed to more important positions until he retired in 1858 as chief of the office. Apart from the continuing impact of his father, and the passing influence of thinkers such as Coleridge and Comte, there was one other major influence in Mill's undramatic life. This was his long friendship with Mrs Harriet Taylor whom he first met when he was twenty-three, but could only marry in 1851. Although Mill sat in the House of Commons between 1865 and 1868, he had little influence as a parliamentarian although he supported reform issues such as the extension of the franchise in 1867, Irish land reform and women's suffrage. His great influence in the nineteenth century as a philosopher, liberal political thinker and economic theorist derives from his major works which include: *A System of Logic* (1843), partly written while he was attracted to Comte's positivism; *Principles of Political Economy* (1848); *On Liberty* (1859); *Considerations on Representative Government* (1861); *Utilitarianism* (1863); and *On the Subjection of Women* (published in 1869 but written between 1860-61). In later years Mill somewhat modified his early utilitarian position. He spent the last fifteen years of his life partly at Avignon in France, where his wife died in 1858, and partly in London. The writing of his *Autobiography,* published in 1873 shortly after his death, was begun in the late 1850s. It ends with his failure to be returned to parliament in the 1868 election.

COUNT CHARLES MONTALEMBERT (1810-70) was born and educated in England until he was nine years old, and then in France at the *Collège de Sainte-Barbe* where he was shocked by the religious unbelief among his fellow students. In 1830 he joined Lamennais and the liberal movement and contributed to *L'Avenir.* His friendship with Lamennais lasted until 1834 when, following the papal condemnation of liberal catholicism, Montalembert chose to submit to the Pope whereas Lamennais was excommunicated. During the years of his association with Lamennais, Montalembert attacked the State monopoly of education and attempted to set up a free catholic school in Paris. He was arrested, prosecuted and fined following his trial by the Chamber of Peers. As he had succeeded to his father's title, Montalembert became a hereditary member of that Chamber in 1835. After the February Revolution of 1848, Montalembert was elected to the Constituent Assembly as a moderate republican; but he had little regard for democracy, although he favoured nationalist and catholic movements in Poland and Ireland. His appointment to the French Embassy in London in 1848 was vetoed by Lord Palmerston. Montalembert welcomed the *Loi Falloux* of 1850 which gave the Church a share in education; and initially he supported Louis Napoleon after the *coup d'état* of December 1851. Subsequently, as a member of the legislative body during the Second Empire, Montalembert was both catholic and liberal in his sympathies. He was also made a member of the French Academy. Although in 1858 he was fined for publishing a criticism of the government in *Des Intérêts catholiques au Dix-neuvième Siècle*, he continued to call for freedom for the Church (cf. his speech at Malines in 1863). His other writings include: *Des Devoirs des Catholiques sur la Question de la Liberté de l'Enseignement* (1843); *De l'Avenir politique de l'Angleterre* (1855); *L'Eglise libre dans l'Etat libre* (1863); and *Le Pape et la Pologne* (1864).

CHARLES-LOUIS DE SECONDAT, BARON DE MONTESQUIEU (1689–1755) was born at the castle of La Brède near Bordeaux, into the French nobility of the robe. Marriage into a wealthy family enabled him to devote most of his time to study. In 1716 he inherited the presidency (*Président à mortier*) of the *Parlement* of Bordeaux from an uncle. He began writing the *Persian Letters* in 1717. They rank as the first great contemporary criticism of the *ancien régime*. At the time when the book was published in Holland in 1721, Montesquieu moved in court circles and in Parisian society. The later 1720s were years of travel for him following the sale of the Bordeaux presidency in 1726 and his election to the French Academy in 1727. He visited Austria, Italy, Germany and Holland between 1728 and 1729; and then stayed in England until 1731, where he moved in the leading circles of the Establishment. He enjoyed the friendship of Henry St John Bolingbroke and of Lord Chesterfield, and was elected to the Royal Society. After his return to France in 1731, Montesquieu was engaged on the long and arduous task of adding knowledge gained from reading to the observations he had already made in England and elsewhere in Europe. He also prepared a discussion of the English constitution in 1734 and this was later used in *L'Esprit des Lois*. A study of the history of the Roman Republic led to the publication in Amsterdam of his *Considerations sur les causes de la grandeur des Romains et leur décadence* (1734). It was in the same year too that Montesquieu decided to write the work that was eventually to be known as *L'Esprit des Lois*. Completed in 1747 and published in Geneva in October 1748, it was the first great study of comparative government and a truly seminal work. Although Montesquieu continued to practise the Catholic faith, he can probably be best described as a deist. After attacks on him by the clergy, *L'Esprit des Lois* was placed on the Index in 1751.

COUNT DE MONTLOSIER (1755–1838) was born at Clermont-Ferrand and educated at a Sulpician seminary. Although as a young man he passed through a period of religious scepticism, and of pantheism, he was later a strict catholic. In 1789 he was elected to the States-General as a Deputy for the nobility of the Auvergne; but from then onwards he never identified himself with any one party. In the National Assembly he sided with the liberal monarchists, but he opposed the abolition of the privileges of the nobility and disagreed with some of the Assembly's decisions on Church property and the religious orders. During the constitutional debates of 1790–91 he favoured a bi-cameral parliament in which the nobility would form an upper house. Montlosier was then a political publicist as well as a Deputy. In September 1791 Montlosier went into exile, first to Germany and then to England where he edited an émigré paper *Courrier de Londres*. He returned to France in 1801 to an appointment in the Foreign Ministry and acted as political correspondent to Napoleon until 1812. In 1813 Napoleon sent Montlosier on a mission to Italy. Montlosier welcomed Napoleon's return from Elba in 1815. After the Bourbon restoration Montlosier withdrew to the Auvergne, studied philosophy and worked at restoring his estates. Politically he was then a conservative but he opposed the clerical influences which he thought were becoming increasingly powerful under Louis XVIII and Charles X. As a Gallican, Montlosier believed he had a mission to oppose Ultramontanism, the Congregations and the Jesuits and so prevent the Church from increasing its power at the expense of the State. The climax of his campaign was the publication of his biting *Memoire à consulter sur un système religieux et politique tendant à renverser la religion, la société et le trône* (1826). Montlosier was later created a peer by Louis Philippe. His many publications include: *De la nécessité d'une contre-révolution en France* (1791); *De la monarchie française depuis son etablissement jusqu'a nos jours* (1814); *Histoire de la monarchie* (1821–24); and *Memoires sur la révolution française, le consulat, l'empire et la restauration* (1830).

(GEORGE) GILBERT MURRAY (1866–1957) was born in Sydney, Australia; his father, Sir Terence Aubrey Murray, then being President of the Legislative Council of New South Wales. At the age of eleven Gilbert Murray was sent to the Merchant Taylor's School in London, and in 1884 he entered St John's College, Oxford. He achieved an outstanding academic record in classics and he became a Fellow of New College, Oxford in 1888. At the age of twenty-three he was appointed Professor of Greek at Glasgow University. He held that position until 1899, when he returned to New College. In 1908 he was appointed Regius Professor of Greek in the University of Oxford. He continued in that chair until his retirement in 1936. He was a Trustee of the British Museum from 1914 to 1948 and a Fellow of the Royal Academy. The Order of Merit was conferred on him in 1941. Gilbert Murray enjoyed a world-wide reputation as a classical scholar. Through his English translations of Greek literature, particularly of Euripides, Sophocles and Aeschylus and to a lesser extent of Aristophanes, he reached a very wide public. During his long and active career Gilbert Murray took a lively interest in political issues. He contributed to *Liberalism and the Empire* (1900); he supported the women's suffrage movement; and, although he abhorred war, he fully backed Sir Edward Grey's policy in July and August 1914. After the First World War Gilbert Murray became a zealous missionary for the League of Nations in Great Britain. He was a very active chairman of the League of Nations Union from 1923 to 1938. Among his political writings are: *The Foreign Policy of Sir Edward Grey* (1915); *Faith, War and Policy* (1918); *The Problem of Foreign Policy* (1921); *The Ordeal of This Generation* (1929); and *Liberality and Civilization* (1938).

FRIEDRICH NAUMANN (1860–1919), Protestant social thinker and democratic liberal politician, was attracted as a young man by the ideas of Adolf Stöcker, the Berlin court preacher. In 1881 Naumann helped Stöcker to found the German Student Association which was nationalistic and antisemitic in its aims. From 1886 to 1890 Naumann was a pastor, finally at Frankfurt-on-Main. Deeply influenced by Max Weber's inaugural lecture at Freiburg in 1895, Naumann's outlook lost its Christian emphasis. Instead he began to concentrate on the problem of the working class in the modern State. In 1896 he founded the National Social Union as a means of reconciling the interests of the monarchy, the middle classes and the working class in a modern mass society. Naumann then described himself as 'a Christian, a Darwinist and an Imperialist', but dropped antisemitism. He attracted large audiences as a speaker and as a persuasive writer, although his influence was strongest among educated Pan-German liberals. From 1895 onward he was the editor of the weekly *Die Hilfe* which had the sub-title 'God's help, self-help, brotherly help'. This phase of Naumann's career was epitomized in the publication of *Demokratie und Kaisertum* (1900). Like some other liberal intellectuals in the Second Reich, Naumann sought to infuse both State and society with moral principles. In 1903 Naumann gave up the attempt to unite monarchical, national and working-class forces into one movement. He was elected to the Reichstag in 1907 as a supporter of the *Freisinnige Vereinigung*, but later joined another left-liberal group, the *Fortschrittliche Volkspartei*. His book *Mitteleuropa*, a blue-print for a new order in Central Europe under German leadership, was published late in 1915. Naumann did not share the views of the extreme annexationists during the war. After the revolution of November 1918 he worked with Theodor Wolff, Max Weber and Hugo Preuss to provide a democratic basis for the new republican constitution and to define individual rights. As one of the founders of the German Democratic Party, Naumann became its leader in the National Assembly until his untimely death in 1919.

THOMAS PAINE (1737–1809), republican pamphleteer and political idealist, was born in Thetford, Norfolk. His father was a Quaker; and, despite the family's poverty, Thomas was educated at the local Grammar

School until he was thirteen. He left home at nineteen, and for the next seventeen years he tried a variety of occupations. In October 1774 Paine arrived in Philadelphia with letters of introduction from Benjamin Franklin, and a career as a writer and journalist soon opened to him. He first became well-known in January 1776 through the publication of his pamphlet *Common Sense* in which he presented arguments in favour of the separation of the American Colonies from Great Britain. The *American Crisis* papers followed (December 1776–77), and Paine also held several short-term official appointments. In 1787 he left the United States and spent the next two years in England and France. Late in 1789 he went to France again, and for the next three years he was a propagandist for revolution in England as well as in France. When late in 1790 Edmund Burke condemned what had happened in France since May 1789, Paine replied early in 1791 with the first part of *The Rights of Man*. The second part, which was far more radical, appeared the following year. Since Paine then called on the English people to overthrow their monarchical government, *The Rights of Man* was suppressed and its author forced to flee the country in order to avoid arrest on a charge of treason. In August 1792 Paine was made a French citizen by the Legislative Assembly and in the following month he was elected as a member of the Convention. He was closely associated with Condorcet until the fall of the Girondins in June 1793. While imprisoned in France from December 1793 to November 1794, he wrote the first part of *The Age of Reason*, an exposition of his deist faith. The second part was published in 1796. Paine returned to the United States in 1802 but lost all political influence. His deism and free-thought were condemned as atheism, and he was socially ostracised. He died in abject poverty.

PIUS IX (Giovanni Maria Mastai-Ferretti, 1792–1878) was elected to the papal throne in 1846, having held the important bishopric of Imola since 1832. In 1840 he had been made a cardinal. At the time of his election he was generally regarded as being liberal in his outlook; and at first he followed a moderately liberal policy on temporal matters in the Papal States. A limited constitution was granted there in 1847. During the revolutions of 1848 in the Italian States, Pius IX refused to lead a war to expel the Austrians from Italy; and following the murder of Rossi in Rome which led to a popular rising, the Pope was forced to leave the city in November 1848 for Gaeta (in the Kingdom of Naples). Pius IX became increasingly reactionary in outlook. He returned to Rome in April 1850 with the support of the French troops in occupation of the city. Following the withdrawal of the Austrians from Lombardy in 1859, the Pope's temporal power over the Papal States was lost in 1860 when the people of those States decided to form part of the new Kingdom of Italy. Pius IX's growing conservatism led to the promulgation of the

Syllabus Errorum in 1864, hostile to all modern trends. Earlier Pius IX had indicated his intention of summoning a General Council of the Church which should strengthen not only the spiritual power of the Church but also restore its temporal power. Before the Council met in December 1869 the hope was expressed that it would unanimously support a declaration of the Pope's infallibility in pronouncing on spiritual matters; but in the final vote two members refused to accept the declaration while 35 bishops had not attended the session. When French troops were finally withdrawn from Rome in 1870, following the outbreak of the Franco-Prussian War, the city was occupied by Italian forces. When it became the capital of the Kingdom of Italy, Pius IX still refused to recognise it as such and, although he remained in Rome, he was restricted to the Vatican until he died in 1878.

DAVID RICARDO (1772–1823) was born in London, the son of a stockbroker of Dutch-Jewish origin. He entered his father's business as a youth. His early interest in science turned to economics in 1799 when he read Adam Smith's *Wealth of Nations*. Ricardo was wealthy as well as successful in business, particularly in his activities on the Stock Exchange. In 1807 he met James Mill and his circle of friends widened to include Malthus, J. R. McCulloch and other economists. Ricardo first established his reputation as an economist through an article on the bullion controversy in 1809 which he later expanded into *The High Price of Bullion* (1810). His major economic treatise *On the Principles of Political Economy and Taxation* was published in 1817. He entered the House of Commons in 1819 and was an effective and influential member on economic and financial matters. Ricardo also supported parliamentary reform through an extension of the franchise and the gradual removal of the Corn Laws in the interests of freedom of trade.

EUGEN RICHTER (1838–1906) was born in Düsseldorf and educated at the universities of Bonn, Heidelberg and Berlin. He tried to enter the Prussian government service, but when he was elected burgomaster of Neuwied in 1864 his election was not confirmed by the government. He then became a political publicist. In the 1860s Richter was a disciple of the radical liberal, Hermann Schulze-Delitsch. He was first elected to the Reichstag in 1867 and throughout the 1870s and 1880s remained in opposition to Bismarck. He was a formidable critic of the annual budgets of the German Reich, of increases in the army, and of the increasing power of the State. During the crisis over the Army Bill in 1874 Richter attempted, in vain, to win parliamentary control over the Reich budget. From 1875 onwards he was the leader of the Progressive Party in the Reichstag and also the party's main publicist. He appealed to the petty bourgeoisie and to the commercial middle class for political support. Richter formed the *Deutsche freisinnige* party in 1884 and founded the *Freisinnige Zeitung* in 1885 as its party organ. The *Freisinnige* party was again split by him in 1893 as a result of his opposition to a new Army Bill. Richter then formed the *Freisinnige Volkspartei*. By then he had become rather doctrinaire in adhering to the classical liberal principles which he had proclaimed since the 1860s. Although Richter opposed Bismarck's anti-socialist legislation in 1878, he remained critical of workers' movements.

KARL VON ROTTECK (1775–1840) was born and educated in Freiburg-im-Breisgau. The son of a professor, he was brought up in the philosophy of the Josephine enlightenment in addition to his being attracted by Kant and Rousseau. After studying law and history at Freiburg, Karl von Rotteck was appointed Professor of World History at Freiburg in 1798. In 1818 he became Professor of Political Science in the Faculty of Law. In 1819 he represented the University in the upper house of the Baden Diet. He used the opportunity to advocate political reform. Between 1812 and 1826 he published the ten volumes of his *Allgemeine Weltgeschichte* (*Universal History*) which became a popular work and was translated into English, French, Italian, Danish and Polish. In 1829 he published his *Lehrbuch des Vernunftsrechts* (*Manual of the Law of Reason*). Rotteck was elected to the second chamber of the Baden Diet in 1831; but a year later he was forced to resign his chair on account of his liberal political views. Although not an original political thinker, his political ideas reflected the outlook of the upper middle class in south Germany. His political writings, based on the south German constitutional experience, became text books for German liberals. Rotteck placed political liberty before the achievement of German national unity. He admired the United States, and regarded the French constitution of 1791 as the model for a constitutional monarchy. Between 1834 and 1844 he collaborated with K. T. Welcker in compiling the *Staatslexikon* (*Political Dictionary*), which became the most influential organ of political liberalism in Germany before 1848. Rotteck favoured a constitutional monarchy as a middle ground between the extremes of revolution and reaction.

JEAN-JACQUES ROUSSEAU (1712–78), the son of a watchmaker and citizen of Geneva, began a life of wandering in Savoy, Italy and France at the age of sixteen. Although he first arrived in Paris in 1741, he only took up residence there from 1743 onwards. His literary talents were then encouraged through his friendship with Diderot, one of the leading encyclopaedists. Rousseau first achieved some recognition with

779

his *Discourse on the Sciences and the Arts*, the prize-winning essay which he wrote for the Dijon Academy in 1750. From that time onwards Rousseau was torn between maintaining contact with people from his own lower middle-class background and his desire for fame and acceptance by the aristocratic and literary world of Paris. At the same time, because of his strong individualism, he disliked being regarded as the dependent or the servant of his social superiors. His next major work, the *Discourse on Inequality*, appeared in 1755, to be followed by the novel *Julie, ou la Nouvelle Héloïse* in 1760, his outstanding political treatise *The Social Contract* (which was printed in Holland) and the novel *Emile* in 1762. *Emile* was seized and publicly burnt; and in order to avoid arrest Rousseau fled to Switzerland. When both *The Social Contract* and *Emile* were also burnt in Geneva in 1763, Rousseau renounced his rights as a burgess and citizen of Geneva. He engaged in a literary controversy with Voltaire. His political views were further defined in the constitution which he drew up for Corsica (drafted in 1765), and in *Considerations sur le Gouvernement de Pologne et sur sa Réformation Projetée* (written in 1771 and published in 1782). Rousseau visited England in 1766. He took up residence again in Paris in 1770. From then on he was tolerated by the authorities. He suffered increasing ill-health until his death in 1778. His *Confessions*, first published in 1783, are autobiographical and include a frank analysis of his inner life.

PIERRE PAUL ROYER-COLLARD (1763–1845) was born at Sompuis near Vitry-le-Français. As a lawyer he practised at the bar before the *Parlement* of Paris. He first became politically active during the early months of the revolution in 1789. He was elected to the municipal council of Paris and acted as its secretary from 1791 to 1792. Having been a member of the Convention in 1792, he went into retirement during the Jacobin dictatorship. During that time he studied philosophy. In 1797 he was elected for the Marne to the Council of the Five Hundred and attempted unsuccessfully to bring about a restoration of the monarchy. From 1811 to 1814 he held the chair of philosophy at the Sorbonne, and during this period he exercised an influence on Guizot and Victor Cousin. Although he supported the Napoleonic regime, he retained some sympathy for Louis XVIII. He became more active politically after the Restoration. In 1815 he was elected deputy for the Marne. Known as the 'theorist of the *Charte*', he belonged to the group known as the *Doctrinaires* or constitutionalists, which also included Guizot. Like him Royer-Collard was particularly inspired by the British constitutional experience. In 1817 and 1818 he supported a restricted franchise. He was a Councillor of State after the Restoration. He became a member of the French Academy in 1827, and President of the Chamber of Deputies in 1828. After the July Revolution in 1830, he continued as a member of the Chamber of Deputies until 1842 when he retired from politics. He was renowned as a great orator in the Chamber where he constantly emphasized the need for safeguarding four freedoms: religion, press, parliament and the immovability of the judiciary. His major speeches are included in *La Vie politique de M. Royer-Collard,* ed. Barante (1861).

JEAN BAPTISTE SAY (1767–1832), born in Lyons, originated from a Protestant merchant family. After having had some business experience in England, he became an enthusiastic supporter of the Revolution on his return to France. In 1799 he was appointed as a member of the *Tribunat* but was dismissed in 1804. The first edition of his *Treatise on Political Economy* was published in 1803. Between 1806 and 1813 he established and ran a cotton-spinning factory in northern France. After the fall of Napoleon, he was sent by the newly-restored Bourbon government to study economic conditions in England. In 1815 he began to teach political economy; and subsequently he was appointed in 1817 to a chair of industrial economy at the *Conservatoire des Arts* at Métiers, and in 1830 to the first chair of political economy at the *Collège de France.* Works published during those years include *Catéchisme d'économie politique* (1817), *Lettres à Malthus* (1820) and *Cours complète d'économie politique* (1828–30).

ADAM SMITH (1723–90) was born in Kirkcaldy. He studied at the University of Glasgow, where he was a pupil of Francis Hutcheson, from 1737 to 1740. He then went to Balliol, Oxford, until 1746. The following two years were spent at Kirkcaldy. From 1748 to 1751 Smith gave public lectures at the University of Edinburgh on rhetoric, belles-lettres and jurisprudence. In 1751 he was elected professor of logic at Glasgow University, but later in the same year he took the chair of moral philosophy. Among his friends was the philosopher David Hume. Smith's first book, *The Theory of Moral Sentiments,* was published in 1759. Between 1764 and 1766 he was in France as tutor to the Duke of Buccleuch, the step-son of Charles Townshend. In Paris Smith made contact with several of the leading physiocrats and philosophes, and in Geneva he met Voltaire. After his return to England Smith acted as adviser for several months to Charles Townshend who was then Chancellor of the Exchequer. As Smith received a generous pension from the Duke of Buccleuch, he was able to work quietly at Kirkcaldy from 1767 until 1773 on the book that was to make him famous. After working three more years on it in London, *The Wealth of Nations** was published in

---

* Its full title is *An Inquiry Into The Nature and Causes of the Wealth of Nations.*

781

March 1776. Appointed in 1778 as Commissioner of Customs at Edinburgh, Smith then lived in Edinburgh until his death in July 1790. In addition to his two major works, he wrote several essays, three of which were published between 1755 and 1761 and others in 1795 after his death.

JOHN PRINCE SMITH (1809–74), the son of a London barrister, was educated at Eton for a short while. Later he was an apprentice clerk in a London warehouse and then a banker's clerk, before he took up reporting and journalism. In 1830 he went to Germany, first to Hamburg in connection with an English newspaper, and then in 1831 to the small port of Elbing in East Prussia as a teacher. Here he found an opportunity to take up the cause of free trade. In 1840 he gave up teaching for political and literary work. He published articles and pamphlets in German, e.g. *Uber Handelsfeindseligkeit* (1843), and he also became a naturalized Prussian citizen. In 1846 Prince Smith moved to Berlin, married the daughter of a wealthy banker and became a burgess of Berlin. In 1847 he was among the founders of a Free Trade Union in Berlin; and before long similar societies and free-trade newspapers came into existence in other leading German commercial towns. From 1858 onwards the free-trade movement was linked with the liberal political movement in Prussia and other German states through the Congress of German Economists in which Prince Smith played a leading part. In the early 1860s the Congress strongly supported the extension of free trade in Germany through the Prussian *Zollverein*. From 1862 to 1866 Prince Smith was a deputy for Stettin in the Prussian Landtag, and in 1870 he was elected to the German Reichstag.

HERBERT SPENCER (1820–1903), the son of a schoolmaster, was born in Derby. As a young man he spent a short time as a teacher and in 1837 he became a railway engineer. Despite his upbringing in a strict non-conformist family, Spencer turned into a religious sceptic. He was self-educated in the natural sciences. As he upheld the natural rights of the individual and condemned State intervention, Spencer was in some respects an anti-Benthamite radical. He was also influenced by Darwin's theory of evolution. Out of these elements Spencer formed a view of society in its final form, a view founded on individualism and on belief in economic and social progress, cf. *The Proper Sphere of Government* (1843); *Social Statics* (1851); and *Progress: its Law and Cause* (1857). From 1848 to 1853 Spencer was a sub-editor of *The Economist*. For the greater part of his career as a writer Spencer was concerned with producing the series of books which make up *Synthetic Philosophy*. These include: *The Principles of Psychology* (1855); *First Principles* (1862); *The*

Biographical List

Principles of Biology (2 vols. 1864–67); *The Principles of Sociology* (3 vols. 1876–96); and *The Principles of Ethics* (2 vols. 1892–93). In *The Man Versus the State* (1884) Spencer still stubbornly upheld individualism against the contrary trends that he saw in Gladstonian liberalism. He condemned the growing power of State bureaucracy. His influence as a social philosopher was most effective in the 1860s and 1870s particularly in the United States, Great Britain and Russia. Among his friends were T. H. Huxley, J. S. Mill, G. H. Lewes and Marian Evans (George Eliot), and Richard Potter, the father of Beatrice Webb.

(ANNE LOUISE) GERMAINE DE STAEL (1766–1817) was the daughter of the Swiss financier Jacques Necker, Controller-General for Louis XVI of France from 1776 to 1781 and again from 1788 to July 1789; but she won far greater fame in her own right as a novelist and to some extent as a political writer. In January 1786 she married a Swedish diplomat, Baron Staël von Holstein. Her first book *Lettres de J. J. Rousseau* appeared in 1788. Mme de Staël took an early interest in the Revolution; but in 1790 she left Paris and went to 'Coppet', the Necker family estate on Lake Geneva. This was the first of many journeys between Paris and Switzerland. She was active in politics in Paris from 1791 to 1792 and again between 1795 and 1797. Her long and stormy association with Benjamin Constant began in Switzerland in 1794–95 and continued until 1814. Mme de Staël was in Paris in November 1799 when Napoleon Bonaparte seized power; but in the following year she began to oppose Napoleon and the journeyings between Paris and Switzerland were resumed. Her husband died in 1802. Mme de Staël's novel *Corinne, ou Italie* was published in 1807. Her famous book on Germany (*De l'Allemagne*) was suppressed by Napoleon in 1810 and did not appear until 1813. In it Mme de Staël contrasted the romantic character of modern German literature with the classical approach of French literature. During the latter years of the Napoleonic régime Mme de Staël left Switzerland for Russia and Stockholm (1812–13), and later in 1813 she arrived in England. She was in Paris again between 1814 and 1815; but returned to 'Coppet' while she was writing her *Considérations sur les principaux événements de la Révolution française* (first published in 1818 after her death). The book is a defence of the principles of 1789 and a fresh exposition of French classical liberalism. The last months of Mme de Staël's life were spent in Paris. She was buried at 'Coppet' with her parents.

783

HEINRICH VON SYBEL (1817–95) was born in Düsseldorf. He studied history at the University of Berlin under Ranke between 1834 and 1838. After lecturing at the University of Bonn in the early 1840s, he was appointed to a chair at Marburg in 1846. By that time he had already published a history of the first crusade (*Geschichte des ersten Kreuzzugs*) in 1841 and a study of the origin of German kingship (*Entstehung des deutschen Königtums*) in 1844. Later he held chairs at Munich (1856) and Bonn (1861). He was also active in politics as a member of the Hessian Landtag (1848–49), as a member of the Pre-Parliament at Frankfurt in 1848 and of the Erfurt Parliament in 1850. In 1859 he became one of the founders of the *Historische Zeitschrift* in Munich. He joined the Nationalverein in 1859 and in the early 1860s he favoured a constitutional and national policy based on the influence of the middle class while fearing the impact of popular political pressures. As a deputy in the Prussian Landtag (1862–64) he was critical of Bismarck's policy during the Prussian constitutional crisis. Yet he became a strong supporter of Bismarck after Prussia's victory over Austria in 1866 and after Bismarck's concessions to the Liberals by way of the Indemnity Bill. He was much impressed by Bismarck's achievement of German unity. Sybel was a vocal National Liberal in the Reichstag in 1867 and again in the Second Empire from 1874 to 1880. In 1875 Bismarck appointed him Director of the Prussian Archives. His two major historical works, which clearly reflect his political views, are a well-documented history of the French Revolution between 1789 and 1795 (*Geschichte der Revolutionszeit von 1789 bis 1795*) published in 5 vols between 1853 and 1879, and a detailed and very approving study of the founding of the Second German Empire under William I (*Die Begründung des deutschen Reiches durch Wilhelm I*) (7 vols. between 1889 and 1894). An English translation appeared between 1890 and 1898).

ADOLPHE THIERS (1797–1877), French statesman, journalist and historian, was born in Marseilles. While practising law in the 1820s he began contributing to the liberal *Constitutionnel*. His interest in the French Revolution led to his ten-volume *Histoire de la Révolution française* (1823–27). This work established Thiers' reputation as a historian. As a liberal he opposed the policies of Charles X and supported the July Revolution of 1830. His theory of constitutional monarchy at that time was expounded in articles in *Le National*. Thiers held ministerial office under Louis Philippe between 1832 and 1836 and for two brief periods, in 1836 and again in 1840, he was Prime Minister and Minister for Foreign Affairs. Later in the 1840s Thiers became a liberal opponent of Louis Philippe. He then began work on his massive *Histoire* *de consulat et de l'empire* (20 vols. published between 1845 and 1862). Following the February Revolution and the creation of the Second Republic, Thiers was elected to the Constituent Assembly as Deputy for Rouen. By that time he had become rather conservative in his political views. Thiers spent the earlier years of the Second Empire in exile. In 1863 he was elected to the Legislative Body as Deputy for the Seine. A shrewd debater in the chamber, he was critical of the Emperor's policies. He was particularly critical of Napoleon III's foreign policy. After the French defeat in 1870 and the proclamation of the Third Republic, Thiers was nominated 'Chief of the Executive Power of the French Republic' by the National Assembly in February 1871. He negotiated the Treaty of Frankfurt with Bismarck; and he ordered the suppression of the Paris Commune in May 1871. In the early years of the Third Republic Thiers became the symbol of a 'conservative republic'; and as President of the French Republic from August 1871 he was able to dominate the National Assembly until March 1873 when his downfall was brought about by the clerical and monarchist right.

ALEXIS CLEREL DE TOCQUEVILLE (1805–59) was a member of a Catholic and aristocratic Norman family. His father was in government service under Charles X. After studying law Alexis de Tocqueville was appointed as a magistrate in the Versailles law courts. In April 1831 he went with a friend to the United States to examine the American penal system and used the opportunity to study the manifold aspects of a democratic State and its society. On his return to France Tocqueville left the judiciary service and spent the next two years writing *Democracy in America* (published in 1835). He also made a visit to England in 1833. The final part of *Democracy in America* appeared in 1840. On the basis of this work alone Tocqueville ranks as one of the greatest of modern political thinkers. He was a Deputy in the French Chamber as an Independent from 1839 to 1851; and for the most part he sided with the 'constitutional opposition' until the February Revolution of 1848. During the short-lived Second Republic Tocqueville was a member of the Constituent Assembly, and he became Foreign Minister for a short time in 1849 until he was dismissed by Louis Napoleon. During the next two years he wrote his important, critical *Recollections* of the end of the July monarchy and the Second Republic (first published in 1893). Tocqueville was bitterly disappointed by the trend of events in France which culminated in the *coup d'état* of Louis Napoleon in December 1851. His last work was given to an historical analysis of France in the eighteenth century. The first part appeared as *The Ancien Régime and the Revolution* (1856) but Tocqueville died before completing this masterly study.

HEINRICH VON TREITSCHKE (1834–96), the son of a Saxon officer, was born in Dresden. Already affected by deafness as a boy, he was encouraged to pursue an academic and literary career instead of the army. In 1851 Treitschke went to the University of Bonn and studied under E. M. Arndt and the historian F. C. Dahlmann. From that time onwards he regarded Prussia as the means of unifying Germany. In 1852 he transferred to Leipzig University where he completed his studies in 1855. He began contributing to the new liberal political *Preussische Jahrbücher* in 1857 and became its editor in 1863. After he began lecturing in Leipzig, Treitschke soon established himself as a forceful, stimulating and inspiring teacher. He was appointed Professor of History at the University of Freiburg in 1863. Although convinced that the future of Germany was with Prussia, in the early 1860s he was critical of Bismarck's actions during the Prussian constitutional crisis. In June 1866 Treitschke resigned from his appointment in Freiburg in protest against Baden's pro-Austrian policy during the Austro-Prussian War. After the Prussian victory of 1866, Treitschke, like some other liberals, came to accept Bismarck's policies for Prussia and Germany. He was appointed to the University of Kiel and became a Prussian citizen. In 1867 he accepted the chair of history at Heidelberg. In 1873 he was given the chair of history in Berlin against the opposition of Leopold Ranke. In 1871 he was also elected a member of the German Reichstag as a National Liberal. The first volume of his very readable historical work, *Deutsche Geschichte im 19. Jahrhundert,* appeared in 1879. Four more volumes were published between then and 1894, the last volume taking the story to 1848. Treitschke was a leading historian of the Prussian school of history with its emphasis on the power State and the nation. For twenty years Treitschke's course of lectures on politics was a prominent feature at the University of Berlin. The nationalism and antisemitism of this passionate scholar influenced subsequent generations in Germany until 1945.

ANNE ROBERT JACQUES TURGOT, BARON D'AULNE (1727–81) was born in Paris into an old Norman family, members of which had served in the royal administration. Turgot was intended for the Church, and so he entered the seminary of St Sulpice. He also studied at the Sorbonne. In 1751 he decided against becoming a priest, and in the same year entered the legal branch of the royal administration. In December 1752 he was made *conseiller* to the *Parlement* of Paris; and during the following year he purchased the office of *maître des requêtes.* Turgot had by then become interested in physiocratic ideas, and Dupont de Nemours and Condorcet were among his friends. As a deist he was also an advocate of toleration (cf. his two letters on toleration written in

1754). In 1755 he contributed several articles to the *Encyclopédie*. Between 1753 and 1756 he accompanied Gournay, the Intendant of Commerce, on his tours of inspection. On Gournay's death in 1759, Turgot wrote an *Eloge* which outlined Gournay's life and his physiocratic beliefs. In 1761 Turgot was appointed *Intendant* at Limoges, an office he held for the next thirteen years. During that time he introduced considerable measures of reform into one of the most backward parts of France. Turgot's outstanding work, *Réflexions sur le formation et la distribution des richesses* was written in 1766 and published in 1770. It purported to be destined for two young Chinese students returning home after having been educated in France. Turgot's *Lettres sur la liberté du commerce des grains* also dates from 1770. In August 1774 Turgot was appointed Controller-General of Finances by Louis XVI. He attempted to introduce a programme of far-reaching reforms; but the opposition of privileged circles at court and in the Church to the Six Edicts of 1776 brought about his dismissal when he lost the confidence of the King.

KARL TWESTEN (1820–70), a native of Schleswig-Holstein, was a radical republican in 1848. In the 1850s he entered local government in Berlin as a county judge. Intellectually he was a German follower of Auguste Comte. In 1859 Twesten published a classic statement on German liberalism in a pamphlet with the title *Woran uns gelegen ist* ('What is Fitting for Us'). His aim was to secure individual liberty in the existing State and present form of society; and he looked to a political partnership between the monarchy and the middle class. In 1861 he was elected to the Lower House of the Prussian *Landtag*. In April of that year he published the pamphlet *Was uns noch retten Kann* ('What still can save us') in which he attacked the military cabinet and the Upper House. Its publication led to a duel with General Edwin von Manteuffel. Although Twesten belonged to the Progressive Party in the *Landtag* and opposed Bismarck on the constitutional issue, he was a moderate and averse to political extremes. In 1863 he opposed the war with Denmark over Schleswig-Holstein; but by 1865 he favoured Prussian annexation of the two duchies because he looked to the unification of Germany under Prussian leadership. Early in 1866 Twesten was still in opposition to Bismarck on the Prussian constitutional issue. He was prosecuted on account of speeches he had delivered in the Chamber, and the charges were upheld by the Supreme Court which fined him. By the time of the Seven Weeks' War and Austria's defeat by Prussia, Twesten was willing to support Bismarck on German national issues if the government's internal policy was reversed. He feared that the Progressive Party would lose public support if it continued in opposition to Bismarck. Twesten therefore decided in 1866 to put national power before freedom; and he

Biographical List

was followed by the smaller section of the Progressive Party in voting for Bismarck's Indemnity Bill. Twesten then became one of the founders of the National Liberal Party in 1866. He was elected to the *Reichstag* of the North German Confederation in 1867.

VOLTAIRE, pen-name of **François-Marie Arouet** (1694–1778) was born in Paris of middle-class parents. He attended the Jesuit *Collège Louis-le-Grand* in Paris. By virtue of his education, and later on account of his literary reputation and his wealth, Voltaire could be regarded as belonging to the aristocracy. Within the limited freedom of expression allowed in France at the time the young poet Voltaire became the wit of Parisian society; but in 1717 he was imprisoned briefly in the Bastille for mocking the Regent, the Duc d'Orléans. He worked on the play *Oedipe* (published 1718) during his imprisonment, and this early work was followed by other plays and the long poem *Henriade* (published secretly 1723). In 1726 he was again imprisoned in the Bastille, owing to the enmity of the Duc de Rohan, and only released on the condition that he leave the country. By this time Voltaire's sense of justice had been aroused as well as his religious scepticism and his belief in toleration; consequently he attacked established society and the Church. He migrated to England (1726–29) where he drafted his *Lettres philosophiques* (published 1734). His history of Charles XII of Sweden also belongs to the early 1730s. In 1746 Voltaire was elected to the French Academy. Voltaire and Frederick II of Prussia had long corresponded with each other before Voltaire went to Prussia in 1750 and remained for three years as Frederick's guest; but the visit ended with the rupture of their friendship. *The Age of Louis XIV* was first published in 1751 although parts of it had been written much earlier. From 1754 onwards Voltaire settled at Ferney near Geneva. His house then became the centre of enlightened opinion and many men of letters and other personalities travelled to Ferney to meet him. By the time that Voltaire settled in Ferney he had already begun writing the *Dictionnaire philosophique,* the first volume of which was published in 1764. The publication of his penetrating *Essai sur les moeurs* (1756) also belongs to the vast literary output of the Ferney years. One of his most famous works, *Candide* (written in 1758 and published in 1759), was the result in part of the great Lisbon earthquake of 1755 which shook his belief in optimism and progress. In and after 1762 Voltaire took up the case of the judicial murder of the Huguenot Jean Calas, with a strong plea for justice and religious toleration (cf. *Treatise on Toleration,* published in 1764).

KARL THEODOR WELCKER (1790–1869), the son of a Lutheran pastor, came from Hesse. After studying law his first academic appointment was at Giessen in Hesse-Darmstadt. In 1814 he became professor of law in Kiel. In 1813 Welcker published a work called *The Foundations of Law, State and Penalty* in which he made an early use of the term *Rechtsstaat*. From Kiel he went to Heidelberg, and then in 1819 he was appointed to a chair in Bonn. He was charged and tried for his liberal activities in connection with the *Burschenschaften*, but he was later acquitted. He was then appointed Professor at Heidelberg and later to a chair at Freiburg (1822). He was elected to the second chamber of the Baden Diet in 1831 where he led the opposition together with Karl von Rotteck and put forward demands for the creation of a national German parliament. He was dismissed from his chair in 1832 during a period of reaction. In the 1830s, jointly with Rotteck, he edited the *Staatslexikon* (1834–48). It was through this Political Dictionary and other means that Welcker exercised his main intellectual influence. Unlike Rotteck, Welcker was not a rationalist; he favoured a British type of constitution and he admired the British parliamentary model. Although reappointed to his university post in 1840, he was suspended again in 1841. In 1847 he attended both the Heppenheim and Heidelberg liberal assemblies. Following the revolutionary outbursts in March 1848, Welcker became the Baden envoy to the Federal Assembly in Frankfurt. Later he was an influential member first of the Pre-Parliament and then of the National Assembly at Frankfurt where he played an active role in the Constitutional Commission.

Index

(For categories of ideas *see also* the table of Contents. In this index main references to writers are set in bold type.)

Acton, J. E. E. D-A. Lord, (1834–1902), **749**
  The History of Freedom in Antiquity (1877), doc. 111
  'The History of Freedom' (uncompleted), 599
  corruption of power; freedom achieved by minorities; Liberty the highest political end; civil and religious liberty; British contribution to liberty, **598–600**, doc. 111
  doubt of progress, 36
  tyranny of majority; proportional representation; federal solution; liberty and good govt not always synonymous; historical definition of liberty, **582**, 692, docs 104, 111
agriculture: British (1800), 289n46
  see also land
Alain, E. A. C., (1868–1951), **749–50**
  Élements d'une doctrine radicale, docs 112 a, b
  corruption of power; necessity of political vigilance; *controllers*, not chiefs to be elected, **78–9, 600–1**
Alfieri, Vittoria (1749–1843), *Virtue Unrecognized*, 702
Alfonso XII, King of Spain (1857–85), 416

Allain-Targé, François, R. E., René (1832–1902), 72
Althusius, Johana (1557–1638), 7
America, *see* USA
anarchism: Godwin, 584; Kropotkin, 739; Mannheim, doc. 120
anti-clericalism, 32; defined, 407
  Bastiat, 264; Cavour, 409–11, doc. 76; Ferry, 72; French, 77; German *Kulturkampf*, doc. 95; Mazzini, 411, doc. 77; Montalambert, 408–10, docs 73, 74; *philosophes*, 114; Pius IX denounces, 411–13, doc. 78; Spain, 415–17, doc. 80a; Voltaire, 114–16
anti-semitism and colour prejudice, Murray, doc. 122
Aquinas, St Thomas of (1225–74), 5–6
Argenson, René Louis, Marquis d' 1694–1757, Rousseau on, 60, doc. 8d
Aristocracy, government by:
  Baumgarten, 425–6, doc. 88; Bentham, 243–4; classical economists, 18; Constant, 56; Hansemann, 421–2, docs 50, 56, 84; Malthus, 18; Mill, James, 246; Ricardo, 18; Rousseau, 126, 133; Turgot, 61–4, 579
Arndt, E. M. (1769–1860), **750**

Index

on fatherland and freedom, emancipation of peasants, **419–20**, docs 81,
82
Asquith, H. H., (1852–1928); influence of
Green, 593; social legislation of,
592; and Social Liberalism, 42
assembly, freedom of, 9, 38; Gambetta,
74
association, freedom of: Frankfurt
(1848), 398, doc. 60; French declaration (1789), 155; Gambetta, 74,
doc. 71; Laboulaye, 72, 398;
Lamennais, 395; List, 265–6; Mazzini, 396; Mill, J. S., 276; Napoleon
I bans, 511; Rotteck, doc. 48; Tocqueville, 570–3, doc. 96; Welcker,
397
atheism: Godwin, 12–13; Locke, 113;
Paine, 126; Voigt, 414, 731
Attwood, Thomas, (1783–1856), 47

Bagehot, Walter, (1826–77), on
Philosophical Radicals, 24
Balzac, Honoré de (1799–1850), on indi-
vidualism, 62
Bamberger, Ludwig (1823–99), 85
Barnave, Joseph (1761–93), propertied
suffrage, 58
Barodet, Désiré (1823–1906), 75
Bastiat, Frédéric (1801–50), **750–1**
Sophismes economiques (1846), 262
'The Physiology of Plunder'
Harmonies of Political Economy (1850)
doc. 28
against socialism, free trade, **262–4**
Baumgarten, Hermann (1825–93), **752**
correspondence with Sybel (1863–6),
doc. 87a-d; (1879–81), 426, docs
93b-f; with Max Weber (1878) doc
93a; 'German Liberalism', doc. 88
on Bismark's illiberalism; need to support war agst Austria; dangers of
Vatican; universal suffrage and
radicalism; liberal demonstrations;
(later) conversion to Bismarck and
support for nobility, **425–6**
Bayle, Pierre (1647–1706):
Philosophical Commentary on religious
freedom, **113–14**
Bebel, August (1840–1913), 86, 90
Beccaria, Marquis Cesare de (1738–94),
Treatise of Crime and Punishment
(1764), 244
Bentham, Jeremy (1748–1832), **751–2**,

12, 13
Anarchical Fallacies (1824), doc. 15
Fragment on Government, doc. 19
Introduction to the Principles of Morals
and Legislation (1789), doc. 18
Introductory View of the Rationale of
Evidence, doc, 17
Leading Principles of a Constitutional
Code (1823), docs 20, 36
Plan for Parliamentary Reform (1809,
pub., 1819), 44–5, 172n204
Radicalism not dangerous, (1820), 46
self-interest; utility principle; greatest
happiness of greatest number;
power and wealth; restriction of
govt and law, **159–61, 243–5**
Plan for a Universal Peace (1786–9)
international harmony; agst secret
diplomacy and wars of conquest
and colonialism; for colonial
emancipation, 17, 22, **278–9**
Deonotology, 22
influence of, 24–5, 161–2; on Cavour,
39; on French radicals, 70; 'greatest happiness' principle, 20–1;
Keynes on, 681; liberty and security, on, 21; radicalism of, 22;
'renovation' rather than 'innovation', 44; representation, on, 581;
rotten boroughs, 46; self-interest
as motivation, 25–6; socialism,
and, 19; Spencer and, 583; State
intervention, 20–1; universal suffrage, 19, 288n16; utility principle,
146;
Benthamites and economic policy, 17
Bethmann-Hollweg, Chancellor
Theobald von (1856–1921), 576
Beveridge, William (1879–1963), **753**
Report on Social Insurance and Allied
Services (1941–2)
Full Employment in a Free Society
(1944)
Why I am a Liberal (1945), doc. 117
Power and Influence (autobiography,
1953)
freedom from want, unemployment,
war; 'Free Society' defined; areas
for state intervention; planning for
freedom; essential and lesser liber-
ties, 677, **682–4**
Biedermann, Karl (1812–1901), social
liberalism, 40
Bildung defined, 26, 272

Index

Bismarck, Prince Otto von (1815–98), 86, **424–6**; Baumgarten and Sybel on, docs 87, 93; constitution of, 34; attitude to programme of the liberal bourgeoisie, 101n19; National Liberal Party and, 38, 86; Reich Press Law (1874), 405; Sonnemann and, 90

Blanc, Louis (1811–82), 11, **71–2**; individualism, 63; rights of workers, 76

Boerne, Ludwig, (1786–1837), 403

Bolingbroke, Henry St John, 1st Viscount (1678–1751), influence on Montesquieue, 121

Booth, Charles (1840–1916), social investigations of, 590

Bouvet, Francisque (1799–1871), **752** non-intervention and international jurisdiction, **281**, doc. 42, 292n143

Briand, Aristide (1862–1932), Europeanism, 626

Bright, John (1811–89) **752–3** international harmony and non-intervention, **279–80**, doc. 39; radicalism, 48; repeal of corn laws, free trade, 22–3

Brougham, Henry, 1st Baron (1778–1868), middle classes, 268; Reform Movt, 47

Burckhardt, Jacob (1784–1817), evil of power, 598

Burdett, Sir Francis (1770–1844), 4 suffrage, 45

bureaucracy: Faguet, 66–7, 587, doc. 106; Humboldt, 274; Leroy-Beaulieu, 587–9, doc. 107; Spencer, 583–7, doc. 105; *see also* State

Burke, Edmund (1729–97), *Reflections on the Revolution in France* (1790), 157

Calas, Jean (1698–1762), trial of, and Voltaire, 114–16

Campbell-Bannerman, Sir Henry (1836–1908), social legislation of, 592

Carrel, Armande (ed. *Le National*), 60

Carlyle, A. J., political liberty in Middle Ages, 91n2

Carnot, Hyppolyte (1801–88): Gambetta defeats, 73; universal suffrage, 71

Cartesianism (Descartes), 5

Cartwright, Major John (1740–1824),

'radical aim' of Parliament (1777), 43–4

Castlereagh, Robert S. (1769–1822), 376

Catholic Association of Ireland, 49

Cavour, Camillo di (1810–61), **753** national liberalism, 38–9; chartists and English model of liberty; 'liberty and order', **393**, doc. 57; 'A Free Church in a Free State', 32, 408, **409–11**

Cecil, Lord Robert (1864–1958), 693, 694

Chadwick, Edwin (1809–90), 13, 16; *laissez-faire*, 25

Chamberlain, Joseph (1836–1914), **754** *The Radical Programme*; four freedoms; politics the science of human happiness; State socialism defined; excessive inequality; development of local govt; free education; land reform; tax reform, 49–51; **594–5**, doc. 109

and Birmingham, 590; radicalism, 591–2; suffrage, 46

Chamberlin, W. H., 731

Charles X, King of France (1757–1836), 60; Church and Bourbons, 408, 514; deposed, 405

Charles-Albert, King of Piedmont-Sardinia (1798–1849), and constitution, 33–4

Chartists, 47, 49; and Cavour, 393

Chateaubriand, François René de (1768–1848), 53

Chevalier, Michel (1806–79), **754–5** *History of the Political Economy Taught by the History of Freedom of Labour*, doc. 98: freedom of labour but dangers in trade union powers (British example); liberty leads to equality, **574–5**

Anglo-French Treaty, 254, 282, 574

Leroy-Beaulieu successor to, 587

China: J. S. Mill on mental stagnation of, 579–80

choice, freedom of, in planned society: Hayek, doc. 121; Mannheim, doc. 120

Church: abolition of, Jordan, 414, 79; Bismarck and, doc. 93; Bourbons and, 408, 514; liberalization of, Lamennais, 32

separation of State and:

793

Index

Cavour, 409–11, doc. 75; Combes, 407; Döllinger, 414, doc. 80; French 1789 declaration, 154; Gambetta, 71; Laboulaye, 72; Lamennais, 394–5, doc. 67; Locke, 112; Montalambert, 408–10; Pius IX, *Syllabus Errorum*, 409, 410, 411–13, doc. 78; Prussian const. 1848, 414–15, Tocqueville (democracy in America), 572; Weimar, 10 *see also* anti-clericalism *and in Contents* 'Freedom from the Church and Freedom for the Church'

Churchill, Winston (1874–1965), Keynes on, doc. 116

classical economists defined, 12; their ideas, 12–20

Clemenceau, Georges (1841–1929): radicalism; social measures for workers; recognition of trade unions; agst class struggle, 72, **76–8**

Cobbett, William (1763–1835), *Political Register*, 47

Cobden, Richard (1804–65), 16, **755**
England, Ireland and America (1835), doc. 37
Anglo-French Commercial Treaty (1860), 254, 282, 574; radicalism, 48; Say and, 263; Simon, influence on, 99n17
international harmony through free trade; arbitration, not war; agst International Court, **279–82**, 286–7, 292n130, 382, docs 37, 43
repeal of Corn Laws; free trade and international harmony, **252–4**, doc. 24

Colbert, J. B. (1619–83), 14: protection of industries, 136; and Adam Smith, 141–2

collectivism: Green, 593; Hobhouse, 596–8; Rousseau, 127, 133; *see also* socialism

colonialism: Bentham, 279, doc. 36; Condorcet, 164

colonial wars: agst, Bentham, 278–9, doc. 36; justified, J. S. Mill, 285–6, doc. 41

Combes, Émile (1835–1921), separation of Church and State, 407

communism, on: Hayek, doc. 121; J. S. Mill, 22; Webbs, doc. 122

Comte, August (1798–1857), 72: influence on J. S. Mill, 255

Condorcet, J. A. N. de Caritat, Marquis de (1743–94), 36, 579, **755–6**
Sketch for a Historical Picture of the Progress of the Human Mind (1793–5), doc. 16; belief in progress; equality of nations and individuals; equality in education **162–4**

conscience, freedom of, *see* religious toleration

Constant de Rebecque, Henri Benjamin (1760–1830), 53, 63, 569, **756**
Principes de Politique (1815); *Réflections sur les Constitutions*, 56–7
Cours de Politique Constitutionelle (1818–20), doc. 46
minimal state rights; constitutional monarchy, English example; citizenship for landed and industrial property; freedom of individual, religion and property, thought and press; trial by jury; independent judiciary; emphasis on the middle classes; restricted suffrage, **54–9**
influence in S. Germany, 389; Tocqueville on, 61

constitution, written, Paine, 125–6

constitutional govt, 29–35; *see also* monarchy, constitutional, *and* State

contract, freedom of: Green, 592–4, doc. 108; decline of, Lecky, 573–4, doc. 100

Cooley, C. H., *Social Organisation* (1929), 721

cooperatives: Germany, 88–9; Schultze-Delitzsch, 87–90; and trade unions, Hobhouse, 596–8

Corn Law (1815), 18, 48; repeal of (1846) Gladstone, doc. 266; Ricardo, 15, 251–2, doc. 23; H. Spencer, 583

Coudenhove-Kalergie, Count Richard (1894–1972), pan-Europeanism, 696

Croce, Benedetto (1866–1952), 36, **757**
History as the Story of Liberty, doc. 113; refutes Hegel's disbelief in automatic progress; liberty achieved spasmodically by sacrifice of few, **677–8**
expects revival of true liberalism; for European Union; on J. S. Mill, 693, **695–7**

Index

Dahlmann, Friedrich C. (1785–1860), 80, **757**
Politics Reduced to Fundamentals and the Measure of Existing Conditions (1835, 1847), docs 55, 83
A Word about the Constitution (1815), doc. 54: constitutional monarchy and the English example; taxation, **392**
the right to resistance; national unity before freedom, 77, **420–1**, 429n76
Darwin, Charles (1809–82): Darwinians and social evolution, 583–4, 590–1; Spencer, 583–4; Murray, 739, 740
democracy:
crisis of, Thomas Mann, 685–7, doc. 119
inevitability of: J. S. Mill, 246, 577; Tocqueville, 570–3, doc. 96
liberty and, Hayek, J. S. Mill, Tocqueville, 692
reaction, and, Hobhouse, 640n76
utilitarians and, 21–5
see also representative government *and* suffrage
demonstrations, liberal, Baumgarten and Sybel on, doc. 87
Descartes, René (1596–1650), 164
Cartesian influence, 5
Destutt de Tracy (1754–1836), **758**
Commentary on 'The Spirit of the Laws' of Montesquieu (1814), doc. 45
freedom of the individual and the press; trial by jury, **388**
legitimacy of property, 60–1
Dewey, John (1859–1952), *The Social Frontier* (1935), 730n
Dilke, Sir Charles (1843–1911): radicalism, 48; and trade unions, 81
doctrinaires, see Guizot and Royer-Collard, Döllinger, Ignaz von (1799–1890), **758**
separation of Church and State, 414, doc. 80
Drucker, Peter (1909–), *The End of Economic Man*, 690, 732
Duchâtel, Charles Marie, Comte de Tannegruy (1803–67), 60
Durando, Giacomo (1807–87), on national liberalism, 39
Durham, J. G. Lambton, Lord (1792–1840), and Reform Movt, 47

Eastman, Max, Hayek on, 731
education:
Bentham, 21
equality of, Condorcet, 164, doc. 16
free: Chamberlain, 594–5, doc. 109; Paine, 159; and compulsory, Gambetta, doc. 71
freedom of, 38: Laboulaye, 72; Lamennais, 395, doc. 67; Mazzini omits, 427n9; Offenburg programme, doc. 185; Simon, 73; South German liberals, 83;
illiteracy: French, (1814), 94n7; Spanish, 429n67
reform, Humboldt, 274
rights of, UN declaration, 11
State (national): Frankfurt 1849, doc. 60, Treitschke, 391, doc. 51
elections, free, Thiers, docs 63, 70
emigrate, right to: Frankfurt 1849, doc. 60; Rotteck and Welcker, 389–90
see also movement, freedom of
equality: Chamberlain, 594–5, doc. 109; Chevalier, 574–5, doc. 98; Condorcet, 162–4, doc. 16; French 1789 declaration, 8, 152; Faguet, 66–7, doc. 106; individualism and, 28–9; Lamennais, 394–5, 408–9, docs 59, 73; Madariaga, 696–7; Paine, 158–9, 161–2; Smith, 143–4; South Germans (1849), 85; Trollope, 48
law, equality before the: Frankfurt 1849 const., doc. 60; German Nat. Lib. Party (1867), doc. 90; Hansemann, 421–2, docs 56, 84; Murray, doc. 122; Thiers, doc. 63
liberty and: Mann, 685–7, docs 118, 119; Mannheim, 687–9, doc. 120; Tocqueville, 570–3, doc. 96
social democracy, through, Mann, 685–7, doc. 119
wealth, through distribution of: Condorcet, 164, doc. 16; Hayek, 689–93; doc. 121; Hobhouse, 596–8
see also rights, human
Ernest Augustus, King of Hanover (1771–1851), 33
Europeanism, 696: Briand, 696; Coudenhove-Kalergie, 696
European Union: Croce, 695–7; Murray, 696–7, doc. 123

Fabians and Benthamites, 25

795

Index

Faguet, Émile (1847–1916), **758–9**
Le Liberalisme, doc. 106
small and large states; the State a
necessary evil; limitations of
bureaucratic powers; patriotism;
anti-egalitarianism, **66–7**, 69, **587**
Fawcett, Henry (1833–84), radicalism, 48
Ferdinand VII, King of Spain (1784–
1833), 3
Ferry, Jules (1832–93), 76; anti-
clericalism, 72
Forster, W. E. (1819–86), Elementary
Education Act (1870) of, 589
Fourier, Charles (1772–1837), socialism,
19
Fox, Charles James (1749–1806), 'radical
reform', 44
France:
*Declaration of the Rights of Man and
Citizen* (1789), 8, 122, 146, doc. 13
Bentham on, 247; Locke on, 152–3,
docs 1*a-c*; Smith on 9
French 'Independents', 60–1; 'radical
socialists', 76; Republican Radical
and Radical-Socialist Party
(founded 1901), 77
newspapers and journals: *Globe*
(Duchâtel), 60; *Lanterne* (ed.
Rochefort), 406; *La République
Française* (founded 1871), 75; *le
National* (ed. Thiers and Correl),
60
Franklin, Benjamin (1706–90), liberty
and safety, 691
Frederick II ('the Great') King of Prussia
(1740–86), 272
Frederick III, King of Prussia, later German Emperor (1831–88), 559n
Frederick William III, King of Prussia
(1770–1840), 403
Frederick William IV, King of Prussia
(1795–1861): refusal of imperial
crown, 85, 423
Freedom:
ancient and modern, Laboulaye, doc.
63
defined, Mann, 686; and discipline,
Mannheim 687–9, doc. 120
love of freedom: Mme de Staël, doc. 58
see also individual freedom *under*:
association; education; religious
tolerance, freedom of conscience;
thought, opinion and speech
Free Masons, French, 72, 74–5

Free trade, 14–15; Bastiat, 262–4, 267;
Baumgarten and Sybel, doc. 93e, f;
Bismarck, 426; Bright, 252–4;
Cobden, 280; Colbert, 136, 141–2;
France, in, 155, 282; Germany, in,
282; Gladstone, 254, 257–8,
289–90ns59–64; List, 264–5, doc.
29; Lavelaye, 283–4, doc. 44;
Mazzini, 396, doc. 68; Mill, J. S.,
255–6; Napoleon III, 282; Peel,
258; physiocrats, 136–9; Prince
Smith, 267–8, doc. 30, 283, doc.
38, Ricardo, 251–2; Schulze-
Delitzsch, 282; Smith, 141–5, docs
11a-d; Turgot, 137–9, docs 9, 10;
see also under laissez-faire
Friedrich, Prof. C. J., on Bismarck and
Cavour, 34

Galdos, Perez, *Electra*, 417
Gallicanism, 408
Gambetta, Léon (1838–82), **759**
'Belleville Manifesto', doc. 71
anti-clericalism, 32, 72; free press, 406;
justice, 99n26
freedoms; universal suffrage, 73, **400–1**
speech after 1870, doc. 99: 'prudence'
end of monarchy; participation by
lower classes, **74–6, 575**
Geiger, Baron de, doc. 63
'general will': French 1789 declaration,
154; Rousseau, 126–35, 154
George III, King of G. B., (1738–1820),
and American independence, 147,
148–9
Germany:
Assemblies, constitutions etc
Carlsbad decrees (1817), 403
Congress of German Economists
(1858–60), 282
Constitution of Second German
Empire (1871), 34–5
Hambach Festival (1832), 81–2
Hanover constitution (1834–7), 420
Heppenheim and Offenburg meet-
ings and programmes (1847), 38,
83–4, 422, docs 85, 86
National Assembly in Frankfurt
(1848–9), 33–4, 84–5, 100n3,
419–23; Declaration of the Fun-
damental Rights of the German
People, 9, 397–8, 414–15, doc. 60
Prussian Constitutions (1848–50),
33, 85, 404

Reich Press Law (1874), 405
south German constitutions (1815–19), 33, 82–3, 389
Stein-Hardenberg reforms (1807), 419
Vormärz, (1815–48), 80
Weimar Constitution (1919), 9–10
Zollverein (1860s), 264, 282, 283
Newspapers and journals: *Deutsche Zeitung* (founded 1847), 403; *Frankfurter Zeitung*, 90; *Kladderadatsch*, 405; *Kölnische Zeitung*, 545; *Kreuzzeitung* 404; *Rheinischer Merkur*, 401, doc. 64, 403; *Rheinische Zeitung*: Marx articles in, 404; *Schwäbischer Merkur*, 546; *Simplicissimus*, 405; *Volkszeitung*, 545
political parties and groups: German People's Party, 89–90; Liberal Democrats, decline after 1919, 678–9; National Liberal Party, 69–70, 387, 404–5, and Bismarck, 86, programme of, doc. 90; National Union (*National-Verein*, founded 1857), 86, 404–5, 423; Progressive Party (founded 1861), 86, 89, 387, 404–5, 576, programmes: (1861), 423, doc. 89, (1873) doc. 95; Social Democratic Party (founded 1869), 89; socialists and liberals separate, 86–7; Verein für Sozialpolitik, 40
Gervinus, Georg (1805–71), **759–60**
individualism; demands liberalization after unification, **28–9**, 85, 403, doc. 92
Girardin, Émile de (1806–81), **760**
non-intervention and disarmament, **281**, doc. 40; on Cobden, 292n145
Gladstone, W. E. (1809–98), 41, 738, **760–1**
budget speeches on public expenditure, docs 26*a* and *b*: workers benefit from free trade; govt non-interference
budgets, 289–90ns59–64
free trade, 254; Irish Home Rule, 591, 595; non-intervention (1850), 284; 'principle, not class interest', 736; Second Reform Bill, 589; and Spencer, 583–4
Godwin, William (1756–1836), 12–13; influence on Spencer, 584

Goerres, Joseph, (1776–1848), **761–2**
Rheinischer Merkur, doc. 64: suppressed (1816), 403
Goethe, Johann Wolfgang von (1749–1832): and Humboldt, 272; influence on J. S. Mill, 276; on 'personality', 28
Gournay, Vincent de (1712–59), *see* Turgot, *Éloge de Gournay*, 137–8
Government, *see* State
Great Britain
agriculture (1800), 289n46
Anti-Corn Law League (1839), 49, 252–3; Anti-Slavery Society (1823), 49; Labour Representation Cttee, 51; Liberal Party, decline of (1914–35), 678; London Corresponding Society (1792), 49; National Educational League (1869), 49, 50, 592, 594; National Liberalism, 37–9; National Liberal Federation, 49; National Reform League and Union, 49, 592; 'New Liberalism', 52, 592, 594; 'New Unions' for unskilled workers, 596; Political Union of the Lower and Middle Classes (1829), 47; political unions (circa 1830), 47–8; Progressive Movt, 593–4, 596; *The Radical Programme* (1885), 49–50; Society for Supporting the Bill of Rights (1769, Wilkes), 49; Westminster Radicals, 47
national wealth (1843–53), 290n64
newspapers and journals: *Economist*, 16; *Fortnightly Review* (1883), 50; *Manchester Guardian*, 52, 597, 744: *Nation*, 52
Green, T. H. (1836–82), **762**
Liberal Legislation and Freedom of Contract (1881), doc. 108
Political Obligations (1879–80), 603n60
influence on Progressive Movt, 596; social liberalism, 40–1; utilitarian individualism, 591
'positive freedom'; necessity of State intervention with freedom of contract; influence on Asquith, **592–4**
Gregory XVI, Pope (1765–1846), condemns liberal catholicism, 395
Grey, Charles, Earl (1764–1845), 47, 738
Grimm, Jacob (1785–1863) and Wilhelm (1786–1859), uphold constitution,

Index

420–1
Grotius, Hugo (1583–1645), and Natural Law, 6
groups a threat to democracy: Mannheim, 687–9, doc. 120; Rousseau, 126–35;
see also minorities
Guizot, François (1787–1874), 30, 53, **762–3**
'The History of Civilization in France' (lectures), 63; and British constitution, 31; on the middle classes, 268–9, 271; propertied suffrage, 36; Tocqueville and, 63
History of the Origin of Representative Government in Europe, doc. 97
Memoirs to Illustrate the History of my Times (1815), doc. 65: press freedom, **401–2**
civil and moral rights distinct from political; support for middle classes and for monarch, **58–60**
representative govt defined; middle classes and propertied suffrage, **569–70**

Hague Court, 283
Haldane, Richard Burton, 1st Viscount (1856–1928), 596
Halévy, Élie (1870–1937), 690
Hall, Robert (dissenter, 1764–1831), 4
Hansemann, David (1790–1864), 403–4, 430ns84, 87, **763–4**
Memorandum for King Frederick William of Prussia (1830), doc. 56
Memorandum on Prussia's Position and Politics (1840), docs 33, 50, 84
freedom for middle classes, agst universal suffrage, **270–1**; English const. not model for Prussia; taxation; struggle between aristocracy and democracy, **392**; representation of educated and propertied classes; agst nobility; equality before the law; const. monarchy, **421–2**
happiness, greatest, of greatest number, 12; Bentham, 20–1, 160, docs 17–20, 243–5; J. S. Mill, 27–8, 247–8, 275, doc. 35; Rousseau, 128
of masses: Chamberlain, 51; pursuit of, American declaration, 148
Harcourt, Sir William (1827–1904), 48
Hare, Thomas (1806–91), and proportional representation (1859), 581

Harkort, Friedrich, and working classes, (1793–1880), 40
harmony, international, *see* non-intervention
Häusser, Ludwig (1818–67), 403
Hayek, F. A. (1899–   ), 677, **763–4**
The Road to Serfdom (1944), doc. 121
socialism and liberty; freedom of choice and equal distribution of wealth; communism and fascism; creation of conditions favourable to progress, not to 'plan progress'; 'limited' and 'absolute' security and liberty, **689–93**
Beveridge on, 683–4, 715–17
Mannheim, and, 687
Hecker, Friedrich, (1811–81), 83, 84, 423
Hegel, Georg (1770–1831): and Constant, 388; Croce refutes, 678; Treitschke, 390
Heimann, Prof. Eduard, Hitler and liberalism, 732–3
Heine, Heinrich (1796–1856), 403
Heppenheim programme, 38, 83–4, 422, doc. 86
Himmelfarb, Gertrude, on Acton, 600
Hinsley, F. A. on Liberals and non-intervention, 287
Hobbes, Thomas (1588–1679): *Leviathan* (1651), 6–7; social contract, 106
Hobhouse, L. T. (1864–1929), 40–2, 51, **764**
Democracy and Reaction (1904) 764: imperialism after Boer War, 604n76
Liberalism (1911), docs 110a and b: the State and collective responsibility; 'justice not charity'; 'social obligation and private responsibility'; Liberalism and Socialism, doc. 110a, 'social conception of property'; 'equation of social service and reward', doc. 110b, **596–8**
'New Liberalism', and, 592; Progressive Movt, and, 596; State to acquire land bordering new towns, 604n81; social liberalism, 40–2, 51–2
Social Evolution and Political Theory (1911) 764
The Labour Movement (1893), 764
support of trade unions; cooperation between trade unions and coops; relation of liberty to collective con-

trol; State intervention for better distribution of wealth, **596–8**
Hobson, J. A. (1858–1940), and social liberalism, 51–2
Hugo, Victor (1802–85), and Peace Congress, 281
Huguenots, 114; Edict of Toleration, 117; refugees, 111; toleration of, Turgot, 116
human rights, *see* rights
Humboldt, Alexander von (1769–1859), 272
Humboldt, Wilhelm von (1767–1835), **764–5**
    The Limits of State Action (1792–3), 26, docs 34a, b; *Bildung*; individuality, 26–7, **272–4**
Hume, David (1711–76), élitist suffrage, 18
Hume, Joseph (1777–1855), 47

imperialism, Hobhouse, 604n76
individual: freedom and security of the, 9, 53–5, 392, 394, 407, docs 58–63; Bentham, (liberty and security), 21; Beveridge (social security), 682–5; Destutt, 388; Franklin, 691; Frankfurt 1849, doc. 60; French declaration (1789), 152, doc. 13; Gambetta, doc. 71; Hayek, 689–93, doc. 121; Keynes, 682, docs 115, 116; Montesquieu, 120–1, 167n70; Murray, doc. 122; Offenburg programme, doc. 85; Paine, 124–5, doc. 6; Rotteck, 38, 421; Rousseau, 129, doc. 8a; Smith, 145; Thiers, docs 63, 70; UN declaration, 11
free trade and the individual: Turgot, doc. 9; planned society, in, Mannheim, 687–9, doc. 120; socialism, and, Hayek, doc. 121
rights: Locke, 7; Paine, 125–6, doc. 4; Staël, 395, doc. 58
individualism: Balzac, 62; Blanc, 63; equality and, 28–9; France (mid-19th cent.), in, 62–3; Gervinus, 28–9; Goethe, 28; Green, 591; Humboldt, 26–7, 272–4, docs 34a and b; Lamartine, 62; Lamennais, 62; Madariaga, doc. 123; planned society and, Mannheim, 687–9, doc. 120; Mill, J. S., 27–8, docs 25, 35; Rousseau, 134; Sainte-Beuve,

62; Spencer, 41, 583–7, doc. 105
aesthetic (qualitative) individualism defined, 26; stressed, Humboldt, 26–7, Mill, J. S., 27–8; Treitschke rejects, 390–1;
majority, and, Mazzini, 397, docs 61, 68
personality, cult of, 28–30
International Court: Cobden agst, 278–82, doc. 43; Hague, 283; Laveleye, 283–4, doc. 44
Itzstein, Johann Adam von (1775–1855), 83

Jefferson, Pres. Thomas (1743–1826), and American declaration, 148
Jordan, Sylvester (1792–1861), **765**
separation of Church and State; supremacy of State, 414, doc. 79
judiciary: independence of, 9; Locke, 108, docs 1b, c; Montesquieu, 121–2, doc. 5a
jury, trial by: Constant, 54; Destutt, 388, doc. 45; List, 266; Offenburg and Heppenheim, docs 85, 86
justice: individual, and, Smith, 145; publicity for, List, 266

Kant, Immanuel (1724–1804): and Humboldt, 272; non-intervention, 281
Keith, Sir Arthur (1866–1955), **709–10**
    New Theory of Evolution (1948): social Darwinism; codes of amity and enmity, 739, 740
Keynes, J. M. (1883–1946), **765–6**
    The End of Laissez-faire (1927), doc. 115: Bentham's *Agenda* and *Non-Agenda*; state socialism; self-interest not necessarily enlightened; separation of social and individual services; where state should intervene; élitism, 712–16
    Essays in Persuasion (1931), doc. 116; decline but value of Liberal Party; Labour Party and tyranny of trade unions; rejection of Churchill; 'Economic Efficiency, Social Justice, Individual Liberty', 680–2
Kinkel, Gottfried (1815–82), 85
Kropotkin, Prince Peter (1842–1921), *Mutual Help*, Murray on, 739
Kulturkampf doc. 95

Laboulaye, Edouard (1811–83), 64, 407, **766**

Index

The Liberal Party, its programme and its future (1864): freedoms; separation of Church and State, 72
L'État et ses Limites, doc. 62: power of State; freedom of assocn; English example; democratic Caesarism, **398** Constant, and, 427n13
free press, 406; Treitschke on, 391–2, 451–3
labour: property includes, source of wealth, division of: Locke, 105–10, doc. 16c; List, 264–7, doc. 29; Say, 17, 60, 259–62; Smith, 140–5, docs 11 a-d
see also workers, working class
Lacordaire, J. B. II. (1802–61), 395
La Fayette, M. J. Marquis de (1757–1834), 53, 60
Laffitte, Jacques (1767–1844), 60, 63
laissez-faire: Bastiat, 262–3; Bentham, 25, 45; Bright, 252–4; Chamberlain, 50–1; Cobden, 252–4; Gladstone, 257–8; Hobhouse, Keynes, 680; Leroy-Beaulieu, 67–70, 587–9, doc. 107; Manchester School, 590; Mann, 685, Mannheim, 687; Mill, J. S., 17, 255–7; Physiocrats, 14; Ricardo, 251–2; Smith, 140–5; Spencer, 583–7, doc. 105; Turgot, 135–40; *see also* Free trade
Lamarck, J. B. P. A. de Mouet, Chevalier de (1744–1829), and Spencer, 583–4
Lamartine, Alphonse de (1790–1869), individualism, 62
Lamennais, Abbé Félicité de (1782–1854), **394–5, 766–7**
L'Avenir (1830), doc. 67, 74
Freedom of the Church (1830), doc. 73
Paroles d'un Croyant, doc. 59, six freedoms; egalitarianism; freedom by sacrifice; decentralization, freedom of education, **394–5**, separation of Church and State; freedom of the press; example of Irish Catholics, 408–9, docs 73, 74
freedom of assocn, 397; Mazzini on, 396; individualism, 62; liberalization of Church, 32
land
reform: Chamberlain, 594–5, doc. 109; Heppenheim, doc. 86; physiocrats,

136–9
productive element: Say, 261; Smith, 140–5
State ownership of: Chamberlain, 594; Hobhouse, 604n81
taxation, of: Quesnay, Say, Turgot, 136–9
see also agriculture
Laski, Harold (1893–1950), economic security and liberty, 691
Lassalle, Ferdinand (1825–64), 86
break with Liberals, 87
Laveleye, Émile de (1822–92), **767**
self-interest; free trade and international arbitration; code of international law; International Court of Justice, 283–4, doc. 44
law, rule of, Locke, 106–7, doc. 16
see also justice, and juries, and natural law
League of Nations, Murray, 693
Lecky, W. E. H. (1838–1903), **767**
Democracy and Liberty (1896), doc. 100
reason and liberty; democracy and liberty not identical; centralization of State power; increase in taxation; decline of free contract and trade; restrictive practices of trade unions; dangers of extended franchise, **573–4**
Ledru-Rollin, Alexandre (1807–74), 'ultra radical', 70–2
Leopold I, King of Belgium (1790–1865), and constitution, 31
Leroy-Beaulieu, Paul (1843–1916), **67–70, 587–9, 767–8**
The Modern State in Relation to Society and the Individual, doc. 107
State 'devoid of inventive genius', 'a copyist', subject to volatile majority; its lack of continuity and interest in larger (synthetic) matters; not competitive; bureaucrats lack stimulus; patriotism and security; colonial nationalism, **67–70, 587–9**
Liberales, origin of name Liberal, 3
Liberty, defence of: Acton, 582, docs 104, 111; Mann, 685–7, doc. 118; Mazzini, doc. 61; Montesquieu, 117, docs 5 a, b, c
Liebknecht, Wilhelm (1826–1900), 86, 90
Lippmann, Walter (1899–1974), social-

ism and freedom, 731
List, Friedrich (1789–1846), **768**
*The National System of Political
Economy* (1819), doc. 29: internal,
not external free trade; freedom of
press, speech, assocn, conscience;
trial by jury; publicity for justice;
division of labour and cooperation,
264–7
Liverpool, Robert, Lord (1770–1828), on
limited suffrage (1793), 246
Lloyd-George, David, (later Lord),
(1863–1945), 52, 713
local government: J. Chamberlain, 594–5,
doc. 109; J. S. Mill, 579–82, doc.
103; Tocqueville, 581
Locke, John (1632–1704), 3, 35–6, **769**
Two Treatises of Government (1681–3
and 1690), doc. 1 a-c
*An Essay Concerning the True, Original
Extent and End of Civil Government* (1689) social compact; state
of nature defined; consent of
majority; power of punishment;
rights of property, including
labour; rule of law; power of legislature not arbitrary; taxation by
consent, **105–10,** 113
Letter on Toleration (1689), doc 2,
110–13, 166n32
American declaration, influence on,
147–8, 170n161; and French
declaration, 152–3, docs 1a-c;
Montesquieu, and, 120–1; Rousseau, and, 127–8
Louis XIV, King of France (1638–1715),
revocation of Edict of Nantes, 113
Louis XVI, King of France (1754–93):
gives civil status to protestants,
154; dismisses Turgot (1776), 139;
religious toleration, 116–7; revolution, and, 150
Louis Napoleon, *see* Napoleon III
Louis Philippe, King of the French
(1773–1850): attempt on life of
(1835), 402; Constant, and, 388;
constitution, and, 31; Guizot, and,
choice of Ministers by, 59; press
censorship, 405
Louménie de Brienne, Archbishop
(1727–94), and toleration, 117

Macaulay, Thomas Babington, 1st Baron
(1800–59): middle classes, 268;

universal suffrage, 19
McCulloch, J. R. (1789–1864), 12, 13,
17–18; agst universal suffrage, 19;
repeal of the Combination Laws,
92n8
MacDonald, Ramsay (1866–1937), and
liberalism, 51–2
Machiavelli, Niccolo di (1469–1527),
Rousseau on, doc. 8e
Madariaga, Salvador de (1886–   ), 694,
769–70
Europe and the Liberal Principles
(1948), doc. 123; European union,
696–7
majority
consent of, Locke, 106–10
individuality, and, J. S. Mill, doc. 35
rule, Paine, doc. 7
tyranny of: Acton, 582, J. S. Mill, 579–
82; Spencer, 583–7; Tocqueville,
577–9
Malthus, T. R. (1776–1834): 12–15; aristocratic govt. 18; influence on
Duchâtel, 60; monarchy, 17;
Reform Bill (1832), 18; Say
rejects, 262
Manchester School, 16; and *laissez faire*,
590; and radicalism, 48
Mann, Thomas (1875–1955), **770**
The Problem of Freedom (1939), doc.
118
'The Social Renewal of Democracy'
(1938), doc. 119
freedom defined; liberalism not identical with liberty; reconciliation of
liberty and equality through social
democracy; crisis of democracy;
bourgeois, passive liberalism obsolete, 677, **685–7**
Mannheim, Karl (1893–1947), 692, **771**
*Freedom, Power and Democratic Plan-
ning* (1949), doc. 120; freedom
and discipline; free enterprise;
equality and freedom; planned
society, the individual and freedom
of choice, 677, 685, **687–9**
Manteuffel, Edwin von (1809–85), 560n
Maret, Henry (ed. *Le Radical*), 77
Martineau, Harriet (1802–76), 16
Marx, Karl (1818–83) and *Rheinische
Zeitung*, 404
Marxism and liberals, 51
Massingham, H. W. (ed. *Nation*, 1860–
1924), 52

Index

Mazzini, Giuseppe (1805–72), **771**
'On the Duties of Man', doc. 61
'Rome and the French Government',
doc. 77, all liberties derived from
God; Liberty and Papacy irreconcilable; Liberty a means, not an
end, **396–7**
freedom of education omitted, 427n9
mercantilism, 3; physiocrats agst. 136;
reaction agst, 13–14; Smith, 140–
5, docs 11 a-d
Metternich, Prince Clemens (1773–
1859): Pius IX, and, 410; restricts
press freedom (1817), 403
Mervissen, Gustav von, (1815–99), social
liberalism, 40, 403–4
Michelet, Jules (1798–1874), cult of the
people, 96n5
middle classes, role of: Brougham, 268;
Constant, 57, 59; Guizot, 268–9,
271
mediocrity of, J. S. Mill, doc. 35
superiority of, 268–70; guide post for
the lower orders, James Mill,
Guizot, Hansemann, 268–71, docs
31–3; Guizot, q.v.; Say, 260–1
values, Cobden, 253
see also under suffrage
Mill, James (1773–1836), 12–13, **772**
Essay on Government (1820, doc. 31
representative govt; universal suffrage
(not women) in principle only;
freedom of discussion, 46, **268–9,
271**
'The Church and its Reform' (1835), 23
aristocratic govt, agst, 18; influence on
Cavour, 39; self-interest motivation, 25–6; socialism, and, 19; universal suffrage, 19, 22–3, 45
Mill, J. S. (1806–73), **772–3**, 35–6, 716n
Principles of Political Economy
(1848–52), doc. 25
Autobiography (1873)
non-interference of State; equality of
taxation; defence of individual;
division of labour, **247–9, 255–7**
On Liberty (1859), doc. 35, 291n125
Utilitarianism (1861)
social freedom; in praise of individuality; importance of genius;
mediocrity of middle classes
modified happiness principle; cultural élitism; pluralism of value systems; liberty of conscience,

thought, assocn; limitation of State
interference; support for
minorities (blacks and women);
freedom of opinion 23, **274–8**
A Few Words on Non-Intervention, doc.
41, for non-intervention, exc
colonial wars and with barbarians;
Britain's image abroad; balance of
power, **284–7**
*Considerations on Representative Gov-
ernment*, doc. 103: individuality;
rights of minorities and pluralism;
tyranny of majority; modified universal suffrage; proportional
representation; importance of local
govt to temper centralization;
democracy inevitable; danger of
social democracy, 577, **579–82**
Bentham, on, 245; communism, 22;
cultural élitism, 28; happiness
principle, 27–8; Humboldt's
influence, 26, 272; individualism,
27–8; Mill, James, on, 247; radicalism, 47–8; socialism, 19–20;
Treitschke on, 451–3; universal
suffrage, 23; utilitarianism, 589
Milton, John (1608–74), 7
Areopagitica (1643), 4
Paradise Lost, 6
minorities:
power, and, Acton, 598–600, doc. 111
protection of, Murray, 122
rights: Frankfurt (1848), 398, doc. 60;
Mill, J. S., 276, 579–82, doc. 103
see also groups
Mirabeau, André, Vicomte de (1754–92),
465
Mommsen, Teodor (1817–1903), on
Bismarck constitution, 34
monarchy, 17–18; American independence and, 147–50; Bentham, 45,
159; Gambetta, 575, doc. 99;
Guizot, 58–60, doc. 65, Malthus,
17; Mill, James, 246; Montlosier,
408, doc. 72; Paine, 157–9, doc.
14; physiocrats, 17; Tocqueville,
61, 63;
constitutional: British example, see
Cavour, Dahlmann, Guizot, Hansemann, Laboulaye, Montesquieu,
Nauman, Staël, Treitschke, Welcker
Constant, 56, 388; Dahlmann, 392,
420; *Deutsche Zeitung*, 403; Ger-

man Nat. Lib. Party (1867), doc. 90; Grimms, 420–1; Hansemann, 421–2; Locke, 105–10, docs 1a, b, c; Naumann, 575; Prince Smith, 267, doc. 30; Rotteck and Welcker, 81–3, 389–90, docs 48, 49; Thiers, 31, 65, 399, doc. 70 French, 53, 60; revolution and, 8–9, 150–8; 1814 const. 94n6; 1834, 70; after 1870, 74 republic and, Montesquieu, 118–19, doc. 5a; sovereignty of the people, Rousseau, 130 *see also* republicanism

Mond, Sir Alfred (1868–1930): Keynes on, doc. 116

monopolies, abolition of: French 1789, declaration, 155, 171n170; Smith, 140–5, Turgot, 137–9

Montalambert, Charles de (1810–70), 395, 428n48, **773–4** 'The Free Church in the Free State': freedom of education and conscience; tolerance, 418, **409–10**

Montesquieu, Charles-Louis de (1689–1755), 39, **774** *The Spirit of the Laws* (1748), docs 5 a–c monarchy or republic; British example, Liberty of the subject (security); separation of legislative and executive powers, 29, 30–1, **117–22**, 167ns70, 75 Destutt on, 388, doc. 45 *Persian Letters* (1721), 114 war, and, 372

Montlosier, François-Dominique de (1755–1838), **774–5** *Mémoire à consulter sur un système religieuse et politique* (1826), doc. 72 monarchist; agst Jesuits, ultramontanists, priests, **408**

Morley, John, 1st Viscount (1838–1923), radicalism, 48, 596

Morley, Samuel (1809–86), radical, 48 movement, freedom of, 83; Frankfurt 1848, 398, doc. 60; Mazzini, 396; UN declaration, 11

Murray, Gilbert (1866–1957), **775–6** *The Meaning of Freedom*, doc. 122 decline of liberalism due to war; call for 'principle, not class interest'; national self-determination; codes

of amity and enmity; socialism dogmatic; League of Nations; scepticism on Human Rights declaration, cooperation between the nations required, but not their independence; liberalism "not a dogma, a process not an end", **679, 693–4**

Napier, Admiral Sir Charles (1786–1860), 359–60

Napoleon 1 (Bonaparte), Emperor of France, (1769–1821), 54 bans free assocns, 511; international 'family', 373

Napoleon III (Louis Bonaparte) Emperor of France (1808–73): coup d'état (1852) of, 72, 450; free trade and, 282; liberal concessions by, 72; 'liberal empire', 64; plebiscitary democracy, 573; Press Law (1852), 406

National-Liberalism, 37–9, docs 85, 86, 90

nationalism, 33, 418–27; Dahlmann and Rotteck, 421; Gervinus, 28–9, doc. 92; Murray, doc. 122; Pfizer, 37, 430n81; Wilson, Pres., 679

nationality, right to, UN declaration, 11

'natural harmony', 14

natural law, 5–6, 14; Grotius, 6; Locke (state of nature), 105–10, docs 1 a–c; Montesquieue (and divine law), doc 5c; Pufendorf, 6; Sieyès (and positive law), 152; Rousseau, 127–9; Voltaire (and intolerance), doc. 3a

natural rights: Bentham, 160; French revolution and, 157; Paine, 158; parliamentary reform and, 24; Rotteck, 390; Spencer, 583–7, doc. 105

Naumann, Friedrich (1860–1919), **776** 'Democracy and Monarchy', (1912), doc. 101, British example of const. monarchy; Germany constitutionally split; democracy to modify conservative Prussia, **575–7**

Newton, Isaac (1642–1727): influence of, 5; model for Say, 260

Nicolaus of Cusa (1400–64), govt by consent, 91n2

non-conformists: and radicalism, 43; religious toleration, and (17th–

Index

18th cent.), 4
non-intervention, international:
Bentham, 278–9; Bouvet, 281,
doc. 42, 292n143; Bright, 279–80,
doc. 39; Cobden, 279–81, doc. 43,
286–7, 292n130; Girardin, 281,
doc. 40; Gladstone, 284; Hinsley,
287; Kant, 281; Mill, J. S., 284–7
see also State, non-intervention

O'Connell, Daniel, (1775–1847), 49
O'Connor, Feargus (1794–1855), chartist, 47
Offenburg programme (1849), 33, 83–4,
422, doc. 85
opinion, freedom of, *see* thought
Owen, Robert (1771–1858), 47; socialism
of, 19

Paine, Thomas (1737–1809), 7, **776–7**
Common Sense (1776), doc. 6
*Dissertation on First Principles of Gov-
ernment* (1795), doc. 7
The Rights of Man (1791 and 1792),
doc. 14
America as an example; security of
individual; majority rule; individual rights; republicanism; separation of powers; written constitution; universal suffrage; revolution; rights of man; atheism; govt.
intervention, 25, **122–6, 157–8**
Age of Reason, 126
influenced by Locke, 109; influence of
Paine, 172n204
Paley, William (1743–1805), 13
Palmerston, Henry, Viscount (1784–
1865), interventionist policy, 279,
280, 284, 359–60; and radicals, 48
Pareto, Vilfredo (1848–1923), on élites,
28
Parkes, Joseph (1796–1865), 47
Parliament, Locke on, 107–8
peace, *see* non-intervention
Peace Congresses, 281–2
Peel, Sir Robert (1788–1850), free trade,
258
Pelletan, Charles Camille (1846–1915),
72, 76
pensions, Paine, 159
Perez Galdos, Benito (1843–1920),
Electra, 417
Pericles (490–429 B.C.), 743–4
Perier, Casimir (banker, 1777–1832), 60

'permissive society', Keynes, 681–2
person, freedom of, *see* individual
Pfizer, P. A. (1801–67), freedom will follow unification, 430n81; national
liberalism, 37
Pfordten, Ludwig Karl von der, (1811–
89), 546n
philhellenists, 272
philosophes, 114, 115; Rousseau on, 127
Philosophical Radicals, 13, 24; and
Reform Bill, 47; suffrage, 45; and
Whigs, 46
physiocrats, 135–9; and *laissez faire*, 14;
and monarchy, 17; refuted by Say,
261; and Smith, 141–3
Pitt, William (1759–1806), and Paine,
159
Pius IX, Pope: *Syllabus Errorum* (1864),
doc. 78; Dogma of Papal Infallibility (1870); 409, 410, **411–13**
condemns Spanish constitution (1876),
416
Place, Francis (1771–1854), 13; and
Reform Movt, 47
plebiscites, Napoleon III, 573
power: desire for, Murray, doc. 122;
wealth and, Bentham, 244, dic, 20;
see also under State
press, freedom of, 9, 38; Cobden, 37;
Constant, 54–8; Destutt, 388;
France, 401–2, 405–6, 428n37;
Germany, 403–5, 428ns30, 34;
Frankfurt 1848, 404, doc. 60;
Gambetta, 406, doc. 71; Goerres,
40, 403–4, doc. 64; Guizot, 401–2,
doc. 65; Italy, 34; Laboulaye, 406;
Lamennais, 408–9; List, 265–6;
Madariaga, doc. 123; Mazzini,
396; Metternich restricts, 403;
Mill, James, 23; Milton, 4; Offenburg and Heppenheim, docs 85,
86; Rotteck, 389, 403; Royer-
Collard, 401–3, 569, doc. 66;
Simon, 73, 406; South German lib-
erals, 83; Staël, doc, 58; Thiers,
406, docs 63, 70; Tocqueville,
570–3; Vacherot, 406; Welcker,
398–90, doc. 68, 403
Preuss, Prof. Hugo, and Weimar const.,
9–10
Prevost-Paradol, L. A. (1829–70), 39
Price, Richard (dissenter, 1723–91)
*Observations on the Nature of Civil Lib-
erty* (1776), 4

804

Priestley, Joseph (dissenter, 1773–1804), 4
Prince Smith, John (1809–74), **782**
'Hostility to Free Trade', doc. 30
'On the political significance of world free trade', doc. 38
for free trade, the entrepreneur, political independence and popular const., **267–8, 283**
private enterprise, Spencer, 583–7, doc. 105
progress:
belief in, 36–7; Condorcet, 162–4, 599; Mazzini, 411, doc. 61; Mill, J. S., 579–80, doc. 103; Rotteck, 36; Turgot, 36, 162–4; Welcker, 36
scepticism, Acton, 36; Croce, 677–8, doc. 113; Hayek, doc. 121; Voltaire, 115, 162–4, 166n44
property, rights of, 9; Bentham, 45, 46; Chamberlain, 595; classical economists, 18; Destutt, 60–1; Frankfurt, 1849, doc. 60; French 1789 declaration, 152, doc. 13; French Independents, 60; Mannheim, 724; Montesquieu, doc. 5c; socialism and, 19; Weimar, 10
inequality, and, Rousseau, 129
labour value, Locke, 7, 106–10, doc. 1b, c, Paine, 158–9
social conception of, Hobhouse, 596–8, doc. 110b
see also under suffrage
proportional representation: Acton, 582; J. S. Mill, 581
Proudhon, Pierre (1809–65), anti-capitalism, 398
Pufendorf, Samuel von (1632–94), Natural Law, 6

Quesnay, François (1694–1774)
Tableau Économique (1758): land, sole source of wealth, to be taxed; circular flow of wealth; favours 'legal' despotism, **135–7**

radicalism: defined, 43; British, 42–52; French, 59–60, 157n175; German, 80–90;
see Alain, Baumgarten, Bentham, Bright, Cartwright, Chamberlain, J., Cobbett, Dilke, Fawcett, Gambetta, Manchester School, Mazzini,

Mill, J. S., Morley, John and Samuel, non-conformists, Paine, Philosophical Radicals, Trevelyan
Realpolitik, term coined, 423
religious toleration, freedom of conscience:
growth of the idea, 3–5; development, 110–17, docs 2–4
see also Acton, Bayle, Cavour, Chamberlain, Constant, Frankfurt 1849 const., French 1789 declaration, Laboulaye, Lamennais, Lecky, Locke, List, Louménie, Mazzini, Milton, Mill, J. S., Montalambert, Montesquieu, non-conformists, Offenburg, Pius IX, Rotteck, Simon, Staël, Tocqueville, Turgot, Voltaire, Weimar, UN declaration, Welcker
Spain, in, 415–18, doc. 80a; Weimar const., 10
see also anti-clericalism, *and* Church
Rémusat, Charles de (1797–1875), 74–5
Renouvier, Charles (1815–1903), 'science of the moral order', 72
representative government, see Bentham, Guizot, Locke, Mill, James and J. S., Paine, Staël
see also suffrage
republicanism: French, 53, 60; Gambetta, 575; Gervinus, 85, Mazzini, 396, doc. 61; Montesquieu, 117–18, docs 5 b, c; Paine, 157–9, docs 7, 14
research, freedom of: Beveridge, 684–5; Madariaga, doc. 123
revolution:
French (1789), cited by: Bentham, doc. 15; Constant, 57, doc. 96; Faguet, doc. 106; Gambetta, docs 71, 99; Guizot, doc. 32; Laveley, 399, doc. 62; Paine, docs, 7, 15; Staël, doc. 53; Thiers, 400, doc. 63; Young, 171n175
right of: Bentham, 161; Dahlmann, 420–1, doc. 83, 429ns76, 77; Locke, 7, Paine, 124–5, doc. 7
Ricardo, David (1772–1823), **778**
On the Principles of Political Economy and Taxation (1817), doc. 23
repeal of corn laws; free trade; law of comparative advantage, 12, 13, **251–2**
agst aristocratic govt, 18; attacks corn laws, 15, 18; Bastiat rejects, 262;

Index

propertied suffrage, 19; Say disagrees on capitalists, 261
Richter, Eugen (1838–1906), **778–9**
defence of liberalism after unification, doc. 94
rights, human; rights of man, 5–12
American declaration (1776), 46–50, doc. 12; Bill of Rights (1689), 126, Frankfurt const. (1849), doc. 60; French declaration (1789), 8, 122, 146, doc. 13; Paine, 125–6; UN declaration, 10–11, 92ns16–18 Murray on, 122, *see also* individual, natural, women's and workers' rights
Rochau, Ludwig August von (1810–73), 423
Rochefort, Henri (1830–1913), ed. *Lanterne*, 429n36
Roggenbach, Franz von (1825–1907), 545n
Roosevelt, Pres. Franklin D. (1884–1945), on freedoms, 683
Rotteck, Karl von (1775–1840), 80, **389–90, 779**
Staatslexikon (1834–48), doc. 48: const. monarchy; freedoms of press, religion, emigration, assocn, **389–90**
free press, 403; individual freedom before national unity, 38, 421: const. monarchy, **81–3**; progress, belief in, 36; Treitschke on, 391, 451
Rouher, Eugene (1814–84), 406
Rousseau, Jean-Jacques (1712–78), 7, 53, **779–80**
Discourse on Arts and Sciences (1750)
Social Contract (1762), doc. 8a–e
La Nouvelle Héloise (1761)
Émile (1762)
'general will' and French declaration, 154; Guizot on, 569–70; social contract, 6, 106
man born free; social compact; sovereignty indivisible; 'general will'; man 'compelled' to be free; separation of powers; threat of groups and assocns; equality before the law; the 'Legislator'; collectivism and individualism, **126–35**
Rowntree, Joseph (1836–1925), social investigations of, 590

Royer-Collard, Pierre Paul (1763–1845), 53, 55, 59, **780**
doctrinaire; freedom of press, **401–3**, 569; propertied suffrage, 58
Ruggiero, Prof., on Cartesians, 5
Russell, John, Lord (1792–1878), 47, 359–60

Sainte-Beuve, Charles A. (1804–69), on individualism, 62
Saint-Simon, Claude Henri de (1760–1825), 729, 730n; and Chevalier, 574
Say, Jean Baptiste (1767–1832), 12, 13, **781**
Treatise on Political Economy (1803), doc. 27, importance of middle classes; refutes physiocrats on land, Smith on labour value, Ricardo on capitalist; principle of utility; the entrepreneur (290n76); law of markets; freedom of production and trade; minimal State interference, 17, 60, **259–62**
Bastiat pupil of, 262; Chevalier successor to, 574
Schapiro, J. S., 45
Schiller, Johann, C. F. von (1759–1805), and Humboldt, 272
Schulze-Delitzsch, Hermann (1808–83): self-help and workers' assocns; cooperatives, **87–90**; and free trade, 282
Schurz, Carl (1829–1906), 85
Scott, C. P. (ed. *Manchester Guardian*, 1846–1932), 597; and New Liberals, 52
Scott, Sir Walter (1771–1832), on public opinion, 580
self-interest motivation: Bentham, 25–6, 243–5; Keynes, 677–8, 680–2, doc. 115; Lavelaye, 283–4, doc. 44; Mill, James, 25–6; Smith, 140–5, docs 11a–d
Senior, Nassau (1790–1864), 12, 13, 16; agst universal suffrage, 19
Shackleton, Robert, on Montesquieu, 122
Shaftesbury, 3rd Earl of (1671–1713), 94n1; and Humboldt, 27
Siebenpfeiffer, Philip Jacob (1789–1845), 81, 100–1n8
Sieyès, Abbé (1748–1836), *What is the Third Estate?*, natural and positive

Index

law, 152–3
Simon, Jules (1814–96), 64
  La Politique Radicale (1868): 'total liberty', **72–3**; and Leroy-Beaulieu, 588; free press, 406
Sirven, Elizabeth, death of and Voltaire, 115
Smith, Adam (1723–90), 12–13, **140–5, 781–2**
  The Theory of Moral Sentiments
  The Wealth of Nations, docs 11a–d division of labour; labour the source of wealth; market economy and abolition of monopolies; wealth and the rent of land; three 'orders of society'; self-interest and monopolies; functions of govt, **140–5**
  French 1789 declaration, 9; physiocrats, and, 135, 136; Ricardo, and, 252; Say, influence on, 60, 259–61, doc. 27; State responsibilities, 15, 16
Smith, Prince, *see* Prince Smith
Smuts, Jan (1870–1950), 'the true liberal', 739
social contract (compact); Bentham, 160; Locke, 105–10, docs 1a–c; Paine, 124, 158; Rotteck, 390; Rousseau, 6, 106, 128
social democracy: Mann, 685–7, docs 118, 119; Mill, J. S., dangers of 577
Social-Liberalism, 39–42
socialism: Bastiat, 262–4, doc. 28; Bentham, classical economists, Fourier, 19; Hayek, 689–93, doc. 121; Hobhouse, 596–8, doc. 110b; liberal radicals, 51; Lippmann, 731; Mann, doc. 122; Mannheim, doc. 120; Mill, James and J. S., 19–20; Owen, 19; Proudhon, 398; Spender, 679–80; Spengler, 690; Tocqueville, 727; TUC, 727
  State: J. Chamberlain, 49–51, 594–5, doc. 109; Keynes, 677–8, 680–2, docs 115, 116
Sonnemann, Leopold (1831–1909): founder of *Frankfurter Zeitung*; workers' education and assocns, **90**
Spencer, Herbert (1820–1903), **782**
  Social Statistics (1851)
  'Over Legislation (1868), doc. 105
  The Coming Slavery (1884)
  social Darwinism and *laissez faire*; rejection of Bentham; a priori

natural rights of individual; agst State intervention; for private enterprise; tyranny of majority and sins of bureaucracy, 41, **583–7**
  influence on Leroy-Beaulieu, 68
Spender, Stephen (1909–), *Forward from Liberalism*, 679–80, 689
Spengler, Oswald (1880–1936), *Decline of the West* (1918, 1922), 690
Staël, Germaine de (1766–1817), **783**
  Considérations sur les principes événements de la Revolution Française (1818), docs 52, 53, 58: English model; dangers of standing army; representative govt and chamber of peers; press freedom; religious toleration; freedom of individual, 53–4, **392, 394**, 407
State:
  inadequacies of, Leroy-Beaulieu, 587–9, doc. 107
  intervention by the State, 7; Arndt, 419–20, docs 81, 82; Bentham, 20–1, 244–5; Beveridge, 682–5, doc. 117; Faguet, 67; Gladstone, 257–8, doc. 26b, 284, 289ns59–64; Green, 592–4, doc. 108; Hobhouse, 596–8, doc. 110a; Jordan, 414, doc. 79; Keynes, doc. 115; Leroy-Beaulieu, 68, 69; Mill, J. S., 255–7, doc. 25, 276; Murray, doc. 122; Prince Smith, 15, 16, 142–5, doc. 11b–d; Say, 259–62; Spencer, 583–7, doc. 105; Treitschke, 390–1, doc. 51
  power: Simon, 73; French radicals, 70
  centralization of: Lecky, 573–4, doc. 100; Mill, J. S., 581–2
  corruption of: Acton, 598–600, doc. 111; Alain, 78–9, 600–1, docs 112a, b
  evils of: Burckhardt, 598
  necessary evil of: Faguet, 587, doc. 106; Paine, 124–6
  limitations of, Constant, 55
  separation of powers: Bentham, 161; Paine and US const., 124; supremacy of, Jordan, 414, doc. 79
  should wither away, Simon, 588
  Welfare: Beveridge, 682–3, doc. 117; Humboldt agst., 273–4
Stein, Lorenz von, 588, 645
Stoics, 5–6
Struve, Gustav von (1805–70), 83–5, 88

807

Index

suffrage:
  restricted élitist, propertied, educated, etc. 18–19, 35–6; Barnave, 58; Britain and France, in, 31–2; Constant, 388–9, doc. 46; Guizot, 569–70, doc. 97; Hansemann, 270–1, doc. 33; 421, docs 56, 84; Hume, 18; Lord Liverpool, 246; McCulloch, 19; Mill, James, 246–7; Mill, J. S., 246–8; Offenburg, doc. 85, Ricardo, 19; Royer-Collard, 58; Senior, 19
  universal manhood (for and agst), 45, 248, 591; achievements of, 42; Alain, 78, Bentham, 19, 45, 288n16; Bismarck and Baumgarten, 425–6, doc. 93f; Carnot, 71; Condorcet, 164; Gambetta, 73–4, doc. 71, 575, doc. 99; Germany, in (over 25), 34; German National Liberal Party (1867), doc. 90; Guizot, 269–70, doc. 32; Lamennais, 395, doc. 67; Lecky, 573–4, doc. 100; Macaulay, 19; Mill, James, 19, 22–3, 45, 246–7; Mill, J. S., 579–82, doc. 103; Paine, 125; Philosophical Radicals, 45; Treitschke, 391, doc. 51; utilitarians, 21–5; Wilkes, 44
  women's: Mill, James, 23, 247; Mill, J. S., 276, UN Declaration, 92n17
Switzerland, Neue Züricher Zeitung, 744n
Sybel, Heinrich von (1817–95), 784
  correspondence with Baumgarten, q.v.
Syllabus Errorum, doc. 78; see Pius IX

Talmon, Prof, J. L., 245
Tawney, R. H. (180–1962), social liberalism, 51–2
taxation, Chamberlain, 594–5, doc. 109; Dahlmann, doc. 54; Lecky, 573–4, doc. 100; Ricardo, 251–2, doc. 23; equality of: Gladstone, 257–8; Mill, J. S., 257; Offenburg and Heppenheim, docs, 85, 86; Paine, 159; South German liberals, 83
  land: Quesnay, Say, Turgot, 136–9
  uniformity, French declaration, 1789, doc. 154
Thiers, Adolphe (1797–1877), 60, 74, 427n17, 784–5
  const. monarchy; five indispensible freedoms; on bourgeoisie, 64–5, 398, 399–400; agst press freedom,

406; as ldr of opposition, 31
thought, opinion and speech, freedom of, 164, 727; Beveridge, 684–5; Constant, 54–8; Frankfurt declaration, doc. 60; French declaration, 1789, 154; Hayek (for minority), 691–2, doc. 121; List, 265–6; Mazzini, 396; Mill, James ('discussion'), 245–7, 268–9, 271, doc. 31; Mill, J. S., 276–7; Milton, 4; UN declaration, 11–12
  see also under religion
Tocqueville, Alexis de (1805–59), 785
  Democracy in America (1835), docs 96, 102
  The Ancien Regime and the Revolution (1856)
  USA and France; responsibility of aristocracy; suffrage; equality and political freedom, 61–4
  inevitability of democracy; dangers of uniformity; equality and freedom; religious freedom and free press and assocn., 570–3
  tyranny of majority, tempered by lawyers; conformism of individuals; liberty and political rights, 31, 577–9
  French and English radicals, 70–1; local govt, 581; progress, scepticism on, 36; socialism, 727; Treischke on, 453
Tooke, John Horn (1736–1812), 'radical reform', 44
Torrens, Robert, 12–13
Toynbee, Arnold (1852–83), 591
Trade Union Congress, support for Liberal radicalism, 51
trade unions: repeal of Combination Laws, 92n8; Chevalier, 574–5, doc. 98; Hobhouse, 595–8; Lecky, 573–4, doc. 100
  rights: France, 76, 77; UN declaration, 11
  tyranny of, in Labour Party, Keynes, doc. 116
Treitschke, Heinrich von (1834–96), 389, 559n, 786
  Die Freiheit (1861): rejects aesthetic individualism and social contract; 'politically limited freedom'; 'State an end in itself'; social justice and national education, 390–1
Trevelyan, Sir Charles (1807–86), radical-

ism, 48
Trollope, Anthony (1815–82), on liberals and equality, 42
Turgot, A. R. J. (physiocrat, 1727–81), **786–7**
Éloge de Gournay (1759), doc. 9
Letter to the Abbé Terray 'sur les marques des fers' (1773), doc. 10
Memorial to the King 'On Toleration' (1775), doc. 4, religious tolerance, **116–17**
freedoms of labour and trade; freeing land from feudalism (169n128); abolition of guilds; taxation of land, **137–40**
progress belief in, 36, 162
Twesten, Karl (1820–70), **787–8**
'Draft of the foundation programme for the National Liberal Party' (1867), doc. 91, 424

ultramontanes, 407–8
UN: Universal Declaration of Human Rights (1948), 10–11, 92ns 16–18; Murray on, doc. 122
International Covenant on Economic, Social and Cultural Rights (1966), 11
unemployment, *see* work, right to
USA: Declaration of Independence (1776), 7–8, doc. 12; influenced by Locke, 109–10, 147–8, 170n161
Constitution (1787), influence of, 29–30; 122, 150
utilitarianism, 20–5; defined, 12–13; ideas, 20–5;
Bentham, q.v.; Green, 591; Mill, J. S., 247–8, 255, 589; Say, 261; Whigs and Tories (19th cent.), 591

Vacherot, Étienne (1809–97), 64; free press, 406
Valéry, Paul (1871–1945), on necessity of war, 741
Vaughan, C. E., on Rousseau, 127, 134
Voigt, F. A., 414, 731
Voltaire (1694–1778), **788**
Candide (1759)
Philosophical Dictionary (1764)
Treatise on Toleration (1764)
natural law and religious toleration, **114–16**; Mazzini on, doc. 77; belief, later doubt of progress; religion of, 166n44

Wallas, Graham (1858–1932), and social liberalism, 51–2
war: Bentham, 278–9; Baumgarten (Austrian war), 425; Beveridge (freedom from), 682–5, doc. 117; Bouvet, doc. 42; Montesquieu, 372; Valéry (necessity of), 741
see also non-intervention
Webb, Beatrice (1858–1943) and Sidney (1859–1947), 596; belief in Russian communism, Murray, doc. 122; hope for extinction of Liberal Party, 735
Welcker, Karl Theodor (1790–1869), **789**
Staatslexikon (1834–48), doc. 49
const. monarchy; ministerial responsibility; English example, **389–90**
const. monarchy, 81; free press, 403; progress, belief in, 36
Wilberforce, William (1759–1833), and slavery, 49
Wilkes, John (1727–97), 49; democratic suffrage, 44
William I, King of Prussia and 1st Emperor of Germany (1797–1888), appoints Bismarck, 424
Wilson, James (*The Economist*), 16
Wilson, Pres. Woodrow (1856–1924), national self-determination, 679
Wolff, Christian, (1679–1754), 7
women: rights for, Condorcet, 164; Mill, J. S., 11, 276; UN Declaration, 11; suffrage: James Mill, 23, 247; UN Declaration, 92n17
work, right to, 11; Beveridge, 682–5, doc. 117; Faguet, 66; France (1848), 155
workers':
associations and cooperatives, Schulze-Delitsch, 88–9
rights: Arndt (emancipation of peasants), 419, doc. 82, 538; Blanc, 76; France (1791), right to strike forbidden, 155; French radicals, 76–7; Gambetta, 76, 575, doc. 99; physiocrats, 136–9; Simon agst fixing hours and wages, 73; Turgot, 137–9
working class: bourgeoisie, and, Lassalle, 87; classical economists, 15–16; classless society, Spender, 679; class war, Keynes agst, 680–1; Constant, doc. 46; economic freedom for, Hayek, 689–93, doc. 121;

Index

exploitation of, J. S. Mill, 255; free trade benefit for: Cobden, 253; Gladstone, 257–8, doc. 160; German industrialists and, 40; liberal vote, Chamberlain, 594–5; threat to const. liberty, Lecky, 573–4, doc. 100; utilitarians, 25

Young, Arthur (1741–1820), and French revolution (1789), 171n175